TRIUMPH

C000298731

 **Published by
BL Cars Limited**

TRIUMPH
TR7

REPAIR OPERATION MANUAL

Publication Part No. AKM 3079B including supplement AKM 3079/1

SPECIFICATION

Purchasers are advised that the specification details set out in this Manual apply to a range of vehicles and not to any one. For the specification of a particular vehicle, purchasers should consult their Distributor or Dealer.

The Manufacturers reserve the right to vary their specifications with or without notice, and at such times and in such manner as they think fit. Major as well as minor changes may be involved in accordance with the Manufacturer's policy of constant product improvement.

Whilst every effort is made to ensure the accuracy of the particulars contained in this Manual, neither the Manufacturer nor the Distributor or Dealer, by whom this Manual is supplied, shall in any circumstances be held liable for any inaccuracy or the consequences thereof.

COPYRIGHT

© BL Cars Limited, 1980
All rights reserved. No part of this publication may be reproduced, stored in a retrieval system or transmitted in any form, electronic, mechanical, photocopying, recording or other means without prior written permission of Rover Triumph, Service Division, Allesley, Coventry.

© Copyright BL Cars Limited 1980
and Brooklands Books Limited 1988, 2006 and 2015

This book is published by Brooklands Books Limited and based upon text and illustrations protected by copyright and first published in 1980 by BL Cars Limited and may not be reproduced transmitted or copied by any means without the prior written permission of Rover Group Limited and Brooklands Books Limited.

Whilst every effort is made to ensure the accuracy of the particulars contained in this Workshop Manual the Manufacturing Companies will not, in any circumstances, be held liable for any inaccuracies or the consequences thereof.

Brooklands Books Ltd., P.O. Box 146, Cobham, Surrey KT11 1LG, England
Phone: (44) 1932 865051
E-mail: sales@brooklands-books.com   www.brooklands-books.com

ISBN 9781855202726   Part No. AKM 3079B   Ref: T172WH   10T5/2471

CONTENTS

INTRODUCTION

The purpose of this manual is to assist skilled mechanics in the efficient repair and maintenance of Triumph TR7 vehicles. Using the appropriate service tools and carrying out the procedures as detailed will enable the operations to be completed in the time stated in the 'Repair Operations Times'.

Indexing
The contents page lists the titles and reference numbers of the divisions in numerical order. A complete index of operations, together with their page numbers, is given from pages 6 onwards.

Operation Numbering
A master index of numbered operations has been compiled for universal application to all vehicles manufactured by the BL Cars and, therefore, because of the different specifications of various models, continuity of the numbering sequence cannot be maintained throughout this manual.

Each operation described in this manual is allocated a number from the master index and cross-refers with an identical number in the 'Repair Operations Times'. The number consists of six digits arranged in three pairs.

Each instruction within an operation has a sequence number and, to complete the operation in the minimum time, it is essential that the instructions are performed in numerical sequence commencing at 1 unless otherwise stated. Where applicable, the sequence numbers identify the relevant components in the appropriate illustration.

Service Tools
Where performance of an operation requires the use of a service tool, the tool number is quoted under the operation heading and is repeated in, or following, the instruction involving its use. An illustrated list of all necessary tools is included in 'SERVICE TOOLS'.

References
References to the left- or right-hand side in the manual are made when viewing from the rear. With the engine and gearbox assembly removed, the 'timing cover' end of the engine is referred to as the front. A key to abbreviations and symbols is given on page 5.

Where the specification of the vehicle is varied, the operation will detail which variant is concerned, i.e. USA and Canada for full emission vehicles. The fuel system and gearbox sections have alternative footlines to cater for the major variations, i.e. 4 and 5 speed gearbox; and the axle is similarly termed 4 and 5 speed to denote with which gearbox the axle is fitted.

REPAIRS AND REPLACEMENTS

When service parts are required it is essential that only genuine Triumph or Unipart replacements are used.

Attention is particularly drawn to the following points concerning repairs and the fitting of replacement parts and accessories.

Safety features embodied in the car may be impaired if other than genuine parts are fitted. In certain territories, legislation prohibits the fitting of parts not to the vehicle manufacturer's specification. Torque wrench setting figures given in the Repair Operation Manual must be strictly adhered to. Locking devices, where specified, must be fitted. If the efficiency of a locking device is impaired during removal it must be renewed. Owners purchasing accessories while travelling abroad should ensure that the accessory and its fitted location on the car conform to mandatory requirements in their country of origin.

The car warranty may be invalidated by the fitting of other than genuine manufacturer's parts or parts approved by the manufacturer. All Unipart replacements have the full backing of the factory warranty. BL Cars Distributors and Dealers are obliged to supply only genuine service parts.

ABBREVIATIONS AND SYMBOLS

Across flats (bolt size)	A.F.	Miles per gallon	m.p.g.
After bottom dead centre	A.B.D.C.	Miles per hour	m.p.h.
After top dead centre	A.T.D.C.	Millimetres	mm
Alternating current	a.c.	Millimetres of mercury	mmHg
Amperes	amp	Minimum	min.
Ampere-hour	Ah	Minus (of tolerance)	-
Atmospheres	Atm	Minute (of angle)	'
Before bottom dead centre	B.B.D.C.	Negative (electrical)	-
Before top dead centre	B.T.D.C.	Newton Metres	Nm
Bottom dead centre	B.D.C.	Number	No.
Brake horse-power	b.h.p.		
Brake mean effective pressure	b.m.e.p.	Ohms	ohm
British Standards	B.S.	Ounces (force)	ozf
		Ounces (mass)	oz
Carbon monoxide	CO	Ounce inch (torque)	ozf in
Centigrade (Celsius)	C	Outside diameter	o.dia.
Centimetres	cm	Overdrive	O/D
Cubic centimetres	cm^3		
Cubic inches	in^3	Paragraphs	para.
Cycles per minute	c/min	Part Number	Part No.
		Percentage	%
Degree (angle)	deg. or °	Pints (Imperial)	pt
Degree (temperature)	deg. or °	Pints (U.S.)	U.S.pt
Diameter	dia.	Plus or minus	±
Direct current	d.c.	Plus (tolerance)	+
		Positive (electrical)	+
Fahrenheit	F	Pounds (force)	lbf
Feet	ft	Pounds (mass)	lb
Feet per minute	ft/min	Pounds feet (torque)	lbf ft
Fifth	5th	Pounds inches (torque)	lbf in
Fig. (illustration)	Fig.	Pounds per square inch	lb/in^2
First	1st		
Fourth	4th		
		Radius	r
Gallons (Imperial)	gal.	Ratio	:
Gallons (U.S.)	U.S. gal	Reference	ref.
Grammes (force)	gf	Revolutions per minute	rev/min
Grammes (mass)	g	Right-hand	R.H.
		Right-hand steering	R.H.Stg.
High compression	h.c.		
High tension (electrical)	h.t.	Second (angle)	"
Horse-power	hp	Second (numerical order)	2nd
Hundredweight	cwt	Single carburetter	SC
		Society of Automobile Engineers	S.A.E.
Inches	in	Specific gravity	sp. gr.
Inches of mercury	inHg	Square centimetres	cm^2
Independent front suspension	i.f.s.	Square inches	in^2
Internal diameter	i.dia.	Standard	std.
		Standard wire gauge	s.w.g.
Kilogrammes (force)	kgf	Synchronizer/synchromesh	synchro
Kilogrammes (mass)	kg		
Kilogramme centimetre	kgf cm	Third	3rd
Kilogramme metres	kgf m	Twin carburetters	TC
Kilogrammes per square centimetre	kg/cm^2		
Kilometres	km	United Kingdom	UK
Kilometres per hour	km/h		
Kilovolts	kV	Volts	V
King pin inclination	k.p.i.		
		Watts	W
Left-hand	L.H.		
Left-hand steering	L.H. Stg.	Screw threads	
Left-hand thread	L.H. Thd.	American Standard	
Low compression	l.c.	Taper Pipe	N.P.T.F.
Low tension	l.t.	British Association	B.A.
		British Standard Fine	B.S.F.
Maximum	max.	British Standard Pipe	B.S.P.
Metres	m	British Standard Whitworth	B.S.W.
Microfarad	mfd	Unified Coarse	U.N.C.
Miniature Edison Screw	MES	Unified Fine	U.N.F.

INDEX

ENGINE

FUEL SYSTEM - UK & EUROPE

FUEL SYSTEM - USA & CANADA - CARBURETTERS

FUEL SYSTEM - USA AND CANADA - FUEL INJECTION

GENERAL SPECIFICATION DATA

ENGINE

Type	In line — inclined at 45°
Number of cylinders	4
Bore	3.56 in (90,3 mm)
Stroke	3.07 in (78,0 mm)
Capacity	122 in³ (1998 cm³)
Valve operation	Single overhead camshaft

Crankshaft bearing

Main journal diameter	2.1260 to 2.1265 in (54,000 to 54,013 mm)
Minimum regrind diameter	2.0860 to 2.0865 in (52,984 to 52,997 mm)
Crankpin journal diameter	1.7500 to 1.7505 in (44,450 to 44,463 mm)
Minimum regrind diameter	1.7100 to 1.7105 in (43,434 to 43,447 mm)
Crankshaft end thrust	Taken on thrust washers at centre main bearing
Crankshaft end float	0.003 to 0.011 in (0,07 to 0,28 mm)

Main bearings

Number	5
Diametrical clearance	0.0012 to 0.0022 in (0,030 to 0,058 mm)
Undersizes	0.010 in 0.020 in 0.030 in 0.040 in (0,254 mm 0,508 mm 0,762 mm 1,016 mm)

Connecting rods

Small end bush fitted internal diameter	0.9377 to 0.9380 in (23,818 to 23,825 mm)
Bush external diameter	1.0015 to 1.0025 in (25,438 to 25,464 mm)
Small end diameter less bush	0.9995 to 1.0005 in (25,387 to 25,413 mm)
Big end diameter less shells	1.8955 to 1.8960 in (48,146 to 48,158 mm)
Length between centres	5.123 to 5.127 in (130,12 to 130,23 mm)
Maximum bend	0.0015 in (0,038 mm) for length of the gudgeon pin
Maximum twist	0.0015 in (0,038 mm) per inch length of gudgeon pin

Big end bearings

Diametrical clearance	0.0008 to 0.0023 in (0,020 to 0,058 mm)
End float on crankpin	0.006 to 0.013 in (0,15 to 0,33 mm)
Undersizes	0.010 in 0.020 in 0.030 in 0.040 in (0,254 mm 0,508 mm 0,762 mm 1,016 mm)

Pistons

Clearance in bore measured at bottom of skirt at right angles to gudgeon pin	0.0005 to 0.0015 in (0,013 to 0,039 mm)
Top compression ring groove width	0.0705 to 0.0713 in (1,790 to 1,810 mm)
Second compression ring groove width	0.0700 to 0.0709 in (1,780 to 1,800 mm)
Oil control ring groove width	0.1579 to 0.1587 in (4,010 to 4,030 mm)

Piston rings

Number one (top) compression ring	Chrome periphery
Gap in bore	0.015 to 0.025 in (0,40 to 0,65 mm)
Clearance in groove	0.0019 to 0.0039 (0,050 to 0,082 mm)
Number two compression ring	Upper face marked "TOP"
Gap in bore	0.015 to 0.025 in (0,40 to 0,65 mm)
Clearance in groove	0.0015 to 0.0025 in (0,040 to 0,065 mm)
Oil control — rails	
Gap in bore	0.015 to 0.055 in (0,40 to 1,40 mm)
Oil control — expander	
Gap in bore	Ends to abut

Gudgeon pins

Length	2.626 to 2.638 in (66,70 to 67,00 mm)
Diameter	0.9374 to 0.9376 in (23,811 to 23,815 mm)
Clearance in con rod	0.0001 to 0.0006 in (0,002 to 0,015 mm)
Clearance in piston	Zero to 0.0004 in (0,010 mm)

Camshaft

Location	Overhead
Bearings	Non-serviceable
Timing chain	0.375 in (9,52 mm) pitch x 106 pitches

Oil pump

Outer ring end-float	0.004 in (0.1 mm)
Inner ring end-float	0.004 in (0.1 mm)
Outer ring to pump body diametrical clearance	0.008 in (0.2 mm)
Rotor lobe clearance	0.010 in (0.25 mm)
Relief valve spring free length	1.70 in (43.18 mm)

Valve timing

Inlet valves open	16° B.T.D.C.
Close	56° A.B.D.C.
Exhaust valves open	56° B.B.D.C.
Close	16° A.T.D.C.

Valves

Inlet

Overall length	4.259 to 4.269 in (108,17 to 108,43 mm)
Head diameter	1.560 in (39,62 mm)
Angle of face	45°
Stem diameter	0.3107 to 0.3113 in (7,881 to 7,907 mm)
Stem to guide clearance	0.0017 to 0.0023 in (0,043 to 0,058 mm)

Exhaust

Overall length	4.254 to 4.258 in (108,05 to 108,15 mm)
Head diameter	1.280 in (32,51 mm)
Angle of face	45°
Stem diameter	0.3100 to 0.3106 in (7,87 to 7,89 mm)
Stem to guide clearance	0.0014 to 0.0030 in (0,035 to 0,076 mm)

Valve seats

Outside diameter: Inlet	1.6695 to 1.6705 in (42,405 to 42,430 mm)
Exhaust	1.3335 to 1.3345 in (33,870 to 33,896 mm)
Angle of seat	42½°

Valve springs

Free length	1.600 in (40,40 mm)
Fitted length	1.440 in (36,57 mm)
Number of working coils	3¾

Lubrication

System	Wet sump, pressure fed
Oil warning light extinguishes at	3 to 5 lbf/in² (0,21 to 0,35 kgf/cm²)
Oil filter	Full-flow, replaceable element
Oil pump type	Hobourn-Eaton
Oil pressure relief valve	
Type	Non-adjustable

FUEL SYSTEM

Carburetter	Refer to 'ENGINE TUNING DATA'
Fuel pump	Mechanically-operated, diaphragm-type
Operating pressure	2.5 to 3.5 lbf/in² (0,17 to 0,24 kgf/cm²)
Fuel injection	Bosch, analogue, electronic
Fuel pump	Electrical
Operating pressure	Approximately 36 lbf/in² (2.5 kgf/cm²)

COOLING SYSTEM

Type	Pressurized spill return with thermostat control, pump and fan-assisted
Type of pump	Centrifugal
Thermostat	
Up to Engine No. CL 1468	82°C (180°F)
From Engine No. CL 1469	88°C (190°F)
Pressure cap	15 lbf/in² (1,05 kgf/cm²)

CLUTCH

Make/type	Borg & Beck, diaphragm-type
Clutch plate diameter	8.5 in (215.9 mm)
Facing material	2124F
Clutch release bearing	Ball journal
Clutch fluid	Refer to 'LUBRICANTS'

GEARBOX — 4 speed

Type	Single helical, constant mesh
Speeds	4 forward, 1 reverse
Synchromesh	All forward speeds

Ratios:

Fourth (Top)	1.00 : 1
Third	1.25 : 1
Second	1.78 : 1
First	2.65 : 1
Reverse	3.98 : 1 Earlier Models
	3.05 : 1 Later Models

Overall ratios:

Fourth (Top)	3.63 : 1
Third	4.56 : 1
Second	6.47 : 1
First	9.62 : 1
Reverse	10.95 : 1 Earlier Models
	11.08 : 1 Later Models

GEARBOX — 5 speed

Type	Single helical, constant mesh
Speeds	5 forward, 1 reverse
Synchromesh	All forward speeds

Ratios:

Fifth (Top)	0.83 : 1
Fourth	1.00 : 1
Third	1.40 : 1
Second	2.09 : 1
First	3.32 : 1
Reverse	3.43 : 1

Overall ratios:

Fifth (Top)	3.24 : 1
Fourth	3.90 : 1
Third	5.46 : 1
Second	8.15 : 1
First	12.95 : 1
Reverse	13.38 : 1

GEARBOX — AUTOMATIC

Type ... Borg Warner 65

	3rd	2nd	1st	Rev.
Transmission conversion range	1.00–1.91	1.45–2.77	2.39–4.57	2.09–3.99
Overall ratios to 1	3.27–6.25	4.74–9.05	7.82–14.95	6.85–13.08
Road speed corresponding to 1000 engine r.p.m. m.p.h.	20.0–10.5			
km.p.h.	32.0–16.8			

AUTOMATIC TRANSMISSION SHIFT SPEEDS

Throttle Position	Zero throttle	Light throttle		Part throttle	
Selector	1	2	D	D	2
Shift	2–1	1–2	2–3	3–2	1–2
Road speed m.p.h.	30–38	8–12	12–16	30–40	38–44
km.p.h.	48–61	13–19	23–26	48–64	61–71

Throttle Position	Kickdown					
Selector	D	D	D	1	D	2
Shift	1–2	2–3	3–2	2–1	3–1	2–1
Road speed m.p.h.	38–44	65–71	58–66	42–50	30–38	30–38
km.p.h.	61–71	105–114	93–106	68–81	48–61	48–61

PROPELLER SHAFT

Type	One piece straight tube
Universal joints	Constant velocity at both ends
Overall length, face to face, fully compressed	936 mm (36.85 in)

FINAL DRIVE — Used with 4 speed gearbox and Automatic transmission

Type	Hypoid
Ratio	3.63 : 1

FINAL DRIVE — Used with 5 speed gearbox

Type	Hypoid
Ratio	3.90 : 1

SUSPENSION

Front .... Independent. McPherson strut telescopic damper units with co-axial coil springs and anti-roll bar

Coil springs

Vehicles with Manual or Automatic Transmission and Heater

Up to Commission Nos. ACG13000/ACW7000 and from Commission Nos. ACG25001/ACW30001

Wire Diameter	0.448 in (11.38 mm)
Number of working coils	5.25
Free length	13.74 in (349 mm)
Rate	88 lbf/in (15.4 N/mm)
Identification	One green stripe

From Commission Nos. ACG13001/ACW7001 to Commission Nos. ACG25000/ACW30000

Wire diameter	0.448 in (11.38 mm)
Number of working coils	5.25
Free length	13.30 in (338 mm)
Rate	88 lbf/in (15.4 N/mm)
Identification	One white stripe and one blue stripe.

Vehicles with Manual or Automatic Transmission and Air Conditioning

Up to Commission Nos. ACG13000/ACW7000 and from Commission Nos. ACG25001/ACW30001

Wire diameter	0.46 in (11.68 mm)
Number or working coils	5.5
Free length	13.85 in (352 mm)
Rate	93.7 lbf/in (16.4 N/mm)
Identification	One red stripe

From Commission Nos. ACG13001/ACW7001 to Commission Nos. ACG25000/ACW30000

Wire diameter	0.46 in (11.68 mm)
Number of working coils	5.5
Free length	13.39 in (340 mm)
Rate	93.7 lbf/in (16.4 N/mm)
Identification	One white stripe and one yellow stripe

Rear .... Four link system. Lower trailing arms, upper trailing radius rods with telescopic damper units, coil springs and anti-roll bar

Coil springs

Up to Commission Nos. ACG13000/ACW7000

Wire diameter	0.463 in (11.76 mm)
Number of working coils	5
Free length	10.71 in (272 mm)
Rate	165 lbf/in (28.9 N/mm)
Identification	One white stripe

From Commission Nos. ACG13001/ACW7001

Wire diameter	0.463 in (11.76 mm)
Number of working coils	5
Free length	10.27 in (261 mm)
Rate	165 lbf/in (28.9 N/mm)
Identification	One white stripe and one red stripe

STEERING

Make/type	Alford & Alder, rack and pinion
Steering wheel diameter:	
Earlier models	14.5 in (368 mm)
Later models	14.0 in (355 mm).
Steering wheel turns, lock-to-lock	3.875

Steering angles and dimensions:

Front wheel alignment	Zero to 0.062 in (1,5 mm) toe-in
Camber angle	¼° negative ± 1°
Castor angle	3½° positive ± 1°
King pin inclination	11¼° ± 1°

{ Check with the vehicle in the kerb condition

BRAKES

Foot brake

Type	Divided hydraulic system with discs at front and drums at rear
Operation	Hydraulic, servo-assisted, boost ratio 2.3 : 1 nominal

Front brake

Type	Hub-mounted discs with two pistons
Disc diameter	9.75 in (247,6 mm)
Disc thickness	0.375 in (9,5 mm)
Front pad area	16.6 in^2 (107 cm^2)
Front swept area	183.5 in^2 (1182 cm^2)
Pad material:	
Earlier models	DON 227
Later models	Ferodo 2241 FG

Rear brake

Type	....	Drums, hand brake actuated, self-adjusting

	4 speed specification	5 speed specification and Automatic Transmission
Drum internal diameter	7.995 to 8.000 in (203.20 to 203.33 mm)	8.995 to 9.000 in (228.47 to 228.60 mm)
Drum maximum worn dia	8.050 in (204.47 mm)	9.050 in (229.87 mm)
Shoe arrangement	One leading & one trailing	One leading & one trailing
Shoe lining width	1.50 in (38.1 mm)	1.75 in (44.5 mm)
Lining material	DON 202 GG	
Rear lining area	46.9 in² (303 cm²)	60.4 in² (390 cm²)
Rear swept area	75.4 in² (486 cm²)	98.9 in² (638 cm²)

Hand brake

Type	....	Mechanical, operation on rear shoes

WHEELS

Size/type	....	5½J x 13 in dia pressed steel rims

TYRES AND TYRE PRESSURES

Size:

4 Speed and Automatic Transmission	175/70 SR13
5 Speed Transmission	185/70 HR13

Pressures (all loading conditions):

Front	24 lbf/in², 1.6 kgf/cm², 1.7 bar
Rear	28 lbf/in², 1.97 kgf/cm², 2.0 bar

ELECTRICAL EQUIPMENT

System	12 volt, negative earth
Fuses	See 86.70.00
Battery capacity	40 amp-hour at 20 hr rate
Alternator	Lucas 17ACR or 20ACR when air conditioning is fitted, or 25ACR
Starter motor	Lucas 2M 100 PE
Wiper motor	Lucas 16 W
Windscreen washer pump	Lucas 103 J
Headlamp actuator	Lucas 15 W
Distributor	See 86.35.00
Bulb chart	See 86.00.00

CAPACITIES (NOMINAL)

	USA	Imperial	Metric
Fuel tank (except Federal and California)	16.6 gals	12.0 gals	54.5 litres
Fuel tank (California and Federal)	14.6 gals	12.1 gals	55.3 litres
Engine sump and filter	9.5 pts	8.0 pts	4.5 litres
Engine sump – drain/refill	8.4 pts	7.0 pts	4.0 litres
Gearbox from dry (4 speed)	2.4 pts	2.0 pts	1.1 litres
Gearbox from dry (5 speed)	3.3 pts	2.7 pts	1.5 litres
Rear axle from dry (4 speed)	2.7 pts	2.25 pts	1.3 litres
Rear axle from dry (5 speed)	2.4 pts	2.0 pts	1.1 litres
Cooling system, including reservoir and heater — Expansion tank system	15.6 pts	13 pts	7.4 litres
— Header tank system	16.1 pts	13.4 pts	7.6 litres
Automatic transmission with oil cooler	11.4 pts	9.5 pts	5.4 litres

GENERAL DIMENSIONS (APPROXIMATE)

Overall length	160.0 in (4065 mm) 164.3 in (4173 mm) U.S.A. 1978, 1979 and 1980 Model Years
Overall width	66.2 in (1681 mm)
Overall height	49.4 to 49.9 in (1255 to 1268 mm) depending on market, model year and load condition
Wheelbase	85.0 in (2160 mm)
Track, front	55.5 in (1409 mm)
Track, rear	55.3 in (1404 mm)
Ground clearance	3.5 to 4.5 in (90 to 114 mm) depending on market, model year and load condition
Turning circle: Between kerbs	29.0 feet (8.8 m)
Between walls	31.5 feet (9.5 m)

WEIGHTS (APPROXIMATE)

*Showroom: Minimum	2240 lb (1016 kg)
Maximum	2282 lb (1035 kg)
*Unladen: Minimum	2341 lb (1062 kg)
Maximum	2509 lb (1138 kg)
*Gross vehicle weight	2866 to 2954 lb (1300 to 1340 kg)
Roof rack capacity	110 lb (50 kg)
*Max. axle load: Front	1477 lb (670 kg)
Rear	1389 lb (630 kg)
Towing capacity – braked trailer	1680 lb (762 kg)

*These figures must be taken as a guide only and vary according to market, model year and equipment fitted.

PAINT AND TRIM CODING SYSTEM

The Commission number plate bears symbols for identification of the vehicle's exterior and trim colours.

Colour Code

The basic colours are allocated a letter as shown in the table. Shades of these colours are allocated two suffix letters. For example, a commission number plate stamped 'Paint JAA. Trim PAA, denotes that the vehicle is painted 'French Blue' and trimmed 'Black'.

Basic Colour	Basic Colour Letter	Paint Trim Code					
Brown/Buff	A	AAA Beige (trim)	AAB Sand Fleck (trim)	AAC Maple	AAD Chestnut (trim)	AAE Russet Brown	
Bronze	B						
Red/Maroon	C	CAA Carmine	CAB Pimento	CAE Vermilion			
Pink	D						
Orange	E	EAA Topaz					
Yellow	F	FAA Mimosa	FAB Inca Yellow				
Gold	G						
Green	H	HAA British Racing Green	HAD Tara Green	HAE Brooklands Green			
Blue	J	JAA French Blue	JAB Delft	JAC Ice Blue	JAD Shadow Blue (trim)	JAF Astral Blue	JAG Pageant Blue
Mauve/Purple/Violet	K						
Grey	L	LAA Birch Grey (trim)	LAB Grey (trim)				
Silver/Aluminium	M						
White/Ivory/Cream	N	NAA White (trim)	NAC Sebring White (trim)	NAD Honeysuckle	NAF Leyland White		
Black	P	PAA Black (trim)	PAB Black (matt)	PAC Black (gloss)	PAD Black (rally)		
Multi-coloured	R	RAA Red/Black	RAB Green/Black				

ENGINE TUNING DATA – UK & Europe

ENGINE

Type	O.h.c. in line 4 cylinder
Capacity	122 in³ (1998 cm³)
Compression ratio	9.25 : 1 (2 valve)
Firing order	1 – 3 – 4 – 2
Number one cylinder	Front
Idle speed	650 to 850 rev/min
Fast idle speed (engine hot)	1500 to 1700 rev/min
Ignition timing:	
Static	10° B.T.D.C.
Dynamic (with vacuum pipe connected)	10° B.T.D.C. at 650 to 850 rev/min
Location of ignition timing marks	Scale on front cover – notch on pulley
Valve clearance (engine cold):	
Inlet	0.008 in (0.2 mm)
Exhaust	0.018 in (0.5 mm)
Valve clearance adjustment	Pallets between valve and cam follower
Valve timing	Inlet opens 16° B.T.D.C. Inlet closes 56° A.B.D.C. Exhaust opens 56° B.B.D.C. Exhaust closes 16° A.T.D.C.

IGNITION DISTRIBUTOR — See 86.35.00

SPARK PLUGS

Make/Type	Champion N12Y
Gap	0.024 to 0.026 in (0.61 to 0.66 mm)

IGNITION COIL

Make/type	Lucas 15C6
Primary resistance at 20°C (68°F)	1.3 to 1.5 ohms

CARBURETTERS

Make/type	Twin SU HS6
Needle	BDM

ENGINE TUNING DATA – USA Markets

ENGINE

Type	O.h.c. in line 4 cylinder
Capacity	122 in³ (1998 cm³)
Compression ratio	8.0 : 1
Firing order	1 – 3 – 4 – 2
Number one cylinder	Front
Idle speed	800 ± 100 rev/min

Ignition timing:

	Federal Carburetter Engines	California Carburetter Engines	California Carburetter Engines and Fuel Injection Engines
Static	10° B.T.D.C.	10° B.T.D.C.	10° B.T.D.C.
Dynamic at idle			2° A.T.D.C.

Location of ignition timing marks	Scale on front cover – notch on pulley
Valve clearance (engine cold):	
Inlet	0.008 in (0.2 mm)
Exhaust	0.018 in (0.5 mm)
Valve clearance adjustment	Pallets between valve and cam follower
Valve timing	Inlet opens 16° B.T.D.C Inlet closes 56° A.B.D.C. Exhaust opens 56° B.B.D.C. Exhaust closes 16° A.T.D.C.

IGNITION DISTRIBUTOR — See 86.35.00

SPARK PLUGS

Make/Type	Champion N12Y
Gap	0.024 to 0.026 in (0.61 to 0.66 mm)

IGNITION COIL

Make/type	Lucas 15C6
Primary resistance at 20°C (68°F)	1.3 to 1.5 ohms

CARBURETTERS

Make	Twin Zenith Stromberg
Type :	
1975/76 Model Years – Federal Specification	175 CD SEVX
California Specification	175 CD 4 TV.
1977 Model Year	175 CDFEVX
1978/79 Model Years	175 CDFVX
Needle:	
1975/76 Model Years	45C
1977/78/79 Model Years – Federal Specification	B1 DH
1977 to 1979 California Specification and 1980 Model Year Federal Specification	B1 EP

FUEL INJECTION

Make/Type	Bosch, analogue, electronic

TORQUE WRENCH SETTINGS

ENGINE

Operation	Description	Nm	lbf ft	kgf m
Air Cleaner to Carburetter	5/16" UNC Setscrew	11	8	1,1
Air Pump Adjusting Link and Mounting Bracket to Block	5/16" UNF Bolt	27	20	2,7
Air Pump Bracket and Alternator Adjusting Link to Block	5/16" UNF Bolt	27	20	2,7
Air Pump Adjusting Link Attachment	5/16" UNF Bolt	27	20	2,7
Air Pump to Mounting Bracket	5/16" UNF Bolt	27	20	2,7
Alternator to Mounting Bracket	5/16" UNF Bolt	27	20	2,7
Alternator Mounting Bracket to Bracing Link	5/16" UNF Bolt	27	20	2,7
Alternator Adjusting Link and Timing Cover to Block	5/16" UNF Bolt	27	20	2,7
Bearing Caps to Block	7/16" UNF Bolt	88	65	8,9
Camshaft Chain Wheel Attachment	¼" UNF Setscrew	14	10	1,38
Camshaft Cover Attachment	¼" UNC Pan Hd. Setscrew	7	5	0,69
Camshaft Bearing Cap Attachment	5/16" UNF Stud	19	14	1,9
Camshaft Bearing Cap and Cover Attachment	5/16" UNF Stud	3	2	0,27
Carburetter Flexible Mounting to Inlet Manifold	5/16" UNC Setscrew	19	14	1,9
Carburetter to Flexible Mounting	5/16" UNF Stud	19	14	1,9
Clutch to Flywheel	5/16" UNF Setscrew	30	22	3,0
Clutch Housing to Rear Engine Plate	3/8" UNF Dowel Bolt	46	34	4,7
Clutch Housing to Rear Engine Plate	5/16" UNF Bolt	27	20	2,7
Clutch Housing and Front Engine Support Bracket to Rear Engine Plate	5/16" UNF Bolt	27	20	2,7
Clutch Housing to Block	5/16" UNF Bolt	27	20	2,7
Connecting Rod Bolt	3/8" Bolt	61	45	6,2
Crankshaft Pulley Attachment	5/8" UNF Bolt	160	120	16,5
Cylinder Head to Block	7/16" UNC Bolt	75	50	6,9
Cylinder Head to Block	7/16" UNC Stud	75	50	6,9
Distributor to Block	¼" UNF Setscrew	12	9	1,2
Diverter Valve to Mounting Bracket	¼" UNF Setscrew	14	10	1,38
Drive Plate to Crank	3/8" UNF Bolt	61	45	6,2
Engine Stay Bracket to Block	5/16" UNF Bolt	27	20	2,7
Engine Stay Attachment	3/8" UNF Jam Nut	46	34	4,7
Engine Support to Block (R.H.)	5/16" UNF Setscrew	27	20	2,7
Evaporative Loss Canister Mounting Bracket to Body	6 mm Setscrew	10	7	0,9
Fan to Holset Coupling	¼" UNF Bolt	12	9	1,2
Fan Pulley Bearing Housing to Timing Cover	5/16" UNC Setscrew	19	14	1,9
Injector clamp plates to manifold	6 mm × 16 mm Setscrew	10	7	0,9
Lambda (oxygen) sensor to exhaust manifold	18 mm	60	44	6,0
Pressure regulator to fuel rail	14 mm	28	21	2,9
Temperature sensor to manifold	12 mm	15	11	1,4
Thermo time switch to manifold	14 mm	28	21	2,9
Flywheel to Crankshaft	3/8" UNF Bolt	61	45	6,2
Front Lifting Eye to Block	3/8" UNF Setscrew	46	34	4,7
Fuel Pump to Block	5/16" UNF Setscrew	19	14	1,9
Gearbox Adaptor Attachment	5/16" UNF Stud	27	20	2,7
Heater By-Pass Pipe to Inlet Manifold	11/16" Union Nut	19	14	1,9
Hot Air Manifold to Exhaust Manifold	5/16" UNF Setscrew	27	20	2,7
Inlet Manifold to Carburetter Flex Mounting	5/16" UNC Setscrew	27	20	2,7
Inlet Manifold Attachment	5/16" UNC Setscrew	27	20	2,7
Idler Shaft Chainwheel Attachment	3/8" UNF Setscrew	51	38	5,2
Oil Pump to Cylinder Block	5/16" UNF Bolt	27	20	2,7
Oil Seal Housing Attachment	¼" UNF Setscrew	12	9	1,2
Oil Seal Housing Attachment	¼" Setscrew	12	9	1,2
Oil Sump Drain Plug	3/8" Dryseal Plug	34	25	3,4
Oil Sump to Block	5/16" UNF Bolt	27	20	2,7
Oil Sump to Block	5/16" UNF Bolt	27	20	2,7
Oil Sump to Timing Cover	5/16" UNF Screw	27	20	2,7
Oil Suction Pipe to Block	¼" UNF Bolt	12	9	1,2
Oil Suction Pipe to Block	¼" UNF Setscrew	12	9	1,2
Oil Transfer Adaptor to Block	3/8" UNF Bolt	46	34	4,7
Rear Engine Mounting to Crossmember	8 mm Setscrew	28	21	2,9
Rear Engine Mounting Bracket to Block	12 mm Setscrew	80	59	8,1
Rear Engine Mounting Bracket to Gearbox	8 mm Setscrew	28	21	2,9
Rear Engine Mounting Crossmember to Body	8 mm Setscrew	28	21	2,9
Rear Engine Plate to Block	5/16" UNF Setscrew	27	20	2,7
Right Hand Front Engine Mounting Bracket to Body	8 mm Setscrew	28	21	2,9
Right Hand Front Engine Mounting to Engine Bracket	8 mm Setscrew	28	21	2,9
Right Hand and Left Hand Engine Mounting Attachment	10 mm	50	37	5,1
Starter Motor to Clutch Housing	3/8" Bolt	46	34	4,7
Throttle Linkage and Mounting Bracket Assembly to Inlet Manifold	¼" UNC Setscrew	10	7	0,9
Timing Chain Tensioner to Block	¼" UNF Bolt	12	9	1,2
Timing Chain Support Bracket and Guides to Block	5/16" UNF Setscrew	27	20	2,7
Timing Cover to Cylinder Block	5/16" UNF Bolt	27	20	2,7
Timing Cover to Cylinder Head	5/16" UNC Setscrew	27	20	2,7
Water Outlet Elbow to Inlet Manifold	5/16" UNF Setscrew	27	20	2,7
Water Pump Cover to Block	5/16" UNF Bolt	27	20	2,7
Water Pump Impeller Retaining	5/16" UNC Setscrew	19	14	1,9
Water Transfer Housing to Cylinder Head	5/16" UNC Setscrew	27	20	2,7

FUEL INJECTION SYSTEM

Operation	Description	Nm	lbf ft	kgf m
Air meter support plate/bracket	8 mm Stud/Setscrew	28	21	2,9
Auxiliary air valve to water pump cover	6 mm × 12 mm Setscrew	7	5	0,7
	14 mm/13 mm dia.	0,68	6 lbf in	0,07
Fuel rail to injectors	5/16" UNC Setscrew	19	14	1,9

Operation	Description	Nm	lbf ft	kgf m
EXHAUST SYSTEM				
Exhaust Manifold Attachment	3/8" UNF Setscrew	46	34	4,7
Exhaust Pipe to Manifold	10 mm Stud	50	37	5,1
Exhaust Pipe to Brackets on Gearbox and Clutch Housing	8 mm Setscrew	28	21	2,9
Exhaust Silencer to Front Exhaust Pipe	8 mm Bolt	10	7	0,9
Exhaust Silencer to Rear Silencer and Tail Pipe	8 mm Bolt	10	7	0,9
Exhaust Support Bracket to Pipe	8 mm Setscrew	28	21	2,9
Rear Silencer Strap to Support Bracket	8 mm Bolt	28	21	2,9
Rear Silencer Support Bracket to Floor	8 mm on Mounting Rubber	28	21	2,9
CLUTCH, 4 SPEED GEARBOX AND PROPELLER SHAFT				
Boss to Clutch Housing	5/16" UNF Setscrew	27	20	2,7
Clutch and Brake Pedal Mounting Bracket Attachment	8 mm Setscrew	28	21	2,9
Clutch Housing to Gearbox Case	3/8" UNF Wedgelock Bolt	43	32	4,4
Clutch Housing to Gearbox Case	3/8" UNF Setscrew	43	32	4,4
Clutch Housing to Rear Engine Plate	3/8" UNF Dowel Bolt	43	32	4,4
Clutch Housing to Rear Engine Plate	5/16" UNF Bolt	27	20	2,7
Clutch Housing and Front Exhaust Support Bracket to Rear Engine Plate	5/16" UNF Bolt	27	20	2,7
Clutch Housing to Cylinder Block	5/16" UNF Bolt	27	20	2,7
Clutch Master Cylinder to Dash	8 mm Setscrew	28	21	2,9
Cover to Gearbox Case	1/4" UNF Setscrew	12	9	1,2
Cover Plate to Top Cover	1/4" UNF Setscrew	12	9	1,2
Exhaust Pipe Support Bracket Attachment	5/16" UNF Setscrew	27	20	2,7
Flange to Mainshaft	5/8" UNF Nut	163	120	16,5
Magnetic Drain Plug	3/8" Dryseal Plug	34	25	3,4
Oil Filler Plug	3/8" NP Taper Plug	34	25	3,4
Oil Sump Coupling Plate to Clutch Housing	10 mm Setscrew	50	37	5,1
Overdrive Adaptor Fixings	5/16" UNF Setscrew	27	20	2,7
Pipe, Clutch Master Cylinder to Slave Cylinder	12 mm Tube Nut	12	9	1,2
Prop Shaft to Gearbox and Rear Axle	3/8" UNF Bolt	46	34	4,7
Prop Shaft Safety Strap Attachment	8 mm Bolt	28	21	2,9
Reverse Idler Spindle Locating Screw	5/16" UNF Pointed Setscrew	19	14	1,9
Selector Shaft to Forks	5/16" UNF Taper Setscrew	13	10	1,4
Slave Cylinder to Boss	5/16" UNF Bolt	12	9	1,2
Slave Cylinder to Clutch Housing	8 mm Bolt	28	21	2,9
Slave Cylinder Attachment	5/16" UNF Setscrew	27	20	2,7
Sump Coupling Plate to Clutch Housing	10 mm Setscrew	50	37	5,1
Top Cover to Gearbox Case	1/4" UNF Bolt	13	10	1,3
Top Cover to Gearbox Case	1/4" UNF Setscrew	13	10	1,3

Operation	Description	Nm	lbf ft	kgf m
GEARBOX — 5 speed				
Driving flange to mainshaft	18 mm nyloc nut	200	150	20,4
Dustcap assembly to extension housing	6 mm x 12 mm Setscrew	10	7	0,9
Extension and centre plate to main case	8 mm x 55 mm bolt	28	21	2,9
Fifth gear selector fork pivot bracket to centre plate	8 mm x 25 mm	28	21	2,9
Front cover to maincase	8 mm x 25 mm Setscrew	28	21	2,9
Interlock spool retainer to gearbox case	6 mm x 16 mm Setscrew	10	7	0,9
'J' coupling pin to main selector shaft	8 mm on pin	20	15	1,8
Mounting bracket upper fixing	8 mm x 20 mm Setscrew	28	21	2,9
Mounting bracket lower fixing	8 mm x 30 mm Bolt	28	21	2,9
Magnetic drain plug	16 mm Plug	35	26	3,5
Oil pump body to rear extension	6 mm x 20 mm screw	10	7	0,9
Oil inlet access hole blanking	8 mm x 8 mm socket Locwel Setscrew	20	15	1,8
Reverse lever mounting pin to centre plate	10 mm on pin	28	21	2,9
Reverse baulk plate to gearbox extension	6 mm x 40 mm Bolt	10	7	0,9
Remote control housing to gearcase rear extension	8 mm x 40 mm Setscrew	20	15	1,8
Speedo cable clip to gearbox	6 mm x 20 mm Setscrew	10	7	0,9
Torsion spring brackets to gearbox extension	6 mm x 20 mm Setscrew	10	7	0,9
Torsion spring adjuster screw locking	8 mm x 25 mm Setscrew	20	15	1,8
REAR AXLE — 4 SPEED GEARBOX				
Crown Wheel Attachment	3/8" UNF Bolt	62	46	6,3
Drain Plug	3/8" Plug	34	25	3,4
Hub to Axle Shaft	5/8" UNF on Axle	160	120	16,5
Hypoid Housing to Axle Casing	5/16" UNF Bolt	27	20	2,7
Hypoid Housing Bearing Cap Retention	3/8" UNF Bolt	52	38	5,2
Hypoid Flange to Pinion	5/8" on Pinion	Tighten to obtain correct pre load as specified in Division 51.		
Wheel Attachment	12 mm Stud	100	75	10,3
Alloy Wheel Attachment	12 mm Stud	120	88	12,2

TORQUE WRENCH SETTINGS

(continued)

Operation	Description	Nm	lbf ft	kgf m
REAR AXLE – 5 SPEED GEARBOX				
Rear cover to axle case	8 mm Setscrew	28	21	2,9
Pinion oil seal housing to axle case	10 mm Setscrew	50	37	4,0
Differential unit bearing caps to axle case		100	75	10,2
Crown wheel to differential unit (with Loctite)	12 mm Bolt	122	90	12,2
Pinion Flange to pinion	16 mm Myloc nut	160	120	16,5
Axle shafts/backplates to axle casing	10 mm Setscrew	50	37	5,1
FRONT SUSPENSION				
Anti-Roll Bar Clamp Bolts	10 mm Bolt	40	30	4,0
Anti-Role Bar to Crossmember	10 mm Bolt	50	37	5,1
Anti Roll Bar to Lower Link	12 mm on Bar	80	59	8,1
Sub-frame Attachment Front Fixing	12 mm Bolt	80	59	8,1
Sub-frame Attachment Rear Fixing	12 mm Bolt	80	59	8,1
Damper Unit Closure Nut	1.781" x 24 UNF	100	74	10,2
Hub to Stub-Axle	9/16" UNF on Axle	Tighten to 5 lbf ft (0,69 kgf m) unscrew one flat and insert pin		
Lower Link to Crossmember	12 mm Bolt	80	59	8,1
Lower Link to Strut Assembly	1/2" UNF on Ball Joint	61	45	6,2
Strut Mounting to Body	8 mm on Mounting Studs	28	21	2,9
Strut to Mounting	12 mm on Cartridge	60	44	6,0
Tie Rod Lever to Stub Axle	12 mm Bolt	100	74	10,2
Wheel Attachment	12 mm Stud	100	74	10,2
Alloy Wheel Attachment	12 mm Stud	120	88	12,2
REAR SUSPENSION				
Anti Roll Bar to Lower Link	10 mm x 30 Bolt	50	37	5,1
	Clamp Nut	27	20	2,7
Damper to Trailing Arm	3/8" UNF on Damper	19	14	1,9
	Lock Nut	27	20	2,7
Lower Link to Body and Axle	7/16" UNF Bolt	65	48	6,6
Upper Link to Body and Axle	7/16" UNF Bolt	65	48	6,6
STEERING				
Rack (Pinion Side) to Crossmember	10 mm Bolt	40	30	4,0
Rack to Crossmember	10 mm Bolt	40	30	4,0
Steering Column Clamp to Upper Column	8 mm Bolt	10	7	0,9
Steering Column Lock Shear Head Bolt	Shear Bolt	Tighten to shear		
Steering Column to Body	Shear Bolt	Tighten to shear		
Steering Column Clamp Locating Plate Attachment	7/16" UNF Grub Screw	20	15	2,0
Steering Column Clamp Locating Plate Attachment	7/16" UNF Jam Nut	50	37	5,1
Steering Column Clamp to Column	1/4" Bolt	12	9	1,2

Operation	Description	Nm	lbf ft	kgf m
STEERING (continued)				
Steering Column Rail to 'A' Post	6 mm Screw	10	7	0,9
Steering Column Support Rail to Tunnel Bracket	6 mm Screw	10	7	0,9
Steering Wheel to Column	11/16" Steering Wheel Nut	50	37	5,1
Tie Rod End Ball Joint Assembly	12 mm on Ball Joint	50	37	5,1
Tie Rod End Ball Joint to Tie-Rod	14 mm Locknut	50	37	5,1
Tube to Support Rail	6 mm Screw	10	7	0,9
Tube to Dash and Pedal Bracket	6 mm Screw	10	7	0,9
Universal Joint Assembly to Upper and Lower Columns and Rack	8 mm Bolt	28	21	2,9
BRAKES				
Brake and Clutch Pedal Mounting Bracket Attachment	8 mm Setscrew	28	21	2,9
Brake Master Cylinder Attachment	8 mm Stud	14	10	1,3
Caliper Assembly Attachment	12 mm Bolt	100	74	10,2
Disc to Hub	3/8" UNC Bolt	43	32	4,4
Disc Shield Assembly to Stub Axle	6 mm Setscrew	10	7	0,9
Front Hose to Caliper	10 mm Nut	15	11	1,4
Hand Brake Cable to Lever on Backplate	5/16" UNF Fork End	10	7	0,9
Hand Brake Compensator Lever to Abutment Boss	6 mm Setscrew	10	7	0,9
Hand Brake Fulcrum Compensator	8 mm Nut	28	21	2,9
Hand Brake Mounting Bracket and Clamp Plate to Floor	6 mm Setscrew	10	7	0,9
Master Cylinder to Pressure Reducing Valve	10 mm Male tube nut	12	9	1,2
Pipe, Pressure Reducing Valve to Front Hoses	10 mm Female pipe nut	12	9	1,2
Pipe, Pressure Reducing Valve to Rear Hoses	10 mm Male tube nut	12	6	1,2
Pipe, Pressure Reducing Valve and Bracket to Turret	10 mm Female pipe nut / 8 mm Bolt	28	21	2,9
Rear Brake Backplate Attachment	5/16" UNF Bolt	19	14	1,9
Rear Brake Drum to Hub	1/4" UNF Setscrew	10	7	0,9
Rear Hose to R.H. Rear Wheel Cylinder	10 mm Female pipe nut	12	9	1,2
R.H. Rear Wheel Cylinder to	10 mm Male tube nut	12	9	1,2
L.H. Rear Wheel Cylinder	10 mm Female pipe nut / 10 mm Male tube nut	12	9	1,2
BODY				
Accelerator Pedal to Mounting Bracket	6 mm Setscrew	10	7	0,9
Accelerator Mounting Bracket to Dash	6 mm Setscrew	10	7	0,9
Bonnet Buffer Fixing	8 mm Jam Nut	12	9	1,2
Bonnet Hinge to Front Panel Assembly	6 mm Setscrew	10	7	0,9
Bonnet Lock Striker to Bonnet	8 mm Setscrew	28	21	2,9
Bonnet Lock to Body	8 mm Setscrew	28	21	2,9
Bonnet Release Cable to Fascia Support Rail Bracket	1/2" UNF Jam Nut	12	9	1,2
Body Side to Front End Assembly	6 mm Setscrew	10	7	0,9

Operation	Description	Nm	lbf ft	kgf m
Bonnet Striker Pin	3/8" UNF on striker pin	19	14	1,9
Dash Assembly	6 mm Weld Stud	8	6	0,8
Deflector to Re-inforced Steering Column Support Rail	6 mm Setscrew	10	7	0,9
Door Division Channel to Door	6 mm Setscrew	10	7	0,9
Door Glass Run Channel to Door	6 mm Setscrew	10	7	0,9
Door Hinge to Door	8 mm Stud on Hinge Assembly	28	21	2,9
Door Lock Attachment	6 mm Setscrew Csk.	10	7	0,9
Door Striker to 'B' Post	6 mm Setscrew	10	7	0,9
Fascia Attachment Brackets (Upper) to Dash Top	6 mm Setscrew	10	7	0,9
Fascia Support Bracket (Lower) to Support Rail	6 mm Setscrew	6	4.5	0,6
Fascia to Dash	6 mm Setscrew	10	7	0,9
Front Bumper Cover Assembly to Front Bumper Bar	6 mm Setscrew	3	2.2	0,3
Front Bumper Assembly to Body	8 mm Weld Bolt	14	10	1,4
Front Tie Down Bracket to Front Crossmember Panel	8 mm Setscrew	28	21	2,9
Front Upper Assembly to Front Fenders	6 mm Setscrew	10	7	0,9
Fuel Tank Attachment	10 mm Stud	50	37	5,1
Mirror Mounting Bracket to Door	6 mm Setscrew	10	7	0,9
Mirror Mounting Bracket to Door Inner Panel	6 mm Setscrew	10	7	0,9
Plenum Panel Fixing	6 mm Pan Head Screw	6	4.5	0,6
Radiator Crossmember to Longitudinal Members	8 mm Setscrew	28	21	2,9
Radiator Fan Guard to Radiator Attachment	8 mm Setscrew	28	21	2,9
Radiator Mounting Bracket to Bonnet Hinge Mounting Panel	8 mm Weld Bolt	14	10	1,4
Rear Bumper to Body	8 mm Weld Bolt	20	15	2,0
Rear Bumper Assembly to Body	8 mm Weld Bolt	14	10	1,4
Rear Bumper Corner Struts to Body	8 mm Setscrew	28	21	2,9
Rear Bumper Cover to Rear Bumper	6 mm setscrew	3	2.2	0,3
Rear Bumper Corner Struts to Rear Bumper	8 mm Weld Bolt	20	15	2,0
Relay Plate to Bracket on Dash Front	6 mm Setscrew	10	7	0,9
Seat Belt Buckle Assembly to Seat Slide	7/16" UNF Setscrew	43	32	4,4
Seat Belt (Inner to Seat Slide)	7/16" UNF Setscrew	43	32	4,4
Seat Belt to Wheel Arch	7/16" UNF Setscrew	43	32	4,4
Seat Belt to Mounting Bracket	7/16" UNF Setscrew	43	32	4,4
Seat Belt Warning Switch to Gearbox	3/8" UNC Switch	20	15	2,0
Seat Slides to Floor	8 mm Cap Screw	28	21	2,9
Seat Slides to Seat Frame	6 mm Cap Screw	10	7	0,9

Operation	Description	Nm	lbf ft	kgf m
Side Lamp and Head Lamp Cables to Radiator closing Panel	6 mm Setscrew	10	7	0,9
Trunk Lid Hinges to Trunk Lid	8 mm Setscrew	28	21	2,9
Trunk Lid Hinges to Body	6 mm Setscrew	10	7	0,9
Trunk Lid Support to Support Bracket Tonneau	6 mm Setscrew	10	7	0,9
Trunk Lock to Lid	6 mm Setscrew	10	7	0,9
Trunk Lock Striker to Body	1/4" UNF Setscrew	12	9	1,2
Window Regulator Attachment	1/4" UNF Setscrew	12	9	1,2

ELECTRICAL

NOTE: Refer to Section 86 for additional torque settings on proprietary items

Operation	Description	Nm	lbf ft	kgf m
Battery Attachment	1/4" on Fixing Rod	3	2	0,27
Battery Earth to Body	6 mm Setscrew	10	7	0,9
Headlamp Box to Hinge Arm	6 mm Weld Bolt	6	4.5	0,6
Headlamp Hinge Arm to Pivot Bracket	10 mm	40	30	4,0
Headlamp Hinge Arm to Bracket Assemblies	8 mm Setscrew	20	15	2,0
Headlamp Hinge Arm to Pivot Pin	8 mm	20	15	2,0
Headlamp Mechanism to Body	8 mm Weld Bolt	14	10	1,4
Headlamp Mechanism Crank Arm to Gearbox	6 mm Nut	15	11	1,4
Headlamp Raising Link Adjustment	6 mm Jam Nut	6	4.5	0,6
Headlamp Tension Spring Attachment	6 mm Shouldered Bolt	8	6	0,8
Heater Mountings	6 mm Setscrew	10	7	0,9
Horn Attachment	6 mm Setscrew	10	7	0,9
Ignition Coil to Mounting Plate	6 mm Setscrew	10	7	0,9

AIR CONDITIONING

Operation	Description	Nm	lbf ft	kgf m
Compressor Mounting Bracket to Cylinder Head	5/16" UNF Bolt	27	20	2,7
Compressor Mounting Bracket to Cylinder Block	5/16" UNF Bolt	27	20	2,7
Compressor Mounting Bracket to Cylinder Block	5/16" UNF Setscrew	27	20	2,7
Compressor Mounting Bracket to Compressor	3/8" UNC Setscrew	40	30	4,0
Compressor Mounting Bracket to Compressor	3/8" UNC Stud	32	24	3,2
Compressor Belt Tension Adjustment	3/8" UNF Locknut	19	14	1,9
Condenser Fan Motor Attachment	5 mm Setscrew	3	2	0,27
Hose — Compressor to Condenser	3/4" Crimp Back Nut	40	30	4,0
Hose — Condenser to Receiver Driver	5/8" Crimp Back Nut	28	21	2,9
Hose — Evaporator to Compressor	7/8" Crimp Back Nut	50	37	5,1
Hose — Evaporator to Receiver Drier	5/8" Crimp Back Nut	28	21	2,9
Ranco Valve to Receiver Drier	7/16" Flare Nut	12	9	1,2
Rotalock Valve to Compressor	1" UNS	50	37	5,1

RECOMMENDED LUBRICANTS & ANTI-FREEZE SOLUTIONS – BRITISH ISLES – ALL SEASONS
(THE PRODUCTS RECOMMENDED ARE NOT LISTED IN ORDER OF PREFERENCE)

COMPONENT	BP	CASTROL	DUCKHAMS	ESSO	MOBIL	PETROFINA	TEXACO	SHELL
Engine Carburetter Dashpots and Oil can — Oils must meet Leyland Cars Specification BLS.OL.02	BP Super Visco-Static 20–50	Castrol GTX	Duckhams Q Motor Oil	Esso Uniflo 15W/50	Mobil Super 15W–50	Fina Super grade Motor Oil S.A.E. 20W–50	Havoline Motor Oil 20W–50	Shell Super Multigrade 20W–50
Manual Gearbox – 4 Speed*	BP Gear Oil S.A.E. 90 EP	Castrol Hypoy	Duckhams Hypoid 90	Esso Gear Oil GX 85W/140	Mobilube HD 90	Fina Pontonic MP S.A.E. 90	Texaco Multigear Lubricant EP 90	Shell Spirax 90 EP
Manual Gearbox – 5 Speed†	BP Gear Oil S.A.E. 80 EP	Castrol Hypoy B 75	Duckhams Hypoid 75	Esso Gear Oil GP 80W	Mobilube HD 80	Fina Pontonic MP SAE 80	Texaco Multigear Lubricant EP 80	Shell Spirax HD 75/80W — Shell Donax TF
Rear Axle	BP Gear Oil S.A.E. 90 EP	Castrol Hypoy	Duckhams Hypoid 90	Esso Gear Oil GX 85W/140	Mobilube HD 90	Fina Pontonic MP S.A.E. 90	Texaco Multigear Lubricant EP 90	Shell Spirax 90 EP
Rear Hubs, Brake Cables, Grease Gun‡	BP Energrease L 2	Castrol LM Grease	Duckhams LD 10 Grease	Esso Multi-Purpose Grease H	Mobilgrease MP or MS	Fina Marson HTL 2 Grease	Marfak All Purpose Grease	Shell Retinax A
Automatic Transmission and Power Steering	BP Autran G	Castrol TQF	Duckhams 'Q'-Matic	Esso Glide (Type 'G')	Mobil ATF 210	Fina Purfimatic 33F	Texamatic Type 'G'	Shell Donax TF
Clutch and Brake Reservoirs	Unipart Universal Brake Fluid or other brake fluids having a minimum boiling point of 260°C (500°F) and complying with FMVSS DOT 3 or SAE J1703 specification.							
Approved Anti-Freeze	Unipart Universal Anti-Freeze.							

* Manual gearbox, if drained, MUST be refilled with Hypoid 75W gear oil.

† Manual gearbox, if drained, MUST be refilled with Hypoid 75W gear oil. For service top-up use Hypoid 75W gear oil, or where this oil is not available, the Hypoid 80W oils shown above may be used.

‡ Front hub grease — Mobilgrease MS or Super.

RECOMMENDED LUBRICANTS AND ANTI-FREEZE SOLUTIONS – OVERSEAS MARKETS

	SERVICE CLASSIFICATION	AMBIENT TEMPERATURE °C (-30, -20, -10, 0, +10, +20)
ENGINE	Oils must meet Leyland Cars' Specification BLS.OL.02 and/or the European Motor Manufacturers' requirements and/or A.P.I.–SE Performance Level	5W/20, 5W/30, 5W/40; 10W/30; 10W/40, 10W/50; 15W/40, 15W/50; 20W/40, 20W/50
FINAL DRIVE	A.P.I. – GL5 / MIL-L-2105B	HYPOID 90
MANUAL GEARBOX* –4 SPEED	A.P.I. – GL4 / MIL-L-2105	HYPOID 80W / HYPOID 90
MANUAL GEARBOX† – 5 SPEED	A.P.I. – GL4 / MIL-L-2105	HYPOID 80 / HYPOID 75W
AUTOMATIC GEARBOX POWER STEERING	ATF TYPE G	
HUBS‡ AND CHASSIS GREASE POINTS	N.L.G.I.–2 Multi-purpose Grease	
BRAKE & CLUTCH RESERVOIRS – USA	LOCKHEED 3295 UNIVERSAL BRAKE FLUID or other brake fluids having a minimum boiling point of 260°C (500°F) and complying with FMVSS 116 DOT3 specifications.	
– except USA	UNIPART UNIVERSAL BRAKE FLUID or other brake fluids having a minimum boiling point of 260°C (500°F) and complying with FMVSS 116 DOT3 or S.A.E. J1703d specifications.	
ANTI-FREEZE	Permanent type ethylene glycol base with suitable inhibitor for MIXED METAL ENGINES.	
WINDSHIELD WASHER	Windshield Washer Anti-Freeze Fluid (Proprietary Brands).	

* Manual gearbox, if drained, MUST be refilled with Hypoid 75W gear oil.
† Manual gearbox, if drained, MUST be refilled with Hypoid 75W gear oil. For Service top-up use Hypoid 75W gear oil, or where this oil is not available, Hypoid 80W oils may be used.
‡ Front hub grease = N.L.G.I. No. 2 high melting-point grease.

ANTI-FREEZE SOLUTIONS

ANTI-FREEZE CONCENTRATION		25%	30%	35%	50%
SPECIFIC GRAVITY OF COOLANT AT 15.5° C (60° F)		1.039	1.048	1.054	1.076
ANTI-FREEZE QUANTITY EXPANSION TANK SYSTEM	US pints UK pints Litres	3.875 3.25 1.85	4.65 3.9 2.22	5.425 4.55 2.59	7.75 6.5 3.7
ANTI-FREEZE QUANTITY HEADER TANK SYSTEM	US pints UK pints Litres	4.02 3.35 1.9	4.82 4.02 2.28	5.628 4.69 2.66	8.04 6.7 3.8
DEGREE OF PROTECTION	**Complete** Car may be driven away immediately from cold	−12° C 10° F	−16° C 3° F	−20° C −4° F	−36° C −33° F
	Safe Limit Coolant in mushy state. Engine may be started and driven away after short warm-up period	−18° C 0° F	−22° C −8° F	−28° C −18° F	−41° C −42° F
	Lower Protection Prevents frost damage to cylinder head, block and radiator. Thaw out before starting engine.	−26° C −15° F	−32° C −26° F	−37° C −35° F	−47° C −53° F

LUBRICATION — Carburetter engined vehicles

NOTE: Figures in italics refer to U.S.A. market specification vehicles.

NOTE: Ensure that the vehicle is standing on a level surface when checking the oil levels.

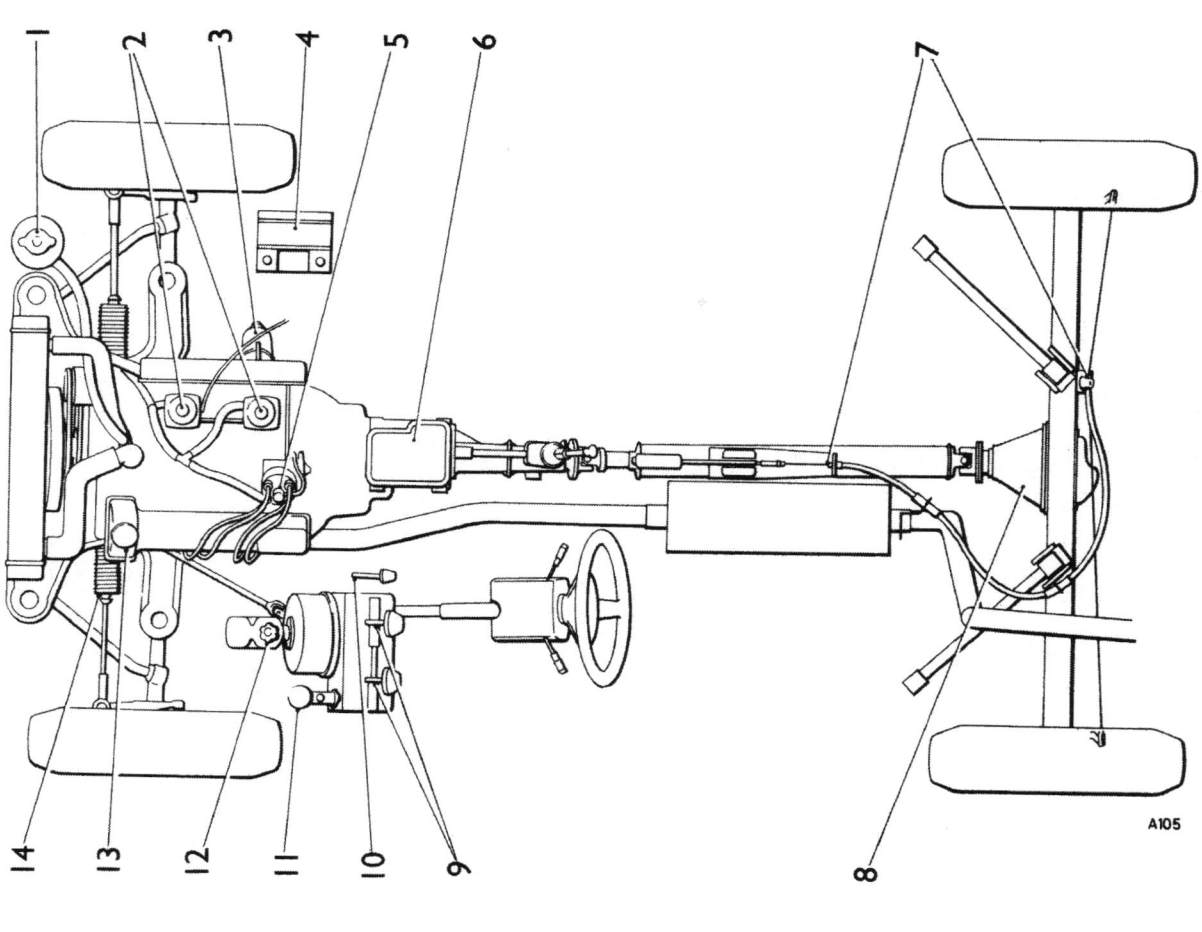

Weekly or before a long journey
1   Check/top up cooling system level.
13 Check engine oil level.

Every 3,000 Miles (5,000 km) — *3, 9, 16, 22, 28, 34, 41, 47 miles x 1000*
1   Check/top up cooling system level.
11 Check/top up clutch fluid reservoir.
12 Check/top up brake fluid reservoir.
13 Check/top up engine oil level.

Every 6,000 Miles (10,000 km) — *6, 19, 31, 44 miles x 1000*
1   Check/top up cooling system.
3   Renew oil filter.
4   Clean and grease battery connections.
6   Check/top up level of gearbox oil.
7   Lubricate handbrake linkage and cable guides.
8   Check/top up level of final drive oil.
10 Lubricate accelerator linkage/pedal fulcrum.
11 Check/top up clutch fluid reservoir.
12 Check/top up brake fluid reservoir.
13 Drain engine oil and refill.
14 Lubricate steering rack and pinion.
    Lubricate all locks, door hinges, strikers and bonnet release.

Every 12,000 Miles (20,000 km) —*12.5, 25, 37.5, 50 miles x 1000*
1   Check/top up cooling system.
2   Check/top up carburetter piston dampers.
3   Renew oil filter.
4   Clean and grease battery connections.
5   Lubricate distributor.
6   Check/top up level of gearbox oil.
7   Lubricate handbrake linkage and cable guides.
8   Check/top up level of final drive oil.
9   Lubricate brake and clutch pedal pivots.

10 Lubricate accelerator linkage/pedal fulcrum.
11 Check/top up clutch fluid reservoir.
12 Check/top up brake fluid reservoir.
13 Drain engine oil and refill.
14 Lubricate steering rack and pinion.
    Lubricate all locks, door hinges, strikers and bonnet release.

For Fuel injection vehicles refer to Maintenance Summary in Section 10

MAINTENANCE SUMMARY, U.K & EUROPE

OPERATION No.	MILEAGE × 1000	KILOMETRES × 1000
10.10.03	1	1.6
10.10.06	3, 9, 15, 21, 27, 33, 39, 45	5, 15, 25, 35, 45, 55, 65, 75
10.10.12	6, 18, 30, 42	10, 30, 50, 70
10.10.24	12, 24, 36, 48	20, 40, 60, 80

Operation Description

Operation Description	1000 Miles / 1600 km	10.10.06	10.10.12	10.10.24
ENGINE				
1 Check/top up engine oil	X	X	X	X
2 Check/top up cooling system	X	X	X	X
3 Check/adjust operation of all washers and top up reservoirs	X		X	X
4 Renew engine oil	X	X	X	X
5 Renew engine oil filter	X	X	X	X
6 Lubricate accelerator control linkage (and pedal pivot) – check operation	X		X	X
7 Check cooling and heater system for leaks and hoses for security and condition	X	X	X	X
8 Check for oil leaks	X	X	X	X
9 Check/adjust torque of cylinder head nuts/bolts	X			
10 Check driving belts, adjust or renew	X		X	X
11 Check security of engine mountings	X		X	X
12 Check/adjust carburetter idle settings	X		X	X
13 Top up carburetter piston dampers	X		X	X
14 Renew carburetter air cleaner element				X
15 Clean fuel pump filter	X			X
IGNITION				
16 Clean/adjust spark plugs			X	X
17 Renew spark plugs				X
18 Check distributor points: adjust or renew	X		X	X
19 Lubricate distributor				X
20 Check/adjust ignition timing using electronic equipment	X		X	X

OPERATION No.	1000 Miles / 1600 km	10.10.06	10.10.12	10.10.24
TRANSMISSION				
21 Check for oil leaks	X	X	X	X
22 Check/top up gearbox oil	X	X	X	X
23 Check/top up rear axle/final drive oil				X
24 Check tightness of propeller shaft coupling bolts				X
25 Check clutch pipes for leaks and chafing	X	X	X	X
26 Check/top up clutch fluid reservoir	X	X	X	X
27 Lubricate clutch pedal pivots				X
28 Check/top up automatic transmission fluid			X	X
29 Lubricate automatic gearbox exposed selector Linkage				X
STEERING AND SUSPENSION				
30 Check steering rack/gear for oil/fluid leaks	X	X	X	X
31 Check security of suspension fixings	X		X	X
32 Check condition and security of steering unit, joints and gaiters	X	X	X	X
33 Check/adjust front wheel alignment	X			
34 Adjust front hub bearing end float				
35 Lubricate steering rack and pinion			X	X
36 Check shock absorbers for fluid leaks			X	X
BRAKES				
37 Inspect brake pads for wear and discs for condition		X	X	X
38 Inspect brake linings/pads for wear and drums/discs for condition	X	X	X	X
39 Check/top up brake fluid reservoir(s)	X		X	X
40 Check foot-brake operation: adjust to manufacturer's instructions (Self-adjusting)				
41 Check handbrake operation, adjust to manufacturer's instructions	X		X	X
42 Lubricate brake pedal pivot(s)			X	X
43 Lubricate handbrake mechanical linkage and cable guides (lever pivot)			X	X
44 Check visually hydraulic hoses, pipes and unions for chafing, cracks, leaks and corrosion	X	X	X	X
45 Check brake servo hose(s) for security and condition	X	X	X	X
ELECTRICAL				
46 Check function of original equipment, i.e. interior and exterior lamps, horns, wipers and warning indicators	X	X	X	X
47 Check/top up battery electrolyte	X	X	X	X
48 Clean and grease battery connections			X	X
49 Check/adjust headlamps alignment				X
50 Check, if necessary renew, wiper blades	X		X	X

PREVENTIVE MAINTENANCE

In addition to the recommended periodical inspection of brake components it is advisable as the car ages and as a precaution against the effects of wear and deterioration to make a more searching inspection and renew parts as necessary.

It is recommended that:

1   Disc brake pads, drum brake linings, hoses and pipes should be examined at intervals no greater than those laid down in the Maintenance Summary Chart.

2   Brake fluid should be changed completely every 18,000 miles (30,000 km) or 18 months whichever is the sooner.

3   All fluid seals in the hydraulic system should be renewed and all flexible hoses should be examined and renewed if necessary every 36,000 miles (60,000 km) or 3 years whichever is the sooner. At the same time the working surfaces of the pistons and bores of the master cylinder, wheel cylinders and other slave cylinders should be examined and new parts fitted where necessary.

Care must be taken always to observe the following points:

a   At all times use the recommended brake fluid.

b   Never leave fluid in unsealed containers, it absorbs moisture quickly and can be dangerous if used in the brake system in this condition.

c   Fluid drained from the system or used for bleeding should be discarded.

d   The necessity for absolute cleanliness throughout cannot be over-emphasized.

Replacing brake shoes

When it becomes necessary to renew the brake-shoes it is essential that only genuine shoes, with the correct grade of lining, are used. Always fit new shoes as complete sets, never individually or as a single wheel set. Serious consequences could result from out-of-balance braking due to the mixing of lining.

OPERATION No.	1000 Miles / 1600 km	10.10.06	10.10.12	10.10.24
EXHAUST AND FUEL PIPES				
51 Check exhaust system for leaks and security	x	x	x	x
52 Check fuel system for leaks, pipes and unions for chafing and corrosion	x	x	x	x
WHEELS AND TYRES				
53 Check/adjust tyre pressures including spare	x	x	x	x
54 Check that tyres comply with manufacturer's specification	x	x	x	x
55 Check tightness of road wheel fastenings	x	x	x	x
56 Check tyres for external cuts in tyre fabric, exposure of ply or cord structure, lumps or bulges	x	x	x	x
57 Check tyres for tread depth and visually for external cuts in tyre fabric, exposure of ply or cord structure, lumps or bulges	x		x	x
Important: If tyres do not conform with legal requirements report to owner				
BODY				
58 Lubricate all locks, hinges and door check mechanism (not steering lock)	x	x	x	x
59 Check condition and security of seats and seat belts	x	x	x	x
60 Check rear view mirrors for cracks and crazing	x	x	x	x
61 Check operation of all door, bonnet and boot locks	x	x	x	x
62 Check operation of seat belt warning system	x	x	x	x
63 Check operation of seat belt inertia reel mechanism	x	x	x	x
64 Check operation of window controls	x	x	x	x
65 Check tightness of sub frame/body mountings	x			x
66 Ensure cleanliness of controls, door handles and steering wheel	x	x	x	x
ROAD TEST				
67 Road/roller test and check function of all instrumentation	x	x	x	x
68 Report additional work required	x	x	x	x

At 36,000 miles (60,000 km) or 3 years (whichever is the sooner).

Renew the air filter in the brake servo unit.

MAINTENANCE SUMMARY – UK & Europe

The Maintenance Summary list gives details of mileage intervals for the following operations. The figure in parentheses to the left of each heading refers to the item number on the summary list.

ENGINE

(1) Check/top up engine oil level

NOTE: Allow time for the oil to drain back into the sump after running the engine.

1 Stand the vehicle on level ground.
   Withdraw the dipstick, wipe it clean and push fully home again before withdrawing it for reading.

2 Add oil via the filler cap until the level reaches the 'High' mark on the dipstick.
   DO NOT OVERFILL and ensure that the dipstick and filler cap are replaced.

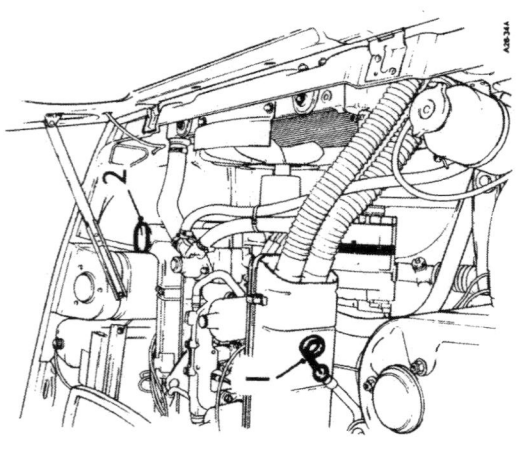
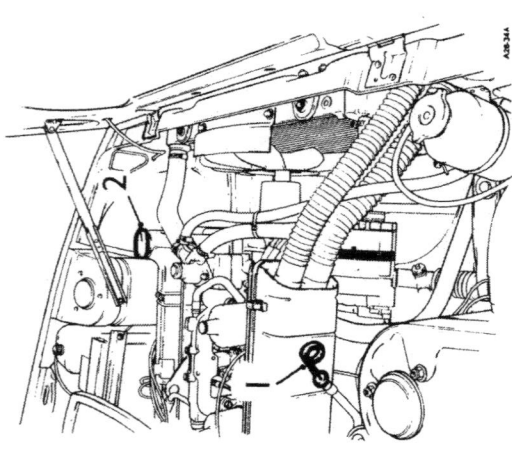

(2) Check/top up cooling system

WARNING: Do NOT remove cooling system filler caps or plugs when engine is hot.

1 Slowly turn the pressure cap anti-clockwise until the resistance of the safety stop is felt. Leave the cap in this position until all pressure is released. Press the cap downwards against the spring to clear the safety stops and continue turning until it can be lifted off.

2 Maintain the level of the coolant. See 26.10.01.

NOTE: Ensure that the specific gravity of the coolant is maintained, see 'LUBRICANTS, FLUIDS & FUEL'.

(3) Check/adjust operation of all washers and top up reservoirs

1 Replenish the container with clean soft water. The addition of a small amount of mild detergent will prevent smearing on the windscreen.

2 During freezing conditions it is beneficial to fill the container with a mixture of one part methylated spirits (wood alcohol) to two parts of water. This will assist in the dispersal of snow and ice from the screen.

3 Do not add anti-freeze solutions to the container as this will discolour the paintwork and damage wiper blades and sealing rubber.

(4) Renew engine oil

NOTE: This operation is best carried out when the engine is warm and with the vehicle standing level on a ramp or over a pit.

1 To drain the sump, unscrew the drain plug three complete turns to direct the oil stream into a receptacle while the engine is warm. When the rate of flow lessens remove the plug completely. Refit the plug and refill the sump with the appropriate grade of engine oil. The use of additives is unnecessary.

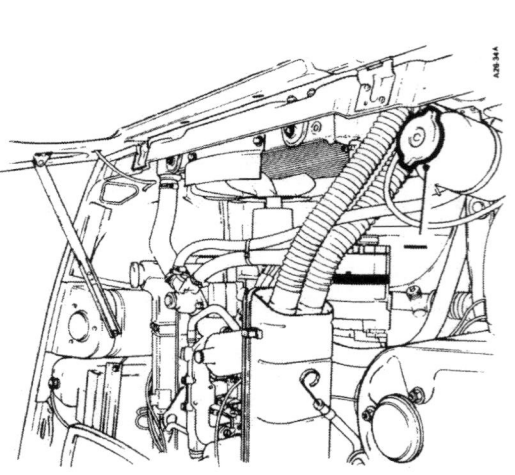

(5) Renew engine oil filter

See 12.60.02.

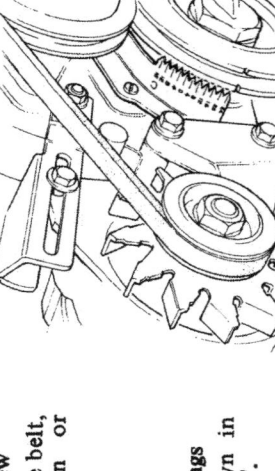

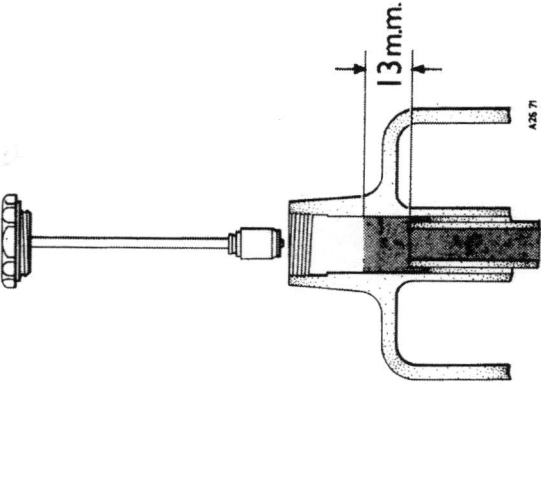

13 m.m.

(6) Lubricate accelerator linkage/pedal fulcrum and check operation

Lubricate
Use an oil can, lubricate the accelerator linkage on the carburetter and the accelerator pedal pivot. Wipe away any surplus oil to avoid drips or any possibility of staining the carpet inside the car.

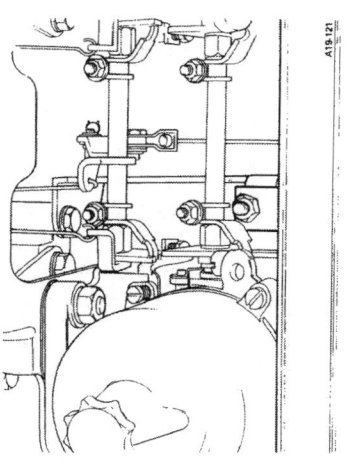

Check operation
Check carburetter throttle response to initial movement of the accelerator pedal. If required, adjust the throttle cable at the carburetter.
Check carburetter throttle position with accelerator pedal fully depressed, by observing that the carburetter lever(s) move to a positive stop.
If the throttle movement is not satisfactory, investigate the cause and rectify as necessary, proceeding in the following order.
Check that the throttle pedal movement is not restricted by floor mats or carpet etc. Check the carburetter lever(s) for correct position and settings, see 19.15.02.
Check the throttle cable location and condition.

(9) Check/adjust torque of cylinder head nuts/bolts
See 12.29.27.

(10) Check driving belt; adjust or renew
Check and adjust alternator drive belt, see 86.10.05; if visibly worn or damaged, renew.

(11) Check security of engine mountings
Using the torque figures shown in 'TORQUE WRENCH SETTINGS'.

(12) Check/adjust carburetter idle speed
See 19.15.02.

(7) Check cooling and heater systems for leaks and hoses for security and condition
1 Check for leaks from engine and radiator drain taps/plugs (where fitted).
2 Check for leaks from the water hose joints.
3 Check for leaks from the water hoses through damage or porosity.
4 Check for leaks from the water pump, thermostat housing, radiator and heater unit.
5 Report any leaks found.

(8) Check/report oil/fuel/fluid leaks
1 Check for oil leaks from the engine and transmission.
2 Check for fuel leaks from the pump, carburetter pipes, joints and unions.
3 Check for fluid leaks from the brake master cylinder, pipes, joints and unions.
4 Check for fluid leaks from the clutch master cylinder, pipes, joints and unions.
5 Report any leaks found.

(13) Top up carburetter piston dampers
1 Unscrew and remove the damper assembly from the top of the carburetter.
2 Top up with clean engine oil to bring the level 13 mm (½ in) above the top of the hollow piston rod.
3 Push the damper assembly back into position and screw the cap firmly into the reservoir.
NOTE: Under no circumstances should a heavy-bodied lubricant be used.

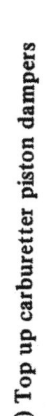

(14) Renew carburetter air cleaner element

See 19.10.08.

(15) Clean fuel pump filter

1 Remove the centre bolt from the fuel pump top cover.
2 Withdraw the filter gauge and wash it in clean fuel.
3 Using a small screwdriver, loosen any sediment in the chamber.
4 Blow out the dirt using a low pressure air line.
5 Renew the gasket if necessary and refit the filter gauge and cover.

NOTE: Leakage of air at the gasket or centre bolt will prevent the pump from functioning correctly.

IGNITION

(16) Clean/adjust spark plugs

For each spark plug in turn:

1 Remove the ignition high tension lead from the plug.
2 Unscrew the plug from the engine using a special plug spanner or a box type spanner. See (17) for method of removal.
3 Wipe clean the ceramic body of the plug.
4 Visually check the plug body for cracks and renew the plug if any cracks are present.
5 Unscrew the end terminal cap from the plug.
6 Clean the plug terminal threads with a wire brush.
7 Clean the cap threads using a low pressure air line.
8 Screw the end terminal cap firmly into position on the plug.
9 Clean the electrode area and the plug threads with a wire brush or sand blasting machine.
10 Visually check the electrode for damage and renew the plug if there are any signs of damage.
11 Check the electrode gap, which if correct will just allow 0.025 in (0.64 mm) feeler gauge to slide slowly between the electrodes under light pressure.
12 If adjustment is necessary
  a Using a suitable tool, carefully move the side electrode.
  b Check the gap, repeat this procedure until the gap is correct.
13 Refit the plug to the engine and tighten to the correct torque.
14 Refit the high tension lead to the plug.

(17) Renew spark plugs

For each plug in turn:

1 Remove the ignition high tension lead from the plug.
2 Unscrew the plug from the engine using a special plug spanner or a suitable box spanner.
3 Discard the plug.
4 Visually check the new plug for damage to the body and electrodes, discard the plug if there are any signs of damage.
5 Check the electrode gap on the new plug which when correct will just allow a 0.025 in (0.64 mm) feeler gauge to slide slowly between the electrodes under light pressure.
  If adjustment is necessary, using a suitable tool carefully move the side electrode. Re-check the gap and repeat this procedure until the gap is correct.
6 Fit the new plug to the engine.
7 Tighten the plug to the correct torque.
8 Refit the high tension lead to the plug.

(18) Check distributor points: Adjust or renew

See 86.35.14.

(19) Lubricate distributor

See 86.35.18.

(20) Check/adjust ignition timing using electronic equipment

See 86.35.15.

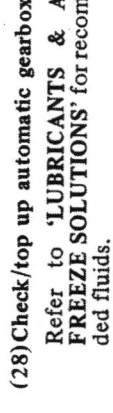

TRANSMISSION

(21) Check for oil leaks

See Maintenance Operation No. 8.

(22) Check/top up gearbox oil

1 With the vehicle standing in a level position, remove the oil level/filler plug and using a suitable dispenser filled with the correct grade oil, see 'LUBRICANTS & ANTI-FREEZE SOLUTIONS', top up the gearbox until the oil is level with the bottom of the filler hole threads.

2 Allow surplus oil to drain away, then refit the filler plug and wipe clean.

(23) Check/top up level of rear axle/final drive oil

1 With the vehicle standing in a level position, remove the oil level/filler plug and top up the final drive unit with the correct grade oil, see 'LUBRICANTS & ANTI-FREEZE SOLUTIONS', until the oil is level with the bottom of the filler hole threads.

2 Allow surplus oil to drain away, then refit the filler plug and wipe clean.

(24) Check tightness of propeller shaft coupling bolts

Refer to 'TORQUE WRENCH SETTINGS'.

(25) Check clutch pipes for leaks and chafing, check visually

1 Clutch pipes, hoses and unions for chafing, leaks and corrosion.

2 Report any defects found.

(26) Check/top up clutch fluid reservoir

Top up when required with new fluid of the type recommended, see 'LUBRICANTS & ANTI-FREEZE SOLUTIONS'.

(27) Lubricate clutch pedal pivots

1 Using an oil can lubricate the clutch pedal pivot.

2 Wipe away the surplus oil to prevent staining the carpet.

(28) Check/top up automatic gearbox fluid

Refer to 'LUBRICANTS & ANTI-FREEZE SOLUTIONS' for recommended fluids.

(29) Lubricate automatic gearbox exposed selector linkage

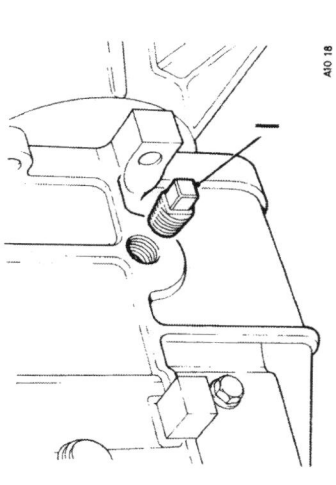

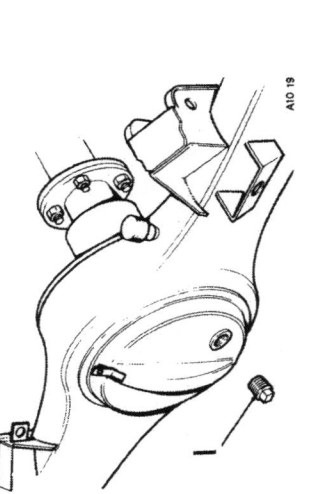

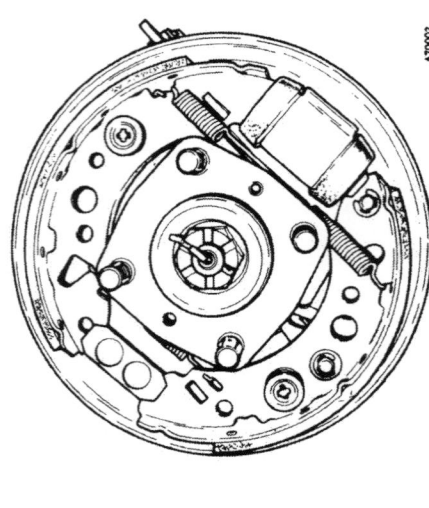

STEERING AND SUSPENSION

(30) Check steering rack/gear for oil fluid leaks

See Maintenance Operation No.8.

(31) Check security of suspension fixings

Refer to 'TORQUE WRENCH SETTINGS'.

(32) Check condition and security of steering unit, joints and gaiters

1 Check security of steering unit mounting and steering joints – refer to 'TORQUE WRENCH SETTINGS'.
2 Check steering for backlash.
3 Check condition of steering gaiters.
4 Report any defects found.

(33) Check/adjust front wheel alignment

See 57.65.01.

(34) Adjust front hub bearing end-float

1 Remove the road wheel.
2 Check the hub for end-float.
3 If any adjustment is required, remove the grease cap, split pin, and nut retaining cap.
4 Tighten the slotted nut as required to eliminate the end-float.
NOTE: A torque of 5 lbf ft (0.691 kgf m) must not be exceeded or damage may be caused to the bearings and the bearing tracks.
5 Refit the nut retaining cap.
6 Insert and lock the split pin.
7 Clean grease cap and refit.
8 Fit the road wheel.

(35) Lubricate steering rack and pinion

1 Wipe clean the plug and surrounding area.
2 Remove the plug.
3 Fit a suitable grease nipple in place of the plug.
4 Apply a grease gun, filled with the correct grade of grease, see 'LUBRICANTS & ANTI-FREEZE SOLUTIONS', to the grease nipple and give five strokes only.

3-5

2-6

A10 20

CAUTION: Over greasing can cause damage to the protective bellows.
5 Remove the grease nipple.
6 Refit the plug.
7 Wipe away any surplus grease.

(36) Check shock absorbers for fluid leaks

Report any fluid leaks found.

BRAKES

(37) Inspect brake pads for wear and discs for condition

1 Jack up the front of the car and place safely onto stands before removing the disc brake pads (see 70.40.02).
CAUTION: Do NOT depress the brake pedal while the pads are removed.
2 Report pad condition if the friction lining has been reduced to 0.125 in (3 mm) or if there is not sufficient material to provide a thickness of 0.125 in (3 mm) at the completion of a further 3,000 miles (5,000 km) motoring.
3 Check the brake discs for excessive scoring and run out and report this if present.
4 Refit the pads, road wheels and lower the car.
5 Firmly depress the footbrake several times to correctly locate the friction pads.

(38) Inspect brake linings/pads for wear and drums/discs for condition

1 Jack up the rear of the car and support the body on stands.
2 Remove the rear road wheels.
3 Remove the rear brake drum, see 70.10.03.
4 Check the brake linings for wear, report if they are excessively worn, damaged or contaminated by oil or grease. Remove any surplus oil or grease and dust linings and drums.
5 Remove the brake drum, see 70.10.03.
6 Fit the rear road wheels and lower the car.
7 See Maintenance No. 35 for the front brake pads and discs inspection.

(39) Check/top up brake fluid reservoir(s)

1 Wipe clean the reservoir cap and surrounding area.
2 Remove the reservoir cap.
3 Check the fluid level against the mark on the side of the reservoir.
4 If necessary, add fluid to bring the level up to the mark on the side of the reservoir.

WARNING: Use only new fluid of the correct specification, see 'LUBRICANTS & ANTI-FREEZE SOLUTIONS'. DO NOT use fluid of unknown origin, or fluid that has been exposed to the atmosphere, or fluid that has been discharged during bleeding operations.

5 Replace the reservoir cap.
6 Remove any spilled fluid with a clean cloth.

CAUTION: Paintwork can be damaged by direct contact with brake fluid.

(40) Check footbrake operation, adjust to manufacturer's instructions (Self-adjusting)

1 With the handbrake off, check the brake pedal for spongy operation.
2 If the pedal has spongy operation, bleed and adjust the brakes, see 70.25.02 and 70.25.03.

(41) Check handbrake operation, adjust to manufacturer's instructions

1 If the handbrake travel is excessive, adjust the handbrake, see 70.35.10.

(42) Lubricate brake pedal pivot(s)

1 Using an oil can, lubricate the brake pedal pivot.
2 Wipe away the surplus oil to prevent staining the carpet.

(43) Lubricate handbrake mechanical linkage and cable guides (lever pivot)

1 Lubricate the handbrake pivot.
2 Smear grease around the handbrake lever cable connection, working it well into the clevis.
3 Smear grease around the brake drum cable connections, working it well into the clevis pin.
4 Grease the exposed section of the inner cable to combat corrosion.

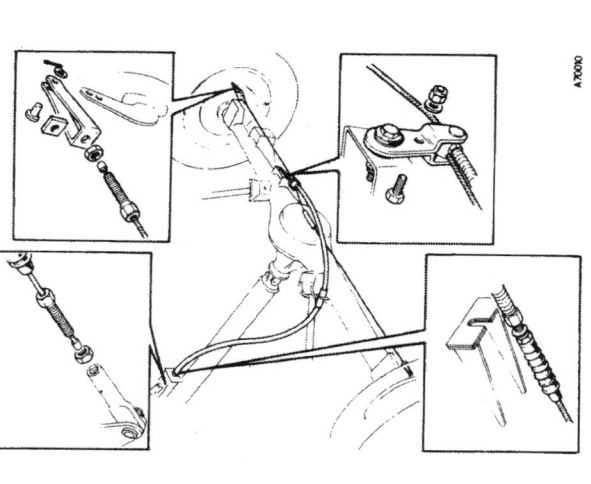

A7000

(44) Check visually hydraulic hoses, pipes and unions for chafing, cracks, leaks and corrosion.

Report any defects found.

(45) Check brake servo hose(s) for security and condition

ELECTRICAL

(46) Check function of original equipment i.e. interior and exterior lamps, horns, wipers and warning indicators

In sequence, check operation of:

1 Side, tail and headlamps (including dip/main beam and 'Flash' control).
2 Instrument panel illuminations.
3 Interior light.
4 Horns.
5 Auxiliary lights.

With ignition circuits energised, check operation of:

6 All warning lights:
7 Fuel lever indicator.
8 Heater blower motor.
9 Windscreen washers.
10 Windscreen wipers
11 Direction indicators.
12 Brake lights.
13 Reversing lights.
14 Start engine and note that the oil pressure warning light has extinguished.

Check operation of:

15 Charging system warning light in relation to engine speed.
16 Temperature indicator.
17 Switch off the engine and return the ignition switch to the auxiliary position, then re-check the function of any fitted accessories e.g. a radio, that are supplied with power from this switch position.
18 Report any defects found.

(47) Check/top up battery electrolyte

Using DISTILLED WATER ONLY top up; the electrolyte level is correct when it just covers the separators.

(48) Clean and grease battery connections

1 Check the battery and surrounding area for corrosion from battery chemicals.
2 Clean off any corrosion found.
3 Check visually for cracks in the battery case and report on any case cracks found.
4 Check security of terminal connections.
5 Coat terminals with petroleum jelly (vaseline).

(49) Check/adjust headlamp alignment

See 86.40.17, Headlamp beam aiming.

(50) Check, if necessary renew, wiper blades

1 Examine each wiper blade in turn for damage.
2 With the wiper blades in position and the windscreen wet, operate the wiper motor.
3 Check the wiper blade operation for smearing and adequate removal of dirt.
4 Stop the wiper motor.
5 If the checks in procedures 1 and 3 are not satisfactory replace the wiper blades as necessary. See 84.15.06 or 84.15.07.

EXHAUST AND FUEL PIPES

(51) Check exhaust system for leaks and security

1 Check the security of the exhaust pipe to the manifold nuts, correct tightening torque is 37 lbf ft (5.1 kgf m).

2 Check the security of the exhaust pipe joint clips.

3 Check the security of the exhaust system mounting bolts.

4 Using a second operator, run the engine at fast idle speed.

5 Check the exhaust system joints for leaks.

6 Check the exhaust pipes for leaks arising from damage or deterioration.

7 Check the exhaust silencers for leaks arising from damage or deterioration.

8 Stop the engine.

9 Report any defects found.

(52) Check fuel system for leaks, pipes and unions for chafing and corrosion

Report any defects found.

WHEELS AND TYRES

(53) Check/adjust tyre pressures including spare

Refer to Driver's Handbook for pressure settings.

WARNING: It can be dangerous :

a To use a car fitted with tyres in a damaged condition.

b To mix cross ply and radial ply tyres on the same axle or to fit radial ply tyres to the front wheels only.

c To use a car fitted with tyres that have a tread depth of less than 0.039 in (1.0 mm) over three-quarters of the tread width for the entire circumference of the tyre.

d To use a car with the tyres inflated to a pressure that is not suitable for the use to which the vehicle is put.

If the tyres do not conform with legal requirements report to the owner.

(54) Check that tyres comply with manufacturer's specifications

See 'GENERAL SPECIFICATION DATA'.

Report any deviations that may influence the car's performance or the accuracy of the speedometer.

(55) Check tightness of road wheel fastenings

Refer to 'TORQUE WRENCH SETTINGS'.

(56) Check tyres for external cuts in the fabric, exposure of ply or cord structure, lumps or bulges.

(57) Check tyres for tread depth and visually for external cuts in tyre fabric, exposure of ply or cord structure, lumps or bulges

BODY

(58) Lubricate all locks and hinges (not steering lock)

Using an oil can sparingly, lubricate all locks, door hinges, strikers and bonnet release. Wipe away any surplus oil to avoid staining paintwork or interior fittings.

(59) Check condition and security of seat and seat belts

(60) Check rear view mirror for cracks and crazing

(61) Check operation of all door, bonnet and boot locks

(62) Check operation of seat belt warning system

(63) Check operation of seat belt inertia reel mechanism

(64) Check operation of window controls

(65) Check tightness of sub-frame/body mountings

Refer to 'TORQUE WRENCH SETTINGS'.

(66) Ensure cleanliness of controls, door handles and steering wheel

ROAD TEST

(67) Road/roller test and check function of all instrumentation

(68) Report additional work required

At 36,000 miles (60,000 km) or 3 years, whichever is the sooner. Renew the air filter in the brake servo unit.

FAULT FINDING CHART—North American Federal Specification—excluding California Specification Vehicles

This chart indicates the possible areas of fault causes. Progressively work through the 'possible causes' cross referring to the key.

Possible causes shown in brackets only relate to the condition bracketed in the fault column.

FAULT	POSSIBLE CAUSES IN ORDER OF CHECKING
Noisy air injection pump	44, 46, 45
Engine cuts out or stalls (at idle)	17, 18, (30), 35, 4, 11, 13, 15, 12, 26, 24, 25, 6, 20, 27, 36, 38, 39, 40, 41, 43, 49, 22, 23, 29, 52, 51, 50, 48, 14, 42, 3

FAULT	POSSIBLE CAUSES IN ORDER OF CHECKING
Will not start	1, 2, 17, 18, 9, 10, 11, 12, 22
Poor or erratic idle	17, 30, 21, 26, 21, 11, 12, 13, 36, 38, 39, 40, 41, 6, 4, 20, 18, 31, 19, 23, 33, 34, 35, 24, 22, 29, 25, 27, 43, 42, 32, 45, 14, 47, 51, 52
Hesitation or flat spot (cold engine)	17, 18, 28, 50, 26, 33, 5, 23, 24, 25, 11, 15, 12, 35, 4, 6, 20, 27, 36, 38, 39, 40, 41, 43, 47, 49, 52, 51, 50, 48, 22, 29, 3, 14, 42
Excessive fuel consumption	19, 31, 24, 5, 26, 25, 22, 35, 4, 11, 13, 15, 12, 47, 49, 52, 51, 50, 48, 43, 6, 20, 27, 36, 38, 39, 40, 41, 29, 3, 14, 42
Lack of engine braking or high idle speed	33, 30, 32, 12, 26, 5, 22, 24, 25
Lack of engine power	17, 18, 34, 5, 35, 11, 13, 15, 12, 26, 24, 25, 22, 4, 47, 49, 52, 51, 50, 48, 43, 6, 20, 27, 36, 38, 39, 40, 41, 29, 14, 3, 42
Engine overheating	7, 12, 51, 50, 48, 26, 25, 8, 14, 42
Engine misfires	17, 18, 11, 13, 15, 12, 35, 4, 26, 24, 25, 6, 20, 27, 36, 38, 39, 40, 41, 49, 14, 3
Fuel smells	19, 31, 24, 39, 37, 38, 40, 41, 26, 25, 35
Engine 'runs on'	17, 30, 33, 32, 38, 7, 12, 51, 50, 48, 26, 25, 8, 14, 42
Engine knock or 'pinking'	17, 12, 7, 51, 50, 48, 26, 25, 14, 8, 42
Arcing at plugs	13, 15
Lean running (low CO)	26, 17, 18, 24, 25, 6, 20, 27, 36, 38, 39, 40, 41, 43, 49
Rich running (excess CO)	26, 40, 24, 25, 52, 51, 50, 48, 44, 46, 45
Backfiring in exhaust	17, 18, 35, 4, 6, 12, 20, 36, 43, 27, 32

KEY TO POSSIBLE CAUSES

Basic Engine Checks
1 Low battery condition or poor connections.
2 Starter system deficient.
3 Poor compressions.
4 Exhaust system leaking or blocked.
5 Faults on areas of the vehicle other than engine.
6 Air leaks at inlet manifold.
7 Cooling system blocked or leaking.
8 Cylinder head gasket leaking.

Ignition System Checks
9 H.T. circuit faults.
10 L.T. power faults.
11 L.T. switching faults.
12 Ignition timing incorrect.
13 System deterioration.
14 Advance mechanism faults.
15 Spark plug faults.
16 Distributor failure.

Fuel System Checks
17 Insufficient or incorrect fuel.
18 Fuel starvation.
19 Fuel leaks.

Carburetter checks
20 Air leak at carburetter/manifold joints.
21 Diaphragm uncorrectly located or damaged.
22 Air valve sticking.
23 Obstructed float chamber or diaphragm vent holes.
24 Incorrect fuel level in float chamber.
25 Metering needle faults.
26 Mixture incorrectly set.
27 Leakage at throttle spindles.
28 Piston damper inoperative.
29 Air valve spring missing, or incorrect.
30 Idle speed incorrectly set.
31 Leakage from fuel connection joints or seals.
32 Incorrectly set or faulty by-pass valve.
33 Sticking throttle.
34 Throttle linkage inhibited or incorrectly set.
35 Dirty or blocked air cleaner.

Evaporative & Crankcase Ventilation System Checks
36 Engine oil filler cap loose or leaking.
37 Fuel filler cap defective.
38 Restrictors missing or blocked.
39 Hoses blocked or leaking.
40 Adsorption canister restricted or blocked.
41 Vapour separator blocked.
42 E.G.R. valve malfunction.
43 Leaks at E.G.R. vacuum control lines.
44 Incorrectly tensioned air pump driving belt.
45 Relief valve malfunction or insufficient + pump pressure.
46 Check valve sticking.
47 Hot air inlet hose loose, adrift or blocked.
48 Flap valve jammed.
49 Vacuum pipes disconnected or leaking.
50 One way (low leak) valve faults.
51 Temperature sensor faulty, leaking or jammed.
52 Flap valve diaphragm leaking.

POSSIBLE CAUSE	CHECK AND REMEDIAL ACTION
1 Low battery condition or poor connections.	Check battery condition with hydrometer. Recharge, clean and secure terminals or renew as necessary. (if battery is serviceable but discharged, trace and rectify cause of flat battery. e.g. short circuit or insufficient charge from alternator).
2 Starter system deficient.	If starter fails to turn engine briskly, check engagement circuit and connections. Check and clean main starter circuit and connections.
3 Poor compressions.	Check compressions with proprietary tester. If compressions are low or uneven, remove cylinder head for further examination and rectification.
4 Exhaust system leaking or	Check and rectify as necessary.
5 Faults on areas of vehicle other than engine.	Check for binding brakes, slipping clutch etc.
6 Air leaks at inlet manifold.	Check inlet manifold/cylinder head joint. Remake with new gasket if necessary. Check manifold tappings for leaks-seal as necessary.
7 Cooling system blocked or leaking.	Flush system and check for blockage. Check hoses and connections for security and leakage. Renew as necessary. Check thermostat and renew if faulty.
8 Cylinder head gasket leaking.	Check cylinder block/head joint for signs of leakage. Renew gasket if necessary.
9 H.T. circuit faults.	Disconnect king lead at distributor and position the end approximately 3/16" (5 mm) from earthed metal. Switch on ignition, disconnect white/blue lead and check for spark at king lead end each time white/blue lead is disconnected. If spark is non-existent or weak, renew king lead and retest. If spark is satisfactory, check H.T. leads for fraying, deterioration and security, distributor cap for cracks, tracking, dirt or condensation, distributor rotor for deterioration and spark plugs. Renew leads, cap, rotor or plugs as necessary.
10 L.T power faults.	a) Ensure ignition switch on and check supply voltage. If less than 11 volts, check ignition switch, wiring and connections. If more than 11 volts, check voltage at coil "+ve" terminal. If this is in the range 4–8 volts, proceed to (b) below. If it is not 4–8 volts renew the ballast resistance wire.
11 L.T switching faults.	b) Check voltage at coil "−ve" terminal. If less than 2 volts, proceed to (c) below. If more than 2 volts, check the drive resistor (8–11 ohms) and renew if necessary. c) Disconnect the white/blue lead and recheck the coil "−ve" terminal voltage. If this is more than 9 volts, check the coil by substitution. If less than 9 volts, disconnect coil "−ve" lead and again check voltage on coil "−ve" terminal. If the voltage is then 9 volts, check the coil by substitution, but, if more than 9 volts, refer to 16. Ensure ignition off and check pick-up gap in distributor. This should to 0.014 to 0.016 in (0.36 to 0.41 mm). Adjust if necessary.
12 Ignition timing incorrect.	Check ignition timing and adjust as necessary.
13 System deterioration.	Check ignition wiring for fraying, chafing and deterioration. Check distributor cap and rotor for cracks and tracking and rotor for condition. Renew leads, cap or rotor as necessary.
14 Advance mechanism faults.	Check operation of advance mechanism against figures using a stroboscopic timing light. Lubricate or renew as necessary.
15 Spark plug faults.	Remove plugs, clean, reset gap and test on proprietary spark plug testing machine. Renew if in doubt.
16 Distributor failure.	a) Ensure that the distributor is earthed. b) With the distributor cap removed, crank the engine and check that the distributor shaft rotates. If not, investigate and rectify. c) Recheck as detailed in 9, 10, 11, and 15. d) As the last resort, renew the distributor complete.
17 Insufficient or incorrect fuel.	Ensure that the fuel tank has an adequate amount of the correct type and grade of fuel. NOTE: It is essential that unleaded fuels are used in this vehicle otherwise serious damage can be caused to the catalytic converter.
18 Fuel starvation.	Insert a pressure gauge into the pump to carburetter fuel line and check the pressure with the engine running. If not

POSSIBLE CAUSE	CHECK AND REMEDIAL ACTION
	satisfactory, check fuel feed and breather pipes for leaks or blockage. Renew connectors if damaged or deteriorated. If contamination of fuel is discovered, flush fuel system and clean or renew the tank filter. If necessary, renew the pump to rectify low pressure.
19 Fuel leaks.	Check fuel system for leaks and rectify as necessary. Renew any doubtful connectors.
20 Air leak at carburetter/manifold joints.	Check joints. Remake with new gaskets if necessary. Check CO.
21 Diaphragm incorrectly located or damaged.	Remove air valve cover and check location of diaphragm – piston depression holes should be in line with and face towards the throttle spindle. Renew diaphragm if damaged or deteriorated.
22 Air valve sticking.	Clean air valve and guide and reassemble. Check free movement by hand-unit should move freely and return, to carburetter bridge with an audible 'click'.
23 Obstructed float chamber, or diaphragm vent holes.	Ensure that gaskets, piping or dirt are not blocking the holes.
24 Incorrect fuel level in float chamber.	Reset float height and clean or renew needle valve and/or float as necessary.
25 Metering needle faults.	Check that needle is correct type. Ensure that shoulder of needle is flush with face of air valve and that needle bias is correct. Check/adjust CO at idle.
26 Mixture incorrectly set.	Check spindles and seals – renew as necessary.
27 (After considerable service) leakage at throttle spindles.	
28 Piston damper inoperative.	Check/top up damper oil level. Check damper operation by raising piston by hand. Resistance should be apparent.
29 Air valve spring missing, or incorrect.	Check that spring is correct (colour code) and refit/renew as necessary.
30 Idle speed incorrectly set.	Check/adjust idle speed.
31 Leakage from fuel connection, joints or seals.	Check fuel inlet connection – renew connector if necessary. Inspect float chamber joint and sealing plug 'O' ring seal – renew if necessary.
32 Incorrectly set or faulty.	Reset or renew by-pass valve as a unit.
33 Sticking throttle.	Check throttle operation – free off and reset as necessary.
34 Throttle linkage inhibited or incorrectly set	Check that throttle linkage and accelerator pedal are not inhibited by carpets, mats, sound insulation pads etc. and that full throttle is obtainable. Lubricate and reset if necessary.
35 Dirty or blocked air cleaner.	Inspect air cleaner element. Fit new element of correct type if necessary.

POSSIBLE CAUSE	CHECK AND REMEDIAL ACTION
36 Engine oil filler cap loose or leaking.	Check cap for security. Renew cap if seal is deteriorated.
37 Fuel filler cap defective.	Check seal for condition – renew if deteriorated. Check filler cap for security – rectify or renew as necessary.
38 Restrictors missing or	Check and clear or renew as necessary.
39 Hoses blocked or leaking.	Check and clear as necessary. Renew any deteriorated hoses.
40 Adsorption canister restricted	Inspect and renew if necessary.
41 Vapour separator blocked	Check and clear or renew as necessary.
42 E.G.R valve malfunction.	Check the function of the E.G.R valve on the vehicle. If not satisfactory, remove and clean valve and pipework. Renew valve if spring is broken, diaphragm ruptured or other fault obvious.
43 Leaks at E.G.R vacuum control lines.	Check security and condition of control lines. Renew connectors or lines as necessary.
44 Incorrectly tensioned air pump driving belt.	Check/adjust belt tension. Renew belt if necessary.
45 Relief valve malfunction or insufficient + pump pressure	Check that the relief valve operates at the correct pressure by using a pressure guage between the relief valve and outlet pipe to measure the point at which air pressure ceases to rise with engine speed. If any deviation is apparent, renew the pump/valve assembly. If the pump does not produce enough pressure to operate the relief valve check 44. and renew pump if necessary.
46 Check valve sticking.	Disconnect air hose at check and blow through valve. If the valve obstructs flow from the pump to the manifold or allows flow from the manifold towards the pump, renew the valve after checking hoses for blockage.
47 Hot air inlet hose loose, adrift or blocked.	Check hot air inlet hose for condition and security. Renew if necessary.
48 Flap valve jammed.	Check operation of flap valve. Renew flap valve if performance is unsatisfactory.
49 Vacuum pipes disconnected or leaking.	Check vacuum pipes for security of connections and deterioration. Renew if necessary.
50 One way (low leak) valve faults.	Blow through valve to check "one-way" action. If the valve leaks, fit a new valve.
51 Temperature sensor faulty leaking or jammed.	Check and renew if necessary.
52 Flap valve diaphragm leaking.	Check with a distributor vacuum test unit. If leakage is apparent, renew servo motor and cover unit.

FAULT FINDING CHART—North American California Specification

This chart indicates the possible areas of fault causes. Progressively work through the 'possible causes' cross referring to the key. Possible causes shown in brackets only relate to the condition bracketed in the fault column.

FAULT	POSSIBLE CAUSES IN ORDER OF CHECKING
Rich running (excess CO)	27, 44, 25, 38, 26, 56, 55, 54, 52, 48, 50, 49
Backfiring in exhaust	18, 19, 36, 4, 6, 12, 15, 21, 39, 47, 28, 33
Noisy air injection pump	48, 50, 49
Engine cuts out or stalls (at idle)	18, 19, (31), (37), 36, 4, 11, 13, 16, 12, 38, 27, 25, 26, 6, 21, 15, 28, 39, 42, 43, 44, 45, 47, 53, 23, 24, 30, 56, 55, 54, 52, 14, 46, 3

FAULT	POSSIBLE CAUSES IN ORDER OF CHECKING
Will not start (warm engine)	1, 2, 18, 19, 37, (38), 9, 10, 11, 12, 23
Poor or erratic idle	18, 31, 22, 27, 16, 10, 11, 12, 15, 13, 39, 42, 43, 44, 45, 6, 4, 21, 19, 32, 20, 24, 34, 35, 36, 25, 38, 23, 30, 26, 24, 28, 47, 46, 33, 49, 14, 51, 55, 56, 52, 8, 3
Hesitation or flat spot (cold engine)	18, 19, 29, (37), (54), 27, 34, 5, 24, 25, 30, 26, 11, 13, 16, 12, 15, 36, 4, 6, 21, 28, 39, 42, 43, 44, 45, 47, 51, 53, 56, 55, 54, 52, 23, 30, 3, 14, 46
Excessive fuel consumption	20, 32, 25, 5, 27, 38, 26, 23, 36, 4, 11, 13, 16, 12, 15, 51, 53, 56, 55, 54, 52, 47, 6, 21, 28, 39, 42, 43, 44, 45, 30, 3, 14, 46
Lack of engine braking or high idle speed	34, 31, 15, 33, 12, 27, 5, 23, 25, 38, 26
Lack of engine power	18, 19, 35, 5, 36, 11, 13, 16, 12, 27, 25, 38, 26, 23, 4, 51, 53, 56, 55, 54, 52, 47, 6, 21, 15, 28, 39, 42, 43, 44, 47, 30, 14, 3, 46
Engine overheating	7, 12, 15, 55, 54, 52, 27, 26, 8, 14, 46
Engine misfires	18, 19, 11, 13, 16, 12, 36, 4, 27, 25, 38, 26, 6, 21, 15, 28, 39, 42, 43, 44, 45, 53, 14, 3
Fuel smells	20, 32, 25, 43, 40, 42, 44, 45, 38, 27, 26, 36
Engine 'runs on'	18, 31, 34, 33, 42, 41, 7, 12, 27, 55, 54, 52, 27, 26, 38, 8, 14, 46
Engine knock or 'pinking'	18, 12, 15, 7, 55, 54, 52, 27, 26, 14, 8, 46
Arcing at plugs	13, 16
Lean running (low CO)	27, 18, 19, 25, 26, 6, 21, 15, 28, 39, 42, 43, 44, 45, 47, 53

KEY TO POSSIBLE CAUSES

Engine checks
1 Low battery condition or poor connections.
2 Starter system deficient.
3 Poor compressions.
4 Exhaust system leaking or blocked.
5 Faults on areas of vehicle other than engine.
6 Air leaks at inlet manifold.
7 Cooling system blocked or leaking.
8 Cylinder head gasket leaking.

Ignition System Checks
9 H.T. circuit faults.
10 L.T. power faults.
11 L.T. switching faults.
12 Ignition timing incorrect.
13 System deterioration.
14 Advance mechanism faults.
15 Vacuum system faults.
16 Spark plug faults.
17 Distributor failure.

Fuel System Checks
18 Insufficient or incorrect fuel.
19 Fuel starvation.
20 Fuel leaks.

Carburetter Checks
21 Air leak at carburetter/manifold joints.
22 Diaphragm incorrectly located or damaged.

23 Air valve sticking.
24 Obstructed float chamber or diaphragm vent holes.
25 Incorrect fuel level in float chamber.
26 Metering needle faults.
27 Mixture incorrectly set.
28 Leakage at throttle spindles (after considerable service).
29 Piston dampers inoperative.
30 Air valve spring missing or incorrect.
31 Idle speed incorrectly set.
32 Leakage from fuel connection joints or seals.
33 Incorrectly set or faulty by-pass valve.
34 Sticking throttle.
35 Throttle linkage inhibited or incorrectly set.
36 Dirty or blocked air cleaner.
37 Choke inoperative.
38 Choke sticking on.

Evaporative & Crankcase Ventilation System Checks
39 Engine oil filler cap loose or leaking.
40 Fuel Filler cap defective.
41 Anti-run on valve inoperative.
42 Restrictors missing or blocked.
43 Hoses blocked or leaking.
44 Adsorption canister restricted or blocked.
45 Vapour separator blocked.

E.G.R. System Checks
46 E.G.R. valve malfunction.
47 Leaks at E.G.R. vacuum control lines.

Air Injection System Checks
48 Incorrectly tensioned air pump driving belt.
49 Relief valve malfunction or insufficient + pump pressure.
50 Check valve sticking.

Miscellaneous
51 Hot air inlet hose loose, adrift or blocked.
52 Flap valve jammed.
53 Vacuum piped disconnected or leaking.
54 One way (low leak) valve faults.
55 Temperature sensor faulty, leaking or jammed.
56 Flap valve diaphragm leaking.

POSSIBLE CAUSE

1 Low battery condition or poor connections.

2 Starter system deficient.

3 Poor compressions.

4 Exhaust system leaking or blocked.

5 Faults on areas of vehicle other than engine.

6 Air leaks at inlet manifold.

7 Cooling system blocked or leaking.

8 Cylinder head gasket leaking.

9 H.T. circuit faults.

10 L.T. power faults.

11 L.T. switching faults.

12 Ignition timing incorrect.

13 System deterioration.

14 Advance mechanism faults.

16 Spark plug faults.

17 Distributor failure.

CHECK AND REMEDIAL ACTION

Check battery condition with hydrometer. REcharge, clean and secure terminals or renew as necessary. (if battery is serviceable but discharged, trace and rectify cause of flat battery e.g. short circuit or insufficient charge from alternator).

If starter fails to turn engine briskly, check engagement circuit and connections. Check and clean main starter circuit and connections.

Check compressions with proprietary tester. If compressions are low or uneven, remove cylinder head for further examination and rectification.

Check and rectify as necessary.

Check for binding brakes, slipping clutch etc.

Check inlet manifold/cylinder head joint. Remake with new gasket if necessary. Check manifold tappings for leaks-seal as necessary.

Flush system and check for blockage. Check hoses and connections for security and leakage. Renew as necessary. Check thermostat and renew if faulty.

Check cylinder block/head joint for signs of leakage. Renew gasket if necessary.

Disconnect king lead at distributor and position the end approximately 3/16" (5 mm) from earthed metal. Switch on ignition, disconnect white/blue lead and check for spark at king lead end each time white/blue lead is disconnected. If spark is non-existent or weak, renew king lead and retest. If spark is satisfactory, check H.T. leads for fraying, deterioration and security, distributor cap for cracks, tracking, dirt or condensation, distributor rotor for deterioration and spark plugs (16). Renew leads, cap, rotor or plugs as necessary.

a) Ensure ignition switch on and check supply voltage. If less than 11 volts, check ignition switch, wiring and connections. If more than 11 volts, check voltage at coil "+ve" terminal. If this is in the range 4–8 volts, proceed to (b) below. If it is not 4–8 volts renew the ballast resistance wire.

b) Check voltage at coil "—ve" terminal. If less than 2 volts, proceed to (c) below. If more than 2 volts, check the drive resistor (8–11 ohms) and renew if necessary.

c) Disconnect the white/blue lead and recheck the coil "—ve" terminal voltage. If this is more than 9 volts, check the coil by substitution. If less than 9 volts, disconnect coil "—ve" lead and again check voltage on coil "—ve" terminal. If the voltage is then 9 volts, check the coil by substitution, but, if more than 9 volts, refer to 17.

Ensure ignition off and check pick-up gap in distributor. This should to 0.014 to 0.016 in (0.36 to 0.41 mm). Adjust if necessary.

Check ignition timing and adjust as necessary

Check ignition wiring for fraying, chafing and deterioration. Check distributor cap for cracks and tracking and rotor for condition. Renew leads, cap or rotor as necessary.

Check operation of advance mechanism against figures using a stroboscopic timing light. Lubricate or renew as necessary.

Remove plugs, clean, reset gap and test on proprietary spark plug testing machine. Renew if in doubt.

a) Ensure that the distributor is earthed.

b) With the distributor cap removed, crank the engine and check that the distributor shaft rotates. If not, investigate and rectify.

c) Recheck as detailed in 9, 10, 11, and 16.

d) As the last resort, renew the distributor complete.

POSSIBLE CAUSE	CHECK AND REMEDIAL ACTION
18 Insufficient or incorrect fuel.	Ensure that the fuel tank has an adequate amount of the correct type and grade of fuel. NOTE: It is essential that unleaded fuels are used in this vehicle otherwise serious damage can be caused to the catalytic converter.
19 Fuel starvation.	Insert a pressure gauge into the pump to carburetter fuel line and check the pressure with the engine running. If not satisfactory, check fuel feed and breather pipes for leaks or blockage (see also 32 and 24). Renew connectors if damaged or deteriorated. If contamination of fuel is discovered, flush fuel system and clean or renew the tank filter. If necessary, renew the pump to rectify low pressure.
20 Fuel leaks.	Check fuel system for leaks and rectify as necessary. Renew any doubtful connectors. Check joints. Remake with new gaskets if necessary. Check CO.
21 Air leak at carburetter/manifold joints.	Remove air valve cover and check location of diaphragm – piston depression holes should be in line with and face towards the throttle spindle. Renew diaphragm if damaged or deteriorated.
22 Diaphragm incorrectly located or damaged.	
23 Air valve sticking.	Clean air valve and guide and reassemble. Check free movement by hand-unit should move freely and return, to carburetter bridge with an audible 'click'.
24 Obstructed float chamber or diaphragm vent holes.	Ensure that gaskets, piping or dirt are not blocking the holes.
25 Incorrect fuel level in float chamber.	Reset float height and clean or renew needle valve and/or float as necessary.
26 Metering needle faults.	Check that needle is correct type. Ensure that shoulder of needle is flush with and face of air valve and that needle bias is correct.
27 Mixture incorrectly set.	Check/adjust CO at idle.
28 (After considerable service) leakage at throttle spindles.	Check spindles and seals – renew as necessary.
29 Piston damper inoperative.	Check/top up damper oil level – Check damper operation by raising piston by hand. Resistance should be apparent.
30 Air valve spring missing, or incorrect.	Check that spring is correct (colour code) and refit/renew as necessary.
31 Idle speed incorrectly set.	Check/adjust idle speed.
32 Leakage from fuel connection, joints or seals.	Check fuel inlet connection – renew connector if necessary. Inspect float chamber joint and sealing plug 'O' ring seal – renew if necessary.
33 Incorrectly set or faulty by-pass valve.	Reset or renew by-pass valve as a unit.
34 Sticking throttle.	Check throttle operation – free off and reset as necessary.
35 Throttle linkage inhibited or incorrectly set.	Check that throttle linkage and accelerator pedal are not inhibited by carpets, mats, sound insulation pads etc. and that full throttle is obtainable. Lubricate and reset if necessary.
36 Dirty or blocked air cleaner.	Inspect air cleaner element. Fit new element of correct type if necessary.
37 Choke inoperative.	Check connections and seals of mixture feed pipe at inlet manifold and autochoke. Check connections of water feed pipes and bleed autochoke system. Check electrical connections, at cut-out switch on inlet manifold, and autochoke. If still unsatisfactory renew autochoke. Bleed autochoke.
38 Choke sticking on.	Check cap for security. Renew cap if seal is deteriorated.
39 Engine oil filler cap loose or leaking.	Check seal for condition – renew if deteriorated. Check filler cap for security. – rectify or renew as necessary.
40 Fuel filler cap defective.	
41 Anti-run on valve inoperative	Apply current to the run on valve solenoid with the engine running. If the engine does not stop, the valve is suspect – renew valve and retest. If the engine does not stop, check wiring between valve, control (oil pressure) switch and the ignition switch.
42 Restrictors missing or blocked.	Check and clear or renew as necessary.
43 Hoses blocked or leaking.	Check and clear as necessary. Renew any deteriorated hoses.
44 Adsorption canister restricted or blocked.	Inspect and renew if necessary.
45 Vapour separator blocked.	Check and clear or renew as necessary.
46 E.G.R. valve malfunction.	Check the function of the E.G.R. valve on the vehicle. If not satisfactory, remove and clean valve and pipework. Renew valve if spring is broken, diaphragm ruptured or other fault obvious.
47 Leaks at E.G.R. vacuum control lines.	Check security and condition of control lines. Renew connectors or lines as necessary.
48 Incorrectly tensioned air pump driving belt.	Check/adjust belt tension. Renew belt if necessary.
49 Relief valve malfunction. or insufficient + pump pressure.	Check that the relief valve operates at the correct pressure by using a pressure gauge between the relief valve and outlet pipe to measure the point at which air pressure ceases to rise with engine speed. If any deviation is apparent, renew the pump/valve assembly. If the pump does not produce enough pressure to operate the relief valve check 48 and renew pump if necessary.

POSSIBLE CAUSE

50 Check valve sticking.

51 Hot air inlet hose loose, adrift or blocked.

52 Flap valve jammed.

53 Vacuum pipes disconnected or leaking.

54 One way (low leak) valve faults.

55 Temperature sensor faulty, leaking or jammed.

56 Flap valve diaphragm leaking.

CHECK AND REMEDIAL ACTION

Disconnect air hose at check and blow through valve. If the valve obstructs flow from the pump to the manifold or allows flow from the manifold towards the pump, renew the valve after checking hoses for blockage.

Check hot air inlet hose for condition and security. Renew if necessary.

Check operation of flap valve. Renew flap valve if performance is unsatisfactory.

Check vacuum pipes for security of connections and deterioration. Renew if necessary.

Blow through valve to check "one-way" action. If the valve leaks, fit a new valve. Check and renew if necessary.

Check and renew if necessary.

Check with a distributor vacuum test unit. If leakage is apparent, renew servo motor and cover unit.

MAINTENANCE SUMMARY, USA Market Specification —

Carburetter engined vehicles

OPERATION No.	MILEAGE × 1000	KILOMETRES × 1000
10.10.03	1	1.6
10.10.14	3, 9, 16, 22, 28, 34, 41, 47	5, 15, 35, 45, 55, 65, 75
10.10.26	6, 19, 31, 44	10, 30, 50, 70
10.10.28	12.5, 37.5	20, 60
10.10.50	25, 50	40, 80

OPERATION No.	10.10.03	10.10.14	10.10.26	10.10.28	10.10.50
ENGINE					
1 Check/top up engine oil	X				
2 Check/top up cooling system	X	X	X	X	X
3 Check/adjust operation of all washers and top up reservoir	X	X			X
4 Renew engine oil	X	X	X	X	X
5 Renew engine oil filter	X		X	X	X
6 Lubricate accelerator control linkage and pedal pivot – check operation	X		X		
7 Check cooling/heater systems for leaks and hoses for security and condition	X		X	X	X
8 Check for oil leaks	X	X	X	X	X
9 Check/adjust torque of cylinder head nuts/bolts	X				
10 Check driving belts, adjust or renew	X			X	
11 Check security of engine mountings	X				X
12 Check/adjust carburetter idle settings	X			X	
13 Top up carburetter, piston dampers	X			X	X
14 Renew carburetter/air intake, air cleaner element				X	X
15 Check/adjust deceleration by-pass valve	X			X	X
16 Check security of E.G.R. valve operating lines	X			X	
17 Check E.G.R. System 1975 and 1976 models Later models – 50,000 miles					X

ENGINE / IGNITION / TRANSMISSION

OPERATION No.	10.03	10.14	10.26	10.28	10.50
18 Check air-intake temperature control system				X	X
19 Check crankcase breathing and evaporate loss control system hoses for security					
20 Check crankcase breathing and evaporative loss control systems. Check hoses/pipes and restrictors for blockage, security and condition	X				
21 Check air injection system hoses/pipes for security and condition				X	X
22 Check/top up air conditioning compressor fluid				X	X
23 Renew adsorption canister					50 only
24 Renew catalytic converter					50 only
IGNITION					
25 Check security of distributor vacuum unit and operation of vacuum unit	X				
26 Lubricate distributor					
27 Check/adjust ignition timing using electronic equipment	X				
28 Check ignition wiring for fraying, chafing and deterioration	X	X		X	X
29 Clean distributor cap, check for cracks and tracking			X	X	X
30 Renew spark plugs			X	X	X
31 Check coil performance on oscilloscope			X	X	X
TRANSMISSION					
32 Check/top up gearbox oil	X			X	X
33 Check/top up rear axle/final drive oil	X			X	X
34 Check for oil leaks		X		X	X
35 Check tightness of propeller shaft coupling bolts				X	X
36 Check/top up automatic gearbox fluid	X		X	X	X
37 Lubricate automatic gearbox exposed selector linkage			X	X	X

CLUTCH / STEERING AND SUSPENSION / BRAKES

OPERATION No.	10.03	10.14	10.26	10.28	10.50
38 Check clutch pipes for leaks and chafing	X	X	X	X	X
39 Check/top up clutch fluid reservoir	X	X	X	X	X
40 Lubricate clutch pedal pivots				X	X
STEERING AND SUSPENSION					
41 Check steering rack for oil leaks	X	X	X	X	X
42 Check security of suspension fixings	X		X	X	X
43 Check condition and security of steering unit joints and gaiters	X	X	X	X	X
44 Check/adjust front wheel alignment	X		X	X	X
45 Adjust front hub bearing end float					
46 Lubricate steering rack and pinion			X	X	X
47 Check shock absorber for fluid leaks	X	X	X	X	X
BRAKES					
48 Inspect brake pads for wear and discs for condition			X	X	X
49 Inspect brake linings/pads for wear, and drums/discs for condition		X	X	X	X
50 Check/top up brake fluid reservoir		X	X	X	X
51 Check footbrake operation; adjust to manufacturer's instructions (self-adjusting)	X	X	X	X	X
52 Check handbrake security and operation; adjust to manufacturer's instructions	X		X	X	X
53 Lubricate brake pedal pivot			X	X	X
54 Lubricate handbrake mechanical linkage and cable guides				X	X
55 Check visually, hydraulic hoses, pipes and unions for chafing, cracks, leaks and corrosion		X	X	X	X
56 Check brake servo hoses for security and condition		X	X	X	X

BODY & GENERAL

OPERATION No.	10.10.03	10.10.14	10.10.26	10.10.28	10.10.50
BODY					
72 Lubricate all locks, hinges and door check mechanism (not steering lock)	X			X	X
73 Check condition and security of seats and seat belts	X		X	X	X
74 Check rear view mirrors for security, cracks and crazing		X	X	X	X
75 Check operation of all door, bonnet and boot locks	X		X	X	X
76 Check operation of seat belt warning system	X			X	X
77 Check operation of seat belt inertia real mechanism	X	X	X	X	X
78 Check operation of window controls	X	X	X	X	X
79 Check tightness of sub frame/body mountings	X				
80 Ensure cleanliness of controls, door handles, steering wheel	X	X	X	X	X
GENERAL					
81 Road/roller test and check function of all instrumentation	X		X	X	X
82 Report additional work required	X	X	X	X	X

Renew air filter in brake servo unit

At 37,500 miles or 3 yrs whichever is the sooner –

ELECTRICAL, EXHAUST AND FUEL PIPES, WHEELS AND TYRES

OPERATION No.	10.10.03	10.10.14	10.10.26	10.10.28	10.10.50
ELECTRICAL					
57 Check function of original equipment, i.e. interior and exterior, lamps, horns, wipers and warning indicators	X				X
58 Check/top up battery electrolyte	X	X	X	X	X
59 Clean and grease battery connections		X	X	X	X
60 Check/adjust headlamp alignment	X	X	X	X	X
61 Check, if necessary renew wiper blades		X	X	X	X
62 Check output of charging system	X	X	X	X	X
63 Check brake system warning light	X		X	X	X
EXHAUST AND FUEL PIPES					
64 Check exhaust system for leaks and security	X	X	X	X	X
65 Check fuel system for leaks, pipes and unions for chafing and corrosion	X	X		X	X
66 Check condition of fuel filler cap seal			X	X	X
WHEELS AND TYRES					
67 Check/adjust tyre pressures including spare	X	X	X	X	X
68 Check that tyres comply with manufacturer's specification		X	X	X	X
69 Check tightness of road wheel fastenings	X	X	X	X	X
70 Check tyres for external cuts in tyre fabric, exposure of ply or cord structure, lumps or bulges	X	X			
71 Check tyres for tread depth and visually for external cuts in fabric, exposure of ply or cord structure, lumps or bulges	X	X	X	X	X
IMPORTANT: If tyres do not conform with legal requirements report to the owner					

ADDITIONAL WORK FOR CANADIAN MARKET SPECIFICATION VEHICLES

1 Check/adjust choke settings (manual choke) — operation Nos. 10.10.03, 10.10.28, 10.10.50.
2 Check operation of distributor vacuum unit — operation Nos. 10.10.28, 10.10.50.

(1) Check/adjust choke settings (manual choke)

1 Maintain the engine at normal running temperature.
2 Check that the mixture control cam lever on both carburetters returns to its stop.
3 Check and if necessary adjust the mixture control cable so that there is free movement.
4 Pull-out the mixture control cable knob on the control cowl approximately ¼ in until the fast idle cams are correctly engaged with the ball locators.
5 Slaken the fast idle screw lock-nut on both carburetters, start the engine and rotate the screw head (on both carburetters) against the cam until the engine revolutions reach a steady 1600 rev/min.
6 Use the air flow meter to check that the carburetters are in balance at 1600 rev/min. if necessary adjust the fast idle screws as required.
7 Tighten the fast idle screw lock-nut on both carburetters and push the mixture control knob fully home.

NOTE: An engine set to 1600 rev/min. while hot is equivalent to a fast idle speed of approximately 1300 rev/min. when cold.

(2) Check operation of distributor vacuum unit.

1 Check security of distributor vacuum unit operating line.
2 Start the engine and warm to normal running temperature.
3 When the engine is idling steadily, disconnect the vacuum pipe at the distributor.

4 A noticeable rise in engine speed (approximately 500 rev/min) should be apparent if the vacuum unit is functioning, otherwise overhaul or renew the distributor.
5 When satisfied that the vacuum unit is operating correctly, reconnect the vacuum unit pipe, ensuring a secure connection.

MAINTENANCE SUMMARY — North American Specification

The Maintenance Summary gives details of mileage intervals for the following operations. The figure in parenthesis to the left of each heading refers to the item number on the summary list.

ENGINE

(1) Check/top up engine oil

NOTE: Allow time for oil to drain back into sump after running engine. Stand vehicle on level ground.

1 Withdraw the dipstick, wipe it clean and push fully home again before withdrawing it for reading.
2 Add oil via the filler cap until the level reaches the 'High' mark on the dipstick. DO NOT OVERFILL and ensure that the dipstick and filler cap are replaced.

(2) Check/top up cooling system

WARNING: Do NOT remove cooling system filler caps or plugs when engine is hot.

1 Slowly turn the pressure cap anti-clockwise until the resistance of the safety stop is felt. Leave the cap in this position until all pressure is released. Press the cap downwards against the spring to clear the safety stops and continue turning until it can be lifted off.
2 Maintain the level of the coolant, see 26.10.01.

NOTE: Ensure that the specific gravity of the coolant is maintained — see 'LUBRICANTS, FLUIDS AND FUEL'.

(3) Check/adjust operation of all washers and top up reservoirs.

1 Replenish the container with clean soft water. The addition of a small amount of mild detergent will prevent smearing on the windscreen.
2 During freezing conditions it is beneficial to fill the container with a mixture of one part methylated spirits (wood alcohol) to two parts of water. This will assist in the dispersal of snow and ice from the screen.
3 Do not add anti-freeze solutions to the container as this will discolour the paintwork and damage wiper blades and sealing rubber.

(4) Renew engine oil

NOTE: This operation is best carried out when the engine is warm and with the vehicle standing level on a ramp or over a pit.

To drain the sump, unscrew the drain plug three complete turns to direct the oil stream into a receptacle while the engine is warm. When the rate of flow lessens, remove the plug completely. Refit the plug and refill the sump with the appropriate grade of engine oil. The use of additives is unnecessary.

(5) Renew oil filter element

See 12.60.02.

(6) Lubricate accelerator linkage/pedal pivot — check operation

Lubricate

Using an oil can, lubricate the accelerator linkage on the carburetter and the accelerator pedal pivot. Wipe away any surplus oil to avoid drips or any possibility of staining the carpet inside the car.

Check operation

Check carburetter throttle response to initial movement of the accelerator pedal. If required, adjust the throttle cable at the carburetter.

Check carburetter throttle position with accelerator pedal fully depressed, by observing that the carburetter lever(s) move to a positive stop.

If the throttle movement is not satisfactory, investigate the cause and rectify as necessary, proceeding in the following order.

Check that the throttle pedal movement is not restricted by floor mats or carpet etc. Check the carburetter lever(s) for correct position and settings — see 19.15.01 or 19.15.02, as applicable. Check the throttle cable location and condition — see 19.20.06.

(7) Check cooling/heater systems for leaks and hoses for security and condition

1 Check for leaks from engine and radiator drain taps/plugs (where fitted).
2 Check for leaks from water hose joints.
3 Check for leaks from water hoses through damage or porosity.
4 Check for leaks from the water pump thermostat housing, radiator and heater unit.
5 Report any leaks found.

(8) Check for oil leaks

Report any found.

(9) Check/adjust torque of cylinder head nuts/bolts

See 12.29.27.

(10) Check driving belts, adjust or renew

Check condition where belt is visibly worn or damaged. Fit new belt if necessary. Check and adjust:
a Alternator drive belt — see 86.10.05.
b Air pump drive belt — see 17.25.13.
c Compressor drive belt (where applicable) — see 82.10.01.

(11) **Check security of engine mountings**

Check the security of the following engine fixings using the data in 'TORQUE WRENCH SETTINGS'.

1 Inlet manifold and exhaust manifold.
2 Cam cover.
3 Air cleaner and carburetters.
4 Air pump.
5 Sump.
6 Timing cover.
7 E.G.R. valve.
8 Engine and gearbox mountings.
9 Alternator.

(12) **Check/adjust carburetter idle settings**

See 19.15.02.

(13) **Top up carburetter piston dampers**

1 Release the two toggle clips securing the outer section of the air cleaner housing.
2 Pivot the outer section about the hot air intake hose to gain access to the air cleaner element. Take care that the air intake control vacuum pipe is not disturbed.
3 Remove the carburetter damper assembly from the carburetter by unscrewing the hexagonal plug in top of the carburetter.
4 Raise the piston by inserting a finger into the carburetter air intake hole. With the piston raised top up the hollow damper guide with a recommended engine oil, until the oil level is ¼" (6 mm) below the top of the guide.
5 Release the piston and refit the damper assembly, screwing down the plastic plug.
6 To ensure correct location of the oil retaining cup in the damper guide, again raise and lower the piston.

NOTE: A certain amount of pressure will be felt when lifting the piston, but it is essential that the piston is lifted to its maximum height to ensure correct location of the oil retaining cup.

(14) **Renew carburetter/air intake air cleaner element**

See 19.10.08.

(15) **Check/adjust deceleration by-pass valve**

See 19.15.02.

(16) **Check security of E.G.R. valve operating lines**

Check E.G.R. valve operating pipe lines for security of push fit connections at the following units:
a E.G.R. valve.
b Cut-off valve.
c Tee-piece (Canada only).
d Fuel trap.
e Carburetter.
Renew any pipes that show signs of deterioration.

(17) **Check E.G.R. system**

1 Disconnect the vacuum pipe from the top of the E.G.R. valve.
2 Remove the two bolts securing the E.G.R. valve to the inlet manifold and withdraw the valve.
3 Clean the base of the valve with a wire brush.
4 Use a standard spark plug machine to clean the valve seat and pintle. Insert the valve opening into the machine and lift the diaphragm evenly by using two fingers. Blast the valve for approximately 30 seconds, remove the inspect. If necessary, repeat until all carbon deposits are removed. Use compressed air to remove all traces of carbon grit from the valve.
5 Examine the E.G.R. ports in the manifold. Light deposits are not detrimental to system function and should not be disturbed. Heavy deposits must be cleared by removing the inlet manifold and cleaning the ports.
CAUTION: Do not attempt to clean the ports with the manifold in position.
6 Using a new gasket, refit the E.G.R. valve and two securing bolts.
7 Reconnect the vacuum pipe to the top of the E.G.R. valve.
8 Check E.G.R. valve operating lines for security of push fit connections at E.G.R. valve, cut-off valve, tee-piece, fuel trap and carburetter. Renew any pipes that show signs of deterioration.

9 Check function of E.G.R. valve as follows:
Start and run the engine until normal operating temperature is attained. Ensure that the choke control knob is pushed fully in. Open and close the throttle several times and observe or feel the E.G.R. valve, which should open and close with the changes in engine speed. The valve should close instantly when the throttle is closed.
10 If the operation of the valve does not appear completley satisfactory, check the valve by connecting the vacuum pipe of a distributor vacuum test unit to the valve. Ensure that the valve is actuated, held, and that there is no leak of vacuum, otherwise, fit a new E.G.R. valve complete.

(18) **Check air intake temperature control system, excluded on catalytic converter vehicles**

See 17.30.01.

(19) **Check crankcase breathing and evaporative loss system hoses for security**

1 Visually check the following hoses for security, and rectify as necessary.
1 Crankcase purge line.
2 Carburetter float chamber vent pipe.
3 Carburetter float chamber vent pipe.
4 Adsorption canister purge line.
5 Fuel tank vent pipe.
6 Manifold vacuum line.

(20) **Check crankcase breathing and evaporative loss control systems**
Check hoses and restrictors for blockage, security and condition

1 Inspect all hoses illustrated for condition and renew any hoses that show signs of deterioration, including slackness or cracking.
2 Completely disconnect the crankcase purge line and the adsorption canister purge line, then using a low pressure air supply, blow through these hoses to check for blockage. Investigate and clear any blockage, paying particular attention to the restrictors.
3 Refit the purge lines, ensuring that all connections are secure and tight. Renew any doubtful hose.

(21) **Check air injection system, hoses pipes for security and condition**

(22) **Check/top up air conditioning compresser fluid**

(23) **Renew adsorption canister**
See 17.15.13.

(24) **Renew Catalytic converter Excluded on Non Catalytic Converter Vehicles**
See 17.50.01.
Reset Catalytic Converter service interval indicator, using special key.

IGNITION

(25) **Check security of distributor vacuum unit line and operation of vacuum unit (California and Canadian Market only)**

1 Check security of distributor vacuum unit operating line connections at carburetter, fuel trap and distributor.
2 Start the engine and warm it to normal running temperature.
3 When the engine is idling steadily, disconnect the vacuum unit pipe at the distributor.
4 A noticeable rise in engine speed (approximately 500 rev/min) should be apparent if the vacuum unit is functioning.
5 When satisfied that the vacuum unit is operating correctly, reconnect the vacuum unit pipe to the distributor, ensuring a secure connection.

(26) **Lubricate distributor**

1 Remove the distributor cap and rotor arm. Using an oil can, apply three drops of a clean, recommended engine oil into the reservoir in the rotor carrier.
2 Remove flash-over shield and lubricate pick-up centre bearing plate with a drop of the same oil in each of the two holes provided. DO NOT disturb the screw securing the base plate. Refit the flash-over shield.

(27) **Check/adjust ignition timing using electronic equipment**
See 86.35.15.

(28) Check ignition wiring for fraying, chafing and deterioration

Low tension circuit

1 Check connections of the ballast resistor wire, drive resistor, distributor, coil and ignition switch.
2 Check ignition coil connections.
3 Check wiring between coil and distributor.
4 Check distributor external connections.
5 Remove distributor cap and check internal wiring.
6 Check distributor internal connections.
7 Refit distributor cap.

High tension circuit.

8 Check lead between coil and distributor.
9 For each spark plug in turn: Check lead between plug and distributor.
10 Check high tension lead connections.
11 Report wiring condition.

(29) Clean distributor cap, check for cracks and tracking

1 Using a nap-free cloth, wipe the distributor cap and rotor arm clean. Inspect the cap and rotor, internally and externally, for cracks and any trace of tracking.
2 Refit the rotor arm and cap if serviceable, otherwise, fit new components as necessary.

(30) Renew spark plugs

For each plug in turn

1 Withdraw ignition high tension lead from plug.
2 Unscrew plug from engine using a special plug spanner or a suitable tube spanner.
3 Discard the plug.
4 Visually check new plug for damage to body and electrodes, discard plug if damaged.
5 Check electrode gap on new plug, which when correct, will just allow a 0.025 in (0.64 mm) feeler gauge to slide slowly between the electrodes under light pressure.
6 If adjustment is necessary, using a suitable tool, carefully move the side electrode. Recheck the gap is correct. this procedure until the gap is correct.
7 Check sealing washer for cracks and distortion, and renew washer if necessary.
8 Fit new spark plug to engine.
9 Tighten plug to 20 lbf ft (2,8 kgf m).
10 Refit the high tension lead to the plug.

(31) Check coil performance on oscilloscope

1 Using proprietary electronic testing equipment, in accordance with the equipment instructions, check the resistance of the ignition coil primary winding, which must be 1.2 to 1.5 ohms. If necessary, fit a new ignition coil.

TRANSMISSION

(32) Check/top up gearbox oil

1 With the vehicle standing in a level position, remove the oil level/filler plug and, using a suitable dispenser filled with the correct grade oil, see 'LUBRICANTS & ANTI-FREEZE SOLUTIONS', top up the gearbox until the oil is level with the bottom of the filler hole threads.
2 Allow surplus oil to drain away, then refit the filler plug and wipe clean.

(33) Check/top up rear axle/final drive oil

1 With the vehicle standing in a level position, remove the oil level/filler plug and top up the final drive unit with the correct grade of oil, see 'LUBRICANTS & ANTI-FREEZE SOLUTIONS', until the oil is level with the bottom of the filler hole threads. Allow surplus oil to drain away, then refit the filler plug and wipe clean.

(34) Check for oil leaks

Report any found.

(35) Check tightness of propeller shaft coupling bolts

Refer to 'TORQUE WRENCH SETTINGS' for data.

(36) Check/top up automatic gearbox fluid

Refer to 'LUBRICANTS & ANTI-FREEZE SOLUTIONS' for recommended fluids.

(37) Lubricate automatic gearbox selector linkage

(38) Check clutch pipes for leaks and chafing

(39) Check/top up clutch fluid reservoir

(40) Lubricate clutch pedal pivots

STEERING AND SUSPENSION

(41) Check steering rack/for oil/leaks

Report any found

(42) Check security of suspension fixings

Refer to 'TORQUE WRENCH SETTINGS' for data.

(43) Check condition and security of steering unit joints and gaiters

Refer to 'TORQUE WRENCH SETTINGS' for data, report any defects found.

(44) Check/adjust front wheel alignment

See 57.65.01.

(45) Adjust front hub bearing end float

1 Remove road wheel.
2 Check hub for end float.
3 If adjustment is required, remove hub cap and split pin.
4 Tighten slotted nut as required to eliminate end float. A torque of 5 lbf ft (0,691 kgf m) must not be exceeded or damage may be caused to bearings and bearing tracks. Slacken nut to permit entry of split pin.
5 Insert and lock split pin.
6 Clean hub cap and refit.
7 Fit road wheel.

(46) Lubricate steering rack and pinion

1 Wipe clean the plug and surrounding area.
2 Remove the plug.
3 Fit a suitable grease nipple in place of the plug.
4 Apply a grease gun, filled with the correct grade of grease, see 'LUBRICANTS & ANTI-FREEZE SOLUTIONS', to the grease nipple and give five strokes only.
CAUTION: Over-greasing can cause damage to the protective bellows.
5 Remove the grease nipple.
6 Refit the plug.
7 Wipe away any surplus grease.

(47) Check shock absorbers for fluid leaks

Report any found

BRAKES

(48) Inspect brake pads for wear and discs for condition

1 Jack up the front of the car and place safely onto stands before removing the disc pads (see 70.40.02).
CAUTION: Do NOT depress the brake pedal while the pads are removed.
2 Report pad condition if the friction lining has been reduced to 0.125 in (3 mm) or if there is not sufficient material to provide a thickness of 0.125 in (3 mm) at the completion of a further 3,000 miles (5,000 km) motoring.
3 Check the brake discs for excessive scoring and run out and report this if present.

(49) Inspect brake lining/pads for wear, drums/discs for condition

1 Jack up the car and place safely onto stands before removing the road wheel (held by 4 nuts) and the brake drum (see 70.10.03).
2 Check the brake linings for wear and report if they are excessively worn, damaged or contaminated by oil or grease. Remove surplus oil or grease and any brake lining dust before replacing the brake drum.
3 For discs see Maintenance Operation 48 for front pads and disc inspection.

(50) **Check/top up brake fluid reservoir**

Top up when required with new fluid of the correct type recommended — see 'LUBRICANTS & ANTI-FREEZE SOLUTIONS.' Do not allow the fluid level to drop below the danger mark on the reservoir.

WARNING: Use only new brake fluid of the correct specification. DO NOT use fluid of unknown origin, or fluid that has been exposed to the atmosphere, or discharged during bleeding operations. If significant topping is required, check the hydraulic system for leaks.

CAUTION: Paintwork can be damaged by direct contact with brake fluid.

(51) **Check footbrake operation, adjust to manufacturers instructions (self adjusting)**

1 With the handbrake off, check the brake pedal for spongy operation.
2 If the pedal has spongy operation, bleed and adjust the brakes, see 70.25.02 and 70.25.03.

(52) **Check handbrake operation; adjust to manufacturers instructions**

1s If the handbrake travel is excessive, adjust the handbrake, see 70.35.10.

(53) **Lubricate brake pedal pivot**

1 Using an oil can, lubricate the brake pedal pivot.
2 Wipe away the surplus oil to prevent staining the carpet.

(54) **Lubricate handbrake mechanical linkage and cable guides**

1 Smear grease around the handbrake compensator, working it well into the clevis pins.
2 Smear grease around the rear brake-drum clevis pins.
3 Grease all exposed sections of the inner cable to resist corrosion.

(55) **Check visually, hydraulic pipes and unions for chafing, leaks and corrosion**

(56) **Check brake servo hoses for security and condition.**

ELECTRICAL

(57) **Check function of original equipment, i.e. interior and exterior lamps, horns, wipers and warning indicators**

In sequence, check operation of:
1 Side, tail and headlamps (including dip/main beam and 'Flash' control) also number plate illumination lamp.
2 Instrument panel illumination.
3 Interior light(s).
4 Horns.
5 Auxiliary lights.
With ignition circuits energised check operation of:
6. All warning lights.
7. Fuel level indicator.
8. Heater blower motor.
9. Windscreen washers.
10. Windscreen wipers.
11. Direction indicators.
12. Brake lights.
13 Reversing lights.
14 Start engine and note that the oil pressure warning has extinguished.
Check operation of:
15 Charging system warning light in relation to engine speed.
16 Temperature indicator.
17 Switch off the engine and return the auxiliary ignition switch to the ignition position, then re-check the function of any fitted accessories e.g. a radio, that are supplied with power from this switch position.
18 Report any defects found.

(58) **Check/top up battery electrolyte**

Using DISTILLED WATER ONLY top up; the electrolyte level is correct when it just covers the separators.

(59) **Clean and grease battery connections**

1 Check the battery and surrounding area for corrosion from battery chemicals.
2 Clean off any corrosion found.
3 Check visually for any cracks in the battery case and report on any case cracks found.
4 Check security of terminal connections.
5 Coat terminals with petroleum jelly.

(60) **Check/adjust headlamp alignment**

See 86.40.17.

(61) **Check, if necessary renew wiper blades**

1 Examine each wiper blade in turn for damage before wetting the windscreen and operating the wiper motor control.
2 Replace wiper blades if they are damaged or if the screen is smeared.

(62) **Check output of charging system**

(63) **Check brake system warning light**

EXHAUST AND FUEL PIPES

(64) **Check exhaust system for leaks and security**

1 Check security of exhaust pipe to manifold nuts, correct tightening torque is 30 to 37 lbf ft (4,2 to 5,1 kgf m).
2 Check security of exhaust pipe joint clips.
3 Check security of exhaust system mounting bolts.
4 Using a second operator, run engine at fast idle speed.
5 Check exhaust system joints for leaks. Check exhaust pipes for leaks arising from damage or deterioration.
6 Check exhaust silencers for leaks arising from damage or deterioration.
7 Stop engine.
8 Report any defects found.

(65) **Check fuel system for leaks, pipes and unions for chafing and corrosion**

Report any defects found.

(66) **Check condition of fuel filler cap seal**

1 Make a visual check of the seal for the fuel tank filler cap.
2 Renew the seal if its condition is doubtful.

WHEELS AND TYRES

(67) **Check/adjust tyre pressures including spare**

Refer to Driver's Handbook for pressure settings.

(68) **Check that tyres comply with manufacturers specification**

See Driver's Handbook.
Report any deviations that may influence the car's performance or the accuracy of the speedometer.

(69) **Check tightness of road wheel fastenings**

Refer to 'TORQUE WRENCH SETTINGS' for data.

(70) **Check tyres for external cuts in tyre fabric, exposure of ply or cord structure, lumps or bulges**

(71) **Check tyres for tread depth and visually for external cuts in fabric, exposure or ply or cord structure, lumps or bulges.**

WARNING
It can be dangerous
a To use a car fitted with tyres in a damaged condition.
b To mix cross ply and radial ply tyres on the same axle or to fit radial ply tyres to the front wheels only.
c To use a car fitted with tyres that have a tread depth of less than 0.039 in (1.0 mm) over three-quarters of the tread width for the entire circumference of the tyre.
d To use a car with the tyres inflated to a pressure that is not suitable for the use to which the vehicle is put.

If the tyres to do not conform with legal requirements report to the owner.

BODY

(72) Lubricate all locks and hinges (not steering lock)

(73) Check condition and security of seats and seat belts

(74) Check rear view mirror for cracks and crazing

(75) Check operation of all door, bonnet and boot locks

(76) Check operation of seat belt warning system

(77) Check operation of seat belt inertial reel mechanism

(78) Check operation of window controls

(79) Check tightness of subframe/body mountings

Refer to 'TORQUE WRENCH SETTINGS' for data.

(80) Ensure cleanliness of controls, door handles, steering wheel

GENERAL

(81) Road/roller test and check function of all instrumentation

(82) Report additional work required

PREVENTIVE MAINTENANCE

In addition to the recommended periodical inspection of brake components it is advisable as the car ages and as a precaution against the effects of wear and deterioration to make a more searching inspection and renew parts as necessary. It is recommended that:

1 Disc brake pads, drum brake linings, hoses and pipes should be examined at intervals no greater than those laid down in the Maintenance Summary Chart.

2 Brake fluid should be changed every 18 months or 19,000 miles whichever is the sooner.

3 All fluid seals in the hydraulic system should be renewed and all flexible hoses should be examined and renewed if necessary every 3 years or 37,500 miles whichever is the sooner. At the same time the working surface of the piston and of the bores of the master cylinder, wheel cylinders and other slave cylinders should be examined and new parts fitted where necessary.

Care must be taken always to observe the following points:

a At all times use the recommended brake fluid.

b Never leave fluid in unsealed containers. It absorbs moisture quickly and can be dangerous if used in your braking system in this condition.

c Fluid drained from the system or used for bleeding should be discarded.

d The necessity for absolute cleanliness throughout cannot be overemphasized.

Replacing brake-shoes

When it becomes necessary to renew the brake-shoes, it is essential that only genuine shoes, with the correct grade of lining, are used. Always fit new shoes as complete sets, never individually or as a single wheel set. Serious consequences could result from out-of-tolerance braking due to the mixing of lining.

MAINTENANCE SUMMARY — USA Market Specification — Fuel Injection Engined Vehicles

Operation No.	Miles × 1000	Kilometres × 1000	Service
10.10.03	1	1-6	A
10.10.15	7.5, 22.5, 37.5, 57.5, 72.5, 87.5, 102.5, 117.5, 132.5	12, 36, 60, 92, 116, 140, 164, 188, 212	B
10.10.30	15, 45, 65, 95, 125	24, 72, 104, 152, 200	C
10.10.60	30, 80, 110, 140	48, 128, 176, 224	D
10.10.99	50, 100	80, 160	E

To meet USA legislative requirements
Items marked thus † are applicable up to 50,000 miles only
Items marked thus †† are applicable at 50,000 miles and onwards

ENGINE

Operation	A	B	C	D	E
Renew engine oil	x	x	x	x	x
Check for oil leaks	x	x	x	x	x
Renew engine oil filter		x	x	x	x
Lubricate accelerator control linkage (and pedal pivot); check operation					
Renew fuel filter(s)	†	†	†	†	
Renew air intake air cleaner element		††	††	††	††
Check/adjust all driving belts		x	x	x	x
Check/adjust all driving belts; renew as necessary					
Check cooling and heater systems for leaks and hoses for security and condition	x	x	x	x	x
Check/adjust torque of cylinder head nuts/bolts	x	x	x	x	x
Check/adjust operation of all washers and top up reservoirs		x	x	x	x
Check crankcase breathing and evaporative loss control systems					
Check hoses/pipes and restrictors for blockage, security and condition	†			††	††
Check/adjust engine idle speed	x	x	x	x	x
Check/top up cooling system					

IGNITION

Operation	A	B	C	D	E
Lubricate distributor (Lucas only)				x	x
Check/adjust ignition timing using electronic equipment			††	††	††
Clean/adjust spark plugs; renew as necessary			††	††	††
Renew spark plugs				†	
Check security of distributor vacuum line and operation of vacuum unit			††	††	††
Check ignition wiring (including electric fuel pump wiring) for security, fraying, chafing and deterioration				†	
Check ignition wiring (including electric fuel pump wiring) for security, fraying, chafing and deterioration			††	††	††

TRANSMISSION

Operation	A	B	C	D	E
Check for oil leaks	x	x	x	x	x
Check/top-up gearbox oil	x	x	x	x	x
Check/top-up automatic gearbox oil	x	x	x	x	x
Renew automatic gearbox oil and filter			x	x	x
Check clutch pipes for cracks, chafing, leaks and corrosion	x	x	x	x	x
Check/top-up rear axle/final drive oil	x	x	x	x	x
Check/top-up clutch fluid reservoir	x	x	x	x	x
Check tightness of propeller shaft coupling bolts	x	x	x	x	x

STEERING AND SUSPENSION

Operation	A	B	C	D	E
Check condition and security of steering unit, joints and gaiters	x	x	x	x	x
Check steering rack/gear for oil/fluid leaks	x	x	x	x	x
Check/top-up fluid in power steering reservoir		x	x	x	x
Check/adjust front wheel alignment	x	x	x	x	x
Check shock absorbers for fluid leaks		x	x	x	x
Check power steering system for leaks, hydraulic pipes and unions for chafing and corrosion	x		x	x	x
Check/adjust front hub bearing end float			x	x	x
Lubricate steering rack and pinion			x	x	x

Operation	Service	A	B	C	D	E
BRAKES						
Check visually hydraulic pipes and unions for cracks, chafing, leaks and corrosion		X	X	X	X	X
Check/top-up brake fluid reservoir(s)		X	X	X	X	X
Inspect brake pads/linings for wear, discs/drums for condition; adjust brakes as necessary		X	X	X	X	X
Check brake servo hose(s) for security and condition		X	X	X	X	X
Renew hydraulic brake fluid		22,500 miles (36,000 km) or 18 months whichever is the sooner.				
Renew air filter in brake servo unit		37,500 miles (60,000 km) or 3 years whichever is the sooner.				
ELECTRICAL						
Check function of original equipment, i.e. interior and exterior lamps, horns, wipers and all warning indicators		X	X	X	X	X
Check/adjust headlamp alignment			X	X	X	X
Check, if necessary renew, wiper blades			X	X	X	X
Check/top up battery electrolyte		X	X	X	X	X
Clean and grease battery connections			X	X	X	X
FUEL AND EXHAUST SYSTEMS						
Check exhaust system for leaks and security		X	X	X	X	X
Check fuel system for leaks, pipes and unions for chafing and corrosion		X	X	X	X	X
Check condition of fuel filler cap seal				X	X	X
Renew Lambda (oxygen) sensor and reset service interval counter					X	X
WHEELS AND TYRES						
Check/adjust tyre pressures including spare		X	X	X	X	X
Check tightness of road wheel fastenings		X	X	X	X	X
Check that tyres comply with manufacturer's specification		X	X	X	X	X
Check tyres for tread depth and visually for external cuts in fabric, exposure of ply or cord structure, lumps or bulges		X	X	X	X	X

Operation	Service	A	B	C	D	E
BODY						
Lubricate all locks, hinges and door check mechanisms (not steering lock)		X		X		X
Check operation of all door, bonnet luggage compartment and steering column locks		X	X	X	X	X
Check condition, security and operation of seats and seat belts		X	X	X	X	X
Check operation of window controls		X	X	X	X	X
GENERAL						
Road/roller test. Check brake operation and function of all instrumentation		X	X	X	X	X
Report additional work required		X	X	X	X	X

ADDITIONAL RECOMMENDATIONS

In addition to the recommended periodical inspection of brake components it is advisable as the car ages and as a precaution against the effects of wear and deterioration to make a more searching inspection and renew parts as necessary.

It is recommended that:

1 Disc brake pads, drum brake linings, hoses and pipes should be examined at intervals no greater than those laid down in the Maintenance Summary.

2 Brake fluid should be changed completely every 18 months or 22,500 miles (36 000 km) whichever is the sooner.

3 All fluid seals in the hydraulic system and all flexible hoses should be examined and renewed if necessary every three years or 37,500 miles (60 000 km) whichever is the sooner. At the same time the working surface of the pistons and of the bores of the master cylinder, wheel cylinders and other slave cylinders should be examined and new parts fitted where necessary.

Care must be taken always to observe the following points:

a At all times use the recommended brake fluid.

b Never leave fluid in unsealed containers; it absorbs moisture quickly and can be dangerous if used in the braking system in this condition.

c Fluid drained from the system or used for bleeding should be discarded.

d The necessity for absolute cleanliness throughout cannot be over-emphasized.

ENGINE

Renew engine oil

NOTE: This operation is best carried out when the engine is warm and with the vehicle standing level on a ramp or over a pit.

1 To drain the sump, unscrew the drain plug three complete turns to direct the oil stream into a receptacle while the engine is warm. When the rate of flow lessens remove the plug completely. Refit the plug and refill the sump with the appropriate grade of engine oil. The use of additives is unnecessary.

Check for oil leaks

Renew engine oil filter

See 12.60.02.

Lubricate accelerator control linkage (and pedal pivot); check operation

Renew fuel filter(s)

A single or twin filters may be fitted. They are located at the right-hand rear of the vehicle, mounted beneath the floor, forward of the rear axle. A cover may be fitted on later models, see 19.25.03.

The fuel system must be depressurized before commencing this operation, see 19.50.02.

1 Disconnect the fuel pipes from each end of the filter(s).
2 Slacken the clip securing the filter(s).
3 Withdraw and discard the filter(s).
4 Fit the new filter with the end marked 'IN' connected to the fuel supply pipe. (Alternative arrow markings denote fuel flow direction.)
5 Tighten the securing clip and fuel connections.

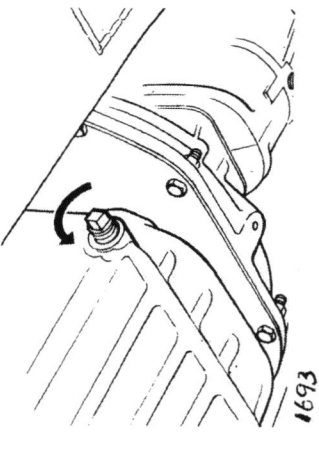

1693

Renew air intake air cleaner element

Refer to Operation 19.10.08.

Check/adjust all driving belts

Check/adjust all driving belts; renew if necessary

Check condition where belt is visibly worn or damaged. Fit new belt if necessary. Check and adjust:
a Alternator drive belt, see 86.10.05.
b Compressor drive belt (where applicable), see 82.10.01.

Check cooling/heating systems for leaks and hoses for security and condition

1 Check for leaks from engine and radiator drain taps/plugs (where fitted).
2 Check for leaks from water hose joints.
3 Check for leaks from water hoses through damage or porosity.
4 Check for leaks from the water pump thermostat housing, radiator and heater unit.
5 Report any leaks found.

Check/adjust torque of cylinder head nuts/bolts

See 12.29.27.

Check/adjust operation of all washers and top-up reservoirs

1 Replenish the container with clean soft water. The addition of a small amount of mild detergent will prevent smearing on the windscreen.
2 During freezing conditions it is beneficial to fill the container with a mixture of one part methylated spirits (wood alcohol) to two parts of water. This will assist in the dispersal of snow and ice from the screen.
3 Do not add anti-freeze solutions to the container as this will discolour the paint-work and damage wiper blades and sealing rubber.

Check crankcase breathing and evaporative loss control systems

Check hoses and restrictors for blockage, security and condition

1 Inspect all hoses for condition and renew any hoses that show signs of deterioration, including slackness or cracking.
2 Completely disconnect the crankcase purge line and the adsorption canister purge line, then using a low pressure air supply, blow through these hoses to check for blockage. Investigate and clear any blockage, paying particular attention to the restrictors.
3 Refit the purge lines, ensuring that all connections are secure and tight. Renew any doubtful hose.

Check/adjust engine idle speeds

See 19.20.18.

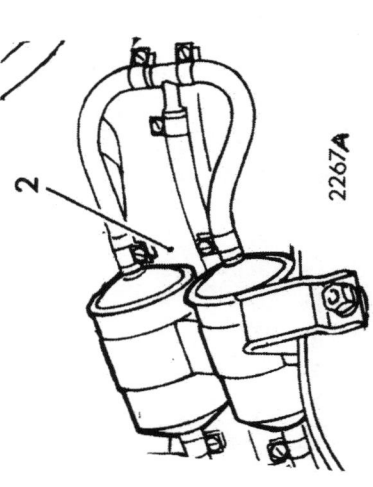

2267A

Check/top-up cooling system

WARNING: When it is necessary to remove the pressure/filler cap from a hot engine, exercise great care by protecting the hands against escaping steam. Slowly turn the pressure cap anti-clockwise until resistance of the safety stop is felt. Leave the cap in this position until all pressure is released. Press the cap downwards against the spring to clear the safety stops, and continue turning until it can be lifted off.

The pressurized cooling system incorporates a header tank which provides a single point for coolant filling and level checking.

The coolant level should be maintained at 1 inch (25 mm) below the neck of the header tank.

If the cooling system has been drained the procedure for refilling the system is as follows:

1　Remove the header tank filler cap.
2　Set the interior heater controls to the maximum heat position.
3　Fill the system until the coolant level is 1 inch (25 mm) below the neck of the header tank.
4　Refit the header tank filler cap and run the engine at approximately 1500 rev/min until the coolant temperature rises sufficiently to open the thermostat.
5　Stop the engine and, observing the caution above, remove the header tank filler cap.
6　Top-up the coolant level as necessary until it is 1 inch (25.4 mm) below the header tank filler neck.
7　Refit the filler cap.

IGNITION

Lubricate distributor (Lucas only)

1　Remove the distributor cap and rotor arm. Using an oil can, apply three drops of a clean, recommended engine oil into the reservoir in the rotor carrier.
2　Remove flash-over shield and lubricate pick-up centre bearing plate with a drop of the same oil in each of the two holes provided. DO NOT disturb the screw securing the base plate. Refit the flash-over shield.

Check/adjust ignition timing using electronic equipment

See 86.35.15.

Clean/adjust spark plugs

For each spark plug in turn:
1　Remove the ignition high tension lead from the plug.
2　Unscrew the plug from the engine using a special plug spanner or a box type spanner.
3　Wipe clean the ceramic body of the plug.
4　Visually check the plug body for cracks and renew the plug if any cracks are present.
5　Unscrew the end terminal cap from the plug.
6　Clean the plug terminal threads with a wire brush.
7　Clean the cap threads using a low pressure air line.

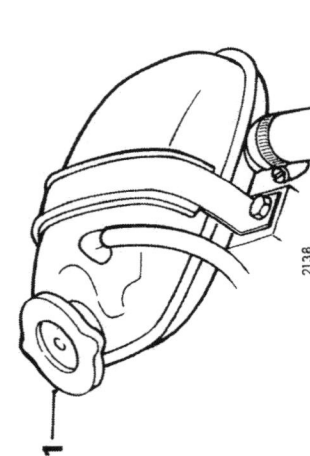

Renew spark plugs

For each plug in turn:
1　Remove the ignition high tension lead from the plug.
2　Unscrew the plug from the engine using a special plug spanner or a suitable box spanner.
3　Discard the plug.
4　Visually check the new plug for damage to the body and electrodes, discard the plug if there are any signs of damage.
5　Check the electrode gap on the new plug which when correct will just allow a 0.025 in (0.64 mm) feeler gauge to slide slowly between the electrodes under light pressure.
If adjustment is necessary, using a suitable tool carefully move the side electrode. Recheck the gap and repeat this procedure until the gap is correct.
6　Fit the new plug to the engine.
7　Tighten the plug to the correct torque.
8　Refit the high tension lead to the plug.

Check security of distributor vacuum line and operation of vacuum unit

1　Check security of distributor vacuum unit operating line connections.
2　Start the engine and warm it to normal running temperature.
3　When the engine is idling steadily, disconnect the vacuum unit pipe at the distributor.
4　A noticeable rise in engine speed (approximately 500 rev/min) should be apparent if the vacuum unit is functioning.
5　When satisfied that the vacuum unit is operating correctly, reconnect the vacuum unit pipe to the distributor ensuring a secure connection.

Check ignition wiring (including electric fuel pump wiring) for security, fraying, chafing and deterioration

TRANSMISSION

Check for oil leaks

Check/top-up gearbox oil

With the vehicle standing on level ground:
1　Remove the oil level plug.
2　Using a suitable dispenser such as a pump-type oil can with flexible nozzle filled with a recommended lubricant, top up the gearbox until the oil is level with the bottom of the filler plug threads.
3　Allow surplus oil to drain away before refitting the level plug and wiping clean.

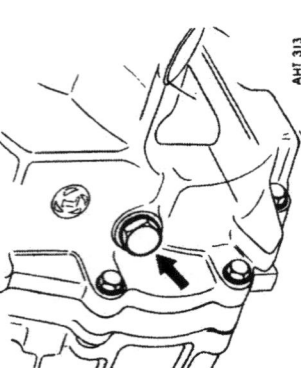

AHT 313

STEERING AND SUSPENSION

Check condition and security of steering unit, joints and gaiters

Refer to Section 06 as applicable.

Check steering rack/gear for oil/fluid leaks

Check/top-up fluid in power steering reservoir

1   Wipe clean the reservoir cap and surrounding area.
2   Unscrew the reservoir cap and dipstick.
3   Wipe the dipstick clean and replace it in position.
4   Withdraw the dipstick again and note the fluid level.

If topping-up is necessary:

5   Add recommended fluid via the filler cap to bring the level just below the high mark on the dipstick. **Do not overfill.**
6   Replace the reservoir cap.

/1679

Check/top-up clutch fluid reservoir

1   Wipe clean the area around the reservoir cap.
2   Unscrew the cap.
3   If necessary, top-up the reservoir to within ¼ in (6 mm) of the top with new brake fluid taken from a sealed container.
4   Replace the reservoir cap.

AHT 296

Renew automatic gearbox oil and filter

1   Remove the automatic gearbox sump, see 44.24.04.
2   Remove and discard the filter.
3   Fit a new filter.
4   Replace the sump, see 44.24.04.
5   Refill the gearbox with new oil.
6   Run the engine, prime the automatic gearbox and check for oil leaks.

Check clutch pipes for cracks, chafing, leaks and corrosion

Check/top-up rear axle/final drive oil

1   Remove the oil level plug.
2   Top-up the rear axle until the oil is level with the bottom of the filler plug thread.
3   Allow surplus oil to drain before fitting the plug and wiping clean.

AHT 293

Check tightness of propeller shaft coupling bolts

Check the following fastenings for tightness:
Propeller shaft to gearbox and rear axle:
10 mm bolt 50 Nm (37 lbf ft).

Check/top-up automatic gearbox oil

1   Stand the car on level ground and apply the handbrake firmly. Start the engine from cold and, with the footbrake firmly applied, run the engine at idle speed for 2 to 3 minutes, passing the selector lever through the complete range of positions to ensure that the transmission is primed.
2   Select the 'P' (Park) position and apply the handbrake. Leave the engine running at idle speed.
3   Remove the transmission dipstick and wipe it with a clean, non-fluffy cloth.
4   Replace the dipstick, ensuring that it is pushed fully into the tube and withdraw it immediately for reading.
5   Check the fluid level on the side of the dipstick marked 'COLD' and, if necessary, add fluid; see 'Lubrication Recommendations'.
6   Repeat instructions 1 to 5 until the fluid level is correct. DO NOT OVERFILL THE TRANSMISSION.

AHT 294

Where the reverse side of the dipstick carries marks denoted 'HOT', the fluid level check may be carried out with the transmission at normal operating temperature. The procedure is as described above except that the vehicle must be driven for 15 to 20 miles (25 to 30 km) to warm the transmission. The check is then carried out using the 'HOT' side of the dipstick.

Check/adjust front wheel alignment

Refer to Operation 57.65.01.

Check shock absorbers for fluid leaks

Check power steering system for leaks, hydraulic pipes and unions for chafing and corrosion

Check/adjust front hub bearing end float

Refer to Operation 60.25.13.

Lubricate steering rack and pinion

Using a recommended grease, lubricate the steering rack and pinion as follows:

1 Wipe clean the plug and surrounding area.

2 Remove the grease nipple plug, taking care not to disturb the larger damper plug.

3 Fit a suitable grease nipple in place of the plug.

4 Turn the steering wheel to full right-hand lock.

5 Apply a grease gun to the grease nipple and give five strokes only.

CAUTION: Overgreasing can cause damage to the protective gaiters and/or seals.

6 Remove the grease nipple and refit the plug.

7 Wipe away any surplus grease.

A57002

BRAKES

Check visually hydraulic pipes and unions for cracks, chafing, leaks and corrosion

Check/top-up brake fluid reservoir

Top-up when required with new fluid of the correct type recommended — see 'LUBRICANTS & ANTI-FREEZE SOLUTIONS'. Do not allow the fluid level to drop below the danger mark on the reservoir.

WARNING: Use only new brake fluid of the correct specification. DO NOT use fluid of unknown origin, or fluid that has been exposed to the atmosphere, or discharged during bleeding operations. If significant topping is required, check the hydraulic system for leaks.

CAUTION: Paintwork can be damaged by direct contact with brake fluid.

Inspect brake pads/linings for wear, discs/drums for condition, adjust brakes as necessary

Front brakes

1 Remove the brake pads, see 70.40.02.

2 Renew the pads if the lining thickness is likely to be below 3 mm (⅛ in) before the next service.

Rear brakes

1 Remove the brake drum, see 70.10.03.

2 Renew the brake linings if they are likely to have worn near the rivets or be less than 1.5 mm (¹⁄₁₆ in) thick before the next service.

Brake-shoe renewal

When it becomes necessary to renew the brake-shoes, it is essential to use only genuine shoes, with the correct grade of lining. Always fit new shoes as complete sets, never individually or as a single wheel set. Serious consequences could result from out-of-balance braking due to the mixing of linings.

Adjustment

The front and rear brakes are self-adjusting, but the handbrake may be adjusted following instructions in Operation 70.35.10.

Check brake servo hose(s) for security and condition

Renew hydraulic brake fluid

Refer to notes following 'Check/top-up brake fluid reservoir'.

Renew air filter in brake servo unit

Refer to Operation 70.50.25.

ELECTRICAL

Check function of original equipment i.e. interior and exterior lamps, horns, wipers and all warning indicators

Check/adjust headlamp alignment

Refer to Operation 86.40.17.

Check, if necessary renew, wiper blades

Refer to Operation 84.15.06/07.

Check/top-up battery electrolyte

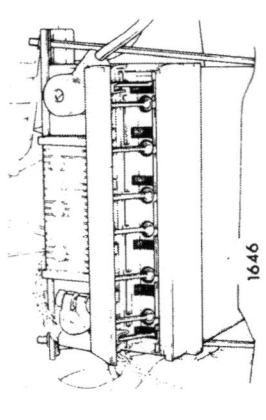

1646

1 Lift the cover.

2 Check the electrolyte level, which if correct should just cover the separators.

3 Add distilled water as necessary.

Clean and grease battery connections

FUEL AND EXHAUST SYSTEMS

Check exhaust system for leaks and security

1 Place the car on a ramp or over a pit.
2 Check the exhaust system fixings for security, paying particular attention to heat shields, flexible mounting plates and clamps.
3 Using a second operator, run the engine at fast idle speed.
4 Check exhaust system joints for leaks.
5 Check exhaust pipes for leaks arising from damage or deterioration.
6 Check exhaust silencers for leaks arising from damage or deterioration.
7 Stop the engine.
8 Report any defects found. Silencers or pipes found to be leaking or badly corroded should be renewed.
9 Fit new parts as necessary.

Check fuel system for leaks, pipes and unions for chafing and corrosion

Visually check the fuel feed system for leaks as follows:

1 Check for leaks from fuel system connections.
2 Check the fuel pipes for chafing, corrosion and damage.
3 Check for leaks from the fuel and expansion tanks, pump, rails and injectors.
4 Renew any items which show signs of deterioration.

Check condition of fuel filler cap seal

Renew Lambda (oxygen) sensor and reset service interval counter

1 Disconnect the electrical lead from the sensor.
2 Unscrew the sensor from the exhaust manifold, taking care not to strain the exhaust system.
3 Lubricate the threads of the new sensor and fit it to the exhaust manifold. Tighten the sensor sufficient to make a gas-tight seal, but do not overtighten.
4 Reconnect the electrical leads to the sensor.
5 Reset the service interval counter using the special tool necessary for this purpose.

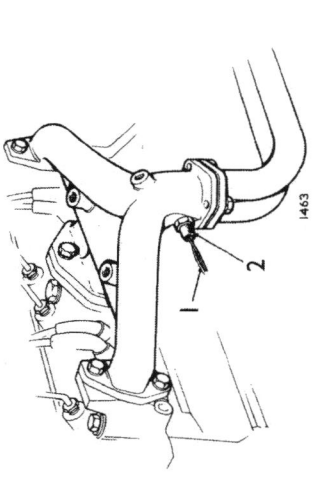

WHEELS AND TYRES

Check/adjust tyre pressures, including spare

Refer to Section 04.

Check tightness of road wheel fastenings

If correct, these will be tightened to a torque of 75 lbf ft (10.3 kgf m).

Check that tyres comply with manufacturer's specification

Refer to Section 04.

Check tyres for tread depth and visually for external cuts in fabric, exposure of ply or cord structure, lumps or bulges

BODY

Lubricate all locks, hinges and door check mechanisms (not steering lock)

Check operation of all door, bonnet, tailgate and steering column locks

Check operation of window controls

Check condition, security and operation of seats and seat belt

The seat belt inertia reel mechanism may be checked using the following procedure:

1 IMPORTANT: The following road test must be carried out only under maximum safe road conditions, i.e. on a dry, straight, traffic-free road.
   With the safety harness fitted to the driver and front seat passenger drive the car at 5 mph (8 km/h); ensuring that it is safe to do so, brake sharply. The safety harness should lock automatically, holding both driver and passenger securely in position.

   It is important when braking that the reactions of both driver and passenger are normal, i.e. the body must not be thrown forward in anticipation, thus causing a 'snatching' action of the belt which would operate the locking mechanism.

2 *Snatch test:* Whilst seated, fasten the seat belt and grip the shoulder belt at approximately shoulder level with the opposite hand. Pull the belt sharply in a downwards direction, the belt should lock.
   If the belt fails to lock on either test, the seat belt should be replaced, see 76.73.10.

GENERAL

Road/roller test. Check brake operation and function of all instrumentation

Brake operation
The operation of the footbrake and handbrake independently should be sufficient to stop the vehicle without pull to one side, within a distance required by any local territory legislation.

In addition the footbrakes and/or the handbrake must prevent vehicle movement on a steep incline. Again reference should be made to any applicable local territory legislation.

Report additional work required

ENGINE

The operations in this Section deal mainly with basic engine units. Where emission control, fuel injection, air conditioning or other equipment is fitted it may be necessary to refer to Sections 17, 19, 82, etc., of this Manual as appropriate.

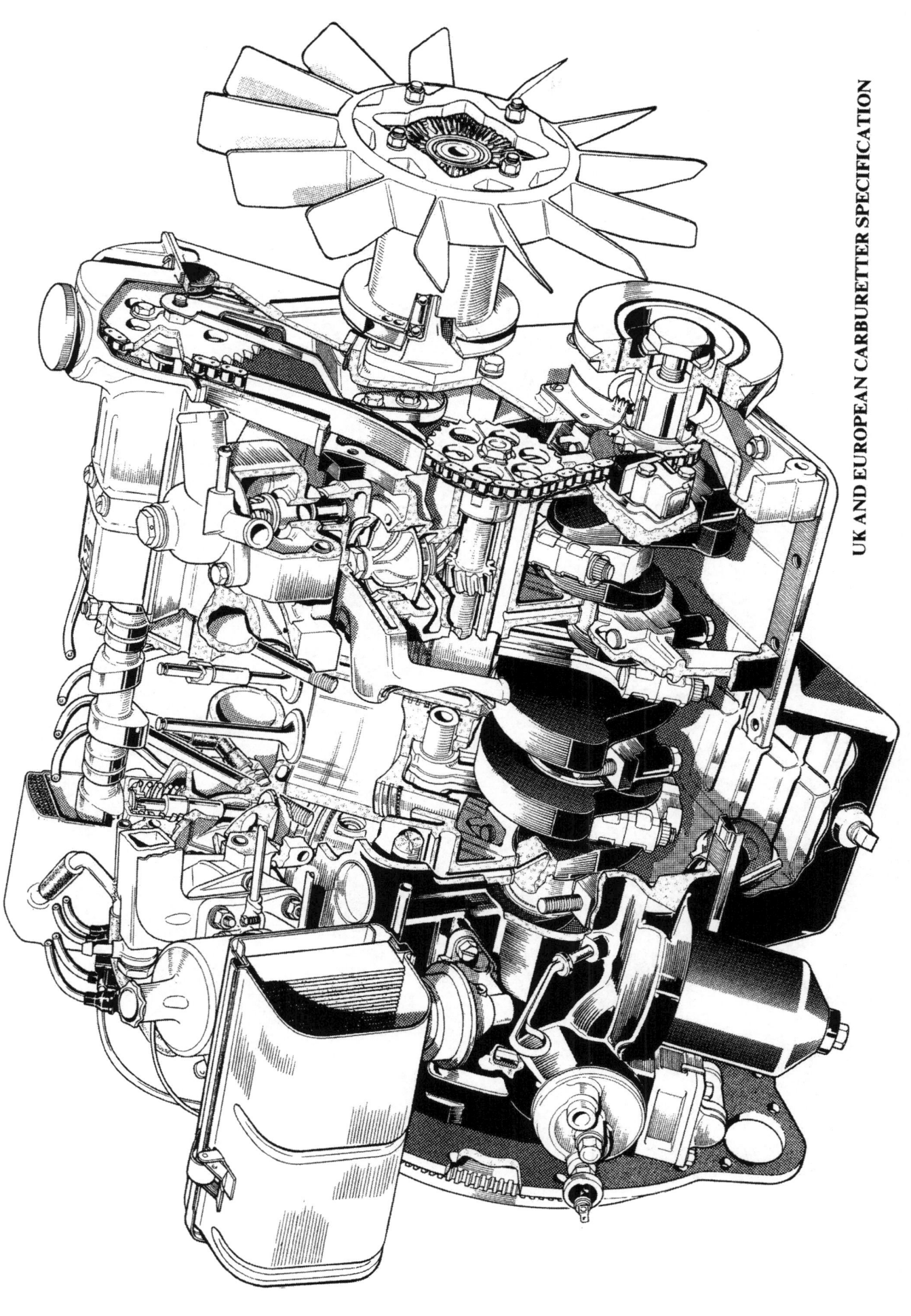

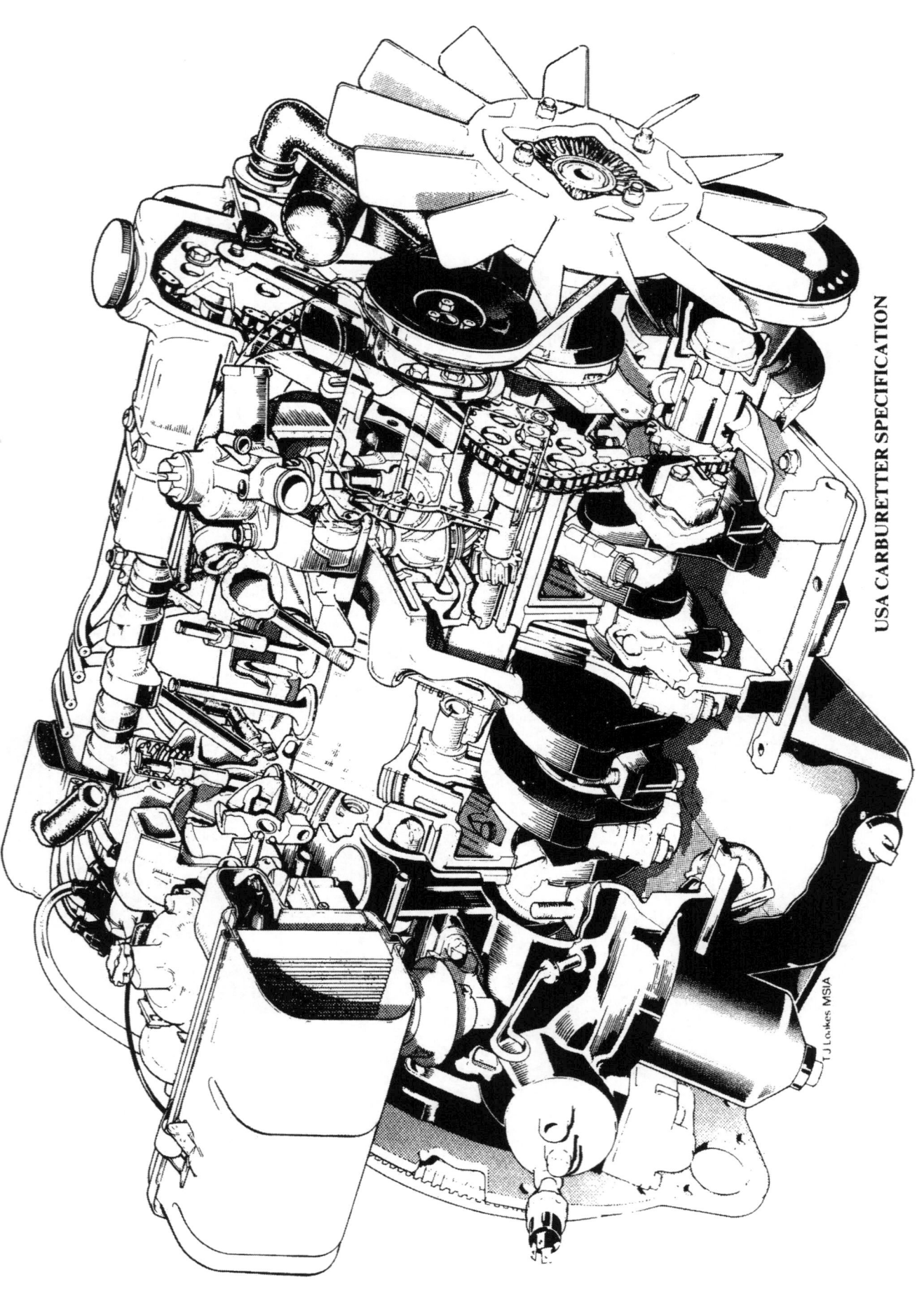

USA CARBURETTER SPECIFICATION

T J Lakes MSIA

JACKSHAFT

Remove and refit   12.10.14

Removing

1 Disconnect the battery.
2 Remove the fresh air duct. 80.15.31.
3 Remove the radiator. 26.40.01.
4 Remove the air conditioning condenser 82.15.10 (if fitted).
5 Remove the timing chain cover. 12.65.01.
6 Remove the inlet manifold complete with carburetters or fuel rail.
7 Remove the water pump cover. 26.50.01.
8 Remove the impeller. 26.50.01.
9 Remove the petrol pump. 19.45.08.
10 Remove the camshaft cover. 12.29.42.
11 Turn the engine over so that the timing mark on the camshaft flange is in line with the groove on the camshaft front bearing cap.
12 Remove the distributor cap and check that the rotor arm points to the last manifold bolt hole in the cylinder head thus indicating that the engine is at T.D.C. number one cylinder firing.
13 Remove the distributor.
14 Remove the hydraulic timing chain tensioner. 12.65.28.

15 Remove the adjustable timing chain guide. 12.65.50.
16 Remove the two Allen screws and withdraw the jackshaft keeper plate.
17 Lift the timing chain clear of the sprocket and withdraw the jackshaft complete with the sprocket.
18 Hold the jackshaft in a vice and remove the sprocket retaining bolt, tab washer and sprocket.

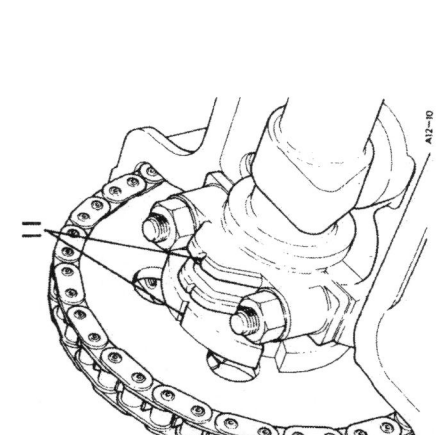

A12-64   USA Specification

Refitting

19 Fit the sprocket to the jackshaft using a new tab washer.
20 Insert the jackshaft into the cylinder block and secure with the keeper plate and two Allen screws.
21 Turn the jackshaft so that the scribed line across the sprocket is equidistant between the lower bolt securing the camshaft sprocket support bracket and the timing cover centre retaining bolt hole. Fit the chain whilst holding the jackshaft in this position.
22 Fit the adjustable chain guide and leave the bolt slack.
23 Fit the hydraulic timing chain tensioner, see 12.65.28, instructions 7 to 19.
24 Fit the petrol pump ensuring that the lever rides on top of the jackshaft cam.
25 Fit the water pump impeller and cover, see 26.50.01, instructions 9 to 14.
26 Fit the distributor and line-up the rotor as in instruction 12 and check the timing. 86.35.15.
27 Fit the timing chain cover. 12.65.01.
28 Fit the camshaft cover.

29 Fit the air conditioning condenser 82.15.10.
30 Fit the radiator. 26.40.01.
31 Fit the inlet manifold complete with carburetters or fuel rail.
32 Fit the fresh air duct. 80.15.31.
33 Check that the cooling system has been filled and connect the battery.

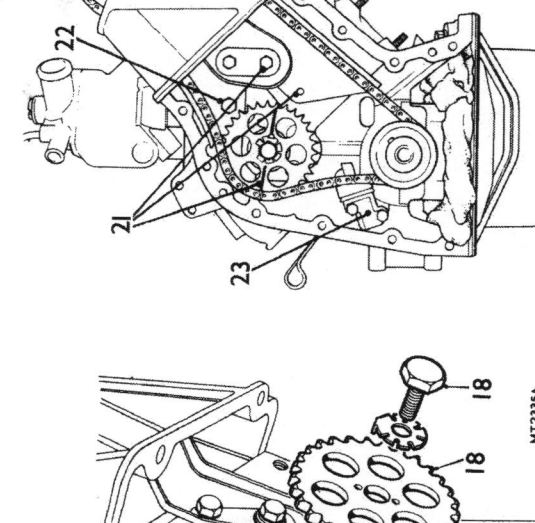

MT2335A

UK and Europe Specification

A12-93

CAMSHAFT   12.13.01

Remove and refit

Removing

1 Disconnect the battery.
2 Remove the fresh air duct. 80.15.31.
3 Remove the camshaft cover. 12.29.42.
4 Turn the engine over so that the timing mark on the camshaft flange is 180° distant from the groove in the camshaft front bearing cap to gain access to the lower bolt.
5 Anchor the camshaft sprocket to the support bracket using a 'slave' nut.
6 Unlock and remove the exposed camshaft sprocket lower retaining bolt.
7 Turn the engine over so that the timing mark on the camshaft flange is exactly in line with the groove in the camshaft front bearing cap.
8 Unlock and remove the remaining sprocket retaining bolt and lock washer.
9 Evenly slacken-off the ten camshaft bearing cap nuts and remove them complete with plain washers.
10 Check that the bearing caps are numbered for identification i.e. starting at the front of the engine, number one is recognized by the timing grooves and the remainder are numbered 2 to 5.
11 Withdraw the caps and remove the camshaft.

Refitting

12 Clean and lubricate the camshaft journals and corresponding bearings in the cylinder head and fit the camshaft.
13 Lubricate and fit the bearing caps in their correct order.

CAUTION: Before commencing instruction 14 ensure that the timing mark on the camshaft flange is approximately in line with the groove in the front bearing cap to avoid damage being caused to the pistons by the valve heads.

14 Fit and tighten the bearing cap nuts and washers evenly to the correct torque figure – see section 06.

NOTE: At this stage in the operation the valve clearances may be checked if desired – see 12.29.48 but it is vital that before doing so the crankshaft is turned 90° so that the pistons are not at T.D.C. and therefore not in danger of being damaged by the valve heads.

15 Finally adjust the position of the camshaft timing mark in relation to the groove in the front bearing cap by turning the shaft by means of a spanner on the hexagon at the rear of the shaft.
16 Secure the camshaft sprocket to the camshaft using a new lock washer – do not at this stage fully tighten or lock the bolt.
17 Turn the engine over so that the remaining bolt may be fitted.
18 Tighten both bolts to the correct torque figure – see section 06 and bend over the lock tabs.
19 Remove the 'slave' nut holding the sprocket to the support bracket.
20 Fit the semi-circular sealing rubber to the cylinder head.
21 Fit the camshaft cover. 12.29.42.
22 Fit the fresh air duct. 80.15.31.
23 Reconnect the battery.

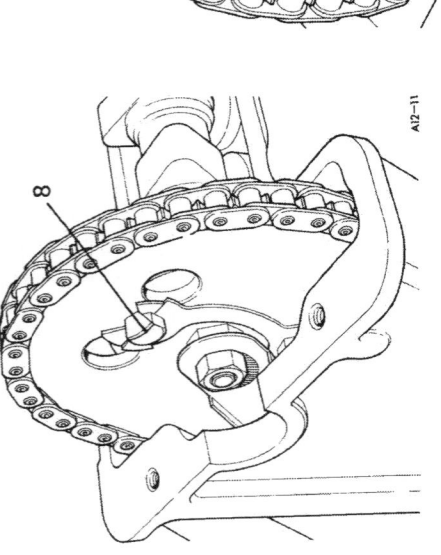
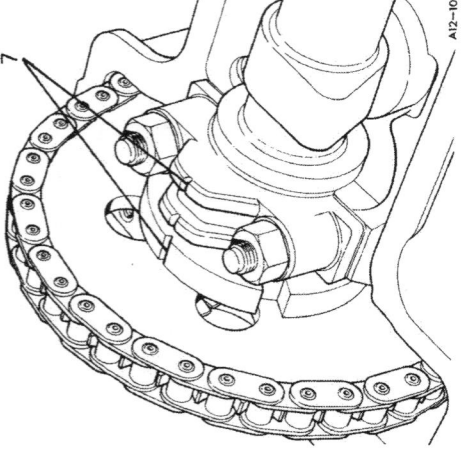
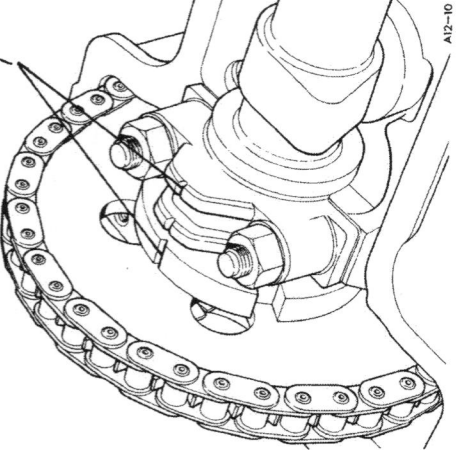

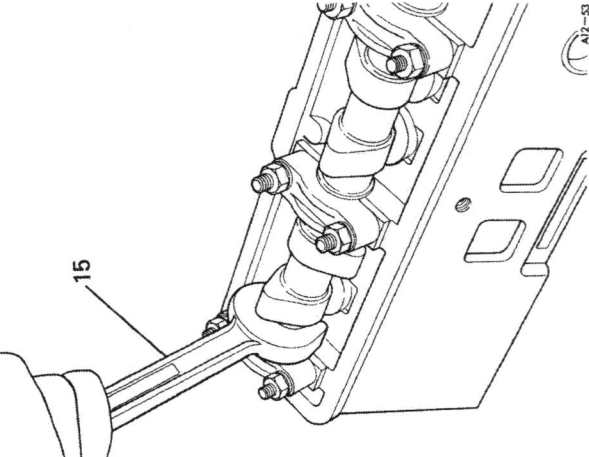
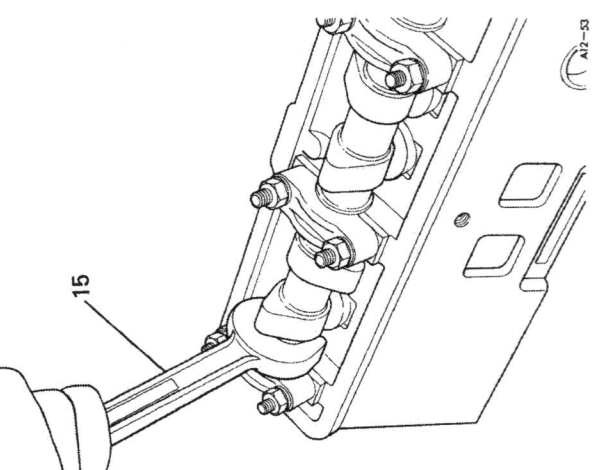

CONNECTING RODS AND PISTONS

Remove and refit   12.17.01

Special tool: 38 U3

CAUTION: Do not mix any components during this operation.

Removing

1 Drive the car onto a ramp and disconnect the battery.
2 Remove the inlet manifold complete with carburetters or fuel rail.
3 Remove the cylinder head. 12.29.10.
4 Remove the sump. 12.60.44.
5 Check the identification numbers on the connecting rods and caps.
6 Turn the crankshaft to bring numbers 1 to 4 pistons to T.D.C. and remove the nuts of numbers 2 and 3 connecting rods.

7 Withdraw the bearing caps and lower shells and fit plastic or rubber sleeves over the connecting rod bolts to prevent damage to the crankpins.
8 Push the piston and connecting rod assemblies upwards and withdraw through the top of the bores and remove the upper shells.
9 Turn the crankshaft to bring numbers 1 and 4 connecting rod bolts to an accessible position and remove the bearing caps nuts and withdraw the bearing caps and lower shells.
10 Push the piston and connecting rod assemblies upwards and withdraw as instruction 8.

Refitting

11 Stagger the piston ring gaps.
12 Lubricate the pistons and rings and compress the rings with special tool number 38 U3.
13 Insert the connecting rod and piston assemblies into their respective bores ensuring that the raised flat part of the piston crown and the valve head recesses are towards the right-hand side of the engine (as from the driver's position).

NOTE: Some pistons may have arrows stamped on both sides of the skirt, on the gudgeon pin bore side, to indicate the direction of the gudgeon pin off-set. Ensure that when fitting the piston assemblies to the bores that these arrows point to the right-hand side of the engine also. Alternatively some pistons may have an arrow on the crown and the piston assemblies must be fitted with the arrow pointing to the front of the engine.

14 Fit the upper bearing shells to the connecting rods ensuring that the keeper tags locate correctly in the connecting rod recesses.
15 Fit the lower bearing shells to the caps ensuring that the keeper tags locate in the recesses.
16 Pull the connecting rods onto the crankpins and fit the bearing caps to their respective connecting rods making sure that the identification numbers coincide and are adjacent. Note also that the bearing keeper recesses in the connecting rods and the caps are on the same side.
17 Secure the bearing caps with NEW nuts and tighten evenly to the correct torque – see 'TORQUE WRENCH SETTINGS'.
18 Fit the oil sump. 12.60.44.
19 Fit the cylinder head. 12.29.10.
20 Fit the inlet manifold complete with carburetters or fuel rail.
21 Refill the sump with the recommended grade of oil to the high mark on the dip-stick.
22 Refill the cooling system, see 26.10.01.
23 Reconnect the battery.

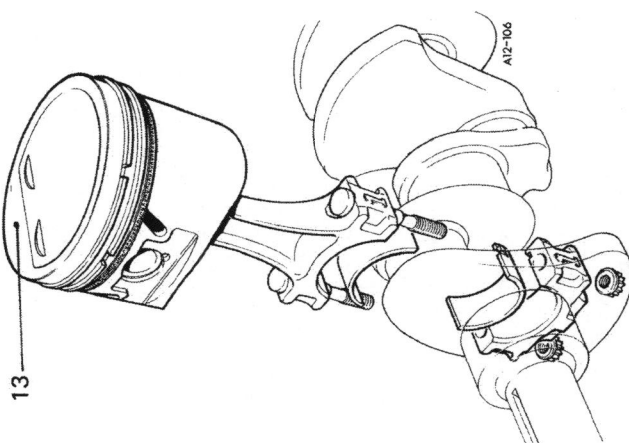

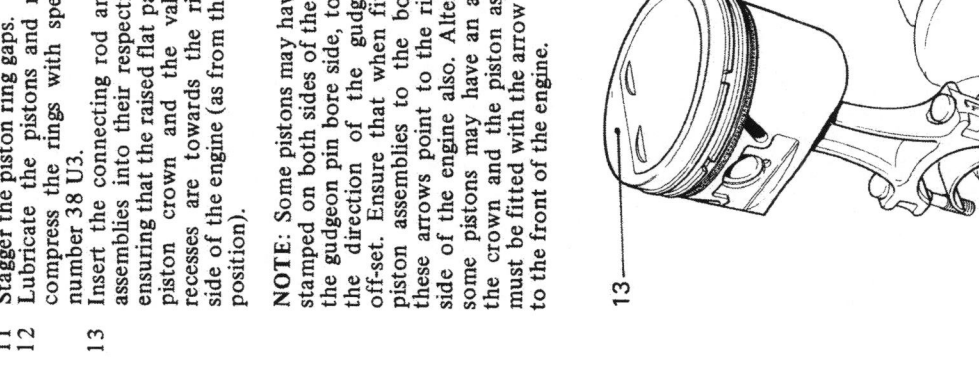

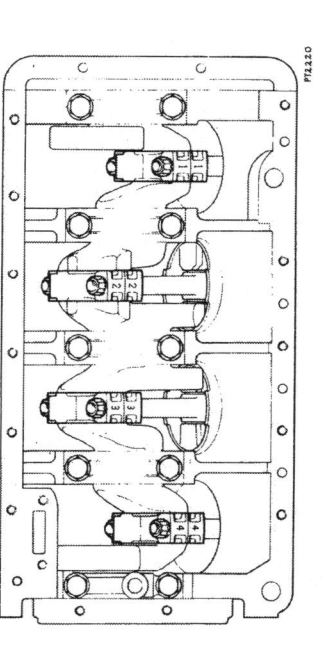

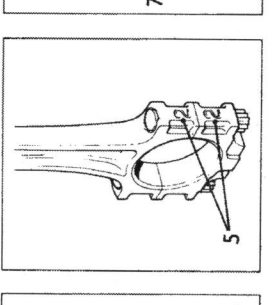

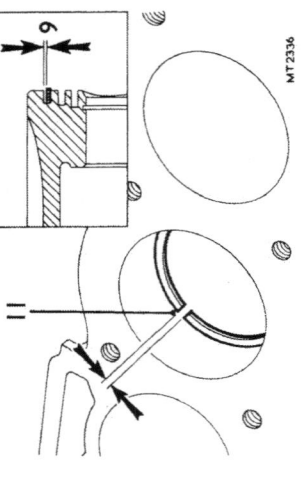

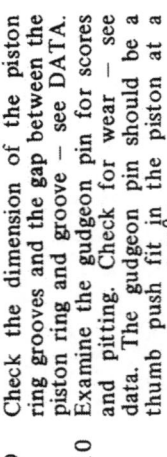

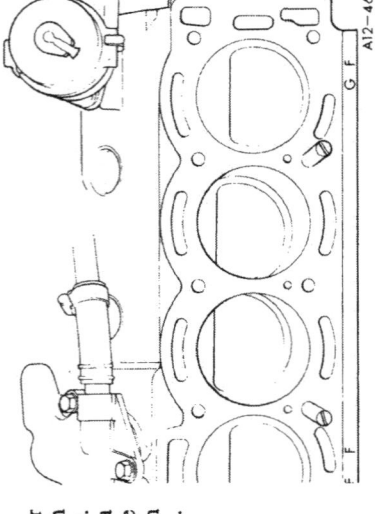

USA Specification

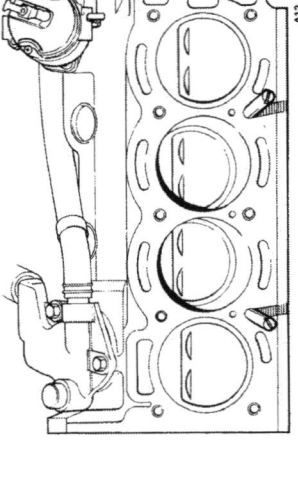

UK & Europe Specification

9 Check the dimension of the piston ring grooves and the gap between the piston ring and groove – see DATA.

10 Examine the gudgeon pin for scores and pitting. Check for wear – see data. The gudgeon pin should be a thumb push fit in the piston at a temperature of 68°F.

11 Check the top and scraper piston ring gaps when inserted squarely into the bores – see DATA.

NOTE: Two grades of standard piston designated F and G are fitted to new engines built on production. The cylinder block is stamped on the L.H. side as illustrated to indicate the individual bore grade. The grade of the corresponding piston is stamped on the crown.

Whilst these pistons are not supplied for service purposes, a single standard piston 0.001 in (0,0254 mm) oversize is available. Therefore should it be necessary to fit a new piston to a standard bore, the bore must be honed to accommodate the piston with the specified clearance – see DATA.

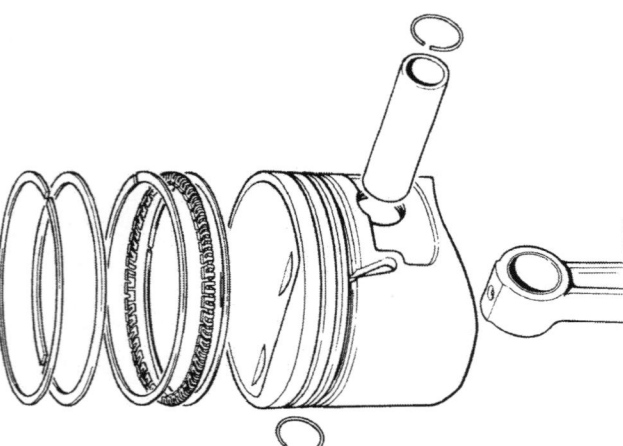

CONNECTING RODS AND PISTONS

Overhaul   12.17.10

Gudgeon pin bush – each –
– remove and refit   12.17.13

Special tool: 335

CAUTION: Do not mix the components during this operation.

Removing

1 Remove the connecting-rods and pistons. 12.17.01.

Dismantling

2 Remove the two gudgeon pin retaining circlips.

3 Push out the gudgeon pin and separate the piston from the connecting-rod.

4 Remove the top, scraper and oil control rings.

5 Repeat instructions 2 to 4 on the remaining pistons and connecting-rod assemblies.

6 De-grease all components and remove carbon deposits from the pistons.

Examination – Pistons and Gudgeon Pins

7 Examine the pistons for damage, scoring and cracks.

8 Determine the maximum clearance that exists between the pistons and their respective bores as follows:

a Measure the piston across the skirt – dimension A – at right angles to the gudgeon pin.

b Using a cylinder bore measuring gauge determine the maximum cylinder bore wear.

c Subtract (a) from (b) and compare the result with the clearance given in data for a new engine.

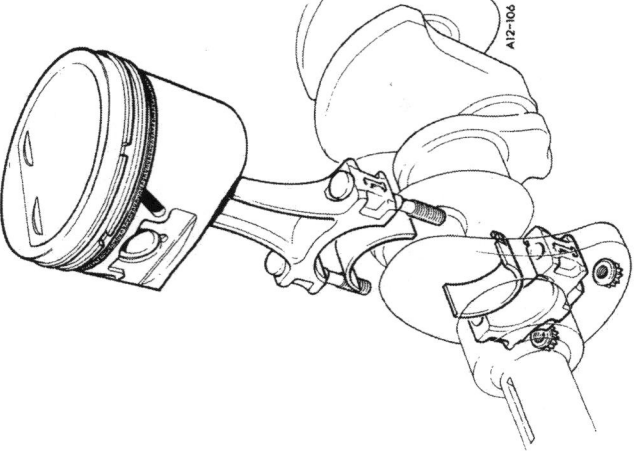

Examination — Connecting-rods

12 Using special tool 335 check the connecting-rods for:
  A. Bend
  B. Twist.
  Rods that exceed the tolerances in data should be realigned or renewed.

13 Check the gudgeon pin bush for wear and if necessary remove the old bush and fit a new one using a suitable press. Ensure that the oil hole in the bush corresponds exactly with the hole in the connecting-rod. Ream the new bush to size — see DATA.

Reassembling

14 Fit the piston rings in the following order:

NOTE: The oil control ring comprises three parts, A, B and C, namely the centre expander rail, flanked by two identical chrome rails.

A. Fit the expander rail into the bottom groove ensuring that the ends butt, not overlap.
B. Fit the bottom chrome rail to the bottom groove.
C. Fit the top chrome rail to the bottom groove.
D. Fit the scraper ring to the centre groove in the piston with the word 'TOP' uppermost.
E. Fit the top compression chrome ring to the top groove.

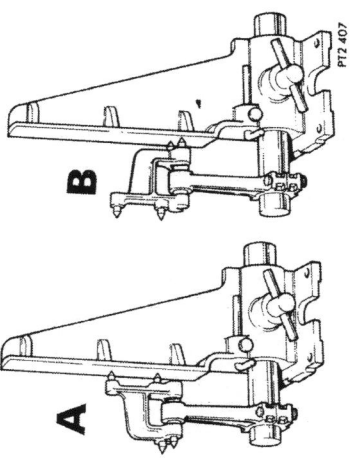

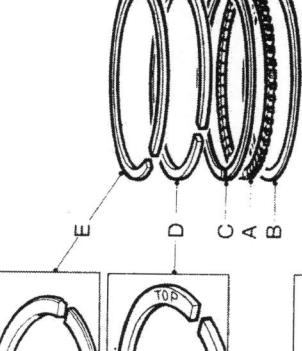

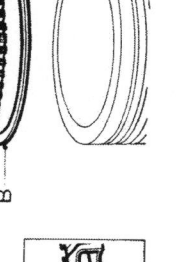

15 Refit the pistons to the connecting-rods so that the identification numbers and the shell bearing keeper recesses are on the opposite side to the raised part of the piston crown.

16 Locate the gudgeon pin with the two circlips ensuring that they fit properly in the grooves.

17 Fit the connecting-rods and pistons to the engine — instructions 10 to 21 12.17.01 ensuring that the sump is refilled with oil to the high mark on the dipstick.

18 Refill the cooling system before connecting the battery.

DATA

Cylinder bore size . . . . 3.56 in (90,3 mm)
Piston clearance in bore measured at bottom of skirt at right angles to the gudgeon pin . . . . 0.0005 to 0.0015 in (0,013 to 0,039 mm)

Pistons
Top compression ring groove width . . . 0.0705 to 0.0713 in (1,790 to 1,810 mm)
Second compression ring groove width . . 0.0700 to 0.0709 in (1,780 to 1,800 mm)
Oil control ring groove width . . . . . . 0.1579 to 0.1587 in (4,010 to 4,020 mm)

Piston rings
Top compression — gap in bore . . . . . 0.015 to 0.025 in (0,40 to 0,65 mm)
Top compression — clearance in groove . 0.0019 to 0.0039 in (0,050 to 0,082 mm)
Second compression ring — gap in bore . 0.015 to 0.025 in (0,40 to 0,65 mm)
Second compression ring — clearance in groove . . . . 0.0015 to 0.0025 in (0,040 to 0,065 mm)
Oil control rails — gap in bore . . . . . 0.015 to 0.055 in (0,40 to 1,40 mm)
Oil control expander — gap in bore . . . ends to butt
Oversize rings . . . . 0.010 to 0.020 in (0,254 to 0,508 mm)

Connecting rods
Small end bush fitted internal diameter . . 0.9377 to 0.9380 in (23,818 to 23,825 mm)
Bush external diameter . . . . 1.0015 to 1.0025 in (25,438 to 25,464 mm)

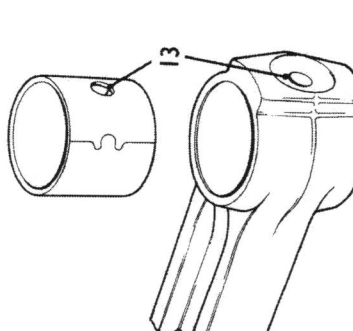

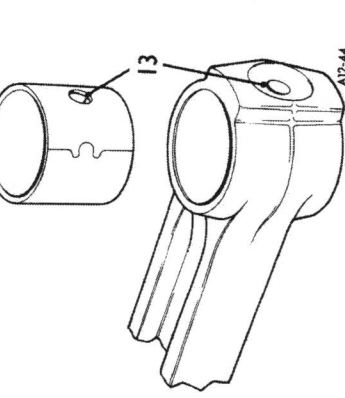

CONNECTING ROD BEARINGS

Remove and refit — set	12.17.16
— one	12.17.17
— extra each	12.17.18

Removing
1 Drive the car onto a ramp.
2 Disconnect the battery.
3 Drain the sump oil, and remove the dipstick.
4 Remove the sump. 12.60.44.
5 Turn the engine until numbers 1 and 4 big-end bearings are in an accessible position.
6 Check that the connecting-rods and caps are numbered correctly.

CAUTION: Do not mix components whilst carrying out the following instructions.

7 Remove the two special nuts securing each big-end cap and withdraw the caps complete with lower shells.

8 Push the connecting rod upwards sufficiently to enable the upper shell bearing to be removed.
9 Fit rubber or plastic sleeves over the big-end bolts to prevent damage being caused to the crankpins.
10 Turn the crankshaft sufficiently to bring numbers 3 and 4 big-end bearings to an accessible position.
11 Repeat instructions 6 to 9 on numbers 2 and 3 big-ends.

Refitting
12 Clean numbers 2 and 3 crankpins and corresponding bearings and caps.
13 Fit the upper bearing shell to the connecting-rod ensuring that the keeper tag locates in the connecting-rod recess and pull the rod onto the crankpin.
14 Fit the lower bearing shell to the cap ensuring that the keeper tag locates correctly in the connecting-rod recess.

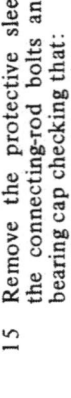

15 Remove the protective sleeves from the connecting-rod bolts and fit the bearing cap checking that:
  a The correct number cap is being fitted to the connecting-rod concerned.
  b The keeper tags are adjacent — i.e. on the same side of the bearing.
16 Fit and evenly tighten new nuts to the correct torque figure — see 'TORQUE WRENCH SETTINGS'.
17 Turn the crankshaft to bring numbers 1 and 4 big-ends to an accessible position.
18 Repeat instructions 12 to 18 on numbers 1 and 4 big-ends.
19 Fit the sump. 12.60.44.
20 Lower the ramp and fill the sump to high mark on the dipstick with oil of a recommended grade.
21 Reconnect the battery.
22 Drive the car from the ramp.

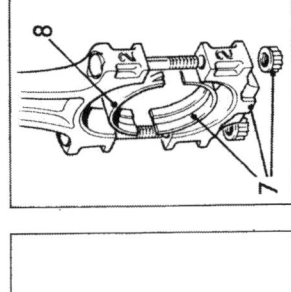
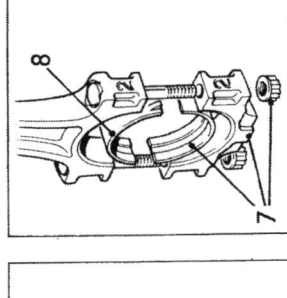
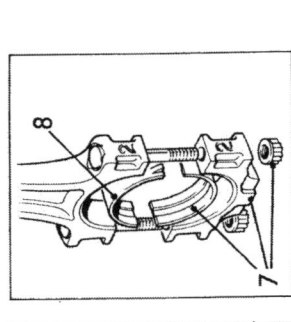
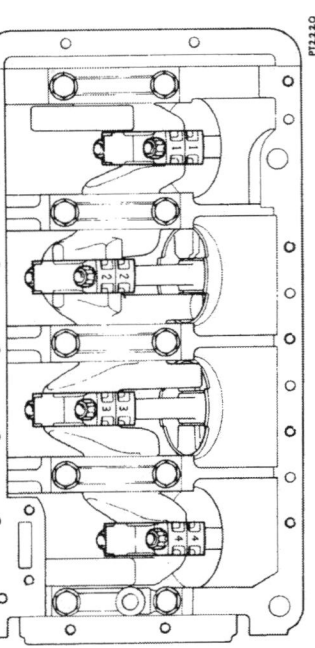

CRANKSHAFT PULLEY   12.21.01

Remove and refit

Removing
1 Drive the car on to a ramp.
2 Disconnect the battery.
3 Slacken the alternator drive belt tension and slip it from the crankshaft pulley.
4 Place the car in gear and put the handbrake 'on'.
5 Raise the ramp.
6 Turn the special bolt — securing the pulley . to the crankshaft — anti-clockwise and remove together with the washer.
7 Withdraw the crankshaft pulley.

Refitting
8 Ensure the key is in position in the crankshaft.
9 Lubricate the crankshaft and fit the pulley.

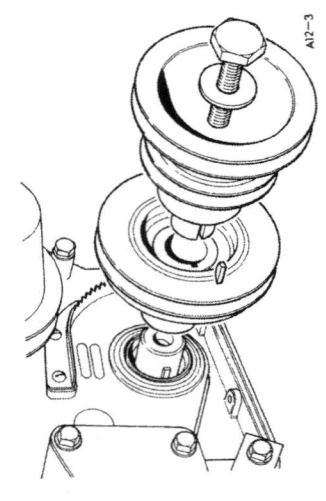

10 Secure the pulley with the special bolt and washer, and tighten to the correct torque figure — see 'TORQUE WRENCH SETTINGS'.
11 Lower the ramp, fit and tension the drive belt.
12 Put the gear lever in the 'neutral' position and re-connect the battery and drive the car off the ramp.

CRANKSHAFT PULLEY AND AUXILIARY DRIVES – USA Specification

Remove and refit   12.21.02

Removing

1. Drive the car onto a ramp, and disconnect the battery.
2. Remove the fan blades. 26.25.06.
3. Slacken the compressor adjustment bolts, and slip the belt from the pulley, see operation 82.10.02 instructions 1 to 3.
4. Slacken the alternator – fan drive belt adjustment bolts and release the belt from the pulley.
5. Place the car in gear and put the hand brake on.
6. Raise the ramp.
7. Remove the special bolt and washer securing the pulleys to the crankshaft.
8. Withdraw the auxiliary pulley cluster.
9. Remove the crankshaft pulley.

Refitting

10. Lubricate the crankshaft pulley boss and fit it to the crankshaft locating on the crankshaft key.
11. Fit the auxiliary pulley cluster locating on the crankshaft key.
12. Secure the assembly with the special bolt and washer and tighten to the correct torque figure see section 06.
13. Lower the ramp and put the gear lever in neutral.
14. Fit the alternator – fan drive belt and adjust the tension see operation 86.10.05 instructions 4 to 7.
15. Fit the compressor drive belt to the pulleys and adjust the tension see operation 82.10.01 instructions 7 to 11 and lower ramp.
16. Refit the fan blades, see 26.25.06, instructions 6 to 8.
17. Reconnect the battery and remove the car from ramp.

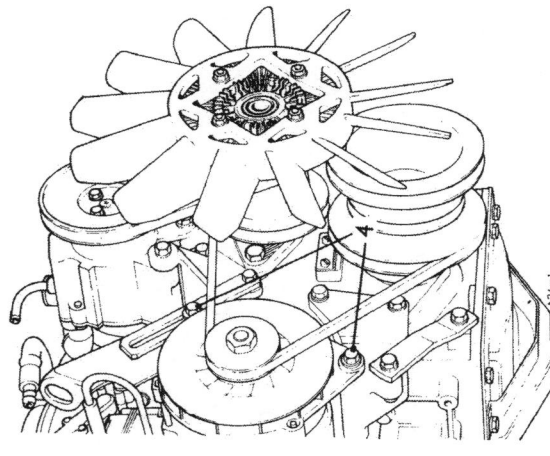

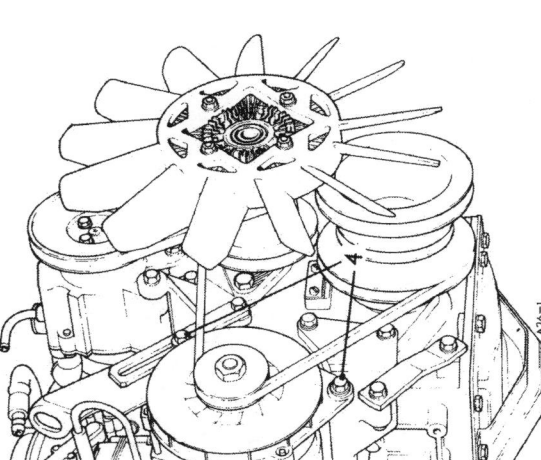

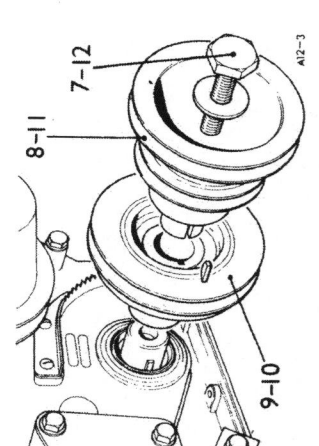

CRANKSHAFT REAR OIL SEAL

Remove and refit   12.21.20

Removing

1. Drive the car onto a ramp.
2. Disconnect the battery.
3. † Remove the gearbox. 37.20.01.
4. † Remove the clutch. 33.10.01.
5. Remove the flywheel. 12.53.07.
6. Remove the two rear sump bolts.
7. Slacken the two rear-most R.H. side sump bolts.
8. Slacken the L.H. side sump rear-most nut and bolt.
9. Remove the six bolts securing the crankcase oil seal housing to the crankcase.
10. Press out the oil seal from the housing.

Refitting

11. Lubricate the outer diameter of a new seal and press it squarely into the housing so that the lip faces the crankshaft.
12. Clean the crankcase and seal housing mating faces and using sealing compound fit a new gasket.
13. Lubricate the crankshaft and carefully ease the seal into position locating the housing on the two dowels.
14. Fit the six housing retaining bolts loosely noting that the two lower opposing bolts are longer.
15. Evenly tighten the bolts to the correct torque figure – see section 06.
16. Fit and tighten the two rear sump to seal bolts.
17. Tighten the R.H. side sump bolts.
18. Tighten the L.H. side nuts and bolts.
19. Fit the flywheel, see 12.53.07.
20. † Fit the clutch assembly. 33.10.01.
21. † Fit the gearbox. 37.20.01.
22. Reconnect the battery and remove the car from ramp.

† When automatic transmission is fitted refer to operations 44.20.01 and 44.17.01/07.

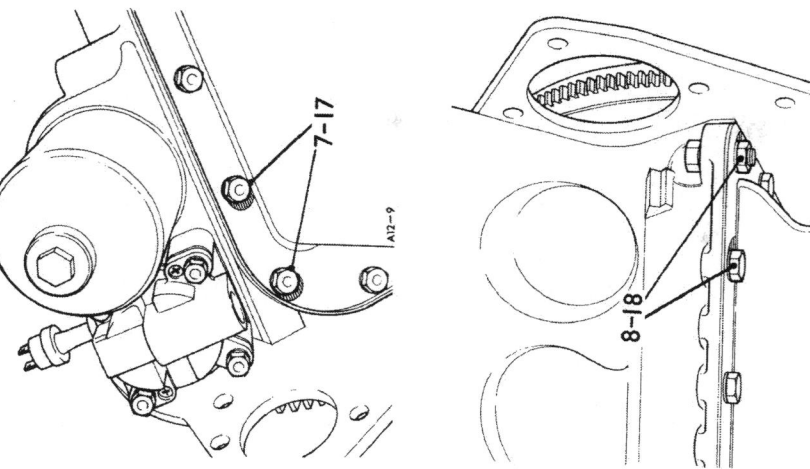

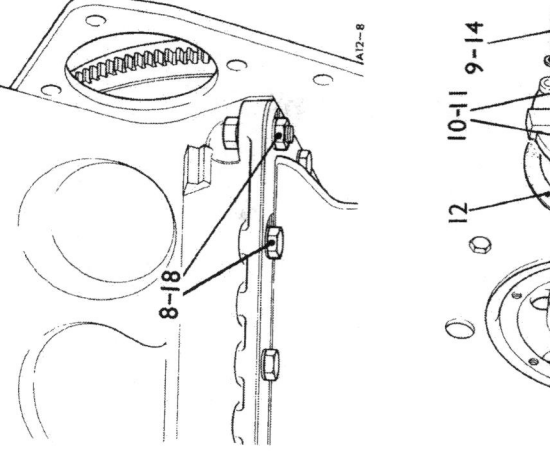

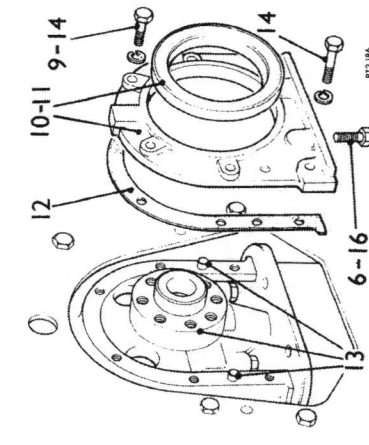

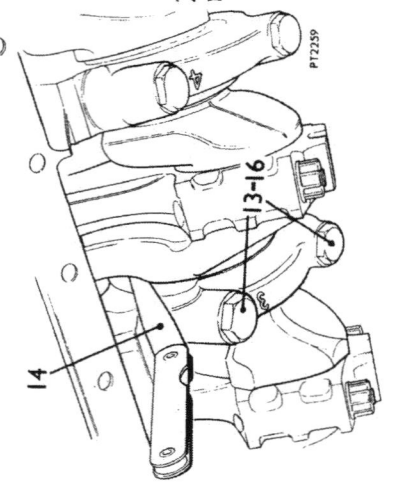

CRANKSHAFT END-FLOAT

Check and adjust   12.21.26

Checking
1 Raise the car on a ramp.
2 Disconnect the battery.
3 Attach the magnetic base of a dial gauge stand to the underside of the sump and arrange the dial gauge so that the stylus rests in a loaded condition on the front face of the crankshaft pulley.
4 Lever the crankshaft rearwards.
5 Zero the dial gauge and lever the crankshaft forward and note the reading.
6 Repeat instructions 4 and 5 several times until a constant reading is achieved – see DATA.
7 Remove the dial gauge and magnetic base.

Adjusting
8 Drain the sump oil and remove the dipstick.
9 Remove the sump. 12.60.44.
10 Remove two bolts and withdraw number 3 main bearing cap and lower shell.
11 Using the blade of a thin screwdriver and taking care not to damage the crankshaft, remove the two crankshaft thrust bearings.

12 Lubricate and feed the thrust bearings of the appropriate size into the channel, reversing the method of removal. Ensure however, that the two grooves in the thrust bearing face outwards away from the bearing cap.
13 Fit the main bearing cap and lower shell noting that the keeper recesses in the cap and crankcase are adjacent. Temporarily tighten the two retaining bolts.
14 Using a feeler gauge or clock gauge check the crankshaft end-float by levering the crankshaft forwards or rearwards.
15 Repeat instructions 10 to 14 if necessary to achieve the correct end-float.
16 Finally tighten the number 3 main bearing cap bolts to the correct torque figure – see section 06.
17 Refit the sump. 12.60.44.
18 Refill the sump to the high mark on the dipstick with oil of a recommended grade.
19 Lower the car.
20 Connect the battery.

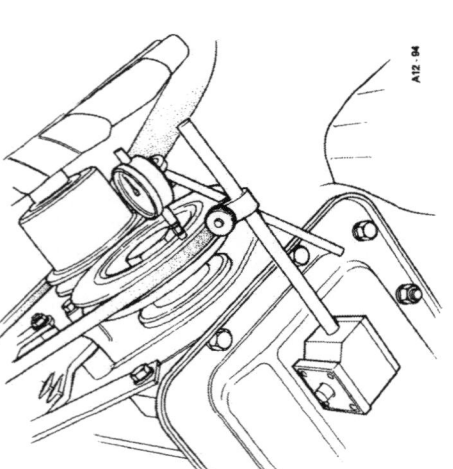

DATA
Crankshaft end-float . . . .   0.003 to 0.011 in (0,07 to 0,28 mm)
Adjustment   . . . .   By selective thrust bearings 0.005 in
                                                 (0,127 mm)

CRANKSHAFT

Remove and refit   12.21.33

Removing

1 Remove the engine and gearbox assembly from the car. 12.37.01.
2 Drain the sump.
3 † Remove the gearbox, noting the position of the remaining bell housing bolts to assist refitting.
4 † Remove the clutch.
5 Remove the flywheel — 12.53.07 instructions 4 to 6.
6 Remove the engine rear adaptor plate.
7 Remove the sump, and dipstick.
8 Remove the crankshaft rear main oil seal — 12.21.20 instruction 9.
9 Remove the timing chain cover —12.65.01
10 Remove the oil pick-up strainer.
11 Remove the oil thrower.
12 Remove the crankshaft sprocket.
13 Remove the drive key and shims.
14 Remove the connecting rod bearing caps and lower shells, and push the pistons up the bores just sufficiently to clear the crankshaft journals. 12.17.16.

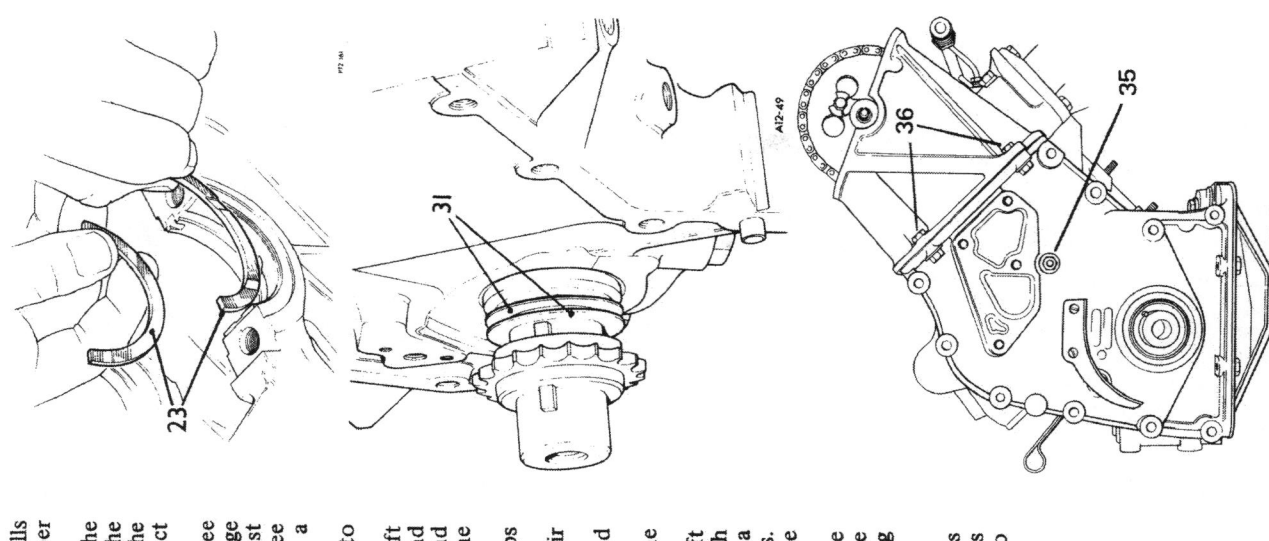

15 Fit plastic or rubber sleeves over the connecting rod bolts to prevent damage to the crankshaft journals.
16 Remove the timing chain 12.65.14 instructions 2 to 15.
17 Remove the ten bolts retaining the main bearing caps.
18 Withdraw the five main bearing caps and lower shells.
19 Lift out the crankshaft.
20 Remove the spigot bush (earlier models) or needle roller bearing (later models).
21 Remove the upper shells and thrust washers from the crankcase.

Refitting

22 Fit the upper shells to the crankcase ensuring that the keeper tags locate in the recesses.
23 Fit the thrust washers to number three main bearing noting that the grooves face outwards.
24 Clean and lubricate the main bearing journals and lower the crankshaft into the crankcase.

25 Clean and fit the main bearing shells to the caps ensuring that the keeper tags locate in the cap recesses.
26 Fit the main bearing caps to the crankcase partially tightening the securing bolts and ensuring that the caps are fitted to their correct crankcase bearings.
27 Check the crankshaft end-float — see DATA — by inserting a feeler gauge between the crankshaft and the thrust washers in number three bearing, see 12.21.26 instruction 14, or using a dial gauge.
28 Tighten the ten main bearing bolts to the correct torque.
29 Clean and lubricate the crankshaft journals, pull the connecting rods and upper shells onto the journals and remove the protective sleeves from the bolts.
30 Clean and fit the connecting rod caps ensuring:
   a The caps are fitted to their correct connecting rods.
   b The keeper tags in the rods and caps are adjacent.
   c The nuts are tightened to the correct torque.
31 Temporarily fit the crankshaft sprocket and check its alignment with the jackshaft sprocket using a straight-edge across the two sprockets. Adjust by fitting shims between the crankshaft and sprocket.
32 Check that the timing mark on the camshaft flange is in line with the groove on the camshaft front bearing cap.

CAUTION: While the timing chain is disconnected do not allow the pistons to reach T.D.C. otherwise damage to the valves and pistons may result.

continued

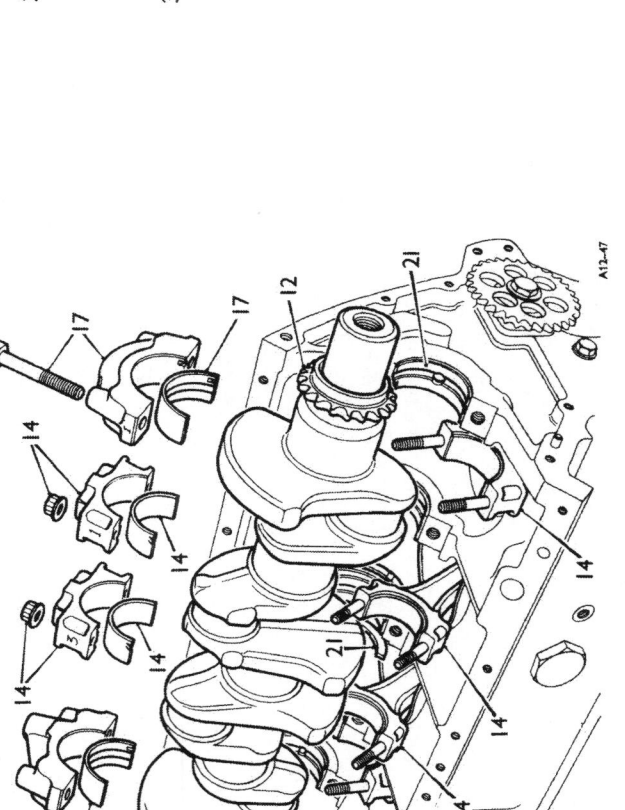

MAIN BEARINGS

Remove and refit — set   12.21.39
Remove and refit — each   12.21.40

Removing

1 Drive the car on to a ramp.
2 Disconnect the battery.
3 Drain the oil sump and remove the dipstick.
4 Remove the sump. 12.60.44.

CAUTION: It is important that during the following instructions the bearing caps, shells and bolts are not mixed but are kept identified with their respective bearings. It will be noted that the bearing caps are numbered 1 to 5 commencing at the front of the engine.

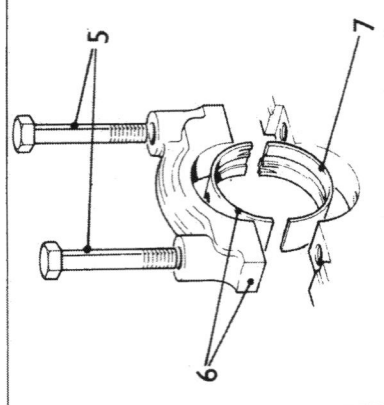

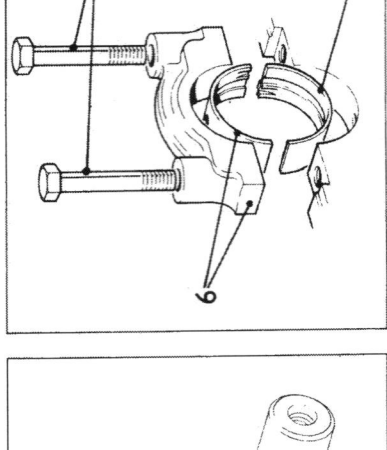

5 Remove the two bolts securing the bearing cap to the crankcase.
6 Withdraw the bearing cap complete with the lower shell.
7 With the tag end leading, carefully slide the upper shell bearing out from between the crankshaft journal and crankcase.
8 Remove the lower shell bearing from the bearing cap.
9 Repeat instructions 5 to 8 on the remaining bearings.

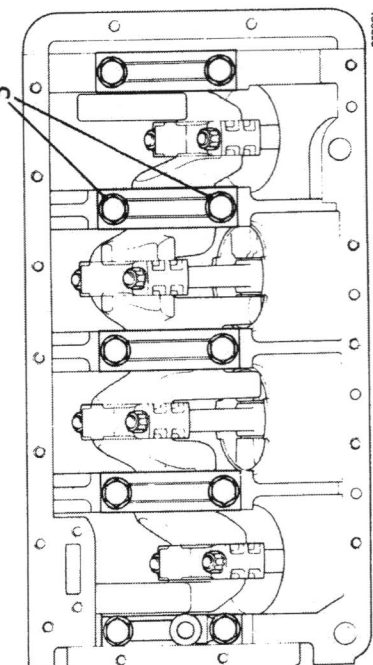

33 Fit the timing chain. 12.65.14.
34 Fit the oil thrower — dished face outwards.
35 Using a new gasket fit the timing chain cover locating it over the dowels. Secure with the centre retaining bolt, noting that it has a fibre washer under the head.
36 Fit the two nuts and bolts securing the timing cover to the cylinder head.
37 Fit the crankshaft pulley.
38 Fit the fan pulley assembly.
39 Fit the alternator mounting bracket. 12.25.21.
40 Fit the alternator and drive belt and adjust the tension. 86.10.02.
41 Fit a new crankshaft rear main oil seal 12.21.20 instructions 11 to 15.
42 Fit the engine rear adaptor plate 12.53.03 instructions 6 and 7.
43 Fit the oil pick-up strainer.
44 Fit the sump and dipstick.
45 Fit the spigot bush, (earlier models) or needle roller bearing (later models).
46 Fit the flywheel, see 12.53.07, instructions 7 to 11.
47† Fit the clutch. 33.10.01.
48† Fit the gearbox.
49 Fit the engine and gearbox to the car. 12.37.01.
50 Fill the sump with oil of a recommended grade to the high mark on the dipstick.
51 Fill the cooling system. 26.10.01.
52 Connect the battery.
53 Check and if necessary adjust the ignition timing. 86.35.15.

† Where automatic transmission is fitted refer to operations 44.20.01 and 44.17.01/07.

DATA

Main bearing journal diameter	2.1260 to 2.1265 in (54,000 to 54,013 mm)
Crankpin diameter	1.7500 to 1.7505 in (44,450 to 44,463 mm)
Minimum re-grind diameter	
— main bearings	2.0860 to 2.0865 in (52,984 to 52,997 mm)
— crankpins	1.7100 to 1.7105 in (43,434 to 43,447 mm)

SPIGOT BUSH

Remove and refit   12.21.45

Note: From Engine No. CG8894, CL36771 and CV10 a needle roller bearing was fitted in place of the spigot bush shown. This bearing may be removed and refitted using the procedure below.

Removing
1 † Remove the gearbox. 37.20.01.
2 † Remove the clutch assembly. 33.10.01.
3   Remove the eight flywheel retaining bolts.
4   Remove the spigot bush retaining plate.
5   Withdraw the spigot bush.

Refitting
6   Insert the spigot bush into the crankshaft bore.
7   Fit the spigot bush retaining plate and the eight flywheel retaining bolts and tighten to the correct torque figure – see 'TORQUE WRENCH SETTINGS'.
8 † Refit the clutch assembly. 33.10.01.
9 † Refit the gearbox. 37.20.01.

† Where automatic transmission is fitted, refer to operations 44.20.01 and 44.17.01/07.

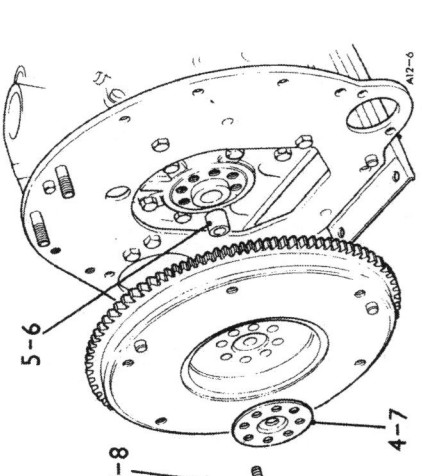

Refitting
10 Lubricate with clean engine oil all bearing shells.
11 With the tag end trailing, feed the upper shell bearing between the crankshaft journal and the crankcase. Ensure that the keeper tag locates properly in the crankcase recess.
12 Fit the lower shell bearing into the bearing cap ensuring that the keeper tag locates correctly in the cap recess.
13 Fit the cap to the crankcase noting that the keeper tag is fitted adjacent to its counterpart in the crankcase.
14 Secure the cap with the bolts and tighten evenly to the correct torque figure see 'TORQUE WRENCH SETTINGS'.
15 Repeat instructions 11 to 14 on the remaining bearings.
16 Check and if necessary adjust the crankshaft end-float. 12.21.26.
17 Fit the sump. 12.60.44.
18 Lower the ramp and fill the sump with oil of a recommended grade to the high mark on the dipstick.
19 Reconnect the battery.
20 Drive the car from the ramp.

CYLINDER BLOCK DRAIN PLUG

Remove and refit   12.25.07

Removing

WARNING: This operation must only be carried out when the engine is cold.

1   Drive the car onto a ramp and disconnect the battery.
2   Raise the ramp and using a long extension with a universal joint and socket remove the drain plug slowly to allow the coolant to drain.
3   Remove the plug completely when the coolant flow lessens.

Refitting
4   Reverse instructions 1 to 3, using a new washer.

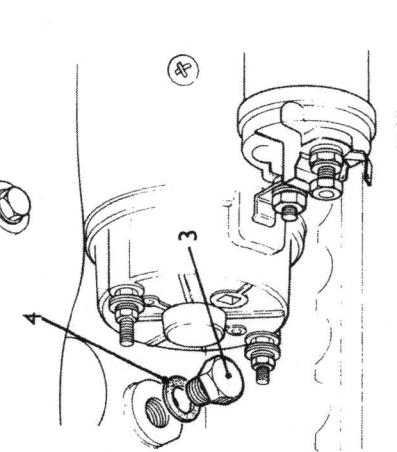

PT2 261

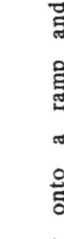

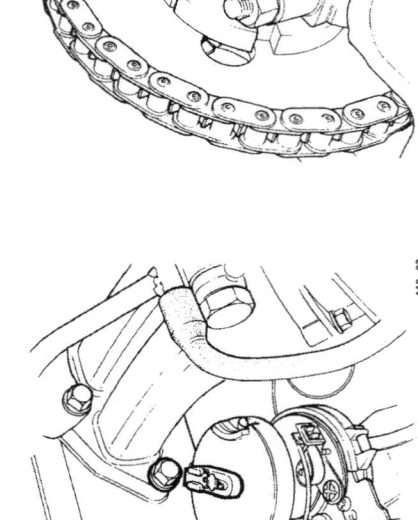

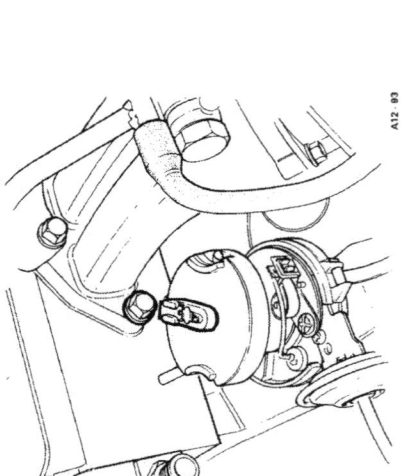

ALTERNATOR CARRIER BRACKET

Remove and refit   **12.25.21**

Removing

1 Disconnect the battery.
2 Remove the alternator. 86.10.02.
3 Remove the four bolts securing the carrier bracket to the engine.
4 Remove the support strap from the bracket.

Refitting

5 Secure the bracket to the engine with the two front bolts.
6 Fit the rear bolt ensuring that the correct thickness of washer is used between the bracket and engine.
7 Fit the support strap.
8 Refit the alternator and tension the belt. 86.10.02.
9 Reconnect the battery.

CYLINDER HEAD GASKET — UK and Europe Specification

Remove and refit   **12.29.02**

Removing

1 Drive the car onto a ramp and disconnect the battery.
2 Drain the cooling system. 26.10.01.
3 Remove the air duct. 80.15.31.
4 Remove the air cleaner.
5 Remove the inlet manifold complete with carburetters. 19.15.15.
6 Remove the camshaft cover.
7 Remove the distributor cap.
8 Remove the semi-circular grommet.
9 Turn the engine over so that the camshaft sprocket bottom bolt is accessible.
10 Unlock and remove the bottom bolt.
11 Anchor the camshaft sprocket to the support bracket.
12 Turn the engine over so that the timing mark on the camshaft flange is in line with groove in the camshaft front bearing cap and the distributor rotor arm points to the manifold rear attachment hole in the cylinder head.
13 Unlock and remove the camshaft sprocket top retaining bolt.

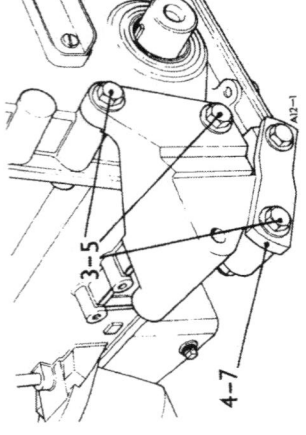

80   ENGINE

14 Disconnect the pipe from the water transfer housing.
15 Raise the ramp and disconnect the exhaust front pipe from the manifold flange.
16 Lower the ramp and remove the two cylinder head bolts to timing cover nuts and bolts.
17 Slacken the cylinder head retaining nuts and bolts in the reverse order as shown in operation 12.29.27.
18 Remove the five cylinder head studs and five bolts.
19 Withdraw the cylinder head complete with exhaust manifold.
20 Remove the cylinder head gasket.

Refitting
21 Clean the cylinder block and cylinder head mating faces.
22 Insert two guide studs in the cylinder block bolt holes as illustrated, to facilitate fitting the cylinder head and gasket.

NOTE: Suitable guide studs may be made to the dimensioned drawing and to enable the studs to be inserted and withdrawn a slot to accommodate a screwdriver blade should be made in one end.

23 Check that number 1 and 4 pistons are at T.D.C. and that the distributor rotor arm is in the same position as in instruction 12.
24 Fit the cylinder head gasket.
25 Fit the cylinder head locating it over the two guide studs.
26 Fit the five cylinder head studs.
27 Remove the two guide studs.
28 Fit and finger tighten only the five cylinder head bolts and washers.
29 Fit and finger tighten the five cylinder head nuts, washers and the two brackets for locating the spark plug leads.
30 Tighten the nuts and bolts to the correct torque – see 'TORQUE WRENCH SETTINGS' – in the sequence shown in operation 12.29.27.

31 Fit the lock washer and camshaft sprocket top retaining bolt.
32 Turn the engine over to enable the bottom bolt to be fitted.
33 Tighten and lock the two bolts.
34 Remove the 'slave' nut from the camshaft sprocket.
35 Fit the semi-circular grommet to the cylinder head.
36 Fit the two timing covers to the cylinder head nuts and bolts.
37 Fit the camshaft cover.
38 Connect the heater hose to the water transfer housing.
39 Fit the plug leads and the distributor cap.
40 Raise the ramp and connect the exhaust down-pipe to the manifold flange.
41 Lower the ramp and fit the inlet manifold complete with carburetters.
42 Fit the air cleaner. 19.10.02.
43 Fit the air duct. 80.15.31.
44 Fill the cooling system. 26.10.01.
45 Connect the battery and drive the car off the ramp.

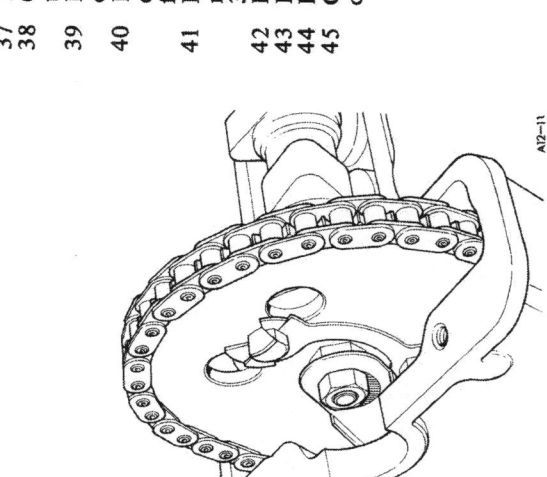

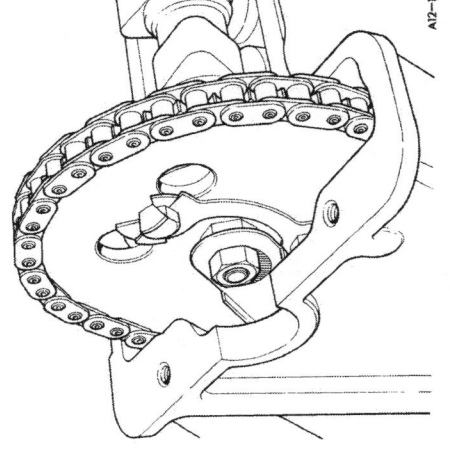

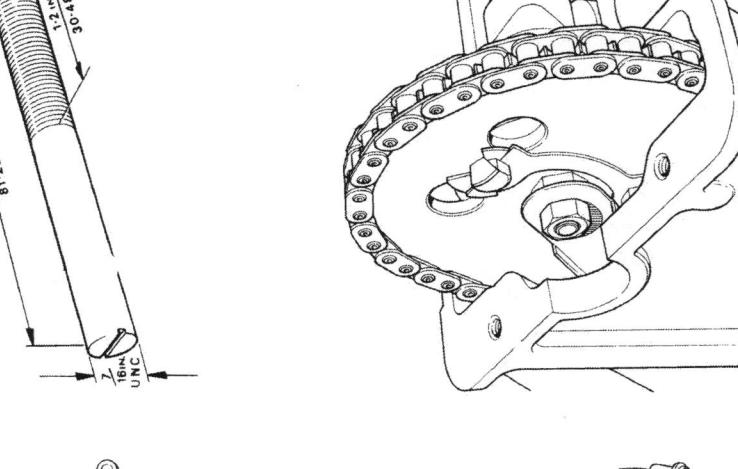

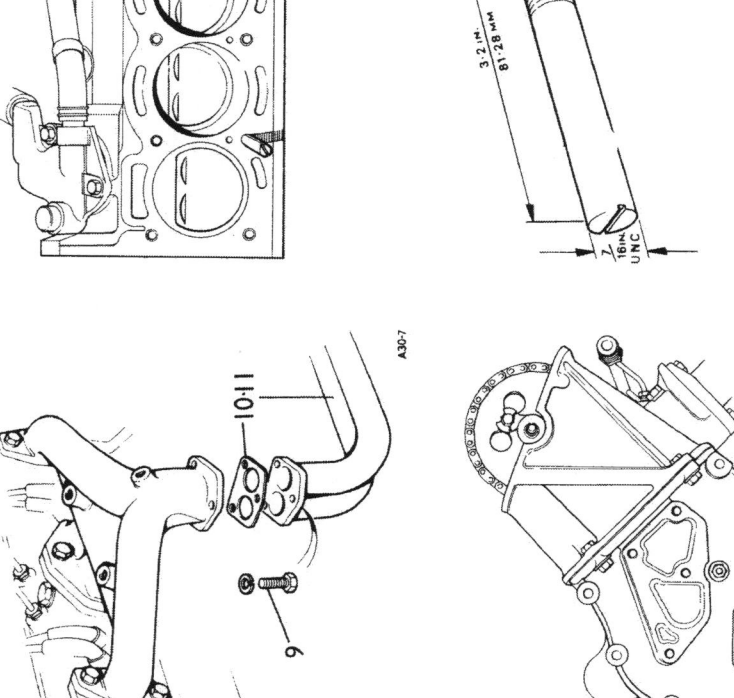

CYLINDER HEAD GASKET – USA Specification

Remove and refit   12.29.02

* *Applicable to carburetter engines only*

** *Applicable to fuel injection engines only*

Removing

1 Drive the car onto a ramp and disconnect the battery.
2 Drain the cooling system. 26.10.01.
3 Remove the air duct. 80.15.31.
4* Remove the air cleaner.
5 Remove the inlet manifold complete with carburetters or fuel rail.
6 Remove the camshaft cover.
7 Remove the distributor cap.
8 Remove the semi-circular grommet.
9 Turn the engine over so that the camshaft sprocket bottom bolt is accessible.
10 Unlock and remove the bottom bolt.
11 Anchor the camshaft sprocket to the support bracket.
12 Turn the engine over so that the timing mark on the camshaft flange is in line with groove in the camshaft front bearing cap and the distributor rotor arm points to the manifold rear attachment hole in the cylinder head.
13 Unlock and remove the camshaft sprocket top retaining bolt.

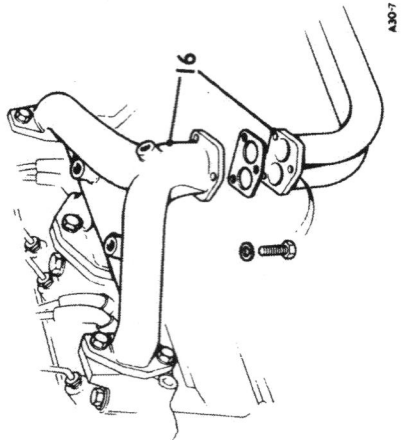

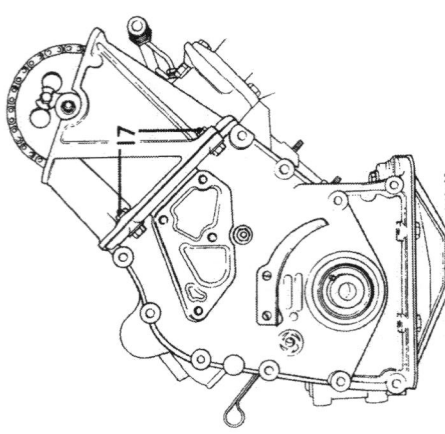

14* Disconnect the pipe to the check valve.

or

** Disconnect the electrical lead to the Lambda (oxygen) sensor.

15 Disconnect the pipe from the water transfer housing.
16 Raise the ramp and disconnect the exhaust front pipe from the manifold flange.
17 Lower the ramp and remove the two cylinder head bolts to timing cover nuts and bolts.
18 Slacken the cylinder head retaining nuts and bolts in the reverse order as shown in operation 12.29.27.
19 Remove the five cylinder head studs and five bolts.
20 Withdraw the cylinder head complete with exhaust manifold.
21 Remove the cylinder head gasket.

Refitting

22 Clean the cylinder block and cylinder head mating faces.
23 Insert two guide studs in the cylinder block bolt holes as illustrated, to facilitate fitting the cylinder head and gasket.
NOTE: Suitable guide studs may be made to the dimensioned drawing and to enable the studs to be inserted and withdrawn a slot to accommodate a screwdriver blade should be made in one end.
24 Check that number 1 and 4 pistons are at T.D.C. and that the distributor rotor arm is in the same position as in instruction 12.
25 Fit the cylinder head gasket.
26 Fit the cylinder head locating it over the two guide studs.
27 Fit the five cylinder head studs.
28 Remove the two guide studs.
29 Fit and finger tighten only the five cylinder head bolts and washers.
30 Fit and finger tighten the five cylinder head nuts, washers and the two brackets for locating the spark plug leads.
31 Tighten the nuts and bolts to the correct torque — see 'TORQUE WRENCH SETTINGS' — in the sequence shown in operation 12.29.27.

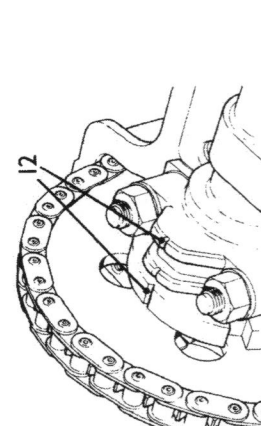

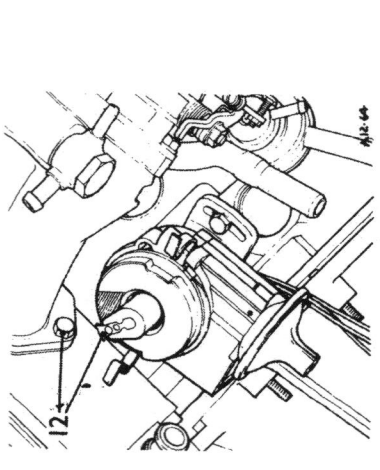

32 Fit the lock washer and camshaft
   sprocket top retaining bolt.
33 Turn the engine over to enable the
   bottom bolt to be fitted.
34 Tighten and lock the two bolts.
35 Remove the 'slave' nut from the
   camshaft sprocket.
36 Fit the semi-circular grommet to the
   cylinder head.
37 Fit the two timing covers to cylinder
   head nuts and bolts.
38 Fit the camshaft cover.
39 Connect the heater hose to the water
   transfer housing.
40* Connect the hose to the check valve.
   or
** Connect the electrical lead to the Lambda
   (oxygen) sensor.
41 Fit the plug leads and the distributor
   cap.
42 Raise the ramp and connect the
   exhaust down-pipe to the manifold
   flange.
43 Lower the ramp and fit the inlet manifold
   complete with carburetters or fuel rail.
44* Fit the air cleaner. 19.10.02.
45 Fit the air duct. 80.15.31.
46 Fill the cooling system. 26.10.01.
47 Connect the battery and drive the car
   off the ramp.

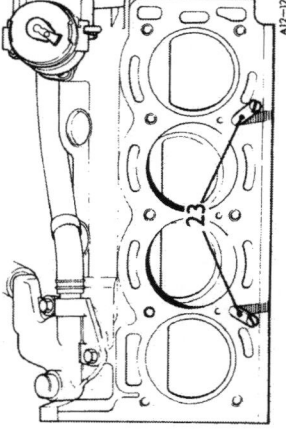

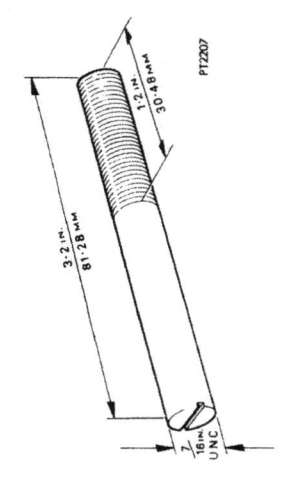

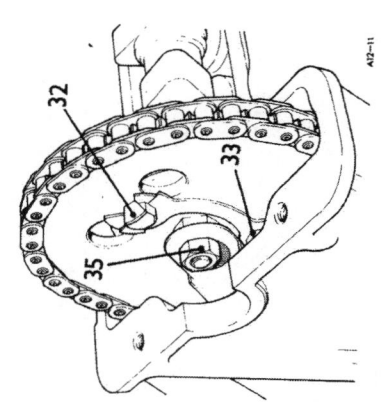

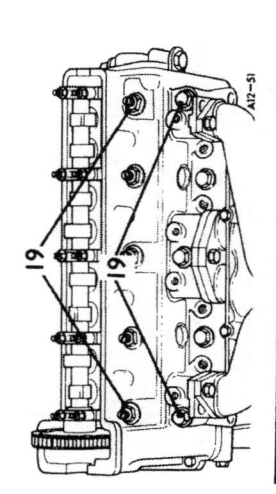

WATER TRANSFER HOUSING

Remove and refit   **12.29.04**

Removing

1 Disconnect the battery.
2 Drain the cooling system. 26.10.01.
3 Remove the fesh air duct. 80.15.31.
4 Disconnect the heater hose from the housing.
5 Remove the five bolts and plain washers securing the housing to the cylinder head.

Refitting

6 Clean the cylinder head and housing mating faces.
7 Using a new gasket fit the housing and secure with the five bolts and plain washers.
8 Connect the heater hose to the housing.
9 Fit the fresh air duct.
10 Fill the cooling system. 26.10.01.
11 Reconnect the battery.

A12-22

CYLINDER HEAD

Remove and refit   **12.29.10**

This operation is covered under CYLINDER HEAD GASKET 12.29.02.

CYLINDER HEAD

Overhaul   **12.29.18**

Which includes:

Valves — exhaust	
— remove and refit	12.29.60
Valves — inlet and exhaust	
— remove and refit	12.29.62
Valves — inlet	
— remove and refit	12.29.63
Valve guide — inlet	
— remove and refit	12.29.70
Valve guide — exhaust	
— remove and refit	12.29.71
Inlet valve seat	
— remove and refit	12.29.76
Exhaust valve seat	
— remove and refit	12.29.77

Special tools: S352, S60A-8 with 60A and 560A-2

Dismantling

1 Remove the cylinder head. 12.29.10.
2 Remove the exhaust manifold.
3 Remove the camshaft. 12.13.01 instructions 8 to 10.
4 Remove the tappets and pallets keeping them in their correct order.
5 Compress each valve spring in turn using special tool S352 and extract the collets, collars, springs, spring seats and valves.

NOTE: Keep all components in sets for reassembly in their original positions unless new items are to be fitted.

6 Remove all carbon deposits from the combustion chambers, exhaust ports and cylinder head face.

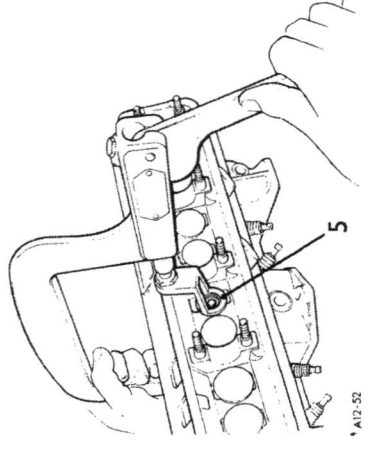

A12-52

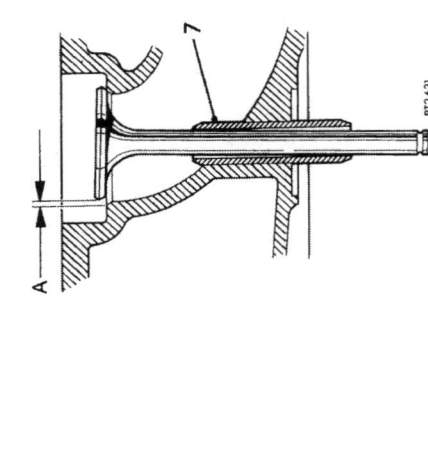

A12-95

Valve guides – checking

7 Check the inlet and exhaust valve guides for wear by inserting a new valves in each guide and tilting it. If movement across the valve seat – dimension 'A', 0.20 in (5.08 mm) – is exceeded, the valve guide should be renewed.

Valve guides – removing inlet and exhaust

8 Position main tool S60A on the top face of the cylinder head and using adaptor S60A-2 withdraw any worn guides.

Valve guides – fitting inlet and exhaust

9 Apply graphite grease to the new valve guides. Assemble main tool S60A and adaptors S60A-2 and S60A-8 on the combustion face of the cylinder head and draw-in the new guides.

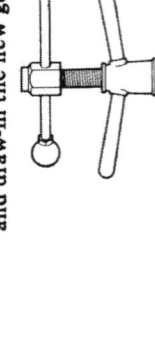

PT2631

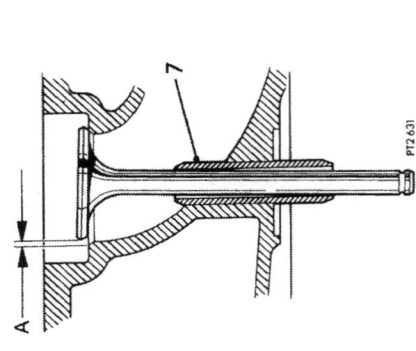

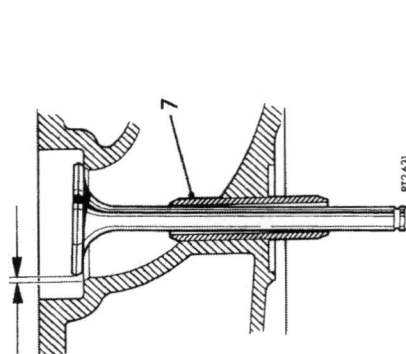

Valve guides – reaming inlet and exhaust

10 Ream out the newly fitted guides using a 0.3125 in (7,95 mm) reamer.

11 Re-cut the valve seats and grind-in the valves where new guides have been fitted.

Valves

12 Examine the valves and discard any with worn or bent stems and badly pitted or burnt heads. Valves with the head thickness reduced below dimension 'A' should be renewed. Valves in an otherwise satisfactory condition may be refaced.

Valve springs

13 Examine the valve springs for cracks and distortion. Check the springs against the information in data and discard any that do not meet these requirements.

Valve seat inserts

14 Examine the valve seat inserts for wear pits, scores and pocketing. Reface where necessary, removing only the minimum of material to obtain a gas tight seal and a correctly seating valve.
A Correctly seating valve.
B Incorrectly seating valve.

15 Valve seat inserts that cannot be restored by machining to provide a correctly seating valve must be renewed as follows:
Machine-out the existing inserts taking care not to damage the insert bores in the cylinder head.

16 Machine the INLET valve seat bore in the cylinder head – dimension C to 1.665 to 1.666 in (42.29 to 42.32 mm).

17 Machine the EXHAUST valve seat bore – dimension B to 1.329 to 1.330 in (33.75 to 33.78 mm).

18 Heat the cylinder head uniformly to a temperature of 180°C and immediately fit the new inlet and exhaust valve seats squarely into the cylinder head.

19 Allow the cylinder head to cool and machine the inlet and exhaust seats to an inclusive angle of 89° – dimension D.

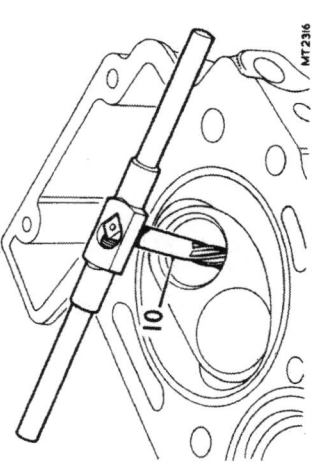

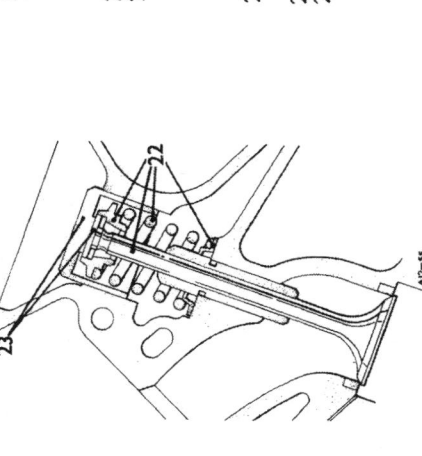

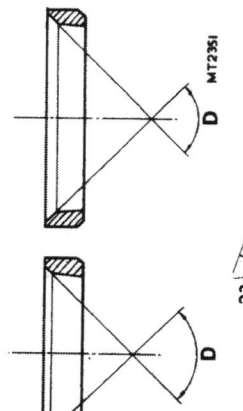

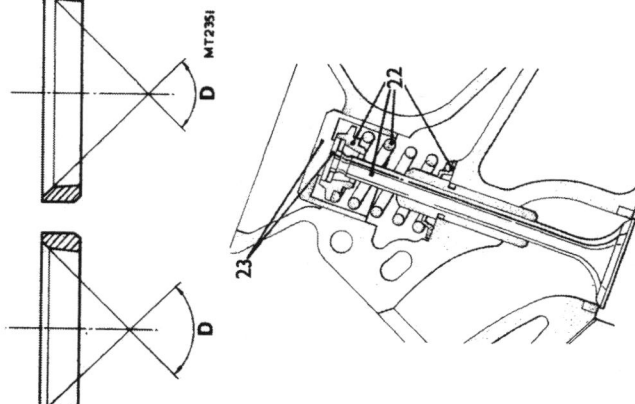

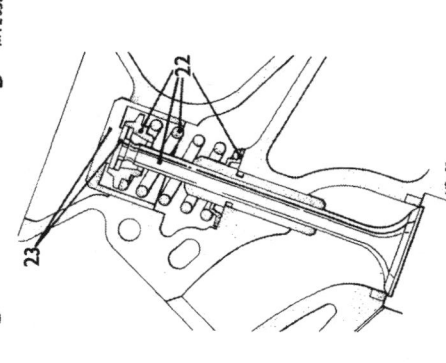

Lapping-in the valves

20 Insert each valve, in turn in its guide and lap-in using coarse followed by fine carborundum compound, until a continuous narrow band is obtained round the valve face and its seating.

21 Clean off all traces of compound from the valves and inserts.

Reassembling

22 Using the valve spring compressor S352, fit the valves, spring seats, spring collars, and secure with the split collets.

23 Fit the pallets and tappets.

24 Fit the camshaft and bearing caps ensuring that they are fitted in their correct positions and tighten the nuts to the correct torque – see 'TORQUE WRENCH SETTINGS'.

25 Check and if necessary adjust the valve clearances. 12.29.48.

26 Fit the exhaust manifold.

27 Fit the cylinder head. 12.29.10.

DATA

Valves

Inlet:

Overall length	4.259 to 4.269 in (108,17 to 108,43 mm)
Head diameter	1.560 in (39,62 mm)
Angle of face	45°
Stem diameter	0.3107 to 0.3113 in (7,881 to 7,907 mm)
Stem to guide clearance.	0.0017 to 0.0023 in (0,043 to 0,058 mm)

Exhaust:

Overall length	4.264 to 4.543 in (108.30 to 115,4 mm)
Head diameter	1.280 in (32,51 mm)
Angle of face	45°
Stem diameter	0.3100 to 0.3106 in (7,87 to 7,89 mm)
Stem to guide clearance.	0.0014 to 0.0030 in (0,035 to 0,076 mm)

Valve springs

Free length	1.600 in (40,40 mm)
Fitted length	1.440 in (36,57 mm)
Number of working coils	3¾

Valve seat inserts

Outside diameter – Inlet	1.6695 to 1.6705 in (42,405 to 42,430 mm)
– Exhaust	1.3335 to 1.3345 in (33,870 to 33,896 mm)
Angle of seat	42½°

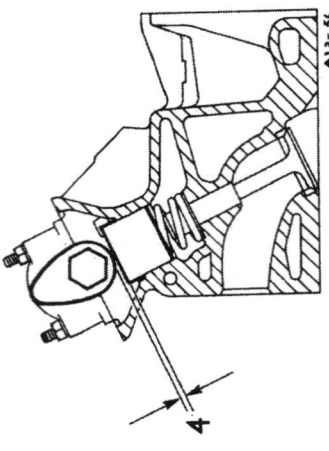

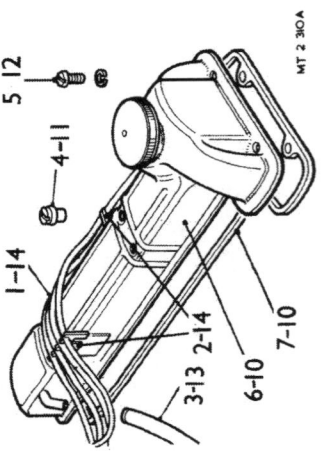

MT 2 310A

```
5 12
4-11
1-14
3-13  2-14
6-10
7-10
```

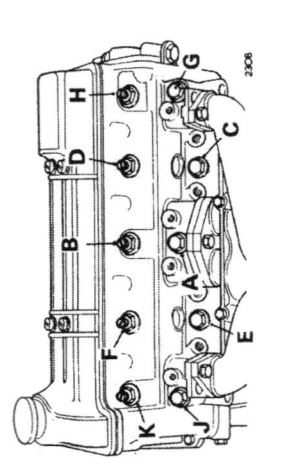

2308

CYLINDER HEAD NUTS AND BOLTS

Tighten   12.29.27

1   To avoid distortion of the cylinder head it is important that the retaining nuts and bolts are tightened in the following alphabetical order, as illustrated, to the correct torque — see 'TORQUE WRENCH SETTINGS'.

   A. B. C. D. E. F. G. H. I. J.

2   When releasing the nuts and bolts, prior to removing the cylinder head, the above sequence must be reversed i.e.

   J. I. H. G. F. E. D. C. B.A.

3   When checking the torque loading of the nuts and bolts they should first be slackened off to overcome static friction and then re-tightened to the correct torque figure.

CAMSHAFT COVER

Remove and refit   12.29.42

Removing

1   Disconnect the H.T. leads from the spark plugs.

2   Disconnect the H.T. leads from the retainers on the camshaft cover and move the leads away.

3   Pull off the breather hose from the camshaft cover.

4   Remove the four slotted sleeve nuts and sealing washers.

5   Remove the two screws and washers.

6   Remove the camshaft cover.

7   Remove the gasket.

Refitting

8   Clean the camshaft cover and cylinder head mating faces.

9   Lightly smear both sides of a new gasket with grease.

10 Fit the gasket and camshaft cover, locating over the four studs.

11 Fit the four slotted sleeve nuts using, if necessary new:

   a   Washers

   b   Sealing rings.

12 Fit the two screws and spring washers.

13 Fit the breather hose.

14 Connect the H.T. leads to the spark plugs and attach the lead clips to the retainers.

VALVE CLEARANCE

Check and adjust   12.29.48

NOTE: This operation may be carried out with the cylinder head on the engine or on the bench. When on the bench turn the camshaft using a spanner on the hexagon at the rear of the shaft.

Checking

1   Disconnect the battery.

2   Remove the camshaft cover. 12.29.42.

3   Slacken off the camshaft bearing cap nuts and re-tighten to the correct torque — see 'TORQUE WRENCH SETTINGS'.

4   Rotate the engine and check and record the maximum clearance of each valve, in turn, using a feeler gauge between the cam heel and tappet. The maximum clearance exists when the cam is vertical to the cylinder head.

NOTE: If all the valve clearances are correct to that given in DATA, refit the camshaft cover and reconnect the battery. Should adjustments be necessary continue with the following instructions.

Adjusting

5 Remove the camshaft. 12.13.01.
6 Withdraw each tappet and pallet where the clearance requires adjustment and keep them in their numbered sequence.
7 Using a micrometer, measure and record the thickness of each pallet.
8 The following calculations should be followed, as an example, to select a new pallet of the appropriate thickness to give a correct valve clearance.

Excessive clearance (exhaust valve used for example)

Valve clearance recorded	0.023 in
Valve clearance required	0.018 in
Valve clearance excess	+ 0.005 in
Plus pallet thickness recorded	0.090 in
= Pallet thickness required	0.095 in

Insufficient clearance (inlet valve used for example)

Valve clearance recorded	0.005 in
Valve clearance required	0.008 in
Insufficient clearance	− 0.003 in
Pallet thickness recorded	0.100 in
Pallet thickness required	0.097 in

9 Fit the new pallets where necessary and refit the tappets 12.29.57 instructions 5 to 7.
10 Refit the camshaft. 12.13.01.
11 Fit the camshaft cover. 12.29.42.

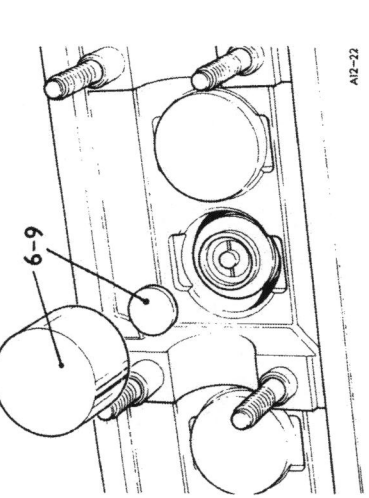

6-9

A12-22

TAPPETS

Remove and refit   12.29.57

Removing

1 Disconnect the battery.
2 Remove the camshaft cover. 12.29.42.
3 Remove the camshaft. 12.13.01.
4 Lift out the tappets and pallets, and identify them for reassembly.

Examination

5 Check the tappets for wear, scoring and pitting and discard as necessary.

Refitting

6 Fit the pallets into the valve collars.
7 Fit the tappets to the same valve assemblies renewing any faulty ones.
8 Refit the camshaft 12.13.01 ensuring that the valve clearances are checked and if necessary adjusted.
9 Fit the camshaft cover. 12.29.42.
10 Reconnect the battery.

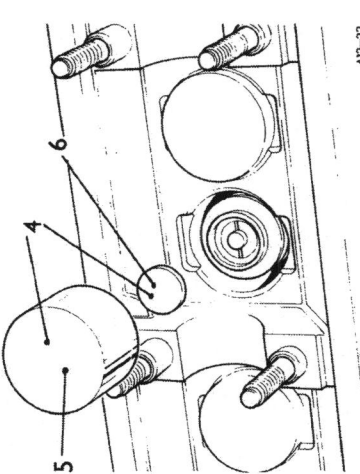

4
6
5
A12-22

DATA
Valve clearances

Inlet	0.008 in (0.2 mm)
Exhaust	0.018 in (0.5 mm)

ENGINE AND GEARBOX ASSEMBLY — UK and Europe Specification

Remove and refit   12.37.01

Removing

1 Disconnect the battery.
2 Remove the bonnet. 76.16.01.
3 Remove the fresh air duct.
4 Remove the radiator. 26.40.01.
5 Disconnect, from the engine, the heater hoses.
6 Disconnect the overflow hose from thermostat housing.
7 Pull off the air intake hoses from the air cleaner.
8 Disconnect the brake servo hose from the engine.
9 Disconnect the oil pressure lead from the switch.
10 Disconnect the H.T. and L.T. leads from the distributor.
11 Disconnect the water temperature transmitter lead from the thermostat housing switch.
12 Disconnect the harness plug from the alternator.
13 Remove the fuel pipe from the pump inlet, and blank-off the pipe and pump.
14 Disconnect the throttle cable.
15 Disconnect the mixture control cable.
16 Pull-off the float chamber spill pipe from the rear carburetter.
17 Remove the bonnet lock. 76.16.21.
18 Remove the exhaust front pipe. 30.10.09.
19 Remove the gear selector lever, see 37.16.04 or 44.15.04.
20 Jack up the front of the car and lower onto axle stands.
21 Jack up the rear of the car and lower onto axle stands.
22 Mark the relationship of the propshaft to the gearbox drive flange and disconnect it from the gearbox.
23 Disconnect the two reverse light (and starter inhibitor) snap connectors.
24 Disconnect the speedometer cable from the gearbox.
25 Remove the clutch slave cylinder (where fitted) and move to one side.
26 Remove the engine L.H. mounting retaining nut.

27 Remove the stabiliser — where fitted. 12.45.16.
28 Remove starter motor shield.
29 Remove the battery lead from the starter motor solenoid.
30 Disconnect the Lucar connector from the starter motor solenoid.
31 Remove the bolt securing the battery earth lead to the bell housing.
32 Remove the propshaft guard.
33 Lower the propshaft.
34 Fit slings to engine lifting hooks and hoist to take the weight of the engine.
35 Support the gearbox with a trolley jack.
36 Remove the four nuts retaining the rear mounting to the body.
37 Remove the R.H. engine mounting nut.
38 Lower the jack supporting the gearbox.
39 Hoist the engine and gearbox assembly and manoeuvre from the engine bay.

Refitting

40 Fit slings to the engine lifting eyes, hoist engine and gearbox assembly and manoeuvre into the engine bay.
41 Place a trolley jack under the gearbox.
42 Lower the engine to line-up the L.H. mounting with its sub-frame location.
43 Continue lowering, so that the engine R.H. rubber mounting stud locates in the slot in the body bracket.
44 Raise the gearbox and connect up the cross member to the body locating studs.
45 Fit the nut and washer to the R.H. engine mounting stud.
46 Fit the nut and washer to the engine L.H. mounting stud.
47 Remove slings from engine lifting eyes.
48 Remove the jack from beneath gearbox.
49 Secure the propshaft to the gearbox lining up the identification marks. Tighten the nuts to the correct torque — see 'TORQUE WRENCH SETTINGS'.
50 Fit the stabiliser — where fitted. 12.45.16.
51 Fit the propshaft guard.
52 Secure R.H. harness to its retaining clip.
53 Connect the reverse light (and starter inhibitor) snap connectors.

54 Fit the clutch slave cylinder (where fitted).
55 Secure the L.H. harness to its retaining clip.
56 Connect the negative earth lead from the battery to the bell housing.
57 Fit battery lead to starter motor solenoid.
58 Fit Lucar connector to the starter motor solenoid.
59 Fit the starter motor shield.
60 Fit the speedometer cable to the gearbox.
61 Fit the exhaust front pipe. 30.10.09.
62 Jack up rear of car and remove axle stands
63 Jack up front of car and remove axle stands.
64 Fit and align the bonnet lock. 76.16.21.
65 Fit spill pipe to the rear carburetter.
66 Fit the heater hoses to the engine connections.
67 Remove the blanking and fit the fuel pipe to the pump.
68 Fit the oil pressure warning light Lucar to the switch.
69 Connect the L.T. and H.T. leads to the distributor.
70 Connect the harness plug to the alternator.
71 Connect the coolant temperature transmitter lead.
72 Fit the vacuum hose to the engine.
73 Fit and adjust the throttle cable
74 Fit the mixture control cable.
75 Fit the air intake hoses to the air cleaner.
76 Connect the overflow hose to the thermostat housing.
77 Fit the radiator. 26.40.01.
78 Fit the fresh air duct.
79 Fit the bonnet. 76.16.01
80 Fit the gear selector lever, see 37.16.04 or 44.15.04.
81 Check the coolant level.
82 Check and if necessary top up the sump with oil of a recommended make and grade.
83 Check and if necessary top up the gearbox oil level — see 'MAINTENANCE'.
84 Connect the battery.
85 Start the engine and run until normal operating temperature is reached

86 whilst checking for coolant and oil leaks.
86 Check and adjust the ignition timing. 86.35.15.
87 Check and if necessary tune and adjust the carburetters. 19.15.02.
88 Road test the car.

ENGINE AND GEARBOX ASSEMBLY — USA and Canada Specification

Remove and refit   12.37.01

*   *Applicable to carburetter engines only*
** *Applicable to fuel injection engines only*

Removing

1 Disconnect the battery.
2 Disconnect the bottom hose at the radiator and allow the collant to drain.
3 Remove the bonnet. 76.16.01.
4 Remove the radiator. 26.40.01.
5 Remove the fresh air hose.
6 Remove the hot air hose.
7 Disconnect the heater hoses at the bulkhead connections.
8 Disconnect the brake servo hoses at the inlet manifold/plenum chamber connection.
9 Disconnect two hoses from the adsorption canister.
10 Disconnect the cooling system expansion hose from the thermostat housing.
11* Disconnect the vacuum hose from the inlet manifold to the anti-run-on valve.
12 Disconnect the electrical leads from the following as applicable:
  a The oil pressure switch.
  b Alternator.
  c Temperature transmitter.
  d Temperature sensor.
  e Thermotime switch.
  f Anti-run-on valve.
  g L.T. leads from ignition coil.
  h Lead from alternator to the throttle jack.
  j H.T. lead from the coil to the distributor.
13 Disconnect the main fuel feed from the pump to the carburetter fuel line or fuel rail.
continued

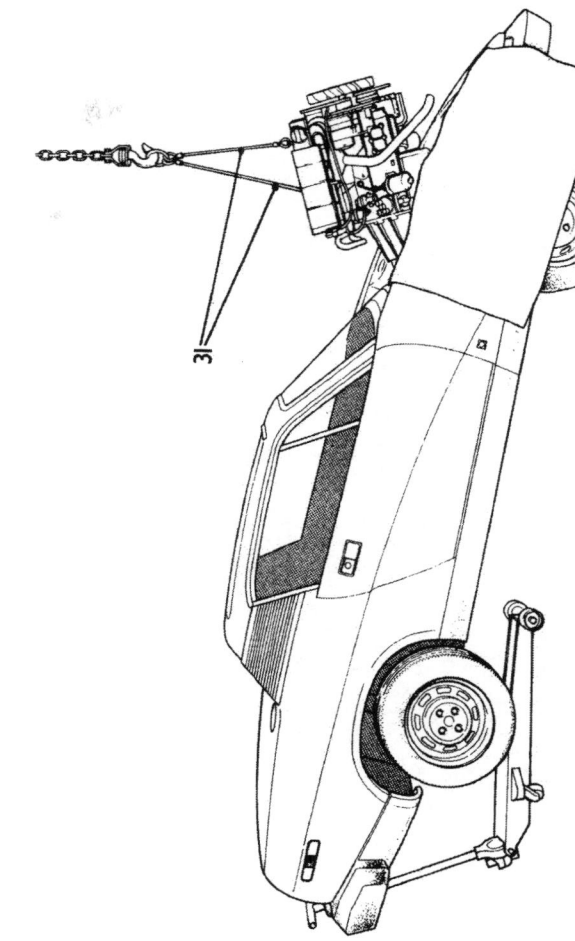

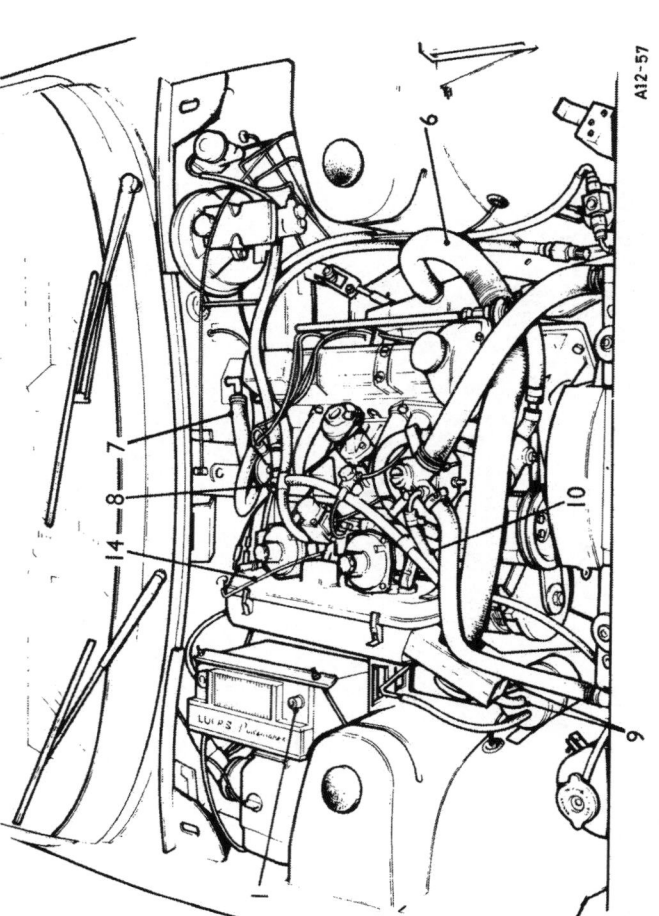

14* Disconnect the choke cable from the rear carburetter.

15 Disconnect the throttle cable from the throttle linkage.

16 Remove the gear selector lever assembly. 37.16.04 or 44.15.04.

17 Jack-up the front and rear of the car and lower onto chassis stands.

18 Disconnect the propeller shaft from the gearbox.

19 Disconnect the reverse light (starter inhibitor) and seat belt interlock wires at the multiway connector.

20 Remove the exhaust down-pipe. 30.10.09. and

** Disconnect the electrical lead to the Lambda (oxygen) sensor.

21 Disconnect the speedometer cable from the gearbox.

22 Remove the clutch slave cylinder (where fitted) see 33.35.01.

23 Remove the engine stabilizer complete (where fitted). 12.45.16.

24 Remove the nut securing the L.H. engine mounting rubber to the subframe.

25 Disconnect the starter motor leads.

26 Release the harness from the bell housing clips.

27 Remove bell housing bolts necessary to remove the clips and release the clutch hydraulic pipe (as applicable).

28 Disconnect the main positive earth lead.

29 Remove the bonnet lock from the bulkhead. 76.16.21.

30 De-pressurize the air conditioning system – where fitted – and disconnect the hoses from the compressor. 82.30.05.

31 Using a sling with a 23 in leg to the rear lifting eye and an 18 in leg to the front eye or similar ratio raise the hoise to take the weight of the engine.

32 Disconnect the R.H. engine mounting rubber from the engine bracket.

33 Remove the five bolts and release the engine rear mounting cross-member from the body, complete with the tie bar and restraint cable – nut A.

34 Raise the rear end of the car.

35 Hoist the engine and remove the L.H. engine mounting.

36 Continue hoisting the engine and manoeuvre it from the car.

37 Lower the rear end of the car.

Refitting

38 Using a sling as in instruction 31 hoist the engine and gearbox assembly to a position over the engine bay.

39 Fit the L.H. engine mounting rubber to the sump cross-member.

40 Raise the rear end of the car and lower the engine unit into the car.

41 When the rear engine mounting is approximately 8 in from the floor lower the rear end of the car and jack-up the gearbox.

continued

42 Continue lowering the engine whilst guiding the L.H. engine mounting stud into its sub-frame location.
43 Remove the slings from the engine.
44 Connect up the R.H. engine mounting to the engine bracket.
45 Bolt the engine and gearbox assembly rear mounting to the body with the four bolts.
46 Connect the propeller shaft to the gearbox.
47 Fit the clutch slave cylinder (as applicable).
48 Fit the bell housing bolts and secure the clutch hydraulic pipe over the bell housing with the clips, with an earth wire (as applicable).
49 Fit the L.H. engine mounting retaining nut.
50 Connect the gearbox harness to the multi-way connector.
51 Connect up the main earth lead to the bell housing.
52 Fit the engine stabilizer and adjust to the correct setting — where fitted. 12.45.16.
53 Fit the starter motor heat shield.
54 Fit the exhaust down-pipe. 30.10.09.
and
** Connect the electrical lead to the Lambda (oxygen) sensor.

55 If fitted connect the air conditioning hoses to the compressor.
56 Connect up the compressor electro-magnet clutch lead.
57 Fit the heater pipes to the bulkhead connections. 80.25.07.
58 Fit the brake servo hose to the manifold/plenum chamber.
59 Fit the mixture control cable.
60 Fit the throttle cable to the carburetter/throttle linkage.
61* Fit the anti-run-on vacuum pipe to the manifold.
62 Fit the main-line fuel pipe to the inlet side of the pump or the fuel rail.
63 Connect up the electrical leads — reversing instruction 12.
64 Fit the cooling system expansion pipe to the thermostat housing.

65 Fit the pipes to the adsorption canister.
66 Connect the H.T. lead to the distributor.
67* Remove the blanking plug and fit the fuel pipe to the pump.
68 Fit the fresh air duct. 80.15.31.
69 Fit the radiator and connect the top and bottom hoses. 26.40.01.
70 Fit the hot air hose.
71 Fit the bonnet. 76.16.01.
72 Fit the gear selector lever assembly, see 37.16.04 or 44.15.04.
73 Fill the cooling system. 26.10.01.
74 Fill the sump with oil of the correct grade to the high mark on the dipstick.
75 Check the gearbox oil level.
76 Connect the battery.

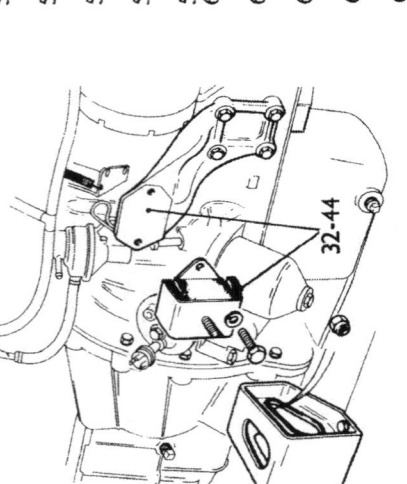

A12-30

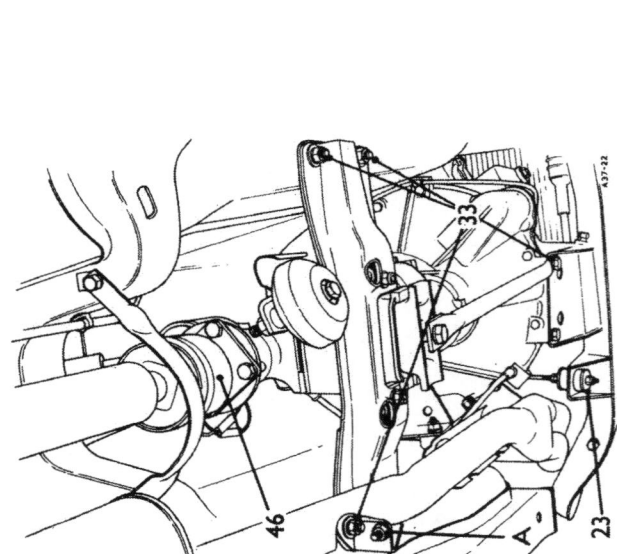

A37-22

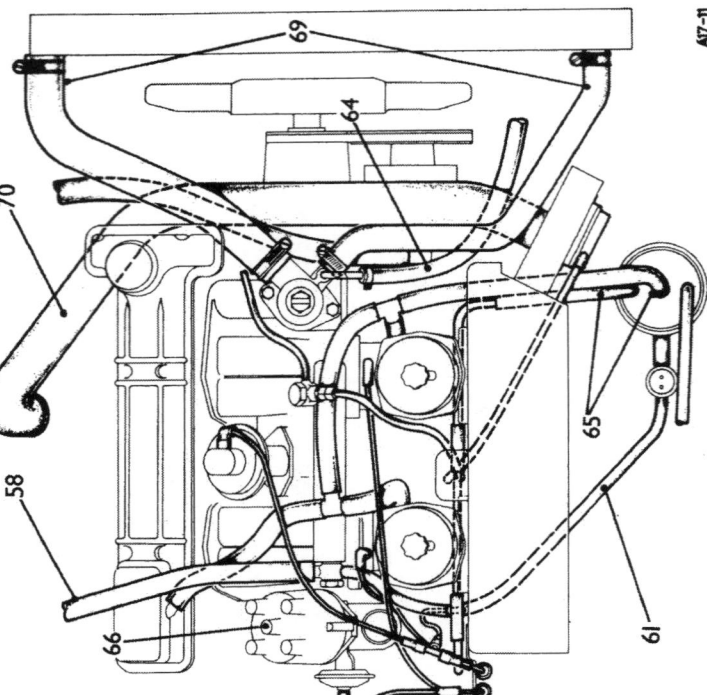

A37-11

A12-58

ENGINE ASSEMBLY – UK & Europe Specification

Strip and rebuild   12.41.05

Special tool: 38 U3

Stripping

1. Remove the engine and gearbox assembly from the car 12.37.01 and drain the sump.
2. Remove the gearbox – noting the position of the remaining bolts for refitting.
3. Drain the cylinder block.
4. Remove the starter motor.
5. Remove the clutch.
6. Remove the inlet manifold complete with carburetters, air cleaner and dipstick and tube.
7. Remove the water pump and remove the bottom hose
8. Remove the fuel pump.
9. Remove the distributor.
10. Remove the R.H. engine mounting bracket.
11. Remove the alternator complete with bracket.
12. Remove the alternator link.
13. Remove the exhaust manifold.
14. Remove the fan pulley and viscous coupling.
15. Remove the water pump.
16. Remove the spark plugs.
17. Remove the flywheel – 12.53.07 instructions 4 to 6.
18. Remove the oil pressure switch.
19. Remove the crankshaft pulley.
20. Remove the front lifting eye.
21. Remove the oil filter bowl and sealing ring.
22. Remove the oil pump and hexagon drive.
23. Remove the oil transfer housing.
24. Withdraw the six bolts and remove the rear adaptor plate.
25. Remove the camshaft cover.
26. Unlock and remove one of the camshaft sprocket retaining bolts.
27. Anchor the sprocket with a 'slave' nut to the support bracket and unlock and remove the remaining bolt.
28. Remove the two nuts and bolts securing the timing cover to the cylinder head.
29. Slacken the cylinder head retaining nuts and bolts in the reverse order as shown in operation 12.29.27.
30. Remove the five cylinder head studs and five bolts.
31. Withdraw the cylinder head complete with the camshaft and discard the gasket.
32. Remove the sump.
33. Remove the oil pick-up strainer.
34. Withdraw the remaining bolts – noting their positions and remove the timing cover.
35. Remove the oil thrower.
36. Remove the two retaining bolts and withdraw the timing chain tensioner.
37. Remove the three bolts securing the two chain guides and support bracket.
38. Remove the guides and support bracket complete with the chain and camshaft sprocket.

continued

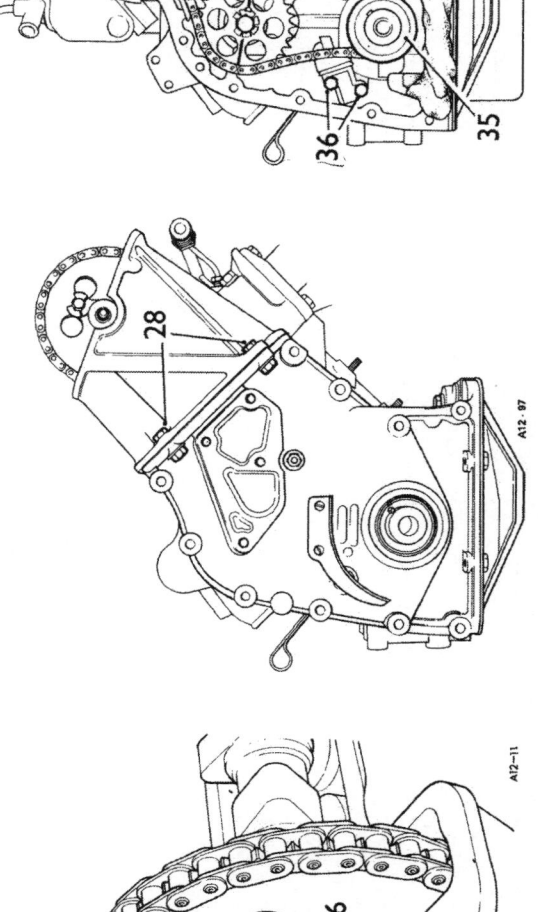

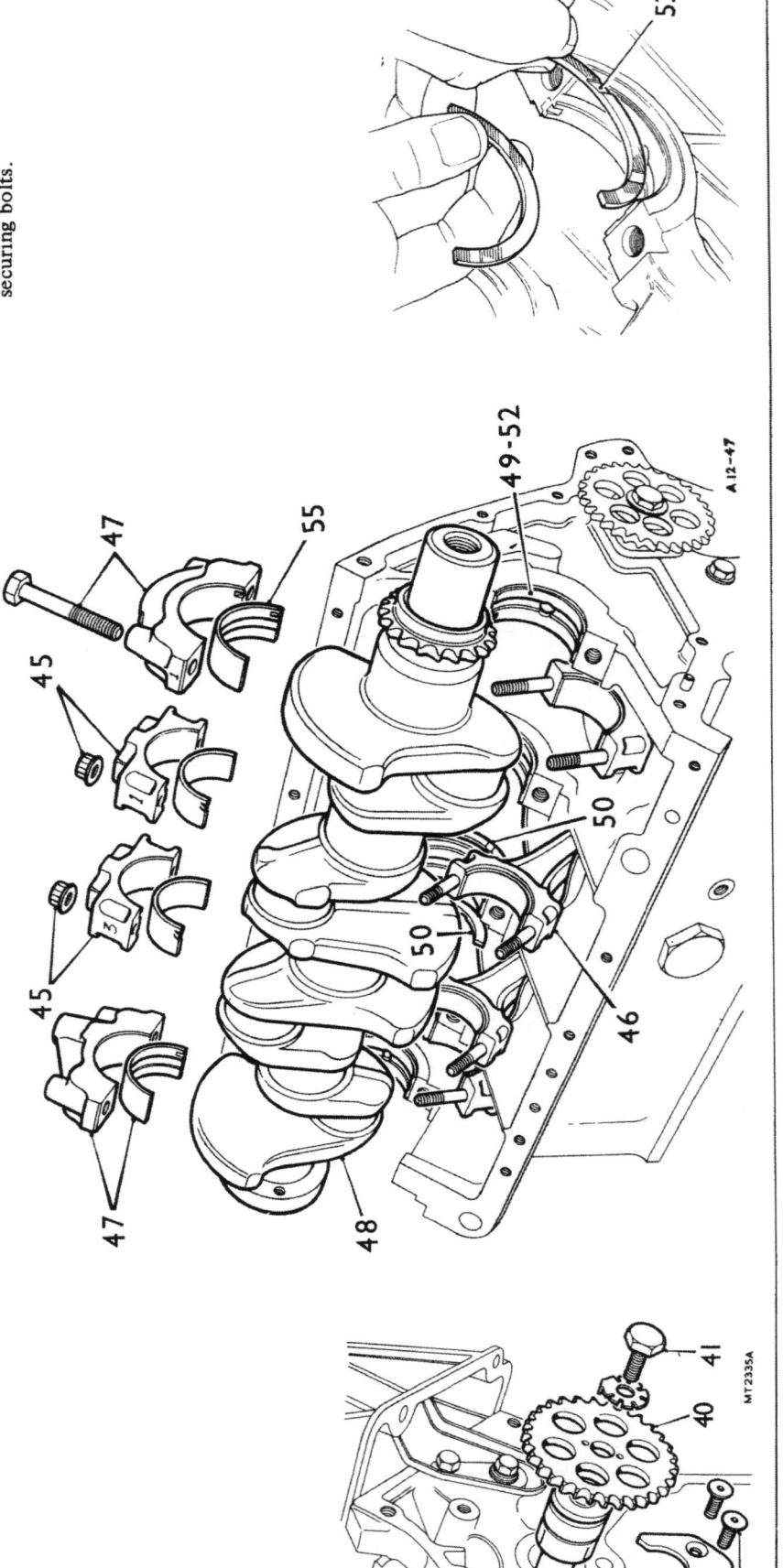

NOTE: The following rebuilding instructions assume that all the individual components and assemblies have been examined, worn parts renewed and assemblies overhauled. Moreover, all joint faces are clean and parts lubricated before assembly.

52 Fit the five main bearing upper shells ensuring that the keeper tags locate in the recess.

53 Fit the crankshaft thrust washers to number 3 main bearing noting that the oil grooves face outwards.

54 Lower the crankshaft into the crankcase.

55 Fit the lower shells to the main bearing caps and fit them to the crankcase. Partially tighten the securing bolts.

48 Lift out the crankshaft.

49 Remove the upper shells from the crankcase.

50 Remove the thrust washers from number three main bearing.

51 Withdraw the spigot bush from the crankshaft.

45 Remove the nuts securing the connecting rod bearing caps and withdraw the caps and lower shells ensuring that if the shells are to be refitted they are kept identified with their respective caps.

46 Push the connecting rods upwards and withdraw the piston assemblies through the top of the bores, keeping the shells identified with their respective connecting-rods.

47 Remove the ten bolts securing the five main bearing caps and withdraw the caps and lower shells.

39 Turn the jackshaft sprocket to expose the two Allen screws retaining the jackshaft keeper plate. Remove the screws and withdraw the plate.

40 Withdraw the jackshaft and sprocket from the cylinder block.

41 Unlock the tab washer and remove the bolt and sprocket from the jackshaft.

42 Withdraw the crankshaft sprocket.

43 Remove the drive key and shims from the crankshaft.

44 Remove the six bolts and remove the rear main oil seal and housing.

56 Using either a dial gauge or feelers check the crankshaft end-float – see data.

57 Tighten the main bearing cap bolts to the correct torque – see 'TORQUE WRENCH SETTINGS'.

58 Stagger the piston ring gaps, avoiding a gap on the thrust side and compress the rings using special tool number 38 U3.

59 Turn the crankshaft to position numbers 2 and 3 crankpins at B.D.C. Insert the respective connecting rod and piston assemblies into the bores and tap the pistons home noting that the flat raised part and the valve head recesses on the piston crown are fitted to the L.H. side of the engine.

60 Fit the upper bearing shells to the connecting rods ensuring that the keeper tags locate in the recesses and pull the connecting rods onto the journals.

61 Fit the lower bearing shells to the connecting rod caps ensuring that the keeper tags locate in the recesses and fit them to the connecting rods. Tighten new nuts to the correct torque – see 'TORQUE WRENCH SETTINGS'.

62 Repeat instructions 58 to 61 on numbers 1 and 2 pistons and connecting rod assemblies.

63 Fit a new seal to the rear main oil seal housing (lip towards the crankshaft) and using a new gasket and jointing compound fit the housing locating it over two dowels. Secure with the six bolts and spring washers noting that the two longer bolts are fitted at the bottom.

64 Fit the rear adaptor plate locating it on two dowels and secure with the six bolts.

65 Fit the spigot bush to the crankshaft.

66 Fit the flywheel – lining up the punch marks – if the original flywheel or crankshaft is being refitted.

67 Secure with the spigot bush retaining plate and eight bolts and tighten to the correct torque – see 'TORQUE WRENCH SETTINGS'.

68 Check the flywheel for run-out using a dial gauge – see DATA.

continued

69 Fit the clutch driven and pressure plates locating the pressure plate assembly over the three dowels.

70 Centralize the driven plate using a dummy primary shaft and evenly tighten the six bolts and spring washers to the correct torque. See 33.10.01.

71 Fit the sprocket to the jackshaft locating it over the single dowel and secure with bolt and new lock washer.

72 Fit the jackshaft to the cylinder block, locate it with the keeper plate and secure the plate with the two Allen screws.

73 Fit the water pump impeller and cover assembly checking the clearance as described in the refitting instructions. 26.50.01.

74. Fit the oil transfer adaptor ensuring that new 'O' rings are fitted and correctly located. Secure with the single bolt.

75 Ensure that the pistons are **not** at T.D.C. see cautionary note below.

76 Fit two 'slave' guide studs to the bolt holes in the cylinder block to facilitate the fitting of the cylinder head and gasket.

NOTE: See 12.29.02 for dimensional drawing of suitable studs.

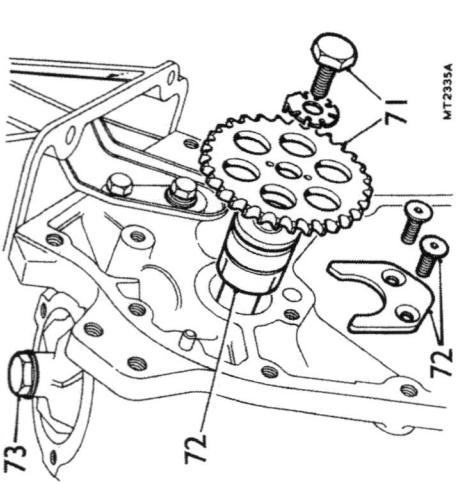

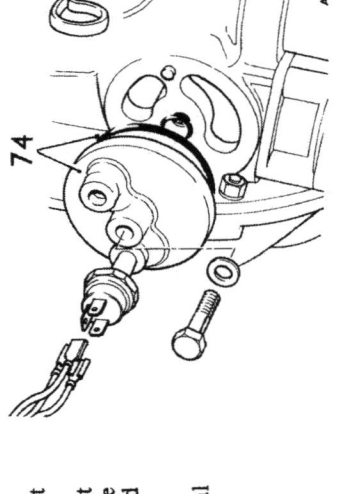

77 Fit the cylinder head gasket locating it over the studs.

78 Fit the cylinder head easing it over the guide studs.

79 Fit the five cylinder head studs.

80 Remove the two 'slave' studs and fit the five cylinder head retaining bolts and plain washers.

81 Fit the nuts and plain washers to the cylinder head studs.

82 Tighten the nuts and bolts to the correct torque and in the correct sequence. 12.29.27.

CAUTION: Once the pistons are fitted care must be taken to ensure that the crankshaft is not allowed to turn a complete revolution until the valve timing has been completed, otherwise damage to the valves and pistons will occur.

83 Temporarily fit the crankshaft sprocket and check its alignment with the jackshaft sprocket by placing a straight edge across the two sprockets.

84 Adjust any misalignment by removing the crankshaft sprocket and fitting shims of suitable thickness between it and the crankshaft. Ensure that the sprocket is pushed fully home when checking the alignment.

85 Remove the sprocket, fit the crankshaft drive key and refit the sprocket.

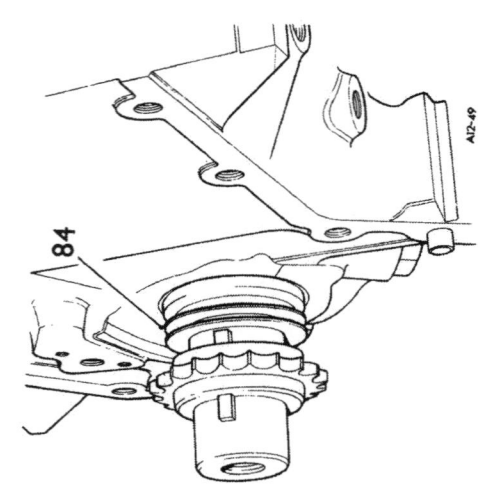

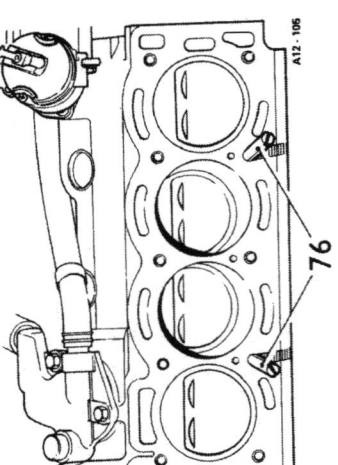

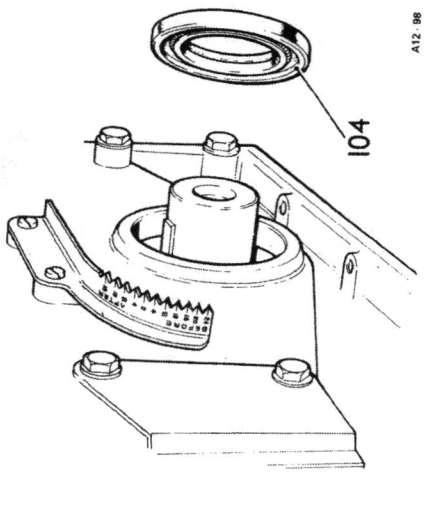

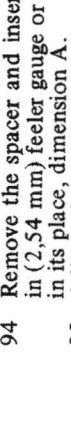

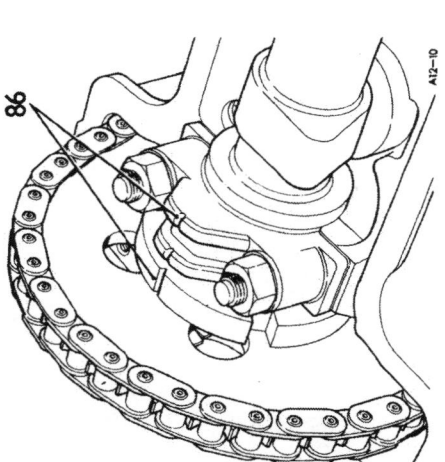

86 Turn the camshaft until the timing mark on the flange is in line with the groove on the camshaft front bearing cap.

87 Temporarily locate the timing cover and crankshaft pulley and turn the crankshaft (having regard for the above CAUTION) until number 1 and 4 pistons are at T.D.C. Remove the pulley and timing cover.

88 Turn the jackshaft until the scribed line across the sprocket is equidistant between bolt A and hole B with the dowel to the left. Remove the pulley and timing cover.

89 Encircle the camshaft sprocket with the timing chain and insert through the cylinder head aperture. Locate the sprocket on the camshaft flange and secure with the lock plate and one bolt

90 Keeping the chain taut on the drive side (i.e. the run between the camshaft and crankshaft sprockets) fit the chain to the crankshaft and jackshaft sprockets. Check and if necessary make any adjustment to the position of the jackshaft sprocket to maintain it in its correct position as in instruction 88.

91 Fit and loosely secure the guides as follows:
a   The adjustable guide.
b   The straight fixed guide.
c   The support bracket.

92 Fit a 'slave' bolt to the lower hole in the fixed guide to ensure alignment when fitting the timing cover centre bolt.

93 Fit the timing chain hydraulic tensioner and secure with the two bolts and spring washers. 12.65.28.

NOTE: To prevent the tensioner releasing while fitting, fit a spacer between the tensioner body and the back of the slipper.

94 Remove the spacer and insert a 0.100 in (2,54 mm) feeler gauge or slip gauge in its place, dimension A.

95 Adjust the chain tension by applying pressure, in the direction of the arrow, to the adjustable guide while tightening the clamp bolt.

96 Remove the gauge and check that the scribed line on the jackshaft sprocket is still correctly positioned.

97 Tighten all the guide retaining bolts and remove the 'slave' bolt.

98 Turn the engine sufficiently to enable the remaining camshaft sprocket retaining bolt to be fitted and locked.

99 Check that the threaded spigot on the camshaft sprocket does not foul the support bracket.

100 Fit the oil thrower with the dished face outwards.

101 Using sealing compound fit a new timing cover gasket and position the timing cover over the two dowels.

102 Secure the cover with the centre bolt noting that it has a fibre washer under the head

103 Fit the two nuts and bolts retaining the timing cover to the cylinder head.

104 With the lip face leading press-in a new timing cover oil seal flush with the outer face of the cover.

continued

105 Fit the crankshaft pulley.
106 Turn the crankshaft to bring numbers 1 and 4 pistons to T.D.C. with the timing mark on the camshaft flange in line with the groove on the front bearing cap.
107 Fit the distributor so that the vacuum advance unit is pointing directly rearward and the rotor arm is in line with the manifold rear retaining bolt hole in the cylinder head.
108 Temporarily tighten the distributor retaining bolts pending final adjustment when the engine is installed.
109 Fit the camshaft cover.
110 Fit the oil pick-up strainer.
111 Fit the sump.
112 Fit the fuel pump using a new gasket and ensuring that the actuating lever rides on top of the jackshaft cam.
113 Fit the fan pulley assembly and the drive belt on the pulley.
114 Fit the alternator complete with bracket and adjusting link.
115 Fit the front lifting eye.
116 Fit and adjust the alternator belt tension. 86.10.05.
117 Fit the exhaust manifold.
118 Fit the hexagon drive and oil pump using a new sealing ring.
119 Fit the oil pressure switch.
120 Insert a new filter element in the filter bowl and fit the assembly with a new sealing rubber.
121 Fit the R.H. engine mounting bracket noting that the long bolts are fitted to the top two holes.
122 Fit the water pump to heater and inlet manifold pipe and hose.
123 Fit the bottom hose to the water pump cover.

124 Fit the inlet manifold complete with carburetters 19.15.15 and the rear lifting eye.
125 Connect the fuel pump to carburetter hose.
126 Connect the engine breather pipes.
127 Fit the dipstick.
128 Fit the spark plugs.
129 Fit the distributor cap and connect the H.T. leads to the plugs (firing order 1, 3, 4, 2 distributor turns anti-clockwise).
130 Fit the gearbox.
131 Fit the starter motor.
132 Fit the engine and gearbox assembly to the car 12.37.01.
133 Check and if necessary adjust the ignition timing 86.35.15.

ENGINE ASSEMBLY – USA & Canada Specification   12.41.05

Strip and rebuild
Special tool: 38 U3

*   Applicable to carburetter engines only
** Applicable to fuel injection engines only

Stripping

1 Remove the engine and gearbox assembly from the car 12.37.01 and drain the sump.
2 Remove the gearbox – noting the position of the remaining bolts for refitting.
3 Drain the cylinder block.
4 Remove the starter motor.
5 Remove the clutch (as applicable).
6 Remove the inlet manifold complete with carburetters and air cleaner or fuel rail.
7 Remove the water pump and remove the bottom hose.
8* Remove the fuel pump.
9 Remove the distributor.
10 Remove the R.H. engine mounting bracket.
11 Remove the alternator complete with bracket.
12 Remove the alternator link.
13* Remove the air distribution manifold complete with diverter and relief valve, check valve and hoses.
14 Remove the exhaust manifold.

15 Remove the air conditioning compressor – where fitted – complete with brackets.
16* Remove the air pump.
17 Remove the fan pulley and torquatrol assembly.
18 Remove the water pump.
19 Remove the spark plugs.
20 Remove the flywheel – 12.53.07 instructions 4 to 6.
21 Remove the oil pressure switch.
22 Remove the dipstick.
23 Remove the auxiliary and crankshaft pulleys. 12.21.01.
24 Remove the front lifting eye.
25 Remove the oil filter bowl and sealing ring.
26 Remove the oil pump and hexagon drive.
27 Remove the oil transfer housing.
28 Withdraw the six bolts and remove the rear adaptor plate.
29 Remove the camshaft cover.
30 Unlock and remove one of the camshaft sprocket retaining bolts.
31 Anchor the sprocket with a 'slave' nut to the support bracket and unlock and remove the remaining bolt.
32 Remove the two nuts and bolts securing the timing cover to the cylinder head.

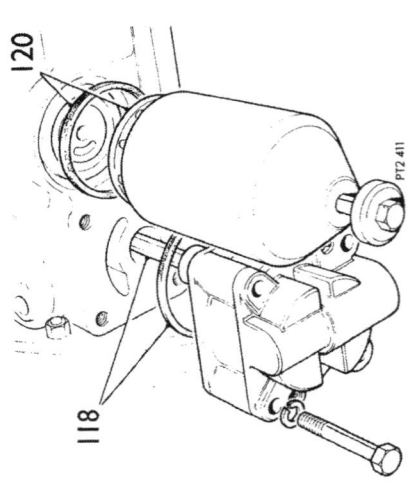

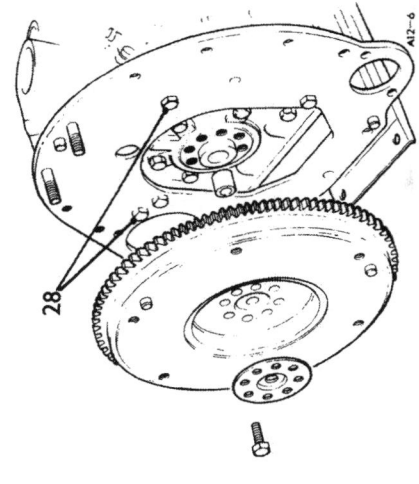

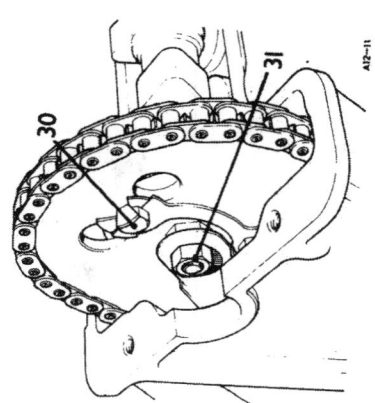

33 Slacken the cylinder head retaining nuts and bolts in the reverse order as shown in operation 12.29.27.

34 Remove the five cylinder head studs and five bolts.

35 Withdraw the cylinder head complete with the camshaft and discard the gasket.

36 Remove the sump.

37 Remove the oil pick-up strainer.

38 Withdraw the remaining bolts — noting their positions and remove the timing cover. Remove the oil seal.

39 Remove the oil thrower.

40 Remove the two retaining bolts and withdraw the timing chain tensioner.

41 Remove the three bolts securing the two chain guides and support bracket.

42 Remove the guides and support bracket complete with the chain and camshaft sprocket.

43 Turn the jackshaft sprocket to expose the two Allen screws retaining the jackshaft keeper plate. Remove the screws and withdraw the plate.

44 Withdraw the jackshaft and sprocket from the cylinder block.

45 Unlock the tab washer and remove the bolt and sprocket from the jackshaft.

46 Withdraw the crankshaft sprocket.

47 Remove the drive key and shims from the crankshaft.

48 Remove the six bolts and remove the rear main oil seal and housing.

49 Remove the nuts securing the connecting rod bearing caps and withdraw the caps and lower shells ensuring that if the shells are to be refitted they are kept identified with their respective caps.

50 Push the connecting rods upwards and withdraw the piston assemblies through the top of the bores, keeping the shells identified with their respective connecting-rods.

51 Remove the 10 bolts securing the five main bearing caps and withdraw the caps and lower shells.

52 Lift out the crankshaft.

53 Remove the upper shells from the crankcase.

54 Remove the thrust washers from number 3 main bearing.

55 Withdraw the spigot bush bearing from the crankshaft.

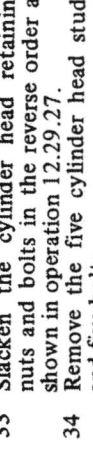

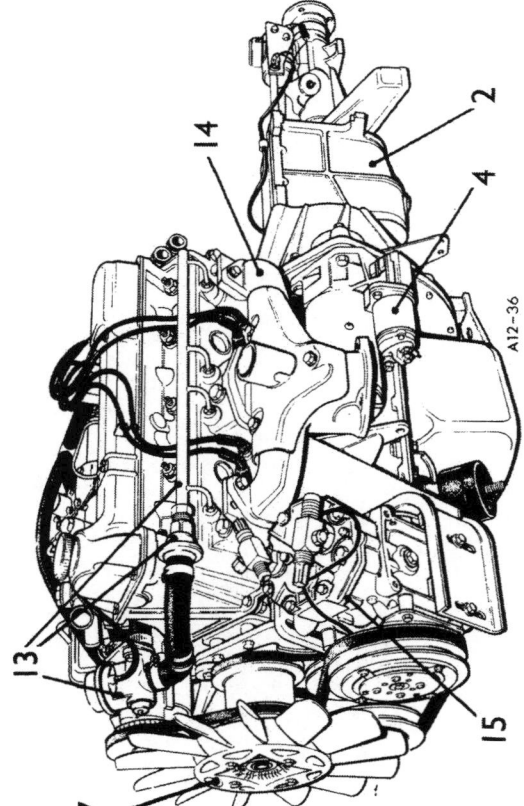

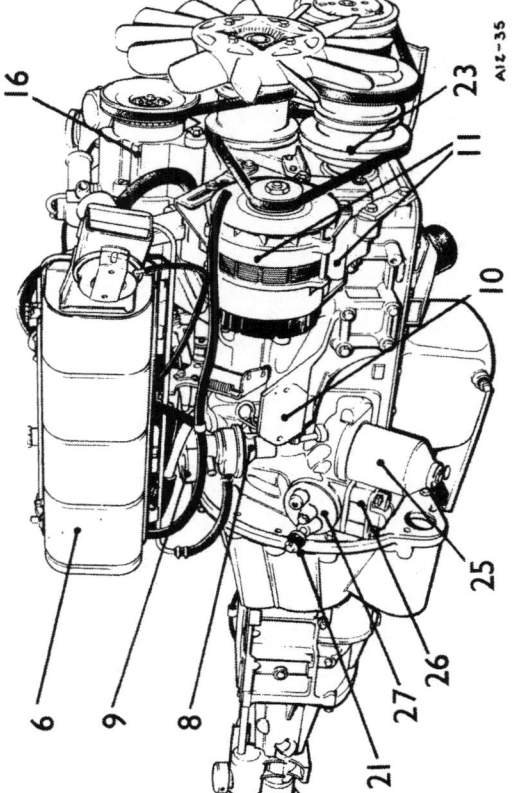

60 Using either a dial gauge or feelers check the crankshaft end-float — see DATA.

61 Tighten the main bearing cap bolts to the correct torque — see section 06.

62 Stagger the piston ring gaps, avoiding a gap on the thrust side and compress the rings using special tool number 38 U3.

63 Turn the crankshaft to position numbers 2 and 3 crankpins at B.D.C. Insert the respective connecting rod and piston assemblies into the bores and tap the pistons home noting that the flat raised part of the piston crown is fitted to the L.H. side of the engine.

64 Fit the upper bearing shells to the connecting rods ensuring that the keeper tags locate in the recesses and pull the connecting rods onto the journals.

65 Fit the lower shells to the connecting rod caps ensuring that the keeper tags locate in the recesses and fit them to the connecting rods. Tighten new nuts to the correct torque — see 'TORQUE WRENCH SETTINGS'.

66 Repeat instructions 62 to 65 on numbers 1 and 2 pistons and connecting rod assemblies.

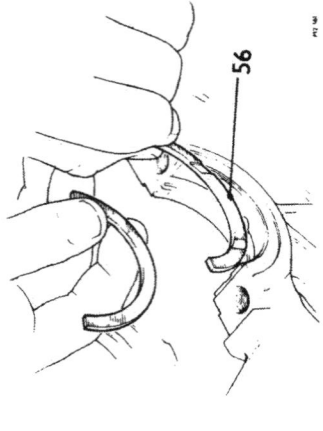

Rebuilding

NOTE: The following rebuilding instructions assume that all the individual components and assemblies have been examined, worn parts renewed and assemblies overhauled. Moreover, all joint faces are clean and parts lubricated before assembly.

56 Fit the five main bearing upper shells ensuring that the keeper tags locate in the recesses.

57 Fit the crankshaft thrust washers to number 3 main bearing noting that the oil grooves face outwards.

58 Lower the crankshaft into the crankcase.

59 Fit the lower shells to the main bearing caps and fit them to the crankcase. Partially tighten the securing bolts.

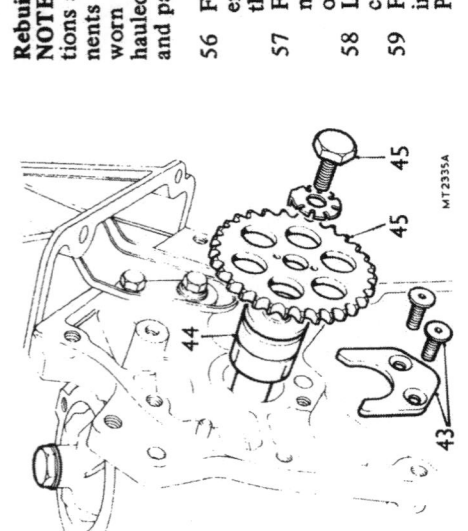

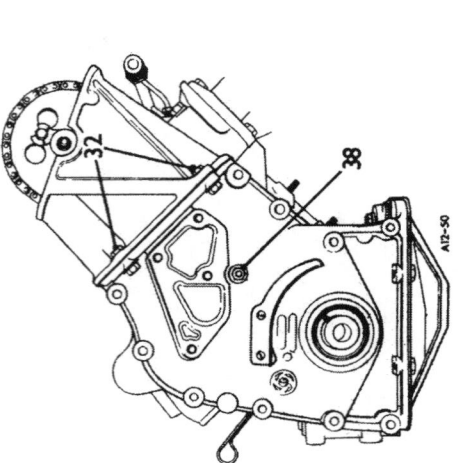

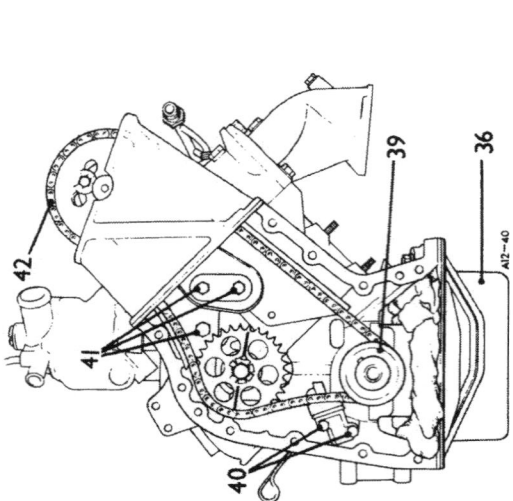

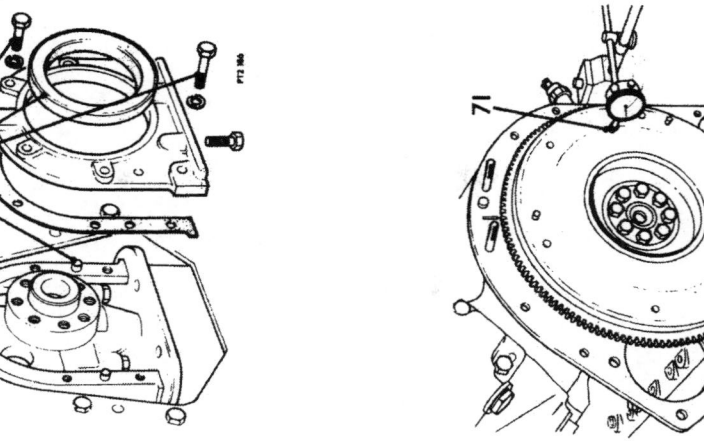

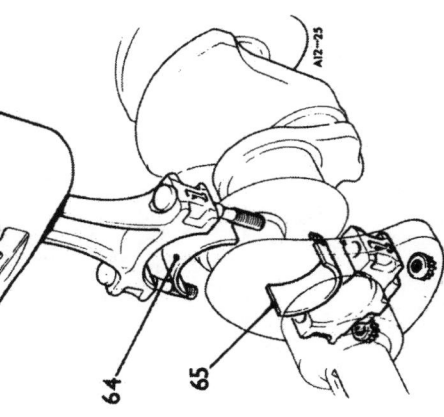

continued

67 Fit a new seal to the rear main oil seal housing (lip towards the crankshaft) and using a new gasket and jointing compound fit the housing locating it over two dowels. Secure with the six bolts and spring washers noting that the two longer bolts are fitted at the bottom.

68 Fit the rear adaptor plate locating it on two dowels and secure with the six bolts.

69 Fit the spigot bush bearing to the crankshaft.

70 Fit the flywheel – lining up the punch marks – if the original flywheel or crankshaft is being fitted. Secure with the spigot bush retaining plate and eight bolts and tighten to the correct torque – see 'TORQUE WRENCH SETTINGS'.

71 Check the flywheel run-out using a dial gauge – see DATA.

72 Fit the clutch driven and pressure plates locating the pressure plate assembly over the three dowels.

73 Centralize the driven plate using a dummy primary shaft and evenly tighten the six bolts and spring washers to the correct torque. See 33.10.01.

74 Fit the sprocket to the jackshaft locating it over the single dowel and secure with bolt and new lock washer.

75 Fit the jackshaft to the cylinder block, locate it with the keeper plate and secure the plate with the two Allen screws.

76 Fit the water pump impeller and cover assembly checking the clearance as described in the refitting instructions 26.50.01.

77 Fit the distributor mounting plate.

78 Fit the oil transfer adaptor ensuring that new 'O' rings are fitted and correctly located. Secure with the single bolt.

79 Ensure that the pistons are not at T.D.C. see cautionary note.

80 Fit two 'slave' guide studs to the bolt holes in the cylinder block to facilitate the fitting of the cylinder head and gasket.

NOTE: See 12.29.02 for dimensional drawing of suitable studs.

81 Fit the cylinder head gasket locating it over the studs.

82 Fit the cylinder head easing it over the guide studs.

83 Fit the five cylinder head studs.

84 Remove the two 'slave' studs and fit the five cylinder head retaining bolts and plain washers.

85 Fit the nuts and plain washers to the cylinder head studs.

86 Tighten the nuts and bolts to the correct torque and in the correct sequence. See 12.29.27.

CAUTION: Once the pistons are fitted care must be taken to ensure that the crankshaft is not allowed to turn a complete revolution until the valve timing has been completed, otherwise damage to the valves and pistons will occur.

87 Temporarily fit the crankshaft sprocket and check its alignment with the jackshaft sprocket by placing a straight edge across the two sprockets.

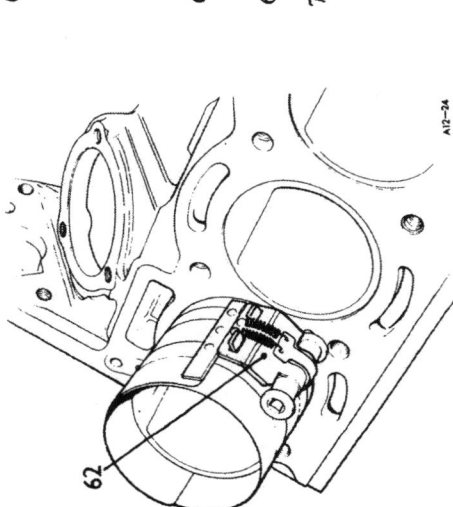

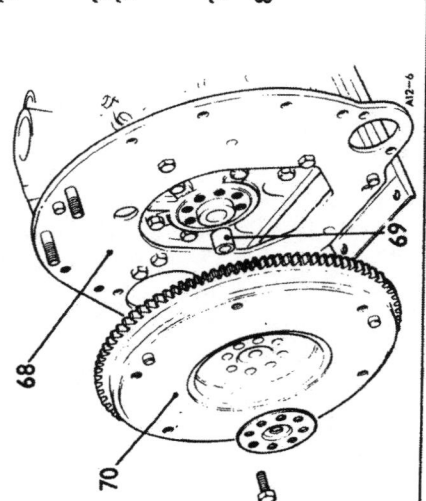

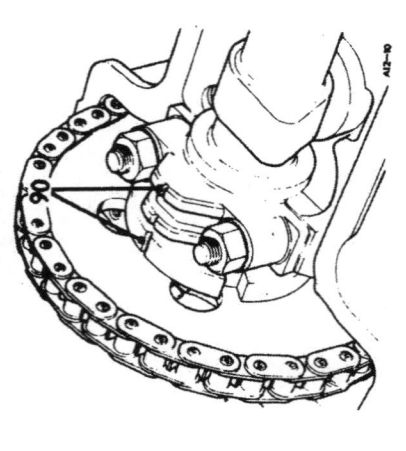

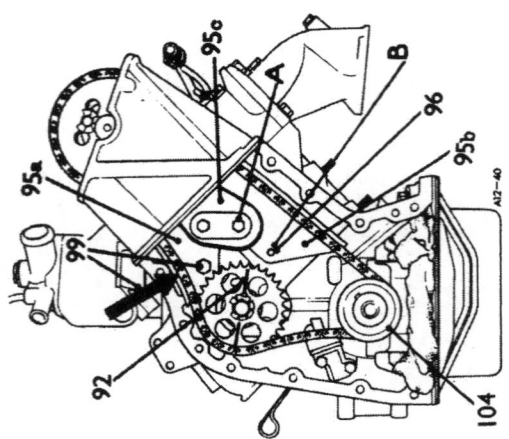

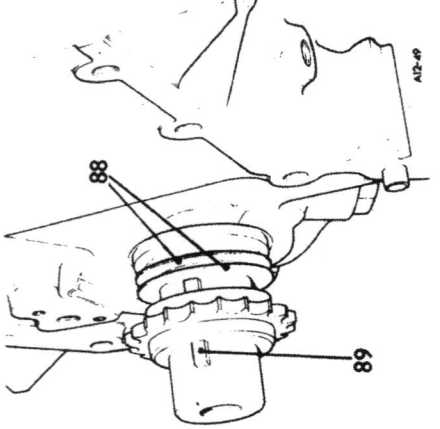

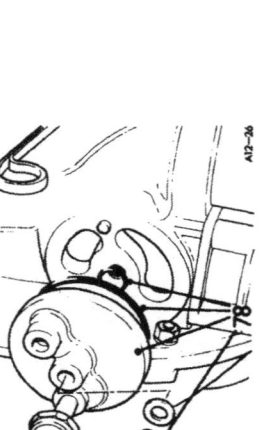

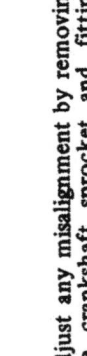

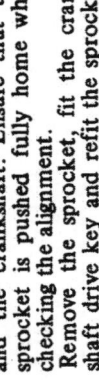

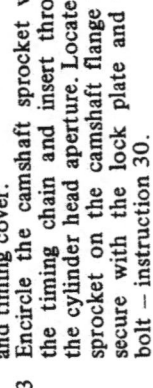

88 Adjust any misalignment by removing the crankshaft sprocket and fitting shims of suitable thickness between it and the crankshaft. Ensure that the sprocket is pushed fully home when checking the alignment.

89 Remove the sprocket, fit the crankshaft drive key and refit the sprocket.

90 Turn the camshaft until the timing mark on the flange is in line with the groove on the camshaft front bearing cap.

91 Temporarily locate the timing cover and crankshaft pulley and turn the crankshaft (having regard for the preceding CAUTION) until number 1 and 4 pistons are at T.D.C. Remove the pulley and timing cover.

92 Turn the jackshaft until the scribed line across the sprocket is equidistant between bolt A and hole B with the dowel to the left. Remove the pulley and timing cover.

93 Encircle the camshaft sprocket with the timing chain and insert through the cylinder head aperture. Locate the sprocket on the camshaft flange and secure with the lock plate and one bolt — instruction 30.

94 Keeping the chain taut on the drive side fit the chain to the crankshaft and jackshaft sprockets. Check and if necessary make any adjustment to the position of the jackshaft sprocket to maintain it in its correct position as in instruction 92.

95 Fit and loosely secure the guides as follows:
a   The adjustable guide.
b   The straight fixed guide.
c   The support bracket.

96 Fit a 'slave' bolt to the lower hole in the fixed guide to ensure alignment when fitting the timing cover centre bolt.

97 Fit the timing chain hydraulic tensioner and secure with the two bolts and spring washers. 12.65.28.

NOTE: To prevent the tensioner releasing while fitting, fit a spacer between the tensioner body and the back of the slipper.

98 Remove the spacer and insert a 0.100 in (2,54 mm) feeler gauge or slip gauge in its place, dimension A.

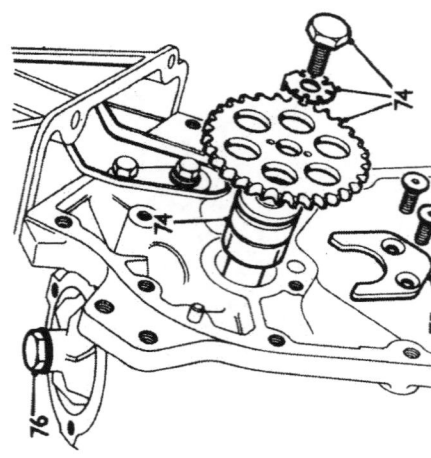

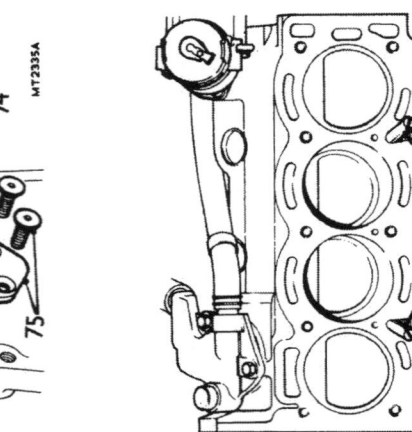

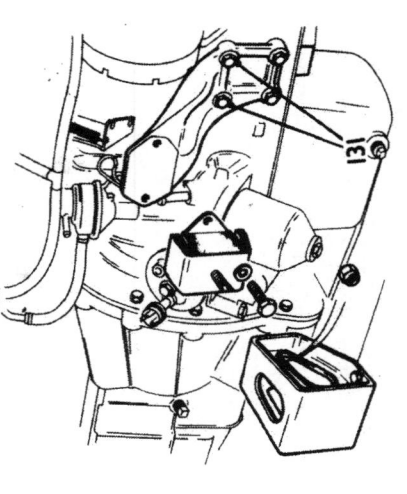

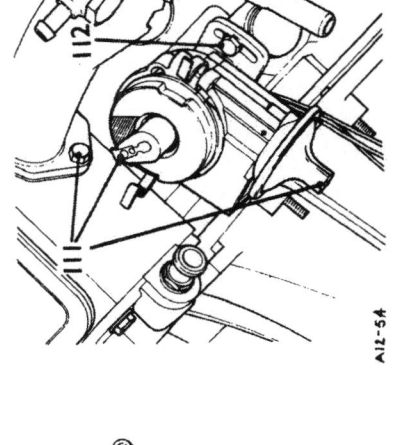

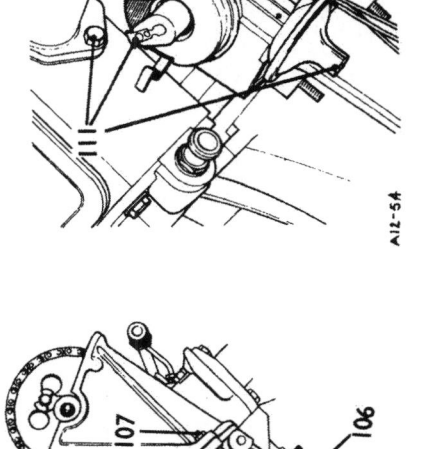

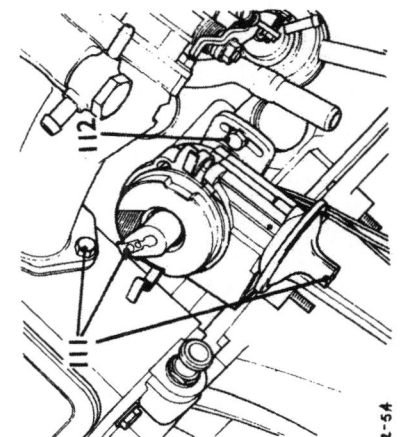

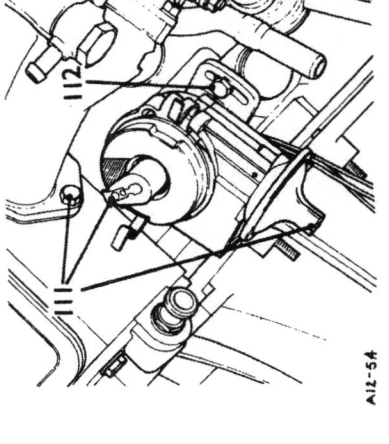

A12-30

A12-61

A12-54

A12-3

A12-50

continued

99 Adjust the chain tension by applying pressure, in the direction of the arrow, to the adjustable guide while tightening the clamp bolt.

100 Remove the gauge and check that the scribed line on the jackshaft sprocket is still correctly positioned.

101 Tighten all the guide retaining bolts and remove the 'slave' bolt.

102 Turn the engine sufficiently to enable the remaining camshaft sprocket retaining bolt to be fitted and locked.

103 Check that the threaded spigot on the camshaft sprocket does not foul the support bracket.

104 Fit the oil thrower with the dished face outwards.

105 Using sealing compound fit a new timing cover gasket and position the timing cover over the two dowels.

106 Secure the cover with the centre bolt noting that it has a fibre washer under the head.

107 Fit the two nuts and bolts retaining the timing cover to the cylinder head.

108 Wit the lip face leading press-in a new timing cover oil seal flush with the outer face of the cover.

109 Fit the crankshaft and auxiliary pulleys.

110 Turn the crankshaft to bring numbers 1 and 4 pistons to T.D.C. with the timing mark on the camshaft flange in line with the groove on the front bearing cap.

111 Fit the distributor so that the vacuum retard unit is pointing directly rearward and the rotor arm is in line with the manifold rear retaining bolt hole in the cylinder head.

112 Temporarily tighten the distributor retaining bolts pending final adjustment when the engine is installed.

113 Fit the camshaft cover.

114 Fit the oil pick-up strainer.

115 Fit the sump.

116*Fit the fuel pump using a new gasket and ensuring that the actuating lever rides on top of the jackshaft cam.

117 Fit the fan pulley assembly and hang the drive belts on the pulleys.

118 Fit the alternator complete with bracket and adjusting link.

119 Fit the front lifting eye.

120*Fit the air pump.

121* Fit the diverter and relief valve complete with the air distribution manifold and hoses.
122* Fit the air pump to diverter and relief valve hose.
123* Fit and adjust the air pump drive belt tension, see 17.25.13, see instructions 4 to 6.
124 Fit and adjust the alternator belt tension, see 86.10.05.
125 Install the air conditioning compressor and brackets — if fitted.
126 Adjust air conditioning compressor drive belt tension, see 82.10.01.
127 Fit the exhaust manifold.
128 Fit the hexagon drive and oil pump using a new sealing ring.
129 Fit the oil pressure switch.
130 Insert a new filter element in the filter bowl and fit the assembly with a new sealing rubber.
131 Fit the R.H. engine mounting bracket noting that the long bolts are fitted to the top two holes.
132 Fit the water pump to heater and inlet manifold pipe and hose.
133 Fit the bottom hose to the water pump cover.
134 Fit the inlet manifold complete with carburetters, see 19.15.15, instructions 19 to 23 or the fuel rail and the rear lifting eye.
135** Connect the fuel pump to carburetter hose.
136 Connect the engine breather pipes.
137 Fit the dipstick.
138 Fit the spark plugs.
139 Fit the distributor cap and connect the H.T. leads to the plugs (firing order 1, 3, 4, 2 distributor turns anti-clockwise).
140 Connect the vacuum pipe to the diverter and relief valve.
141 Fit the gearbox.
142 Fit the starter motor.
143 Fit the engine and gearbox assembly to the car 12.37.01.
144 Check and if necessary adjust the ignition timing 86.35.15.

ENGINE MOUNTING — FRONT L.H.

Remove and refit   12.45.01

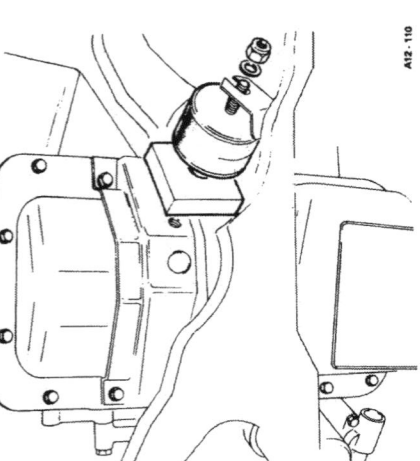

A12·110

Removing
1 Disconnect the battery.
2 Remove the fan guard.
3 Remove the fresh air duct. 80.15.31.
4 Raise the car on a ramp.
5 Remove the engine stabilizer. 12.45.16.
6 Remove the single nut securing the engine mounting to the sub-frame.
7 Place a jack to support the engine, under the sump coupling plate.
8 Remove the engine R.H. mounting retaining nut.
9 Jack up the engine sufficiently to enable the L.H. rubber mounting to be unscrewed from the sump cross-member threaded hole.
10 Remove the mounting.
11 Remove the packing piece — where fitted.

Refitting
12 Screw the mounting into the sump cross-member, inserting the packing piece — where fitted.
13 Lower the jack and tighten the engine R.H. mounting nut.
14 Remove the jack and fit and tighten the single nut securing the L.H. engine mounting to the sub-frame.
15 Fit and adjust the engine stabilizer. 12.45.16.
16 Lower the ramp.
17 Fit the fan guard.
18 Fit the fresh air duct. 80.15.31.
19 Connect the battery.

ENGINE MOUNTING — FRONT R.H.

Remove and refit   12.45.03

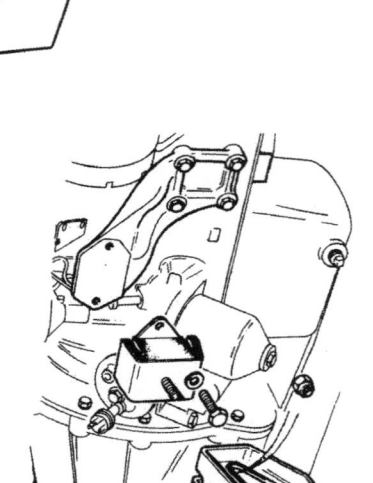

A12·96

Removing
1 Disconnect the battery.
2 Support the weight of the engine under the sump coupling plate.
3 Remove the single nut securing the mounting to the body bracket.
4 Remove the two bolts retaining the rubber mounting to the engine bracket.
5 Withdraw the mounting.

Refitting
6 Fit the mounting to the engine bracket with the two bolts and spring washers.
7 Secure the mounting to the body bracket with the single nut and plain washer.
8 Remove the engine support.
9 Connect the battery.

ENGINE MOUNTING – REAR CENTRE – UK and Europe Specification

Remove and refit   12.45.08

Removing

1 Drive the car onto a ramp and disconnect the battery.
2 Raise the ramp and place a jack in support under the gearbox.
3 Remove the two nuts and bolts retaining the rear mounting assembly to the gearbox extension.
4 Remove the two distance plates.
5 Remove the four bolts retaining the mounting cross-member to the body and remove the assembly from the car.
6 Remove the centre bolt and nut washer.
7 Remove the bracket.
8 Remove the distance piece.
9 Remove the restrictor plate.
10 Remove the two nuts and bolts securing the rubber mounting to the cross-member.
11 Remove the rubber mounting rubber from the cross-member.

Refitting

12 Fit the rubber mounting to the cross-member with the two nuts and bolts.
13 Reverse instructions 6 to 9 leaving the centre bolt and nut slack.
14 Fit the rear mounting assembly to the gearbox extension with the two nuts and bolts and four plain washers (one under the head of each bolt and one under the nut). Ensure that the two distance plates are fitted between the bracket and gearbox extension.
15 Fit the cross-member to the body with the four nuts.
16 Tighten the centre nut and bolt.
17 Remove the jack, lower the car and connect the battery.

ENGINE MOUNTING – REAR CENTRE – USA and Canada Specification

Remove and refit   12.45.08

Removing

1 Drive the car onto a ramp and disconnect the battery.
2 Raise the ramp and place a jack in support under the gearbox.
3 Disconnect the restraint cable from the crossmember.
4 Remove the two nuts securing the mounting assembly to the gearbox extension.
5 Disconnect the tie bar from the sump coupling plate.
6 Remove the four bolts retaining the mounting crossmember to the body and remove the assembly from the car, complete with the tie bar.
7 Remove the centre bolt.
8 Remove the tie bar.
9 Remove the distance piece.
10 Remove the restrictor plate.
11 Remove the two nuts and bolts securing the rubber mounting to the crossmember.

Refitting

12 Fit the rubber mounting to the crossmember with the two nuts and bolts.
13 Reverse instructions 7 to 11 leaving the centre bolt slack.
14 Fit the cross-member to the body with the four bolts.
15 Fit the assembly to the gearbox extension with the two nuts.
16 Connect the tie bar to the sump coupling plate.
17 Tighten the centre bolt.
18 Connect and adjust the restraint cable 37.20.01 instruction 29.
19 Remove the jack, lower the car and connect the battery.

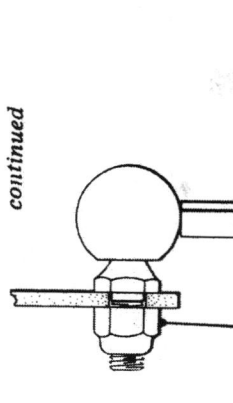

ENGINE STABILIZER – Early Models

Remove and refit   12.45.16

Removing

1 Raise the car on a ramp.
2 Remove the nyloc nut securing the engine stabilizer to the cylinder block bracket.
3 Remove the nyloc nut securing the stabilizer to the sub-frame and withdraw:
   a The lower washer.
   b The lower rubber.
   c The nylon distance piece.
4 Remove the stabilizer complete with:
   a The top rubber.
   b The top washer.
   c The top retaining nut.
   d The lock nut.

continued

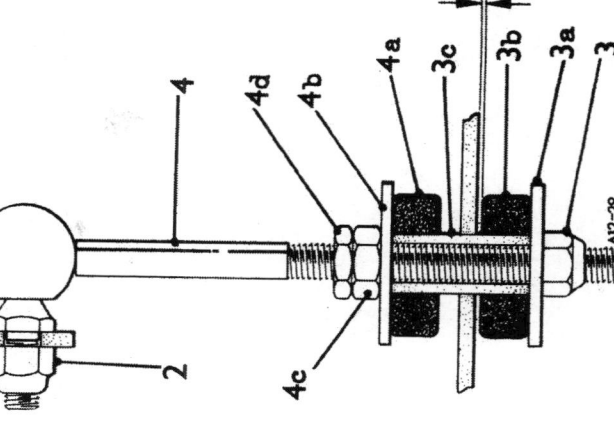

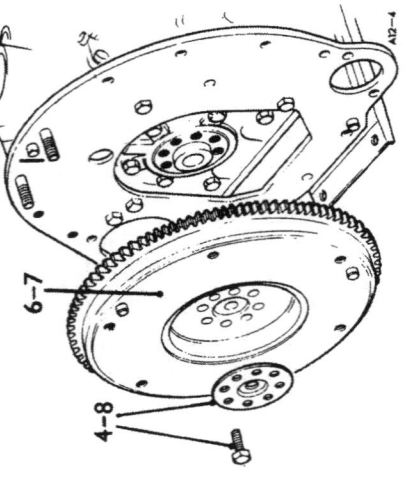

Refitting

5 Slacken off the lock nut and upper retaining nut.

6 Insert the stabilizer into the sub-frame location complete with the upper retaining nut and its lock-nut and upper washer and rubber.

7 Locate the stabilizer in the cylinder block bracket and secure with the nyloc nut.

8 Fit the nylon distance piece.

9 Fit the lower rubber washer and nyloc nut.

10 Tighten the lower nyloc nut until a gap of 0.040 in (1.0 mm) – dimension A – exists between the sub-frame and lower rubber.

11 Tighten the top retaining nut down until the upper washer just nips the nylon distance piece and tighten the lock nut.

12 Check the dimension A and lower the ramp.

ENGINE REAR ADAPTOR PLATE

Remove and refit   12.53.03

Removing

1 Remove the gearbox, see 37.20.01 or 44.20.01.

2 Remove the clutch assembly (as applicable).

3 Remove the flywheel, see 12.53.07, instructions 4 to 6.

4 Remove the six bolts securing the adaptor plate to the cylinder block.

5 Withdraw the rear adaptor plate.

Refitting

6 Clean the engine and adaptor plate mating faces and locate the plate on the engine over the dowels and studs.

7 Secure the plate with the six bolts.

8 Fit the flywheel 12.53.07 – instructions 7 to 11.

9 Fit the clutch (as applicable).

10 Fit the gearbox, see 37.20.01 or 44.20.01.

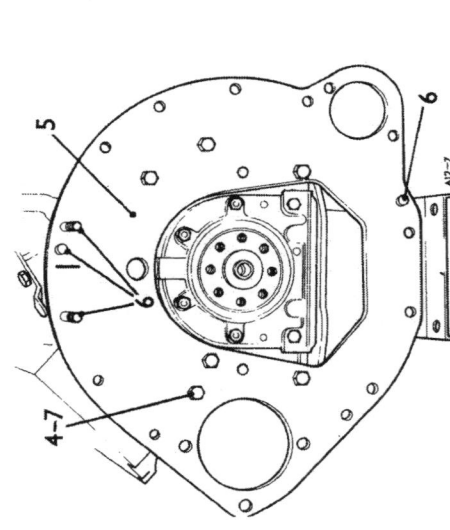

FLYWHEEL

Remove and refit   12.53.07

Removing

1 Isolate the battery.

2 Remove the gearbox, see 37.20.01 or 44.20.01.

3 Remove the clutch assembly (as applicable).

4 Remove the eight bolts and spigot bush retaining plate.

5 Mark for reassembly the relationship between the flywheel hub and crankshaft flange.

6 Withdraw the flywheel and ring gear assembly.

Refitting

7 Locate the flywheel assembly on the crankshaft so that the identification marks line up.

8 Secure the flywheel to the crankshaft with the eight bolts and retaining plate. Tighten the bolts to the correct torque – see 'TORQUE WRENCH SETTINGS'.

9 If a new flywheel has been fitted, turn the engine over so that numbers 1 and 4 pistons are at T.D.C. with number 1 cylinder firing.

10 Mark a chisel mark on the outside edge of the flywheel in line with the vertical mark on the engine rear adaptor plate.

11 Using a dial gauge check the flywheel for run-out – see DATA.

12 Refit the clutch (as applicable).

13 Refit the gearbox, see 37.20.01 or 44.20.01.

14 Reconnect the battery.

DATA

Flywheel run-out maximum .... 0.002 (0,050 mm) at a radius of 4 in (101 mm) on the friction face.

STARTER RING GEAR

Remove and refit   12.53.19

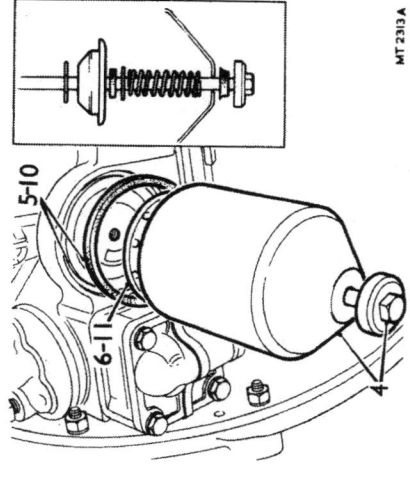

Removing

1 Remove the flywheel. 12.53.07.
2 Drill a hole approximately 0.375 in (10 mm) between the root of any tooth and inner rim of the ring gear. Drill sufficiently to weaken the ring gear without damaging the flywheel.
3 Secure the flywheel in a soft-jawed vice.
4 Place a heavy cloth over the ring gear for protection against flying fragments when splitting the ring gear.

WARNING: Take adequate precaution to avoid injury from flying fragments when splitting the ring gear.

5 Place a chisel immediately above the drilled hole and strike sharply to split the gear.

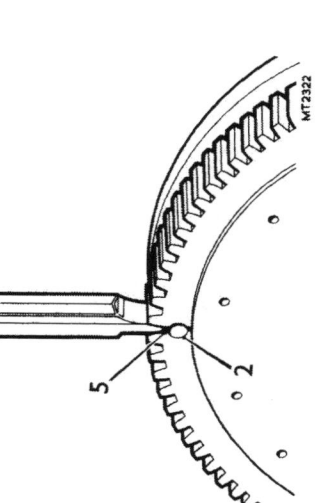

Refitting

6 Place the flywheel friction face downwards on a flat surface.
7 Heat the ring gear uniformly between 170° and 175°C (338° to 347°F) but do not exceed this temperature.
8 Locate the ring gear on the flywheel and retain it in position until it contracts sufficiently to grip the flywheel.
9 Allow the gear to cool gradually to avoid distortion. A maximum permissible gap of 0.025 in (0,6 mm) is allowed between the flywheel and ring gear in any one length of 6 in (15 cm) only of the circumference.
10 Fit the flywheel. 12.53.07

OIL FILTER ELEMENT

Remove and refit   12.60.02

Overhauling filter assembly — instructions 6 to 9   12.60.08

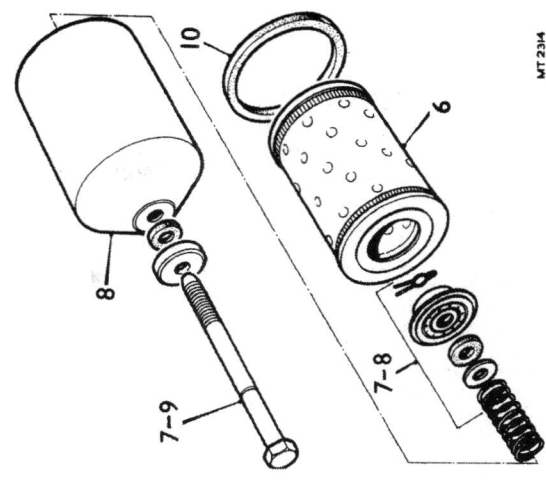

Removing

1 Drive the car onto a ramp.
2 Disconnect the battery and raise the ramp.
3 Place a suitable receptacle under the filter bowl to catch surplus oil.
4 Remove the filter bowl centre retaining bolt, and withdraw the assembly.
5 Extract the seal from the annular groove in the crankcase.

Overhauling

6 Remove the element and discard.
7 Dismantle the centre bolt assembly and clean all components including the bowl.
8 Assemble the centre bolt assembly to the bowl as illustrated, using new seals and if necessary renew the spring.
9 Secure the assembly with the retaining clip ensuring that it locates properly in the annular groove in the bolt.

Refitting

10 Clean the crankcase mating face and annular groove and fit a new seal to the groove ensuring that it seats properly and is not twisted.
11 Insert a new element into the filter bowl and secure the assembly to the crankcase and whilst tightening the centre bolt rotate the bowl to ensure that it seats correctly in the groove. Tighten the bolt to the correct torque — see 'TORQUE WRENCH SETTINGS'.
12 Reconnect the battery, start the engine and check for oil leaks.
13 Stop the engine and lower the ramp.
14 Allow sufficient time for the oil to drain back into the sump, check the oil level and top-up to the high mark on the dipstick with oil of a recommended make and grade.

OIL TRANSFER HOUSING

Remove and refit   12.60.14

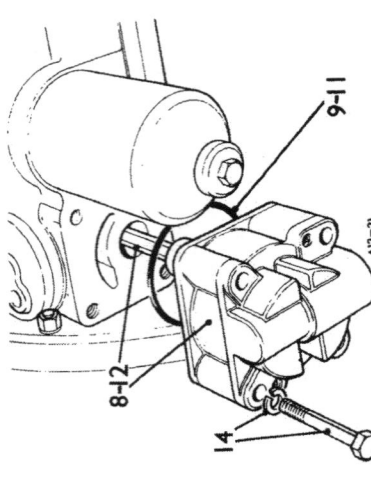

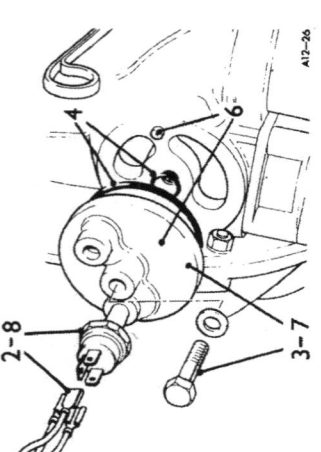

Removing

1 Disconnect the battery.
2 Disconnect the three Lucar leads from the oil pressure switch.
3 Remove the centre retaining bolt and withdraw the transfer housing.
4 Remove the 'O' ring seals from the housing.

Refitting

5 Clean the transfer housing and crankcase mating faces.
6 Using new 'O' ring seals fit the transfer housing engaging the dowel in the crankcase in the hole in the housing.
7 Fit and tighten the centre retaining bolt and plain washer.
8 Reconnect the three electrical leads to the correct connectors. 86.65.30.
9 Reconnect the battery.

OIL PUMP

Remove and refit   12.60.26

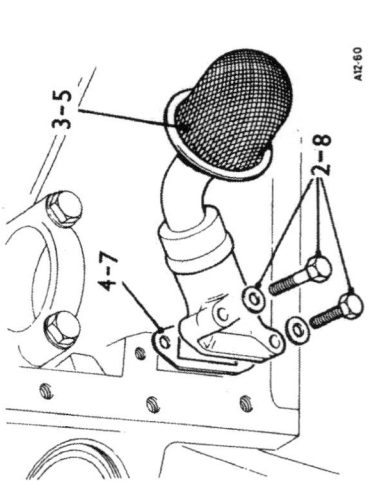

Removing

1 Drive the car onto a ramp and disconnect the battery.
2 Raise the ramp.
3 Remove the two bolts securing the clutch slave cylinder to the bell housing.
4 Carefully withdraw the clutch slave cylinder, complete with fluid pipe.
5 Withdraw the slave cylinder completely and secure it in a convenient position to gain access to the oil pump.
6 Remove the bell housing nut and bolt.
7 Remove the four oil pump retaining bolts and spring washers.
8 Withdraw the pump complete with the hexagonal drive shaft.
9 Remove the 'O' sealing ring.

Refitting

10 Clean the oil pump and crankcase mating faces.
11 Fit a new 'O' ring to the groove in the oil pump.
12 Engage the hexagonal drive shaft in the oil pump rotor.
13 Fit the oil pump ensuring that the drive shaft engages with the distributor.
14 Fit and evenly tighten the four oil pump retaining bolts and spring washers to the correct torque – see 'TORQUE WRENCH SETTINGS'.
15 Fit the bell housing nut and bolt.
16 Fit the clutch slave cylinder ensuring that the push rod enters the hole in the rubber boot.
17 Tighten the two retaining bolts and spring washers.
18 Lower the ramp and reconnect the battery.
19 Run the engine for three minutes, raise the ramp and check for oil leaks.

OIL PICK-UP STRAINER

Remove and refit   12.60.20

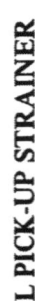

Removing

1 Remove the sump. 12.60.44.
2 Remove the two bolts and plain washers.
3 Withdraw the strainer.
4 Remove the gasket.

Refitting

5 Clean the strainer gauge.
6 Clean the strainer and crankcase mating faces.
7 Fit a new gasket.
8 Fit the strainer and secure with the two bolts and plain washers.
9 Refit the sump. 12.60.44.

OIL PUMP

Overhaul   12.60.32

Dismantling

1 Remove the oil pump. 12.60.26.
2 Withdraw the hexagonal drive shaft.
3 Remove the two screws and lift off the pump cover from the pump body.
4 Remove the rotors.
5 Remove the 'O' sealing ring from the pump body.
6 Remove the split pin from the oil pump cover.
7 Remove the locating plug, spring and relief valve.
8 Remove the 'O' sealing ring from the locating plug.

Inspecting

9 Clean all components
10 Install the rotors in the pump body, ensuring that the chamfered edge of the outer rotor is at the driving end of the rotor pocket.
11 Check the end-float of the inner and outer ring.
12 Check the outer ring to pump body diametrical clearance.
13 Check the rotor lobe clearances.
14 Check the length of the relief valve spring.
15 Check the relief valve and its bore for scoring or damage.
16 Renew the pump assembly if the clearances or end-floats measured in operations 11 to 13 exceed the figures given in DATA.
17 Check the bush in the pump cover, renew if scored or worn.

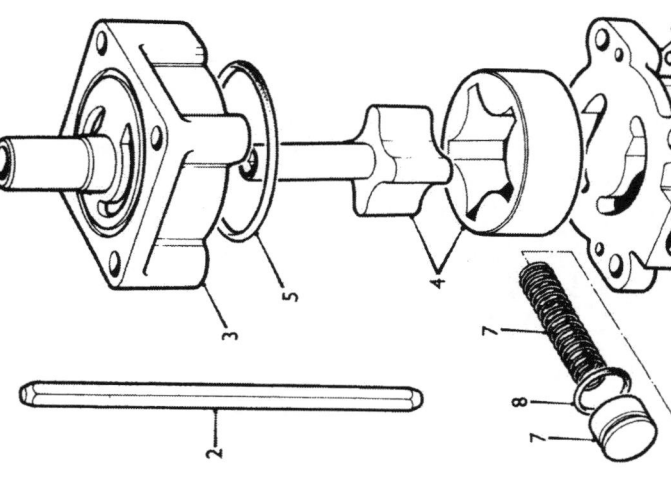

Reassembling

18 Lubricate all parts in clean engine oil before assembling.
19 Reverse the procedure in 1 to 8, noting:
  a Fit the relief valve with its large diameter first, so that its small spigot will engage with spring.
  b Fit a new 'O' sealing ring to the oil pressure relief valve locating plug.
  c Ensure that the outer rotor is installed in the pump body with its chamfered edge towards the driving end.
  d Fit a new 'O' sealing ring to the pump body.
20 Check the pump for freedom of action.
21 Fit the oil pump. 12.60.26.

DATA

Oil pump – Hobourn-Eaton

Outer ring end-float	0.004 in (0.1 mm)
Inner ring end-float	0.004 in (0.1 mm)
Outer ring to pump body diametrical clearance	0.008 in (0.2 mm)
Rotor lobe clearance	0.010 in (0.25 mm)
Relief valve spring free length	1.70 in (43.18 mm)

OIL SUMP

Remove and refit   12.60.44

Removing

1 Drive the car onto a ramp and disconnect the battery.
2 Remove the fresh-air duct.
3 Remove the fan guard.
4 Raise the ramp.
5 Drain the sump oil and refit the drain plug.
6 Remove the coupling plate bolts.
7 Remove the engine stabilizer. 12.45.16. (Where fitted).
8 Make up a support bracket from angle-iron in accordance with the dimensional drawing.

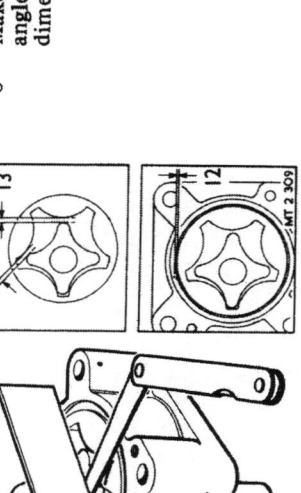

continued

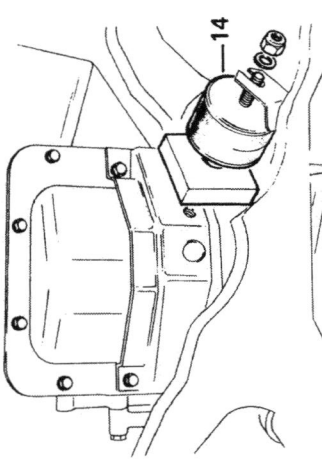

9 Remove the alternator support strap bolt and move the link away.

10 Remove the opposite timing cover lower bolt.

11 Using these bolts attach the support bracket to the timing cover.

12 Support the engine under the bracket with a jack.

13 Remove the two engine R.H. mounting bolts.

14 Remove the engine L.H. mounting to sub-frame nut.

15 Remove the sump nuts and bolts.

16 Raise the engine sufficiently to enable the sump complete with the L.H. engine mounting and cross-member to be withdrawn.

Refitting

17 Using a new gasket, manoeuvre the sump into position on the crankcase and loosely secure in position with a few bolts.

18 Fit the cross-member with mounting to the sump and fit and tighten the remaining sump retaining nuts and bolts.

19 Lower the engine and secure the L.H. rubber mounting to the sub-frame.

20 Connect the R.H. side engine mounting.

21 Fit the engine stabilizer. 12.45.16. (Where fitted).

22 Remove the jack, and the support bracket and refit the timing cover bolts and alternator strap.

23 Fit the coupling plate bolts.

24 Lower the ramp.

25 Fit the fan guard.

26 Fit the fresh air duct.

27 Fill the sump with engine oil of recommended make and grade to the high mark on the dipstick.

28 Reconnect the battery, run the engine and check for leaks.

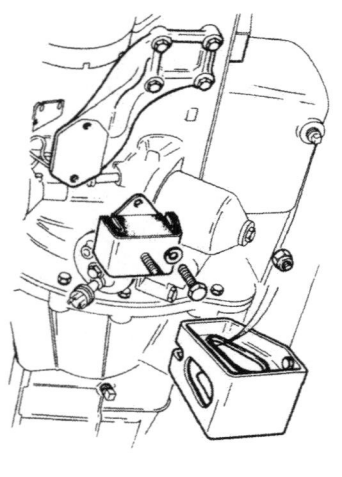

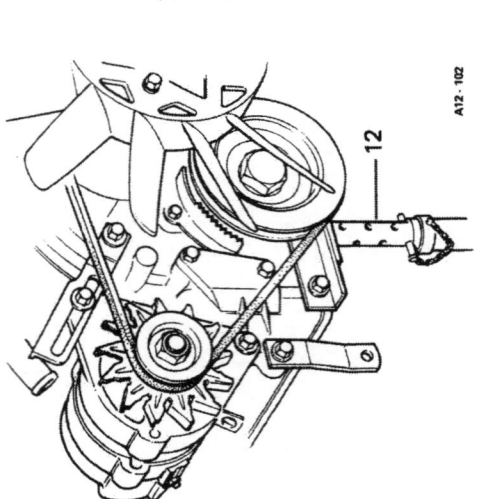

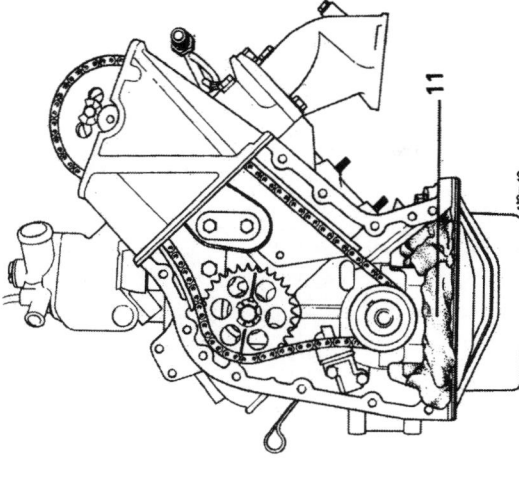

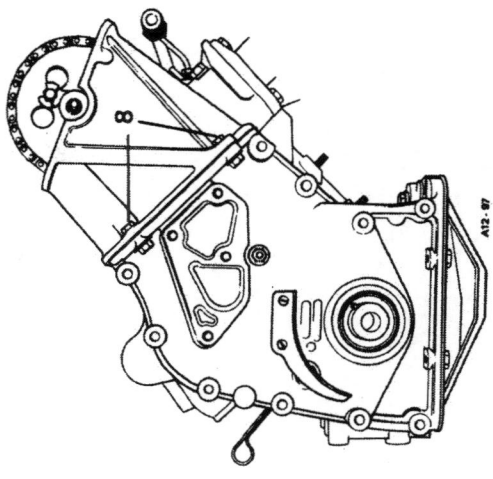

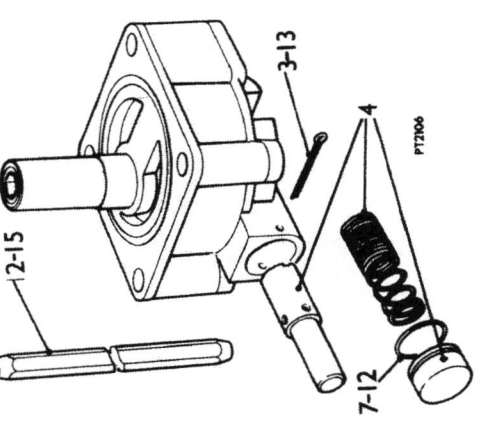

OIL PRESSURE RELIEF VALVE 12.60.56

Remove and refit

Removing
1 Remove the oil pump. 12.60.26.
2 Withdraw the hexagonal drive shaft.
3 Remove the split pin from the oil pump casing.
4 Remove the locating plug, spring and plunger by tapping the pump cover.

NOTE: Since in some instances the 'O' ring on the locating plug may stick to the bore, in order to accomplish instruction 4 the pump cover will have to be removed and the plug tapped out from the underside of the cover. Follow instructions 5 and 6 if this is necessary.

5 Remove the two screws securing the pump cover to the main body and lift off the cover.
6 Using a suitable soft drip tap out of the plug from the underside of the pump cover.
7 Remove the 'O' ring from the locating plug.

Examination
8 Examine the plunger and its bore for scores or wear.
9 Check the plunger spring length and renew if not in accordance with data.

Refitting
10 Observing absolute cleanliness fit the plunger to the pump cover ensuring that it moves freely in its bore.
11 Fit the spring over the plunger spigot end noting that the close coiled end is inserted first.
12 Fit a new 'O' ring to the locating plug and insert the plug.
13 Fit a new split pin.
14 Fit the cover to the pump and secure with the two screws.
15 Fit the hexagonal shaft to the crankcase.
16 Refit the oil pump to the engine. 12.60.26.

DATA
Relief valve spring free length . . . . .
1.70 in (43,18 mm)

TIMING CHAIN COVER — UK & Europe Specification

Remove and refit 12.65.01

Removing
1 Remove the bonnet, drive the car on ramp and disconnect the battery.
2 Remove the crankshaft pulley. 12.21.02.
3 Remove the alternator. 86.10.02.
4 Remove the alternator mounting bracket. 12.25.21.
5 Remove the alternator adjusting link.
6 Remove the two front sump bolts and one each side.
7 Remove the fan and viscous coupling assembly. 26.25.21.
8 Remove the two bolts and nuts securing the timing cover to the cylinder head.
9 Remove the remaining timing cover retaining bolts, including the centre bolt.
10 Withdraw the timing cover and gaskets.
11 Place a piece of rag over the access to the sump to prevent items falling in by accident.

Refitting
12 Remove the protective rags.
13 Clean the engine and timing cover mating faces and place new gaskets in position on the timing cover.
14 Locate the timing cover on the engine over the dowels and fit and tighten the centre retaining bolt, noting that it has a fibre washer under the head.
15 Fit the fan and viscous coupling unit.
16 Fit, but leave loose, the cylinder head to timing cover nuts and bolts.
17 Fit, but leave slack, the alternator adjusting link bracket.
18 Fit the alternator mounting bracket.
19 Fit the alternator but leave slack.
20 Connect the alternator harness plug to the alternator.
21 Loosely place in position the alternator drive belt.
22 Finally tighten the cylinder head to timing cover nuts and bolts.
23 Raise the ramp and fit and tighten the sump bolts.
24 Fit the crankshaft pulley.
25 Adjust the alternator drive belt tension. 86.10.05.
26 Secure the radiator with the two top brackets and four nuts.
27 Fit the fan guard.
28 Fit the bonnet.
29 Reconnect the battery.

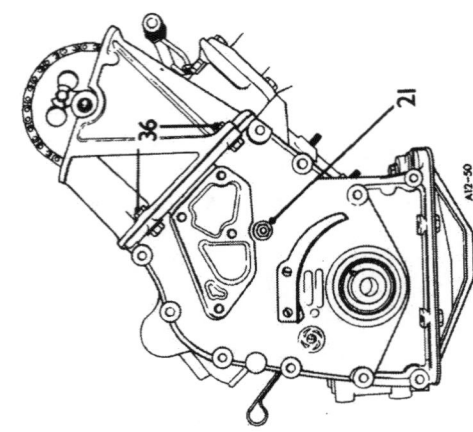

TIMING CHAIN COVER –
USA & Canada Specification

Remove and refit   12.65.01

* *Applicable to carburetter engines only*

Removing
1 Remove the bonnet, drive car on ramp and disconnect the battery.
2 Remove the crankshaft pulleys.
3 Remove the alternator. 86.10.02.
4 Remove the alternator mounting bracket. 12.25.21.
5 Remove the alternator adjusting link.
6 * Remove the air pump, see 17.25.07.
7 * Remove the 'diverter and relief valve' complete with attachment bracket.
8 * Remove the air pump bracket and lifting eye, see 17.25.07.
9 * Remove the air conditioning compressor steady bracket.
10 Remove the two bolts and nuts securing the timing cover to the cylinder head.
11 Slacken the four bolts securing the air conditioning compressor carrier bracket to the engine.

12 Remove the three air conditioning compressor adjusting bolts.
13 Remove the air conditioning compressor adjusting bracket.
14 Remove the two front sump bolts and one each side.
15 Remove the timing cover centre attachment bolt and bottom left hand bolt (looking at engine from front).
16 Remove the fan and Torquatrol assembly – instructions 6 to 9. 26.25.21.
17 Withdraw the timing cover and gaskets.
18 Place a piece of rag over the access to the sump to prevent items falling in by accident.

Refitting
19 Remove the protective rags.
20 Clean the engine and timing cover mating faces and place new gaskets in position on the timing cover.
21 Locate the timing cover on the engine over the dowels and fit and tighten the centre retaining bolt, noting that it has a fibre washer under the head.
22 Fit the fan and torquatrol assembly securing it to the timing cover with the two uncommitted bolts.
23 Fit the air conditioning compressor adjustment bracket securing it with the rear bolt but leaving it slack.
24 Fit, but leave loose, the cylinder head to timing cover nuts and bolts.
25 Fit the air conditioning compressor steady bracket and tighten the bolts.
26 Tighten the air conditioning compressor adjustment bracket rear bolt.
27 Fit the air conditioning compressor to the adjustment bracket but leave the bolts slack.
28* Fit the air pump bracket together with the lifting hook.
29* Fit the diverter and relief valve bracket complete with valve.
30 Fit, but leave slack, the alternator adjusting link bracket.
31 Fit the alternator mounting bracket.
32 Fit the alternator but leave slack.
33 Connect the alternator harness plug – instructions 16 and 17. 86.10.02.
34* Fit the air pump, but leave slack.

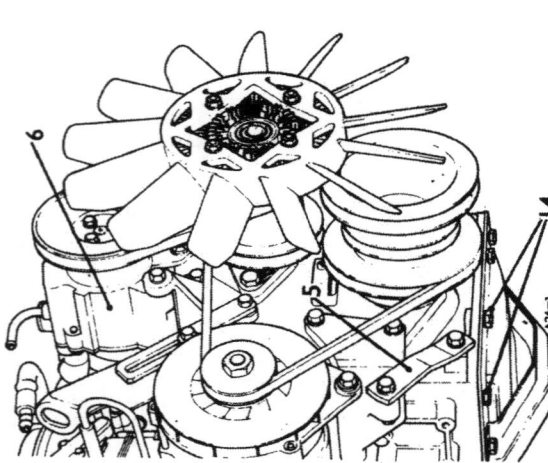

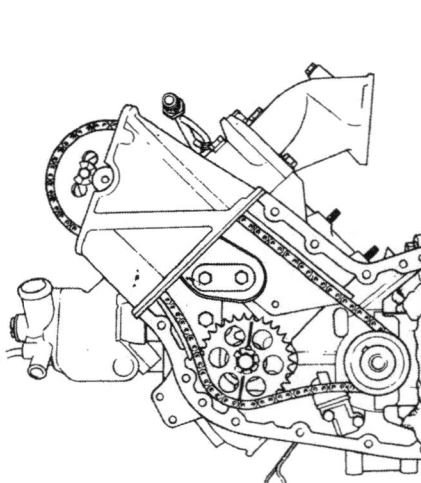

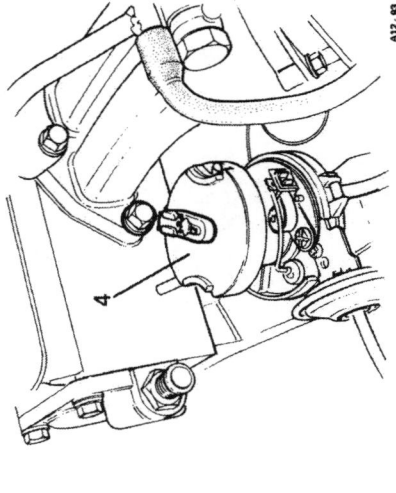

A12-100

A12-83

35 Loosely place in their correct relative positions the following:
  a The alternator drive belt.
  b* The air pump drive belt.
  c The air conditioning compressor drive belt.
36 Finally tighten the cylinder head to timing cover nuts and bolts.
37 Raise the ramp and fit and tighten the sump bolts.
38 Fit the crankshaft and auxiliary pulleys – instructions 9 to 11. 12.21.02.
39 Tighten the four air conditioning compressor to carrier engine bolts.
40 Fit air conditioning compressor drive belt to the pulleys and adjust tension.
41 Adjust the alternator drive belt tension, see 86.10.05.
42* Adjust air pump drive belt tension, see 17.25.13.
43* Connect air pump hose to 'diverter and relief valve'.
44 Fit the fan blades to the Torquatrol unit.
45 Secure the radiator with the two top brackets and four nuts.
46 Fit the fan guard.
47 Fit the bonnet.
48 Reconnect the battery.

VALVE TIMING –
UK and Europe Specification

Check and adjust   12.65.08

Checking
1 Disconnect the battery.
2 Turn the engine over until the timing mark on the crankshaft pulley coincides with the zero mark on the timing cover scale.
3 Remove the fresh air duct. 80.15.31.
4 Remove the distributor cap and check that the rotor arm points to the rear bolt securing the inlet manifold to the cylinder head.
5 Remove the camshaft cover. 12.29.42.
6 The valve timing is correct when the timing mark on the camshaft flange is in line with the corresponding groove in the camshaft front bearing cap.
7 Refit the distributor cap.
8 Refit the camshaft cover. 12.29.42.
9 Refit the fresh air duct. 80.15.31.
10 Reconnect the battery.

continued

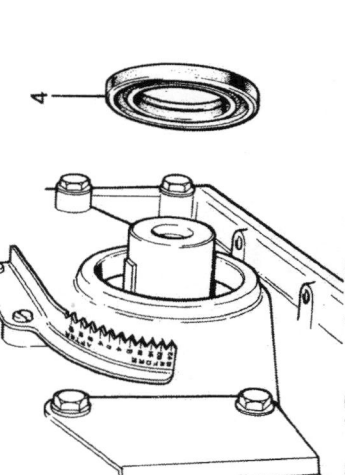

A12-70

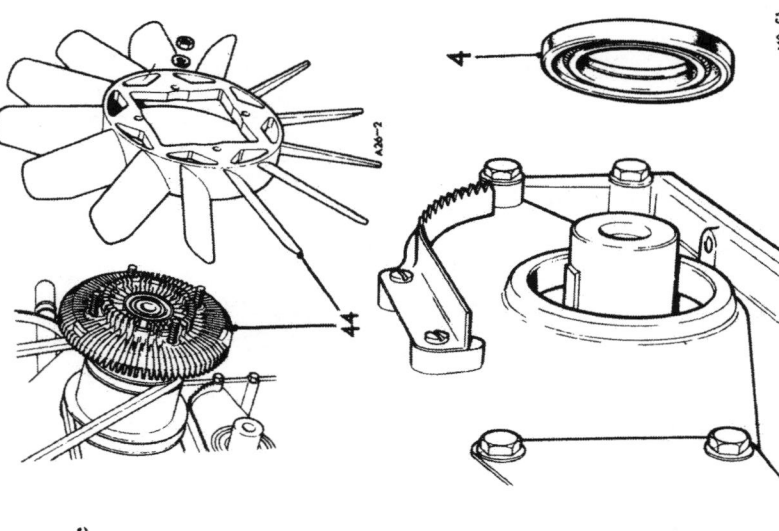

A36-2

A12-61

USA Specification

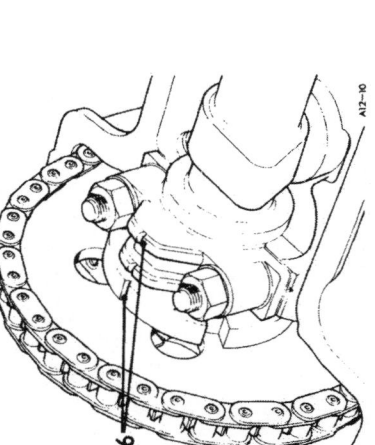

A12-96

UK and Europe Specification

TIMING COVER OIL SEAL

Remove and refit   12.65.05

Removing
1 Disconnect the battery.
2 Remove the crankshaft pulleys. 12.21.02.
3 Lever out the old seal.

Refitting
4 Dip a new seal in engine oil and with the lip face leading tap it squarely into its housing until flush with the outside of the timing cover. Check by placing a straight edge across the face of the seal and timing cover.
5 Refit the crankshaft pulleys. 12.21.07.
6 Reconnect the battery.

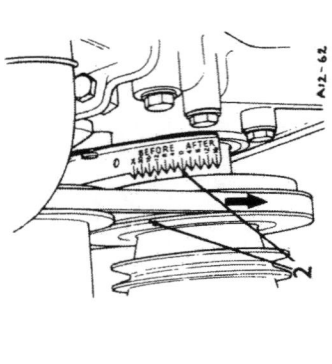

A12-62

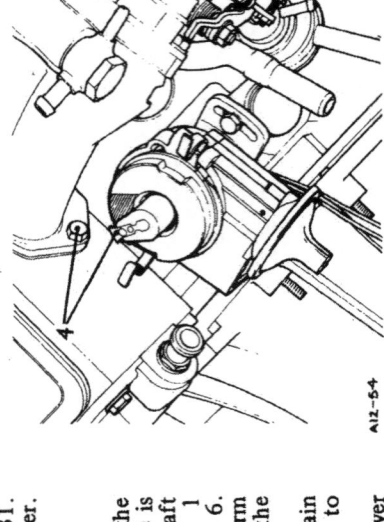

A12-54

USA & Canada Specification

Adjusting

11 Disconnect the battery.
12 Remove the fresh air duct. 80.15.31.
13 Remove the timing chain cover. 12.65.01.
14 Remove the distributor cap.
15 Remove the camshaft cover.
16 Turn the engine over so that the timing mark on the camshaft flange is in line with the groove in the camshaft front bearing cap, i.e. number 1 cylinder T.D.C. firing – instruction 2.
17 Check that the distributor rotor arm points to the rear bolt securing the inlet manifold – instruction 4.
18 Remove the hydraulic timing chain tensioner. 12.65.28 instructions 2 to 4.
19 Fit a 'slave' bolt to the timing cover centre hole in the cylinder block to ensure alignment when refitting the cover.
20 Remove the two bolts securing the adjustable chain guide.
21 Slacken the remaining guide bolt.
22 Remove the adjustable guide.
23 Slip the timing chain from the jackshaft and crankshaft sprockets.
24 Temporarily fit the timing chain cover locating it on the two dowels.
25 Temporarily fit the crankshaft pulley.
26 Turn the crankshaft until the timing mark on the crankshaft pulley coincides with the zero figure on the timing cover scale – instruction 2.
27 Remove the timing cover and pulley.
28 Fit the timing chain to the sprockets keeping it taut on the drive side, i.e. the run between the camshaft and the crankshaft sprockets.
29 Since the jackshaft sprocket may have been moved, whilst disconnecting the chain, re-set to its correct position by turning the sprocket until the scribed line is equidistant between bolts A and B and the distributor rotor arm points to the rear bolt head securing the inlet manifold to the cylinder head.
30 Fit the adjustable guide locating it loosely with the two bolts – noting that the locking bolt has a plain and spring washer.
31 Fit the hydraulic timing chain tensioner. 12.65.28 instructions 12 to 20.
32 Remove the 'slave' bolt.
33 Refit the timing chain cover. 12.65.01.

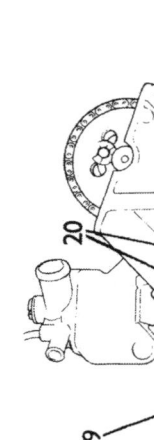
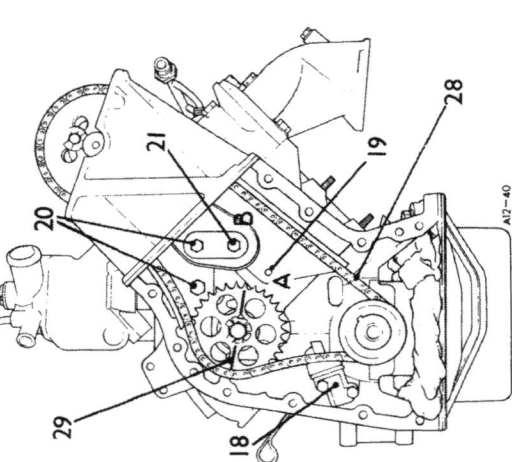

A12-40

DATA

Valve timing

Inlet valves open	16° B.T.D.C.
Inlet valves close	56° A.B.D.C.
Exhaust valves open	56° B.B.D.C.
Exhaust valves close	16° A.T.D.C.

VALVE TIMING — USA & Canada Specification

Check and adjust   12.65.08

Checking

1 Disconnect the battery.
2 Turn the engine over until the timing mark on the crankshaft pulley coincides with the zero mark on the timing cover scale.
3 Remove the fresh air duct. 80.15.31.
4 Remove the distributor cap and check that the rotor arm points to the rear bolt securing the inlet manifold to the cylinder head.
5 Remove the camshaft cover. 12.29.42.
6 The valve timing is correct when the timing mark on the camshaft flange is in line with the corresponding groove in the camshaft front bearing cap.
7 Refit the distributor cap.
8 Refit the camshaft cover. 12.29.42.
9 Refit the fresh air duct. 80.15.31.
10 Reconnect the battery.

Adjusting

11 Disconnect the battery.
12 Remove the fresh air duct. 80.15.31.
13 Remove the timing chain cover. 12.65.01.
14 Remove the distributor cap.
15 Remove the camshaft cover.
16 Turn the engine over so that the timing mark on the camshaft flange is in line with the groove in the camshaft front bearing cap, i.e. number 1 cylinder T.D.C. firing – instruction 6.
17 Check that the distributor rotor arm points to the rear bolt securing the inlet manifold – instruction 4.
18 Remove the hydraulic timing chain tensioner. 12.65.28 instructions 2 to 4.
19 Fit a 'slave' bolt to the timing cover centre hole in the cylinder block to ensure alignment when refitting the cover.
20 Remove the two bolts securing the adjustable chain guide.
21 Slacken the remaining guide bolt.
22 Remove the adjustable guide.
23 Slip the timing chain from the jackshaft and crankshaft sprockets.

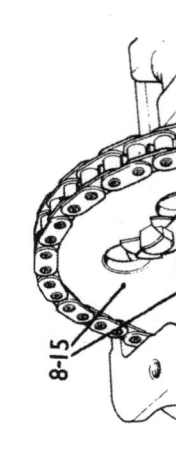
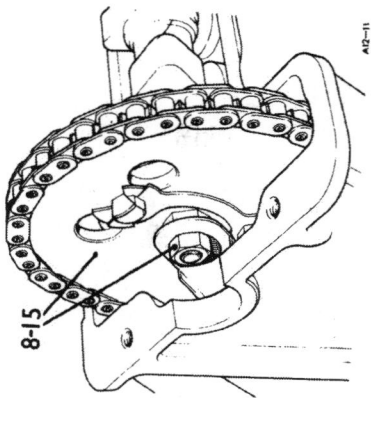

3–9
2–10
5
4–14
7–12
6

8–15

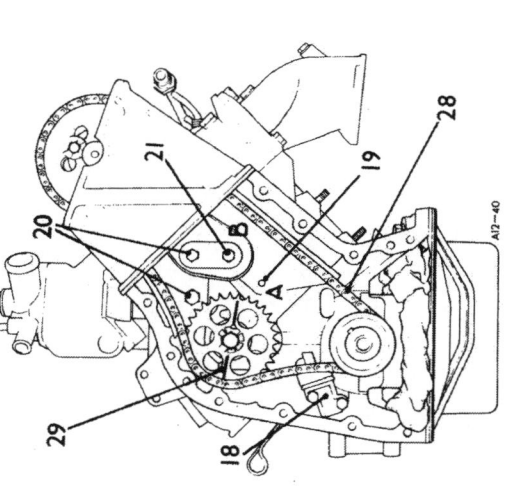

TIMING CHAIN AND SPROCKETS

Remove and refit 12.65.12

Removing

1 Remove the timing chain. 12.65.14.
2 Unlock and remove the jackshaft retaining bolt.
3 Withdraw the jackshaft sprocket.
4 Remove the oil thrower.
5 Remove the crankshaft sprocket.
6 Remove the crankshaft key.
7 Remove the sprocket alignment shims.
8 Detach the camshaft sprocket from the support bracket.

Refitting

9 Using a new locking washer, fit the jackshaft sprocket, ensuring that it locates correctly over the dowel.
10 Fit and tighten the retaining bolt to the correct torque, see 'TORQUE WRENCH SETTINGS', and lock it.
11 Temporarily fit the crankshaft sprocket and check its alignment with the jackshaft sprocket by using a straight edge across the two sprockets as illustrated.
12 Adjust any misalignment by the addition of shims behind the crankshaft sprocket.
13 Remove the crankshaft sprocket, fit the crankshaft key and refit the sprocket.
14 Fit the oil thrower noting that the dished side faces outwards away from the engine.
15 Attach the camshaft sprocket to the support bracket with a 'slave' nut.
16 Refit the timing chain. 12.65.14.

24 Temporarily fit the timing chain cover locating it on the two dowels.
25 Temporarily fit the crankshaft pulley.
26 Turn the crankshaft until the timing mark on the crankshaft pulley coincides with the zero figure on the timing cover scale – instruction 2.
27 Remove the timing cover and pulley.
28 Fit the timing chain to the sprockets keeping it taut on the drive side, i.e. the run between the camshaft and crankshaft sprockets.
29 Since the jackshaft sprocket may have been moved, whilst disconnecting the chain, re-set to its correct position by turning the sprocket until the scribed line is equidistant between the bolts A and B and the distributor rotor arm points to the rear bolt head securing the inlet manifold to the cylinder head.
30 Fit the adjustable guide locating it loosely with the two bolts – noting that the locking bolt has a plain and spring washer.
31 Fit the hydraulic timing chain tensioner 12.65.28 instructions 12 to 20.
32 Remove the 'slave' bolt.
33 Refit the timing chain cover 12.65.01 instructions 19 to 48.

6

21
20
29
18
19
28

DATA

Valve timing

Inlet valves open	. . 16°	B.T.D.C.
Inlet valves close	. . 56°	A.B.D.C.
Exhaust valves open	. . 56°	B.B.D.C.
Exhaust valves close	. . 16°	A.T.D.C.

TIMING CHAIN

Remove and refit   12.65.14

Removing

1 Remove the timing chain cover. 15.65.01.

2 Remove the camshaft cover.

3 Remove the distributor cap.

4 Turn the engine over so that the timing mark on the camshaft is at the bottom i.e. 180° distant from the groove in the camshaft front bearing cap, to enable instruction 5 to be carried out.

5 Unlock and remove the exposed camshaft retaining bolt.

6 Turn the engine over until the mark on the camshaft flange is in line with the groove on the camshaft front bearing cap.

7 Check that the distributor rotor arm points to the head of the rear bolt securing the inlet manifold i.e. T.D.C. number 1 cylinder firing.

8 Secure the camshaft sprocket to the support bracket with a 'slave' nut.

9 Unlock and remove the remaining bolt retaining the camshaft sprocket.

10 Remove the hydraulic timing chain tensioner and guide plate.

11 Remove the locking bolt from the adjustable chain guide.

12 Remove the common bolt securing the adjustable guide and camshaft sprocket support bracket.

13 Remove the adjustable guide.

14 Remove the bolt securing the camshaft support bracket and fixed guide whilst holding the camshaft sprocket.

15 Remove the fixed guide and release the chain from the jackshaft and camshaft sprockets and withdraw upwards the camshaft sprocket and bracket together with the timing chain.

Refitting

16 Encircle the camshaft sprocket with the timing chain and insert it through the aperture with the support bracket and pass the chain over the jackshaft and crankshaft sprockets.

17 Fit the fixed guide and support bracket and loosely secure with the common bolt and spring washer.

18 Fit the adjustable guide and loosely secure with the two bolts noting that the locking bolt has a plain and spring washer.

19 Fit a slave bolt to the timing cover centre retaining bolt hole.

20 Secure the camshaft sprocket to the camshaft with one bolt and a new tab washer.

21 Turn the jackshaft sprocket so that the scribed line across it is equidistant between the 'slave' bolt A and bolt 'B'.

22 Check that the distributor arm is in the position as described in instruction 7.

23 Fit the hydraulic timing chain tensioner 12.65.28 reversing instructions 2 to 4 ensuring that the three retaining bolts for the chain guides are tightened and that the position of the jackshaft sprocket has not altered.

continued

NOTE: If it is suspected that the crankshaft may have been turned, temporarily fit the timing cover and crankshaft pulley and check that the timing mark on the pulley coincides with the zero figure on the timing cover scale.

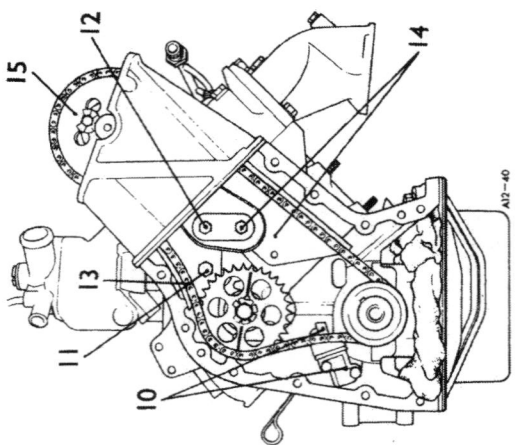

A12-10

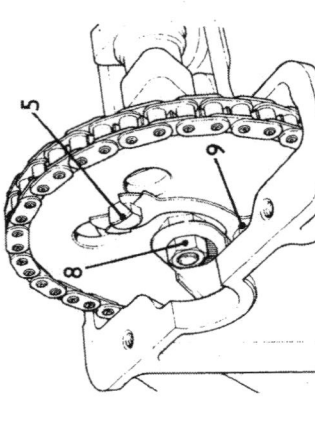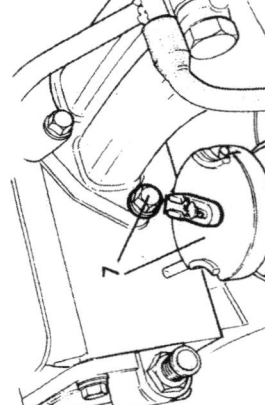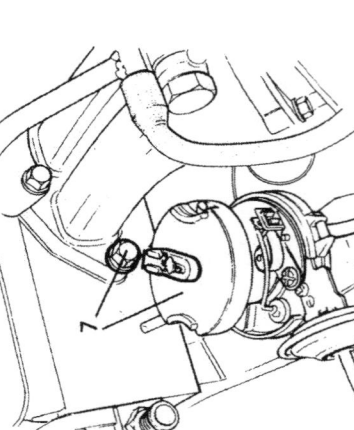

A12-40

A12-11

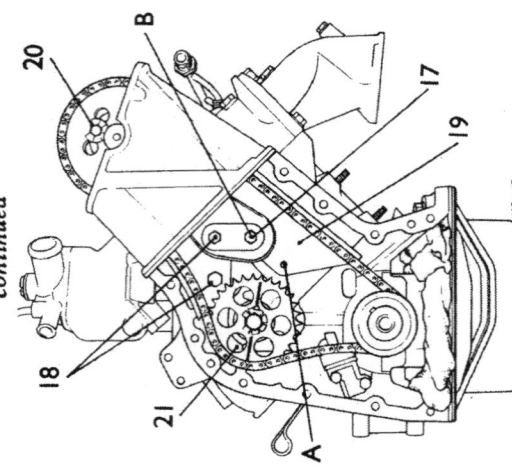

A12-83

A12-54

USA & Canada Specification   **UK & Europe Specification**

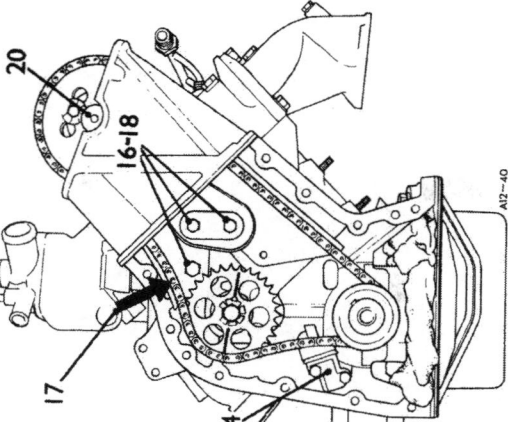

Reassembling

12 Insert the slipper into the bore.

13 Fit the ratchet into the bore and turn it clockwise with an Allen key to lock it in a retracted position.

NOTE: To prevent the tensioner releasing while fitting, insert a spacer between the tensioner body and the back of the slipper.

Refitting

14 Fit the tensioner assembly and back plate to the cylinder block taking care not to allow the tensioner to release. Secure with the two bolts and spring washers. Remove the spacer.

15 Insert a 0.100 in (2.54 mm) feeler or slip gauge between the slipper and tensioner body – dimension A.

16 Slacken the three chain guide retaining bolts.

17 Press down, in the direction of the arrow, on top of the adjustable chain guide until the feeler or slip gauge is a sliding fit.

18 Whilst holding the guide in this position tighten the adjustable guide bolt first, and then the two remaining bolts.

19 Remove the feeler or slip gauge.

20 Remove the camshaft cover and check that the camshaft spigot is positioned centrally in the support bracket and does not foul when the camshaft is revolved.

21 Refit the timing chain cover. 12.65.01.

DATA

Tensioner spring free length . . . . 2.750 in (69,8 mm)

---

24 Remove the 'slave' nut supporting the camshaft sprocket and ensure that the threaded spigot does not foul in the support bracket hole.

25 Turn the engine over sufficiently to enable the remaining camshaft sprocket retaining bolt to be fitted.

26 Tighten and lock the bolt and turn the engine back again and finally tighten and lock the first bolt.

27 Fit the camshaft cover.

28 Fit the distributor cap.

29 Fit the timing chain cover. 19.65.01.

TIMING-CHAIN SPROCKETS 12.65.22

Remove and refit

This operation is covered under operation 12.65.12.

TIMING CHAIN TENSIONER 12.65.28

Remove and refit

Removing

1 Remove the timing chain cover. 12.65.01.

2 Remove the tensioner retaining bolts.

3 Remove the tensioner from the engine.

4 Remove the backplate between the tensioner body and cylinder block.

Dismantling

5 Press-in the slipper and remove it from the tensioner body.

6 Remove the ratchet and spring.

Examination

7 Check the slipper pad for wear and renew if necessary.

8 Renew the ratchet if worn.

9 Check the spring and renew if it is not in accordance with DATA.

10 Examine the tensioner body and check that the oil inlet hole is clear.

11 Ensure that the oil outlet hole is clear.

TIMING CHAIN GUIDES

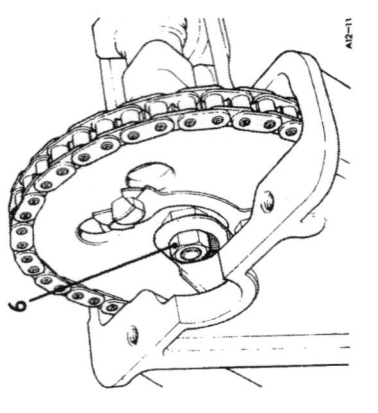

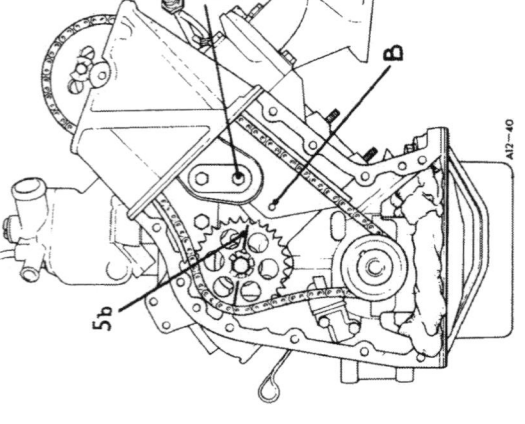

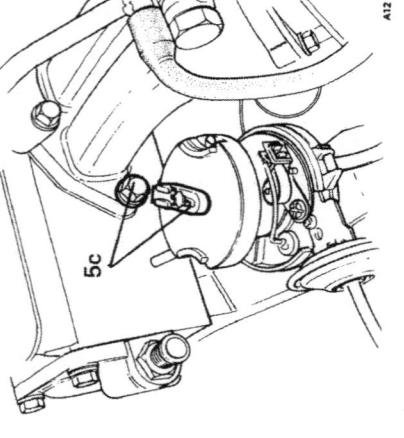

UK & Europe Specification

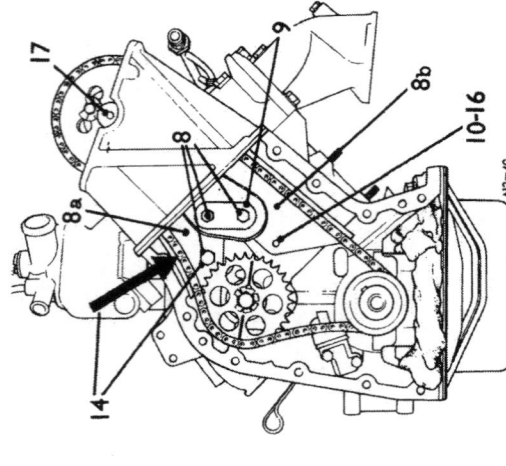

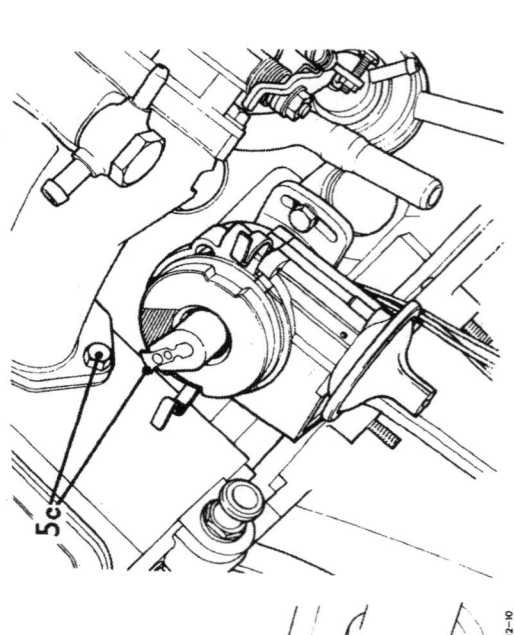

USA & Canada Specification

Remove and refit   **12.65.50**

Removing

1 Remove the timing chain cover. 12.65.01.
2 Remove the fresh air duct. 80.15.31.
3 Remove the camshaft cover.
4 Remove the distributor cap.
5 Turn the engine over until the following conditions are achieved:
   a The timing mark on the camshaft flange is in line with the groove in the camshaft front bearing cap.
   b The scribed line across the jackshaft sprocket is equal distance between bolt A and hole B.
   c The distributor rotor arm points to the head of the rear bolt securing the inlet manifold to the cylinder head.

6 Secure the camshaft sprocket to the support bracket with a 'slave' nut.
7 Insert a 0.100 slip gauge between the body of the hydraulic tensioner and the back of the slipper to prevent the tensioner releasing when the chain pressure is released, and remove the tensioner.
8 Remove the three chain guide retaining bolts and withdraw:
   a The adjustable guide.
   b The fixed guide.

Refitting

9 Fit the fixed guide and support bracket securing it loosely with the common bolt.
10 Fit a 'slave' bolt to the timing cover centre retaining bolt to facilitate refitting the cover.
11 Fit the adjustable guide retaining it loosely with the two bolts, noting that the locking bolt has a plain and spring washer.
12 Fit the timing chain tensioner.
13 Insert a 0.100 in feeler gauge between the body of the tensioner and the back of the slipper.

14 Press downwards on the adjustable guide whilst tightening the locking bolt.
15 Tighten the two remaining bolts.
16 Remove the 'slave' bolt.
17 Remove the 'slave' nut and ensure that the threaded spigot does not foul in the support bracket hole.
18 Check that the position of the jackshaft sprocket has not altered as described in instruction 5b.
19 Refit the timing chain cover — 12.65.01 – instructions 19 to 48.
20 Refit the camshaft cover.
21 Refit the distributor cap.

EMISSION AND EVAPORATIVE LOSS CONTROL

TR7 vehicles are fitted during manufacture with various items of emission and evaporative loss control equipment to meet individual territory requirements. Therefore some operations in this section of the Manual may not be applicable to all vehicles and some operations will be specific to selected markets and/or a model year manufacture only.

In addition, and where fitted, the electronic fuel injection system contributes to the exhaust emission control characteristics of the engine and reference should be made, as necessary, to the section of the Manual covering this equipment.

Unauthorized replacement or modification of the emission or evaporative loss control equipment may contravene local territory legislation and render the vehicle user and/or repairer liable to legal penalties.

EMISSION AND EVAPORATIVE LOSS CONTROL

CRANKCASE EMISSION CONTROL

Description   **17.00.00**

Crankcase breathing and evacuation of 'blow by' gases is achieved by utilizing the characteristic partial vacuum in the constant depression carburetter. By this method crankcase emissions are burned in the engine combustion process. A wire gauze strainer in the engine top cover acts as an oil separator/flame trap.

On fuel injection engines a depression is maintained in the crankcase under all operating conditions by connecting the crankcase breathing housing to a point between the air meter flap and the throttle plate (i.e. a constant depression region).

CRANKCASE BREATHING AND CANISTER PURGE SYSTEMS — USA MARKET 1975 AND 1976 MODEL YEARS AND LATER CANADIAN MARKET SPECIFICATIONS

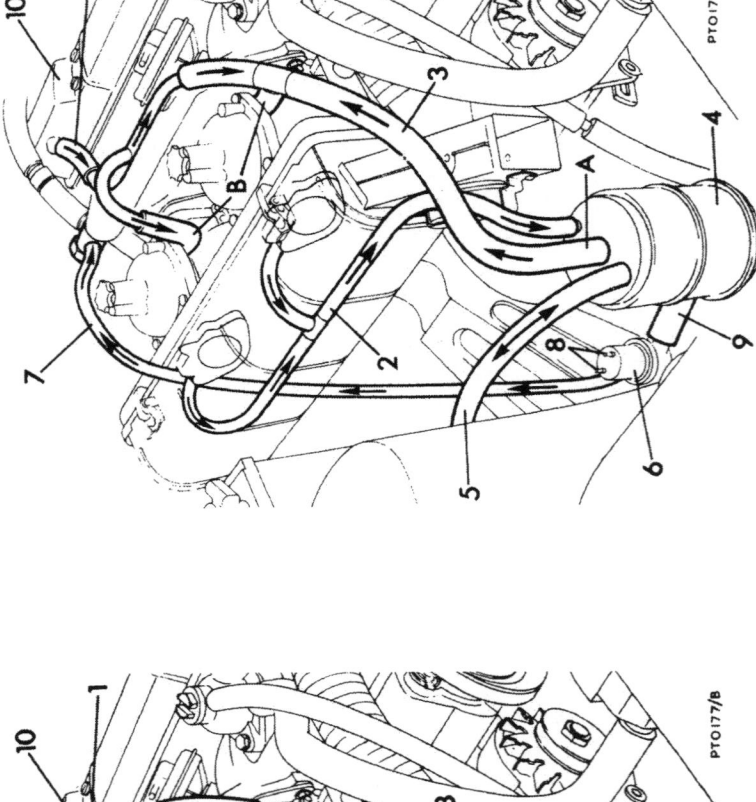

USA Federal and Canadian Market Specifications

California Market Specification

1 Crankcase purge line
2 Carburetter float chamber vent pipe
3 Canister purge line
4 Adsorption canister
5 Fuel tank vent pipe
6 Anti-run-on valve
7 Manifold vacuum line
8 Electrical connections for anti-run-on valve
9 Purge air to canister
10 Flame arrestor
A. $\frac{3}{32}$ in restrictor
B. $\frac{5}{16}$ in restrictor

CRANKCASE BREATHING AND CANISTER PURGE SYSTEMS — USA MARKET 1977 MODEL YEAR

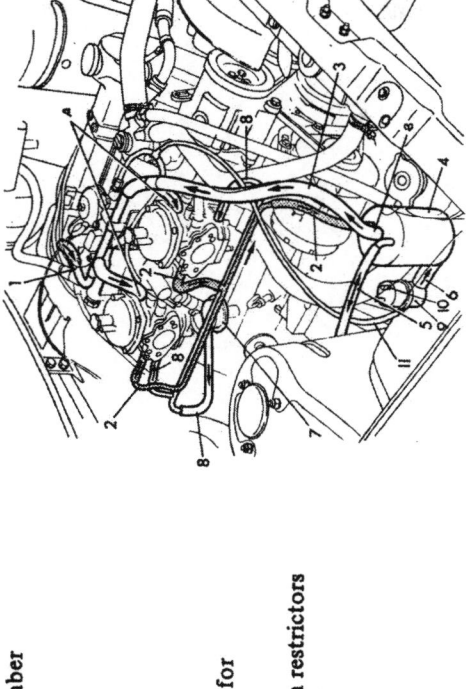

California Market Specification

1 Crankcase purge line
2 Carburetter float chamber
  vent pipe
3 Canister purge pipe
4 Adsorption canister
5 Fuel tank vent pipe
6 Purge air to canister
7 Fuel pump
8 Fuel pipe
9 Anti-run-on valve
10 Electrical connections for
   anti-run-on valve
11 Manifold vacuum line
   A. 0.280 to 0.300 in restrictors
   B. 3/32 in restrictor

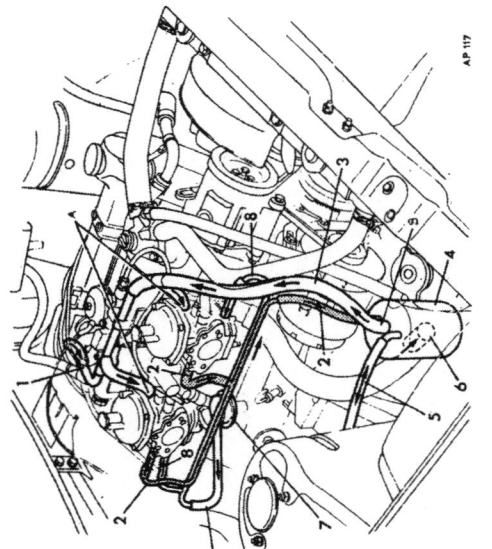

Federal Market Specification

CRANKCASE BREATHING AND CANISTER PURGE SYSTEMS — USA MARKET 1978, 1979 AND 1980 MODEL YEARS

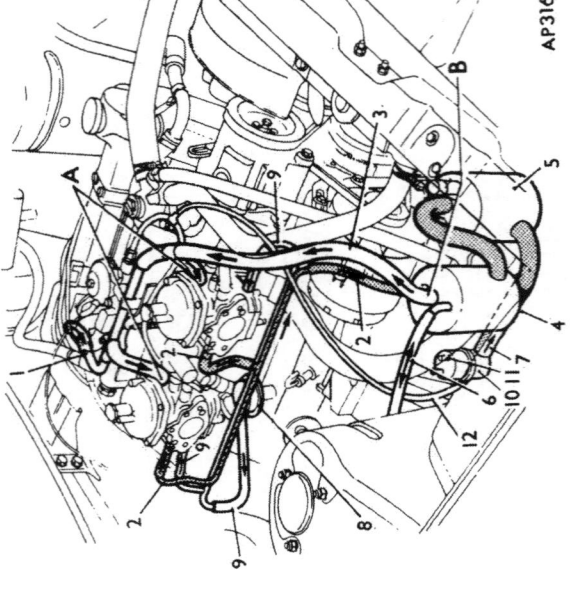

1 Crankcase purge line
2 Carburetter float chamber vent pipe
3 Canister purge pipe
4 Primary canister
5 Secondary canister
6 Fuel tank vent pipe
7 Purge air to canister
8 Fuel pump
9 Fuel pipe
10 Anti-run-on valve
11 Electrical connections for anti-run-on valve
12 Manifold vacuum line
   A. 0,280 to 0.300 in restrictors
   B. $\frac{3}{32}$ in restrictor

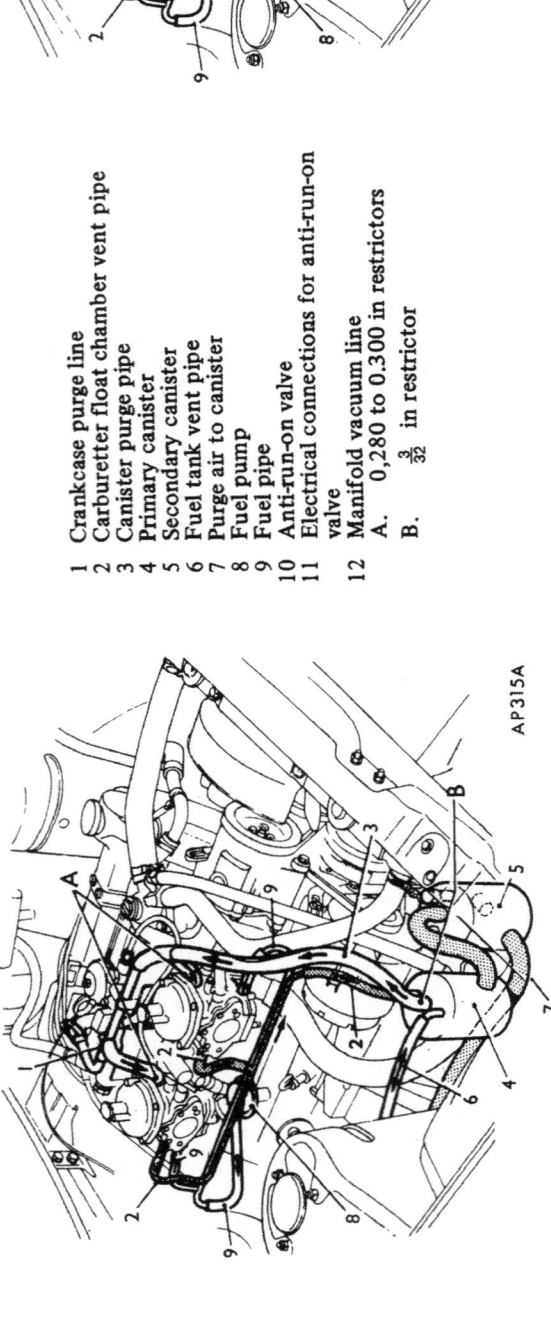

AP315A

Federal Market Specification — 1978 and 1979

AP316A

California Market Specification — 1978 and 1979

Federal Market Specification — 1980

1. Crankcase purge line
2. Canister purge line
3. Charcoal canisters
4. Fuel tank vent pipe
5. Purge air to canister
6. Crankcase and canister purge line
  A 0.433 inch restrictor
  B $\frac{3}{32}$ inch restrictor

AP 459

California Market Specification — 1980

EVAPORATIVE LOSS CONTROL SYSTEM

Description   17.15.00

The system is designed to prevent the emission to atmosphere of fuel vapour. The vapour collected from the fuel tank and carburetters is stored in an adsorption canister while the engine is at rest. Once the engine is running the vapour is purged from the canister and passed to the combustion chambers.

On some models twin canisters are fitted.

Fuel tank

When the fuel tank filler cap is correctly fitted the system is sealed and venting of the tank can only take place via a vapour separator to the adsorption canister(s).

To ensure that sufficient space is available to accommodate fuel displaced by expansion due to increased temperatures, a fuel filling restrictor is incorporated in the vapour separator which prevents the tank being completely filled with fuel.

Adsorption canister(s)

The adsorption canister provides a means of storing fuel vapour whilst the car is parked. The canister, which is not serviceable, contains active charcoal granules. Vapour tubes from the fuel tank, carburetter float chambers (where applicable) and the purge pipe from the engine breathing system are connected to ports on top of the canister. The manifold vacuum pipe can be connected to an anti-run on valve at the base of the canister.

Fuel vapour entering the canister through the vapour pipes is adsorbed by the charcoal granules. When the engine is started air is drawn by the engine breather system through the purge tube, at the bottom of the canister. The resulting purging action by the air passing over the granules carries the vapours through the engine breather system to the combustion chambers.

Vapour separator and restrictor

Vapour from the tank passes into the vapour separator and through two breather notches in a seat on which a taper plug rests. These small notches by virtue of their size allow only a limited flow of vapour as would be the case under normal running and stationary conditions. When the tank is being filled, however, the vapour air flow increases and the small notches create a restriction. Once the fuel has reached a level just above the filler tube this restriction and resulting pressure limits the quantity of fuel that the tank will accommodate to a predetermined maximum level.

Anti-run-on valve

The purpose of the valve is to prevent the engine 'running-on' once the ignition has been switched off.

The solenoid operated valve is connected by a hose to the base of the adsorption canister. The manifold vacuum hose is connected to the opposite side of the valve. The solenoid is connected electrically by two leads, one to the oil pressure switch and the other to the ignition switch.

When the ignition is turned-off a contact in the switch closes and energizes the solenoid thus opening the valve to manifold vacuum. At the same instant the purge vent to atmosphere closes.

Since the throttle is now closed the carburetter vent valve has opened the passage to the float chamber. Partial vacuum has now been transferred from the base of the adsorption canister, via the float chamber vent pipe, to the float chamber thus preventing fuel entering the carburetter jet.

When the engine stops revolving the drop in oil pressure activates the oil pressure switch, opens the circuit and de-energizes the solenoid valve.

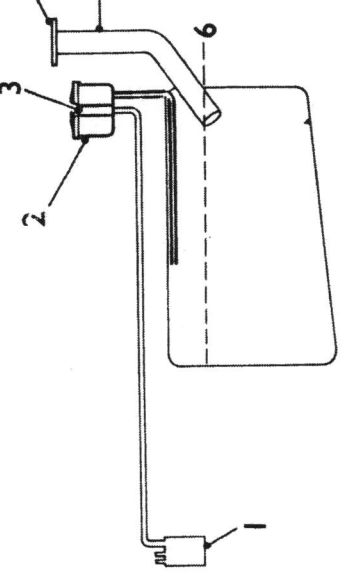

PTO44

1 Adsorption canister.
2 Fuel vapour separator.
3 Fuel fill restrictor.
4 Sealed cap.
5 Fuel filler pipe.
6 Maximum fuel level.

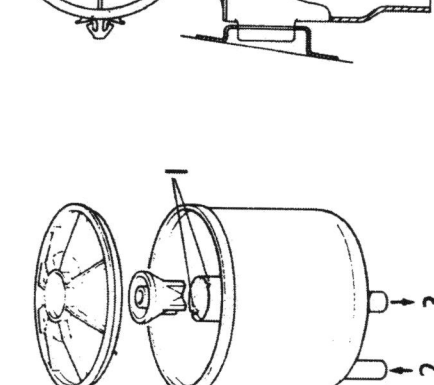

1 Breather notches.
2 Fuel tank pipe connection.
3 Adsorption pipe connection.

1 Engine.
2 Carburetter vent valve.
3 Adsorption canister.
4 Fuel tank.
5 Ignition switch.
6 Oil pressure switch.
7 Manifold vacuum.
8 Solenoid valve.

EVAPORATIVE LOSS CONTROL SYSTEM
USA MARKETS UP TO 1978 MODEL YEAR

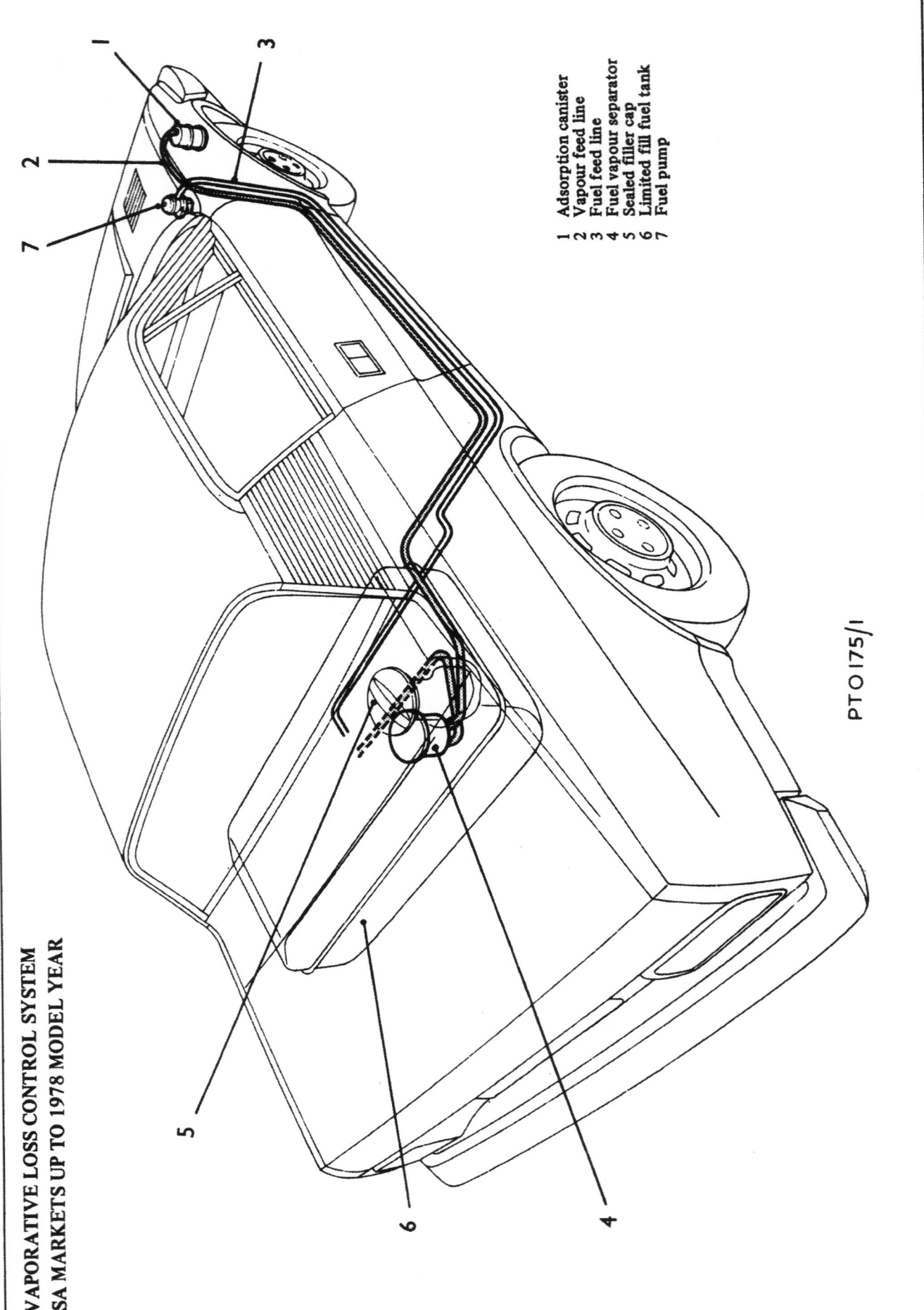

1 Adsorption canister
2 Vapour feed line
3 Fuel feed line
4 Fuel vapour separator
5 Sealed filler cap
6 Limited fill fuel tank
7 Fuel pump

PTO 175/1

EVAPORATIVE LOSS CONTROL SYSTEM
USA MARKETS — 1978, 1979 AND 1980 MODEL YEAR
(EXCLUDING CALIFORNIA MARKET 1980 MODEL YEAR)

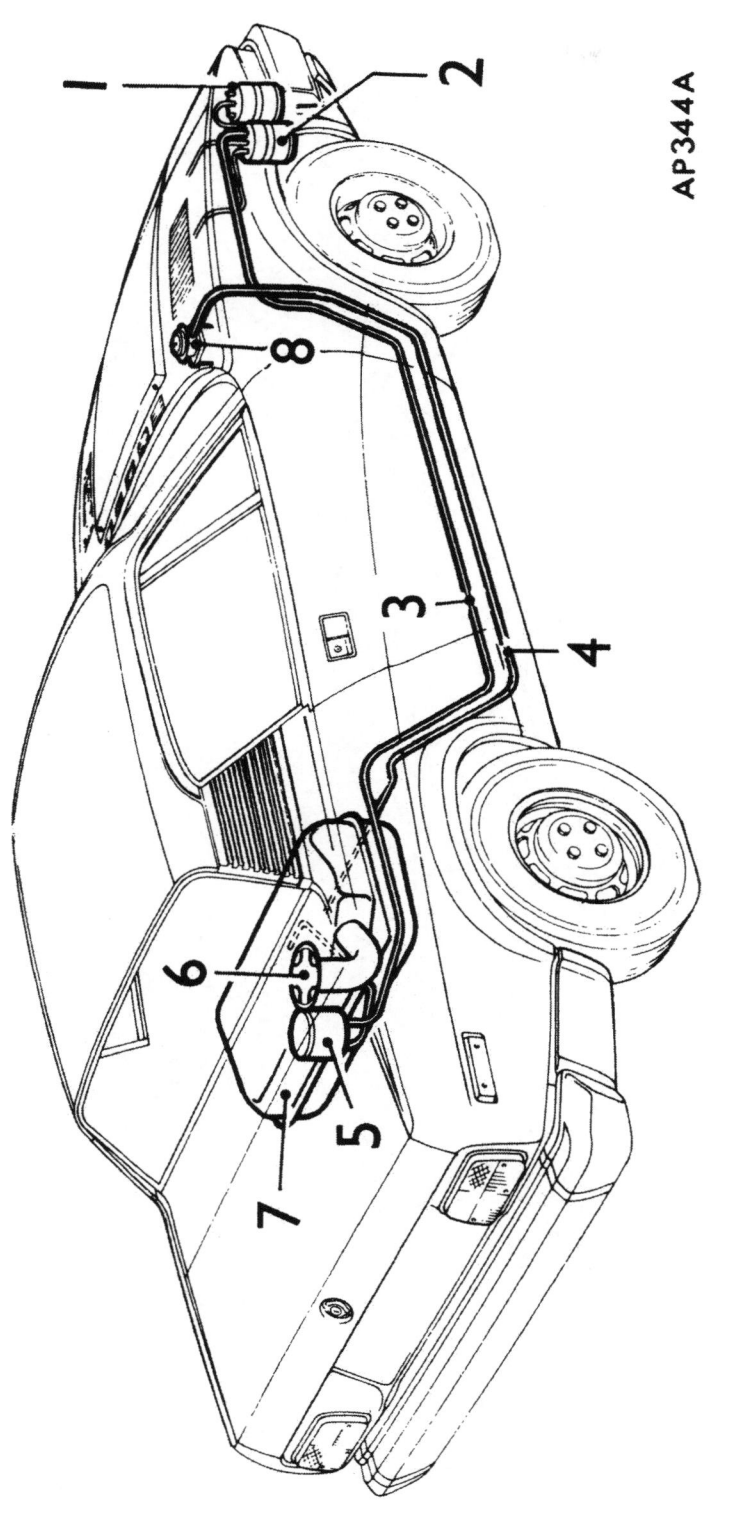

AP344A

1 Primary canister
2 Secondary canister
3 Vapour feed line
4 Fuel feed line
5 Fuel vapour separator
6 Sealed filler cap
7 Limited fill fuel tank
8 Fuel pump

EVAPORATIVE LOSS CONTROL SYSTEM
USA CALIFORNIA MARKET — 1980 MODEL YEAR

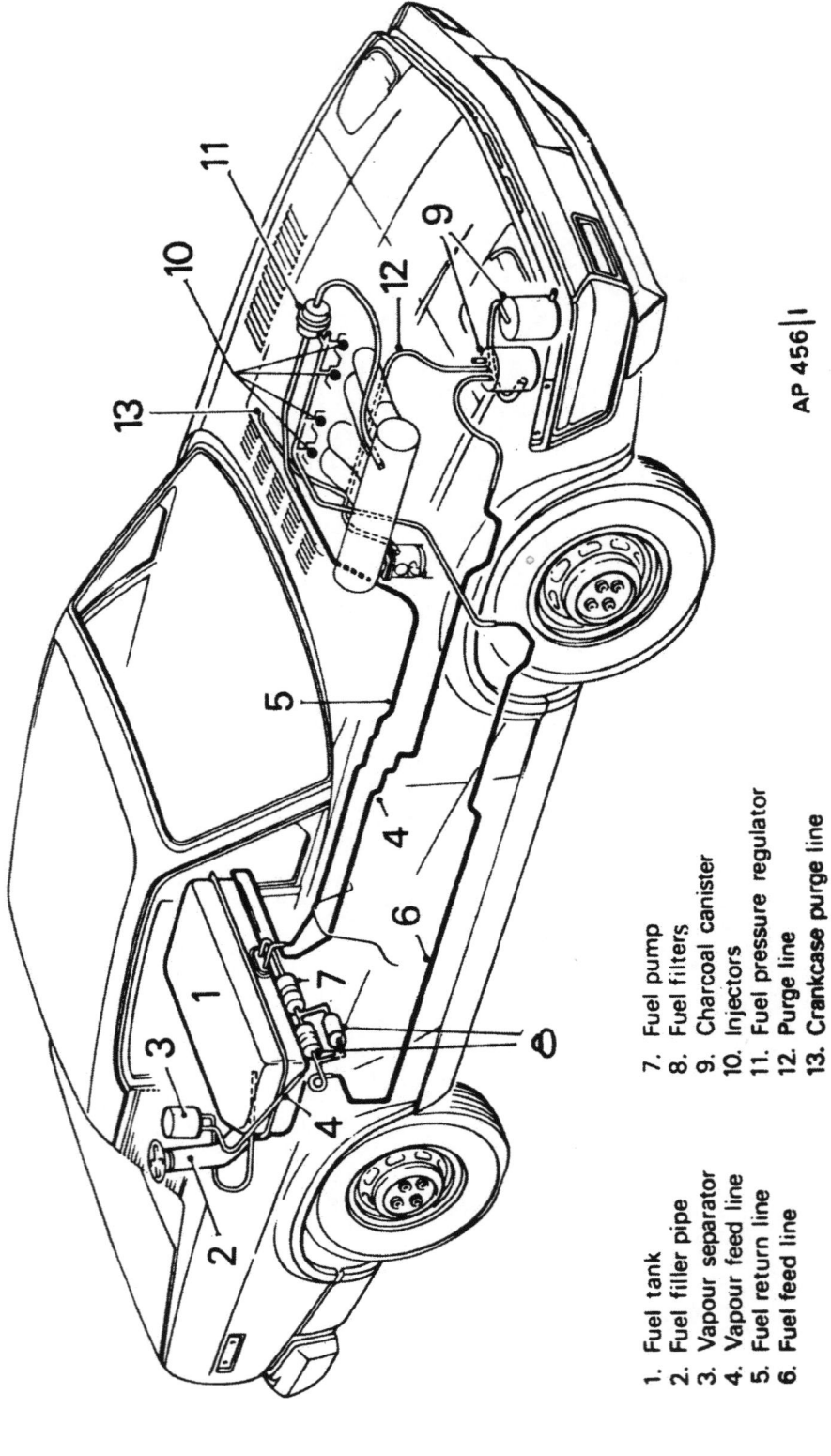

AP 456|1

1. Fuel tank
2. Fuel filler pipe
3. Vapour separator
4. Vapour feed line
5. Fuel return line
6. Fuel feed line
7. Fuel pump
8. Fuel filters
9. Charcoal canister
10. Injectors
11. Fuel pressure regulator
12. Purge line
13. Crankcase purge line

ADSORPTION CANISTER
Single Canister Specification

Remove and refit   17.15.13

Removing
1. Disconnect the canister to run-on valve pipe. (where fitted).
2. Disconnect from the canister:
   a. The canister to fuel tank pipe.
   b. The canister purge pipe.
   c. Carburetter vent pipe.
3. Slacken the clamp nut.
4. Remove the canister.

Refitting
5. Secure the canister in the clamp.
6. Reverse instructions 1 to 3.

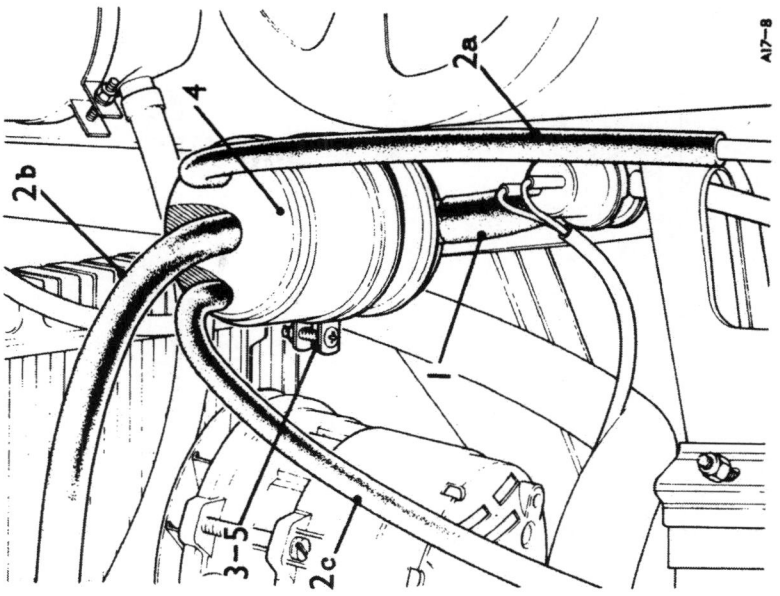

A17—8

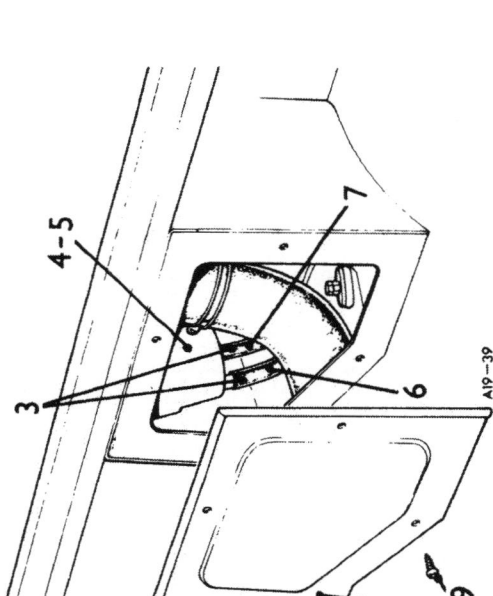

A19—39

VAPOUR SEPARATOR

Remove and refit   17.15.02

1. Open the boot and remove the four screws retaining the access panel.
2. Remove the fuel filler cap and filler assembly. 19.55.08.
3. Pull-off the two hoses from the vapour separator.
4. Pull the vapour separator laterally from its retaining clip.

Refitting
5. Push the vapour separator into its retaining clip.
6. Fit the hose from the tank to the L.H. connection.
7. Fit the hose to the adsorption canister to the R.H. connection.
8. Fit the fuel filler assembly and cap. 19.55.08.
9. Refit the access panel.

ADSORPTION CANISTERS —
Twin Canister Specification

Remove and refit   17.15.13

Removing
1. Disconnect from the primary canister:
   a. The canister purge pipe.
   b. The carburetter float chamber vent pipe.
   c. The fuel tank vent pipe.
   d. The connecting pipe from the lower canister.
2. Slacken the clamp nut.
3. Remove the canister.
4. Remove the connecting pipe between the primary and secondary canisters.
5. Remove the purge air canister pipe from the secondary canister.
6. Slacken the clamp nut.
7. Remove the canister.

Refitting
8. Reverse instructions 1 to 7.

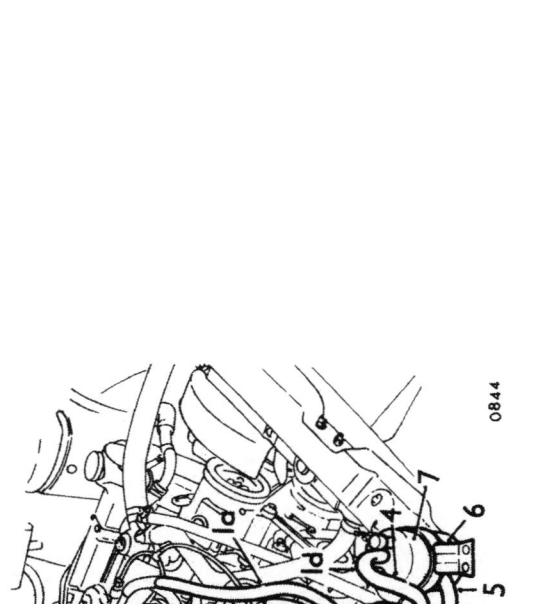

0844

AIR INJECTION SYSTEM

Description   **17.20.00**

Air pump

The rotary vane type air pump is fitted at the front of the engine and driven by a belt from a crankshaft pulley.

The pump delivers air under pressure to each of the four exhaust ports via a diverter and relief valve, check valve and air inlet manifold.

The pressurized air combines with the exhaust gases to continue and assist in making more complete the oxidization process in the exhaust system.

1   Inlet port.
2   Exhaust port.
3   Vanes.
4   Rotor.
5   Carbon sealing shoes.
6   Bearings.

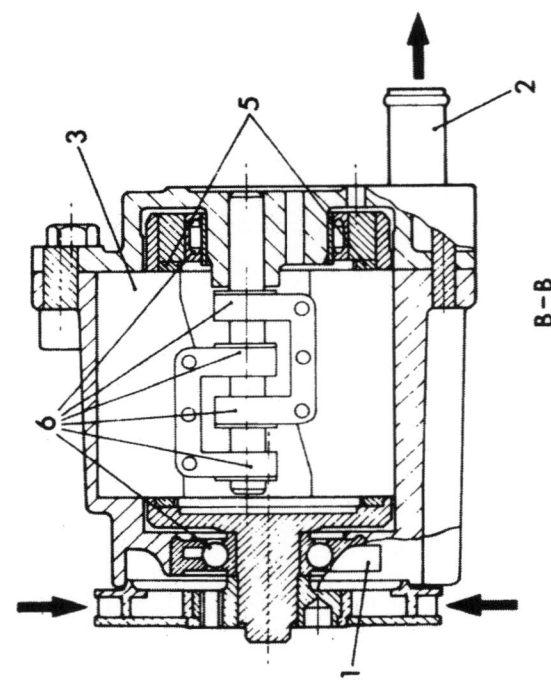

B – B

Diverter and Relief valve

Fitted to earlier models only.
Later models have a relief valve incorporated into the air pump.

This combined valve is incorporated to divert the air from the pump during deceleration to prevent backfire. The relief valve allows excessive air pressure at high engine speeds to discharge to the atmosphere.

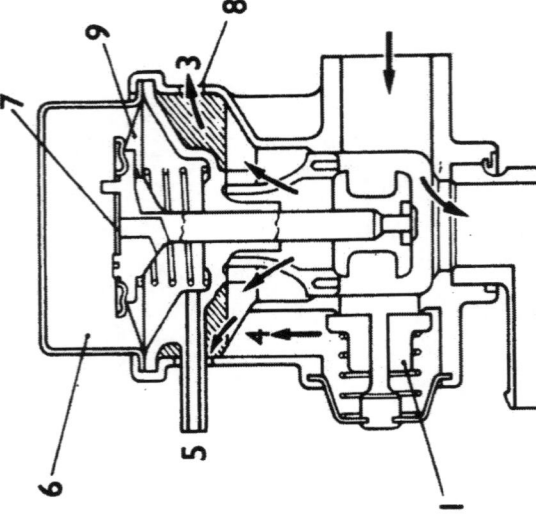

1   Relief valve.
2   Normal flow from air pump.
3   Diverted air.
4   Relief valve air.
5   Manifold vacuum.
6   Timed vacuum.
7   Timing feature.
8   Diverter and relief valve ports.
9   Diaphragm.

Check valve

The check valve is a one-way valve positioned between the diverter and relief valve and the air manifold. Its purpose is to protect the pump from back-flow of exhaust gases. The valve closes if the pump pressure falls while the engine is running, should, for example, the drive belt break.

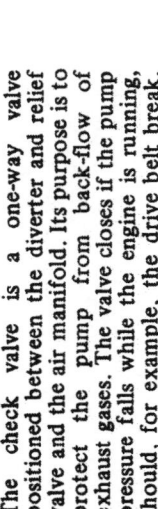

QTO 110

1 Valve diaphragm.
2 Direction of flow.

Air Manifold

The air manifold is finally responsible for delivering the pumped air directly into the exhaust ports through four small branch pipes.

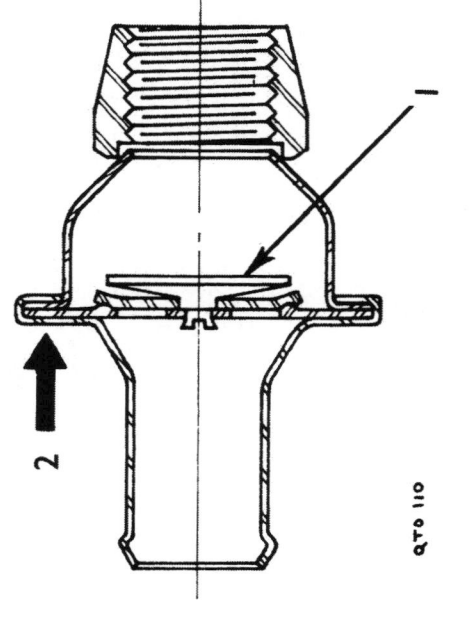

AP 119/1

TR7 AIR INJECTION SYSTEM

1 Air pump
2 Air rail
3 Check valve
4 Exhaust manifold

AIR PUMP

Remove and refit   17.25.07

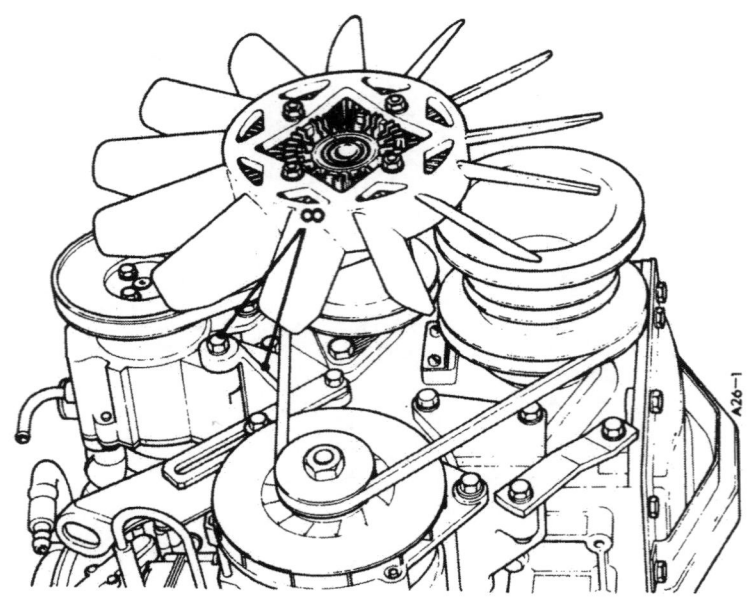

Removing

1 Disconnect the battery.
2 Disconnect the hose from the air pump.
3 Remove the adjusting nut and bolt.
4 Remove the pivot bolt and nut.
5 Remove the belt from the pump pulley.
6 Withdraw the pivot bolt until the head contacts the radiator.
7 Remove the pump.

Refitting

8 Fit the pump to its carrier bracket and loosely secure with the pivot nut and bolt.
9 Fit the adjusting nut and bolt.
10 Fit the belt onto the pulleys and correctly tension the belt. 17.25.13.
11 Reconnect the hose.
12 Reconnect the battery.

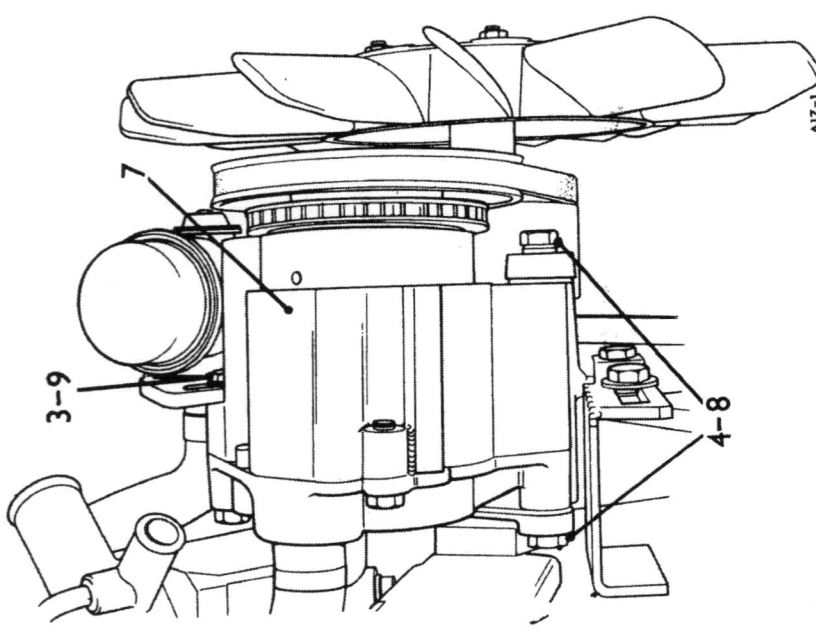

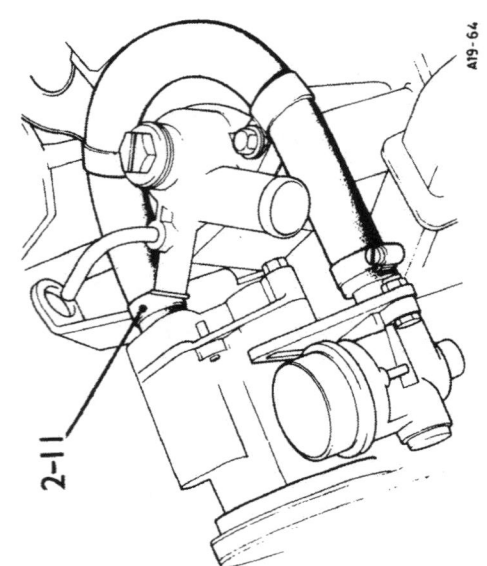

AIR PUMP DRIVE BELT

Tensioning 17.25.13

1 Disconnect the battery.
2 Slacken the adjusting nut and bolt.
3 Slacken the pivot bolt and nut.
4 With care use a lever on the pump to tension the belt and tighten the adjusting nut and bolt.
5 Tighten the pivot bolt.
6 Check the belt tension which is correct when 3/8 in. (9.5 mm) overall lateral movement is possible at the mid-point of the run.
7 Reconnect the battery.

AIR PUMP DRIVE BELT

Remove and refit 17.25.15

Removing

1 Disconnect the battery.
2 Remove the fan guard.
3 Remove the fan blades. 26.25.06.
4 Slacken off air pump belt tension.
5 Remove drive belt from the pulleys.

Refitting

6 Feed the belt onto the pulleys.
7 Tension the drive belt. 17.25.13.
8 Fit the fan blades. 26.25.06.
9 Reconnect the battery.

AIR DISTRIBUTION MANIFOLD

Remove and refit 17.25.17

Removing

1 Disconnect the hose from the diverter and relief valve.
2 Unscrew the four union nuts securing the air injection tubes into the exhaust ports.
3 Withdraw the air distribution manifold complete with the check valve.
4 Hold the air distribution manifold in a vice by the hexagon and remove the check valve.

Refitting

5 Reverse instructions 1 to 4.

CHECK VALVE

Remove and refit 17.25.21

Removing

1 Disconnect the air hose from the diverter and relief valve from the check valve.
2 Using two open-ended spanners – one on the air distribution manifold hexagon, to support the manifold, and the other to remove the check valve anti-clockwise.

CAUTION: Do not impose any strain on the air manifold.

Refitting

3 Reverse instructions 1 and 2.

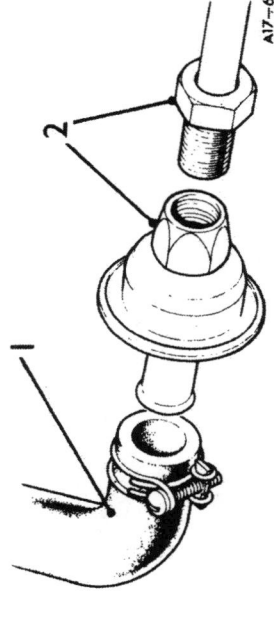

A17–6

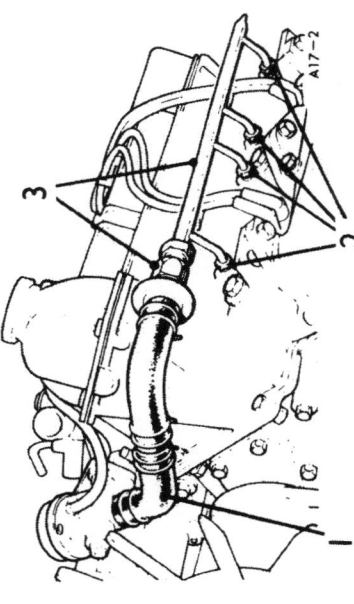

A17–2

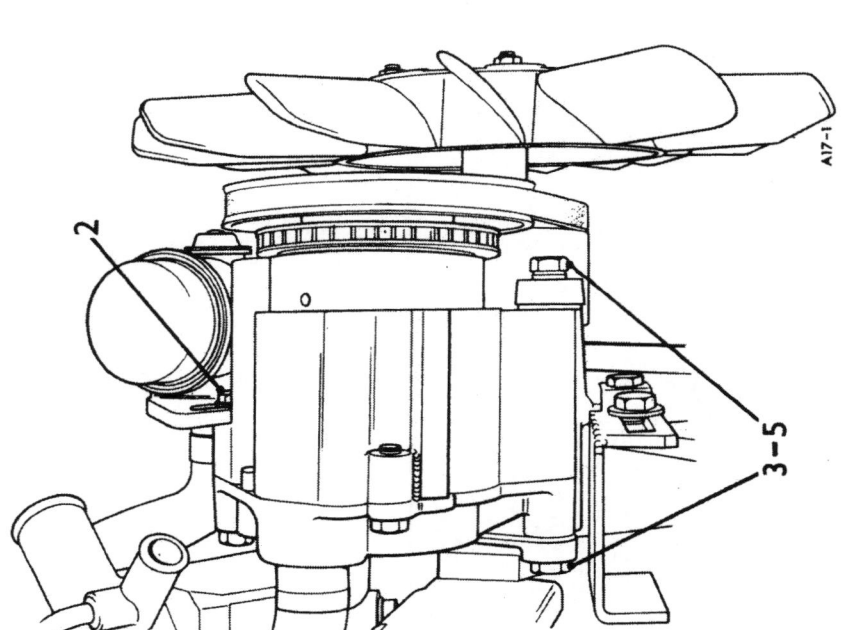

A17–1

CHECK VALVE

Test
17.25.22

Testing
CAUTION: Do not use a pressure air supply for this test.

1 Remove the check valve. 17.25.21.
2 Blow through the valve orally in both directions in turn. Air should only pass through the valve when blown from the hose connection end. Should air pass through the valve when blown from the air manifold end, renew the valve.
3 Refit the check valve. 17.25.21.

DIVERTER AND RELIEF VALVE
Earlier Models Only

Remove and refit
17.25.25

Removing
1 Disconnect the battery.
2 Disconnect the pump to valve hoses.
3 Disconnect the air hose from the valve to the check valve.
4 Disconnect the diverter valve triggering vacuum pipe.
5 Remove the air pump adjusting nut and bolt.
6 Remove the bolt securing the common bracket holding the valve and air pump drive belt adjustment.
7 Remove the valve complete with bracket.
8 Remove the two nuts and bolts retaining the valve to the bracket.
9 Remove the valve and gasket.

Refitting
10 Fit the valve to the bracket using a new gasket.
11 Fit the bracket complete with valve to the engine.
12 Fit the drive belt tensioning nut and bolt.
13 Connect the check valve to diverter air hose.
14 Connect the air pump to diverter valve hose.
15 Connect the diverter air valve triggering vacuum pipe to the valve.
16 Check and if necessary adjust the air pump drive belt tension.
17 Reconnect the battery.

AI7—5

AIR INTAKE TEMPERATURE CONTROL SYSTEM

Description   17.30.00

The carburetters are tuned to function most efficiently at an air intake temperature of 100°F (38°C).

Earlier Models

The temperature is maintained by a sponge rubber flap valve which seals off the air cleaner cold air intake, permitting only warm air drawn from around the exhaust manifold to enter the engine after it is started up from cold. As the engine temperature rises, the flap valve moves under the influence of a bi-metal strip to first allow a mixture of warm air and air at ambient temperature to enter the air cleaner, and finally sealing off the warm air intake when the engine has reached operating temperature.

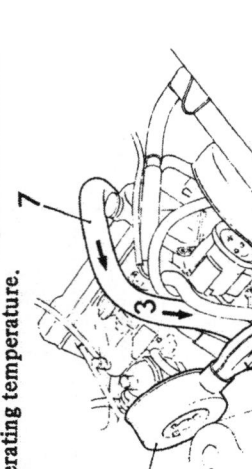

1 Air cleaner   5 Bi-metal
2 Air cleaner cover   6 Sponge rubber seal
3 Hot air intake   7 Hot air pipe
4 Cold air intake

Later models

The temperature is maintained by a sensing device incorporated in the air cleaner. The sensor allows inlet manifold vacuum to operate a flap valve in the air cleaner intake. The valve controls the entry of cold air at under bonnet temperature and hot air drawn from a duct on the exhaust manifold.

In order to maintain full vacuum influence on the flap valve when the manifold depression is temporarily destroyed during sudden throttle openings, a one-way valve is fitted in the vacuum line from the inlet manifold to the temperature sensor.

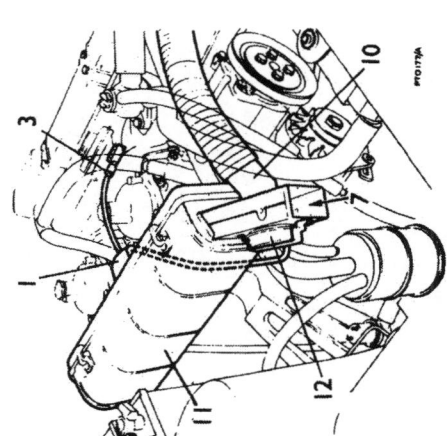

1 Temperature sensor   10 Hot air hose
3 One-way valve   11 Air cleaner cover
7 Cold air intake   12 Motor case

AIR INTAKE TEMPERATURE CONTROL SYSTEM

Function test   17.30.01

Earlier models

1. With the engine and air cleaner in a cold condition check that the sponge rubber valve effectively closes the aperture to atmosphere at the front of the intake.

2. Start the engine and check that the valve progressively closes the aperture to the hot air supply as the engine running temperature increases.

Later models

1 Inspect the condition and security of the following:
   a Hot air inlet hose.
   b The vacuum hose from the one-way valve to the temperature sensor unit.
   c The vacuum hose from the temperature sensor unit to the servo motor in the air cleaner outer cover.

2 With the engine and air cleaner cold i.e. below 100°F (38°C) check that the flap valve is in the cold air position i.e. parallel with the rectangular air intake – illustration A thus allowing cold air (ambient) only to enter the air cleaner.

3 Start the engine and allow it to idle for a few seconds. The flap valve should move immediately to the hot air position – illustration B thereby permitting only hot air via the hot air hose to enter the air cleaner.

4 With the flap valve in the hot air position – illustration B, attempt to lower the engine vacuum by increasing the engine speed suddenly and holding for a few seconds and check that the flap valve has remained in the hot air position.

5 Run the engine until normal operating temperature is reached and under bonnet temperature is above 100°F (38°C) and check that the flap valve has moved to the cold air position – illustration A.

continued

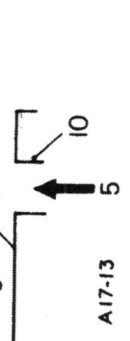

A

B

A17-13

1 Temperature sensor
2 Inlet manifold
4 Valve diaphragm
5 Hot air intake
6 Flap valve
7 Cold air intake
8 Vacuum side of motor
9 Return spring
10 Hot air hose

AIR INTAKE TEMPERATURE CONTROL – FAULT FINDING

SYMPTOM	POSSIBLE CAUSE	ACTION
Poor or erratic idle Hesitation or flat spot (cold engine) Excessive fuel consumption Lack of power Engine overheating	Hot air inlet hose loose, adrift or blocked	Check hot air inlet hose for condition and security. Renew if necessary
Poor or erratic idle Hesitation or flat spot (cold engine) Excessive fuel consumption Lack of power Engine cuts-out or stalls (at idle) Engine 'runs-on' Engine 'knocks or pinks' Rich running (excess CO)	Flap valve jammed	Check operation of flap valve 17.30.01 If fault cannot be rectified renew air cleaner outer cover which includes flap valve. See 19.10.01
Poor or erratic idle Hesitation or flat spot (cold engine) Excessive fuel consumption Lack of engine power Engine cuts-out or stalls (at idle) Engine misfires Lean running (low CO)	Vacuum pipes disconnected or leaking*	Check the vacuum pipes for security and deterioration. Renew if necessary*

SYMPTOM	POSSIBLE CAUSE	ACTION
Hesitation or flat spot (cold engine) Excessive fuel consumption Lack of power Engine overheating Engine cuts-out or stalls (at idle) Engine 'runs-on' Engine knocks or pinks Rich running (excess CO)	One-way valve faulty*	Blow through valve to check 'one way' action. If the valve leaks fit a new valve. 17.30.05.*
Poor or erratic idle Hesitation or flat spot (cold engine) Excessive fuel consumption Lack of power Engine overheating Engine cuts-out or stalls (at idle) Engine 'runs-on' Engine knocks or pinks Rich running (excess CO)	Temperature sensor faulty, leaking or jammed*	Check and renew if necessary. 17.30.10.*
Poor or erratic idle Hesitation or flat spot (cold engine) Excessive fuel consumption Lack of power Engine cuts-out or stalls Rich running	Flap valve diaphragm leaking	Check with a distributor vacuum test unit. If leakage is apparent, renew air cleaner outer cover which includes the servo motor*

*These operations are not applicable to earlier type air cleaners

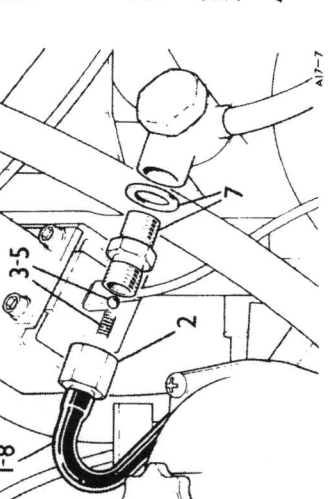

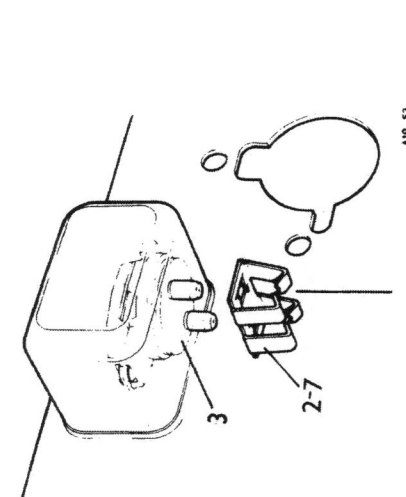

ONE-WAY VALVE

Remove and refit   17.30.05

Removing

1 Disconnect the pipe from the one-way valve.
2 Remove the one-way valve, complete with union nut, from the brass banjo union.
3 Separate the union nut from the valve body taking care not to lose the ball and spring.

Refitting

4 Clean the valve internally and ensure the hole is clear.
5 Insert the spring and ball.
6 Fit and tighten the union nut.
7 Fit the valve assembly to the banjo union using a new fibre washer.
8 Reconnect the pipe to the one-way valve.

RUNNING-ON CONTROL VALVE

Remove and refit   17.40.01

Removing

1 Disconnect the solenoid electrical leads.
2 Disconnect the vacuum control pipe.
3 Disconnect the canister to run-on valve pipe.
4 Twist the valve and withdraw it from its retaining bracket.

Refitting

5 Reverse instructions 1 to 4.

TEMPERATURE SENSOR UNIT

Remove and refit   17.30.10

Removing

1 Remove the air cleaner. 19.10.08.
2 Prise off the clip securing the temperature sensor unit to the air cleaner back-plate.
3 Remove the temperature sensor unit.
4 Remove the felt washer.

Refitting

5 Fit the felt washer to the sensor unit.
6 Fit the sensor unit to the back-plate noting that it can only be fitted in one position.
7 Secure the unit with the spring clip.
8 Refit the air cleaner, 19.10.08, ensuring that the two vacuum pipes are correctly positioned on the sensor unit i.e.

a The pipe from the one-way valve is fitted to the connection closest to the back-plate.
b The pipe from the air inlet temperature control unit furthest from the back-plate.

EXHAUST GAS RECIRCULATION SYSTEMS – USA FEDERAL MARKET 1975 AND 1976 MODEL YEAR AND LATER. CANADIAN MARKET SPECIFICATIONS

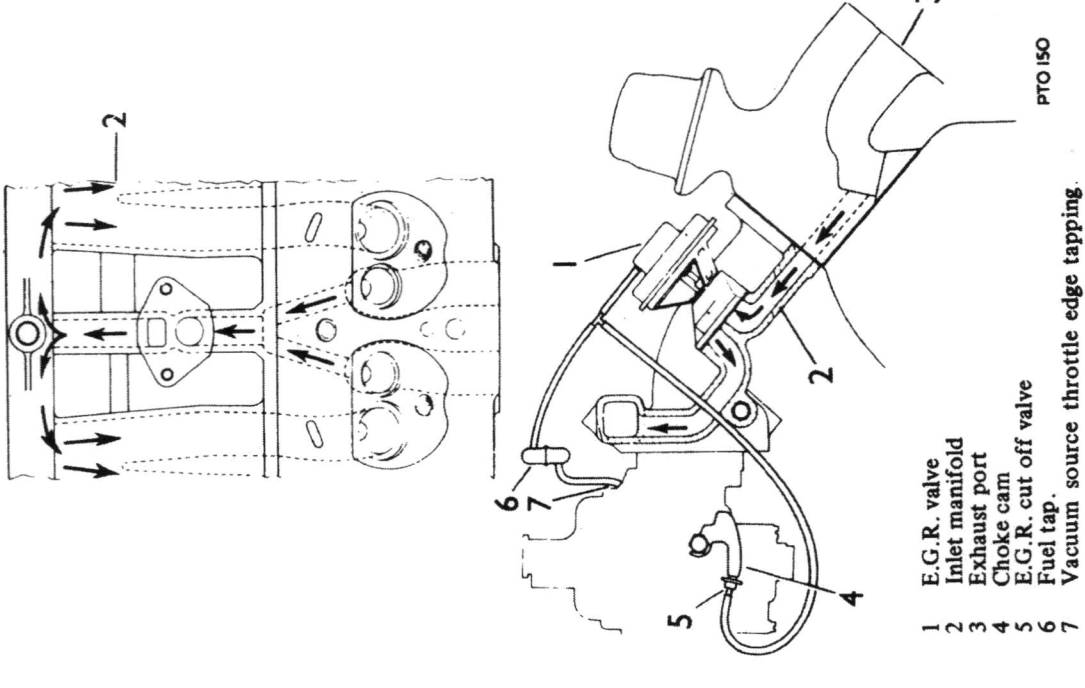

PTO 150

1 E.G.R. valve
2 Inlet manifold
3 Exhaust port
4 Choke cam
5 E.G.R. cut off valve
6 Fuel tap.
7 Vacuum source throttle edge tapping

EXHAUST GAS RECIRCULATION SYSTEM

Description   17.45.00

Exhaust gas recirculation system
Exhaust gas is taken from numbers 2 and 3 cylinders by two drillings to each side of the cylinder head. An exhaust gas recircula-tion valve (E.G.R. valve) mounted on a passage on the inlet manifold controls the flow to the balance pipe on the inlet manifold. The control signal is taken from a throttle-edged tapping which gives no recirculation at idle speed or full load, but gives an amount of recirculation dependent on the vacuum signal and metering profile of the valve. An E.G.R control valve cuts the signal to the E.G.R. valve when the choke is in operation by opening an air bleed into the vacuum line.

E.G.R Control valve
This valve is attached to the rear carburetter and is actuated by a heel on the fast idle cam. The choke knob on the facia must be pulled out approximately ¼ in. before the control valve operates and must be pushed-in within 1/10 in. or fully home before the E.G.R. valve is operational.

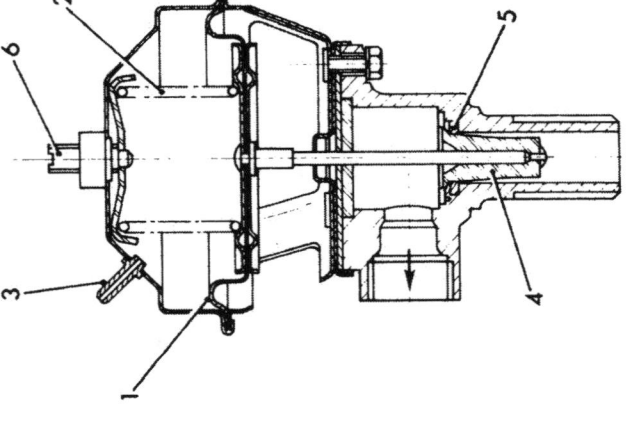

PTO 492

1 Diaphragm
2 Spring
3 To vacuum source
4 Metering pintle
5 Valve seat
6 Production adjustment – sealed after setting

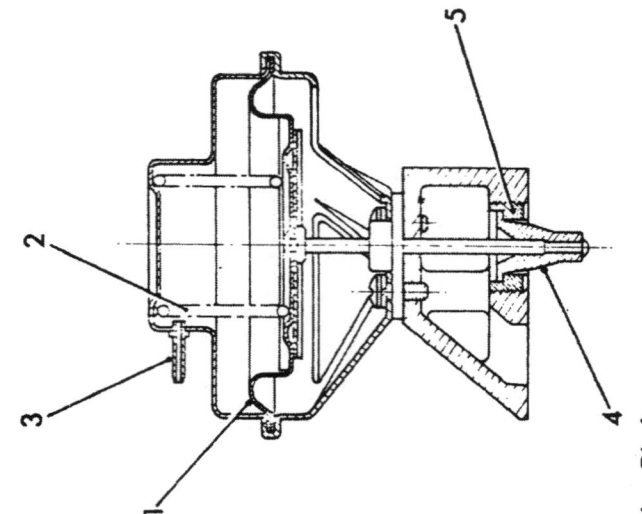

1 Diaphragm
2 Spring
3 To vacuum source
4 Metering pintle
5 Valve seat adjustable for production setting and sealed

EXHAUST GAS RECIRCULATION SYSTEMS

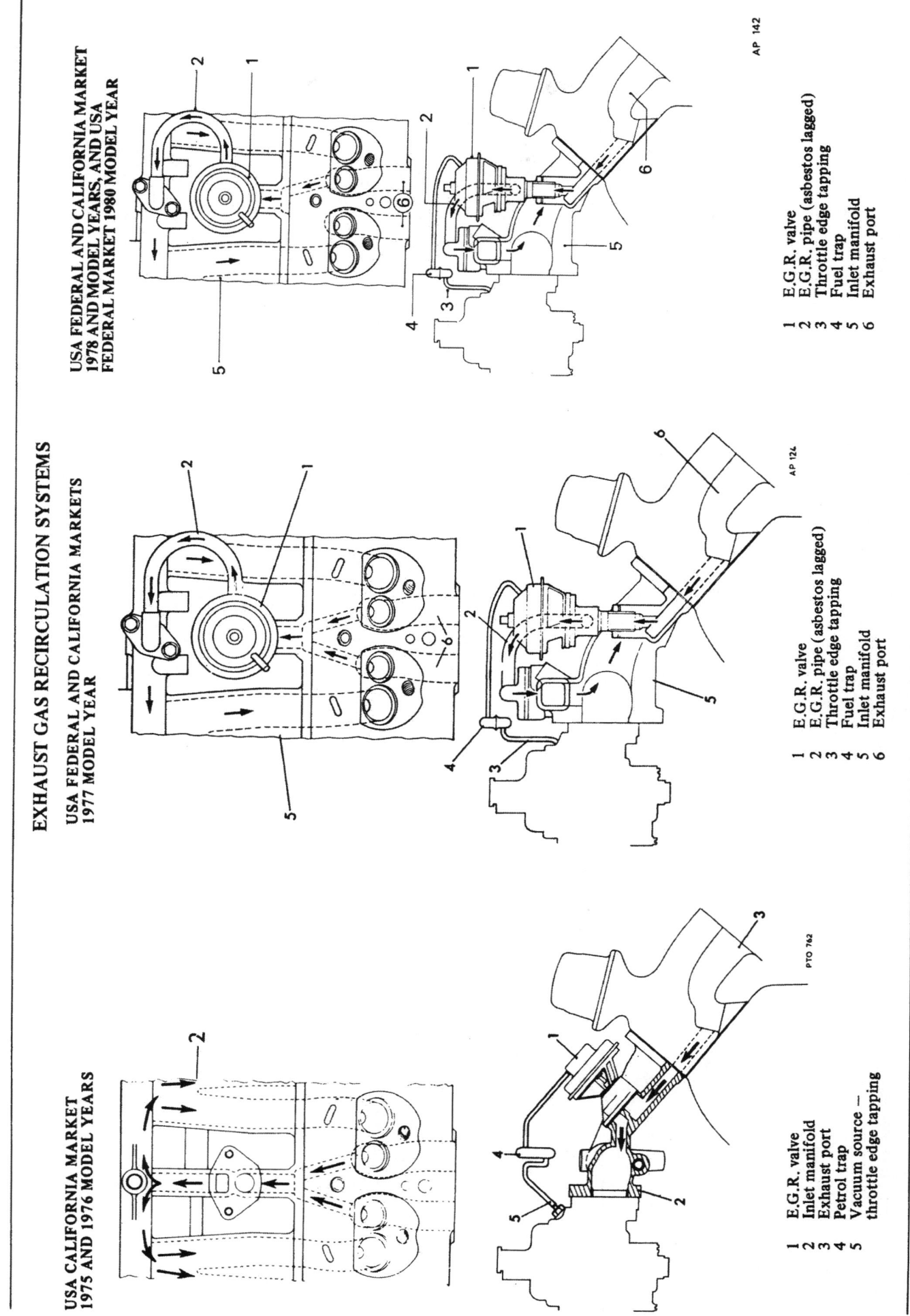

**USA CALIFORNIA MARKET
1975 AND 1976 MODEL YEARS**

1 E.G.R. valve
2 Inlet manifold
3 Exhaust port
4 Petrol trap
5 Vacuum source —
   throttle edge tapping

PTO 762

**USA FEDERAL AND CALIFORNIA MARKETS
1977 MODEL YEAR**

1 E.G.R. valve
2 E.G.R. pipe (asbestos lagged)
3 Throttle edge tapping
4 Fuel trap
5 Inlet manifold
6 Exhaust port

AP 124

**USA FEDERAL AND CALIFORNIA MARKET
1978 AND MODEL YEARS, AND USA
FEDERAL MARKET 1980 MODEL YEAR**

1 E.G.R. valve
2 E.G.R. pipe (asbestos lagged)
3 Throttle edge tapping
4 Fuel trap
5 Inlet manifold
6 Exhaust port

AP 142

EXHAUST GAS RECIRCULATION VALVE 17.45.01

Remove and refit

Earlier Models

Removing

1 Remove the vacuum pipe.
2 Remove the two bolts securing the valve to the manifold location.
3 Lift off the valve complete with gasket.

Refitting

4 Clean the valve port and the valve to manifold mating faces.
5 Place a new gasket in position ensuring that it is fitted with the correct face towards the manifold as stamped on the gasket i.e. 'MANIFOLD SIDE'.
6 Secure the valve with the two bolts and plain washers.
7 Connect the vacuum pipe.

Later models

Removing

1 Disconnect the vacuum pipe from the valve.
2 Disconnect the asbestos lagged pipe from the valve.
3 Unscrew the valve from the manifold.

Refitting

4 Reverse instructions 1 to 3, ensuring that the valve is securely sealed to the manifold.

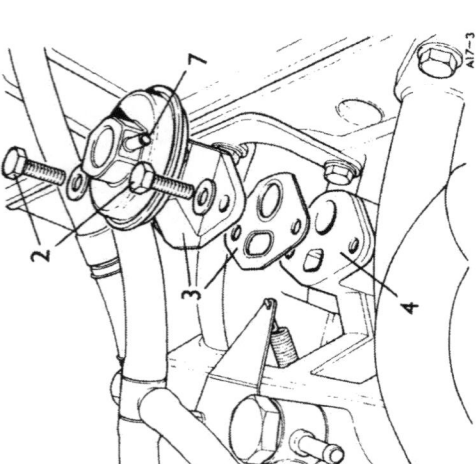

A17—3

EXHAUST GAS RECIRCULATION CONTROL VALVE 17.45.05

Remove and refit

Removing

1 Disconnect the pipe from the valve.
2 Remove the screw and shake proof washer securing the valve bracket to the rear carburetter.
3 Remove the bracket and valve complete.

Refitting

4 Reverse instructions 1 to 3.

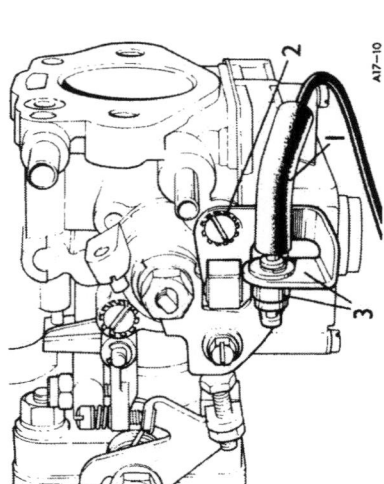

A17—10

CATALYTIC CONVERTER 17.50.01

Remove and refit

Removing

1 Disconnect the battery and raise the car on a ramp, and allow converter to cool.
2 Remove the three nuts and bolts at both ends of the converter.
3 Ease converter and extract the olives from the exhaust pipe.
4 Withdraw the converter.

Refitting

5 Position the olives in the down-pipe and main pipe.
6 Ease the two pipes apart and insert the catalyst converter ensuring that the deflection plate is facing towards the front of the car.
7 Secure the converter with three nuts and bolts at both ends of the converter.
8 Lower the ramp and reconnect the battery.

TAMPERPROOF CARBURETTERS (Non USA Markets)

Description   19.00.00

Later vehicles may be fitted with tamper-proof carburetters and the amount of attention that can be given to these units can be the subject of legislation in various territories.

They can be identified by a sealed mixture control nut (A), throttle return springs (B) acting directly on the throttle butterfly spindles and may have incorporated in them a capstat temperature compensated jet (C), a ball bearing suction chamber assembly (D), and a sealed slow-running adjustment screw (E).

The purpose of these carburetters is to control more stringently the air/fuel mixture entering the engine combustion chambers and, in consequence, the exhaust gas emissions leaving the engine.

For this reason the only readily accessible external adjustment on these carburetters is to the throttle settings for fast idle speed, using the screw (F).

Dismantling the carburetters

Should it be necessary, the float-chamber cover may be removed for access to the float or the float-chamber needle valve, refer to operation 19.15.24.

Otherwise, dismantling these carburetters is normally limited to removing the piston damper assembly, removing the suction chamber, and withdrawing the piston complete with needle assembly, for the purpose of cleaning these components or replacing the needle assembly.

CAUTION: Dismantling the carburetter unit beyond that described above, or un-authorized breaking of the mixture control or slow-running control seals and adjust-ment of the settings; or the fitting of an incorrect needle assembly, may render the vehicle user liable to legal penalties according to local territory legislation.

Should it be unavoidable and be permitted by local territory legislation, the mixture and slow-running adjustments may be al-tered. Remove the respective seals and adhere strictly to operation 19.15.02. Use an approved type CO meter as a final emissions level check and fit new sealing devices as required by local territory legis-lation.

Needle assembly

The needle is of a specific type, and with its related components is an assembly which may be peculiar to the model. Therefore it should always be replaced as an assem-bly.

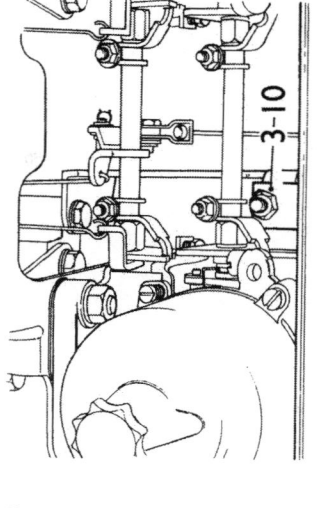

0077

AIR CLEANER

Remove and refit   19.10.01

Later vehicles may be fitted with an air cleaner incorporating air intake temperature control similar to the USA and Canada later carbur-etter specification.

Removing

1 Disconnect the two air inlet hoses from the front of the air cleaner.
2 Disconnect the engine dipstick support from the air cleaner.
3 Slacken the nut securing the throttle linkage bracket to the air cleaner.
4 Release the two air cleaner cover clips and remove the cover.
5 Withdraw the filter element.
6 Remove the six bolts and spring washers (three each carburetter) secur-ing the air cleaner body to the car-buretters.
7 Remove the air cleaner body and gaskets.

Refitting

8 Offer up the air cleaner body to the carburetters ensuring that the rear support lug engages the throttle

bracket bolt and that the carburetter flange gaskets are correctly positioned.
9 Fit the six securing bolts and spring washers to the carburetter flanges.
10 Tighten the nut securing the throttle bracket to the air cleaner body.
11 Install the filter element (metal frame to carburetters).
12 Fit the cover and secure with the two clips.
13 Fit the air inlet pipes.
14 Attach the dipstick guide to the cover.

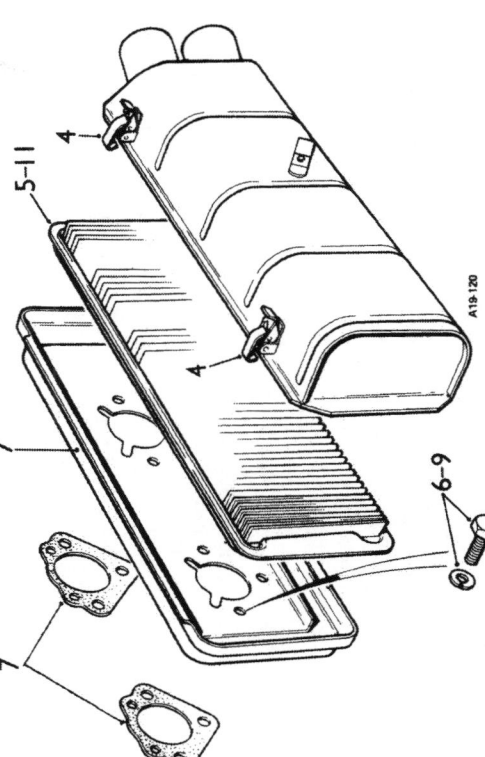

A19-121

3-10

5-11

4

4

7

7

7

6-9

A19-120

A19-095

MT2 297

AIR CLEANER

Renew element   19.10.08

Note: Later vehicles may be fitted with an air cleaner incorporating air intake temperature control similar to the USA and Canada later carburetter specification.

1   Disconnect the two air inlet pipes.
2   Remove the screw and nut securing the engine dipstick to the filter cover.
3   Release the two filter cover clips and remove the cover.
4   Withdraw the filter element.
5   Thoroughly clean interior of filter body and cover.
6   Install new filter element (metal frame to carburetters).
7   Fit the cover.
8   Fit the air inlet pipes.
9   Secure the dipstick clip to the cover.

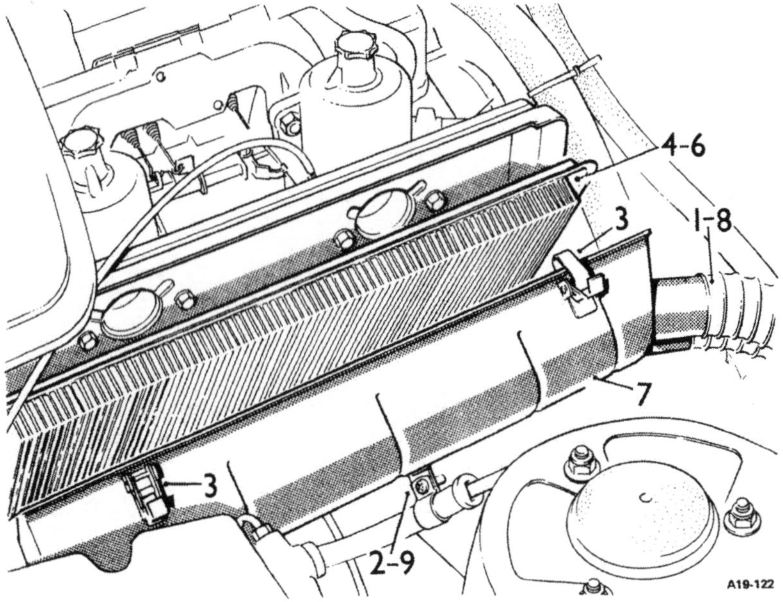

CARBURETTERS

Tune and adjust   19.15.02

Where tamperproof carburetters are fitted, refer to 19.00.00.

1   Remove the air cleaner, see 19.10.02.
2   Check the throttle for correct operation ensuring that it does not stick.
3   Turn the fast idle adjusting screws anti-clockwise until well clear of the cams, and disconnect the mixture control cable at the trunnion.
4   Turn the throttle adjusting screws until just clear of the throttle levers with the throttles closed, then turn the screws 1½ turns clockwise.
5   Raise the piston of each carburetter in turn (use the lifting pin if fitted) and check that it falls freely onto the carburetter bridge. If either piston shows any tendency to stick, remove and clean the piston and suction chamber, see 19.15.30.
6   Lift and support the piston clear of the carburetter bridge so that the jet is visible.

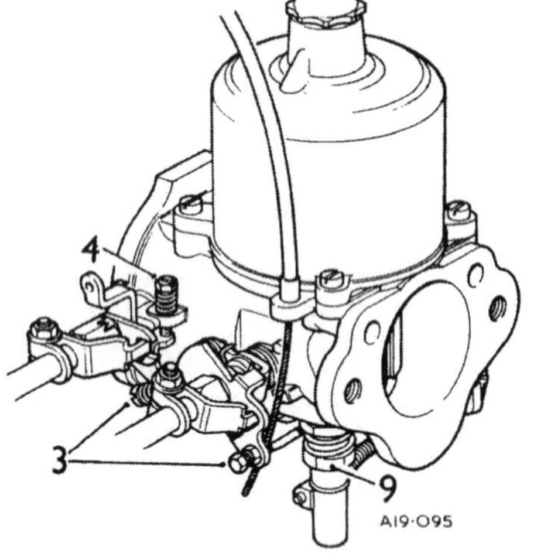

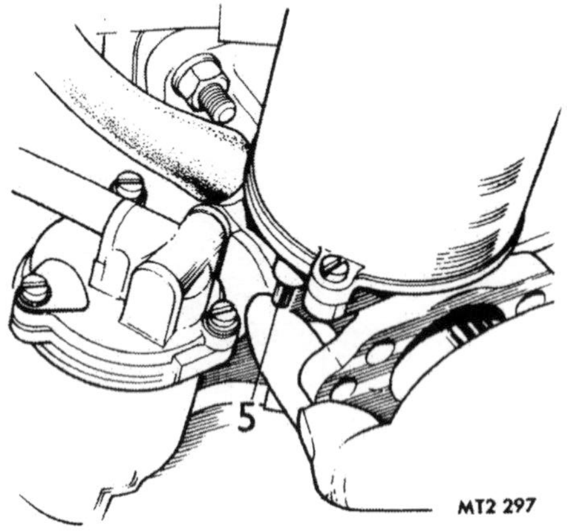

A19-122

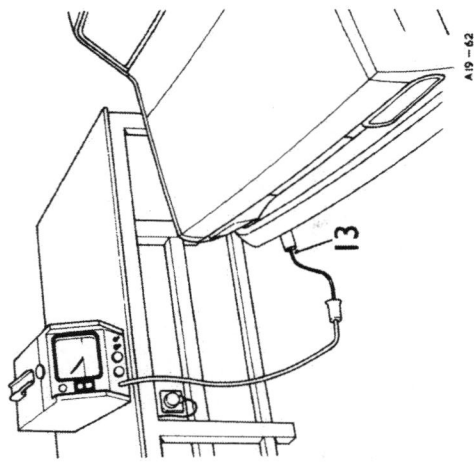

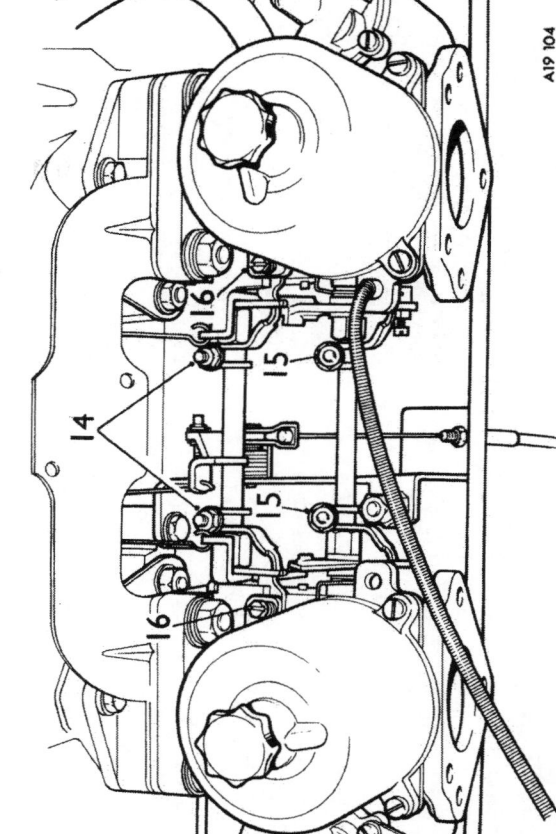

11 Start the engine and run at a fast idle speed until it attains normal running temperature and continue for a further five minutes.

12 Increase the engine speed to 2500 r.p.m. for thirty seconds.

13 Using an exhaust gas analyser insert the probe into the exhaust pipe in accordance with the manufacturers instructions.
NOTE: Tuning can now commence, but if adjustments cannot be achieved within three minutes increase the engine speed to 2500 r.p.m. and then continue. Repeat this clearing procedure at three minute intervals until tuning is complete.

14 Slacken both clamping nuts and bolts on the throttle spindle inter-connections.

15 Slacken both nuts and bolts on the jet control interconnections.

16 Using a balancing meter check the carburetters for balance and adjust by turning the throttle adjusting screws whilst maintaining the correct idling speed – see DATA.

continued

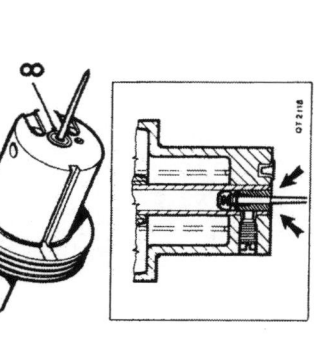

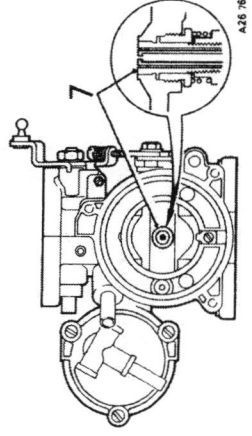

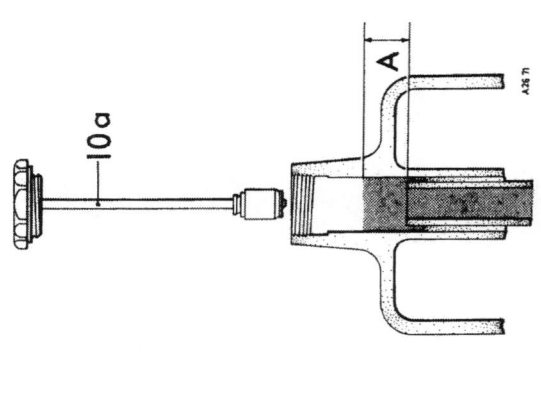

7 Turn the jet adjusting nuts to bring the jets flush with the carburetter bridge.

8 Check that the needle shank is flush with the underside of the piston.

9 Turn the jet adjusting nuts down two turns.

10 Check the piston damper oil level as follows:

a Unscrew the cap and withdraw the damper.

b Top-up the hollow piston rod with S.A.E. 20 oil until the level is ½ in (13 mm) above the top of the hollow piston rod – dimension A.

17 Turn the jet adjusting nut on each carburetter down to enrich or up to weaken the mixture by the same amount until the fastest speed is indicated on the tachometer.

18 Turn each adjusting nut up one flat at a time until the engine speed just commences to fall.

19 Turn the adjusting nuts down by the minimum amount until the fastest speed is regained.

20 Check the idle speed and adjust if necessary by turning the throttle adjusting screws by the same amount.

21 Check that the CO reading on the exhaust gas analyser is within the accepted limits at idling, see DATA.

22 If the CO reading falls outside the limits, reset both jet adjusting nuts by the minimum amount necessary.

NOTE: If an adjustment exceeding three flats or half a turn is required to achieve this the carburetters must be removed and overhauled.

Throttle and mixture control linkage setting

23 Hold the throttle lever against its stop.

24 Rotate the lever pins on the throttle interconnection shaft until a gap of 0.010 in (0.25 mm) exists between the pins and the lower arm of the forks.

25 Ensure that the link rod is at the top of the elongated hole in throttle shaft actuating lever.

26 Whilst maintaining the positions in instructions 24 and 25 tighten the lever pin clamping nuts and bolts on both carburetters.

27 Adjust the throttle cable to take-up any slack.

28 Check and if necessary adjust the accelerator pedal stop to ensure full throttle opening.

29 Using the balancing meter re-check the carburetters for balance by running the engine at 1500 r.p.m.

30 With the fast idle cams against their respective stops tighten the jet control interconnection clamps, so that both cams begin to move simultaneously.

31 Connect the mixture control cable to the trunnion and ensure that there exists a $\frac{1}{16}$ in (1.5 mm) free movement of the cable before the cams move.

32 Pull out the mixture control knob until the linkage is about to move the jet.

33 Using the balancing meter to ensure equal adjustment turn the fast idle adjusting screws to give the correct fast idle speed — see DATA — and tighten the lock nuts.

Automatic kick-down

34 Where applicable, adjust the kick-down cable so that there is no slack, but that a gap of 0.020 to 0.025 in (0.050 to 0.63 mm) exists between the ferrule and the cable adjuster.

35 Fit the air cleaner, see 19.10.02.

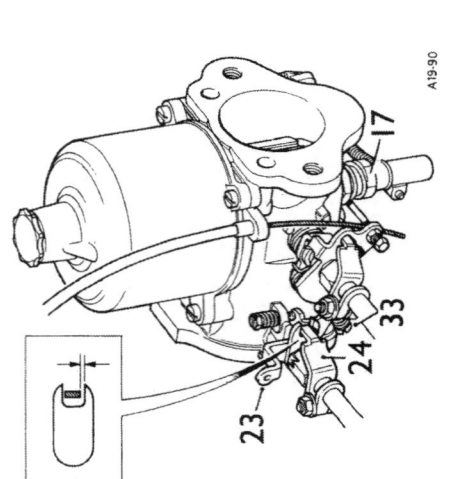

A19-90

CARBURETTERS 19.15.11

Remove and refit

Removing

1 Disconnect the battery.

2 Remove the air cleaner complete, see 19.10.01.

3 Remove the fresh air duct.

4 Disconnect the mixture control cable from the front carburetter.

5 Pull-off the fuel over-flow pipes from the front and rear float chambers.

6 Pull-off the vacuum pipe from the rear carburetter to the distributor advance capsule.

7 Disconnect the engine breather pipes from the carburetters.

8 Disconnect the fuel feed pipes to the carburetters.

9 Disconnect the vertical link from the throttle interconnection shaft.

10 Disconnect the three throttle shaft return springs.

11 Remove the eight (four per carburetter) nuts, plain and spring washers securing the carburetters to the inlet manifold.

12 Withdraw the carburetters complete.

13 Remove and discard the gaskets.

Refitting

14 Clean the carburetter and flexible mounting mating faces and fit new gaskets.

15 Fit the carburetters ensuring that the mixture control pins are located in their respective forks.

16 Fit the plain and spring washers and evenly tighten, to the correct torque, the eight retaining nuts.

17 Reverse instructions 1 to 10.

18 Tune and adjust the carburetters, see 19.15.02.

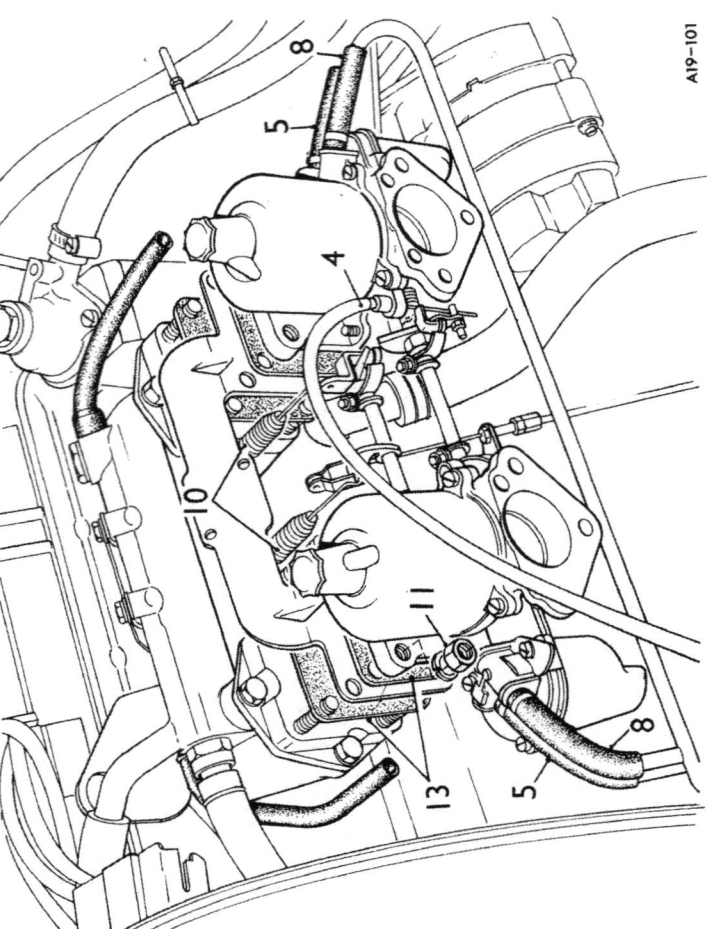

A19-101

DATA

Idling speed	650 to 850 r.p.m.
Fast idling speed	1100 to 1300 r.p.m.
CO level at idling speed	2.0 to 4.5%

CARBURETTERS

Overhaul and adjust   19.15.17

Where tamperproof carburetters are fitted refer to 19.00.00

Dismantling

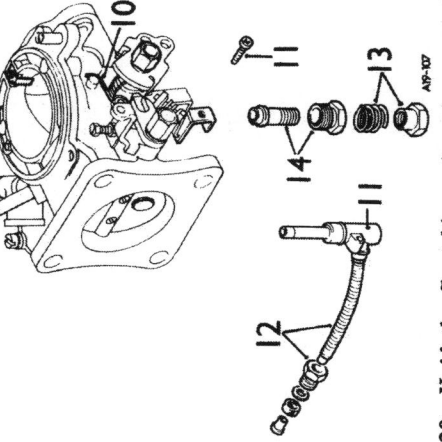

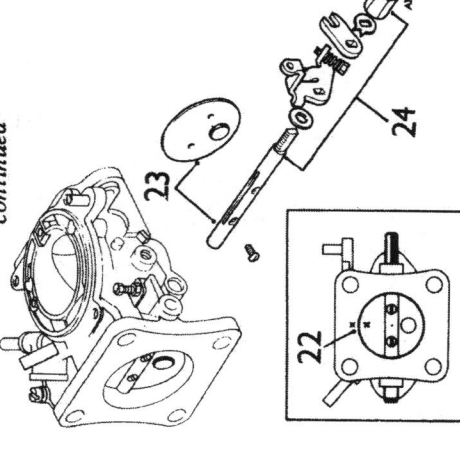

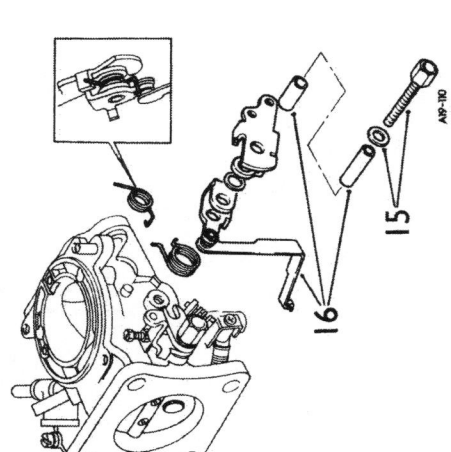
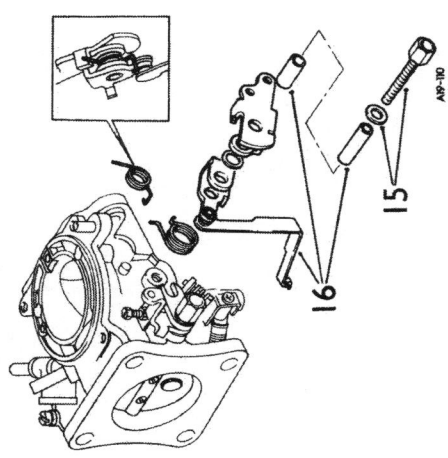
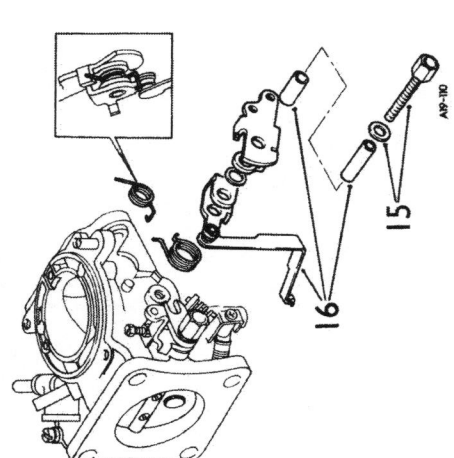

1 Remove the carburetter assembly, see 19.15.11.
2 Thoroughly clean the outside of the carburetter.
3 Mark the suction chamber to ensure it is refitted to the same body.
4 Remove the damper and its washer.
5 Unscrew the suction chamber securing screws and lift off the chamber.
6 Remove the piston spring.
7 Carefully lift out the piston assembly and empty the oil from the piston rod.
8 Remove the guide locking screw and withdraw the needle assembly, taking care not to bend the needle. Withdraw the needle from the guide and remove the spring from the needle.
9 Where fitted, push the piston lifting pin upwards, detach its securing circlip and washers and withdraw the pin and spring downwards.
10 Release the pick-up lever return spring from its retaining lug.
11 Support the plastic moulded base of the jet and remove the screw retaining the jet pick-up link and link bracket.
12 Unscrew the flexible jet tube sleeve nut from the float-chamber and withdraw the jet assembly. Note the gland, washer and ferrule at the end of the jet tube.
13 Remove the jet adjusting nut and spring.
14 Unscrew the jet locking nut and detach the nut and jet bearing; withdraw the bearing from the nut.
15 Unscrew and remove the lever pivot bolt and spacer.
16 Detach the lever assembly and return springs, noting the pivot bolt tubes and the location of the cam and pick-up lever springs.
17 Unscrew the securing bolt and remove the float chamber and spacer.
18 Mark the float chamber lid location.
19 Remove the lid securing screws and detach the lid with its joint washer and float. Retain the part number tag.

20 Hold the float hinge pin at its serrated end and withdraw the pin and float.
21 Extract the float needle from its seating and unscrew the seating from the lid.
22 Close the throttle and mark the relative position of the throttle disc and the carburetter flange.
23 Press the split ends of the disc retaining screws together and remove the screws. Open the throttle and remove the disc from its slot in the throttle spindle.
24 Release the lock washer tabs securing the spindle nut; remove the nut and detach the fork lever, lever arm, washer and throttle spindle; note the location of the lever arm in relation to the spindle and carburetter body.

continued

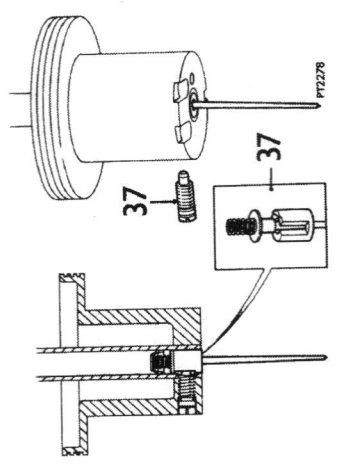

37 Fit the spring and guide to the needle and insert the assembly into the piston (with the shoulder of the needle guide flush with the underside face of the piston) and the needle positioned adjacent to the needle guide locking screw. Fit a new guide locking screw.

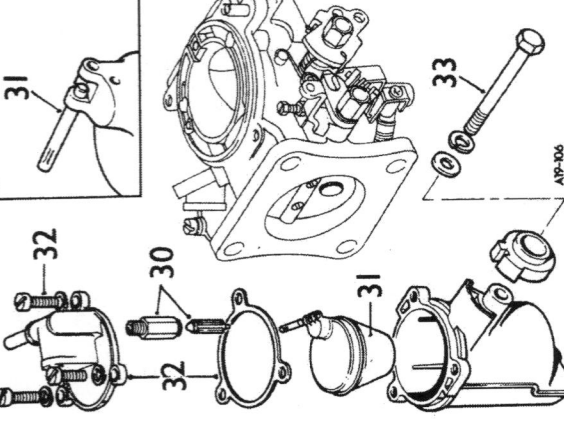

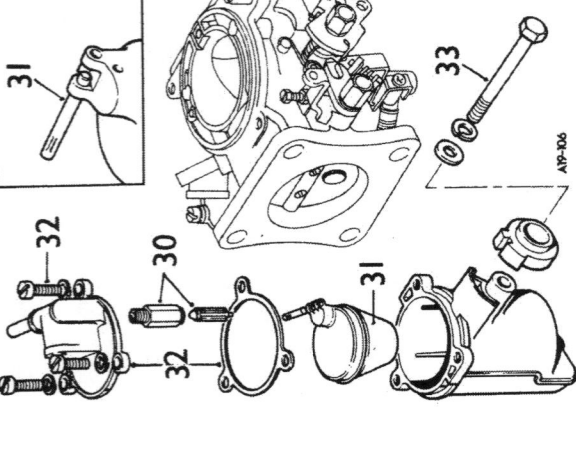

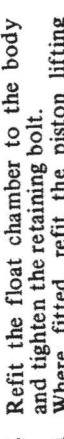

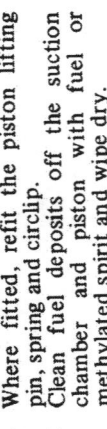

Inspecting

25 Examine the components as follows:

a Check the throttle spindle in the body for excessive play, and renew if necessary.

b Examine the float needle for wear; i.e. small ridges or grooves in the seat of the needle, and ensure that the spring-loaded plunger on the opposite end operates freely. Replace the needle and seating if necessary.

c Inspect all other components for wear and damage; renew unserviceable components.

Reassembling

26 Refit the spindle to the body, with the countersunk holes in the spindle facing outwards.

27 Assemble the spacing washer, lever, fork lever, lock washer and securing nut, ensure that the idling stop on the lever is against the idling screw abutment on the body in the closed throttle position. Tighten the spindle nut and lock with tab washer.

28 Insert the throttle disc into the spindle slot; not the markings for reassembling. Manoeuvre the disc in the spindle until the throttle can be closed, snap the throttle open and closed to centralize it in the bore of the carburetter.

29 Fit new disc retaining screws but do not fully tighten, check that the disc closes fully and adjust its position as necessary. Tighten the screws fully and spread their split ends just enough to prevent them turning.

30 Screw the seating into the float chamber lid; do not overtighten. Insert the needle coned-end first into the seating.

31 Refit the float to the chamber lid and insert the hinge pin.

32 Refit the float chamber lid with a new joint washer, noting the assembly markings, tighten the securing screws evenly.

33 Refit the float chamber to the body and tighten the retaining bolt.

34 Where fitted, refit the piston lifting pin, spring and circlip.

35 Clean fuel deposits off the suction chamber and piston with fuel or methylated spirit and wipe dry.

CAUTION: Do not use an abrasive.

36 Check the operation of the suction chamber and piston (without the spring fitted) as follows:

a Refit the damper and washer to the suction chamber; temporarily plug the piston transfer holes with rubber plugs or Plasticine and insert the piston fully into the suction chamber.

b Secure a large flat washer to one of the fixing holes with a screw and nut so that it overlaps the bore.

c With the assembly upside-down, hold the piston and check the time taken for the suction chamber to fall the full extent of its travel. The time taken should be five to seven seconds; if this time is exceeded, check the piston and chamber for cleanliness and mechanical damage. Renew the assembly if the time taken is still not within these limits.

38 Check the piston key in the body for security.
39 Refit the jet bearing; fit and tighten the jet locking nut.
40 Refit the spring and jet adjustment nut; screw the nut up as far as possible.
41 Insert the jet into the bearing, fit the sleeve nut, washer and gland to the end of the flexible tube (if removed). The tube must project a minimum of ³⁄₁₆ in (4.8 mm) beyond the gland. Tighten the sleeve nut until the gland is compressed; over-tightening can cause leakage.
42 Refit the piston, spring and suction chamber to the body (noting the assembly marks) and tighten the securing screws evenly.
43 Reverse the procedure in 15 and 16.
44 Hold up the choke lever to relieve pressure on the jet pick-up link, refit the link bracket; support the end of the moulded jet and tighten the securing screw.
45 Screw the jet adjusting nut down two complete turns (12 flats) to provide the initial setting.
46 Refit the carburetters, see 19.15.11.
47 Tune and adjust the carburetters, see 19.15.02.

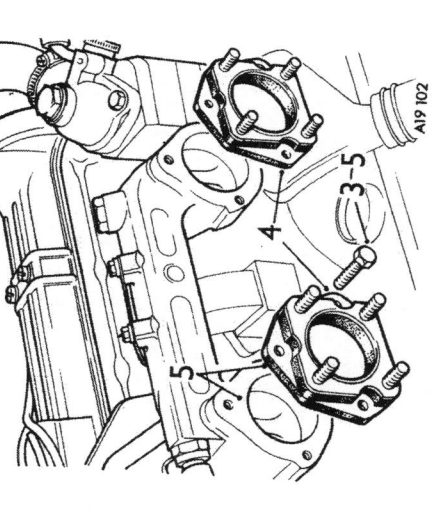

CARBURETTER FLEXIBLE MOUNTINGS   19.15.19

Remove and refit

Removing
1 Remove the air cleaner, see 19.10.01.
2 Remove the carburetters, see 19.15.11.
3 Remove the six bolts (three per manifold) securing the mountings to the intakes.
4 Remove the mountings.

Refitting
5 Clean the manifold intake and flexible mounting faces and secure the mounting with the bolts and spring washers.
6 Fit the carburetters and tune, see 19.15.11.
7 Fit the air cleaner, see 19.10.01.

FLOAT CHAMBER NEEDLE AND SEAT   19.15.24

Remove and refit

Removing
1 Remove the fresh air duct for rear carburetter, see 80.15.31.
2 Disconnect the fuel over-flow pipe.
3 Disconnect the fuel feed pipe to the float chamber.
4 Disconnect the breather hose from the carburetter.
5 Mark the lid and float-chamber for assembly.
6 Remove the lid securing screws and detach the lid.
7 Hold the float hinge pin at its serrated end and withdraw the pin and float.
8 Extract the float needle from its seating.

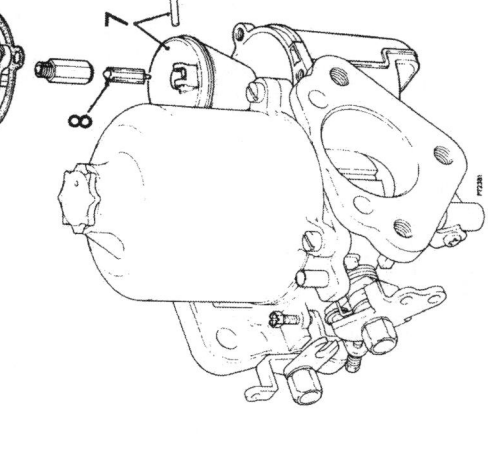

Inspecting
9 Examine the float needle for wear, i.e. small ridges or grooves in the seat of the needle, also check that the spring-loaded plunger on the opposite end operates freely. Renew the needle and seating if the needle is worn.

Refitting
10 Clean any sediment from the float-chamber, and fit a new joint washer if required.
11 Reverse instructions 1 to 9.

PISTON AND SUCTION CHAMBER   19.15.30

Remove, clean and refit

Where tamperproof carburetters are fitted refer to 19.00.00.

Removing
1 Remove the fresh air duct—for rear carburetter only, see 80.15.31.
2 Mark the relative position of the suction chamber and the carburetter body.
3 Remove the damper and its washer.
4 Unscrew the suction chamber securing screws and lift off the chamber.

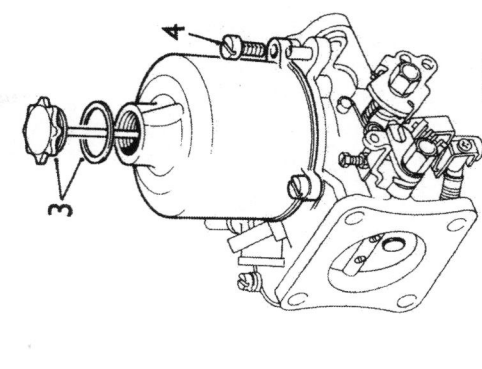
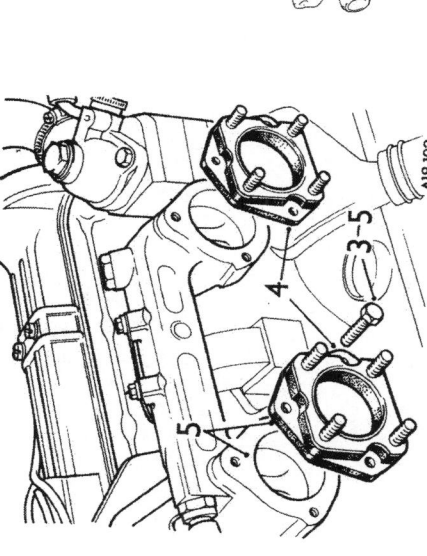

continued

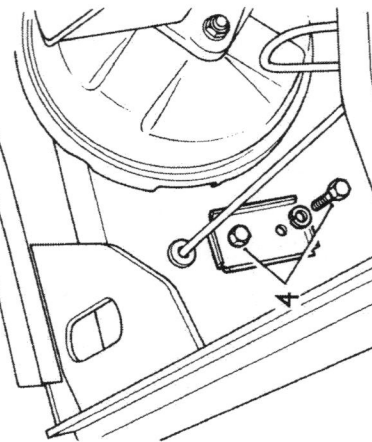

A19 14

THROTTLE PEDAL ASSEMBLY 19.20.01

Remove and refit

Removing
1 Disconnect the battery.
2 Working from inside the car remove the spring clip securing the throttle cable.
3 Remove the cable from the pedal.
4 Open the bonnet and remove the two bolts securing the pedal assembly to the bulkhead.
5 Remove the pedal assembly from the car.
6 Strip the pedal assembly, and discard worn parts.

Refitting
7 Locate the spring in the bracket.
8 Fit the pedal to the bracket.
9 Insert the clevis pin.
10 Fit the anti-rattle washer.
11 Fit the plain washer.
12 Secure the assembly with a new split pin.
13 Fit the pedal to the bulkhead and secure with the two bolts.
14 Fit the cable to the pedal and retain with the spring clip.
15 Re-connect the battery.

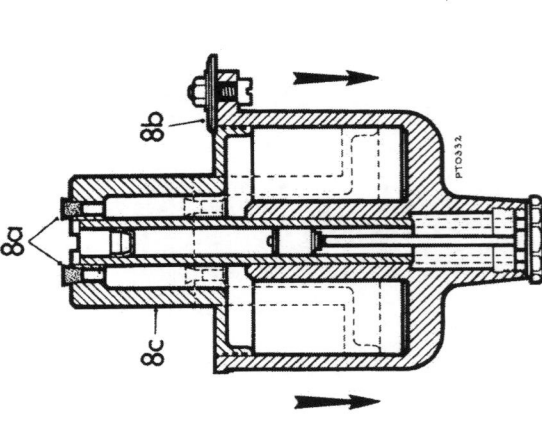

A19 054

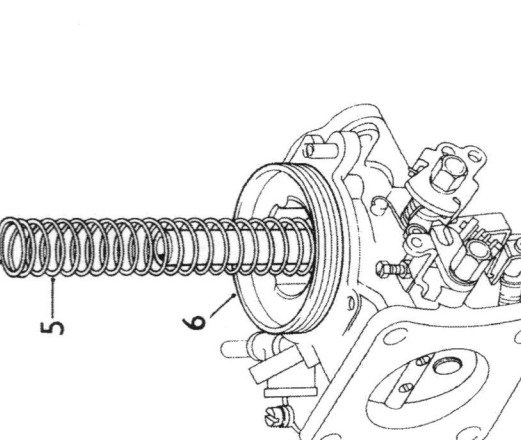

A19 – 124

PT0332

5 Remove the piston spring.
6 Carefully lift out the piston assembly and empty the oil from the piston rod.
7 Clean fuel deposits off the suction chamber and piston with fuel or methylated spirit and wipe dry.

CAUTION: Do not use abrasives.

8 Check the operation of the suction chamber and piston (without the spring fitted) as follows:
a Refit the damper and washer to the suction chamber, temporarily plug the piston transfer holes with rubber plugs or Plasticine and insert the piston fully into the suction chamber.
b Secure a large flat washer to one of the fixing holes with a screw and nut so that it overlaps the bore.
c With the assembly upside-down, hold the piston and check the time taken for the suction chamber to fall the full extent of its travel. The time taken should be five to seven seconds, if this time is exceeded, check the piston and chamber for cleanliness and mechanical damage. Renew the assembly if the time taken is still not within these limits.

Note: This operation is not applicable to tamperproof carburetters.

Refitting
9 Refit the piston, spring and suction chamber to the carburetter (noting the assembly marks) and tighten the screw evenly.
10 Top up each piston damper with a recommended engine oil until the level is ½ in (13 mm) above the top of the hollow piston rod.
11 Refit each piston damper with its washer.

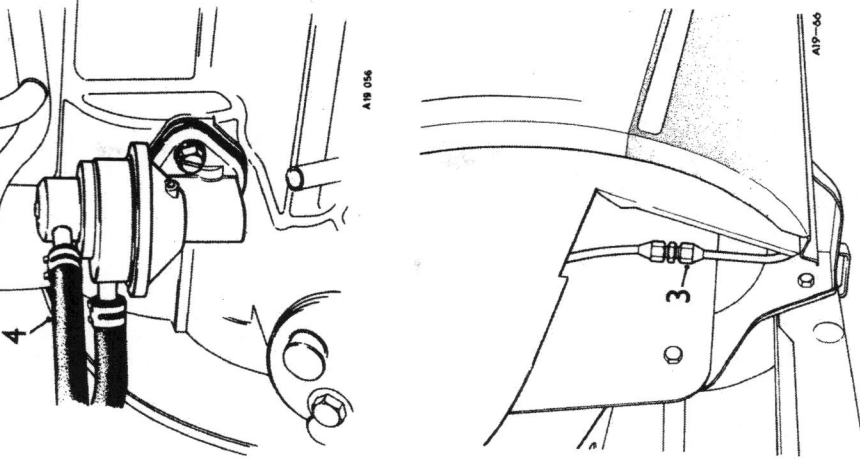

4 Pull off the rubber hose connecting engine-end section to the fuel pump.
5 Remove the pipe from the retaining clips.

Refitting
6 Reverse instructions 3 to 5.
7 Start the engine and checks for leaks.
8 Stop the engine and lower the ramp.

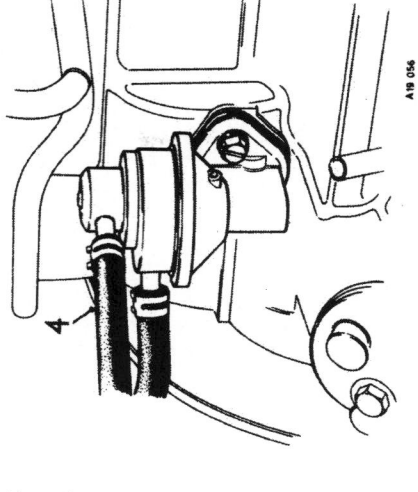

MIXTURE CONTROL CABLE ASSEMBLY

Remove and refit   19.20.13

Inner cable — instructions   19.20.14
1 to 2

Removing
1 Disconnect the exposed inner cable from the carburetter trunnion.
2 Working inside the car, pull the mixture control knob and withdraw the inner cable complete.
3 Pull-off the choke indicator Lucar from the switch.
4 Slacken the outer cable retaining nut.
5 Unscrew the bezel from the outer cable.
6 Remove the outer cable complete from the bracket and car.
7 Slacken the grub screw and remove the choke indicator switch from the cable.

Refitting
8 Reverse instructions 1 to 7 ensuring that the choke indicator switch is fitted correctly, see 86.65.53.

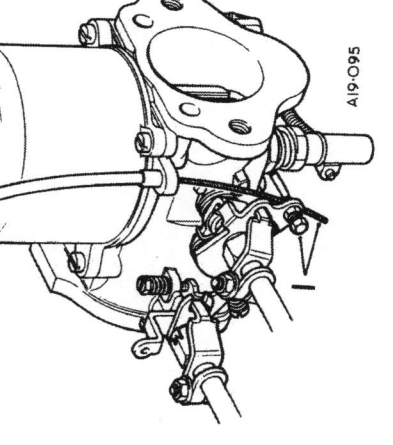

PETROL PIPE – MAIN LINE – TANK END SECTION

Remove and refit   19.40.02

Removing
1 Drive the car on to a ramp and raise.
2 Drain the petrol tank.
3 Pull off the rubber connection from the tank.
4 Release the tank-end section from the engine-end section at the union (right-hand rear wing).
5 Release the pipe from the retaining clips and remove from the car.

Refitting
6 Clip the pipe into position.
7 Connect the pipe to the engine-end section at the union.
8 Connect the pipe to the tank with the rubber connector.
9 Lower the ramp and refill the tank.

PETROL PIPE – MAIN LINE – ENGINE END SECTION

Remove and refit   19.40.04

Removing
1 Drive the car onto a ramp.
2 Raise the ramp and drain the petrol tank.
3 Disconnect the engine-end section from the petrol tank-end section at the union (right-hand wing).

HOSE – FILLER TO TANK 19.40.19

Remove and refit

Removing
1. Open the boot and remove the access panel.
2. Remove the filler cap assembly, see 19.55.08.
3. Release the hose clip securing the filler hose to the fuel tank, visible through the access aperture.
4. Pull off the filler hose.

Refitting
5. Fit the filler hose to the tank and secure with the hose clip.
6. Fit the fuel filler cap assembly – instructions 7 to 10, see 19.55.08.
7. Fit the access panel.

FUEL PUMP

Clean filter 19.45.05

1. Remove the fresh air duct, see 80.15.31.
2. Remove the pump cover retaining screw using a long shafted screw driver.
3. Lift off the cover.
4. Remove the sealing ring.
5. Lift out the filter.
6. Clean sediment from the cover.
7. Clean and examine the filter and refit.
8. Fit a new sealing ring – if necessary.
9. Fit the cover and secure it with the screw and a new washer.

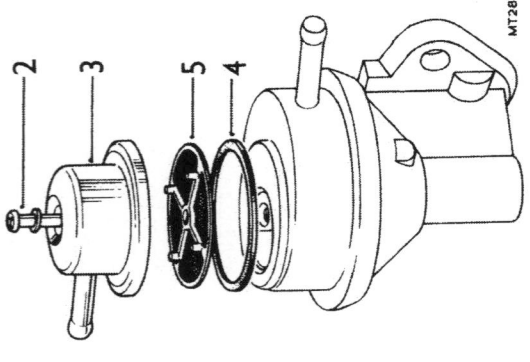

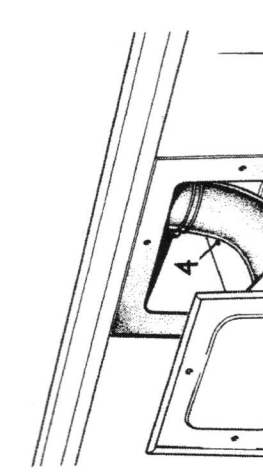

FUEL TANK 19.55.01

Remove and refit

Removing
1. Drive the car onto a ramp and disconnect the battery.
2. Remove the fuel filler cap assembly, see 19.55.08.
3. Raise the ramp and unclip the fuel tank breather hose from the LH side of the rear chassis member.
4. Drain the fuel tank.
5. Support the body with jacks both sides of the car forward of the trailing arm attachment points.
6. Disconnect the dampers at their lower attachment to the axle.
7. Disconnect the tank unit electrical leads.
8. Pull off the rubber connection to the main fuel line.
9. Disconnect the R.H. radius rod from the body bracket.
10. Remove the L.H. radius rod from the car.

FUEL PUMP 19.45.08

Remove and refit

Removing
1. Remove the air cleaner outer cover and element.
2. Disconnect the pipe from the fuel tank to the pump inlet connection.
3. Disconnect the outlet pipe from the pump.
4. Remove the bolts securing the pump to the cylinder block.
5. Remove the pump.
6. Remove the gasket.

Refitting
7. Clean the pump and cylinder block mating faces.
8. Fit a new gasket.
9. Fit the pump ensuring that the actuating arm rides on top of the cam.
10. Fit and tighten the retaining nuts and spring washers.
11. Fit the fuel inlet and outlet pipes.

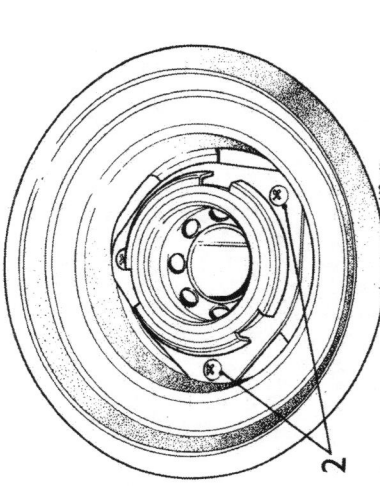
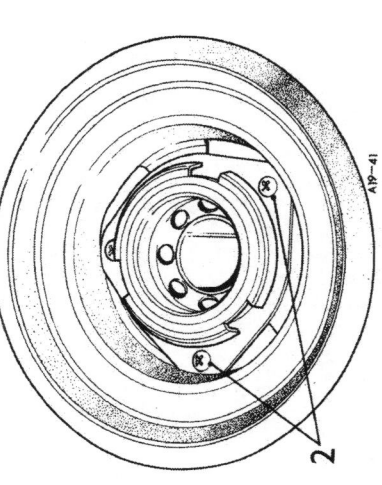

FUEL FILLER CAP AND FILLER ASSEMBLY   19.55.08

Removing

1 Turn the fuel filler cap anti-clockwise and withdraw.
2 Remove the three screws securing the filler tube assembly to the body.
3 Open the boot and remove the access panel—four screws.
4 Slacken the top hose clip.
5 Withdraw the filler tube.
6 Remove the finisher.

Refitting

7 Place the finisher in position.
8 Insert the filler tube into the filler hose and secure with the three screws.
9 Refit the filler cap.
10 Tighten the filler hose top clip.
11 Refit the access panel and close the boot.

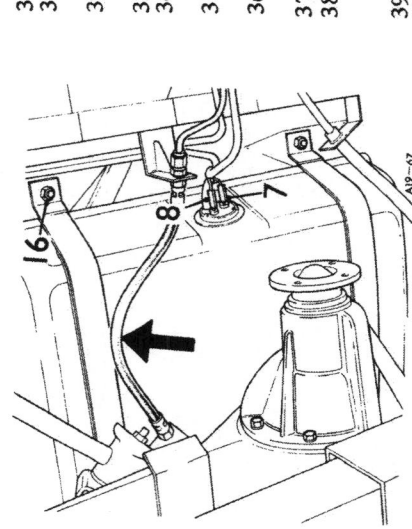

11 Jack up the body sufficiently to remove both road springs.

CAUTION: Care must be taken to ensure that whilst jacking up the body the brake hydraulic system jump hose is not stretched—shown arrowed.

12 Remove the L.H. rear road wheel and allow the axle to drop having regard for the above cautionary note.
13 Support the axle with a jack to relieve any tension in the hydraulic jump hose.
14 Remove the tail pipe and silencer assembly, see 30.10.22.
15 Remove the L.H. bump stop.
16 Remove the four nuts and tank retaining straps.
17 Withdraw the tank from the L.H. side of the car.
18 Remove the filler hose.
19 Remove the breather hose.
20 Remove the tank unit, see 88.25.32 instructions 6 to 8.

NOTE: Instructions 18 to 20 are only necessary if the tank is to be renewed.

Refitting

NOTE: If the tank is not being renewed ignore instructions 18 to 22. However, renew all hoses if any deterioration exists.

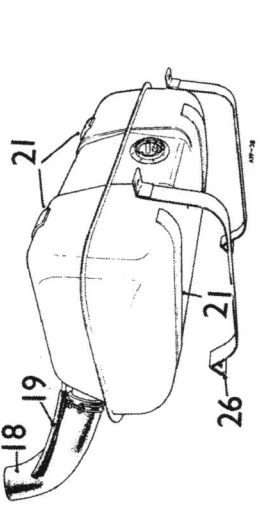

21 Using adhesive fit new cushion strips to the tank noting that thicker strips are fitted to the top of the tank.
22 Fit the filler hose.
23 Fit the breather hose.
24 Fit the tank unit – reversing instructions 6 to 8, see 88.25.32.
25 Manoeuvre the tank into position from the L.H. side of the car.
26 Fit the supporting straps noting that the elongated holes in the straps are fitted to the rear studs in the body.
27 Fit and tighten the four retaining nuts.
28 Fit the L.H. radius rod to the axle—including the handbrake cable bracket—leaving the body-end free for the time being.
29 Fit the springs and jack-up the axle both sides and connect the dampers to their axle locations.
30 Fit the L.H. bump stop.
31 Fit the L.H. and R.H. radius rods to their body locations.
32 Fit the tail pipe and silencer assembly, see 30.10.22.
33 Fit the L.H. rear road wheel.
34 Lower and remove the body and axle jacks.
35 Connect the fuel tank to the main line pipe with the rubber connector.
36 Fit the electrical leads to the tank unit—instruction 10, see 88.25.32.
37 Fit the breather pipe.
38 Lower the ramp and fit the fuel filler assembly, see 19.55.08 instructions 7 to 10.
39 Fit the access panel.
40 Refill the fuel tank, connect the battery, start the engine and check for leaks.

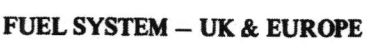

AIR CLEANER

Remove and refit   19.10.01

Earlier Models

Removing

1 Disconnect the emission control pipes from the clips attached to the air cleaner back plate.

2 Disconnect the hot air hose from the air cleaner intake.

3 Remove the two bolts, plain and rubber washers, securing the air cleaner to the carburetter.

4 Withdraw the air cleaner complete with the air temperature control unit.

5 Slacken the hose clip and remove the air temperature control unit.

Refitting

6 Reverse instructions 1 to 5, using a new gasket between the air cleaner and carburetter intake.

Earlier Models

Removing

1 Disconnect the hot air pipe from the air cleaner.

2 Remove the vacuum pipe from air inlet temperature control unit.

3 Release the two retaining clips.

4 Separate the air cleaner outer cover from the backplate and withdraw the element.

5 Remove the outer cover.

6 Remove the two fuel traps from the clips.

7 Disconnect the vacuum pipe from the temperature sensor unit.

8 Remove the single retaining nut behind the back-plate.

9 Remove the six bolts securing the back-plate to the carburetter intakes.

10 Withdraw the back-plate complete with gaskets.

Refitting

11 Using new gaskets reverse instructions 1 to 10.

A19-48

AIR CLEANER

Renew element   19.10.08

Earlier Models

1 Remove the air cleaner see 19.10.01, omitting instruction 5.

2 Separate the air cleaner back plate from the container.

3 Remove the used element and rubber sealing rings.

4 Clean the back plate and container.

5 Assemble the new element and sealing rings into the container.

6 Fit the back plate, ensuring that the peg on the container locates in the back plate slot.

7 Refit the air cleaner see 19.10.01, using a new gasket.

Later Models

1 Disconnect the hot air pipe from the air cleaner.

2 Release the two retaining clips and hinge back the outer cover from the back-plate.

3 Withdraw the air cleaner element.

4 Clean the inside of the box and insert a new element noting that it is fitted with the rubber seal towards the engine.

5 Hinge forward the outer cover and secure with the two clips.

6 Connect the hot air pipe.

7 Check that the vacuum pipe is connected to the temperature sensor unit at one end and the air inlet temperature control unit at the other.

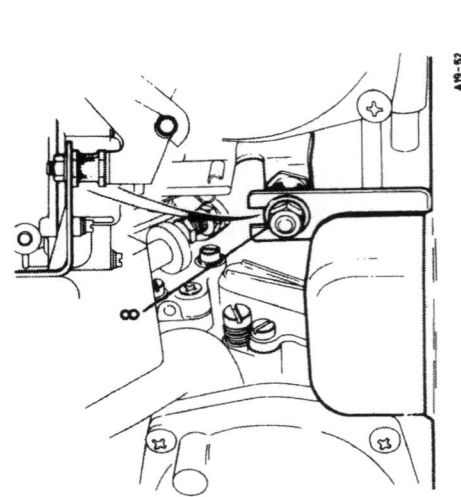

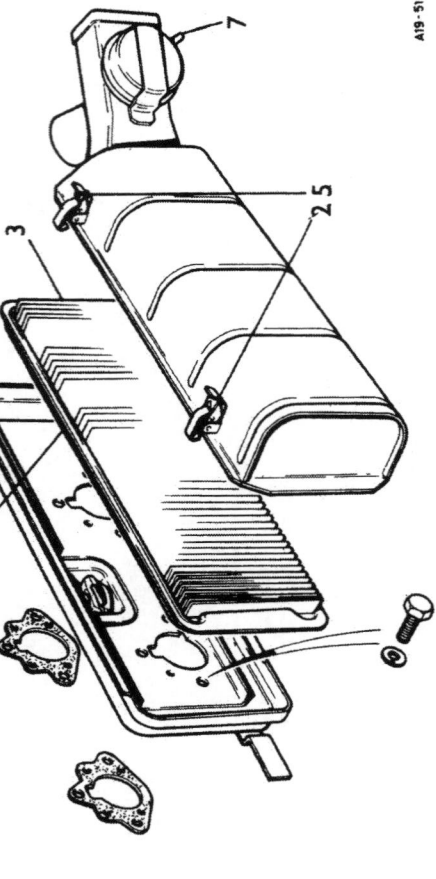

A19-51

A19-52

AHT 83

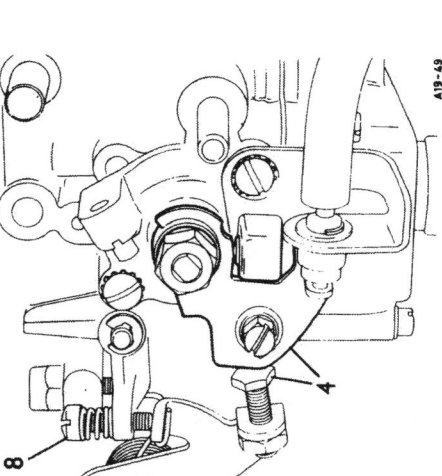

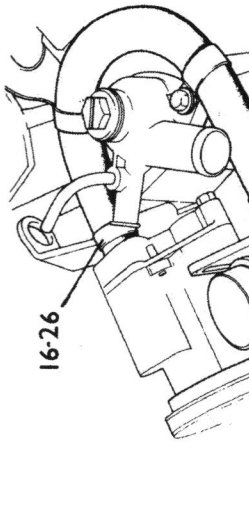

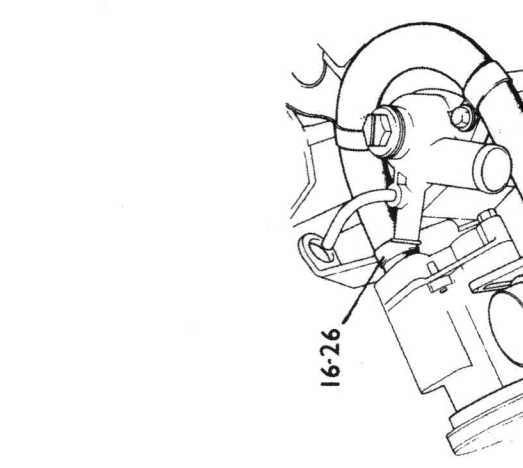

CARBURETTERS

Tune and adjust   19.15.02

Special tools: Non dispersive infra-red exhaust gas analyser and mixture adjusting tool S353.

CAUTION: To ensure compliance with exhaust emission legislative requirements the following items must not be changed or modified in any way:
The fuel jet assembly.
The piston assembly.
The depression cover.

The following items must not be adjusted in service but should be replaced completely by factory-set units:
The temperature compensator.
The piston assembly return spring.
The starter assembly.

NOTE: During the course of the following instructions do not allow the engine to idle for longer than three minutes without a 'clear-out' burst of one minute duration at 2000 r.p.m.

1 Remove the fresh air duct – 80.15.31.
2 Run the engine until normal operating temperature is reached.
3 Remove the air cleaner. 19.10.01.

Adjusting idle speed and air flow for balance

4 Ensure that the fast idle screw is clear of the fast idle cam.
5 Using an air flow meter check that the air flow through both carburetters is the same. If not, adjust as follows:
6 Hold the roller into the corner of the progression lever. – (Canadian Specification only).
7 Adjust the spring loaded screws equally until the adjusting bar is in the centre of both forks.
8 Unscrew the throttle adjusting screws on both carburetters to permit the throttles to close completely.
9 Rotate the throttle adjusting screws so that they just touch the throttle levers and give a further half-turn to provide a datum setting.

10 Continue rotating the screws by equal amounts while holding an air flow meter to each carburetter intake in turn, until a balanced air flow is achieved at an engine speed of 800 r.p.m.
11 Hold the roller into the corner of the progression lever. – (Canadian Specification only).

Canadian Specification Vehicles only
12 Adjust the spring loaded screws to give a gap of 0.010 in. (0,25 mm) dimension A between the forks and the adjusting bar.
13 If necessary turn the throttle adjusting screws on both carburetters an equal amount to maintain the idle speed of 800 r.p.m.
14 Increase the engine speed to 1600 r.p.m. and check the balance with the air flow meter. If necessary turn the throttle adjusting screws by equal amounts to achieve a balance.
15 Re-check the air flow balance at idle speed.

Checking and adjusting CO level at idle — all vehicles

16 Disconnect and plug the outlet hose from the air pump.
17 Maintain the engine at normal operating temperature, and check that the idle speed is 800 r.p.m.
18 Check and if necessary adjust the ignition timing. 86.35.15.
19 Re-check the idle speed.
20 Insert the gas analyser probe as far as possible into the exhaust pipe.
21 Check the CO reading against the emission control decal on the car (under the bonnet lid).
22 Adjust the mixture if necessary — see mixture adjustment.
23 Check and if necessary adjust the idle speed.
24 Withdraw the analyser probe.
25 Switch off the ignition.
26 Unplug air injection hose and reconnect to the pump.

NOTE: Do not allow the engine to idle for longer than 3 minutes without a 'clear out burst' of 1 minute at 2000 rev/min.

continued

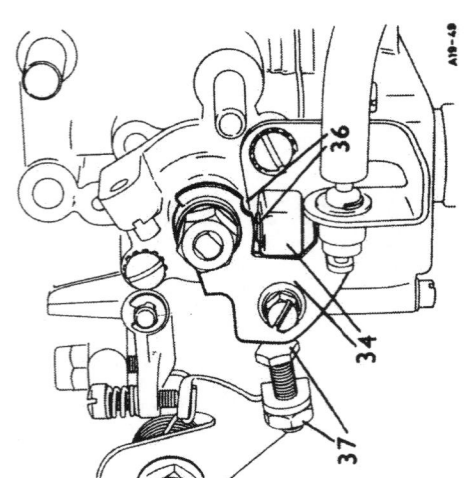

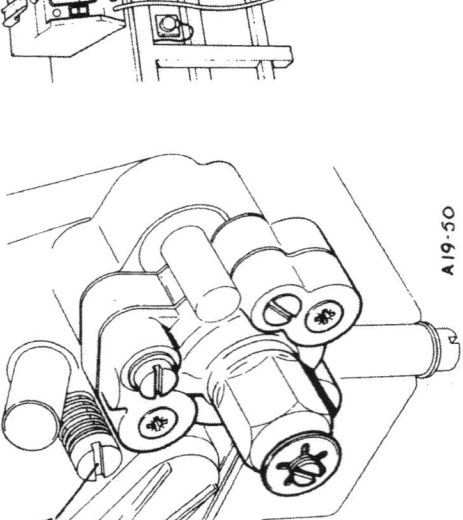

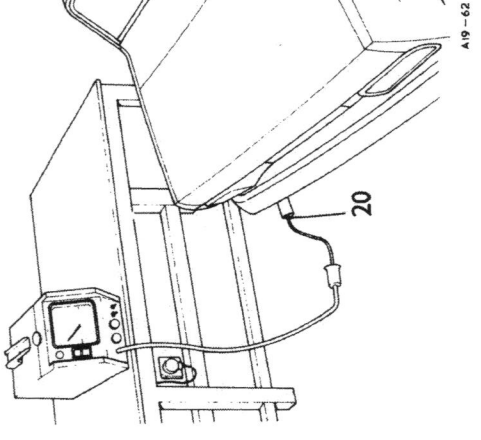

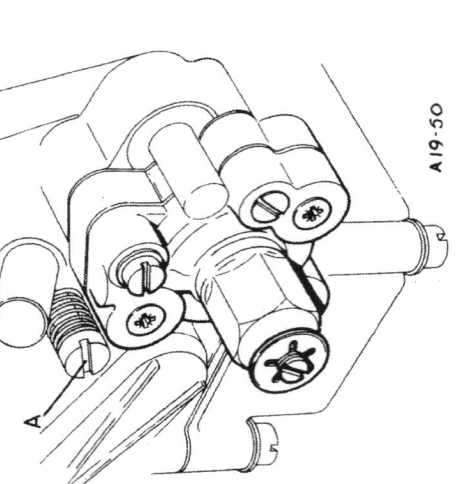

Mixture adjustment

NOTE: If the CO reading is only slightly outside the permitted limits, adjust the idle trim screw A on both carburetters by equal amounts until the CO reading is to within the limits.

CAUTION: The setting MUST ALWAYS be checked by means of a non-dispersive infra-red exhaust gas analyser.

For significant deviation outside the specified CO limits the mixture should be adjusted as follows:

27 Remove the piston damper from both carburetters.

28 Carefully insert special tool S353 into the dashpot until the outer tool engages in the air valve and the inner tool engages the hexagon in the needle adjuster plug.

CAUTION: The outer tool must be correctly engaged and held in position otherwise damage to the diaphragm may result.

29 Holding the outer tool turn the inner tool:
  a Clockwise to enrich the mixture.
  b Anti-clockwise to weaken.

30 Repeat instruction 28 and 29 on the remaining carburetter ensuring that the adjustment made is by the same amount.

31 Top-up the carburetter dampers, ensuring that the special instructions in 'MAINTENANCE' are followed.

32 Re-check the CO reading — instructions 16 to 26 and if necessary repeat instructions 27 to 30 until the CO reading is within the specified limits.

Checking and adjusting fast idle speed —
Canadian Specification Vehicles only

33 Maintain the engine at normal running temperature.

34 Check that the mixture control cam lever on both carburetters returns to its stop.

35 Check and if necessary adjust the mixture control cable so that there is free movement.

36 Pull-out the mixture control cable knob on the control cowl approximately ¼ in. until the fast idle cams are correctly engaged with the ball locators.

37 Slacken the fast idle screw lock-nut on both carburetters, start the engine and rotate the screw head (on both carburetters) against the cam until the engine revolutions reach a steady 1600 r.p.m.

38 Use the air flow meter to check that the carburetters are in balance at 1600 r.p.m. if necessary adjust the fast idle screws as required.

39 Tighten the fast idle screw lock-nut on both carburetters and push the mixture control knob fully home.

NOTE: An engine set to 1600 r.p.m. while hot is equivalent to a fast idle speed of approximately 1300 r.p.m. when cold.

Checking and adjusting deceleration by-pass valves –
California and Canadian Specification Vehicles only

40 Maintain the engine at normal running temperature.

41 With the engine idling, disconnect the vacuum pipe from the distributor and place a finger over the end of the pipe.

42 If the valves are correctly adjusted the engine idle speed should increase to approximately 1300 r.p.m.

43 Should one or both of the valves be 'floating' and therefore out of adjustment the engine revolutions will increase quickly to approximately 2000–2500 r.p.m. Furthermore if the throttle is momentarily opened the resulting increase in r.p.m. will be slow to fall.
If adjustment is required continue with the following instructions:

44 Without removing the circular spring clip, turn the by-pass valve adjusting screw anti-clockwise fully on to its seat on the carburetter NOT being adjusted.

NOTE: This procedure prevents the one by-pass valve from working while the valve on the other carburetter is being adjusted. It is not however, necessary to repeat this procedure when adjusting the valve on the second carburetter.

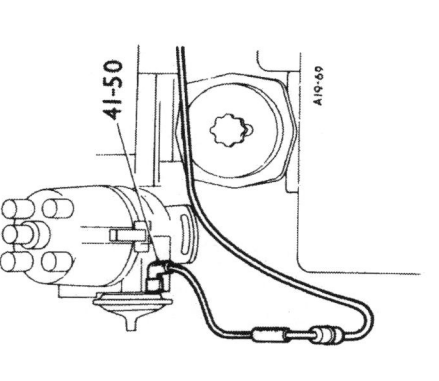
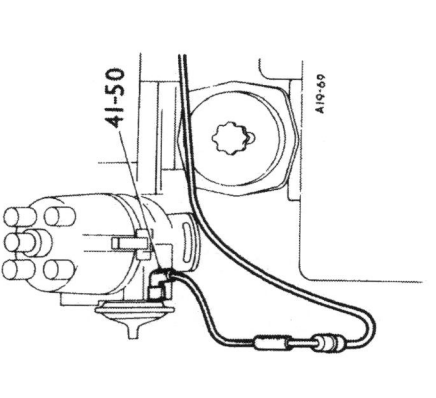

41-50

A19-69

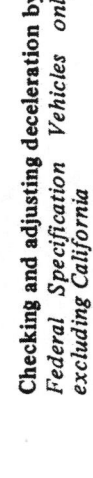

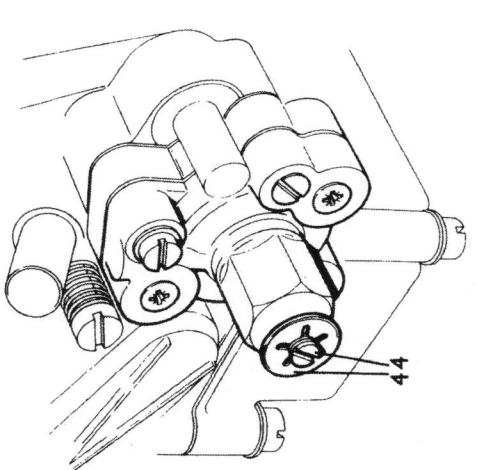

44

45 Remove and plug the vacuum pipe from the distributor.

46 With the engine running turn the by-pass valve clock-wise until the engine speed increases abruptly to approximately 2000 to 2500 r.p.m. thereby causing the valve to 'float' on its seat.

47 Turn the adjustment screw anti-clockwise until the engine speed falls to approximately 1300 r.p.m.

48 Using the throttle, momentarily increase the engine speed and immediately release the throttle. If the valve is correctly adjusted the engine speed should fall to approximately 1300 r.p.m. If not, the valve is still floating and the above adjusting sequence must be repeated.

49 When a correct adjustment has been achieved on both carburetters, turn the by-pass valve adjustment screw, on both carburetters, anti-clockwise half a turn to finally seat the valves.

50 Unplug the vacuum pipe and connect it to the distributor.

Checking and adjusting deceleration by-pass
Federal Specification Vehicles only – excluding California

51 Maintain the engine at normal running temperature and idling speed.

52 Slowly turn the rear carburetter by-pass valve adjusting crew clockwise from the fully loaded position until the engine revolutions begin to increase.

53 Turn the by-pass valve adjusting screw anti-clockwise 3 full revolutions.

54 Repeat operation No. 1 on the front carburetter by-pass valve adjusting screw.

55 Turn the front carburetter adjusting screw anti-clockwise 2 full revolutions.

56 Turn the rear carburetter adjusting screw anti-clockwise 1 full revolution.

CAUTION: Renewal of the by-pass valves, should it be necessary, must only be done as complete units.

57 Refit the air cleaner.
58 Refit the fresh air duct. 80.15.31.

CARBURETTERS – CAR SET

Remove and refit   19.15.11

Which includes:
Carburetter rubber mountings—remove and refit omitting instructions 13, 17 and 25

Removing
1 Disconnect the battery.
2 Remove the fresh-air duct. 80.15.31.
3 Remove the hot air hose from the air cleaner.
4 Remove the air cleaner. 19.10.02.
5 Disconnect all the piping from the carburetters.
6 Disconnect the fuel feed pipe.
7 Disconnect the throttle return spring.
8 Disconnect the throttle link.
9 Remove the eight nuts, plain and spring washers (four per carburetter) securing the carburetters to the manifold.
10 Withdraw the carburetters complete with gaskets.
11 Vehicles with air conditioning and automatic transmission only: Remove the electrical leads from the throttle jack.
12 Vehicles with air conditioning and automatic transmission only: Remove the throttle jack mounting bracket.
13 Remove the six bolts and spring washers (three per mounting) securing the carburetter rubber mountings to the manifold.
14 Remove the throttle interconnection linkage and separate the carburetters.

Refitting
15 Fit the carburetter rubber mountings securing with the six (three each side) bolts and spring washers.
16 Vehicles with air conditioning and automatic transmission only: Fit the throttle jack mounting bracket.
17 Vehicles with air conditioning and automatic transmission only: Connect the electrical leads to the throttle jack.
18 Join the carburetters together keeping the interconnection clamps slack.
19 Clean the carburetter mating faces and fit new gaskets.
20 Fit the carburetters and secure with the eight nuts, plain and spring washers (four per carburetter) tightening the nuts evenly to the correct torque figure.
21 Connect the throttle link.
22 Connect the fuel feed pipe.
23 Connect the mixture control cable.
24 Connect the throttle return spring.
25 Connect all the piping to the carburetters.
26 Tune and adjust the carburetters. 19.15.02.
27 Refit the air cleaner. 19.10.02.
28 Refit fresh air duct.

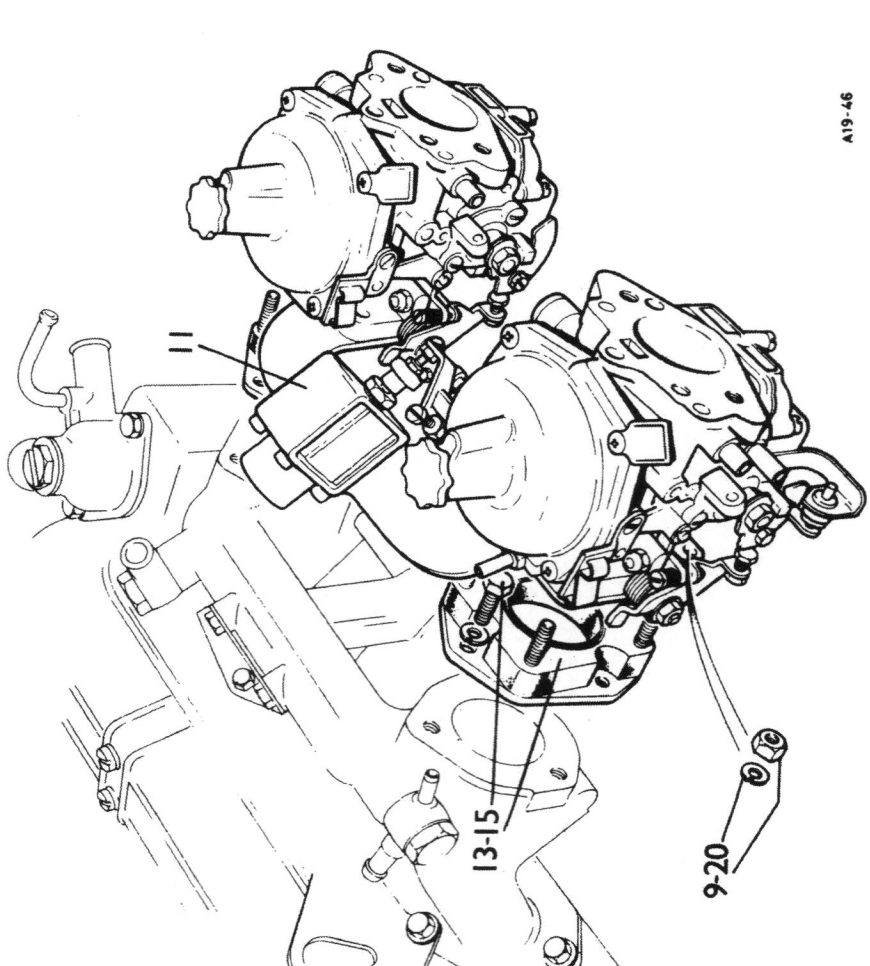

A19-46

INLET MANIFOLD COMPLETE WITH CARBURETTERS

Remove and refit   19.15.15

Removing

1 Disconnect the battery.
2 Drain the cooling system including the cylinder block. 26.10.01.
3 Remove the fresh air duct. 80.15.31.
4 Remove the air cleaner. 19.10.02.
5 Disconnect the top water hoses from the engine.
6 Disconnect all emission control hoses.
7 Remove water temperature transmitter lead. 88.25.20. Instruction 3.
8 Disconnect petrol main feed pipe to carburetters.
9 Disconnect brake servo pipe from manifold connection.
10 Disconnect the mixture control cable from the carburetters.

11 Disconnect the throttle cable from the carburetters.
12 Remove the distributor cap.
13 Remove the six manifold attachment bolts.
14 Disconnect the heater pipe at the union.
15 Lift the manifold complete with carburetters from the cylinder head.
16 Remove the 'O' ring.
17 Remove the water pump connecting tube, and 'O' rings.
18 Remove the gasket.

Refitting

19 Fit a new 'O' ring to the manifold.
20 Fit two new 'O' rings to the connecting tube and insert into the pump cover.

NOTE: Early engines may be fitted with a moulded type tube, in which case ignore instruction 20 and follow instructions 32 and 33.

21 Clean the cylinder head and manifold mating faces and using a new gasket fit the manifold complete with carburetters ensuring that the connecting tube is properly located. Fit the manifold retaining bolts but leave slack.
22 Connect the heater pipe to the union but leave the nut slack.
23 Tighten the manifold attachment bolts evenly to the correct torque figure and finally tighten the heater union nut.
24 Fit the distributor cap.
25 Fit the petrol feed pipe to the carburetters.
26 Connect the throttle cable and adjust.
27 Connect the mixture control cable.
28 Connect the lead to the water temperature sensor.
29 Reconnect the emission and evaporative control pipe work.
30 Fit the air cleaner. 19.10.02.
31 Fit the brake servo pipe to the manifold connection.

continued

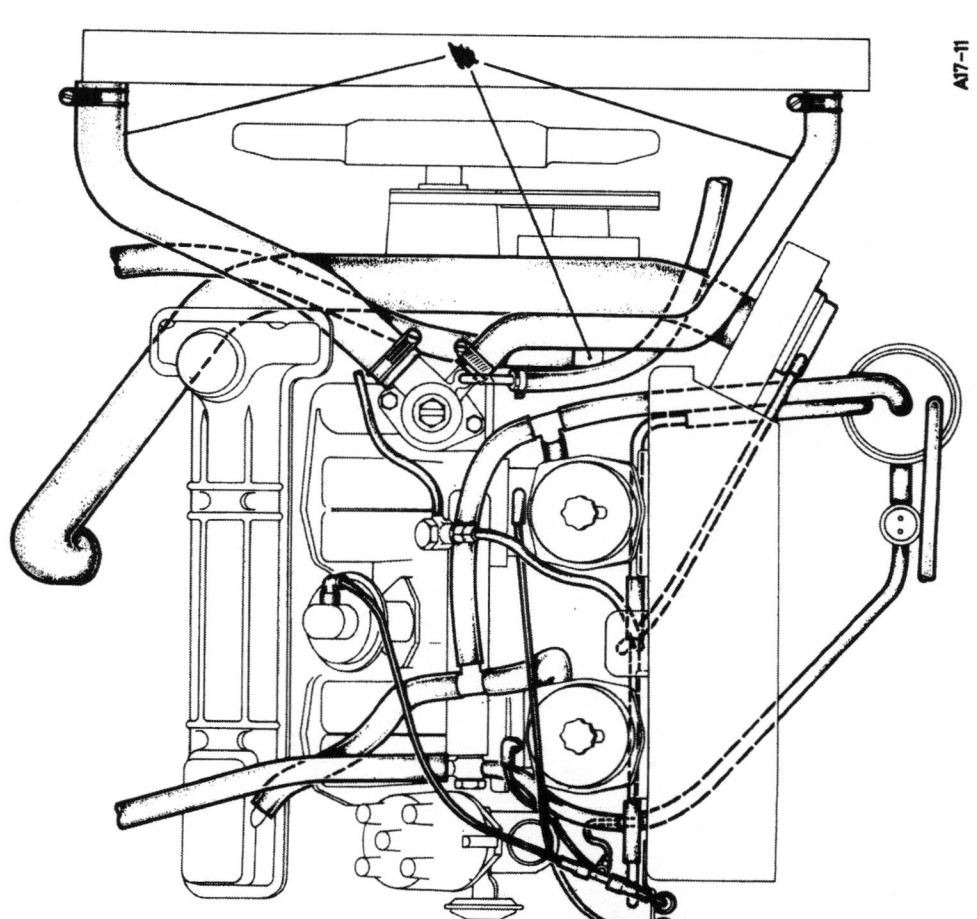

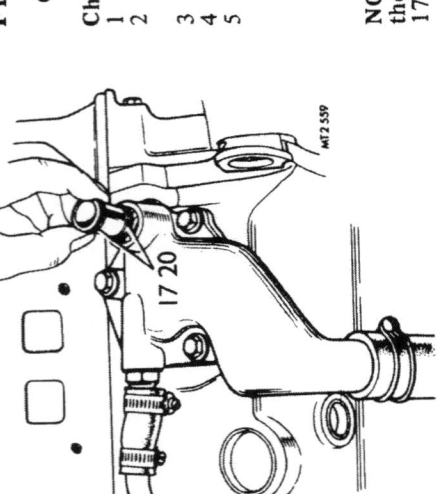

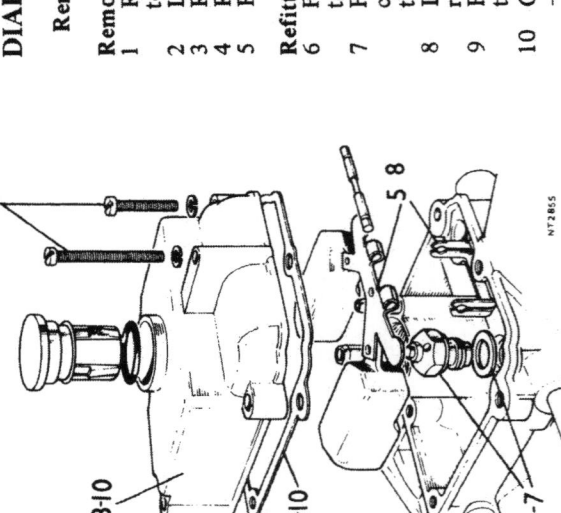

FLOAT CHAMBER LEVELS 19.15.32

Check and adjust

Check
1 Remove the carburetters. 19.15.11.
2 Remove the six screws securing the float chamber to the body.
3 Remove the float chamber.
4 Remove the gasket.
5 With the carburetter in the inverted position check the distance between the gasket face on the carburetter body to the highest point of each float A.

NOTE: The height of both floats must be the same i.e. 0.625 to 0.627 in. (16 to 17 mm).

Adjust
6 Bend the tab that contacts the needle valve but ensure that it sits at right angles to the valve to prevent the possibility of sticking.
7 Fit a new gasket and reverse instructions 1 to 3.

DIAPHRAGM 19.15.35

Remove and refit

Removing
1 Remove the four screws securing the top cover to the carburetter body.
2 Lift off the top cover.
3 Remove the diaphragm spring.
4 Remove the diaphragm retaining plate.
5 Remove the diaphragm.

Refitting
6 Fit the diaphragm, locating the inner tag in the air valve recess.
7 Fit the retaining plate and ensure the correct diaphragm seating and tighten the screws.
8 Locate the diaphragm outer tag in the recess in the carburetter body.
9 Fit the top cover and evenly tighten the screws.
10 Check and if necessary top up damper — see special instructions in 'MAINTENANCE'.

---

sctions 32 and 33 should owed if a moulded type conve is fitted.

move the thermostat housing and ermostat and push the connecting tube fully home.
33 Refit the thermostat and housing using a new gasket.
34 Reconnect the top water hoses.
35 Refit the fresh air duct. 80.15.31.
36 Refill the cooling system. 26.10.01.
37 Reconnect the battery.
38 Run the engine and check for coolant leaks.

CARBURETTER RUBBER MOUNTINGS 19.15.19

Remove and refit

This operation is included in Operation 19.15.11

FLOAT CHAMBER NEEDLE VALVE 19.15.24

Remove and refit

Removing
1 Remove the carburetters. 19.15.11.
or
2 Remove the six screws securing the float chamber to the body.
3 Remove the float chamber.
4 Remove the gasket.
5 Remove the float assembly by gently prising the spindle from the locating clips.
6 Remove the needle valve and washer.

Refitting
7 Fit the needle valve and renew the washer.
8 Fit the float assembly.
9 Check and if necessary, adjust the height of both floats. Instruction 5. 19.15.32.
10 Renew the gasket and refit the float chamber.
11 Refit the carburetters.

153

AUTOMATIC CHOKE (Fully Automatic Starter Device)

Remove and refit   19.15.38

CAUTION: The automatic choke must be renewed as a complete unit.

Removing
1 Remove the air cleaner. 19.10.01.
2 Slacken the clip securing the auto-choke fuel mixture outlet pipe hose, to the inlet manifold.
3 Disconnect the lead from the auto-choke heater.
4 Remove the carburetters. 19.15.11.

NOTE: The automatic choke is fitted to the front carburetter only.

5 Remove the 3 setscrews securing the auto-choke to the carburetter.
6 Remove the gasket and auto-choke assembly.

Refitting
7 Reverse instructions 1 to 6.

STARTER ASSEMBLY — Canadian Specification Vehicles

Remove and refit   19.15.52

CAUTION: This component must only be renewed as a complete unit.

Removing
1 Remove the fresh air duct. 80.15.31.
2 Remove the air cleaner. 19.15.01.
3 Disconnect the mixture control cable (depending upon whether it is the front or rear carburetter).
4 Remove the two screws securing the starter assembly to the carburetter body.
5 Remove the exhaust gas recirculation control valve (rear carburetter only).
6 Withdraw the starter assembly.

Refitting
7 Clean the carburetter and starter mating faces.
8 Reverse instructions 1 to 6.

TEMPERATURE COMPENSATOR

Remove and refit   19.15.59

CAUTION: This component must only be renewed as a complete new unit.

Removing
1 Remove the air cleaner assembly. 19.10.01.
2 Remove the two screws and shakeproof washers securing the temperature compensator to the carburetter.
3 Withdraw the compensator complete.
4 Remove and discard the outer rubber washer.
5 Remove the inner rubber washer from the carburetter body and discard.

Refitting
6 Clean the carburetter and temperature compensator mating faces.
7 Insert a new inner rubber washer into the bore in the carburetter body.
8 Fit a new outer rubber washer.
9 Fit the compensator to the carburetter and secure with the two screws and shakeproof washers.
10 Refit the air cleaner.

DECELERATION AND BY-PASS VALVE

Remove and refit   19.15.64

CAUTION: This component must only be renewed as a complete unit.

Removing
1 Remove the carburetters. 19.15.11.
2 Remove the two cheese headed screws and the single countersunk slotted screw (not cross slotted) securing the by-pass valve assembly to the carburetter.
3 Withdraw the valve assembly complete.
4 Remove the gasket.

Refitting
5 Clean the carburetter and valve assembly mating faces.
6 Using a new gasket fit the assembly to the carburetter with the three screws and washers.
7 Refit the carburetters to the engine — less the air cleaner and fresh air duct.
8 Check and if necessary adjust the deceleration and by-pass valves — 19.15.02 instructions 40 to 52.

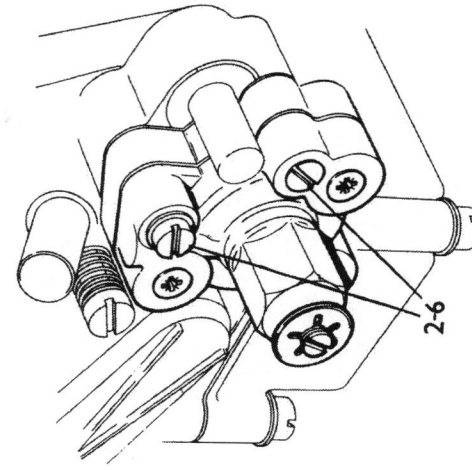

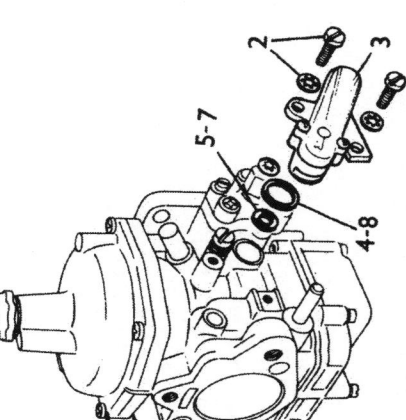

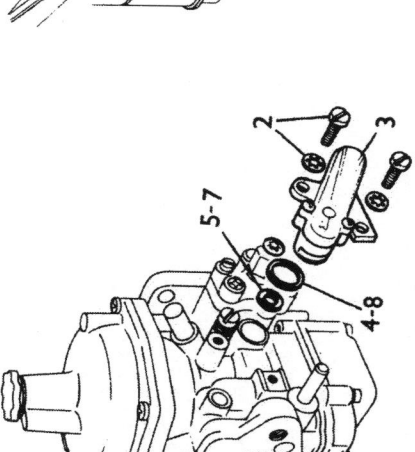

THROTTLE PEDAL ASSEMBLY

Remove and refit   19.20.01

Removing

1 Disconnect the battery.
2 Working from inside the car remove the spring clip securing the throttle cable.
3 Remove the cable from the pedal.
4 Open the bonnet and remove the two bolts securing the pedal assembly to the bulkhead.
5 Remove the pedal assembly from the car.
6 Strip the pedal assembly, and discard worn parts.

Refitting

7 Locate the spring in the bracket.
8 Fit the pedal to the bracket.
9 Insert the clevis pin.
10 Fit the anti-rattle washer.
11 Fit the washers (plain).
12 Secure the assembly with a new split pin.
13 Fit the pedal to the bulkhead and secure with the two bolts.
14 Fit the cable to the pedal and retain with the spring clip.
15 Re-connect the battery.

PETROL PIPE – MAIN LINE – TANK END SECTION

Remove and refit   19.40.02

Removing

1 Drive the car on to a ramp and raise.
2 Drain the petrol tank.
3 Pull off the rubber connection between the tank and main line pipe.
4 Release the tank-end section from the engine-end section at the union (right-hand rear wing).
5 Release the pipe from the retaining clips and remove from the car.

Refitting

6 Clip the pipe into position.
7 Connect the pipe to the engine-end section at the union.
8 Connect the pipe to the tank with the rubber connector.
9 Lower the ramp and refill the tank.

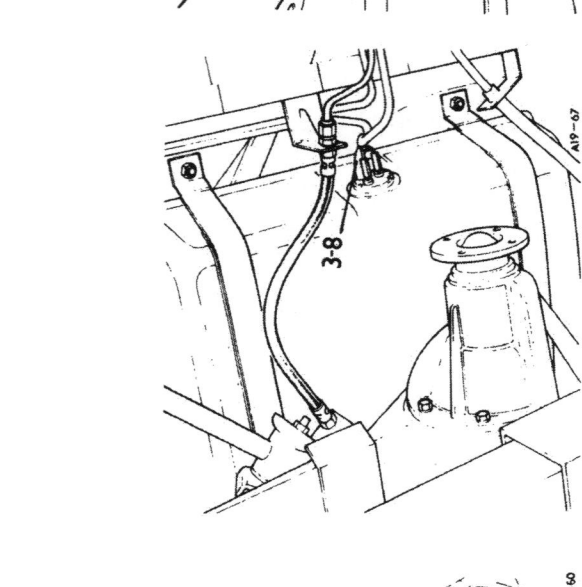

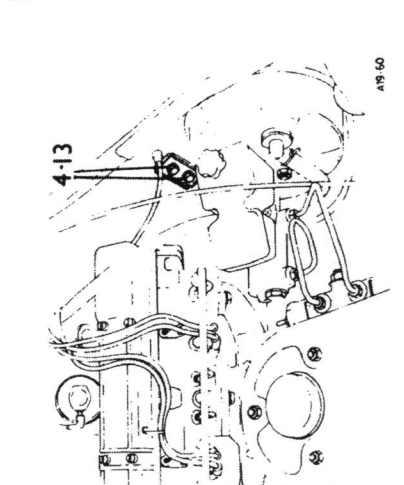

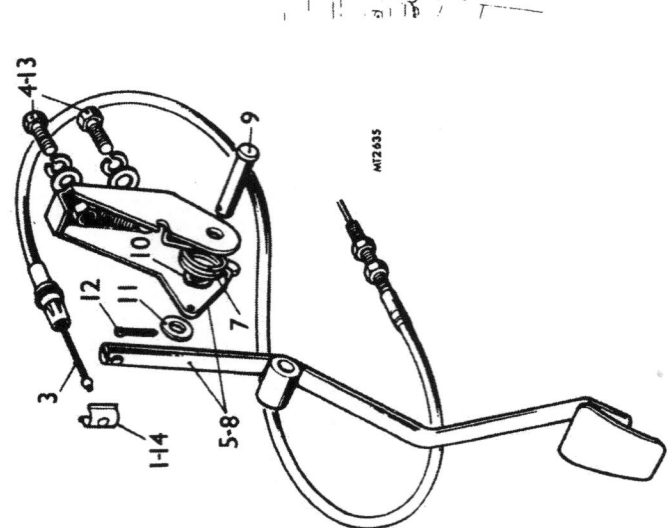

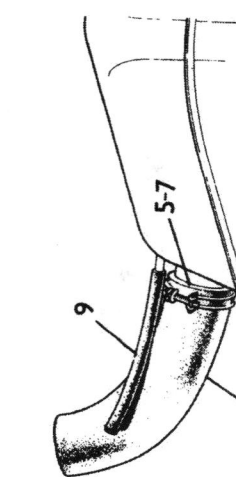
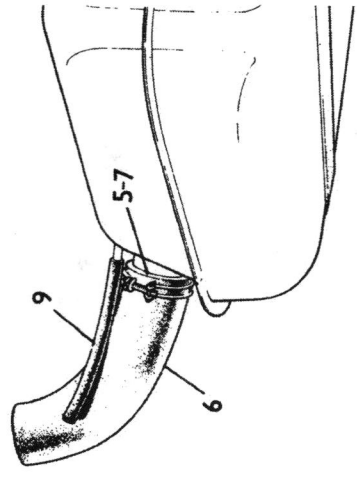

PETROL PIPE – MAIN LINE – ENGINE END SECTION

– Remove and refit   **19.40.04**

Removing

1 Drive the car onto a ramp.
2 Raise the ramp and drain the petrol tank.
3 Disconnect the engine-end section from the petrol tank-end section at the union (right-hand wing).
4 Pull off the rubber hose connecting the engine-end section to the fuel pump.
5 Remove the pipe from the retaining clips.

Refitting

6 Reverse instructions 3 to 5.
7 Start the engine and check for leaks.
8 Stop the engine and lower the ramp.

HOSE – FILLER TO TANK

– Remove and refit   **19.40.19**

Removing

1 Open the boot and remove the access panel.
2 Remove the filler cap assembly. 19.55.08.
3 Remove the hoses from the vapour separator.
4 Remove the vapour separator by pulling it laterally from its retaining clip.
5 Release the hose clip securing the filler hose to the fuel tank, visible through the access aperture.
6 Pull off the filler hose.

Refitting

7 Fit the filler hose to the tank and secure with the hose clip.
8 Fit the vapour separator by pushing it laterally into its retaining clip.
9 Fit the tank breather hose to the vapour separator L.H. connection.
10 Fit the hose to the adsorption canister pipe run to the R.H. connection on the vapour separator.
11 Fit the fuel filler cap assembly – instructions 7 to 10. 19.55.08.
12 Fit the access panel.

FUEL PUMP

Clean filter   19.45.05

1 Remove the fresh air duct. 80.15.31.
2 Remove pump cover retaining screw.
3 Lift off the cover.
4 Lift out the filter.
5 Clean sediment from the filter and cover.
6 Refit the cover renewing, if necessary the rubber seal.
7 Secure the cover with the retaining screw and fit, if necessary, a new fibre washer under the screw head.
8 Refit the fresh air duct.

FUEL PUMP

Remove and refit   19.45.08

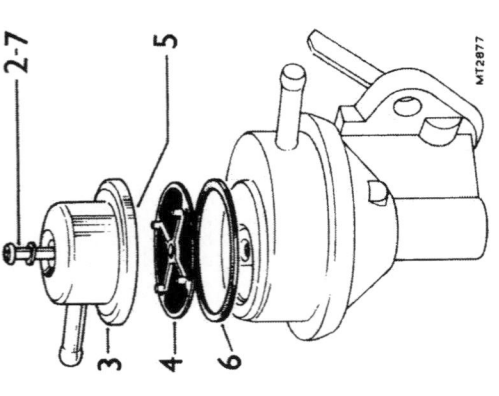

Removing

1 Remove the fresh air duct. 80.15.31.
2 Remove the inlet hose to the pump.
3 Remove the outlet hose from the pump.
4 Remove the two fuel pump retaining bolts and plain washers.
5 Withdraw the pump complete with gasket.

Refitting

6 Reverse instructions 1 to 5 ensuring that when fitting, the pump actuating lever rides on top of the jackshaft cam.

FUEL TANK

Remove and refit   19.55.01

Removing

1 Drive the car onto a ramp and disconnect the battery.
2 Remove the fuel filler cap assembly. 19.55.08.
3 Disconnect the pipe from the tank to the vapour separator.
4 Raise the ramp and drain the fuel tank.
5 Support the body with jacks both sides of the car forward of the trailing arm attachment points.
6 Disconnect the dampers at their lower attachment to the axle.
7 Disconnect the tank unit electrical leads.
8 Pull off the rubber connection to the main fuel line.
9 Disconnect the R.H. radius rod from the body bracket.
10 Remove the L.H. radius rod from the car.
11 Jack up the body sufficiently to remove both road springs.

CAUTION: Care must be taken to ensure that whilst jacking up the body the brake hydraulic system jump hose is not stretched—shown arrowed.

12 Remove the L.H. rear road wheel and allow the axle to drop having regard for the above cautionary note.
13 Support the axle with a jack to relieve any tension in the hydraulic jump hose.
14 Remove the tail pipe and silencer assembly. 30.10.22.
15 Remove the L.H. bump stop.
16 Remove the four nuts and tank retaining straps.
17 Withdraw the tank from the L.H. side of the car.
18 Remove the filler hose.
19 Remove the breather hose.
20 Remove the tank unit – 88.25.32 instructions 6 to 8.

NOTE: Instructions 18 to 20 are only necessary if the tank is to be renewed.

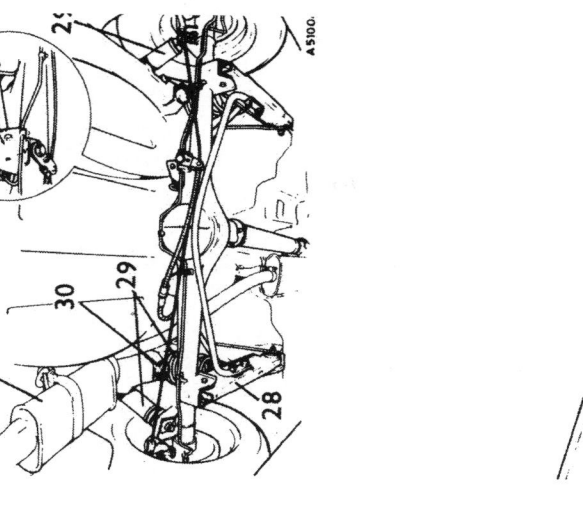

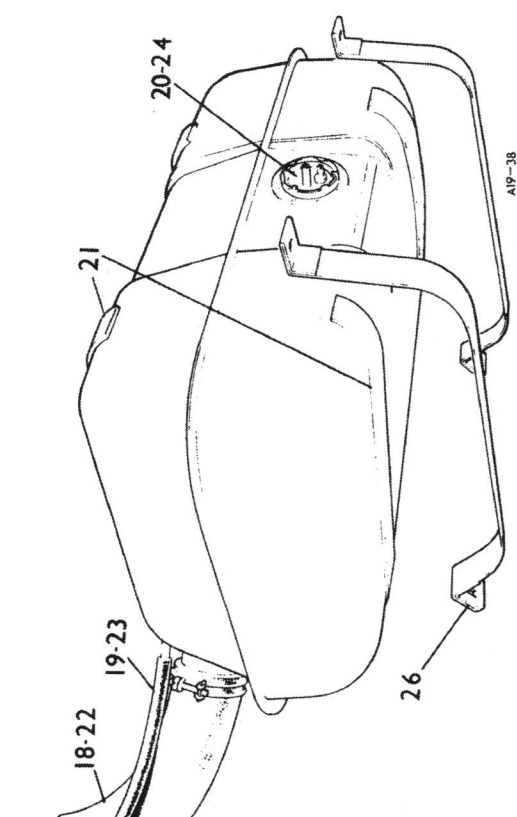

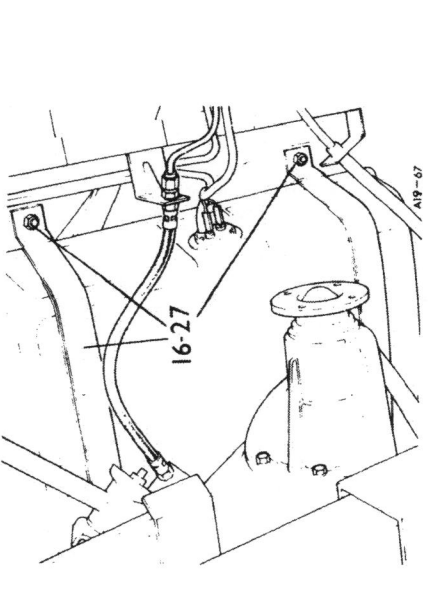

Refitting

NOTE: If the tank is not being renewed ignore instructions 19 to 22. However, renew all hoses if any deterioration exists.

21 Using adhesive fit new cushion strips to the tank noting that thicker strips are fitted to the top of the tank.

22 Fit the filler hose.

23 Fit the breather hose.

24 Fit the tank unit – reversing instructions 6 to 8. 88.25.32.

25 Manoeuvre the tank into position from the L.H. side of the car.

26 Fit the supporting straps noting that the elongated holes in the straps are fitted to the rear studs in the body.

27 Fit and tighten the four retaining nuts.

28 Fit the L.H. radius rod to the axle – including the handbrake cable bracket – leaving the body-end free for the time being.

29 Fit the springs and jack-up the axle both sides and connect the dampers to their axle locations.

30 Fit the L.H. bump stop.

31 Fit the L.H. and R.H. radius rods to their body locations.

32 Fit the tail pipe and silencer assembly. 30.10.22.

33 Fit the L.H. rear road wheel.

34 Lower and remove the body and axle jacks.

35 Connect the fuel tank to the main line pipe with the rubber connector.

36 Fit the electrical leads to the tank unit – instruction 10. 88.25.32.

37 Fit the breather pipe from the tank to the L.H. connection on the vapour separator.

38 Lower the ramp and fit the fuel filler assembly. 19.55.08 instructions 7 to 10.

39 Fit the access panel.

40 Refill the fuel tank, connect the battery, start the engine and check for leaks.

FUEL FILLER CAP AND FILLER ASSEMBLY

Remove and refit   19.55.08

Removing

1   Turn the fuel filler cap anti-clockwise and withdraw.
2   Remove the three screws securing the filler tube assembly to the body.
3   Open the boot and remove the access panel – four screws.
4   Slacken the top hose clip.
5   Withdraw the filler tube.
6   Remove the finisher.

Refitting

7   Place the finisher in position.
8   Insert the filler tube into the filler hose and secure with the three screws.
9   Refit the filler cap.
10 Tighten the filler hose top clip.
11 Refit the access panel and close the boot.

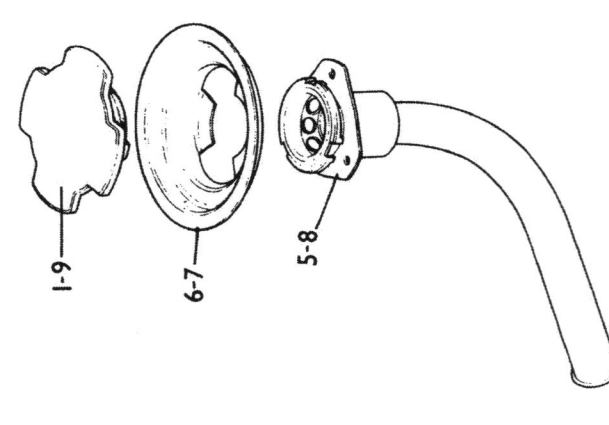

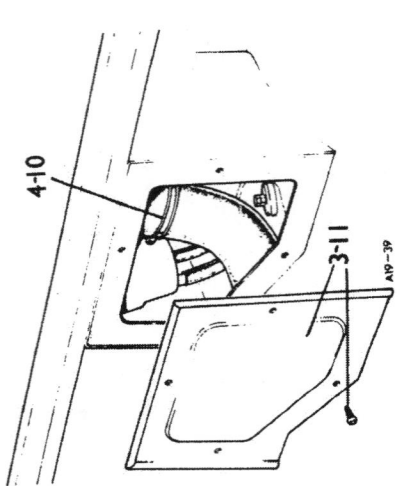

2-8

1-9

6-7

5-8

4-10

3-11

ELECTRONIC FUEL INJECTION SYSTEM

Description

19.00.00

The electronic fuel injection system, fitted as an alternative to carburetters, comprises of two parts: a fuel injection system and an electronic control for the fuel injection system.

Fuel injection system components

Fuel is drawn from a tank at the rear of the vehicle and pressurized to approximately 36 lbf/in² (2.5 kgf/cm²) by an electric fuel pump located beneath the car floor. The fuel pump will only operate when the ignition and/or the starter motor circuits are energized. From this pump fuel passes through fuel filters located beneath the car floor to a pressure regulator, the spring chamber of which is connected to the engine intake manifold. As a result, the difference between the intake manifold pressure and the fuel pressure is held constant, excess fuel being returned to the fuel tank via an anti-surge pot.

A fuel rail links the pressure regulator with the fuel injectors, one injector being fitted to each inlet manifold spur. The injectors may be either 'open' or 'closed' and are solenoid operated. The injector solenoids are energized through a relay actuated by the ignition circuit and are pulsed to 'open' by the electronic control unit (E.C.U.) completing a circuit to 'earth'. When 'open', the injectors spray fuel into the inlet manifold to be drawn into the engine cylinders at the next induction stroke of the working cycle.

Therefore there needs to be no fixed relationship between the injector timing and the engine ignition or valve timing.

The injectors are programmed to 'open' as a bank of four, in unison, twice per engine operating cycle (two revolutions). The time that the injectors are 'open' governs the amount of fuel supplied to the engine and this 'open' time is computed by the electronic control unit from the input it receives from various sensors.

To assist cold starting, a separate cold start injector sprays a fine jet of fuel against the air stream entering the plenum chamber before fuel is added to it by the main injectors. The cold start injector is energized from the engine starter motor circuit and has in series with it a thermotime switch. This switch is dual activated by engine coolant temperature (heat) and a heater coil around a bi-metal strip (time), the coil being again energized from the starter motor circuit. The purpose of the thermotime switch is to ensure that the cold start injector will not be energized when the engine is at normal operating temperature or should the starter motor be used for prolonged periods when the engine is below normal operating temperature. Thus the switch prevents extra fuel being supplied to the engine when it is not required. The switch will isolate the cold start injector after approximately 8 to 12 seconds at −20°C (−4°F) decreasing this time as the engine approaches its normal operating temperature.

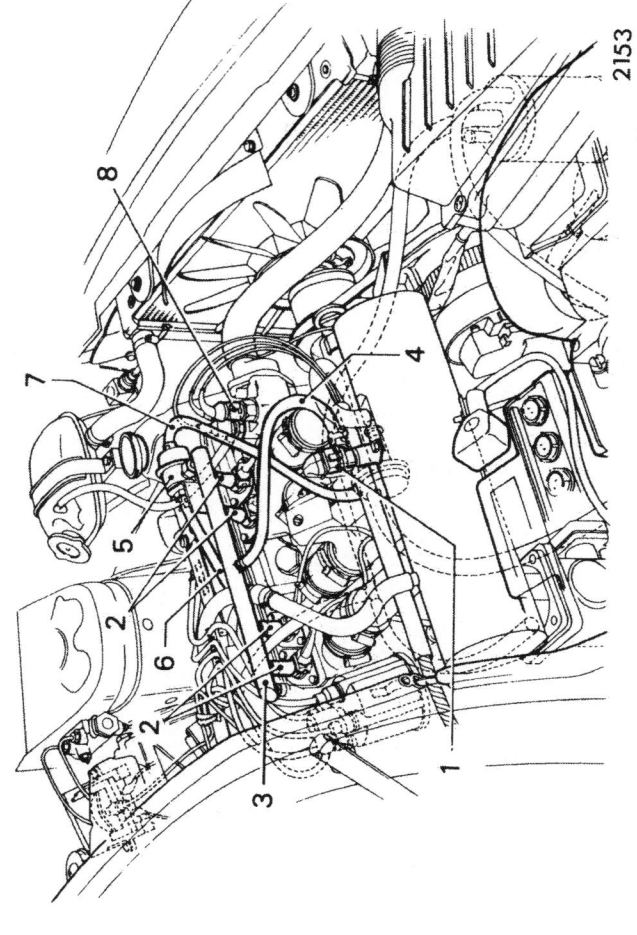

2153

Fuel injection system components

1 Cold start injector
2 Injectors
3 Fuel rail
4 Cold start injector—fuel feed pipe
5 Fuel pressure regulator
6 Return line to fuel tank
7 Pipe to plenum chamber
8 Thermotime switch

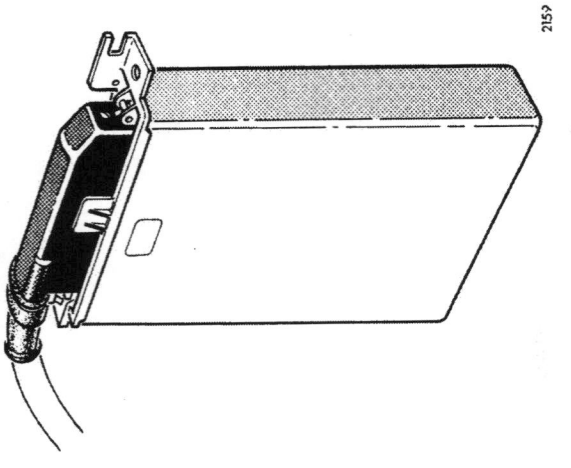

Electronic control unit

Electronic control of the fuel injection system

At the heart of the electronic control system is the electronic control unit (E.C.U.) which is a box approximately $9 \times 7 \times 2$ inches ($23 \times 18 \times 5$ cm) located under the glove box. The E.C.U. receives input signals from various sensors and computes from these an output signal to the fuel injector solenoid circuits. When activated, the solenoids 'open' the injectors to spray fuel into the engine inlet manifold, the injectors remaining open for between 1.5 and 10 milliseconds depending upon engine running conditions.

The electronic control unit is sealed; it requires no maintenance and should not be opened or tampered with.

Engine speed

This input is very simply obtained by taking a tapping from the ignition coil low tension circuit output (–ive). Thus the ignition low tension circuit pulses are passed to the E.C.U. to be computed into an engine speed input.

Electric fuel pump operation

The fuel pump is energized independently of the electronic control unit, from an output terminal on the combined relay. The combined relay is the component that provides an interface between the main vehicle electrical harness and those items that are specifically related to the electronic fuel injection system. An inertia switch is included in the circuit to isolate the fuel pump and prevent it from operating in the event of an impact-type accident. The circuit is also routed through the electronic control system air-flow meter where a simple contact switch ensures that the fuel pump cannot operate when no air is flowing into the engine, i.e. the engine is not running. This contact switch is by-passed when the starter motor circuit is energized.

Once the engine is running a circuit from the ignition switch passes through a relay to 'earth', via the electronic control unit. When energized, this relay permits a circuit to be made to the air-flow meter contact switch. Providing the contact switch is closed, a circuit is completed through a second relay to 'earth'. When energized this second relay completes the circuit to operate the fuel pump.

Under engine starting conditions the air-flow meter contact switch would normally isolate the fuel pump as no air is flowing into the engine. To overcome this an input is taken direct from the starter motor circuit to energize the second relay and thus permit the fuel pump to operate during the engine starting operation.

Electric fuel pump

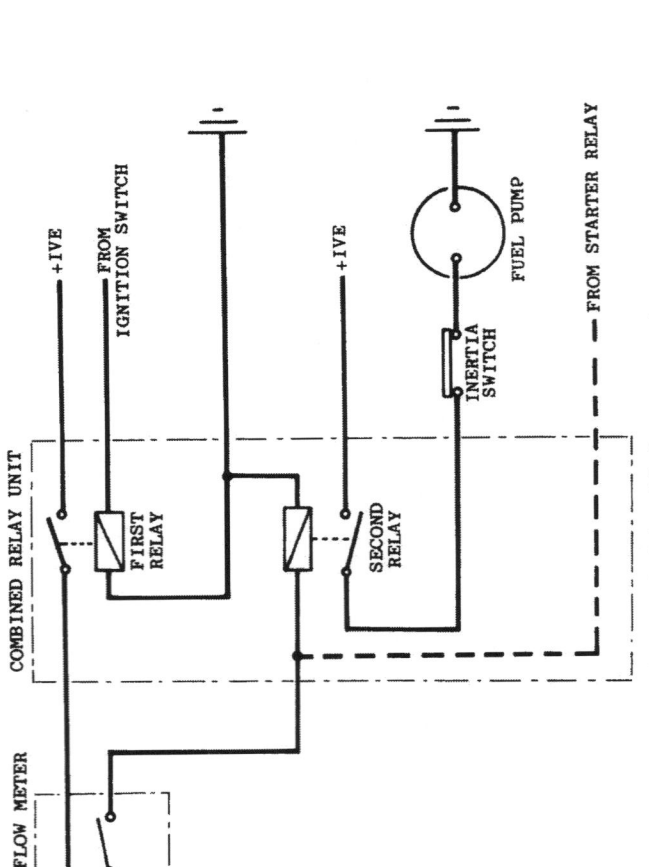

Circuit principles of fuel pump operation

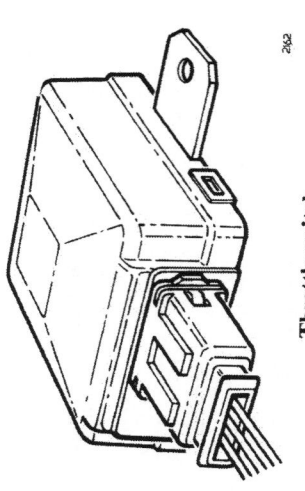

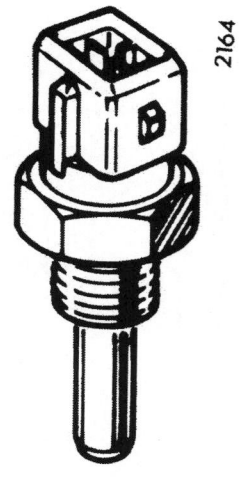

Throttle switch

Coolant temperature sensor

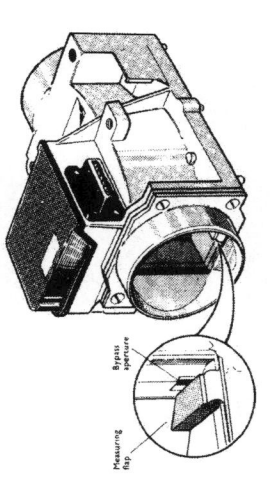

Air-flow meter

Schematic view of air-flow meter

Air outlet
Compensating flap
Adjustment screw
Spiral spring
Idle air bypass
Pump switch
Measuring flap
Potentiometer
Air temperature sensor
Air inlet

Air-flow meter

To measure the air-flow into the engine an air-flow meter is fitted in the engine compartment between the air cleaner and a plenum chamber above the engine. The plenum chamber acts as a collecting box for the ingoing air and helps to smooth out any rapid fluctuations in air-flow that might upset the air-flow meter signals.

The air-flow meter itself is basically a short tube in which there is a pivoted measuring flap that is moved by air flowing past it into the engine. To reduce excessive fluttering of this flap, such as would be caused by sudden changes or pulses in the air-flow, a compensating flap is fitted as part of the same casting as the measuring flap. The position of the measuring flap is controlled by the air drawn into the engine and the action of a coil return spring. The mass of air drawn into the engine at any time is indicative of the engine load and a signal, proportional to the flap position, is passed to the E.C.U.

However, the air mass is related to air density which in turn is dependent upon air temperature. Therefore an **air temperature sensor** is incorporated into the air-flow meter and this sends a separate electrical signal to the E.C.U.

Due to the action of the coil return spring, the air-flow meter measuring flap is almost closed when the engine is idling and an idle air by-pass channel is provided to assist the engine to breathe at this low speed. Air passing through the by-pass channel is not registered by the air-flow meter measuring flap. An adjustment screw is fitted into the by-pass channel to regulate the air-flow, thus providing some adjustment for the engine slow running speed, and in particular to the air/fuel ratio, and hence the exhaust gas CO level at idle speed. This adjustment screw is normally sealed by a coloured plug in the screw recess and adjustment of the screw settings and resealing is subject to normal legislative requirements.

Throttle switch

A throttle switch forms part of the electronic control for the fuel injection system and provides the E.C.U. with information on throttle operating conditions.

This switch is of the contact type and is located on the throttle body in the engine compartment. The switch contacts close when the accelerator pedal is fully depressed, signalling to the E.C.U. to lengthen the time that the main injectors are 'open', thus supplying extra fuel for the acceleration required.

Coolant temperature sensor

This sensor is located at the side of the engine and provides coolant temperature information to the E.C.U. The signal from the sensor serves two purposes. First, it causes the E.C.U. to slightly lengthen the time that the main injectors are 'open', reducing this time as the engine warms up and cutting it off when normal engine operating temperature is reached. Second, it completes an 'earth' return circuit in the E.C.U. for the heater element in the extra air valve when the engine is running below normal operating temperature. In practice the sensor functions by modifying an output voltage from the E.C.U. through an 'earth' return circuit.

Extra air valve

This valve is mounted above a water passage in the inlet manifold and registers the same temperature as the engine coolant. Its purpose is to provide the additional air required to maintain satisfactory engine idle speed until the engine reaches normal operating temperature. This air is taken from a point before the throttle butterfly (but after the air-flow meter, so that the air is registered by the E.C.U.) and returned to the plenum chamber after the throttle butterfly.

To allow air to pass through the valve, and thus by-pass the throttle butterfly, an opening in a rotatable metal disc is aligned with the inlet and outlet tubes on the valve. The position of this disc is controlled by a bi-metal strip which deflects according to the temperature it experiences. As the bi-metal strip heats up it rotates the metal until its opening no longer lines up with the air valve tubes and the extra air source is reduced and finally terminated as normal engine operating temperature is reached. The bi-metal strip is heated from two sources, the coolant temperature and a heater coil around the strip. The heater coil is energized from the ignition circuit and comes into operation whenever the coolant temperature sensor causes the E.C.U. to complete the heater coil circuit to 'earth'.

Over-run valve

This second air-flow control device bleeds air into the engine inlet manifold, via the plenum chamber, when the manifold depression is high and thus maintains combustion during engine over-run.

The valve operates independently of the electronic control system and is incorporated in the throttle butterfly connecting the constant depression region between the throttle and the air-flow meter measuring flap.

Lambda sensor

A single sensor is located in the exhaust system near to the catalyst and, like the catalyst, requires only UNLEADED fuel to be used to prevent damage to it.

The internal working surfaces of the sensor are coated with a thin platinum layer which is permeable to gas. A special ceramic layer protects the electrodes against corrosion and this becomes conductive to oxygen atoms at about 600°C (1112°F). If the concentration of oxygen inside the sensor (from the exhaust gases) differs from that outside the sensor (atmosphere) a voltage is developed between the two surfaces that changes when the outer electrode has catalytic activity. This voltage is passed to the E.C.U. which compares it against a reference voltage for ideal combustion and adjusts the main injector 'open' time accordingly to permit more or less fuel to be used by the engine. More fuel will use up the excess oxygen in the exhaust gas, less fuel will allow more oxygen, and so the ideal oxygen content is supplied to permit the catalyst to operate at its best efficiency.

By using Lambda Sensors to monitor the exhaust gases in this way a feed back 'closed loop' type of control system can be introduced for the fuel injection operation. Should for any reason the Lambda Sensors become inoperative or be disconnected the electronic control system will continue to function as an 'open loop' system without the fine tuning effect of the sensors.

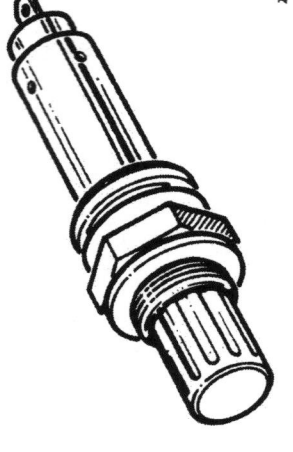

2166

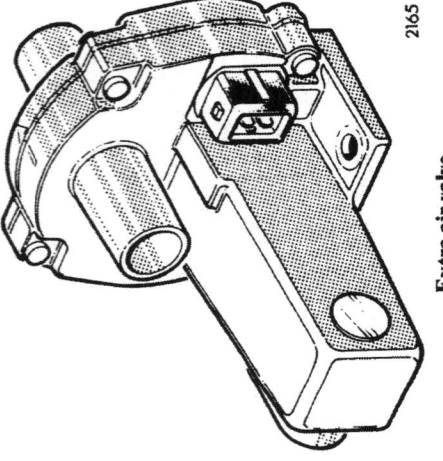

2165

Extra air valve

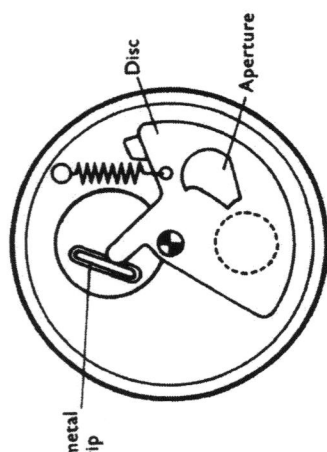

(i) By-pass channel closed

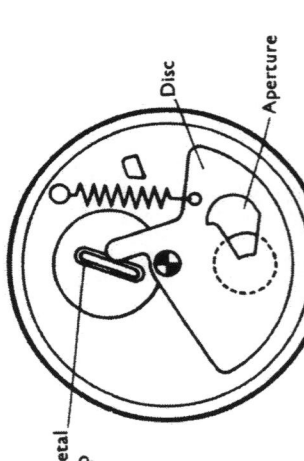

(ii) By-pass channel partly open

Extra air valve operation

Lambda (oxygen) sensor

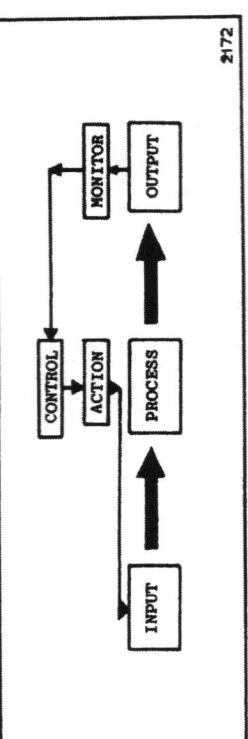

2172

The general 'closed loop' feed back control system

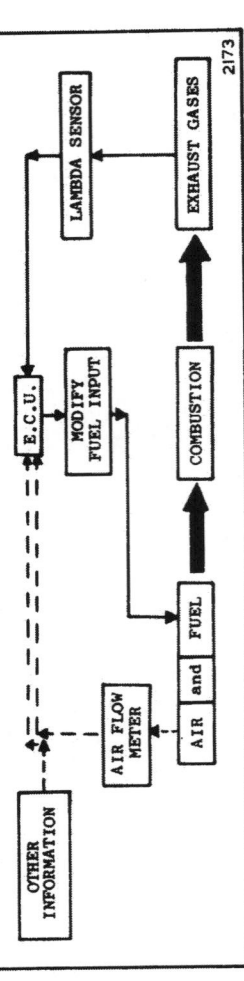

2173

Electronic fuel injection 'closed loop' feed back control system

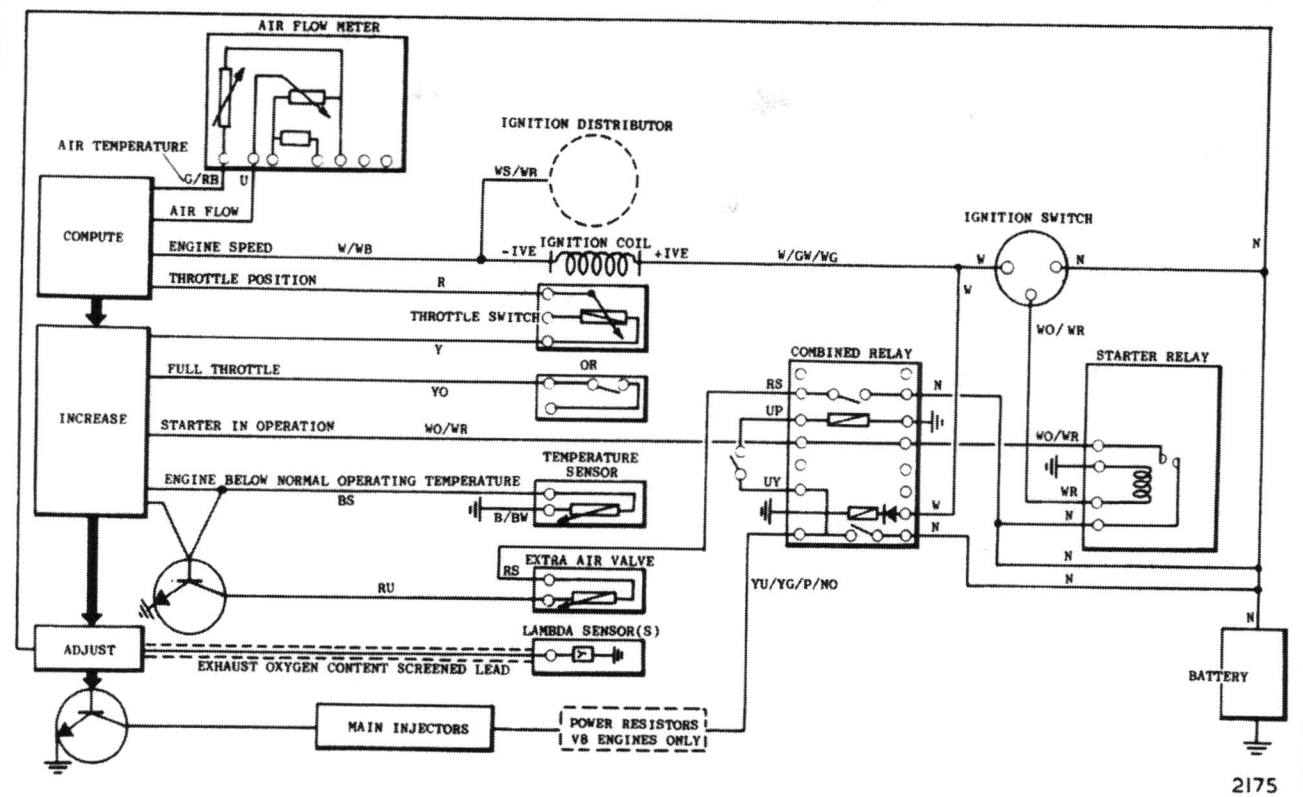

Schematic wiring diagram of electronic fuel injection system components

2175

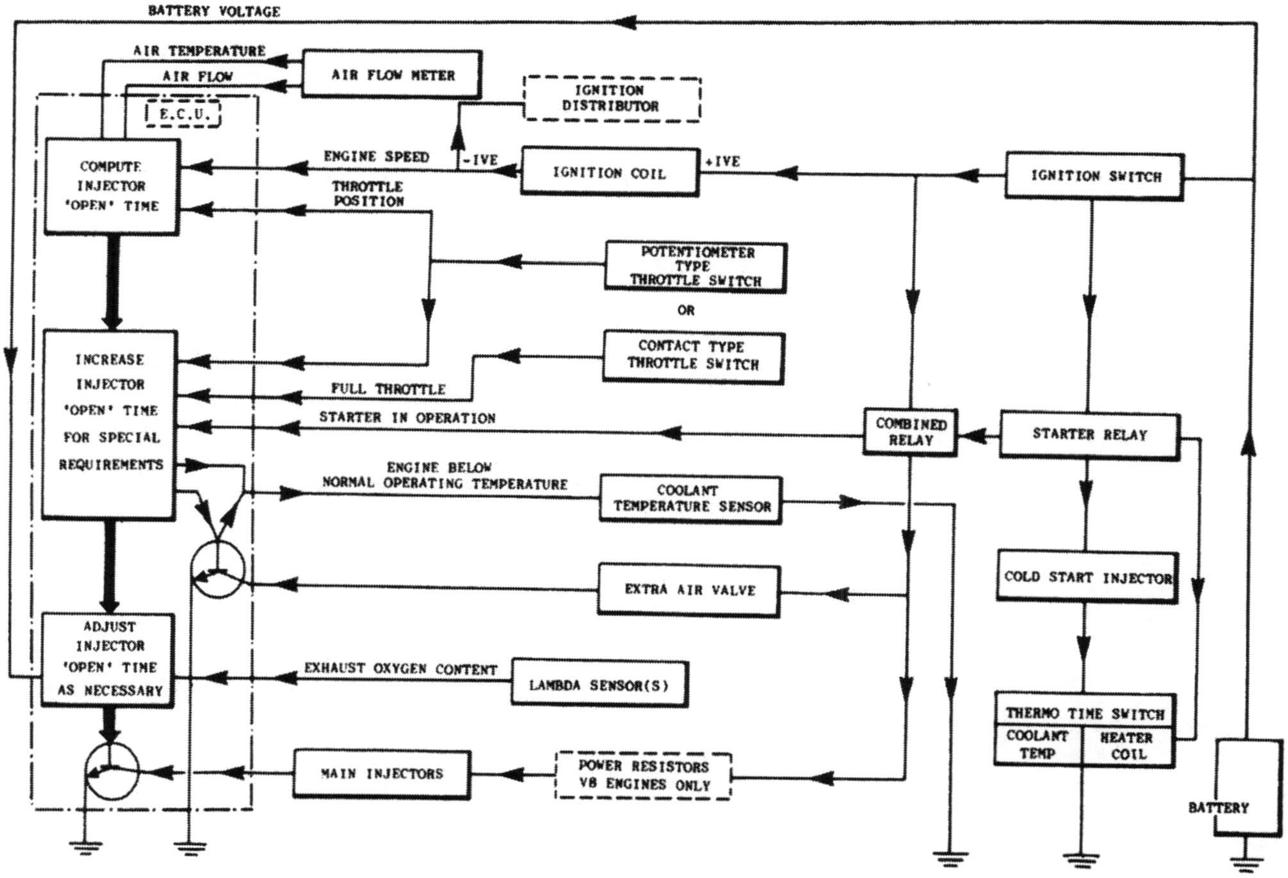

Function diagram of electronic fuel injection system components

2141

THROTTLE PEDAL ASSEMBLY   19.20.01

Remove and refit

Removing

1   Disconnect the battery.
2   Working from inside the car remove the spring clip securing the throttle cable.
3   Remove the cable from the pedal.
4   Open the bonnet and remove the two bolts securing the pedal assembly to the bulkhead.
5   Remove the pedal assembly from the car.
6   Strip the pedal assembly, and discard worn parts.

Refitting

7   Locate the spring in the bracket.
8   Fit the pedal to the bracket.
9   Insert the clevis pin.
10   Fit the anti-rattle washer.
11   Fit the washers (plain).
12   Secure the assembly with a new split pin.
13   Fit the pedal to the bulkhead and secure with the two bolts.
14   Fit the cable to the pedal and retain with the spring clip.
15   Reconnect the battery.

THROTTLE CABLE   19.20.06

Remove and refit

Removing

1   Remove the plenum chamber for access.
2   Release the outer cable from the throttle body bracket.
3   Release the inner cable from the throttle body bracket.
4   From inside the car remove the clip and disconnect the inner cable from the accelerator pedal.
5   Remove the cable into the engine compartment.

Refitting

6   Reverse instructions 1 to 5.

AIR CLEANER   19.10.01

Remove and refit

Removing

1   Locate the air cleaner at the front right-hand side of the engine compartment forward of the front suspension turret.
2   Remove the air cleaner element.
3   Disconnect the air cleaner case from the air-flow meter.
4.   Remove four bolts connecting the case to the body and lift off the case.

Refitting

5   Reverse instructions 1 to 4.

AIR CLEANER   19.10.08

Renew element

1   Remove the air intake pipe from the air cleaner case.
2   Remove eight screws to release the two halves of the air cleaner case.
3   Carefully lift off the top half of the case to expose the element.
4   Remove and discard the element, noting its position for refitting.
5   Clean the interior of the air cleaner case and fit a new element.
6   Reverse instructions 1 to 3.

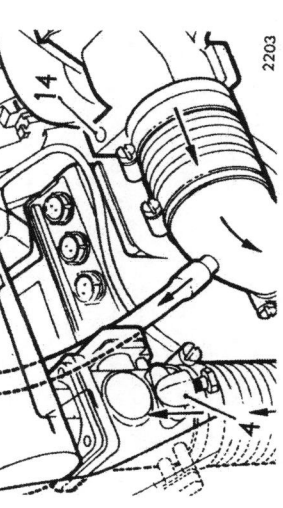
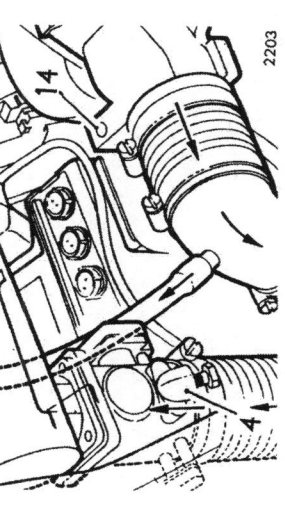

2283

EXTRA AIR VALVE

Remove and refit　　　　19.20.16

CAUTION: This operation should only be completed on a cold or cool engine.

Removing
1　Remove the plenum chamber for access.
2　Disconnect the electrical multi-pin plug from the valve.
3　Disconnect two air hoses from the valve.
4　Remove two mounting bolts securing the valve to the inlet manifold.
5　Lift off the valve.

Refitting
6　Clean the mating faces on the valve and manifold.
7　Reverse instructions 1 to 5.

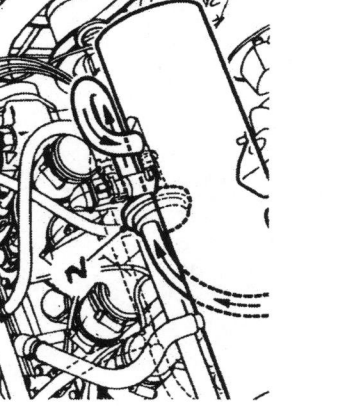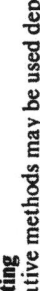

2202

EXTRA AIR VALVE

Test　　　　19.20.17

1　Remove the electrical connector from the valve.
2　Connect a voltmeter across the terminals of the connector.
3　Crank the engine over; battery voltage should be obtained. If there is no voltage there is a fault in the electrical system and the wires should be checked for leakage and deterioration. When it has been established that power is reaching the valve, the heating coils resistance should be checked.
4　Connect an ohmmeter between the terminals of the air valve. A resistance of 33 ohms should be obtained. If there is no resistance, the valve should be replaced.

Idle fuel setting

Two alternative methods may be used depending on the equipment available.

Approved type exhaust gas analyser
5　Insert analyser probe into exhaust pipe.
6　Check analyser CO reading which must not exceed that given in Section 05, Engine Tuning Data.
7　If adjustment is necessary follow instructions 13 to 15 below.
8　Remove analyser probe.

Approved type fuel setting indicator
9　Connect the instrument to the fuel setting diagnostic connector, located behind the right-hand glove box.
10　Check the instrument reading which, if correct, will show lamp No. 2 in rows A or B alight.
11　If adjustment is necessary follow instructions 13 to 15 below.
12　Disconnect the instrument.

Idle fuel setting adjustment
13　Remove the blanking plug from the air flow meter to expose the recessed adjustment screw.
14　Turn the adjustment screw until the required reading is obtained.
15　Reseal the adjustment screw as required by local territory legislation.

2203

IDLE SPEED

Adjust　　　　19.20.18

1　Run the engine until it has been working at normal operating temperature for at least two minutes.
NOTE: Before, and every three minutes during, the fuel setting procedure below the engine should be given a clear outburst by running it at approximately 2000 rev/min on light load for a minimum of 30 seconds to maintain normal operating temperature.
2　Ensure that the engine ignition timing is correct (refer to Section 05, Engine Tuning Data) and that the throttle linkage is correctly set.

Idle speed
3　Using a separate proprietary tachometer, connected following the manufacturer's instructions, or if necessary the vehicle fitted tachometer, check the engine idle speed; refer to Section 05, Engine Tuning Data.
4　If adjustment is necessary, slacken the locknut and turn the idle adjustment bolt (clockwise to decrease speed, anti-clockwise to increase speed). Retighten the locknut.

LAMBDA (OXYGEN) SENSOR

Remove and refit   19.22.16

Removing
1 Disconnect the electrical lead from the
   sensor.
2 Unscrew the sensor from the exhaust pipe,
   taking care not to strain the exhaust
   system.

Refitting
3 Lubricate the threads of the sensor and fit
   it to the exhaust pipe.
4 Reconnect the electrical leads to the
   sensor.
5 Reset the service interval counter, using
   the special service tool key.

COOLANT TEMPERATURE SENSOR

Remove and refit   19.22.18

Removing
CAUTION: Before commencing this procedure ensure that the cooling system is depressurized. Remove the cooling system header
tank filler cap taking care to avoid scalding;
refer to Section 26, Cooling System.

1 Locate the sensor, referring to the illustration and the vehicle wiring diagram.
2 Disconnect the electrical leads from the
   sensor.
3 Unscrew the sensor from the engine.

Refitting
4 Reverse instructions 2 and 3, ensuring
   that the sensor is sufficiently tightened to
   prevent water leaks without over straining
   the threads.
5 Check/top-up the cooling system water
   level.

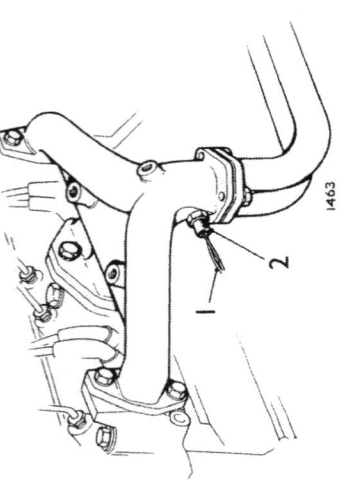

COOLANT TEMPERATURE SENSOR

Test   19.22.19

1 Disconnect battery.
2 Pull connector from temperature sensor.
3 Connect suitable ohmmeter between terminals; note resistance reading. The reading is subject to change according to
   temperature, and should closely approximate to the relevant resistance value given
   in the table.
4 Disconnect ohmmeter.
5 Check resistance between each terminal
   in turn and body of sensor. A very high
   resistance reading (open circuit) must be
   obtained.
6 Re-connect cable.
7 Re-connect battery.

Coolant Temperature (°C)	Resistance (kilohms)
−10	9.2
0	5.9
+20	2.5
+40	1.18
+60	0.60
+80	0.325

THERMOTIME SWITCH

Remove and refit   19.22.20

Removing
CAUTION: Before commencing this procedure ensure that the cooling system is depressurized. Remove the cooling system header
tank filler cap taking care to avoid scalding;
refer to Section 26, Cooling System.

1 Locate the switch, referring to the illustration and the vehicle wiring diagram.
2 Disconnect the electrical leads from the
   switch.
3 Unscrew the switch from the engine.

Refitting
4 Reverse instructions 2 and 3, ensuring
   that the switch is sufficiently tightened to
   prevent water leaks without over-strain-
   ing the threads.
5 Check/top-up the cooling system water
   level.

THERMOTIME SWITCH

Test   19.22.21

Equipment required: Stop watch, ohmmeter,
single-pole switch, jump lead for connecting
switch to battery and Thermotime switch, and
a thermometer.
NOTE: Check coolant temperature with thermometer and note reading before carrying out
procedures detailed below. Check rated value
of Thermotime switch (stamped on body flat).

1 Disconnect battery earth lead.
2 Pull electrical connector from Thermotime switch.

**'A' Coolant temperature higher than switch
rated value**

3 Connect ohmmeter between terminal 'W'
   and earth. A very high resistance reading
   (open circuit) should be obtained.
4 Renew switch if a very low resistance
   reading (short circuit) is obtained.

**'B' Coolant temperature lower than switch
rated value**

5 Connect ohmmeter between terminal 'W'
   and earth. A very low resistance reading
   (closed circuit) should be obtained.
6 Connect 12V supply via isolating switch
   to terminal 'G' of Thermotime switch.
7 Using stop watch, check time delay
   between making isolating switch and
   indication on ohmmeter changing from
   low to high resistance. Delay period must
   closely approximate to time indicated in
   table, see table for specific coolant temperature (noted above).
8 Renew Thermotime switch if necessary.
9 Re-connect Thermotime switch.
10 Re-connect battery earth lead.

Coolant Temperature	Delay
−20°C	8 sec.
0°C	4½ sec.
+10°C	3½ sec.
+35°C	0

AIR TEMPERATURE SENSOR

Remove and refit   19.22.22

The air temperature sensor is integral with the air-flow meter and as such cannot be replaced as a separate item.

AIR TEMPERATURE SENSOR

Test   19.22.23

1 Disconnect the battery.
2 Remove the multi-pin electrical connector from air-flow meter.
3 Connect a suitable ohmmeter between terminals 6 and 27 of the air-flow meter.

Ambient Air Temperature (°C)	Resistance (kilohms)
−10	9.2
0	5.9
+20	2.5
+40	1.18
+60	0.60

4 Note the resistance reading. The reading is subject to change according to the temperature and should closely approximate to the relevant resistance value given in the table above.
5 Disconnect the ohmmeter.
6 Re-connect the multi-pin connector.
7 Re-connect the battery.

AIR-FLOW METER

Remove and refit   19.22.25

Removing
1 Remove the air cleaner for access.
2 Disconnect the air outlet pipe from the air-flow meter.
3 Disconnect the electrical multi-pin plug from the meter.
4 Remove four bolts securing the meter to the body.
5 Lift out the meter.

Refitting
6 Reverse instructions 1 to 5.

ELECTRONIC CONTROL UNIT (E.C.U.)

Remove and refit   19.22.34

Removing
1 Locate the E.C.U. below the passenger glove box inside the car and remove the cover (if fitted).
2 Peel back the passenger footwell carpet for access.
3 Disconnect the electrical multi-pin plug from the E.C.U.
4 Remove three bolts securing the E.C.U. and lower it into the footwell.

Refitting
5 Reverse instructions 1 to 4.

THROTTLE SWITCH

Remove and refit   19.22.36

Removing
1 Locate the throttle switch on the throttle bracket at the left-hand end of the plenum chamber.
2 Pull the electrical connector from the throttle switch.
3 Remove the two screws, plain and shakeproof washers securing the throttle switch and lift the switch from the spindle.

Refitting
4 Locate the switch on the spindle.
5 Secure the switch with the two screws, plain and shakeproof washers.

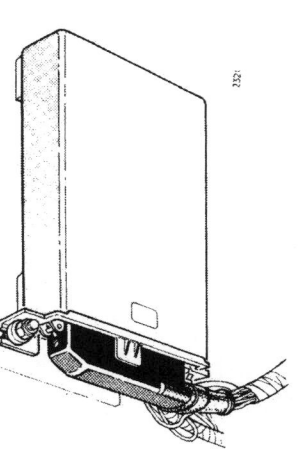

THROTTLE SWITCH

Test   19.22.37

NOTE: Before commencing the following tests ensure that the throttle linkage is correctly adjusted.

1 Disconnect the battery.
2 Remove the electrical connector from the throttle switch.
3 Connect a powered test lamp between terminals 3 and 18 of the throttle switch.
4 Open the throttle; the bulb should light up when the throttle nears the wide open position.
6 If the bulb does not light, replace the throttle switch.
7 Refit the electrical connector to the switch.
8 Re-connect the battery.

PLENUM CHAMBER

Remove and refit   **19.22.46**

Removing

NOTE: If a water-heated plenum chamber is NOT fitted, instructions 1 and 2 should be omitted.

1   Partially drain the cooling system, see 26.10.01.

2   Disconnect the water pipes from the plenum chamber.

3   Remove the battery for access.

4   Release the throttle bracket from the side of the chamber.

5   Release the engine oil dipstick tube from the plenum chamber bracket.

6   Release the interconnecting pipes from the plenum to the inlet manifold.

7   Disconnect from the plenum chamber the brake servo vacuum pipe, the extra air valve pipe, the pressure regulator vacuum pipe and the cold start injector.

8   Remove five bolts to release the chamber from the throttle housing and lift off the chamber.

Refitting

9   Reverse instructions 1 to 8.

FUEL SYSTEM

WARNING: The fuel in the system is pressurized by the fuel pump to approximately 36 lbf/in² (2.5 kgf/cm²) whilst the engine is running and experience has shown that this pressure has a very slow decay rate. Therefore it is essential to depressurize the fuel system, following the procedure under 19.50.02 before disconnecting any component in the system.

WARNING: During all operations connected with the fuel system make provision to minimize any risk of fire or explosion.

FUEL LINE FILTER(S)

Remove and refit   **19.25.03**

NOTE: A single filter or twin filters may be fitted, and later vehicles have a protective shield over the filter(s).

Removing

1   Depressurize the fuel system, see 19.50.02.

2   Locate the filter(s) on the right-hand underside of the body, forward of the rear axle, just below the fuel pump.

3   Where fitted, remove four screws and lift off the filter cover.

4   Disconnect the input fuel pipe(s) and plug them to prevent fuel loss.

5   Disconnect the output fuel pipe(s) and plug them to prevent fuel loss.

6   Remove the filter retaining clamp bolt and nut and manoeuvre the filter(s) off the car.

Refitting

7   Reverse instructions 2 to 6.

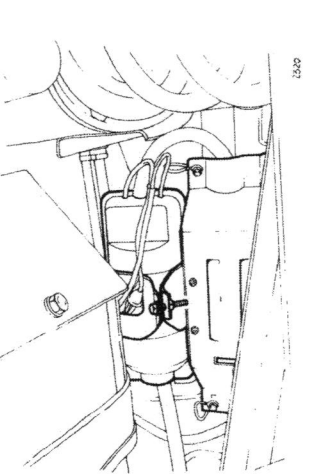

FUEL PIPES

Petrol pipe — main line — engine end section — remove and refit   **19.40.02**

Petrol pipe — main line — tank end section — remove and refit   **19.40.04**

Petrol pipe — fuel return valve to petrol tank — remove and refit   **19.40.54**

FUEL PUMP

Remove and refit   **19.45.08**

Removing

1   Depressurize the fuel system, see 19.50.02.

2   Locate the fuel pump on the right-hand underside of the body, forward of the rear axle.

3   Disconnect the electrical leads to the fuel pump.

4   Clamp the input fuel pipe to the pump to prevent the fuel tank draining when it is disconnected. Disconnect the pipe.

5   Disconnect the output fuel pipe from the pump and plug it to prevent fuel loss.

6   Remove the single bolt and nut securing the clamping bracket.

7   Manoeuvre the pump from the car.

Refitting

8   Reverse instructions 2 to 7.

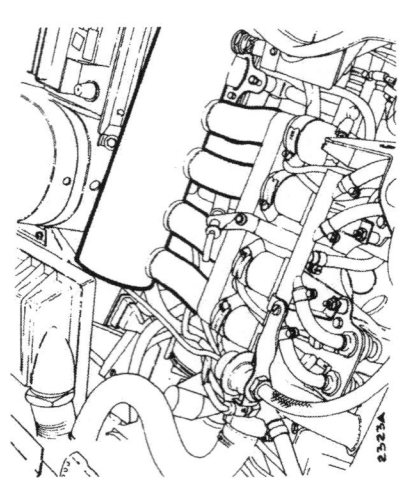

FUEL PRESSURE REGULATOR

Remove and refit   19.45.11

Removing

1 Depressurize the fuel system, see 19.50.02.
2 Disconnect the vacuum pipe from the regulator.
3 Disconnect and plug the fuel inlet pipe.
4 Remove the screw and nut securing the regulator bracket.
5 Using two spanners release the regulator from the fuel rail, taking care not to strain the rail.

Refitting

6 Reverse instructions 2 to 5.

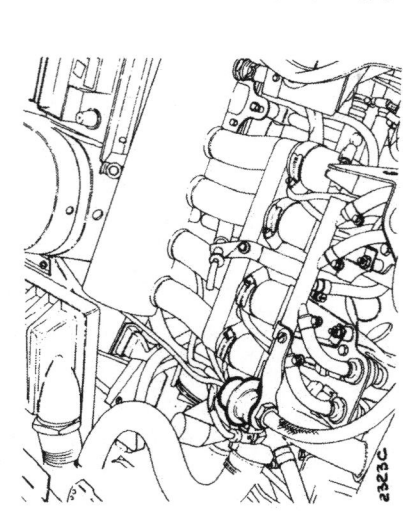

2323C

FUEL PRESSURE REGULATOR

Test   19.45.12

1 Depressurize the fuel system, see 19.50.02.
2 Slacken pipe clip securing cold start injector supply pipe to fuel rail and pull pipe from rail.
3 Connect pressure gauge pipe to fuel rail and tighten pipe clip.
   CAUTION: Pressure gauge must be checked against an approved standard at regular intervals.
4 Pull '–ve' L.T. lead from ignition coil and switch ignition on.
   Check reading on pressure gauge; reading must be 36.25 ± 0.725 lbf/in^2 ($2,55 \pm 0,05$ kgf/cm^2).
   NOTE: The pressure reading may slowly drop through either the regulator valve seating or the pump non-return valve. A slow, steady drop is permissible; a rapid fall MUST be investigated.
   If satisfactory results have been obtained, depressurize the fuel system and continue with operations 5 to 9. If satisfactory results have not been obtained, replace the regulator with a new unit.
5 Slacken pipe clip and remove pressure gauge from fuel rail.
6 Re-connect cold start injector supply pipe and secure pipe clip.
7 Re-connect the '–ve' L.T. lead to ignition coil.
8 Switch ignition on and check for leaks.
9 Switch ignition off.

FUEL SYSTEM

Depressurize   19.50.02

CAUTION: The fuel system MUST always be depressurized before disconnecting any fuel system components.

1 Remove the fuel pump earth lead.
2 Switch on and crank engine for a few seconds.
3 Switch the ignition off and re-connect the pump to earth.

Pressure test, see operation 19.45.12.

ALTERNATIVELY: The fuel cut-off inertia switch may be used to disconnect the fuel pump before cranking the engine.

FUEL TANK

Remove and refit   19.55.01

Follow the instructions for carburetter fitted vehicles, operation 19.55.01, noting that the fuel return pipe from the pressure regulator must additionally be disconnected and reconnected to the fuel tank.

INJECTORS

Injector winding check　　　19.60.02

1　Use ohmmeter to measure resistance value of each injector winding, which should be 2.4 ohms at 20°C (68°F).

2　Check for short-circuit to earth on winding by connecting ohmmeter probes between either injector terminal and injector body. Meter should read infinity. If any injector winding is open-circuited or short-circuited, replace the injector.

FUEL RAIL

Remove and refit　　　19.60.05

Removing

1　Depressurize the fuel system, see 19.50.02.

2　Remove the pressure regulator, see 19.45.11.

3　Release the fuel pipe connections to the rail.

4　Remove two bolts securing the rail to the inlet manifold and lift off the rail.

Refitting

5　Reverse instructions 2 to 4.

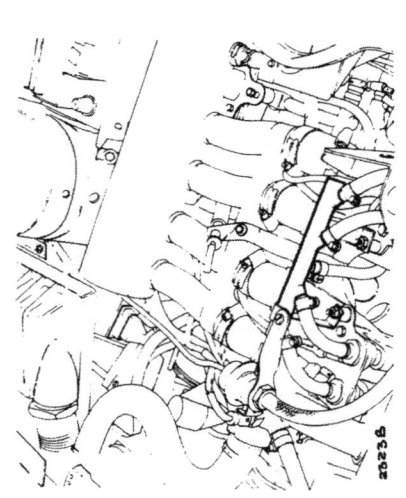

COLD START INJECTOR

Remove and refit　　　19.60.06

Removing

1　Depressurize the fuel system, see 19.50.02.

2　Locate the injector beneath the plenum chamber.

3　Disconnect the electrical leads from the injector.

4　Remove the injector clamp bracket screws and withdraw the injector and bracket.

Refitting

5　Renew the sealing ring and reverse instructions 2 to 4.

INJECTORS

Remove and refit　　　19.60.10

Removing

1　Depressurize the fuel system, see 19.50.02.

2　Disconnect the electrical lead from the injector.

3　Disconnect the fuel feed pipe to the injector.

4　Remove the injector clamp bracket securing screws and lift off the bracket.

5　Withdraw the injector.

Refitting

6　Renew the sealing ring and reverse instructions 2 to 5.

FAULT FINDING

Within the following pages are suggested procedures for tracing faults associated with poor engine running and failure to start.

In these circumstances and before suspecting, checking or changing fuel injection system components, it is recommended that common engine malfunction/failure to start causes are checked out, including, for example:

a. the presence and quality of fuel in the fuel tank;

b. the adequate and correct functioning of the ignition system up to the point of a good spark at *each* spark plug;

c. correct ignition and valve timing and adequate compression in *each* cylinder;

and, in the case of an engine failing to start:

d. that the battery has sufficient power reserve to operate the starter motor, supply the ignition system and power the fuel injection components.

SECTION 1. ENGINE FAILS TO START

	PROCEDURE	RESULT	ACTION
	If the engine fails to crank	Engine does not turn over	Check battery leads for security and cleanliness; battery, for state of charge
B	Ignition ON. Attempt to start engine	Engine starts	Go to N
		Engine fails to start	Go to C
C	Check that coolant temperature sensor is correctly connected	Connected	Go to D
		Disconnected	Re-connect sensor. Start engine and drive away
D	Check for spark at No. 1 spark plug lead. Disconnect lead from plug and hold end approx. 1/8 in from bare metal of engine block and crank engine	Good spark	Go to E
		No spark	Check ignition system
E	Ignition ON. Check fuel tank contents	Fuel in tank	Go to F
F	Ensure fuel cut-off inertia switch is closed	Switch closed	Go to G
		Switch open	Close switch by pressing button on top of switch. Start engine and drive away
G	Switch ignition OFF. Switch ignition ON. Crank engine and listen for fuel pump running	Pump does not run	Go to M
		Pump runs	Go to K
H	Switch ignition OFF. Remove cover from inertia switch and ensure cables are connected. If cables secure, disconnect and short together. Switch ignition ON. Pump should run when engine cranked	Pump does not run	Go to J
		Pump runs	Secure cables together and make safe with insulating tape etc. Start engine and drive away. Contact Dealer or Distributor as soon as possible

	PROCEDURE	RESULT	ACTION
J	Re-connect inertia switch. Ensure fuel injection system 12 volt cable is connected. Check connections	Loose or detached connections	Secure connections. Start engine and drive away
		All connections secure	Contact Dealer or Distributor
K	Crank engine in neutral gear position. Listen carefully to ensure all injectors click	Injectors click	Go to M
		Injectors do not click	Go to L
L	Check electrical connections to relay and ignition coil check multi-pin connectors to E.C.U. and air meter	Loose or disconnected connectors or wires	Re-connect, secure connectors and drive away
		Connectors secure	Go to M
M	Check for possible air leakage into manifold	Loose or disconnected	Secure. Start engine and drive away
		Connections secure	Go to O Contact Dealer or Distributor
N	Engine starts and runs	Normally	Drive away
		Unevenly	Check following connections for condition and security. Coolant temperature sensor. Auxiliary air valve. Throttle switch and all injector plugs. If all in order go to Section 2
O	Check for free movement of air meter control flap after removing hose at rear of air meter	Operates normally	Contact Dealer or Distributor
		Sticking	Free flap. Drive away. Contact Dealer or Distributor

SECTION 2.   ENGINE CUTS OUT, RUNS UNEVENLY OR LOSES POWER

	PROCEDURE	RESULT	ACTION
A	Vehicle operating normally	Engine cuts out	Pull to side of road, switch OFF ignition. Go to C of Section 1
		Engine runs unevenly or loses power	Pull to side of road, leave engine running. Go to B
B	Engine running, car at standstill. Ensure manual transmission cars are in neutral, automatic cars have either 'N' or 'P' selected and handbrake applied	Engine idles normally	Go to D
		Engine idles unevenly	Go to C
C	Ignition OFF Check—Spark plug leads Injector connectors Start engine	Engine runs normally	Drive away
		Engine runs unevenly	Go to F and return if necessary to C. Stop engine. Check for excessive oil fumes at breather or exhaust. Contact Distributor or Dealer as soon as possible
D	Apply pressure to throttle pedal and increase engine revolutions slowly	Engine runs normally	Go to E
		Engine runs unevenly	Go to F
E	Engage forward gear and drive at moderate speed	Engine runs unevenly	Go to F
		Engine runs normally	Fuel filter or supply pipe probably obstructed. Drive away, contact Distributor or Dealer as soon as possible
F	Check for possible air leakage into manifold. 1. Convolute hose 2. Induction elbow 3. Auxiliary air valve, top No. 13 and bottom hose	Loose or disconnected	Secure. Start engine and drive away
		Connections secure	Return to C

POSSIBLE CAUSES IN ORDER OF CHECKING

SYMPTOMS

Will not start*

Difficult cold start

Difficult hot start

Starts but will not run

Misfires and cuts out

Runs rough

Idle speed to fast

Hunting at idle

Low power and top speed

High fuel consumption

* Before proceeding with checks, hold throttle fully open and attempt a start. If the engine then starts and continues to run, no further action is necessary.

PROCEDURES FOR RECTIFICATION OF CAUSES SHOWN IN TABLE

Temperature Sensors — If either sensor is short-circuited, starting improves with higher engine temperature. Engine will run very weak, improving as temperature rises, but still significantly weak when fully hot. If a sensor is open-circuit, or disconnected, engine will run very rich, becoming worse as temperature rises. Engine may not run when fully hot, and will almost certainly not restart if stalled. Effort of air temperature sensor will be less marked than coolant temperature sensor. .

Auxiliary Air Valve — Check opening throttle. If engine immediately starts, unscrew idle speed adjustment, and re-check start with closed throttle. Re-set idle speed when engine hot. Check cold start. Check throttle return springs and linkage for sticking or maladjustment as a sticking throttle may have enforced incorrect idle speed adjustment on a previous occasion.

Throttle Switch — Check operation of throttle switch. Incorrect function or sequence of switching will give this fault.

Throttle Butterfly — Check adjustment of the throttle butterfly valve, ensure return springs correctly fitted, and throttle not sticking open.

Compression — Low compressions; a general lack of engine tune could cause this fault. Check engine tune, ignition timing, and function of ignition system complete. If necessary, check valve condition.

Idle Fuel Control Setting — Check exhaust gas CO level. If necessary adjust. CAUTION: This MUST NOT be moved unless correct test equipment and skilled personnel are in attendance to monitor changes made.

Air Filters — Remove air cleaner element and check for choked filter element.

Throttle Linkage — Check throttle linkage adjustment and ensure that throttle butterfly valves can be fully operated.

Battery — Battery depleted, giving insufficient crank speed or inadequate spark. Check battery condition with hydrometer. Re-charge, clean and secure terminals, or renew as necessary.

Connections — Ensure all connector plugs are securely attached. Pull back rubber boot and ensure plug is fully home. While replacing boot press cable towards socket. Ensure electronic control unit (E.C.U.) multi-pin connector is fully made. Ensure all ground connections are clean and tight.

Ignition System — Check ignition system as detailed in electrical section of Repair Operations Manual.

Fuel System — Open filler cap of fuel tank. Check for fuel pipe failure (strong smell of fuel) and retention of in-line fuel pressure. Check inertia switch closed. If necessary, clear fuel tank vents or supply pipe.

Cold Start System — Fault conditions could cause cold start system to be inoperative on a cold engine, or operative on a hot engine. If engine is either very hot, or cold, these particular faults will cause the engine to run very rich. Check cold start system.

E.C.U./Amplifier — If the E.C.U. is faulty it is possible that injectors will be inoperative. The E.C.U. may also be responsible for any degree of incorrect fuelling. Before suspecting the E.C.U. for fuelling problems, however, all other likely components should be proved good.

Air Leaks — Ensure all hose and pipe connections are secure. Engine is, however, likely to start more easily with air leaks if cold, as air leaking augments that through the auxiliary air valve. A leak, or failed air valve is shown up, however, by a very high idle speed when the engine is warm and air valve main passage should be closed.

COOLING SYSTEM

Description   26.00.00

Two types of cooling system have been fitted to TR7 models, the change taking place during the 1979 Model Year manufacture.

Earlier vehicles are fitted with an expansion tank, later models have a header tank. Both are 'no loss' systems allowing for coolant expansion and contraction.

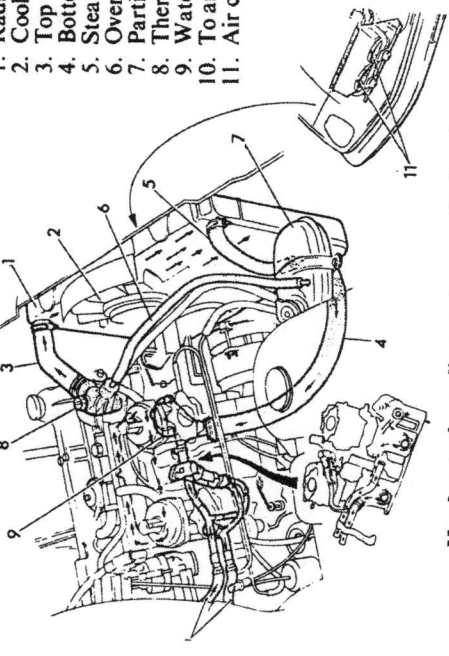

1. Radiator
2. Cooling fan
3. Top hose
4. Bottom hose
5. Steam bleed
6. Overflow pipe
7. Partial flow tank
8. Thermostat
9. Water pump
10. To and from heater
11. Air conditioning fans

Header tank cooling system — Carburetter engines

1. Radiator
2. Cooling fan
3. Top hose
4. Bottom hose
5. Steam bleed
6. Overflow pipe
7. Expansion bottle
8. Thermostat
9. Water pump
10. To and from heater

Expansion tank cooling system — Carburetter engines

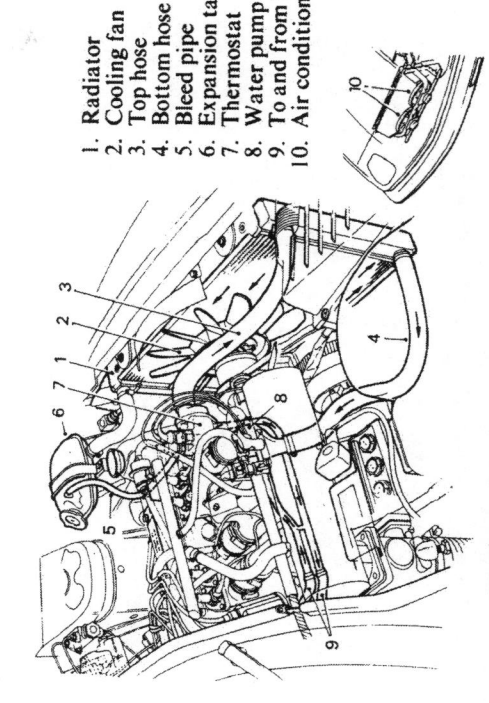

1. Radiator
2. Cooling fan
3. Top hose
4. Bottom hose
5. Bleed pipe
6. Expansion tank
7. Thermostat
8. Water pump
9. To and from heater
10. Air conditioning fans

AP 458

Header tank cooling system — Fuel Injection engines

COOLANT

Drain and refill   26.10.01

Draining

WARNING: This operation must only be carried out when the engine is cold.

1 Disconnect the battery.
2 Place a suitable container beneath the radiator bottom hose connection.
3 Remove the thermostat housing filler plug.
4 Disconnect the bottom hose at the radiator and allow the coolant to drain.
5 Remove the cylinder block drain plug. 12.25.07.

Refilling (earlier models with expansion tank)

6 Fit and tighten the cylinder block drain plug using a new washer.
7 Connect the bottom hose to the radiator.
8 Check that the expansion tank is half-full.
9 Set the heater control to 'HOT'.
10 Fill the system through the thermostat housing to the bottom of the threads, with the correct mixture of a recommended anti-freeze solution see 'LUBRICANTS & ANTI-FREEZE SOLUTIONS'.
11 Refit the thermostat housing filler plug carefully; do not overtighten.
12 Remove the pressure cap from the expansion tank.
13 Run the engine for three minutes at approximately 1200 rev/min.
14 Stop the engine.
15 Refit the expansion tank pressure cap.
16 Remove the filler plug from the thermostat housing.
17 Gently squeeze the large top hose between the thermostat housing and radiator to expel any trapped air in the hose.
18 Top up the system to the bottom of the filler plug threads in the thermostat housing.
19 Refit the filler plug using a new sealing washer if necessary. Do not overtighten.
20 Recheck the expansion tank coolant level, and top up to half full if necessary.

NOTE: Subsequent topping-up of the cooling system should be carried out, when the engine is cool, via the expansion tank which must be maintained at half full.

Refilling (later models with header tank)

1 Fit the bottom hose, cylinder block drain plug and thermostat housing filler plug.
2 Remove the header tank filler cap.
3 Set the interior heater controls to the maximum heat position.
4 Fill the system until the coolant level is 1 inch (25 mm) below the neck of the header tank.
5 Refit the header tank filler cap and run the engine at approximately 1500 rev/min until the coolant temperature rises sufficiently to open the thermostat.
6 Stop the engine and, taking care to avoid scalding, remove the header tank filler cap.
7 Top up the coolant level as necessary until it is 1 inch (25 mm) below the header tank filler neck.
8 Refit the filler cap.

NOTE: The coolant level should be maintained at 1 inch (25 mm) below the neck of the header tank (1).

HEADER TANK–LATER MODELS   26.15.01

Remove and refit

Removing

WARNING: This operation must only be carried out when the engine is cold.

1 Disconnect the lower hose from the tank and drain the coolant into a suitable container.
2 Disconnect the upper hose and overflow hose from the tank.
3 Remove two bolts securing the tank to the mounting bracket.
4 Lift off the header tank.

Refitting

5 Reverse instructions 1 to 4 and refill the cooling system, see 26.10.01.

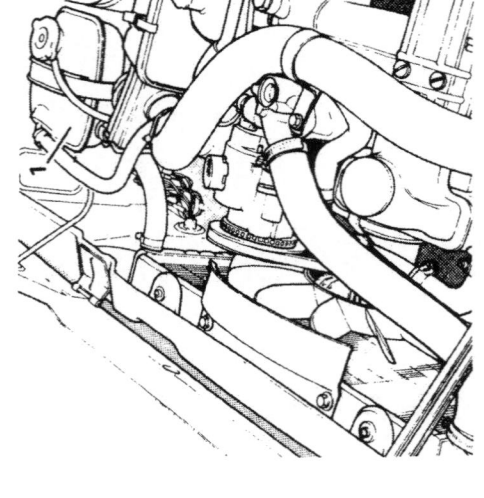

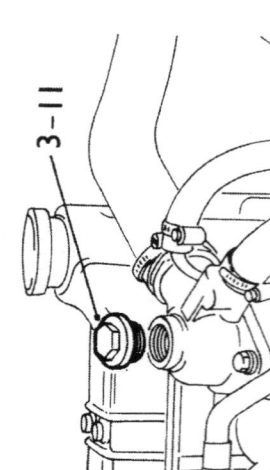
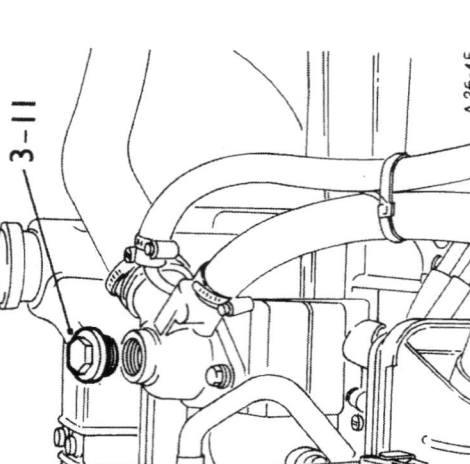

A26-45

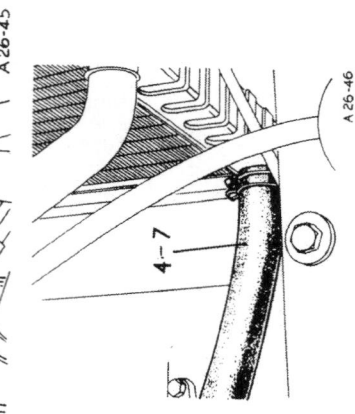

A26-46

   COOLING SYSTEM

EXPANSION TANK – EARLIER MODELS

Remove and refit   26.15.01

Removing

WARNING: This operation must only be carried out when the engine is cold or cool.

1. Disconnect the expansion pipe from the thermostat housing.
2. Remove the expansion tank pressure cap and allow the coolant to drain into a suitable clean container.
3. Remove the expansion pipe from the expansion tank.
4. Slacken the expansion tank retaining clamp nut and bolt.
5. Withdraw the expansion tank.
6. Remove the overflow pipe from the tank.

Refitting

7. Fit the tank into the clamp and secure.
8. Fit the overflow pipe.
9. Fit the expansion pipe to the tank and thermostat housing.
10. Half-fill the expansion tank with the correct mixture of anti-freeze and water.
11. Refit the pressure cap.
12. Refill the cooling system, see 26.10.01.

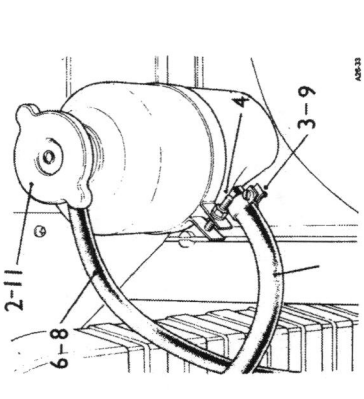

FAN AND ALTERNATOR DRIVE BELT – UK and Europe

Remove and refit   26.20.07

Removing

1. Disconnect the battery.
2. Slacken the alternator adjustment bolts and move the alternator towards the engine.
3. Slip the belt from the pulleys and feed it over the fan blades to remove it from the engine.

Refitting

4. Reverse instructions 1 to 3 ensuring that the drive belt is correctly tensioned. 86.10.05.

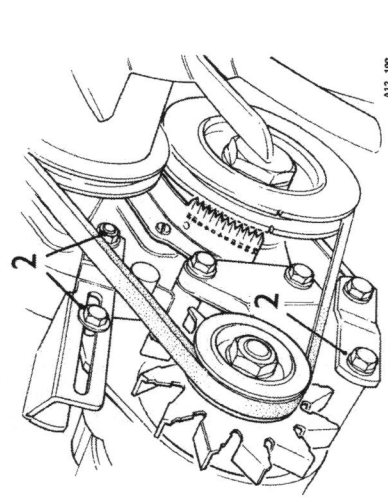

FAN AND ALTERNATOR DRIVE BELT – USA Specification Vehicles

Remove and refit   26.20.07

Removing

1. Disconnect the battery.
2. Raise the car and slacken off the air conditioning compressor belt adjustment bolts—see operation 82.10.02 instructions 1 to 3.
3. Remove the fan guard—two bolts.
4. Slacken off the four fan blade attachment nuts and bolts to provide a clearance for removing the belt.
5. *Carburetter vehicles only:* Slacken off the air pump adjustment (see operation 17.25.13) and remove the belt from the pump pulley only.
6. Slacken off the alternator adjustment bolts and remove the drive belt, feeding it over the air pump and compressor belts.

Refitting

7. Refit the alternator–fan drive belt– reversing instruction 6 and correctly tension the belt. 86.10.05.
8. *Carburetter vehicles only:* Fit the air pump belt and correctly tension, see 17.25.13.
9. Fit and adjust the compressor belt, see operation 82.10.01. instructions 7 to 11.
10. Tighten the fan blade attachment bolts.
11. Refit the fan guard.
12. Reconnect the battery.

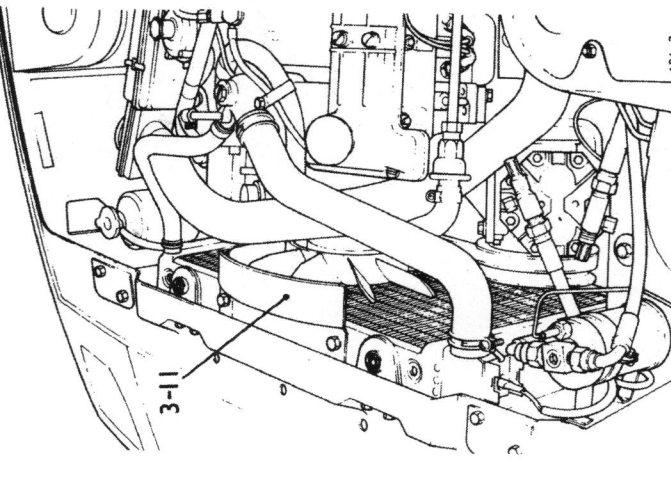

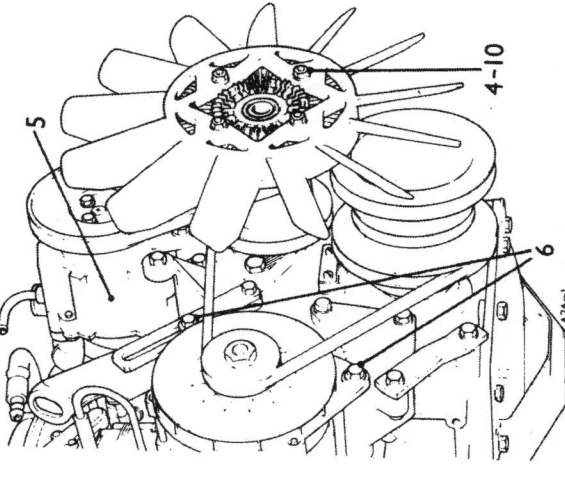

FAN BLADES

Remove and refit   26.25.06

Removing

1. Disconnect the battery.
2. Remove the fan blade shield.
3. Slacken off the nuts securing the radiator top support brackets sufficiently to move the radiator forward–away from the engine.
4. Remove the four nuts and bolts securing the blades to the viscous coupling.
5. Move the radiator forward whilst withdrawing the fan blades vertically.

Refitting

6. Fit the fan blades to the Torquatrol unit and tighten the retaining nuts and bolts evenly.
7. Tighten the four radiator support bracket nuts.
8. Refit the fan blade shield.
9. Reconnect the battery.

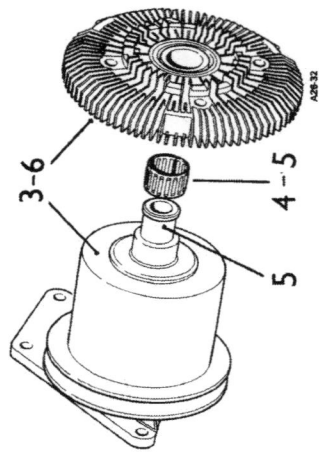

4–6

A28-31

VISCOUS COUPLING

Remove and refit   26.25.19

Removing

1. Remove the fan blades and pulley assembly. 26.25.21.
2. Remove the fan blades. 26.25.06.
3. Place a support at the back of the torquatrol unit as close to the centre as possible and using a suitable press tool, press the pulley assembly from the viscous coupling.
4. Remove the tolerance ring.

3–6

4–5

5

A28-32

Refitting

5. Fit a new tolerance ring in position on the pulley bearing shaft.
6. Compress the tolerance ring with the fingers whilst locating the viscous coupling on the bearing shaft. Ensure that the coupling is fitted the correct way round – see illustration.
7. Press the unit squarely onto the shaft keeping the tolerance ring compressed.
8. Refit the fan blades.
9. Fit the fan blades and pulley assembly to the engine. 26.25.21.

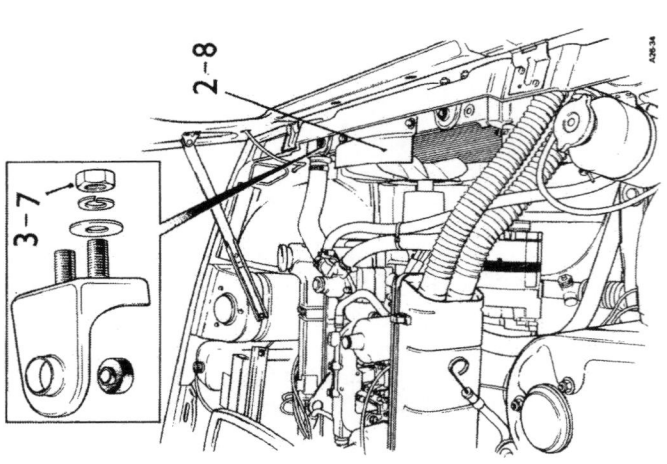

3–7

2–8

A28-34

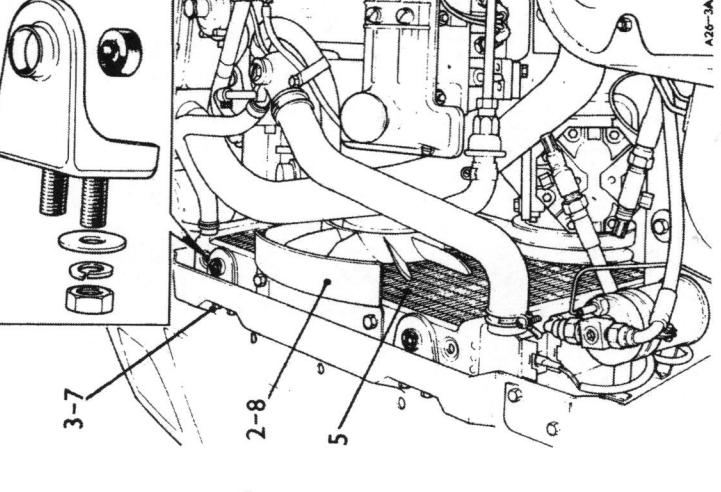

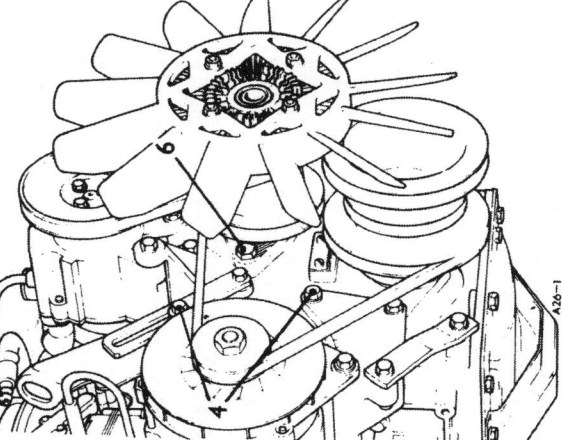

FAN PULLEY AND BLADE ASSEMBLY – UK and Europe   26.25.21

Remove and refit

Removing

1. Disconnect the battery.
2. Slacken the alternator adjustment and slip the belt from the pulleys.
3. Remove the four bolts retaining the pulley assembly to the timing cover.
4. Withdraw the pulley assembly from the left-hand side of the engine.

Refitting

5. Reverse instructions 1 to 4.

FAN PULLEY AND BLADE ASSEMBLY – USA Specification   26.25.21

Remove and refit

Removing

1. Disconnect the battery.
2. Remove the bonnet. 76.16.01.
3. *Carburetter vehicles only:* Remove the air pump, see 17.25.07.
4. Slacken the alternator adjustment and slip the belt from the pulleys.
5. Remove the five bolts securing the air compressor steady bracket.
6. Remove the remaining two bolts securing the pulley assembly to the timing chain cover, i.e. one on L.H. side and one on R.H. side of pulley assembly.
7. Remove the fan blade guard (two bolts).

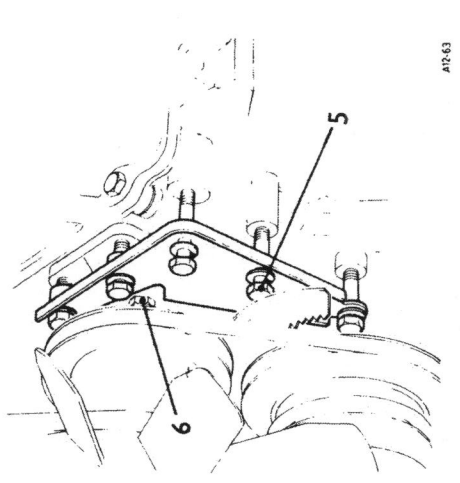

8. Slacken the four bolts securing the radiator top location brackets sufficiently to enable the radiator to be moved forward.
9. Pull the radiator forward–away from the engine–and withdraw the fan pulley assembly complete with fan blades and Torquatrol unit.

Refitting

NOTE: Before refitting the assembly ensure that the alternator and air pump drive belts are in their correct relative positions.

10. Place the drive belt on the fan pulley and offer the assembly to the engine.
11. Locate the assembly with the two short bolts, i.e. those not common to securing the compressor bracket and fan pulley assembly.
12. Fit the steady bracket and tighten the remaining five bolts.
13. *Carburetter vehicles only:* Fit the air pump and correctly tension the drive belt.
14. Tighten the radiator top location brackets.
15. Fit the fan guard.
16. Fit the bonnet. 76.16.01.
17. Reconnect the battery.

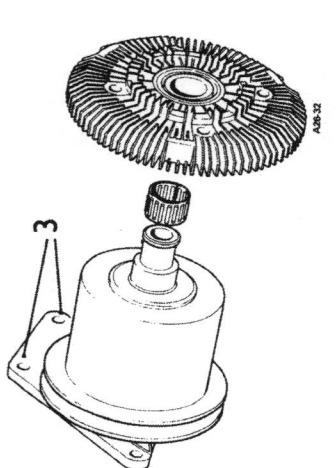

RADIATOR TOP HOSES

Remove and refit   26.30.01

Removing

WARNING: This operation must only be carried out when the engine is cold or cool.

1 Disconnect the battery.
2 Partially drain the radiator.
3 Disconnect and remove the two top hoses.

Refitting

4 Fit the two hoses and tighten the clips.
5 T o p - u p   t h e   c o o l i n g system—26.10.01—with the correct mixture of anti-freeze.
6 Reconnect the battery.
7 Check for leaks after the engine has been run and attained normal operating temperature.

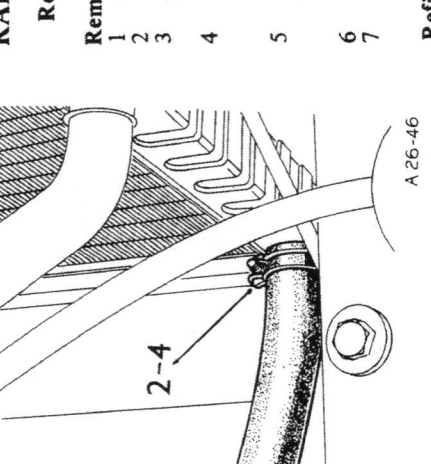
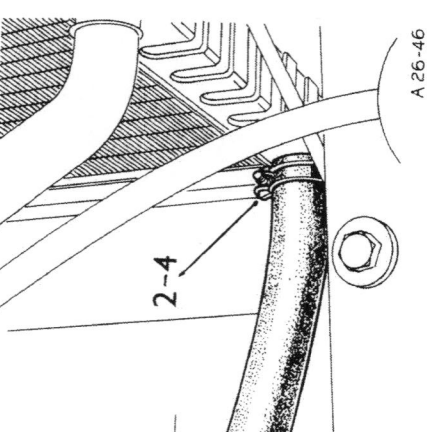

RADIATOR BOTTOM HOSE

Remove and refit   26.30.07

Removing

WARNING: This operation must only be carried out when the engine is cold or cool.

1 Disconnect the battery.
2 Place a suitable container below the hose connection to the radiator, disconnect the hose from the radiator and allow the coolant to drain.
3 Disconnect and remove the hose from the water pump cover connection.

Refitting

4 Place the hose clips over the hose and fit the hose to the pump and radiator. Tighten the clips.
5 Connect the battery.
6 Refill the cooling system. 26.10.01.

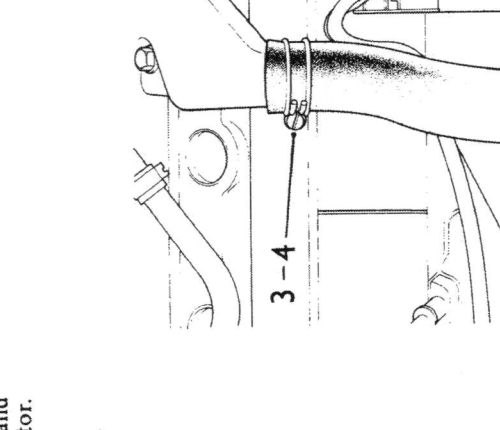
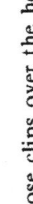

RADIATOR

Remove and refit   26.40.01

Removing

1 Disconnect the battery.
2 Drain the cooling system. 26.10.01.
3 Disconnect from the radiator the two top hoses.
4 Remove the temperature sensor leads from the L.H. side of the radiator. —Air conditioning specification vehicles.
5 Remove the four nuts and washers securing the two radiator attachment brackets.
6 Remove the brackets.
7 Withdraw the radiator vertically.

Refitting

8 Ensure that the four radiator mounting rubbers are in position on the radiator—two top, two bottom.
9 Lower the radiator into position ensuring that the bottom mounting rubbers locate properly in the holes in the radiator support crossmember.
10 Refit the radiator top support brackets.
11 Refit the top hoses.
12 Reconnect the bottom hose. 26.30.07
13 Refill the cooling system. 26.10.01.
14 Reconnect the temperature sensor leads.
15 Reconnect the battery.

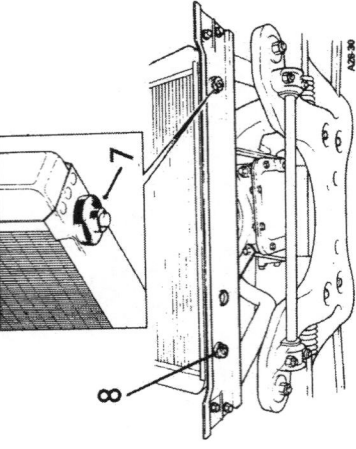

CONNECTING TUBE

Remove and refit   26.30.25

See Operation 30.15.02

THERMOSTAT

Remove and refit   26.45.01

WARNING: This operation must only be carried out when the engine is cold.

Carburetter engines

Removing

1 Disconnect the battery.
2 Partially drain the cooling system.
3 Remove the two bolts securing the thermostat housing dome.
4 Lift off the dome and withdraw the thermostat.

Refitting

5 Locate the thermostat in the housing.
6 Using a new gasket fit the domed cover and evenly tighten the retaining bolts.
7 Reconnect the battery.
8 Top-up and check the cooling system.

THERMOSTAT

Test   26.45.10

1 Remove the thermostat. 26.45.01.
2 Note the temperature stamped on the thermostat at which it should be fully open.
3 Place the thermostat and a centigrade thermometer in a laboratory beaker and heat the water, observe the temperature at which the thermostat opens.
4 Refit or renew the thermostat as necessary, see 26.45.01, instructions 5 to 8.

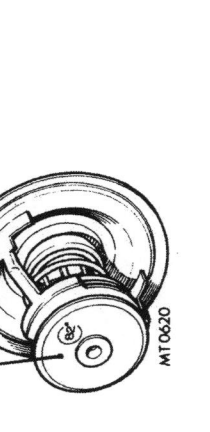

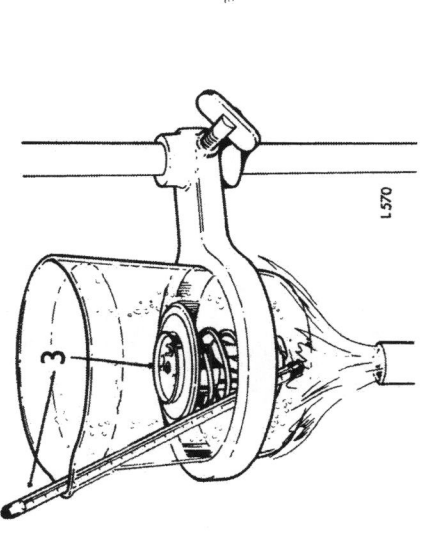

WATER PUMP

Remove and refit   26.50.01

Service tools S4235A/10, 4235A.

WARNING: This operation must only be carried out when the engine is cool.

1 Disconnect the battery.
2 Remove the inlet manifold complete with carburetters. 30.15.02.
3 Remove the connecting tube from the water-pump cover.
4 Disconnect the bottom hose from the water pump cover.
5 Remove the three bolts securing the pump cover to the cylinder block.
6 Lift off the pump cover complete with gaskets.
7 Using a spanner on the impeller centre bolt turn clockwise until either:
  a the water pump is released from the jackshaft gear and can be withdrawn.
  or
  b the centre bolt is removed.
8 If (b) applies fit special tool S4235A/10 and 4235A impact tool and adaptor to remove the pump.

continued

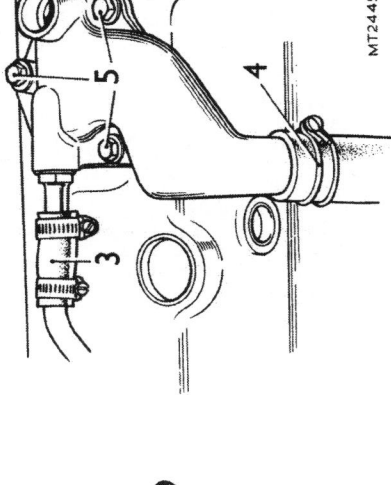

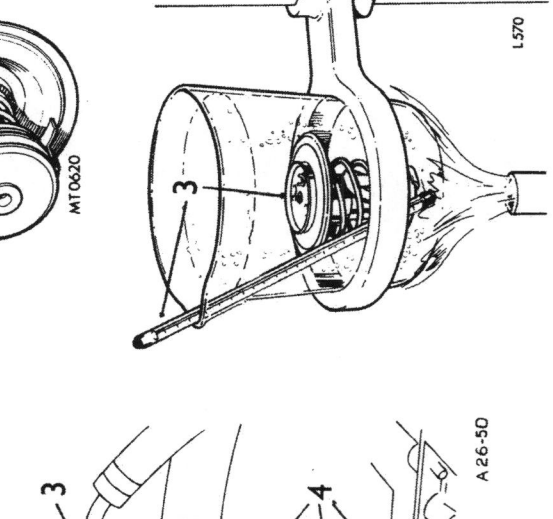

Fuel injection engines
The thermostat is located at the radiator top hose connection on the inlet manifold. The thermostat cover is secured by two bolts. The thermostat is removed and refitted following the procedure above.

WATER PUMP

Overhaul   **26.50.06**

Service Tool Kit: S348

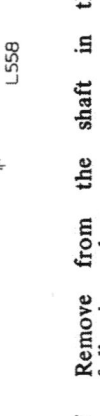

L558

Dismantling

1. Remove the water pump. 26.50.01.
2. Remove the centre bolt—noting that it has a left-hand thread.
3. Insert the assembly into the large hole of special tool S348/1.
4. Using a special tool S348/6 drift the unit from the impeller.
5. Insert the assembly, gear uppermost, into the small hole of tool S348/1.
6. Drift the unit from the housing.

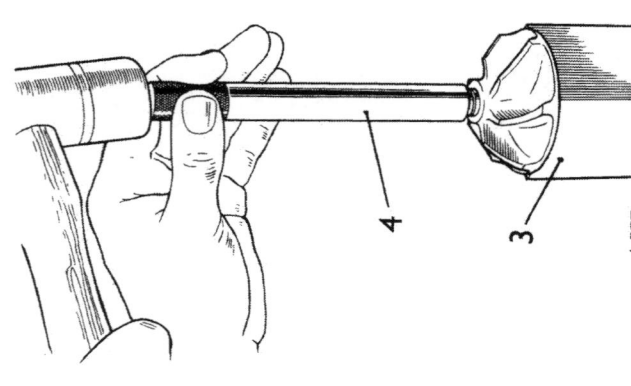

L557

7. Remove from the shaft in the following order:
   a 'O' ring.
   b graphite seal.
   c water flinger.
   d oil seal.
   e circlip.

Refitting

MT2443A

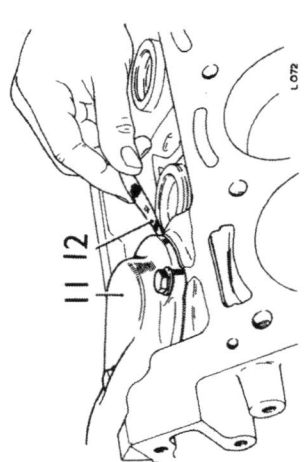

L072

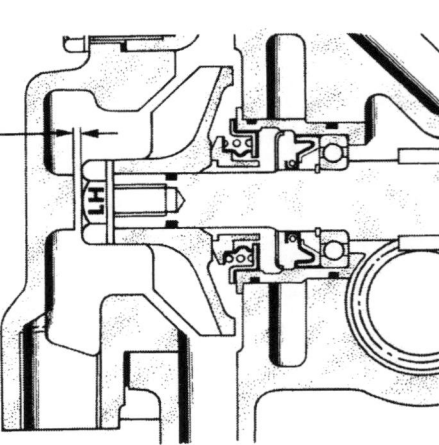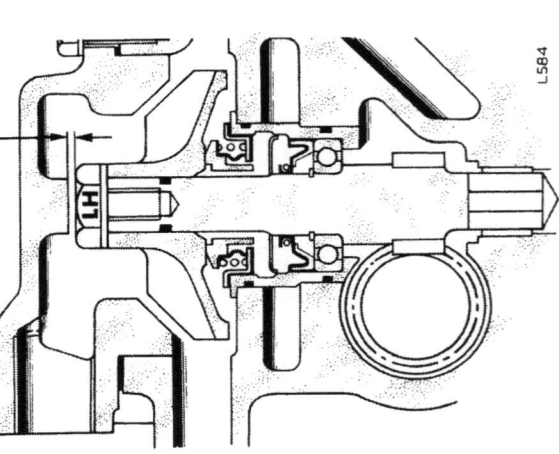

L584

9. Fit the pump into the cylinder block housing, ensuring that the pump and jackshaft gears mesh correctly and that the pump is properly seated. Check by turning the impeller centre bolt anti-clockwise.
   CAUTION: The use of force or impact to seat the pump will damage the pump and graphite seal.
10. Ensure that the cylinder block housing and mating faces are clean.
11. Temporarily fit the pump cover leaving the three bolts finger tight.
12. Using feeler gauges check and note that the gap between the pump cover and cylinder block is equal. Equalize the gap by adjusting the bolts.
13. Select water pump gaskets to equal the gap noted in instruction 12 plus

    Six bladed impeller: 0.010 in to 0.025 in (0.25 to 0.63 mm);
    Twelve bladed impeller: 0.012 in to 0.020 in (0.30 to 0.50 mm), to obtain the correct running clearance.

    NOTE: Water pump gaskets are available in the following thicknesses, 0.010, 0.020, 0.030 in.

    The six bladed impeller and twelve bladed impeller with their respective covers are interchangeable in sets only.
14. Remove the pump cover, fit the selected gaskets, fit the cover and tighten the bolts evenly to the correct torque figure—see section 06.
15. Refit the inlet manifold complete with carburetters. 30.15.02.

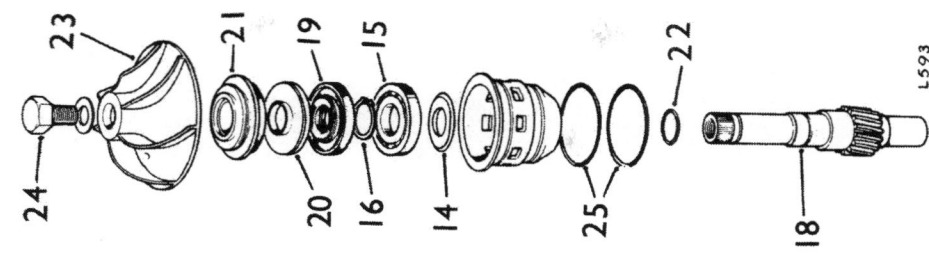

L593

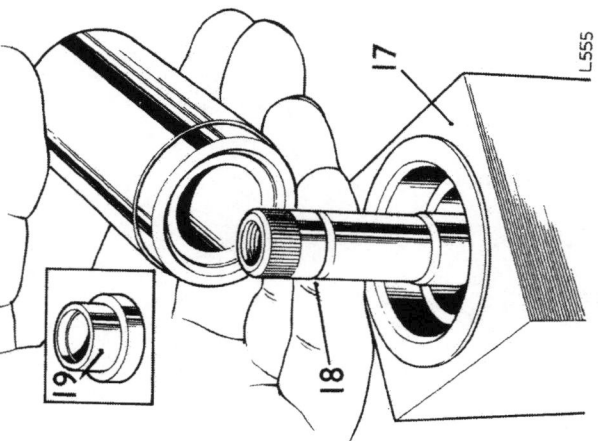

L555

L554

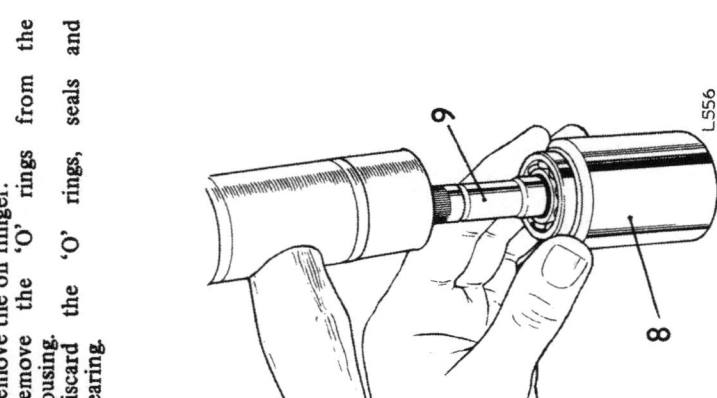

L556

8   Insert the shaft, gear downwards, into tool S348/7.
9   Drift the shaft from the bearing.
10 Remove the oil flinger.
11 Remove the 'O' rings from the housing.
12 Discard the 'O' rings, seals and bearing.

Examination

13 Inspect the shaft, housing and impeller for serviceability and renew if necessary.

Assembling

14 Fit the oil flinger to the shaft dished face towards the gear.
15 Fit the bearing to the shaft using tool S348/7.
16 Fit the circlip ensuring that it seats correctly.
17 Fit the water pump body into the small hole in tool S348/1.
18 Fit the shaft unit, gear downwards, into the housing and using tool S348/2 gently drift into position.
19 Fit the oil seal, flat face towards the bearing.

20 Fit the water flinger, dished face towards the bearing using tool S348/2.
   CAUTION: The water flinger will seat on the shoulder of the shaft. Excessive force applied when fitting, will cause distortion and fouling of the water-pump body.
21 Fit the graphite seal, flat face downwards, over the shaft and seating in the housing.
22 Fit the 'O' ring to the shaft.
23 Press the impeller on to the shaft.
24 Fit the centre bolt and washer (left-hand thread) and tighten to the correct torque — see 'TORQUE WRENCH SETTINGS'.
25 Fit the two 'O' rings to the water pump housing, smaller one nearest to the gear.
26 Refit the water pump. 26.50.01.

EXHAUST SYSTEM

Description   30.00.00

The general arrangement exhaust system shown may differ in detail according to market specification and model year build.

These differences will include the fitting of a single or twin front pipe and slight visual changes in the silencer or mountings.

However, skilled personnel should experience no difficulties when following the general information given under each operation heading.

Fuel injection engines are fitted with a catalyst unit in the front pipe. The catalyst heat shield is a simple bolt-on fixing.

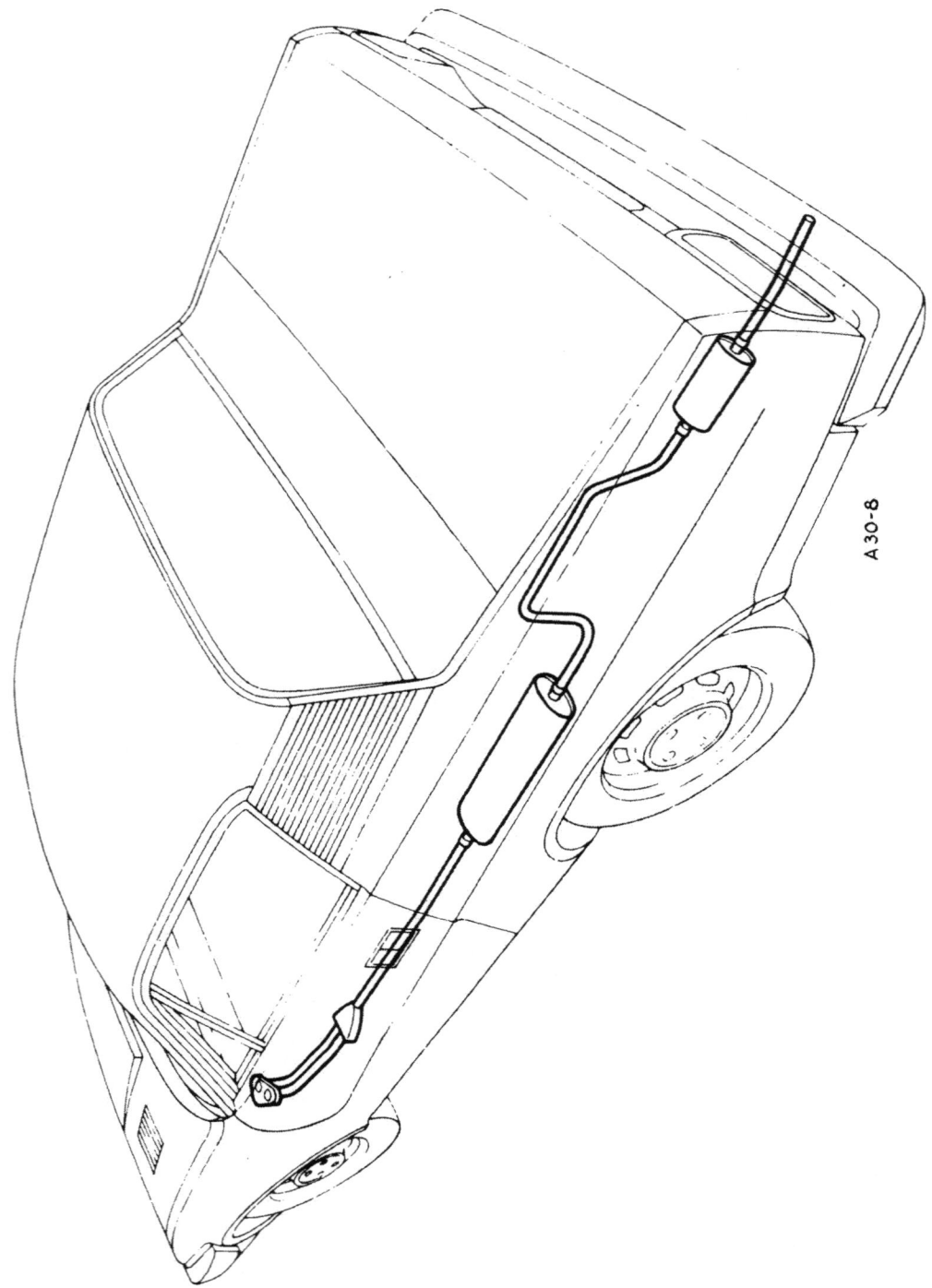

A 30-8

FRONT PIPE

Remove and refit   30.10.09

Removing

1 Drive the car on to a ramp.
2 Raise the ramp.
3 Slacken the silencer to down-pipe clamp bolt.
4 Un-hook the silencer from its body hanger.
5 Un-hook the tail-pipe from its hanger.
6 Drive the silencer from the down-pipe.
7 Remove the nut and bolt securing the rear-end of the down pipe.
8 Remove the two nuts and bolts retaining the front end of the pipe.
9 Remove the three bolts securing the down-pipe to the manifold flange.
10 Remove the pipe complete with gasket.

Refitting

11 Fit the down pipe to the manifold flange using a new gasket.
12 Secure the pipe to the front bracket using the two nuts and bolts.
13 Connect the pipe to its rear mounting with the single nut and bolt.
14 Fit the silencer to the down-pipe leaving the clamp slack.
15 Fit the silencer to its body hanger.
16 Secure the tail pipe to its hanger.
17 Tighten the silencer front clamp bolt.
18 Lower the ramp.

SILENCER – FRONT

Remove and refit   30.10.14

Removing

1 Raise the car on a ramp.
2 Release the clips clamping the silencer to the tail and down-pipes.

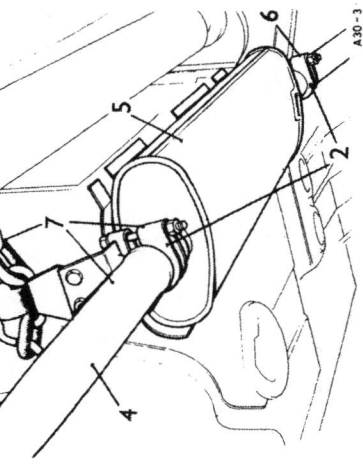

A30-3

3 Disconnect the tail pipe from the body.
4 Withdraw the tail pipe assembly from the silencer.
5 Withdraw the silencer from the front-pipe.

Refitting

6 Fit the silencer to the front-pipe and tighten the retaining clip.
7 Fit the tail pipe assembly to the silencer and attach it to the body.
 Tighten the tail-pipe to silencer clip.
8 Lower the ramp.

TAIL-PIPE AND REAR SILENCER

Remove and refit   30.10.22

Removing

1 Raise the car on a ramp.
2 Release the clip clamping the tail-pipe to the silencer.
3 Unhook the tail-pipe from its forward hanger.
4 Unhook the tail-pipe from its rear hanger.
5 Withdraw the tail-pipe from the silencer.
6 Remove the two nuts and bolts securing the hanger bracket assembly to the tail-pipe bracket, and separate the two assemblies.

Refitting

7 Fit the hanger bracket assembly to the tail-pipe bracket with the two nuts and bolts.
8 Fit the tail-pipe to the silencer.
9 Hang the tail-pipe to its forward and rear hanger brackets using, if necessary, new rubbers.
10 Tighten the silencer-to-tail-pipe clamp bolt.
11 Lower the ramp.

A30-7

FRONT PIPE FLANGE GASKET

Remove and refit   30.10.26

Removing
1. Raise the car on a ramp.
2. Remove the three front-pipe to manifold flange retaining bolts.

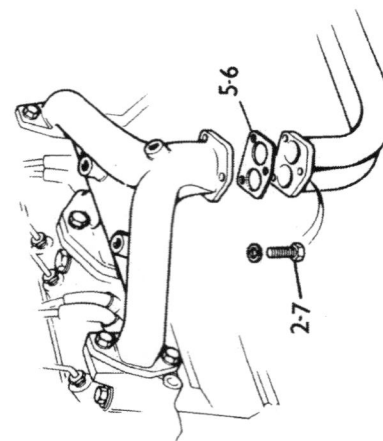

3. Remove the two nuts and bolts securing the down-pipe to its suspension bracket.
4. Remove the nut and bolt securing the intermediate pipe to its bracket.
5. The down-pipe will now drop sufficiently to remove the gasket.

Refitting
6. Insert the gasket into position.
7. Fit the flange manifold bolts but leave slack.
8. Fit the two nuts and bolts securing the down-pipe to its bracket, but leave slack.
9. Fit and tighten the nut and bolt retaining the intermediate pipe to its bracket.
10. Tighten the flange bolts to the correct torque – see 'TORQUE WRENCH SETTINGS'.
11. Tighten the front-pipe bracket bolts.
12. Lower the ramp.

EXHAUST MANIFOLD –
UK and Europe

Earlier models – remove and refit 30.15.01

Later models have a hot air collection pressing fitted around the manifold similar to U.S.A. market specification.

Removing
1. Drive the car on to a ramp and disconnect the battery.
2. Raise the ramp and remove the three bolts securing the exhaust front-pipe to the manifold.
3. Remove the four manifold lower retaining bolts.
4. Lower the ramp.
5. Remove the three manifold top retaining bolts and lift-off the manifold.

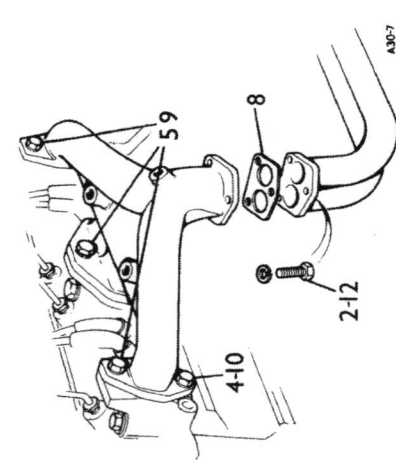

A30-7

Refitting
6. Place a new front pipe to manifold gasket in position.
7. Fit the manifold securing it loosely with the three top bolts.
8. Raise the ramp and fit the four lower retaining bolts.
9. Finally tighten the manifold bolts evenly to the correct torque – see 'TORQUE WRENCH SETTINGS'.
10. Fit and tighten the three front-pipe to manifold bolts.
11. Lower the ramp and reconnect the battery.

EXHAUST MANIFOLD –
USA & Canada Specification Vehicles

Remove and refit   30.15.01

Removing
1. Drive the car on to a ramp and disconnect the battery.
2. Raise the ramp and remove the three bolts securing the exhaust front-pipe to the manifold.
3. Remove the manifold four lower retaining bolts.
4. Lower the ramp and remove the hot air hose from the manifold.
5. Remove the three manifold top retaining bolts and lift-off the manifold.
6. Withdraw the three bolts and remove the hot air collection pressing. Note that later models have a vertical outlet from the hot air collection pressing.

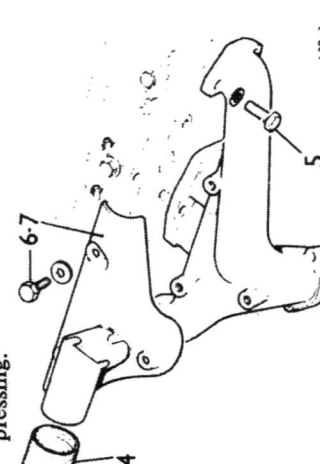

A30-:

Refitting
7. Fit the hot air collection pressing to the manifold.
8. Place the new front pipe to manifold gasket in position.
9. Fit the manifold securing it loosely with the three top bolts.
10. Raise the ramp and fit the four lower retaining bolts.
11. Finally tighten the manifold bolts evenly to the correct torque – see 'TORQUE WRENCH SETTINGS'.
12. Fit and tighten the three front-pipe to manifold bolts.
13. Lower the ramp and fit the hot air hose.
14. Reconnect the battery.

INDUCTION MANIFOLD — CARBURETTER ENGINES

Remove and refit   30.15.02

Removing

1 Disconnect the battery.
2 Drain the cooling system. 26.10.01.
3 Remove the fresh air duct. 80.15.31.
4 Remove the air cleaner. 19.10.02.
5 Disconnect the top water hoses from the engine.
6 Disconnect the water temperature transmitter lead.
7 Disconnect the main fuel feed to the carburetters.
8 Disconnect the brake servo hose from the manifold.
9 Disconnect the mixture control cable from the front carburetter. – Not U.S.A.
10 Pull-off the spill pipe from the rear carburetter float chamber.
11 Disconnect the throttle cable from the carburetter linkage.
12 Pull-off the breather hose from the camshaft cover.
13 Remove the distributor cap.
14 Pull-off the distributor vacuum pipe from the rear carburetter.
15 Remove the six manifold attachment bolts and remove the engine lifting bracket.
16 Disconnect the heater pipe at union with the induction manifold.
17 Lift the manifold complete with carburetters from the engine.
18 Remove the 'O' ring between manifold and cylinder head.
19 Remove the connecting tube.
20 Remove the gasket.
21 Disconnect the engine breather pipes from the carburetters.
22 Disconnect the throttle linkage springs from the manifold bracket.
23 Remove the bolts retaining the throttle linkage bracket to the manifold.
24 Remove the eight nuts securing the carburetters to the manifold (four per carburetter).
25 Withdraw the carburetters and gaskets.
26 Remove the throttle jack bracket.
27 Remove the rubber mountings and gaskets.

NOTE: If the manifold is to be renewed remove the following items:—

28 Remove the two bolts and lift-off the thermostat housing cover.
29 Withdraw the thermostat.
30 Remove the two bolts and remove the common throttle spring and breather pipe bracket.
31 Remove the water temperature transmitter.
32 Remove the brake servo pipe banjo.
33 Remove the banking plug.

Refitting

34 Reverse instructions 28 to 33.
35 Using new gaskets fit the rubber mountings.
36 Fit the throttle jack bracket.
37 Fit the carburetters using new gaskets, and secure with eight nuts and spring washers.
38 Fit the throttle linkage bracket to the manifold.
39 Connect the throttle linkage springs.
40 Connect the engine breather pipes to the carburetters.
41 Place a new gasket in position on the manifold face.
42 Fit a new 'O' ring to the manifold.
43 Fit the manifold complete with carburetters and engine lifting bracket and secure with the six bolts, tightening evenly to the correct torque.
44 Connect the heater pipe at the union with the induction manifold.
45 If fitted, remove the thermostat housing cover and withdraw the thermostat.
46 Insert the connecting tube squarely through the thermostat housing until fully home.
47 Refit the thermostat and cover using a new gasket.
48 Reverse instructions 1 to 14.

INDUCTION MANIFOLD — FUEL INJECTION ENGINES

Remove and Refit   30.15.02

Removing

1 Disconnect the battery.
2 Drain the cooling system, see 26.10.01.
3 Remove the plenum chamber, see 19.22.46, disconnecting the air pipes at the manifold.
4 Disconnect the temperature sensor, temperature switch and Thermotime switch from the inlet manifold, noting their connections for refitting. If required, unscrew the units from the manifold.
5 Depressurize the fuel system, see 19.50.02.
6 Remove the fuel rail, see 19.60.05.
7 Remove the fuel injectors, see 19.60.10.
8 Disconnect the radiator top hose and outlet water pipes from the manifold.
9 Remove the thermostat, see 26.45.01.
10 Remove four bolts and lift off the manifold.

Refitting

11 Clean all mating faces on the manifold and cylinder head. Replace any gasket that is suspect or damaged.
12 Reverse instructions 1 to 4 and 5 to 9.

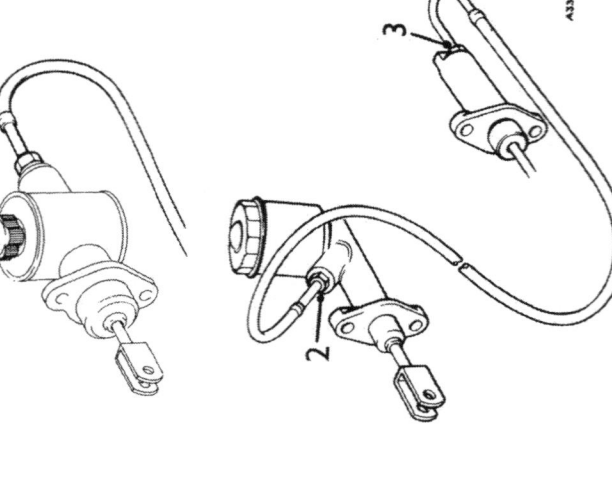

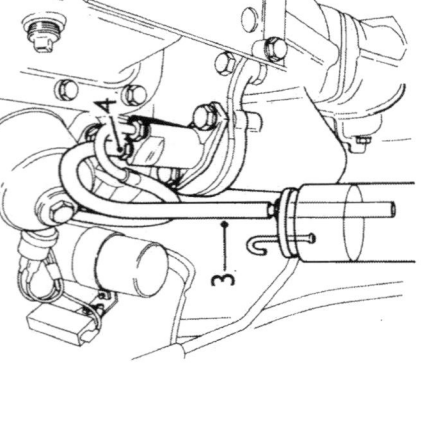

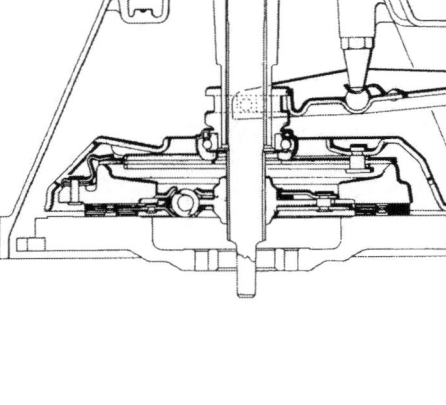

CLUTCH ASSEMBLY

Remove and refit 33.10.01

Removing
1 Remove the gearbox. 37.20.01
2 Evenly slacken and remove the six bolts and spring washers securing the clutch to the engine flywheel.
   NOTE: If the clutch is to be refitted, scribe or mark clutch and flywheel to identify original relationship.
3 Remove the clutch assembly and drive plate.

Refitting
4 Using a substitute first motion shaft offer up the drive plate to the flywheel. Note that the longer boss of the drive plate must be adjacent to the gearbox.
5 Engage the clutch assembly on the flywheel dowels. Fit the six securing bolts and spring washers and tighten evenly to the correct torque – see 'TORQUE WRENCH SETTINGS'.
6 Remove the substitute first motion shaft.
7 Fit the gearbox. 37.20.01.

HYDRAULIC SYSTEM

Bleeding 33.15.01

1 Thoroughly clean the areas in the vicinity of the master cylinder reservoir filler cap and the slave cylinder bleed nipple.
2 Ensure that the master cylinder reservoir is topped up.
3 Attach one end of a bleed tube to the slave cylinder bleed nipple and immerse the other end in a transparent vessel containing brake fluid.
4 Open the bleed nipple approximately three-quarters of a turn. Depress and release the clutch pedal, pausing momentarily at each down stroke until fluid free of air issues from the slave cylinder. Close the bleed nipple with pedal depressed and release the pedal.
   Care must be taken to ensure that the level of fluid in the master cylinder reservoir is never permitted to fall to less than half capacity.
5 Remove the bleed tube and top up the reservoir.

FLUID PIPE

Remove and refit 33.15.09

Removing
1 Drain the hydraulic system.
2 Unscrew the pipe from the master cylinder.
3 Unscrew the pipe from the slave cylinder.
4 Remove the pipe from the car.

Refitting
5 Align the new pipe in the approximate position in the car.
6 Screw the pipe into the master cylinder.
7 Screw the pipe into the slave cylinder.
8 Top up the master cylinder with new brake fluid.
9 Bleed the system. 33.15.01.

DRIVE PLATE

Remove and refit 33.10.02

As operation 33.10.01.

MASTER CYLINDER

Remove and refit   33.20.01

Removing

1 Unscrew the pipe from the master cylinder.
   CAUTION: Plug the master cylinder outlet and the end of the pipe to prevent spillage of fluid.
2 Remove the split pin, washer and clevis pin securing the push rod to the clutch pedal.
3 Remove the two nuts, spring washers and bolts securing the master cylinder to the body.
4 Withdraw the master cylinder.

Refitting

5 Reverse instructions 1 to 4.
6 Bleed the system. 33.15.01.

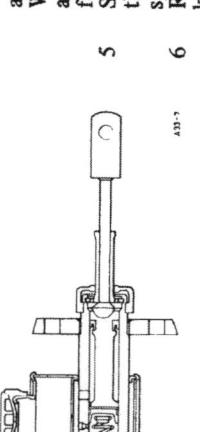

MASTER CYLINDER (Earlier Models)

Overhaul   33.20.07

Dismantling

1 Remove the master cylinder, see 33.20.01.
2 Slide the rubber boot clear of the mounting flange to expose the push-rod retaining circlip.
3 Remove the circlip and withdraw the push-rod assembly. Remove the rubber boot.
4 Extract the piston and rear cup seal, front cup seal and washer, spring and spring retainer button.

Inspection

5 Discard the rubber boot, front and rear cup seals and thoroughly clean remaining components in clean brake fluid or methylated spirit.
6 Carefully examine the piston and cylinder bore. Renew either or both components if there is evidence of corrosion or scoring.

Reassembling

7 Fit a new rear cup to the piston. Lubricate the cylinder bore with clean brake fluid.
8 Insert the spring (larger diameter leading) and spring retainer button into the cylinder.
9 Insert the front cup (cup lips leading) into the cylinder.
10 Insert the dished spring washer.
11 Insert the piston complete with rear cup.
12 Fit a new rubber boot to the push-rod assembly and smear the ball-end and shaft with disc brake lubricant or rubber grease.
13 Fit the push-rod assembly and retaining circlip.
14 Slide the rubber boot into position on the master cylinder.
15 Install the master cylinder on the car, see 33.20.01.
16 Bleed the circuit.

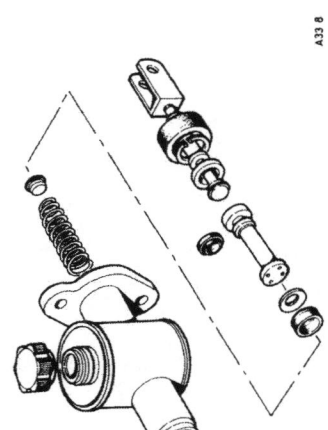

4 Withdraw the piston spring and seal assembly from the master cylinder. Withdrawal may be facilitated by applying a compressed air line to the fluid outlet union.
5 Straighten the prong of the spring thimble and remove the thimble and spring from the piston.
6 Release the valve stem from the keyhole slot in the thimble.
7 Slide the valve seal spacer along the valve stem.
8 Remove the valve seal from the valve stem and fit a new seal.

9 Assemble the spacer, spring and thimble to the valve stem.
10 Remove the seal from the piston and fit a new seal (seal lip towards the spring).
11 Engage the spring thimble on the piston and carefully depress the thimble prong.
12 Lubricate the bore of the master cylinder with clean brake fluid and insert the seal assembly spring and piston.
13 Fit a new rubber to the push-rod.
14 Fit the push-rod and washer to the master cylinder and secure with the clip.
15 Slide the rubber into position on the master cylinder.
16 Refit the master cylinder. 33.15.01.
17 Bleed the system. 33.15.01.

MASTER CYLINDER (Later Models)

Overhaul   33.20.07

1 Remove the master cylinder. 33.20.01.
2 Slide the rubber along the push-rod.
3 Remove the circlip from the end of the master cylinder and withdraw the push-rod and washer.

 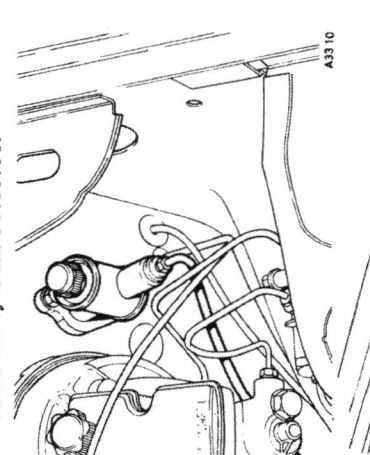 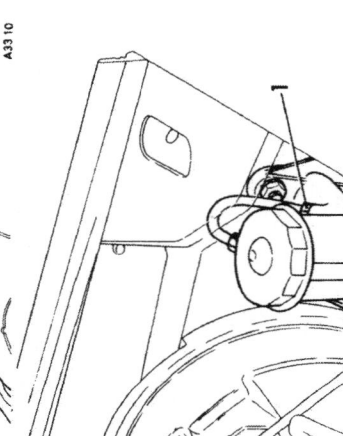

RELEASE BEARING ASSEMBLY   33.25.12

Remove and refit

Service tools: ST 1136

Removing
1 Remove the gearbox. 37.20.01.
2 Using Tool ST 1136 unscrew the clutch release lever pivot bolt from the clutch housing.
3 Withdraw the release lever complete with pivot bolt and the release bearing.
4 Detach the release bearing from the release lever.

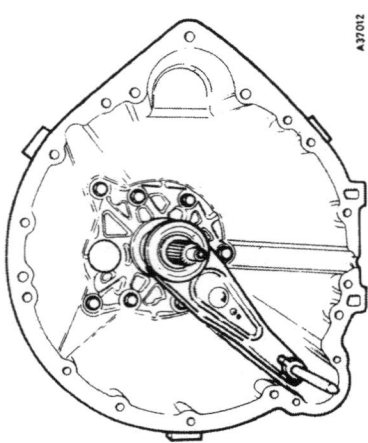

A37012

Refitting
5 Offer up the release bearing to the release lever ensuring that the rectangular slippers engage the collar.
6 Slide the bearing complete with release lever and pivot bolt into position in the clutch housing.
7 Engage the pivot bolt in the clutch housing.
8 Using Tool ST 1136, tighten the pivot bolt.
9 Fit the gearbox to the car. 37.20.01.

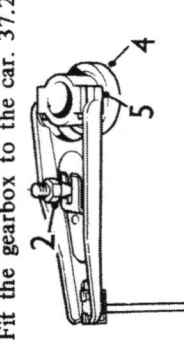

A37—014

RELEASE BEARING   33.25.17

Overhaul

Removing
1 Remove the release bearing assembly. 33.25.12.
2 Mount the assembly in a press and extract the sleeve from the bearing.

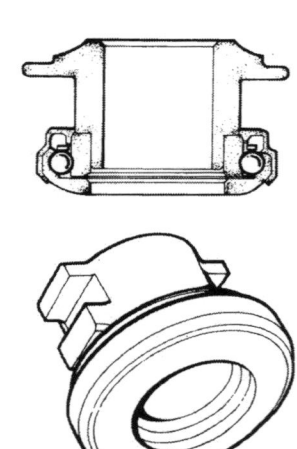

A33 9

CLUTCH AND BRAKE PEDAL ASSEMBLY   33.30.01

Remove and refit

As operation 70.35.03.

CLUTCH PEDAL RETURN SPRING   33.30.03

Remove and refit

Removing
1 Release the spring ends from the clutch pedal and pedal bracket.

Refitting
2 The longer leg of the spring attaches to the clutch pedal. Engage the spring hook in the pedal bracket then clip the other hook through the drilling in the clutch pedal.

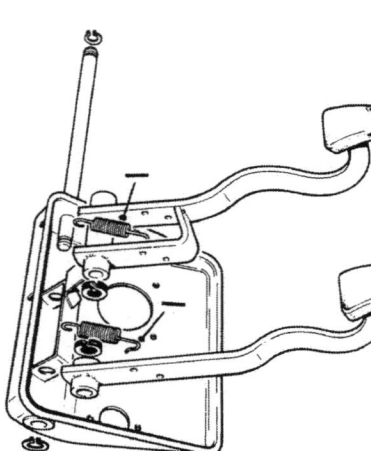

A70008

Refitting
3 Stand the sleeve on its collar end and evenly engage the new release bearing on the sleeve. (Release face of bearing uppermost.)
4 Press the bearing onto the sleeve until it abuts against the sleeve shoulder. CAUTION: The bearing *must not* be assembled to the sleeve by applying a load to the outer race.
5 Fit the release bearing assembly to the gearbox. 33.25.12.

CLUTCH AND BRAKE PEDAL ASSEMBLY   33.30.06

Overhaul

As operation 70.35.04.

SLAVE CYLINDER   33.35.01

Remove and refit

Removing
1 Raise or jack up the car and support securely.
2 Clean the slave cylinder removing all loose mud etc. in the vicinity of the fluid pipe and nipple.
3 Disconnect the fluid pipe and plug the cylinder and pipe union.
4 Remove the two bolts and nuts securing the slave cylinder to the engine.
5 Gently withdraw the slave cylinder. CAUTION: When the slave cylinder is removed do not attempt to move the operating push rod in a forward direction as this may cause the clutch release lever to be dislodged, necessitating the removal of the gearbox to permit refitting of the release lever.

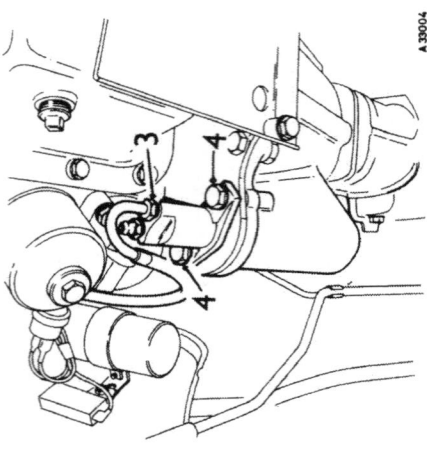

A33004

Refitting
6 Reverse instructions 3 to 5. The slave cylinder must be mounted with the bleed nipple *above* the fluid pipe.
7 Bleed the system. 33.15.01.
8 Lower the car.

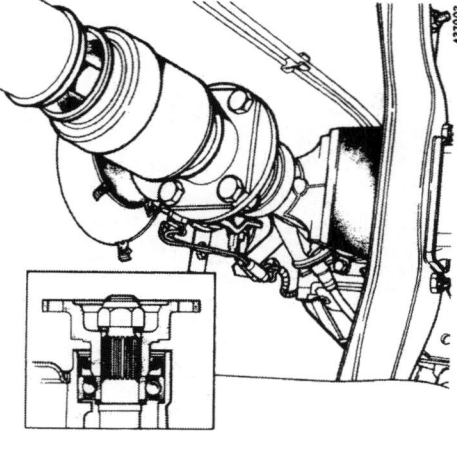

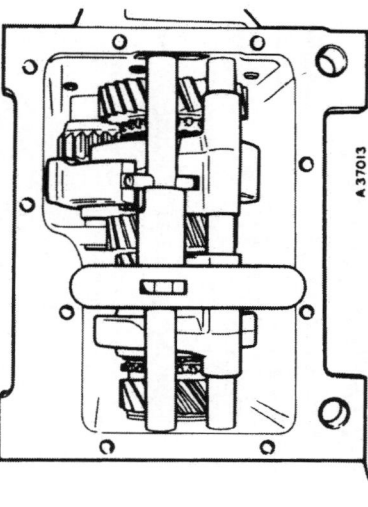

SLAVE CYLINDER

Overhaul   33.35.07

Dismantling
1   Remove the slave cylinder. 33.35.01.
2   Remove the rubber boot.
3   Extract the circlip piston, cup and spring.

Inspection
4   Discard the rubber boot and cup and clean remaining components in clear brake fluid or methylated spirit.
5   Carefully examine the piston and cylinder bore. Renew either or both components if there is evidence of corrosion or scoring.

Assembling
6   Fit a new cup to the piston.
7   Lubricate the cylinder bore with clean brake fluid.
8   Fit the smaller diameter of the spring to the piston and fit the spring (larger diameter leading) piston and cup into the cylinder. Fit the circlip.
9   Smear the piston and bore with disc brake lubricant or rubber grease.
10 Fit the rubber boot.
11 Refit the slave cylinder. 33.35.01.
12 Bleed the system. 33.15.01.

DRIVE FLANGE

Remove and refit   37.10.01

Service tools: S337 or 18G 1205

Removing
1   Raise the car and support securely.
2   Slacken one bolt securing the propeller shaft safety strap and remove the remaining bolt. Swing the strap clear of the propeller shaft.
3   Scribe the relationship of the propeller shaft and gearbox flanges and remove the four securing nuts and bolts.
4   Release the propeller shaft from the driving flange.
5   Using tool S337 to prevent rotation of the driving flange remove the securing nut and washer.
6   Withdraw the driving flange.

Refitting
7   Reverse instructions 1 to 6.
    The drive flange nut should be torqued to: 90-120 lbf ft (12.44-16.60 kgf m).
    Propeller shaft bolts to: 26-34 lbf ft (3.60-4.70 kgf m).

REAR EXTENSION

Remove and refit   37.12.01

Service tools : S337 or 18G 1205

Removing
1   Raise the car, drain the gearbox and refit the drain plug.
2   Remove the gearbox from the car, see 37.20.01.
3   Support the gearbox in a vice by means of the drain plug and remove the seat belt interlock switch and reverse switch.
4   Remove the clutch housing and gasket, see 37.12.07.
5   Withdraw the three springs from the layshaft front thrust washer.
6   Carefully drift out the roll pin from the selector rod.
7   Remove the speedometer drive pinion, see 37.25.05.
8   Using tool S337 to prevent rotation of the driving flange remove the securing nut and washer.
9   Withdraw the driving flange.
10 Remove the gearbox top cover, gasket and spool plate.
11 Locate the gear selector in the reverse gear position and ensure that the selector shaft pins clear the interlock spool and the gear selector forks.

continued

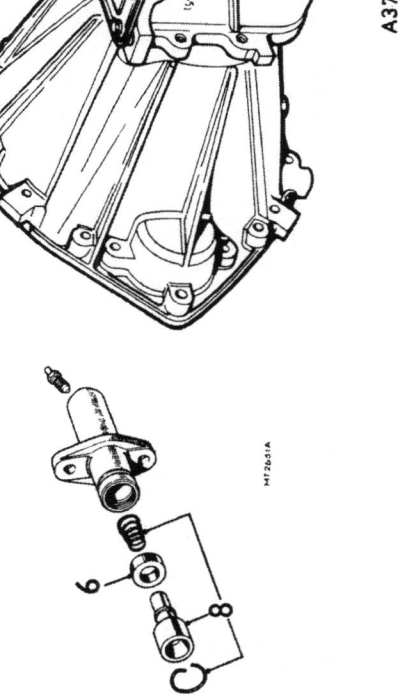

CLUTCH/BELL HOUSING 37.12.07

Remove and refit

Removing

1 Remove the gearbox from the car, see 37.20.10.

2 Withdraw the clutch release lever and release bearing, see 33.25.12.

3 Tape the splines of the first motion shaft to prevent damage to the oil seal when the clutch housing is withdrawn.

4 Remove the seven bolts and washers securing the clutch housing to the gearbox. Note that the lower bolt is fitted with a copper washer; the remaining bolts are fitted with spring washers.

5 Withdraw the clutch housing and gasket. Observe that three compression springs are inserted in the front of the gearbox casing to provide a thrust load for the layshaft front bearing.

Refitting

6 Reverse instructions 2 to 5.

7 Remove the tape from the splines of the first motion shaft.

8 Fit the gearbox to the car, see 37.20.01.

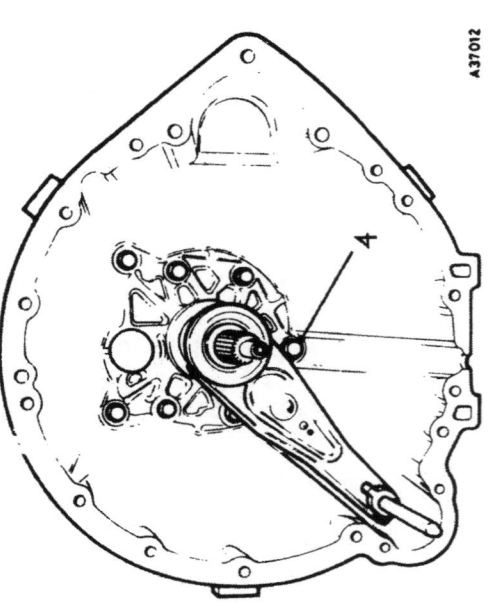

A37-014

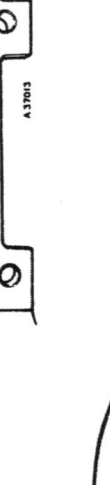

A37013

A37007

28 Refill the gearbox with fresh lubricant. Ensure drain plug is tight.

29 Fit the interlock spool plate, gasket and top cover.

30 Fit the gearbox to the car, see 37.20.01.

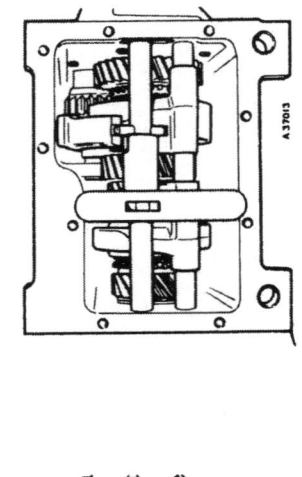

A37012

12 Remove the bolts and spring washers securing the rear extension to the gearbox and remove the rear extension exhaust bracket.

13 Remove the rear extension from the gearbox. Ensure that the selector pins do not foul and that the layshaft is not displaced. Lift out the interlock spool as the rear extension and selector shaft are withdrawn.

14 Remove the gasket.

15 Remove the distance washer from the mainshaft.

16 Remove the oil seal and bearing from the rear extension case.

Refitting

17 Ensure that the mating faces of the gear case and rear extension housing are clean.

18 Locate a new gasket in position on the rear of the gear case.

19 Fit the distance washer to the mainshaft.

20 Offer up the rear extension to the gear case and guide the selector rail into position remembering to fit the selector spool.

21 Fit the rear extension securing bolts and washers and exhaust bracket and lock plate.

22 Fit the rear bearing and a new oil seal to the extension casing. The lip of the seal must be fitted towards the gearbox. When installed the seal should be flush with the casing.

23 Lubricate the seal lip and running surface of the drive flange. Fit the drive flange, washer and nut. Using tool S337 to prevent flange rotation, torque the nut to 90-120 lbf ft (12.44-16.60 kgf m).

24 Fit the roll pin to the front end of the selector rail. This pin must be positioned centrally.

25 Fit the speedometer drive pinion, see 37.25.05.

26 Fit the seat belt interlock switch and reverse switch.

27 Fit the clutch housing, gasket, clutch release fork and bearing, see 37.12.07.

194   MANUAL GEARBOX — 4 SPEED

MAIN CASE

Remove and refit   37.12.40

As operation 37.20.04 but excluding instructions 21 to 25, 27 to 35, and 38.

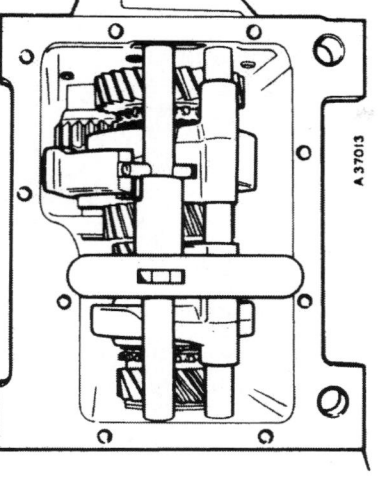

A37013

GEAR CHANGE SELECTORS

Remove and refit   37.16.31

Service tools: S337 or 18G 1205

Removing

1   Remove the gearbox rear extension, see 37.12.01.
2   Withdraw the selector fork shaft.
3   Lift out the selectors.

Refitting

4   Fit the selectors to the gears.
5   Fit the selector shaft.
6   Fit the gearbox rear extension, see 37.12.01.

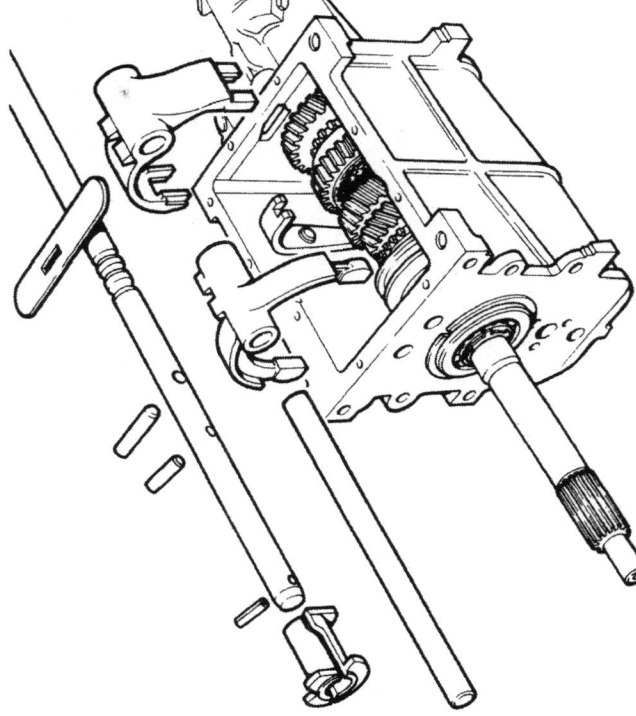

A37011

GEAR CHANGE LEVER

Remove and refit   37.16.04

Removing

1   Select neutral and unscrew and remove the gear lever knob.
2   Remove the two screws securing the gear lever gaiter and top panel assembly to the rear of the console.
3   Remove the gear lever gaiter and panel assembly.
4   Remove the four screws retaining the gear lever draught excluder and flange assembly.
5   Slide the draught excluder flange to the left to clear the console and lift off.
6   Release the bayonet cap securing the gear lever to the gearbox extension and lift out the gear lever. Care must be taken not to lose the nylon plunger and spring (anti-rattle) from the gear lever ball swivel.

Refitting

7   Reverse instructions 1 to 6.

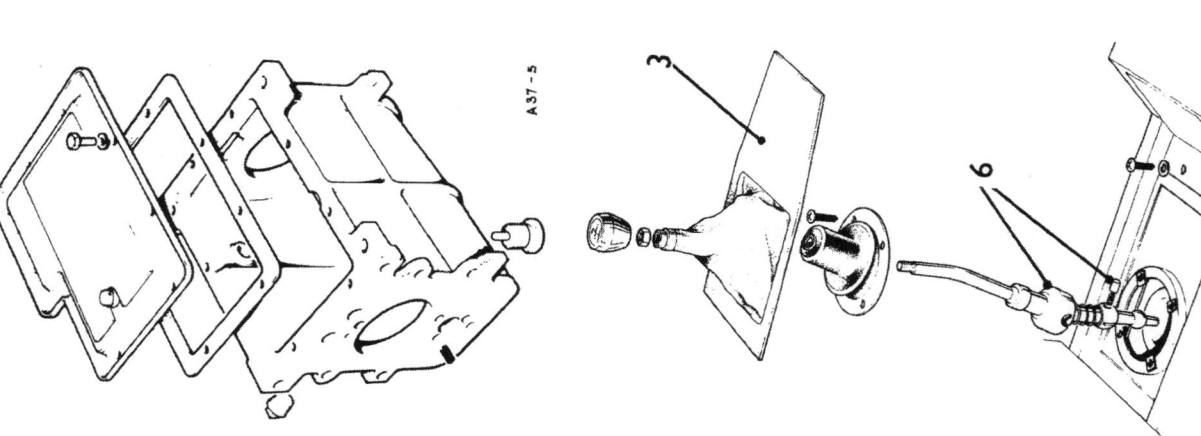

A37 – 5

A37 – 016

GEAR CHANGE LEVER DRAUGHT EXCLUDER

Remove and refit   37.16.05

As operation 37.16.04 instructions 1 to 5.

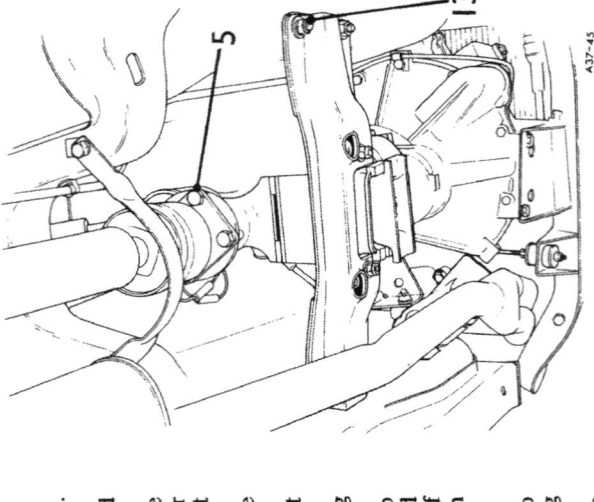

A37-45

A37-43

GEAR SELECTOR MECHANISM AND HOUSING 37.16.37

Remove and refit

Service tools: S337 or 18G 1205

Removing

1 Remove the gearbox rear extension, see 37.12.01.
2 Slide the selector shaft rearward until it contacts the rear blanking plug.
3 Gently tap the selector shaft to remove the blanking plug.
4 Slide the selector shaft rearward until the selector shaft yoke is exposed.

5 Remove the roll pin securing the yoke to the shaft and withdraw the yoke.
6 Withdraw the selector shaft, moving it towards the front of the rear extension. Ensure that the roll pin hole at the rear of the selector shaft is maintained in an horizontal position to prevent the selector plunger trapping the shaft as it is withdrawn.
7 Remove the nylon plug, plunger, spring and 'O' ring from the rear extension casing.

Refitting

8 Reverse instructions 1 to 7.

GEARBOX ASSEMBLY 37.20.01

Remove and refit

Removing

1 Disconnect the battery.
2 Remove the gear lever, see 37.16.04.
3 Remove the radiator fan guard.
4 Raise the car on a ramp or jack up and support securely.
5 Disconnect the propeller shaft at the gearbox flange and tie the propeller shaft so that it will not obstruct gearbox withdrawal.
6 Remove the exhaust down pipe, see 30.10.09.
7 Disconnect the speedometer cable at the gearbox.
8 Disconnect the electrical harness plug to the gearbox.
9 Position a jack under the engine sump and support the engine. To avoid damage to the sump a suitable piece of wood should be interposed between the jack pad and the sump.
10 Remove the starter motor.
11 Remove the clutch slave cylinder. Do not allow the cylinder to hang suspended by the fluid pipe.
12 Remove the two bolts securing the sump stiffening plate to the clutch housing.
13 Remove the four bolts and nuts securing the gearbox rear mounting bracket to the body.
14 Carefully lower the jack to permit access to the clutch housing bolts. Ensure that the water hoses and the engine stabiliser are not strained.
15 Remove the bolts and nuts securing the clutch housing to the engine. Note the location of the fitted bolt adjacent to the clutch slave cylinder.
16 Carefully withdraw the gearbox ensuring that weight and stress are not imparted to the clutch driving plate.
17 Remove the gearbox mounting bracket.

Refitting

18 Reverse instructions 1 to 17.

A37008

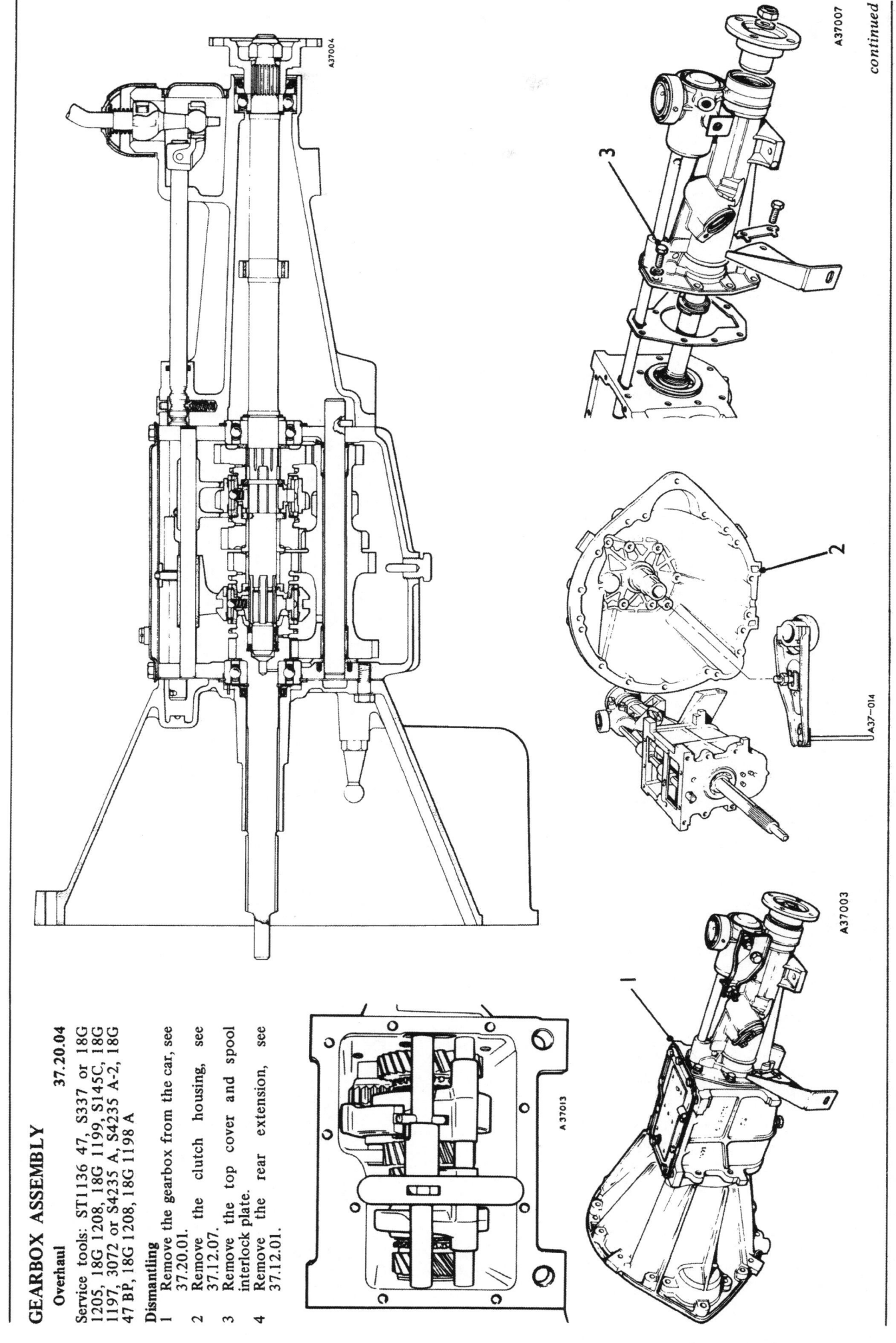

GEARBOX ASSEMBLY

Overhaul 37.20.04

Service tools: ST1136 47, S337 or 18G 1205, 18G 1208, 18G 1199, S145C, 18G 1197, 3072 or S4235 A, S4235 A-2, 18G 47 BP, 18G 1208, 18G 1198 A

Dismantling

1 Remove the gearbox from the car, see 37.20.01.

2 Remove the clutch housing, see 37.12.07.

3 Remove the top cover and spool interlock plate.

4 Remove the rear extension, see 37.12.01.

continued

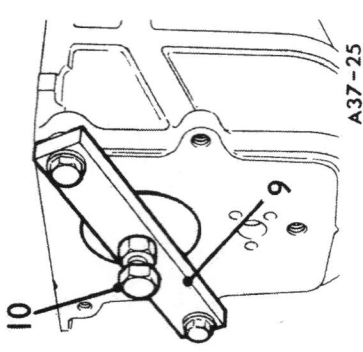
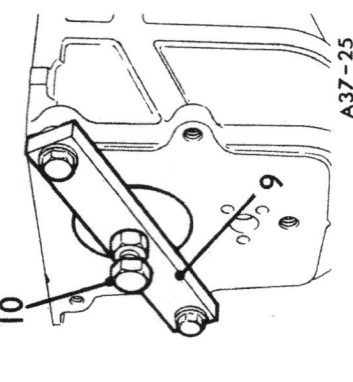

A37-25

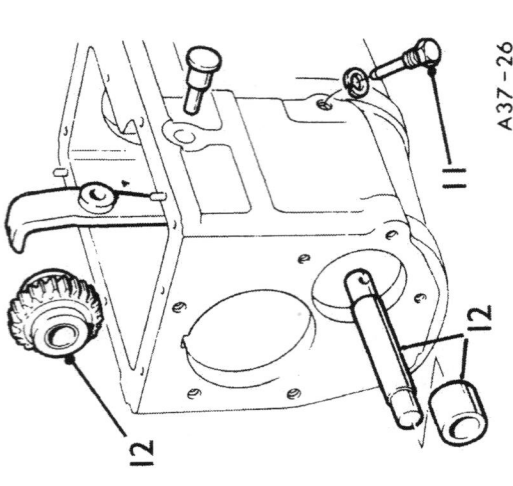

A37-26

9 Fit the steady bracket of 18G 47 BP to the front of the gear case using two clutch housing bolts. Ensure that the centre adjusting bolt and locknut are fully released before tightening the tool securing bolts.

10 Adjust the centre bolt to locate and support the mainshaft spigot. Tighten the locknut.

11 Remove the bolt and spring washer securing the reverse/idler gear spindle.

12 Withdraw the reverse/idler gear spindle, and spacer and remove the reverse/idler gear.

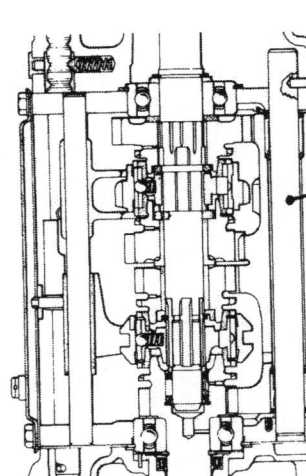

A37011

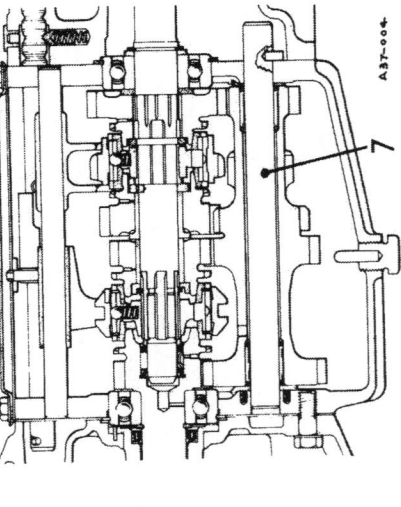

A37-004

5 Remove the gear selector mechanism, see 37.16.37.

6 Remove the selector shaft and selector forks.

7 Using tool 18G 1208 displace and remove the layshaft, allowing the laygear to drop to the bottom of the gear case.

8 Remove the first motion shaft, see 37.20.16.

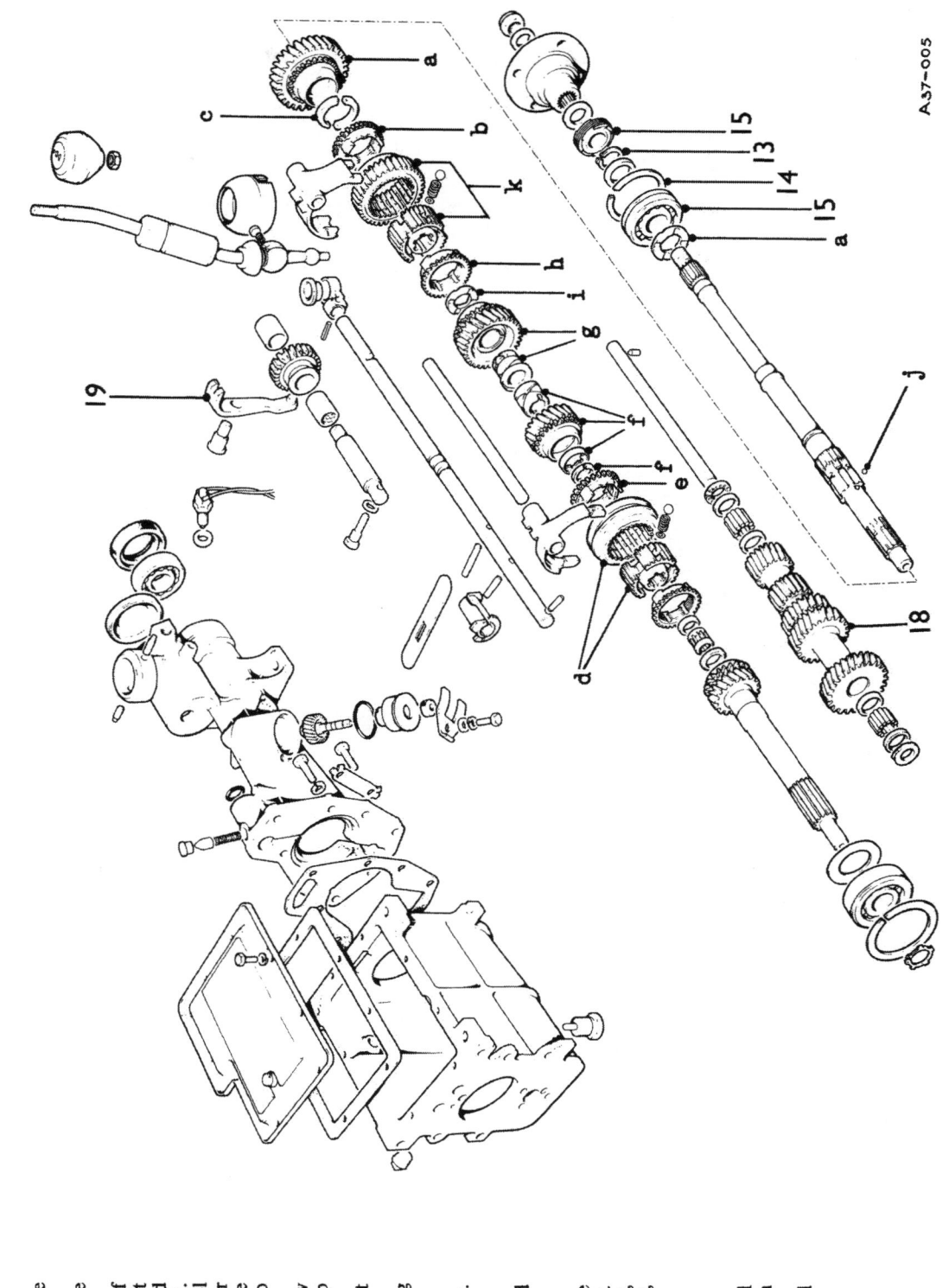

A.37-005

13　Release the circlip securing the mainshaft bearing to the mainshaft.

14　Remove the snap ring fitted to the mainshaft bearing.

15　Using tool 47 and bearing remover of 18G 47 BP, remove the mainshaft bearing, selective washer, circlip and speedometer gear from the mainshaft.

16　Remove the steady bracket of tool 18G 47 BP from the front of the gear case. Do not alter the setting of the centre bolt and locknut prior to reassembly.

17　Tilt the mainshaft and withdraw complete with gears through the top cover aperture.

18　Remove the laygear and thrust washers.

19　Remove the reverse gear operating lever.

20　Remove from the mainshaft.

　a　Thrust washer and 1st speed gear.
　b　1st speed synchro – cup.
　c　Two, split collars.
　d　3rd/4th speed synchro-hub and sleeve assembly.
　e　3rd speed synchro-cup.
　f　Using tool 18G 1199 expand the circlip retaining 3rd speed gear. Carefully lever off 3rd speed gear, and bush, thrust washer, circlip, and tool.
　g　2nd speed gear and bush.
　h　2nd speed synchro-cup.
　i　Selective washer.
　j　Using a magnet extract the ball locating the selective washer from its recess in the mainshaft.
　k　1st/2nd speed synchro-hub and sleeve assembly.

continued

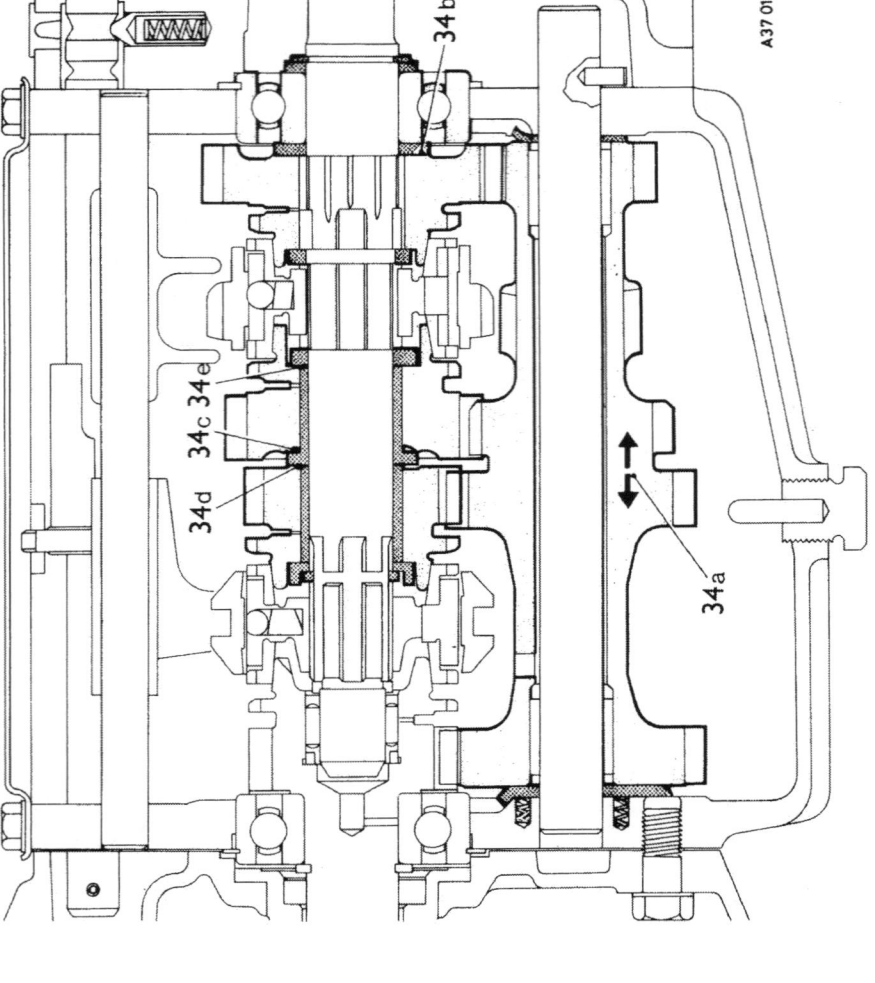

A37 017A

34b
34e
34c
34d
34a

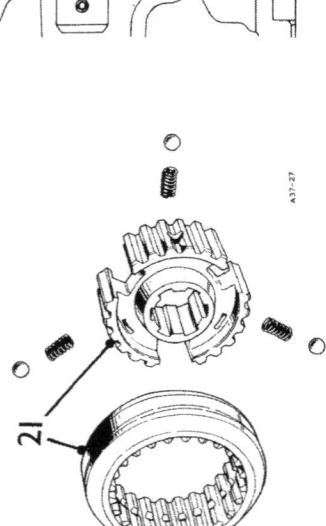

A37-27

21

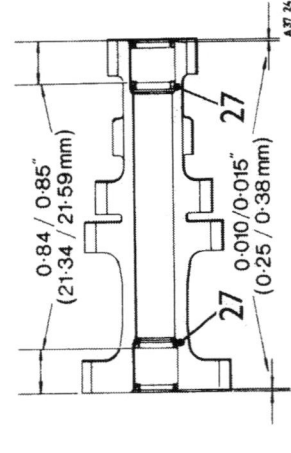

0·84 / 0·85"
(21·34 / 21·59mm)

27

27

0·010/0·015"
(0·25 / 0·38mm)

A37 24

21 Scribe the sleeve and synchro-hub assemblies of 1st/2nd and 3rd/4th speeds to ensure reassembly in the original locations. Separate the sleeves from the hubs ensuring that care is taken to capture the three balls and springs in each assembly.
Note: In some instances shims may be fitted below the springs.

22 Remove the 25 needle rollers from each end of the laygear cluster.

23 Remove the needle roller retaining rings from the laygear (only if renewal is intended).

24 Press out the bush from the reverse/idler gear.

25 Remove the reverse operating lever pivot pin from the gear case (only if renewal is intended).

Preparation for reassembly

26 Thoroughly clean and examine all components. Obtain new parts as necessary. Renew all gaskets and seals.

27 If required fit new needle roller retaining rings to the laygear to the dimensions shown. Care must be taken not to damage the laygear bore.

28 Using grease install the needle rollers (25 each side) in the laygear. Fit dummy layshaft, tool 18G 1208.

29 Fit the shims (if removed), springs and balls to the 1st/2nd speed synchro-hub and slide the sleeve into position observing the scribe marks made prior to dismantling. The teeth of the outer member must be fitted adjacent to the larger boss of the synchro-hub.

30 Check the load required to shift the sleeve in either direction. This should be within 19-27 lb (8.7-12.2 kg).
Add or remove shims to obtain required effort.

31 Fit the shims (if removed), springs and balls to the 3rd/4th speed synchro-hub and slide the sleeve into position observing the scribe marks made prior to dismantling.

32 Check the load required to shift the sleeve in either direction. This should be within 19-21 lb (8.7-9.5 kg). Add or remove shims to obtain required effort.

33 Fit a new brush to the reverse/idler gear. The bush should be flush with the boss opposite the collar of the operating lever. Ream the bush within 0.6585-0.6592 in diameter (16.7279-16.8011 mm).

34 Check that the following requirements obtain:
a Laycluster end-float — 0.007-0.015 in (0.178-0.381 mm).
b 1st gear end-float (between split collars and thrust washer) — 0.004-0.013 in (0.102-0.33 mm).
c 2nd gear end-float (on bush) 0.002 in (0.051 mm).
d 3rd gear end-float (on bush) 0.002-0.006 in (0.051-0.152 mm).
e Mainshaft bushes (2nd and 3rd gears) — 0-0.006 in (0-0.051 mm). Adjust clearances by means of selective washer. Four alternative washers are available in 0.003 in (0.076 mm) steps.

35 Renew the first motion shaft bearing, see 37.20.17.

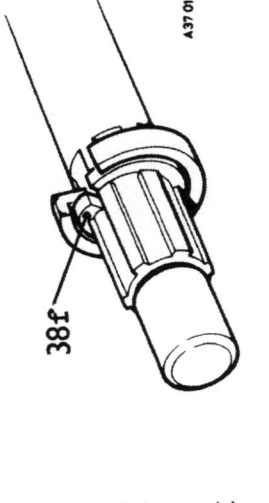

A37-25

41

A 37 018

38f

45

A 37 30

40·48

48

A37-26

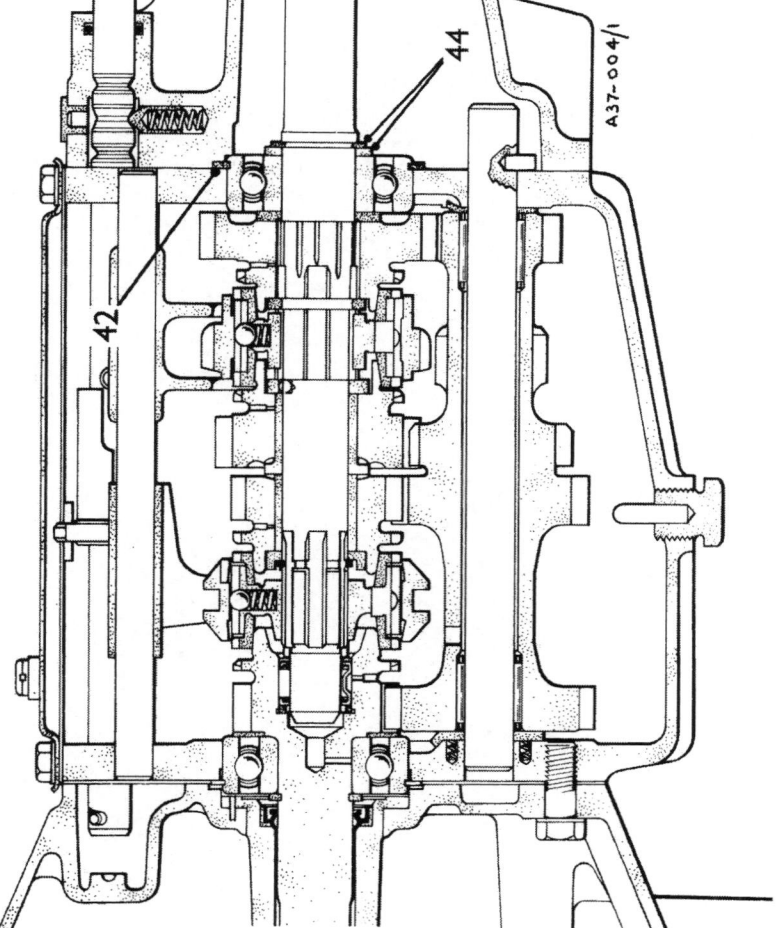

44

42

A37-004/1

Reassembling

36 Locate the laygear front and rear thrust washers in position ensuring that their respective tabs engage in the casing slots.

37 Place the laygear cluster complete with dummy shaft in the bottom of the gear case. (Large gear to front of case.)

38 Fit the following components to the mainshaft.

   a 1st/2nd speed synchro assembly (larger hub boss to front of gearcase).

   b 2nd speed synchro-cup.

   c Locating ball for selective washer.

   d Selective washer, ensuring groove on washer inner diameter aligns with ball.

   e 2nd gear and bush (bush collar to front of gearbox), 3rd gear and bush, and thrust washer (rim of washer to front of gearbox).

   f Using tool 18G 1198 fit the retaining circlip ensuring that the inclined end of the clip faces forward and the clip end aligns with the edge of the mainshaft spline.

   g 3rd gear synchro-cup, 3rd gear synchro assembly (larger boss to hub of front of gearbox).

   h 1st speed synchro-cup, split collars, 1st gear and thrust washer.

39 Tilt the mainshaft (rear end leading) into position through the top cover aperture.

40 Place the reverse gear in the bottom of the gear case and fit the reverse operating lever.

41 Fit the steady bracket of 18G 47 BP to the front of the gear case engaging the mainshaft spigot.

42 Fit the snap ring to the mainshaft centre bearing and slide the bearing (snap ring trailing) on to the mainshaft.

43 Drive the bearing into position using tool 18G 1197 and the bearing replacer of 18G 47 BP.

44 Fit the selective washer and circlip. Four selective washers are available in 0.003 in (0.076 mm) steps. Mainshaft end-float should not exceed 0.002 in (0.051 mm).

45 Fit the speedometer gear.

46 Remove the steady bracket of 18G 47 BP from the front of the gear case and fit spigot bearing and rings, 4th speed synchro-cup, and the 1st motion shaft.

47 Fit the layshaft, removing the dummy shaft in the process.

48 Fit the reverse gear, reverse gear shaft and spacer.

continued

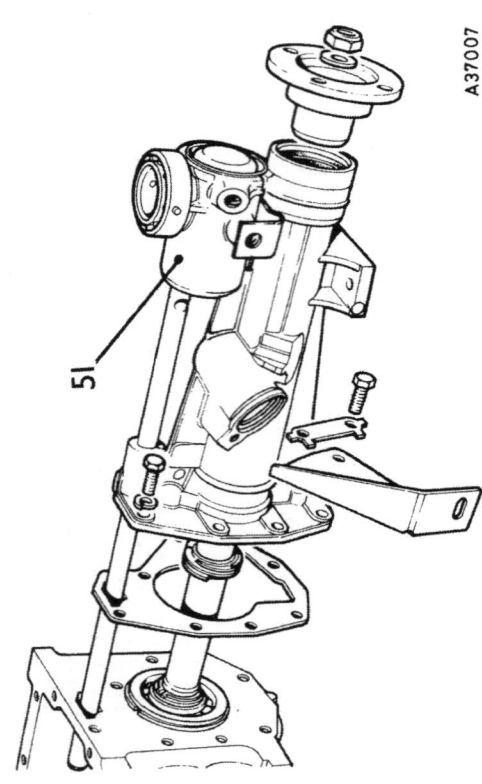

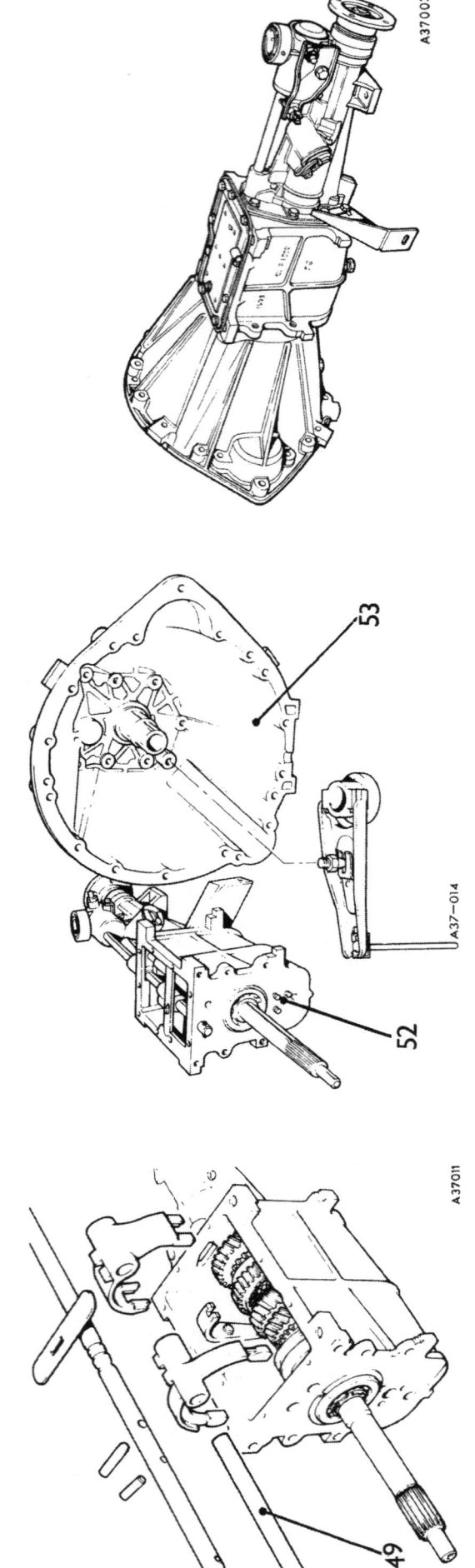

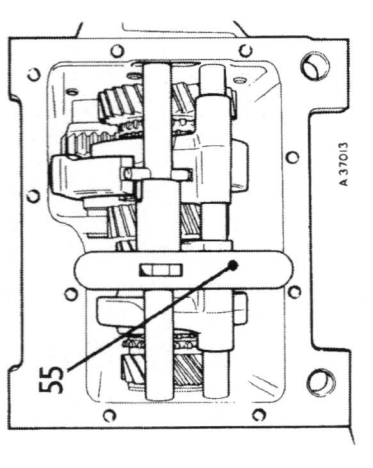

49 Fit the selector forks and shaft.
50 Fit the gear selector mechanism, see 37.16.37.
51 Fit the rear extension and drive flange, see 37.12.01.
52 Fit the three thrust springs to the laygear front bearing.
53 Fit the clutch housing gasket, clutch housing, clutch release fork and bearing, see 37.12.07. Ensure splines of 1st motion shaft do not damage seal.
54 Fit the gear case drain plug and fill to level plug with fresh oil.
55 Fit the spool interlock plate, gasket and top cover.

SYNCHRONIZER ASSEMBLIES

Remove and refit   37.20.07

Service tools: Refer operation 37.20.04

Removing
Instructions 1 to 17 and 20a to 20h.

Refitting
Instructions 38 to 40, 42 to 50 and 52 to 55.

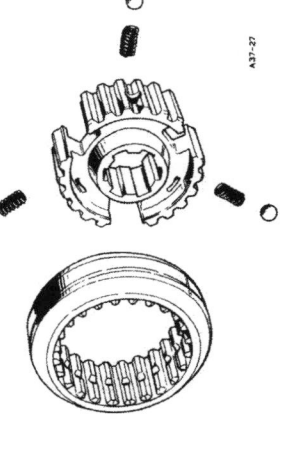

A37-27

FIRST MOTION SHAFT   37.20.16

Remove and refit

Service tools: 18G 1208, 3072 or S4235 A, S4235 A - 2

Removing
1 Remove the gearbox from the car, see 37.20.01.
2 Remove the rear extension, see 37.12.01.
3 Remove the clutch housing, see 37.12.07.
4 Insert tool 18G 1208 and push out the layshaft.
5 Allow the laygear with tool 18G 1208 to drop to the bottom of the gearbox case.
6 Fit tool 3072 and adaptor S4235 A - 2 to the first motion shaft.
7 Extract the first motion shaft from the gearbox.
8 Remove the spigot bearing and spacers (2).
9 Remove the 4th gear synchromesh cup.

Refitting
10 Reverse instructions 1 to 9.

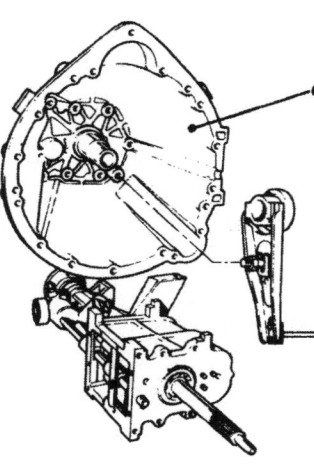

A37-014

3

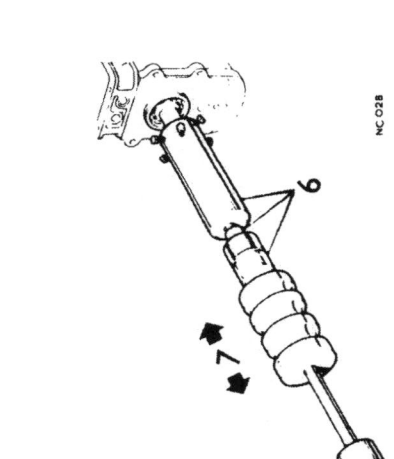

NC 028

7
6

FIRST MOTION SHAFT BEARING

Remove and refit   37.20.17

Service tools 18G 1208, 3072 or S4235 A, S4235-2

Removing
1 Remove the first motion shaft, see 37.20.16.
2 Remove the bearing circlip.
3 Remove the bearing snap ring.
4 Using tool S4235 A and adaptor S4235 A-2 remove the bearing from the shaft.
5 Remove the oil flinger.

Refitting
6 Reverse instructions 1 to 5. Use grease to retain the oil flinger when fitting the bearing to the shaft.

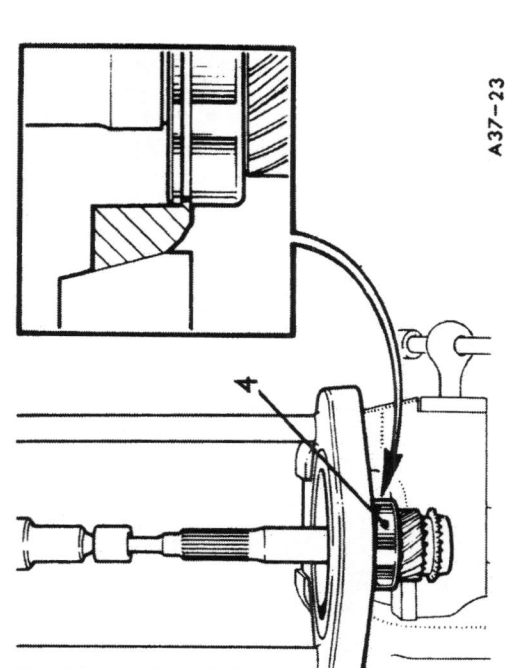

4

A37-23

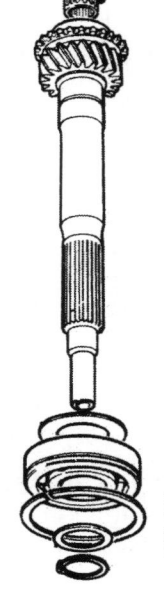

8

A37-041

I NC 028

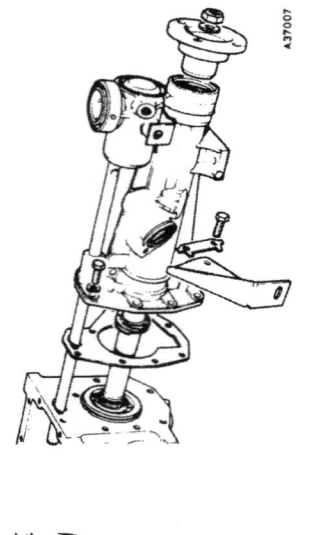

LAYSHAFT

Remove and refit   37.20.19

Service tools: S337 or 18G 1205, 18G 1208

Removing
1. Remove the gearbox from the car, see 37.20.01.
2. Remove the clutch housing, see 37.12.07.
3. Remove the top cover and spool interlock plate.
4. Remove the rear extension, see 37.12.01.
5. Using tool 18G 1208 displace and remove the layshaft.

Refitting
6. Reverse instructions 1 to 5.

MAINSHAFT BEARING

Remove and refit   37.20.26

Service tools: S337 or 18G 1205, 18G 1208, 18G 1197.

Removing
As operation 37.20.04 Instructions 1 to 4 and 6 to 16.

Refitting
As operation 37.20.04 Instructions 42 to 48, 50, and 52 to 55.

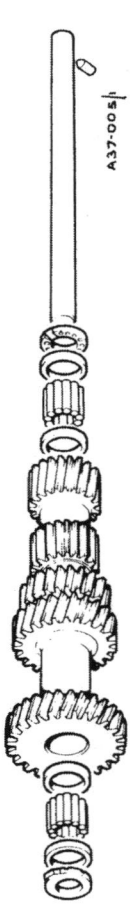

LAYSHAFT BEARING

Remove and refit   37.20.22

Service tools: S337 or 18G 1205, 18G 1208, 18G 1199, S145 C, 18G 1197, 3072 or S4235 A, S4235 A - 2

As operation 37.20.04 instructions 1 to 10, 13 to 18, 22, 23, 27, 28, 36, 37 and 41 to 55.

REAR OIL SEAL

Remove and refit   **37.23.01**

Service tools: S337 or 18G 1205

Removing
1 Raise the car.
2 Remove the drive flange, see 37.10.01.
3 Prise out the oil seal.

Refitting
4 Evenly install the new seal in the gearbox rear extension ensuring that it is flush with the rear face of the extension housing. Note that the seal lips must be towards the gearbox.
5 Lubricate the seal lips and driving flange seal contact area.
6 Fit the drive flange, see 37.10.01.
7 Lower the car.

FIRST MOTION SHAFT OIL SEAL

Remove and refit   **37.23.04**

Removing
1 Remove the gearbox from the car, see 37.20.01.
2 Remove the clutch housing, see 37.12.07.
3 Remove the oil seal.

Refitting
4 Evenly install a new oil seal ensuring that the seal lips are towards the clutch.
5 Lubricate the seal lips and ensure that the splines of the first motion shaft are protected by tape to prevent damage to the seal lip when the clutch housing is fitted.
6 Fit the clutch housing, see 37.12.07.
7 Remove the tape from the splines of the first motion shaft.
8 Fit the gearbox to the car, see 37.20.01.

GEAR CHANGE ROD OIL SEAL

Remove and refit   **37.23.10**

Service tools: S337 or 18G 1205

As operation 37.16.37.

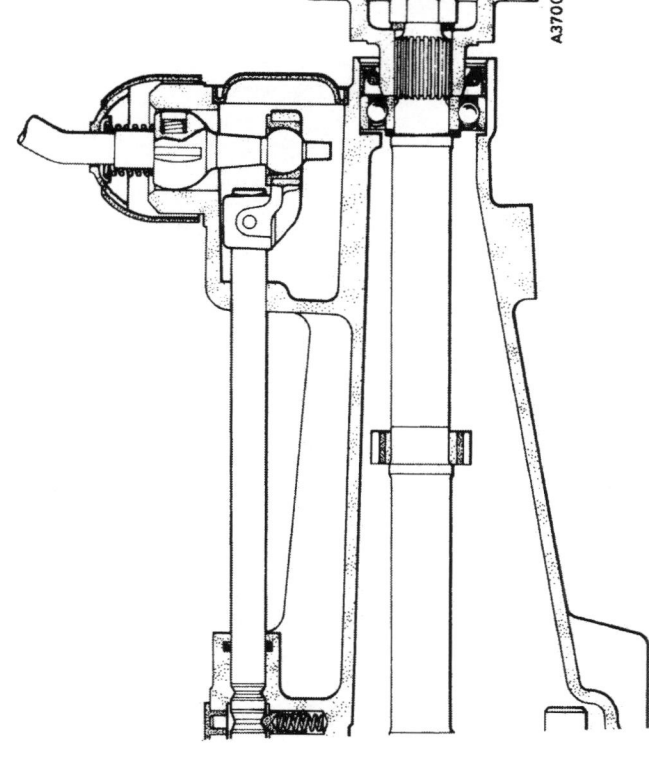

SPEEDOMETER DRIVE GEAR 37.25.01

Remove and refit

Service tools: S337 or 18G 1205, 18G 1197

Removing

1   Remove the gearbox from the car, see 37.20.01.
2   Remove the rear extension, see 37.12.01.
3   Remove the speedometer drive gear.

Refitting

4   Using tool 18G 1197 drive the speedometer gear into position on the mainshaft ensuring that it registers against the step on the mainshaft.
5   Reverse instructions 1 and 2.

A37007

SPEEDOMETER DRIVE PINION 37.25.05

Remove and refit

Removing

1   Remove the bolt and spring washer retaining the speedometer cable clamp plate.
2   Release the speedometer cable from the drive pinion.
3   Remove the pinion housing and pinion from the gearbox rear extension.

Refitting

4   Reverse instructions 1 to 3. Renew the pinion housing 'O' ring if necessary.

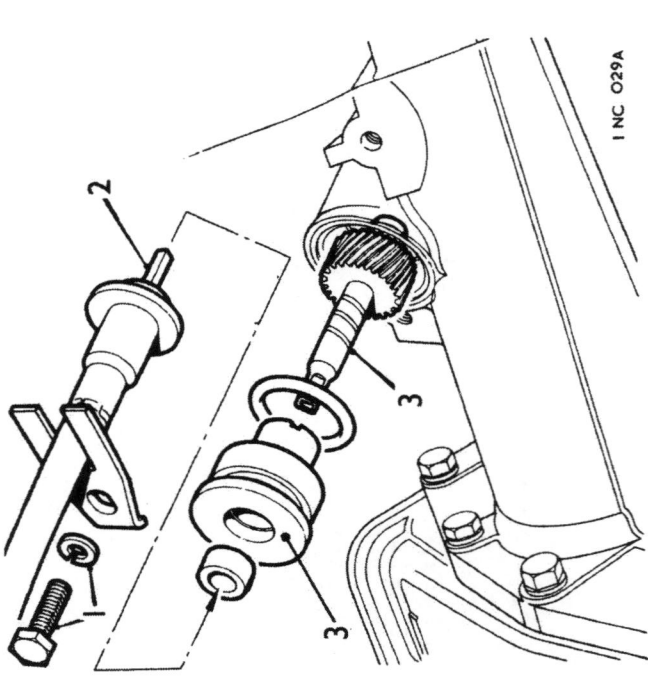

1 NC O29A

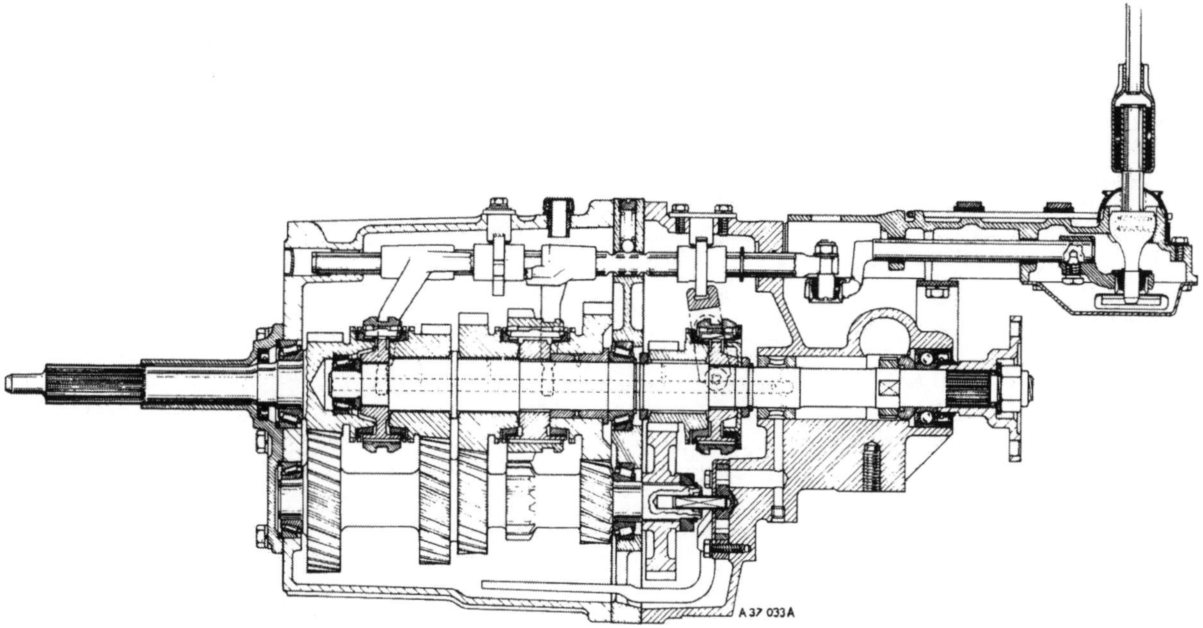

GEARBOX—5-SPEED

CLUTCH/BELL HOUSING 37.12.07

Remove and refit

Service tools: ST 1136

Removing

1 Remove the gearbox from the car, see 37.20.10/55.
2 Withdraw the clutch release lever and release bearing, see 33.25.12.
3 Remove the six bolts, plain and spring washers securing the clutch housing to the gearcase.
4 Remove the clutch housing.

Refitting

5 Reverse instructions 1 to 4.

REAR COVER 37.12.42

Remove and refit

Service tools: RG 421 or 18G 1205

Removing

1 Disconnect the battery.
2 Remove the gear lever.
3 Raise the car on a ramp or jack and support securely.
4 Remove one bolt from the propeller shaft safety strap, slacken the remaining bolt and swing the strap aside.
5 Disconnect the propeller shaft from the gearbox.
6 Tie the propeller shaft to the vehicle in a position where it allows access to the gearbox.
7 Release the rubber rings securing the exhaust system.
8 Detach the exhaust system from the manifold down-pipe.
9 Remove the gearbox drain plug and drain the oil.
10 Disconnect the speedometer cable and remove the speedometer drive pinion and housing, see 37.25.05.
11 Using tool RG 421 or 18G 1205 to prevent shaft rotation remove the nut and washer securing the gearbox drive flange.
12 Withdraw the drive flange.

continued

DRIVE FLANGE 37.10.01

Remove and refit

Service tools: RG 421 or 18G 1205

Removing

1 Raise the car and support securely.
2 Slacken the bolt securing the propeller shaft strap and remove the remaining bolt. Swing the strap clear of the propeller shaft.
3 Scribe the relationship of the propeller shaft and gearbox flanges and remove the four securing nuts and bolts.
4 Release the propeller shaft from the gearbox flange.

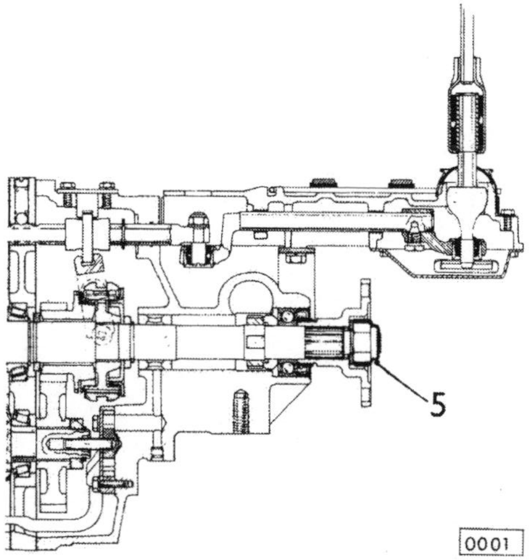

5 Using tool RG 421 or 18G 1205 to prevent rotation of the gearbox driving flange remove the securing nut and washer.
6 Withdraw the driving flange.

Refitting

7 Reverse instructions 1 to 6. The gearbox flange nut should be torqued to: 90-120 lbf ft (12.44-16.60 kgf m). Propeller shaft bolts to: 26-34 lbf ft (3.60-4.70 kgf m).

A37 033A

0001

13 Locate the jack under the engine flywheel and support the weight of engine and gearbox.
14 Remove the four bolts, spring washers and plate washers securing the gearbox rear crossmember to the body.
15 Carefully lower the jack slightly to facilitate access to the top of the gearbox.
16 Remove the nut, washer and pin securing the remote control linkage to the gearbox selector rod and detach the reverse switch lead.
17 Remove the two bolts and spring washers securing the flange of the fifth gear spool locating boss.
18 Withdraw the fifth gear spool locating boss.

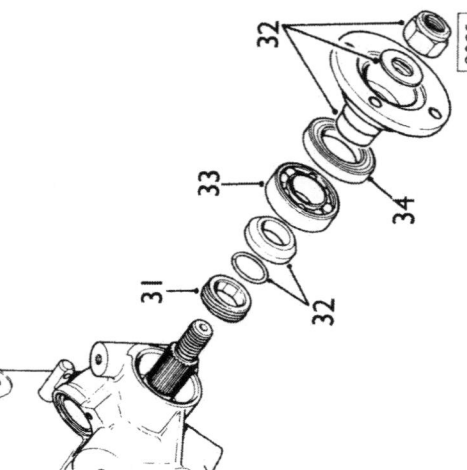

0003

19 Place a container under the gearbox centre plate/rear cover to catch residual oil when the rear cover is disturbed.
20 Remove the bolts and spring washers securing the rear cover to the gearbox.
21 Withdraw the rear cover and gasket ensuring that the centre plate is not disturbed.
22 Fit temporary slave bolts to retain the centre plate in position.
23 Remove the oil pump drive shaft.
24 Remove the rear oil seal, bearing, spacer, ring and speedometer driving gear from the rear cover.

Refitting
25 Remove the slave bolts from the gearbox centre plate.
26 Ensure that the centre plate and rear cover mating faces are clean and fit a new gasket to the centre plate.

0002

27 Engage the oil pump drive shaft in the layshaft.

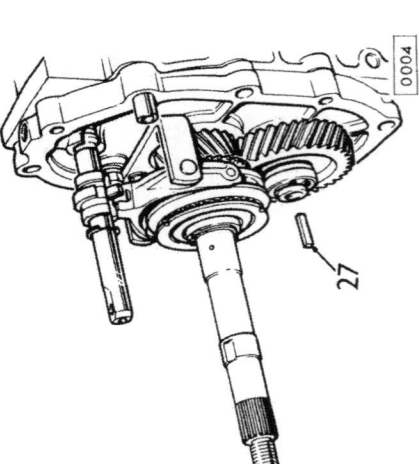

0004

28 Note the radial relationship of the square oil pump drive and align the oil pump gear centre.
29 Offer up the rear cover to the gearbox mainshaft and slide carefully into position. Ensure that the oil pump shaft engages the oil pump.
30 Fit and tighten the rear cover securing bolts.

0005

31 Fit the speedometer driving gear ensuring that it properly engages the flats on the mainshaft and that the tapered head of the gears is to the rear.
32 Fit the circlip and the spacer, (machined recess in spacer towards the circlip).
33 Fit the rear bearing.
34 Fit a new oilseal. Lubricate the seal lip.
35 Lubricate the seal contact area on the driving flange and fit the flange, washer and nut.
36 Fit the 5th gear spool locating boss.
37 Fit the pin, washer and nut securing the remote control linkage to the gearbox selector rod. Connect the reverse switch lead.
38 Raise the jack supporting the engine and bolt the gearbox crossmember to the body.

39 Remove the engine jack.
40 Connect the propeller shaft to the gearbox.
41 Fit the propeller shaft safety strap.
42 Connect up the exhaust system.
43 Fit and tighten the gearbox drain plug.
44 Refill the gearbox with fresh oil.
45 Lower the car.
46 Fit the gear lever.
47 Connect the battery.

OIL PUMP

Remove and refit   37.12.47

Removing
1 Remove the rear cover, see 37.12.42.
2 Remove the four bolts and spring washers securing the oil pump cover to the gearbox rear cover.
3 Withdraw the oil pump cover and oil intake pipe.
4 Remove the internal and external toothed gears.

Refitting
5 Reverse instructions 1 to 4.

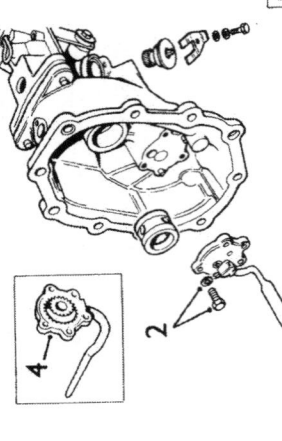

0006

OIL PUMP

Test
37.12.50

1 Ensure that the gearbox oil level is correct.
2 Start the engine and allow to idle.
3 Remove the threaded plug in the rear cover, a steady flow of oil should be expelled.
4 Switch off the engine.
5 Prime the plug with 'Locquic Primer Grade T' then applying 'Loctite 270' immediately prior to assembly, refit the threaded plug.
6 Check and top up the gearbox level.

GEAR CHANGE LEVER

Remove and refit
37.16.04

Removing

1 Select neutral and unscrew and remove the gear lever knob.
2 Slacken the two screws securing the gear lever gaiter and top panel assembly to the rear of the console.
3 Remove the gear lever gaiter and panel assembly.
4 Remove the four screws retaining the gear lever draught excluder and flange assembly.
5 Withdraw the draught excluder and flange assembly.
6 Remove the dome cover securing the gear lever to the correct extension housing.
7 Remove the countersunk screw and bolt securing the bias spring rear bridge, and withdraw the bridge and liner.
8 Carefully prise the bias spring legs clear of the gear lever pins.
9 Gently lift out the gear lever taking care not to lose the nylon plunger and spring (anti-rattle) from the gear lever pivot ball.

Refitting

10 Reverse instructions 1 to 9.

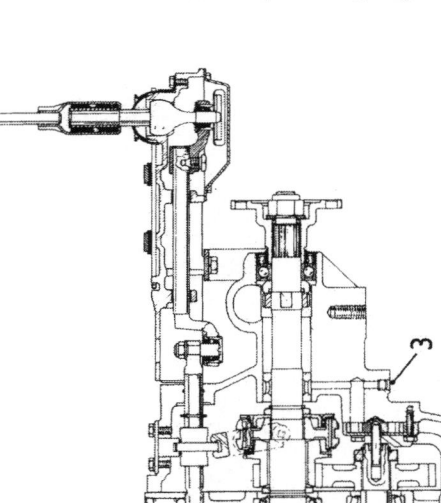

GEAR CHANGE REMOTE CONTROL ASSEMBLY

Remove and refit
37.16.19

Removing

1 Disconnect the battery.
2 Remove the gear lever, see 37.16.04/55.
3 Raise the car on a ramp, or jack up the rear of the vehicle and support securely.
4 Remove one bolt from the propeller shaft safety strap and slacken the remaining bolt and swing the strap aside.
5 Disconnect the propeller shaft from the gearbox.
6 Tie the propeller shaft to the vehicle in a position where it allows access to the gearbox.
7 Release the rubber rings securing the exhaust system.
8 Detach the exhaust system from the manifold down pipe.

9 Locate a jack under the gearbox and support weight.
10 Disconnect the two reverse light switch leads.
11 Disconnect the speedometer cable at the gearbox.
12 Remove the four bolts securing the gearbox rear mounting bracket.
13 Carefully lower the jack and gearbox sufficient to obtain access to the remote control assembly.
14 Disconnect the nut, washer and pin securing the gearbox selector shaft to the remote control shaft.
15 Remove the four bolts, spring and plain washers securing the remote control assembly to the gearbox rear cover.
16 Withdraw the remote control assembly.

Refitting

17 Reverse instructions 1 to 16.

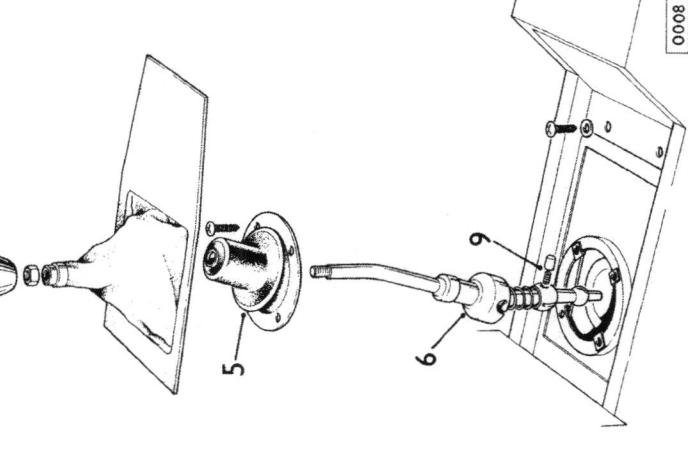

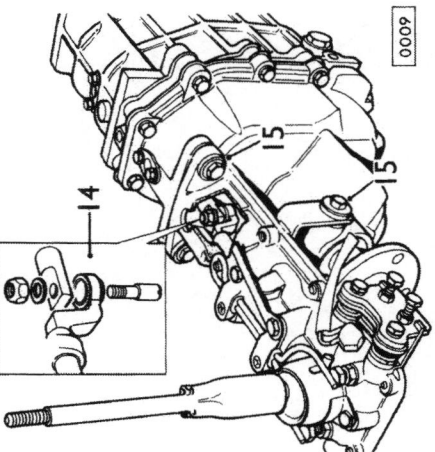

GEAR CHANGE REMOTE CONTROL ASSEMBLY

Overhaul   37.16.20

Dismantling

1 Remove the remote control assembly from the gearbox.

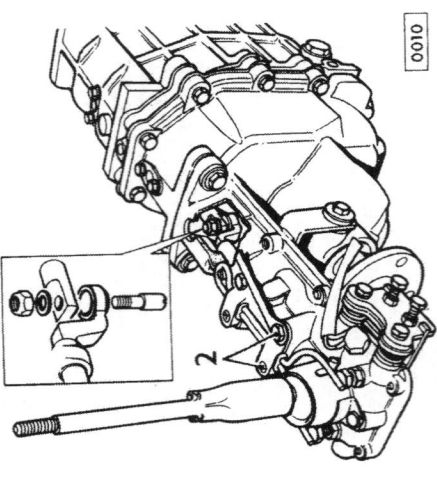

2 Remove the two bolts and two countersunk screws securing the bias spring bridge plates.
3 Remove the two bridge plates, bridge plate liners and the bias spring.
4 Remove the bias spring adjusting bolts and locknuts.
5 Remove the two bolts and washers securing the reverse baulk plate assembly and withdraw the reverse baulk plate, springs and spacers.
6 Remove the four bolts and washers securing the bottom cover plate.
7 Remove the bottom cover plate.
8 Remove the reverse light switch and locknut.
9 Remove the square-headed pinchbolt securing the selector shaft elbow.
10 Remove the selector shaft elbow.
11 Withdraw the selector shaft.
12 Press out the two selector shaft bushes in the remote control casing.
13 Remove the circlips securing the pivot ball and bushes in the selector shaft elbows and press out the bushes and pivot balls.

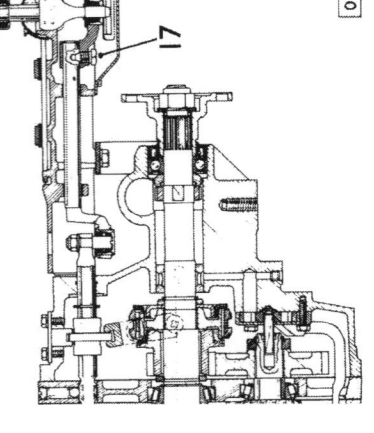

Assembling

14 Press in new selector shaft bushes in the remote control casing.
15 Fit new bushes, pivot balls and circlips to the selector shaft elbow.
16 Fit the selector shaft to the casing.
17 Fit the rear elbow and secure with the square-headed pinchbolt.
18 Fit the baulk plate assembly.
19 Fit the reverse switch and locknut.
20 Fit the bottom cover plate.
21 Fit the bias spring adjusting bolts and locknuts.
22 Fit the bias spring, bridge plate liners and bridge plates.
23 Fit the remote control assembly to the gearbox.
    Operations to be carried out following the fitting of the remote control assembly to the gearbox.
24 Fit the gear lever.

Adjusting the reverse baulk plate

Adjustment of the reverse baulk plate must be carried out on a complete gearbox assembly.

25 Remove the bottom cover plate of the gear lever remote control assembly.
26 Locate the gear lever in neutral in a vertical position.
27 Slacken the baulk plate adjusting bolts and locknuts until the baulk plate is in contact with the backing plate.
28 Tighten the adjusting bolts *equally* until they just start to move the baulk plate out of contact with the backing plate.
29 Using a straight edge and feeler gauge move the adjusting bolts equally until a clearance of 0.050 to 0.060 in (1,27 to 1,42 mm) exists between (a) the lower face of the gear lever and the underside of the baulk plate. Tighten the locknuts. Note also that (b) a minimum clearance of 0.10 in (0,254 mm) must exist between the upper face of the baulk plate and the lower edge of the gear lever bush.

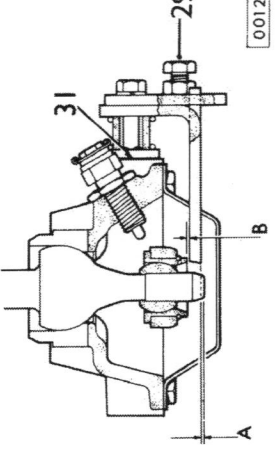

Adjustment of 1st/2nd gate stop

This operation must be carried out following the adjustment of the reverse baulk plate.

30 Engage 1st plate.
31 Check the clearance between the side of the gear lever and the edge of the baulk plate. This should be 0.004 to 0.012 in (0,10 to 0,30 mm). Adjust by adding or removing shims as necessary.
32 Check clearance between baulk plate edge and gear lever with 1st and 2nd gears engaged.
33 Fit bottom cover plate.

Adjustment of gear lever bias spring

34 Unit completely assembled, engage 3rd gear.
35 Adjust the screws to position both legs of spring 0.5 mm clear of lever crosspin.
36 Apply a light load to gear lever in L.H. direction taking up play. Adjust R.H. screw downward until R.H. spring leg just makes contact with crosspin.
37 Repeat instruction 36 on the other side. Play will still be present but at extremes of gear lever travel the crosspin should make contact with the spring legs.
38 Return lever to neutral and rock across gate several times. Lever should return to 3rd/4th gate.
39 Tighten the locknuts.
40 Adjust the reverse switch, see 86.65.20.

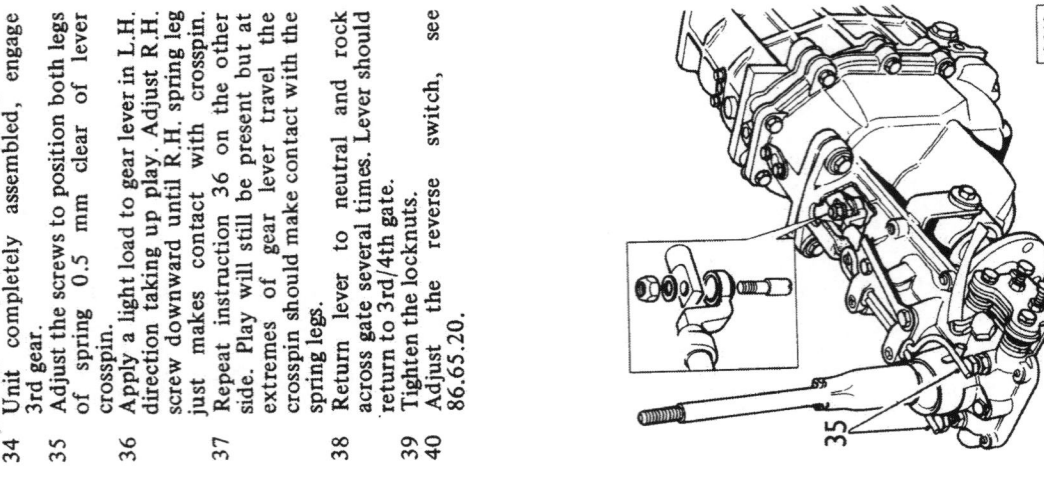

GEARBOX

Remove and refit   **37.20.01**

Removing

1 Disconnect the battery.

2 Remove the gear lever, see 37.16.04.

3 Raise the car on a ramp, or jack up and support securely.

4 Remove the propeller shaft safety strap.

5 Disconnect the propeller shaft at the gearbox flange and tie the propeller shaft so that it will not obstruct gearbox withdrawal.

6 Disconnect the electrical connections at the reverse switch.

7 Release the speedometer cable at the gearbox.

8 Remove the exhaust down pipe.

9 Withdraw the starter motor heat shield. (Spring clips to solenoid.)

10 Position a jack under the engine sump and support the engine. To avoid damage to the sump a suitable piece of wood should be interposed between the jack pad and the sump.

11 Remove the two bolts securing the clutch slave cylinder to the clutch housing and withdraw the slave cylinder. Do not allow the weight of the cylinder to hang suspended on the fluid hose.

12 Remove the two bolts securing the engine sump stiffening plate to the clutch housing.

13 Remove the four nuts securing the gearbox rear crossmember to the body.

14 Lower the jack located under the engine sump ensuring that radiator hoses are not strained. Ensure also that the gear lever remote control housing does not foul the brake pipe.

15 Disconnect the wires to the starter motor and remove the starter motor.

16 Remove the bolts and nuts securing the clutch housing to the engine. Note the location of the dowel bolt adjacent to the lower bolt of the clutch slave cylinder mounting flange and the positions of the clips for the electrical harness.

17 Carefully withdraw the gearbox and clutch housing assembly ensuring that weight and stress are not imparted to the clutch driving plate. Mention of the fact that the dry weight of the gearbox and clutch housing assembly is approximately 60.5 lb (27.5 kg) provides some idea of the effort required to handle this unit.

Refitting

18 Reverse instructions 1 to 17.

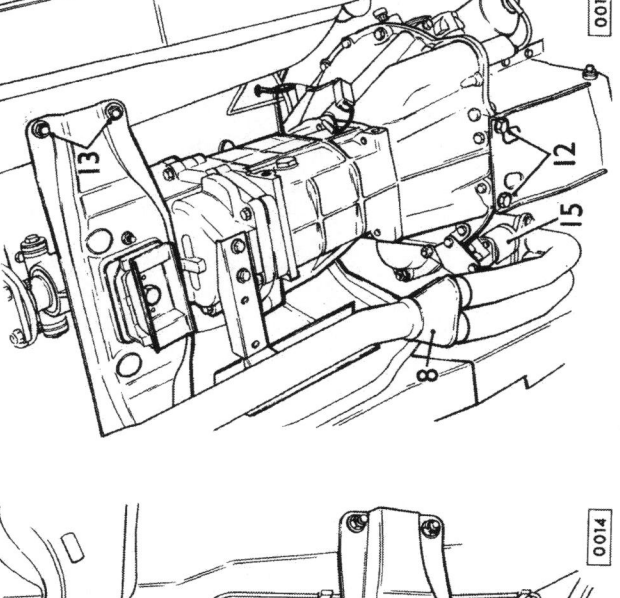

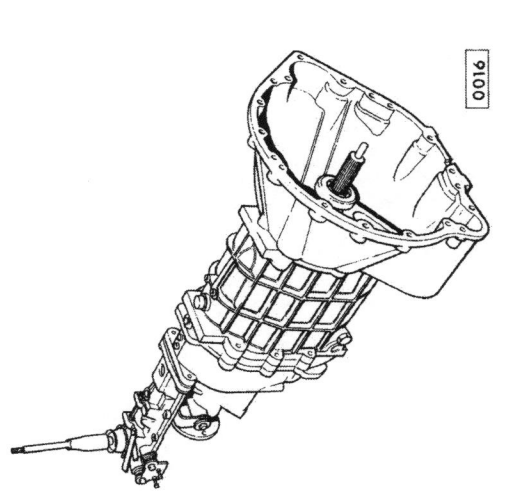

GEARBOX ASSEMBLY

Overhaul   37.20.04

Service tools: 47, 284, 18G 705-1, RG 421 or 18G 1205, RTR 47-23, LC 370-2, 18G 705 or S323, 18G 284 AAH, ST 1136

Dismantling

1   Place the gearbox on a bench or a gearbox stand ensuring that the oil is first drained.

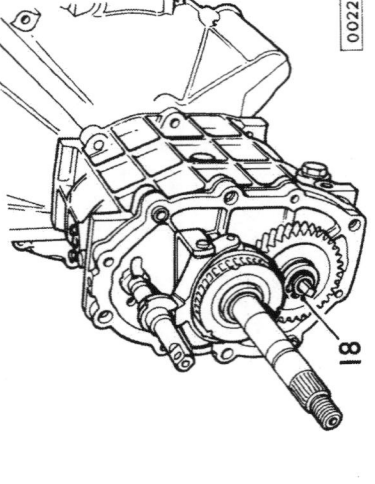

0017

2   Using tool ST 1136 unscrew the clutch release lever pivot bolt and withdraw the clutch release lever complete with pivot bolt and release bearing slippers.

3   Detach the release bearing and slippers.

4   Remove the six bolts, plain and spring washers securing the bell housing to the gearcase and remove the bell housing.

5   Remove the nut and connecting pin linking the selector shaft to the remote control shaft.

6   Remove the four bolts, spring and plain washers (2 top, 1 either side) securing the remote control housing to the gearcase rear cover.

7   Remove the nut and plain washer securing the drive flange to the mainshaft. Use tool RG 421 or 18G 1205 to prevent shaft rotation.

8   Withdraw the driving flange.

9   Remove the speedometer driven gear and housing.

10   Remove the two bolts and spring washers securing the locating boss for the selector rear spool and withdraw the locating boss.

11   Remove the ten bolts, spring and plain washers securing the rear cover to the gearcase and withdraw the rear cover and gasket.

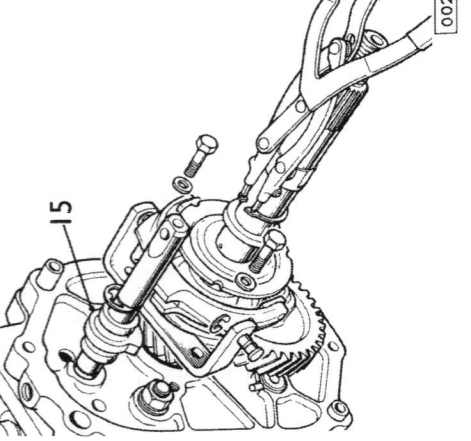

0019

12   Withdraw the oil pump drive shaft.

13   Remove the fifth gear selector fork and bracket (two bolts and spring washers).

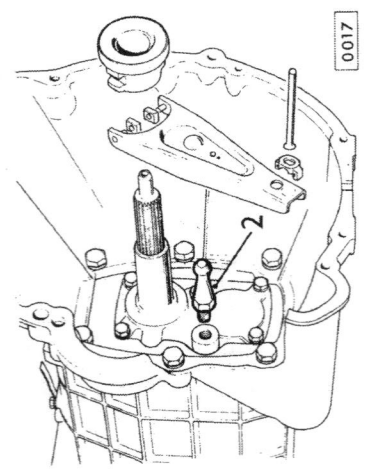

0018

14   Remove the circlip from the selector shaft.

15   Withdraw the fifth gear selector spool. Note that the longer cam of the spool is fitted towards the bottom of the gearbox.

16   Remove the circlip retaining the fifth gear synchro assembly to the mainshaft.

0020

17   Withdraw the synchro assembly, fifth gear (driven) and spacer from the mainshaft.

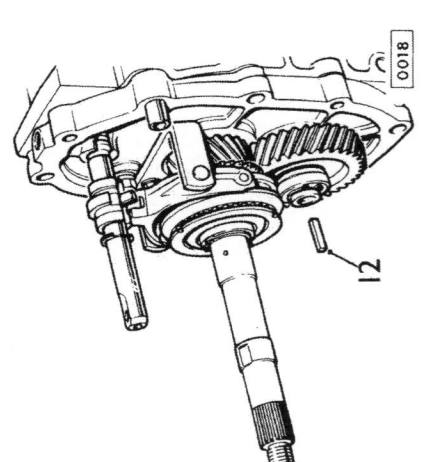

0021

18   Remove the circlip retaining the fifth gear (driving) from the layshaft.

19   Using tool 18G 705 and adaptors 18G 705-1 remove the fifth gear and spacer from the layshaft.

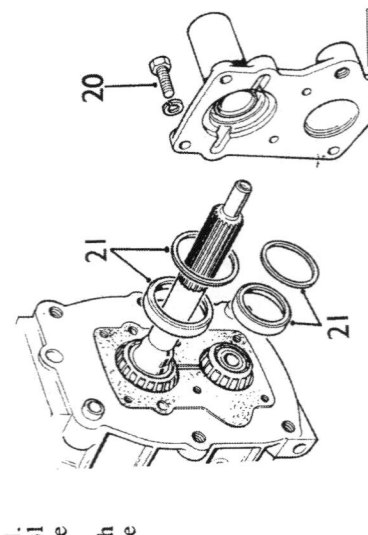

0022

20   Remove the front cover and gasket (six bolts and spring washers).

21   Remove the input shaft selective washer, bearing track, layshaft selective washer and bearing track from the gearcase.

22   Remove the two bolts and spring washers securing the locating boss for the selector shaft front spool and withdraw the locating boss.

23   Remove the selector plug, spring and ball from centre plate.

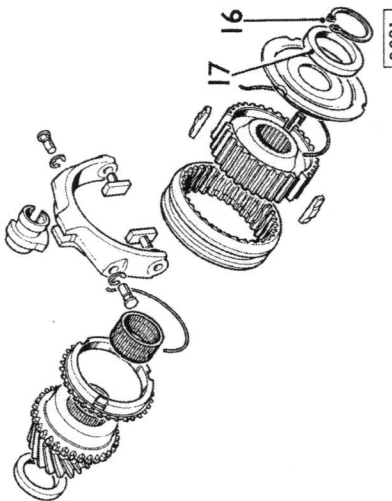

0023

A37-070

24 Supporting the gearbox on the centre plate withdraw the gearcase.
25 Remove the input shaft and 1st gear synchro cone.
26 Withdraw the layshaft cluster.

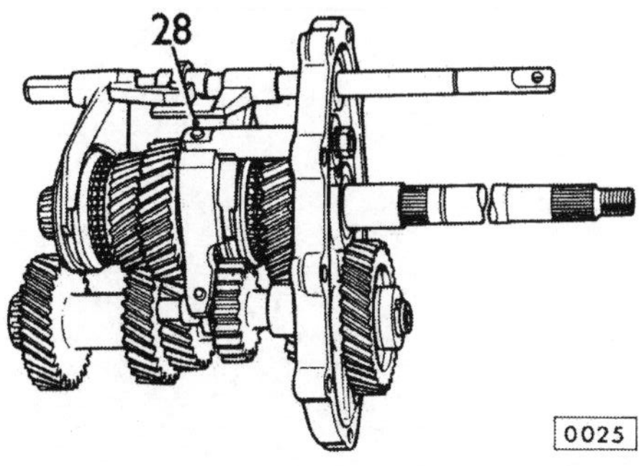

0024

27 Support the centre plate complete with gears in protected vice jaws.
28 Remove the reverse lever pivot pin circlip and pivot pin.

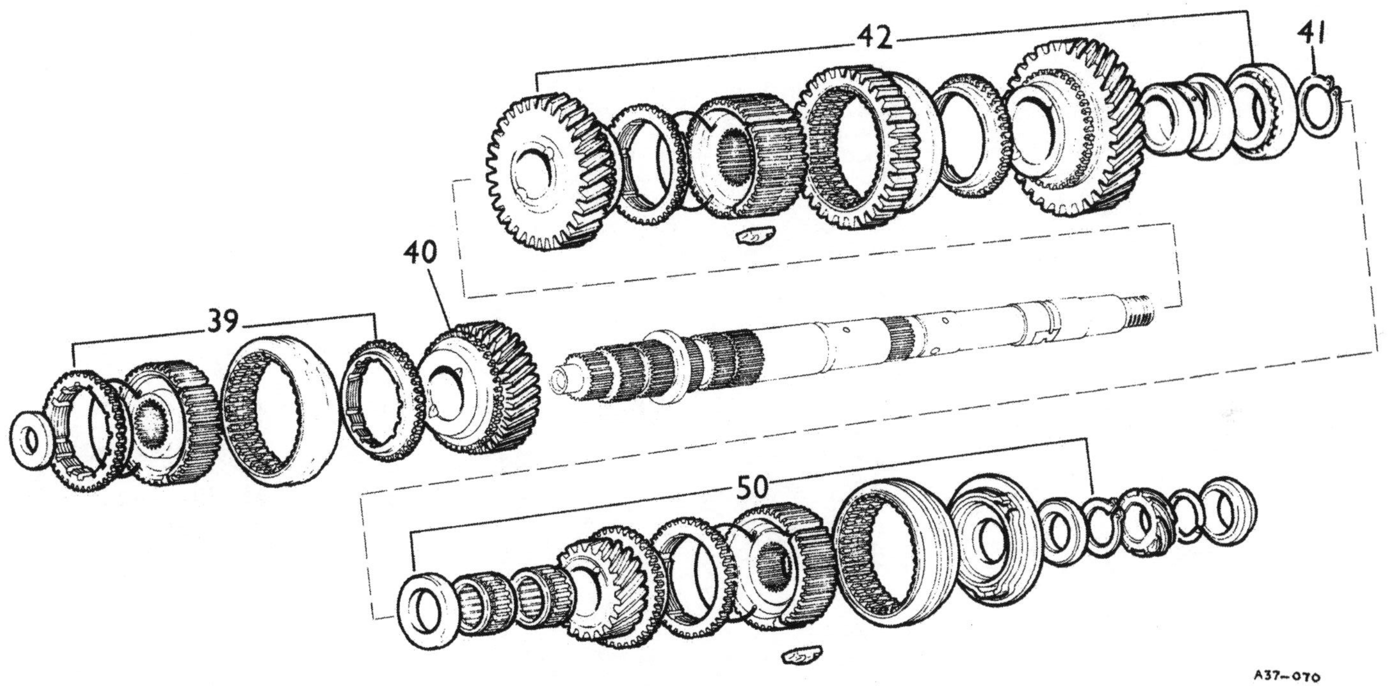

0025

29 Remove the reverse lever and slipper pad.
30 Slide the reverse shaft rearwards and withdraw the reverse gear spacer, mainshaft, selector shaft, selector shaft fork and spool in a forward direction clear of the centre plate.
31 Withdraw the selector fork and spool. Note that the shorter cam of the spool is fitted towards the bottom of the gearbox.
32 Remove the nut and spring washers securing the reverse gear pivot shaft and remove the pivot shaft (only if renewal of the pivot shaft and/or the centre plate is intended).
33 Remove the centre plate from the vice and extract the two dowels (only if dowels and/or centre plate renewal is intended).

Input Shaft and Front Cover
34 Using tool RTR 47-23 remove the external bearing.

35 Using tools 18G 284 AAH and 284 withdraw the internal bearing track.
36 Remove the oil seal from the front cover.

Layshaft
37 Using tools LC 370-2 remove the layshaft bearings.

Mainshaft
38 Remove the pilot bearing and spacer.
39 Remove the 3rd and 4th speed synchroniser hub and sleeve.
40 Remove the 3rd speed gear.
41 Remove the circlip securing the mainshaft bearing.
42 Remove the bearing, 1st gear and bush, 1st and 2nd speed hub, sleeve and synchromesh cones, and 2nd gear.

Rear Cover
43 Remove the oil seal, bearing, speedo gear, circlip and sleeve and oil sleeve. Remove the oil pump drive, pump cover and gears.
44 Thoroughly clean and examine all components. Obtain new parts as necessary.

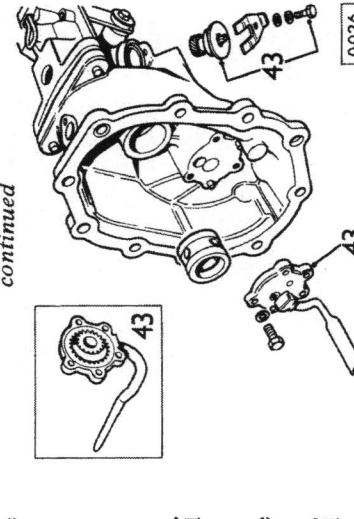

continued

0026

MANUAL GEARBOX — 5 SPEED   213

Layshaft

45 Fit the bearings to the layshaft.

Mainshaft

46 *Synchro Assemblies.* With the outer sleeve held, a push-through load applied to the outer face of the synchro hub should register 18 – 22 lb (18.2 – 10 kgm) to overcome spring detent in either direction.

47 *Checking 1st speed bush end-float.* Fit 2nd gear, 1st/2nd speed synchro hub and 1st gear bush to the mainshaft.

Manufacture a spacer to the dimensions illustrated and slide the spacer on the mainshaft.

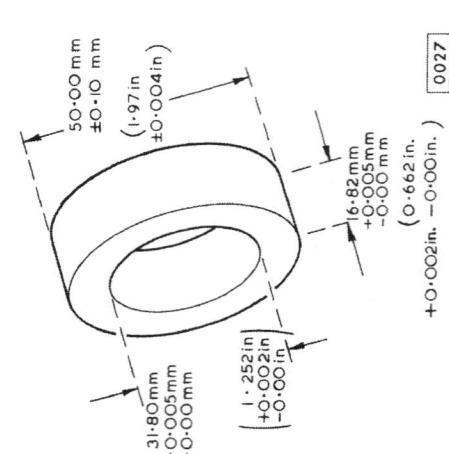

50·00 mm ±0·10 mm (1·97in ±0·004in)

16·82mm +0·005mm −0·00 mm (0·662in. −0·00in.)

31·80mm +0·005mm −0·00mm (1·252in +0·002in −0·00in) +0·002in. −0·00in.

0027

Using an oil circlip and feeler gauges check the clearance existing between the spacer and the circlip, which should be within 0.005 to 0.055 mm (0.0002 to 0.002 in). The first speed bush is available with collars of different thickness. Select a 1st speed bush with a collar which will give the required end-float.

48 Remove the circlip, spacer, bush, synchro hub and 2nd gear from the mainshaft.

49 *Checking 5th gear end-float.* Fit the 5th gear assembly to the mainshaft, i.e. front spacer, 5th gear, synchro hub, rear plate and spacer. Fit an old circlip and using feeler gauges check the end-float which should be within 0.005 to 0.055 mm (0.0002 to 0.002 in). The rear spacer is available in a range of sizes. Select a rear spacer which will ensure the required clearance.

50 Remove the circlip spacer and 5th gear assembly.

Assembly

51 It is important that 1st/2nd synchro is assembled correctly (short splines on inner member) towards 2nd gear. Fit 2nd gear, baulk ring, synchro hub and sleeve (selector fork annulus to rear of gearbox), baulk ring, 1st gear and selective bush, bearing and a *new* circlip. When fitting the circlip care must be taken to ensure that it is not stretched (opened) beyond the *minimum* necessary to obtain entry over the shaft. The internal diameter of an expanded circlip *must not* exceed 32.30 mm.

52 Fit 3rd gear, baulk ring, and synchro hub and sleeve (longer boss of synchro hub to front of gearbox) to the mainshaft.

53 Fit the spacer and bearing to front of mainshaft.

54 Fit the layshaft bearing track to the centre plate.

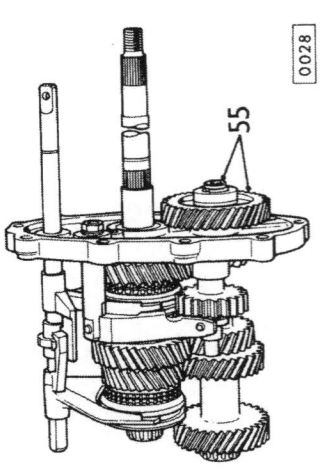

55

0028

55 Fit the layshaft to the centre plate and fit the fifth gear, spacer and a new circlip. When fitting the circlip care must be taken to ensure that it is not stretched (opened) beyond the *minimum* necessary to obtain entry. The internal diameter of an expanded circlip *must not* exceed 22.5 mm.

56 Fit the mainshaft bearing track to the centre plate.

57 Locate the centre plate in protected vice jaws.

58 Take the selector shaft complete with 1st and 2nd selector fork, front spool and 3rd and 4th selector fork and engage both forks in their respective synchro sleeves on the mainshaft. Simultaneously engage the selector shaft and mainshaft assemblies in the centre plate.

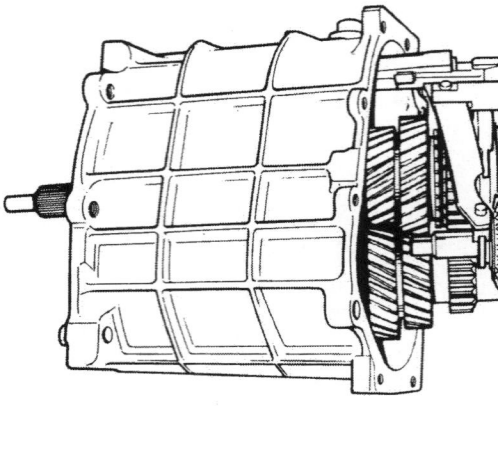

0029

59 Fit the spacer, 5th gear, baulk ring, synchro hub and sleeve end-plate, selective spacer (instruction 48), and a new circlip. When fitting the circlip care must be taken to ensure that it is not stretched (opened) beyond the *minimum* necessary to obtain entry. The internal diameter of an expanded circlip *must not* exceed 27.63 mm.

60 Fit the reverse gear (lip for slipper pad to front of box) front and rear spacers and the reverse shaft.

61 Fit the reverse lever, slipper pad, pivot pin and circlip. If a new reverse gear pivot shaft is to be fitted it is necessary to ensure that its radial location is consistent with reverse pad slipper engagement/clearance. Radial location is determined on assembly. Secure with spring washer and nuts, subsequently checking movement of reverse lever and ensuring slipper pad is properly engaged.

62 Remove the centre plate and gear assembly from the vice and locate on a suitable stand with the front of the mainshaft vertically uppermost. Ensure that the reverse shaft does not slide out of position.

63 Fit the centre plate front gasket.

64 Fit the external bearing and internal bearing track to the input shaft.

65 Fit the input shaft to the gearcase.

0030

66 Carefully slide the gearcase and input shaft into position over the gear assemblies. Do not use force. Ensure that the centre plate dowels and selector shaft are engaged in their respective locations.

FIRST MOTION SHAFT OIL SEAL

Remove and refit 37.23.04

Service tools: ST 1136

Removing

1 Remove the gearbox, see 37.20.01.

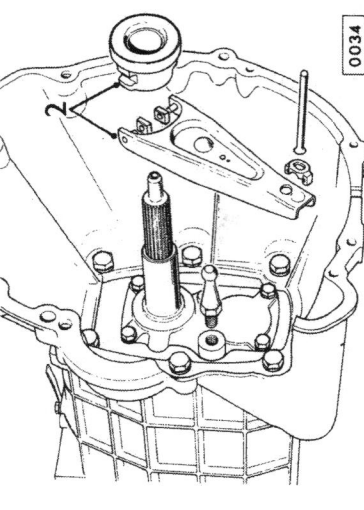

2 Using tool ST 1136 remove the clutch release fork and bearing.
3 Remove the bolts and washers securing the front cover to the gearbox.
4 Remove the front cover and gasket.
5 Remove the oil seal from the front cover. Ensure that the spacers for the first motion shaft and layshaft bearings are not intermixed.

continued

67 Fit the layshaft and input shaft bearing outer tracks.
68 Using seven slave bolts and plain washers to prevent damaging the rear face of the centre plate evenly draw the gearcase into position on the centre plate.
69 Place a layshaft spacer of nominal thickness (0.040 in, 1.02 mm) on the layshaft bearing track, and fit the front cover and gasket, securing with six bolts.
70 Using a dial gauge check layshaft end-float.
71 Remove the front cover and provisional spacer. The required layshaft end-float is 0.005 to 0.055 mm (0.0002 to 0.002 in). Check the thickness of the provisional spacer. Spacer thickness required is: provisional spacer thickness, plus end-float obtained, minus 0.055 mm (0.002 in).
72 Again fit the front cover and gasket, this time with the correct spacer arrived at in instruction 71.
73 Check layshaft end-float to ensure it is within the limits specified in instruction 71.
74 Place a ball bearing in the centre of the input shaft. This facilitates checking mainshaft end-float using a dial gauge.
75 Mount the dial gauge on the gearcase with the stylus resting on the ball. Zero the gauge.
76 Check the mainshaft and input shaft combined end-float. Care must be taken when checking dial gauge readings to ensure that end-float only – as distinct from side movement of the input shaft – is recorded. If difficulty is encountered in differentiating between end-float and side movement remove the front cover and wrap the plain portion of the input shaft below the splines with six turns of masking tape. Refit the front cover and again check end-float ensuring that rise and fall of the input shaft is not restricted by the tape.
77 Having ascertained end-float select the spacer required as follows:
End-float minus 0.055 mm (0.002 in) – spacer thickness required. Fit the spacer thus determined and again check end-float which must be within 0.005 to 0.055 mm (0.0002 to 0.002 in).
78 Remove the front cover and tape (if employed).

79 Fit the oil seal to the front cover and lubricate the seal lips.
80 Mask the splines and fit the front cover, applying Loctite to the bolts. Remove the splines masking.
81 Place the gearbox on a bench or stand and remove the slave bolts and washers from the centre plate.
82 Fit the 5th gear spool and circlip to the selector shaft. NOTE: The longer cam of the spool is fitted towards the bottom of the gearbox.
83 Fit the 5th gear selector fork and bracket.
84 Renew the selector shaft 'O' ring in the rear cover and fit the oil ring bush.
85 Fit the rear gasket to the centre plate and engage the oil pump shaft in the layshaft.
86 Fit the oil pump gears and cover to the gearbox rear cover.
87 Fit the rear cover ensuring that the oil pump shaft engages the oil pump.
88 Fit the selector shaft ball, spring and plug to the centre plate.
89 Fit the spool locating bosses (2) to the 1st/2nd spool and 5th gear spool.
90 Fit the speedometer driving gear to the mainshaft ensuring that it properly engages the mainshaft flats.
91 Fit the circlip and sleeve and ball race to the mainshaft.
92 Fit the rear oil seal. Lubricate seal lip.
93 Fit the driving flange, washer and nut.
94 Fit the speedometer driven gear and housing.
95 Fit the bell housing.
96 Fit the clutch release bearing and withdrawal lever.
97 Fit the remote control housing.

Refitting

6 Fit a new oil seal to the front cover (seal lip towards gearbox).
7 Lubricate the oil seal and fit the front cover and gasket, applying Loctite to the bolts.
8 Fit the clutch release fork and bearing.
9 Fit the gearbox to the car, see 37.20.01.

SPEEDOMETER DRIVE GEAR   37.25.01

Remove and refit

As Operation 37.12.42.

SPEEDOMETER DRIVE PINION

Remove and refit   37.25.05

Removing

1 Remove the bolt and washer securing the speedometer clamp plate.
2 Release the speedometer cable from the drive pinion.
3 Withdraw the pinion housing and pinion from the gearbox.
4 Remove the pinion from the housing.

Refitting

5 Reverse instructions 1 to 4. Renew the pinion housing 'O' ring if necessary.

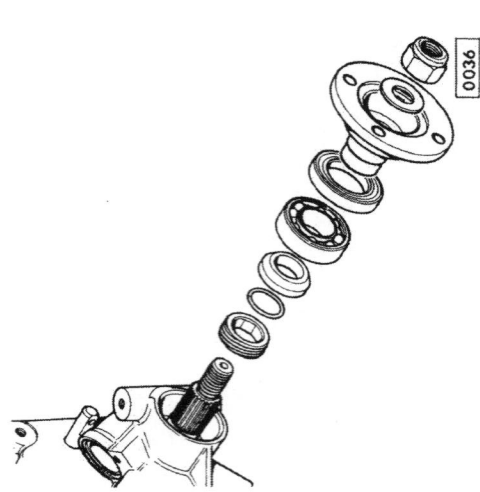

0036

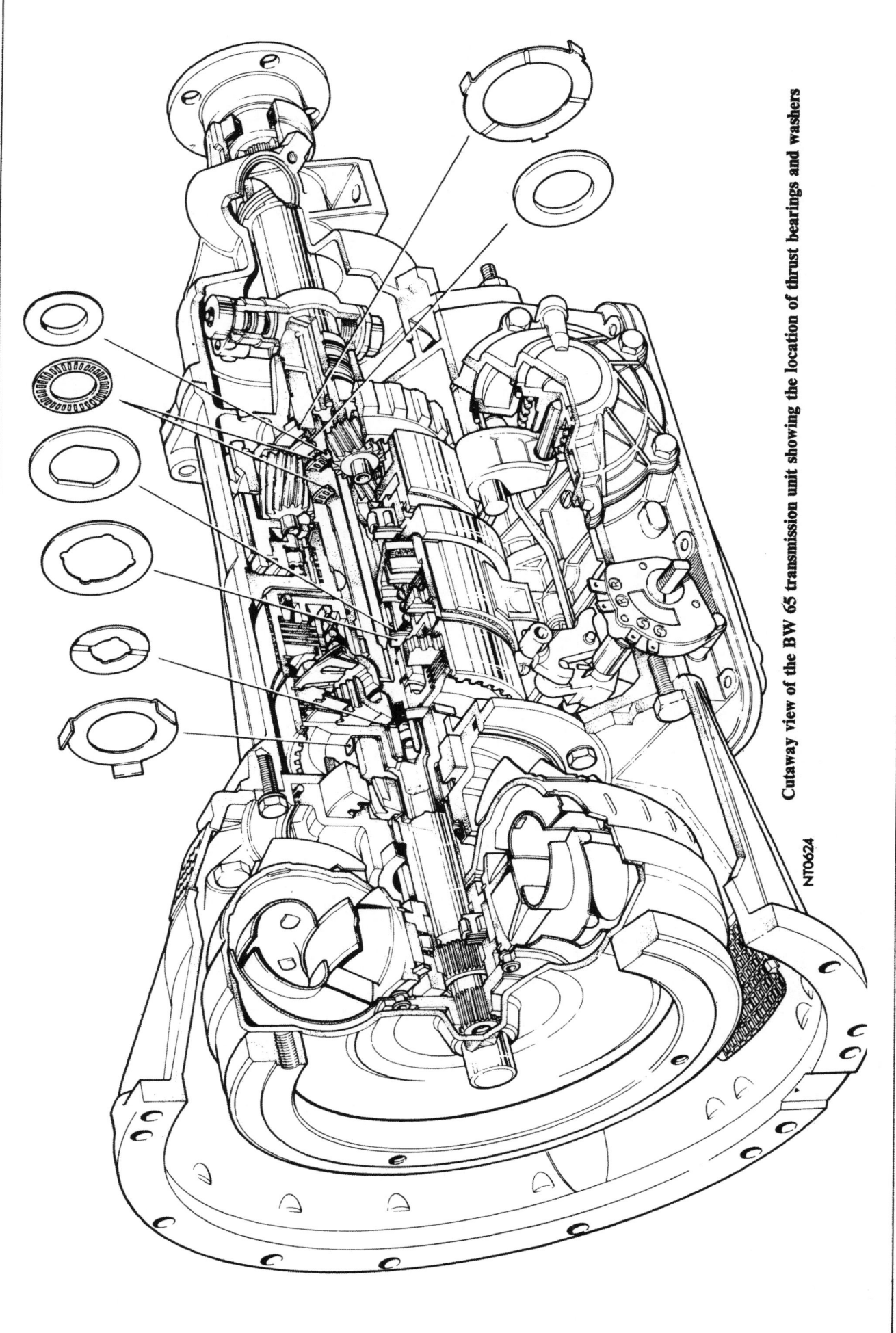

Cutaway view of the BW 65 transmission unit showing the location of thrust bearings and washers

NT0624

IMPORTANT

Under agreements existing between Borg-Warner Limited and the car manufacturers, the former does NOT undertake the servicing of automatic transmission units, nor do they supply spare parts or service tools. All matters appertaining to service or spares must therefore be dealt with by Triumph Distributors or Dealers within the organisation.

TYPE – Borg-Warner 65 Unit – P.R.N.D.2.1. System

UNIT IDENTIFICATION

A serial number prefix 027 appears on a dark admiralty grey nameplate on the left hand side of the transmission case.

AUTOMATIC TRANSMISSION – SHIFT SPEEDS

Throttle Position	Zero Throttle	Light Throttle		Part Throttle			KICK-DOWN				
		2	D	2	D	D	D	1	D	2
Selector	−1										
Shift	2−1	1−2	2−3	3−2	1−2	2−3	3−2	2−1	3−1	1−2	2−1
Road Speed M P H	30−38	8−12	12−16	30−40	38−44	65−71	58−66	42−50	30−38	38−44	30−38
KM/H	48−61	13−19	19−26	48−64	61−71	105−114	93−106	68−81	48−61	61−71	48−61

Capacity 5.3 Litres (9¼ pints) including cooler of 0.3 litres (½ pint)

TRANSMISSION DATA

	TOP (3rd)	Intermediate (2nd)	Low (1st)	Reverse
Gearbox ratios	1:1	1.45:1	2.39:1	2.09:1
Convertor reduction (1.91)	Infinitely variable between 1 – 1.91:1 operating in all gears			
OVERALL RATIOS	3.27:1	4.74:1	7.82:1	6.85:1

217 K Convertor – dia 242 mm (9½″) – RATIO 1.91:1

EXAMINATION OF COMPONENTS

Transmission Case and Servo Covers
Check for cracks and obstructions in passages.

Front and Rear Pump
Check for scoring and excessive wear.

Shafts
Check bearing and thrust faces for scoring.

Clutch Plates
Check for warping, scoring, overheating and excessive wear.

Bands
Check for scoring, overheating and excessive wear.

Drums
Check for overheating and scoring.

Gears
Check teeth for chipping, scoring, wear and condition of thrust faces.

Uni-directional Clutch and Races
Check for scoring, overheating and wear.

Valve Block and Governor
Check for burrs, crossed or stripped threads, and scored sealing faces.

Impeller Hub and Front Pump Drive Gear
Check for pitting and wear. Ensure good contact.

Thrust Washers
Check for burrs, scoring and wear.

White Metal Bushes
Check for scoring and loss of white metal.

Lip Seals
Check for cuts, hardening of rubber, leakage past outer diameter.

Rubber 'O' Rings and Seals
Check for hardening, cracking, cuts or damage.

Cast Iron Sealing Rings
Check fit in groove and wear (evident by lip overhanging the groove).

Teflon Sealing Rings
Check for cracking, cuts or damage.

SERVICING REQUIREMENTS

1 For all operations high standards of cleanliness are essential.

2 Rags and cloths must be clean and free from lint; nylon cloths are preferable.

3 Prior to assembly all components must be cleaned thoroughly with petrol, paraffin or an industrial solvent.

4 All defective items must be renewed.

5 Components should be lubricated with transmission fluid before assembly.

6 New joint washers should be fitted where applicable.

7 Where jointing compound is required, the use of Hylomar SQ32M, Hermetite or Wellseal is approved.

8 All screws, bolts and nuts must be tightened to the recommended torque figure.

9 Thrust washers and bearings should be coated with petroleum jelly to facilitate retaining them in position during assembly operations. Grease should not be used as it may be insoluble in the transmission fluid and could subsequently cause blockage of fluid passages and contamination of brake band and clutch facings.

IMPORTANT: Metric threads are used throughout most of the transmission unit and it is therefore essential that fastenings, and especially lock washers, are segregated into sets and not intermixed with those from other parts of the vehicle.

FRONT BRAKE BAND

Remove and refit   44.10.01

Service tools: CBW 60, CBW 547A-50

Removing

1. Remove the transmission unit. 44.20.01.
2. Wash the exterior of the unit in clean petrol or paraffin, invert it and place on a bench cradle CBW 60. Remove the switch. 44.15.15.
3. Unscrew the bolts securing the torque converter housing.
4. Remove the torque converter housing.
5. Unscrew 12 bolts.
6. Remove the oil pan, joint washer and magnet.
7. Pull out the five oil tubes.
8. Release the downshift inner cable from the downshift cam.
9. Take out three bolts and washers.
10. Lift off the valve block.
11. Unscrew two bolts.
12. Remove the oil tube locating plate.
13. Pull out the oil tubes. (Note the 'O' ring on the pump section tube.)
14. Take out five bolts.

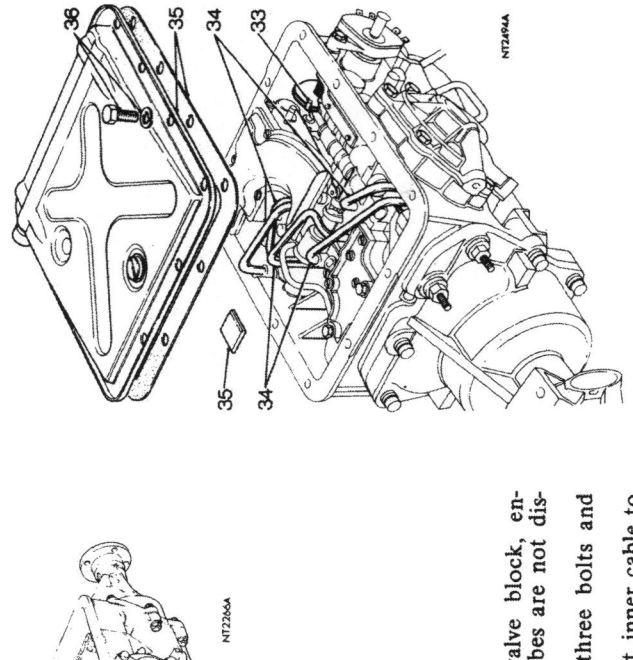

15. Remove the pump and joint washer.
16. Remove the thrust washer.
17. Withdraw the front clutch.
18. Remove the thrust washers.
19. Withdraw the rear clutch and forward sun gear.
20. Squeeze together the ends of the front brake band and remove it together with the strut.

31. Carefully refit the valve block, ensuring that the oil tubes are not distorted.
32. Fit and tighten the three bolts and washers.
33. Connect the downshift inner cable to the downshift cam.
34. Refit the five oil tubes.
35. Replace the magnet and refit the oil pan and joint washer.
36. Fit and tighten 12 bolts.

Refitting

21. Squeeze together the ends of the front brake band and fit it in position together with the strut.
22. Refit the rear clutch and forward sun gear assembly.
23. Using petroleum jelly, stick the thrust washers to the rear clutch assembly (phosphor bronze towards the front clutch).
24. Refit the front clutch assembly.
25. Using petroleum jelly, stick the thrust washer to the pump assembly.
26. Refit the pump assembly and joint washer.
27. Fit and tighten the bolts.
28. Refit the oil tubes. (Note the 'O' ring on the pump suction tube.)
29. Refit the oil tube locating plate.
30. Fit and tighten the two bolts.

37. Locate the torque converter housing in place.
38. Fit and tighten four bolts securing the torque converter housing.
39. Refit the switch 44.15.15.
40. Refit the transmission unit.

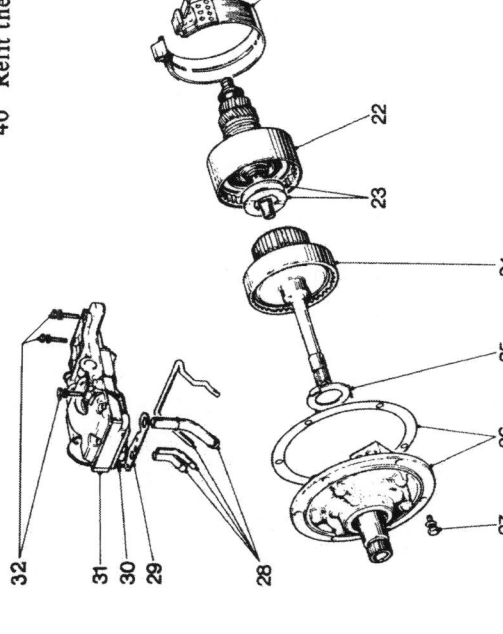

REAR BRAKE BAND   44.10.09

Remove and refit

Service tools: CBW 60, CBW 547A-50

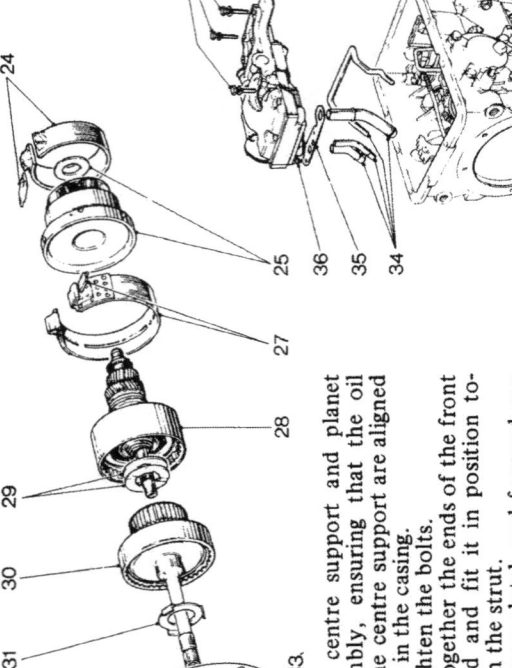
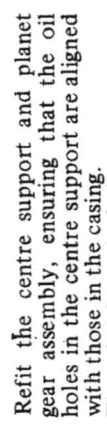
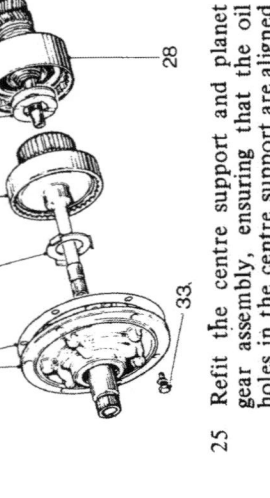
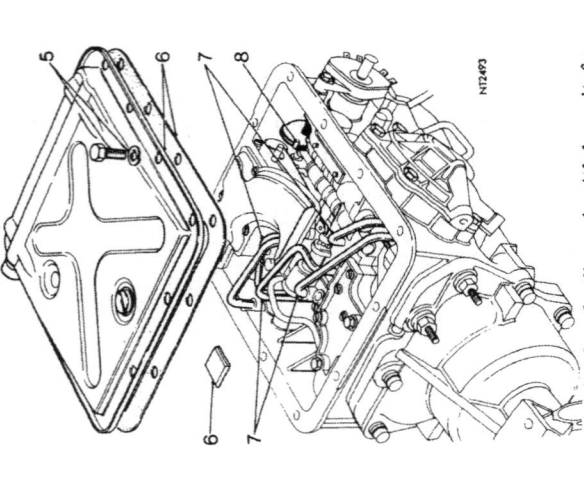
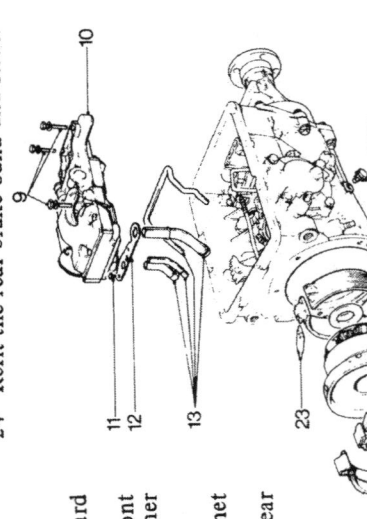
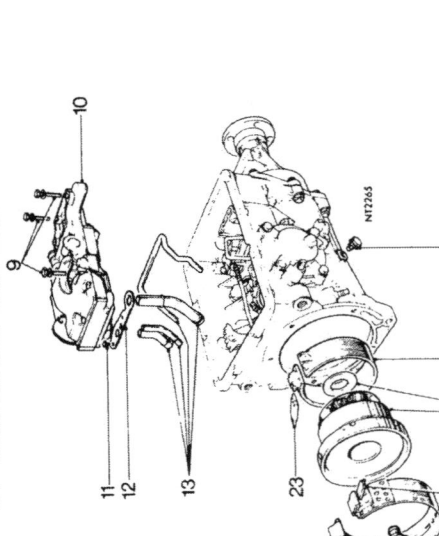
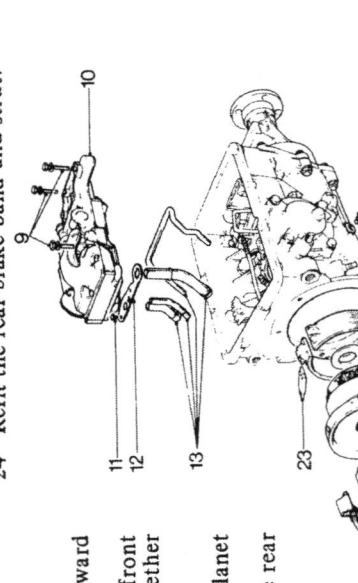
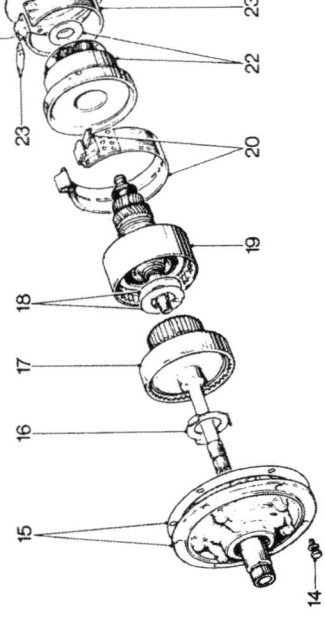

Removing

1 Remove the transmission unit. 44.20.01.
2 Wash the exterior of the unit in clean petrol or paraffin, invert it and place on a bench cradle CBW 60. Remove the switch. 44.15.15.
3 Unscrew the bolts securing the torque converter housing.
4 Remove the torque converter housing.
5 Unscrew 12 bolts.
6 Remove the oil pan, joint washer and magnet.
7 Pull out the oil tubes.
8 Release the downshift inner cable from the downshift cam.
9 Lift off the valve block.
10 Unscrew two bolts.
11 Unscrew two bolts.
12 Remove the oil tube locating plate.
13 Pull out the oil tubes. (Note the 'O' ring on the pump suction tube.)
14 Take out five bolts.
15 Remove the pump and joint washer.
16 Remove the thrust washer.
17 Withdraw the front clutch.
18 Remove the thrust washers.
19 Withdraw the rear clutch and forward sun gear.
20 Squeeze together the ends of the front brake band and remove it together with the strut.
21 Unscrew the bolts.
22 Withdraw the centre support/planet gear assembly and thrust race.
23 Squeeze together the ends of the rear brake band, tilt and withdraw it from the casing together with the strut.

Refitting

24 Refit the rear brake band and strut.
25 Refit the centre support and planet gear assembly, ensuring that the oil holes in the centre support are aligned with those in the casing.
26 Fit and tighten the bolts.
27 Squeeze together the ends of the front brake band and fit it in position together with the strut.
28 Refit the rear clutch and forward sun gear assembly.
29 Using petroleum jelly, stick the thrust washers to the rear clutch assembly (phosphor bronze towards the front clutch).
30 Refit the front clutch assembly.
31 Using petroleum jelly, stick the thrust washer to the pump assembly.
32 Refit the pump assembly and joint washer.
33 Fit and tighten the bolts.
34 Refit the oil tubes. (Note the 'O' ring on the pump suction tube.)
35 Refit the oil tube locating plate.
36 Fit and tighten the two bolts.
37 Carefully refit the valve block, ensuring that the oil tubes are not distorted.
38 Fit and tighten the three bolts and washers.
39 Connect the downshift inner cable to the downshift cam.
40 Refit the oil tubes.
41 Replace the magnet and refit the oil pan and joint washer.
42 Fit and tighten 12 bolts.
43 Locate the torque converter housing in place.
44 Fit and tighten four bolts securing the torque converter housing.
45 Refit the switch. 44.15.15.
46 Refit the transmission unit. 44.20.01.

FRONT CLUTCH

Remove and refit   44.12.04

Service tools: CBW 60, CBW 547A-50

Removing

1 Remove the transmission unit. 44.20.01.
2 Wash the exterior of the unit in clean petrol or paraffin, invert it and place on a bench cradle CBW 60. Remove the switch. 44.15.15.
3 Unscrew the bolts securing the torque converter housing.
4 Remove the torque converter housing.
5 Unscrew 12 bolts.
6 Remove the oil pan, joint washer and magnet.
7 Pull out the oil tubes.
8 Release the downshift inner cable from the downshift cam.
9 Take out three bolts and washers.
10 Lift off the valve block.
11 Unscrew two bolts.
12 Remove the oil tube locating plate.
13 Pull out the oil tubes. (Note the 'O' ring on the pump suction tube.)
14 Take out five bolts.
15 Remove the pump joint washer.
16 Remove the thrust washer.
17 Withdraw the front clutch.
18 Remove the thrust washers.

Refitting

19 Using petroleum jelly, stick the thrust washers to the rear clutch assembly (phosphor bronze towards the front clutch).
20 Refit the front clutch assembly.
21 Using petroleum jelly, stick the thrust washer to the pump assembly.
22 Refit the front assembly and joint washer.
23 Fit and tighten the bolts.
24 Refit the oil tubes. (Note the 'O' ring on the pump suction tube.)
25 Refit the oil tube locating plate.
26 Fit and tighten the two bolts.
27 Carefully refit the valve block, ensuring that the oil tubes are not distorted.
28 Fit and tighten the three bolts and washers.
29 Connect the downshift inner cable to the downshift cam.
30 Refit the oil tubes.
31 Replace the magnet and refit the oil pan and joint washer.
32 Fit and tighten the 12 bolts.
33 Locate the torque converter housing in place.
34 Fit and tighten four bolts securing the torque converter housing.
35 Refit the switch. 44.15.15.
36 Refit the transmission unit. 44.20.01.

REAR CLUTCH

Remove and refit   **44.12.07**

Service tools: CBW 60, CBW 547A-50

Removing

1. Remove the transmission unit. 44.20.01.
2. Wash the exterior of the unit in clean petrol or paraffin, invert it and place on a bench cradle CBW 60. Remove the switch. 44.15.15.
3. Unscrew the bolts securing the torque converter housing.
4. Remove the torque converter housing.
5. Unscrew 12 bolts.
6. Remove the oil pan, joint washer and magnet.
7. Pull out the oil tubes.
8. Release the downshift inner cable from the downshift cam.
9. Take out three bolts and washers.
10. Lift off the valve block.
11. Unscrew two bolts.
12. Remove the oil tube locating plate.
13. Pull out the oil tubes. (Note the 'O' ring on the pump suction tube.)
14. Take out five bolts.
15. Remove the pump and joint washer.
16. Remove the thrust washer.
17. Withdraw the front clutch.
18. Remove the thrust washers.
19. Withdraw the rear clutch and forward sun gear.
20. Separate the forward sun gear assembly from the rear clutch.

Refitting

21. Assemble the forward sun gear to the rear clutch.
22. Refit the rear clutch and forward sun gear assembly.
23. Using petroleum jelly, stick the thrust washers to the rear clutch assembly (phosphor bronze towards the front clutch).
24. Refit the front clutch assembly.
25. Using petroleum jelly, stick the thrust washer to the pump assembly.
26. Refit the pump assembly and joint washer.
27. Fit and tighten the bolts.
28. Refit the oil tubes. (Note the 'O' ring on the pump suction tube.)
29. Refit the oil tube locating plate.
30. Fit and tighten the two bolts.
31. Carefully refit the valve block, ensuring that the oil tubes are not distorted.
32. Fit and tighten the three bolts and washers.
33. Connect the downshift inner cable to the downshift cam.
34. Refit the oil tubes.
35. Replace the magnet and refit the oil pan and joint washer.
36. Fit and tighten 12 bolts.
37. Locate the torque converter housing in place.
38. Fit and tighten four bolts securing the torque converter housing.
39. Refit the switch. 44.15.15.
40. Refit the transmission unit. 44.20.01.

FRONT CLUTCH

Overhaul 44.12.10

Service tool: BW 42

1 Remove the front clutch. 44.12.04.

Dismantling

2 Remove the circlip.
3 Withdraw the input shaft.
4 Remove the thrust washer.
5 Remove the hub.
6 Take out the inner and outer friction plates.
7 Remove the pressure plate.
8 Remove the circlip.
9 Take out the spring.
10 Remove the spring bearing.
11 Withdraw the piston. (If necessary, blank off the bores of the clutch drum and apply a compressed air line to the piston valve hole.)
12 Remove the seal from the piston.
13 Remove the 'O' ring from the drum.

Reassembling

14 Refit the 'O' ring to the drum.
15 Refit the seal to the piston.
16 Fit the piston into tool no. BW 42 and place the tool in the drum. Push the piston into the drum and remove the tool.
17 Locate the spring bearing in position.
18 Refit the spring.
19 Fit the circlip.
20 Refit the pressure plate.
21 Refit the hub.
22 Fit the inner and outer friction plates in alternate sequence.
23 Using petroleum jelly, stick the thrust washer to the hub.
24 Locate the input shaft in position.
25 Refit the circlip.
26 Refit the front clutch. 44.12.04.

REAR CLUTCH

Overhaul 44.12.13

Service tools: CBW 37A, BW 41

1 Remove the rear clutch. 44.12.07.

Dismantling

2 Remove the circlip.
3 Take out the pressure plate.
4 Remove the inner and outer friction plates.
5 Using tool BW 37A as shown, compress the spring and remove the spring seat circlip. Remove the tool.
6 Take out the spring seat.
7 Remove the spring.
8 Withdraw the piston.
9 Remove the rubber sealing ring from the piston.
10 Remove the rubber 'O' ring from the drum.

Reassembling

11 Fit the 'O' ring to the drum.
12 Fit the sealing ring to the piston drum.
13 Fit the piston assembly into tool BW 41 and locate the tool in the drum. Push the piston into the drum. Remove the tool.
14 Refit the spring.
15 Refit the spring seat.
16 Using tool BW 37A, compress the spring and fit the circlip. Remove the tool.
17 Refit the inner and outer clutch plates in alternate sequence.
18 Fit the pressure plate.
19 Refit the circlip.
20 Refit the rear clutch. 44.12.07.

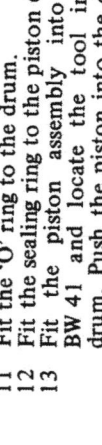

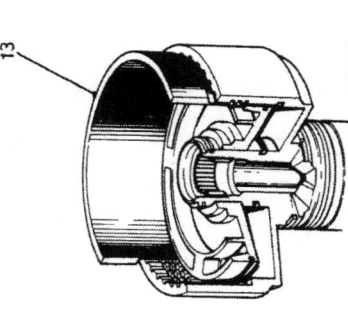

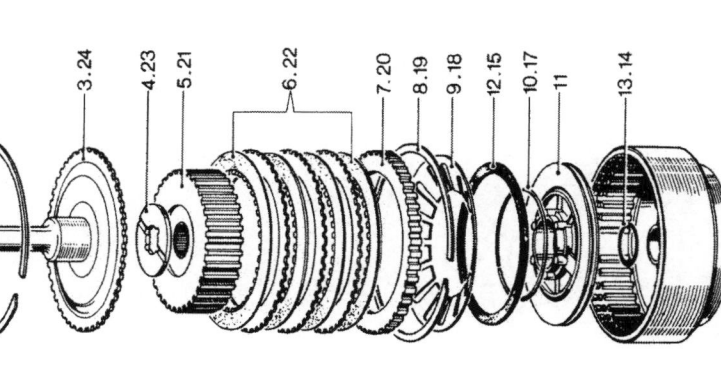

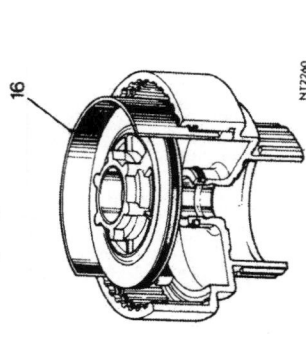

AUTOMATIC GEARBOX 223

UNI-DIRECTIONAL CLUTCH

Remove and refit   44.12.16

Service tools: CBW 60, CBW 547A-50

Removing

1. Remove the transmission unit. 44.20.01.
2. Wash the exterior of the unit in clean petrol or paraffin, invert it and place on a bench cradle CBW 60. Remove the switch. 44.15.15.
3. Unscrew the bolts securing the torque converter housing.
4. Remove the torque converter housing.
5. Unscrew 12 bolts.
6. Remove the oil pan, joint washer and magnet.
7. Pull out the oil tubes.
8. Release the downshift inner cable from the downshift cam.
9. Take out three bolts and washers.
10. Lift off the valve block.
11. Unscrew two bolts.
12. Remove the oil tube locating plate.
13. Pull out the oil tubes. (Note the 'O' ring on the pump suction tube.)
14. Take out five bolts.
15. Remove the pump and joint washer.
16. Remove the thrust washer.
17. Withdraw the front clutch.
18. Remove the thrust washer.
19. Withdraw the rear clutch and forward sun gear.

20. Squeeze together the ends of the front brake band and remove it together with the strut.
21. Unscrew the bolts.
22. Withdraw the centre support/planet gear assembly.
23. Separate the centre support from the planet gear assembly.
24. Withdraw the uni-directional clutch.
25. Remove the circlip.
26. Remove the uni-directional clutch outer race.

Refitting

27. Refit the uni-directional clutch outer race to the rear drum.
28. Refit the circlip.
29. Refit the uni-directional clutch.
30. Assemble the centre support and planet gear assembly.
31. Refit the assembly, ensuring that the oil and locating holes in the centre support align with those in the casing.
32. Fit and tighten three bolts.
33. Squeeze together the ends of the front brake band and fit it in position together with the strut.
34. Refit the rear clutch and forward sun gear assembly.
35. Using petroleum jelly, stick the thrust washer to the rear clutch assembly (phosphor bronze towards the front clutch).

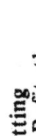
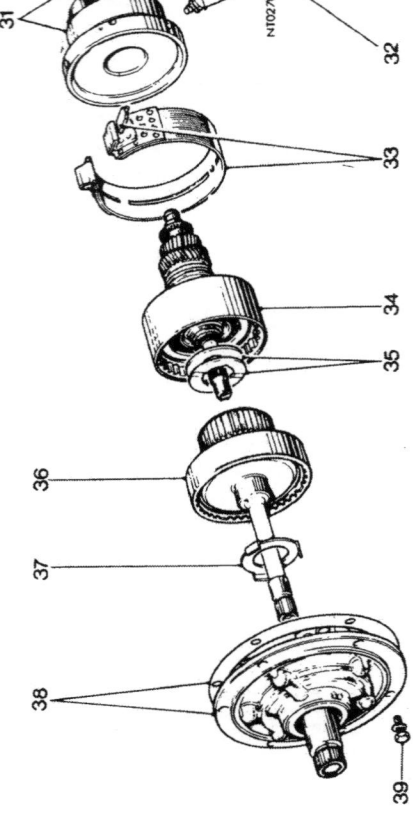
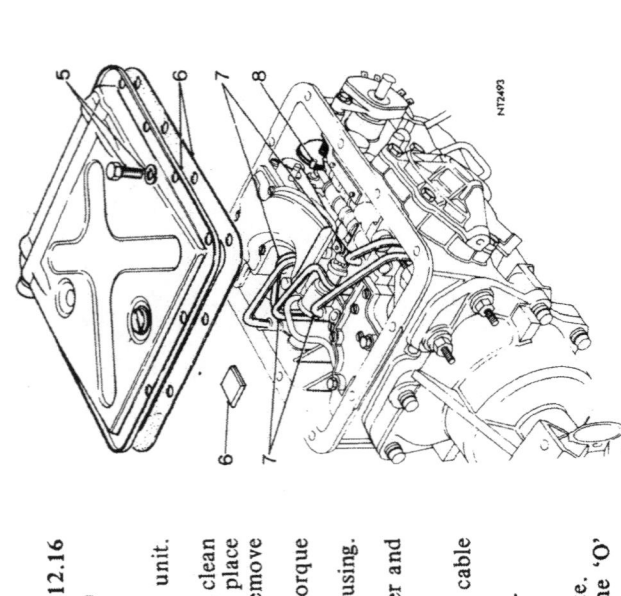
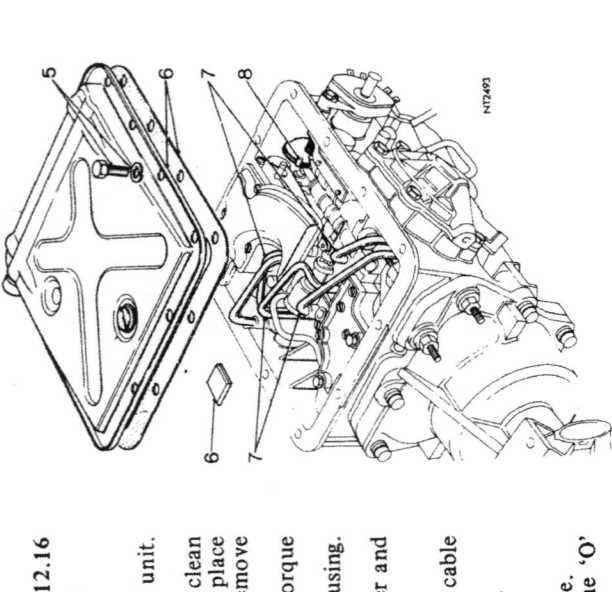
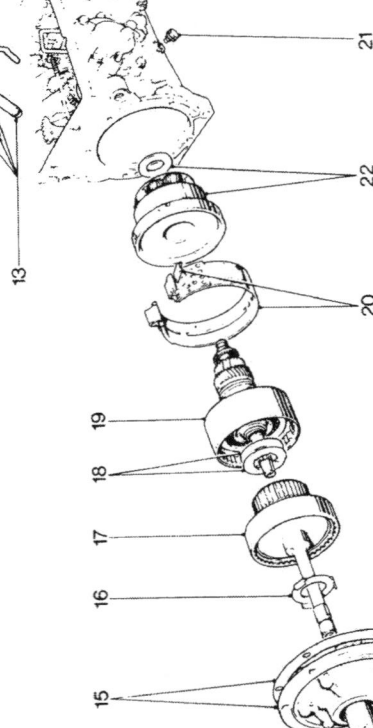

36 Refit the front clutch assembly.
37 Using petroleum jelly, stick the thrust washer to the pump assembly.
38 Refit the pump assembly and joint washer.
39 Fit and tighten the bolts.
40 Refit the oil tubes. (Note the 'O' ring on the pump suction tube.)
41 Refit the oil tube locating plate.
42 Fit and tighten the two bolts.
43 Carefully refit the valve block, ensuring that the oil tubes are not distorted.
44 Fit and tighten three bolts and washers.
45 Connect the downshift inner cable to the downshift cam.
46 Refit the oil tubes.
47 Replace the magnet and refit the oil pan and joint washer.
48 Fit and tighten 12 bolts.
49 Locate the torque converter housing in place.
50 Fit and tighten four bolts securing the torque converter housing.
51 Refit the switch. 44.15.15.
52 Refit the transmission unit. 44.20.01.

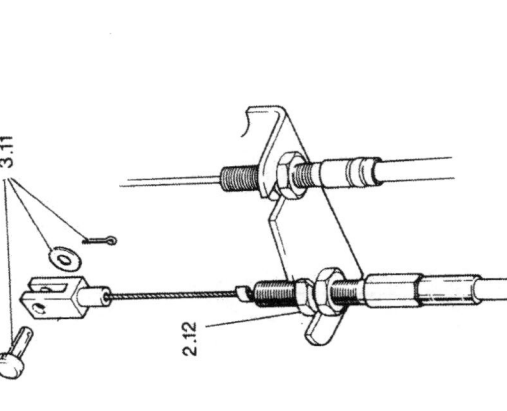

HAND SELECTOR LEVER 44.15.04
Remove and refit

Removing
1 Remove the push button cap.
2 Remove the push button securing screw.
3 Remove the push button and spring.
4 Unscrew and remove the gear knob.
5 Remove the two screws securing the gear lever surround.

continued

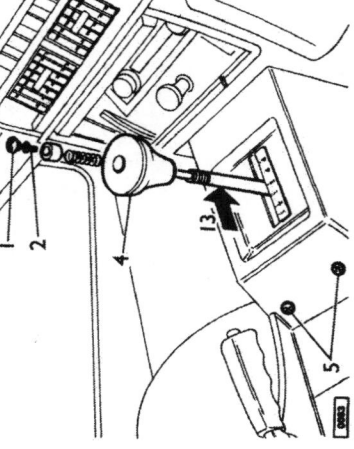

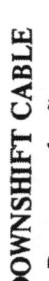

11 Refit the clevis pin, washer and split pin.
12 Refit the locknut and adjust the cable. 44.30.01.
13 Refill the unit with transmission fluid.

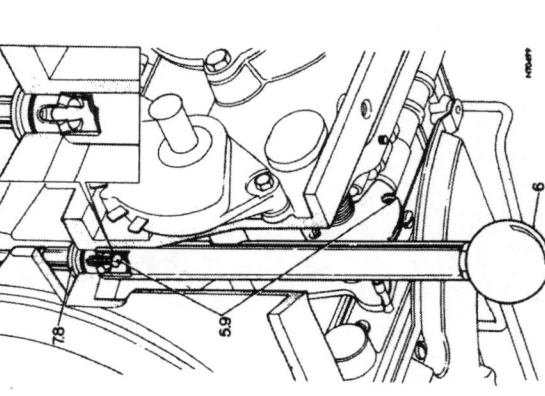

DOWNSHIFT CABLE 44.15.01
Remove and refit
Service tool: CBW 62

Removing
1 Drive the vehicle onto a ramp, select 'N', chock the wheels and open the bonnet.
2 Unscrew the locknut and remove the cable from the bracket.
3 Remove the split pin, washer and clevis pin.
4 Raise the ramp and remove the transmission sump pan. 44.24.04.
5 Disconnect the downshift inner cable from the cam.
6 Using tool no. CBW 62, remove the downshift outer cable from the gearbox casing.
7 Remove the downshift cable assembly.

Refitting
8 Clip the downshift outer cable into the gearbox casing.
9 Connect the inner cable to the downshift cam.
10 Refit the sump pan and lower the ramp.

HAND SELECTOR LEVER 44.15.05

Overhaul

1 Remove the hand selector lever. 44.15.04.
2 Pull out the inner lever.
3 Clean, inspect and regrease the inner lever.
4 Refit the inner lever.
5 Refit the hand selector lever.

HAND LEVER TURRET ASSEMBLY 44.15.06

Overhaul

1 Jack up front of the vehicle and place on two axle stands.
2 Disconnect the clip securing the selector rod to the turret lever.
3 Disconnect the selector rod from the turret lever.
4 Remove the hand selector lever assembly. 44.15.04.
5 Remove the two screws securing the hand brake lever surround.
6 Carefully remove the hand brake surround over the hand brake lever.
7 With the centre glove box open, remove the two screws securing the glove box catch to the centre console.
8 Remove the glove box catch.
9 Remove the four screws and rear plate securing the centre console.

6 Disconnect the quadrant illumination light from the surround.
7 Remove the gear lever surround.
8 Disconnect the gear indication light from the socket.
9 Remove the steel cover by operating the gear lever to each extreme.
10 Remove the two bolts securing the roller assembly.
11 Remove the roller assembly.
12 Remove the two bolts securing the gear lever to the turret shaft and remove the lever.

Refitting

13 Reverse 1–12.
(To facilitate the refitting of the push button securing screw, pull out the inner lever and hold in position against the quadrant stop.)

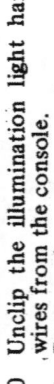

10 Unclip the illumination light harness wires from the console.
11 Remove the centre console.
12 Remove the screws securing the turret assembly to the transmission tunnel.
13 Lift out the turret assembly.
14 Remove the two nuts and bolts securing the quadrant to the turret.

15 Remove the quadrant.
16 Remove the circlip and washer retaining the turret shaft in the tunnel.
17 Remove the turret shaft.
18 Clean and inspect all parts including the hand selector lever.
19 Grease all bearing surfaces.
20 Reverse 4–17.
21 Select 'P–Park' position on the lever.
22 Select 'P–Park' position on the gearbox selector lever.
23 Check/adjust the selector rod as necessary. 44.30.04.
24 Reconnect the selector rod to the turret lever.
25 Engage the securing clip.
26 Lower the vehicle.

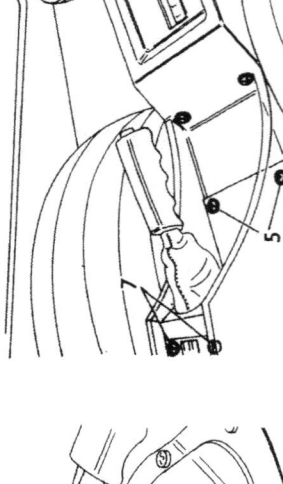

SELECTOR ROD 44.15.08

Remove and refit

Removing

1 Drive the vehicle onto a ramp, lock the selector lever in 'N' and apply the hand brake.
2 Raise the ramp.
3 Push the clips clear of the levers.
4 Remove the selector rod from the gearbox selector and hand lever.

Refitting

5 Slacken the selector rod locknut.
6 Ensure that the gearbox selector lever and the hand lever are both in position 'N'.
7 Fit the selector rod to the gearbox selector lever.
8 Fit the clip onto the selector lever.
9 Alter the length of the rod by adjusting the turn-buckle until the end of the rod can be located in the hand lever.
10 Tighten the locknut.
11 Push the clip onto the lever and secure the rod.
12 Lower the ramp.

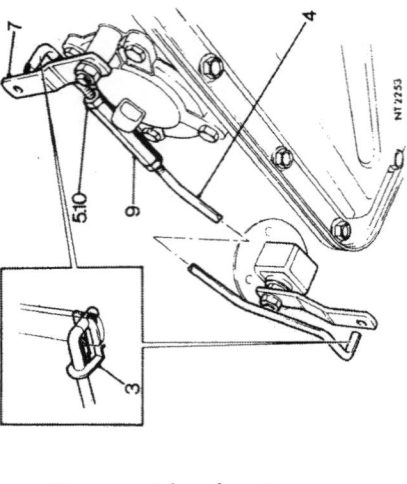

GEARBOX SELECTOR LEVER 44.15.09

Remove and refit

Removing

1 Drive the vehicle onto a ramp, select 'N' and apply the hand brake.
2 Raise the ramp.
3 Push the clip rearward.
4 Disconnect the selector rod from the lever.
5 Unscrew the nut and washer.
6 Remove the lever.

Refitting

7 Fit the lever to the shaft.
8 Fit and tighten the nut and washer.
9 Move the selector into the neutral position.
10 Connect the selector rod to the lever.
11 Push the clip onto the lever and secure the rod.
12 Lower the ramp.

STARTER INHIBITOR/REVERSE LAMP SWITCH 44.15.15

Remove and refit

Removing

1 Drive the vehicle onto a ramp, chock the wheels and raise the ramp.
2 Remove the three bolts securing the heat shield to the transmission sump.
3 Remove the heat shield and spacers.
4 Disconnect the switch from the block connector on the wiring harness.
5 Remove the thread protector (if fitted).
6 Remove the bolt securing the switch to the transmission unit.
7 Remove the switch.

Refitting

8 Reverse 1–7.

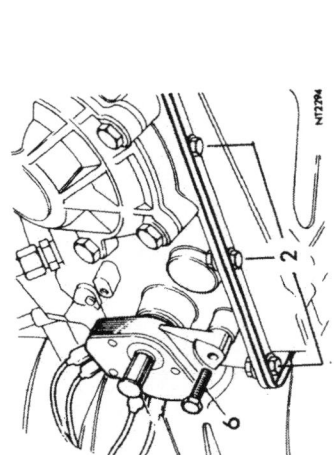
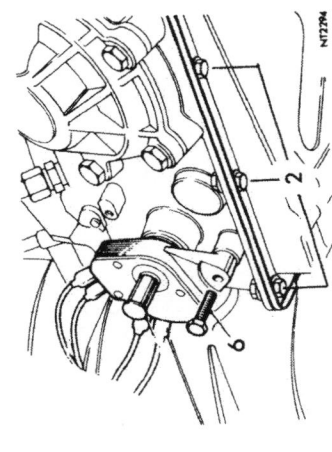

TORQUE CONVERTER HOUSING 44.17.01

Remove and refit

Service tool: CBW 547A-50 — Torque Wrench.

Removing

1 Remove the gearbox. 44.20.01.
2 Unscrew the four bolts securing the torque converter housing to the transmission.
3 Remove the housing.

Refitting

4 Place the torque converter housing in position.
5 Fit and tighten the four bolts using Service tool CBW 547A-50.
6 Refit the gearbox. 44.20.01.

GEARBOX 44.20.01

Remove and refit

Removing

1 Drive the vehicle onto a ramp, select 'N' and chock the wheels.
2 Remove the split pin, washer and clevis pin and undo the cable lock nut.
3 Release the downshift cable from the throttle linkage.
4 Raise the ramp.
5 Remove the exhaust front pipe. 30.10.09.
6 Disconnect the dipstick tube from the transmission sump and drain the fluid into a suitable receptacle.
7 Disconnect the selector lever from the selector shaft.
8 Disconnect the breather hose from the gearbox.
9 Disconnect the starter inhibitor/reverse light switch at the block connector on the wiring harness.
10 Disconnect the cooler pipes.
11 Remove the clamp and disconnect the speedometer cable.
12 Remove the propshaft bolts and disconnect the propshaft.
13 Remove the four bolts securing the torque converter to the engine drive plate.
14 Using a suitable jack under the engine sump, support the engine and gearbox assembly.
15 Remove the centre bolt and plate from the rear mounting.

continued

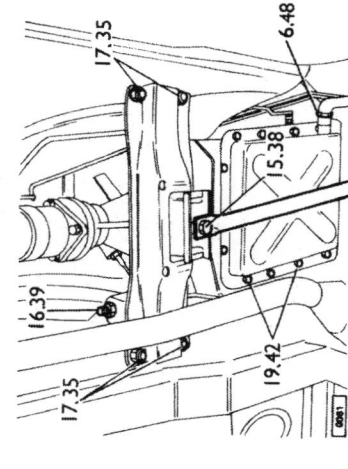

TORQUE CONVERTER 44.17.07

Remove and refit

Service tool: CBW 547A-50

Removing

1 Remove the transmission unit. 44.20.01.
2 Remove the torque converter from the transmission unit.

Refitting

3 Relocate the torque converter in the transmission unit.
4 Refit the gearbox. 44.20.01.

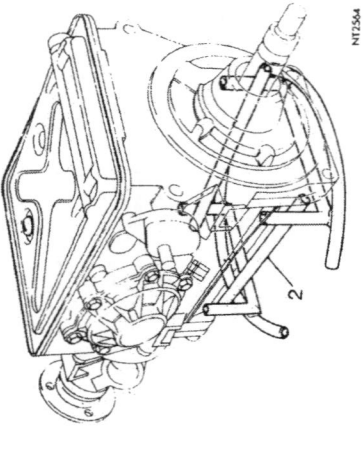

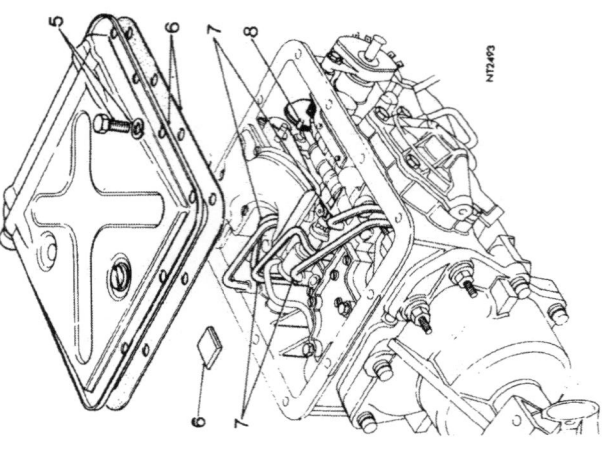

GEARBOX

Overhaul 44.20.06

Service tools: CBW 60, CBW 33, CBW 34, CBW 62, CBW 547A-50, CBW 547A-50-2A, RG 421 or S 337, CBW 33

1 Remove the transmission unit. 44.20.01.
2 Wash the exterior of the unit in clean petrol or paraffin, invert it and place on a bench cradle CBW 60.

Dismantling

3 Unscrew the bolts securing the torque converter housing.
4 Remove the torque converter housing.
5 Unscrew 12 bolts.
6 Remove the oil pan, joint washer and magnet.
7 Pull out the oil tubes.
8 Release the downshift inner cable from the downshift cam.
9 Take out three bolts and washers.
10 Lift off the valve block.
11 Unscrew two bolts.
12 Remove the oil tube locating plate.
13 Pull out the oil tubes. (Note the 'O' ring on the pump suction tube.)

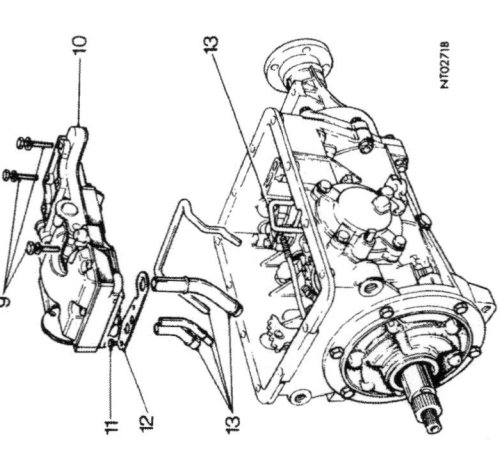

31 Reposition the starter motor, earth leads, dipstick tube and harness clips to the converter housing.
32 Fit and tighten the remaining securing bolts.
33 Refit the exhaust bracket and tighten the fixing bolts.
34 Raise the engine and gearbox assembly into the mounting position.
35 Position the rear cross member and tighten the four securing bolts.
36 Remove the engine support jack and unit lift.
37 Position the rear mounting centre plate and steady bar (if fitted).
38 Tighten the rear mounting centre bolt.
39 Reconnect the steady cable (if fitted).
40 Fit and tighten the four bolts securing the torque converter to the engine drive plate.
41 Reconnect the propshaft and tighten the four bolts.
42 Fit the spacers, heat shield and securing bolts.
43 Reconnect and secure the speedo cable.
44 Reconnect the cooler pipes to the gearbox and tighten the union nuts.
45 Reconnect the starter inhibitor/reverse light switch at the block connector on the wiring harness.
46 Reconnect the breather pipe.
47 Reconnect the selector lever.
48 Reconnect and tighten the dipstick tube to the transmission sump.
49 Reposition the radiator and tighten the four bolts securing the lower mounting.
50 Clip the cooler pipes to the radiator.
51 Refit the exhaust front pipe.
52 Lower the ramp.
53 Reconnect the downshift cable to the throttle linkage.
54 Fill the gearbox with fluid. 44.24.02.

16 Remove the steady bar and disconnect the cable (if fitted).
17 Remove the four nuts securing the rear cross member.
18 Remove the cross member.
19 Remove the three bolts, heat shield and spacers.
20 Position the unit lift and support the gearbox.
21 Remove the four bolts securing the radiator lower mounting.
22 Detach the cooler pipes from the securing clips.
23 Detach the radiator from the upper mountings and withdraw forwards.
24 Remove the exhaust support bracket.
25 Lower the unit and remove all the bolts and nuts securing the bell housing and starter motor to the engine unit.
26 Remove the dipstick tube.
27 Remove the earth leads and all the harness securing clips.
28 Lower the gearbox rearwards on the unit lift.

Refitting

29 Raise the gearbox into position using the unit lift.
30 Fit and tighten the dowel bolt and nuts securing the bell housing to the engine.

228 **AUTOMATIC GEARBOX**

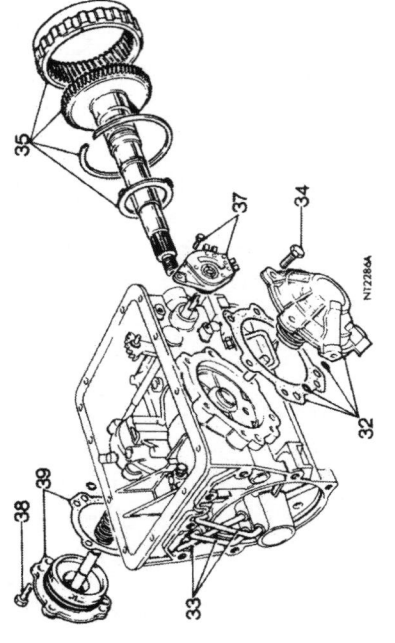

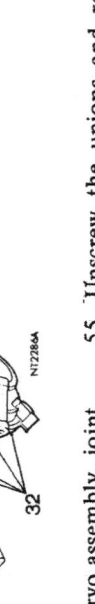

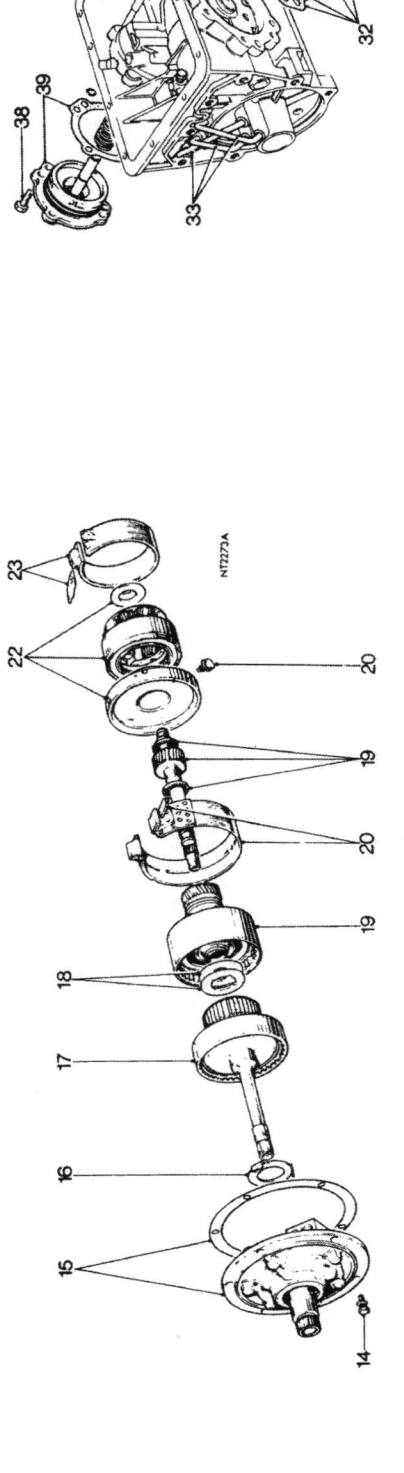

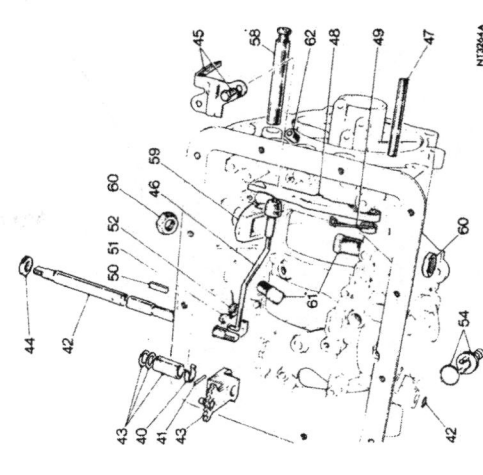

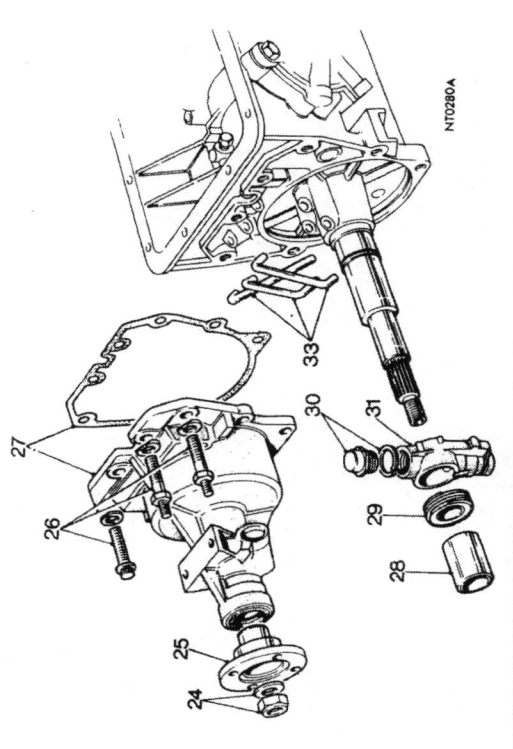

14 Take out five bolts.
15 Remove the pump and joint washer.
16 Remove the thrust washer.
17 Withdraw the front clutch.
18 Remove the thrust washers.
19 Withdraw the rear clutch and forward sun gear.
20 Squeeze together the ends of the front brake band and remove it together with the strut.
21 Unscrew the three bolts.
22 Withdraw the centre support/planet gear assembly.
23 Squeeze together the ends of the rear brake band, tilt and withdraw it together with the strut.
24 Using tool no. RG 421 or S 337 to hold the flange, unscrew the nut.
25 Withdraw the flange.
26 Unscrew the bolts.
27 Remove the rear extension and joint washer.
28 Remove the clamp tube.
29 Withdraw the speedometer drive gear.
30 Unscrew the counterweight.
31 Withdraw the governor assembly.
32 Withdraw the output shaft assembly and thrust washer.
33 Remove the oil tubes.
34 Unscrew the bolts.

35 Remove the rear servo assembly, joint washer and 'O' rings.
36 Unscrew the nut and remove the selector lever.
37 Unscrew the bolt and remove the switch.
38 Unscrew the bolts.
39 Remove the front servo and joint washer.
40 Remove the spring clip.
41 Withdraw the pin.
42 Withdraw the cross-shaft and remove the 'O' ring.
43 Remove the detent lever, collar, washers and 'O' ring.
44 Remove the oil seal.
45 Unscrew two screws and remove the cam plate.
46 Remove the parking brake rod assembly.
47 Withdraw the parking brake pawl pivot pin.
48 Remove the parking brake pawl.
49 Remove the spring.
50 Remove the relay lever pivot pin.
51 Remove the relay lever.
52 Remove the torsion spring.
53 Using tool no. CBW 62, remove the downshift cable assembly.
54 Using tool no. CBW 62, remove the breather adaptor.

55 Unscrew the unions and remove the bridge pipe.
56 Unscrew the adaptor.
57 Unscrew the return valve.
58 Withdraw the rear servo lever pivot pin.
59 Remove the rear servo lever.
60 Unscrew the locknuts.
61 Unscrew the adjusting screws.
62 Unscrew the pressure take-off plug.

continued

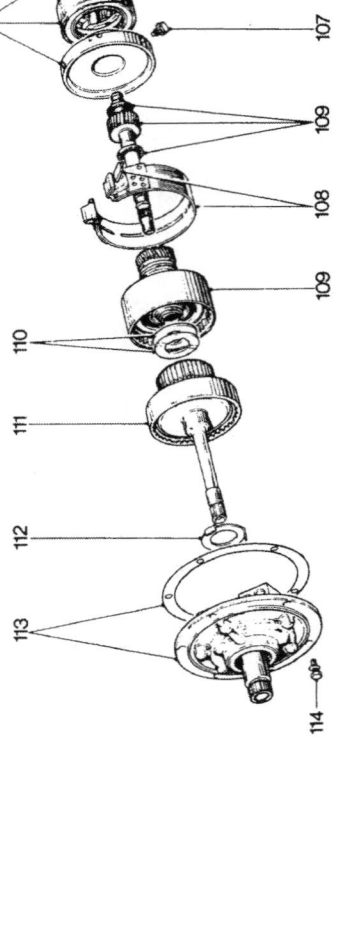

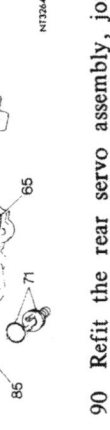

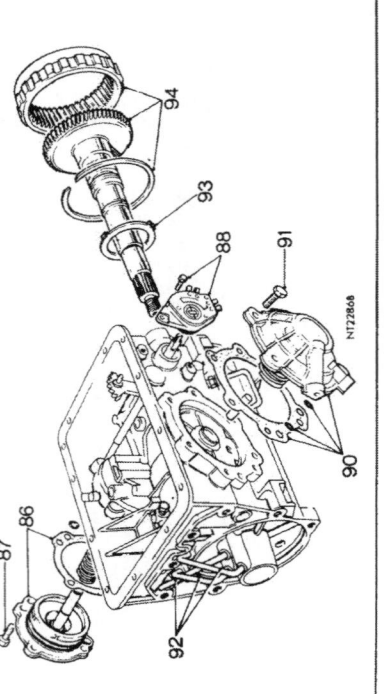

Reassembling

63 Fit the pressure take-off plug.
64 Refit the adjusting screws.
65 Loosely refit the locknuts.
66 Replace the rear servo lever.
67 Refit the rear servo lever pivot pin.
68 Fit the oil return valve.
69 Fit the adaptor.
70 Refit the bridge pipe and tighten the unions.
71 Refit the breather adaptor.
72 Refit the downshift cable.
73 Replace the relay lever and torsion spring.
74 Refit the relay lever pivot pin.
75 Replace the parking brake pawl and spring.
76 Refit the parking brake pawl pivot pin.
77 Refit the parking brake rod.
78 Refit the cam plate, ensuring that the tag end locates in the groove in the rear servo lever pivot pin.
79 Fit and tighten the bolts.
80 Fit a new cross-shaft oil seal.
81 Locate the cross-shaft through the oil seal and fit the washers.
82 Fit the collar and detent lever and push the cross-shaft fully home.
83 Refit the pin.
84 Refit the clip.
85 Refit the 'O' ring.
86 Refit the front servo and joint washer.
87 Fit and tighten the bolts.
88 Refit the switch and secure with the bolt.
89 Refit the selector lever and secure with the nut.

90 Refit the rear servo assembly, joint washer and 'O' rings, retaining them in position using petroleum jelly.
91 Fit and tighten the bolts.
92 Refit the oil tubes, ensuring that they are correctly located.
93 Locate the thrust washer on the end wall of the casing, using petroleum jelly.
94 Carefully refit the output shaft assembly.
95 Refit the governor assembly.
96 Fit and tighten the counterweight.
97 Refit the speedometer drive gear.
98 Refit the clamp tube.
99 Refit the rear extension housing and joint washer.

100 Fit and tighten the bolts.
101 Tap the drive flange into position.
102 Fit the washer and nut; using tool no. RG 421 or S 337 to hold the flange, tighten the nut to the correct torque.
103 Squeeze together the ends of the rear brake band, tilt and locate it in position.
104 Refit the rear brake band strut.
105 Using petroleum jelly, locate the thrust race on the rear drum spigot.
106 Refit the centre support/planet gear assembly, ensuring the oil and locating holes align with those in the casing.
107 Fit and tighten the three bolts.

108 Squeeze together the ends of the front brake band and fit it in position together with the strut.
109 Refit the rear clutch and forward sun gear assembly.
110 Using petroleum jelly, stick the thrust washers to the rear clutch assembly (phosphor bronze towards the front clutch).
111 Refit the front clutch assembly.
112 Using petroleum jelly, stick the thrust washer to the pump assembly.
113 Refit the pump assembly and joint washer.
114 Fit and tighten the bolts.

REAR EXTENSION HOUSING

Remove and refit   44.20.15

Service tool: RG 421 or S337

Removing

1 Drive the vehicle onto a ramp, select 'N', chock the road wheels and raise the ramp.
2 By removing one of the bolts and slackening the other, swing the prop guard clear of the propshaft.
3 Remove the four nuts and bolts securing the propshaft to the drive flange and disconnect the propshaft.

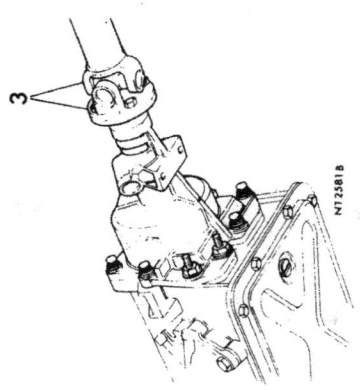

4 Using Service tool RG 421 or S337 remove the nut securing the drive flange.
5 Remove the drive flange.
6 Using a ramp jack and suitable wooden block, support the transmission unit under the sump pan.
7 Remove the centre gearbox mounting bolt and plate.
8 Remove the steady bar and disconnect the cable (if fitted).
9 Remove the four nuts securing the cross-member.
10 By raising the L.H. captive bolts, release the cross-member and remove.

continued

115 Using tool no. CBW 33, check the gear train end-float, and if necessary, adjust the selective use of the thrust washer fitted between the pump and the front clutch.
Recommended end-float 0.25 mm to 0.75 mm (0.010 to 0.030 in).

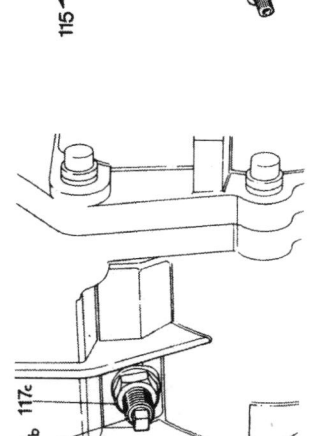

116 Adjust the front band as follows:
   a   Slacken the adjusting screw and locknut.
   b   Tighten the adjusting screw to 0.7 kgf m (5 lbf ft) and back off three-quarters of a turn.
   c   Tighten the locknut.

117 Adjust the rear band as follows:
   a   Slacken the adjusting screw and locknut.
   b   Tighten the adjusting screw to 0.7 kgf m (5 lbf ft) and back off three-quarters of a turn.
   c   Tighten the locknut.

118 Refit the oil tubes. (Note the 'O' ring on the pump suction tube).
119 Refit the oil tube locating plate.
120 Fit and tighten the two bolts.
121 Carefully refit the valve block, ensuring that the oil tubes are not distorted.
122 Fit and tighten the three bolts and washers.
123 Connect the downshift inner cable to the downshift cam.
124 Refit the oil tubes.
125 Replace the magnet and refit the oil pan and joint washer.
126 Fit and tighten 12 bolts.
127 Locate the torque converter housing in place.
128 Fit and tighten four bolts securing the torque converter housing.
129 Refit the transmission unit.

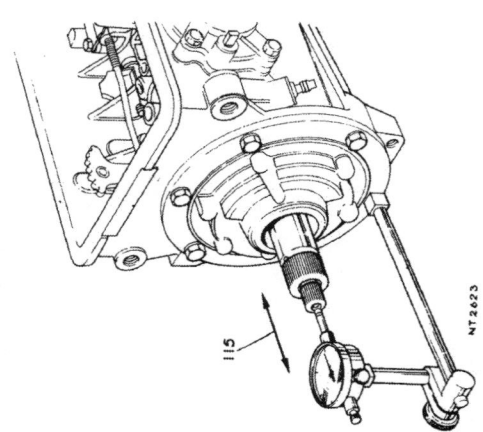

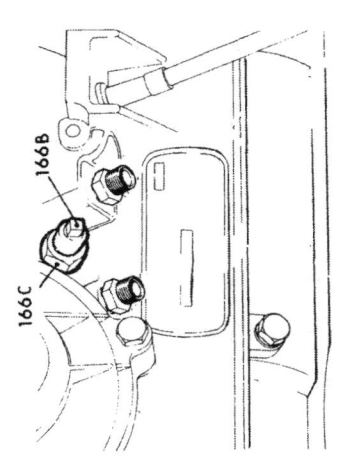

GOVERNOR 44.22.04

Overhaul

Dismantling
1. Pull off the retainer.
2. Withdraw the weight.
3. Withdraw the stem.
4. Remove the spring.
5. Withdraw the valve.

Reassembling
6. Insert the valve.
7. Refit the spring onto the stem.
8. Refit the stem and spring.
9. Refit the weight.
10. Refit the retainer.

GOVERNOR 44.22.01

Remove and refit

Removing
1. Remove the rear flange, rear extension and speedometer drive gear. 44.38.07.
2. Unscrew the counterweight.
3. Note the position and withdraw the governor assembly.

Refitting
4. Slide the governor assembly into the noted position.
5. Locate and secure the counterweight.
6. Refit the speedometer drive gear, rear extension and drive flange. 44.38.07.

REAR OIL SEAL 44.20.18

Remove and renew

Removing
1. Drive vehicle onto a ramp, select 'P', chock the road wheels and raise the ramp.
2. Remove the four nuts and bolts securing the propshaft to the drive flange.
3. Disconnect the propshaft.
4. Remove the nut securing the drive flange.
5. Remove the drive flange.
6. Prise out the oil seal.
7. Clean the area surrounding the oil seal.

Renewing
8. Carefully fit the new oil seal into the rear extension.
9. Lubricate the lip of the oil seal.
10. Refit the drive flange and securing nut.
11. Reconnect the propshaft.
12. Refit and tighten the prop bolts and nuts.
13. Lower the ramp.

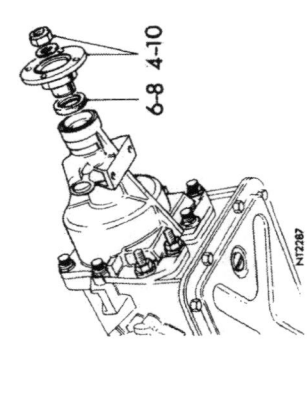

11. Remove the clamp bolt and clamp and disconnect the speedo cable.
12. Remove the nut and bolt securing the exhaust pipe to the mounting bracket.
13. Remove the two nuts securing the bracket to the rear extension housing and remove the bracket and spacers.
14. Remove the eight bolts securing the rear extension to the transmission case.
15. Withdraw the rear extension housing.

Refitting
16. Reverse 1–15.

DIPSTICK/FILLER TUBE

Remove and refit   44.24.01

Removing

1 Drive the vehicle onto a ramp, select 'P'.'Park', apply the hand brake and open the bonnet.
2 Withdraw the dipstick.
3 Raise the ramp.
4 Release the filler tube from the engine/ transmission flange.
5 Unscrew the union nut from the sump pan, and release the filler pipe from the sump.
6 Withdraw the filler tube from below the vehicle.

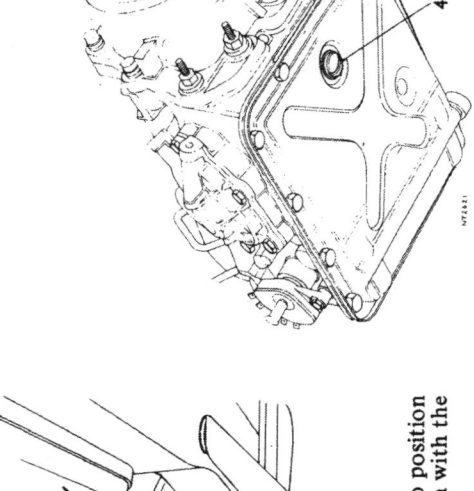

Refitting

7 Manoeuvre the filler tube into position and secure it to the sump pan with the union nut.
8 Secure the filler tube to the engine/ transmission flange.
9 Lower the ramp.
10 Refill the unit with fluid. 44.24.02.

TRANSMISSION FLUID

Drain and refill   44.24.02

Draining

1 Drive the vehicle onto a ramp, select 'P'.'PARK' and apply the hand brake.
2 Raise the ramp.
3 Place a tray under the drain plug.
4 Unscrew the plug.
5 Drain the fluid into the tray.
   NOTE: It is not possible to drain the torque converter.

Filling

If the sump has been drained it will be necessary to replenish the transmission unit until the fluid level is no higher than the 'cold high' mark 'C' (third mark down from top).

Check the level (hot) as follows:

6 Drive the vehicle for approximately 30 km (20 miles) until the transmission unit has reached its normal operating temperature.
7 Park the vehicle on level ground, apply the hand brake and select 'P'-'PARK'. Leave the engine running at idle speed.
8 Raise the bonnet and wipe clean around the dipstick/filler orifice.
9 Withdraw the dipstick and wipe it clean, using clean paper or a non-fluffy cloth.
10 Push the dipstick home and again withdraw it for reading. The fluid level should be at the top mark 'A' ('Hot high').
   DO NOT OVERFILL THE TRANS-MISSION.

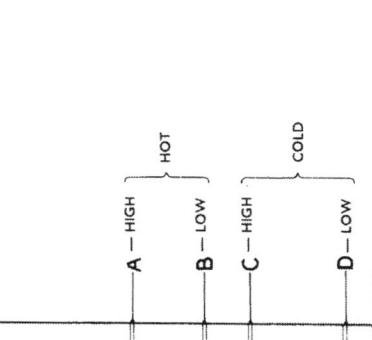

	HOT
A — HIGH	
B — LOW	
C — HIGH	COLD
D — LOW	

TRANSMISSION SUMP

Remove and refit   44.24.04

Removing

1 Unscrew the filler pipe union and drain the transmission unit.
2 Remove the bolts securing the heat shield.
3 Remove the heat shield spacers.
4 Remove the steady bar (if fitted).
5 Unscrew the bolts securing the sump.
6 Remove the sump and joint washer.

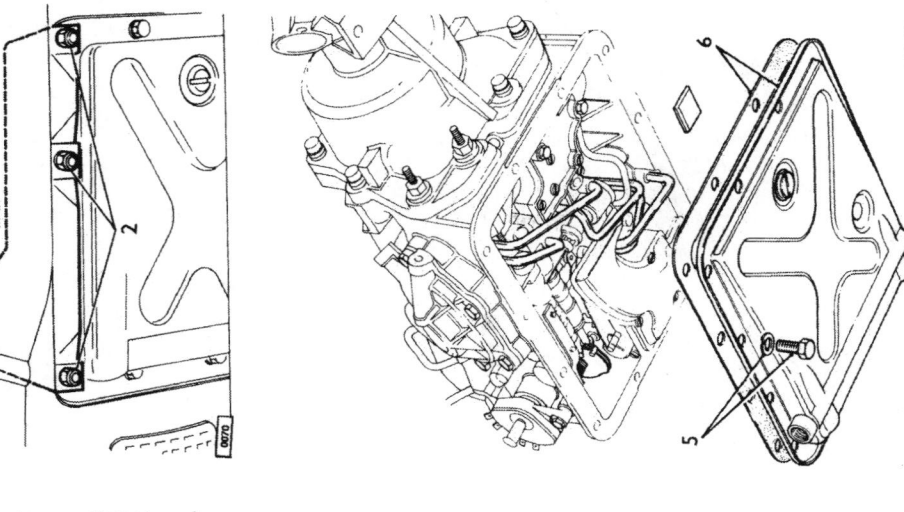

Refitting

7 Reverse 1–6.
8 Fill the transmission unit with fluid. 44.24.02.

OIL/FLUID FILTER 44.24.07

Remove and refit

Removing

1 Remove the transmission sump. 44.24.04.
2 Remove the four screws securing the filter in position.
3 Remove the filter.

Refitting

4 Reverse 1–3.

OIL/FLUID COOLER 44.24.10

Remove and refit

Removing

1 Drive the vehicle onto a ramp, select 'P'-'Park', chock the road wheels and raise the ramp.
2 Detach the cooler pipes from the securing clip beneath the radiator.
3 Undo the cooler pipe union nuts.
4 Disconnect the cooler pipes.
5 Remove the two bolts securing the cooler to the body.
6 Remove the cooler.

Refitting

7 Reverse 1–6
8 Check/top up the transmission fluid.

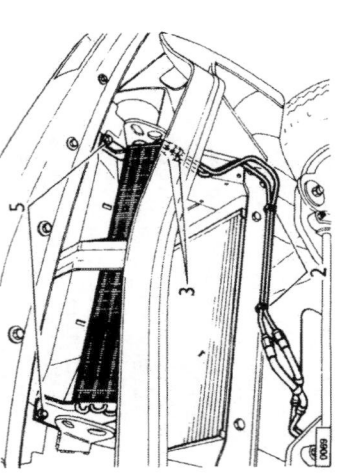

DOWNSHIFT CABLE 44.30.01

Initial setting

1 Check that the carburetter slow running and fast idle settings are satisfactory.
2 Slacken the locknut.
3 Adjust the outer cable in the bracket until the crimped stop is 1.5 mm (1/16 in) from the end of the outer cable ferrule.
4 Tighten the locknut.
5 Road test the vehicle and check the gear shift speeds.

DOWNSHIFT CABLE 44.30.02

Adjust

1 Drive the vehicle onto a ramp, apply the hand brake and chock the wheels.
2 Start the engine, select 'D' and adjust the idling speed to 750 rev/min. Stop the engine.
3 Slacken the locknut.
4 Adjust the outer cable to 1.5 mm (1/16 in) from the stop. 44.20.01 (para. 3).
5 Remove the sump pan. 44.24.04.

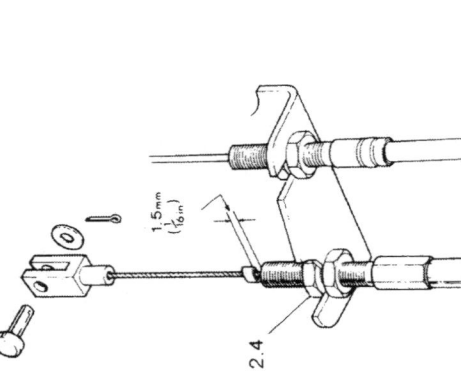

6 Check that the downshift cam is in the idling position.
7 With the aid of an assistant in the driving seat, fully open the throttle and check that the downshift cam is in the kick-down position.
8 If necessary, adjust the outer cable until the idling and kick-down positions can be correctly obtained on the downshift cam. Tighten the locknut.
9 Refit the sump. 44.24.04.

DOWNSHIFT CABLE 44.30.03

Pressure check

Service tools: CBW 1C and CBW 1C-2

1 Start and run the engine until the transmission reaches its normal operating temperature.
2 Drive the vehicle onto a ramp and check that the engine idling speed is approximately 750 rev/min. Stop the engine.

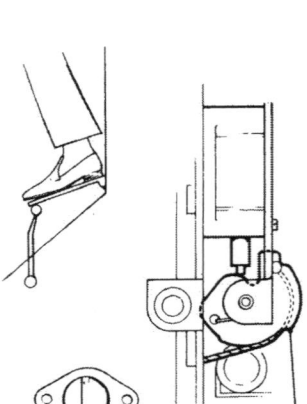
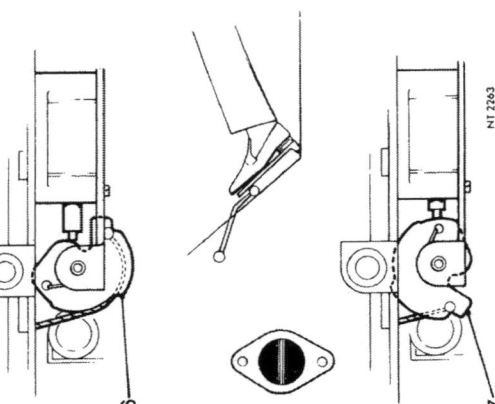

3 Raise the ramp.
4 Remove the plug.
5 Connect the pressure gauge to the transmission unit.
6 Lower the ramp, chock the wheels and apply the hand brake and foot brake.
7 Start the engine and select 'D'.

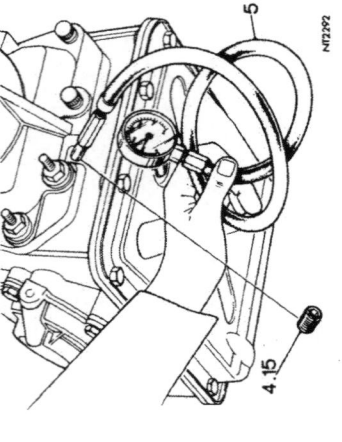

8 With the engine idling at 750 rev/min, note the pressure gauge reading which should be 4.2 to 5.3 kgf/cm^2 (60 to 75 lbf/in^2).
9 Increase the engine speed to 1,000 rev/min and note the pressure increase which should be 1.0 to 1.4 kgf/cm^2 (15 to 20 lbf/in^2).
10 Stop the engine.
11 If the pressure increase is less than 1.0 kgf/cm^2 (15 lbf/in^2), increase the effective length of the outer cable. If the pressure increase is more than 1.4 kgf/cm^2 (20 lbf/in^2), decrease the effective length of the outer cable.
12 Repeat operations 7 to 11 until the pressure increase is correct.
13 Raise the ramp.
14 Disconnect the pressure gauge.
15 Refit the plug.
16 Lower the ramp.

SELECTOR ROD

Adjust 44.30.04

1 Drive the vehicle onto a ramp, select P – 'Park', lock the selector lever in 'N' and apply the hand brake.
2 Raise the ramp.
3 Slacken the locknut.
4 Push the clip off the hand lever.
5 Disconnect the selector rod and check that the gearbox selector lever is in the neutral position.
6 Alter the length of the selector rod by adjusting the turnbuckle until the end of the rod can be located in the hand lever.
7 Tighten the locknut.
8 Push the clip onto the lever and secure the rod.
9 Lower the ramp.

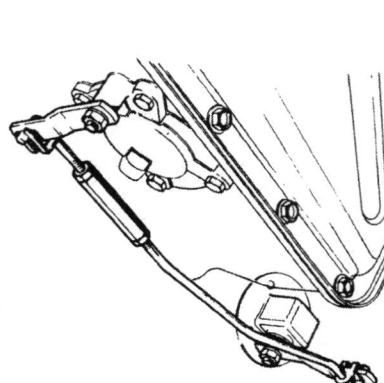

FRONT BRAKE BAND

Adjust 44.30.07

Service tools: 18G 307

1 Drive the vehicle onto a ramp, select P – 'Park', apply the hand brake and raise the ramp.
2 Slacken the locknut.
3 Tighten the adjusting screw to 0.41 kgf m (36 lbf in) and back off three-quarters of a turn.
4 Tighten the locknut to 3.1 kgf m (22 lbf ft).
5 Lower the ramp.

REAR BRAKE BAND

Adjust 44.30.10

Service tools: 18G 307

1 Drive the vehicle onto a ramp, select P – 'Park', apply the handbrake and raise the ramp.
2 Slacken the locknut.
3 Tighten the adjusting screw to 0.41 kgf m (36 lbf in) and back off three-quarters of a turn.
4 Tighten the locknut to 3.1 kgf m (22 lbf ft).
5 Lower the ramp.

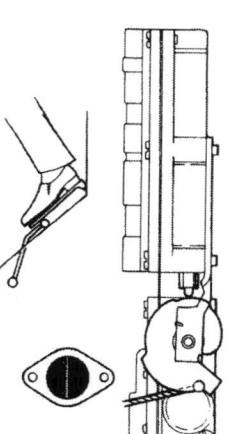

STALL TEST

44.30.13

The function of a stall test is to determine that the torque converter and gearbox are operating satisfactorily.

1 Check the condition of the engine. An engine which is not developing full power will affect the stall test readings.
2 Allow the engine and transmission to reach correct working temperatures.
3 Chock the wheels and apply the hand brake and foot brake.
4 Select '1' or 'R' and depress the throttle to the 'kick-down' position. Note the reading on the tachometer which should be 2,200 rev/min. If the reading is below 1,400 rev/min, suspect the converter for stator slip. If the reading is down to 1,600 rev/min, the engine is not developing full power. If the reading is in excess of 2,400 rev/min, suspect the gearbox for brake band or clutch slip.
NOTE: Do not carry out a stall test for a longer period than 10 seconds, otherwise the transmission will become overheated.

ROAD TEST

44.30.17

Throughout the road test procedure the term 'full throttle' is equivalent to approximately seven-eighths of the available pedal movement and 'kick-down' is equivalent to the full movement.

Procedure

1 Check that the starter motor will operate only with the selector lever in 'PARK' or 'N' and that the reverse lights operate only in 'R'.
2 Apply the hand brake and with the engine idling select 'N–D', 'N–2', 'N–R'. Engagement should be positive. A cushioned 'thump' under fast idling conditions is normal.
3 With the transmission at normal running temperatures, select 'D', release the brakes and accelerate with minimum throttle. Check the 1–2 and 2–3 shift speeds and the quality of change.
4 Stop the vehicle, select 'D' and re-start using 'full throttle'. Check 1–2 and 2–3 shift speeds and the quality of change.
5 At 40 m.p.h. (65 km/h) apply 'full throttle'. The vehicle should accelerate in third gear and should not downshift to second.
6 At a maximum speed of 56 m.p.h. (90 km/h) 'kick-down', fully. The transmission should downshift to second gear.
7 At a maximum speed of 35 m.p.h. (56 km/h) 'kick-down', fully. The transmission should downshift to first gear.
8 Stop the vehicle, select 'D' and re-start using 'kick-down'. Check the 1–2 and 2–3 shift speeds.
9 At 35 m.p.h. (56 km/h) select 2 and release the throttle. Check the 3–2 downshift.
10 At 30 m.p.h. (50 km/h) select 1 and release the throttle. Check the 2–1 downshift.

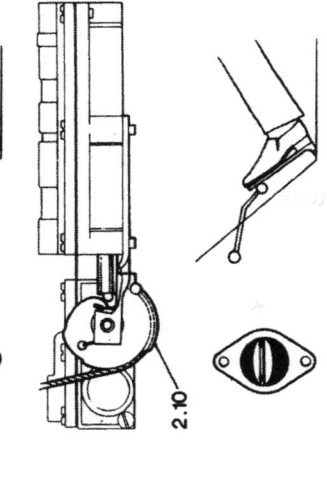

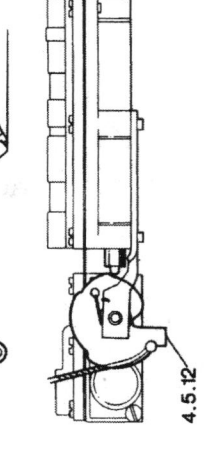

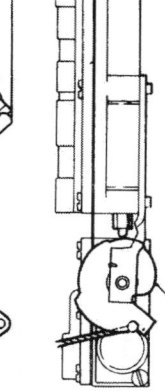

ROAD TEST – FAULT DIAGNOSIS CHART

NOTE: The numbers indicate the recommended sequence of investigation

Diagnosis	Engagement of 1, 2, D or R			Take off						Upshifts				Upshift Quality						Downshifts					Downshift Quality			
	None	Delayed	Bumpy	Slip	Squawk	No neutral	Seizure reverse	None reverse	None forward	Below normal speed	Above normal speed	No 2-3	No 1-2	Siezure 2-3	Siezure 1-2	Rough 2-3	Rough 1-2	Slip 2-3	Slip 1-2	Below normal speed	Above normal speed	Involuntary 3-2	No 3-2	No 2-1	Rough 3-2	Rough 2-1	Slip 3-2	Slip 2-1
SYMPTOM																												
ADJUSTMENT FAULTS																												
Fluid level insufficient	1	1	2	1							1		1					1	1		1	1	1	1				
Downshift cable incorrectly assembled or adjusted					2													2	2	1			1	1	1			
Manual linkage incorrectly assembled or adjusted	2	3	1					1	2			1	1					3	3									
Incorrect engine idling speed										1						2	2										1	1
Incorrect front band adjustment	2	2					1						2	1	1			4	4									
Incorrect rear band adjustment	3							1							1			3				1						
HYDRAULIC CONTROL FAULTS																												
Oil tubes incorrectly installed, missing or leaking	4	3			7		7	3	3	8	8	8	8					8	9	2			3	3	6	7	3	
Sealing ring missing or broken	7	4					6	6	2	9	8	9	9	5	5			9	10	5	5		2	2	8	5		
Valve block screws missing or loose	6	5	5			3	5	5		10	9	10	10	3	6	10		10	11	6	6		7		4	3		
Primary regulator valve sticking	5	6	3									6	6	4		3	3	6	7	4			8	3	5	4		
Throttle valve sticking			4							2	10	7	7			4	4	7	8	2	7							
Modulator valve sticking											2					4	5			2	7							
Governor valve sticking, leaking or incorrectly assembled											3	3	2				6			3	2		3	2		3	2	
Orifice control valve sticking							3		3			2	3										2	2				
1-2 shift valve sticking									4		4		4								3							
2-3 shift valve sticking											5	3									5		7				3	
2-3 shift valve plunger sticking											6	4	6								6		8	3				2
Converter 'out' check valve sticking or missing	13																			4	4		3	3				
Check valve sticking or missing	8																											
MECHANICAL FAULTS																												
Front clutch slipping	9	6		4					4			5	5			9		5		3			4			9		2
Front clutch seized or plates distorted	10	7			9	2																				9	6	
Rear clutch slipping						2										5	2	5				3						7
Rear clutch seized or plates distorted					6																							
Front band slipping due to faulty servo or worn band																		6	6			5				2	2	8
Rear band slipping due to faulty servo or worn band	11							8									7						5	4				
Uni-directional clutch slipping or incorrectly installed									5								8								1	1		
Uni-directional clutch seized	7													3	4													
Input shaft broken	8	12																										
Front pump drive tangs on converter hub broken	9																											
Front pump worn																												
Converter blading and/or uni-directional clutch failed	10																											

11 With 1 still engaged, stop the vehicle and using 'kick-down' accelerate to over 40 m.p.h. (65 km/h). Check for 'slip', 'squawk', and the absence of upshifts.

12 Stop the vehicle and select 'R'. Reverse using 'full throttle' if possible. Check for 'slip' and 'squawk'.

13 Stop the vehicle on a gradient. Apply the hand brake and select 'P'-'PARK'. Release the hand brake and check the parking pawl hold. Check that the selector lever is held firmly in the gate in 'P'.

CONVERTER DIAGNOSIS

Inability to start on steep gradients, combined with poor acceleration from the rest and low stall speed (1,400 rev/min) indicates that the converter stator uni-directional clutch is slipping. This condition permits the stator to rotate in an opposite direction to the impeller and turbine, and torque multiplication cannot occur.

Poor acceleration in third gear above 30 m.p.h. (50 km/h) and reduced maximum speed, indicates that the stator uni-directional clutch has seized. The stator will not rotate with the turbine and impeller and the 'fluid flywheel' phase cannot occur. This condition will also be indicated by excessive overheating of the transmission although the stall speed will be correct.

PUMP

Remove and refit   44.32.01

Service tools: CBW 60, CBW 547A-50

Removing

1 Remove the transmission unit. 44.20.01.
2 Wash the exterior of the unit in clean petrol or paraffin, invert it and place on a bench cradle CBW 60. Remove the switch. 44.15.15.
3 Unscrew the bolts.
4 Remove the torque converter housing.
5 Unscrew 12 bolts.
6 Remove the oil pan, joint washer and magnet.
7 Pull out the oil tubes.
8 Release the inner downshift cable from downshift cam.
9 Take out three bolts and washers.
10 Lift off the valve block.
11 Unscrew two bolts.
12 Remove the oil tube locating plate.
13 Pull out the oil tubes. (Note the 'O' ring on the pump suction tube.)
14 Take out five bolts.
15 Remove the pump and joint washer.
16 Remove the thrust washer.

Refitting

17 Using petroleum jelly, stick the thrust washer to the pump assembly.
18 Refit the pump assembly and joint washer.
19 Fit and tighten the bolts.
20 Refit the oil tubes. (Note the 'O' ring on the pump suction tube.)
21 Refit the oil tube locating plate.
22 Fit and tighten the two bolts.
23 Carefully refit the valve block, ensuring that the oil tubes are not distorted.

24 Fit and tighten the three bolts and washers.
25 Connect the downshift inner cable to the downshift cam.
26 Refit the oil tubes.
27 Replace the magnet and refit the oil pan and joint washer.
28 Fit and tighten 12 bolts.
29 Locate the torque converter housing in place.
30 Fit and tighten four bolts.
31 Refit the switch. 44.15.15.
32 Refit the transmission unit.

PUMP

Overhaul   44.32.04

Service tool: CBW 547A-50

1 Remove the pump. 44.32.01.

Dismantling

2 Unscrew the bolts.
3 Take out the locating screw.
4 Separate the stator support from the pump body assembly.
5 Mark the outside faces of the gears to facilitate correct assembly.
6 Remove the gears.
7 Remove the 'O' ring.
8 Extract the seal.

Reassembling

9 Renew the seal.
10 Refit the 'O' ring.
11 Fit the gears into the pump body.
12 Lightly lubricate the gears and the 'O' ring.
13 Refit the stator support.
14 Fit and tighten the locating screw and lock washer.
15 Fit and tighten the bolts and lock washers.
16 Refit the front pump. 44.32.01.

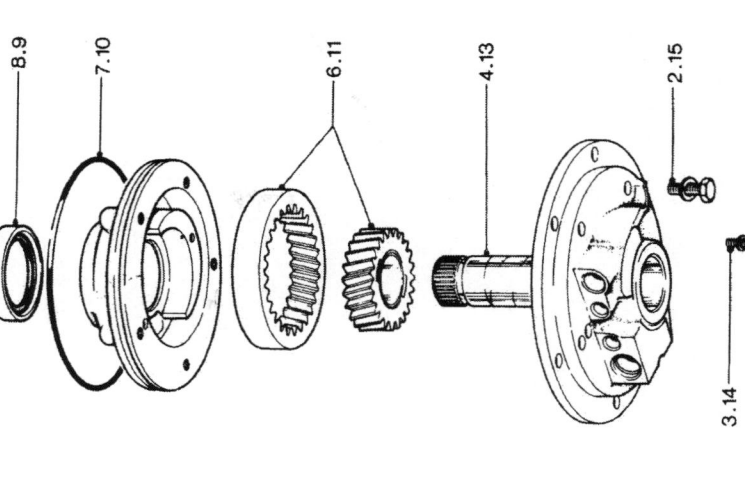

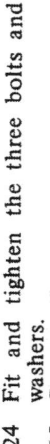

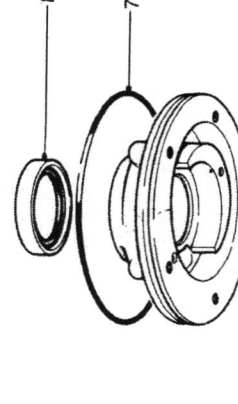

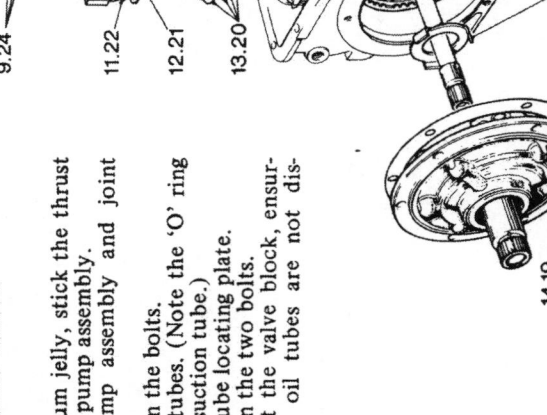

FRONT SERVO

Remove and refit   44.34.07

Service tool: CBW 547A-50

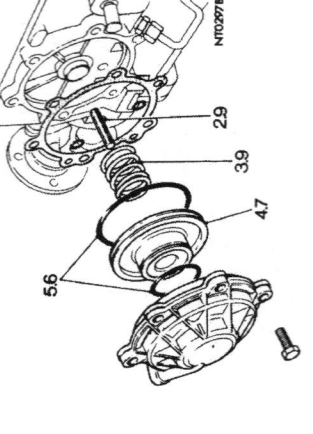

Removing
1. Drive the vehicle onto a ramp, select 'N' and apply the hand brake.
2. Disconnect the gearbox selector lever.
3. Take out the four bolts.
4. Withdraw the front servo assembly, spring and joint washer.

Refitting
5. Locate the joint washer onto the servo body flange.
6. Refit the servo and spring.
7. Fit the tighten the bolts using CBW 547A-50.

FRONT SERVO

Overhaul   44.34.10

1. Remove the front servo. 44.34.07

Dismantling
2. Remove the spring.
3. Withdraw the piston using air pressure.
4. Remove the 'O' rings from the body.
5. Remove the 'O' rings from the piston.

Reassembling
6. Fit the 'O' rings to the piston.
7. Fit the 'O' rings to the body.
8. Refit the piston.
9. Fit the spring.
10. Refit the servo assembly.

REAR SERVO

Remove and refit   44.34.13

Service tool: CBW 547A-50

1. Remove the exhaust front pipe. 30.10.09.

Removing
2. Unscrew the six bolts.
3. Withdraw the servo and joint washer together with 'O' rings, spring and push-rod.

Refitting
4. Locate the 'O' rings and joint washer onto the gearbox casing.
5. Fit the servo assembly, spring and push-rod.
6. Fit and tighten the six bolts using CBW 547A-50.
7. Refit the exhaust front pipe. 30.10.09.

REAR SERVO

Overhaul   44.34.16

1. Remove the rear servo. 44.34.13.

Dismantling
2. Remove the push-rod.
3. Remove the spring.
4. Withdraw the piston using air pressure.
5. Remove the 'O' rings.

Reassembling
6. Fit the 'O' rings to the piston.
7. Refit the piston.
8. Refit the spring.
9. Refit the push-rod.
10. Refit the rear servo.

OUTPUT SHAFT

Remove and refit   44.36.01

Service tools: CBW 60, RG 421 or S 337, CBW 547A-50

Removing

1 Remove the transmission unit. 44.20.01.
2 Wash the exterior of the unit in clean petrol or paraffin, invert it and place on a bench cradle CBW 60. Remove the switch. 44.15.15.
3 Unscrew the bolts securing the torque converter housing.
4 Remove the torque converter housing.
5 Unscrew 12 bolts.
6 Remove the oil pan, joint washer and magnet.
7 Pull out the oil tubes.
8 Release the downshift inner cable from the downshift cam.
9 Take out three bolts and washers.
10 Lift off the valve block.
11 Unscrew two bolts.
12 Remove the oil tube locating plate.
13 Pull out the oil tubes. (Note the 'O' ring on the pump suction tube.)
14 Take out five bolts.
15 Remove the pump and joint washer.
16 Remove the thrust washer.
17 Withdraw the front clutch.
18 Remove the thrust washers.
19 Withdraw the rear clutch and forward sun gear.
20 Squeeze together the ends of the front brake band and remove it together with the strut.

21 Unscrew the three bolts.
22 Withdraw the centre support/planet gear assembly and needle thrust assembly.
23 Squeeze together the ends of the rear brake band, tilt and withdraw together with the strut.
24 Using tool no. RG 421 or S 337 to retain the flange, unscrew the nut.
25 Withdraw the flange.
26 Unscrew the bolts.

27 Withdraw the rear extension and joint washer.
28 Remove the clamp tube.
29 Withdraw the speedometer drive gear.
30 Unscrew the counterweight and remove the governor.
31 Withdraw the output shaft assembly.
32 Remove the thrust washer.
33 Remove the circlip.
34 Detach the outer annulus from the output shaft.

continued

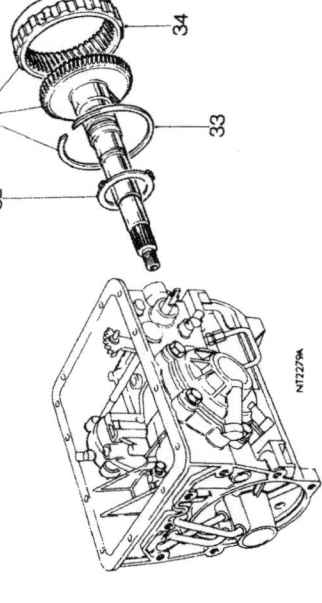

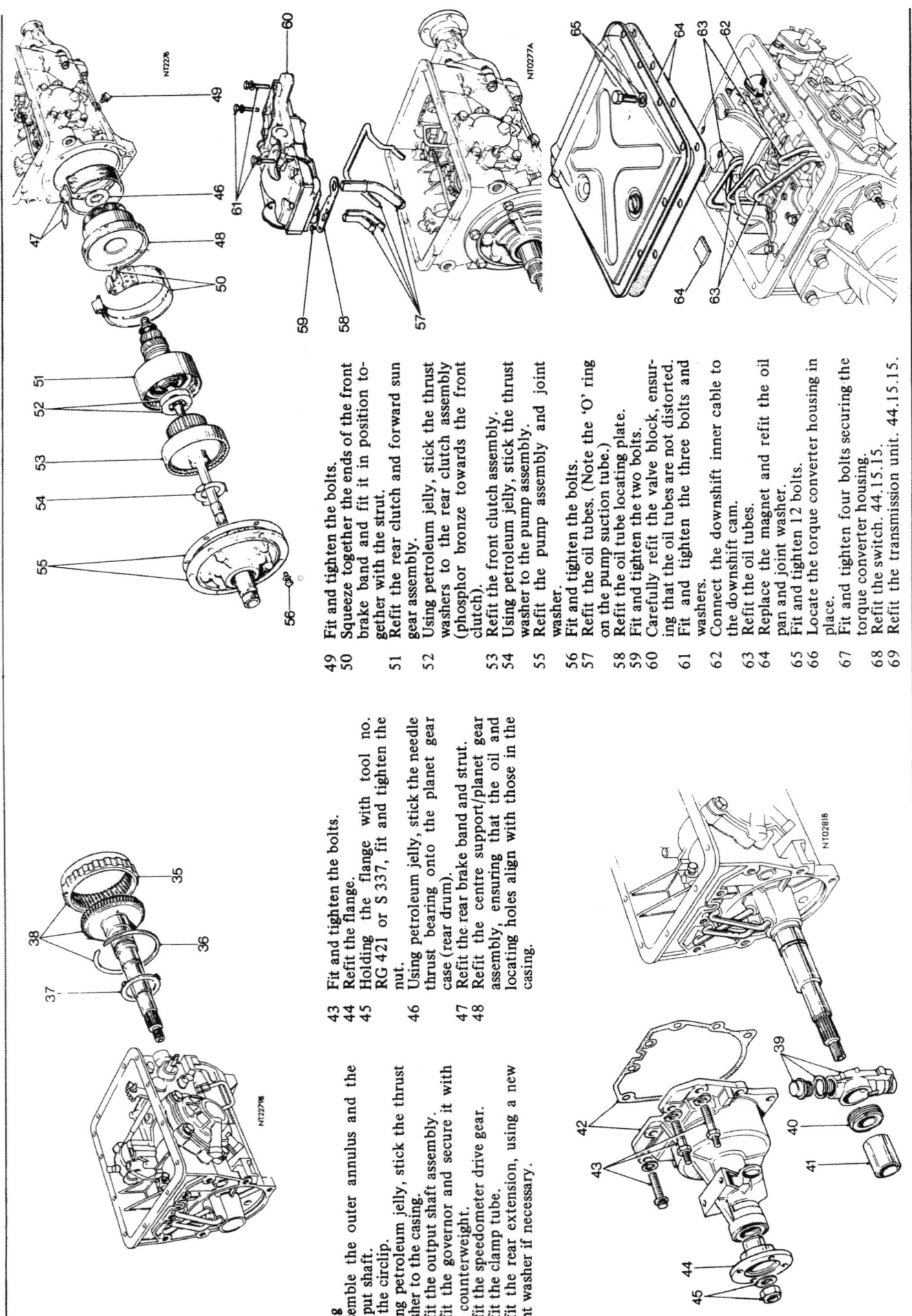

Refitting

35 Assemble the outer annulus and the output shaft.

36 Fit the circlip.

37 Using petroleum jelly, stick the thrust washer to the casing.

38 Refit the output shaft assembly.

39 Refit the governor and secure it with the counterweight.

40 Refit the speedometer drive gear.

41 Refit the clamp tube.

42 Refit the rear extension, using a new joint washer if necessary.

43 Fit and tighten the bolts.

44 Refit the flange.

45 Holding the flange with tool no. RG 421 or S 337, fit and tighten the nut.

46 Using petroleum jelly, stick the needle thrust bearing onto the planet gear case (rear drum).

47 Refit the rear brake band and strut.

48 Refit the centre support/planet gear assembly, ensuring that the oil and locating holes align with those in the casing.

49 Fit and tighten the bolts.

50 Squeeze together the ends of the front brake band and fit it in position to-gether with the strut.

51 Refit the rear clutch and forward sun gear assembly.

52 Using petroleum jelly, stick the thrust washers to the rear clutch assembly (phosphor bronze towards the front clutch).

53 Refit the front clutch assembly.

54 Using petroleum jelly, stick the thrust washer to the pump assembly.

55 Refit the pump assembly and joint washer.

56 Fit and tighten the bolts.

57 Refit the oil tubes. (Note the 'O' ring on the pump suction tube.)

58 Refit the oil tube locating plate.

59 Fit and tighten the two bolts.

60 Carefully refit the valve block, ensur-ing that the oil tubes are not distorted.

61 Fit and tighten the three bolts and washers.

62 Connect the downshift inner cable to the downshift cam.

63 Refit the oil tubes.

64 Replace the magnet and refit the oil pan and joint washer.

65 Fit and tighten 12 bolts.

66 Locate the torque converter housing in place.

67 Fit and tighten four bolts securing the torque converter housing.

68 Refit the switch. 44.15.15.

69 Refit the transmission unit. 44.15.15.

PLANET GEARS AND REAR DRUM ASSEMBLY

Remove and refit 44.36.04

Service tools: CBW 60, CBW 547A-50

Removing

1   Remove the transmission unit. 44.20.01.
2   Wash the exterior of the unit in clean petrol or paraffin, invert it and place on a bench cradle CBW 60. Remove the switch. 44.15.15.
3   Unscrew the bolts securing the torque converter housing.
4   Remove the torque converter housing.
5   Unscrew 12 bolts.
6   Remove the oil pan, joint washer and magnet.
7   Pull out the oil tubes.
8   Release the downshift inner cable from the downshift cam.
9   Take out three bolts and washers.
10 Lift off the valve block.
11 Unscrew two bolts.
12 Remove the oil tube locating plate.
13 Pull out the oil tubes. (Note the 'O' ring on the pump suction tube.)
14 Take out five bolts.
15 Remove the pump and joint washer.
16 Remove the thrust washer.
17 Withdraw the front clutch.
18 Remove the thrust washers.
19 Withdraw the rear clutch and forward sun gear.
20 Squeeze together the ends of the front brake band and remove it together with the strut.
21 Take out three bolts.
22 Withdraw the centre support/planet gear assembly.
23 Separate the centre support from the planet gear assembly.
24 Withdraw the uni-directional clutch.
25 Remove the circlip.
26 Detach the uni-directional clutch outer race.

Refitting

27 Fit the uni-directional clutch outer race to the rear drum assembly.
28 Fit the circlip.
29 Refit the uni-directional clutch.
30 Assemble the centre support and planet gear assembly.
31 Refit the centre support/planet gear assembly, ensuring that the oil and locating holes align with those in the casing.
32 Fit and tighten the bolts.
33 Squeeze together the ends of the front brake band and fit it in position together with the strut.
34 Refit the rear clutch and forward sun gear assembly.
35 Using petroleum jelly, stick the thrust washers to the rear clutch assembly (phosphor bronze towards the front clutch).

continued

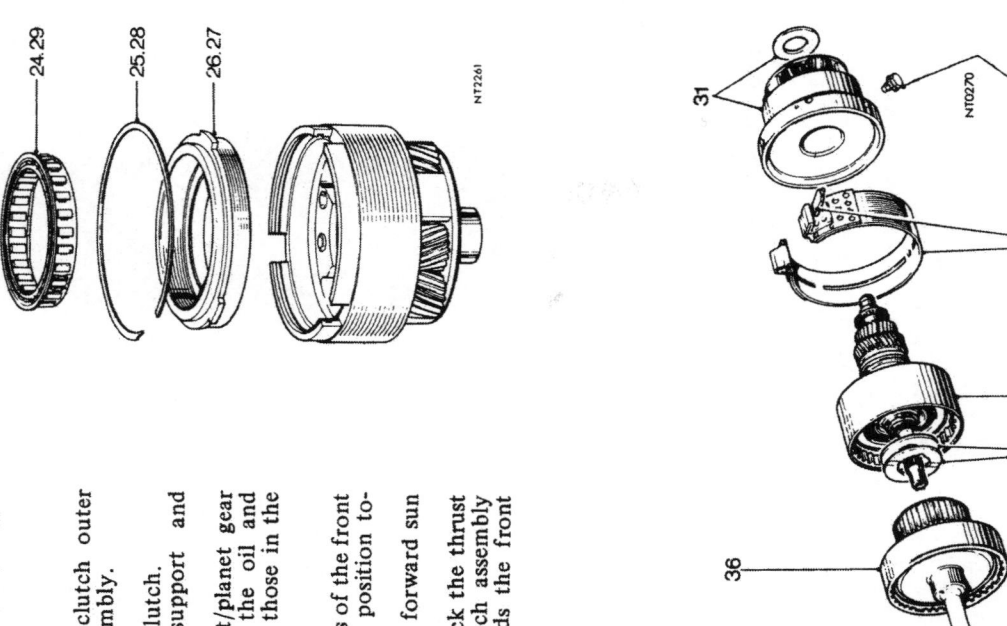

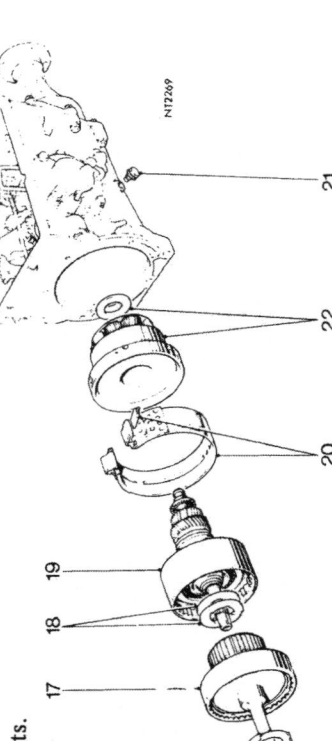

36 Refit the front clutch assembly.
37 Using petroleum jelly, stick the thrust washer to the pump assembly.
38 Refit the pump assembly and joint washer.
39 Fit and tighten the bolts.
40 Refit the oil tubes. (Note the 'O' ring on the pump suction tube.)
41 Refit the oil tube locating plate.
42 Fit and tighten the two bolts.
43 Carefully refit the valve block, ensuring that the oil tubes are not distorted.
44 Fit and tighten the three bolts and washers.
45 Connect the downshift inner cable to the downshift cam.
46 Refit the oil tubes.
47 Replace the magnet and refit the oil pan and joint washer.
48 Fit and tighten 12 bolts.
49 Locate the torque converter housing in place.
50 Fit and tighten four bolts securing the torque converter housing.
51 Refit the switch. 44.15.15.
52 Refit the transmission unit.

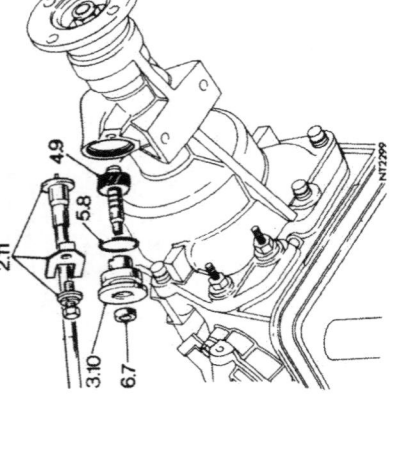

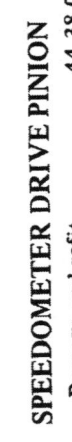

VALVE BLOCK

Remove and refit   44.40.01

Removing

1 Remove the sump pan, 44.24.04, and remove the switch. 44.15.15.
2 Remove the magnet.
3 Pull out the oil connector pipes.
4 Disconnect the downshift cable from the cam.
5 Take out three bolts.
6 Release the valve block.

Refitting

7 Ensure that the pipes are correctly located.
8 Fit the valve block to the unit.
9 Secure with three bolts.
10 Attach the downshift cable to the cam, ensuring that the cam is correctly located on the manual valve.
11 Refit the oil connector pipes.
12 Attach the magnet to one end of the bolt heads.
13 Refit the switch. 44.15.15.
14 Replace the sump pan. 44.24.04.

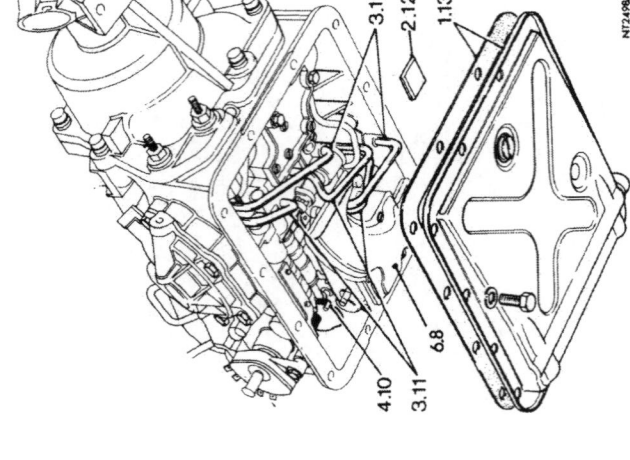

SPEEDOMETER DRIVE GEAR

Remove and refit   44.38.07

Removing

1 Remove the rear extension. 44.20.15.
2 Remove the clamp tube.
3 Withdraw the speedometer drive gear.

Refitting

4 Fit the speedometer drive gear.
5 Refit the clamp tube.
6 Refit the rear extension. 44.20.15.

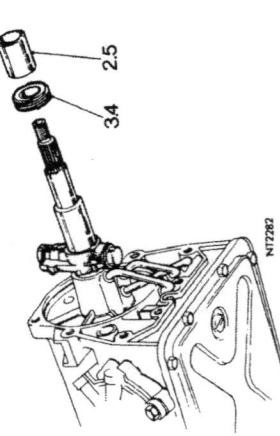

SPEEDOMETER DRIVE PINION

Remove and refit   44.38.04

Removing

1 Drive the vehicle onto a ramp, apply the hand brake and raise the ramp.
2 Disconnect the speedometer cable from the gearbox.
3 Carefully prise the speedometer pinion housing out of the extension.
4 Withdraw the pinion from the housing.
5 Remove the 'O' ring.
6 Extract the seal.

Refitting

7 Press a new seal into the housing.
8 Fit a new 'O' ring to the housing.
9 Fit the drive pinion into the housing.
10 Press the housing into the rear extension.
11 Refit the speedometer cable.
12 Lower the ramp.

VALVE BLOCK

Overhaul 44.40.04

Service tool: CBW 548

Dismantling

1 Remove the valve block. 44.40.01.
2 Take out two screws.
3 Remove the downshift cam assembly.
4 Take out four screws.
5 Remove the oil strainer and gasket.
6 Take out screw.
7 Remove detent spring and spacer.
8 Take out eight screws.
9 Remove upper valve body.
10 Take out eight screws.
11 Remove the oil tube collector.
12 Take out four screws.
13 Remove the governor line plate.
14 Remove the separating plate.
15 Remove the check valve.
16 Remove the check valve ball and spring.
17 Remove the servo orifice control valve spring and stop.
18 Remove the throttle valve stop and return spring.
19 Remove the throttle valve plate.
20 Withdraw the manual control valve.
21 Withdraw the downshift valve.
22 Withdraw the throttle valve spring.
23 Withdraw the throttle valve.
24 Tap out the dowel pin, applying light pressure to the plug.
25 Withdraw the modulator plug.
26 Withdraw the modulator valve.
27 Withdraw the modulator valve spacer.
28 Withdraw the modulator valve spring.
29 Withdraw the servo orifice control valve.
30 Slacken progressively the three screws.
31 Carefully remove the end plate.
32 Remove the spring.
33 Withdraw the sleeve.
34 Take out the primary regulator valve.
35 Remove the spring.
36 Withdraw the secondary regulator valve.
37 Remove the screws from the upper valve body.

38 Remove the front end plate.
39 Take out three screws.
40 Remove the rear end plate.
41 Withdraw the 2-3 shift valve from the rear.
42 Remove the spring.
43 Withdraw the plunger.
44 Withdraw the 1-2 shift valve from the rear.
45 Remove the spring.
46 Withdraw the plunger.

Reassembling

47 Insert the 1-2 shift valve.
48 Insert the 2-3 shift valve.
49 Replace the rear end plate.
50 Fit and tighten the three screws.
51 Insert the 1-2 shift valve plunger.
52 Insert the 2-3 shift valve spring.
53 Insert the 1-2 shift valve spring.
54 Insert the 2-3 shift valve plunger.
55 Locate the front end plate in position.
56 Fit and tighten three screws.
57 Insert the secondary regulator valve into the lower valve body.
58 Refit the spring.
59 Insert the primary regulator valve.
60 Insert the sleeve.
61 Insert the spring.
62 Hold the end plate in position.
63 Fit and tighten the three screws.
64 Insert the servo orifice control valve.
65 Insert the spring.
66 Depress the spring and fit the stop.
67 Insert the modulator control valve spring.
68 Insert the spacer.
69 Insert the modulator control valve.
70 Insert the plug.
71 Fit the dowel pin.
72 Insert the throttle valve.
73 Insert the spring.
74 Insert the downshift valve.
75 Insert the manual control valve.
76 Insert the throttle valve return spring and stop.
77 Refit the throttle valve plate.
78 Refit the check valve ball and spring.
79 Refit the check valve.
80 Place the separating plate in position.
81 Hold the governor line plate in position.
82 Fit and loosely tighten the four screws.
83 Replace the oil tube collector.
84 Fit and loosely tighten eight screws.
85 Replace the upper valve body.
86 Fit and tighten the eight screws.
87 Refit the oil strainer and gasket.
88 Fit and tighten four screws.
89 Refit the detent spring and spacer.
90 Fit and tighten the screw.
91 Tension the downshift cam and refit the assembly.
92 Fit and tighten two screws.
93 Refit the valve block. 44.40.01.

NT2272A

PROPELLER SHAFT   47.15.01

Remove and refit

Removing

1 Scribe the gearbox flange, rear axle flange, and propeller shaft flanges to enable reassembly in original locations.
2 Remove the guard strap, as applicable.
3 Remove the four bolts and nyloc nuts securing the propeller shaft and gearbox flanges.
4 Remove the four bolts and nyloc nuts securing the propeller shaft and rear axle pinion flanges.
5 Remove the propeller shaft.

Refitting

6 Reverse instructions 1 to 5.

UNIVERSAL JOINT (Early types)

Remove and refit   47.15.18

Removing

1 Remove the propeller shaft, see 47.15.01.
2 Remove paint, rust, etc., from the vicinity of the bearing cups and circlips.
3 Remove the circlips.
4 Tap the bearing yokes to eject the bearing cups.
5 Withdraw the bearing cups and spider.

Refitting

6 Remove the bearing cups from the new spider.
7 Check that all needles are in place.
8 Fit the spider to the yoke.

9 Engage the spider trunnion in the bearing cup and insert the cup in the yoke ensuring that the needle bearings are not displaced.
10 Fit the opposite bearing cup to the yoke and carefully press both cups into position ensuring that the spider trunnions engage both cups and that the needle bearings are not displaced.
11 Using two flat-faced adaptors of slightly smaller diameter than the bearing cups press the cups into the yoke until they reach the lower land of the circlip grooves. Do not press the cups below this point or damage may be caused to the cups and seals.
12 Fit the circlips.

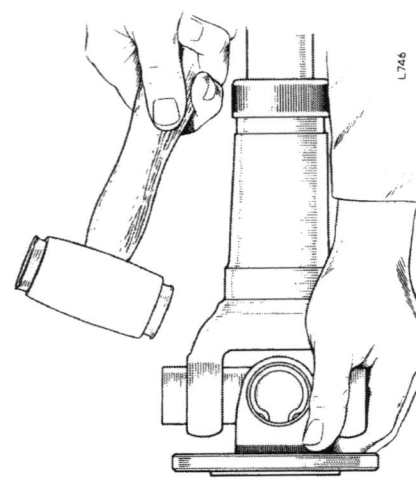

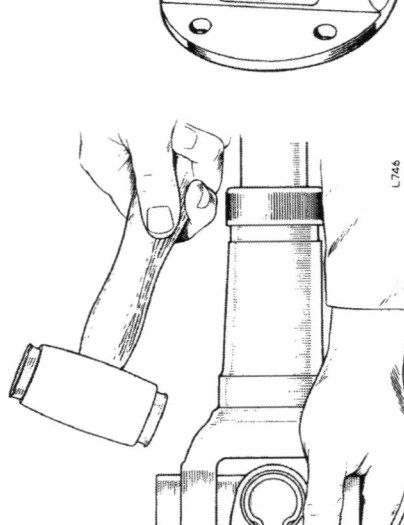

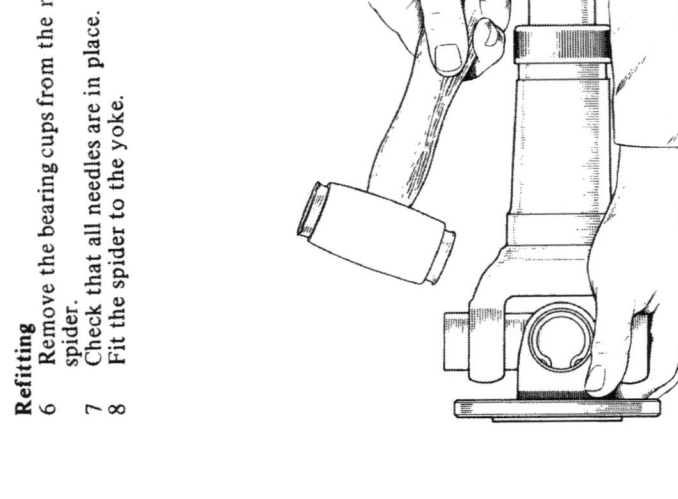

Early type shown –

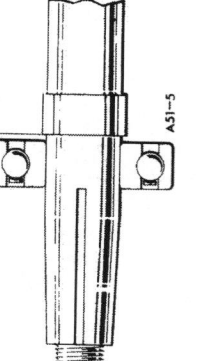

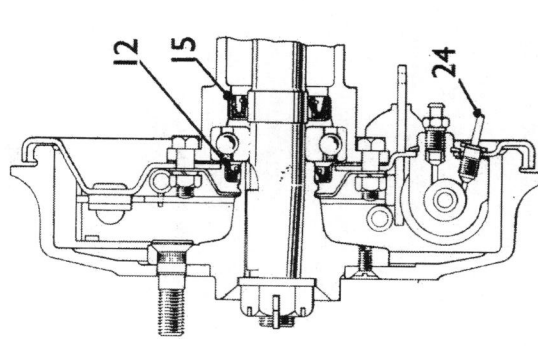

HALF SHAFT

Remove and refit   51.10.01

Service tools: S4235A, S4235A—1

Removing

1. Raise and support the rear of the car.
2. Remove the road wheel.
3. Remove the split pin, nut and washer securing the hub to the half shaft.
4. Remove the brake drum.
5. Remove the clevis pin linking the handbrake cable to the wheel cylinder operating lever.
6. Disconnect the brake pipe(s) from the wheel cylinder. Seal or blank off the pipe(s) and wheel cylinder to prevent the ingress of dirt.
7. Remove the four nuts, spring washers and bolts securing the backplate to the axle flange.
8. Using Tool S4235A and adaptor S4235A—1 withdraw the half shaft complete with hub, backplate, oil catcher plate, oil seal and housing and bearing retaining plate.

Refitting

9. Pack the half shaft bearing with a lithium base grease.
10. Fit the half shaft complete with hub, backplate, oil catcher plate, and oil seal and housing to the axle casing.
11. Align the holes in the oil seal housing plate, bearing retainer plate, backplate and oil catcher. Ensuring that the oil drain hole in the oil seal housing corresponds with the drain hole in the axle flange. Note that the trough of the oil catcher plate must be fitted below the half shaft.
12. Fit the four bolts, spring washers and nuts securing the backplate to the axle casing.
13. Fit the hub securing washer and nut and torque to 100—110 lbf ft (13,83—15,21 kgf m).
14. Connect the brake pipe(s).
15. Connect the hand brake cable.
16. Fit the brake drum
17. Fit the road wheel.
18. Bleed the brakes.
19. Lower the car.

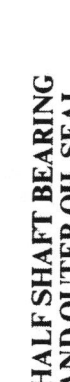

HALF SHAFT BEARING AND OUTER OIL SEAL

Remove and refit   51.10.02

Service tools: S356C, S4235A, S4235A—1

Removing

1. Raise and support the rear of the car.
2. Remove the road wheel.
3. Remove the nut and washer securing the hub to the half shaft.
4. Remove the brake drum.
5. Withdraw the hub from the half shaft using Tool S356C.
6. Remove the clevis pin and release the handbrake cable from the wheel cylinder operating lever.
7. Disconnect the brake pipe(s) from the wheel cylinder. Seal or blank off the pipe(s) and wheel cylinder connections to prevent the ingress of dirt.
8. Remove the four nuts, spring washers and bolts securing the backplate to the axle flange.

9. Remove the oil catcher plate. Note that the elongated area of the plate aligns with drain holes in the backplate, oil seal housing and axle casing flange.
10. Remove the backplate.
11. Remove the hub oil seal housing and gasket. Note that the drain hole aligns with a corresponding hole in the axle casing flange.
12. Remove the oil seal from the housing.
13. Remove the key from the half shaft.
14. Withdraw the half shaft and bearing using Tool S4235A, S4235A-1.
15. Remove the inner oil seal from the axle casing.
16. Press the bearing from the half shaft.

Refitting

17. Install a new inner seal in the axle casing. The lips of the seal must be towards the differential. Lubricate the seal lips.
18. Fit a new hub seal to the housing and lubricate the seal lips. The seal lips must be towards the differential.
19. Pack the half shaft bearing with a lithium-base grease and fit the bearing to the half shaft (shielded side of bearing to hub).
    CAUTION: The bearing must not abut against the collar on the half shaft. A minimum clearance of 0.16 in (4,1 mm) between the bearing inner track and the half shaft collar is required. (The final, installed position of the ... it is fully tightened).
20. Fit the half shaft, hub seal housing and gasket, backplate and oil catcher. Ensure oil drain holes align with the axle casing flange.
21. Fit the half shaft key.
22. Fit the hub washer and nut and torque to 100—110 lbf ft (13,83—15,21 kgf m).
23. Fit the brake drum.
24. Connect the brake pipe(s).
25. Connect the handbrake cable.
26. Fit the road wheel and hub cap.
27. Bleed the brakes.
28. Lower the car.

REAR HUB

Remove and refit   **51.10.18**

Service tool: S356C

Removing

1 Raise and support the rear of the car.
2 Remove the road wheel.
3 Remove the nut and washer securing the hub to the half shaft.
4 Remove the brake drum.
5 Withdraw the hub from the half shaft using Tool S356C and the nuts supplied. The standard wheel nuts must not be used for this purpose.

Refitting

6 Reverse instructions 1 to 5. The nut securing the hub to the half shaft must be torqued to 100–110 lbf ft (13,83–15,21 kgf m).

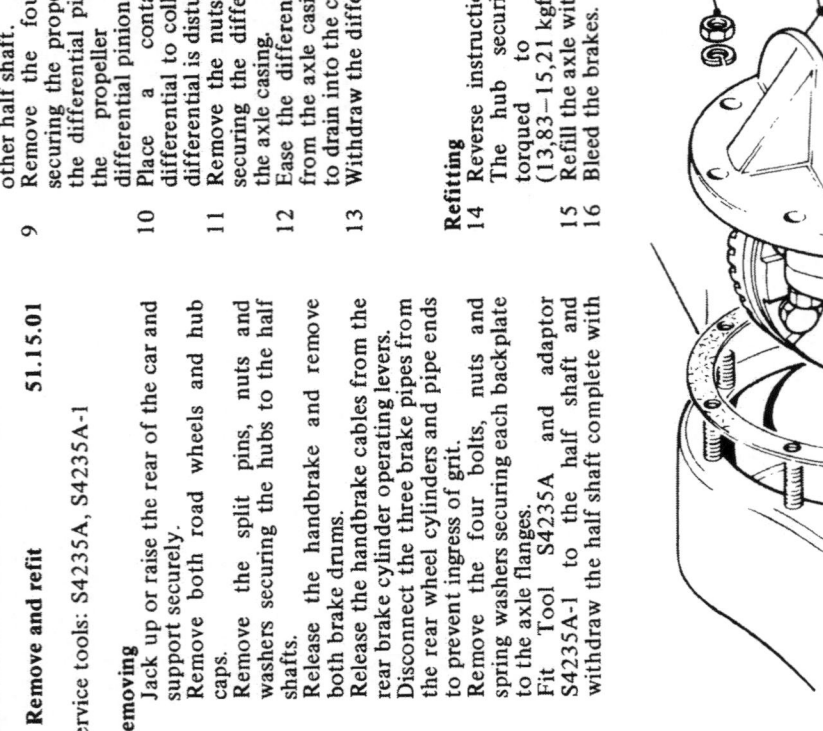

REAR HUB WHEEL STUDS

Remove and refit   **51.10.19**

Service tool: S356C

Removing

1 Raise the rear of the car and support securely.
2 Remove the rear hub. 51.10.18.
3 Drive out the wheel studs.

Refitting

4 Ensure that mating, tapered faces of studs and wheel hub are clean.
5 Enter the stud in the hub ensuring splines engage.
6 Drive or press the stud into position.
7 Fit the rear hub. 51.10.18.
8 Lower the car.

hub, backplate and bearing. Repeat on other half shaft.

9 Remove the four bolts and nuts securing the propeller shaft flange to the differential pinion flange. Release the propeller shaft from the differential pinion.

DIFFERENTIAL ASSEMBLY

Remove and refit   **51.15.01**

Service tools: S4235A, S4235A-1

Removing

1 Jack up or raise the rear of the car and support securely.
2 Remove both road wheels and hub caps.
3 Remove the split pins, nuts and washers securing the hubs to the half shafts.
4 Release the handbrake and remove both brake drums.
5 Release the handbrake cables from the rear brake cylinder operating levers.
6 Disconnect the three brake pipes from the rear wheel cylinders and pipe ends to prevent ingress of grit.
7 Remove the four bolts, nuts and spring washers securing each backplate to the axle flanges.
8 Fit Tool S4235A and adaptor S4235A-1 to the half shaft and withdraw the half shaft complete with
10 Place a container under the differential to collect the oil when the differential is disturbed.
11 Remove the nuts and spring washers securing the differential assembly to the axle casing.
12 Ease the differential assembly flange from the axle casing and allow the oil to drain into the container.
13 Withdraw the differential assembly.

Refitting

14 Reverse instructions 1 to 13. Note: The hub securing nuts must be torqued to 100–110 lbf ft (13,83–15,21 kgf m).
15 Refill the axle with fresh lubricant.
16 Bleed the brakes.

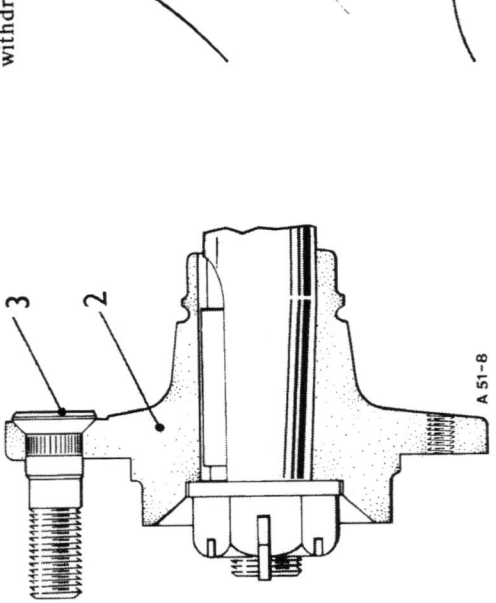

DIFFERENTIAL ASSEMBLY

Overhaul 51.15.07

Service tools: 47, 18G 47BD, S337 or 18G 1205, S4221A-17, 550, 18G 134DH, 18G 191, 18G 191M, S101

Dismantling

1 Remove the differential assembly. 51.15.01.

Crown wheel and differential unit

2 Place the differential assembly in a vice (crown wheel uppermost).
3 Mark the bearing caps to identify original locations.
4 Remove the bearing cap bolts and spring washers. (4).
5 Remove the bearing caps.
6 Carefully lever the crown wheel and differential unit clear of the assembly housing.
7 Lift out the crown wheel and differential unit complete with carrier bearings and shims.
8 Using press 47 and adaptor 18G 47BD withdraw the carrier bearings.
9 Remove the eight bolts and spring washers securing the crown wheel to the differential unit and withdraw the crown wheel.
10 Drive out the pin retaining the differential pinion pin.
11 Remove the differential pinion pin.
12 Rotate the differential sun wheels to bring the planet wheels and their respective selective thrust washers clear of the differential unit.
13 Remove the two planet wheels and thrust washers.
14 Remove the two sun wheels and thrust washers.

Pinion and bearings

15 Locate the differential assembly housing horizontally in the vice.
16 Remove the cap from the differential pinion flange.
17 Using Tool S337 to hold the pinion flange remove the pinion shaft nut and washer.
18 Withdraw the pinion flange.

19 Using a hardwood block carefully tap out the pinion complete with pinion head bearing, selective washer and collapsible spacer.
20 Carefully drive out the pinion outer bearing and oil seal.
21 Evenly drift out both bearing outer tracks.
22 Using press 47 and adaptor S4221A-17 remove the pinion head bearing and selective washer.
23 Thoroughly clean all components.

Assembling

Crown wheel and differential unit

24 Using Tool 550 and 18G 134DH fit the carrier bearings to the differential unit. (Tapered face of bearings towards half shafts.)
25 *Lightly* lubricate the carrier bearings and locate the differential unit in the differential casing.
26 Rotate the differential unit to allow the bearings to settle and push the differential unit complete with bearings to one side of the differential casing.
27 Using a dial gauge mounted against the crown wheel mounting flange check for 'run-out'. If 'run-out' is found to exceed 0.003 in (0,08 mm) it will be necessary to remove the carrier bearings and renew the differential unit housing. Ensure before discarding the differential unit housing that the excessive 'run-out' reading obtained is not due to improperly seated bearing cups. If 'run-out' is within 0.003 in (0,08 mm) proceed as follows:
28 Ensuring that the bearing cups are properly in contact with the bearings, float the differential unit laterally until it butts against the bearing seats in either direction. Using the dial gauge measure this lateral free movement. Call the measurement Dimension 'A'. Record Dimension 'A' as it will be used later to determine the required shim pack for the carrier bearings and to obtain correct pinion backlash.

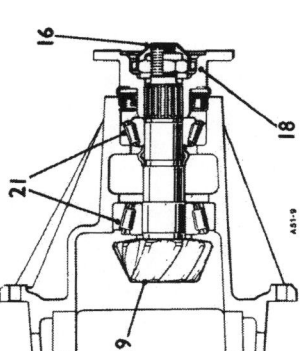

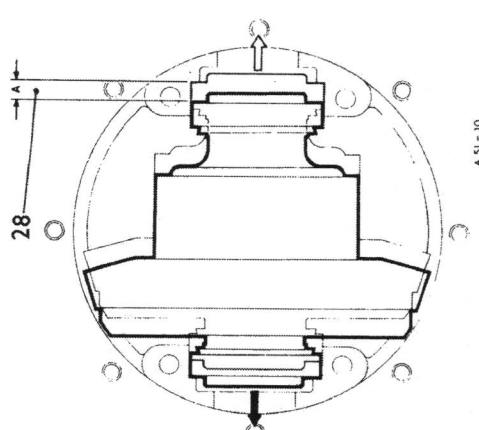

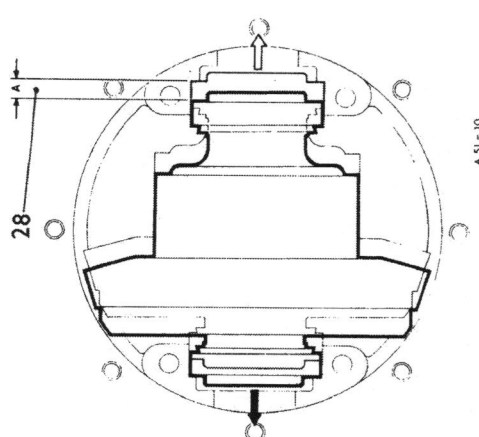

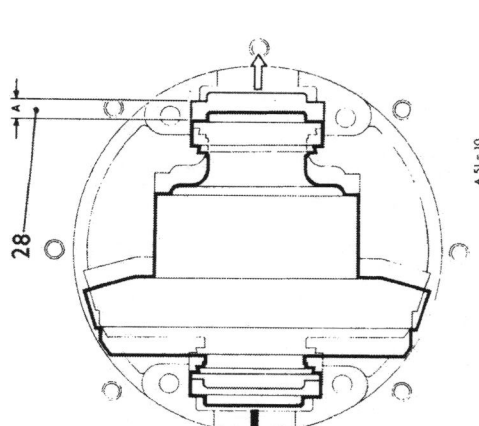

continued

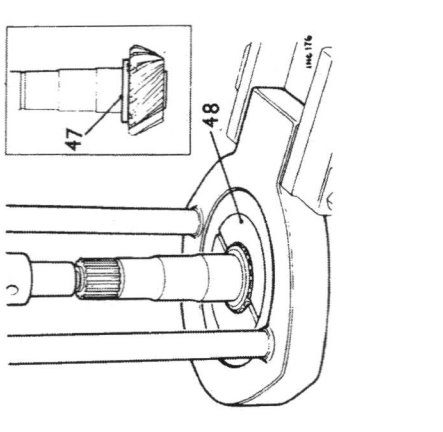

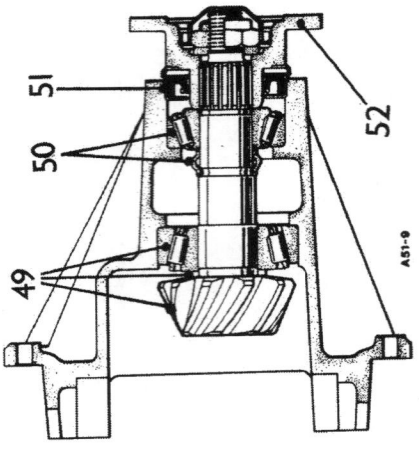

29 Remove the differential unit complete with bearings.
30 Lightly lubricate the sun wheel thrust faces and thrust washers and install them in the differential unit.
31 Mesh the planet wheels with the sun wheels ensuring the planets are diametrically opposite and rotate both sun wheels to bring the planets into their position in the differential unit casing.
32 Fit the differential pinion pin.
33 Check and assess the planet end-float.
34 Remove the pinion pin and rotate both sun wheels to bring the planets clear of the differential unit casing.
35 Lubricate the planet thrust washers selected and slide the planets and washers into position. Fit the pinion pin and again check the planets for end-float and backlash. Zero backlash is required. Choose thrust washers as appropriate from the nine thicknesses available.
36 Fit the retaining pin to the pinion pin and stave the casing.
37 Fit the crown wheel.
38 Smear the threads of the crown wheel securing bolts with 'Locquic' grade 'T' primer and 'Locquic 75' compound. Fit the bolts and spring washers and evenly tighten to the recommended torque.

Pinion and bearings
39 Fit the pinion inner bearing to the dummy pinion 18G 191M. *The standard pinion head spacer 0.077 in (1,95 mm) is incorporated in the dimensions of the dummy pinion.*
40 Lightly lubricate the bearings and fit the dummy pinion, bearings spacer, washer and nut.
41 Gradually tighten the nut until a bearing pre-load of 15 to 18 lbf in (0,17 to 0,21 kgf m) is obtained. This can be measured using a lbf in (kgf m) scale torque wrench and a suitable size socket spanner.
42 Ensure the face of the dummy pinion is clean. Position the dial gauge foot of 18G 191 on the dummy head and zero the gauge on to the head.

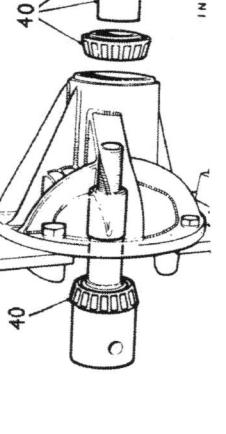

43 Move the gauge foot over the centre of one differential bearing bore. Note the indicated measurement. Repeat for the opposite bearing bore.
44 *Add the two measurements and divide by two.*
45 Twenty-two pinion head washers are available ranging from 0.075 to 0.096 in (1,91 to 2,44 mm).
46 Remove the dummy pinion 18G 191M and dismantle.

Calculating pinion head spacer size
Example
Sum of each bore measurement divided by two . . .0.002 in (0,051 mm)
Plus dummy pinion spacer allowance . . . .0.077 in (1,956 mm)
Required size of pinion head spacer . . .0.079 in (2,007 mm)

NOTE: Etched + or − markings will be found on the pinion face.
These markings should be ignored since they are allowed for in the design and method of using the dummy pinion.

47 Fit the correct pinion head spacer to the pinion.
48 Fit the inner bearing to the pinion using S4221A-17.
49 Insert the pinion, spacer and bearing in the differential casing.
50 Fit a new collapsible spacer and the outer bearing to the pinion shaft.
51 Fit a new oil seal (lips towards pinion). The seal should be soaked in clean oil for one hour before fitting.
52 Fit the flange, washer and nut to the pinion shaft.
53 Gradually tighten the nut checking the bearing pre-load.
54 Rotate the flange to settle the bearings. Using an in/lb (kg/m) torque wrench or S98A check the torque required to rotate the flange.
55 Tighten the nut as required to obtain a torque (flange rotation) of 13 to 20 lbf in (1,80 to 2,77 kgf m).
CAUTION: If the pinion nut is overtightened and the above torque figure exceeded it will be necessary to *renew* the collapsible spacer and repeat instructions 53 to 55.

56 Place the differential unit/crown wheel assembly complete with bearing cups into position in the differential casing.
57 Move the crown wheel fully into mesh with the pinion and zero the dial gauge on the rear of the crown wheel.
58 Move the crown wheel and differential unit fully in the opposite direction. Note the gauge reading. This is the 'IN-OUT' of mesh clearance. Call this dimension 'B'.

Setting Crown Wheel Backlash

Example
'IN-OUT' of mesh' clearance (Dimension B)
Instruction 58 .... 0.025 in (0,63 mm).

Minus required backlash
0.005 in .... 0.005 in (0,127 mm)
                 0.020 in (0,503 mm)

Plus required carrier bearing pre-load divided by two 0.004 in

$$\frac{0.004 \text{ in}}{2} \ldots 0.002 \text{ in } (0,051 \text{ mm})$$

                 0.022 in (0,554 mm)

This equals shims required for crown wheel side carrier bearing.

Total side clearance (Dimension A)
Instruction 28 .... 0.060 in (1,52 mm)
Minus above calculation for crown wheel side shims .. 0.022 in (0,554 mm)
                 0.038 in (0,976 mm)

Plus carrier bearing pre-load divided by two 0.004 in

$$\frac{0.004 \text{ in}}{2} \ldots 0.002 \text{ in } (0,051 \text{ mm})$$

                 0.040 in (2,027 mm)

This equals shims required for carrier bearing opposite crown wheel.

59 Allocate the shims calculated for each carrier bearing. Shims are available in sizes 0.003 in (0,076 mm), 0.005 in (0,127 mm), 0.010 in (0,25 mm), and 0.020 in (0,50 mm).

60 Fit the spreading Tool S101 to the differential casing.

61 Carefully stretch the differential casing to permit the differential unit complete with bearings and their respective shim packs to be placed in position.
IMPORTANT: Do not stretch more than is necessary or damage will be caused to the differential casing. Each flat on the turnbuckle is numbered. Do not exceed a stretch beyond three to four flats. The maximum permissible stretch is 0.008 in (0,20 mm). Do not lever against the stretcher.

62 Remove the stretcher.

63 Fit the bearing caps and the four securing bolts and spring washers. Evenly tighten the four bolts.

64 Fit the differential assembly to the axle casing. 51.15.01.

PINION OIL SEAL

Remove and refit   **51.20.01**

Service tools: S337 or 18G 1205

Removing

1 Raise the rear of the car and support securely.

2 Scribe the propeller shaft rear flange and differential pinion flange to identify original relationship.

3 Remove the four bolts and nuts securing the propeller shaft rear flange.

4 Release the propeller shaft from the differential pinion.

5 Remove the nut shield from the differential pinion flange.

6 Using a centre punch carefully mark the flange, pinion shaft and nut to identify original position.

7 Using Tool S337 to hold the differential pinion flange, unscrew and remove the nut and washer. Count the number of turns required for nut removal.

8 Withdraw the differential pinion flange.

9 Extract the pinion oil seal.

Refitting

10 Fit a new pinion oil seal (lip of seal towards axle).
Note: This seal should be soaked in engine oil for one hour before installation.

11 Fit the differential pinion flange, aligning the flange marking (instruction 6) to the mark in the pinion shaft.

12 Fit the washer and nut. Count the number of turns and using Tool S337 to hold the pinion flange, tighten the nut until the pop marks are aligned.

13 Fit the nut shield to the flange.

14 Fit the propeller shaft noting the flange alignment marks.

15 Fit and tighten the shaft four securing bolts and nuts.

16 Lower the car.

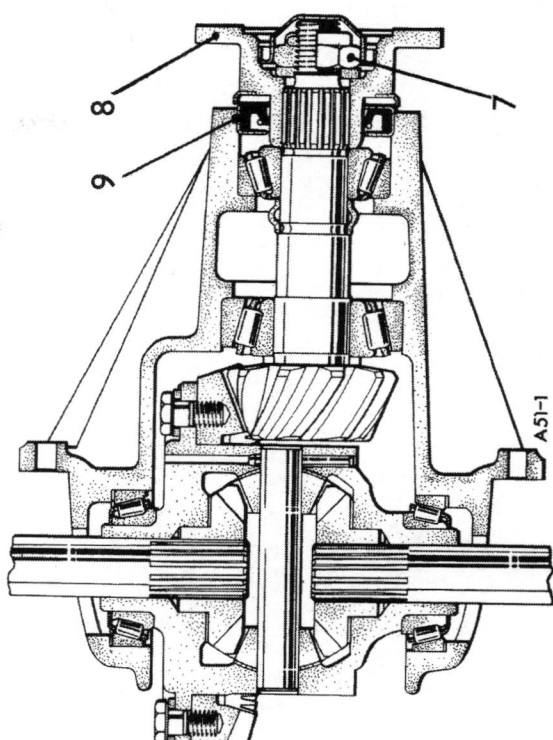

A5]–1

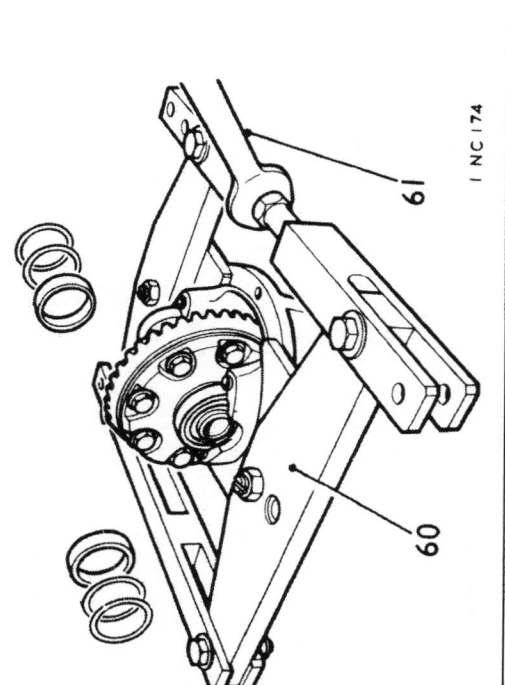

I NC 174

HALF SHAFT INNER OIL SEAL

Remove and refit   51.20.14

Removing
1 Remove the half shaft assembly. 51.20.14.
2 Remove the half shaft inner oil seal.

Refitting
3 Evenly install a new half shaft inner oil seal in the axle casing to lips of seal towards differential.
4 Lubricate the lips of the seal.
5 Refit the half shaft assembly. 51.20.14.

REAR HUB OIL SEAL

Remove and refit   51.20.17

Service tool: S356C

Removing
1 Raise the car and support securely.
2 Remove the rear hub. 51.10.18.
3 Disconnect the handbrake cable from the rear wheel cylinder operating lever.
4 Disconnect the brake pipe(s) from the rear wheel cylinder, seal the pipe end(s) and cylinder to prevent ingress of dirt.
5 Remove the four bolts and nuts securing the backplate to the axle flange.
6 Withdraw the oil catcher plate, backplate and the hub oil seal housing and gasket.
7 Extract the hub oil seal from its housing. Renew the housing gasket.

Refitting
8 Fit a new oil seal to the seal housing (seal lips towards differential).
9 Lubricate the seal lips and reverse instructions 1 to 6.
10 Bleed the brakes.
11 Lower the car.

REAR AXLE ASSEMBLY

Remove and refit   51.25.01

Removing
1 Locate a trolley jack under the rear axle, raise the car and support the body securely on stands.
2 Remove the rear wheels.
3 Disconnect the propeller shaft at the rear axle.
4 Disconnect the forward end of the flexible rear brake hose.
5 Disconnect the handbrake cable forks at the backplate.
6 Remove the nut and bolt clamping the handbrake compensator and release the handbrake cables and trunnion. Withdraw the cables clear of the differential bracket.
7 Disconnect the rear dampers at the axle casing bracket.
8 Lower the jack and remove the rear road springs.
9 Remove the two bolts and nuts securing the radius rods to the axle and detach the handbrake cable bracket from the left hand side.
10 Remove the two bolts and nuts securing the axle to the rear suspension arms.
11 Lower the jack and release the radius rods from the axle brackets.
12 Lift the axle clear of the suspension arms and anti-roll bar and remove from the car.

Refitting
13 Reverse instructions 1 to 12.
14 Bleed the brakes.

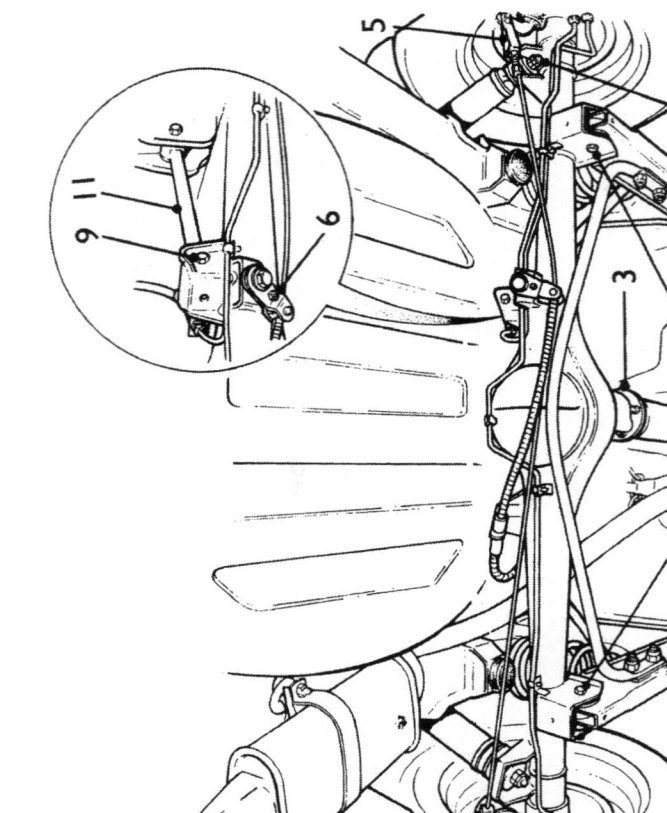

A51004

REAR AXLE CASING

Remove and refit   **51.25.04**

Service tools: S356C, S4235A, S4235A-1

Removing

1   Raise the rear of the car and support the body securely, on stands.
2   Remove the rear axle assembly. 51.25.01.
3   Remove the differential assembly. 51.15.01 (exclude instructions 1 and 2).
4   Detach the brake pipes from the five nylon clips.
5   Unscrew and remove the breather.
6   Remove the filler/level plug.

Refitting

7   Remove the brake pipe nylon clips (3 single, 2 double).
8   Renew the half shaft inner seals.
9   Reverse instructions 1 to 6.
10   Refill the casing with fresh lubricant.
11   Bleed the brakes.

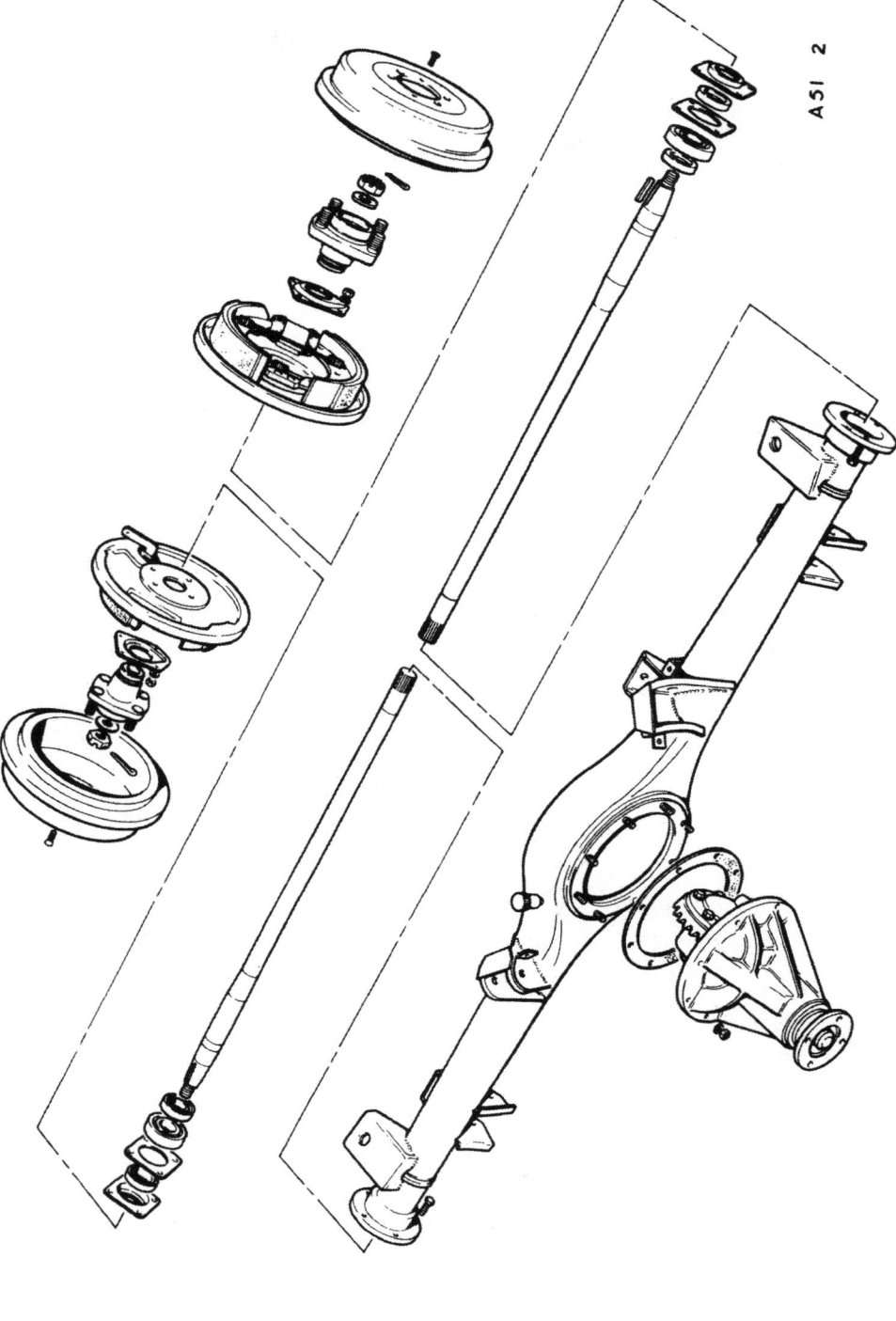

A 51   2

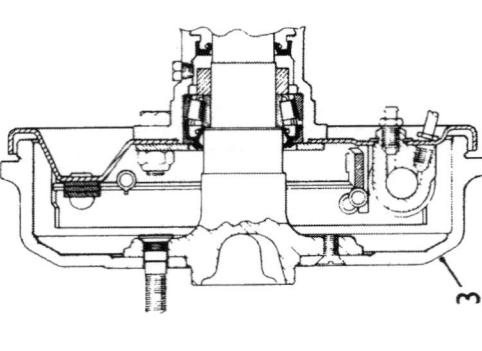

HALF SHAFT BEARING AND OUTER OIL SEAL

Remove and refit 51.10.02

Service Tools: 18G 284 AR and 284

Removing
1 Jack up the rear of the car and support securely.
2 Remove the half shaft. 51.10.12
3 Using a drill, bore the retaining collar to weaken it.
CAUTION: Do not allow the drill to penetrate the collar as damage will be caused to the half shaft.

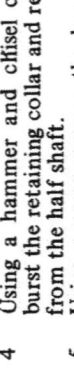

4 Using a hammer and chisel carefully burst the retaining collar and remove it from the half shaft.
5 Using a press remove the bearing, oil seal and retaining plate.
6 Using tools 18G 284 AR and 284 remove the half shaft bearing outer track from the axle casing.

Refitting
7 Fit the half shaft outer bearing track to the axle casing.
8 Fit the retaining plate to the half shaft (welded member adjacent to the shaft flange).
9 Lubricate the lip of the oil seal.
10 Slide the seal into position on the shaft.
11 Fit the bearing (tapered face of bearing towards the half shaft splines).
12 Wipe the shaft in front of the bearing clean of grease.
13 Smear the shaft in front of the bearing with Loctite 602 compound and also the bore of the new retaining collar.
14 Fit the new retaining collar and press the collar home until it butts against the bearing.
CAUTION: A force of not less than three tons should be required to slide the retaining collar into position over the last 0.125 in (3.175 mm) of its travel. If it is found that the interference fit of the collar is such that it can be fitted using a force of less than three tons the collar must be removed and another fitted.
15 Smear the bearing oil seal and the rear axle tube with a lithium base grease. See NOTE Operation No. 7 – 51.10.12.
16 Fit the half shaft. 51.10.12.
17 Lower the car.

HALF SHAFT ASSEMBLY

Remove and refit 51.10.12

Service Tools: 18G 284-1 and 284. (4235 or 3072 with S4235A-1 may be used in lieu of 284).

Removing
1 Jack up the rear of the car and support securely.
2 Remove the rear road wheel.
3 Release the handbrake and remove the brake drum.
4 Remove the four bolts and nuts securing the half shaft assembly and the back plate to the axle tube flange.
5 Using tools 18G 284-1 and 284 withdraw the half shaft.

Refitting
6 Smear the interior of the axle tube/half shaft bearing area with a lithium base grease.
7 Similarly grease the half shaft bearing and oil seal.

Crown wheel differential unit

8 Check or mark the carrier bearing caps to establish original locations. Bearing caps must not be interchanged.

9 Remove the four bolts securing the bearing caps.

10 Remove the bearing caps.

11 Carefully lever the crown wheel and differential unit clear of the axle casing. If difficulty is experienced a spreader, tool S101 and S101-1 should be employed.

12 Lift out the crown wheel and differential unit complete with carrier bearings and shims.

continued

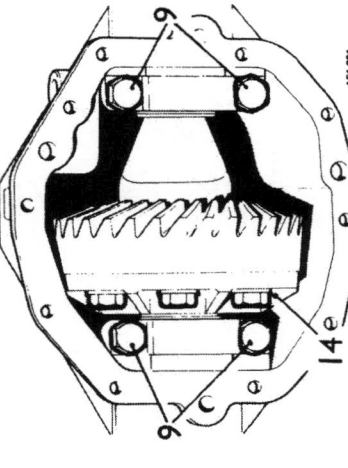

DIFFERENTIAL ASSEMBLY

Overhaul   51.15.07

Service Tools: S101, S101-1, 47, S4221A-16, 18G 191, 18G 191M, S98A, 18G 47AJ, 18G 1272, 6312, 18G 1273

1 Remove the rear axle assembly from the car. 51.25.01.

2 Remove the brake pipes.

3 Support the axle on stands.

Dismantling

4 Remove the differential rear cover and drain the oil.

5 Remove the half shafts and brake backplates. 51.10.12.

6 Remove the nyloc nut securing the drive flange and remove the flange.

7 Remove the four bolts securing the pinion oil seal housing to the axle case.

HALF SHAFT INNER OIL SEAL

Remove and refit   51.10.14

Service Tool: 18G 1271

Removing

1 Jack up the rear of the car and support securely.

2 Remove the half shaft assembly. 51.20.12.

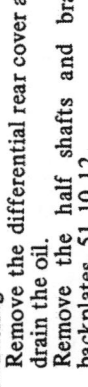

3 Remove the half shaft inner oil seal using tool 18G 1271

Refitting

4 Evenly install a new half shaft inner oil seal in the axle casing (lip of seal towards differential).

5 Lubricate the seal lip.

6 Fit the half shaft assembly.

7 Lower the car.

NOTE: On initial build, when lubricating the half shaft bearing using a grease-gun, the shaft should be rotated during the operation to ensure that the bearing is properly 'primed'.
On initial assembly, a total of 40 g of grease must be used.

8 Enter the half shaft in the axle tube and engage the differential splines.

9 Carefully slide the half shaft into position. Ensure that the bearing and the oil seal enter the axle tube squarely.

10 Fit the four securing bolts and nuts. Tighten them evenly.

11 Carefully wipe off surplus grease to prevent contamination of the brake linings.

12 Fit the brake drum.

13 Fit the road wheel.

14 Lower the car.

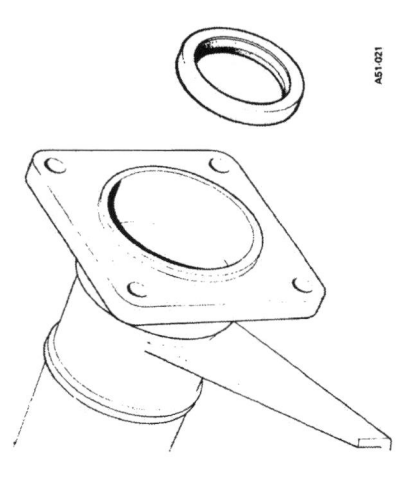

13 Using press 47 and adaptors S4221A-16 withdraw the carrier bearings.

14 Remove the eight bolts securing the crown wheel to the carrier flange and withdraw the crown wheel.

15 Withdraw the ball locating the differential pinion pin.

16 Remove the differential pinion pin.

17 Rotate the differential sun wheels to bring the two planet wheels and their respective thrust washers clear of the casing.

18 Remove the planet wheels and thrust washers.

19 Remove the two sun wheels and thrust washers.

Pinion and Bearings

20 Using tools 18G 1272 and S98A remove the pinion shaft nut.

21 Using a hardwood block carefully tap out the pinion complete with selective spacer, pinion head bearing and collapsible spacer.

22 Remove the pinion outer bearing from the axle casing.

23 Evenly drift out the pinion inner and outer bearing tracks from the axle casing. Care must be taken not to damage the axle casing.

24 Remove the collapsible spacer from the pinion shaft.

25 Using tool 47 and adaptor 18G 47AJ remove the pinion head bearing and spacer.

Assembling
Crown Wheel and Differential Unit

26 Fit the carrier bearings to the differential unit.

27 Lightly lubricate the carrier bearings, fit the bearing outer tracks and place the differential unit in the axle casing.

28 Slide the differential unit to one side of the axle casing and rotate the unit to allow the bearings to centralise.

29 Using a dial gauge check the crown wheel mounting flange for 'run-out'. 'Run-out' should not exceed 0.003 in (0.08 mm). Ensure that the bearing tracks are properly seated. When satisfied that 'run-out' is correct proceed as follows:

30 With the differential unit and bearings pressed to one side of axle casing note the reading on the dial gauge.

31 Slide the differential unit and bearings to the other side of the casing. Note this lateral travel registered on the dial gauge. Record this lateral travel (dimension 'A') as it is subsequently used to determine the shim pack required for the carrier bearings.
CAUTION: The lateral travel in some cases may be found to be restricted due to a foul condition between the axle case and the short side of the differential unit. In the event of this, a nominal shim should be used between the case and the bearing on the short side of the differential unit. The value of this shim should be added to the lateral travel.

32 Remove the differential complete with bearings.

33 Lightly lubricate the sun wheel thrust washers and install the sun wheel and thrust washers in the differential unit.

34 Mesh the planet wheels with the sun wheels ensuring that the planet wheels are diametrically opposite. Rotate the sun wheels to bring the planet wheels into position in the differential unit casing.

35 Fit the differential pinion pin.

36 Check and assess planet wheel end-float.

37 Remove the pinion pin and rotate both sun wheels to bring the planet wheels clear of the differential unit casing.

38 Lubricate the planet wheel thrust washers selected and slide the planet wheels and thrust washers into position. Fit the pinion pin ensuring that the groove aligns with the location for the retaining ball and again check the planet gears for backlash and end-float. Zero backlash is required. Choose thrust washers as necessary from the selection available.

39 Fit the crown wheel and the ball retaining the pinion pin.

40 Smear the threads of the crown wheel securing bolts with 'Locquic T' grade primer and 'Loctite 601' compound. Fit the bolts and evenly tighten. (See Torque Wrench Settings.)

Pinion and Bearings

41 Fit the pinion shaft inner and outer bearing tracks to the axle casing.

42 Fit the pinion inner bearing to the dummy pinion 18G 191-1.
NOTE: The dimension of the dummy pinion incorporates a built-in allowance for the maximum pinion head bearing spacer available, 0.0492 in (1.25 mm).

43 Lightly lubricate the bearings and fit the dummy pinion, bearings, spacer, washer and nut.

44 Tighten the dummy pinion nut until a bearing pre-load of 15 to 18 lbf in (0.17 to 0.21 kgf m) is obtained. This can be checked using a lbf in (kgf m) scale torque wrench and a socket.

45 Mount a dial gauge (tool 18G 191) on the dummy pinion and zero the gauge using the dummy pinion head as a base.

46 Move the gauge stylus over the centre of one carrier bearing bore. Note the indicated measurement. Repeat for the opposite carrier bearing bore.

47 Add the two measurements and divide by two.

48 Remove the gauge and dummy pinion.

49 Calculating the spacer required for the pinion head bearing.
Example:
Sum of carrier bearing bore readings
= 0.002 in (0.051 mm) + 0.002 in (0.051 mm)
= 0.004 in (0.102 mm)
Divide by two

$$\frac{0.004 \text{ in } (0.102 \text{ mm})}{2} = 0.002 \text{ in } (0.051 \text{ mm})$$

Add dummy pinion spacer allowance. 0.049 in (1.25 mm) (Inbuilt in dummy pinion dimensions)
= 0.002 in (0.051 mm) + 0.049 in (1.25 mm)
= 0.051 in (1.301 mm)
Examine the markings on the pinion head. Three markings will be found. These are:

X Identification for matched crown wheel/pinion set.

Y Variation in pinion head thickness from nominal.

Z This is a 'boxed' figure which indicates the variation from nominal setting to obtain the best running position. This dimension must be used when calculating the thickness of the pinion head spacer. If the 'boxed' figure Z is plus, subtract this value (+0.003 in) from the previous calculation. In the example 0.051 in (1.301 mm) − 0.003 in (0.076 mm) = 0.048 in (1.225 mm) = pinion head spacer required. If the 'boxed' figure Z is minus, add this value to the previous calculation. In the example 0.051 in (1.301 mm) + 0.003 in (0.076 mm) = 0.054 in (1.337 mm) = pinion head spacer required.

50 Fit a spacer of the required thickness to the pinion.

51 Fit the pinion head (inner) bearing to the pinion.

52 Fit a new collapsible spacer to the pinion and enter the pinion in the axle casing.

53 Fit the outer bearing, washer and nut. Using tools 18G 1272 and S98 A carefully tighten the nut, periodically checking the torque required to rotate the pinion. Rotation torque should be within 13 to 20 lbf in (0.91 to 1.41 kgf m).

54 IMPORTANT: Should the nut be over-tightened so that a torque reading exceeding 20 lbf in (1.41 kgf m) is obtained it will be necessary to renew the collapsible spacer and repeat instructions 51 to 53. Under no circumstances must the nut be slackened to obtain the required torque.

Crown wheel and differential unit

55 Place the crown wheel and differential unit complete with outer bearing tracks into position in the axle casing.

56 Slide the unit towards the pinion until the crown wheel and pinion are fully meshed.

57 Zero a dial gauge on the rear (plain face) of the crown wheel ensuring that the crown wheel remains in contact with the pinion.

58 Slide the crown wheel and differential unit complete with bearings fully in the opposite direction. Note the reading indicated on the dial gauge. Call this dimension 'B'.
CAUTION: Refer to Caution in Operation Number 31.

59 To calculate the shim pack thickness required for each carrier bearing the following information is necessary:
Required crown wheel/pinion backlash:
0.004 to 0.006 in (0.102 to 0.15 mm)
Required carrier bearing pre-load
0.002 to 0.004 in (0.051 to 0.102 mm)
Carrier bearing shims are available in 0.0016 in (0.04 mm) steps from 0.112 in (2.85 mm) to 0.136 in (3.45 mm).

60 Shim thickness required for carrier bearing on toothed side of crown wheel = Dimension 'A' (Instruction 31) minus Dimension 'B' (Instruction 58) plus

$$\frac{\text{carrier bearing preload}}{2}$$

Example:
Using the mean value of 0.003 in for carrier bearing pre-load and assumed values of 0.240 in for dimension 'A' the calculation is:

$$\frac{0.240 \ (\text{dimension 'A'}) - 0.115 \ (\text{dimension 'B'})}{2} + .003 \ (\text{bearing pre-load})$$

= 0.240 − 0.115 + 0.0015
= 0.1265 in (3.21 mm) = thickness of shims required.

61 Shim thickness required for carrier bearing on plain side of the crown wheel = Dimension 'B' (Instruction 58) minus crown wheel backlash

$$\text{plus} \ \frac{\text{carrier bearing pre-load}}{2}$$

Example:
Using the mean values of 0.005 in for the crown wheel backlash, 0.003 in for carrier bearing pre-load and an assumed valve of 0.115 in for dimension 'B' the calculation is:

$$\frac{0.115 \ (\text{dimension 'B'}) - 0.005 \ (\text{backlash})}{2} + \frac{0.003 \ (\text{preload})}{2}$$

= 0.115 − 0.005 + 0.0015
= 0.1115 in (2.8321 mm) = thickness of shim required.
In the example quoted the required shim thickness falls outside the shim sizes available. The nearest shim thickness is 0.112 in (2.85 mm). It is thus thicker by 0.0005 in (0.028 mm) than the calculated requirement. Since the calculation was made using the mean values for backlash and bearing pre-load and the increased thickness of the shim available falls within the tolerance specified (Instruction 60) the 0.112 in (2.85 mm) shim is acceptable.

62 Allocate the selected shims to their respective carrier bearings. Ensure the shims are not interchanged.

63 Fit the spreading tool S101 and S101-1 to the axle casing.

64 Carefully expand the spreading tool to allow the crown wheel/differential unit to be placed in position complete with carrier bearing shims. Do not expand more than is necessary or irreparable damage will be caused to the axle casing. Do not exceed a stretch exceeding three or four flats of a finger tight turnbuckle. Do not lever against the spreader.

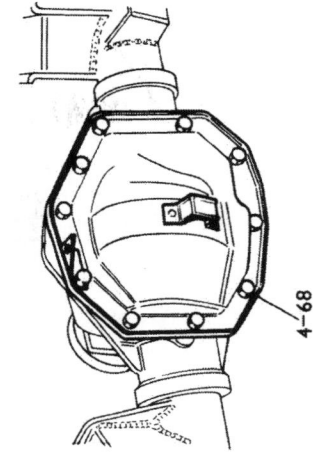

65 Remove the spreading tool.

66 Fit the carrier bearing caps to their original marked position and the four securing bolts. Evenly tighten the bolts—see 'TORQUE WRENCH SETTINGS'.

continued

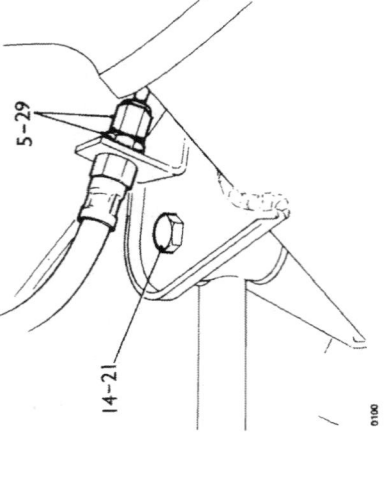

5-29

14-21

0100

REAR AXLE ASSEMBLY 51.25.01

Remove and refit

Removing

1 Jack up the rear of the vehicle and support the body securely on two stands.

2 Remove the rear wheels and release the handbrake.

3 Co-relate the drive flanges and remove the four rear propshaft securing nuts and bolts.

4 Fit a brake pipe clamp to the flexible brake hose.

5 Undo the fixed brake pipe and union nut and displace the flexible hose from the axle.

0098

6 Remove the split pins and clevis pin from the handbrake cable clevis forks.

7 Slacken the compensator pinch bolt.

8 Remove the compensator trunion.

9 Feed the handbrake cables through the rear bracket on the axle.

10 Support the axle on a jack.

11 Disconnect the rear dampers from their lower fixing brackets.

12 Lower the axle on the jack.

13 Remove the rear road springs.

14 Remove the nuts and bolts securing the radius arms to the axle.

15 Displace the handbrake cables and bracket to one side.

16 Remove the nuts and bolts securing the trailing arms to the axle.

17 Manoeuvre the axle over the anti-roll bar and clear of the vehicle.

Refitting

18 Position the jack and manoeuvre the axle into position over the anti-roll bar.

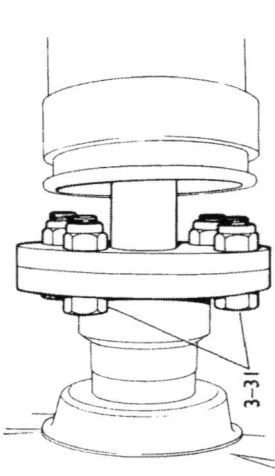

3-31

0101

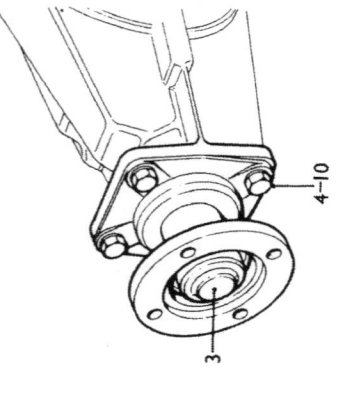

4-10

3

67 Check crown wheel/pinion backlash.

68 Fit the rear cover and gasket to the axle casing.

69 Fit the halfshafts and backplate assemblies, 51.10.12.

Pinion oil seal housing

70 Remove the old oil seal from the pinion seal housing and fit a new seal (tool 6312, seal lip facing away from the front face of the seal housing).

71 Using a strip of masking tape place it over the machined step on the pinion shaft as illustrated. This protects the seal when the housing is eased into position. Apply the tape marginally to facilitate tape removal.

72 Lubricate the seal lip and masking tape.

73 Enter the seal housing in the axle casing and tap gently into position. Remove the masking tape.

74 Fit the brake pipes.

75 Fill the axle to the level of the filler plug with fresh oil.

76 Fit the axle to the car. 51.25.01

77 Bleed the brakes.

78 Lower the car.

DIFFERENTIAL PINION OIL SEAL 51.20.01

Remove and refit

Service tools: 6321 and 18G 1273 18G 1205

Removing

1 Jack up the rear of the vehicle and support securely on stands.

2 Remove the four bolts securing the rear propshaft coupling.

3 Remove the nut securing the drive flange and remove the flange.

4 Remove the four bolts and spring washers securing the pinion oil housing to the axle case.

5 Remove the pinion oil seal (Tool 6312).

Refitting

6 Fit a new oil seal to the housing ensuring that the lip of the seal faces away from the front face of the housing (Tool 18G 1273).

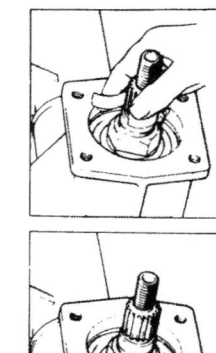

A51027A

7 Wrap a narrow strip of masking tape over the machined step on the pinion shaft. This prevents damage to the seal when fitting. Apply the tape marginally to facilitate tape removal.

8 Lubricate the seal lip and the masking tape.

9 Fit the seal and housing, evenly entering the housing in the axle casing. Gently and evenly tap into position.

10 Fit and tighten the four bolts and spring washers securing the pinion oil seal housing to the axle case.

11 Refit the flange and nyloc nut and washer.

12 Tighten the flange nut.

13 Refit and tighten the rear propshaft coupling bolts.

14 Lower the vehicle.

15 Check the oil level.

19 Grease all bushes with rubber grease.
20 Refit and tighten the trailing arm securing bolts and nuts.
21 Reposition the handbrake cable bracket and refit and tighten the radius arm securing bolts and nuts.
22 Refit the rear road springs.
23 Jack up the axle and locate the dampers in their lower fixing brackets.
24 Fit the damper rubbers and washers and tighten the securing nuts and lock nuts.
25 Lower the jack.

26 Feed the handbrake cables through the rear bracket and refit the compensator trunion.
27 Tighten the pinch bolt.
28 Connect the handbrake cable clevis forks, pins and split pins.
29 Refit the flexible brake hose to the axle and connect the fixed brake pipe.
30 Remove the brake pipe clamp.
31 Refit the propshaft and tighten the four nuts and bolts.
32 Bleed the brakes.
33 Refit the rear wheels.
34 Remove the stands and lower the rear of the vehicle.
35 Check the axle oil level.

TORQUE FIGURES FOR REAR AXLE

	Nm	lbf ft
Rear cover to axle case	22–28	16–21
Pinion oil seal housing to axle case	40–50	30–37
Differential unit bearing caps to axle case	80–100	60–75
Crown wheel to differential unit (with Loctite)	108–122	80–90
Pinion flange to pinion	120–160	90–120
Axle shafts/backplates to axle casing	40–60	35–40
Oil capacity	1.60 pts	0.91 litres

Loctite specification – axle shaft collars and crown wheel bolts

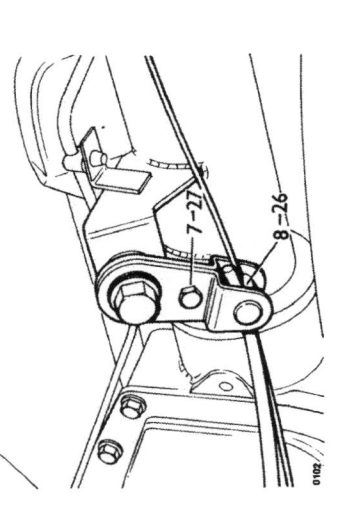

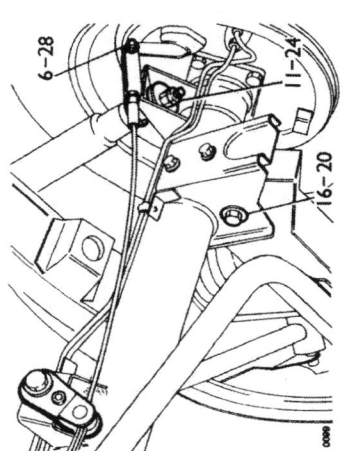

STEERING RACK AND PINION   57.25.01

Remove and refit

Removing

1 Drive the vehicle onto a ramp.
2 Set the road wheels to the straight-ahead position.
3 Raise the ramp.
4 Scribe the pinion shaft and the lower steering coupling to ensure original spline location on refitting. NOTE: This instruction applies only if the pinion and rack are not to be dismantled.
5 Disconnect the rack tie-rod outer ball joints from the steering arms.
6 Remove the pinch bolt securing the steering coupling to the rack pinion.
7 Remove the two bolts, spring washers and plain washers securing the pinion end of the rack to the sub-frame.
8 Remove the two nyloc nuts and plain washers, and withdraw the bolts securing the rack to the sub-frame.
9 Disconnect the lower coupling from the pinion shaft.
10 Withdraw the rack from the driver's side.

Refitting

11 Locate the rack on the sub-frame from the driver's side. With the steering-wheel in the straight-ahead position, align the previously scribed markings and engage the pinion shaft into the lower coupling;

or

If no scribe lines were made, or the rack and pinion were dismantled, it is advised that the rack shaft is centralized before beginning installation on the car. Remove the centre plug from the thrust pad and using a length of stiff wire (e.g. welding rod), locate the dimple in the rack shaft. When the dimple is aligned with the wire, the rack shaft is centred. Fit a bolt to the pinion plug and gently tighten until the pinion shaft is pinched. This will hold the rack shaft in its centred position. The rack assembly can now be offered to the sub-frame.

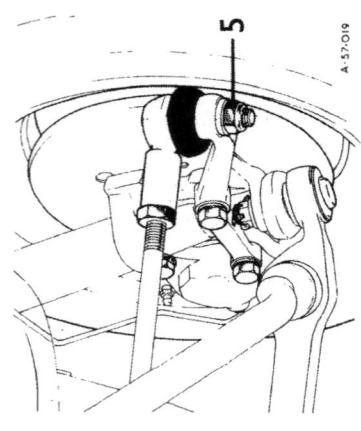

A-57.019

A57004

12 Secure the rack to the sub-frame with the bolts, washers and nyloc nuts.
13 Fit the tie-rod outer ball joints to the steering-arms.
14 Fit and tighten the pinion coupling pinch bolt.
15 Remove the locating bolt used to temporarily lock the pinion shaft, and fit the centre plug.
16 Lower the ramp.
17 Check and adjust the front wheel track as necessary, see 57.65.01.

STEERING RACK GAITERS   57.25.02

Remove and refit

Removing

1 Slacken the locknut securing both tie-rod outer ball joints.
2 Remove the nut and washer securing the tie-rod outer ball joint to the steering-arm.
3 Release the ball joint from the steering-arm.
4 Unscrew the ball joint from the tie-rod and remove the retaining locknut.
5 Remove the inner and outer clips retaining the gaiter to the rack and tie-rod respectively.
6 Withdraw the gaiter.
7 Repeat instructions 2 to 6 on the opposite tie-rod.

Refitting

8 Lubricate the tie-rod inner ball joint with fresh grease.

9 Slide the new gaiter along the tie-rod into position on the rack.
10 With the rack centralized, fit the inner clip to the gaiter and rack housing.
11 Position the outer end of the gaiter on the tie-rod so that it is capable of accommodating movement of the tie-rod from lock to lock.
12 Secure the outer end of the gaiter to the tie-rod end with the clip.
13 Fit the locknut to the tie-rod, locating it as near as possible to its original location.
14 Fit the outer ball joint to the tie-rod.
15 Connect the tie-rod outer ball joint to the steering-arm and secure it with the plain washer and nut.
16 Repeat instructions 8 to 15 on the opposite tie-rod.
17 Check, and re-set the front wheel track as necessary.
18 Tighten the locknut securing the tie-rod outer ball joint.

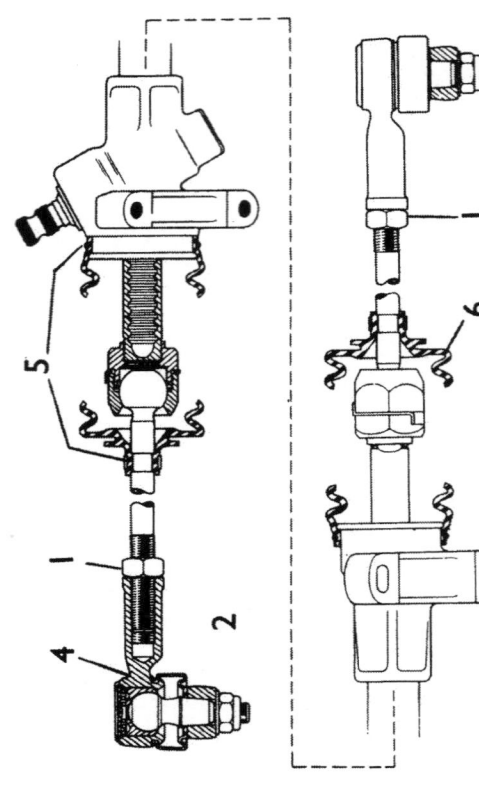

A57001

STEERING RACK AND PINION

Overhaul 57.25.07

Special tool: 18G 1261

Dismantling

1 Remove the rack, see 57.25.01.

Rack damper

2 Remove the plug securing the damper assembly to the rack housing.
3 Withdraw the spring, shim(s) and damper.

Pinion

4 Remove the rubber seal.
5 Remove the pinion retaining plug using the special tool 18G 1261.
6 Withdraw the pinion and bearing from the rack housing.
7 Remove the circlip securing the ball race to the pinion shaft and withdraw the ball race.

Tie-rods and rack shaft

8 Release the clips and tie-wires securing the gaiters to the rack housing and the tie-rods, and slide the gaiter clear of the rack.
9 Slide the pinion end of the rack housing towards its adjacent tie-rod inner ball joint.
10 Grip the exposed rack shaft in protected vice jaws.
11 Unscrew the tie-rod inner ball joint assemblies from both ends of the rack shaft.
12 Withdraw the rack shaft.

Rack housing bush

13 Using a suitable drift, remove the bush from the rack housing.

Reassembling

Rack housing bush

14 Fit a new bush to the rack housing.

Rack shaft and tie-rods

15 Hold the plain (toothless) portion of the rack shaft in protected vice jaws.
16 Fit the tie-rod inner ball joint assembly to the rack shaft, tighten to 35 to 45 lbf ft (4.84 to 6.22 kgf m), and deform the collar to secure the ball joint housing to the rack shaft.

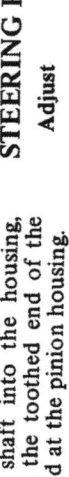

17 Fit the rack shaft into the housing, ensuring that the toothed end of the shaft is located at the pinion housing.
18 Fit the tie-rod assembly to the pinion end of the rack shaft – refer to operation 15.

Pinion

19 Fit the ball race to the pinion and secure it with the circlip. Fit the rubber seal.
20 Position the rack shaft teeth to permit pinion entry and engage the rack with the pinion.
21 Lubricate the pinion shaft, refit and tighten the end plug.
22 Pack the ends of the rack shafts and tie-rod inner ball joints with clean grease.
23 Fit and secure the gaiters.
24 Fit the rack damper, see 57.35.10.
25 Fit the rack to the car, see 57.25.01.

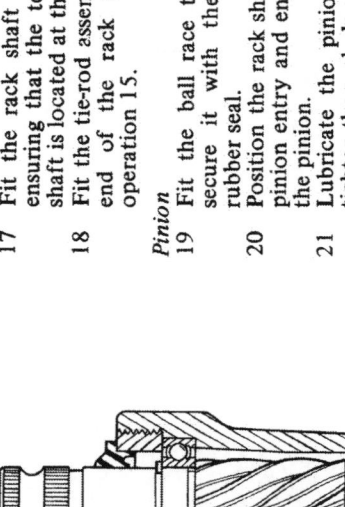

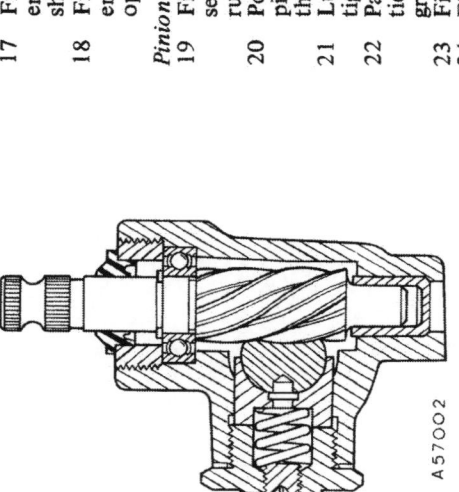

A57002

A57005

STEERING RACK DAMPER

Adjust 57.35.09

1 Remove the rack, see 57.25.01.
2 Locate the rack shaft in mid-position.
3 Remove the centre plug from the damper plug and insert a stylus or dial gauge and check the rack shaft for side movement (90° to shaft axis). Side movement should be within 0.001 to 0.007 in (0.03 to 0.18 mm).
4 Adjust if necessary by removing the damper plug and adding or subtracting shim(s) as required;
 or
4a In the absence of a dial gauge, remove the damper plug and shims.
4b Remove the shims and spring and replace the damper plug.
4c Gently tighten the damper plug until the plunger grips the rack eliminating all side-play.
4d With feeler gauges inserted between the rack pinion housing and the underside of the damper plug flange, check the clearance existing.
4e To the thickness of the feeler gauge pack, add the rack side movement required, 0.001 to 0.007 in (0.03 to 0.18 mm). This gives the thickness of the shims to be fitted under the damper plug flange.
4f Remove the damper plug and fit the required shim pack. Tighten the damper plug to 45 to 60 lbf ft (6.22 to 8.30 kgf m).
5 Refit the rack, see 57.25.01.

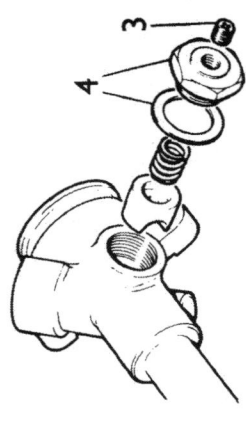

A57006

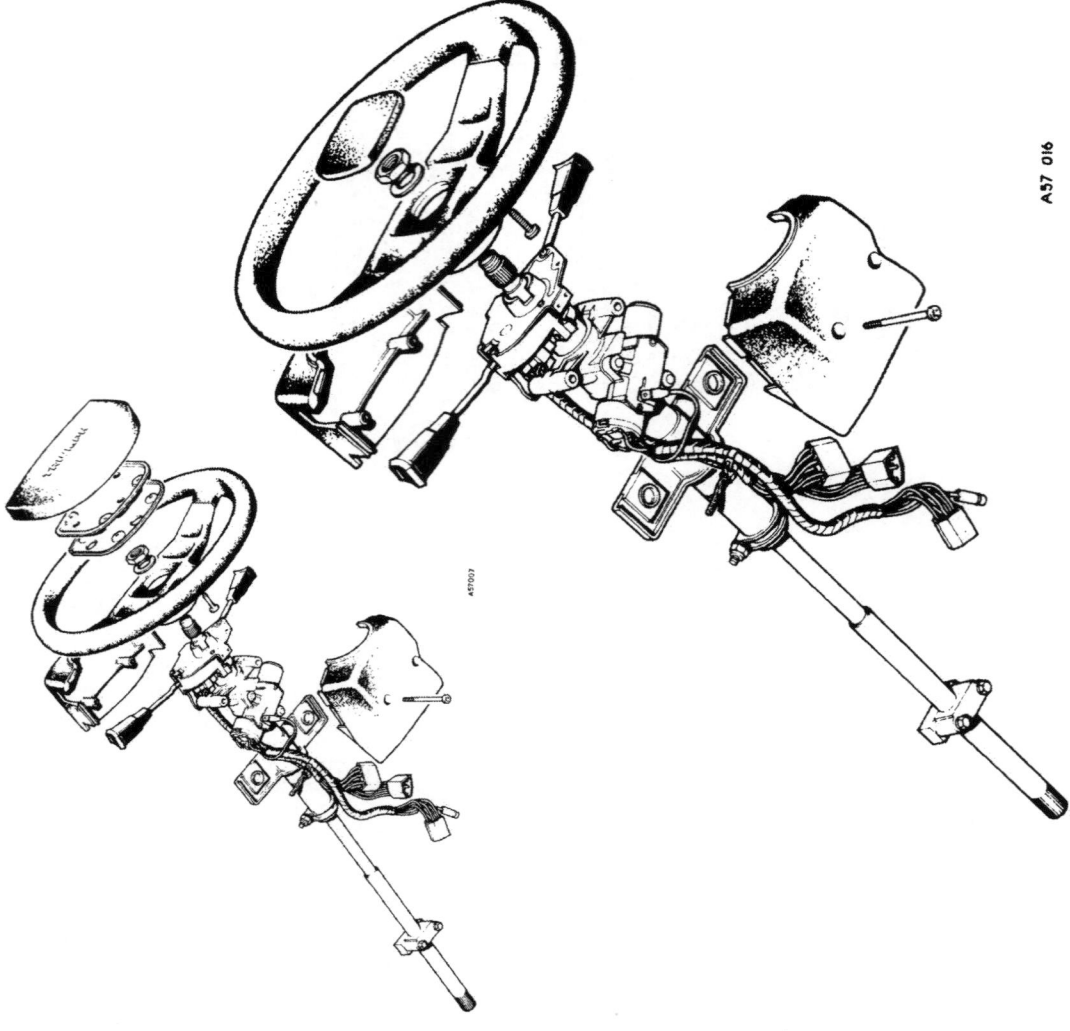

A57 016

A57007

STEERING RACK DAMPER   57.35.10

Remove and refit

Removing

1 Remove the rack, see 57.25.01.
2 Remove the clip and tie-wire securing the gaiter at the pinion end of the rack and slide the gaiter along the tie-rod to expose the rack shaft.
3 Unscrew and remove the damper plug and shims.
4 Withdraw the spring and plunger.

Refitting

5 Locate the rack shaft in mid-position.
6 Fit the plunger and spring.
7 Check, and adjust the rack shaft side movement as required (instructions 4 to 6, operation 57.35.09).
8 Refit the rack, see 57.25.01.

A57002

STEERING-COLUMN ASSEMBLY   57.40.01

Remove and refit

Removing

1 Open the bonnet and disconnect the battery.
2 Remove the pinch bolt securing the upper universal coupling to the steering mast.
3 Remove the cleat securing the electrical harness to the steering-column.
4 Disconnect the plug-in connectors (4) for the ignition/starter, horn/trafficator/lights and windscreen wiper/washer switches.
5 Remove the two screws securing the nacelle to the steering-column. Remove the nacelle.
6 Using a centre-punch, mark the centre of the two shear-head bolts securing the column housing to the body.
7 Using a small chisel, unscrew the shear-head bolts;

or

a If instruction 7 proves to be unsuccessful drill into the shear-head bolts where previously marked by the centre punch and unscrew using an Easiout extractor.
8 With the road wheels in the straight-ahead position, withdraw the steering-column assembly, noting the positions of the flat and wavy washers.

Refitting

9 Enter the steering-column in the lower bush. Ensure that the flat and wavy washers are in position.
10 With the road wheels in the straight-ahead position and the steering-wheel centralized, engage the steering-column splines in the upper universal coupling.
11 Fit and tighten the pinch bolt.
12 Locate the steering-column on the body and align the mounting holes.
13 Fit two new shear-head bolts and tighten evenly until both heads shear.

14 Re-connect the plug in connectors and secure the electrical harness to the steering-column housing with the plastic cleat.
15 Fit the nacelle and secure with the two screws.
16 Connect the battery.

260   **STEERING**

STEERING COLUMN ASSEMBLY   57.40.10

Overhaul

Dismantling

1. Remove the steering-column assembly from the car, see 57.40.01.
2. Remove the steering-wheel centre cover.
3. Slacken and remove the nut and washer securing the steering-wheel hub to the steering-column.
4. Using a suitable extractor, remove the steering-wheel.
5. Slacken the clamping screw and withdraw the steering-column multi-purpose switch assembly from the column.
6. Using a centre-punch, mark the centre of the two shear-head bolts securing the steering lock to the column housing.
7. Using a small chisel, unscrew the shear head bolts;

or

   a. If instruction 7 proves to be unsuccessful, drill into the shear-head bolts where previously marked by the centre-punch and unscrew using an Easiout extractor.
8. Withdraw the column housing off the steering mast.
9. Remove the nut and bolt securing the clamp to the steering mast. Remove the clamp.
10. Using a suitable drift, remove the top and bottom bushes from the steering-column housing.

Reassembling

11. Align the slots in the bushes with the lugs in the column housing. Press in the bushes.
12. Fit the clamp to the steering mast. Fit and tighten the pinch bolt.
13. Fit the steering mast into the housing.
14. Fit the steering lock to the column housing and secure with two new shear-head bolts. Evenly tighten the bolts until the heads shear off.
15. Fit the multi-purpose switch assembly to the column housing and secure by tightening the clamp screw.
16. Align the arrow on the trafficator cancelling collar with the centre of the trafficator stalk.
17. Align the lugs of the steering-wheel with the cut-outs in the cancelling cam. Fit the steering-wheel.
18. Fit and tighten the plain washer and nut securing the steering-wheel hub to the steering-column.
19. Fit the steering-wheel centre cover.
20. Fit the steering-column assembly to the car, see 57.40.01.

A57003

INTERMEDIATE SHAFT   57.40.22

Remove and refit

Removing

1. Remove the pinch bolt securing the intermediate shaft to the upper universal coupling.
2. Remove the pinch bolt securing the intermediate shaft universal joint to the rack pinion.
3. Set the road wheels to the straight-ahead position.
4. Slide the intermediate shaft upwards to disengage the universal joint from the pinion shaft.
5. Withdraw the intermediate shaft downwards and disengage from the upper universal coupling.

Refitting

6. Engage the splines of the intermediate shaft in the upper universal coupling.
7. Ensure that the steering-wheel is in the straight-ahead position and engage the intermediate shaft universal joint in the splines of the rack pinion.
8. Fit and tighten the two pinch bolts.

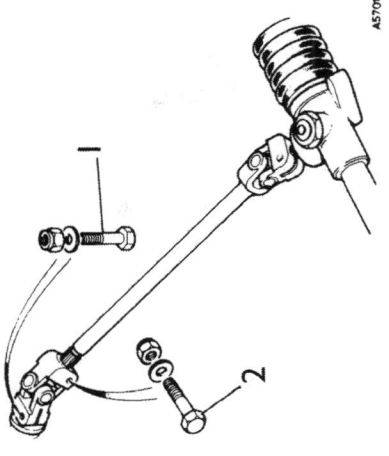

A57013

STEERING-COLUMN UPPER UNIVERSAL COUPLING   57.40.26

Remove and refit

Removing

1. Slacken the pinch bolt securing the upper universal coupling to the steering mast.
2. Remove the pinch bolt securing the upper universal coupling to the intermediate shaft.
3. Turn the steering-wheel to facilitate the removal of the top pinch bolt.
4. Set the road wheels to the straight-ahead position.
5. Slide the upper universal coupling down the intermediate shaft and remove the two washers from the steering mast (noting position for reassembly).
6. Remove the upper universal coupling from the intermediate shaft.

Refitting

7. Engage the upper universal coupling in the splines of the intermediate shaft.
8. Fit the two washers to the steering mast.
9. Ensuring that the steering-wheel and the road wheels are in the straight-ahead position, engage the coupling in the splines of the steering mast.
10. Fit and tighten the two pinch bolts.

A57008

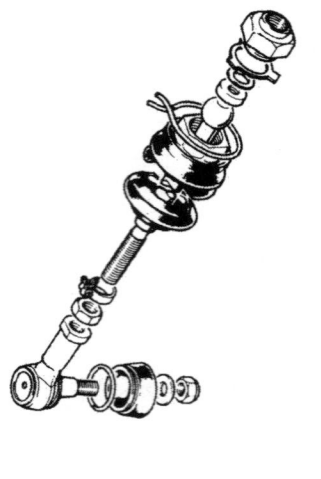

A57009

A57005

TIE-ROD BALL JOINT – OUTER 57.55.02

Remove and refit

Removing

1 Slacken the locknut securing the tie-rod to the outer ball joint.

2 Remove the nut and washer securing the ball joint to the steering-arm.

3 Release the ball joint from the steering-arm.

4 Unscrew the ball joint from the tie-rod.

Refitting

5 Screw the ball joint onto the tie-rod. (The distance between tie-rod ball joint centres [inner to outer] is 13¼ in (338 mm.)

6 Connect the ball joint to the steering-arm and secure with the washer and nut.

7 Check and adjust the front wheel track as necessary.

8 Tighten the tie-rod locknut.

TIE-ROD BALL JOINT – INNER 57.55.03

Remove and refit

Removing

1 Remove the tie-rod outer ball joint, see 57.55.02.

2 Release the wire and clip, and remove the gaiter from the inner ball joint to be renewed.

3 Release the tie-wire and clip, and slide the gaiter along the tie-rod at the opposite end of the rack.

4 Wipe the inner ball joints clean of grease.

5 Unscrew the tie-rod inner ball joint from the rack shaft. To prevent stress being applied to the rack pinion the opposite inner ball joint assembly should be held with a spanner.

Refitting

6 Fit the new inner tie-rod ball joint assembly to the rack shaft and tighten to 35 to 45 lbf ft (4.84 to 8.22 kgf m). To prevent stress being applied to the rack pinion the opposite inner ball joint assembly should be held with a spanner.

7 Using a suitable drift, deform the lock collar to secure the inner ball joint assembly to the rack shaft.

8 Fit the gaiters, tie-wires and clips.

9 Fit the outer ball joint to the tie-rod, see 57.55.02.

10 Check and adjust the front wheel track as necessary.

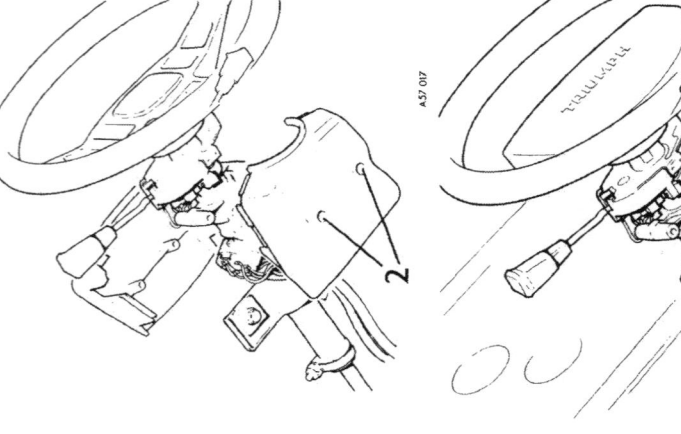

A57 017

STEERING-COLUMN NACELLE 57.40.29

Remove and refit

Removing

1 Withdraw the key from the steering lock/ignition switch.

2 Remove the two screws clamping the nacelle halves.

3 Remove the nacelle halves.

Refitting

4 Reverse instructions 1 to 3.

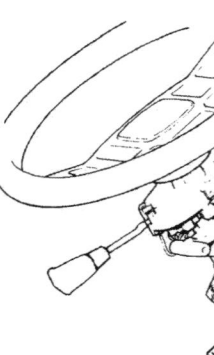

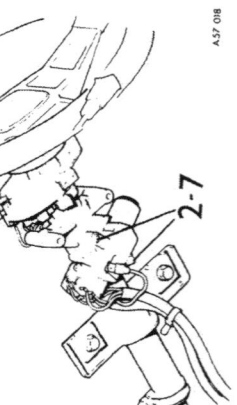

A57 018

STEERING LOCK/IGNITION SWITCH 57.40.31

Remove and refit

Removing

1 Remove the nacelle, see 57.40.29.

2 Using a centre-punch, mark the centre of the two shear-head bolts securing the steering lock to the column.

3 Using a small chisel, unscrew the shear-head bolts;

or

a If instruction 3 proves to be unsuccessful, drill into the shear-head bolts where previously marked by the centre-punch, and unscrew using an Easiout extractor.

4 Disconnect the plug-in connector to the ignition switch.

5 Remove the steering lock.

Refitting

6 Locate the steering lock on the column and align the mounting holes.

7 Fit two new shear-head bolts. Evenly tighten until both heads shear.

8 Connect the plug-in connector for the ignition switch.

9 Fit the nacelle, see 57.40.29.

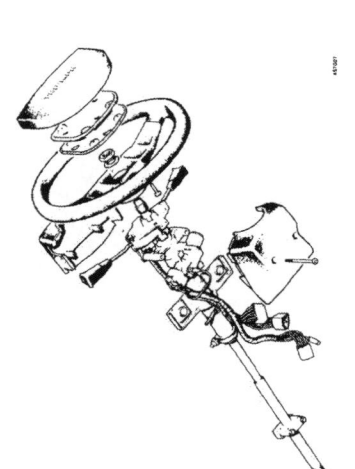

STEERING-WHEEL

Remove and refit 57.60.01

Removing
1 Remove the three screws (underside of the steering-wheel spokes) securing the steering-wheel pad and withdraw the pad.

or

Remove the steering-wheel centre cover.

2 Locate the road wheels in the straight-ahead position.

3 Slacken and remove the nut and washer securing the steering-wheel hub to the steering-column.

4 To ensure that the steering-wheel (hub) will be replaced in its original spline location, scribe both the hub centre and the top of the steering mast.

5 Using a suitable extractor, withdraw the steering-wheel. DO NOT attempt to drive or tap the steering-wheel from the mast.

Refitting
6 Ensure that the arrow on the trafficator cancelling collar aligns with the centre of the trafficator stalk. Reverse instructions 1, 2, 3 and 5. If the steering-wheel was withdrawn without the spline location being marked, set the road wheels to the straight-ahead position and centralize the steering-wheel.

STEERING-WHEEL CENTRE PAD

UK/European models

Remove and refit 57.60.03

Removing
1 Remove the three screws (underside of the steering-wheel spokes) securing the steering-wheel pad.

2 Withdraw the steering-wheel pad.

3 Remove the four screws at the back of the pad and part the two plates securing the pad.

Refitting
4 Reverse instructions 1 to 3.

USA Models

The steering-wheel pad may be carefully prised out of the wheel assembly.

STEERING GEOMETRY

Check 57.65.00

See 'GENERAL SPECIFICATION DATA'.

FRONT WHEEL ALIGNMENT 57.65.01

Check and adjust

Checking
1 Locate the car on level ground and position the front wheels in the straight-ahead position.

2 Using wheel alignment equipment, check the front wheels for toe-in.

Four requirements should be met:

a Centralized steering-wheel.

b Centralized steering-rack.

c Front wheels parallel to $\frac{1}{16}$ in (1.59 mm) toe-in.

d Ball centres of both tie-rods equal.

Adjusting
3 Slacken the outer clips on the rack gaiters.

4 Slacken the locknut at the tie-rod outer ball joints.

5 Shorten or extend both tie-rods by an equal amount to obtain the required setting (0 to $\frac{1}{16}$ in, 0 to 1.59 mm toe-in).

6 Tighten the locknuts at the tie-rod outer ball joints.

7 Tighten the gaiter clips.

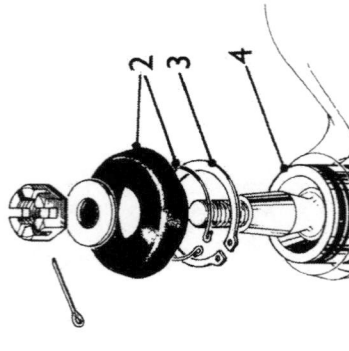

ANTI-ROLL BAR

Remove and refit 60.10.01

Bottom link rubbers
— remove and refit 60.10.06

Removing

1 Raise the car and support securely.
2 Remove the bolts and nyloc nuts (two each side) securing the anti-roll bar brackets to the sub-frame. Remove the distance piece washer (where fitted).

Later models only: Release two additional clamping nuts/bolts. Securing the bar inboard of the brackets.

3 Remove the spring pin, nyloc nut, flat washer, dished washer and outer rubber bush, securing each end of the anti-roll bar to the bottom link.

4 Withdraw the anti-roll bar, adjusting the jacks as necessary to facilitate removal.

5 Remove the inner bush and dished washer from each end of the anti-roll bar.

Refitting

6 Fit the inner dished washer (dish towards the bush) and the inner rubber bush to each end of the anti-roll bar.

7 Offer up the anti-roll bar and align the ends with the mounting holes in each of the bottom links.

8 Fit the outer rubber bush, dish washer, flat washer and nyloc nut to each end of the anti-roll bar.

9 Tighten to stop and fit the spring pin.

10 Position the mounting brackets and secure the anti-roll bar to the sub frame with the bolts and nyloc nuts.

11 Slacken the clamp bolts, push the clamp and washers hard against the inner face of the mounting rubbers and tighten the clamp bolts.

12 Lower the car.

ANTI-ROLL BAR MOUNTING RUBBERS

Remove and refit 60.10.05

Removing

1 Raise the car and support securely.
2 Remove the anti-roll bar. 60.10.01.
3 Cut the old mounting bushes and remove them from the anti-roll bar.

Refitting

4 Ensure that the anti-roll bar is clean throughout its length.
5 Smear the anti-roll bar with the approved rubber grease.
6 Slide the new mounting bushes into position along the anti-roll bar.
7 Fit the anti-roll bar to the car. 60.10.01.
8 Lower the car.

BALL JOINT

Remove and refit 60.15.03

Removing

1 Remove the bottom link. 60.40.02.
2 Remove the plastic boot from the ball joint.
3 Remove the circlip.
4 Press out the ball joint housing.

Refitting

5 Using a short length of suitable bore steel tubing, press a new ball joint and housing squarely into the bottom link. Do not apply pressure to the centre of the housing end cap.
6 Fit the circlip and plastic boot.
7 Fit the bottom link. 60.40.02.

FRONT ROAD SPRING

Remove and refit   60.20.01

Bump stop — remove and refit   60.30.10

Service tools: P.5045, RTR 360

Removing

1. Jack up the car and support the body on stands.
2. Remove the road wheel.
3. Detach the steering arm from the stub axle assembly (two bolts).
4. Slacken the locknut securing the brake hose to the bracket on the damper tube.
5. Remove the remaining bolt securing the brake caliper to the stub axle

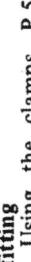

4–27

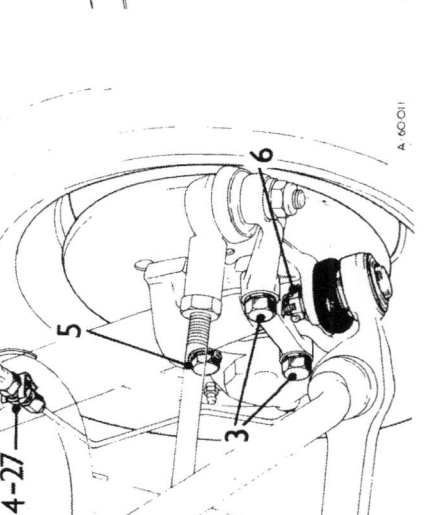

A.60.011

assembly, and support the brake caliper.

6. Remove the split pin, slotted nut and flat washer and release the ball joint from the stub axle assembly.
7. Remove the three nyloc nuts securing the damper and spring to the wing valance.
8. Pull the strut clear of the car.
9. Fit the two clamps P.5045 to the spring and compress coils evenly.
10. Remove the nut from the damper piston rod.
11. Lift off the spring pan complete with the top mounting and swivel assembly.
12. Withdraw the road spring from the damper strut.
13. Progressively slacken the spring clamps.

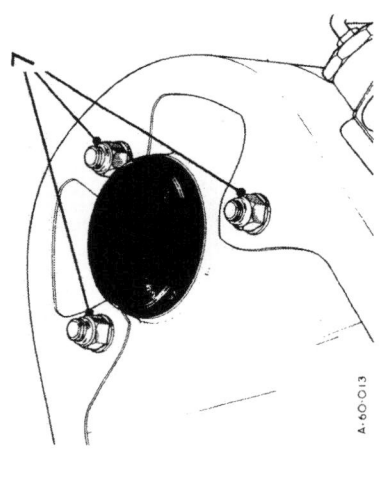

A.60.013

Refitting

14. Using the clamps, P.5045 compress the road spring.
15. Ensure that the bump stop rubber is in position.
16. Extend fully the damper piston rod and fit the lower insulating ring, rubber gaiter, road spring, upper insulating ring and spring pan.
17. Fit the seal to the thrust collar and position on the upper spring pan.
18. Fit the large plain washer (ground surface facing spring pan), smearing it first with a light coating of a general purpose chassis grease containing Molybdenum Disulphide.
19. Fit the rubber mounting to the damper piston rod and secure with the dished washer and nut using the special tool RTR 360. Tighten to the correct torque.

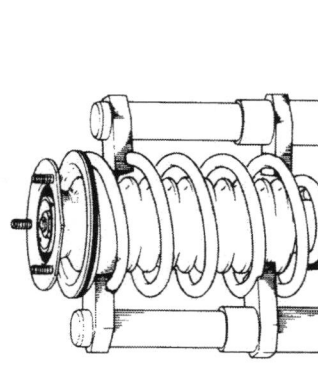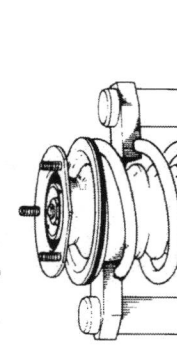

A.60.004

20. Slacken progressively the spring clamps, ensuring correct seating of the spring.
21. Ensure that the rubber gaiter is correctly fitted.
22. Thoroughly clean the spring turret and apply plasti-seal to the damper upper mounting flange.
23. Offer up the damper to the spring turret with the cut out facing outboard.
24. Engage the three studs, fit the plain washers, nyloc nuts and tighten.
25. Fit the ball joint into the stub axle assembly and secure with the flat washer, slotted nut and split pin.
26. Position the brake caliper onto the stub axle assembly and insert the upper bolt – do not tighten at this stage.
27. Position the brake pipe to the bracket on the damper tube.
28. Fit the steering arm to the stub axle assembly (the rear bolt also secures the brake caliper) and tighten to the correct torque.
29. Tighten the brake hose locknut to the fixing bracket.
30. Fit the road wheel and lower the car.

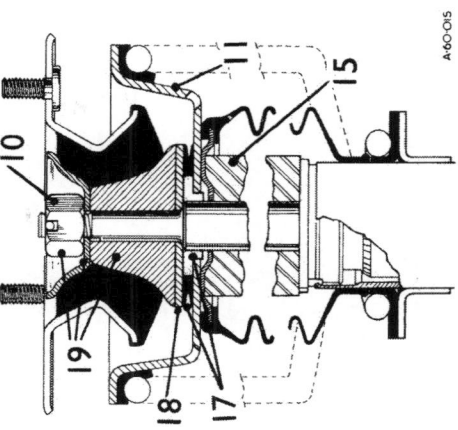

A.60.015

FRONT HUB

Remove and refit 60.25.01

Removing

1. Jack up the car and support the body on stands.
2. Remove the caliper. 70.55.02.
3. Prise off the hub cap and wipe grease from the end of the stub axle.
4. Remove the split pin, nut retaining cap, nut and washer from the stub axle.
5. Withdraw the hub complete with disc, bearings and oil seal.

Refitting

6. Partially pack the hub with fresh grease.
7. Locate the oil seal in the hub and enter the hub and bearings on the stub axle.
8. Fit the washer and slotted nut to the stub axle.
9. Tighten the slotted nut to a torque of 5 lbf ft (0.691 kgf m) back off one flat, fit the nut retaining cap and secure with a split pin.
10. Position the brake pipe to the fixing bracket on the damper tube.
11. Fit the caliper. 70.55.02.
12. Fit the road wheel and lower the car.

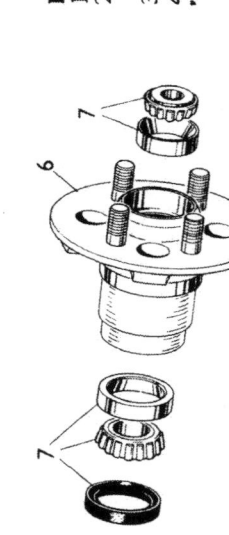

FRONT HUB BEARING END-FLOAT

Check and adjust 60.25.13

1. Remove the road wheel.
2. Check the hub for end-float.
3. If adjustment is required remove hub cap and split pin.
4. Tighten the slotted nut as required to eliminate end-float. A torque of 5 lbf ft (0.691 kgf m) must not be exceeded or damage may be caused to the bearings and bearing tracks. Back off one flat and fit the nut retaining cap.
5. Insert and lock the split pin.
6. Clean the hub cap and refit.
7. Fit the road wheels.

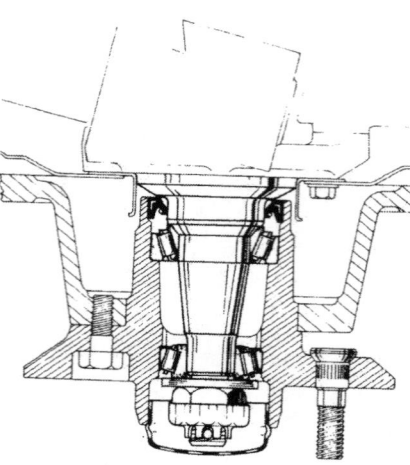

FRONT HUB BEARINGS

Remove and refit 60.25.14

Removing

1. Remove the front hub. 60.25.01.
2. Remove the outer bearing, inner oil seal and inner bearing.
3. Thoroughly clean the hub.
4. Drift the outer and inner bearing tracks from the hub.

Refitting

5. Clean the bearing track recesses in the hub.
6. Install the new tracks in the hub, ensuring that they abut against the machined lip.
7. Fit a new oil seal. 60.25.15.
8. Fit the hub assembly to the car. 60.25.01.

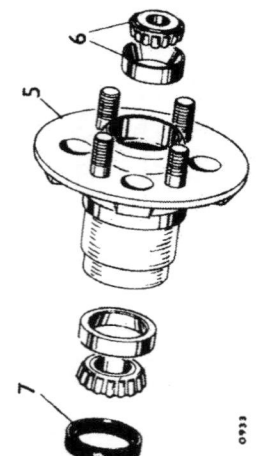

FRONT HUB OIL SEAL

Remove and refit   **60.25.15**

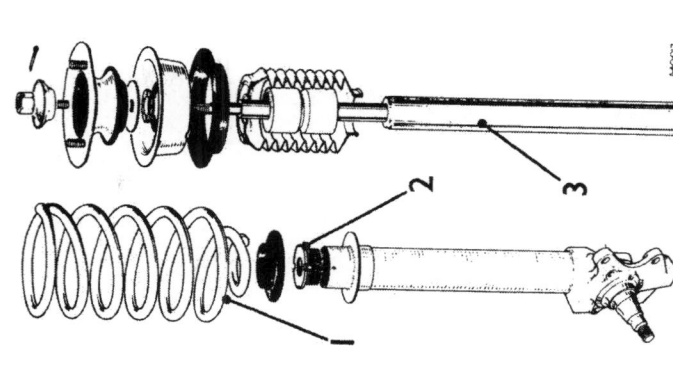

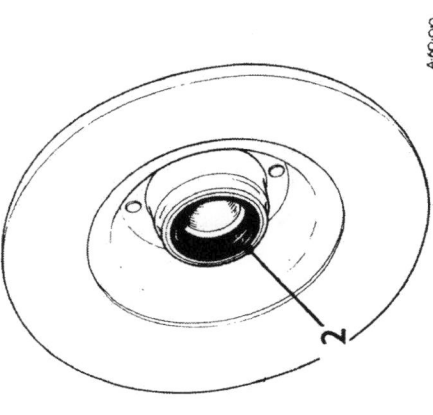

Removing
1 Remove the front hub. 60.25.01.
2 Extract the oil seal from the hub.

Refitting
3 Insert the new oil seal (lip towards bearing) into hub and press or drift evenly into position.
4 Lubricate the seal lip.
5 Ensure that the seal deflector ring, incorporated in the disc shield is not damaged and does not foul the hub.
6 Fit the hub to the car. 60.25.01.

STUB AXLE ASSEMBLY

Remove and refit   **60.25.22**

Removing
1 Remove the road spring. 60.20.01.
2 Remove the front damper cartridge. 60.30.02.
3 Remove the front hub. 60.25.01, instructions 7 to 9.
4 Remove the three bolts securing the disc shield.

Refitting
5 Secure the disc shield with the three bolts and spring washers.
6 Refit the front hub. 60.25.01, instructions 10 to 15.
7 Fit the front damper cartridge. 60.30.02.
8 Fit the road spring to the car. 60.20.01.

WHEEL STUD

Remove and refit   **60.25.29**

Removing
1 Remove the front hub. 60.25.01.
2 Remove the four bolts retaining the hub to the brake disc and remove the hub from the disc.
3 Extract the stud from the hub.

Refitting
4 Ensure that the mating countersunk faces of the stud and the flange are clean.
5 Enter the stud from the rear of the hub flange, align the splines and press into position.
6 Fit the front hub to the disc and evenly tighten the four bolts 25-32 lbf ft (3.46-4.42 kgf m).
7 Fit the front hub to the stub axle. 60.25.01.

FRONT DAMPER

Remove and refit   **60.30.02**

Service tool: RTR 359

Removing
1 Remove the front road spring. 60.20.01.
2 Using the special tool undo the closure nut.
3 Remove the damper cartridge.

Refitting
4 Fit the damper cartridge.
5 Fit the closure nut, and tighten to the correct torque.
6 Fit the road spring. 60.20.01.

FRONT STRUT UPPER SWIVEL ASSEMBLY

Remove and refit   **60.30.04**

As operation 60.20.01.

BOTTOM LINK

Remove and refit   60.40.02

Removing

1   Jack up the car and support the body on stands.
2   Remove the road wheel.
3   Remove the spring pin, nyloc nut, flat washer and outer rubber bush from the end of the anti-roll bar.
4   Remove the two bolts securing the steering arm to the stub axle assembly and push clear.
5   Remove the split pin, slotted nut and plain washer and release the ball joint from the stub axle assembly.
6   Remove the bolt and nyloc nut securing the bottom link to the sub frame. Withdraw the bottom link.

Refitting

7   Locate the anti-roll bar into the mounting hole in the bottom link.
8   Position the bottom link and secure to the sub frame with the bolt and nyloc nut. DO NOT tighten fully until the car is resting on its wheels.
9   Fit the ball joint into the stub axle assembly and secure with the flat washer, slotted nut and split pin.
10   Place the jack under the bottom link and carefully raise the link to locate the outer rubber bush, dished washer, flat washer and nyloc nut onto the end of the anti-roll bar.
11   Tighten the nyloc nut to the stop and fit the spring pin.
12   Lower the jack.
13   Fit the steering arm and tighten the two bolts.
14   Fit the road wheel and lower the car.

BOTTOM LINK

Overhaul   60.40.06

1   Remove the bottom link. 60.40.02.
2   Remove the plastic gaiter and rubber ring from the ball joint.
3   Remove the circlip retaining the ball joint housing to the bottom link.
4   Press or drive out the ball joint and housing.
5   Enter the new ball joint and housing from the underside of the bottom link ensuring that the housing is squarely located.
6   Press the housing into the bottom link taking care not to damage the bottom of the housing. (A short length of suitable diameter tube is recommended.)
7   Fit the circlip, new plastic gaiter and gaiter retaining ring.
8   Press out the rubber bush and sleeve from the fulcrum end of the bottom link.
9   Press the new bush and sleeve into position.

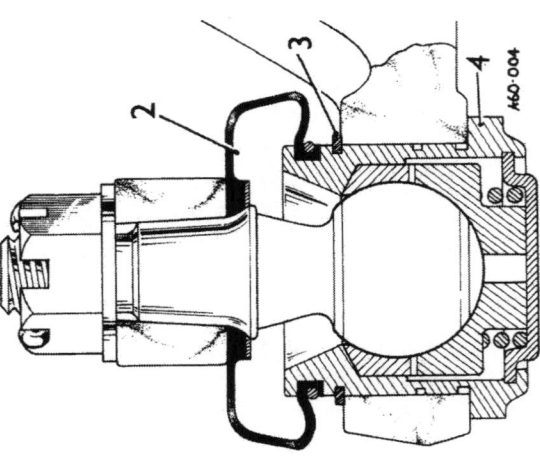

A·60·004

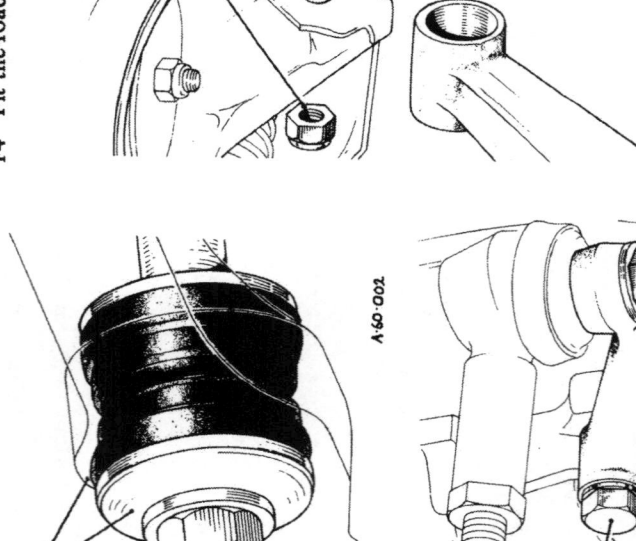

A·60·005

A·60·002

A·60·006

ROAD SPRING

Remove and refit	64.20.01
Insulating rings	64.20.17

Removing

1. Jack up the car and support the body on stands.
2. Remove the road wheel.
3. Transfer the jack to support the suspension arm and partially compress the road spring, taking care not to relieve the weight on the stands.
4. Remove the two nuts and bolts securing one side of the anti-roll bar to the suspension arm.
5. Remove the nut and bolt securing the rear end of the suspension arm to the axle bracket.
6. Carefully lower the jack.
7. Remove the spring and its upper and lower insulating rubbers.

Refitting

8. Ensure that the spring insulating rubbers are correctly positioned and fit the spring.
   NOTE: The spring should be fitted such that the spring end faces the front of the vehicle and is on the centre line of the lower link.
9. Position the jack under the suspension arm.
10. Carefully raise the jack and engage the rear end of the suspension arm in the axle bracket.
11. Fit the bolt and nut.
12. Connect the anti-roll bar to the suspension arm.
13. Fit the road wheel.
14. Remove the stands and lower the car.
15. Tighten the nut and bolt securing the rear end of the suspension arm to the axle bracket.

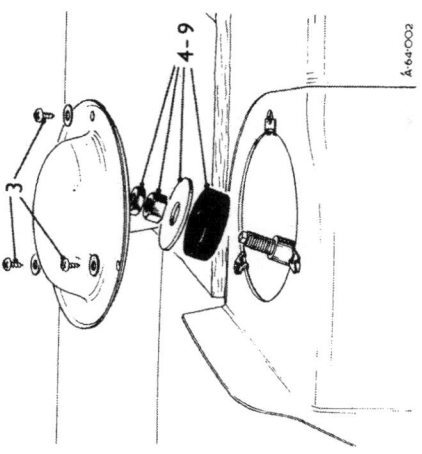

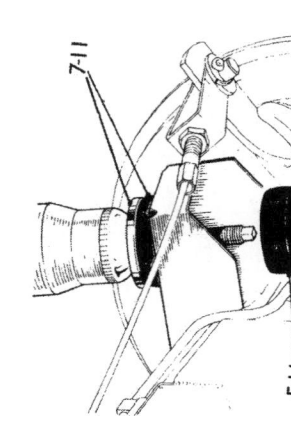

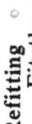

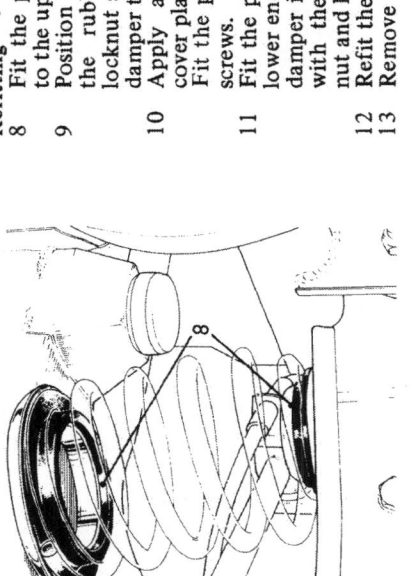

REAR DAMPER LEFT HAND

Remove and refit	64.30.02

Removing

1. Jack up the car and support the body on stands.
2. Remove the rear wheel.
3. Remove the three screws securing the damper access plate to the body in the boot. Remove the plate.
4. Remove the locknut, nut, plain washer and rubber bush securing the upper end of the damper to the body.
5. Remove the locknut, nut, plain washer and rubber bush securing the lower end of the damper to the axle bracket. Withdraw the damper.
7. Remove the rubber and plain washer from each end of the damper.

Refitting

8. Fit the plain washer and rubber bush to the upper end of the damper.
9. Position the damper on the car. Fit the rubber, plain washer, nut and locknut securing the upper end of the damper to the body.
10. Apply a plasti-seal, to the damper cover plate. Fit the plate and secure with the three screws.
11. Fit the plain washer and rubber to the lower end of the dampers. Position the damper in the axle bracket and secure with the rubber, bush, plain washer, nut and locknut.
12. Refit the road wheel.
13. Remove the stands and lower the car.

REAR DAMPER RIGHT HAND 64.30.03

Remove and refit

Removing
1 Jack up the car and support the body on stands.
2 Remove the rear road wheel.
3 Remove the fuel filler cap and filler assembly. 19.55.08.
4 Remove the locknut, nut, plain washer and rubber bush securing the upper end of the damper to the body.
5 Remove the locknut, nut, plain washer and rubber bush securing the lower end of the damper to the axle bracket.
6 Withdraw the damper.
7 Remove the rubber bush and plain washer from each end of the damper.

Refitting
8 Fit the plain washer and rubber bush to the upper end of the damper.
9 Position the damper on the car. Fit the rubber bush, plain washer, nut and locknut, securing the upper end of the damper to the body.
10 Fit the fuel filler cap and filler assembly. 19.55.08.
11 Fit the plain washer and rubber bush to the lower end of the damper. Position the damper in the axle bracket and secure with the rubber bush, plain washer, nut and locknut.
12 Refit the road wheel.
13 Remove the stands and lower the car.

SUSPENSION ARM 64.35.02

Remove and refit

Removing
1 Jack up the car and support the body on stands.
2 Remove the road wheel.
3 Transfer the jack to support the suspension arm and partially compress the road spring, taking care not to relieve the weight on the stands.
4 Remove two nuts and bolts securing the anti-roll bar to the suspension arm.
5 Remove the nut and bolt securing the rear end of the suspension arm to the axle bracket.
6 Carefully lower the jack.
7 Remove the spring.
8 Remove the nut and bolt (and, later models, the washers) securing the forward end of the suspension arm to the body bracket.
9 Detach the suspension arm from the bracket.

Refitting
10 Engaging the forward end of the suspension arm in the body bracket, fit the bolt and nut. Do not tighten at this stage.
11 Place the jack under the suspension arm.
12 Ensure that the spring insulating rubbers are correctly positioned and fit the spring.
13 Raise the jack and engaging the rear end of the suspension arm in the axle bracket, fit the bolt and nut. Do not tighten at this stage.
14 Connect the anti-roll bar to the suspension arm.
15 Fit the road wheel.
16 Remove the stands and lower the car.
17 Tighten the front and rear suspension arm, nuts and bolts.

BUMP STOP 64.30.15

Remove and refit

Removing
1 Remove the bump stop from its mounting.

Refitting
2 Press new bump stop into position.

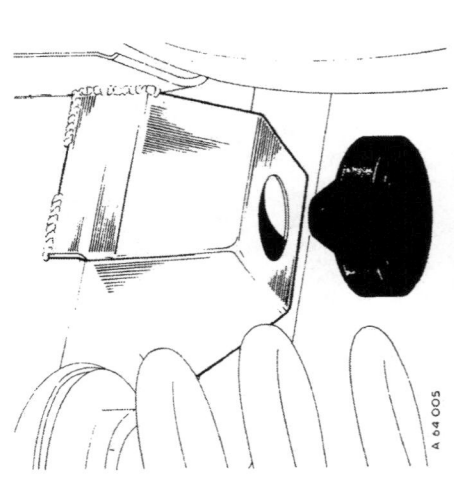

270   **REAR SUSPENSION**

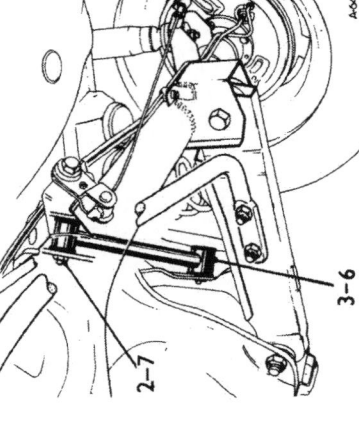

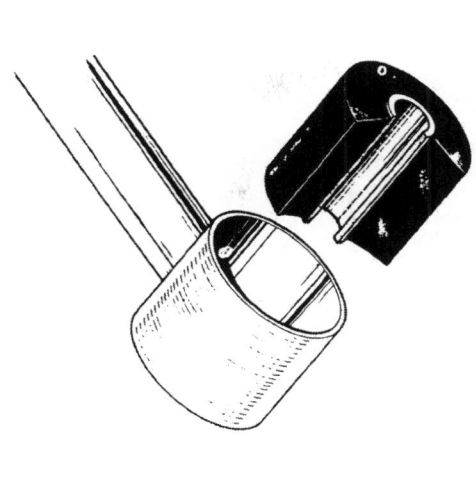

2-7

3-6

RADIUS ROD

Remove and refit 64.35.28

Removing

1 Jack up the car and support the body on stands.
2 Remove the nut and bolt securing the rear end of the radius rod to the rear axle bracket.
3 Remove the nut and bolt securing the forward end of the radius rod to the body bracket.
4 Withdraw the radius rod.

Refitting

5 Refit the radius rod.
6 Engage the forward end of the radius rod in the body bracket and fit the bolt and nut.
7 Engage the rear end of the radius rod in the axle tube bracket. Fit the bolt and nut.
8 Tighten both nuts.
9 Remove the stands and lower the car.

RADIUS ROD BUSHES

Remove and refit 64.35.29

Removing

1 Remove the radius rod from the car. 64.35.28.
2 Press out the bush from the radius rod.

Refitting

3 Fit a new bush to the radius rod.
4 Install the radius rod in the car. 64.35.28.

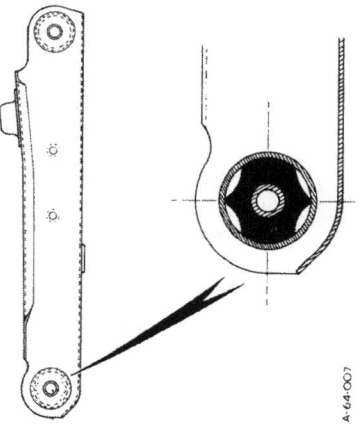
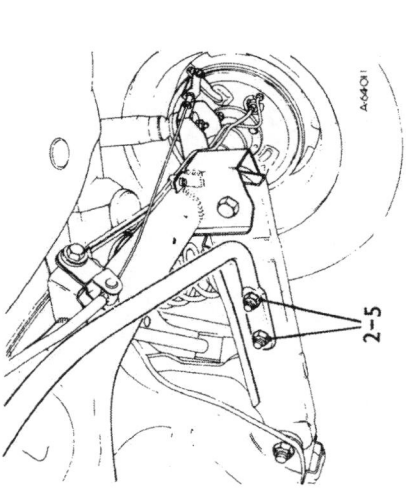

2-5

SUSPENSION ARM BUSHES

Remove and refit 64.35.05

Removing

1 Remove the suspension arm. 64.35.02.
2 Press out the old bushes.

Refitting

3 Press in the new bushes ensuring that they are centralized in the suspension arm. Note that the front bush must be installed in the position illustrated.
4 Fit the suspension arm. 64.35.02.

ANTI-ROLL BAR

Remove and refit 64.35.08

Removing

1 Raise the car and support it safely.
2 Remove the four bolts and nuts (two either side) securing the anti-roll bar to the rear suspension arms.
3 Withdraw the anti-roll bar and shim(s), if fitted.

Refitting

4 Locate the anti-roll bar (and shim(s), if removed) in position on the rear suspension arms.
5 Align the mounting holes and fit and tighten the four securing bolts and nuts.
6 Lower the car.

PRESSURE REDUCING VALVE

Description 70.00.00

The pressure reducing valve is installed in the brake circuit between the master cylinder and the front and rear brakes. Its function is to limit the pressure applied to the rear brakes relative to the pressure applied to the front brakes, thus minimizing the possibility of rear wheel locking. In the event of a failure in the front brake circuit the cut-off pressure is increased and the pressure reduction ratio changes.

Operation

Fluid from the primary chamber of the master cylinder is fed into the pressure reducing valve at port A and out to the front brakes via ports C and D. The master cylinder secondary chamber feeds into port B, through the internal passages in the valve plunger, past the metering valve and out to the rear brakes via port E. The large spring S is pre-loaded to bias the valve plunger to the left. Hydraulic pressure therefore acts on the annular area (a1 – a2) forcing the plunger to the left while the force acting on area a1 and annular area (a4 – a3) tends to move the plunger to the right where it is opposed by spring S. When the net force acting to the right overcomes the pre-load provided by spring S the plunger assembly shifts to the right thereby closing the metering valve F. Pressure at the rear outlet port E therefore falls relative to the input pressure. As pressure is increased at ports A and B the plunger is forced to the left, opening the metering valve F and permitting a small quantity of fluid to be fed to the rear brakes. The resultant increase in pressure acting on area a1 causes the plunger to again shift to the right closing the metering valve. This procedure continues until there is no further increase in pressure from the master cylinder.

The pressure at outlet E is reduced after cut-off in proportion to the areas a2 and the difference between the two annular areas (a1 – a2) and (a4 – a3). The cut-off pressure is equal to the pre-load in the spring S divided by the combined areas a2 and (a4 – a3). Should the front brake circuit fail there will be no pressure acting on annular area (a4 – a3) so that the net force tending to move the plunger to the right will be equivalent to the product of the input pressure and area a2. Thus, as the value of the pre-load spring S is unchanged, the cut-off pressure will increase considerably (approximately threefold).

As the annular area (a4 – a3) is now redundant, the reduction ratio after cut-off changes to a value which is proportional to the areas a1 and (a1 – a2). Should the rear brake circuit fail the pressure reducing valve is completely inoperative and pressure is fed to the front brakes in the normal manner.

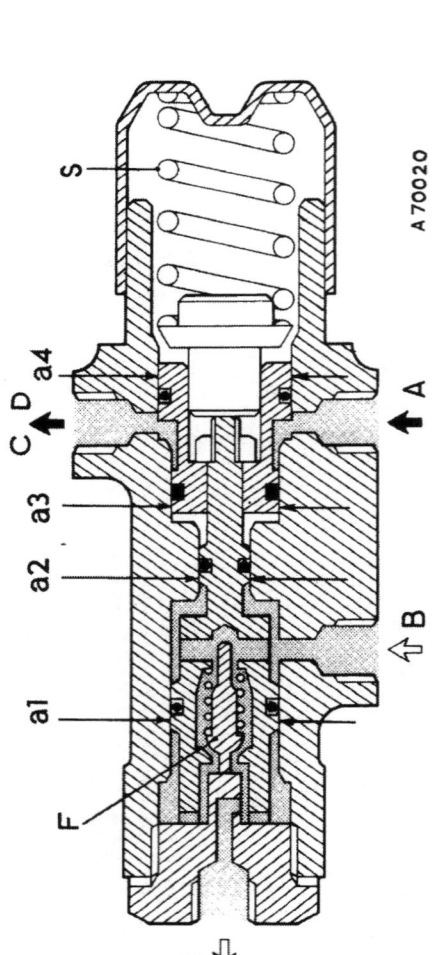

REAR BRAKE-DRUM

Remove and refit 70.10.03

Removing

1 Jack up the car and support the body on stands.
2 Remove the road wheel.
3 Release the hand brake.
4 Remove the countersunk screw(s) securing the brake-drum to the hub and withdraw the brake-drum.

Refitting

5 Align the countersunk hole(s) in the drum with the tapped hole(s) in the hub.
6 Engage the wheel studs in the drum.
7 Slide the drum into position. If the brake-shoes were disturbed, they may require to be centralized on the backplate to allow drum entry.
8 Fit and tighten the countersunk screw(s).
9 Fit the road wheel and lower the jack.
10 Apply the foot brake several times to adjust the rear brakes.

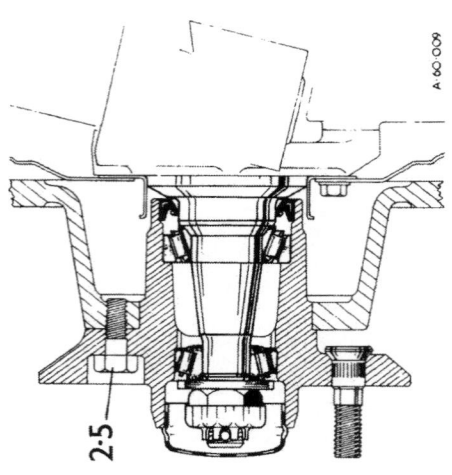

BRAKE DISC

Remove and refit 70.10.10

Removing

1 Remove the front hub, see 60.25.01.
2 Remove the four bolts securing the disc to the hub.
3 Withdraw the disc.

Refitting

4 Offer up the disc to the hub.
5 Fit and evenly tighten to 25 to 32 lbf ft (3.5 to 4.4 kgf m) the four bolts securing the disc to the hub.
6 Fit the front hub to the stub axle and adjust, see 60.25.01.

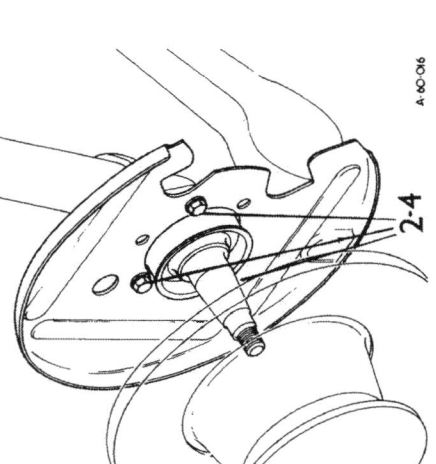
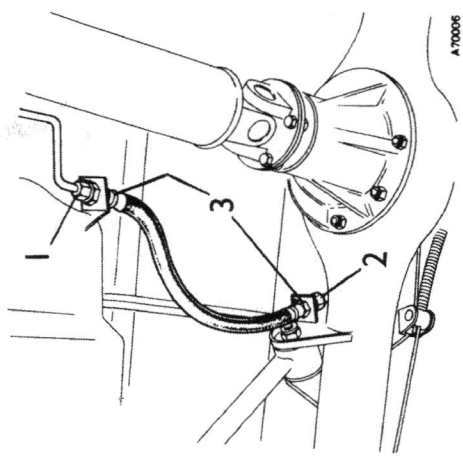

BRAKE HOSE – FRONT

Remove and refit – Left-hand 70.15.02
– Right-hand 70.15.03

Removing
1 Disconnect the brake pipe and union from the inboard end of the flexible hose.
2 Disconnect the brake pipe and union from the outboard end of the flexible hose.
3 Using two spanners, remove the locknuts and washers securing the hose to the support brackets, one on the wheel arch the other on the damper tube, and remove the hose.

Refitting
4 Reverse instructions 1 to 3. Ensure that the hose is neither kinked nor twisted when installed.
5 Bleed the brakes.

BRAKE HOSE – REAR

Remove and refit 70.15.17

Removing
1 Disconnect the brake pipe and union at the front end of the brake hose.
2 Disconnect the brake pipe and union at the rear end of the brake hose.
3 Using two spanners, remove the locknuts and washers securing the hose to the brackets, one on the body, the other on the axle tube. Remove the brake hose.

Refitting
4 Reverse instructions 1 to 3. Ensure that the hose is neither kinked nor twisted when installed.
5 Bleed the brakes.

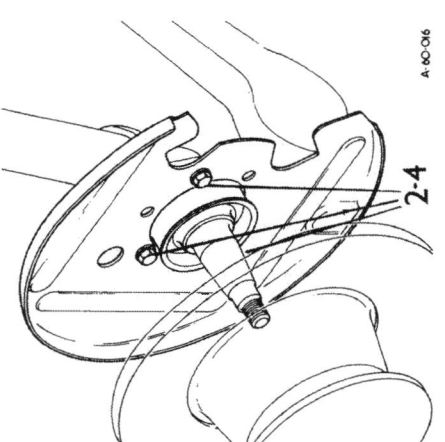

DISC SHIELD 70.10.18

Remove and refit

Removing
1 Remove the front hub, see 60.25.01.
2 Remove the three bolts and spring washers or special screws, securing the disc shield to the vertical link assembly.
3 Remove the disc shield.

Refitting
4 Position the disc shield over the stub axle and secure to the vertical link with the three bolts and spring washers, or three special screws.
5 Fit the front hub to the stub axle and adjust, see 60.25.01.

REAR BRAKE BACKPLATE 70.10.26

Remove and refit

Removing
1 Jack up the car and support the body on stands.
2 Remove the rear road wheel and release the hand brake.
3 Remove the rear hub, see 51.10.18.
4 Remove the clevis pin securing the hand brake cable fork to the back plate lever.
5 Disconnect the fluid feed pipe union at the wheel cylinder (left-hand side only);
or
Disconnect the fluid feed and transfer pipe unions at the wheel cylinder (right-hand side only).
6 Remove four nuts, spring washers, and bolts securing the backplate to the axle casing flange.
7 Withdraw the deflector plate and the backplate.

Refitting
7 Reverse instructions 1 to 7.
8 Bleed the brakes.

HYDRAULIC PIPES

Remove and refit

70.20.00

To aid identification of individual pipes, operation numbers are included in the illustration showing the general arrangement of the brake system. Left-hand-drive vehicles are set out symmetrically opposite at the front end to that shown.

Pipe — master cylinder to pressure reducing valve — front brakes   70.20.44
Pipe — master cylinder to pressure reducing valve — rear brakes   70.20.45
Pipe — pressure reducing valve to L.H. front hose   70.20.02
Pipe — pressure reducing valve to R.H. front hose   70.20.03
Pipe — L.H. front hose to caliper   70.20.04
Pipe — R.H. front hose to caliper   70.20.05
Pipe — Pressure reducing valve to rear hose   70.20.13
Pipe — R.H. rear wheel cylinder to L.H. rear wheel cylinder   70.20.17
Pipe — rear hose to R.H. rear wheel cylinder   70.20.18

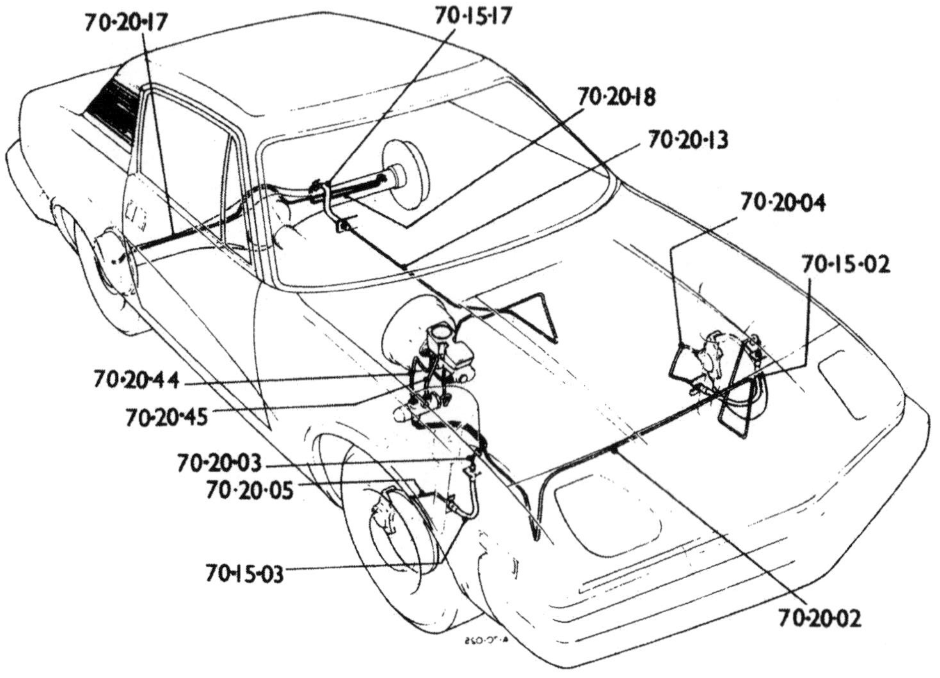

BRAKES

Bleed 70.25.02

Do not allow the fuel level in the reservoir to fall below half capacity. When topping-up during the bleeding process, DO NOT USE aerated fluid exhausted from the system. DO NOT bleed the system with the servo in operation (engine running).

1 Disconnect the wires to the pressure failure switch and remove the pressure failure switch from the underside of the master cylinder.

2 Release the hand brake.

3 Attach the bleed tube to the bleed nipple of the front caliper farthest from the master cylinder, allowing the free end of the bleed tube to hang submerged in brake fluid in a transparent container.

4 Open the bleed nipple (90 to 180 degrees).

5 Fully depress the brake pedal and follow with three rapid successive strokes. Allow the pedal to return. Repeat this procedure until fluid free from air bubbles issues from the wheel cylinder.

6 Depress the brake pedal, close the nipple and release the pedal.

7 Remove the bleed tube.

8 Attach the bleed tube to the opposite front caliper and repeat instructions 4 to 7.

9 Attach the bleed tube to the single nipple on the rear backplate (R.H. Stg. — left-hand backplate; L.H. Stg. — right-hand backplate) and repeat instructions 4 to 7.

10 In order to ensure the efficiency of the brake bleeding operation, the following check should be carried out:
a Start the engine and apply the handbrake.
b With a load of 25 lbf (11.3 kgf) applied to the brake pedal, check that the pedal travel does not exceed 1.90 in (48.26 mm).
c If the pedal travel exceeds this amount, repeat instructions 2 to 9.

11 Fit the pressure failure switch to the master cylinder and connect the wires. The P.D.W.A. shuttle fitted to this vehicle is self-centering.

BRAKES

Adjust 70.25.03

Self-adjusting brakes are fitted to the front and rear. Front adjustment is hydraulically self-compensating to provide for brake pad wear. In the rear brakes a self-adjusting mechanism incorporated in the brake-shoe hand brake linkage maintains a fixed brake liner/drum running clearance; self-adjustment occurs on the application of the footbrake.

PRESSURE REDUCING VALVE 70.25.21

Remove and refit

Removing

1 Slacken the brake pipe unions at the master cylinder.

2 Remove the two inlet pipes from the top of the pressure reducing valve.

3 Remove the rear brake outlet pipe from the end plug of the pressure reducing valve.

4 Remove the two front brake outlet pipes from the underside of the pressure reducing valve. To facilitate removal of the L.H. front brake pipe, first remove the R.H. front brake pipe from the pressure reducing valve and detach the pipe from the clip on the inner wheel arch.

5 Remove the nut, plain washer, spring washer and bolt, and remove the pressure reducing valve with the bracket from the suspension turret.

Refitting

6 Align the lugs on the bracket with the holes in the suspension turret.

7 Fit the pressure reducing valve and secure to the suspension turret with the bolt, plain washer, spring washer and nut.

8 Fit the brake pipes, tighten the pressure reducing valve unions, and attach the R.H. front brake pipe to the clip on the inner wheel arch.

9 Tighten the brake pipe unions at the master cylinder.

10 Bleed the brakes.

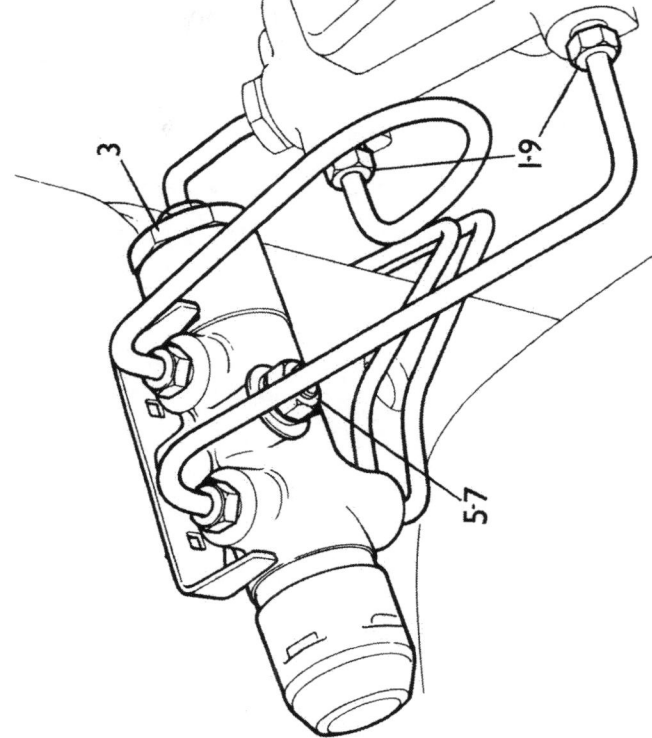

MASTER CYLINDER – TANDEM   70.30.08

Remove and refit

Removing

1 Noting their positions, disconnect the brake pipes at the master cylinder. Plug the master cylinder ports to prevent fluid discharge from the reservoir. Seal the brake pipes to prevent ingress of foreign matter.

2 Disconnect the wires to the pressure failure switch.

3 Remove the two nuts and spring washers securing the master cylinder to the servo and withdraw the master cylinder.

Refitting

4 Reverse instructions 1 to 3.

5 Bleed the brakes.

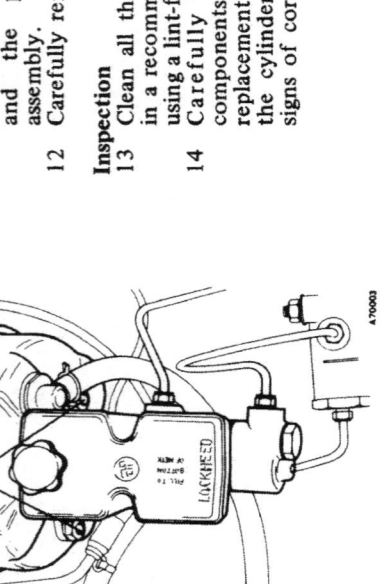

MASTER CYLINDER – TANDEM   70.30.09

Overhaul

Dismantling

1 Remove the tandem master cylinder from the car, see 70.30.08.

2 Drain the fluid from the reservoir.

3 Remove the two screws securing the fluid reservoir to the master cylinder and remove the reservoir.

4 Noting their original positions, remove the two rubber seals from the cylinder body recesses.

5 Remove the metal cap and rubber boot from the end of the master cylinder.

6 Remove the circlip, withdraw the primary piston and return spring.

7 Insert a soft metal rod into the cylinder and depress the secondary piston. This will release the stop pin which is seated adjacent to the secondary piston fluid feed port.

8 Remove the pin and withdraw the secondary piston, the spring retainer and the return spring.

9 Carefully note the sizes and positions of the rubber seals, the piston washers and the spring retainers. Remove the seals using only the fingers.

10 Unscrew the pressure failure switch from the cylinder body.

11 Remove the end plug and copper washer, withdraw the distance piece, and the piston and spring sub assembly.

12 Carefully remove the two rubber seals.

Inspection

13 Clean all the components thoroughly in a recommended brake fluid and dry using a lint-free cloth.

14 Carefully inspect the metal components for faults and wear. A replacement assembly must be fitted if the cylinder bores show the slightest signs of corrosion, ridging or scoring.

15 Ensure that all the ports and drillings in the cylinder body, piston heads and the vent hole in the filler cap are clear of any obstructions.

Reassembly

CAUTION: Scrupulous cleanliness is essential. Immerse all components in a recommended brake fluid and assemble when wet.

16 Fit new seals and washers to the primary and secondary pistons, using only the fingers.

17 Fit the secondary return spring, spring retainer and piston into the cylinder bore, taking care not to bend back the lip of the seal.

18 With a soft metal rod, depress the secondary piston. When the head of the piston passes the secondary fluid feed port, fit the piston stop pin.

19 Fit the primary return spring, spring retainer and piston into the cylinder bore, ensuring that the lip of the seal is not bent back.

20 Fit the circlip at the mouth of the cylinder bore and check that it is correctly seated in the groove.

21 Fit the two rubber seals into the cylinder body recesses.

22 Ensure that the reservoir is clean and fit it to the master cylinder body with the two screws. Tighten to a torque of 5 lbf ft (0.69 kgf m). DO NOT overtighten.

23 Fit two new 'O' rings into the grooves on the P.D.W.A. piston and spring sub-assembly.

24 Insert the piston and spring sub-assembly into its respective bore, taking care not to damage the 'O' rings.

25 Fit the metal distance piece.

26 Fit a new copper washer to the end plug and screw into the bore. Tighten to a torque of 33 lbf ft (4.56 kgf m).

27 Fit the master cylinder to the car, see 70.30.08.

28 Bleed the brakes.

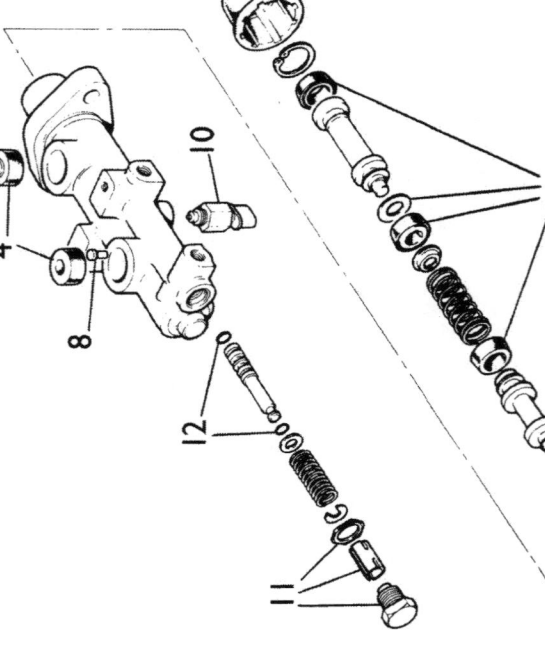

PEDAL BOX

Remove and refit   70.35.03

Removing

1. Disconnect the two spade terminals from the brake stop light switch.
2. Remove the speedo cable from its retaining clip.
3. Remove the clevis pin securing the brake pedal to the brake master cylinder rod.
4. Remove the clevis pin securing the clutch pedal to the clutch master cylinder rod.
5. Remove the four nuts and spring washers securing the servo to the pedal box.
6. Remove the two nuts, bolts and spring washers securing the clutch master cylinder to the pedal box.
7. Remove the cleat securing the harness to the stabilizer bar.
8. Remove the nut and bolt securing the stabilizer bar to the fascia rail.
9. Remove the three bolts and spring washers securing the top of the pedal box to the body.
10. Withdraw the pedal box assembly.

Refitting

11. Reverse instructions 1 to 10.

PEDAL BOX

Overhaul   70.35.04

1. Remove the pedal box from the car, see 70.35.03.
2. Remove the brake stop light switch.
3. Remove the circlip from one end of the pedal pivot rod.
4. Push the rod through the bracket.
5. Remove the brake and clutch pedals and the two anti-rattle springs.
6. Remove and renew the two Teflon coated bushes in each pedal.
7. Remove and renew the pedal pad rubbers.
8. Locate both the clutch and brake pedals in the pedal box, ensuring that the anti-rattle springs are fitted.
9. Push through the pivot rod and secure using the circlip.
10. Fit the brake stop light switch.
11. Fit the pedal box to the car, see 70.35.03.

HANDBRAKE LEVER ASSEMBLY

Remove and refit   70.35.08

Removing

1. Drive the vehicle onto a ramp. Release the hand brake.
2. Raise the ramp.
3. Using a screw jack, raise the body to allow access to the underside of the transmission tunnel.
4. Pull back the rubber gaiter and release the hand brake cable locknut; note original position.
5. Unscrew the hand brake cable from the operating rod.
6. Lower the ramp.
7. Remove the centre console, see 76.25.01.
8. Remove the Lucar connector from the handbrake warning light switch.
9. Remove the four bolts and spring washers securing the hand brake lever assembly to the transmission tunnel.
10. Withdraw the hand brake lever assembly, the lower plate and the rubber gaiter.

Refitting

11. Reverse instructions 1 to 10.
12. Check the adjustment of the hand brake and rectify as necessary, see 70.35.10.

HAND BRAKE CABLES

Adjust   70.35.10

1. Jack up the rear of the vehicle and support the axle on stands.
2. Release the hand brake.
3. Disconnect the hand brake cables from the rear brake backplate levers.
4. Applying light finger pressure, push the brake operating levers inboard to ensure that the operating levers are in contact with the brake-shoe webs.
5. With the compensator 12 mm (½ in) to the left-hand side of its vertical position adjust the cable forks to permit clevis pin entry. Fit the clevis pins. Ensure that the brakes do not drag.
6. (continued)
7. With 25 lbf effort applied to the hand brake, the travel of the lever should be between five and seven notches.

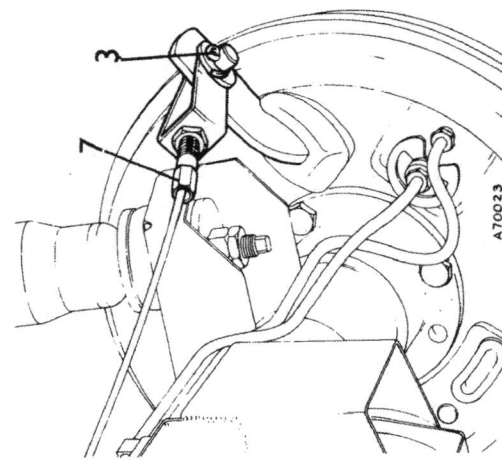

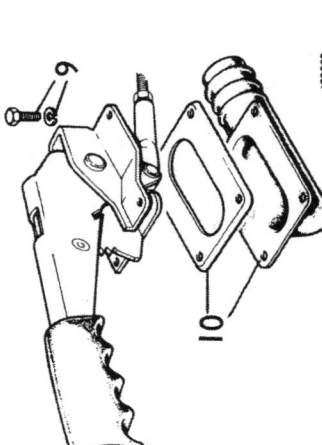
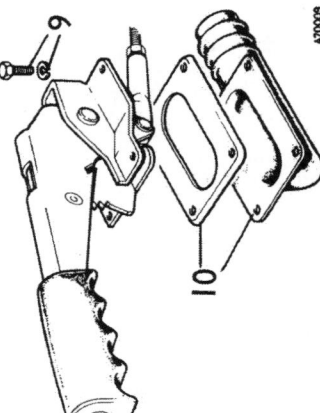

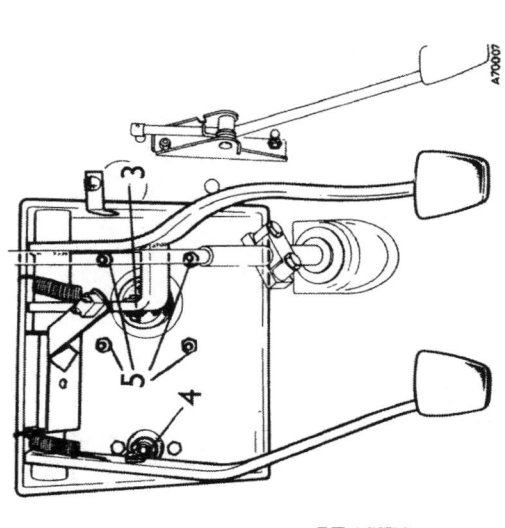

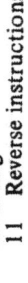

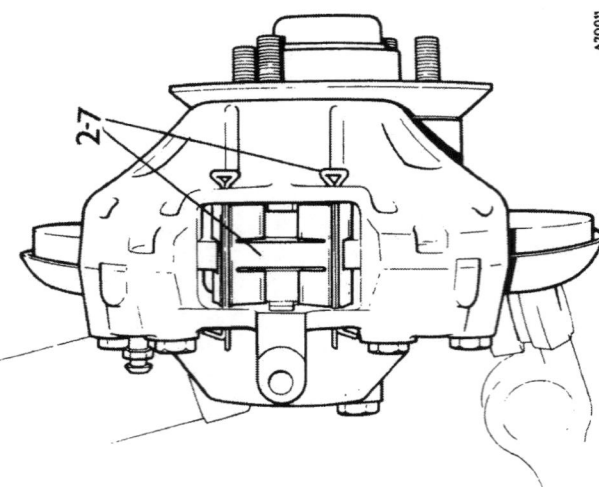

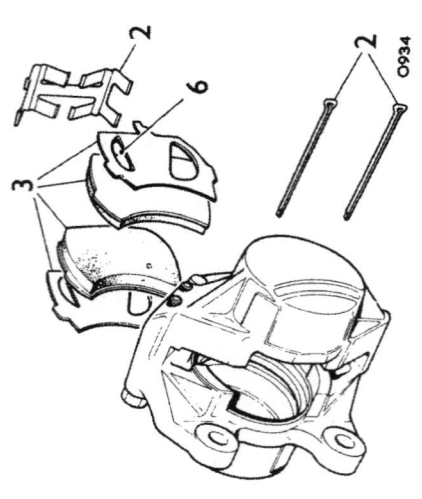

FRONT BRAKE PADS

Remove and refit   70.40.02

Removing

1 Jack up the car and remove the front road wheel.

2 Depress the pad-retaining spring and withdraw the split pins.

3 Taking note of their positions, lift the pads and shims out of the caliper recesses.
   The shims need not be renewed provided they are undamaged and are not corroded.

Refitting

4 Ease the caliper pistons into the bores to provide the extra clearance to accommodate the new unworn brake pads. During this operation brake fluid will be displaced and to prevent the reservoir overflowing, open the caliper bleed screw as pressure is applied to the piston. Close the bleed screw when the piston has moved the required amount. Repeat on the opposite piston in the caliper.

5 Remove dust and clean the brake pad locations in the caliper.

6 Insert the new pads and shims (smaller cut-out uppermost) into the caliper recesses.

7 Fit the new pad-retaining spring and split pins.

8 Firmly depress the footbrake pedal several times to correctly locate the friction pads.

9 Fit the road wheel and lower the car.

10 Check the fluid level in the reservoir and top up as necessary.

HANDBRAKE CABLE ASSEMBLY

Remove and refit   70.35.16

Removing

1 Drive the vehicle onto a ramp. Release the handbrake.

2 Raise the ramp.

3 Using a screw jack, raise the body to allow access to the underside of the transmission tunnel.

4 Pull back the rubber gaiter and release the handbrake cable locknut.

5 Unscrew the handbrake cable from the operating rod.

6 Slacken the nut to release the cable from the abutment bracket.

7 Remove the split pin, washer and clevis pin retaining the cable to each rear brake operating lever.

8 Remove the trunnion locating nut, spring washer and bolt.

9 Slacken the nut securing the compensating levers.

10 Remove the cable assembly from the compensating levers, and the retaining brackets.

Refitting

11 If a new handbrake cable has been fitted the following setting procedure should be carried out:

   a Feed the cable forward through the guide bracket at the left-hand upper link, then through the guide bracket on the heelboard.

   b Locate the cable abutment into the rear of the handbrake bracket but do not tighten the nut.

   c Fit the cable adjuster (complete with jam nut) to the handbrake lever and screw fully into the connection. Lock the jam nut and pull the rubber boot over the joint.

   d Secure the abutment to the bracket.

   e Fit rubber sleeves on the cable into the guide brackets.

   f Pivot the compensator lever on the axle towards the left-hand wheel so that the lever is offset approximately ½ in (12 mm) from vertical.

   g Pull the left-hand operating lever away from the backplate to eliminate free movement and screw the adjuster into the fork-ends with fingers until all slack is removed from the cable.

   h Repeat (g) for the right-hand brake.

   i Apply the handbrake lever five times with a good double-handed pull (equal to approximately 100 lbf or 45 kgf) for a full stroke of the lever on each occasion to compress the handbrake outer cable.

   j Repeat (g) and (h) to finally adjust the fork-ends.

   k Secure the locknuts to the fork-ends.

   l Apply Retinax grease to the fork-ends.

12 Reverse instructions 1 to 10.

13 Adjust the handbrake cable, see 70.35.10.

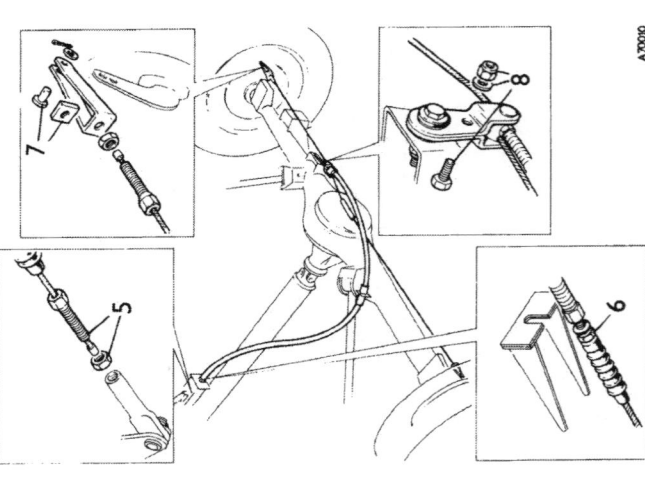

REAR BRAKE-SHOES

Remove and refit   70.40.03

Removing

1 Jack up the car and support the body on stands.

2 Remove the road wheel.

3 Release the hand brake.

4 Remove the two countersunk screws securing the brake-drum and withdraw the brake-drum.
When brake-drum removal is found to be difficult due to wear or ridging, remove the rubber plug on the inboard side of the backplate. Insert a small screwdriver, and engage it in the slotted hole in the small adjusting lever. Press down to release the mechanism.

5 Carefully note the position of the shoes and springs.

6 Remove the shoe steady pin cups and springs and extract the shoe steady pin from the rear of the backplate.

7 Ease the toe of the leading shoe followed by the heel of the trailing shoe out of the slotted piston heads.

8 Unlock the pull-off springs, and the cross lever tension spring and remove the brake-shoes.
To avoid possible ejection of the wheel cylinder pistons restrain them in position with a twist of wire or a suitable clamp. Take care not to damage the rubber boots.

Refitting

9 Insert the cross lever tension spring hook in the cross lever, engage the other end in the leading shoe web in the previously noted hole position. This spring is not interchangeable with the spring on the opposite brake.

10 Ease the brake-shoe and the cross lever towards the backplate, engage the toe of the shoe into the slot in the piston and the heel of the shoe into the abutment.

11 Hold the cross lever and shoe against the backplate, fit the steady pin, spring and cup.

12 Hook the pull-off springs into the holes in the shoe webs. The spring nearest the abutment is fitted on the backplate side of the shoes.

13 Pull the trailing shoe against the resistance of the springs. Position the heel into the slot in the piston and the toe into the abutment. Ensure that the cut-out in the cross lever engages with the slot in the adjuster plate.

14 Fit the remaining steady pin, spring and cup.

15 The functioning of the adjuster can be checked by gently operating the foot brake with the drum removed. Following expansion of the brake-shoes the ratchet will be seen to operate. Brake-shoes expansion can be cancelled by raising the ratchet plate to separate the ratchet teeth and allowing the pull-off springs to retract the shoes.

16 Replace the brake-drum and road wheel. Lower the car.

17 Apply the foot brake heavily several times to centralize and adjust the brake-shoes.

18 Road-test the car. If the operation of the brakes, including the hand brake, is poor, make four brake applications applying moderately high pedal efforts to decelerate the vehicle from 20 m.p.h. to rest. This will ensure correct adjustment of the rear brakes.

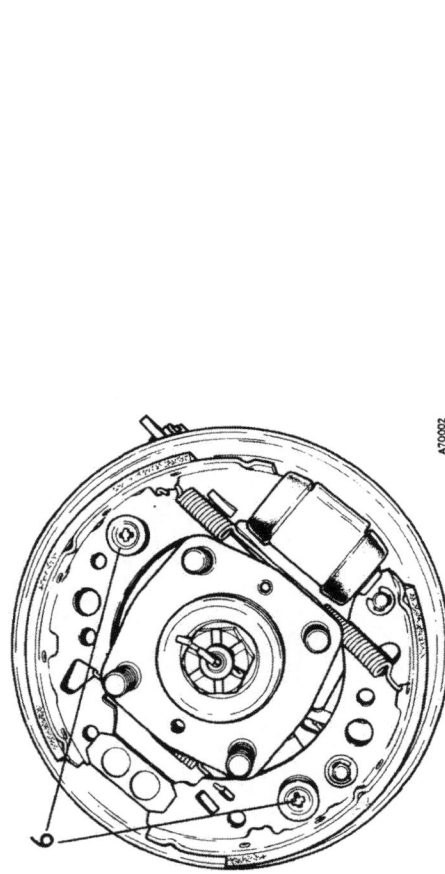

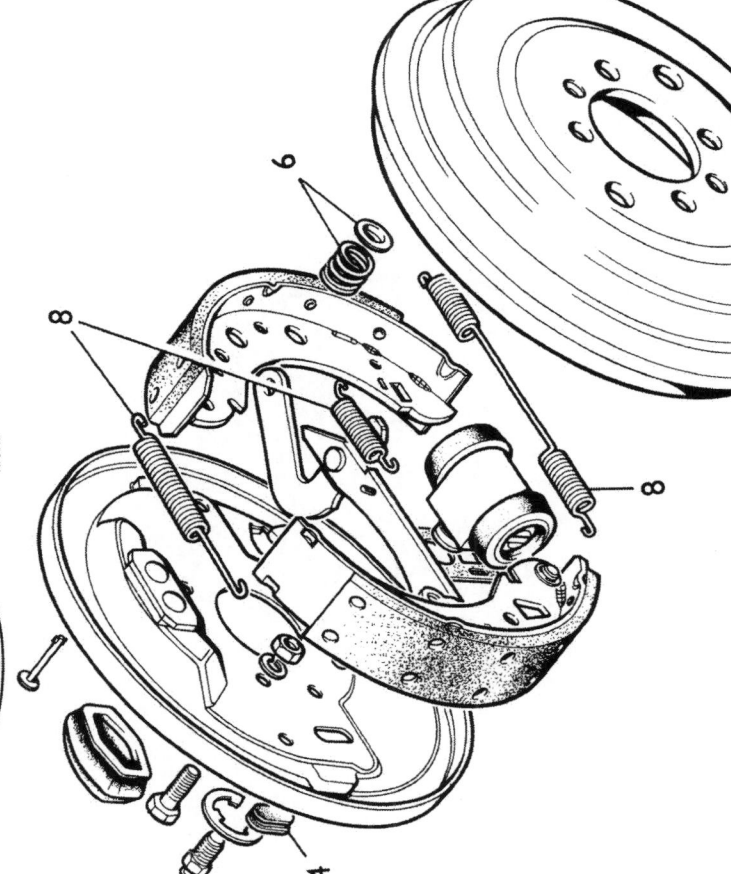

NON-RETURN VALVE 70.50.15

Remove and refit

Removing

1 With the engine stopped, depress the brake pedal to destroy the vacuum in the servo.
2 Release the hose clip securing the vacuum hose to the non-return valve and disconnect the hose.
3 Withdraw the non-return valve from the servo.

Refitting

4 Renew the sealing rubber as necessary, and press the non-return valve into position in the servo.
5 Connect the vacuum hose to the non-return valve and secure with the hose clip.

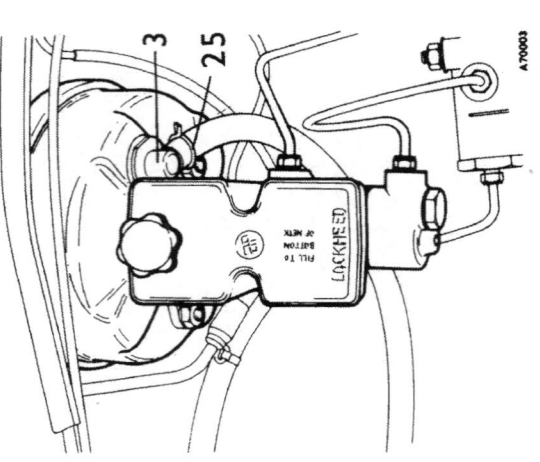

A70003

SERVO 70.50.01

Remove and refit

Removing

1 Remove the master cylinder from the servo, see 70.30.01.
2 Disconnect the vacuum hose from the non-return valve.
3 Remove the clevis pin securing the servo push-rod to the brake pedal.
4 Remove the four nuts and spring washers securing the servo to the pedal bracket.
5 Withdraw the servo.

Refitting

6 Reverse instructions 1 to 5.
7 Bleed the brakes.

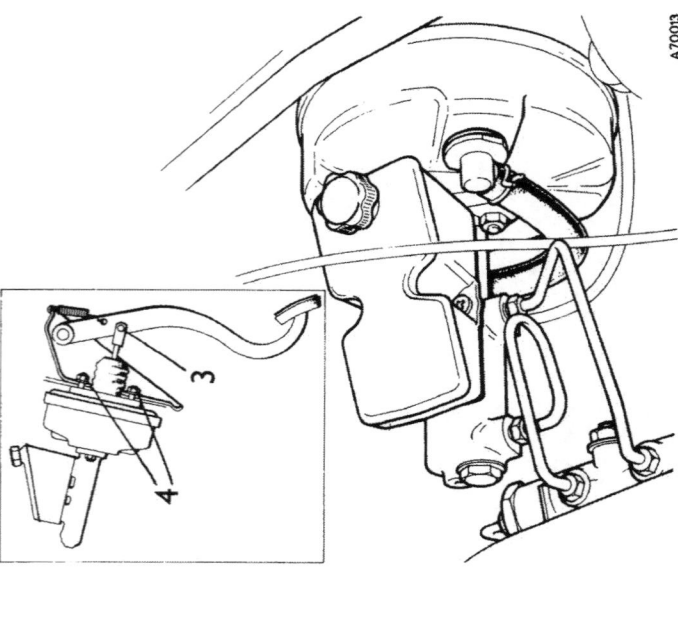

A70013

VACUUM HOSE 70.50.14

Remove and refit

Removing

1 Release the vacuum hose clips at the manifold and the servo non-return valve.
2 Remove the hose from the manifold and the non-return valve.

Refitting

3 Reverse instructions 1 and 2.

A70018

SERVO FILTER

Remove and refit   **70.50.25**

Removing

1. Remove the brake stop light switch.
2. Remove the split pin, plain washer and clevis pin securing the servo rod to the brake pedal.
3. Remove the rubber boot from the push-rod.
4. Withdraw the filter.

Refitting

5. Reverse instructions 1 to 4.

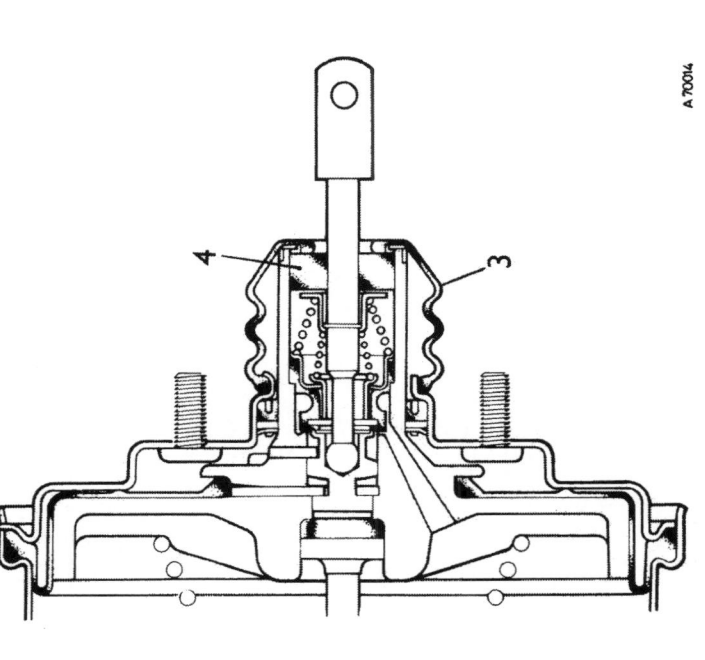

A 70014

BRAKE CALIPER — FRONT

Remove and refit   **70.55.02**

Removing

1. Jack up the car and remove the front wheel.
2. Disconnect the brake union at the caliper and seal the fluid connections to prevent entry of grit.
3. Remove the two bolts and spring washers retaining the steering-arm and the caliper lower mounting lug to the stub axle assembly.
4. Push the steering-arm clear.
5. Remove the bolt and spring washer securing the caliper upper mounting lug to the stub axle assembly.
6. Withdraw the caliper.

Refitting

7. Engage the caliper on the disc and align the locating lugs.
8. Position the upper bolt and spring washer; do not tighten.
9. Fit the steering-arm to the stub axle assembly.
10. Tighten the three bolts.
11. Bleed the brakes.
12. Fit the road wheel and remove the jack.

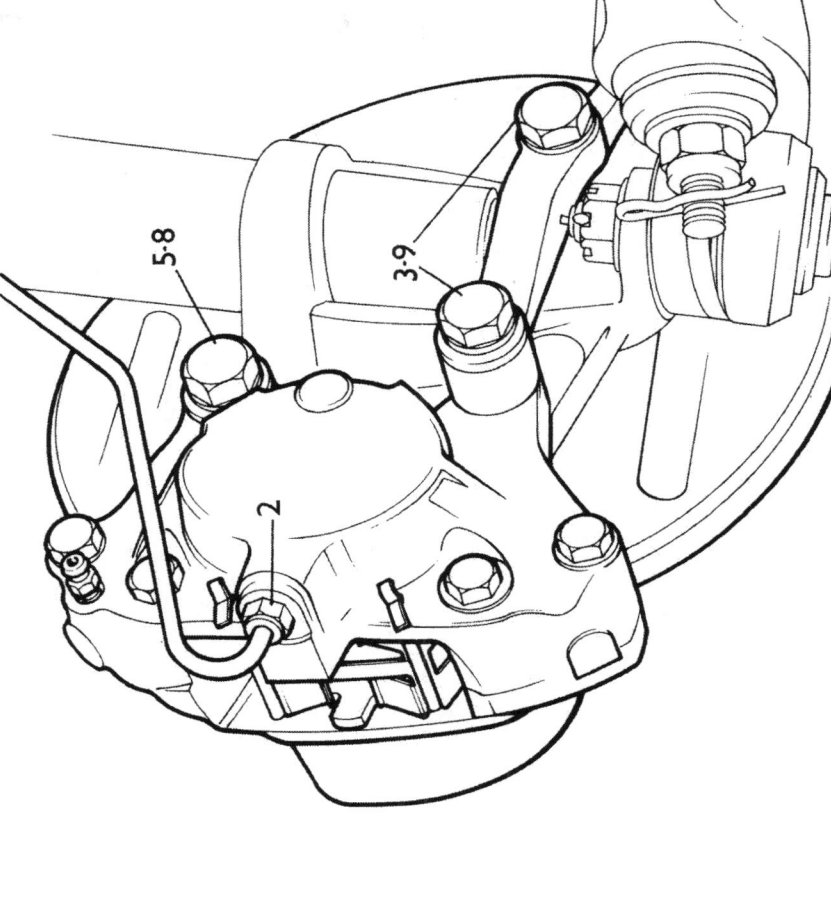

A70015

FRONT CALIPER 70.55.13

Renew seals

Dismantling

1 Remove the caliper from the car, see 70.55.02.
2 Remove the brake pads and shims, see 70.40.02.
3 Extract the caliper pistons. Piston removal may be affected by using a low pressure air line. DO NOT interchange the pistons. If either piston is seized, the whole caliper assembly must be renewed.
4 Using a blunt screwdriver carefully prise out the wiper seal retainers, taking care not to damage the seal grooves in the caliper bores.
5 Extract the wiper dust seal and the fluid seal from each caliper bore.
6 Thoroughly clean the caliper pistons and caliper bores with new clean brake fluid or methylated spirit.
7 Carefully inspect the caliper bores and pistons. If they show any signs of corrosion, fault or wear, the parts affected must be renewed.

Reassembling

8 Fit the new fluid seals, using only the fingers, into the grooves in the caliper bores, ensuring that they are properly located. The fluid seal grooves and the seals are not the same in section, therefore even when located correctly the seal feels proud at the edge farthest away from the mouth of the caliper bore.
9 Lubricate the bores with new, clean brake fluid.
10 Squarely insert the pistons into the caliper bores. Leave approx. ⅜ in (7.94 mm) of each piston projecting from the mouth of each bore.
11 Fit a new wiper seal into each of the seal retainers and slide the assemblies, seal first, carefully into the mouth of each bore using the pistons as a guide.
12 Carefully press home the seals, taking care not to distort the retainers.
13 Push home the pistons.

14 Fit the caliper to the car, see 70.55.02.
15 Fit the brake pads and shim(s), see 70.40.02.
16 Bleed the brakes.

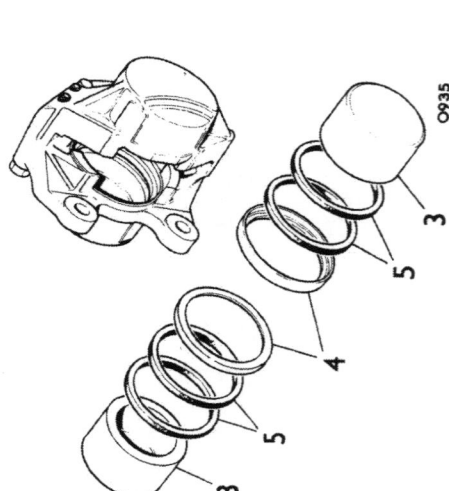

0935

REAR WHEEL CYLINDER 70.60.18

Remove and refit

Removing

1 Jack up the car and support the body on stands.
2 Remove the rear wheel.
3 Remove the brake-drum, see 70.10.03.
4 Remove the brake-shoes, see 70.40.03.
5 Disconnect the hand brake cable at rear of the backplate.
6 Disconnect the fluid feed pipe union at the wheel cylinder and remove the bleed screw (left-hand side only);
or
Disconnect the fluid feed and transfer pipe unions at the wheel cylinder (right-hand side only).

7 Remove the spring clip securing the wheel cylinder to the rear of the backplate.
8 Remove the wheel cylinder and gasket.

Refitting

9 Reverse instructions 1 to 8, fitting a new gasket and circlip.
10 Apply the foot brake several times to adjust the rear brakes.
11 Bleed the brakes.
12 Road-test the car. If the operation of the brakes, including the hand brake, is poor, make four brake applications applying moderately high pedal efforts to decelerate the vehicle from 20 m.p.h. to rest. This will ensure correct adjustment of the rear brakes.

A7002

REAR WHEEL CYLINDER

Overhaul   **70.60.26**

1. Remove the wheel cylinder from the backplate, see 70.60.18.

2. Remove the rubber boots from the cylinder body and remove the pistons.

3. Withdraw the pistons from the bore and retrieve the spring located between the two pistons.

4. Carefully inspect all components for faults and wear. A replacement wheel cylinder assembly must be fitted if, after cleaning, the bore of the old unit shows the slightest signs of corrosion or scoring.

5. Smear the cylinder bore with clean brake fluid.

6. Renew the seal on each piston, carefully fit the seal into the larger groove on each piston, with the lip of the seal facing away from the slotted head.

7. Locate the rubber boots into the smaller groove on each of the pistons.

8. Insert the pistons into the cylinder bore ensuring that the spring locates between them in the counter-bored ends.

9. Refit the wheel cylinder, see 70.60.18.

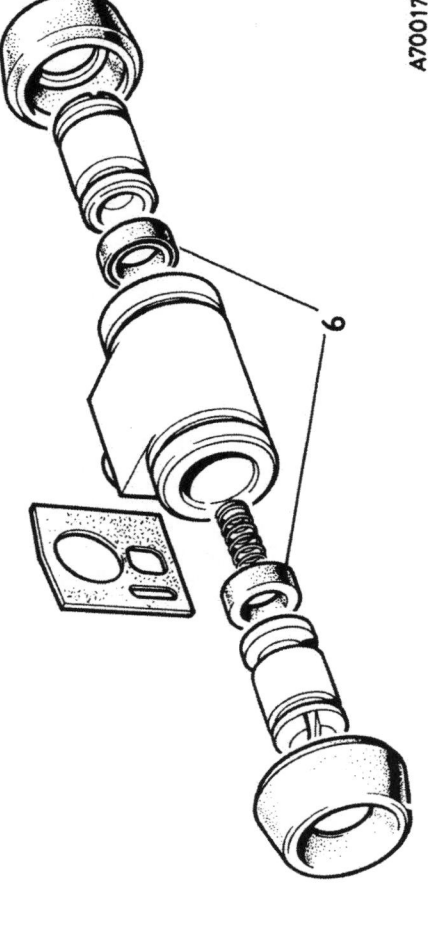

A70017

BODY UNIT

Alignment check   **76.10.01**

1   A preliminary check of the alignment
    should be carried out by dropping a
    plumb-bob from the centre of the
    points A, B, C, D on each side of the
    car.
2   Establish a centre line by means of a
    large pair of compasses at points B and
    D.
3   Check measurements against those
    given in DATA.
4   Construct diagonals.

Incorrect alignment will be evident by the
failure of the diagonals to intersect on the
centre line by considerable deviation from
the dimensions given.

DATA

A	B	C	D
552 mm	594 mm	964 mm	1042 mm
(21.73 in)	(23.38 in)	(37.95 in)	(41.02 in)

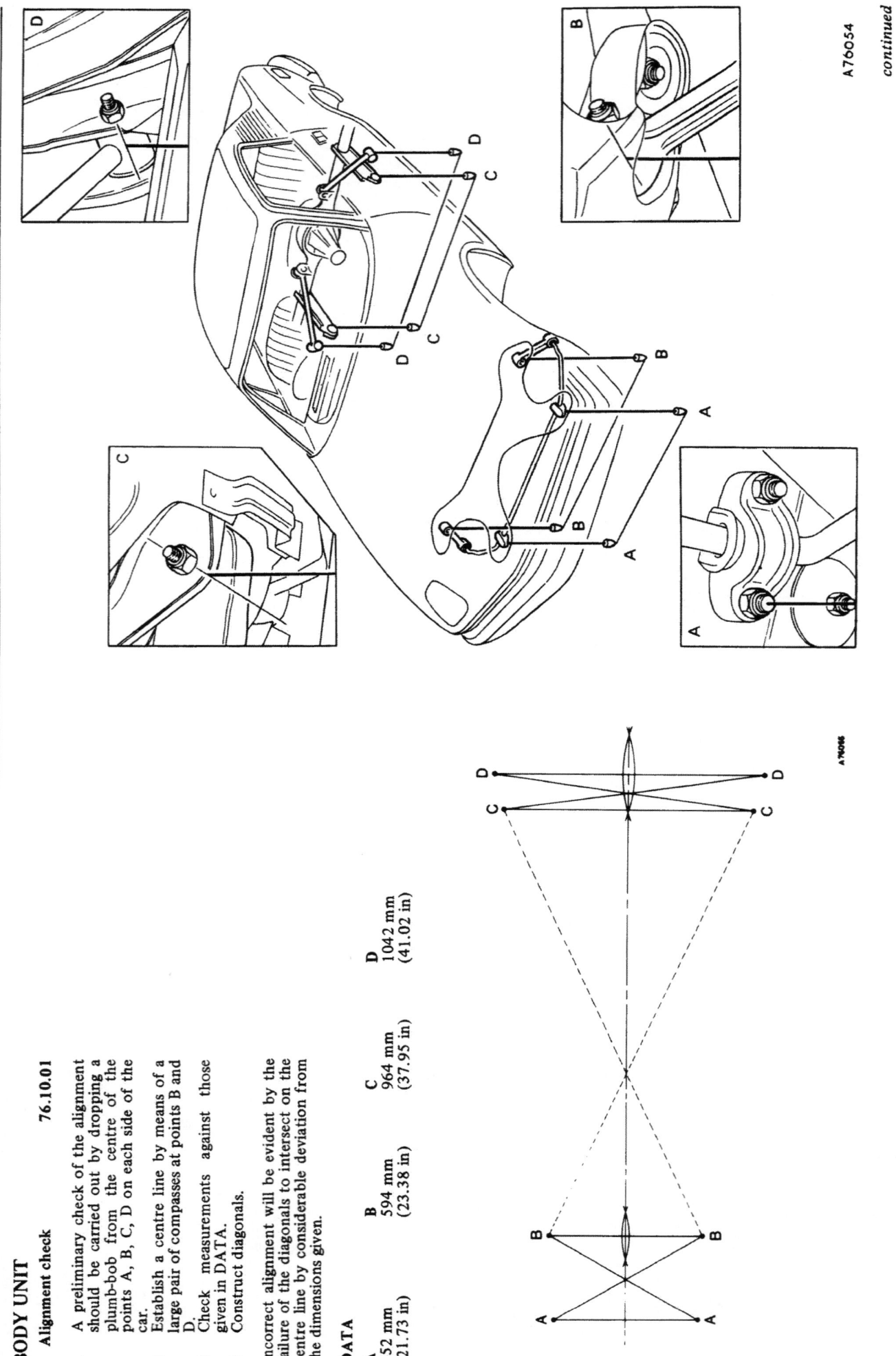

A76054

continued

A76066

Vertical alignment

The dimensions given below are for cars in showroom condition, unladen and without fuel. It should be noted that the important point is the relative positions of the vertical datum points to each other and not their actual height from the wheel hub centres.

Code	Dimension	Location
A	346 mm (13.62 in)	Anti-roll bar front mounting to suspension pod cap
B	141,5 mm (5.57 in)	Rear suspension arm mounting to radius rod mounting
a	33 mm (1.29 in)	Anti-roll bar clamp front fixing bolt to lower link
b	361 mm (14.20 in)	Top of front wheel arch to wheel hub centre — Europe — 4 speed gearbox
	356 mm (14.02 in)	Top of front wheel arch to wheel hub centre — Europe — 5 speed gearbox
	353 mm (13.90 in)	Top of front wheel arch to wheel hub centre — Europe — Automatic transmission
	354 mm (13.96 in)	Top of front wheel arch to wheel hub centre — USA — 4 speed gearbox
	350 mm (13.78 in)	Top of front wheel arch to wheel hub centre — USA — 5 speed gearbox
	347 mm (13.67 in)	Top of front wheel arch to wheel hub centre — USA — Automatic transmission
	356 mm (14.02 in)	Top of front wheel arch to wheel hub centre — USA — 4 speed gearbox — air conditioning
	352 mm (13.88 in)	Top of front wheel arch to wheel hub centre — USA — 5 speed gearbox — air conditioning
	349 mm (13.75 in)	Top of front wheel arch to wheel hub centre — USA — Automatic transmission — air conditioning

Code	Dimension	Location
c	571 mm (22.48 in)	Lower link to front suspension pod cap
d	476.5 mm (18.75 in)	Front suspension pod cap to datum line
e	338 mm (13.3 in)	Top of wheel arch to datum line
f	136 mm (5.35 in)	Rear suspension arm mounting to radius rod mounting
g	95 mm (3.74 in)	Rear suspension arm mounting to datum line
h	319 mm (12.56 in)	Top of rear wheel arch to datum line
j	348 mm (13.71 in)	Top of rear wheel arch to wheel hub centre — Europe — 4 speed gearbox
	350 mm (13.80 in)	Top of rear wheel arch to wheel hub centre — Europe — 5 speed gearbox
	345 mm (13.60 in)	Top of rear wheel arch to wheel hub centre — Europe — Automatic transmission
	346 mm (13.63 in)	Top of rear wheel arch to wheel hub centre — USA — 4 speed gearbox
	348 mm (13.72 in)	Top of rear wheel arch to wheel hub centre — USA — 5 speed gearbox
	343 mm (13.52 in)	Top of rear wheel arch to wheel hub centre — USA — Automatic transmission
Z-Z		Datum line

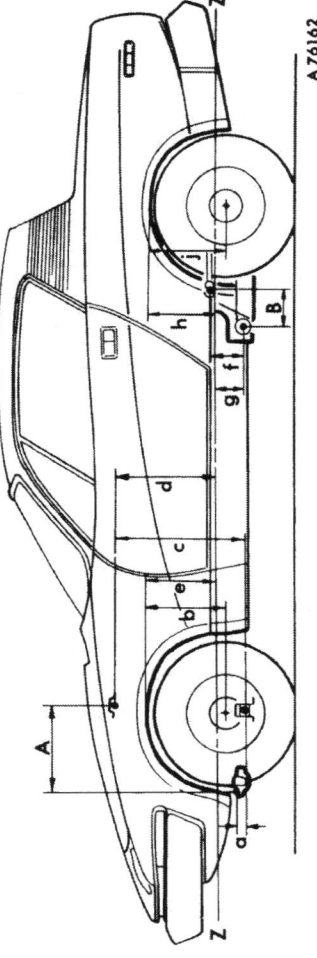

A 76162

BODY UNIT

Alignment check 76.10.01

(Using Churchill 700 or 707 system)

Whilst severe underframe damage is readily detected, less serious damage may cause distortion that is not visually apparent.
If steering or suspension checks indicate a fault which cannot be attributed to anything other than underframe distortion, initial checking should be carried out to determine the area and extent of distortion.

Initial check

1 Clip the location tape to the right-hand side of the jig and make a chalk mark on the floor at each required location for initial checking.
2 Remove the tape to avoid damage.
3 Position the car centrally over the jig with the front wheel centres approximately 76 cm (30 in) from the front of the jig.

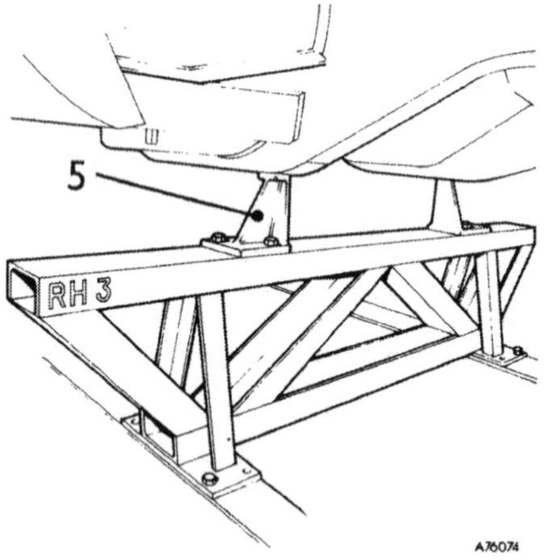

4 Raise the front of the car and fit transverse member number 3 to the jig with the rear mounting holes at tape position 12/7.
5 Fit brackets S700–39/1 (LH) and S700–39/2 (RH) to the transverse member, locating the inner bolt in hole J.

6 Lower the car to locate the bracket pegs in the front tooling holes in the floor side-member.
7 Raise the rear of the car by jacking under the differential.

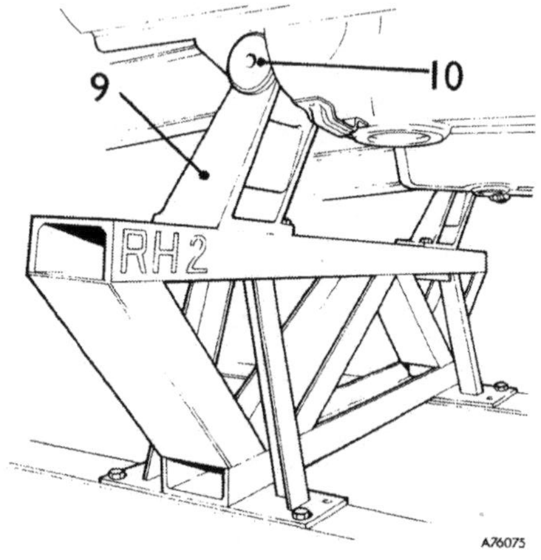

8 Fit transverse member number 2.
9 Fit brackets S700-29/1 (LH) and S700-29/2 (RH) to the transverse member, locating the inner bracket bolts in holes 'L'.
NOTE: These holes are not marked on Churchill 700 systems. Distance across bolt centres should be 819 mm (32.25 in).
10 Lower the car and fit the two bushes S700-29/4 over the trailing arm hanger bolt heads.
11 Fit transverse member number 4 with the rear mounting holes at tape position 18.

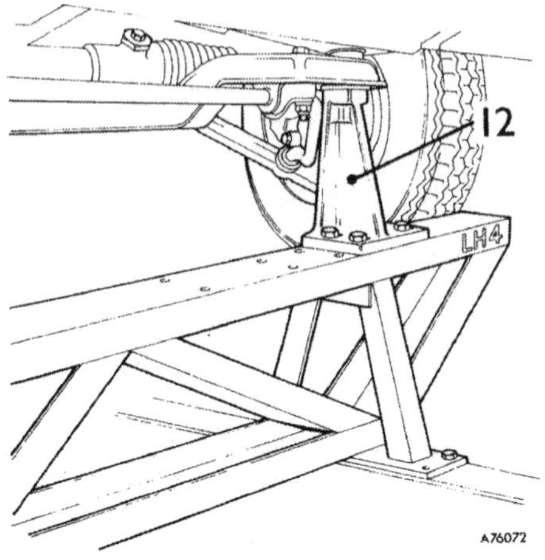

12 Fit bracket S700-401/1 (LH) and S700-401/2 (RH) locating the inner bracket bolts in holes 'G'.

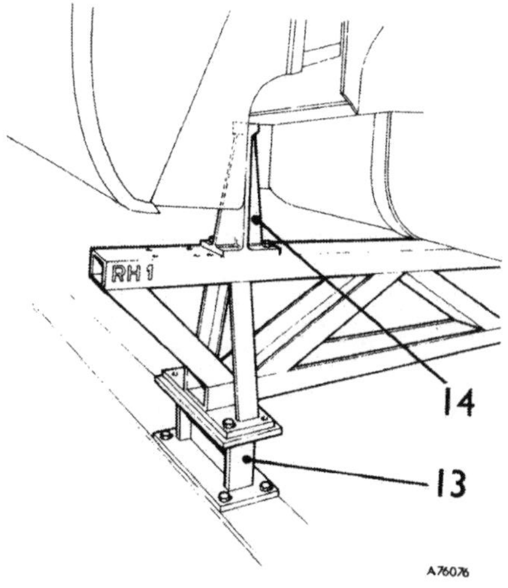

13 Fit risers S700-2B and transverse member number 1 with the rear mounting holes at tape position 4/28.
14 Fit brackets S700-19 (LH) and S700-19/2 (RH) locating the outer bracket bolts in holes 'B'.
NOTE: These holes are not marked on Churchill 700 systems. Distance across bolt centres should be 952 mm (37-50 in).

The following operations are only necessary if repairs are required.

Repair Stage

It may not be necessary to fit the full set of repair brackets. If damage is confined to the front end of the car, repair brackets can be fitted at the front and the initial check brackets retained at the rear or vice-versa in the case of rear end damage.
Where it is necessary to remove sub-assemblies before fitting repair brackets, reference should be made to the appropriate workshop manual section.
For front end repairs, the transverse members and brackets used for initial checking are used again in their original positions with the following additions:-

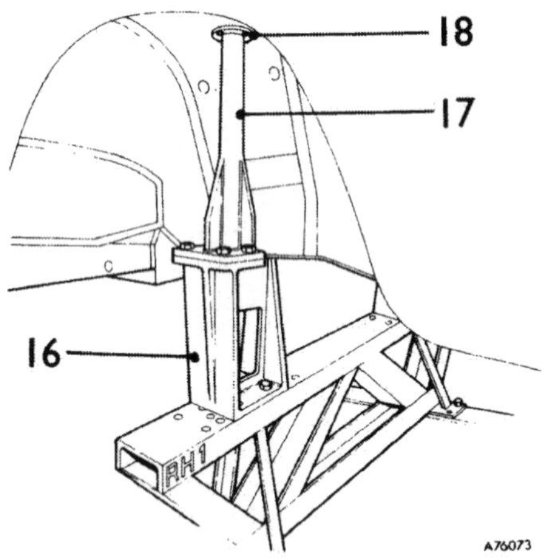

15 Fit transverse member number 1 with the rear mounting holes at tape position 15.

16 Fit risers S700-17/1 (LH) and S700-17/2 (RH).

17 Fit brackets S700-18/1 (LH) and S700-18/2 (RH) to the risers, using the eight screws supplied.

18 Secure the brackets to the spring turrets, using the damper attachment nuts.

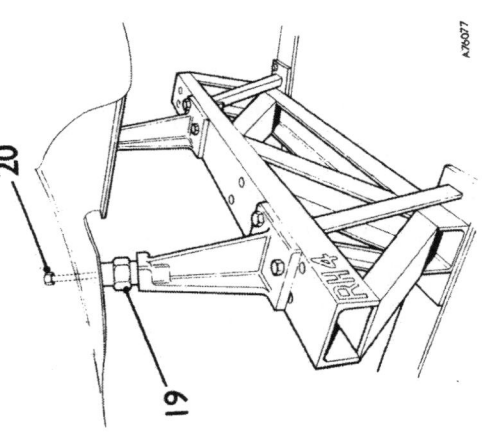

A76078

For rear end repairs:-

21 Remove the two bushes S700-29/4 and the two bolts and nuts from the trailing arm hangers. Refit the bushes and fit the two pins S700-29/5.

A76077

19 Fit adaptors S700-401/3 into brackets S700-401/1 (LH) and S700-401/2 (RH).

20 Install the two original bolts through the sub-frame front mounting holes in the longitudinal members and screw them into the adaptors.

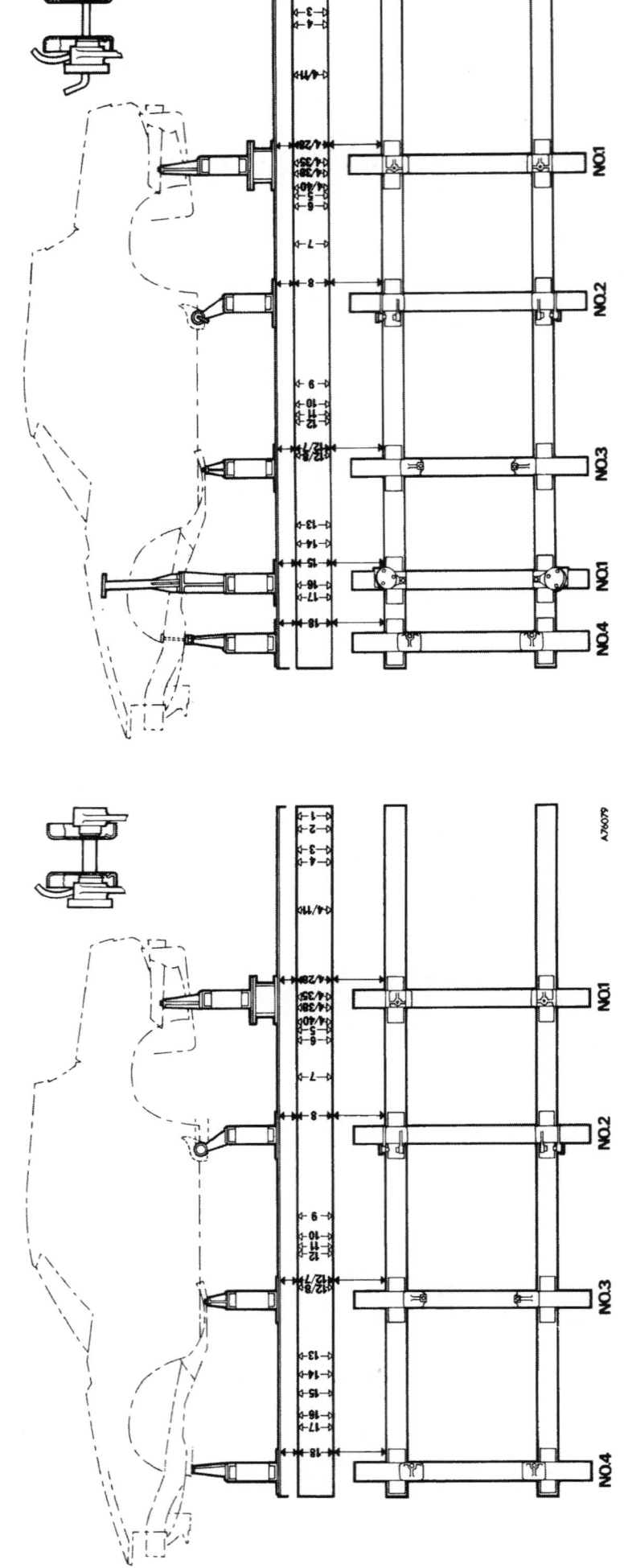

Transverse member locations for repair

Transverse member locations for initial check

SUB FRAME

Alignment check

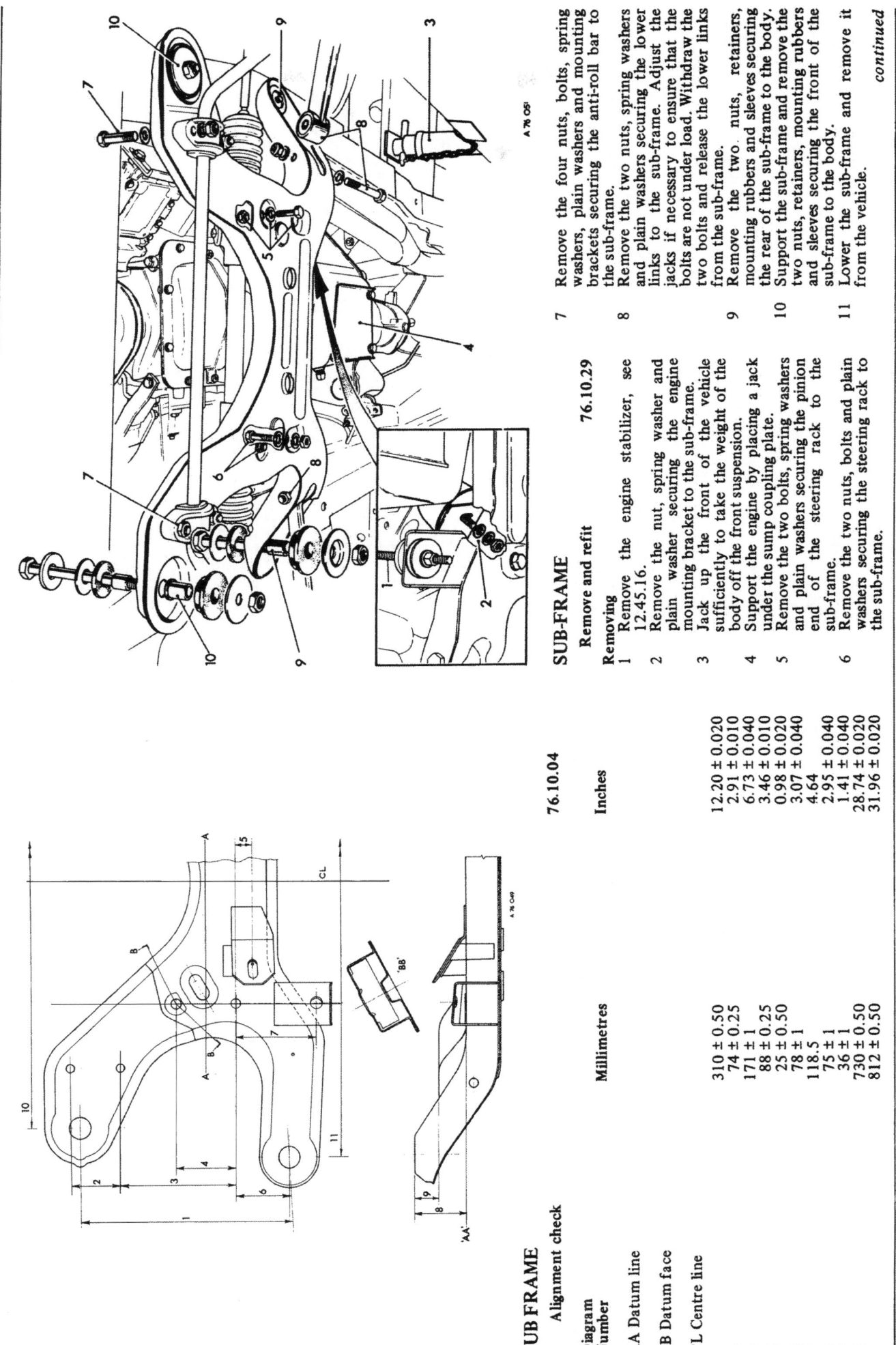

A 76 049

Diagram Number	Millimetres	Inches
AA Datum line		
BB Datum face		
CL Centre line		
1	310 ± 0.50	12.20 ± 0.020
2	74 ± 0.25	2.91 ± 0.010
3	171 ± 1	6.73 ± 0.040
4	88 ± 0.25	3.46 ± 0.010
5	25 ± 0.50	0.98 ± 0.020
6	78 ± 1	3.07 ± 0.040
7	118.5	4.64
8	75 ± 1	2.95 ± 0.040
9	36 ± 1	1.41 ± 0.040
10	730 ± 0.50	28.74 ± 0.020
11	812 ± 0.50	31.96 ± 0.020

76.10.04

A 76 05¹

SUB-FRAME

Remove and refit   76.10.29

Removing

1 Remove the engine stabilizer, see 12.45.16.

2 Remove the nut, spring washer and plain washer securing the engine mounting bracket to the sub-frame.

3 Jack up the front of the vehicle sufficiently to take the weight of the body off the front suspension.

4 Support the engine by placing a jack under the sump coupling plate.

5 Remove the two bolts, spring washers and plain washers securing the pinion end of the steering rack to the sub-frame.

6 Remove the two nuts, bolts and plain washers securing the steering rack to the sub-frame.

7 Remove the four nuts, bolts, spring washers, plain washers and mounting brackets securing the anti-roll bar to the sub-frame.

8 Remove the two nuts, spring washers and plain washers securing the lower links to the sub-frame. Adjust the jacks if necessary to ensure that the bolts are not under load. Withdraw the two bolts and release the lower links from the sub-frame.

9 Remove the two nuts, retainers, mounting rubbers and sleeves securing the rear of the sub-frame to the body.

10 Support the sub-frame and remove the two nuts, retainers, mounting rubbers and sleeves securing the front of the sub-frame to the body.

11 Lower the sub-frame and remove it from the vehicle.

continued

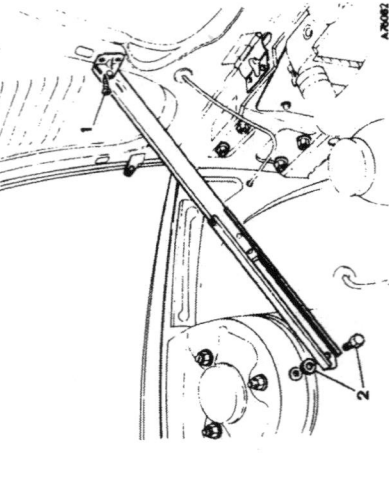

A2082

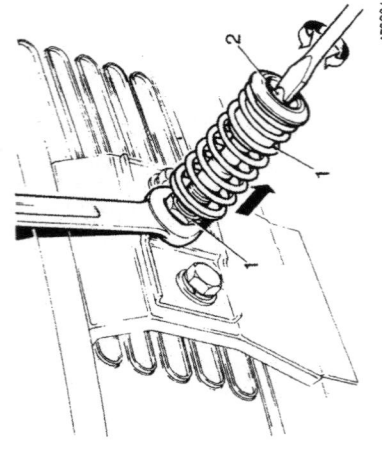

A76004

Refitting

12 Position the sub-frame on the mounting bolts ensuring that the four mounting rubbers and washers are correctly positioned between sub-frame and body.
13 Tighten the nuts 10 and 9 to torque figures given in 'TORQUE WRENCH SETTINGS'.
14 Reverse instructions 2 to 8.
15 Refit and adjust the engine tie-rod, see 12.45.16.

REAR QUARTER TRIM PAD 76.13.12

Remove and refit

Removing

1 Pull the weatherstrip away from the door aperture in the area of the trim pad.
2 Carefully pull the trim pad edging away from the body flange.
3 Remove the cap, screw and retainer.
4 Prise off the trim pad—5 clips.

Refitting

5 Reverse instructions 1 to 4, using Dunlop SP758 adhesive on the mating surfaces of trim pad edging and body flange.

REAR COMPARTMENT TRIM PAD 76.13.20

Remove and refit

Removing

1 Move both seats and seat squabs to the fully forward position.
2 Open the rear console lid and remove the two screws and plain washers securing the console and trim pad to the body.
3 Remove the two screws and cup washers securing the trim pad to the body.
4 Remove the four screws and cup washers securing the parcel tray and the trim pad to the body.
5 Carefully raise the forward edge of the parcel tray, raise the trim pad clear of the console and remove it from the car.

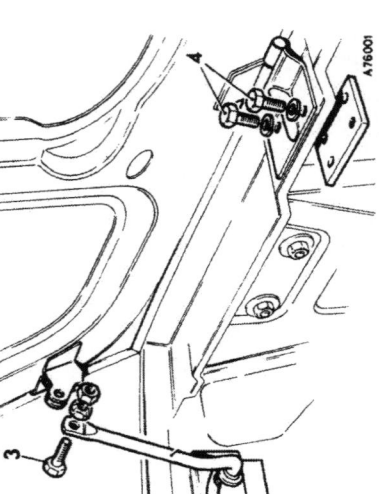

A76001

BONNET

Remove and refit 76.16.01

Removing

1 Pull the tubing from the screenwasher pump; attach a suitable length of string to the end of the tubing to facilitate refitting, and pull the tubing through the holes in the inner wheel arch.
2 Mark the hinge positions on the body.
3 Support the bonnet and remove the single bolt and nut (earlier models) or two screws and spring washers (later models) securing the stay to the bonnet.
4 Remove the four bolts securing the hinges to the adjuster plates and lift off the bonnet.

Refitting

5 Reverse instructions 1 to 4, adjusting if necessary to ensure correct alignment before fully tightening bolts 4.

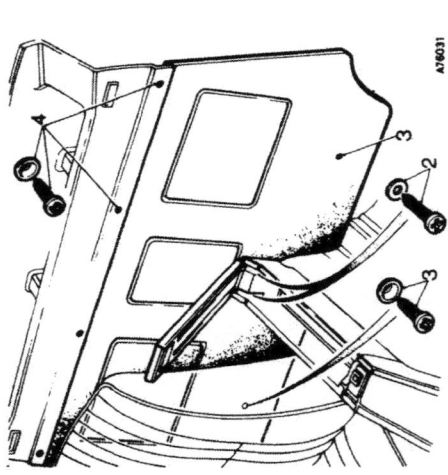

A76031

BONNET CATCH

Adjust 76.16.20

To ensure positive locking and eliminate free movement at the closing face, adjust the bonnet catch as follows:

1 Pull back the spring and slacken the locknut at the base of the shaft.
2 Using a screwdriver, screw the shaft in or out as required.
3 Retighten the locknut.
4 Check the bonnet closing action and repeat instructions 1 to 3 if necessary.

Refitting

3 Reverse instructions 1 and 2.

BONNET STAY

Remove and refit 76.16.14

Removing

1 Support the bonnet and remove the single bolt and nut (earlier models) or two screws and spring washers (later models) securing the stay to the bonnet.
2 Disengage the lower end of the stay from the body (earlier models) or remove the bolt and spring washer securing the lower end of the stay to the body (later models).

Refitting

6 Reverse instructions 1 to 5.

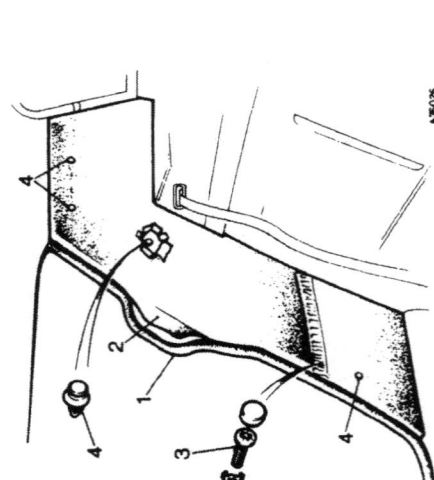

A76026

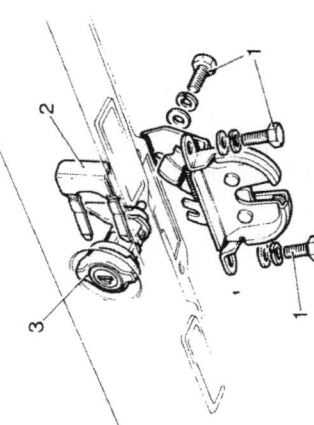

A76008

Refitting
3 Reverse instructions 1 and 2 ensuring correct alignment in the vertical plane before fully tightening bolts 2.

LUGGAGE COMPARTMENT LOCK 76.19.11

Remove and refit

Removing
1 Remove the three bolts, spring washers and plain washers and lift off the latch.
2 Pull the spring clip to one side to disengage it from the lock.
3 Carefully withdraw the lock and gasket.

A76009

Refitting
4 Reverse instructions 1 to 3.

A76010

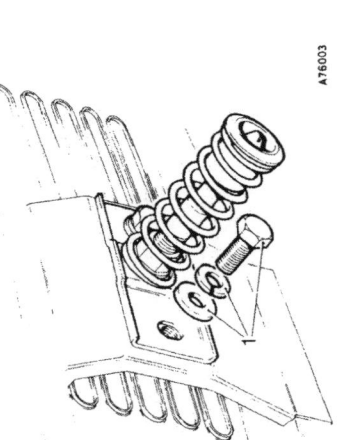

LUGGAGE COMPARTMENT LID 76.19.01

Remove and refit

Removing
1 Mark the hinge positions on the lid.
2 Disconnect the two rear number plate lamp leads from the connector at the R.H. side of the luggage compartment.
3 *Earlier Models:* Support the lid and remove the two bolts securing the stay to the lid.
4 Remove the four bolts, spring washers and plain washers securing the lid to the hinges and lift off the lid.

Refitting
5 Reverse instructions 1 to 3, ensuring correct alignment of the lid in the horizontal plane before fully tightening bolts 4.

LUGGAGE COMPARTMENT LID HINGES 76.19.07

Remove and refit

Removing
1 a Remove the luggage compartment lid, see 76.19.01.
  b *Later models only:* Remove one bolt, nut and washers to release the gas strut from each hinge.
2 Remove (two each side) the four bolts, spring washers and plain washers securing the hinges to the body and lift off the hinges.

Refitting
2 Refit in reverse order and adjust if necessary, see 76.16.20.

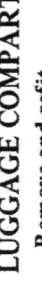

A76006

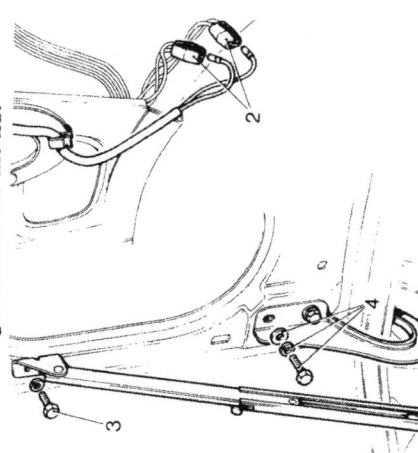

BONNET CATCH 76.16.34

Remove and refit

Removing
1 Remove the two bolts, spring washers and plain washers. Remove the catch from the bonnet.

Refitting
5 Reverse instructions 1 to 4, ensuring that the lock release lever is not pre-loaded by the cable.

A76003

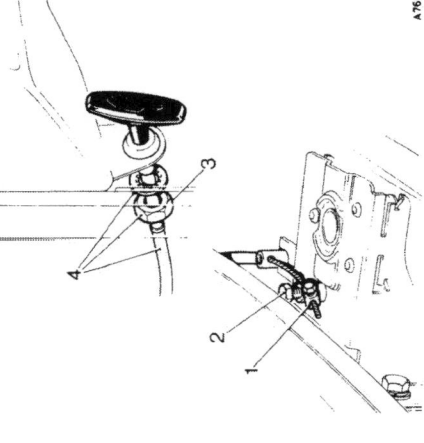

A76005

BONNET LOCK 76.16.21

Remove and refit

Removing
1 Remove the trunnion from the cable.
2 Slacken the pinch bolt and detach the cable from the lock.
3 Remove the four bolts, spring washers and plain washers securing the lock to the body.

Refitting
4 Reverse instructions 1 to 3.

BONNET RELEASE CABLE 76.16.29

Remove and refit

Removing
1 Remove the trunnion from the cable.
2 Slacken the pinch bolt and detach the cable from the lock.
3 Unscrew the nut securing the outer cable to the bracket beneath the facia.
4 Withdraw the cable through the grommet on the bulkhead and collect the nut and shakeproof washer.
CAUTION: Do not close the bonnet with the cable removed or loose.

LUGGAGE COMPARTMENT LOCK STRIKER   76.19.12

Remove and refit

Removing
1 Pull the weatherstrip away from the body panel in the area of the striker.
2 Mark the position of the striker bolts on the body panel.
3 Remove the three bolts, spring washers and plain washers.
4 Withdraw the striker from the body panel aperture.

Refitting
5 Reverse instructions 1 to 4, adjusting the striker in the vertical plane if necessary, before fully tightening bolts 3.

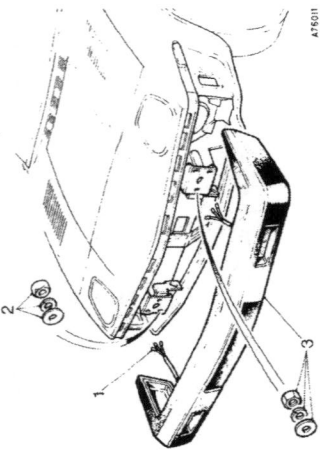

BUMPER—FRONT   76.22.08

Remove and refit

Removing
1 Disconnect the six snap connectors from the parking and flasher lamp leads.
2 Remove the outer four nuts, spring washers and plain washers.
3 Support the bumper and remove the remaining two nuts, spring washers and plain washers. Lift off the bumper.

CONSOLE ASSEMBLY   76.25.01

Remove and refit

Removing
1 Raise the handgrip lever and pull off the grip.
2 Unscrew the gear lever knob.
3 Remove the two screws and lift off the handbrake lever surround trim panel.
4 Prise off the gear lever gaiter—4 fasteners.
5 Remove the two screws and plain washers securing the front console to the transmission tunnel.

Refitting
4 Reverse instructions 1 to 3.

BUMPER—REAR   76.22.15

Remove and refit

Removing
1 Remove the four nuts, spring washers and plain washers securing the side support brackets to the bumpers.
2 Remove the three nuts, spring washers and plain washers and lift off the handling brackets. — U.S.A. models.
3 Support the bumper and remove the remaining two nuts, spring washers and plain washers. Lift off the bumper.

7 Raise the lid/armrest and remove the two screws securing the catch to the consoles. Lift off the catch and the front console.
8 Remove the two screws and plain washers securing the rear console to the rear parcel shelf and body—lift off the rear console.

Refitting
9 Reverse instructions 1 to 8.

CONTROL COWL   76.25.03

Remove and refit

Removing
1 Remove the console assembly, see 76.25.01.
2 Pull the four knobs from the heating and ventilation control levers.
3 Remove the two screws securing the cowl to the control levers.
4 Remove the two screws securing the control illumination panel to the cowl.
5 Remove the screw securing the cowl to the bracket beneath the fascia.
6 Remove the two screws securing the cowl to the bracket on the transmission tunnel.

continued

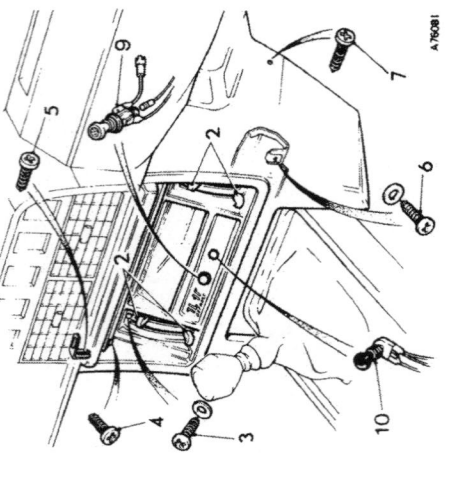

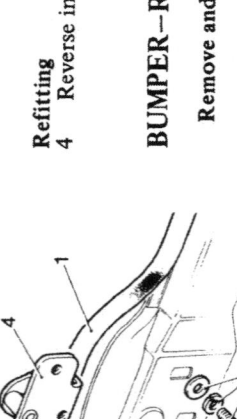

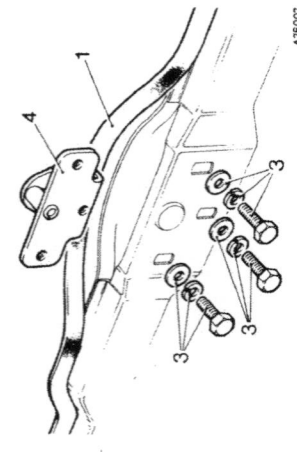

6 Remove the two screws and plain washers securing the consoles and bridge plate to the floor and lift off the bridge plate.

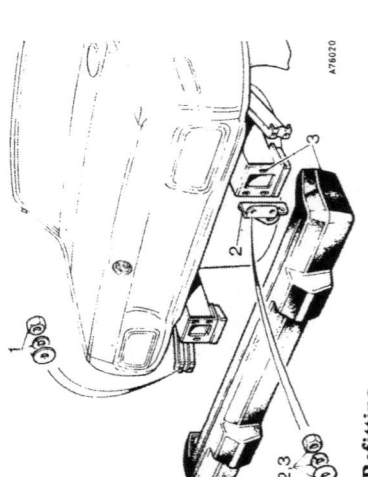

Refitting
4 Reverse instructions 1 to 3.

7 Remove the two screws securing the cowl to the body.
8 Engage top gear and pull the cowl clear of the heater.
9 Disconnect the bulbholder and two leads from the cigar lighter.
10 Disconnect the two lucar connectors from the rheostat.
11 Remove the cowl from the vehicle.

Refitting
12 Reverse instructions 1 to 11.

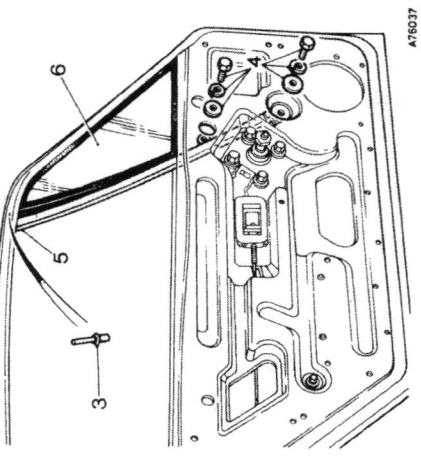

A76037

DOOR

Remove and refit   76.28.01

Removing
1 Isolate the battery.
2 Remove the door trim pad, see 76.34.01.
3 Support the door and remove the six nuts, spring washers, plain washers and two adjuster plates securing it to the hinges. Lift off the door.

Refitting
4 Reverse instructions 1 to 3. Check the door closing action and alignment and adjust if necessary before fully tightening nuts 3.

DOOR HINGE – FRONT UPPER

Remove and refit   70.28.42

The body half of the hinge is welded to the 'A' post and will only be renewed during extensive body repair.
This operation renews the door half of the hinge and the two hinge pins.
To ensure satisfactory retention of the serrated pins, the door half of the hinge and the two hinge pins should always be fitted as an all new set.

Removing
1 Using a chisel under the pin head, drive the upper pin upwards until the serrations are clear of the assembly.
2 Drive the lower pin downwards until the serrations are clear of the assembly.
3 Remove the door, see 76.28.01.
4 Remove the two pins.
5 Remove the door half of the hinge and collect up the spring.

Refitting
6 Apply grease to the bore of the body half of the hinge.
7 Position the spring and the door half of the hinge such that the door adopts its half open position.
8 Compress the spring by hand and fit the two pins finger-tight.
9 Engage the pin serrations either by using a hammer and drift or by pressing both pins in together using a suitable clamp.
10 Fit the door, see 76.28.01.

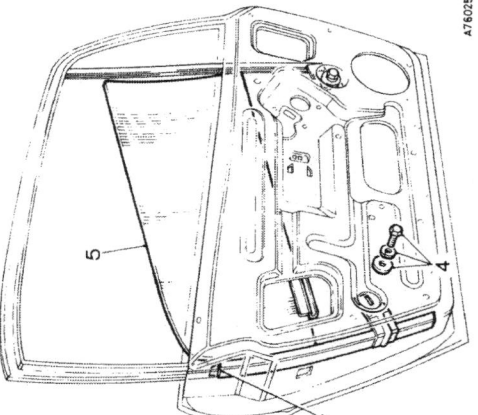

A76025

DOOR GLASS

Remove and refit   76.31.01

Removing
1 Remove the door trim pad, see 76.31.45.
2 Remove the door lock remote control, see 76.37.31
3 Remove the door glass regulator, see 76.31.45.

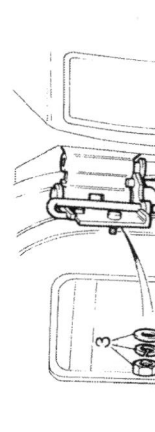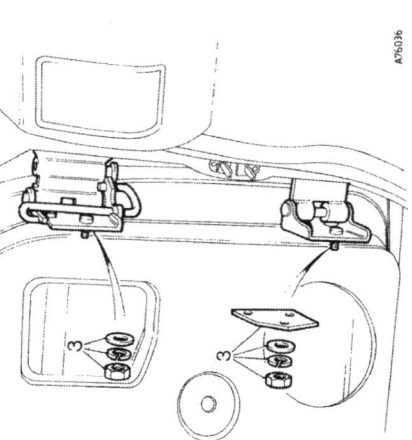

A76036

4 Remove the bolt, spring washer and plain washer securing the rear glass channel to the door. Detach the insert from the channel and carefully withdraw the channel and weather curtain.
5 Turn the glass anti-clockwise until it can be withdrawn through the door aperture. Lift out the glass taking care to avoid scratching it on the seal clips.

Refitting
6 Reverse instructions 1 to 5, ensuring that the glass channel is positioned to enable the glass to be moved freely.

DOOR QUARTER LIGHT

Remove and refit   76.31.29

Removing
1 Fully lower the door glass.
2 Remove the door trim pad, see 76.34.01.
3 Drill out the rivet securing the top of the glass channel to the door.
4 Remove the two bolts and plain washers securing the front glass channel to the door.
5 Pull the top of the glass channel away from the quarter light weatherstrip.

6 Carefully ease the quarter light and weatherstrip rearwards and upwards and remove them from the door.

Refitting
7 Reverse instructions 1 to 6, ensuring that the weatherstrips are correctly positioned.

DOOR GLASS REGULATOR

Remove and refit   76.31.45

Removing
1 Remove the door trim pad, see 76.34.01.
2 Remove the door lock remote control, see 76.37.31.
3 Refit the regulator handle, fully raise the glass and then turn the handle back (anti-clockwise) slightly to ensure that the regulator mounting bolts are not under load. Remove the handle.
4 Support the glass.
5 Remove the four bolts, spring washers and plain washers securing the regulator to the door.
6 Carefully push the regulator handle shaft inside the door aperture and slide the regulator assembly towards the rear of the door, lowering the glass by hand sufficiently to enable the rollers to be disengaged from the glass channels and the channel on the door interior.

continued

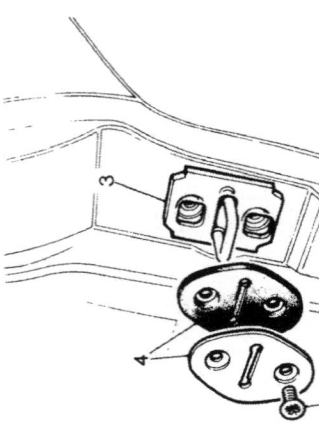

A76021

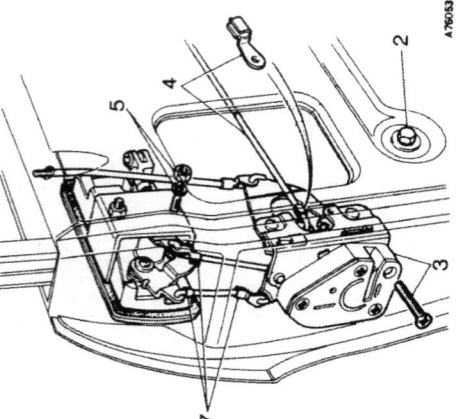

A76053

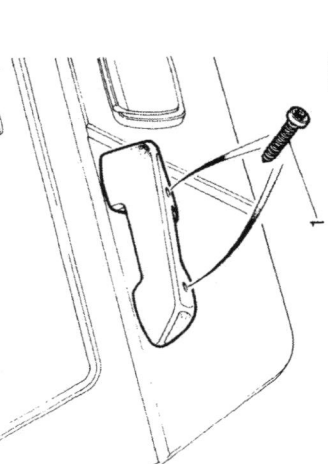

A76012

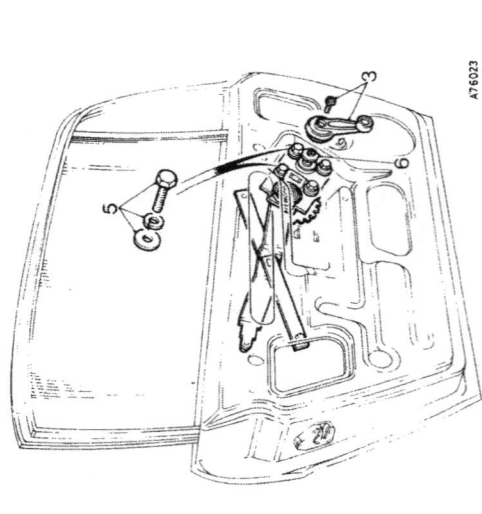

A76023

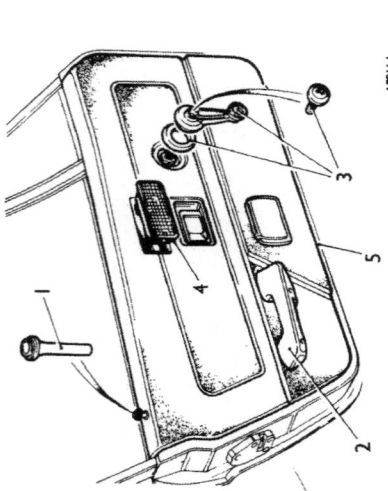

A76104

2 Remove the arm-rest, see 76.34.23.
3 Remove the screw securing the regulator handle. Lift off the handle and bezel.
4 Remove the map/courtesy lamp, see 86.45.10.
5 Using a large screwdriver, carefully prise out the nine clips securing the trim pad to the door.
6 Carefully lift the trim pad over the plunger rod.
7 Later models: Disconnect the two speaker leads.

Refitting
8 Reverse instructions 1 to 7.

7 Manoeuvre the regulator out of the door through the lower aperture, taking care to avoid scratching the glass.

Refitting
8 Reverse instructions 1 to 7.

DOOR TRIM PAD 76.34.01
Remove and refit

Removing
1 Unscrew and remove the plunger knob.

---

3 Withdraw the striker from inside the 'B' post.
4 Lift off the outer striker plate and the seal.

Refitting
5 Reverse instructions 1 to 4.

4 Remove the retaining clip and detach the remote control rod from the lock.
5 Remove the two nuts and spring washers securing the clamp bracket to the outside handle.
6 Manoeuvre the outside handle and seal, together with the door lock, through the handle aperture and out of the door.
CAUTION: Care must be taken to avoid straining locks or linkages.
7 Remove the retaining clips from the door handle and private lock control rods and separate the outside handle and door lock.

Refitting
8 Reverse instructions 1 to 7 ensuring that the plunger rod is correctly located before securing the lock to the door.

DOOR ARM-REST 76.34.23
Remove and refit

The door arm-rest is secured to the door shell by two screws.

DOOR LOCK 76.37.12
Remove and refit

Removing
1 Remove the door trim pad, see 76.34.01.
2 Remove the bolt, spring washer and plain washer securing the rear glass channel to the door. Detach the insert from the channel and carefully withdraw the channel and weather curtain.
3 Remove the four screws securing the lock assembly to the door and lift off the disc latch.

DOOR LOCK STRIKER 76.37.27
Adjust
1 Slacken the two screws.
2 Adjust the striker position as necessary to ensure correct door locking action and alignment.
3 Re-tighten the screws.

DOOR LOCK REMOTE CONTROL 76.37.31
Remove and refit

Removing
1 Remove the door trim pad, see 76.34.01.
2 Remove the retaining clip and detach the control rod from the lock.
3 Remove the screw and lift off the escutcheon.
4 Remove the screw and push the control assembly rearwards to disengage it from the door.

DOOR LOCK STRIKER 76.37.23
Remove and refit

Removing
1 Remove the rear quarter trim pad, see 76.13.12.
2 Remove the two screws securing the striker assembly to the 'B' post.

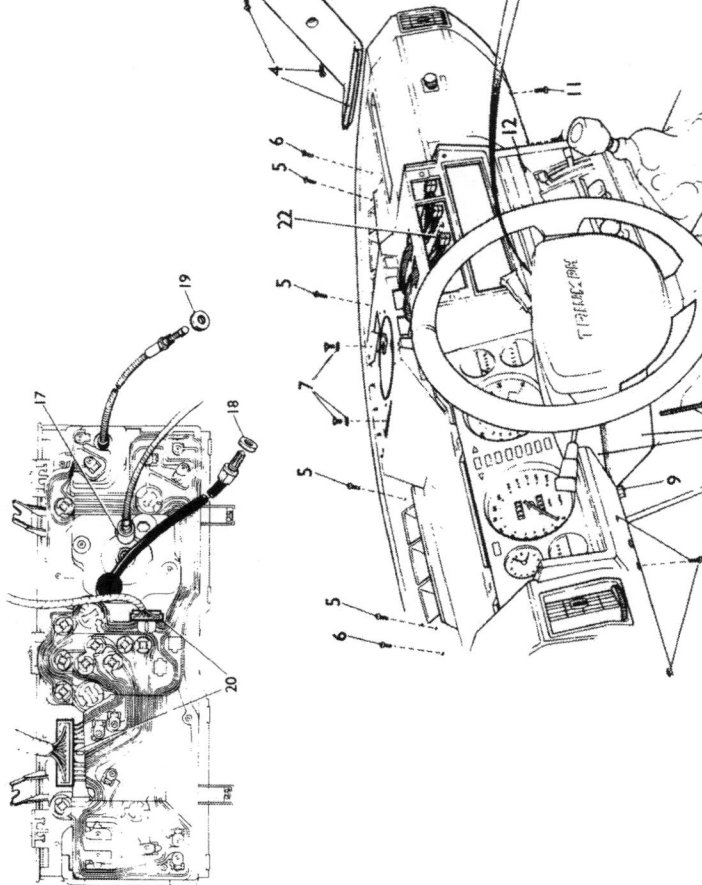

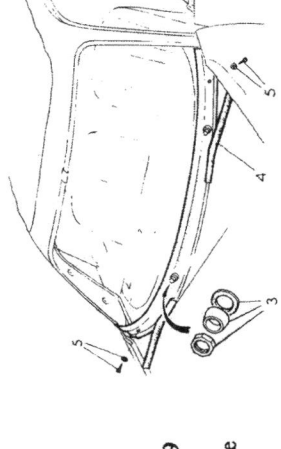

A760 34

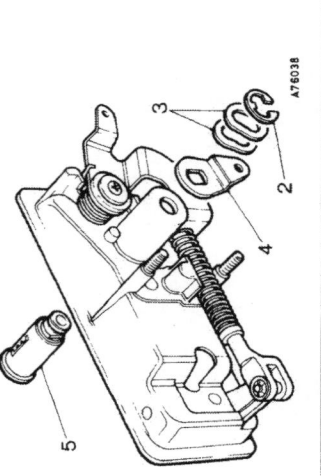

A76024

3 Remove the two spring washers.
4 Remove the locking lever.
5 Push out the lock.

Refitting
6 Reverse instructions 1 to 5.

WINDSCREEN FINISHER–LOWER
Remove and refit   76.43.41

Removing
1 Remove the drivers wiper arm, see 84.15.02.
2 Remove the passengers wiper arm, see 84.15.03.
3 Remove the nut, distance piece and rubber washer from the passenger's side wheelbox spindle.
4 Pull off the two bulkhead weatherstrips.
5 Remove the two screws and plain washers and detach the finisher from the body taking care to avoid scratching the body and windscreen.

5 Withdraw the control assembly from the door.

Refitting
6 Reverse instructions 1 to 5.

DOOR PRIVATE LOCK
Remove and refit   76.37.39

Removing
1 Remove the door outside handle, see 76.58.01.
2 Remove the circlip.

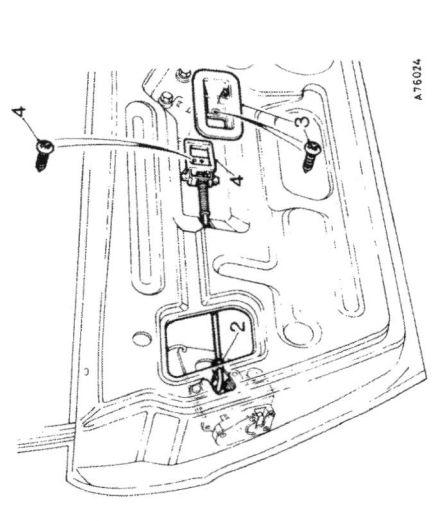

A76038

Refitting
6 Reverse instructions 1 to 5.

FASCIA
Remove and refit   76.46.01

Removing
1 Isolate the battery.
2 Remove the instrument cowl, see 76.46.17.
3 Remove the fascia switch panel, see 86.65.66, noting the positions of the three harness plugs and two switch identification bulb holders for refitting.

4 Remove the two 'A' post trim pads–two screws–together with the fascia corner finishers.
5 Remove the four screws securing the demister vents to the fascia.
6 Remove the two screws securing the fascia to the brackets on the bulkhead
7 Remove the two bolts and plain washers securing the tongues on the fascia to the bulkhead

continued

8 Remove the steering nacelles—two screws.

9 Remove the two shear-head bolts securing the steering column housing to the body. Operation 57.40.01, instructions 6 and 7.

10 Remove the five screws (two each side of the steering column—one below bonnet release) securing the fascia to the support rail beneath the instrument panel.

11 Remove the two screws securing the fascia to the support rail beneath the glovebox.

12 Remove the two screws securing the control illumination panel to the cowl.

13 Remove the screw securing the fascia to the bracket on the control cowl.

14 Remove the lid from the component mounting panel inside the glovebox—two screws.

15 Remove the three screws and two brackets securing the component mounting panel to the fascia.

16 Remove the two screws securing the wiring harness clips to the top of the fascia.

17 Disconnect the cable from the speedometer by depressing the lever to release the catch from the annular groove in the boss.

18 Unscrew the knurled nut and release the speedometer trip reset from the bracket slot.

19 Unscrew the knurled nut and release the clock reset from the bracket slot.

20 Disconnect the two multi-contact harness plugs

21 Ease the fascia rearwards and pull the air hoses from the outer swivelling vents.

22 Carefully manoeuvre the fascia out of the car, simultaneously feeding the three harness plugs and two switch identification bulb holders through the four apertures above the switch panel aperture

Refitting

23 Ensure that the demister vents are correctly positioned.

24 Reverse instructions 1 to 22.

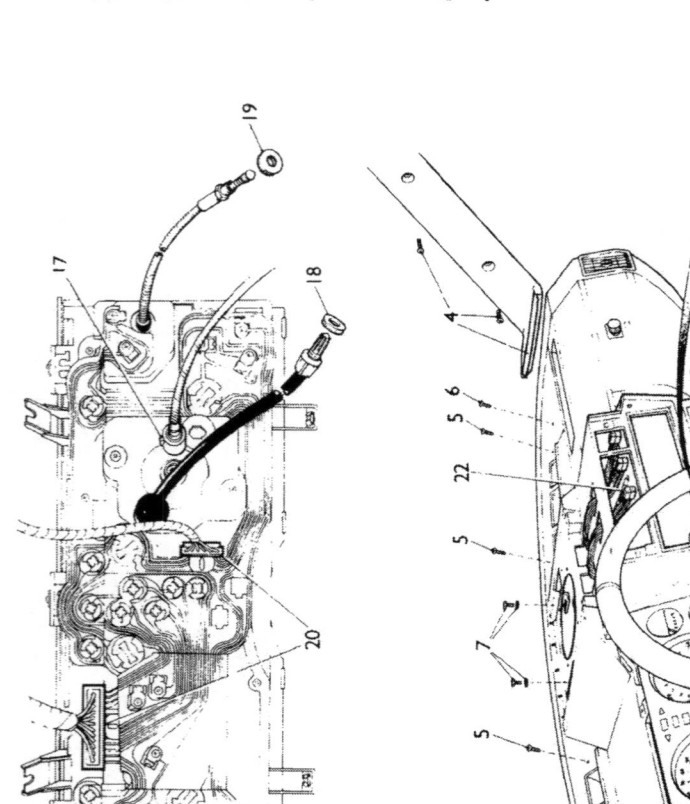

FASCIA INSTRUMENT COWL 76.46.17

Remove and refit

Removing

1 Remove the fascia centre grille, see 76.55.14.

2 Remove the two screws securing the cowl to the fascia above the switch panel.

3 Remove the two screws securing the cowl to the fascia above the instrument panel.

4 Remove the screw securing the underside of the cowl to the bracket above the switch panel.

5 Remove the two screws securing the outer tongues of the cowl to the fascia.

6 Swing the cowl rearwards to disengage the side tongues from the fascia.

7 Remove the cowl.

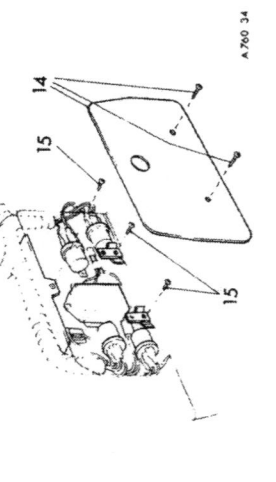
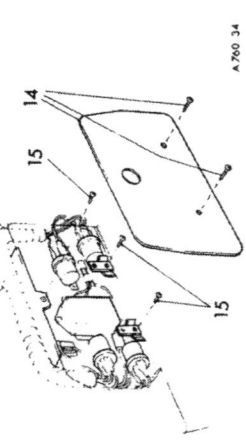

Refitting

8 Reverse instructions 1 to 7.

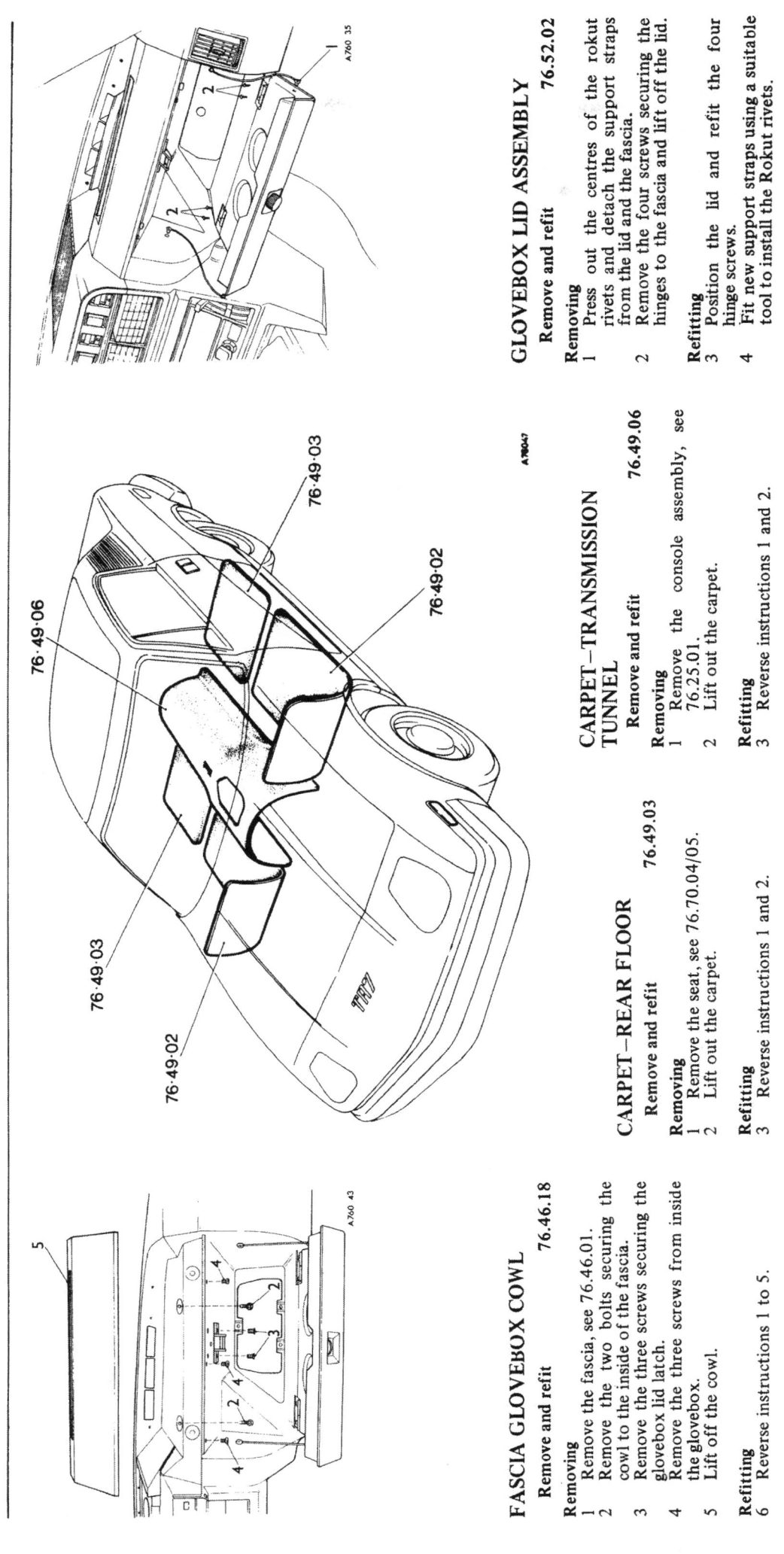

A760 35

A78047

A760 43

FASCIA GLOVEBOX COWL   76.46.18

Remove and refit

Removing

1 Remove the fascia, see 76.46.01.
2 Remove the two bolts securing the cowl to the inside of the fascia.
3 Remove the three screws securing the glovebox lid latch.
4 Remove the three screws from inside the glovebox.
5 Lift off the cowl.

Refitting

6 Reverse instructions 1 to 5.

GLOVEBOX LID ASSEMBLY   76.52.02

Remove and refit

Removing

1 Press out the centres of the rokut rivets and detach the support straps from the lid and the fascia.
2 Remove the four screws securing the hinges to the fascia and lift off the lid.

Refitting

3 Position the lid and refit the four hinge screws.
4 Fit new support straps using a suitable tool to install the Rokut rivets.

CARPET – REAR FLOOR   76.49.03

Remove and refit

Removing

1 Remove the seat, see 76.70.04/05.
2 Lift out the carpet.

Refitting

3 Reverse instructions 1 and 2.

CARPET – TRANSMISSION TUNNEL   76.49.06

Remove and refit

Removing

1 Remove the console assembly, see 76.25.01.
2 Lift out the carpet.

Refitting

3 Reverse instructions 1 and 2.

GLOVEBOX LOCK　　　76.52.08

Remove and refit

Removing

1 Pull off the knob.
2 Remove the two bolts securing the lock to the lid interior and withdraw the lock.
3 Remove the latch if necessary by removing the two screws securing it to the fascia.

Refitting

4 Reverse instructions 1 to 3.

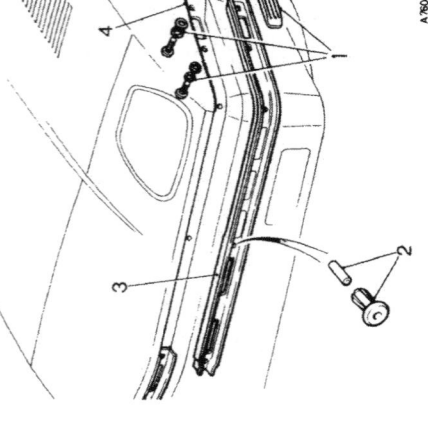

FRONT GRILLE　　　76.55.03

Remove and refit

Removing

1 Remove the blanking plate—two screws.
2 Press out the centres of the three Rokut rivets securing the grille to the body.
3 Remove the grille.

FASCIA CENTRE GRILLE　　　76.55.14

Remove and refit

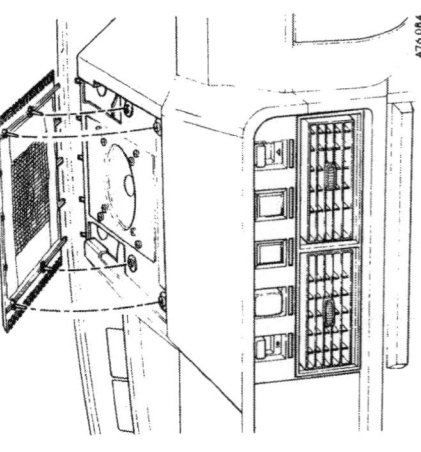

Removing

1 The grille is retained by five forward projections which locate into slots in the fascia and by four plastic spigots which locate into 'snap backs' secured to the fascia.
2 Using a wide bladed screwdriver, carefully prise up the grille adjacent to the spigots.
3 Move the grille rearwards to disengage the forward projections.

Refitting

4 Locate the forward projections into the fascia slots.
5 Locate the spigots into the 'snap backs' and press down into position.

AIR VENT GRILLE　　　76.55.17

Remove and refit

Removing

1 Remove the rear quarter trim pad, see 76.13.12.
2 Remove the four nuts, spring washers, plain washers and two spacers. Note spacer positions for refitting—long spacer on front lower fixing—short spacer on rear lower fixing.
3 Lift off the moulding together with the four 'T' shaped bolts.

Refitting

4 Apply Seelastik to the body area shown.
5 Reverse instructions 1 to 3, using a suitable tool to install the rokut rivets.

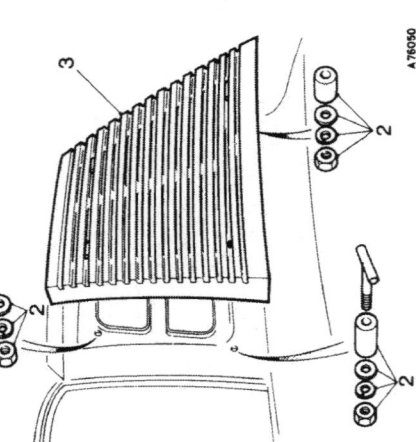

Refitting

4 Reverse instructions 1 to 3.

DOOR OUTSIDE HANDLE　　　76.58.01

Remove and refit

Removing

1 Remove the door trim pad, see 76.34.01.
2 Remove the bolt, spring washer and plain washer securing the rear glass channel to the door. Detach the insert from the channel and carefully withdraw the channel and weather curtain.
3 Remove the four screws securing the lock assembly to the door and lift off the disc latch.
4 Remove the retaining clip and detach the remote control rod from the lock.
5 Remove the two nuts and spring washers securing the clamp bracket to the outside handle.
6 Manoeuvre the outside handle and seal, together with the door lock, through the handle aperture and out of the door.
CAUTION: Care must be taken to avoid straining locks or linkages.
7 Remove the retaining clips from the door handle and private lock control rods and separate the outside handle and door lock.

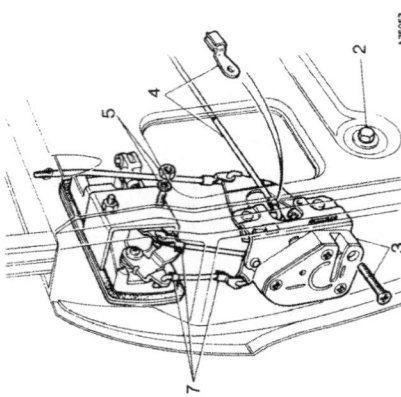

Refitting

8 Reverse instructions 1 to 7 ensuring that the plunger rod is correctly located before securing the lock to the door.

HOOD (USA only)

Remove and refit   76.61.08

Removing

1   Release the front of the hood by turning the levers.

2   Disconnect the eight fasteners securing the sides of the hood to the body.

3   Remove the eight screws securing the rear trimboard to the body and pull the trimboard forwards.

4   Remove the seven nuts securing the hood retaining strip to the rear deck.

5   Remove the two hood linkage covers – three screws each.

6   Lower the hood into the rearmost position ensuring that the hood material does not become damaged.

7   With the aid of an assistant, remove the four bolts, spring washers and plain washers and lift off the hood.

Refitting

8   Install the hood and loosely fit bolts 7.

    Ensure that the hood moves freely, and fully tighten the bolts.

9   Reverse instructions 1 to 6.

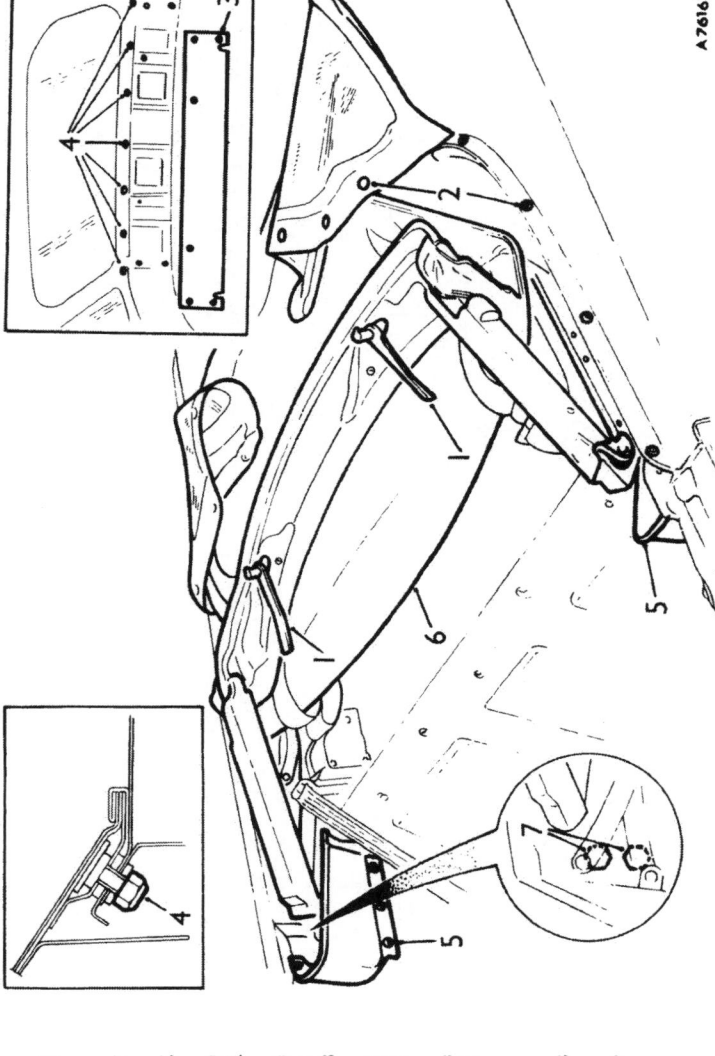

A 76163

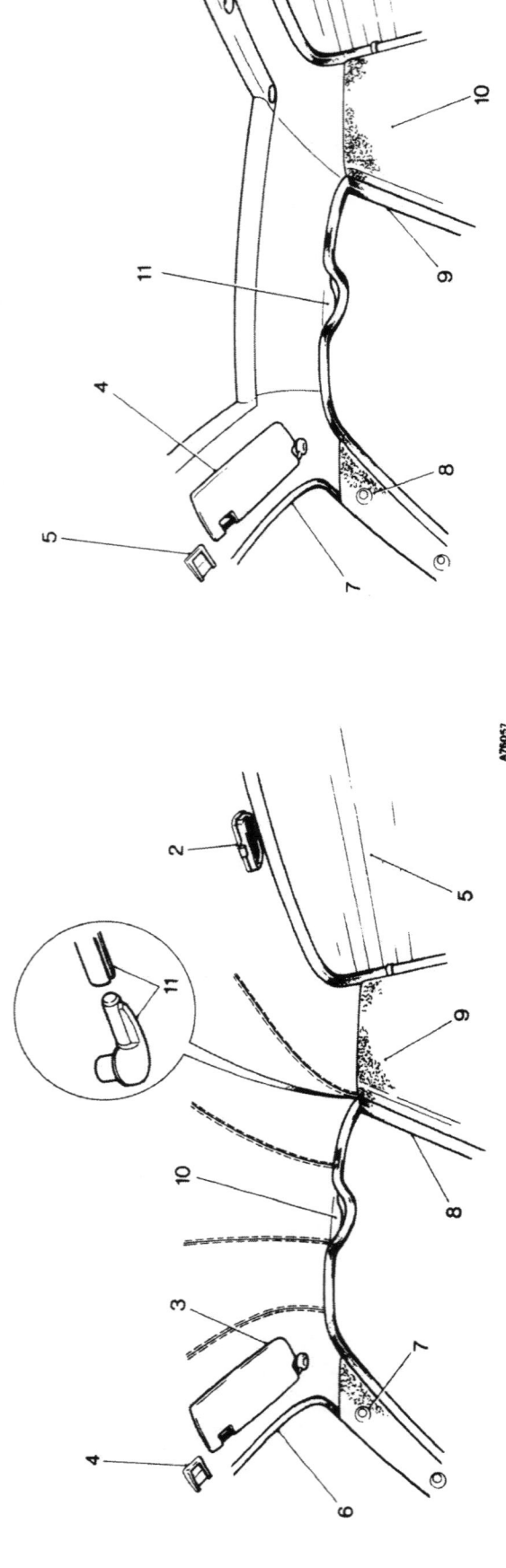

A76042

A76057

HEADLINING

Remove and refit
(Cars without sliding roof)   76.64.01

Removing

1 Isolate the battery.
2 Remove the roof lamp, see 86.45.02.
3 Remove the heated backlight, see 76.81.11.
4 Remove the sun visors and retainers.
5 Remove the interior mirror — two screws.
6 Pull off the windscreen header rail finisher.
7 Remove the two 'A' post trim pads—two screws each.
8 Pull off the door weatherstrips.
9 Remove the rear quarter trim pads, see 76.13.12.
10 Pull the lining edges away from the body flanges.
11 Detach the listing rails and remove the headlining.

Refitting

12 Apply a 2 in border of Dunlop SP 758 adhesive to the headlining, around the roof light aperture, and on the body flanges. Allow ten minutes for the adhesive to become tacky.
13 Reverse instructions 1 to 11, cutting off any excess material, to leave approximately 13 mm (½ in) overlap on all flanges and apertures.

HEADLINING

Remove and refit
(Cars with sliding roof)   76.64.01

Removing

1 Isolate the battery.
2 Remove the sliding roof, see 76.82.01.
3 Remove the roof lamp, see 86.45.02.
4 Remove the heated backlight, see 76.81.11.
5 Remove the sun visors and retainers.
6 Remove the interior mirror — two screws.
7 Pull off the windscreen header rail finisher.
8 Remove the two 'A' post trim pads — two screws each.
9 Pull off the door weatherstrips.
10 Remove the rear quarter trim pads, see 76.13.12.
11 Pull the lining edges away from the body and remove the headlining from the vehicle.

Refitting

12 Apply a 2 in border of Dunlop SP 758 adhesive to the headlining edges and around the roof light and sliding roof apertures. Allow ten minutes for the adhesive to become tacky.
13 Reverse instructions 1 to 11, cutting off any excess material to leave approximately 13 mm (½ in) overlap on all flanges and apertures.

PARCEL TRAY – REAR

Remove and refit   76.67.06

Removing

1 Move both seats and seat squabs to the fully forward position.
2 Remove the two bolts and spring washers securing the seat belt swivel brackets to the seats.
3 Feed the seat belts through the apertures in the parcel tray.
4 Remove the four screws and cup washers securing the parcel tray and rear compartment trim pad to the body.
5 Remove the four screws and cup washers securing the rear of the parcel tray to the body.
6 Carefully manoeuvre the parcel tray upwards and forwards and remove it from the car.

Refitting

7 Install the parcel tray in the car, feeding both seat belts through the apertures before finally positioning it.
8 Reverse instructions 1, 2, and 4 to 6.

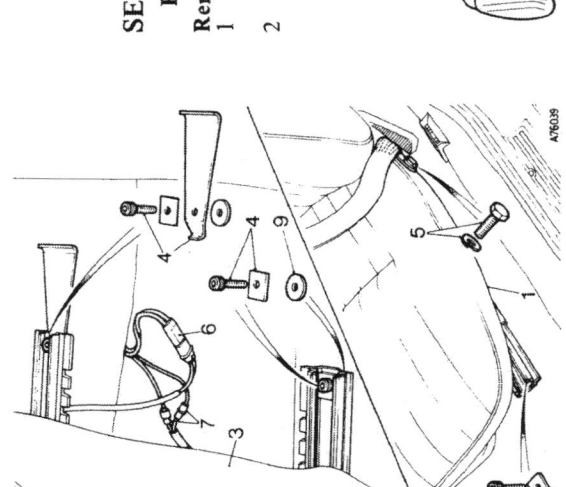

ASHTRAY

Remove and refit   76.67.13

Removing

1 Depress the stubber to release the top edge of the bowl and carefully disengage the retainers on the bottom edge from the surround.
2 Using a small screwdriver carefully prise up the retainers on the surround sufficiently to enable it to be pulled clear of the trim pad.

Refitting

3 Press the surround into the trim pad sufficiently to engage the retainers.
4 Refit the bowl.

SEATS

Remove and refit

Driver's seat   76.70.04
Passenger's seat   76.70.05

Removing

1 Move the seat fully rearwards.
2 Remove the two capscrews (long), and rectangular washers securing the runners to the floor.

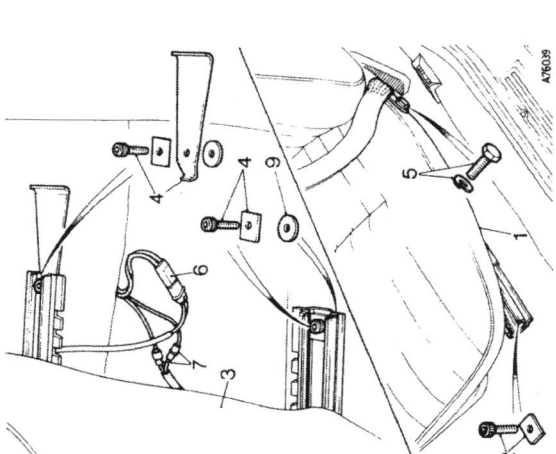

3 Move the seat fully forwards.
4 Remove the two capscrews (short), one rectangular washer and one stop plate securing the seat to the floor.
5 Remove the bolt and spring washer securing the seat belt bracket to the seat.

6 Disconnect the seat belt buckle unit harness plug (if fitted).
7 Disconnect the two seat belt warning light switch harness plugs (if fitted).
8 Lift out the seat complete with runners.

Refitting

9 Ensure that the packing washers are correctly positioned.
10 Reverse instructions 1 to 8.

SEAT RUNNERS

Remove and refit   76.70.21

Removing

1 Remove the seat, see 76.70.04/ 76.70.05.
2 Remove the six capscrews and spring washers securing the runners to the seat, moving the slides as necessary to obtain access.

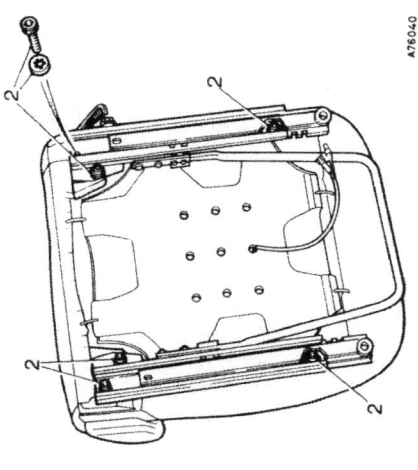

Refitting

3 Reverse instructions 1 and 2.

BODY   301

SEAT BELTS

Remove and refit   76.73.10

Removing

1 Remove the bolt and spring washer securing the swivel bracket to the seat.
2 *Earlier Models:* Feed the seat belt through the aperture in the parcel shelf.
3 *Earlier models:* Working inside the luggage compartment remove the trim panel above the wheel arch—two fasteners.
4 Remove the bolt and spring washer securing the reel unit mounting bracket to the wheel arch.

NOTE: On later models a cover over the reel must be prised up and lifted off to gain acess to the reel securing bolt.

5 Withdraw the seat belt and reel from the vehicle.
6 Remove the seat belt switch if necessary, see 86.65.31/86.65.32.
7 Remove the tongue retainer, if necessary—two screws.

Refitting

8 Reverse instructions 1 to 7.

WINDSCREEN

Introduction   76.81.00

The Thermo Electric Windscreen Sealer is an uncured 'Neoprene' based material supplied in round strip form, which has a thin insulated resistance wire running through its centre core. The compound surrounding the wire also has a heat activated accelerator incorporated in it and has sufficient initial tackiness to adhere it to the painted metal aperture.

The service kit contains a preformed Solbit sealing strip of sufficient length to lap completely around the windscreen aperture flange. Also included are a bottle of primer, wire for cutting out laminated windscreens and two rubber spacers for supporting the new windscreen. The internal resistance wire is exposed at each end of the strip and connected to a low voltage electrical supply. This is obtained by connecting two fully charged 12 volt batteries in series (+ to −) or alternatively using a variable output transformer capable of giving 11 amps at 24 volts. A lower current would be insufficient to effect a satisfactory cure of the Solbit strip. The resistance wire becomes warm and softens the strip, enabling the windscreen and finishers to be bedded into position. Further heat helps to cure the sealer and after 1½ to 2 hours the adhesion is strong enough for the car to be used.

NOTE:
A The aid of an assistant is required for this operation.
B Glass lifters should be used for handling the screen.
C Cleanliness is essential.

WINDSCREEN GLASS

Remove and refit   76.81.01

Removing

1 Cover the fascia and interior trim to protect them from broken glass.
2 Remove the windscreen wiper arms, see 84.15.02/03.
3 Remove the lower windscreen finisher, see 76.43.41.
4 Remove the 'A' post trim pads – two screws, together with the fascia corner finishers.
5 Pull off the header rail finisher.
6 Push the finisher moulding cover to one side to expose the Solbit.

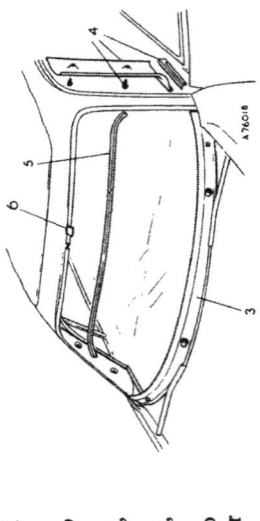

A76018

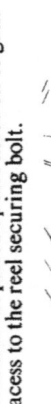

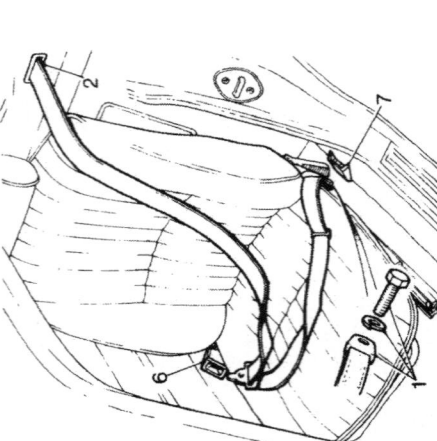

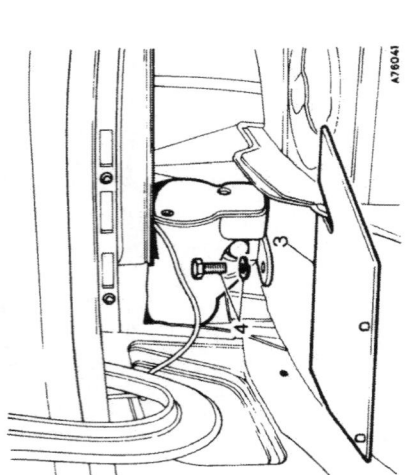

A76041

A76019

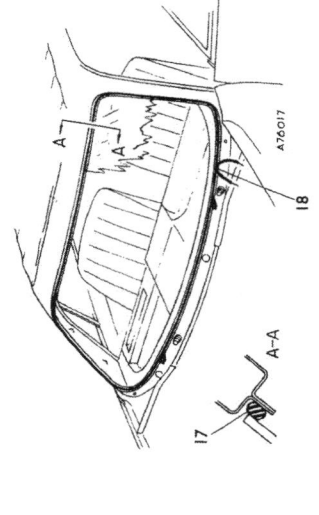

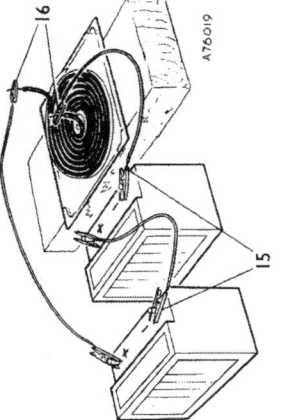

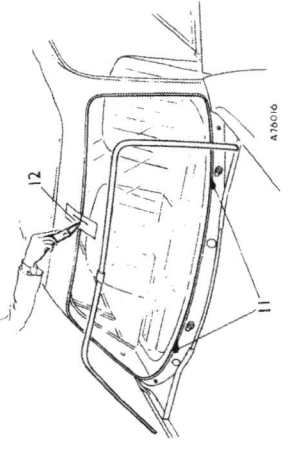

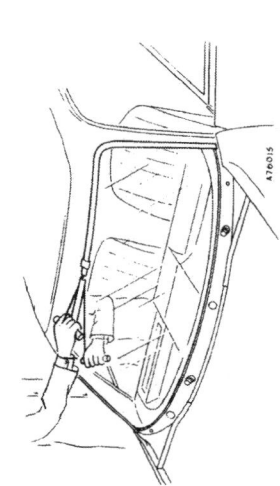

7 From both outside and inside, cut or pierce a hole through the existing Solbit and thread one end of the wire through the hole to an assistant inside the car. At each end of the wire twist on a small piece of wood to act as a handle or form a handle by threading the wire through a small hole drilled in the end of an old screwdriver. By pulling through the Solbit. Use long steady pulls rather than short quick ones otherwise the wire will overheat and break. Narrow the angle of the cut by keeping the wire ends as close as possible to the glass. Ensure that the wire outside the car is pulled along the moulding rather than the painted body otherwise the latter will be damaged.

8 With a sharp knife, cut through the old Solbit remaining on the flange and remove it by a combination of cutting and pulling.

9 Cut away any sharp edges or remaining lumps of old Solbit to ensure an even surface.

10 Cut away and remove Solbit from the finisher mouldings. Avoid distorting the mouldings during the cleaning operation. It may be necessary to obtain replacements. Remove any dirt or loose material from the flange using a clean lint-free cloth moistened with methylated spirit.

Refitting

11 Place the two rubber spacers from the kit on to the bottom flange about 150 mm (6 in) to 225 mm (9 in) from the pillars. Using glass lifters, offer the windscreen up to rest on the spacers; positioning it to give equal gaps all the way round. Position finisher mouldings and join them together at the top with the cover to ensure that they fit well and have not been distorted during removal. Remove the finisher mouldings.
NOTE: If any straightening of the mouldings is necessary, it should be carried out at this stage.

12 Place a piece of masking tape approximately on the top centre of the glass, sticking this across the gap between the glass and the body. Mark the masking tape so as to facilitate location when finally placing the windscreen for fitting. Then cut through the tape between the glass and body and remove the windscreen on to a bench.
NOTE: Take careful note of the size of the gap because when applying the Solbit strip to the flange, there must be sufficient Solbit along the whole length of the gap into which the reveal mouldings are embedded and sufficient Solbit under the glass for a watertight bond line to be made.

13 Apply a thin coat of primer to the remaining Solbit or painted flange using a clean lint-free cloth. Allow to dry for approximately one minute.

14 Clean the new windscreen with a solvent (e.g. methylated spirit) if necessary, and apply a thin coating of primer, no more than 13 mm (½ in) wide, to the periphery of the inner face of the windscreen. Allow to dry for approximately one minute.

15 Connect two *fully charged* 12 volt batteries in series (+ to −).
NOTE: Alternatively a variable output transformer set to give 11 amps at 24 volts may be used.

16 Expose the bared ends of the wire in the Solbit strip whilst in the container pack and connect to the batteries or transformer until the Solbit is just sufficiently tacky to adhere to the flange. This time can vary between 15 and 90 seconds depending on the temperature and age of the Solbit. Disconnect the current.
NOTE: Do not overheat the Solbit as this will make it both difficult to remove from the pack and to handle.
Starting about 75 mm (3 in) from one of the bottom corners of the screen aperture, place the Solbit strip on the flange so that when the windscreen is fitted, there is sufficient exudation of Solbit to the right and the left of the edges of the screen aperture for bonding the glass and for embedding the chrome finishers.

17 Take careful note of the size

18 Cross over the ends of the Solbit, approximately 50 mm (2 in) in length at the lower right corner of the windscreen aperture, having first placed a small strip of masking tape on the body to prevent marking by the ends of the Solbit.
NOTE: Care must be taken with this operation otherwise a hairline crack could be left on the surface of the Solbit after compression.

19 Using glass lifters install the windscreen in the aperture resting the bottom edge on the spacers and taking care to position it exactly where previously marked with the masking tape. Avoid fingering the primed areas. Remove approximately 25 mm (1 in) of the exposed excess Solbit from the wire.

20 Connect the two bared wire ends of the Solbit strip to the 24 volt supply. This will begin to soften the Solbit and after 1½ to 2 minutes, press the glass into the Solbit, starting with pressure in the centre of the glass and out to the pillars. Do not press the glass too far into the Solbit at this stage because, if somewhat proud, the depth can be rectified when the chrome finishers are embedded into the Solbit.

continued

HEATED BACKLIGHT — 76.81.11

Remove and refit

Removing

1 Break the seal, using a suitably blunt tool.
2 Carefully pull the rear edges of the rear quarter trim pads away from the body to expose the Lucar connectors. Disconnect the two Lucar connectors from the backlight.
3 Push the glass outwards.
CAUTION: Take care to avoid scratching the glass, which must be steadied by an assistant.
4 Remove the weatherstrip from the glass.

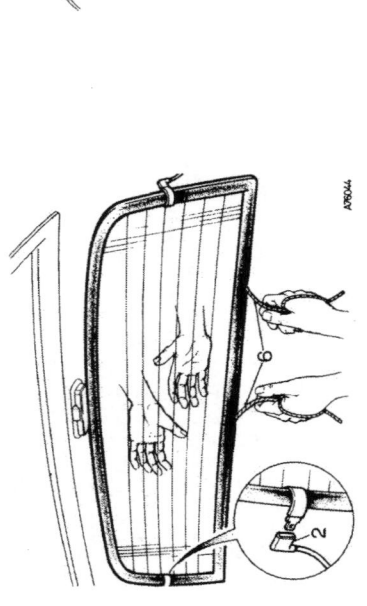

Refitting

5 Reverse instruction 4 using a new weatherstrip if necessary, and apply Seelastik to the glass channel before fitting.
6 Insert a strong cord into the weatherstrip inner channel, allowing the ends to protrude from the lower edge.
7 Have an assistant position the glass centrally in the aperture, and maintain a steady pressure whilst the cord ends are pulled to locate the weatherstrip on the body flange.
8 Seal the outer channel of the weatherstrip to the body using Seelastik.
9 Reconnect the two Lucar connectors and ensure that the rear quarter trim pads are correctly positioned.

21 Inspect the bond line (which should be no less than 7 mm (¼ in) wide) through the glass during early stages of the heating cycle. Potential leak sources can easily be seen and rectified by a little extra pressure in the area while the heat is on or by pressing some of the previously removed excess Solbit into the particular leak source.
22 After 10 minutes position and embed the chrome finishers into the Solbit; very little pressure is required. If at this stage mouldings and windscreen are proud, additional pressure can be applied. Disconnect electrical current after 1½ to 2 hours.
23 Allow the glass to cool down.
24 Test for water leaks.
25 Trim off exposed ends of Solbit and rubber spacers with snips or press out of sight into the rebate.
26 Refit the header rail.
27 Refit the 'A' post trim pads—2 screws, together with the fascia corner finishers.
28 Refit the lower windscreen finisher, see 76.43.41.
29 Refit the windscreen wiper arms, see 84.15.02/03.

SLIDING ROOF — 76.82.01

Remove and refit

Removing

1 Prise out the four chrome caps.
2 Remove the four screws, spring washers and plain washers.
3 Open the roof and carefully pull it rearwards on one side at a time until the four slides are disengaged from the runners. Lift off the roof.
4 Remove the five screws securing one of the side runners to the roof. Remove the runner taking care to avoid breaking the spring when disengaging it. Remove the opposite side runner in the same manner.
5 Remove the five screws securing the rear frame to the roof. Remove the frame.
6 Drill out the four rivets on the vertical face of the front frame.
7 Carefully pull the two hinge brackets outwards to disengage them.
8 Drill out the eight rivets on the top face of the frame. Remove the frame.

Refitting

9 Ensure that the headlining is correctly positioned with an overlap of approximately 13 mm (½ in).
10 Apply Kelseal to the forward top face of the roof aperture.
11 Reverse instructions 3 to 8.
12 Close the roof and adjust if necessary to obtain correct tension before fully tightening screws 2.
13 Replace the four chrome caps.

BODY PANEL REPAIR

PREPARATION AND TECHNIQUES   77.00.01

Description

A body repair can be effected by many methods dependent upon the extent of the damage. These methods range from straightening procedures to the replacement of individual parts or panel assemblies.

The Repairer will select the best and most economic repair, subject to available equipment and labour, but will ensure, at all times, that safety requirements are observed.

This section is intended to advise skilled body repairers on methods by which a damaged vehicle can be restored to an acceptable structural condition.

To reduce the cost of a repair, certain individual panels are available which may be used either in their entirety or cut at a convenient point to reduce the volume of work involved.

Damage may make it impossible, or unnecessary, to remove some of the mechanical and electrical components before carrying out a body repair; but when components are removed and, subsequently, refitted, refer to the appropriate section for detailed instructions.

Equipment

The equipment shown should be used when carrying out repairs described in this section:

A   Pneumatic saw
B   Hand punching tool (5mm dia.)
C   Drilling machine
D   Grinding machine
E   Spot welding gun
F   Metal Inert Gas welding equipment

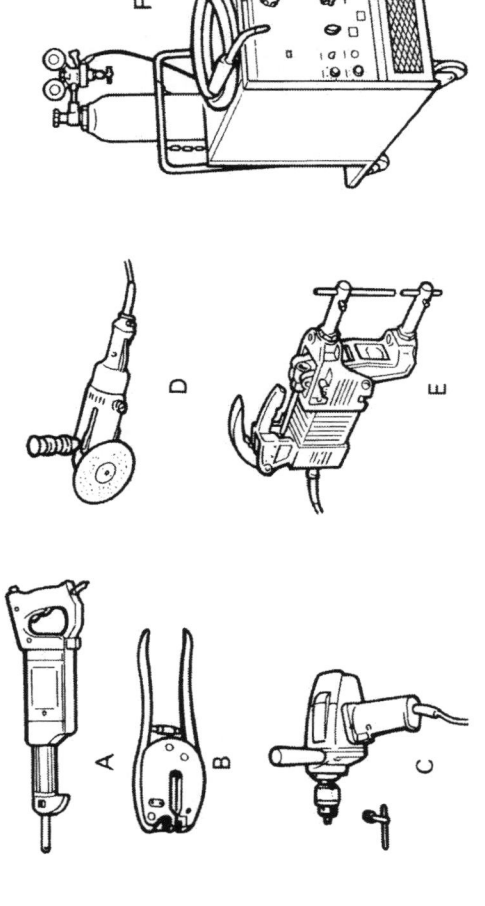

BR 0028

Joints

There are four types of joint to be considered when effecting body repairs which are as follows:

(a) butt joints
(b) lap joints
(c) double lap joints
(d) flanged joints

Welds

1. **Fusion welds** are suitable for butt and lap joints and should also be used for reinforcing corners and notches in flanges. If it is necessary to fusion weld a flange joint ensure that the designed strength of the joint is preserved. A fusion weld along the toe of a flange is not, generally, acceptable unless the flange is cut back.

BR 0029

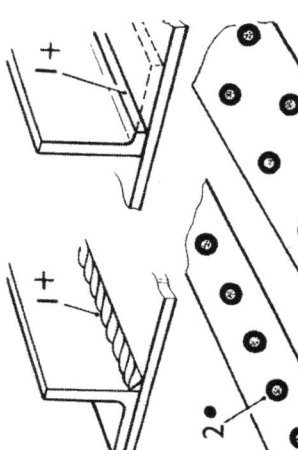

BR 0070

2. **Spot welds** (i.e. resistance spot welds unless otherwise stated) are suitable for lap, double lap and flanged joints. This method can be used either in single or double, staggered rows. For single row spot welding, space the spot welds 13 to 25mm apart. In the case of double row spot welding, space the welds 22 to 31mm apart.

External examination gives little indication of the quality of a spot weld. It is therefore necessary to make a test joint using similar material and then split the test pieces apart. If the metal tears or the weld pulls a hole in one piece the joint is satisfactory. Repeat the test each time the electrodes are re-dressed or changed and each time a change of metal gauge is encountered.

3. **Plug welds** are employed where the area to be welded is only accessible from one side. To make a plug weld, drill a 5 to 8mm hole through the accessible panel and weld the components together through the hole. The components may be clamped together by using drive screws at intervals. After plug welding, the drive screws are removed and the resulting holes plug welded.

Separation of spot welded components

Centre-punch each spot weld. Adjust a spot weld cutter so that it cuts through the thickness of the material to be removed. Holding the cutter square to the material, cut through each spot weld. Always use a pneumatic tool provided with a throttle.

If the new joint is made with spot welds, cut the old spot welds from the component which is to be discarded. If the new joint is to be made with plug welds, cut the old spot welds from the component which is to be retained and use the holes for plug welding.

Welding preparation

Remove all traces of sealer from the area of the joint likely to be affected by heat. Clean both sides of the welding areas, to bare metal, on both existing and new panels. Grind existing welds smooth and dress the panels or flanges to ensure that the welding faces fit closely. Mask the welding areas and paint any areas which will be inaccessible after panels are fitted. Remove all masking before welding.

Prior to spot welding apply zinc rich welding primer to both mating surfaces and spot weld while the primer is still moist.

Finishing

Grind all plug welds and butt welds smooth and fill the surface where necessary. Clean the repair for sealing and painting.

Sealing

After fitting panels seal all joints and apply underseal where required.

Legal requirements

'E' Mark Approval Label

This label is attached to the R.H. front suspension turret. If the label is detached or damaged or if the valance is renewed, a new label should be ordered giving the vehicle, chassis, commission, body shell and engine numbers.

Attach the new label to the R.H. front suspension turret.

Symbols

The following symbols are used on the illustrations in this section to indicate cutting areas and recommended types of weld.

Cutting Symbols

A

1 Saw cut
2 Remove spot weld (minimum number of spot welds quoted)
3 Cut (using hammer, bolster chisel and/or pincers)

Weld/Braze Symbols

B

4 Spot weld
5 MIG weld/continuous MIG weld
6 Braze
7 Gas weld
8 Plug weld

77.01.01

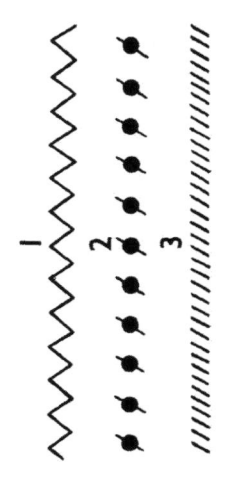

BR0030

HORIZONTAL ALIGNMENT CHECK

1 A preliminary check of the alignment should be carried out by dropping a plumb-bob from the centre of the points A, B, C, D on each side of the vehicle.
2 Establish a centre line by means of a large pair of compasses at points B and D.
3 Check measurements against those given in DATA.
4 Construct diagonals.

Incorrect alignment will be evident by the failure of the diagonals to intersect on the centre line by considerable deviation from the dimensions given.

DATA

A	B	C	D
552mm	594mm	964mm	1042mm

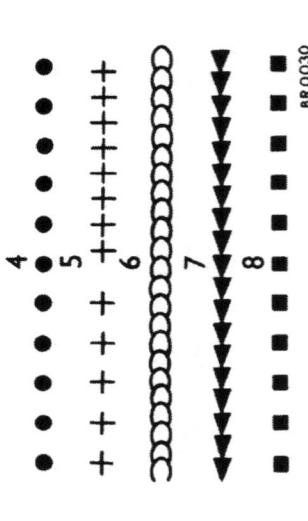

BR0001

77.01.02

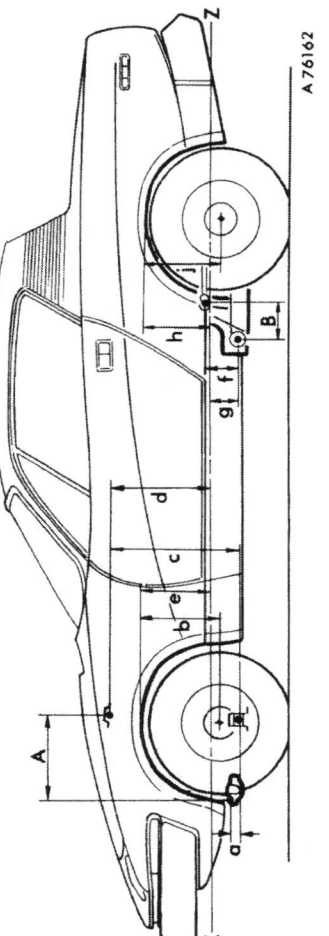

A 76162

Vertical alignment

The dimensions given below are for cars in showroom condition, unladen and without fuel. It should be noted that the important point is the relative positions of the vertical datum points to each other and not their actual height from the wheel hub centres.

Code	Dimension	Location
A	346 mm (13.62 in)	Anti-roll bar front mounting to suspension pod cap
B	141.5 mm (5.57 in)	Rear suspension arm mounting to radius rod mounting
a	33 mm (1.29 in)	Anti-roll bar clamp front fixing bolt to lower link
b	361 mm (14.20 in)	Top of front wheel arch to wheel hub centre — Europe — 4 speed gearbox
	356 mm (14.02 in)	Top of front wheel arch to wheel hub centre — Europe — 5 speed gearbox
	353 mm (13.90 in)	Top of front wheel arch to wheel hub centre — Europe — Automatic transmission
	354 mm (13.96 in)	Top of front wheel arch to wheel hub centre — USA — 4 speed gearbox
	350 mm (13.78 in)	Top of front wheel arch to wheel hub centre — USA — 5 speed gearbox
	347 mm (13.67 in)	Top of front wheel arch to wheel hub centre — USA — Automatic transmission
	356 mm (14.02 in)	Top of front wheel arch to wheel hub centre — USA — 4 speed gearbox — air conditioning
	352 mm (13.88 in)	Top of front wheel arch to wheel hub centre — USA — 5 speed gearbox — air conditioning
	349 mm (13.75 in)	Top of front wheel arch to wheel hub centre — USA — Automatic transmission — air conditioning

Code	Dimension	Location
c	571 mm (22.48 in)	Lower link to front suspension pod cap
d	476.5 mm (18.75 in)	Front suspension pod cap to datum line
e	338 mm (13.3 in)	Top of wheel arch to datum line
f	136 mm (5.35 in)	Rear suspension arm mounting to radius rod mounting
g	95 mm (3.74 in)	Rear suspension arm mounting to datum line
h	319 mm (12.56 in)	Top of rear wheel arch to datum line
j	348 mm (13.71 in)	Top of rear wheel arch to wheel hub centre — Europe — 4 speed gearbox
	350 mm (13.80 in)	Top of rear wheel arch to wheel hub centre — Europe — 5 speed gearbox
	345 mm (13.60 in)	Top of rear wheel arch to wheel hub centre — Europe — Automatic transmission
	346 mm (13.63 in)	Top of rear wheel arch to wheel hub centre — USA — 4 speed gearbox
	348 mm (13.72 in)	Top of rear wheel arch to wheel hub centre — USA — 5 speed gearbox
	343 mm (13.52 in)	Top of rear wheel arch to wheel hub centre — USA — Automatic transmission
Z–Z		Datum line

77.25.33

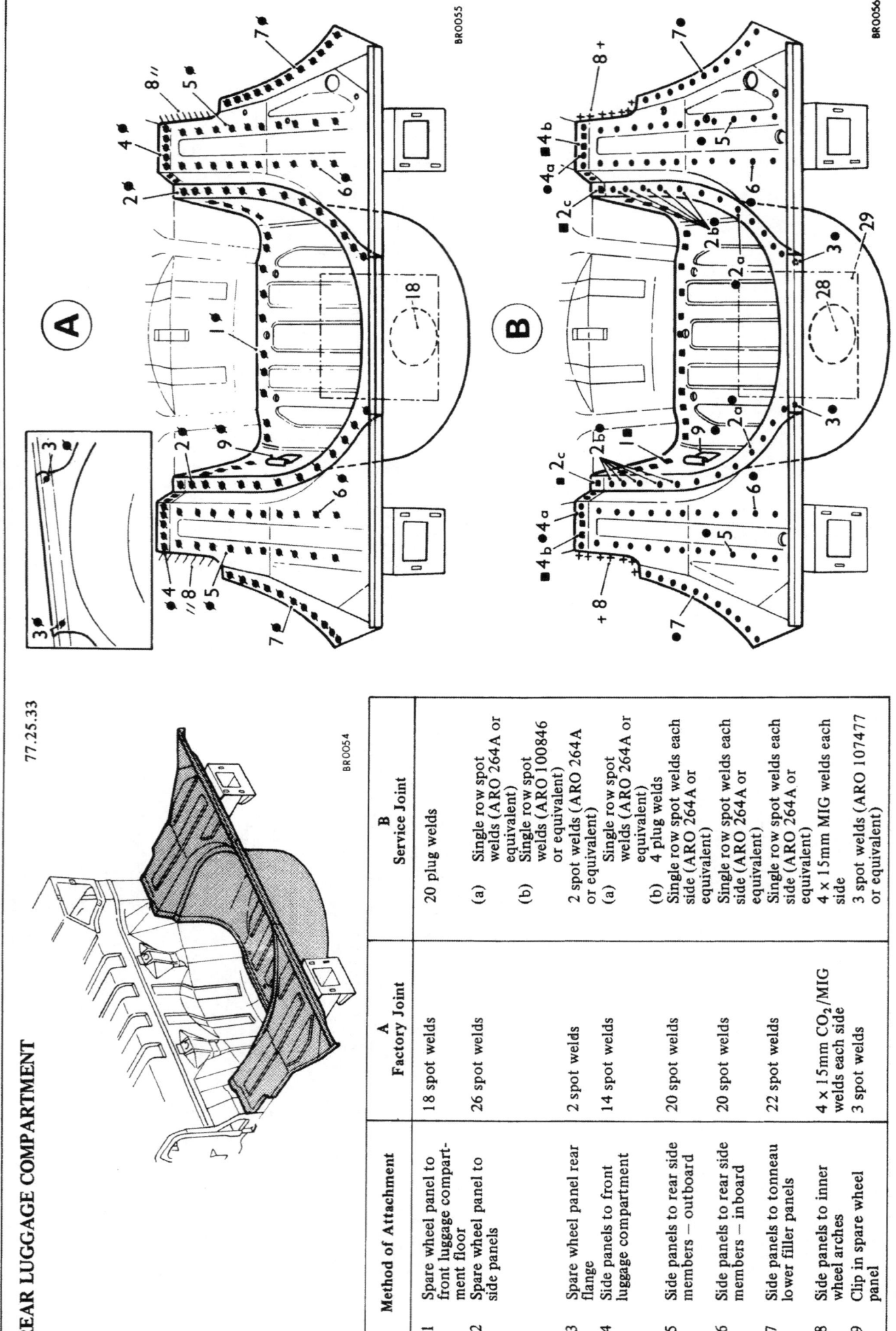

BR0054
BR0055
BR0056

Method of Attachment		A Factory Joint	B Service Joint
1	Spare wheel panel to front luggage compartment floor	18 spot welds	20 plug welds
2	Spare wheel panel to side panels	26 spot welds	(a) Single row spot welds (ARO 264A or equivalent) (b) Single row spot welds (ARO 100846 or equivalent)
3	Spare wheel panel rear flange	2 spot welds	2 spot welds (ARO 264A or equivalent)
4	Side panels to front luggage compartment	14 spot welds	(a) Single row spot welds (ARO 264A or equivalent) (b) 4 plug welds
5	Side panels to rear side members — outboard	20 spot welds	Single row spot welds each side (ARO 264A or equivalent)
6	Side panels to rear side members — inboard	20 spot welds	Single row spot welds each side (ARO 264A or equivalent)
7	Side panels to tonneau lower filler panels	22 spot welds	Single row spot welds each side (ARO 264A or equivalent)
8	Side panels to inner wheel arches	4 x 15mm CO$_2$/MIG welds each side	4 x 15mm MIG welds each side
9	Clip in spare wheel panel	3 spot welds	3 spot welds (ARO 107477 or equivalent)

Removing

10 Disconnect battery.
11 Remove fuel tank.
12 Remove components as necessary to gain access to the rear luggage compartment.
13 Cut spot welds as described in 1, 2 and 3.
14 Remove spare wheel panel.
15 Cut spot welds as described in 4, 5, 6 and 7.
16 Grind off welds at 8.
17 Remove clip described in 9 from spare wheel panel for re-use.
18 Remove blanking disc, laid in with sealant under anti-drum pad, and retain for further use.

Refitting

19 Prepare all mating surfaces (see 'PREPARATION AND TECHNIQUES').

20 Clamp the side panels in position and place the spare wheel panel between to check alignment.
21 Remove spare wheel panel.
22 Make spot welds at 4a, 4b, 5, 6 and 7.
23 Spot weld clip to spare wheel panel at 9.
24 Place spare wheel panel in position.
25 Make spot welds as described in 2a, 2b and 3.
26 Plug weld at 1, 2c and 4b.
27 MIG weld at 8.
28 Replace blanking disc and seal.
29 Replace anti-drum pad.
30 Finish (see 'PREPARATION AND TECHNIQUES') and paint.
31 Reverse instructions 10 to 12.

FRONT PANEL

Removing

5 Disconnect the battery.
6 Remove components as necessary to obtain access to the front panel.
7 Remove bonnet tapping plates.
8 Remove eight bolts, front panel to wings.
9 Cut spot welds in 2 and 3.
10 Cut the welds in 4.

Refitting

11 Prepare new panel (see PREPARATION AND TECHNIQUES').

12 Replace four bolts each side.
13 Place front panel in position and tighten bolts.
14 Replace bonnet tapping plates.
15 Bolt bonnet in position to check alignment.
16 Remove bonnet.
17 Make spot welds in 2a and 3.
18 Spot weld as described in 2b.
19 MIG weld as described in 4.
20 Finish (see 'PREPARATION AND TECHNIQUES') and paint.
21 Refit the components removed in 6 and connect the battery.

77.28.25

BR0007

BR0006

Method of Attachment	A Factory Joint	B Service Joint
1 To wings	8 bolts (10mm)	8 bolts (10mm)
2 To bonnet abutment	16 spot welds	(a) Single row spot welds (ARO 242A or equivalent) (b) 6 spot welds (ARO 100483 or equivalent)
3 Lower attachments	10 spot welds	Single row spot welds (ARO 242A or equivalent)
4 To panel filler	10 x 15mm CO_2/MIG welds	10 x 15mm MIG welds

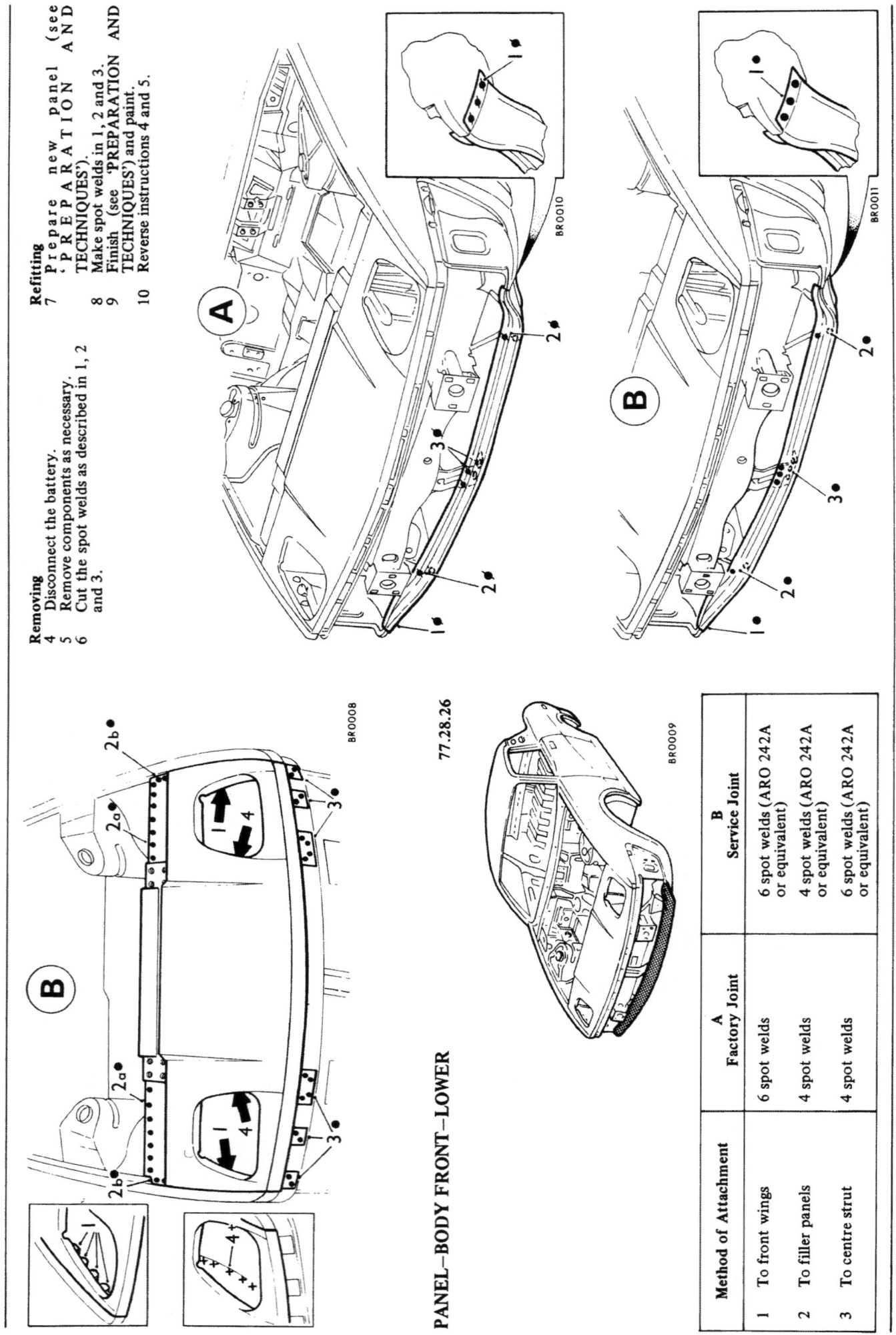

Removing

4 Disconnect the battery.
5 Remove components as necessary.
6 Cut the spot welds as described in 1, 2 and 3.

Refitting

7 Prepare new panel (see 'PREPARATION AND TECHNIQUES').
8 Make spot welds in 1, 2 and 3.
9 Finish (see 'PREPARATION AND TECHNIQUES') and paint.
10 Reverse instructions 4 and 5.

BRO010

BRO011

BRO008

BRO009

77.28.26

PANEL—BODY FRONT—LOWER

Method of Attachment		A Factory Joint	B Service Joint
1	To front wings	6 spot welds	6 spot welds (ARO 242A or equivalent)
2	To filler panels	4 spot welds	4 spot welds (ARO 242A or equivalent)
3	To centre strut	4 spot welds	6 spot welds (ARO 242A or equivalent)

77.28.29

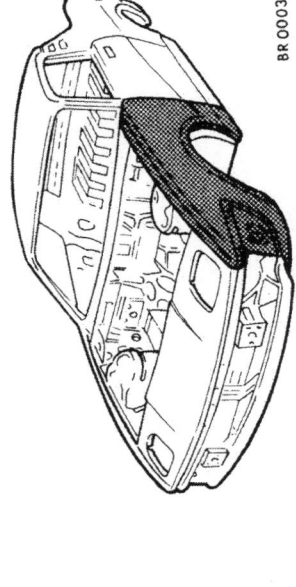

BR 0003

BR 0004

BR 0005

Method of Attachment		A Factory Joint	B Service Joint
1	To front panel	4 bolts (10mm)	4 bolts (10mm)
2	To 'A' post	3 bolts (10mm)	3 bolts (10mm)
3	To valance top flange	17 spot welds	(a) Single row spot welds (ARO 103402 or equivalent) (b) 4 MIG plug welds (c) 2 spot welds (ARO 100843 or equivalent)
4	To sill flange	8 spot welds	Single row spot welds (ARO 105492 or equivalent)
5	To front panel	2 spot welds	2 spot welds (ARO 105492 or equivalent)
6	To lower front panel	3 spot welds	3 spot welds (ARO 242A or equivalent)
7	To wheel arch	24 spot welds	Single row spot welds (ARO 105010 or equivalent)
8	To valance	4 x 10mm MIG	MIG

Method of Attachment	A Factory Joint	B Service Joint
1 To front longitudinal – top	4 spot welds	4 spot welds (ARO 264A or equivalent)
2 To front longitudinal – bottom	4 spot welds	4 spot welds (ARO 264A or equivalent)
3 To front longitudinal – vertical flange	8 spot welds	Single row spot welds each side (ARO 264A or equivalent)

Removing

9 Disconnect battery.
10 Remove components as necessary to obtain access to the wing and wing joints.
11 Remove sill trim strip.
12 Remove four bolts to front panel. Access through headlamp aperture.
13 Remove three bolts to 'A' post.
14 Cut wing away as illustrated.
15 Cut the spot welds described in 3, 4, 5, 6 and 7.
16 Remove remnants of wing panel.
17 Cut the weld at 8.

Refitting

18 Slot bolt holes in new front wing to facilitate assembly.
19 Prepare the panels (see 'PREPARATION AND TECHNIQUES').
20 Fit the three bolts and washers to the 'A' post.
21 Fit the new wing, align it with the door and bonnet and clamp in position.
22 Fit re-inforcing strip and bolt wing to front panel.
23 Attach clamps to wheel arch and tack weld in position.
24 Replace bonnet to check alignment of wing.
25 Remove the bonnet.
26 Make the spot welds described in 3, 4, 5, 6 and 7.
27 MIG weld at 8.
28 Finish (see 'PREPARATION AND TECHNIQUES') and paint.
29 Refit sill trim strip.
30 Replace all components removed in 10 and connect the battery.

Removing

4 Disconnect the battery.
5 Remove components as necessary to gain access.
6 Cut spot welds described in 1, 2 and 3.

Refitting

7 Prepare the replacement cross-member (see 'PREPARATION AND TECHNIQUES').
8 Clamp cross-member in position and align.
9 Make the welds described in 1 to 3.
10 Finish and paint (see 'PREPARATION AND TECHNIQUES').
11 Reverse the procedure in 4 and 5.

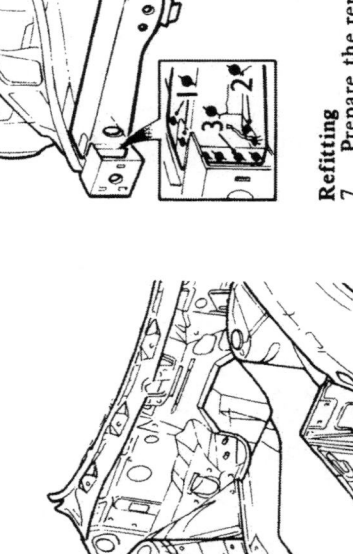

BR0033

BR0032

FRONT CROSS-MEMBER

77.31.29

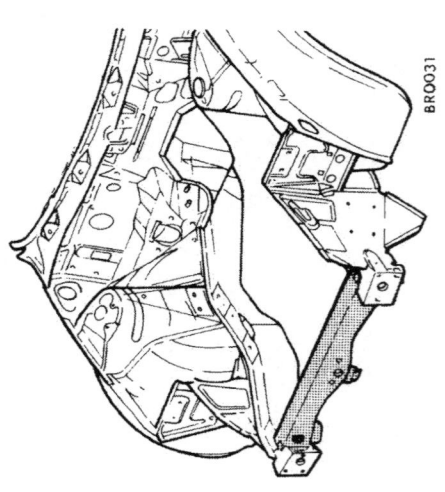

BR0031

FRONT LONGITUDINAL

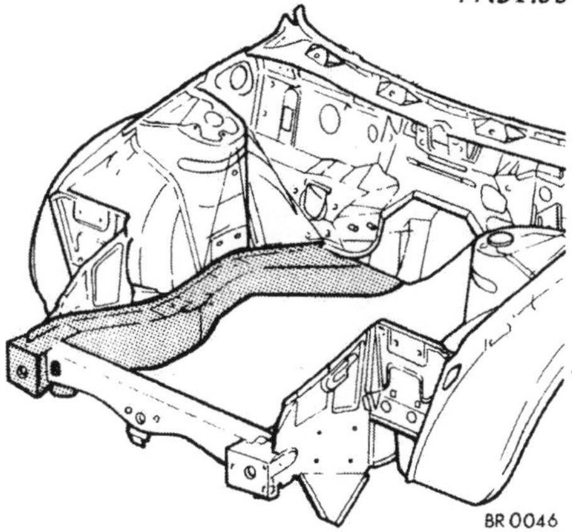

77.31.55

BR0046

A — BR0047

B — BR0048

Method of Attachment	A Factory Joint	B Service Joint
1 Upper flange to bulkhead	2 x 15mm CO_2/MIG welds	2 x 15mm MIG welds
2 To underframe	2 x 15mm CO_2/MIG welds	2 x 15mm MIG welds
3 Toe-board vertical flange	1 spot weld	1 x 15mm MIG weld
4 Longitudinal rear end lug	2 spot welds	1 x 25mm MIG weld
5 Longitudinal rear end flanges	2 x 25mm CO_2/MIG welds	2 x 25mm MIG welds
6 Longitudinal inboard flange at rear	1 x 35mm CO_2/MIG weld	1 x 35mm MIG weld
7 Gearbox reinforcement plate	6 x 10mm CO_2/MIG welds	6 x 10mm MIG welds
8 Longitudinal rear end to toe-board and floor	36 spot welds	40 plug welds
9 Anchor bracket attachment to longitudinal	6 x 20mm CO_2/MIG welds	6 x 20mm MIG welds

Removing

10 Disconnect the battery.
11 Remove components as necessary to gain access to the longitudinal and its joints.
12 Grind off welds described in 1, 2, 5 and 6.
13 Grind away weld at 7 and retain gearbox reinforcing plate for refitting.
14 Cut spot welds at 8.

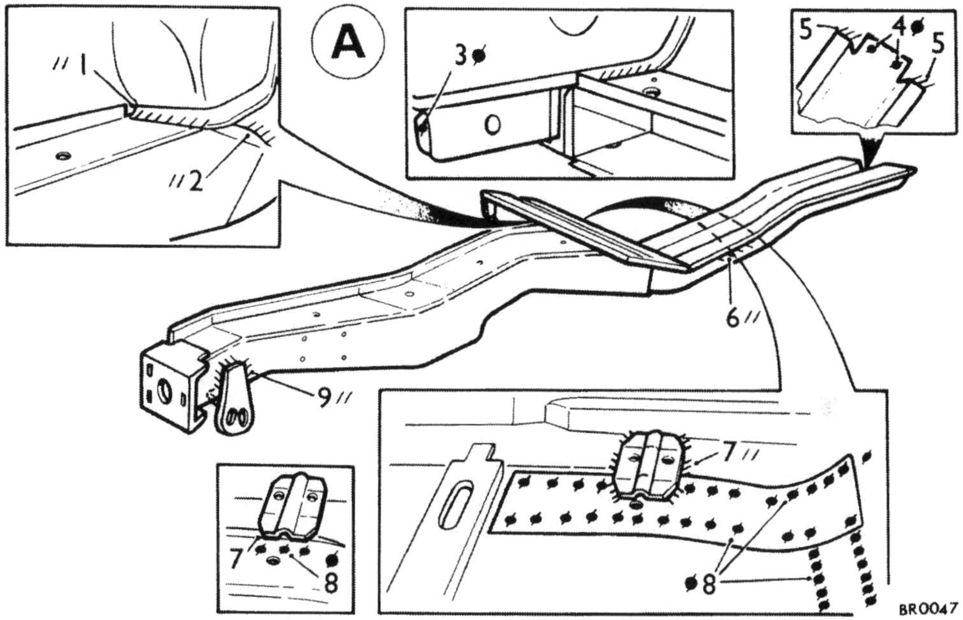

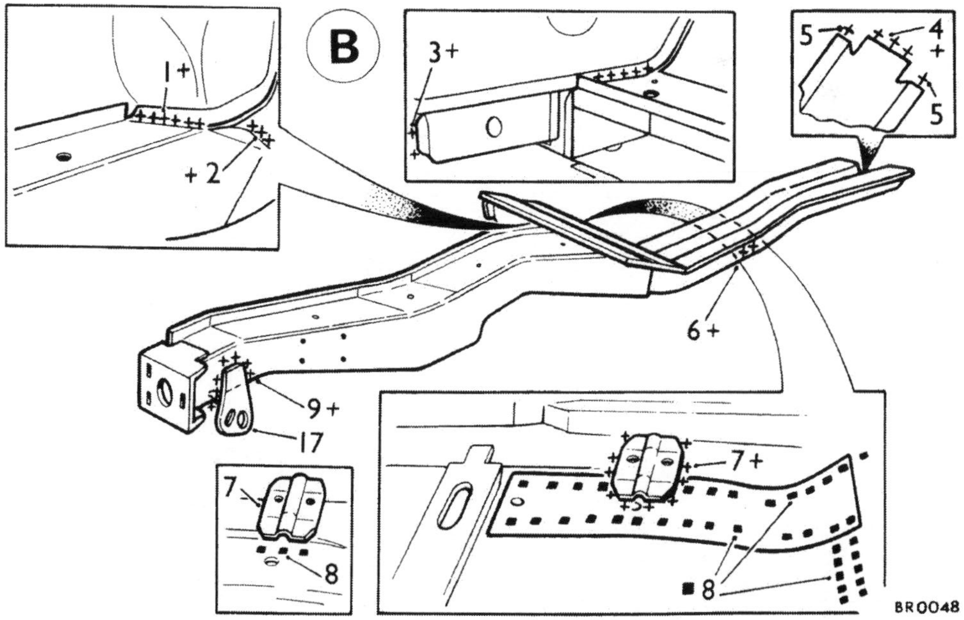

15 Grind off welds at 9 and retain anchor bracket for refitting.

Refitting
16 Prepare the replacement front longitudinal (see 'PREPARATION AND TECHNIQUES').
17 Weld anchor bracket in position on bench as described in 9.
18 Position longitudinal on jig and clamp in position.
19 Tack plug through floor panel to hold alignment.
20 MIG plug through floor panel and toe-board as described in 8.
21 Position gearbox reinforcing plate and MIG weld as described in 7.
22 Make the MIG welds described in 1, 2, 3, 4, 5 and 6.
23 Finish (see 'PREPARATION AND TECHNIQUES') and paint.
24 Reverse instructions 10 and 11.

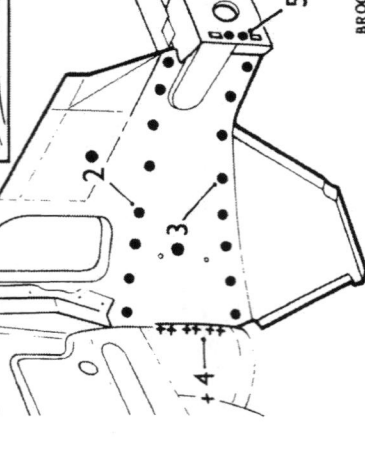

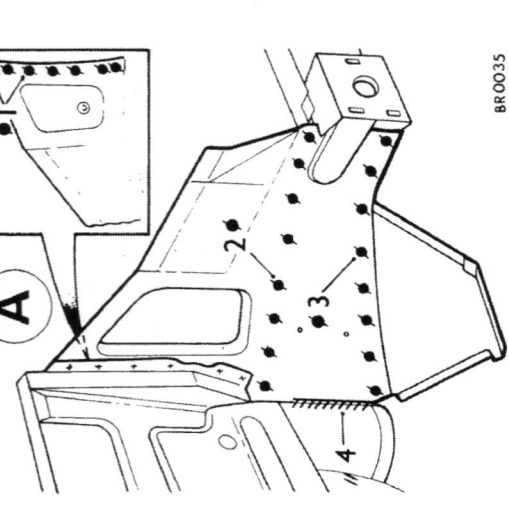

Removing
5 Disconnect the battery.
6 Remove components as necessary to gain access.
7 Cut spot welds described in 1, 2 and 3.
8 Grind off welds described in 4.

Refitting
9 Prepare the replacement panel (see 'PREPARATION AND TECHNIQUES') and all mating surfaces.
10 Clamp closing panel in position and align.
11 Make the spot welds described in 1, 2 and 3.
12 Make MIG welds as described in 4.
13 Finish (see 'PREPARATION AND TECHNIQUES') and paint.
14 Reverse the procedure in 5 and 6.

FRONT LONGITUDINAL CLOSING PANEL

77.31.57

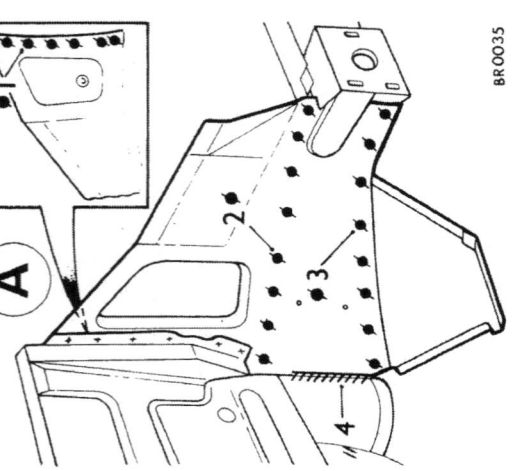

Method of Attachment	A Factory Joint	B Service Joint
1 To headlamp closing panel	6 spot welds	Single row spot welds (ARO 264A or equivalent)
2 To front longitudinal – top flange	8 spot welds	Single row spot welds (ARO 264A or equivalent)
3 To front longitudinal – bottom flange	8 spot welds	Single row spot welds (ARO 264A or equivalent)
4 To front longitudinal – vertical flange	3 x 10mm CO_2/MIG welds	3 x 10mm MIG welds

OUTER WHEEL ARCH FRONT

77.40.04

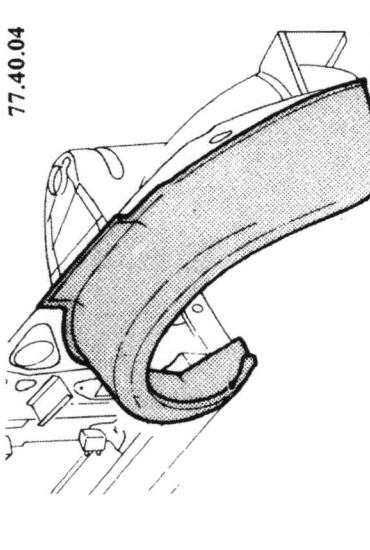

BR0043

Method of Attachment	A Factory Joint	B Service Joint
1	To fender valance — front	11 spot welds	Single row spot welds (ARO 264A or equivalent)
2	To fender valance — top	16 spot welds	Single row spot welds (ARO 264A or equivalent)
3	To fender valance — rear	6 spot welds	Single row spot welds (ARO 264A or equivalent)
4	To sill	8 spot welds	Single row spot welds (ARO 264A or equivalent)
5	Inner flange to fender valance	12 spot welds	Single row spot welds (ARO 264A or equivalent)

Removing

6 Disconnect the battery.

7 Remove components as necessary to gain access.

8 Cut spot welds as described in 1, 2, 3, 4 and 5.

Refitting

9 Prepare the replacement panel (see 'PREPARATION AND TECHNIQUES').

10 Clamp the new outer wheel arch in position and tack weld.

11 Make spot welds described in 1, 2, 3, 4 and 5.

12 Finish (see 'PREPARATION AND TECHNIQUES') and paint.

13 Reverse instructions 6 and 7.

FENDER VALANCE R.H.

77.40.06

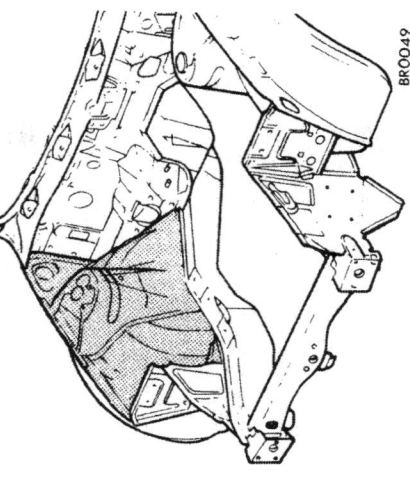

BR0049

Method of Attachment	A Factory Joint	B Service Joint
1	To 'A' post	7 spot welds	Single row spot welds (ARO 264A or equivalent)
2	To front longitudinal — top flange	15 spot welds	(a) Single row spot welds (ARO 264A or equivalent) (b) 11 MIG plug welds
3	To bulkhead	14 spot welds	Single row spot welds (ARO 100486 or equivalent)
4	To front longitudinal — lower flange	20 spot welds	Single row spot welds (ARO 264A or equivalent)
5	To bonnet retention bracket	5 spot welds	Single row spot welds (ARO 264A or equivalent)

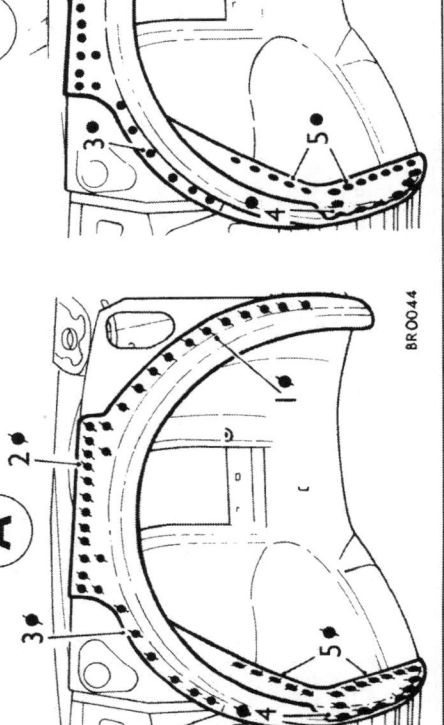

BR0045

BR0044

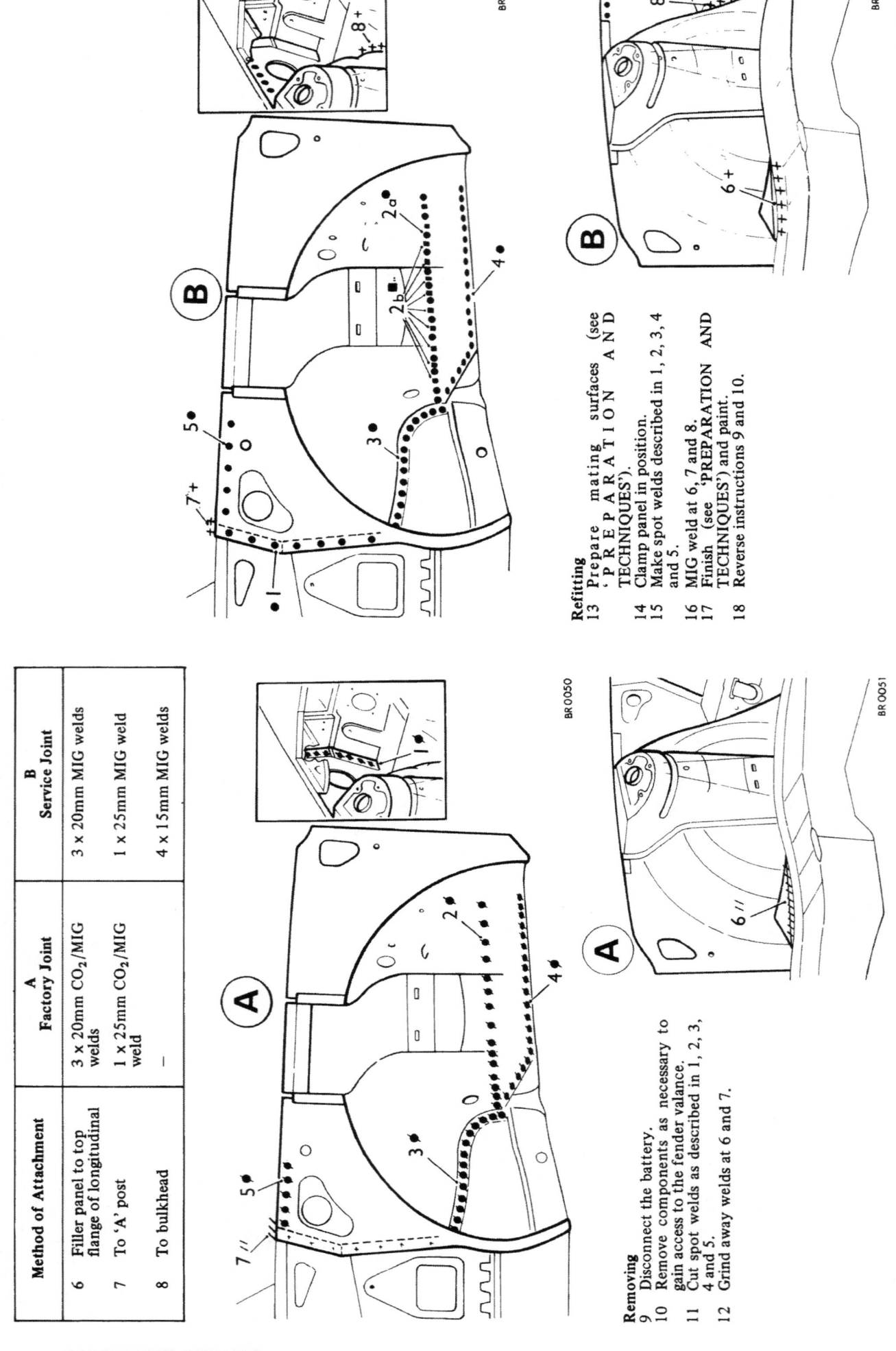

Method of Attachment		A Factory Joint	B Service Joint
6	Filler panel to top flange of longitudinal	3 x 20mm CO₂/MIG welds	3 x 20mm MIG welds
7	To 'A' post	1 x 25mm CO₂/MIG weld	1 x 25mm MIG weld
8	To bulkhead	—	4 x 15mm MIG welds

Removing

9 Disconnect the battery.
10 Remove components as necessary to gain access to the fender valance.
11 Cut spot welds as described in 1, 2, 3, 4 and 5.
12 Grind away welds at 6 and 7.

Refitting

13 Prepare mating surfaces (see 'PREPARATION AND TECHNIQUES').
14 Clamp panel in position.
15 Make spot welds described in 1, 2, 3, 4 and 5.
16 MIG weld at 6, 7 and 8.
17 Finish (see 'PREPARATION AND TECHNIQUES') and paint.
18 Reverse instructions 9 and 10.

FENDER VALANCE—L.H.

77.40.07

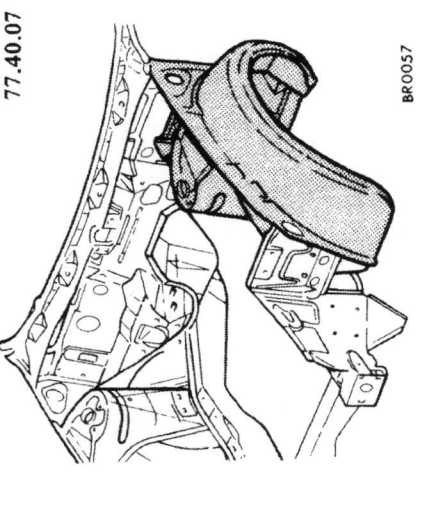

BR0057

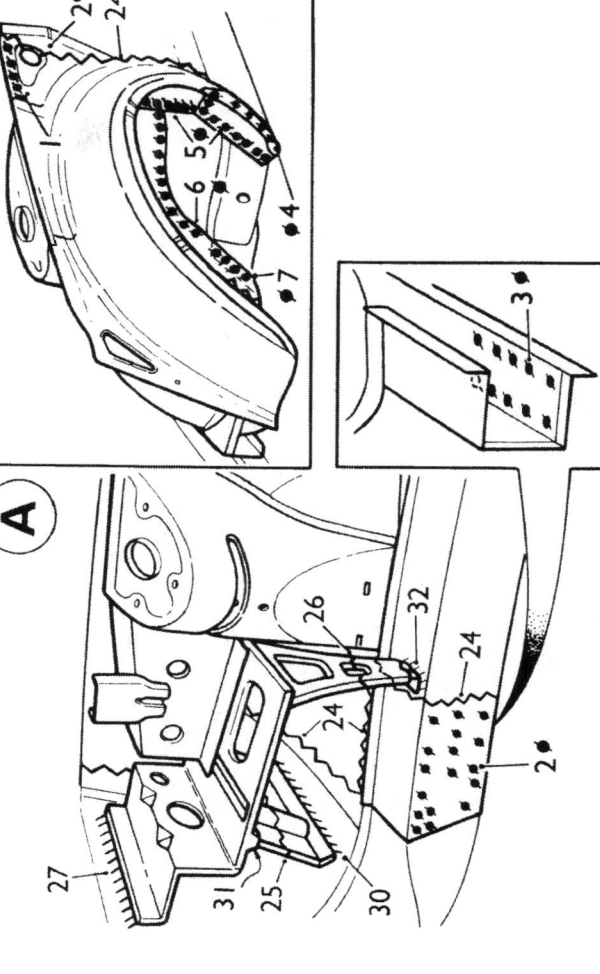

BR0058

Method of Attachment	A Factory Joint	B Service Joint
12 Outer wheel arch top flange	—	Single row spot welds (ARO 264A or equivalent)
13 Outer wheel arch front flange	—	Single row spot welds (ARO 264A or equivalent)
14 To bulkhead	—	4 x 15mm MIG welds
15 Fender valance filler panel to longitudinal top flange	—	3 x 20mm MIG welds
16 Battery tray to support bracket	—	4 spot welds (ARO 264A or equivalent)
17 Support bracket to bulkhead	—	3 x 20mm MIG welds
18 Top flange of battery tray to bulkhead	—	4 x 20mm MIG welds
19 Forward battery strut to attachment bracket	—	2 spot welds (ARO 264A or equivalent)
20 Attachment bracket to longitudinal	—	2 x 10mm MIG welds

Method of Attachment	A Factory Joint	B Service Joint
1 To bonnet retention bracket	5 spot welds	Single row spot welds (ARO 264A or equivalent)
2 Longitudinal front section – vertical face	17 spot welds	17 MIG plug welds
3 Longitudinal front section – bottom face	10 spot welds	10 MIG plug welds
4 To sill outer	8 spot welds	Single row spot welds (ARO 264A or equivalent)
5 Inner flange to fender valance	12 spot welds	(a) 5 spot welds (ARO 264A or equivalent) (b) 4 MIG plug welds
6 Fender valance to bulkhead	10 spot welds	Single row spot welds (ARO 100486 or equivalent)
7 To longitudinal	4 spot welds	4 spot welds (ARO 264A or equivalent)
8 To longitudinal top flange	—	(a) Single row spot welds (ARO 264A or equivalent) (b) 11 MIG plug welds
9 To longitudinal lower flange	—	Single row spot welds (ARO 264A or equivalent)
10 Fender valance to 'A' post	—	Single row spot welds (ARO 264A or equivalent)
11 Outer wheel arch rear flange	—	Single row spot welds (ARO 264A or equivalent)

Removing

21 Disconnect battery.
22 Remove components as necessary to gain access to the panel and its joints.
23 Cut spot welds as described in 1 to 7.
24 Cut through longitudinal and fender valance as shown.
25 Cut through support bracket below battery tray.
26 Cut through forward battery tray strut.
27 Grind off welds on top flange of battery tray.
28 Withdraw fender valance and front section of longitudinal.
29 Remove remnants of panel and forward section of longitudinal.
30 Grind off lower portion of battery tray support bracket.
31 Grind off upper portion of battery tray support bracket and MIG weld to lower portion to incorporate in service repair.

32 Grind off front battery tray support strut attachment angle for re-use.

Refitting

33 Prepare all mating surfaces (see 'PREPARATION AND TECHNIQUES').
34 Offer up front section of longitudinal, place on front jig point and clamp in position.
35 Mark position of anchorage bracket and weld in position on bench.
36 Reposition front section of longitudinal, align front cross-member and clamp in position.
37 Spot weld front cross-member to longitudinal.
38 Plug weld front section of longitudinal to rear section as described in 2 and 3.
39 Offer up fender valance assembly and support in jig at turret.
40 Clamp fender valance in position and make spot welds described in 1, 6, 7, 8, 9 and 10.

41 Offer up outer wheel arch and clamp in position.
42 Spot weld as described in 11, 12, 13, 4 and 5a.
43 MIG plug as described in 5b.
44 MIG weld at 14 and 15.
45 Offer up battery tray rear support and spot weld in position as described in 16.
46 MIG weld as described in 17 and 18.
47 Spot weld at 19.
48 MIG weld as described in 20.
49 Finish (see 'PREPARATION AND TECHNIQUES') and paint.
50 Reverse instructions 21 and 22.

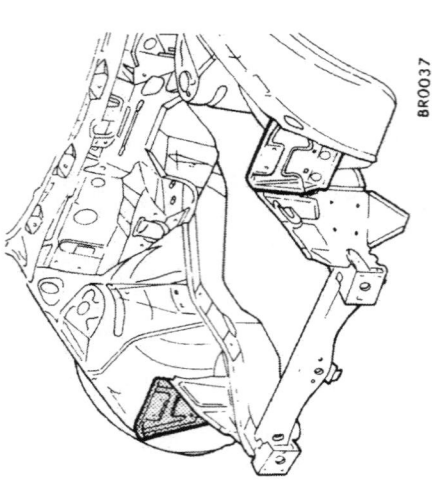

77.40.10

HEADLAMP CLOSING PANEL

Method of Attachment	A Factory Joint	B Service Joint
1 To front longitudinal closing panel	6 spot welds	Single row spot welds (ARO 264A or equivalent)
2 To fender valance closing plate	4 spot welds	4 spot welds (ARO 264A or equivalent)
3 To fender valance	5 spot welds	5 spot welds (ARO 264A or equivalent)

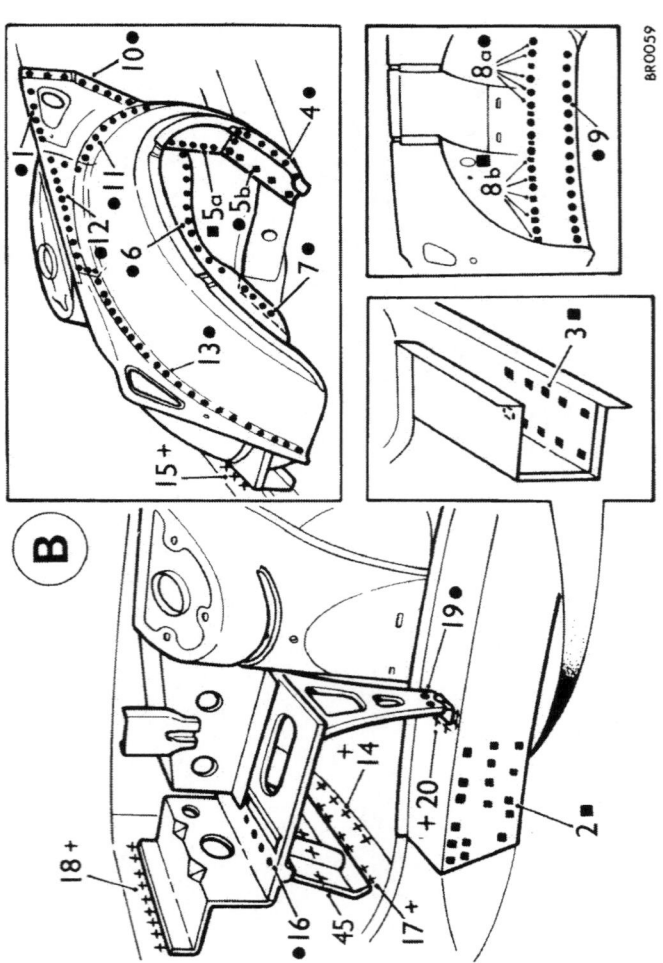

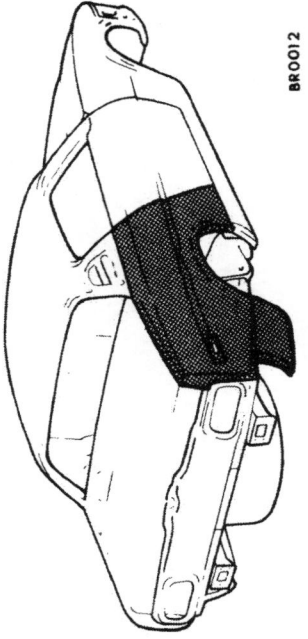

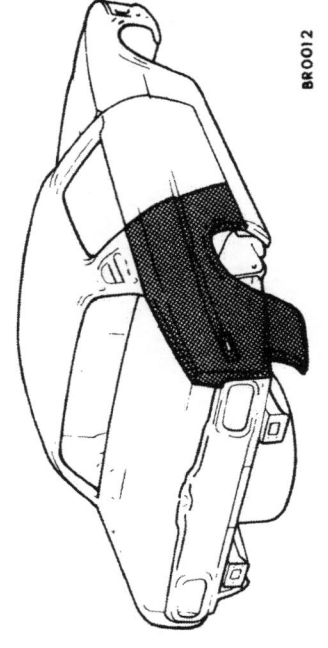

BR0012

TONNEAU SIDE PANEL—R.H.

77.61.01

	Method of Attachment	A Factory Joint	B Service Joint
1	Tonneau side panel to closing panel	3 bolts (10mm)	3 bolts (10mm)
2	Tonneau side panel to 'B' post	12 spot welds	Single row spot welds (ARO 264A or equivalent)
3	Tonneau side panel to wheel arch	16 spot welds	Single row spot welds (ARO 105010 or equivalent)
4	Tonneau side panel to rear upper panel	5 spot welds	Single row spot welds (ARO 103402 or equivalent)
5	Tonneau side panel to sill	6 spot welds	4 MIG plug welds
6	Tonneau side panel to 'B' post closing	4 spot welds	4 MIG plug welds
7	Tonneau side panel to rear quarter panel	10 spot welds	10 MIG plug welds
8	Rear deck to tonneau side panel	1 Pop rivet	—
9	Tonneau side panel to 'B' post closing	MIG	MIG
10a	Rear deck to tonneau side panel	MIG	2 x 15mm MIG welds
10b	Tonneau side panel gutter to rear deck	6 spot welds	4 MIG plug welds

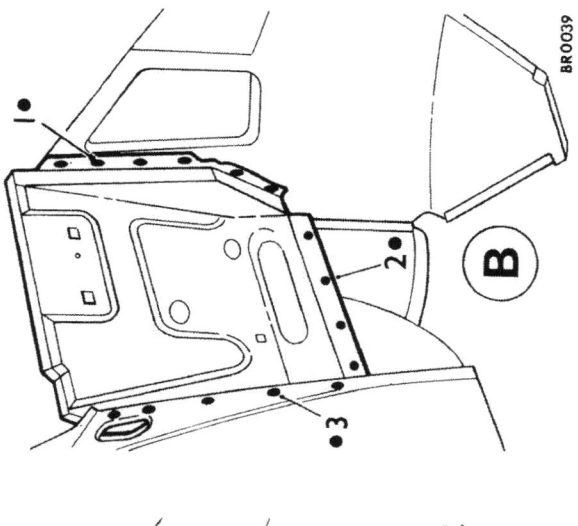

BR0039

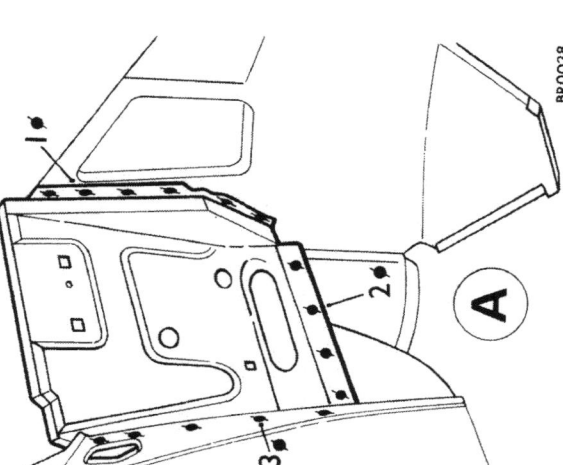

BR0038

Removing
4 Disconnect battery.
5 Remove components as necessary to gain access.
6 Cut spot welds described in 1, 2 and 3.

Refitting
7 Prepare the replacement panel, (see 'PREPARATION AND TECHNIQUES').
8 Clamp closing plate in position and align.
9 Make the spot welds described in 1, 2 and 3.
10 Finish (see 'PREPARATION AND TECHNIQUES') and paint.
11 Reverse the procedure in 4 and 5.

BODY PANEL REPAIRS   319

Method of Attachment	A Factory Joint	B Service Joint
11a Tonneau lower panel rear flange	6 spot welds	Single row spot welds (ARO 105010 or equivalent)
11b Tonneau lower panel front flange	7 spot welds	Single row spot welds (ARO 105010 or equivalent)
11c Tonneau lower panel bottom flange	5 spot welds	Single row spot welds (ARO 105010 or equivalent)
12 Tonneau side panel to luggage compartment floor	4 spot welds	4 MIG plug welds
13 Tonneau side panel to floor	—	MIG
14 Tonneau side panel to tonneau lower panel	6 spot welds	Single row spot welds (ARO 102653 or equivalent)
15 Tonneau side panel gutter to rear upper panel gusset	5 spot welds	Single row spot welds (ARO 103402 or equivalent)
16 Boot lid stay bracket (L.H. side only)	2 spot welds	4 spot welds (ARO 102653 or equivalent)

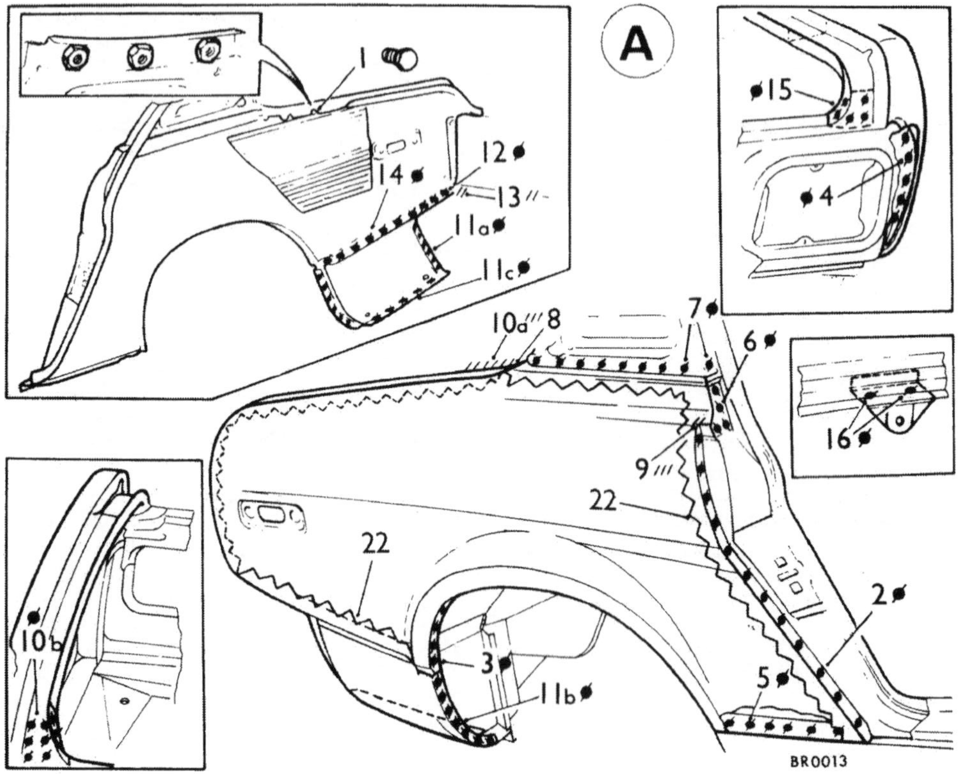

Removing

17 Disconnect the battery.

18 Remove components as necessary to obtain access to the tonneau side panel and its joints.

19 Remove boot lid.

20 Remove three bolts securing tonneau side panel to valance.

21 Cut spot welds described in 2, 3, 4, 5, 6 and 7.

22 Cut tonneau side panel as shown.

23 Cut spot welds at 10b, 12 and 15.

24 Cut welds at 9, 10a and 13.

25 Remove remnants of tonneau side panel.

26 Cut spot welds described in 11a, 11b, 11c and 14.

27 Remove tonneau lower panel.

Refitting

28 Prepare tonneau side panel and tonneau lower panel (see 'PREPARATION AND TECHNIQUES').

29 Offer up the tonneau lower panel and clamp in position.

30 Make spot welds described in 11a, 11b and 11c.

31 Clamp tonneau side panel in position.

32 Locate tonneau side panel on bolts. To facilitate this, slot holes in panel.

33 Check door and boot lid alignment.

BR0013

TONNEAU SIDE PANEL—L.H.

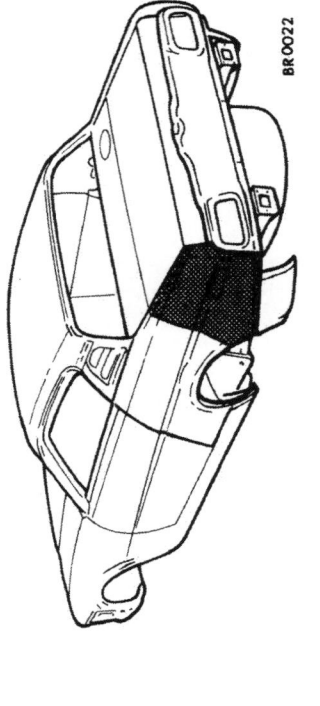

BR0022

Method of Attachment	A Factory Joint	B Service Joint
1 Support stay bracket (L.H. side only)	2 spot welds	4 spot welds (ARO 102653 or equivalent)
2 Tonneau side panel to gutter	10 spot welds	Single row spot welds (ARO 103402 or equivalent)
3 Tonneau side panel to rear upper panel	5 spot welds	Single row spot welds (ARO 103402 or equivalent)
4 Tonneau side panel to wheel arch	5 spot welds	Single row spot welds (ARO 105010 or equivalent)
5 Tonneau side panel to lower panel	9 spot welds	(a) 5 spot welds (ARO 102653 or equivalent) (b) 4 MIG plug welds
6 New part panel to existing panel	—	Continuous MIG
7 Fill in holes in boot floor	—	MIG

Removing
8 Disconnect the battery.
9 Remove the fuel tank.
10 Remove components as necessary to obtain access to the tonneau side panel and its joints.
11 Cut spot welds as described in 1, 2, 3 and 4.
12 Cut through tonneau side panel as shown.
13 Cut through welds at 5 and 7.
14 Remove remnants of panel.

34 Make spot welds described in 2, 3, 4 and 14.
35 MIG plug weld at 5, 6, 7, 10b and 12.
36 MIG plug weld holes at 13.
37 Make spot welds at 15.
38 Spot weld bonnet lid stay bracket in position (L.H. side only).
39 Finish (see 'PREPARATION AND TECHNIQUES') and paint.
40 Refit components removed in 18 and connect battery.

B

BR0014

Refitting

15 Cut new panel to approximately the shape required.

16 Prepare all surfaces (see 'PREPARATION AND TECHNIQUES').

17 Clamp new panel section in position and check alignment.

18 Cut panels to butt.

19 Prepare panel mating surfaces (see 'PREPARATION AND TECHNIQUES').

20 MIG tack weld part panel in position.

21 Continuous MIG weld as described in 6.

22 Align boot lid, rear upper panel and tonneau side panel.

23 Make spot welds in 1, 2, 3, 4 and 5a.

24 Make MIG plug welds in 5b.

25 Finish (see 'PREPARATION AND TECHNIQUES') and paint.

26 Refit components and connect battery.

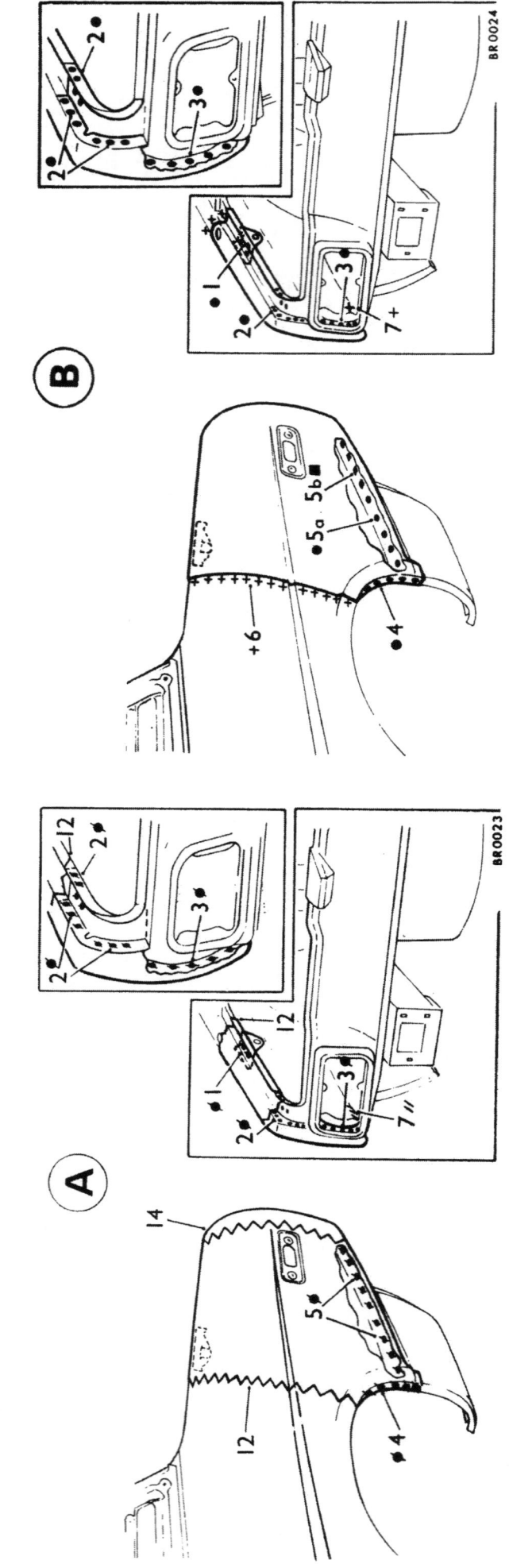

REAR UPPER PANEL

77.61.65

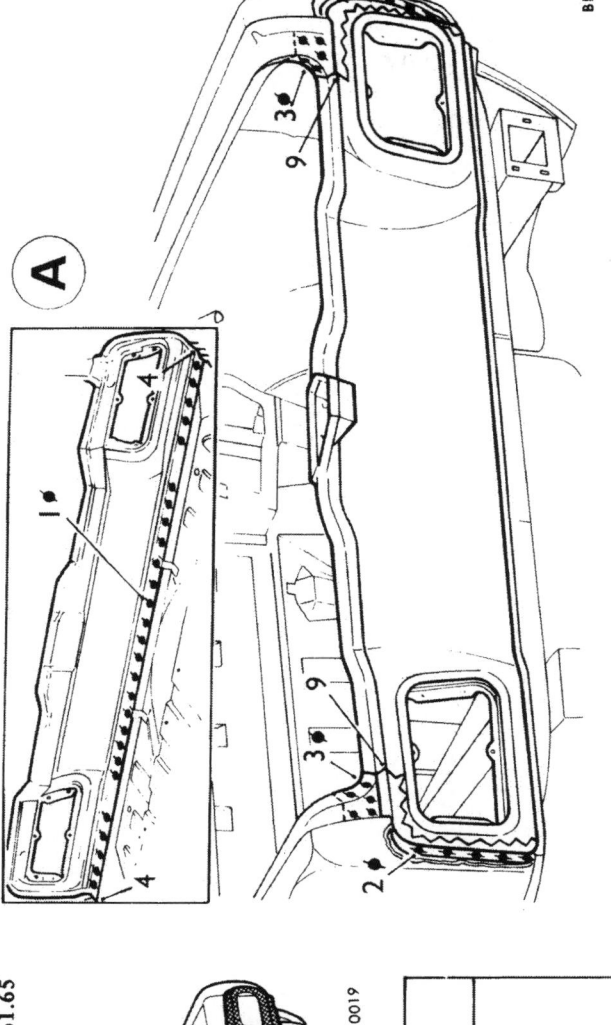

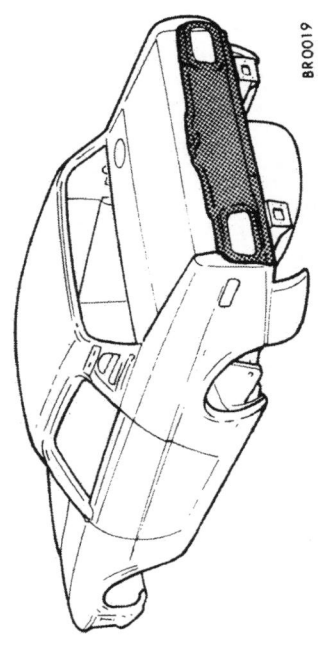

BR0019

BR0020

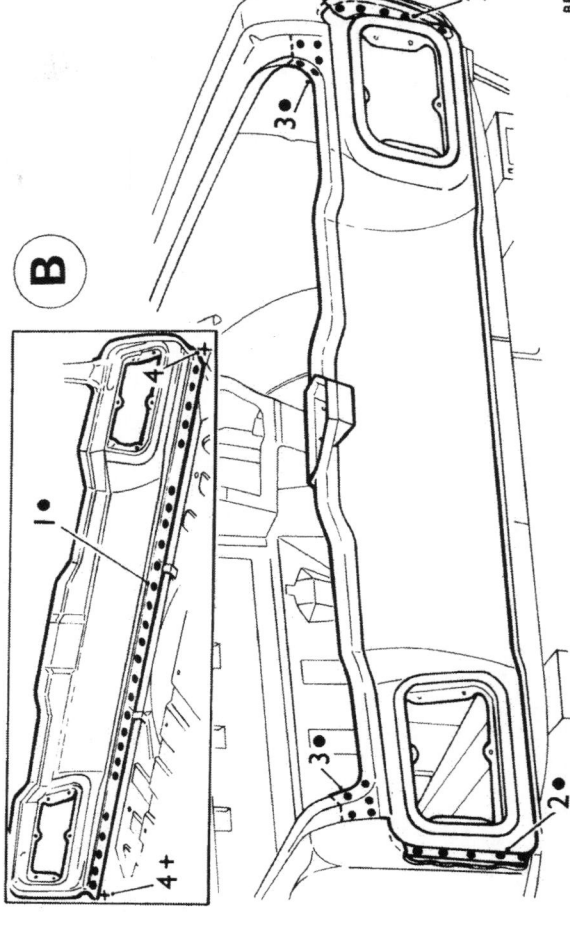

BR0021

Method of Attachment		A Factory Joint	B Service Joint
1	Rear upper panel to side panels and rear luggage compartment floor	27 spot welds	Single row spot welds (ARO 103402 or equivalent)
2	Rear upper panel to tonneau side panels	10 spot welds	Single row spot welds (ARO 103402 or equivalent)
3	Rear upper panel gusset to gutter	10 spot welds	Single row spot welds (ARO 103402 or equivalent)
4	Fill holes in luggage compartment floor	CO_2/MIG	MIG

Removing

5 Disconnect the battery.
6 Remove any components which prevent access to the rear upper panel and its joints.
7 Remove all flammable material from the vicinity of the rear upper panel.
8 Cut the spot welds described in 1.
9 Cut the rear upper panel either side as shown and remove having cut welds at 4.
10 Cut spot welds described in 2 and 3.

Refitting

11 Prepare the panel and all mating joints (see 'PREPARATION AND TECHNIQUES').
12 Fit the rear upper panel and align with drain channels and tonneau side panels.
13 Make spot welds described in 1.
14 Fit boot lid and check alignment.
15 Remove boot lid and make spot welds described in 2 and 3.
16 MIG weld fill holes at intersection of rear upper panel, tonneau side panels and side panels of luggage compartment.
17 Finish (see 'PREPARATION AND TECHNIQUES') and paint.
18 Reverse the procedure in 5 and 7.

REAR SIDE MEMBER

77.64.01

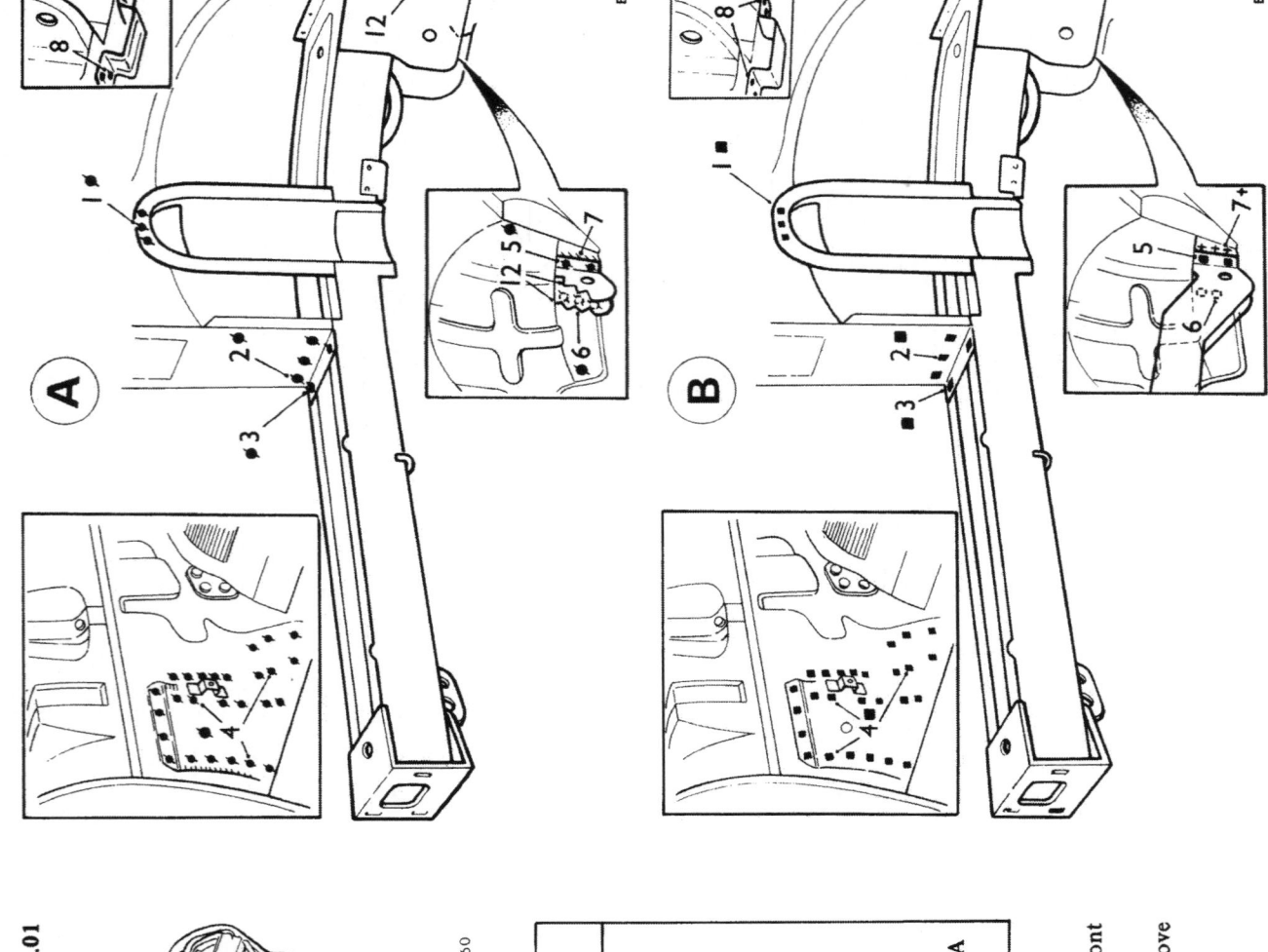

Method of Attachment	A Factory Joint	B Service Joint
1 To spring turret	3 spot welds	3 plug welds
2 To petrol filler duct	3 spot welds	3 plug welds
3 To side-member flanges	2 spot welds	2 plug welds
4 To heelboard	25 spot welds	26 plug welds
5 Side-member forward flange — outboard	2 spot welds	2 plug welds
6 Side-member forward flange — inboard	3 spot welds	2 plug welds
7 To edge of side-member flange — outboard	—	2 x 20mm MIG welds
8 Skid bracket attachment to underframe	4 spot welds	4 spot welds (ARO 264A or equivalent)

Removing

8   Disconnect battery.
9   Remove fuel tank.
10   Remove components as required to gain access to the side-member.
11   Cut spot welds as described in 1, 2, 3 and 4.
12   Cut through rear side-member at front flanges and remove side-member.
13   Cut spot welds at 5 and 6.
14   Grind off flanges at 7 and remove remnants of panel.
15   Cut spot welds at 8.

BR0060

BR0061

BR0062

Method of Attachment	A Factory Joint	B Service Joint
1 To trailing edge of fender valance	20 spot welds	(a) Single row spot welds (ARO 100486 or equivalent) (b) 5 MIG plug welds (c) 4 MIG plug welds
2 To forward flange of sill	6 spot welds	Single row spot welds (ARO 100486 or equivalent)
3 To sill	14 spot welds	14 MIG plug welds
4 Screen surround to upper 'A' post	6 spot welds	(a) 4 spot welds (ARO 242A or equivalent) (b) 2 MIG plug welds
5 To windscreen surround	6 spot welds	6 MIG plug welds
6 To drain channel	CO_2/MIG weld	(a) 4 spot welds (ARO 100486 or equivalent) (b) 3 x 15mm MIG welds
7 'A' post to 'A' post upper	CO_2/MIG weld	Continuous MIG weld
8 Closing panel to sill top flange	CO_2/MIG weld	Continuous MIG weld

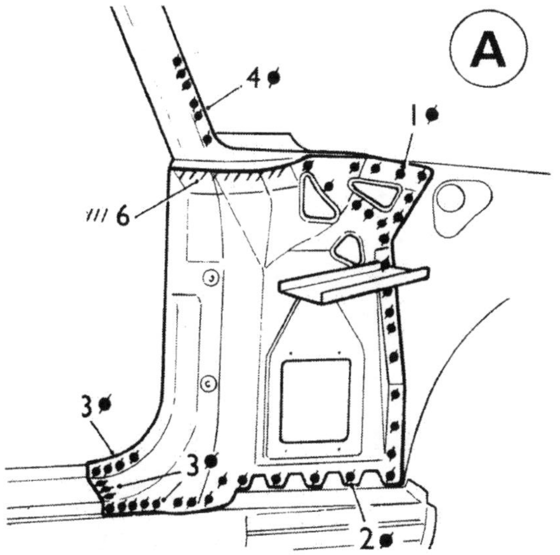

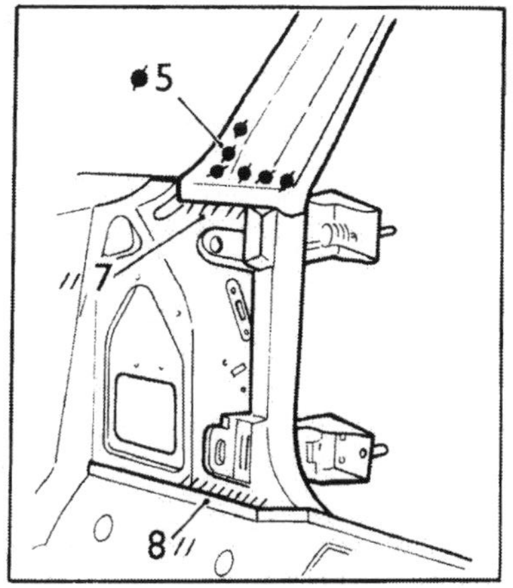

Refitting

16 Prepare all mating flanges (see 'PREPARATION AND TECHNIQUES').

17 Offer up replacement side-member, clamp in position and support in jig.

18 Plug weld as described in 1, 2, 3, 4, 5 and 6.

19 MIG weld at 7.

20 Spot weld as described in 8.

21 Finish (see 'PREPARATION AND TECHNIQUES') and paint.

22 Reverse instructions 8, 9 and 10.

'A' POST

77.70.03

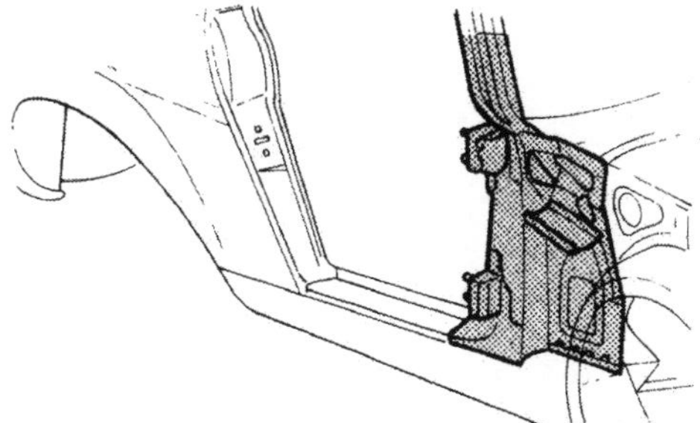

Removing

9 Disconnect the battery.

10 Remove components as necessary to gain access.

11 Cut spot welds as described in 1, 2, 3, 4 and 5.

12 Grind off the welds described in 6, 7 and 8.

Refitting

13 Prepare the replacement panel (see 'PREPARATION AND TECHNIQUES').

14 Clamp the new 'A' post in position.

15 Fit the wing to check alignment.

16 Fit door to check alignment.

17 Remove door and front wing.

18 Tack weld 'A' post in position.

19 Make spot welds described in 1a, 2, 4a and 6a.

20 Make the plug welds described in 1b, 1c, 3, 4b and 5.

21 Make the MIG welds described in 6a, 7 and 8.

22 Finish (see 'PREPARATION AND TECHNIQUES') and paint.

23 Refit the components described in 10 and connect the battery.

BRO040

BRO041

DOOR PANEL

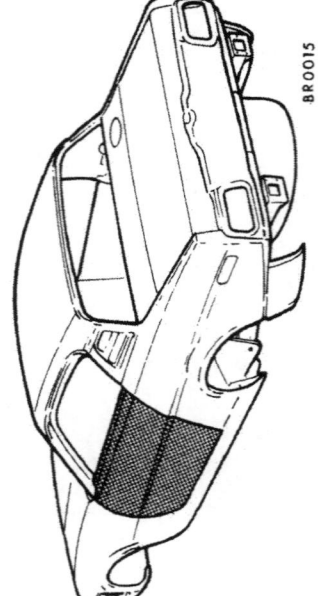

BR0015

Method of Attachment	A Factory Joint	B Service Joint
1 To door frame	1 x 15mm CO_2/MIG 1 x 35mm CO_2/MIG 2 spot welds	1 x 15mm MIG 1 x 35mm MIG 2 spot welds (ARO 100737 or equivalent) 9 tack welds (ARO 242A with electrode 5632)
	Metal-to-metal adhesive	Metal-to-metal adhesive

Removing

2 Remove the door glass and inner components.
3 Remove the door frame.
4 Grind off the edges of the door panel.
5 Cut the spot welds and separate.
6 Cut around the arc welds, break the adhesive joint and remove the panel.
7 Remove remnants of door panel.

Refitting

8 Prepare the panel (see 'PREPARATION AND TECHNIQUES').
9 Apply metal-to-metal adhesive to door flange.
10 Place panel in position on door frame and clamp in position.
11 Tack spot weld around flange of door frame.
12 Dress face welds and paint with zinc based primer around flange.
13 Bend flanges on door panel over edges of door frame.
14 Make spot welds as above.
15 MIG weld around door frame.
16 Finish (see 'PREPARATION AND TECHNIQUES') and paint.
17 Reverse the procedure in 2 and 3.

BR0042

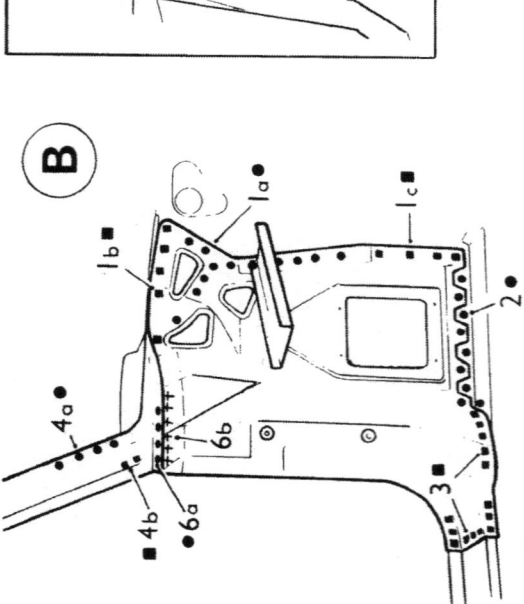

REAR WHEEL ARCH ASSEMBLY

77.70.65

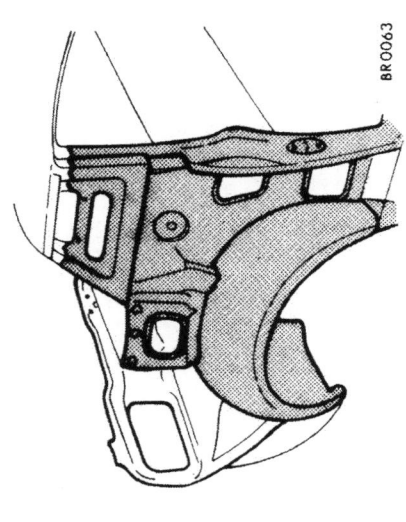

BRO063

Method of Attachment	A Factory Joint	B Service Joint
10 Rear deck to closing panel	1 x 25mm CO$_2$/MIG weld	1 x 25mm MIG weld
11 'B' post closing panel to rear quarter panel	2 spot welds	(a) 1 plug weld (b) 1 x 25mm MIG weld
12 'B' post closing panel to header rail	5 spot welds	5 plug welds
13 'B' post to 'B' post closing panel	24 spot welds	Single row spot welds (ARO 242A or equivalent)
14 'B' post closing to front luggage compartment	—	2 MIG plug welds
15 Top of 'B' post to door aperture	—	Braze
16 Seat belt anchorage in wheel arch outer	4 spot welds	4 spot welds (ARO 264A or equivalent)
17 Outer wheel arch to inner wheel arch	19 spot welds	Single row spot welds (ARO 264A or equivalent)
18 Outer wheel arch to inner wheel arch and tonneau lower filler panel	8 spot welds	Double row spot welds (ARO 264A or equivalent)
19 Outer wheel arch flange to inner wheel arch flange	Roller weld (continuous seam weld 1320mm)	4 x 25mm MIG welds
20 Wheel arch angle to outer wheel arch	—	Single row spot welds (ARO 264A or equivalent)
21 Seat belt bracket to wheel arch	—	7 MIG plug welds
22 Inner wheel arch to heelboard	17 spot welds	Single row spot welds (ARO 264A or equivalent)
23 Inner wheel arch to underframe	8 spot welds	(a) Single row spot welds (ARO 242A or equivalent) (b) 3 MIG plug welds
24 Inner wheel arch vertical webs	14 spot welds	12 MIG plug welds

Method of Attachment	A Factory Joint	B Service Joint
1 Rear flange of rear quarter panel	4 spot welds	4 plug welds
2 Forward flange of rear quarter panel	2 spot welds	4 spot welds (ARO 242A or equivalent)
3 Rear quarter panel to 'B' post closing panel	5 spot welds	2 x single row spot welds (ARO 264A or equivalent)
4 'B' post closing panel to inner sill	6 spot welds	Single row spot welds (ARO 264A or equivalent)
5 'B' post closing panel to wheel arch angle	8 spot welds	Single row spot welds (ARO 264A or equivalent)
6 Wheel arch angle to closing panel	9 spot welds	Single row spot welds (ARO 264A or equivalent)
7 Closing panel to rear deck	3 bolts (10mm)	3 bolts (10mm)
8 Closing panel to 'B' post closing panel	4 spot welds	4 MIG plug welds
9 Seat belt bracket to 'B' post closing panel	6 spot welds	6 spot welds (ARO 100486 or equivalent)

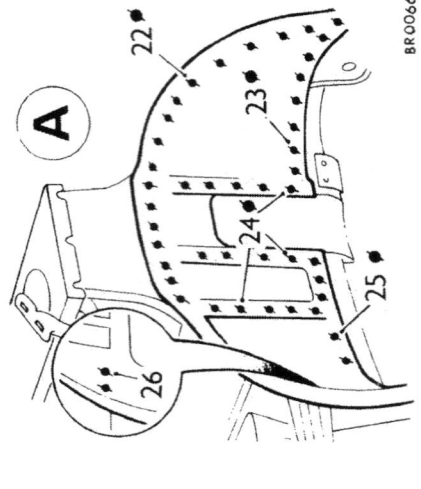

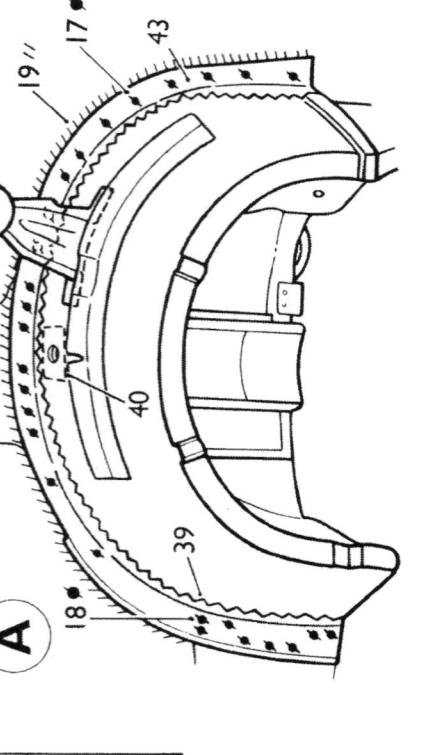

Method of Attachment		A Factory Joint	B Service Joint
25	Inner wheel arch lower flange rear	5 spot welds	(a) 3 spot welds (ARO 242A or equivalent) (b) 1 MIG plug weld
26	Inner wheel arch to side panel	2 spot welds	2 spot welds (ARO 264A or equivalent)

Removing
27 Disconnect the battery.
28 Remove the fuel tank.
29 Remove components as necessary to gain access to the wheel arch and associated panels.
30 Remove all flammable material from the vicinity of the wheel arch.
31 Cut through the rear quarter panel and 'B' post where shown.
32 Cut the spot welds at 1, 2 and 3.
33 Remove the lower portion of rear quarter panel.
34 Cut spot welds at 4, 5, 6 and 8.
35 Grind off weld at 10.
36 Unbolt at 7 and remove filler panel.

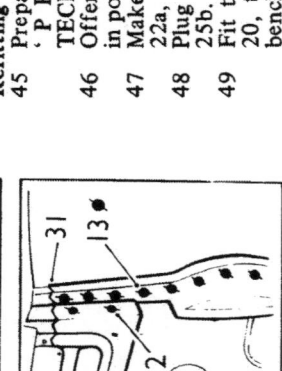

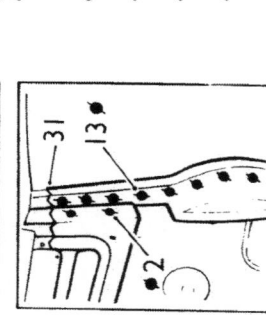

37 Cut spot welds at 9.
38 Cut spot welds at 11, 12 and 13 and remove 'B' post closing panel.
39 Cut through the outer wheel arch as shown.
40 Cut spot welds at 16 and salvage seat belt anchorage plate to use in repair.
41 Cut spot welds at 17 and 18.
42 Grind away seam weld at 19.
43 Remove flange by grinding.
44 Cut spot welds at 22, 23, 24, 25 and 26.

Refitting
45 Prepare the replacement panels (see 'PREPARATION AND TECHNIQUES').
46 Offer up inner wheel arch and clamp in position.
47 Make the spot welds as described in 22a, 23 and 25a.
48 Plug weld as described in 22b, 24 and 25b.
49 Fit the wheel arch angle, described in 20, to the outer wheel arch on the bench.

50 Bench fit the seat belt anchorage plate to the outer wheel arch.
51 Offer up the outer wheel arch and clamp in position.
52 Offer up tonneau side panel to check alignment.

continued

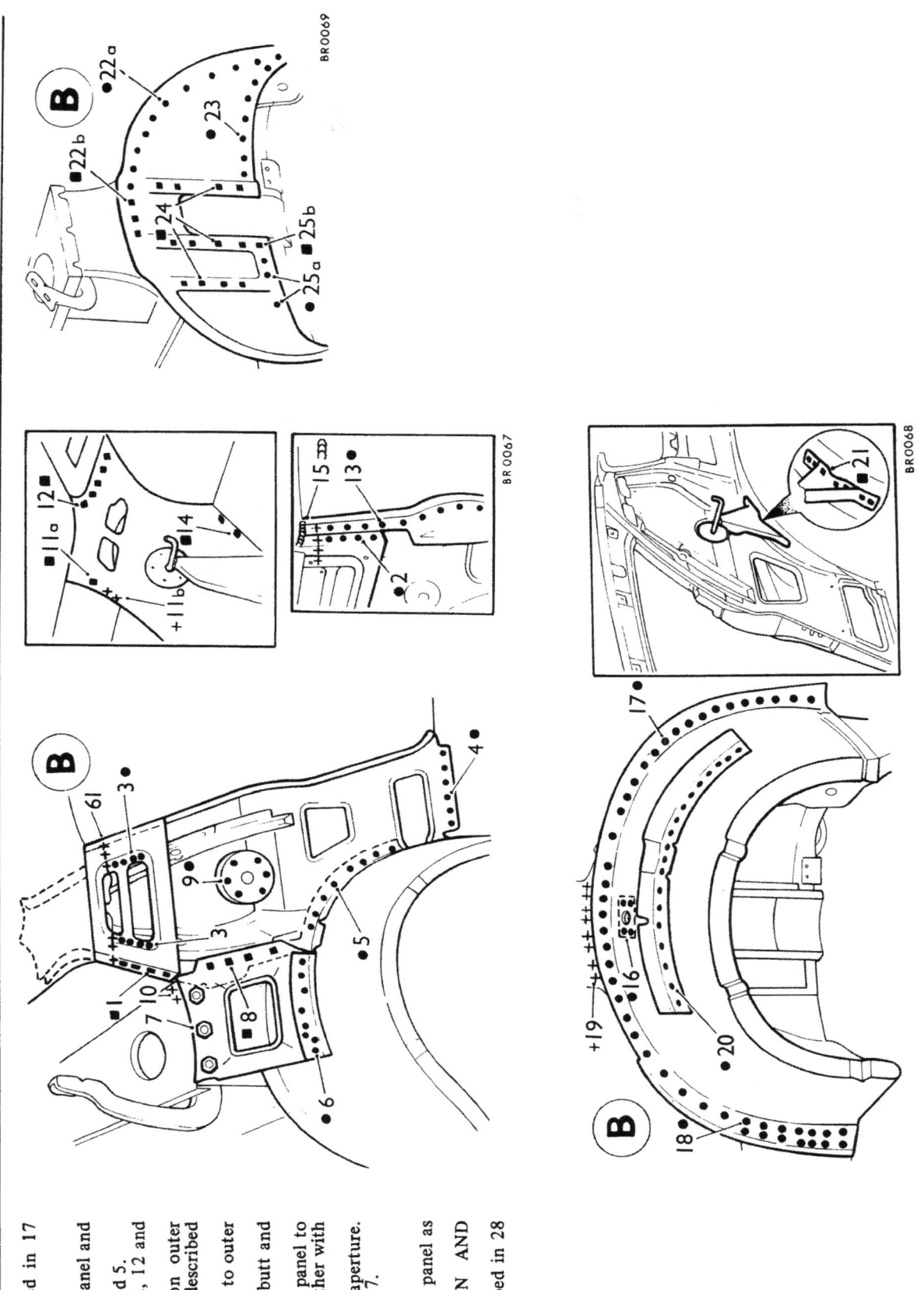

53 Make spot welds as described in 17 and 18.
54 MIG weld as described in 19.
55 Offer up the 'B' post filler panel and clamp in position.
56 Spot weld as described in 4 and 5.
57 Plug weld as described in 11a, 12 and 14.
58 Position seat belt bracket on outer wheel arch and spot weld as described in 9.
59 Plug weld foot of seat bracket to outer wheel arch as described in 21.
60 Cut replacement 'B' post to butt and spot weld as described in 13.
61 Cut replacement rear quarter panel to butt and MIG weld joint together with 'B' post.
62 Braze top of 'B' post to door aperture.
63 Locate filler panel on bolts at 7.
64 Spot weld as described in 6.
65 Plug weld as described in 8.
66 MIG weld rear deck to filler panel as described in 10.
67 Finish (see 'PREPARATION AND TECHNIQUES') and paint.
68 Refit the components described in 28 and 29.
69 Reconnect the battery.

OUTER SILL COMPLETE

77.70.70

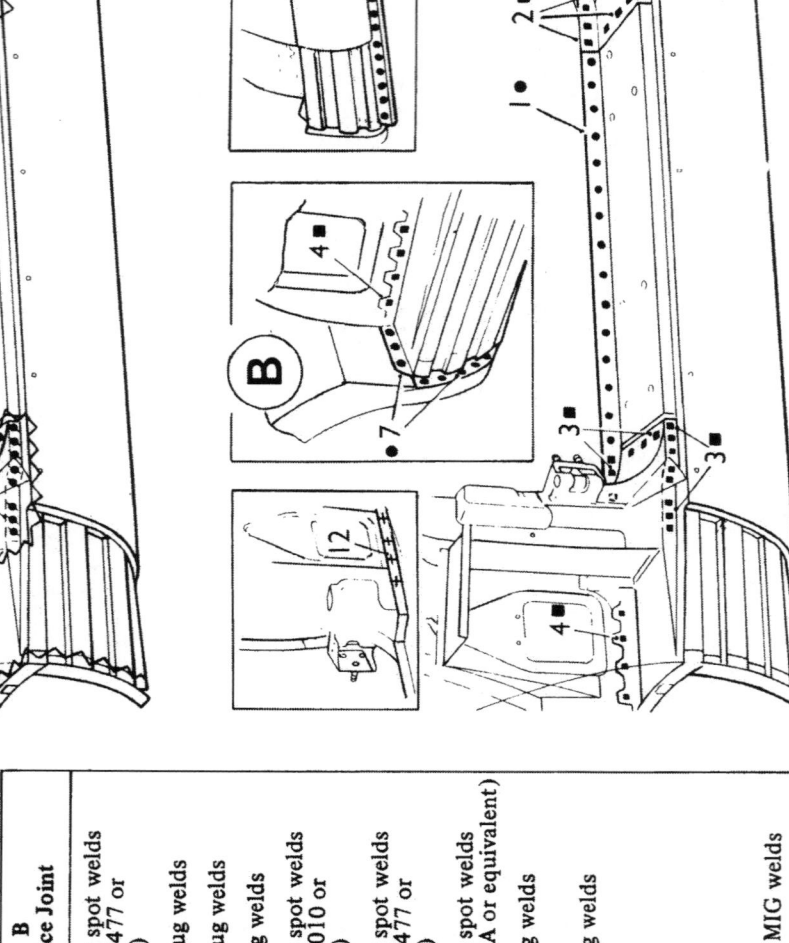

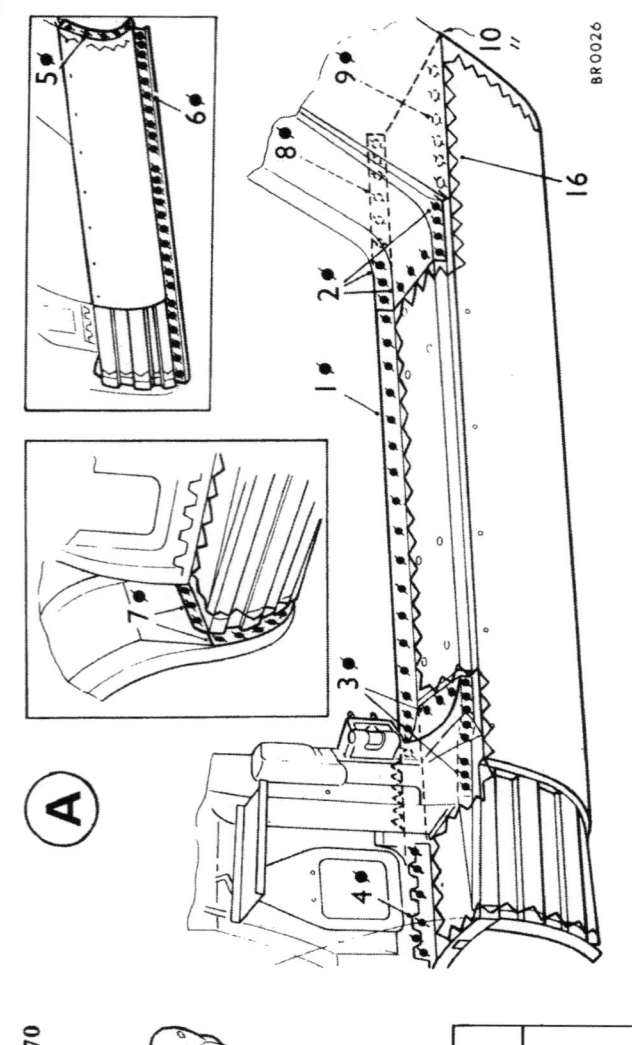

	Method of Attachment	A Factory Joint	B Service Joint
1	Sill top flange	15 spot welds	Single row spot welds (ARO 107477 or equivalent)
2	'B' post to sill	10 spot welds	10 MIG plug welds
3	'A' post to sill	15 spot welds	14 MIG plug welds
4	Sill to 'A' post	6 spot welds	4 MIG plug welds
5	Sill to wheel arch rear	5 spot welds	Single row spot welds (ARO 105010 or equivalent)
6	Sill bottom flange	32 spot welds	Single row spot welds (ARO 107477 or equivalent)
7	Sill to wheel arch front	8 spot welds	Single row spot welds (ARO 242A or equivalent)
8	Sill inner flange to tonneau side panel	6 spot welds	4 MIG plug welds
9	Tonneau side panel to sill	6 spot welds	4 MIG plug welds
10	Sill to wheel arch abutment	CO_2/MIG weld	MIG weld
11	Tonneau side panel abutment to sill	—	Braze
12	'A' post to inner sill	CO_2/MIG weld	3 x 15mm MIG welds

Method of Attachment	A Factory Joint	B Service Joint
1 Sill top flange	13 spot welds	Single row spot welds (ARO 107477 or equivalent)
2 Sill to 'B' post	10 spot welds	10 MIG plug welds
3 Sill bottom flange	17 spot welds	Single row spot welds (ARO 107477 or equivalent)
4 Sill to tonneau side panel	Braze	Braze
5 Sill to wheel arch	4 spot welds	4 spot welds (ARO 105010 or equivalent)
6 Sill top flange to valance	6 spot welds	4 MIG plug welds
7 Sill to wheel arch rear	MIG	MIG
8 Tonneau side panel to sill	6 spot welds	4 MIG plugs
9 New sill to existing sill	–	MIG weld butt joint

Removing

13 Remove front wing as described in 77.28.29.

14 Remove door and all flammable material from area of sill.

15 Cut spot welds as described in 1, 2, 3, 4 and 5.

16 Cut sill as shown.

17 Cut spot welds in 6.

18 Cut sill reinforcing member.

19 Remove remnants of lower flange.

20 Cut spot welds at 7.

21 Cut sill flange at rear of 'A' post.

22 Cut spot welds described in 8 and 9.

23 Remove remnants of panel.

24 Cut and separate top portion of sill reinforcement.

25 Cut the weld described in 10.

Refitting

26 Prepare the panel and mating surfaces (see 'PREPARATION AND TECHNIQUES').

27 Clamp the replacement outer sill in position.

28 Plug tack outer sill with door in position to check alignment.

29 Make spot welds described in 1, 5, 6 and 7.

30 Make MIG plug welds described in 2, 3, 4, 8 and 9.

31 MIG weld at 10 and 12.

32 Braze at 11.

33 Finish (see 'PREPARATION AND TECHNIQUES') and paint.

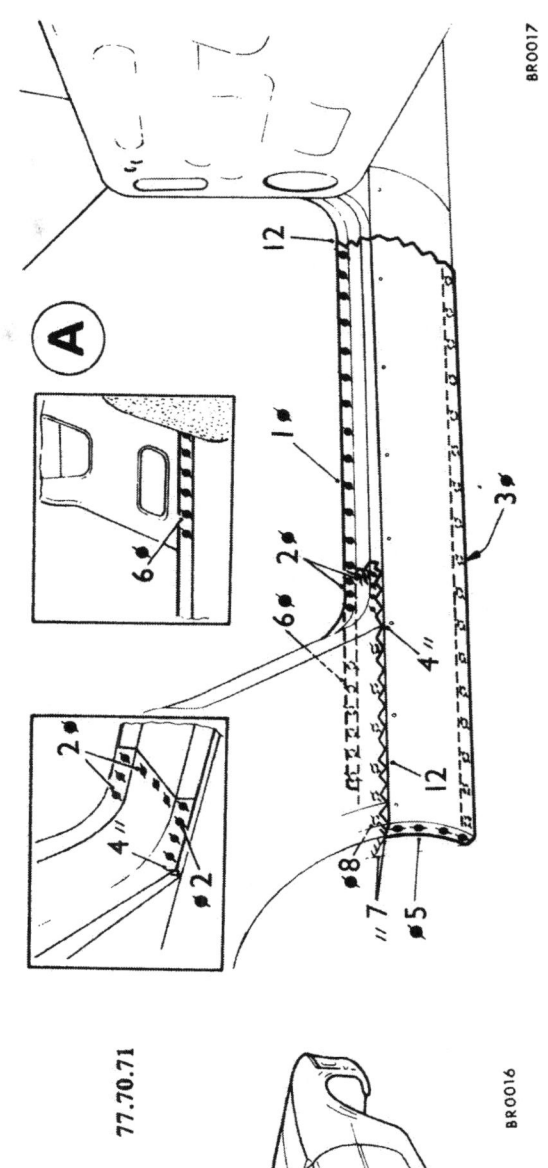

BR0017

OUTER SILL
(Cut rear of 'A' post)

77.70.71

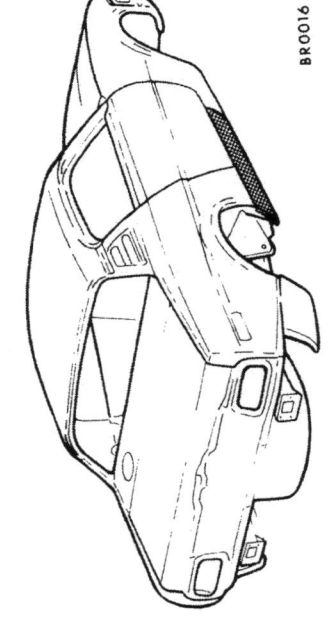

BR0016

BODY PANEL REPAIRS   331

INNER SILL

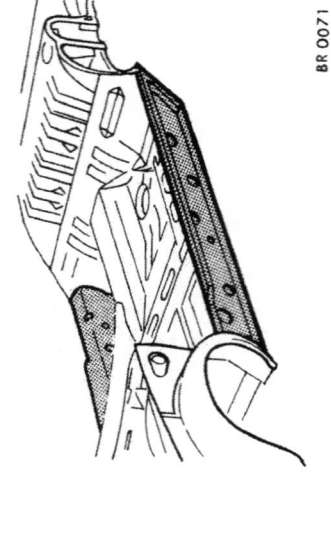

BR 0071

Method of Attachment	A Factory Joint	B Service Joint
1	To 'B' post closing panel	6 spot welds	Single row spot welds (ARO 264A or equivalent)
2	Lower flange	24 spot welds	Single row spot welds (ARO 264A or equivalent)
3	Forward flange	5 spot welds	Single row spot welds (ARO 264A or equivalent)
4	Sill to front floor stiffener	3 spot welds	Single row spot welds (ARO 264A or equivalent)
5	Sill to central floor stiffener	4 spot welds	Single row spot welds (ARO 264A or equivalent)
6	Sill to intermediate floor stiffener	4 spot welds	Single row spot welds (ARO 264A or equivalent)
7	Sill to rear floor stiffener	5 spot welds	Single row spot welds (ARO 264A or equivalent)
8	Rear flange to heel-board	7 spot welds	MIG weld
9	Wheel arch to lower panel	5 spot welds	5 spot welds (ARO 264A or equivalent)

Removing
10 Disconnect the battery.
11 Remove the outer sill, see 77.70.70.
12 Cut spot welds described in 1.
13 Cut spot welds described in 4, 5, 6 and 7.
14 Cut through inner sill panel as shown.
15 Cut spot welds at 2 and 3.

BR0018

BR0018

Removing
10 Disconnect the battery.
11 Disconnect petrol pipe (R.H. side only).
12 Cut through outer sill panel:
  a along the rear edge of the 'A' post to the bottom flange,
  b around the front, outer and rear of the tonneau side panel and 'B' post.
13 Cut the spot welds described in 1 and 6.
14 Cut weld described in 7.
15 Cut the spot welds described in 8 and remove remnants of sill.

Refitting
16 Cut the new outer sill to make butt joints described in 9.
17 Prepare the panels (see 'PREPARATION AND TECHNIQUES').
18 Clamp the outer sill section in position and cut to butt.
19 Check door alignment with sill clamped in position.
20 MIG tack butt joint.
21 Continuous MIG weld butt joint and finish (see 'PREPARATION AND TECHNIQUES').
22 Make spot welds described in 1, 3 and 5.
23 Plug weld as described in 2, 6 and 8.
24 Finish (see 'PREPARATION AND TECHNIQUES') and paint.

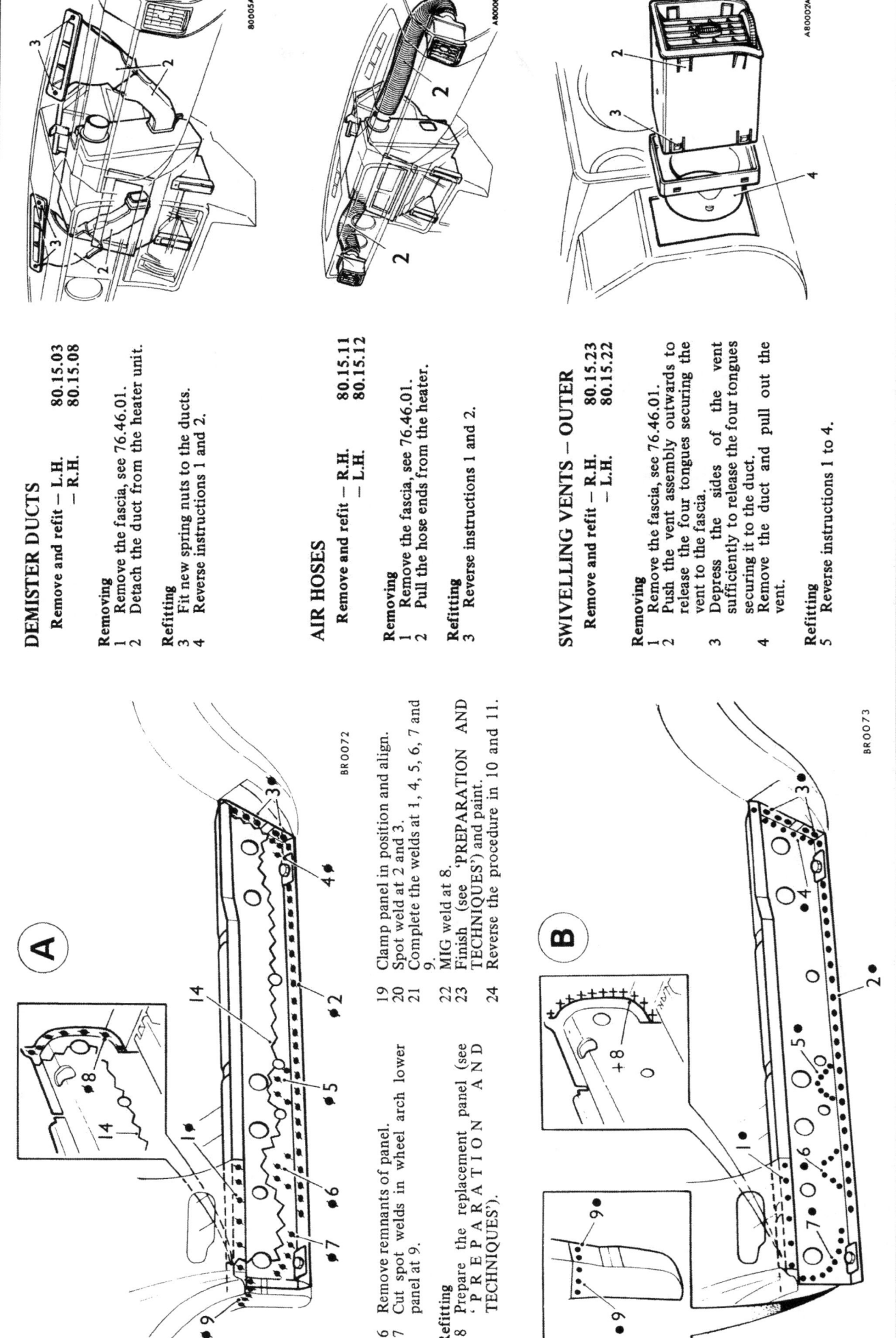

DEMISTER DUCTS

Remove and refit – L.H. 80.15.03
**   – R.H. 80.15.08**

Removing
1 Remove the fascia, see 76.46.01.
2 Detach the duct from the heater unit.

Refitting
3 Fit new spring nuts to the ducts.
4 Reverse instructions 1 and 2.

AIR HOSES

Remove and refit – R.H. 80.15.11
**   – L.H. 80.15.12**

Removing
1 Remove the fascia, see 76.46.01.
2 Pull the hose ends from the heater.

Refitting
3 Reverse instructions 1 and 2.

SWIVELLING VENTS – OUTER

Remove and refit – R.H. 80.15.23
**   – L.H. 80.15.22**

Removing
1 Remove the fascia, see 76.46.01.
2 Push the vent assembly outwards to release the four tongues securing the vent to the fascia.
3 Depress the sides of the vent sufficiently to release the four tongues securing it to the duct.
4 Remove the duct and pull out the vent.

Refitting
5 Reverse instructions 1 to 4.

16 Remove remnants of panel.
17 Cut spot welds in wheel arch lower panel at 9.

Refitting
18 Prepare the replacement panel (see 'PREPARATION AND TECHNIQUES').
19 Clamp panel in position and align.
20 Spot weld at 2 and 3.
21 Complete the welds at 1, 4, 5, 6, 7 and 9.
22 MIG weld at 8.
23 Finish (see 'PREPARATION AND TECHNIQUES') and paint.
24 Reverse the procedure in 10 and 11.

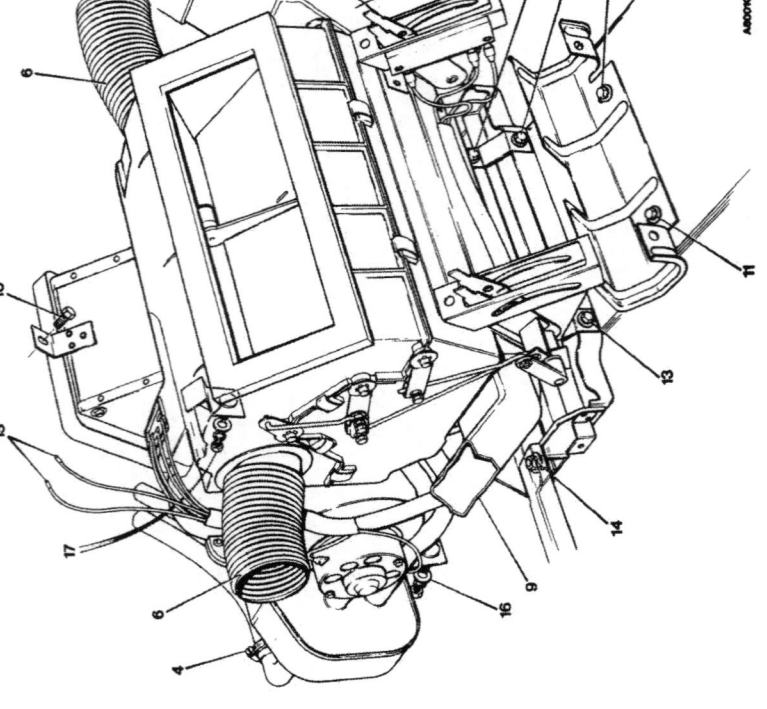

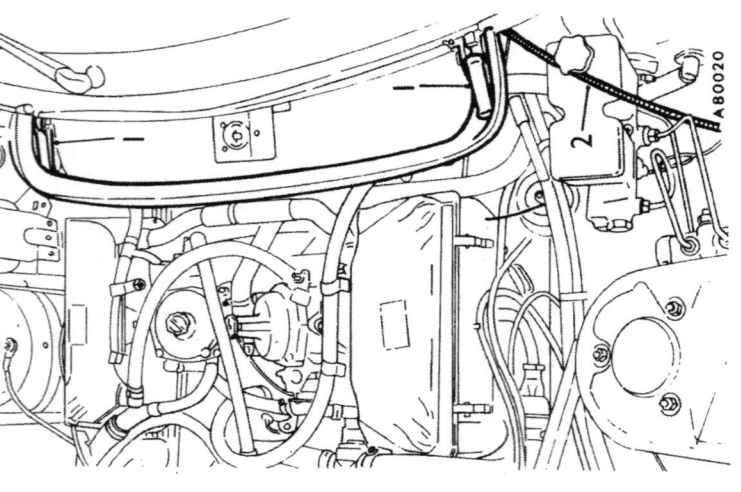

SWIVELLING VENT – CENTRE

– Remove and refit   80.15.24

Removing
1 Depress one side of the vent frame to detach the retaining boss from the surround,
2 Lift out the vent.

Refitting
3 Reverse instructions 1 and 2.

FRESH AIR DUCT

Remove and refit   80.15.31

Removing
1 Release the two clips.
2 Disengage the bonnet lock cable from the duct and carefully manoeuvre the duct clear of the engine compartment.

Refitting
3 Reverse instructions 1 and 2 ensuring that the duct is located in the retaining clips on the bulkhead.

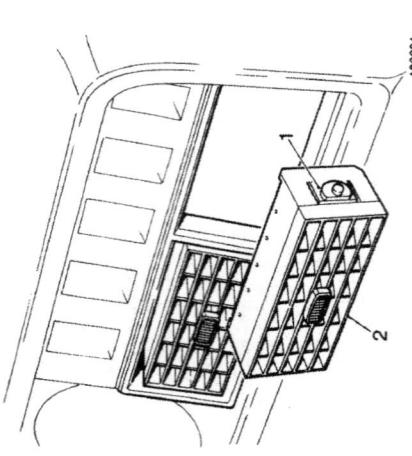

HEATER UNIT

Remove and refit   80.20.01

Removing
1 Isolate the battery.
2 Drain the coolant.
3 Remove the fresh air duct. 80.15.31.
4 Slacken the two clips and disconnect both water hoses from the heater.
5 Remove the fascia. 76.46.01.
6 Remove the two air hoses from the heater.

7 Remove the console assembly. 76.25.01.
8 Remove the control cowl. 76.25.03.
9 Remove the two demister ducts from the heater unit.
10 Remove the one bolt securing the heater air intake to the bulkhead.
11 Remove the control cowl support bracket – two bolts, spring washers and plain washers.
12 Slacken the two bolts securing the heater to the front of the heater support bracket on the transmission tunnel.
13 Remove the two heater support brackets – two bolts, spring washers, and plain washers.

14 Remove the two nuts, bolts, spring washers and plain washers securing the fascia support rails to the support bracket on the transmission tunnel.
15 Disconnect the two leads from the fan motor. (1 Black 1 Green).
16 Remove the nut, spring washer and plain washer securing the water pipe bracket to the bulkhead.
17 Remove the nut, spring washer and plain washer securing the rear of the heater to the bulkhead.
18 Remove the heater from the vehicle taking care to avoid spillage of coolant remaining in the matrix.

Refitting
19 Reverse instructions 1 to 18.

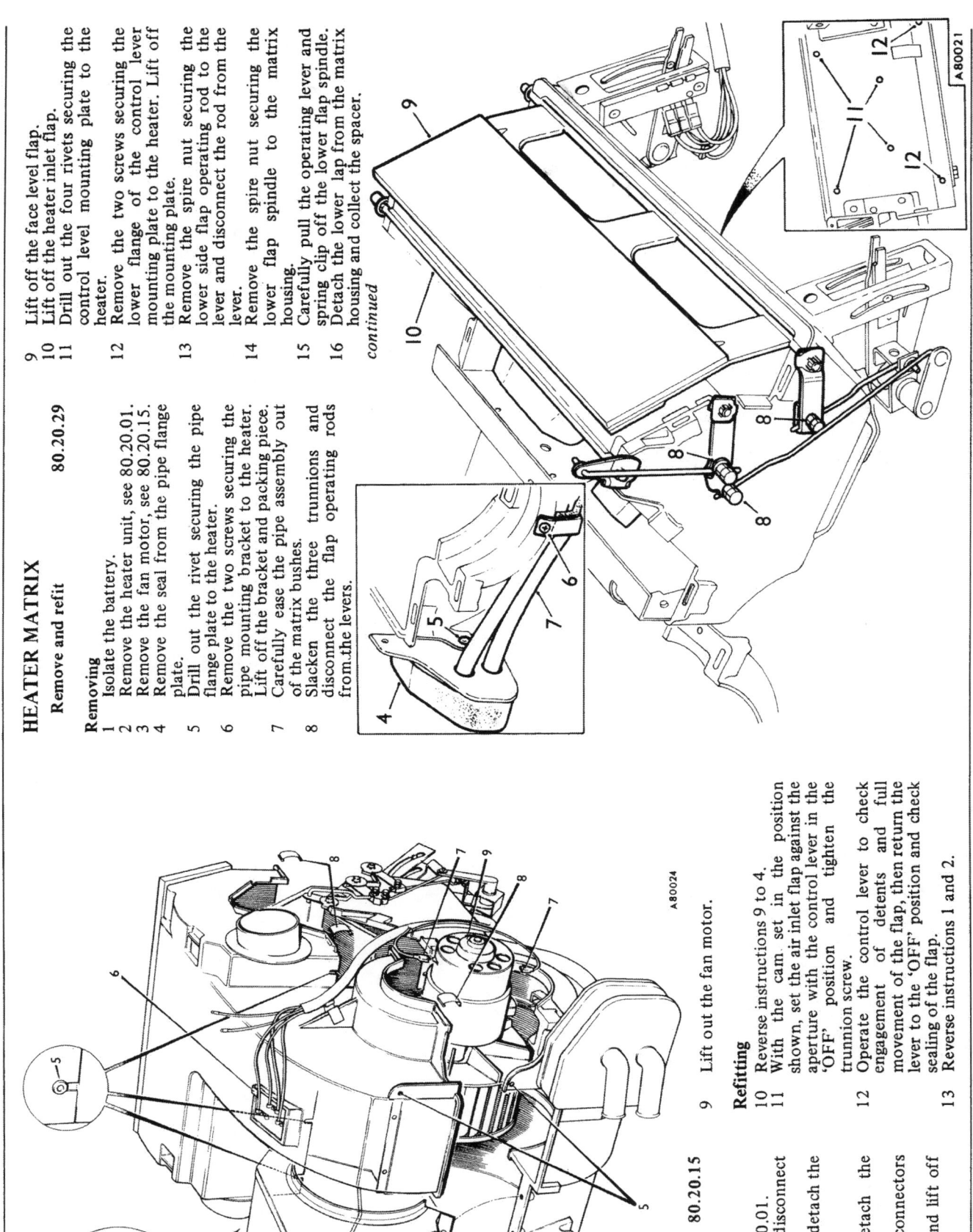

9 Lift off the face level flap.
10 Lift off the heater inlet flap.
11 Drill out the four rivets securing the control level mounting plate to the heater.
12 Remove the two screws securing the lower flange of the control lever mounting plate to the heater. Lift off the mounting plate.
13 Remove the spire nut securing the lower side flap operating rod to the lever and disconnect the rod from the lever.
14 Remove the spire nut securing the lower flap spindle to the matrix housing.
15 Carefully pull the operating lever and spring clip off the lower flap spindle.
16 Detach the lower lap from the matrix housing and collect the spacer.
continued

HEATER MATRIX

Remove and refit　　　80.20.29

Removing
1 Isolate the battery.
2 Remove the heater unit, see 80.20.01.
3 Remove the fan motor, see 80.20.15.
4 Remove the seal from the pipe flange plate.
5 Drill out the rivet securing the pipe flange plate to the heater.
6 Remove the two screws securing the pipe mounting bracket to the heater. Lift off the bracket and packing piece.
7 Carefully ease the pipe assembly out of the matrix bushes.
8 Slacken the three trunnions and disconnect the flap operating rods from the levers.

FAN MOTOR

Remove and refit　　　80.20.15

Removing
1 Isolate the battery.
2 Remove the heater, see 80.20.01.
3 Slacken the trunnion and disconnect the air intake control rod.
4 Remove the six screws and detach the air intake from the heater.
5 Drill out the four rivets.
6 Release the clip and detach the resistor from the heater.
7 Disconnect the two Lucar connectors from the fan motor.
8 Detach the fourteen clips and lift off the upper half of the casing.
9 Lift out the fan motor.

Refitting
10 Reverse instructions 9 to 4.
11 With the cam set in the position shown, set the air inlet flap against the aperture with the control lever in the 'OFF' position and tighten the trunnion screw.
12 Operate the control lever to check engagement of detents and full movement of the flap, then return the lever to the 'OFF' position and check sealing of the flap.
13 Reverse instructions 1 and 2.

17 Drill out the two rivets securing the lower side flap assembly to the heater box.
18 Remove the lower side flap assembly.
19 Drill out the seven rivets securing the matrix housing to the heater box.
20 Remove the matrix complete with housing from the heater box.
21 Remove the matrix from the housing.

Refitting
22 Fit two new pipe seals into the matrix and replace the foam packing piece.
23 Reverse instructions 8 to 21.
24 Lubricate the pipes and seals with an anti-freeze solution.
25 Reverse instructions 7 to 3.
26 With the face level ventilation flap closed against the aperture as shown and the control lever in the 'OFF'

27 position, tighten the trunnion screw. Operate the control lever to check engagement of detents and full movement of the flap, then return the lever to the 'OFF' position and check sealing of the flap.
28 With the lower flap closed against the aperture as shown and the control lever in the 'SCREEN' position tighten the trunnion screw.
29 Operate the control lever to check engagement of detents and full movement of the flap, then return the lever to the 'SCREEN' position, and check sealing of the flap.
30 With the cam in the position shown set the air inlet flap against the aperture with the control lever in the 'OFF' position and tighten the trunnion screw.

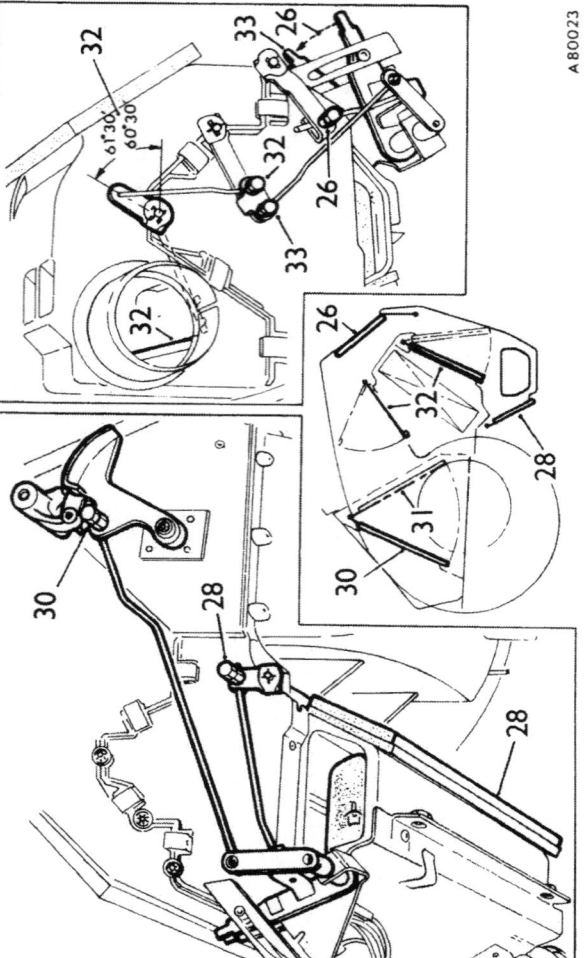

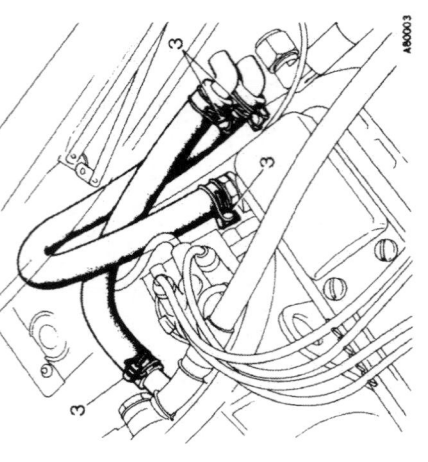

31 Operate the control lever to check engagement of detents and full movement of the flap, then return the lever to the 'OFF' position and check sealing of the flap.
32 With the heater inlet flap set as shown and the outlet flap closed as shown, tighten the trunnion screw.
33 Set the control level in the 'COLD'

position and tighten the trunnion screw.
34 Operate the control lever to check engagement of detents and full movement of both flaps, then return the lever to the 'COLD' position and check sealing of the outlet flap.
35 Reverse instructions 1 and 2.

WATER HOSES

— Remove and refit
  — hose — feed
  — engine to heater   80.25.07
— Hose — return — heater
  to engine return pipe   80.25.12

Removing
1 Drain the cooling system. 26.10.01.
2 Remove the fresh air duct. 80.15.31.
3 Slacken the clips and remove the hoses.

Refitting
4 Reverse instructions 1 to 3.

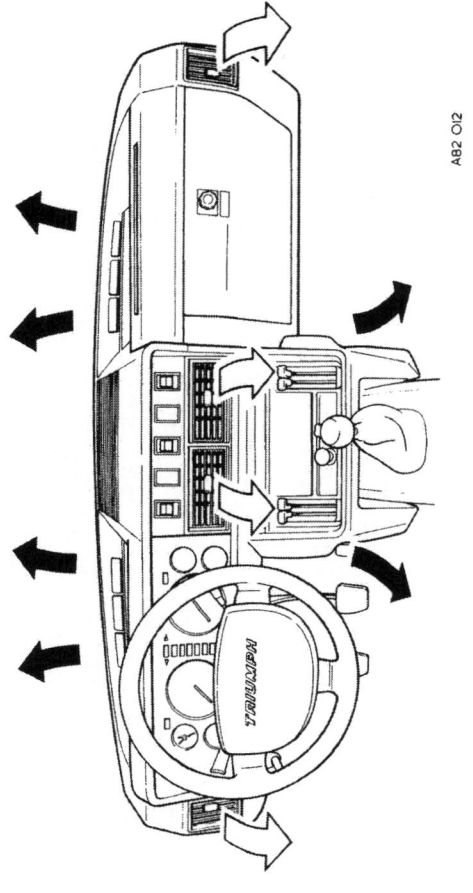

A82 012

Introduction   82.00.00

The air conditioning system is designed to provide a two level output. The upper level provides cool air at face level for increased comfort in hot climates. The lower level provides either cool or warm air at foot level and an air supply available to the screen.

The principal component of the system is the air conditioner unit. It governs all airflows and contains one blower motor and two matrixes. A cold matrix is cooled by the cold refrigerant circuit and a hot matrix heated by the hot water circuit.

All incoming air is accelerated by the blower motor running at one of three speeds. When the blower motor is selected OFF a flap prevents outside air entering the system. All incoming air is first cooled, dehumidified and cleaned by passing through the cold matrix. The air is then passed to the distribution and hot matrix area.

Cold air is delivered from the central fascia vent and the two end fascia vents at a temperature controlled by the cold temperature control system.

Cold air or hot air is delivered from the footwell outlets and screen outlets at a temperature controlled by a combination of both the cold temperature control system and the hot temperature control system.

Air extraction is from two air vent grilles in the vehicle body rear quarter panels.

The refrigerant circuit consists of a compressor at the front of the engine driven from a drive belt and electromagnetic clutch, a condenser with two fans in the nose of the vehicle, a receiver drier cylinder at the front of the engine bay and the cold matrix in the air conditioner unit. Hoses join the components.

The system is filled with refrigerant which must be subject to special precautions. It exists in the circuit both as a liquid and a vapour.

Service personnel who are not familiar with air conditioned vehicles must study Servicing 82.30.00. A full understanding of this section must be obtained before breaking into the system. Failure to observe this instruction may result in severe personal injury.

Hot water circuit

The function of the hot water circuit is to heat the hot matrix. The hot water flow is induced by the engine water pump. Hot water is drawn from the water transfer housing at the rear of the cylinder head and passes through the water flow valve to the hot matrix. From the hot matrix outlet the flow is forward below the carburetters to enter the water pump cover. This entry is on the suction side of the water pump.

Cold refrigeration circuit

Introduction

The function of the refrigeration circuit is to cool the cold matrix. The circuit comprises the following main components:

Compressor
Condenser
Receiver drier
Expansion valve and cold matrix

Hoses are employed to transport the refrigerant between components.

Compressor

The compressor draws vaporized refrigerant from the cold matrix. It is compressed, and thus heated, and passed on to the condenser as a hot, high pressure vapour.

Condenser

The condenser is mounted at the front of the car. Its function is to remove heat from the refrigerant and disperse it into the atmosphere. It is delivered with hot, high pressure vapour. Air flow across the tubes, induced by vehicle movement and assisted by two electric fans, cools the vapour, causing it to condense into a high pressure liquid. As this change of state occurs a large amount of latent heat is released.

Receiver drier

This unit filters, removes moisture, and acts as a reservoir for the liquid. To prevent icing inside the system, extreme precautions are taken during servicing to exclude moisture. The receiver drier should be considered as a second stage insurance to prevent the serious consequences of ice obstructing the flow. A sight glass provided in the unit top enables a visual check to be made of the high pressure liquid flow.

Expansion valve and cold matrix

High pressure liquid refrigerant is delivered to the expansion valve. A severe pressure drop occurs across the valve and as the refrigerant enters the cold matrix space at a temperature of approximately -6° C it boils and vaporizes. As this change of state occurs, a large amount of latent heat is absorbed. The cold matrix is therefore cooled and as a result heat is extracted from the air flowing across the matrix.

Second cycle

Vaporized refrigerant is then drawn from the the cold matrix by the compressor and a second cycle commences.

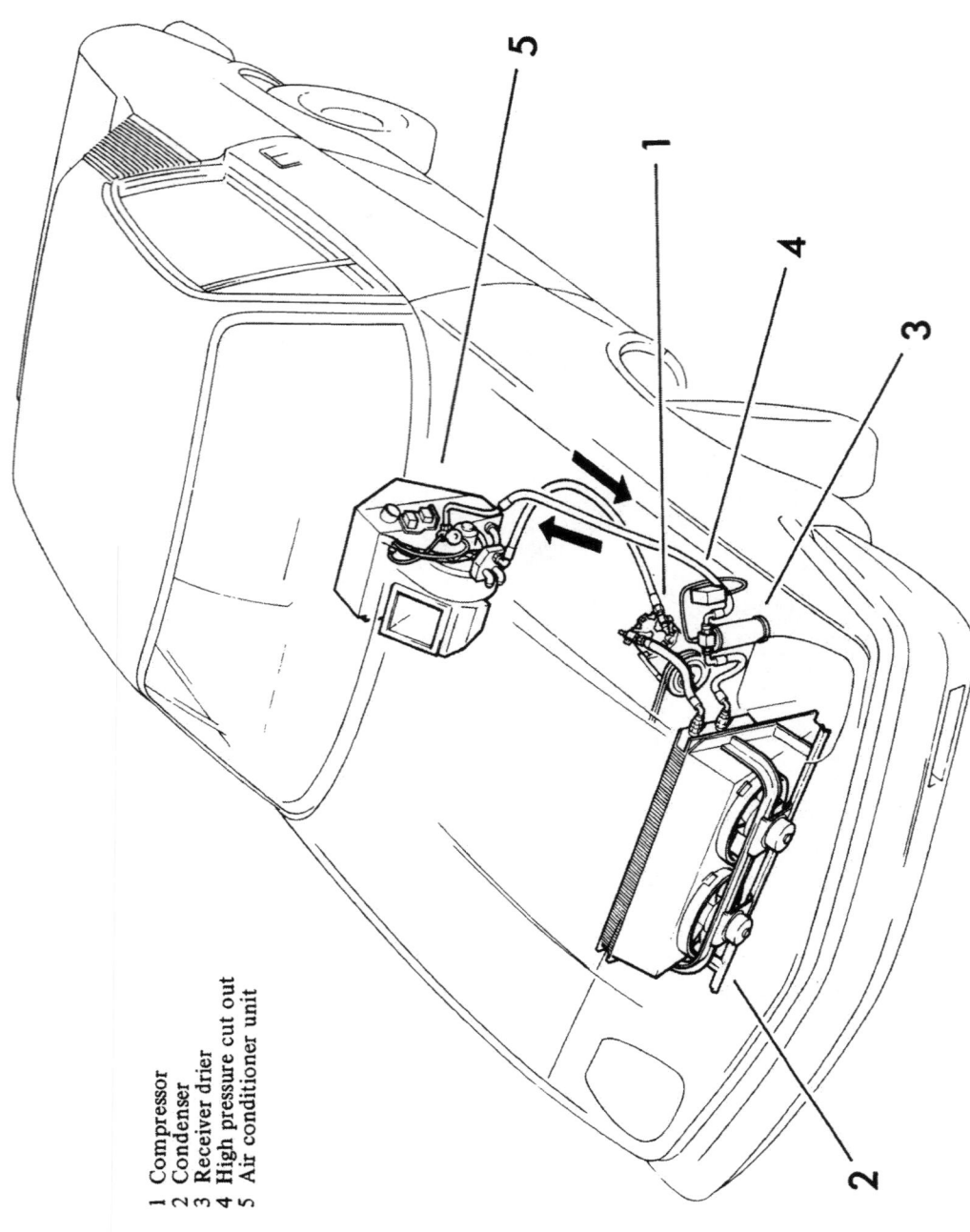

1 Compressor
2 Condenser
3 Receiver drier
4 High pressure cut out
5 Air conditioner unit

A 82 OIO

COMPRESSOR

Data 82.10.00

Compressor

Manufacturer . . . . : York Division of Borg Warner, York, U.S.A.
Model . . . . : 210
Triumph part no. . . . . : RKC 0456

Cylinders . . . . : 2 in line
Capacity . . . . : 10.3 cu in/rev
Bore . . . . : 1.875 in
Stroke . . . . : 1.866 in
Crankcase and liners . . . . . . : Die-cast light alloy with case in cast iron liners
Head . . . . : Die-cast light alloy
Valves and valve plate . . . . . : Two-way non-return valve unit above each cylinder. Assembled onto a common steel valve plate

Front plate, rear plate and base plate . . : Die-cast light alloy
Main bearings . . . . : Two ball bearings
Crankshaft nose tapping . . . : $\frac{5}{16}$ – 24 UNF 1.250 deep
Lubrication . . . . : Refrigerant compressor oil. Distributed by splash and pressure differential

Lubrication plugs . . . . : Two located on crankcase sides.
Mounting tappings . . . . : $\frac{3}{8}$ –16 UNC 0.620 in deep
Maximum permissible speed . . : 6,000 rev/min
Weight . . . . : 14.6 lb

Clutch

Manufacturer . . . . : Warner Electric
Triumph part no. . . . . : TKC 2019

Current . . . . : 4.5 amp.
Pulley nominal diameter . . . . : 6.0 in

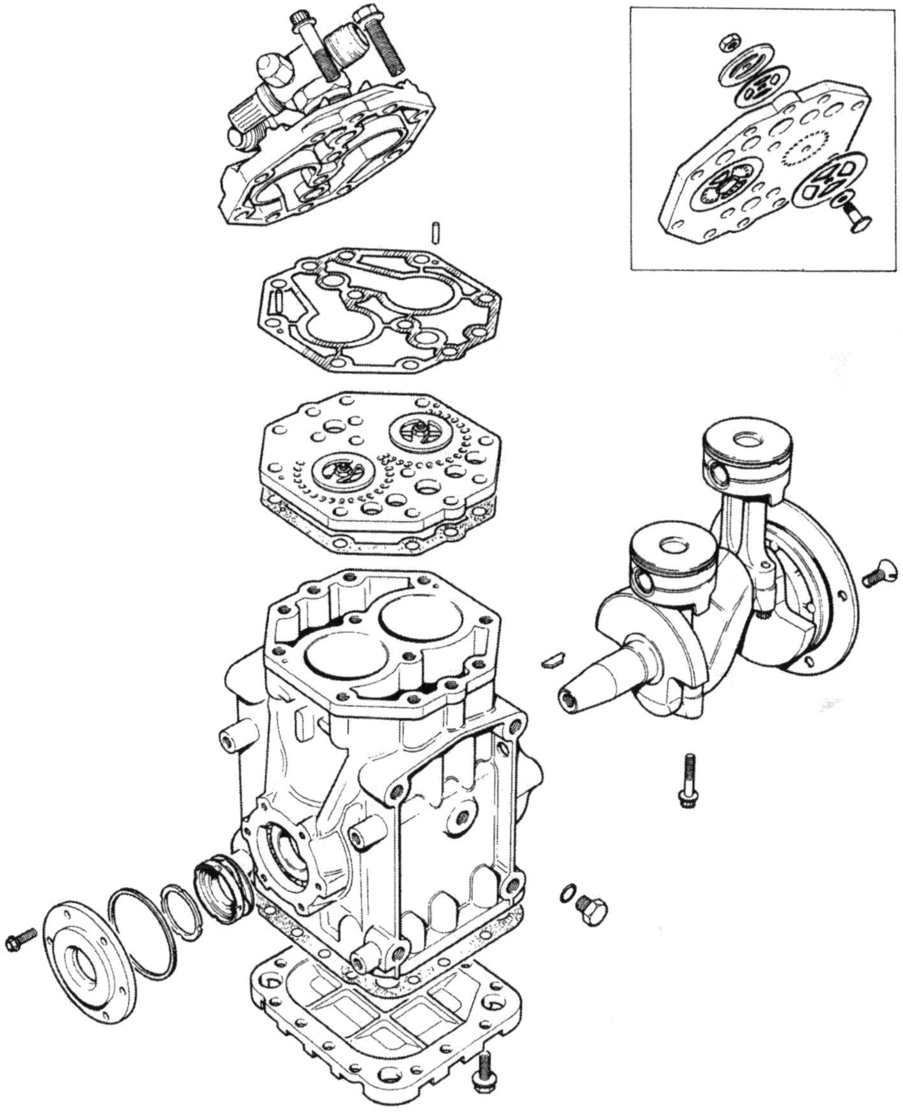

COMPRESSOR

Drive belt — adjust   82.10.01

1   Drive the vehicle onto a ramp.
2   Raise the ramp.
3   At the transverse support bracket slacken two bolt assemblies.
4   At the longitudinal support bracket slacken two bolt assemblies.
5   Lower the ramp.
6   At the exhaust bracket slacken one bolt assembly.
7   Slacken the locknut.
8   Slacken three main mounting nuts.
9   Rotate the adjustment nut — clockwise to tighten the belt or anti-clockwise to slacken the belt.
10   Tighten three main mounting nuts.
11   Check the belt tension. This should be 0.75 to 1.00 in (19 to 25 mm) at the mid-point of the belt run.
12   If a correction is required repeat operations 8 to 11.
13   Tighten the locknut.
14   At the exhaust bracket tighten one bolt assembly.
15   Raise the ramp.
16   At the longitudinal support bracket tighten two bolt assemblies.
17   At the transverse support bracket tighten two bolt assemblies.

COMPRESSOR

Drive belt — remove and refit   82.10.02

Removing

1   Perform 82.10.01, operations 1 to 8.
2   Rotate the adjustment nut anti-clockwise to lower the compressor.
3   Slacken the fan blade bolt assemblies to enable the fan blades to be slid forward to provide the required clearance.
4   Remove the belt. Do not stretch the belt over the wide section of the clutch pulley. Run the belt off the crankshaft pulley.

Refitting

5   Fit the belt.
6   Tighten the fan blade bolt assemblies.
7   Perform 82.10.01, operations 9 to 17.

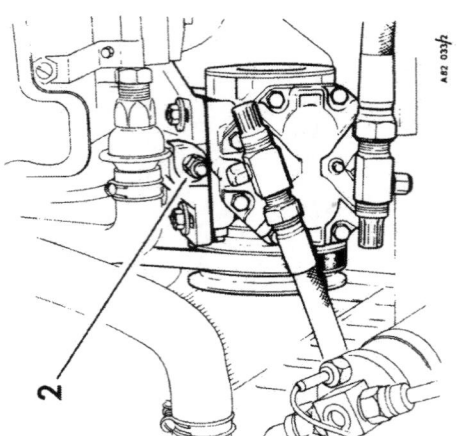

A82 033/h

2

6-14

4-16

7-13

9

8-10

3-17

A82 016/1

COMPRESSOR

Clutch — remove and refit   82.10.08

Removing

1 Remove the radiator, see 26.40.01.
2 Disconnect the clutch electrical connection.
3 Use a slave wire between the battery positive terminal and the clutch electrical connection to energize the clutch. This action will lock the compressor crankshaft to the pulley.

WARNING: Do not energize the clutch through the vehicle harness as this would require the ignition circuit to be energised with the danger of an engine start during the operation.

4 Retain the pulley and remove the centre bolt.
5 Retain the pulley and screw a 0.625 in UNC slave bolt into the thread provided to withdraw the pulley from the tapered shaft.

CAUTION: Take care to screw the slave bolt in square to prevent a 'cross thread' condition.

6 Remove four bolts and lift away the clutch coil.

Refitting

7 Position the clutch coil with the wire emerging upwards. Secure with four bolts.
8 Ensure that the key is fitted to the tapered shaft.
9 Fit the pulley to the tapered shaft.
10 Electrically energise the clutch.
11 Retain the pulley and fit the centre bolt. Torque load to 16 lbf ft (2.2 kgf m).
12 Connect the clutch electrical connection.
13 Adjust the drive belt, see 82.10.01.
14 Fit the radiator, see 26.40.01.

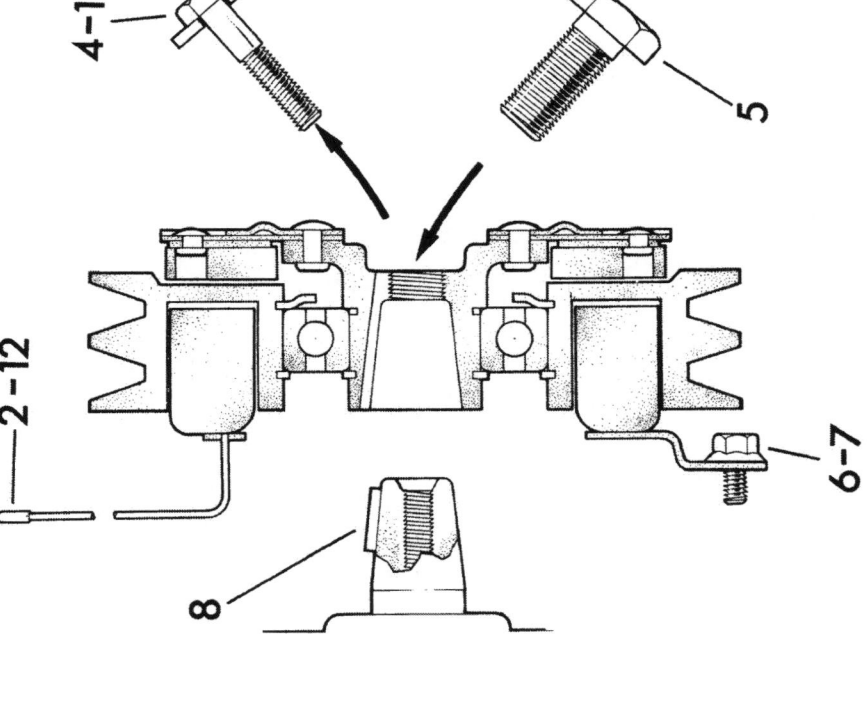

M110/1

COMPRESSOR

Remove and refit   82.10.20

Removing

1 Drive the vehicle onto a ramp.
2 Connect gauge set, see 82.30.01.
3 Discharge – compressor only, see 82.30.20.
4 Protect the eyes with safety goggles and wear gloves during operation 5.
5 Unscrew two service valve union nuts. Blank exposed compressor connections immediately.
6 Remove the fresh air duct, see 80.15.31.
7 Remove two bolts, spring washers and washers. Lift away the fan guard.
8 Raise the ramp.
9 At the transverse support bracket slacken the right-hand bolt assembly and remove the left-hand bolt assembly.
10 At the longitudinal support bracket slacken the upper bolt assembly and remove the lower bolt assembly

Early vehicles only:
11 Remove the engine stabilizer, see 12.45.16.
12 At the front left-hand engine mounting remove one nut and washer.
13 Provide a jack under the engine with a large block of wood to distribute the load under the engine sump.
14 Jack up the engine to the position where the front left-hand engine mounting stud remains just retained in the sub frame bracket.

NOTE: Do not allow the stud to come out of the bracket as insertion may prove difficult.

15 Lower the ramp.
16 At the exhaust bracket remove one bolt assembly.
17 Withdraw the longitudinal support bracket.
18 Slacken the locknut.
19 Slacken three main mounting nuts.
20 Rotate the adjustment nut anti-clockwise to lower the compressor.

21 Remove the belt from the compressor pulley. Do not stretch the belt over the wide section of the clutch pulley. Run the belt rearwards off the crankshaft pulley.
22 Remove three main mounting nuts and washers. Lift the compressor from the vehicle.
23 If necessary detach the following items from the compressor:
   a   Adjustment plate assembly.
   b   One bolt.
   c   One bolt, washer and right angle bracket.
   d   Three studs.
   e   Clutch, see 82.10.08.

Refitting

24 If necessary attach the items listed at operation 23 above to the compressor.

NOTE: Item d, the shorter stud threads screw into the compressor tappings. The lower rear tapping is not fitted with a stud.

25 Position the compressor to the vehicle. Secure with three washers and nuts finger tight.
26 Fit the belt.
27 Adjust the belt, see 82.10.01, operations 9 to 12.
28 Tighten the locknut.
29 Position the longitudinal support bracket.
30 At the exhaust bracket fit one bolt assembly finger tight.
31 Raise the ramp.
32 Lower the jack.
33 At the front left-hand engine mounting fit one washer and nut.

Early vehicles only:
34 Fit the engine stabilizer, see 12.45.16.
35 At the longitudinal support bracket fit and tighten the lower bolt assembly and tighten the upper bolt assembly.
36 At the transverse support bracket fit and tighten the left-hand bolt assembly and tighten the right-hand bolt assembly. Ensure that the right angle bracket is correctly aligned.
37 Lower the ramp.
38 At the exhaust bracket tighten one bolt assembly.

39 Position the fan guard. Secure with two bolts, spring washers and washers.
40 Fit the fresh air duct, see 80.15.31.
41 Connect two service valve union nuts. Use refrigerant compressor oil on all mating surfaces to assist leakage prevention. Position the service valves for the best hose alignment.
42 Evacuate – compressor only, see 82.30.21.
43 Charge – compressor only, see 82.30.23.
44 Perform a leak test on any disturbed joints, see 82.30.09.
45 Functional check, see 82.30.16.
46 Disconnect gauge set, see 82.30.01.

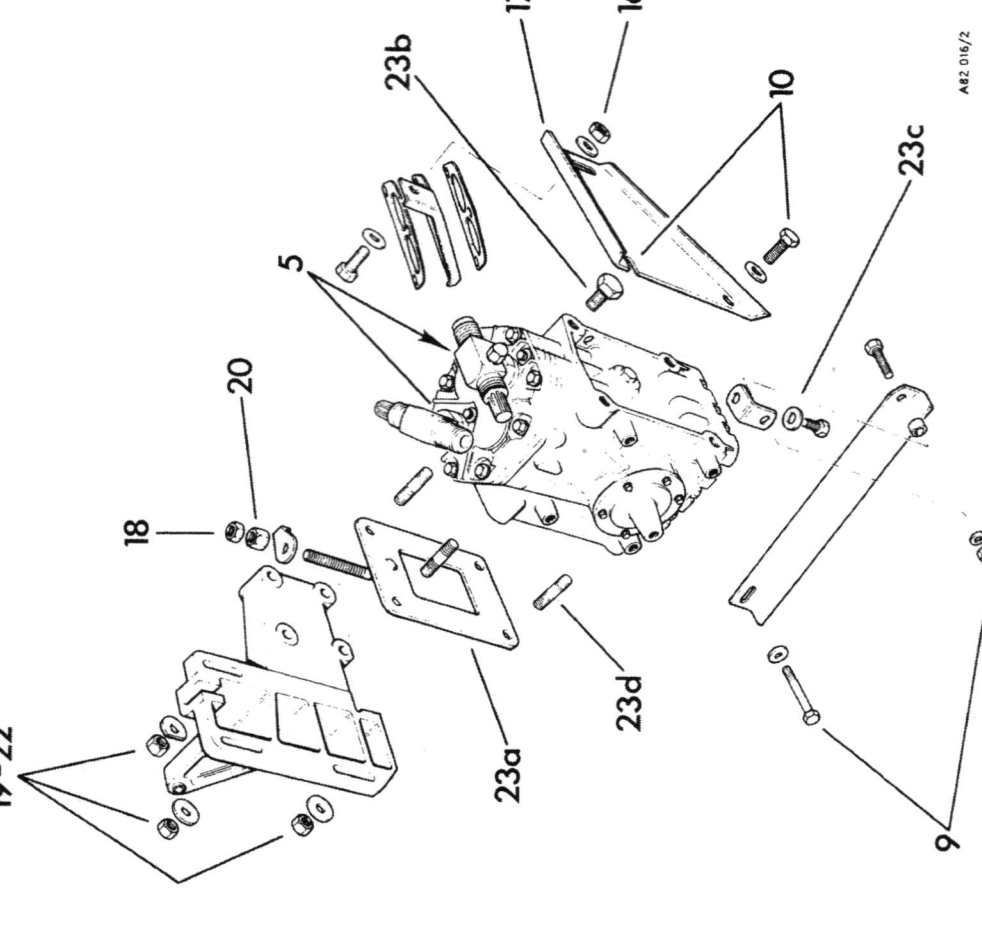

A82 016/2

CONDENSER FAN MOTOR 82.15.01

Remove and refit

Removing

1 Drive the vehicle onto a ramp.
2 Raise the ramp.
3 Using a small screwdriver slacken the grub screw to release the fan.
4 Remove the fan from the motor shaft.
5 Disconnect the fan motor harness plug.
6 Remove three nuts, anti-vibration washers, washers and bolts.
7 Withdraw the fan motor from the mounting assembly. Take care not to damage the wires. To allow the grommet to pass through the aperture tilt the fan motor. If the grommet remains obstructive pull it from the aperture.

8 Remove the fan motor from the vehicle. It may be necessary to slightly bend the vehicle body front cross-member to achieve this operation.

Refitting

9 Ensure that the fan is positioned in the cowling.
10 Reverse 1 to 8. Insert the fan motor to the mounting assembly with the wires emerging downwards for improved water sealing.
Fit the fan to the motor shaft with the grub screw aligned to a motor shaft recess.

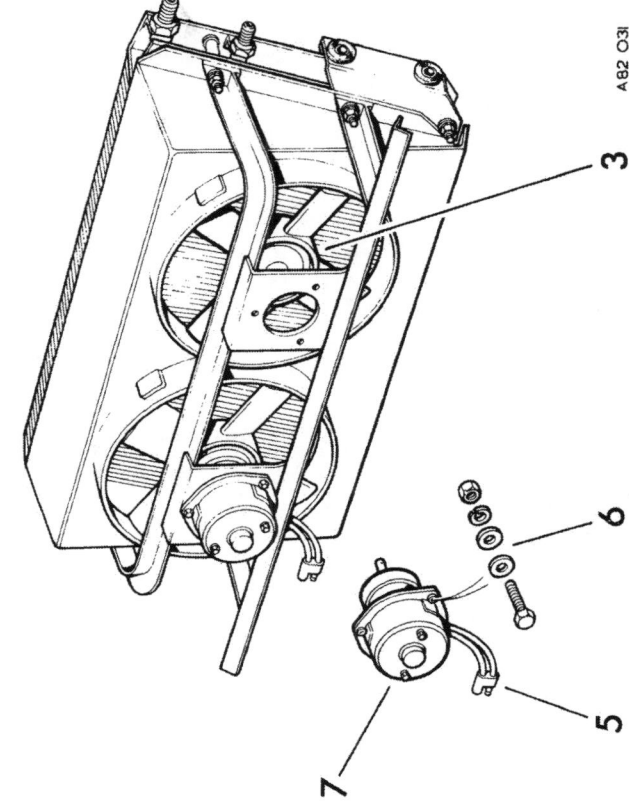

A82 O3I

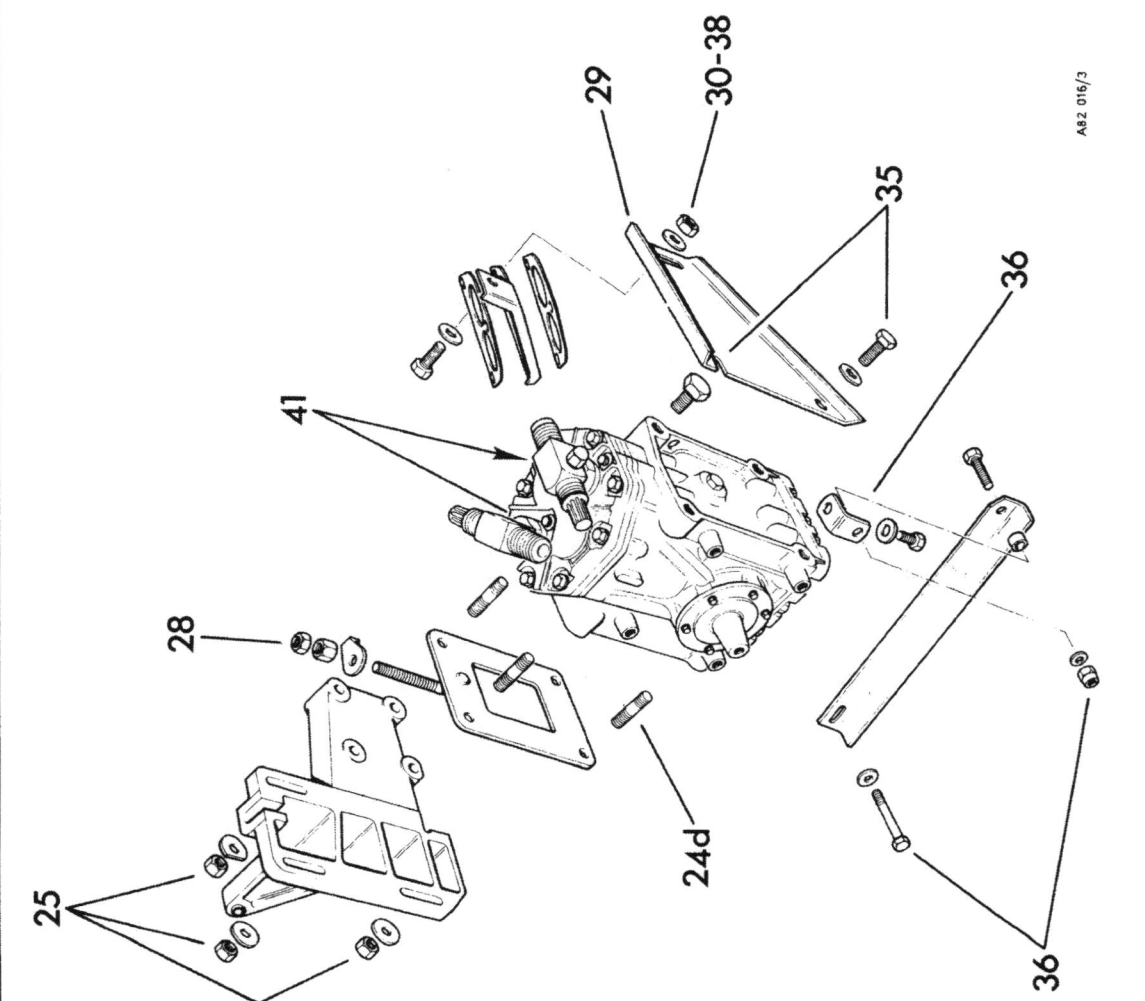

A82 016/3

CONDENSER

Remove and refit 82.15.07

Removing

1 Remove the condenser and fan assembly, see 82.15.10.
2 Remove two top nuts, anti-vibration washers, washers and shorter bolts.
3 Remove two middle nuts, anti-vibration washers, washers, washers and longer bolts.
4 Remove the fan motor mounting assembly.
5 Remove one nut, anti-vibration washer, washer and bolt. Remove the left-hand bracket which includes two mounting rubbers.
6 Remove one nut, anti-vibration washer, washer and bolt. Remove the right-hand bracket which has no mounting rubbers.

Refitting

7 Reverse 1 to 6.

CONDENSER AND FAN ASSEMBLY 82.15.10

Remove and refit 82.15.10

Removing

1 Drive the vehicle onto a ramp.
2 Select the master light switch to raise the headlamps.
3 Isolate the battery to extinguish the headlamps.
4 Connect gauge set, see 82.30.01.
5 Discharge – complete system, see 82.30.05.
6 Remove the radiator, see 26.40.01.
7 Protect the eyes with safety goggles and wear gloves during operation 8.
8 Carefully disconnect two hose connections. Use two spanners at each joint to protect the delicate condenser pipe joints. Blank exposed connections immediately.
9 Raise the ramp.
10 Remove four bolts, lock washers and washers. Remove the radiator mounting cross-member.
11 Disconnect two fan motor harness plugs.
12 Slacken two right-hand bracket bolt assemblies.

NOTE: The right-hand bracket is provided with slots as shown to facilitate withdrawal and positioning of the assembly and to ensure that the brackets are drawn up firmly against the body longitudinal members. Note that the left-hand bracket has no slots.

13 Remove two nuts, lock washers and washers securing the fan motor mounting assembly rail.
14 Remove two left-hand longer side bolts, anti-vibration washers and washers.
15 Collect up the nut plate.
16 Remove two right-hand shorter side bolts, anti-vibration washers and washers.
17 Carefully withdraw the condenser and fan assembly downwards from the vehicle. Handle with care as the fins are easily damaged.

Refitting

18 Ensure that the two right-hand bracket bolt assemblies are slackened.
19 Reverse 9 to 17.
20 Connect two hose connections. Use refrigerant compressor oil on all mating surfaces to assist leakage prevention.
21 Fit the radiator, see 26.40.01.
22 Evacuate – complete system, see 82.30.06.
23 Connect the battery.
24 Charge – complete system, see 82.30.08.
25 Perform a leak test on any disturbed joints, see 82.30.09.
26 Select the master light switch to lower the headlamps.
27 Functional check, see 82.30.16.
28 Disconnect gauge set, see 82.30.01.

Illustration on following page

A82 032

RECEIVER DRIER

Remove and refit   **82.17.01**

CAUTION: Immediate blanking of the receiver drier is important. Exposed life of the unit is only 15 minutes.

Removing

1. Connect gauge set, see 82.30.01.
2. Discharge – complete system, see 82.30.05.
3. Protect the eyes with safety goggles and wear gloves during operations 4 and 5.
4. Carefully disconnect the capillary tube from the receiver drier. Blank exposed connections immediately.
5. Carefully disconnect two hose connections. Use a second spanner to support the squared hose adaptor. Blank exposed connections immediately.
6. Remove the clamp screw, washer, washer and nut.
7. Withdraw the receiver drier from the mounting bracket.

Refitting

8. Insert the receiver drier into the mounting bracket with the inlet and outlet connections correct to the refrigerant circuit flow as shown.
9. Connect two hose connections finger tight. Use refrigerant compressor oil on all mating surfaces to assist leakage prevention.
10. Fit the clamp screw, washer, washer and nut.
11. Tighten two hose connections. Use a second spanner to support the squared hose adaptor.
12. Carefully connect the capillary tube to the receiver drier. Use refrigerant compressor oil on all mating surfaces to assist leakage prevention.
13. Evacuate – complete system, see 82.30.06.
14. Charge – complete system, see 82.30.08.
15. Perform a leak test on any disturbed joints, see 82.30.09.
16. Functional check, see 82.30.16.
17. Disconnect gauge set, see 82.30.01.

A82 002/1

A82 030/1

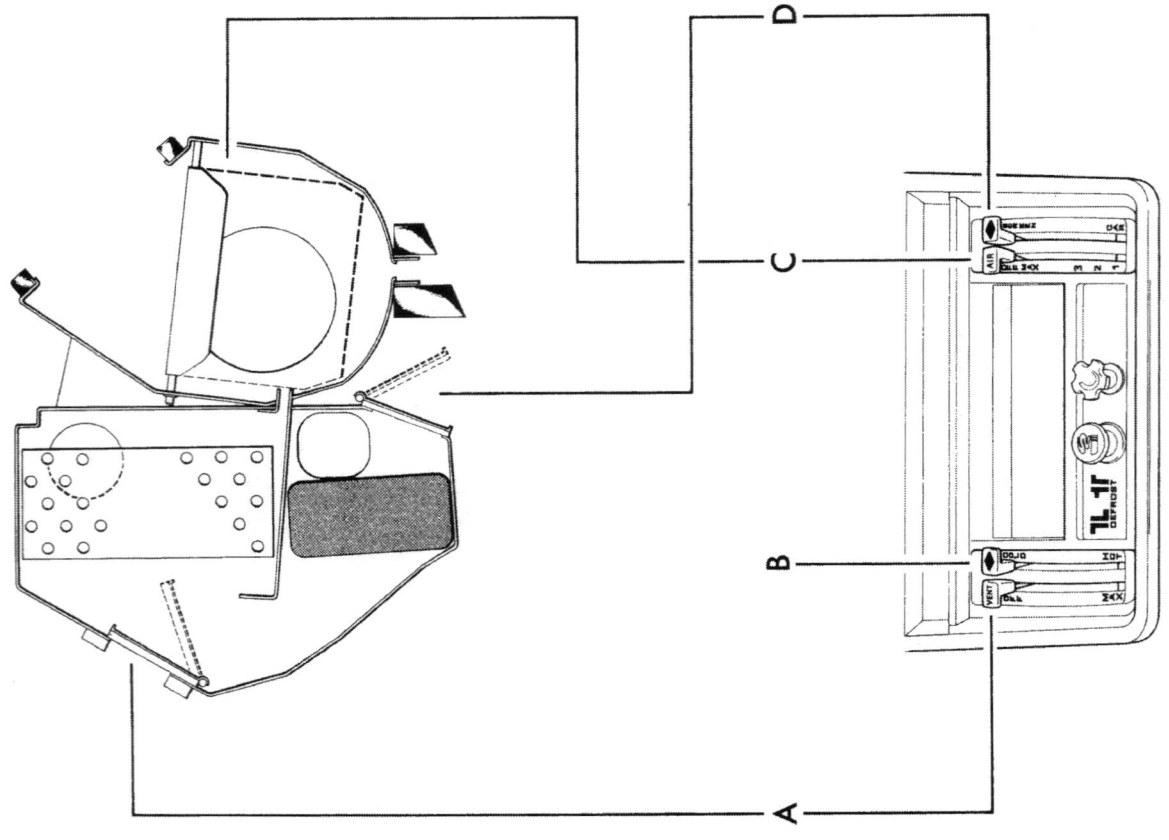

A82 017

CONTROLS

Description   **82.20.00**

Control levers

Lever A — controls the flow of cold air delivered from the central fascia vent. Moving lever A up to the OFF position will terminate the airflow. Moving lever A down to the MAX position will provide the maximum airflow. Any intermediate position may be used. This control operates through the direct linkage A to position flap A.

Lever B — directs the temperature required. Moving lever B up to the COLD position will provide maximum cooling. Moving lever B down to the HOT position will provide maximum heating. Any intermediate position may be used. This control operates through the non-direct linkage B to provide an input to both the cold thermostat and the hot thermostat. Lever B therefore influences the airflow from both the cold outlets and the hot outlets. After setting the position of lever B the cold temperature control system and/or the hot temperature control system will maintain an approximately constant interior temperature.

Lever C—is the master control to bring into action the cold refrigerant circuit and the blower motor. It also selects the input air—either fresh air at ambient temperature through the under bonnet fresh air duct or recirculated air from the vehicle interior.

Moving lever C up to the OFF position will electrically switch off the compressor electro-magnetic clutch, throttle jack (automatic vehicles only) and the two condenser fan motors. Flap C will be in the recirculate position so vehicle movement will not induce an airflow through the system.

Moving lever C slightly down to position MAX will electrically switch on the cold refrigerant circuit and the blower motor at its fastest speed. Flap C will remain in the recirculate position. This selection of lever C will provide the maximum cooling or the maximum heating condition.

Moving lever C further down to position 3 will maintain the cold refrigerant circuit electrically on and the blower motor at its fastest speed. Flap C will be traversed by the non-direct 'quick changeover' linkage C to the fresh position. Any intermediate position between MAX and 3 may be used.

Moving lever C slightly further down to position 2 will maintain the cold refrigerant circuit electrically on and the flap C at the fresh position. The blower motor will drop to its middle speed.

Moving lever C slightly further down to position 1 will maintain the cold refrigerant circuit electrically on and flap C at the fresh position. The blower motor will drop to its slowest speed.

Lever D—controls the flow of cold air or hot air delivered from the screen vents and footwell. Moving lever D up to the SCREEN position will provide the maximum airflow to the screen vents. Moving lever D down to the CAR position will provide the maximum airflow to the footwell. Any intermediate position may be used. This control operates through the direct linkage D to position flap D.

Cold temperature control system

The principal unit of the system is the cold thermostat mounted on the left-hand side of the air conditioner unit. The thermostat receives two inputs. A capillary tube inserted into the air space of the cold matrix senses the cold matrix temperature. The driver's direction of the temperature required is transmitted by lever B and linkage B to position the thermostat lever. The output of the thermostat is an electric switch in the air conditioning electrical circuit. This controls indirectly the on-off switching of the compressor electro-magnetic clutch, throttle jack (automatic vehicles only) and the two condenser fan motors.

Hot temperature control system

The principal unit of the system is the hot thermostat mounted on the left-hand side of the air conditioner unit. The thermostat receives two inputs. A capillary tube mounted against the downstream face of the hot matrix senses the hot matrix temperature. The driver's selection of the temperature required is transmitted by lever B and linkage B to position the thermostat lever. The output of the thermostat is a water valve in the hot water circuit. This controls the flow of hot water from the engine into the hot matrix.

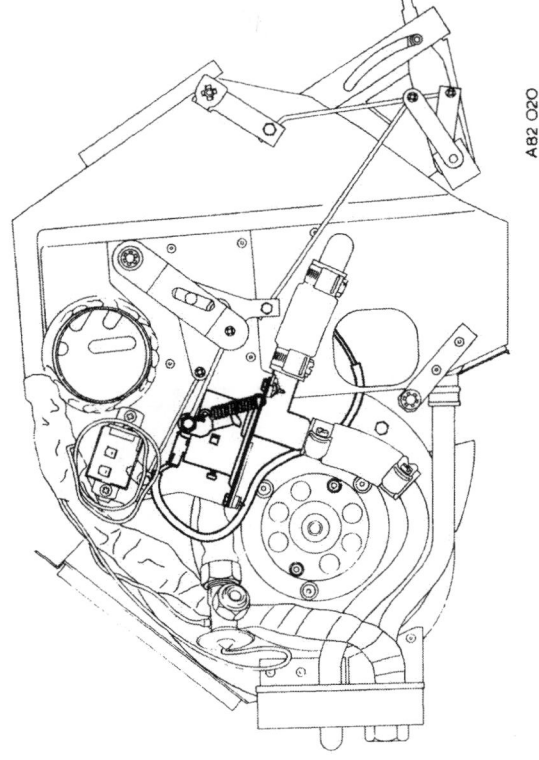

A82 020

Hot thermostat

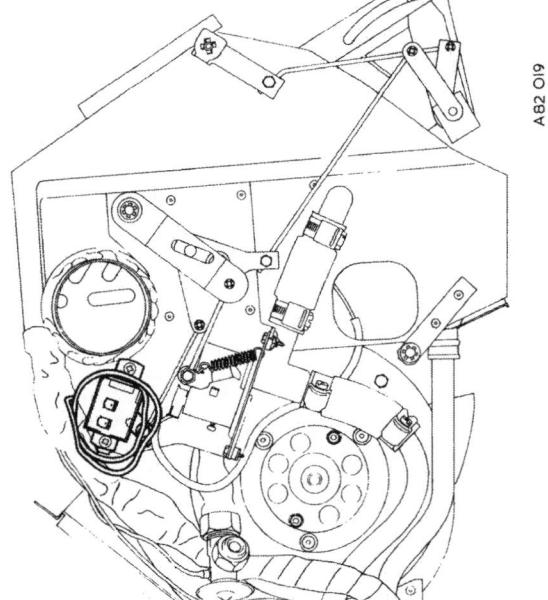

A82 019

Cold thermostat

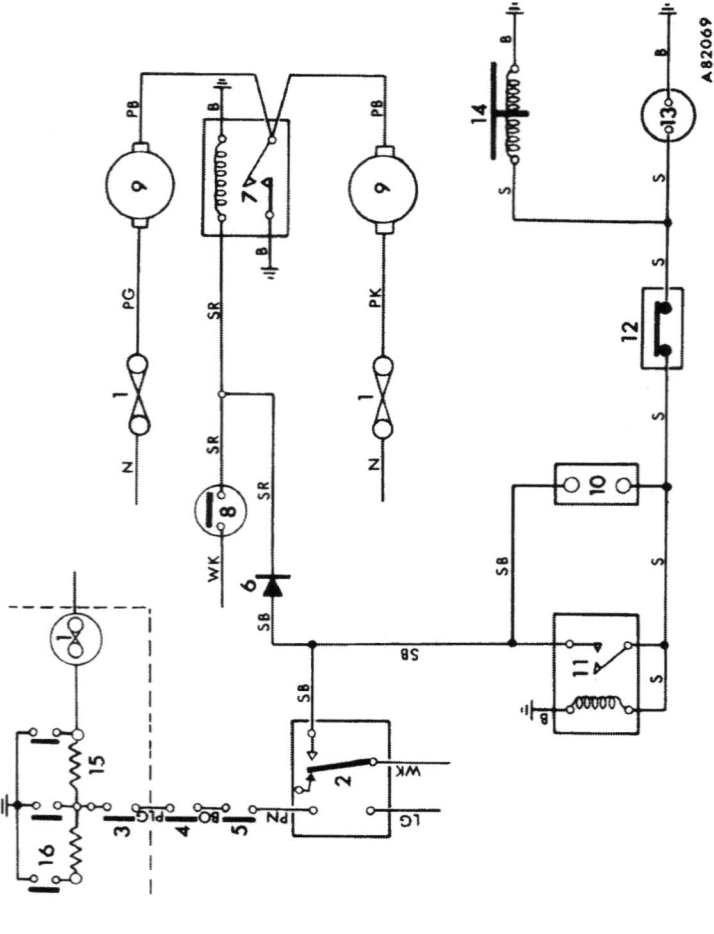

A82069

Electrical circuit

The function of the circuit is to control the on-off switching of the compressor electro-magnetic clutch, throttle jack (automatic vehicles only) and the two condenser fan motors. The circuit may be considered in two sections: the relay control circuit, and the power circuit.

Relay control circuit—Supply to the relay winding is from an ignition-controlled fuse. The earth path may be interrupted by the cold thermostat and by the driver's selection of lever 'C'. With lever 'C' up to the 'OFF' position, the circuit is broken. With lever 'C' selected to any other position, 'MAX', '3', '2' or '1', an earth path exists across the blower motor switch. The relay control circuit current is small, so the introduction of a blower motor speed control resistor in the circuit at positions 'MAX', '3' and '1' will have no consequence.

Power circuit—Actuation of the relay connects supply from the air conditioning fuse to the compressor clutch, throttle jack and the two condenser fan motors.

During the starting sequence the clutch and fan relays are energized when the key is in the No. 2 (Ignition) position. They are not energized when the key is in the 'Auxiliary' or 'Start' positions.

The circuit to the compressor clutch and throttle jack may be interrupted by the dealy circuit as detailed below and by the high pressure cut-out which is a safety feature not subject to continuous cycling. The two condenser fan motors are controlled directly by the relay but these units may also be selected independently by the radiator switch as detailed below.

Delay circuit—This circuit is included to prevent a severe momentary voltage drop in the vehicle electrical system that would occur if the compressor clutch, throttle jack and the two condenser fan motors were allowed to 'cut in' simultaneously.

The circuit allows the two condenser fan motors to 'cut in' when the relay energizes. An acceptable first voltage drop occurs and the recovery is quick as the alternator output is rebalanced to the additional load.

The delay circuit flasher unit also first receives current when the relay energizes. This current heats a metal ribbon causing expansion which finally allows a metal vane to relax and the contacts to close.

The delay circuit relay is energized to hold the condition and the compressor clutch and throttle jack 'cut in'. A second acceptable voltage drop occurs and again recovery is quick as the alternator output is rebalanced to the additional load.

This action is repeated each time the air conditioning circuit is manually selected by lever 'C', or automatically switched on-off by the cold temperature control system.

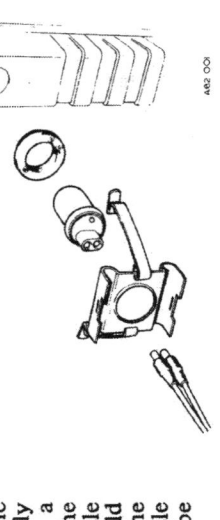

High pressure cut out

The unit is a safety feature to protect the refrigeration circuit from excessive pressure. It is not subject to continuous cycling during normal system operation.

A capillary tube senses the refrigerant pressure at the receiver drier. This pressure governs an electrical switch within the unit.

The switch is included in the electrical circuit. If the refrigerant pressure rises to the 'cut out' pressure the electrical circuit to the compressor clutch and throttle jack (automatic vehicles only) is interrupted. The compressor electro magnetic clutch reverts to the off condition and the refrigerant pressure is prevented from rising further.

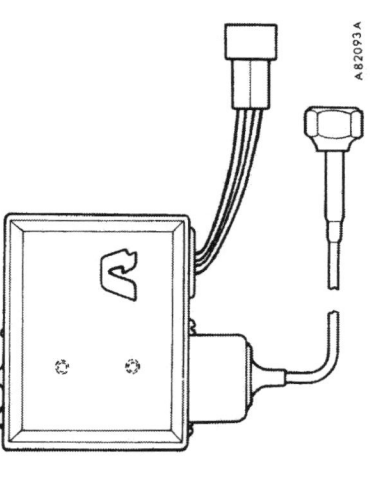

Radiator switch

This item is not strictly a component of the air conditioning system. Its function is to actuate if the engine coolant temperature should reach a high level. Advantage of the two condenser fan motors is then taken to assist in cooling the radiator.

NOTE: As the temperature of the coolant in the upper section of the radiator may reach a high level immediately after the vehicle is parked, and the electrical supply to the radiator switch is direct from a battery control fuse, it is possible for the two fans to start running while the vehicle is parked and unattended. The run should only continue for a short period until the radiator has cooled. Under certain vehicle operating conditions this action may be considered as normal.

Throttle jack

The throttle jack is fitted to vehicles equipped with both air conditioning and automatic transmission.

This unit consists of a solenoid coil and plunger. It is included to maintain an approximately constant engine idle speed both with the compressor clutch free and with the compressor clutch engaged to apply the compressor drive load to the engine.

With the air conditioning system switched out the plunger is retracted to an unemployed position under the action of a spring.

With the air conditioning system switched in the solenoid coil is energised to extend the plunger to provide a new stop position for the carburetter throttle linkage.

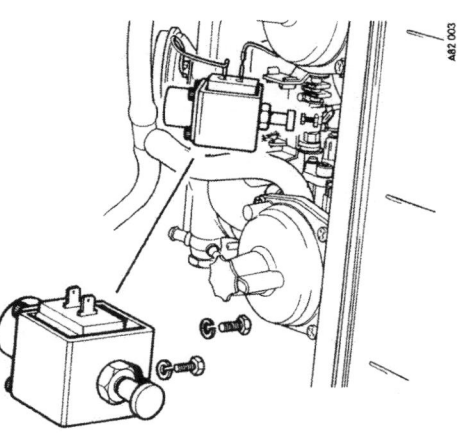

CONTROL SUMMARY

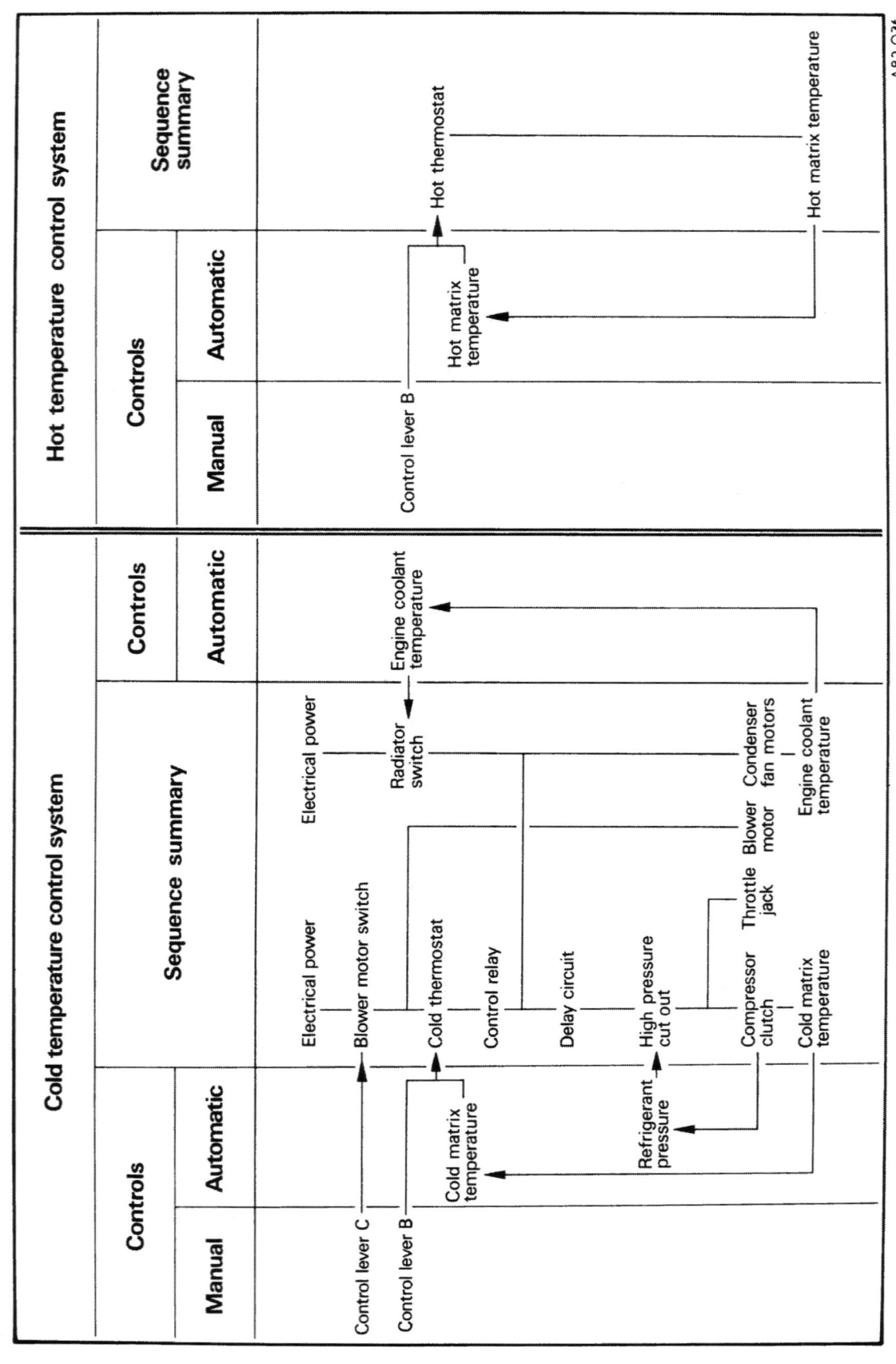

A82 034

CONTROLS

Radiator switch – remove and refit   82.20.09

Removing

1 Isolate the battery.
2 Pull off two electrical connections.
3 Release the rear spring clip from the radiator flange. Swing the bracket forward. Release the front spring clip from the radiator flange.
4 Using a wide blade screwdriver, carefully prise the switch outwards from the rubber seal.
5 Remove the rubber seal.

Refitting

6 Fit the rubber seal. Fit a new rubber seal if available.
7 Insert the switch. Position the electrical connection pedestal forward as shown to facilitate operation 8 below.
8 Engage the front spring clip to the radiator flange. Swing the bracket rearward to align correctly to the switch. Engage the rear spring clip to the radiator flange.
9 Push on two electrical connections. The connections may be fitted either way round.
10 Connect the battery.

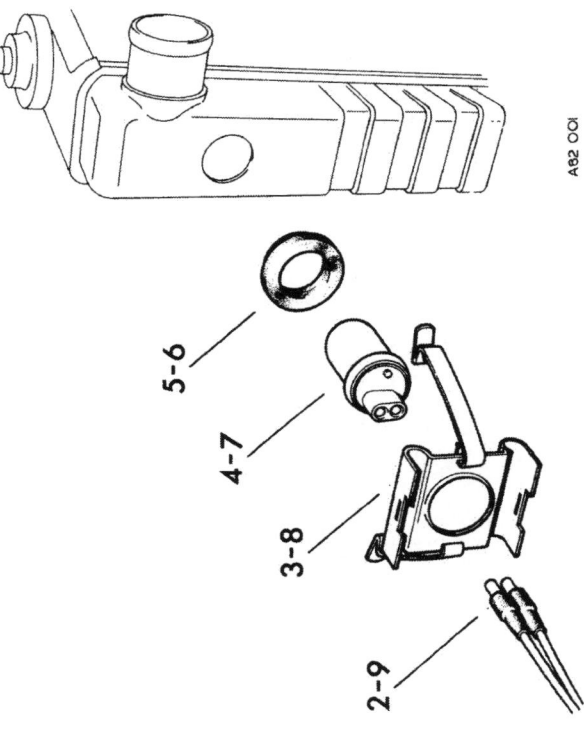

5-6

4-7

3-8

2-9

A82 001

CONTROLS

Cold thermostat — remove and refit   82.20.18

Removing

1 Isolate the battery.
2 Remove the fascia, see 76.46.01.
3 Disconnect two Lucar connectors.
4 Hold the cold thermostat trunnion hexagon and slacken the screw. Detach the control rod.
5 Free the capillary tube from the sealer below the refrigerant outlet pipe.
6 Centre punch and drill out two rivets. Use a ¼ in drill.
7 Carefully withdraw the capillary tube from the air space of the cold matrix.
8 Collect up the split rubber grommet.
9 Remove the cold thermostat from the vehicle.

Refitting

10 Bend the capillary tube of the new cold thermostat to the correct shape. Use the old unit as a guide and bend the end as shown.
11 Fit two spire nuts FJ 2544 to the mounting bracket.
12 Thread the capillary tube between the refrigerant outlet pipe and the case. Insert the capillary tube end into the air space of the cold matrix to achieve the position shown.
13 Fit the split rubber grommet AAP 0165.
14 Coil the surplus length of the capillary tube as shown. Ensure that the coil does not extend outboard of the cold thermostat. Position the cold thermostat against the mounting bracket. Secure with two screws YZ 3404.
15 If necessary restore the sealer below the refrigerant outlet pipe.
16 Attach the control rod. Adjust linkage B, see 82.25.08.
17 Connect two Lucar connectors. The connectors may be fitted either way round.
18 Fit the fascia, see 76.46.01.
19 Connect the battery.
20 Functional check, see 82.30.16.

21 If the operation of the cold thermostat is suspect an adjustment may be made by amending the position of the capillary tube in the air space of the cold matrix.
    Access to achieve this operation may be obtained by removing the fascia centre grille, see 76.55.14.

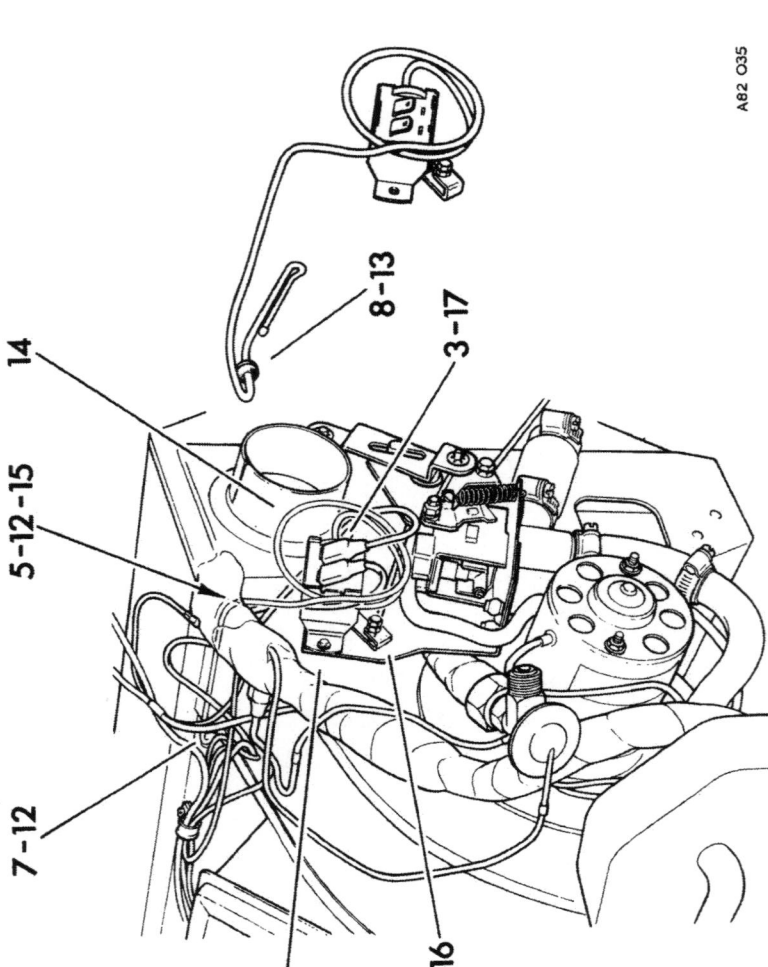

11

14

A82 040

10-12-21

A82 034/1

2·5 in
65 mm

8-13

3-17

14

5-12-15

7-12

4-16

6

A82 035

CONTROLS

High pressure cut out – remove and refit
82.20.20

CAUTION: Immediate blanking of the receiver drier is important. Exposed life of the unit is only 15 minutes.

Removing

1. Connect gauge set, see 82.30.01.
2. Discharge – complete system, see 82.30.05.
3. Protect the eyes with safety goggles and wear gloves during operation 4.
4. Carefully disconnect the capillary tube from the receiver drier. Blank exposed connections immediately.
5. Disconnect the multi-connector.
6. Remove two bolts and spring washers. Lift the high pressure cut out from the vehicle.

Refitting

7. Position the high pressure cut out to the bracket. Secure with two bolts and spring washers.
8. Connect the multi-connector.
9. Carefully connect the capillary tube to the receiver drier. Use refrigerant compressor oil on all mating surfaces to assist leakage prevention.
10. Evacuate – complete system, see 82.30.06.
11. Charge – complete system, see 82.30.08.
12. Perform a leak test on any disturbed joints, see 82.30.09.
13. Functional check, see 82.30.16.
14. Disconnect gauge set, see 82.30.01.

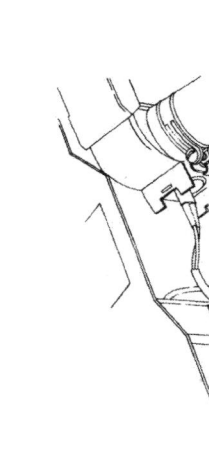

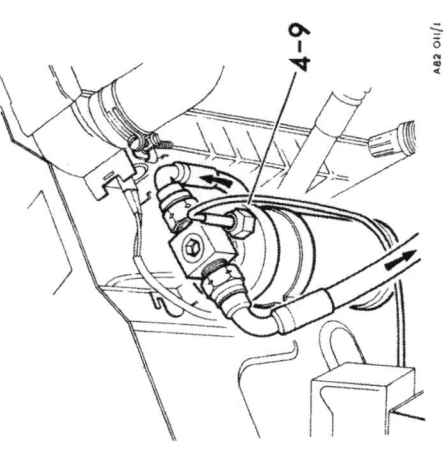

CONTROLS

Hot thermostat — remove and refit   82.20.31

Removing

1 Isolate the battery.
2 Remove the fascia, see 76.46.01.
3 Drain the coolant, see 26.10.01.
4 Note the run of the capillary tube.
5 Cut the metal case between the screen outlet and grommet aperture. This will allow the capillary tube to be withdrawn sideways.
6 Hold the hot thermostat trunnion hexagon and slacken the screw. Detach the control rod.
7 Centre punch and drill out three rivets. Use a short 3⁄16 in drill and right angle drive to remove the forward two rivets. Use a 3⁄16 in drill from below to remove the rear rivet.
8 Slacken four hose clips.
9 Using a wide bladed screwdriver carefully prise the capillary tube loop from the four plastic clips securing it against the face of the hot matrix.
10 Carefully remove the hot thermostat from the vehicle. Maintain the shape of the capillary tube loop as a guide for the new unit.
11 Collect up the split rubber grommet.

Refitting

12 Bend the capillary tube of the new hot thermostat to the correct shape. Use the old unit as a guide.
13 Fit three spire nuts FJ 2544 to the mounting bracket.
14 Insert the capillary tube loop into position against the face of the hot matrix. Secure to the four plastic clips.
15 Manoeuvre the hot thermostat to position the two hose connections and achieve the capillary tube run noted at operation 4 above. Position the hot thermostat on the mounting bracket. Secure with three screws YZ 3404 and washers WP 0005.
16 Tighten four hose clips.
17 Attach the control rod. Adjust linkage B, see 82.25.08.
18 Fit the split rubber grommet.
19 Apply suitable sealer to the cut in the metal case.
20 Refill the coolant, see 26.10.01.
21 Fit the fascia, see 76.46.01.
22 Connect the battery.

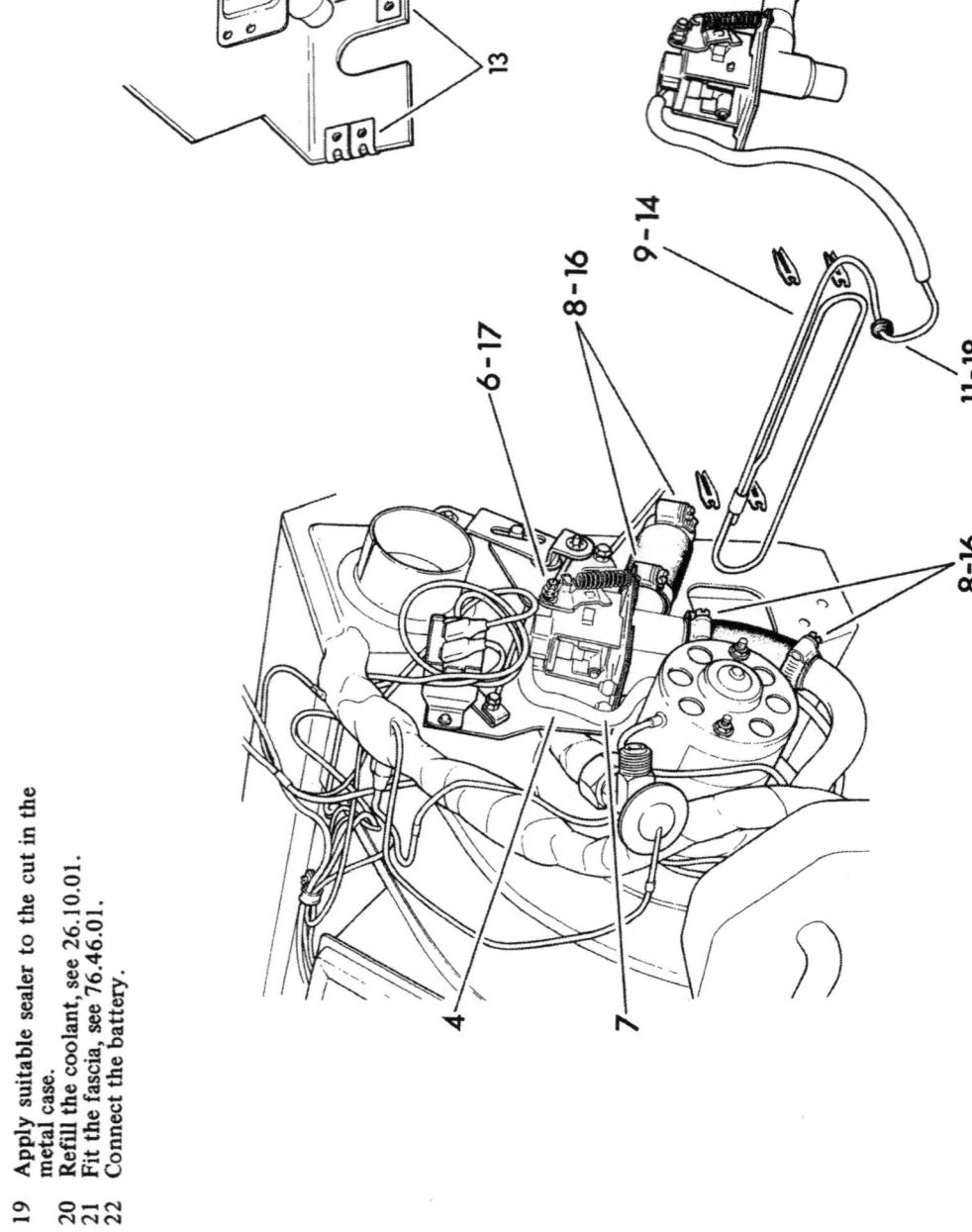

A82 041

A82 037

354   **AIR CONDITIONING**

CONTROLS

Throttle jack — remove and refit   82.20.36

The throttle jack is fitted to vehicles equipped with both air conditioning and automatic transmission.

Carburetter engines

Removing

1   Disconnect two Lucar connectors.
2   Remove two bolts and lock washers.

Refitting

3   Position the throttle jack. Secure with two bolts and lock washers.
4   Connect two Lucar connectors. The connectors may be fitted either way round.
5   Adjust the throttle jack, see 82.20.37.

Fuel Injection engines

The throttle jack is located on the throttle linkage bracket at the rear of the plenum chamber.

To remove, refit and adjust the throttle jack, follow the procedure in 82.30.36 and 82.30.37.

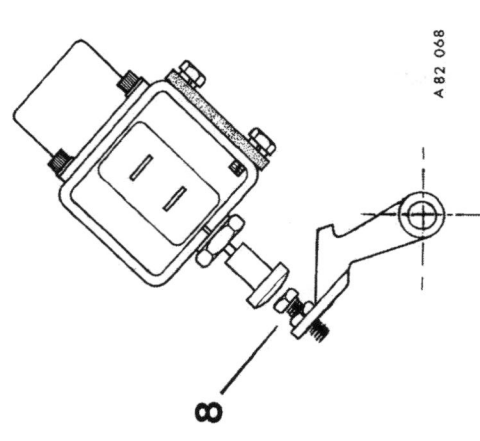

A82 003

CONTROLS

Throttle jack — adjust   82.20.37

The throttle jack is fitted to vehicles equipped with both air conditioning and automatic transmission.

1   Connect a tachometer to the engine as instructed by the manufacturer.

NOTE: The vehicle instrument panel tachometer may be used if no other instrument is available.

2   Run the engine.
3   Select lever C to 'OFF'.

NOTE: This action will switch out the air conditioning system. The compressor clutch will disengage removing the compressor drive load from the engine. The throttle jack plunger will be retracted.

4   The idle speed should now be 650 to 850 r.p.m. Nominal 750 r.p.m.
5   If a correction is required refer to Carburetters — tune and adjust, see 19.15.02.
6   Select lever C to any other position, 1, 2 or 3.

NOTE: This action will switch in the air conditioning system. The compressor clutch will engage applying the compressor drive load to the engine. The throttle jack plunger will be extended.

7   The idle speed should be maintained at 650 to 850 r.p.m. Nominal 750 r.p.m.
8   If a correction is required perform the following: Slacken the lock nut. Rotate the screw to adjust the idle speed. Tighten the lock nut.
9   Check that the correct idle speed has been maintained.

AIR CONDITIONER UNIT

Description 82.25.00

The air conditioner unit is positioned on the centre line of the vehicle between the bulkhead and the fascia/centre console. The function of the unit is to receive air, process and deliver it to the outlets as directed by the control positions.

Controls — to comprehend the system it should be appreciated that control lever 'A' positions flap 'A' via linkage 'A'. Similarly control lever 'B' operates linkage 'B'. Control lever 'C' positions flap 'C' via linkage 'C'. Finally control lever 'D' positions flap 'D' via linkage 'D'.

Intakes — the system draws fresh air at ambient temperature through the fresh air duct, or recirculated air from the vehicle interior, into the blower motor intake. The choice is directed by control lever and flap C.

Blower motor — one blower motor which may be considered as an integral component of the air conditioner unit transfers air into the cold matrix.

Cold matrix — this unit is cooled by the cold refrigeration circuit. All airflow passes across the cold matrix to be conditioned. Cooling is achieved by heat being absorbed by the cold surfaces. Dehumidifying is achieved by moisture carried in the air condensing on the pipes of the cold matrix. Cleaning is achieved by the dust suspended in the air tending to be retained by the moisture. Water drains into a tray below the cold matrix. From the tray it escapes into the air inlet chamber via a short drain pipe. A second drain pipe runs vertically through the mounting rubber to the underside of the vehicle.

Hot matrix — this unit is heated by the hot water circuit. All airflow which is not permitted to escape cold through the three fascia vents is passed through the hot matrix to be heated.

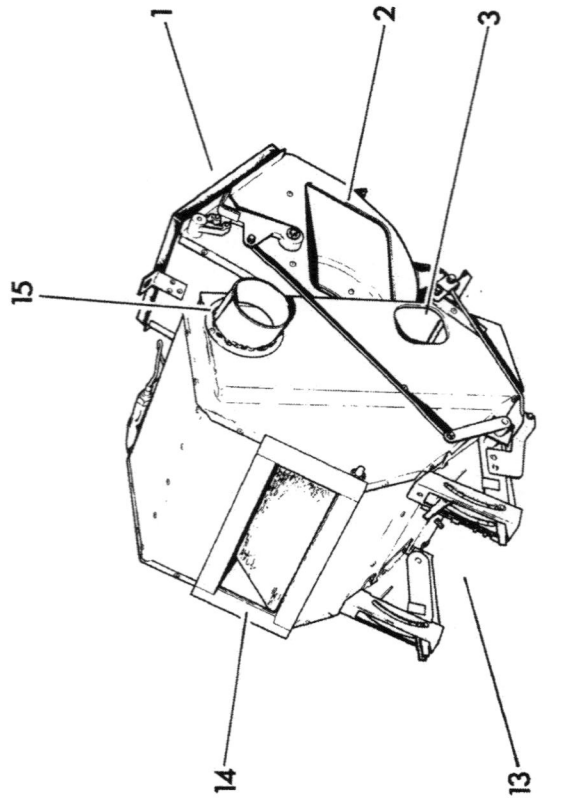

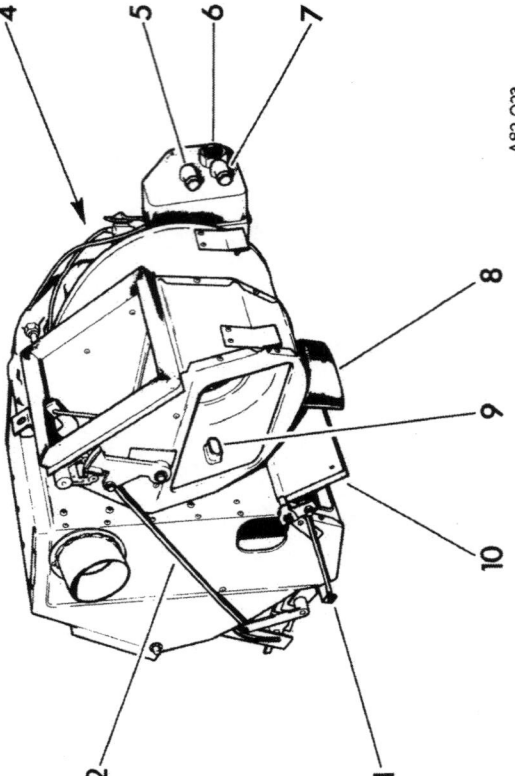

A82 O23

1 Fresh air inlet
2 Recirculated air inlet
3 Screen outlet
4 Refrigerant inlet
5 Water inlet
6 Refrigerant outlet
7 Water outlet
8 Drain pipe
9 Drain pipe
10 Footwell outlet
11 Linkage D
12 Linkage C
13 Control levers
14 Central facia vent outlet
15 End facia vent outlet

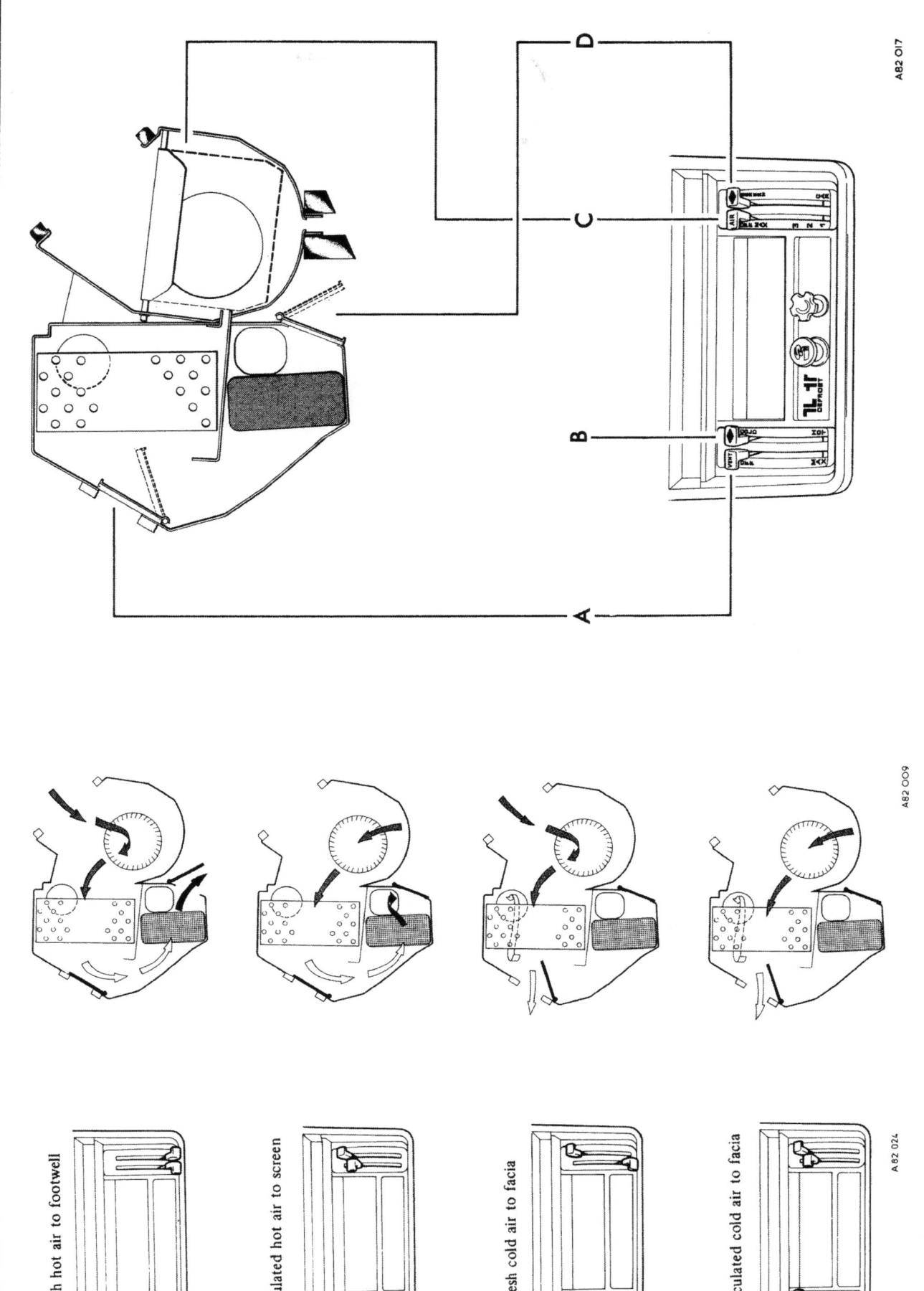

Fresh hot air to footwell

Recirculated hot air to screen

Fresh cold air to facia

Recirculated cold air to facia

AB2 017

A82 009

A82 024

AIR CONDITIONER UNIT

Expansion valve — remove and refit   **82.25.01**

Removing

1. Connect gauge set, see 82.30.01.
2. Discharge — complete system, see 82.30.05.
3. Isolate the battery.
4. Remove the fascia, see 76.46.01.
5. Note the run of the two capillary tubes.
6. Carefully cut and pull back the insulating material to expose the temperature capillary tube clamp and the pressure capillary tube union.
7. Slacken the clamp screw. Carefully withdraw the temperature capillary tube coil.
8. Carefully disconnect the pressure capillary tube union. Blank the exposed connections immediately.
9. Carefully disconnect the hose connection. Blank the exposed connections immediately.
10. Carefully disconnect the expansion valve mounting connection. Use two spanners at the joint to protect the delicate air conditioner unit pipe joint. Note that the larger rearward hexagon is the union to be rotated. Blank the exposed connections immediately.

Refitting

11. Apply refrigerant compressor oil to the mating surfaces of the three connections to assist leakage prevention.
12. Position the expansion valve with the run of the two capillary tubes as noted at operation 5 above. Carefully insert the temperature capillary tube coil in the clamp. Assemble the three connections finger tight.
13. Tighten the expansion valve mounting connection.
14. Tighten the hose connection.
15. Tighten the pressure capillary tube union.
16. Ensure that the temperature capillary tube coil is clean and in good contact with the refrigerant outlet pipe. Tighten the clamp screw.

17. Evacuate — complete system, see 82.30.06.
18. Connect the battery.
19. Charge — complete system, see 82.30.08.
20. Isolate the battery.
21. Perform a leak test on any disturbed joints, see 82.30.09.
22. Restore the insulating material. Ensure that the refrigerant outlet pipe is fully covered.
23. Fit the fascia, see 76.46.01.
24. Connect the battery.
25. Functional check, see 82.30.16.
26. Disconnect gauge set, see 82.30.01.

8-11-12-15   7-16   6-22   7-12-16

9-11-12-14

10-11-12-13

5

A82 038

AIR CONDITIONER UNIT

Linkages – adjust   82.25.08

Linkage A

This is the linkage between control lever A and flap A.

1 Isolate the battery.
2 Remove the front console, see 76.25.01. This is necessary to obtain access to two screws.
3 Remove the control cowl, see 76.25.03.
4 Hold the trunnion hexagon and slacken the screw.
5 Position control lever A up to the OFF position.
6 Hold the flap arm in the close position. Tighten the screw.
7 Fit the control cowl, see 76.25.03.
8 Fit the front console, see 76.25.01.
9 Connect the battery.

Linkage B

This is the linkage between control lever B to the cold thermostat and the hot thermostat.

10 Isolate the battery.
11 Remove the instrument panel, see 88.20.01.
12 Pull the facia end vent hose from the air conditioner unit outlet.
13 Hold the hot thermostat trunnion hexagon and slacken the screw.
14 Hold the cold thermostat trunnion hexagon and slacken the screw.
15 Hold the bell crank trunnion hexagon and slacken the screw.
16 Position control lever B up to the COLD position. Maintain in this position during operations 17 to 19.
17 Hold the bell crank so that the bell crank pin is positioned at the lower end of the swinging link slot. Tighten the screw.
18 Hold the cold thermostat input lever at its rearmost limit of travel. Tighten the screw.
19 Hold the hot thermostat input lever at its rearmost limit of travel with the forward projection against the metal stop. Tighten the screw.
20 Push the facia end vent hose onto the air conditioner unit outlet.
21 Fit the instrument panel, see 88.20.01.
22 Connect the battery.

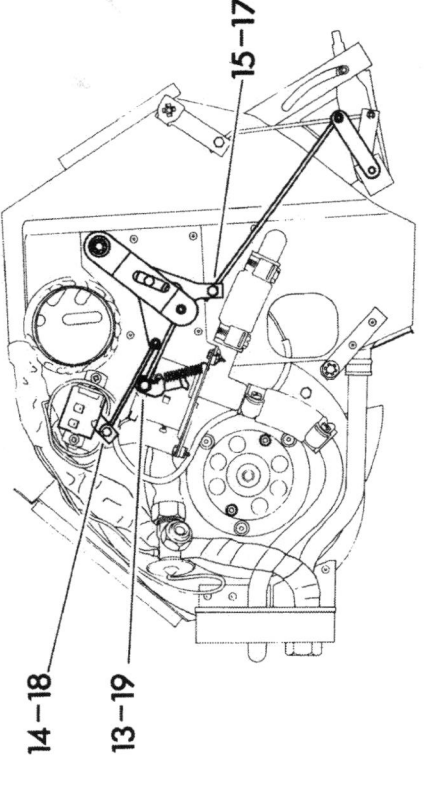

15–17

14–18

13–19

A82 O26/1

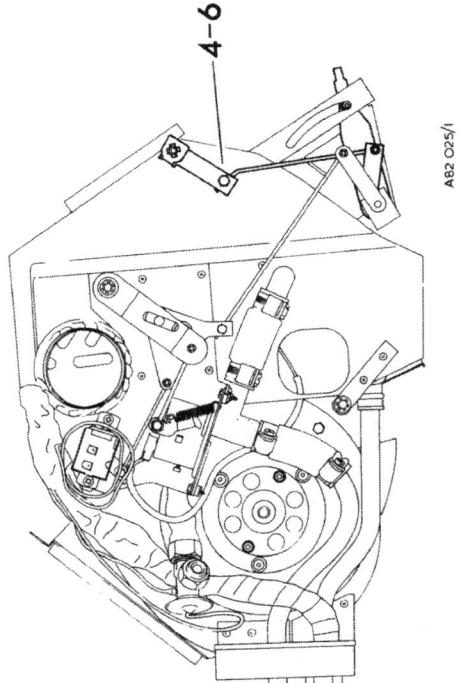

4–6

A82 O25/1

Linkage C

This is the linkage between control lever C and the recirculate/fresh air flap C.

23   Isolate the battery.
24   Remove the facia, see 76.46.01.
25   Hold the trunnion hexagon and slacken the screw.
26   Position control lever C to the MAX position. This is one stop down from the full up position.
27   Hold the position of the 'quick changeover' lever to achieve the dimension shown. This is a nominal dimension of 2.75 mm from the lever reference face to the follower hole centre line. Tighten the screw.
28   Fit the facia, see 76.46.01.
29   Connect the battery.

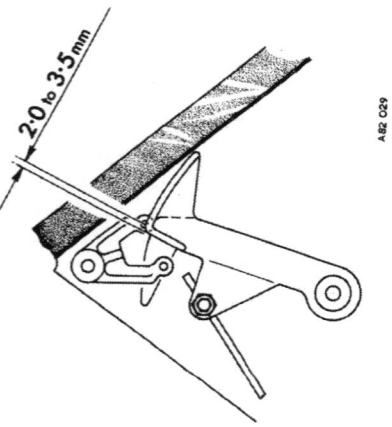

2·0 to 3·5 mm

A82 029

Linkage D

This is the linkage between control lever D and flap D.

30   Isolate the battery.
31   Remove the front console, see 76.25.01. This is necessary to obtain access to two screws.
32   Remove the control cowl, see 76.25.03.
33   Hold the trunnion hexagon and slacken the screw.
34   Position control lever D up to the SCREEN position.
35   Hold the flap arm in the close position. Tighten the screw.
36   Fit the control cowl, see 76.25.03.
37   Fit the front console, see 76.25.01.
38   Connect the battery.

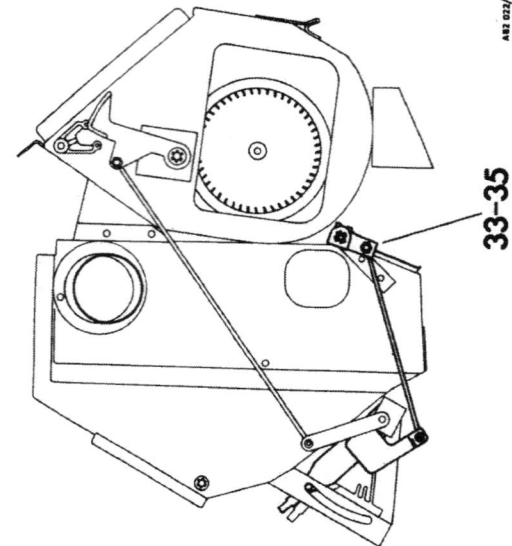

A82 022/A

33–35

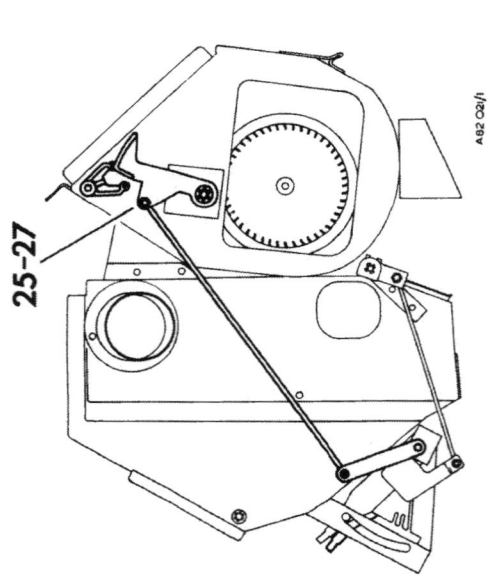

25–27

A82 02/I

SERVICING

82.30.00

WARNING:

The refrigeration circuit must only be disturbed by a qualified refrigeration engineer possessing the required special servicing equipment. Failure to observe this instruction may result in severe personal injury.

When discharging or subsequently breaking open any pipe connections, protect the eyes with safety goggles and wear gloves.

If any liquid refrigerant should contact the eyes, splash with cold water to slowly raise the temperature. Mineral or cod liver oil on the area will reduce the chance of infection. Consult an eye specialist as soon as possible.

Ensure that no refrigerant vapour comes into contact with an open flame. Should this occur a poisonous, corrosive gas may be produced. This vapour may attack metal.

Refrigerant in containers must be protected from heat. Do not expose to radiant heat from the sun. Do not place in water above 50° C (122° F). Do not heat with any flame. Do not carry a container in the vehicle interior.

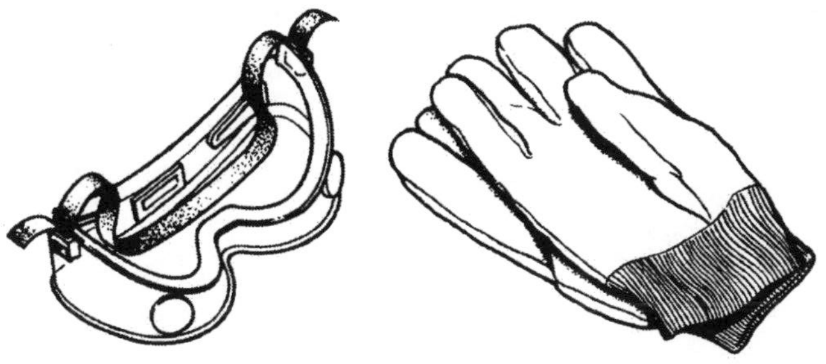

Data

Refrigerant

Type	Refrigerant 12
Approved trade names	Arcton 12
	Freon 12
	Isceon 12
Properties at normal atmospheric pressure and temperature	Vapour
	Odourless
	Colourless
	Heavier than air
	Non-corrosive
	Non-explosive
	Non-inflammable
	Non-poisonous
Dangerous at normal atmospheric pressure and temperature	
— contact with the skin	Liquid refrigerant will freeze anything it contacts. Severe burns may result. Especially dangerous to the eyes. Always protect with safety goggles.
— contact with an open flame	A poisonous, corrosive gas may be produced. This vapour may attack metal.

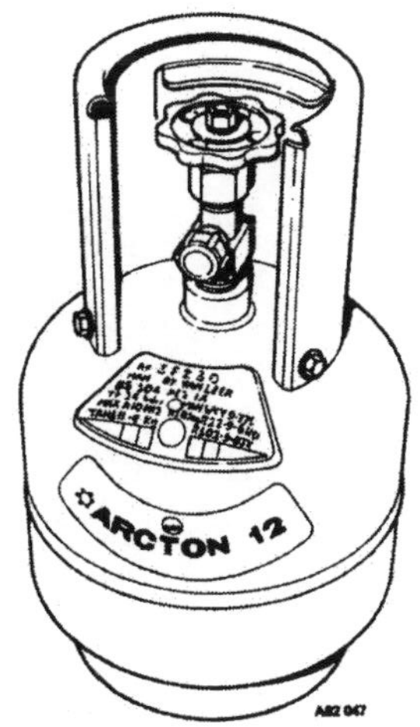

Description 82.30.00

Servicing equipment must include a suitable gauge set or service trolley. Other tools are shown below.

When it is necessary to 'break into' the refrigeration circuit the system must first be discharged.

Either the complete system or the compressor only may be discharged. The choice will depend on the operation to be undertaken. When the compressor only is discharged the remainder of the system stays charged and undisturbed. A saving of refrigerant is also achieved.

To prevent icing or corrosion inside the refrigeration system extreme precautions must be observed during servicing to exclude moisture. Component connections and hose ends must only be open to atmosphere for a brief period. Blanking caps must be fitted immediately to any exposed connections. Replacement components will be supplied sealed and must only be opened immediately prior to making the connections.

After assembly the system must be evacuated. This should remove air, moisture and old refrigerant from the system.

The system should then be immediately charged with fresh refrigerant.

Refrigerant may be provided from single cans, from a multi-can manifold or from a service trolley container. The container should be replenished from a heavy bottle.

A method of calculating the weight of refrigerant introduced into the system is required. This may be by a spring balance or a service trolley container with a graduated scale.

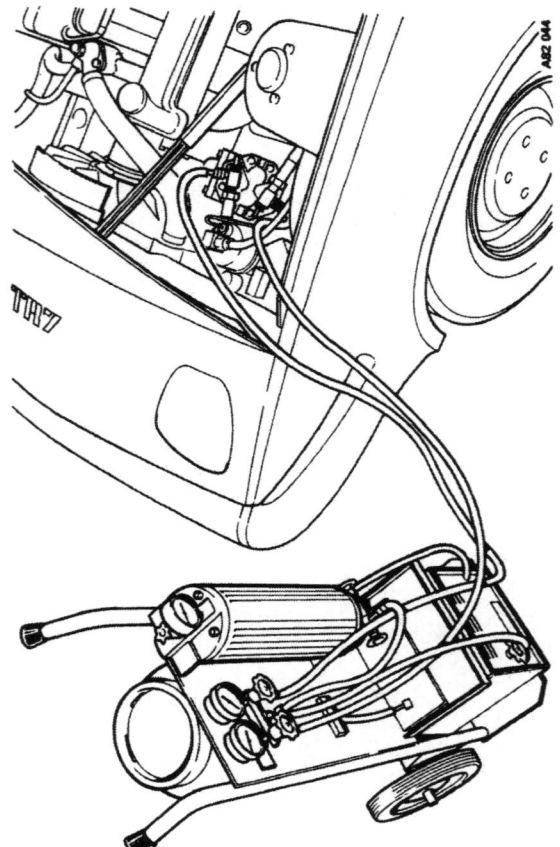

Single can on spring balance

Service trolley

Gauge set

Service valves

Refrigerant is introduced and removed from the refrigeration circuit by way of two service valves located on the compressor top plate.

One service valve communicates with the input side of the compressor and is designated the 'SUCTION' or low side service valve. The other service valve is associated with the compressor output side and is designated the 'DISCHARGE' or high side service valve.

The service valves are controlled by square ended shafts normally covered by protective covers.

Each service valve has three basic positions summarized as follows:

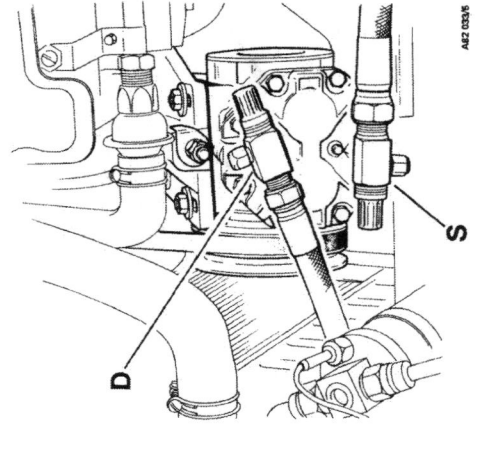

D Discharge valve
S Suction valve

Continued

A82 045/1

1 Goggles
2 Gloves
3 Thermometer
4 Square ¼ AF tool to fit service valve stem.

NOTE: Girling brake adjuster spanner
– Girling Part No. 64947051 –
is ideal for this operation.

5 Spanner ⅞ AF to fit service valve hexagon cap.

SERVICE VALVE POSITIONS

Back seat position	Turn full anti-clockwise	Normal system operating position Compressor communicating with refrigeration circuit. Service port sealed
Mid position	From back seat position turn clockwise 3 turns	Compressor and refrigeration circuit communicating with service port
Front seat position	Turn full clockwise.	Compressor communicating with service port Refrigeration circuit sealed

MO84

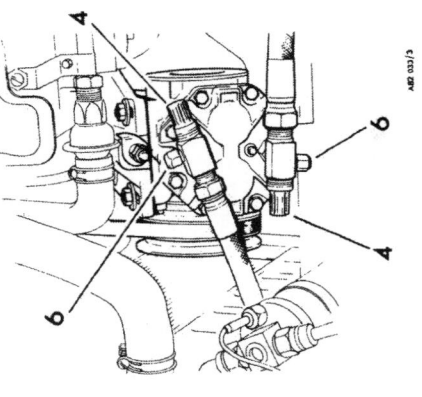

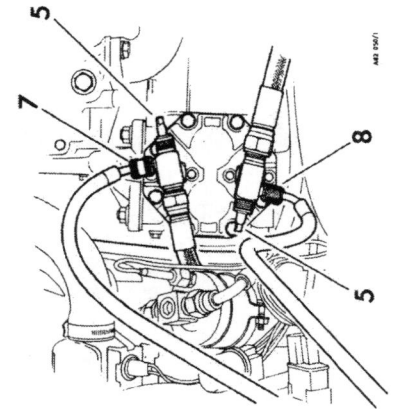

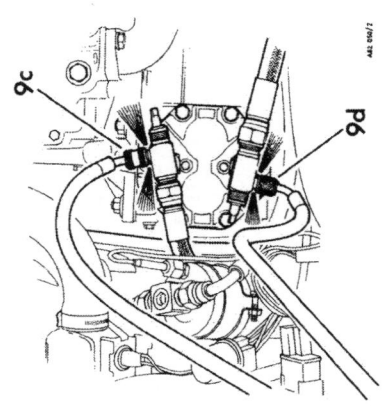

SERVICING

Gauge set – connect   **82.30.01**

1 Position the vehicle in a suitable area. This should be:

   a Well ventilated for the discharge of refrigerant.

   b Away from any naked flame.

   c Suitable for an engine run.

2 Provide a suitable gauge set or service trolley.

3 Close all gauge set or service trolley valves.

4 Remove the two service valve protective covers.

5 Ensure that both service valves are in the back seat position — turn anti-clockwise.

6 Remove the two hexagon caps.

7 Connect the gauge set discharge hose to the discharge service valve.

8 Connect the gauge set suction hose to the suction service valve.

9 Purge the air from the two gauge set hoses as follows:

   a Provide a supply of refrigerant to the gauge set centre manifold hose.

   NOTE: This may be from a single can, from a multi-can manifold or from a service trolley container.

   b Protect the eyes with safety goggles and wear gloves during operations c and d.

   c Loosen the gauge set hose connection to the discharge service valve. Carefully open the gauge set discharge valve. When refrigerant is seen to be escaping tighten the hose connection. Close the gauge set discharge valve.

   d Loosen the gauge set hose connection to the suction service valve. Carefully open the gauge set suction valve. When refrigerant is seen to be escaping tighten the hose connection. Close the gauge set suction valve.

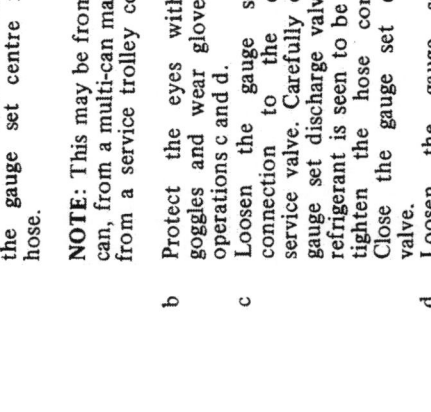

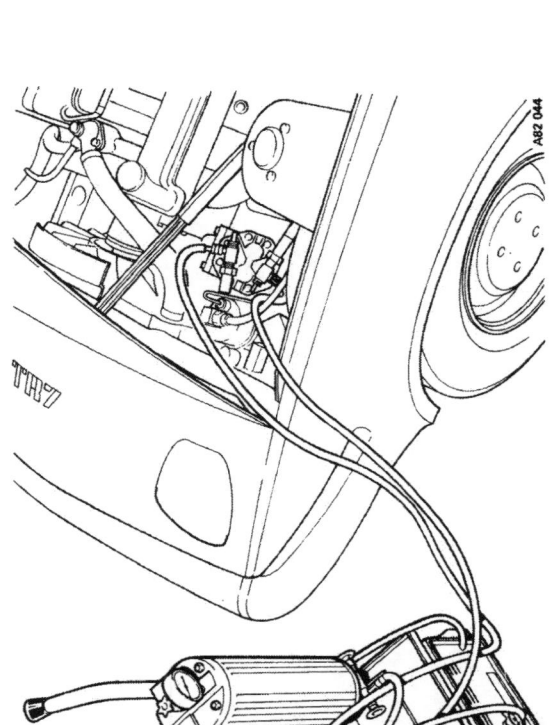

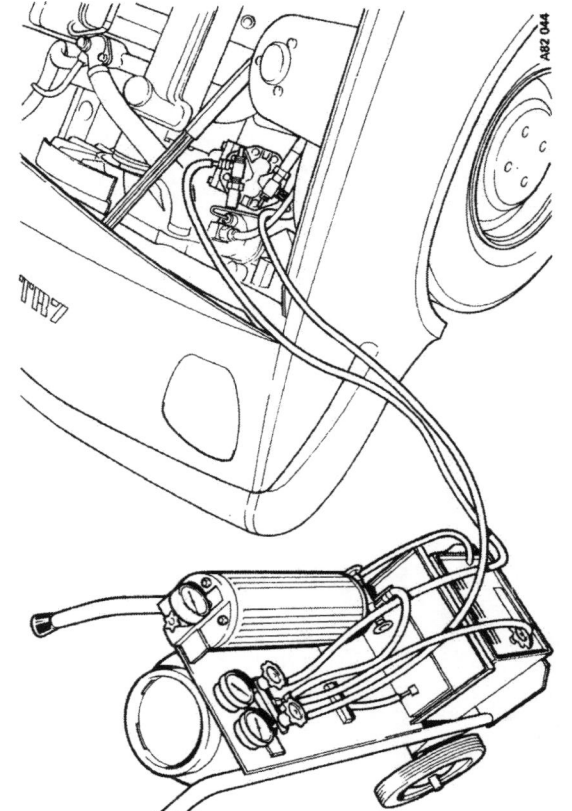

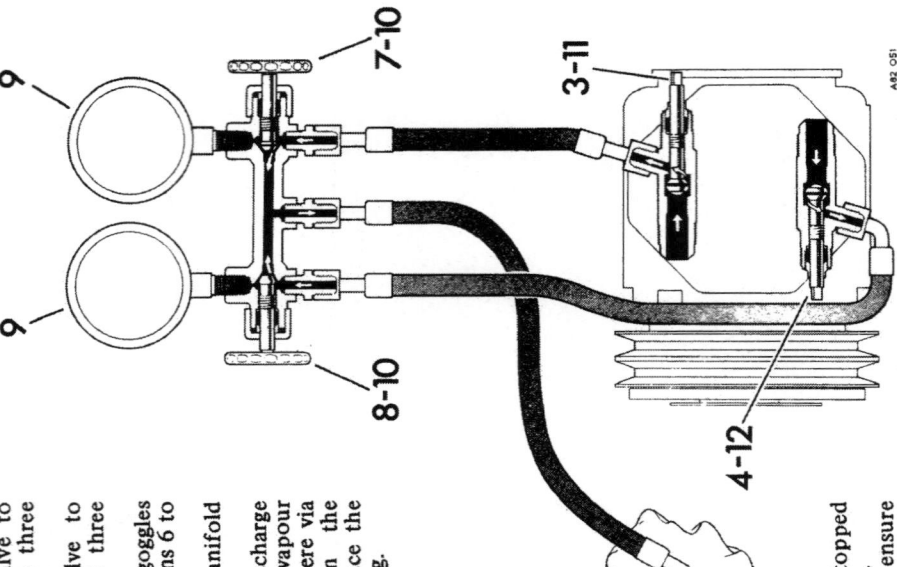

A82 051

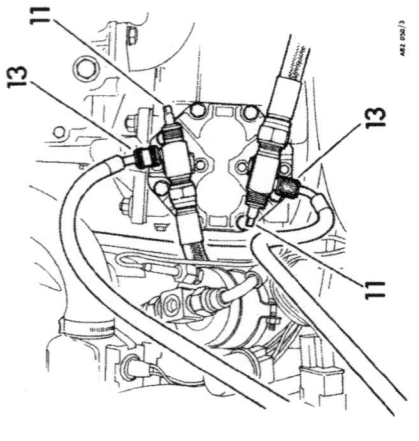

A82 090/3

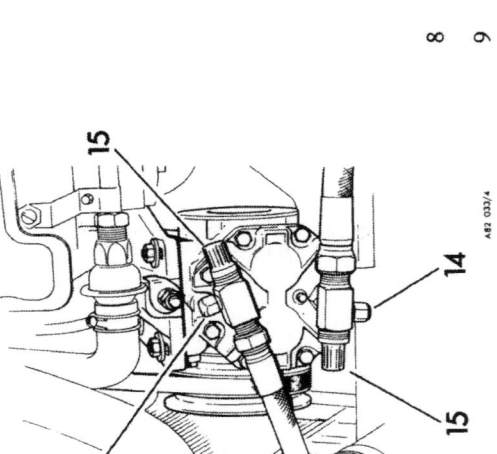

A82 032/4

SERVICING

Discharge — complete system   82.30.05

1 Connect gauge set, see 82.30.01.
2 Immobilize the refrigerant circuit by disconnecting the electrical connection to the compressor clutch.
3 Open the discharge service valve to mid-position — turn clockwise three turns.
4 Open the suction service valve to mid-position — turn clockwise three turns.
5 Protect the eyes with safety goggles and wear gloves during operations 6 to 8.
6 Hold the gauge set centre manifold hose end in a suitable rag.
7 Slightly open the gauge set discharge valve to allow the refrigerant vapour to slowly discharge to atmosphere via the hose end. If oil from the compressor is discharged, reduce the gauge set discharge valve opening.
8 When the discharge has nearly stopped open the gauge set suction valve.
9 When the discharge has stopped ensure that both gauges read zero.
10 Close both gauge set valves.
11 Close the discharge service valve to the back seat position – turn anti-clockwise.
12 Close the suction service valve to the back seat position – turn anti-clockwise.

SERVICING

Gauge set – disconnect   82.30.01

10 Close all gauge set or service trolley valves.
11 Ensure that both service valves are in the back seat position – turn anti-clockwise.
12 Protect the eyes with safety goggles and wear gloves during operation 13.
13 Disconnect both gauge set hoses from the service valves.
14 Fit the two hexagon caps.
15 Fit the two service valve protective covers.

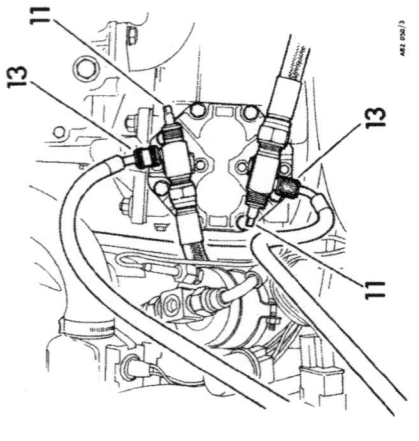

366   **AIR CONDITIONING**

SERVICING

Charge — complete system   82.30.08

CAUTION: Charge with refrigerant 12 of approved trade names:

Arcton 12
Freon 12
Isceon 12

Do not charge with methylchloride refrigerant. This would react undesirably with aluminium parts used in the system.

1 Connect gauge set, see 82.30.01.
2 Discharge — complete system, see 82.30.05.
3 Evacuate — complete system, see 82.30.06
4 Provide a supply of refrigerant to the gauge set centre manifold hose.

NOTE: *This may be from single cans, from a multi-can manifold or from a service trolley container.*

5 If the centre manifold hose contains air purge with refrigerant as follows:

a Protect the eyes with safety goggles and wear gloves during operation b.
b Carefully loosen the gauge set centre manifold hose connection. When refrigerant is seen to be escaping tighten the hose connection.

continued

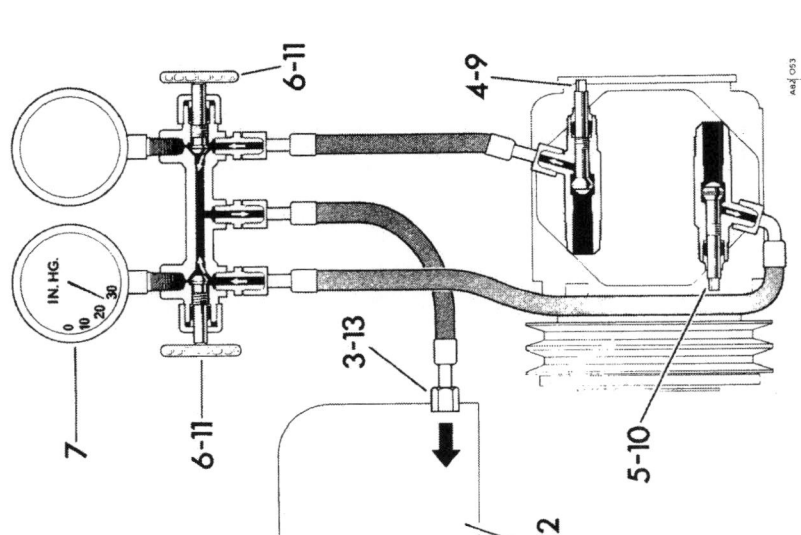

SERVICING

Evacuate — complete system   82.30.06

1 Connect gauge set, 82.30.01.
2 Discharge — complete system, see 82.30.05.
3 Connect a vacuum pump to the gauge set centre manifold hose.
4 Open the discharge service valve to mid-position — turn clockwise three turns.
5 Open the suction service valve to mid-position — turn clockwise three turns.
6 Open both gauge set valves fully.

7 Run the vacuum pump for 20 minutes. A vacuum of 28 in Hg should be indicated on the suction gauge. If this is not achieved, consider the possibility of a system leak.
8 Perform operations 9 to 11 with the vacuum pump running.
9 Close the discharge service valve to the back seat position — turn anti-clockwise.
10 Close the suction service valve to the back seat position — turn anti-clockwise.
11 Close both gauge set valves.
12 Stop the vacuum pump.
13 Disconnect the vacuum pump from the gauge set centre manifold hose.

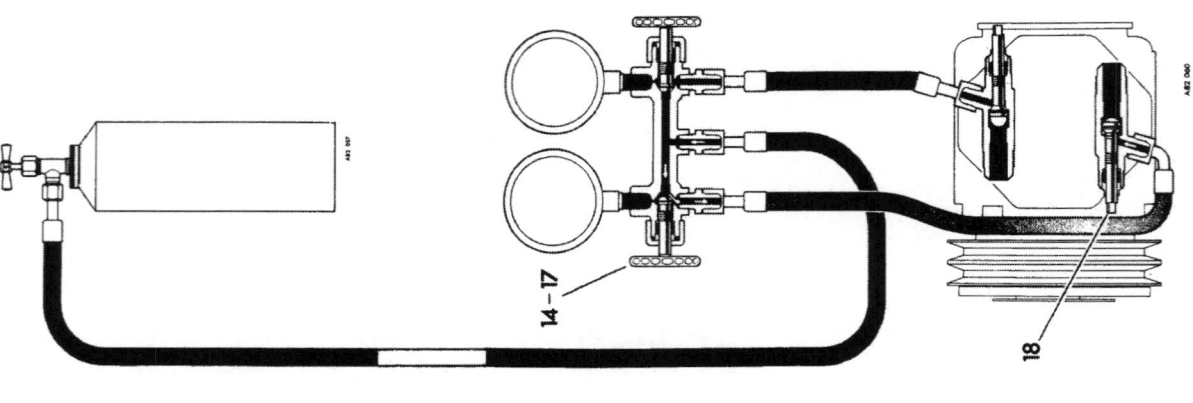

14-17

18

A82 060

A83 057

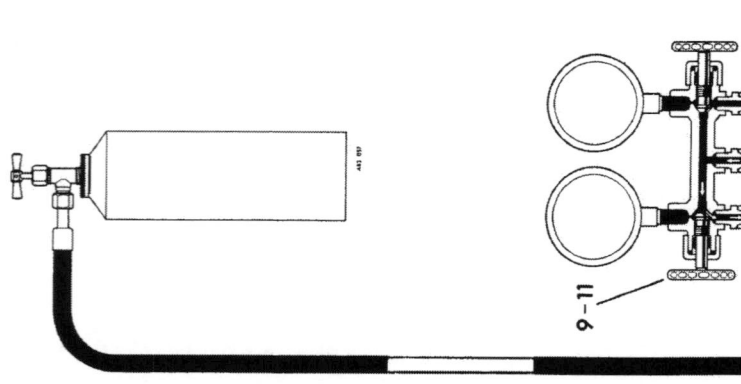

9-11

8-12a

A83 059

A83 057

6 Provide a method of calculating at any time during the operation, the weight of refrigerant put into the system.

NOTE: *A single can or a multi-can manifold may be weighed by hanging from a spring balance. A service trolley container should have a graduated scale.*

7 Note the datum refrigerant weight.

8 Open the suction service valve to mid-position – turn clockwise three turns.

9 Slightly open the gauge set suction valve. Allow approximately ½ lb (230 g) of refrigerant to enter the system. Close the gauge set suction valve.

NOTE: *High pressure liquid refrigerant from the container will vaporize on entering the evacuated low pressure system. Flow will continue until container pressure equals system pressure or until the gauge set suction valve is closed.*

10 Perform a first leak test on any disturbed joints, see 82.30.09.

11 Slightly open the gauge set suction valve. If the pressure differential between the container and the system permits allow the flow to continue until a total of 2½ lb (1130 g) of refrigerant – from the datum weight operation 7 – has entered the system. Close the gauge set suction valve.

NOTE: *High pressure liquid refrigerant from the container will vaporize on entering the evacuated low pressure system. Flow will continue until container pressure equals system pressure or until the gauge set suction valve is closed.*

12 If a total of 2½ lb (1130 g) of refrigerant is in the system perform the following:

a   Close the suction service valve to the back seat position – turn anti-clockwise.

b   Ignore operations 13 to 19.

13 If the container pressure and the system pressure equalize before a total of 2½ lb (1130 g) of refrigerant is in the system perform operations 14 to 19.

14 Ensure that the gauge set suction valve is closed.

15 Connect the electrical connection to the compressor clutch.

16 Run the engine at 1000 to 1500 rev/min for 5 minutes with the control levers set as follows:

Lever A to MAX.
Lever B to COLD
Lever C to 3
Lever D to CAR

This is to warm the engine and stabilize the system.

NOTE: *Warm air from above the engine will enter the fresh air duct to be presented to the cold matrix. This condition will cause the system to operate hard and prevent frequent cutting in and out of the compressor clutch.*

17 Slightly open the gauge set suction valve. Allow the flow to continue until a total of 2½ lb (1130 g) of refrigerant – from the datum weight operation 7 – has entered the system. Close the gauge set suction valve.

NOTE: *Compressor suction will draw further vaporized refrigerant into the system. The refrigeration circuit will commence to function and vapour passed into the condenser will accumulate as liquid refrigerant in the receiver drier.*

18 Close the suction service valve to the back seat position – turn anti-clockwise.

19 Stop the engine.

SERVICING

Leak test   82.30.09

A major leak in the system should be shown up during the evacuate operation prior to charging with fresh refrigerant.

Minor leaks should be searched for as instructed in the charge operation using one of the two basic types of leak testing equipment in common use.

The burner type has a hand held burner connected by hose to a cylinder of gas. A second hose attached to the burner is the search hose which draws in air or refrigerant vapour. This hose is of some length so its end may be positioned close to the unions while the burner is held and observed by a second operator a safe distance from the vehicle. A leak is indicated by the flame changing colour to green or purple. The product of burning gas and refrigerant is a poisonous, corrosive gas which should not be inhaled.

The electronic type may be semi portable with mains electric power or fully portable with batteries. The sensors are sensitive to refrigerant vapour. The sensor may be positioned at the end of a search cable or the air sample may be drawn through a search hose by a small electric air pump to be passed across a sensor in the unit. The sensor signal is amplified. A leak is indicated by audible warning, a light signal or meter reading.

Whether a burner type or electronic type unit is used the equipment should be employed as detailed by the manufacturer. The following instructions are provided to assist leak testing.

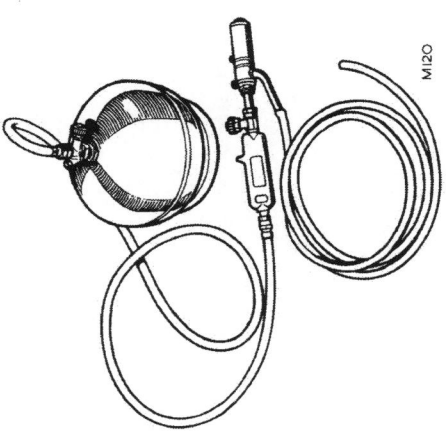

Typical electronic leak tester

M120

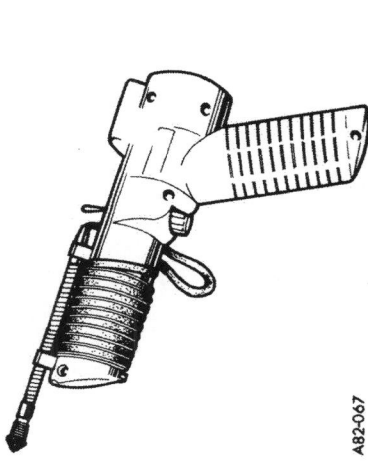

Typical burner leak tester

A82-067

General

Place the vehicle in a well ventilated area or refrigerant may persist in the vicinity and give misleading results.

Strong draughts should be avoided as a leak may be dissipated without detection.

Refrigerant is heavier than air. When checking each union pass the detector slowly round each joint with special attention to the underside.

Compressor

Check two hose connections, service valves, head joint, rear bearing plate joint and base joint.

Check the shaft seal by positioning the detector between the clutch and seal plate. As access is poor, leave the detector in the vicinity for one minute.

Condenser

Check two hose connections. Check all soldered joints and pass detector across underside of unit.

Receiver drier

Check two hose connections and high pressure cut-out capillary.

Expansion valve and air conditioner unit pipes

Check all accessible pipes and joints. If a known leak can not be located it may finally be necessary to perform the following:

Remove the facia. Carefully cut and pull back the insulating material to expose the pipe runs. After the leak test restore the insulating material. Ensure that the refrigerant outlet pipe is fully covered.

Cold matrix

Select lever 'A' to MAX. Insert the probe through the central facia vent.

Select lever 'D' to CAR. Insert the probe into the footwell outlet.

Check below the matrix by positioning the probe into the recirculated air inlet and checking near the drain pipe (see 82.25.00, Item 9).

Functional check 82.30.16

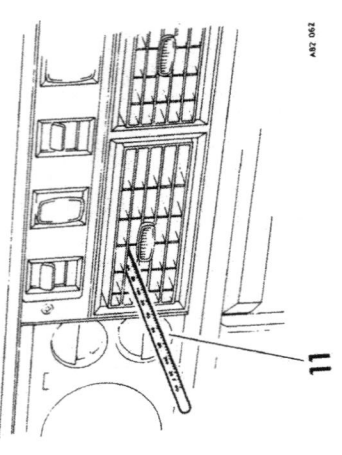

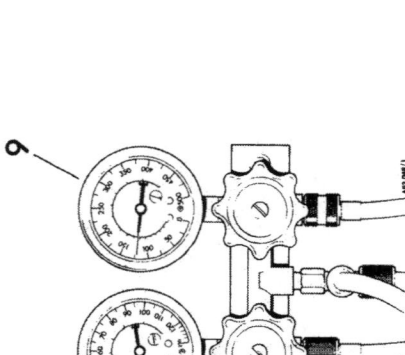

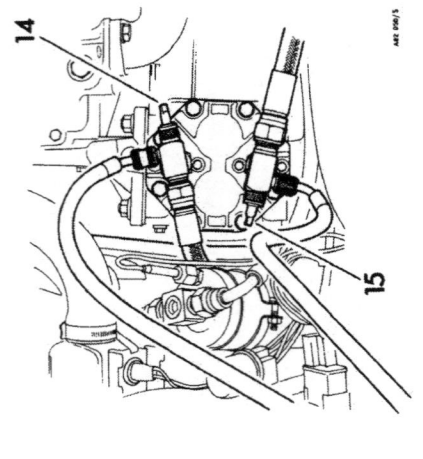

1 Ensure that the compressor drive belt is correctly adjusted, see 82.10.01.

2 Connect gauge set, see 82.30.01.

3 Open the discharge service valve towards mid-position – turn clockwise half a turn.

4 Open the suction service valve forwards mid-position – turn clockwise half a turn.

5 Note the ambient air temperature.

6 Run the engine at 1000 to 1500 rev/min for 5 minutes with the control levers set as follows:

        Lever A to MAX.
        Lever B to COLD

NOTE: *In humid conditions it may be necessary to reduce lever 'B' setting from full 'COLD' towards 'HOT' to prevent icing of the cold matrix. Slightly higher central fascia vent air temperatures should then be expected.*

        Lever C to MAX.
        Lever D to CAR

7 This is to warm the engine and stabilize the system.

Check that the two condenser fan motors run when the compressor clutch pulls in and stop when the compressor clutch drops out.

8 Check that the receiver drier sight glass is clear of bubbles or foam.

9 Note the maximum discharge gauge reading when the compressor clutch is pulled in.

10 Note the minimum suction gauge reading when the compressor clutch is pulled in.

11 Insert a thermometer into the central fascia vent and note the minimum temperature.

12 Stop the engine.

13 Compare all readings with the values given in the table.

14 Close the discharge service valve to the back seat position – turn anti-clockwise.

15 Close the suction service valve to the back seat position – turn anti-clockwise.

16 Disconnect gauge set, see 82.30.01.

Ambient air temperature		Discharge gauge – maximum		Suction gauge – minimum		Central facia vent temperature – minimum	
°F	°C	psi	kg/cm²	psi	kg/cm²	°F	°C
60	16	12 to 20	0.8 to 1.4	80 to 130	5.6 to 9.1	32 to 40	0 to 4
80	27	16 to 25	1.1 to 1.8	130 to 180	9.1 to 12.7	35 to 44	2 to 7
100	38	18 to 28	1.3 to 2.0	200 to 240	14.1 to 16.9	38 to 47	3 to 8
110	43	19 to 29	1.3 to 2.0	240 to 275	16.9 to 19.3	39 to 48	4 to 9

The above figures are not specific to the TR7 installation. All readings obtained should be approximately equal to the values given in the table.

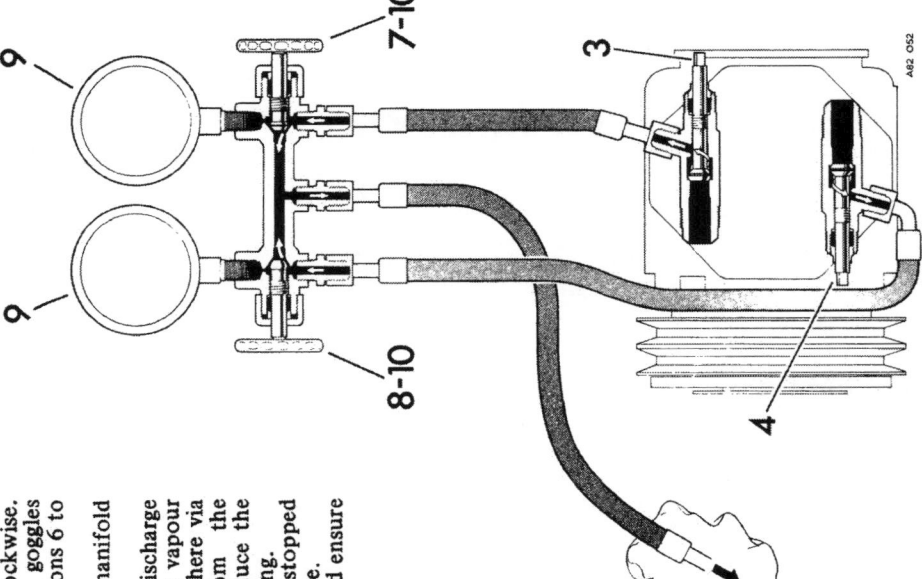

SERVICING

Discharge — compressor only 82.30.20

1 Connect gauge set, see 82.30.01.
2 Immobilize the refrigerant circuit by disconnecting the electrical connection to the compressor clutch.
3 Close the discharge service valve to the front seat position — turn clockwise.
4 Close the suction service valve to the front seat position — turn clockwise.
5 Protect the eyes with safety goggles and wear gloves during operations 6 to 8.
6 Hold the gauge set centre manifold hose end in a suitable rag.
7 Slightly open the gauge set discharge valve to allow the refrigerant vapour to slowly discharge to atmosphere via the hose end. If oil from the compressor is discharged, reduce the gauge set discharge valve opening.
8 When the discharge has nearly stopped open the gauge set suction valve.
9 When the discharge has stopped ensure that both gauges read zero.
10 Close both gauge set valves.

SERVICING

Evacuate — compressor only 82.30.21

1 Connect gauge set, see 82.30.01.
2 Discharge — compressor only, see 82.30.20.
3 Connect a vacuum pump to the gauge set centre manifold hose.
4 Open both gauge set valves fully.
5 Run the vacuum pump for 20 minutes. A vacuum of 28 in Hg should be indicated on the suction gauge. If this is not achieved, consider the possibility of a system leak.
6 Perform operation 7 with the vacuum pump running.
7 Close both gauge set valves.
8 Stop the vacuum pump.
9 Disconnect the vacuum pump from the gauge set centre manifold hose.

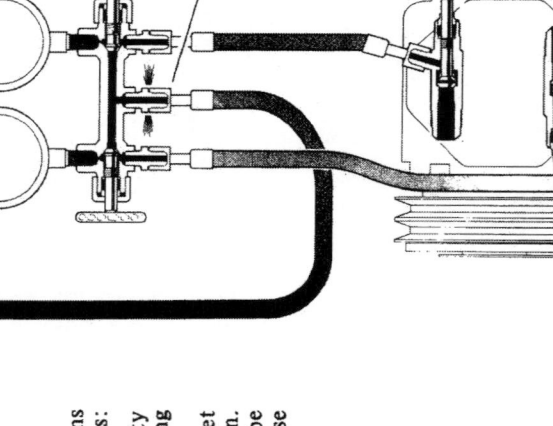

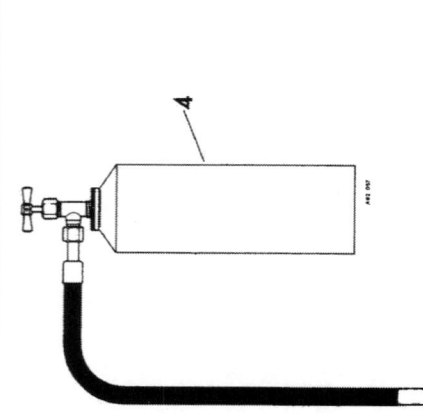

SERVICING

Charge — compressor only   82.30.23

CAUTION: Charge with refrigerant 12 of approved trade names:

       Arcton 12
       Freon 12
       Isceon 12

Do not charge with methylchloride refrigerant. This would react undesirably with aluminium parts used in the system.

1 Connect gauge set, see 82.30.01.
2 Discharge — compressor only, see 82.30.20.
3 Evacuate — compressor only, see 82.30.21.
4 Provide a supply of refrigerant to the gauge set centre manifold hose.

5 If the centre manifold hose contains air purge with refrigerant as follows:

   a Protect the eyes with safety goggles and wear gloves during operation b.
   b Carefully loosen the gauge set centre manifold hose connection. When refrigerant is seen to be escaping tighten the hose connection.

6 Provide a method of calculating at any time during the operation the weight of refrigerant put into the system.

   NOTE: A single can or a multi-can manifold may be weighed by hanging from a spring balance. A service trolley container should have a graduated scale.

7 Note the datum refrigerant weight.
8 Open the discharge service valve to mid-position — turn anti-clockwise five turns.
9 Open the suction service valve to mid-position — turn anti-clockwise five turns.

   NOTE: Operation 8 and 9 will allow high pressure refrigerant in the remainder of the system to enter the evacuated low pressure compressor.

10 Perform a first leak test on any disturbed joints, see 82.30.09.

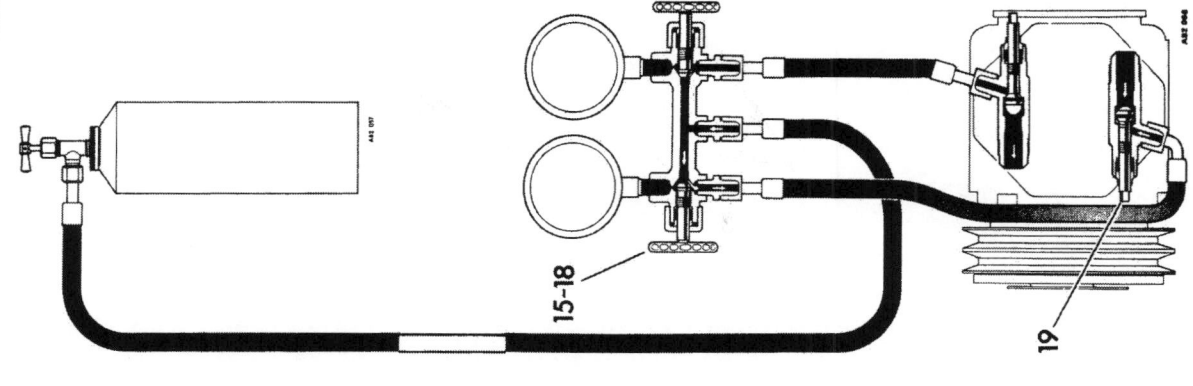

15-18

19

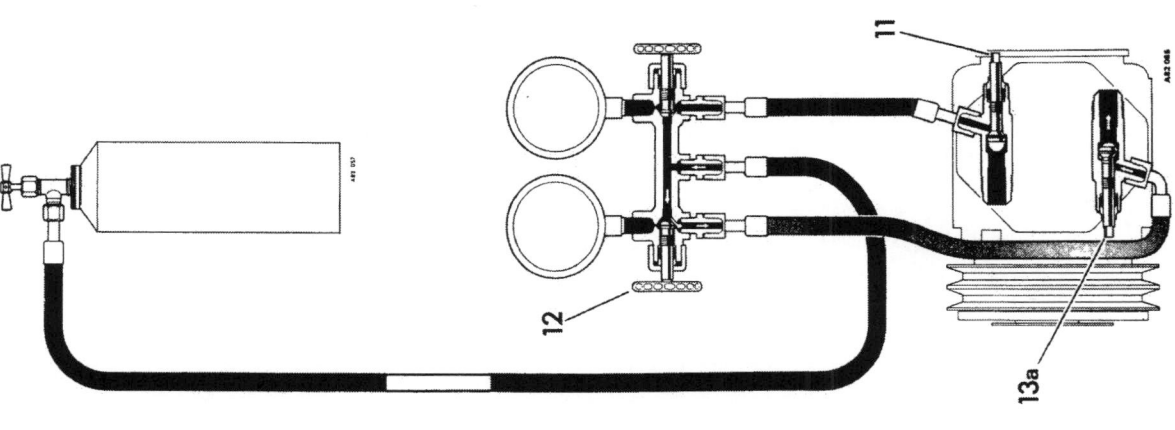
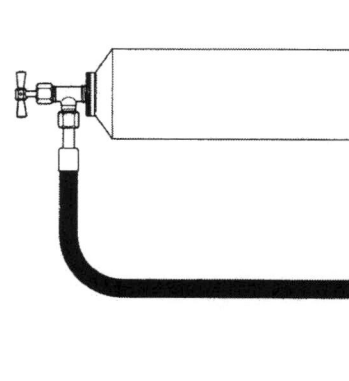
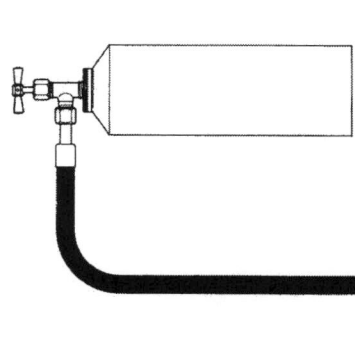

11

12

13a

14 If the container pressure and the system pressure equalize before 6 oz (170 g) of refrigerant has entered the system perform operations 15 to 20.

15 Ensure that the gauge set suction valve is closed.

16 Connect the electrical connection to the compressor clutch.

17 Run the engine at 1000 to 1500 rev/min for 5 minutes with the control levers set as follows:

Lever A to MAX.
Lever B to COLD
Lever C to 3
Lever D to CAR

This is to warm the engine and stabilize the system.

NOTE: *Warm air from above the engine will enter the fresh air duct to be presented to the cold matrix. This condition will cause the system to operate hard and prevent frequent cutting in and out of the compressor clutch.*

18 Slightly open the gauge set suction valve. Allow the flow to continue until 6 oz (170 g) of refrigerant — from the datum weight operation 7 — has entered the system. Close the gauge set suction valve.

NOTE: *Compressor suction will draw further vaporized refrigerant into the system. The refrigeration circuit will commence to function and vapour passed into the condenser will accumulate as liquid refrigerant in the receiver drier.*

19 Close the suction service valve to the back seat position — turn anti-clockwise.

20 Stop the engine.

11 Close the discharge service valve to the back seat position — turn anti-clockwise.

12 Slightly open the gauge set suction valve. If the pressure differential between the container and the system permits, allow the flow to continue until 6 oz (170 g) of refrigerant has entered the system. Close the gauge set suction valve.

NOTE: *High pressure liquid refrigerant from the container will vaporize on entering the system. Flow will continue until container pressure equals system pressure or until the gauge set suction valve is closed.*

13 If 6 oz (170 g) of refrigerant has entered the system perform the following:

a Close the suction service valve to the back seat position — turn anti-clockwise

b Ignore operations 14 to 20.

WINDSCREEN WASHER RESERVOIR   84.10.01

Remove and refit

Removing

1 Pull the windscreen washer reservoir pipe from the windscreen washer pump.
2 Lift the windscreen washer reservoir from the retaining bracket.

Refitting

3 Reverse 1 to 2.

WINDSCREEN WASHER JET   84.10.09

Remove and refit

Removing

1 Pull the pipe from the jet.
2 Remove the nut and anti-vibration washer.
NOTE: Take care not to drop the nut and anti-vibration washer as retrieval may prove difficult.
3 Remove the jet and rubber sealing washer.

Refitting

4 Reverse 1 to 3. Fit the jet with the jet outlet in the correct location to the bonnet.
5 Close the bonnet and operate the pump to check the jet aim.
6. If necessary adjust the jet aim by using a screwdriver in the slot to slightly rotate the jet outlet.

WINDSCREEN WASHER PUMP   84.10.21

Remove and refit

Removing

1 Remove the windscreen washer reservoir, see 84.10.01 to obtain improved access.

2 Disconnect two Lucar connectors.
3 Note the positions of the inlet and outlet pipes. IN and OUT are stamped on the mounting bracket.
4 Pull the outlet pipe from the windscreen washer pump.
5 Remove two Pozidriv screws and washers. Remove the windscreen washer pump.
NOTE: Take care not to drop the two Pozidriv screws and washers as retrieval may prove difficult.

Refitting

6 Position the windscreen washer pump. Secure with two Pozidriv screws and washers.
7 Push the outlet pipe onto the windscreen washer pump in the position noted at operation 3 above.
8 Connect two Lucar connectors as follows:
Light green/black wire to the positive terminal.
Black wire to the negative terminal.
9 Refit windscreen washer reservoir, see 84.10.01.

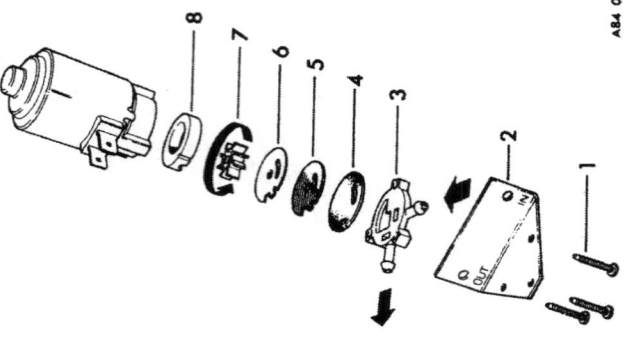

A84 001

WINDSCREEN WASHER PUMP

Overhaul   84.10.24

The motor is a sealed unit and cannot be serviced. It is possible to dismantle and clean the interior of the pump as detailed below.

Dismantling

1 Remove three screws.
2 Lift off the bracket.
3 Remove the pump cover.
4 Remove the rubber disc.
5 Remove the metal disc.
6 Remove the plastic disc.
7 Carefully withdraw the rotor.
8 Withdraw the rotor housing.

Reassembling

9 Reverse 1 to 8. Ensure that all the components are assembled the correct way round as shown.

WINDSCREEN WIPER SYSTEM

Description   84.15.00

The unit consists of a two speed permanent magnet motor and a gearbox unit which drives a cable rack mechanism. Rotation of the motor armature is converted to a reciprocating motion of the cable rack by a single stage worm and gear, a connecting rod and a cross head contained in a guide channel.

Two speed operation is provided by a third brush. When high speed is selected the positive supply is transferred from the normal speed brush to the high speed brush.

A switching feature stops the blades in the park position irrespective of their position when the steering column switch is selected OFF. This is effected by a two stage limit switch unit attached to the gearbox. The contacts are actuated by a straight cam slope on a slider block which is traversed by a projection from the cross head.

When the steering column switch is selected OFF, the motor will continue to run until the limit switch first stage contacts open. A momentary period follows during which no contact is made. The second stage contacts then close causing regenerative braking of the armature which maintains consistent parking of the blades.

DATA

Motor

Manufacturer	Lucas
Type	16W
Running current—after 60 seconds from cold with connecting rod removed:	
Normal speed	1.5 amp
High speed	2.0 amp
Running speed—final gear after 60 seconds from cold with connecting rod removed:	
Normal speed	46 to 52 rev/min.
High speed	60 to 70 rev/min.
Armature end-float	0.002 to 0.008 in. (0.05 to 0.20 mm)
Brush length—normal speed: new	0.380 in. (9.65 mm)
renew if less than	0.180 in. (4.76 mm)
high speed: new	0.380 in. (9.65 mm)
renew if less than	0.280 in. (7.11 mm) (i.e. when narrow section is worn to step into full width section)
earth: new	0.380 in. (9.65 mm)
renew if less than	0.180 in. (4.76 mm)
Brush spring pressure—when compressed so brush bottom is aligned with brushbox slot end	5 to 7 ozf (140 to 200 gf)
Maximum permissible force to move cable rack in tubing—arms and blades removed	6 lbf (3 kgf)

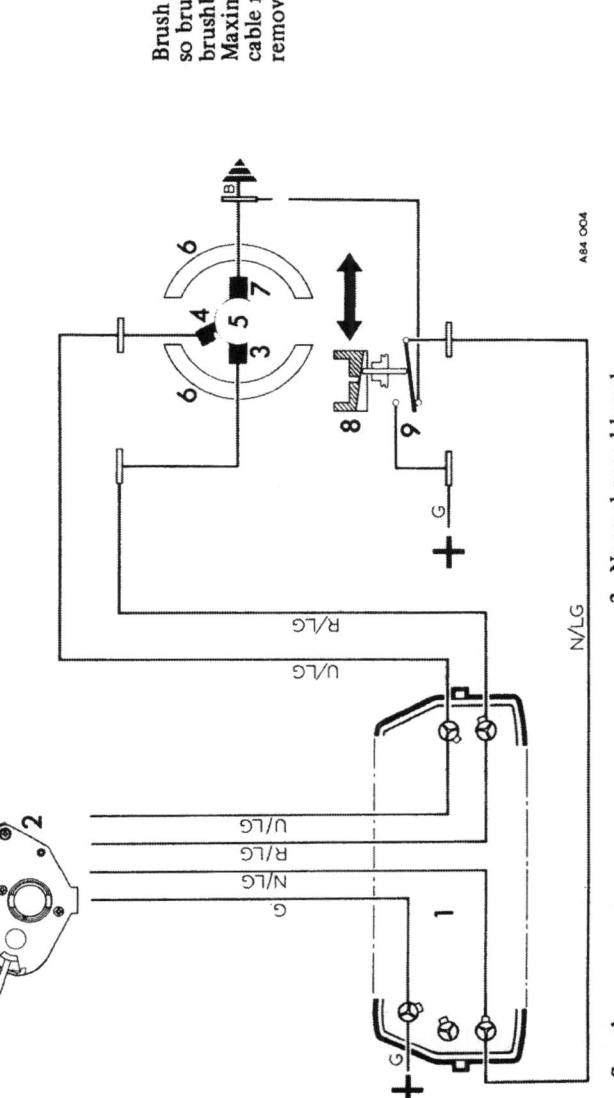

A84 004

+ Supply
1. Steering column harness plug
2. Steering column multi-purpose switch—washer/wiper unit:

2	HIGH SPEED	G to U/LG
1	NORMAL SPEED	G to R/LG
0	OFF	N/LG to R/LG
1	SWEEP WIPE FACILITY	G to R/LG

3. Normal speed brush
4. High speed brush
5. Commutator
6. Permanent magnet
7. Earth brush
8. Slider block
9. Limit switch unit

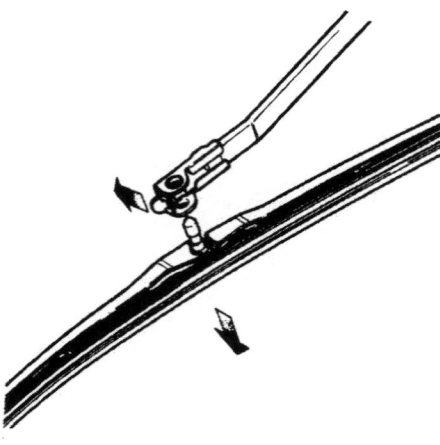

A86 017

WINDSCREEN WIPER BLADE
Driver's — remove and refit 84.15.06
Removing

1 Lift the wiper arm and blade away from the screen.

2 Simultaneously depress the clip and withdraw the blade pin from the pivot block.

CAUTION: If the wiper blade refit is not to take place immediately protect the windscreen glass as follows: Bind the arm end with suitable tape. Isolate the battery to ensure that the wiper motor is not energised.

Refitting

3 Reverse 1 to 2.

A86 014

WINDSCREEN WIPER ARM
Driver's — remove and refit 84.15.02
Removing

1 Position a screwdriver as shown and impart a twisting action to lift the clip from the spindle groove.

2 The arm may now be removed from the spindle by hand.

3 Remove the spindle nut.

4 Remove the distance piece.

5 Remove the wiper arm pivot plate.

Refitting

6 Position the wiper arm pivot plate.

7 Position the distance piece with the tongue correctly located through the pivot plate, rubber gasket and body slot.

8 Fit the spindle nut.

9 Ensure that the spindle is in the 'park' position.

10 Locate the splines for a suitable 'park' position. Push on to engage the clip to the spindle groove.

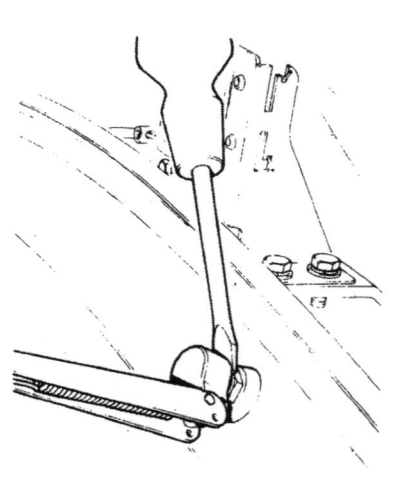

WINDSCREEN WIPER BLADE
Passenger's—remove and refit 84.15.07
Removing

1 Lift the wiper arm and blade from the screen so that it falls into its service position.

2 Simultaneously lift the clip and withdraw the blade pin from the arm.

Refitting

3 Reverse 1 to 2.

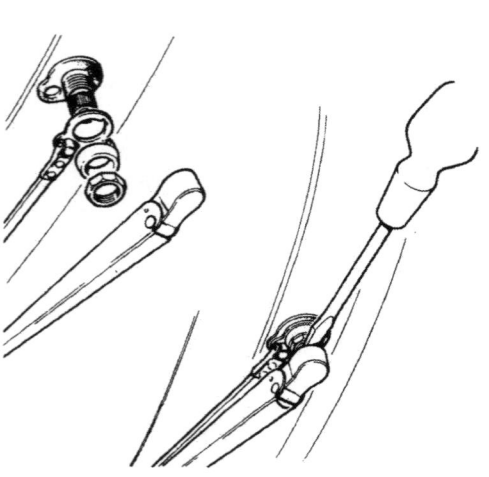

A86 015

WINDSCREEN WIPER ARM
Passenger's — remove and refit 84.15.03
Removing

1 Lift the wiper arm and blade from the screen so that it falls into its service position.

2 Position a screwdriver as shown and impart a twisting action to lift the clip from the spindle groove.

3 The assembly may now be removed by hand.

Refitting

4 Ensure that the spindles are in the 'park' position.

5 Hinge the wiper arm against the spring to adopt its service position.

6 Locate the splines for a suitable 'park' position. Push on to engage the clip to the spindle groove.

7 Lower the wiper arm to the screen.

WINDSCREEN WIPER SYSTEM

**Motor and drive assembly —
remove and refit**   **84.15.10**

Removing

1   Remove the passenger's wiper arm, see 84.15.03.
2   Remove the driver's wiper arm from the wheelbox spindle, see 84.15.02 operations 1 to 2.
3   Remove the fresh air duct, see 80.15.31.
4   Disconnect two 35 amp Lucar connectors from the battery lead connector.
5   Remove the windscreen washer reservoir tank.
6   Remove the battery, see 86.15.01.
7   Disconnect the harness plug.
8   Remove single screw. Disengage the clamp strap from the vehicle body slot.
9   Remove two Pozidriv screws and washers. Withdraw the plate adjacent to the brake master cylinder servo.
10 At the driver's wiper arm remove the spindle nut, distance piece, pivot plate and rubber gasket.
11 At the passenger's wiper arm remove the spindle nut, distance piece and rubber gasket.
12 Manoeuvre the motor and drive assembly from the vehicle.

Refitting

13 Position the motor and drive assembly to the vehicle.
14 At the passenger's wiper arm fit the rubber gasket, distance piece and spindle nut.
15 At the driver's wiper arm fit the rubber gasket, pivot plate, distance piece and spindle nut.
16 Insert the plate adjacent to the brake master cylinder servo. Secure with two Pozidriv screws and washers.
17 Slacken the olive nut.
18 Ensure that the rubber pad is correctly positioned.
19 Position the motor and tubes for the best alignment.
20 Engage the clamp strap to the vehicle body slot. Secure with single screw.
21 Tighten the olive nut.
22 Connect the harness plug.
23 Fit the battery, see 86.15.01.
24 Fit the windscreen washer reservoir tank.
25 Connect two 35 amp Lucar connectors to the battery lead connector.
26 Fit the fresh air duct, see 80.15.31.
27 Run the motor and 'switch off' using the windscreen wiper switch so that the wheelbox spindles assume the park position.
28 Fit the driver's wiper arm to the wheelbox spindle, see 84.15.02 operations 9 to 10.
29 Fit the passenger's wiper arm, see 84.15.03.

WINDSCREEN WIPER SYSTEM

Motor — remove and refit   **84.15.12**

Removing

1 Remove the motor and drive assembly, see 84.15.10.
2 Remove five screws. Lift off the gearbox cover.
3 Remove the crankpin spring clip by withdrawing sideways. Remove the washer.
4 Carefully withdraw the connecting rod. Remove the washer.
5 Lift out the cross-head, rack and tube assembly.

Refitting

6 Lubricate all moving parts of the motor during assembly as instructed on the illustration.
7 Position the slider block with the direction of cam slope as shown.
8 Position the cross-head, rack and tube assembly locating the projection in the slider block slot.
9 Fit the washer. Carefully insert the connecting rod.
10 Fit the washer. Fit the crankpin spring clip by inserting sideways.
11 Position the gearbox cover. Secure with five screws.
12 Fit the motor and drive assembly, see 84.15.10.

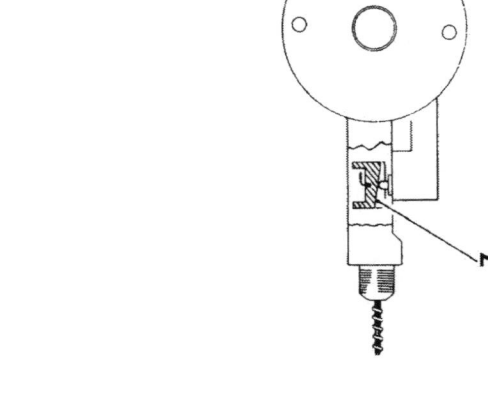

A84 009A

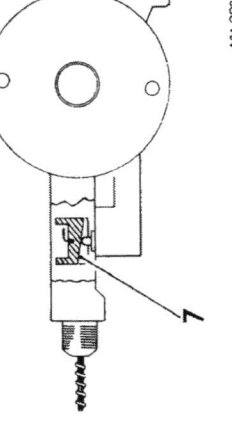

A84 008A

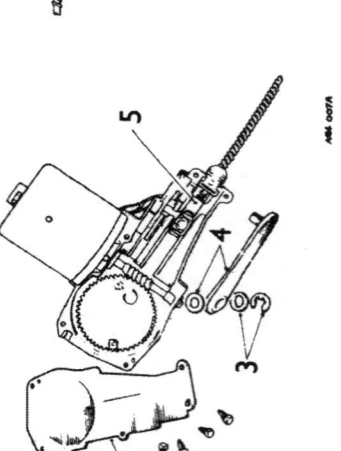

RLG Ragosine Listate grease
ST410 Shell turbo 41 oil

A84 003

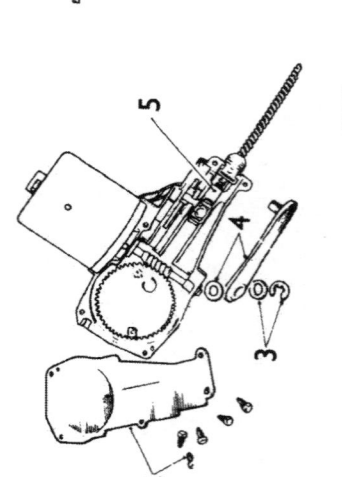

A84 007A

WINDSCREEN WIPER MOTOR

Overhaul   84.15.18

Dismantling

1 Remove five screws. Lift off the gearbox cover.
2 Lift out the slider block.
3 Remove the crankpin spring clip by withdrawing sideways. Remove the washer.
4 Carefully withdraw the connecting rod. Remove the washer.
5 Remove the final gear shaft spring clip by withdrawing sideways. Remove the washer.
6 Ensure that the shaft is burr-free and withdraw it. Remove the dished washer.
7 Remove the thrust screw and locknut.
8 Remove the through bolts.

9 Carefully withdraw the cover and armature about 0.2 in (5 mm). Continue withdrawal allowing the brushes to drop clear of the commutator. Ensure that the three bushes are not contaminated with grease.
10 Pull the armature from the cover against the action of the permanent magnet.
11 Scribe a line round the limit switch to note its position on the gearbox.
12 Remove three screws to release the brush assembly.
13 Remove two screws and washers to release the limit switch.
14 Remove both units joined together by the wires.
15 Remove the plate.

Reassembling

16 Lubricate all moving parts of the motor during assembly as instructed in the text and on the illustration.
17 Position the plate so that the round hole will accommodate the limit switch plunger.
18 Position the limit switch to the scribe lines made at operation 11 above. Secure with two screws and washers.
19 Secure the brush assembly with three screws.
20 Lubricate the cover bearing and saturate the cover bearing felt washer with Shell Turbo 41 oil.
21 Position the armature to the cover against the action of the permanent magnet.
22 Lubricate the self-aligning bearing with Shell Turbo 41 oil.
23 Ensure that the three brush springs and brushes are correctly positioned. Retain in position using slave clips locally made from paper clips or similar wire as shown.
24 Carefully insert the armature shaft through the bearing. Ensure that the brushes are not contaminated with lubricant. Ensure that the commutator clears the brushes.
25 With the brushes over the commutator remove the slave clips.

continued

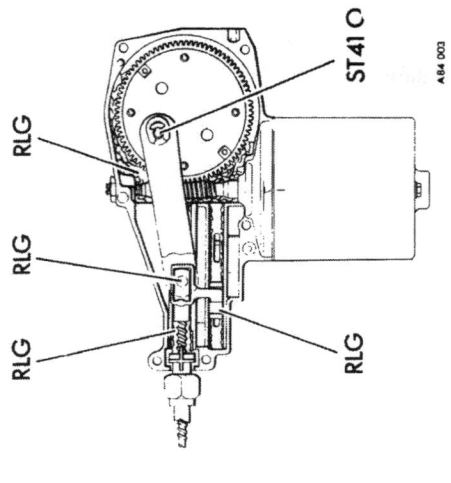

RLG   RLG

RLG   RLG

RLG

RLG

ST41 O

A84 003

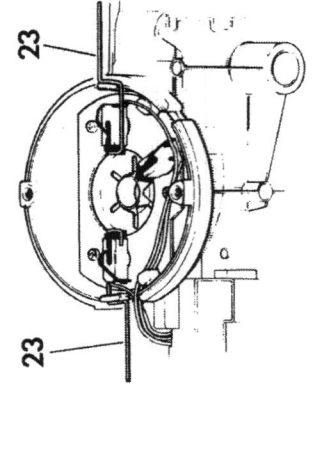

RLG Ragosine Listate grease
ST410 Shell turbo 41 oil

A84 002

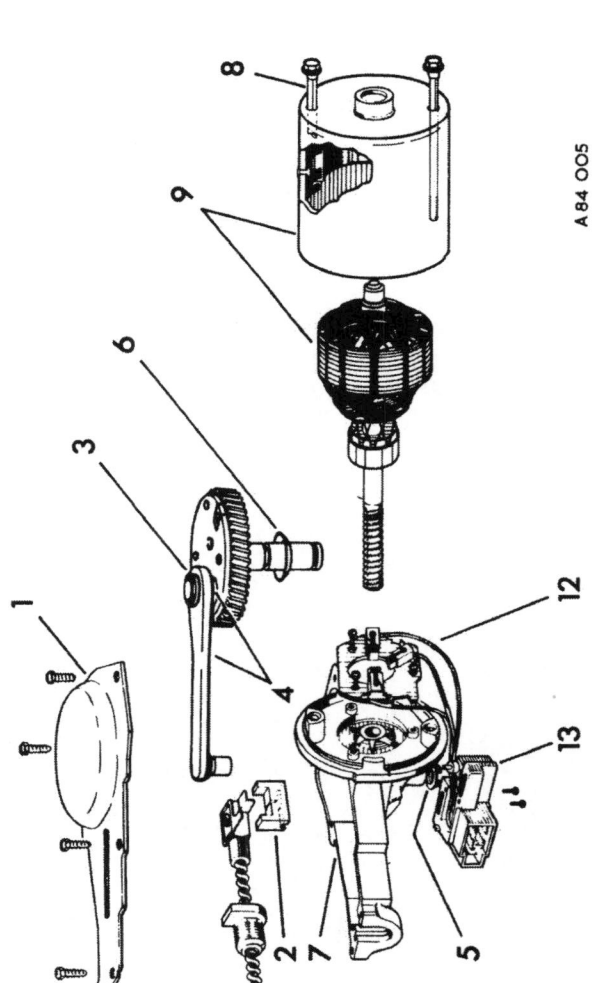

A84 005

WINDSCREEN WIPER SYSTEM

Rack — remove and refit   84.15.24

Removing

1   Remove the motor and drive assembly, see 84.15.10.
2   Remove the motor, see 84.15.12.
3   Withdraw the rack from the tube assembly.
4   Remove the ferrule.

Refitting

5   Fit the ferrule.
6   Lubricate the rack with Ragosine Listate grease.
7   Insert the rack into the tube assembly. If necessary slightly rotate the wheelbox spindles by hand to facilitate rack engagement.
8   Fit the motor, see 84.15.12.
9   Fit the motor and drive assembly, see 84.15.10.

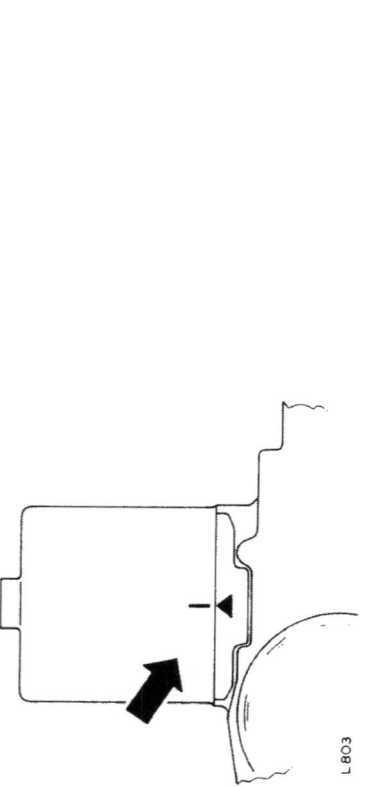

L803

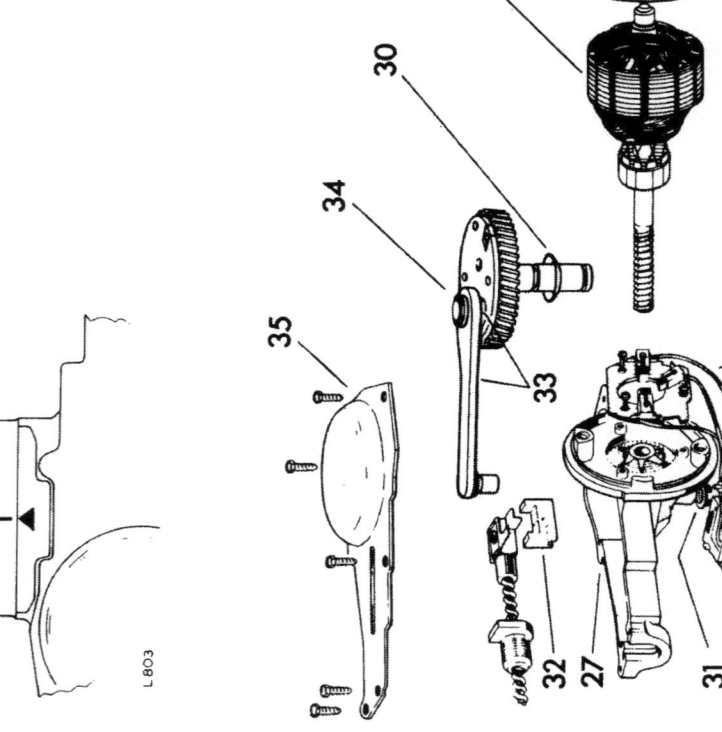

A84 006

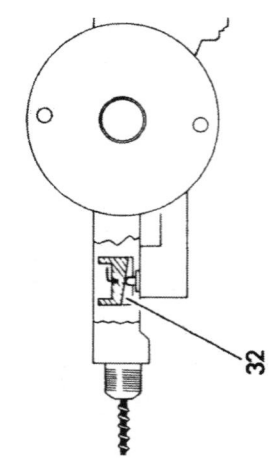

A84 010

26   Seat the cover against the gearbox. Turn the cover to align the marks shown. Fit the through bolts.
27   Fit the thrust screw and locknut.
28   Adjust the armature end-float as follows:
     Slacken the locknut. Screw the thrust screw in until resistance is felt. Screw the thrust screw out a quarter of a turn — maintain in this position and tighten the locknut.
29   Lubricate the final gear bushes with Shell Turbo 41 oil.
30   Fit the dished washer with its concave surface facing the final gear. Insert the shaft.
31   Fit the washer. Fit the spring clip by inserting sideways.
     NOTE: If the motor is to be immediately fitted to the motor and drive assembly, ignore operations 32 to 35. Refit the motor, see 84.15.12. If the motor is to be stored perform the remaining operations.
32   Position the slider block with the direction of cam slope as shown.
33   Fit the washer. Carefully insert the connecting rod.
34   Fit the washer. Fit the crankpin spring clip by inserting sideways.
35   Position the gearbox cover. Secure with five screws.

Wheelbox — driver's — remove and refit 84.15.28

Earlier models

Removing

1 Remove the motor and rack assembly complete, see 84.15.10.
2 Remove two Pozidriv screws and washers. Withdraw the plate adjacent to the brake master cylinder servo.
3 Disengage the tube from the passenger's wheelbox.
4 Remove the spindle nut.
5 Remove the distance piece.
6 Remove the wiper arm pivot plate.
7 Remove the rubber gasket.
8 Withdraw the wheelbox spindle from the vehicle body aperture.
9 Remove the driver's wheelbox and two tubes as an assembly from the vehicle.
10 Note the position of the long tube and the short tube.
11 Scribe a line to note the radial position of the long tube.
12 Remove two nuts and remove the wheelbox plate.
13 Disengage two tubes from the wheelbox.

Refitting

14 Reverse 3 to 13.
15 Ensure that the position of the tube and wheelbox achieves the best alignment.
16 Insert the plate adjacent to the brake master cylinder servo. Secure with two Pozidriv screws and washers.
17 Fit the motor and rack assembly complete, see 84.15.10.

Wheelbox — driver's — remove and refit 84.15.28

Later models

Removing

1 Remove the motor and drive assembly, see 84.15.10.
2 Scribe a line to note the radial position of the tube.
3 Remove the two nuts. Remove the wheelbox plate.
4 Disengage and remove the short straight tube.
5 Disengage and remove the wheelbox.

Refitting

6 If a new wheelbox is to be fitted reproduce the scribe line on the new unit.
7 Fit the wheelbox the correct way round.
8 Lubricate the wheelbox and exposed section of the rack with Ragosine Listate grease.
9 Reverse 1 to 4.

Wheelbox — passenger's — remove and refit 84.15.29

Earlier models

Removing

1 Remove the motor rack assembly complete, see 84.15.10.
2 Disengage the tube from the wheelbox.
3 Remove the spindle nut.
4 Remove the distance piece.
5 Remove the rubber washer.
6 Withdraw the wheelbox spindle from the vehicle body aperture.

Refitting

7 Reverse 1 to 6.

Wheelbox — passenger's — remove and refit 84.15.29

Later models

Removing

1 Remove the motor and drive assembly, see 84.15.10.
2 Scribe two lines to note the radial position of the tube.
3 Remove two nuts. Remove the wheelbox plate.
4 Disengage and remove the tube and far wheelbox assembly.
5 Disengage and remove the wheelbox.

Refitting

6 If a new wheelbox is to be fitted reproduce the scribe lines on the new unit.
7 Fit the wheelbox the correct way round.
8 Lubricate the wheelbox and exposed section of the track with Ragosine Listate grease.
9 Reverse 1 to 4.

AHT 232

1 Alternator
2 Battery
3 Ignition/starter switch
4 Starter inhibitor switch (automatic transmission only)
5 Starter motor relay
6 Starter motor
7 Radio
8 Speaker
9 Headlamp – circuit breaker
10 Master light switch
11a Headlamp – flash relay
11b Headlamp – flash control unit
12 Headlamp – actuator passenger's side
13 Headlamp – actuator driver's side
14 Headlamp – run/stop relay passenger's side
15 Headlamp – run/stop relay driver's side
16 Main/dip/flash switch
17 Dip beam
18 Main beam
19 Main-beam warning light
20 Clock
21 Horn-push
22 Horn relay
23 Horn
24 Fog lamp switch
25 Fog lamp
26 Ballast resistor wire
27 Ignition cowl
28 Ignition distributor
29 Fasten belts warning light
30 Passenger's seat switch
31 Passenger's belt switch
32 Driver's belt switch
33 Fuel indicator
34 Fuel tank unit
35 Fuel warning light delay unit
36 Fuel warning light
37 Ignition warning light
38 Tachometer
39 Battery condition indicator
40 Temperature indicator
41 Temperature transmitter
42 Oil pressure warning light
43 Oil pressure switch

44 Brake warning light
45 Brake line failure switch
46 Handbrake switch
47 Choke warning light
48 Choke switch
49 Cigarette lighter
50 Plate illumination lamp
51 Tail lamp
52 Rear fog lamp switch
53 Rear fog lamp warning light
54 Rear fog lamp
55 In-line fuse
56 Panel rheostat
57 Heater control illumination
58 Instrument illumination
59 Fascia switch panel illumination
60 Cigarette lighter illumination
61 Selector panel illumination (automatic transmission only)
62 Front parking lamp
63 In-line fuse
64 Heated backlight switch
65 Heated backlight warning light
66 Heated backlight

67 Reverse lamp switch
68 Reverse lamp
69 Heater motor
70 Heater resistor
71 Heater switch
72 Washer/wiper switch
73 Wiper motor
74 Washer pump
75 Stop lamp switch
76 Stop lamp
77 Hazard flasher unit
78 Hazard switch
79 L.H. front flasher lamp
80 L.H. rear flasher lamp
81 R.H. front flasher lamp
82 R.H. rear flasher lamp
83 Hazard warning light
84 Turn signal flasher unit
85 Turn signal switch
86 L.H. flasher warning light
87 R.H. flasher warning light
88 Roof lamp
89 Door switch
90 Fuse

COLOUR CODE

B	Black	N	Brown	S	Slate
G	Green	O	Orange	U	Blue
K	Pink	P	Purple	W	White
LG	Light green	R	Red	Y	Yellow

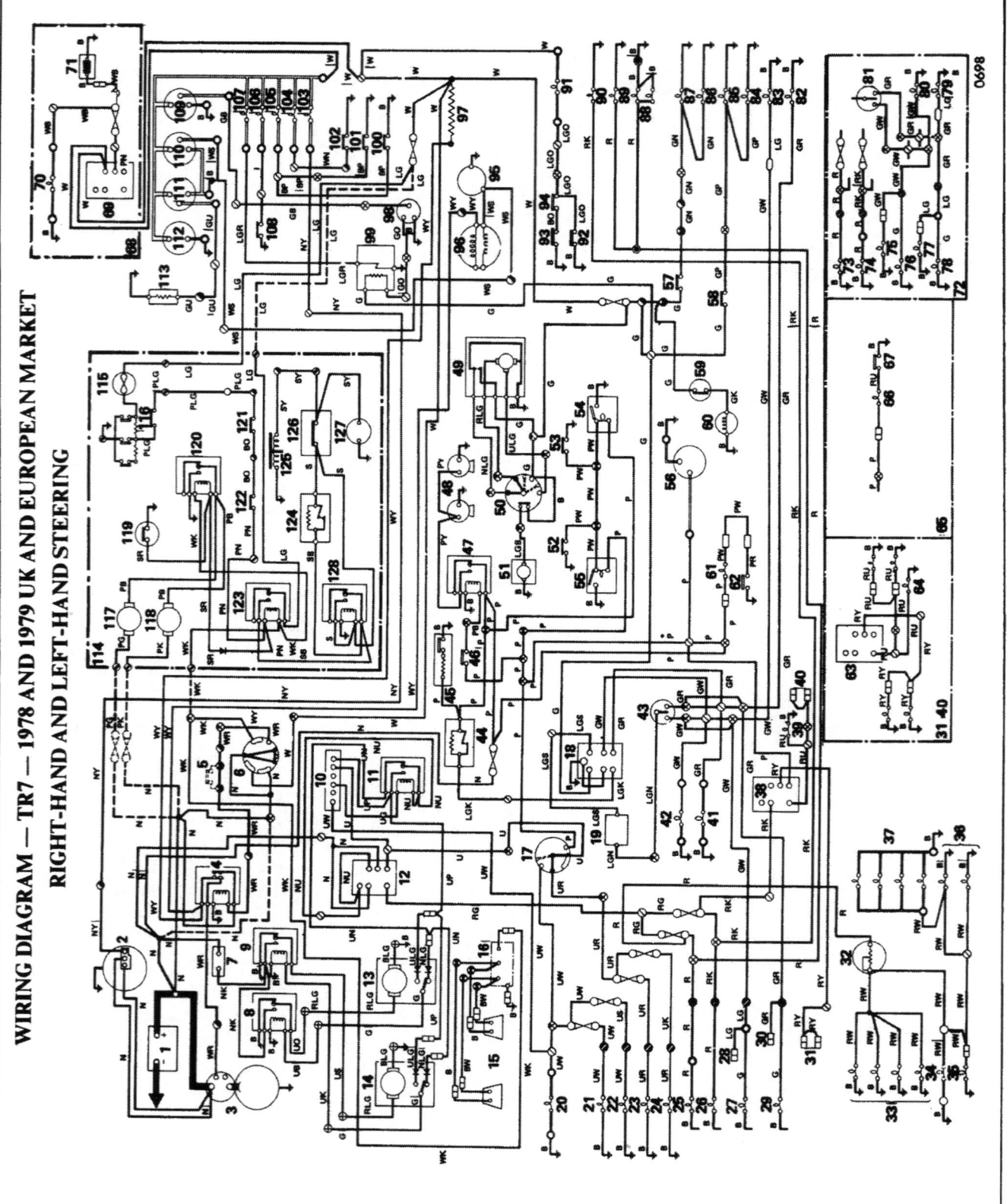

WIRING DIAGRAM — TR7 — 1978 AND 1979 UK AND EUROPEAN MARKET

RIGHT-HAND AND LEFT-HAND STEERING

1 Battery
2 Alternator
3 Starter motor
4 Starter motor relay
5 Start inhibit switch (Automatic)
6 Ignition switch
7 Headlamp motor circuit breaker
8 Headlamp relay
9 Headlamp relay
10 Headlamp flash control
11 Headlamp flash relay
12 Master light switch
13 Headlamp motor
14 Headlamp motor
15 Loudspeakers
16 Radio
17 Main dip flash switch
18 Hazard switch
19 Flasher unit
20 Main beam warning light
21 Main beam
22 Main beam
23 Dip beam
24 Dip beam
25 Sidelight
26 Sidelight
27 Side indicator connection
28 Side repeater connection
29 Side indicator
30 Side repeater connection
31 Front fog lamps junction
32 Panel rheostat
33 Heater control illumination

34 Borg-Warner illumination
35 Cigar lighter illumination
36 Switch panel illumination
37 Panel illumination
38 Fog lamps switch
39 Rear fog lamps warning light
40 Rear fog lamps junction
41 L.H. indicator warning light
42 R.H. indicator warning light
43 Direction indicator switch
44 Hazard unit
45 Cigar lighter
46 Horn-push
47 Horn relay
48 Horns
49 Windscreen wiper motor
50 Windscreen wipe/wash switch
51 Windscreen washer motor
52 Door switch
53 Door switch
54 Courtesy light
55 Courtesy light
56 Clock
57 Reverse light switch
58 Stop light switch
59 Engine thermostat
60 F.A.S.D.
61 Boot lamp
62 Boot lamp switch
63 Fog switch
64 Rear fog lamp warning light
65 Boot lamp and switch wiring assembly — L.H. steering

66 Boot lamp
67 Boot lamp switch
68 Heated rear screen assembly — TR7 coupé
69 Heated rear screen switch
70 Heated rear screen warning light
71 Heated rear screen
72 Wiring condition for front, side and front and rear indicator lights — L.H. steering
73 Sidelight
74 Sidelight
75 Side repeater
76 Side indicator
77 Side repeater
78 Side indicator
79 Rear side indicator
80 Rear side indicator
81 Direction indicator switch
82 Side indicator
83 Side indicator
84 Stop light
85 Stop light
86 Reverse light
87 Reverse light
88 Number-plate lights
89 Tail light
90 Tail light
91 Seat belt warning light
92 Driver's buckle switch
93 Passenger belt switch
93 Passenger seat switch
94 Passenger seat switch
95 Distributor

96 6 volt coil
97 Eureka wire
98 Tank unit
99 Low fuel delay unit
100 Brake pressure differential switch
101 Hand brake switch
102 Oil pressure switch
103 Ignition warning light
104 Oil warning light
105 Brake warning light
106 Choke warning light
107 Low.fuel warning light
108 Choke warning light switch
109 Fuel gauge
110 Tachometer
111 Temperature gauge
112 Battery condition indicator
113 Temperature transmitter
114 Air conditioning blower unit
115 Heater/air conditioning blower unit
116 Thermostat
117 R.H. condenser fan
118 L.H. condenser fan
119 Radiator thermostat
120 Fan relay
121 Full throttle cut-off switch
122 Air conditioning cut-out switch
123 Air conditioning relay
124 Delay unit
125 Throttle jack
126 Ranco valve high pressure cut-out
127 Clutch
128 Delay circuit relay

COLOUR CODE

B	Black	N	Brown	S	Slate
G	Green	O	Orange	U	Blue
K	Pink	P	Purple	W	White
LG	Light green	R	Red	Y	Yellow

WIRING DIAGRAM — TR7 — 1980 UK AND EUROPEAN MARKET
RIGHT-HAND AND LEFT-HAND STEERING

1 Battery
2 Alternator
3 Ignition/starter switch
4 Start inhibit switch (automatic transmission only)
5 Starter relay
6 Starter motor
7 Headlamp motor circuit breaker
8 Headlamp run/stop relay — L.H.
9 Headlamp run/stop relay — R.H.
10 Headlamp actuator — L.H.
11 Headlamp actuator — R.H.
12 Radio
13 Speaker
14 Master light switch
15 Main/dip/flash switch
16 Main beam warning light
17 Main beam
18 Dip beam
19 Headlamp delay unit
20 Headlamp flash relay
21 Front parking lamp
22 Front fog lamp
23 Rear guard lamp
24 Tail lamp
25 Plate illumination lamp
26 Fog switch
27 Rear guard lamp warning light
28 Panel rheostat
29 Heater control illumination

30 Selector panel illumination (automatic transmission only)
31 Cigarette lighter illumination
32 Instrument illumination
33 Switch panel illumination

Air conditioning:
34 Master relay
35 Manual cut-out swich
36 Full throttle cut-out switch
37 Cold thermostat
38 Blower motor switch
39 Blower motor
40 Delay unit
41 Clutch delay relay
42 Ranco valve high pressure cut-out
43 Clutch
44 Throttle jack
45 Condenser fan relay
46 Condenser fan L.H.
47 Condenser fan R.H.
48 Radiator thermostat
49 Diode
50 Diode
51 Hazard flasher unit
52 Hazard switch
53 Hazard warning light
54 Cigarette lighter
55 Horn-push
56 Horn relay

57 Horn
58 Windscreen wash/wipe switch
59 Windscreen wiper motor
60 Windscreen washer pump
61 Map/courtesy lamp
62 Door switch
63 Clock

R.H. steering only:
64 Luggage boot lamp
65 Luggage boot lamp switch

L.H. steering only:
66 Luggage boot lamp
67 Luggage boot lamp switch
68 Coolant low indicator unit
69 Coolant low sensor
70 Coolant low warning light
71 Choke switch
72 Choke warning light
73 Battery condition indicator
74 Temperature indicator
75 Temperature transmitter
76 Tachometer
77 Fuel indicator
78 Tank unit
79 Low fuel delay unit
80 Low fuel warning light
81 Brake warning light
82 Brake pressure differential switch

83 Handbrake warning light
84 Handbrake switch
85 Oil pressure warning light
86 Oil pressure switch
87 Ignition warning light
88 Ballast resistor wire
89 Ignition coil — 6 volt
90 Ignition distributor
91 Heated back-light switch
92 Heated back-light
93 Heated back-light warning light
94 Seat belt warning light
95 Passenger seat switch
96 Passenger belt switch
97 Driver belt switch
98 Reverse lamp switch
99 Reverse lamp
100 Stop lamp switch
101 Stop lamp
101 Stop lamp
102 Turn signal flasher unit
103 Turn signal switch
104 L.H. turn signal warning light
105 R.H. turn signal warning light
106 L.H. front flasher lamp
107 L.H. front flasher repeater lamp
108 L.H. rear flasher lamp
109 R.H. front flasher lamp
110 R.H. front flasher repeater lamp
111 R.H. rear flasher lamp

COLOUR CODE

B	Black	N	Brown	S	Slate
G	Green	O	Orange	U	Blue
K	Pink	P	Purple	W	White
LG	Light green	R	Red	Y	Yellow

WIRE COLOUR CODES OF FLASHER LAMP CIRCUIT

Wire identity	Item	Right-hand steering		Left-hand steering	
		Heater vehicles	Air conditioning vehicles	Heater vehicles	Air conditioning vehicles
*1	L.H. supply	G/LG	GR	LG/G	GR
*2	L.H. front lamp	G/LG	GR	LG/G	GR
*3	L.H. rear lamp	GR		GR and LG	GR and LG
*4	R.H. supply	LG/G	GW	G/LG	GW
*5	R.H. front lamp	LG/G	GW	G/LG	GW
*6	R.H. rear lamp	GW and LG		GW	GW

WIRING DIAGRAM – TR7 – 1975 U.S.A. MARKET

1 Alternator
2 Ignition warning light
3 Battery
4 Battery condition indicator
5 Ignition/starter switch
6 Radio supply
7 Interlock module
8 Interlock starter motor relay
9 Starter motor
10 Ballast resister wire
11 Ignition coil
12 Ignition distributor
13 Drive resistor
14 Battery lead connector
15 Master light switch
16 Actuator – limit switch
17 Circuit breaker
18 Headlamp – run/stop relay
19 Actuator – motor
20 Main dip/flash switch
21 Main beam
22 Main beam warning light
23 Dip beam
24 L.H. door switch
25 Key switch
26 Fasten belts warning light
27 Interlock – gearbox switch
28 Driver's belt switch
29 Driver's seat switch
30 Passenger's belt switch
31 Passenger's seat switch
32 Tachometer
33 Temperature indicator
34 Temperature transmitter
35 Fuel indicator
36 Fuel warning light
37 Fuel tank unit

U.S.A. Federal market vehicles only
38 Choke warning light
39 Choke switch

U.S.A. Calafornia market vehicles only
38 Catalyst service warning light
39 Catalyst service interval indicator

40 Brake warning light
41 Brake line failure switch
42 Handbrake switch
43 Oil pressure warning light
44 Oil pressure switch
45 Anti-run on valve

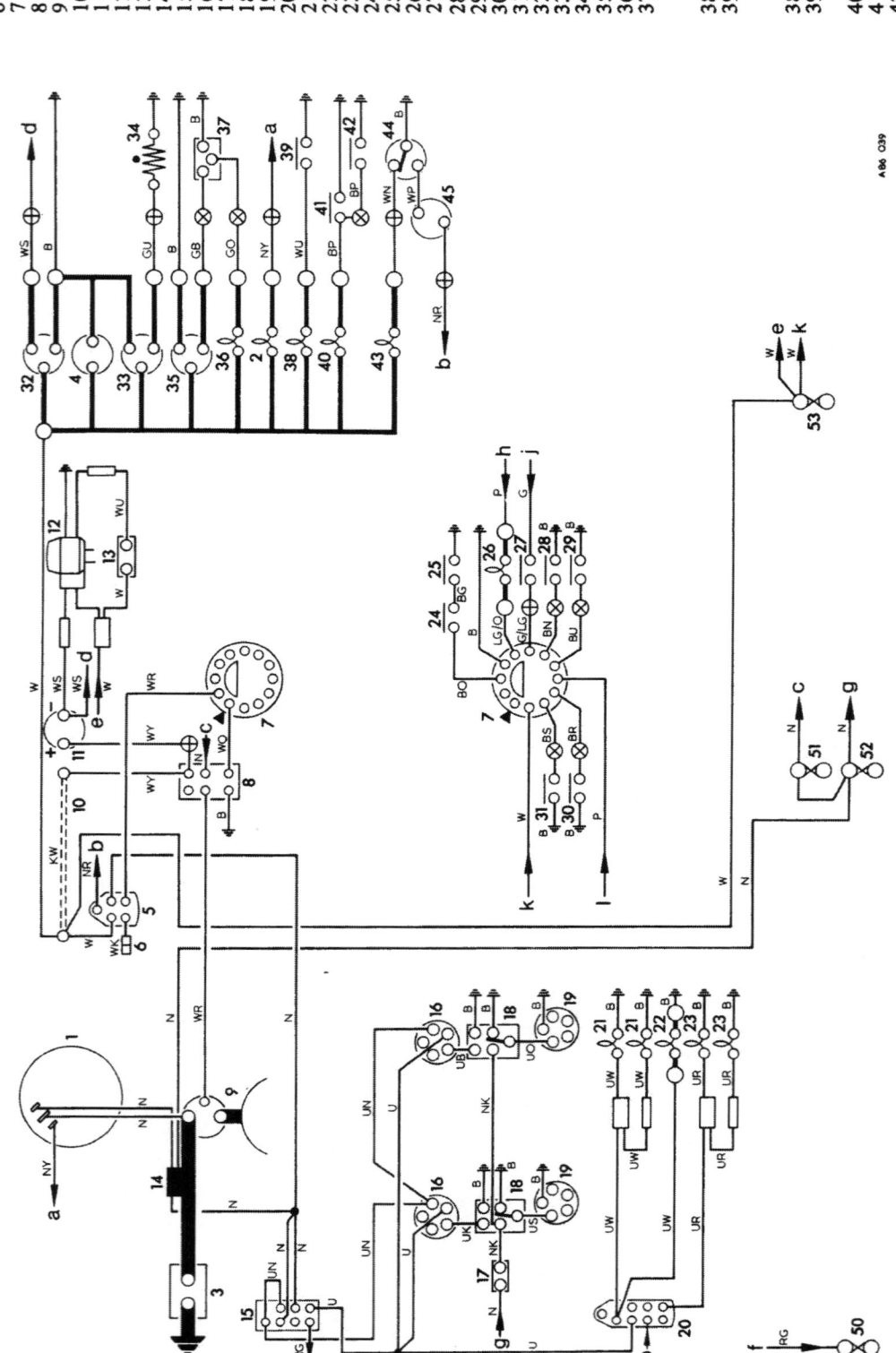

A86 O39

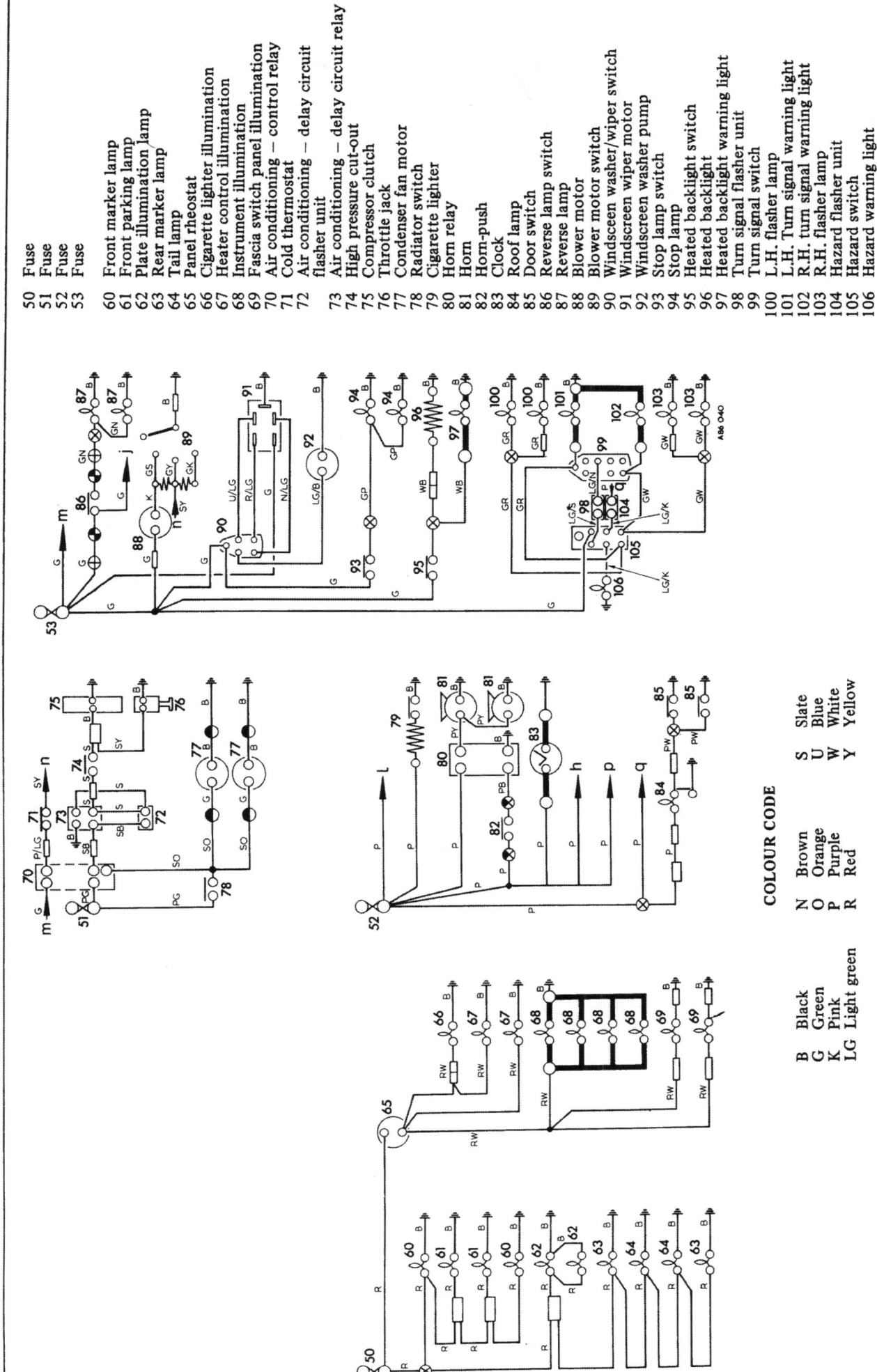

50	Fuse
51	Fuse
52	Fuse
53	Fuse
60	Front marker lamp
61	Front parking lamp
62	Plate illumination lamp
63	Rear marker lamp
64	Tail lamp
65	Panel rheostat
66	Cigarette lighter illumination
67	Heater control illumination
68	Instrument illumination
69	Fascia switch panel illumination
70	Air conditioning — control relay
71	Cold thermostat
72	Air conditioning — delay circuit
	flasher unit
73	Air conditioning — delay circuit relay
74	High pressure cut-out
75	Compressor clutch
76	Throttle jack
77	Condenser fan motor
78	Radiator switch
79	Cigarette lighter
80	Horn relay
81	Horn
82	Horn-push
83	Clock
84	Roof lamp
85	Door switch
86	Reverse lamp switch
87	Reverse lamp
88	Blower motor
89	Blower motor switch
90	Windscreen washer/wiper switch
91	Windscreen wiper motor
92	Windscreen washer pump
93	Stop lamp switch
94	Stop lamp
95	Heated backlight switch
96	Heated backlight
97	Heated backlight warning light
98	Turn signal flasher unit
99	Turn signal switch
100	L.H. flasher lamp
101	L.H. Turn signal warning light
102	R.H. turn signal warning light
103	R.H. flasher lamp
104	Hazard flasher unit
105	Hazard switch
106	Hazard warning light

COLOUR CODE

B	Black	S	Slate
G	Green	U	Blue
K	Pink	W	White
LG	Light green	Y	Yellow
N	Brown		
O	Orange		
P	Purple		
R	Red		

WIRING DIAGRAM – TR7 – 1976 U.S.A. MARKET – AIR CONDITIONING

1 Alternator
2 Ignition warning light
3 Battery
4 Battery condition indicator
5 Ignition/starter switch
6 Radio supply
7 Radio
8 Speaker
9 Starter motor relay
10 Starter motor
11 Ballast resistor wire
12 Ignition coil
13 Ignition distributor
14 Drive resistor
15 Battery lead connector
16 Master light switch
17 Actuator – limit switch
18 Circuit breaker
19 Headlamp – run/stop relay
20 Actuator motor
21 Main/dip/flash switch
22 Dip beam
23 Main beam
24 Main beam warning light
25 Fuse – 35 amp
26 Rear fog lamp switch
27 Rear fog lamp warning light
28 Rear fog lamp
29 Front marker lamp

30 Front parking lamp
31 Plate illumination lamp
32 Rear marker lamp
33 Tail lamp
34 Panel rheostat
35 Heater control illumination
36 Fascia panel switch illumination
37 Selector panel illumination
38 Cigarette lighter illumination
39 Instrument illumination
40 Fuse – 50 amp
41 Buzzer/timer module
42 Driver's belt switch
43 Fasten belt warning light
44 L.H. door switch
45 Key switch
46 Horn-push
47 Horn relay
48 Horn
49 Cigarette lighter
50 Clock
51 Front fog lamp switch
52 Front fog lamp
53 Roof lamp
54 R.H. door switch
55 Service indicator diodes – catalyst vehicles only
56 E.G.R. service indicator

57 E.G.R. service warning light
58 Catalyst service indicator
59 Catalyst warning light
60 Fuse – 50 amp
61 Radiator switch
62 Condenser fan motor
63 Air conditioning – control relay
64 Air conditioning – delay circuit flasher unit
65 Air conditioning – delay circuit relay
66 High pressure cut-out
67 Compressor clutch
68 Throttle jack
69 Air conditioning cut-out switch
70 Cold thermostat
71 Blower motor
72 Blower motor switch
73 Fuse – 35 amp
74 Windscreen washer/wipe switch
75 Windscreen wiper motor
76 Windscreen washer pump
77 Fuse – 50 amp
78 Reverse lamp switch
79 Reverse lamp
80 Stop lamp switch
81 Stop lamp
82 Turn signal flasher unit

83 Turn signal switch
84 L.H. flasher lamp
85 L.H. turn signal warning light
86 R.H. flasher lamp
87 R.H. turn signal warning light
88 Hazard flasher unit
89 Hazard switch
90 Hazard warning light
91 Fuel indicator
92 Fuel tank unit
93 Fuel warning light
94 Fuel delay unit
95 Tachometer
96 Temperature indicator
97 Temperature transmitter
98 Oil pressure warning light
99 Oil pressure switch
100 Anti-run-on valve
101 Brake warning light
102 Brake line failure switch
103 Handbrake switch
104 Choke warning light – non-catalyst vehicles only
105 Choke switch
106 Heated backlight switch
107 Fuse – 15 amp
108 Heated backlight
109 Heated backlight warning light

COLOUR CODE

B	Black	N	Brown	S	Slate
G	Green	O	Orange	U	Blue
K	Pink	P	Purple	W	White
LG	Light green	R	Red	Y	Yellow

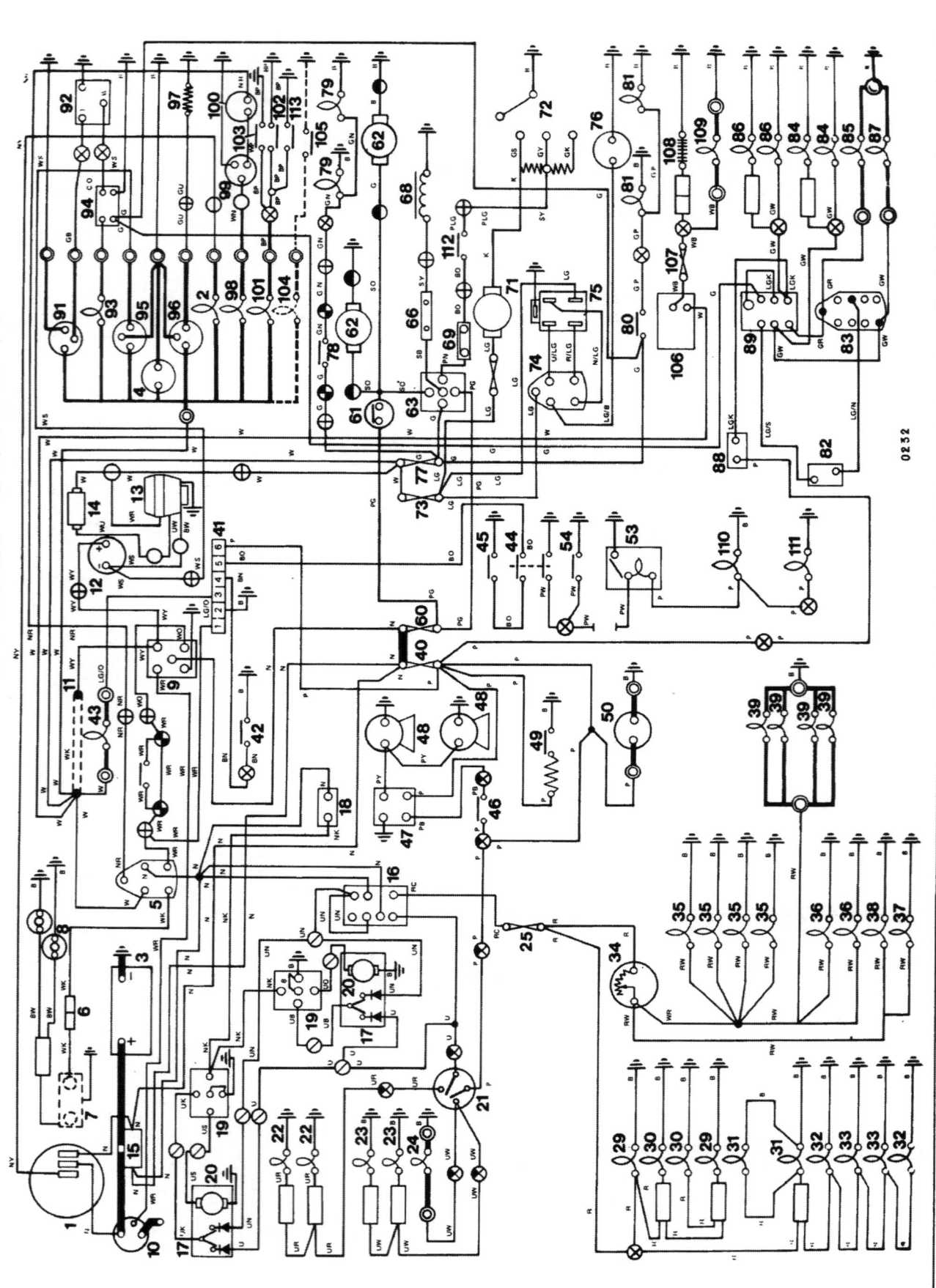

WIRING DIAGRAM — TR7 — 1977 U.S.A. MARKET — AIR CONDITIONING

1 Alternator
2 Ignition warning light
3 Battery
4 Battery condition indicator
5 Ignition starter switch
6 Radio supply
7 Radio
8 Speaker
9 Starter motor relay
10 Starter motor
11 Ballast resistor wire
12 Ignition coil
13 Ignition distributor
14 Drive resistor
15 Battery lead connector
16 Master light switch
17 Actuator – limit switch
18 Circuit breaker
19 Headlamp – run/stop relay
20 Actuator motor
21 Main/dip/flash switch
22 Dip beam
23 Main beam
24 Main beam warning light
25 Fuse – 35 amp
29 Front marker lamp

30 Front parking lamp
31 Plate illumination lamp
32 Rear marker lamp
33 Tail lamp
34 Panel rheostat
35 Heater control illumination
36 Fascia switch panel illumination
37 Selector panel illumination
38 Cigarette lighter illumination
39 Instrument illumination
40 Fuse – 50 amp
41 Buzzer/timer module
42 Driver's belt switch
43 Fasten belt warning light
44 L.H. door switch
45 Key switch
46 Horn-push
47 Horn relay
48 Horn
49 Cigarette lighter
50 Clock
53 Roof lamp
54 R.H. door switch
60 Fuse – 50 amp
61 Radiator switch
62 Condenser fan motor

63 Air conditioning – control relay
66 High pressure cut-out
68 Throttle jack
69 Air conditioning cut-out switch
71 Blower motor
72 Blower motor switch
73 Fuse – 35 amp
74 Windscreen washer
75 Windscreen wiper motor
76 Windscreen washer pump
77 Fuse – 50 amp
78 Reverse lamp switch
79 Reverse lamp
80 Stop lamp switch
81 Stop lamp
82 Turn signal flasher unit
83 Turn signal switch
84 L.H. flasher lamp
85 L.H. turn signal warning light
86 R.H. flasher lamp
87 R.H. turn signal warning light
88 Hazzard flasher unit
89 Hazzard switch and warning light
91 Fuel indicator
92 Fuel tank unit
93 Fuel warning light

94 Fuel delay unit
95 Tachometer
96 Temperature indicator
97 Temperature transmitter
98 Oil pressure warning light
99 Oil pressure switch
100 Anti-run-on valve
101 Brake warning light
102 Brake line failure switch
103 Handbrake switch
104 Choke warning light – non-catalyst vehicles only
105 Choke switch
106 Heated backlight switch
107 Fuse – 15 amp
108 Heated backlight
109 Heated backlight warning light
110 Map light
111 Boot light
112 Full throttle cut-out switch
113 Ignition switch

COLOUR CODE

B   Black
G   Green
K   Pink
LG Light green

N   Brown
O   Orange
P   Purple
R   Red

S   Slate
U   Blue
W   White
Y   Yellow

WIRING DIAGRAM – TR7 – 1978 AND 1979 U.S.A. MARKET – AIR CONDITIONING

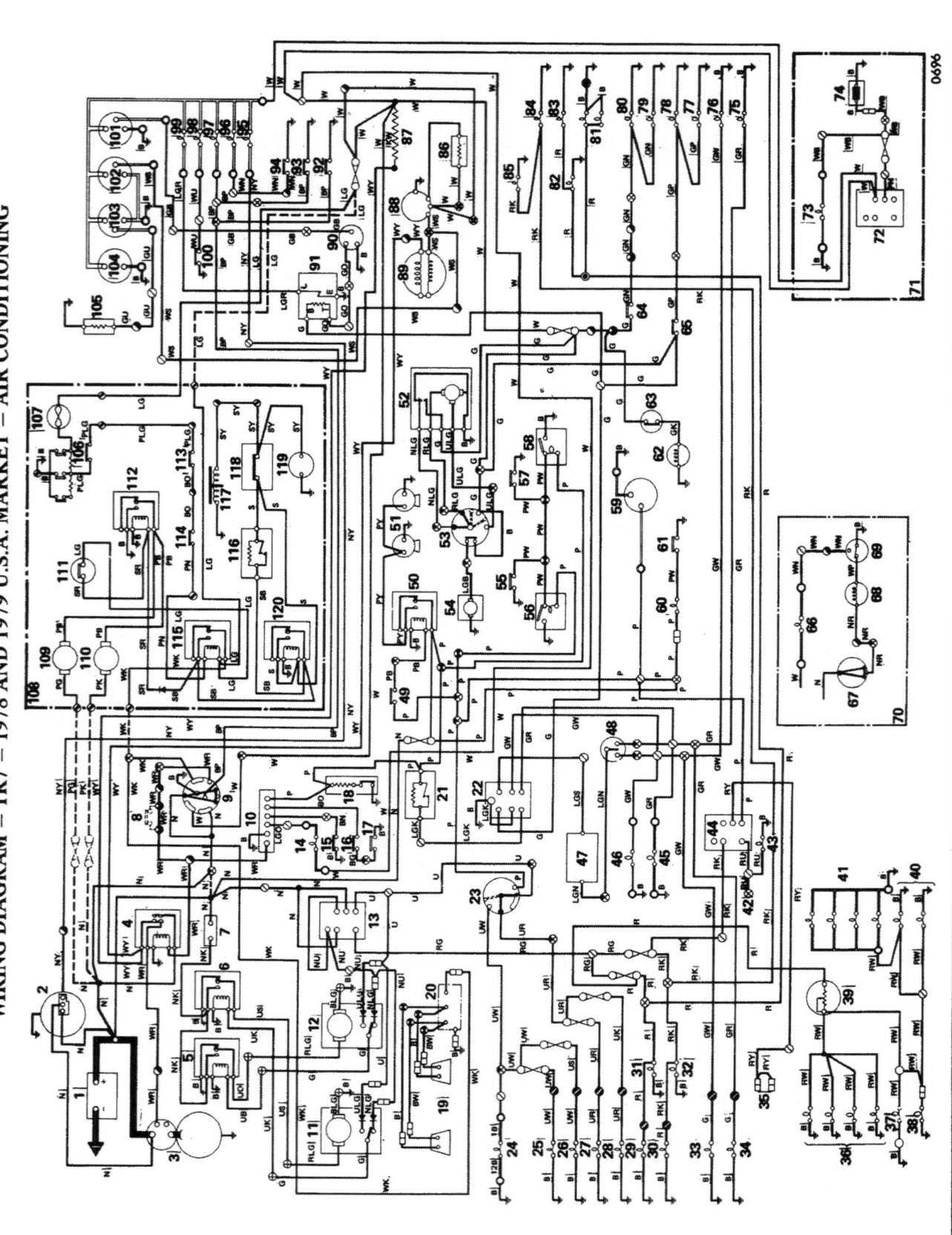

1 Battery
2 Alternator
3 Starter motor
4 Starter motor relay
5 R.H. headlamp relay
6 L.H. headlamp relay
7 Headlamp motor circuit breaker
8 Start inhibit switch (Automatic)
9 Ignition switch
10 Buzzer timer unit
11 L.H. headlamp motor
12 R.H. headlamp motor
13 Master light switch
14 Seat belt warning light
15 Buckle switch
16 Door switch
17 Audible warning
18 Cigar lighter
19 Loudspeakers
20 Radio
21 Hazard unit
22 Hazard switch
23 Main/dip/flash switch
24 Main beam warning light
25 R.H. main beam
26 L.H. main beam
27 R.H. dip beam
28 L.H. dip beam
29 R.H. sidelight
30 L.H. sidelight

31 R.H. side marker
32 L.H. side marker
33 R.H. side indicator
34 L.H. side indicator
35 Front fog lamps junction
36 Heater control illumination
37 Borg-Warner illumination
38 Cigar lighter illumination
39 Panel rheostats
40 Switch panel illumination
41 Panel illumination
42 Rear fog lamps illumination
43 Rear fog lamps warning light
44 Fog lamps switch
45 L.H. indicator warning light
46 R.H. indicator warning light
47 Flasher unit
48 Direction indicator switch
49 Horn-push
50 Horn relay
51 Horns
52 Windscreen wiper motor
53 Windscreen wipe/wash switch
54 Windscreen washer motor
55 Door switch
56 Courtesy light
57 Door switch
58 Courtesy light
59 Clock
60 Boot lamp

61 Boot lamp switch
62 F.A.S.D.
63 Engine thermostat
64 Reverse light switch
65 Stop light switch
66 Oil warning light
67 Ignition switch
68 Anti-run-on valve
69 Oil pressure switch
70 Anti-run-on valve – California market only
71 Heated rear screen – TR7 coupé
72 Heated rear screen switch
73 Heated rear screen warning light
74 Heated rear screen
75 L.H. side indicator
76 R.H. side indicator
77 L.H. stop light
78 R.H. stop light
79 L.H. reverse light
80 R.H. reverse light
81 Number-plate lights
82 R.H. side marker
83 R.H. tail lights
84 L.H. tail lights
85 L.H. side marker
86 Drive resistor
87 Eureka wire (1.3 to 1.5 ohms)
88 Distributor
89 Ignition coil
90 Tank unit

91 Low fuel relay unit
92 Brake pressure differential switch
93 Hand brake switch
94 Oil pressure switch
95 Ignition warning light
96 Oil warning light
97 Brake warning light
98 Choke warning light
99 Low fuel warning light
100 Choke warning light switch
101 Fuel gauge
102 Tachometer
103 Temperature gauge
104 Battery condition indicator
105 Temperature transmitter
106 Thermostat
107 Heater/air conditioning blower unit
108 Air conditioning circuit
109 R.H. condenser fan
110 L.H. condenser fan
111 Radiator thermostat
112 Fan relay
113 Full throttle cut-off switch
114 Air conditioning cut-out switch
115 Air conditioning relay
116 Delay unit
117 Throttle jack
118 Ranco valve high pressure cut-out
119 Clutch
120 Delay circuit relay

COLOUR CODE

B	Black	N	Brown	S	Slate
G	Green	O	Orange	U	Blue
K	Pink	P	Purple	W	White
LG	Light green	R	Red	Y	Yellow

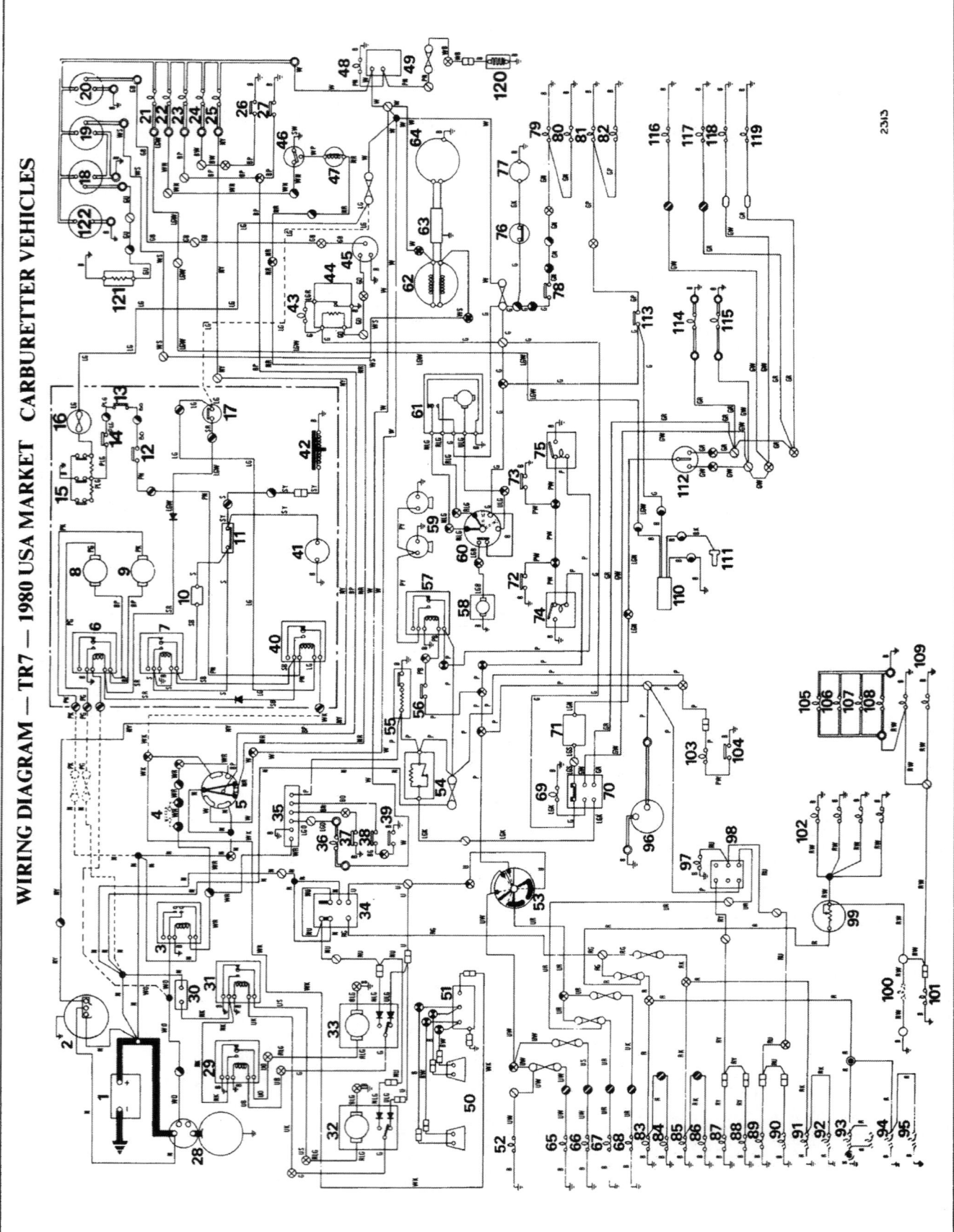

WIRING DIAGRAM — TR7 — 1980 USA MARKET   CARBURETTER VEHICLES

1 Battery
2 Alternator
3 Starter relay
4 Starter inhibitor switch (automatic transmission only)
5 Ignition/starter switch

Air conditioning:
6 Condenser fan relay
7 Clutch delay relay
8 Condenser fan — L.H.
9 Condenser fan — R.H.
10 Delay unit
11 Ranco valve high pressure cut-out
12 Manual cut-out switch
13 Full throttle cut-out switch
14 Cold thermostat
15 Blower motor switch
16 Blower motor
17 Radiator thermostat

18 Temperature indicator
19 Tachometer
20 Fuel indicator
21 Coolant low warning light
22 Oil pressure warning light
23 Brake warning light
24 Handbrake warning light
25 Ignition warning light
26 Handbrake switch
27 Brake pressure differential switch
28 Starter motor
29 Headlamp run/stop relay — R.H.
30 Headlamp motor circuit breaker
31 Headlamp run/stop relay — L.H.
32 Headlamp actuator — L.H.
33 Headlamp actuator — R.H.
34 Master light switch
35 Seat belt timer/buzzer unit
36 Seat belt warning light
37 Belt switch
38 Door switch
39 Key switch

Air conditioning:
40 Master relay
41 Clutch
42 Throttle jack

43 Low fuel warning light
44 Low fuel delay unit
45 Tank unit
46 Oil pressure switch
47 Anti run-on valve
48 Heated back-light warning light
49 Heated back-light switch
50 Speakers
51 Radio
52 Main beam warning light
53 Column light switch
54 Hazard flasher unit
55 Cigarette lighter
56 Horn-push
57 Horn relay
58 Windscreen washer pump
59 Horn
60 Windscreen wash/wipe switch
61 Windscreen wiper motor
62 and
63 Ignition coil and electronic module assembly
64 Ignition distributor
65 Main beam — R.H.
66 Main beam — L.H.
67 Dip beam — R.H.
68 Dip beam — L.H.
69 Hazard warning light
70 Hazard switch
71 Turn signal flasher unit
72 Door switch
73 Door switch
74 Map/courtesy lamp
75 Map/courtesy lamp
76 Engine thermostat
77 Carburetter fuel heater
78 Reverse lamp switch
79 Reverse lamp
80 Reverse lamp
81 Stop lamp
82 Stop lamp
83 Front marker lamp — R.H.
84 Front parking lamp — R.H.
85 Front marker lamp — L.H.
86 Front parking lamp — L.H.
87 Front fog lamp
88 Front fog lamp
89 Rear guard lamp
90 Rear guard lamp
91 Tail lamp — L.H.
92 Rear marker lamp — L.H.
93 Plate illumination lamp
94 Rear marker lamp — R.H.
95 Tail lamp — R.H.
96 Clock
97 Rear guard lamp warning light
98 Fog switch
99 Panel rheostat
100 Selector panel illumination (automatic transmission only)
101 Cigarette lighter illumination
102 Heater control illumination
103 Luggage boot lamp
104 Luggage boot lamp switch
105 Instrument illumination
106 Instrument illumination
107 Instrument illumination
108 Instrument illumination
109 Switch panel illumination
110 Coolant low indicator unit
111 Coolant low sensor
112 Turn signal switch
113 Stop lamp switch
114 Turn signal warning light — L.H.
115 Turn signal warning light — R.H.
116 Front flasher lamp — R.H.
117 Front flasher lamp — L.H.
118 Rear flasher lamp — R.H.
119 Rear flasher lamp — L.H.
120 Heated back-light
121 Temperature transmitter
122 Battery condition indicator

COLOUR CODE

B	Black	N	Brown	S	Slate
G	Green	O	Orange	U	Blue
K	Pink	P	Purple	W	White
LG	Light green	R	Red	Y	Yellow

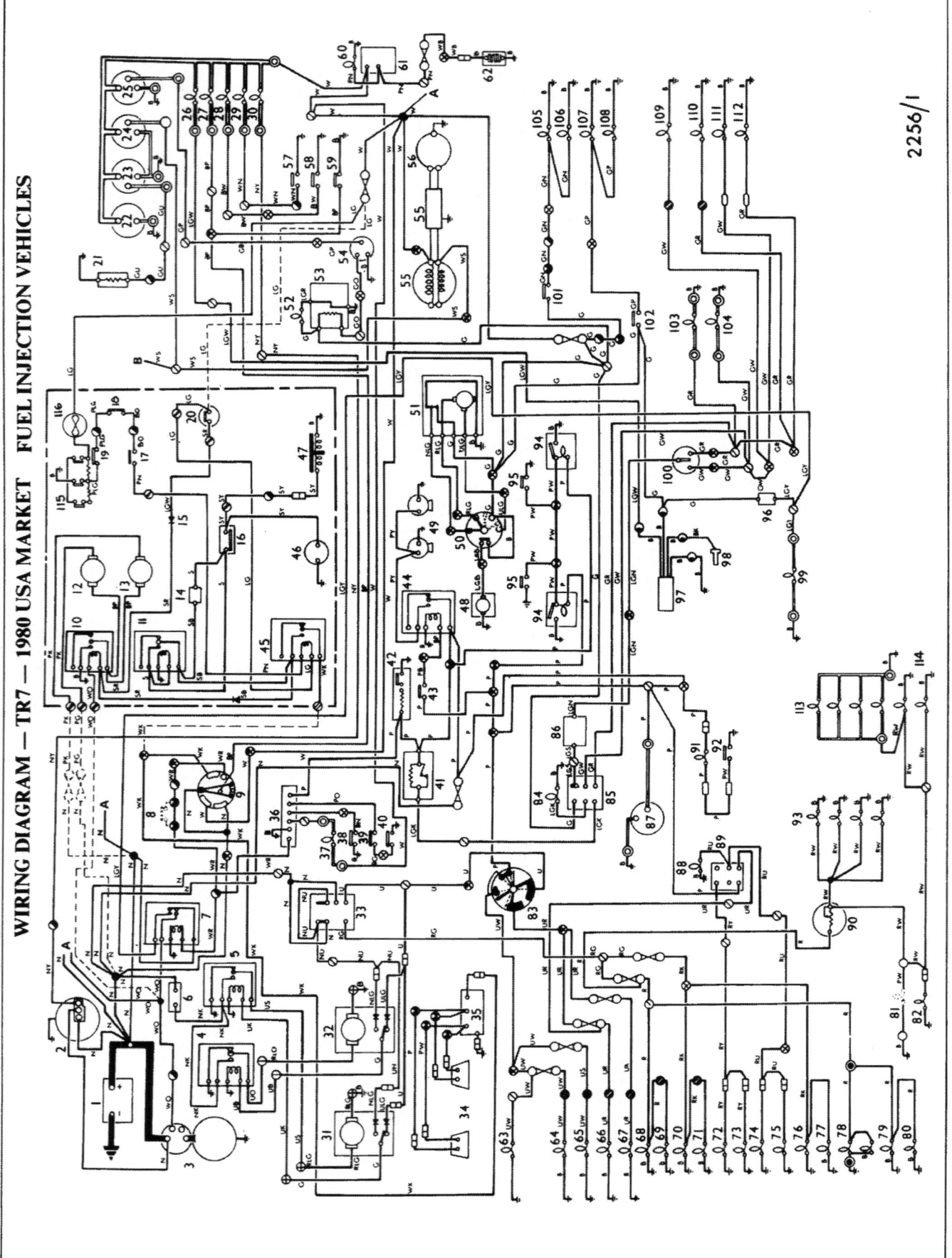

WIRING DIAGRAM — TR7 — 1980 USA MARKET   FUEL INJECTION VEHICLES

2256/1

1 Battery
2 Alternator
3 Starter motor
4 Headlamp run/stop relay — R.H.
5 Headlamp run/stop relay — L.H.
6 Headlamp motor circuit breaker
7 Starter relay
8 Starter inhibitor switch (automatic transmission only)
9 Ignition/starter switch

Air conditioning:
10 Condenser fan relay
11 Clutch delay relay
12 Condenser fan — L.H.
13 Condenser fan — R.H.
14 Delay unit
15 Diode
16 Ranco valve high pressure cut-out
17 Manual cut-out switch
18 Full throttle cut-out switch
19 Cold thermostat
20 Radiator thermostat

21 Temperature transmitter
22 Battery condition indicator
23 Temperature indicator
24 Tachometer
25 Fuel indicator
26 Coolant low warning light
27 Brake warning light
28 Handbrake warning light

29 Oil pressure warning light
30 Ignition warning light
31 Headlamp actuator — L.H.
32 Headlamp actuator — R.H.
33 Master light switch
34 Speakers
35 Radio
36 Seat belt timer/buzzer unit
37 Seat belt warning light
38 Belt switch
39 Door switch
40 Key switch
41 Hazard flasher unit
42 Cigarette lighter
43 Horn-push
44 Horn relay

Air conditioning:
45 Master relay
46 Clutch
47 Throttle jack

48 Windscreen washer pump
49 Horn
50 Windscreen wash/wipe switch
51 Windscreen wiper motor
52 Low fuel warning light
53 Low fuel delay unit
54 Tank unit
55 Ignition coil and electronic module assembly
56 Ignition distributor

57 Oil pressure switch
58 Handbrake switch
59 Brake pressure differential switch
60 Heated back-light warning light
61 Heated back-light switch
62 Heated back-light
63 Main beam warning light
64 Main beam — R.H.
65 Main beam — L.H.
66 Dip beam — R.H.
67 Dip beam — L.H.
68 Front marker lamp — R.H.
69 Front parking lamp — R.H.
70 Front marker lamp — L.H.
71 Front parking lamp — L.H.
72 Front fog lamp
73 Front fog lamp
74 Rear guard lamp
75 Rear guard lamp
76 Tail lamp — L.H.
77 Rear marker lamp — L.H.
78 Plate illumination lamp
79 Rear marker lamp — R.H.
80 Tail lamp — R.H.
81 Selector panel illumination (automatic transmission only)
82 Cigarette lighter illumination
83 Column light switch
84 Hazard warning light
85 Hazard switch
86 Turn signal flasher unit
87 Clock

88 Rear guard lamp warning light
89 Fog switch
90 Panel rheostat
91 Luggage boot lamp
92 Luggage boot lamp switch
93 Heater control illumination
94 Map/courtesy lamp
95 Door switch
96 Service interval counter
97 Coolant low indicator unit
98 Coolant low sensor
99 Oxygen sensor warning light
100 Turn signal switch
101 Reverse lamp switch
102 Stop lamp switch
103 Turn signal warning light — L.H.
104 Turn signal warning light — R.H.
105 Reverse lamp
106 Reverse lamp
107 Stop lamp
108 Stop lamp
109 Front flasher lamp — R.H.
110 Front flasher lamp — L.H.
111 Rear flasher lamp — R.H.
112 Rear flasher lamp — L.H.
113 Instrument illumination
114 Switch panel illumination

Air conditioning:
115 Blower motor switch
116 Blower motor

COLOUR CODE

B Black	N Brown	S Slate	
G Green	O Orange	U Blue	
K Pink	P Purple	W White	
LG Light green	R Red	Y Yellow	

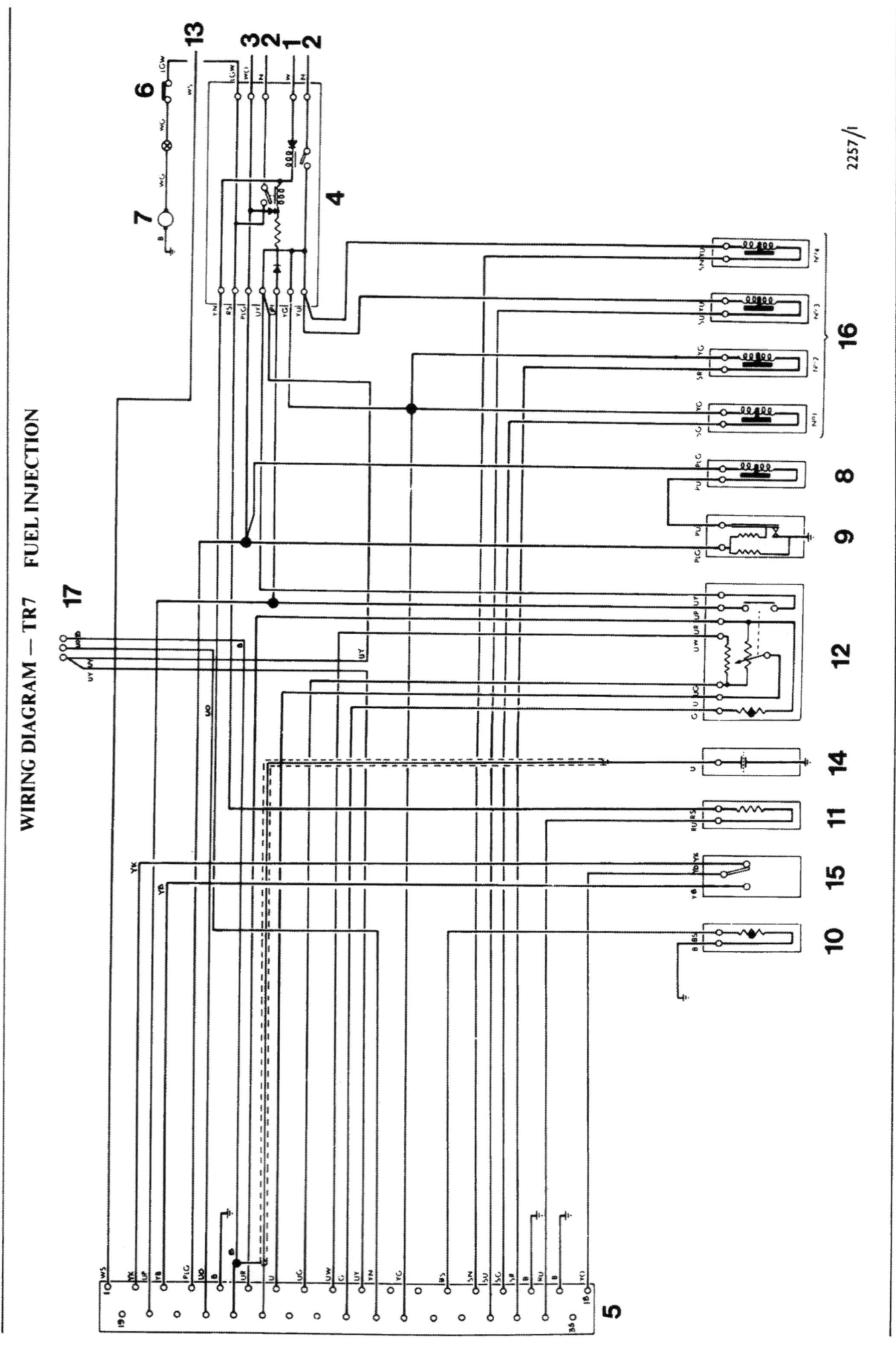

WIRING DIAGRAM — TR7   FUEL INJECTION

2257/1

1   Ignition control input
2   Battery input
3   Start input
4   Relay
5   Electronic control unit — E.C.U.
6   Inertia switch
7   Fuel pump
8   Cold start injector
9   Thermotime switch
10 Water temperature sensor
11 Extra air valve
12 Air flow meter
13 Engine speed — input from ignition coil negative
14 Lambda sensor
15 Throttle switch
16 Injector — 4 off
17 Test facility — feedback monitor plug

COLOUR CODE

B	Black	N	Brown	S	Slate
G	Green	O	Orange	U	Blue
K	Pink	P	Purple	W	White
LG	Light green	R	Red	Y	Yellow

ALTERNATOR WIRING DIAGRAM
Lucas 17ACR Alternator with 14TR Regulator
Lucas Part No. 23796

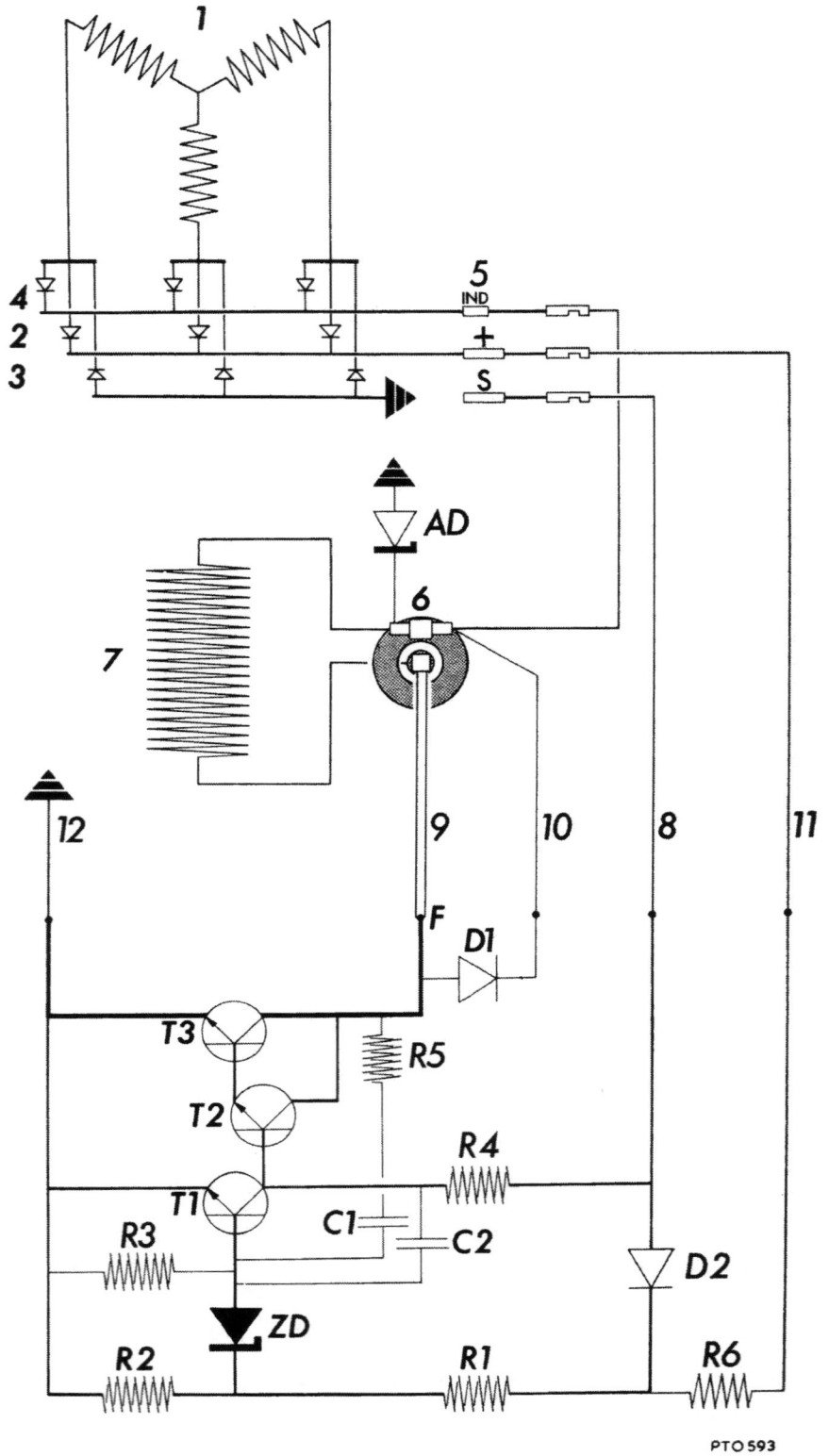

PTO 593

KEY TO ALTERNATOR WIRING DIAGRAM

Lucas 17ACR Alternator with 14TR Regulator
Lucas Part No. 23796

1	Stator windings	
2	Live side output diodes	
3	Earth side output diodes	
4	Field winding supply diodes	
5	European terminations	IND Ignition warning light + Main to battery S Sense to battery
6	Brushes to slip rings	
7	Field winding	
8	Battery sensed lead—white	
R4	Resistor	Restricts T2 base current supplied from 'battery sensed lead'
T2	Intermediate transistor	Controls T3 base current direct
9	Metal connector link	
T3	Output Transistor	Controls field winding earth return circuit
R1 and R2	Resistors	Potential divider—used in normal operation. Senses battery reference voltage
ZD	Zener diode	Voltage sensitive component. Opposes passage of current until breakdown voltage—approximately 8 volts—is reached. Controls T1 base current direct
T1	Input transistor	Controls T2 base current by diverting current passing through R4 to earth when ZD is conducting
C1 and R5	Capacitor and resistor	Prevents transistor overheating by providing positive feedback circuit to ensure quick switching of transistors from 'fully on' to 'fully off'
R3	Resistor	Path for small leakage current which may pass through ZD at high temperatures
10	Surge lead—yellow	
D1	Surge quench diode	Connected across field winding. Protects T3 from field winding high induced voltage surge and smooths field winding current
C2	Condenser	Radio interferance suppression
11	Machine sensed lead—red	
R6	Resistor	Fail-safe component. If main alternator to battery wire disconnects battery sensed lead voltage will fall. Alternator runway voltage is clamped by high voltage on machine sensed lead. Modified potential divider R1, R2 and addition R6
D2	Diode	Fail-safe component. If battery sensed lead disconnects alternator shuts down as supply via R4 to transistors T2 and T3 stops. D2 blocks feed into this circuit from machine sensed lead via R6
AD	Avalanche diode	Protects output transistor from high transient voltage which may occur from faulty charging circuit connectors
12	Earth lead—black	Regulator earth

CAUTION: The alternator contains polarity sensitive components that may be irreparably damaged if subjected to incorrect polarity.

Do not connect or disconnect any part of the charging circuit — including the battery leads — while the engine is running. Run the alternator with all connections made or with the unit disconnected.

Manufacturer Type	Lucas 17 ACR		Lucas 20 ACR		Lucas 25 ACR	
	Lucas Part No.	Triumph Part No.	Lucas Part No.	Triumph Part No.	Lucas Part No.	Triumph Part No.
Part numbers—						
assembly	—	TKC 0863	54021510	TKC 0905	—	RKC 2803
—comprising—						
alternator	23818	TKC 0864	23817	TKC 0906	23859	RKC 2804
fan	54217652	147990	54216943	157069		
pulley	54217767	154334	54201395	157083		154334
Polarity	Negative earth only		Negative earth only		Negative earth only	
Brush length						
— new	0.5 in (12.70 mm)		0.5 in (12.70 mm)		0.5 in (12.70 mm)	
— renew if less than	0.2 in (5.00 mm) protrudes from brushbox when free		0.3 in (8.00 mm) protrudes from brushbox when free		0.3 in (8.00 mm) protrudes from brushbox when free	
Brush spring pressure	9 to 13 oz (255 to 370 g) at face flush with brushbox		9 to 13 oz (255 to 370 g) at face flush with brushbox		9 to 13 oz (255 to 370 g) at face flush with brushbox	
Rectifier pack						
— output rectification	6 diodes (3 live side and 3 earth side)		6 diodes (3 live side and 3 earth side)		6 diodes (3 live side and 3 earth side)	
— field winding supply rectification	3 diodes		3 diodes		3 diodes	
Stator windings	Three phase—star connected		Three phase—delta connected		Three phase—delta connected	
Field winding rotor						
— poles	12		12		12	
— maximum permissible speed	15,000 rev/min		15,000 rev/min		15,000 rev/min	
— shaft thread	9/16 in—18 U.N.F.		M16—1.5		M16—1.5	
Field winding resistance at 20°C	$3.2 \pm 5\%$ ohms		3.5 ohms		3.0 to 3.5 ohms	
Control	Dual sensed—battery sensed with machine sensed safety control		Dual sensed—battery sensed with machine sensed safety control		Dual sensed—battery sensed with machine sensed safety control	
Regulation—type	14 TR		14 TR		14 TR	
Terminations	European		—		BSH	
Adjustment bolt tapping	Metric M8—1.25		—		—	
Nominal output						
— condition	Hot		Hot		Hot	
— alternator speed	6000 rev/min		6000 rev/min		6000 rev/min	
— control voltage	14 volt		14 volt		14 volt	
— amp	36 amp		66 amp		65 amp	

ALTERNATOR

Remove and refit   86.10.02

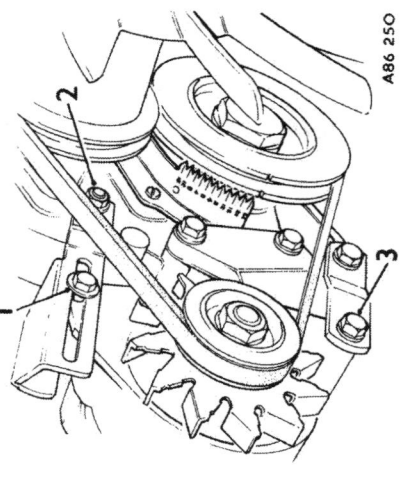

A86 250

Removing
1 Isolate the battery.
2 Disconnect the harness plug.
3 Remove the adjustment bolt and washer.
4 Push the alternator towards the engine and remove the drive belt from the pulley.
5 Remove the nut and washer.
6 Support the weight of the alternator. Withdraw the main mounting bolt and washer. Remove the alternator.

Refitting
7 Tap the bush slightly rearwards to assist assembly.
8 Position the alternator. Insert the main mounting bolt and washer.
9 Fit the nut and washer finger-tight.
10 Push the alternator towards the engine and fit the drive belt to the pulley.
11 Fit the adjustment bolt and washer finger-tight.
12 Adjust the drive belt, see 86.10.05.
13 Connect the harness plug.
14 Connect the battery.

ALTERNATOR

Drive belt adjust   86.10.05

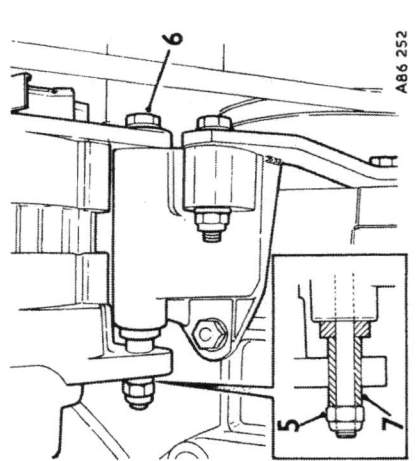

A86 251

A86 252

1 Slacken the adjustment bolt.
2 Slacken the support bracket bolt.
3 Slacken the main mounting bolt.
4 Carefully lever the alternator away from the engine to tension the belt. Tighten the adjustment bolt.
CAUTION: To prevent bearing damage when tensioning the belt use a lever of soft material – preferably wood – applied to the alternator drive end bracket. Do not lever on any other part of the alternator.
5 Check the belt tension. Total movement should be 0.75 to 1.00 in (20 to 25 mm) at the mid-point of the longest run.
6 Tighten the support bracket bolt.
7 Tighten the main mounting bolt.

ALTERNATOR – LUCAS TYPE 17 ACR

Overhaul   86.10.08

This overhaul instruction is specific to alternator Lucas part number 23818. Other units may differ slightly.

Dismantling

1   Remove the moulded cover.
2   Before disturbing any wires note the wire positions and colours.
3   Remove the brushbox, regulator and surge protection diode assembly as follows:
   Remove screw to release surge protection diode. Disconnect four Lucar connectors from the rectifier pack. Remove two screws to release the brushbox. Lift away the assembly.
4   If required, the regulator may be detached from the assembly as follows:
   Remove screw to release one wire eyelet. Remove screw to release the regulator. Disengage two lugs and lift away the regulator. Collect up the spacer.
5   Remove screw to release the radio capacitor.
6   Note the position of the three stator wires on the rectifier pack.
7   Unsolder the three stator wire connections. Do not overheat the diodes or bend the diode pins. Solder quickly and provide a heat sink by gripping the diode pin with pliers.
8   Remove screw to release the rectifier pack earth strip. Slacken the nut and withdraw the rectifier pack.
9   Remove the through-bolts.
10 Provide an extractor tool as shown.

11 To remove the slip-ring end bracket, position the extractor tool to engage with the outer journal of the slip-ring end bearing. Employ a second operator to support the slip-ring end bracket by hand. Carefully tap the extractor tool to drive the bearing from the housing.
   NOTE: It may be necessary to carefully file away surplus solder from the two field winding connections on the slip-ring moulding if the exterior tool will not pass over the moulding.
12 The rubber 'O' ring fitted in the slip-ring end bracket bearing housing may remain *in situ* unless replacement is contemplated.
13 Remove the stator windings from the drive end bracket.
14 Prevent the rotor turning by wrapping a scrap fan belt round the pulley and retaining by hand or vice. Remove the nut, spring washer, pulley and fan. If necessary, use a suitable extractor.
15 Remove the key.
16 Using a suitable press, remove the rotor from the drive end bracket.
   CAUTION: Do not attempt to remove the rotor by applying hammer blows to the shaft end. Such action may burr over and damage the thread.
17 Collect up the thick spacer.
18 Remove the thin spacer from the rotor shaft.

Reassembling

19 Fit the thin spacer to the rotor shaft.
20 Using a suitable press, fit the thick spacer and a suitable tube, fit the rotor to the drive end bracket by applying pressure to the bearing inner journal.
   CAUTION: Do not use the drive-end bracket as a support while fitting the rotor. If the spacer is not employed, the felt ring may be damaged.

21 Fit the key.
22 Fit the fan, pulley, spring washer and nut. Prevent the rotor turning by wrapping a scrap fan belt round the pulley and retaining by hand or vice. Torque load the nut to 25 to 30 lbf ft (3.46 to 4.15 kgf m).
23 Observe the relationship of the stator windings to the drive-end bracket determined by the stator wire connections, the rectifier pack position on the slip-ring end bracket, the alignment of the mounting lugs on the end brackets and the through-bolt clearances on the stator windings.
24 Position the stator windings to the drive-end bracket.
25 Ensure that the rubber 'O' ring is fitted correctly in the slip-ring end bracket bearing housing.
26 Fit the slip-ring end bracket by carefully pushing the bearing into the housing.
27 Fit the through-bolts, tightening evenly.
28. Position the rectifier pack. Fit screw to secure the rectifier pack earth strip. Tighten the nut to secure the rectifier pack.
29 Position three stator wires on the rectifier pack as noted in operation 6.
30 Solder three stator wire connections. Note the precautions stated in operation 7 and use 'M' grade 45-55 resin core solder.
31 Position the radio capacitor. Fit the screw to secure.
32 If required, attach the regulator to the brushbox, regulator and surge protection diode assembly as follows:
   Position the spacer. Position the regulator. Fit screw to secure the regulator. Fit screw to secure one wire eyelet.
33 Fit the brushbox, regulator and surge protection diode assembly as follows:
   Position the assembly. Fit two screws to secure the brushbox, include one earth wire eyelet under one screw head. Connect four Lucar connectors to the rectifier pack. Fit screw to secure surge protection diode.
34 Fit the moulded cover.

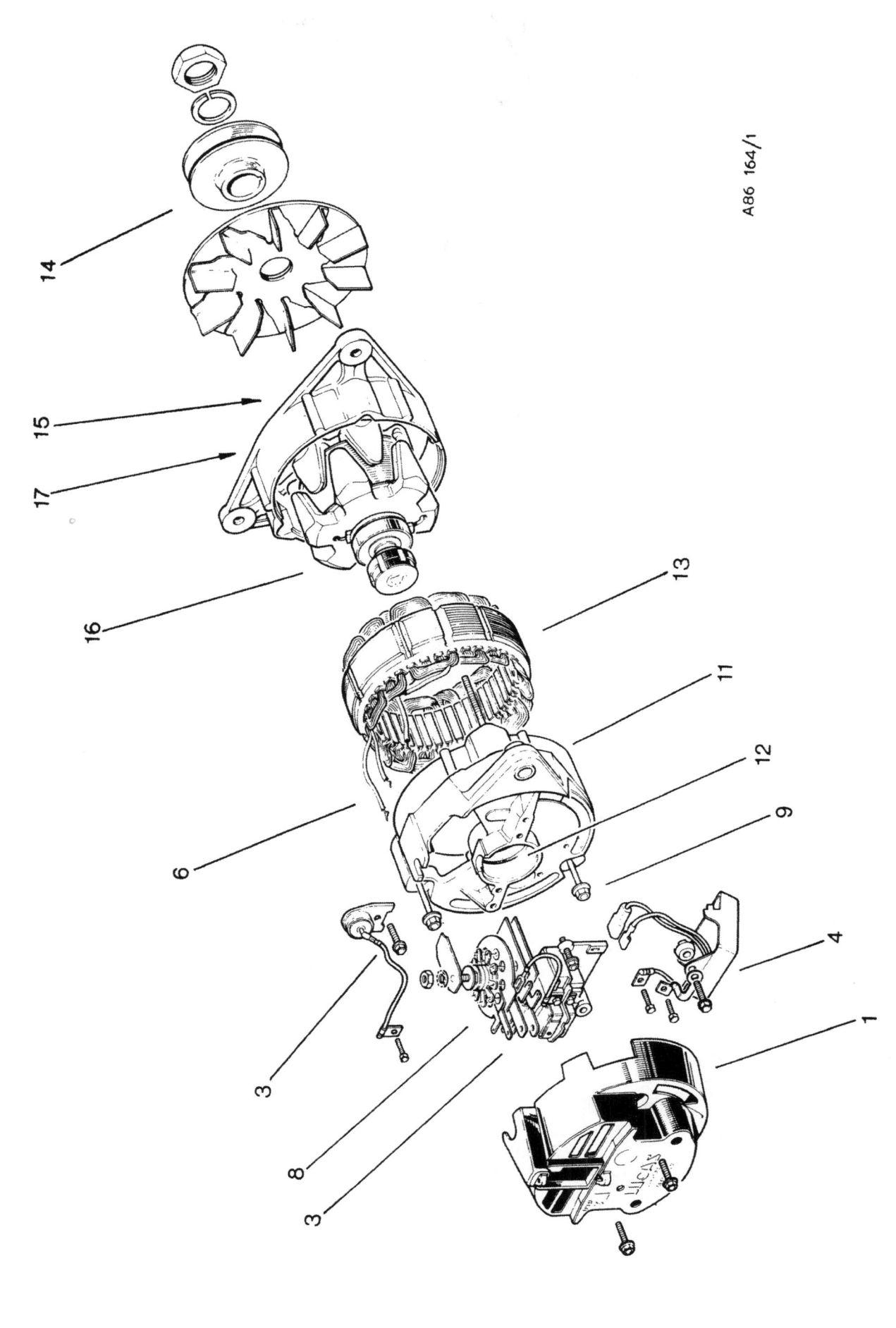

A86 164/1

ALTERNATOR – LUCAS TYPE 20ACR

Overhaul   86.10.08

Dismantling

1 Remove two screws, washers and spring washers. Remove the cover.
2 Note the wire positions and colour codes.
3 Disconnect the red wire small Lucar connector.
4 Disconnect the white wire small Lucar connector.
5 Disconnect the red wire large Lucar connector.
6 Remove the screw, washer and spring washer.
7 Remove the screw and spring washer.
8 Remove the screw, washer and spring washer.
9 Lift out the brushbox, regulator and surge protection diode assembly.
10 If necessary detach the regulator from the brushbox as follows—
Remove the screw to release one wire eyelet. Remove the screw to release the regulator. Bend up the contact strap. Disengage two lugs and lift away the regulator. Collect up the spacer.
11 Remove three Pozidriv screws.
12 Remove the earth strap screw and spring washer.
13 Remove three screws, washers and spring washers.
14 Lift out the rectifier pack.
15 Scribe a line across the slip ring end bracket, stator winding and drive end bracket.

16 Remove three side bolts and spring washers.
17 Collect up three nuts.
18 Provide an extractor tool as shown.
19 To remove the slip ring end bracket, position the extractor tool to engage with the outer journal of the slip ring end bearing. Employ a second operator to support the slip ring end bracket by hand. Carefully tap the extractor tool to drive the bearing from the housing.
NOTE: It may be necessary to carefully file away surplus solder from the two field winding connections on the slip ring moulding if the extractor tool will not pass over the moulding.
20 The rubber 'O' ring fitted in the slip ring end bracket bearing housing may remain in situ unless replacement is contemplated.
21 Remove the stator windings from the drive end bracket.
22 Remove the nut and spring washer. Prevent the rotor turning by wrapping a scrap fan belt round the pulley and retaining by hand or vice.
23 Remove the pulley.
24 Remove the fan.
25 Remove the flanged spacer.
26 Remove the key.
27 Unsolder two field winding connections. Pull the slip ring moulding from the shaft. This operation is necessary to prevent damage to the slip ring moulding during remove and refit of the rotor to the drive end bracket.
28 Using a suitable press remove the rotor from the drive end bracket.
CAUTION: Do not attempt to remove the rotor by applying hammer blows to the shaft end. Such action may burr over and damage the thread.
29 Remove the thin spacer from the rotor shaft.
30 Remove three screws. Remove the plate.
31 Remove the rubber ring.
32 Press the bearing from the drive end bracket.

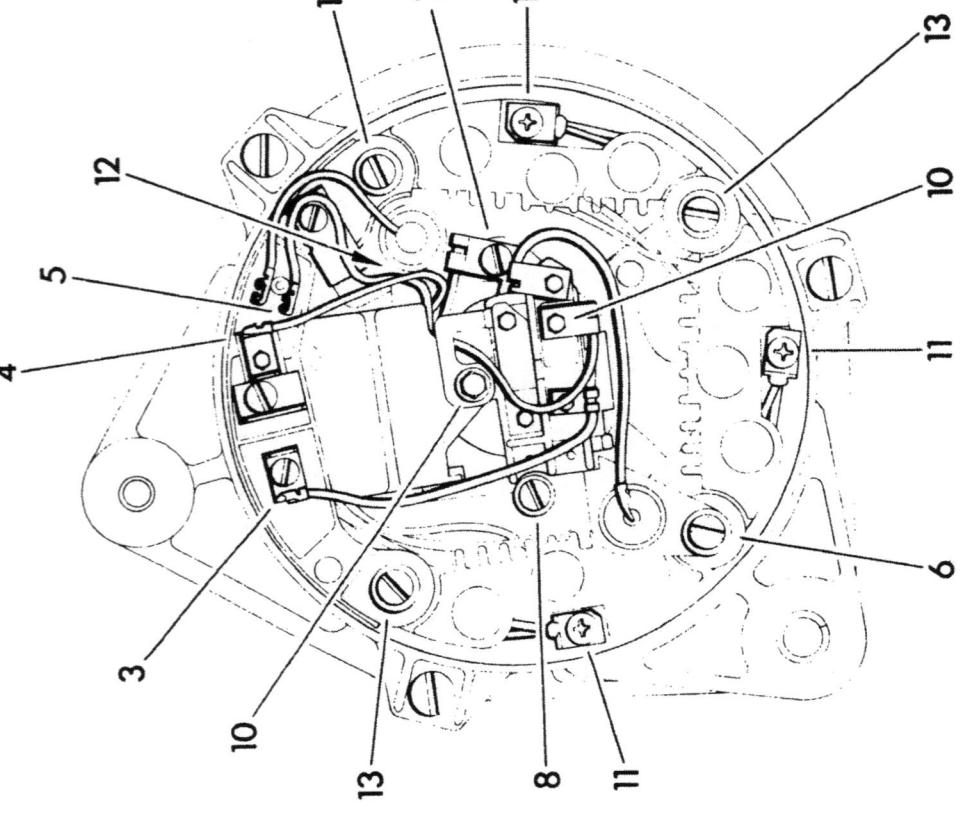

A86·068

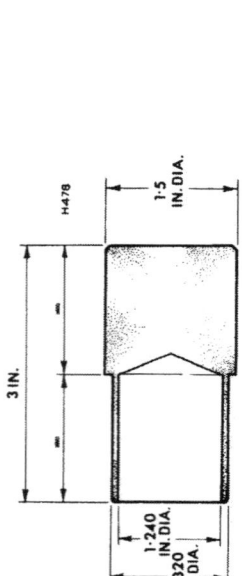

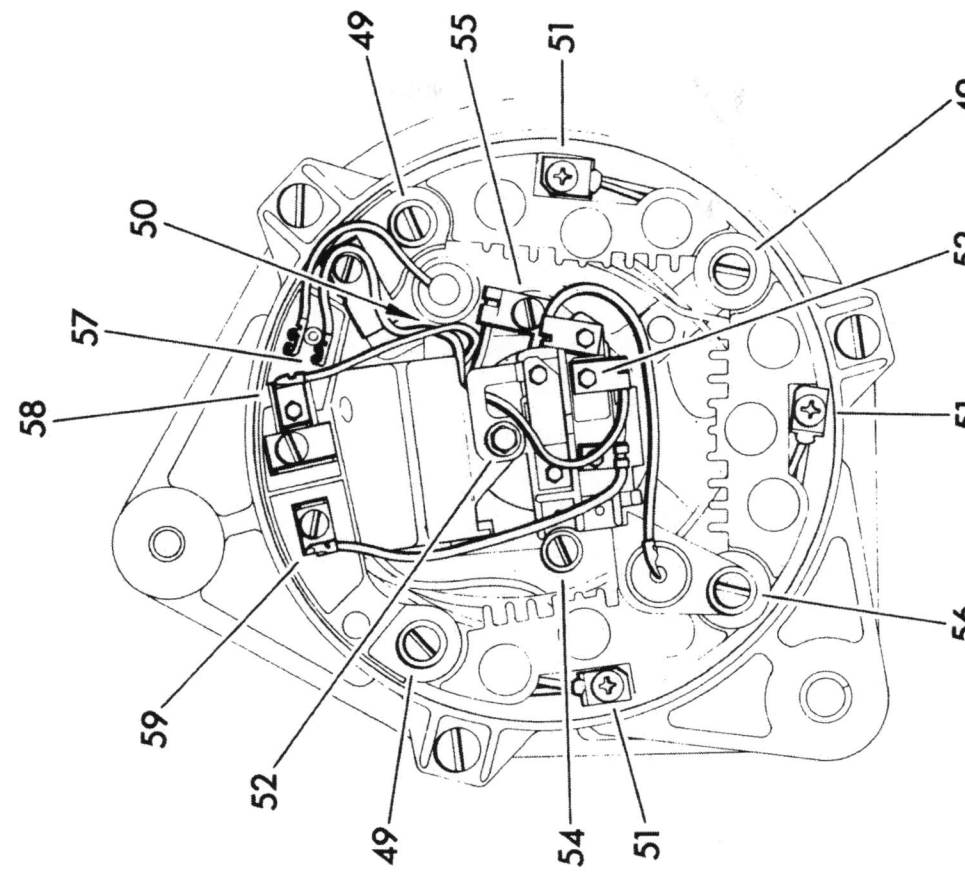

A86 069

Reassembling

33 Press the bearing into the drive and end bracket.

34 Position the rubber ring.

35 Position the plate with the countersinks uppermost. Secure with three screws.

36 Fit the thin spacer to the rotor shaft.

37 Using a suitable press, the flanged spacer and a suitable tube, fit the rotor to the drive end bracket by applying pressure to the bearing inner journal. CAUTION: Do not use the drive end bracket as a support while fitting the rotor.

38 Push the slip ring moulding onto the shaft. Ensure that the moulding tongue engages correctly in the shaft slot. Solder two field winding connections.

39 Fit the key.

40 Fit the flanged spacer with the reduced diameter against the bearing inner journal.

41 Fit the fan with the blades adjacent to the drive end bracket.

42 Fit the pulley with the boss against the fan.

43 Fit the spring washer and nut. Prevent the rotor turning by wrapping a scrap fan belt round the pulley and retaining by hand or vice. Torque load the nut to 30 to 36 lbf ft (4.2 to 4.9 kgf m).

44 Position the stator windings to the drive end bracket. Align the scribe lines made at operation 15 above.

45 Ensure that the rubber 'O' ring is fitted correctly in the slip ring end bracket bearing housing.

46 Fit the slip ring end bracket by carefully pushing the bearing into the housing. Align the scribe lines made at operation 15 above.

47 Fit three side bolts with spring washers under the bolt heads. Secure with three nuts. Tighten evenly.

48 Position the rectifier pack.

49 Fit three screws, washers and spring washers.

50 Fit the earth strap screw and spring washer.

51 Fit three Pozidriv screws.

52 If necessary attach the regulator to the brushbox as follows—
Position the spacer. Position the regulator. Bend down the contact strap. Fit the screw to secure the regulator. Fit the screw to secure one wire eyelet.

53 Position the brushbox, regulator and surge protection diode assembly.

54 Fit the screw, washer and spring washer.

55 Fit the screw and spring washer. Include the capacitor lug and the regulator earth wire eyelet in the assembly.

56 Fit the screw, washer and spring washer. Include the surge protection diode lug in the assembly.

57 Connect the red wire large Lucar connector.

58 Connect the white wire small Lucar connector.

59 Connect the red wire small Lucar connector.

60 Position the cover. Secure with two screws, washers and spring washers.

ALTERNATOR – LUCAS 25ACR

Overhaul 86.10.08

Dismantling

1 Remove two bolts. Remove the cover.
2 Note the wire positions and the colour codes.
3 Disconnect the yellow wire small Lucar connector from the rectifier pack.
4 Remove the screw securing the avalanche diode.
5 Disconnect the white wire Lucar connector from the terminal block.
6 Disconnect the yellow wire Lucar connector from the terminal block.
7 Remove the nut, spring washer and two red wire tags from the terminal block.
8 Remove the two screws. Lift out the brushbox, regulator and avalanche diode assembly.
9 If necessary detach the regulator from the brushbox as follows:
   Remove the screw to release one wire eyelet. Remove the screw to release the regulator. Bend up the contact strap. Disengage two lugs and lift away the regulator.
10 Remove screw and radio capacitor.
11 Remove three through bolts.
12 Provide an extractor tool as shown.

13 To remove the slip-ring end bracket, stator, rectifier and terminal block assembly position the extractor tool to engage with the outer journal of the slip-ring end bearing.
   Employ a second operator to support the slip-ring end bracket and stator by hand. Carefully tap the extractor tool to drive the bearing from the housing.
   NOTE: It may be necessary to carefully file away surplus solder from the two field winding connections on the slip-ring moulding if the extractor tool will not pass over the moulding.
14 The rubber 'O' ring fitted in the slip-ring end bracket bearing housing may remain *in situ* unless replacement is contemplated.
15 If necessary detach the stator, rectifier and terminal block from the slip-ring end bracket as follows:
   Unsolder three wires. At each apply solder iron, bend out centre limb and disconnect wire. Remove stator. Slacken nut and withdraw rectifier. Remove two screws and terminal block.
16 Prevent the rotor turning by wrapping a scrap fan belt round the pulley and retaining by hand or vice. Remove the nut and spring washer.
17 Remove the pulley.
18 Remove the fan.
19 Remove the key.
20 Remove the outer spacer.
21 Using a suitable press remove the rotor from the drive end bracket.
   CAUTION: Do not attempt to remove the rotor by applying hammer blows to the shaft end. Such action may burr over and damage the thread.
22 Remove the inner spacer.
23 Remove three screws. Remove the plate.
24 Press the bearing from the drive end bracket.
25 Collect up the metal retainer and felt washer.

Reassembling

26 Position the felt washer and metal retainer.
27 Press the bearing into the drive end bracket.
28 Position the plate. Secure with three screws.
29 Fit the inner spacer.
30 Using a suitable press, the outer spacer and a slave tube – fit the drive end bracket to the rotor by applying pressure to the bearing inner journal.
   CAUTION: Do not use the drive end bracket as a support while fitting the rotor.
31 Fit the outer spacer.
32 Fit the key.
33 Fit the fan.
34 Fit the pulley.
35 Fit the spring washer and nut. Retain as at instruction 16 and torque load nut to 30 lbf ft (41 Nm).
36 If necessary, assemble the stator, rectifier and terminal block to the slip-ring end bracket as follows:
   Position terminal block and secure with two screws. Insert rectifier and tighten nut. Position stator. Solder three wires using standard resin-cored solder.
37 Ensure that rubber 'O' ring is fitted in the slip-ring end bracket bearing housing.
38 Fit the slip-ring end bracket, stator, rectifier and terminal block assembly by carefully pushing the bearing into the housing. Align the main mounting lugs.
39 Fit three through bolts. Tighten evenly. Torque load to 5 lbf ft (7 Nm).
40 Position radio capacitor. Secure with screw.
41 If necessary, assemble the regulator to the brushbox as follows:
   Position the regulator. Bend down the contact strap. Fit the screw to secure the regulator. Fit the screw to secure yellow wire eyelet.
42 Position the brushbox, regulator and avalanche diode assembly. Secure with two screws. Include the regulator earth wire eyelet under one screw head.
43 Position two red wire tags to the terminal block. Secure with spring washer and nut.

44 Connect the yellow wire Lucar connector to the terminal block.
45 Connect the white wire Lucar connector to the terminal block.
46 Fit the screw to secure the avalanche diode.
47 Connect the yellow wire small Lucar connector to the rectifier pack.
48 Position the cover. Secure with two bolts.

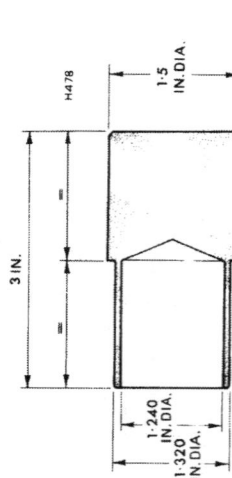

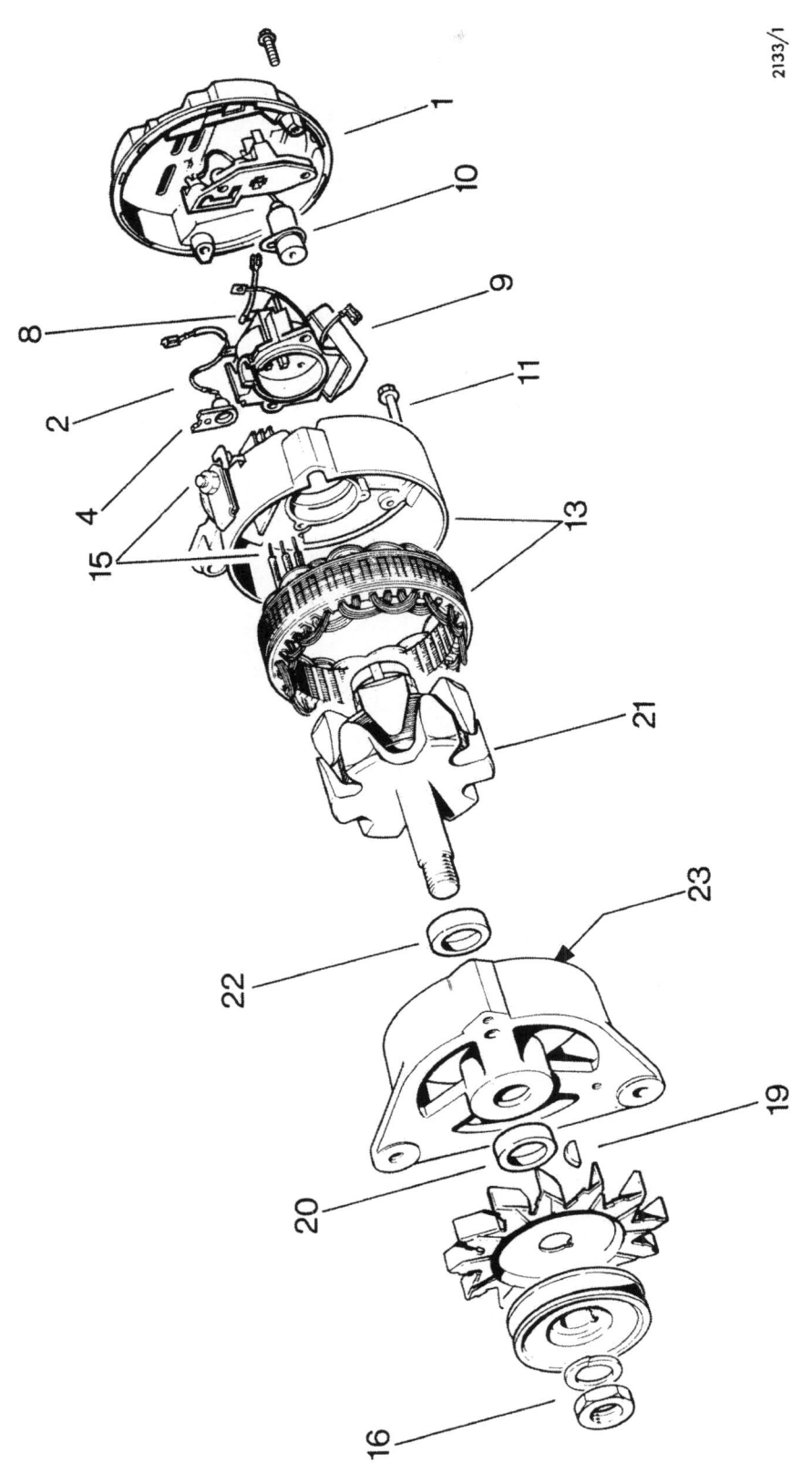

2133/1

IGNITION DISTRIBUTOR APPLICABILITY, IGNITION TIMING AND FEATURES CHART
1975 to 1979

	UK AND EUROPE 1976/77/78/79	U.S.A. MARKET			
		Federal		California	
		1975/76	1977/78/79	1975/76	1977/78/79
Triumph part No.	RKC 0066	TKC 1204	TKC 3328	TKC 1689	TKC 3330
Lucas part No.	X	41601	41701	41603	41700
Delco Remy part No.	7992715	X	X	X	X
Ignition timing — static	10 degrees B.T.D.C.	10 degrees B.T.D.C.	10 degrees B.T.D.C.	10 degrees B.T.D.C.	10 degrees B.T.D.C.
Ignition timing — at idle	See table 86.35.15 Advance pipe disconnected	2 degrees A.T.D.C. Retard pipe connected	10 degrees B.T.D.C.	2 degrees A.T.D.C. Retard pipe connected	2 degrees A.T.D.C. Retard pipe connected
Idle speed	800 rev/min	800 rev/min	800 rev/min	800 rev/min	800 rev/min
Conventional points ignition	✓	X	X	X	X
Electronic ignition	X	✓	✓	✓	✓
Centrifugal advance	✓	✓	✓	✓	✓
Vacuum advance	✓	X	X	X	X
Retard unit	X	✓	X	✓	✓
Micrometer adjustment nut	X	X	X	X	X

IGNITION DISTRIBUTOR APPLICABILITY, IGNITION TIMING AND FEATURES CHART 1980

	UK AND EUROPE	U.S.A. MARKET				CANADA AND AUSTRALIA
		Federal			California	
	Carburetter	Carburetter	Carburetter	Fuel Injection	Fuel Injection	Carburetter
	1980	Cosmetic 1980	1980	1980	1980	1980
Triumph part No.	RKC 0066	TKC 3330	PKC 1333	RKC 3773	RKC 3773	RKC 4722
Lucas part No.	X	41700	X	X	X	X
Delco Remy part No.	7992715	X	9977215	9977120	9977120	9977254
Ignition timing — static	10 degrees B.T.D.C.	10 degrees B.T.D.C.	10 degrees B.T.D.C.	10 degrees B.T.D.C.	10 degrees B.T.D.C.	10 degrees B.T.D.C.
Ignition timing — at idle	See table 86.35.15 Advance pipe disconnected	2 degrees A.T.D.C. Retard pipe connected	2 degrees A.T.D.C. Retard pipe connected	2 degrees A.T.D.C. Retard pipe connected	2 degrees A.T.D.C. Retard pipe connected	2 degrees A.T.D.C. Retard pipe connected
Idle speed	800 rev/min	800 rev/min	800 rev/min	800 rev/min	800 rev/min	800 rev/min
Conventional points ignition	✓	X	X	X	X	X
Electronic ignition	X	✓	✓	✓	✓	✓
Centrifugal advance	✓	✓	✓	✓	✓	✓
Vacuum advance	✓	X	X	X	X	X
Retard unit	X	✓	✓	✓	✓	✓
Micrometer adjustment nut	X	X	X	X	X	X

IGNITION DISTRIBUTOR – DELCO REMY

Data

Manufacturer	AC Delco
Series	D302
Delco Remy part no.	7992715
Stanpart No.	RKC 0066
Contact gap	0.014 to 0.016 in
Rotation — viewed on rotor	Anti-clockwise
Firing angles	90 ± 1 degree
Dwell angle	39 ± 1 degree
Open angle	51 ± 1 degree
Moving contact spring tension	19 to 24 ozf
Condenser capacity	0.18 to 0.23 mfd
Engine firing order	1–3–4–2

Centrifugal advance

Distributor r.p.m.	Degs. distributor advance		Crankshaft r.p.m.	Degs. crankshaft advance	
	Minimum	Maximum		Minimum	Maximum
300	No advance to occur		600	No advance to occur	
500	0	1.00	1000	0	2.0
900	1.85	3.85	1800	3.7	7.7
1200	4.00	6.00	2400	8.0	12.0
1600	5.00	7.00	3200	10.0	14.0
2400	7.00	9.00	4800	14.0	18.0
3000	9.00	9.00	6000	18.0	18.0

Vacuum advance

Ins. of mercury vacuum	Degs. distributor advance		Degs. crankshaft advance	
	Minimum	Maximum	Minimum	Maximum
3	No advance to occur		No advance to occur	
5	1.30	4.67	2.60	9.34
7	6.00	8.00	12.00	16.00
10	6.00	8.00	12.00	16.00
20	8.00	8.00	16.00	16.00

IGNITION DISTRIBUTOR – DELCO REMY

Contact assembly – remove and refit   86.35.13

Remove

1   Remove the fresh air duct, see 80.15.31.
2   Pull the 'king' high tension lead from the distributor cover.
3   Remove the distributor cover and swing to rest across the camshaft cover.
4   Remove two screws and spring washers. Lift off the rotor.
5   Push the moving contact spring away from the terminal post and slip two wire eyelets along the post to release.
6   If necessary rotate the crankshaft to position the weights for the best access to the cross headed screws.
NOTE: The screws are cross headed to provide a choice of screwdriver position.
7   Remove two cross headed screws and spring washers.
8   Lift out the contact assembly.

Refitting

9   Wipe preservative from the new contact faces.
10   Reverse 5 to 8.
11   Adjust contact gap, see 86.35.14.

IGNITION DISTRIBUTOR – DELCO REMY

Contact gap – adjust   86.35.14

1   Remove the fresh air duct, see 80.15.31.
2   Pull the 'king' high tension lead from the distributor cover.
3   Remove the distributor cover and swing to rest across the camshaft cover.
4   Remove two screws and spring washers. Lift off the rotor.
5   Rotate the crankshaft to position the contact heel on a cam peak and position the weights for the best access to the contacts.
6   If the contact gap is correct a 0.015 in (0.38 mm) feeler gauge will fit between the contacts.
7   If the gap is correct operations 8 to 11 may be ignored.
8   Slacken two cross headed screws.
9   Move the fixed contact about the pivot to adjust the gap. This may be facilitated by inserting a screwdriver in the slots and twisting to position the fixed contact.
10   Tighten two cross headed screws.
11   Check that the correct gap has been maintained.
12   Reverse 1 to 4.

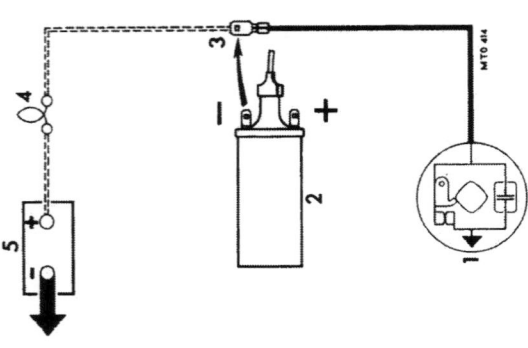

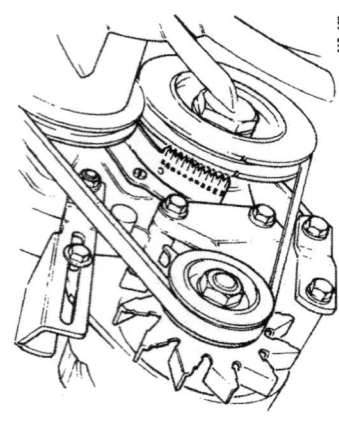

1 Distributor – diagrammatic layout.
2 Ignition coil.
3 Distributor fly lead removed from coil.
4 Test lamp – 12 volt.
5 Vehicle battery.

IGNITION DISTRIBUTOR – DELCO REMY

Ignition timing – adjust   86.35.15

If the engine can be run adjust dynamically as follows. If the engine cannot be run adjust statically as follows:

Dynamic

1 Remove the fresh air duct, see 80.15.31.
2 Pull off the advance unit pipe.
3 Connect a tachometer to the engine as instructed by the manufacturer.
  NOTE: The vehicle instrument panel tachometer may be used if no other instrument is available.
4 Connect a timing light as instructed by the manufacturer. The engine is timed on number one cylinder which is at the front of the engine.
5 Run the engine.
6 Position the timing light to illuminate the crankshaft pulley and timing cover scale.
7 Hold the speed at each of the engine r.p.m. indicated. The ignition timing should be as stated.

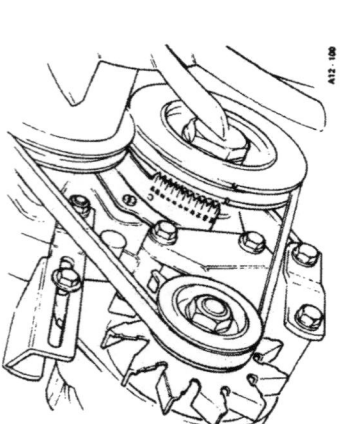

Engine r.p.m.	Static timing	Centrifugal advance – mean	Ignition timing B.T.D.C.
1000	10 degs.	1.0	11.0
1800	B.T.D.C.	5.7	15.7
2400		10.0	20.0

8 Stop the engine.
9 If the ignition timing is correct operations 10 to 13 may be ignored.
10 Use service tool S349 to slacken two distributor mounting bolts.
11 Rotate the distributor body slightly clockwise to advance the timing or anti-clockwise to retard the timing.
12 Tighten two distributor mounting bolts.
13 Repeat operation 5 onwards.
14 Remove the timing light.
15 Remove the tachometer.
16 Push on the advance unit pipe.
17 Fit the fresh air duct, see 80.15.31.

Static

18 Isolate the battery.
19 Disconnect the distributor low tension fly lead from the harness.
20 Provide a test lamp circuit as shown.
21 Rotate the crankshaft in the engine run direction to bring the crankshaft pulley notch to the start of the timing cover scale. The test lamp should now be illuminated.
22 Carefully rotate the crankshaft further until the lamp just goes out.
23 If the timing is correct the pulley notch will be aligned with the 10 degree BEFORE on the scale.
24 If the ignition timing is correct operations 25 to 30 may be ignored.
25 Remove the fresh air duct, see 80.15.31.
26 Use service tool S349 to slacken two distributor mounting bolts.
27 Rotate the crankshaft in the engine run direction to align the pulley notch with the 10 degree BEFORE on the scale.
28 Rotate the distributor body anti-clockwise past the test lamp illumination position. Carefully rotate clockwise until the lamp just goes out.
29 Tighten two distributor mounting bolts.
30 Repeat operation 21 onwards.
31 Remove the test lamp circuit.
32 Connect the distributor low tension fly lead to the harness white/slate wire.
33 Fit the fresh air duct, see 80.15.31.
34 Connect the battery.

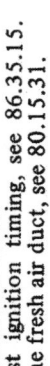

IGNITION DISTRIBUTOR – DELCO REMY

Lubrication   86.35.18

1 Remove the fresh air duct, see 80.15.31.
2 Pull the 'king' high tension lead from the distributor cover.
3 Remove the distributor cover and swing to rest across the camshaft cover.
4 Remove two screws and spring washers. Lift off the rotor.

Vehicles fitted with cam lubrication sponge only:
Perform instructions 6 to 10.

6 Squeeze the two sides of the cam lubrication post together and withdraw the post.
7 Remove the sponge from the post.
8 Work on amount of Shell Alvania No. 2 grease or equivalent into the spong.
9 Fit the sponge to the post.
10 Squeeze the two sides of the post together and insert the post. Ensure that the curved base surface faces outwards.

11 *Vehicles not fitted with cam lubrication sponge only:*
Lightly grease the cam with Shell Alvania No. 2 grease or equivalent.
12 Inject a few drops of engine oil through the OIL hole to lubricate the top bearing.
13 Apply one drop of engine oil to each weight pivot post and each 'cam action' position.
14 Reverse instructions 1 to 4.

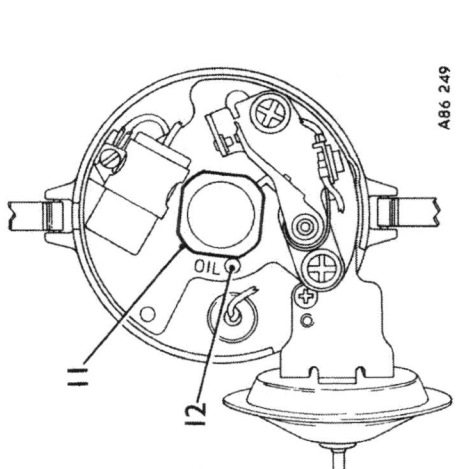

A86 248

A86 249

IGNITION DISTRIBUTOR – DELCO REMY

Remove and refit   86.35.20

Removing

1 Remove the fresh air duct, see 80.15.31.
2 Pull the 'king' high tension lead from the distributor cover.
3 Remove the distributor cover and swing to rest across the camshaft cover.
4 To assist the refit rotate the crankshaft in the engine run direction to bring number one piston to T.D.C. on the firing stroke. This is indicated when the rotor is pointing approximately towards the rear manifold mounting bolt as shown and the mark on the pulley is aligned with the 0 degree on the timing cover scale.
5 Pull off the advance unit pipe.
6 Disconnect the distributor low tension fly lead from the harness.
7 Use service tool S349 to remove two distributor mounting bolts, spring washers and washers.
8 Carefully withdraw and manoeuvre the distributor from the block.

Refitting

9 Ensure that number one piston is at T.D.C. on the firing stroke and the mark on the pulley is aligned with the 0 degree on the timing cover scale.
10 Carefully manoeuvre and insert the distributor into the block with the vacuum unit facing exactly rearwards. Engage the drive gear so that the rotor is finally pointing approximately towards the rear manifold mounting bolt as shown.
11 Fit two distributor mounting bolts, spring washers and washers.
12 Connect the distributor low tension fly lead to the harness white/slate wire.
13 Push on the advance unit pipe.
14 Fit the distributor cover.
15 Push the 'king' high tension lead onto the distributor cover.
16 Adjust ignition timing, see 86.35.15.
17 Fit the fresh air duct, see 80.15.31.

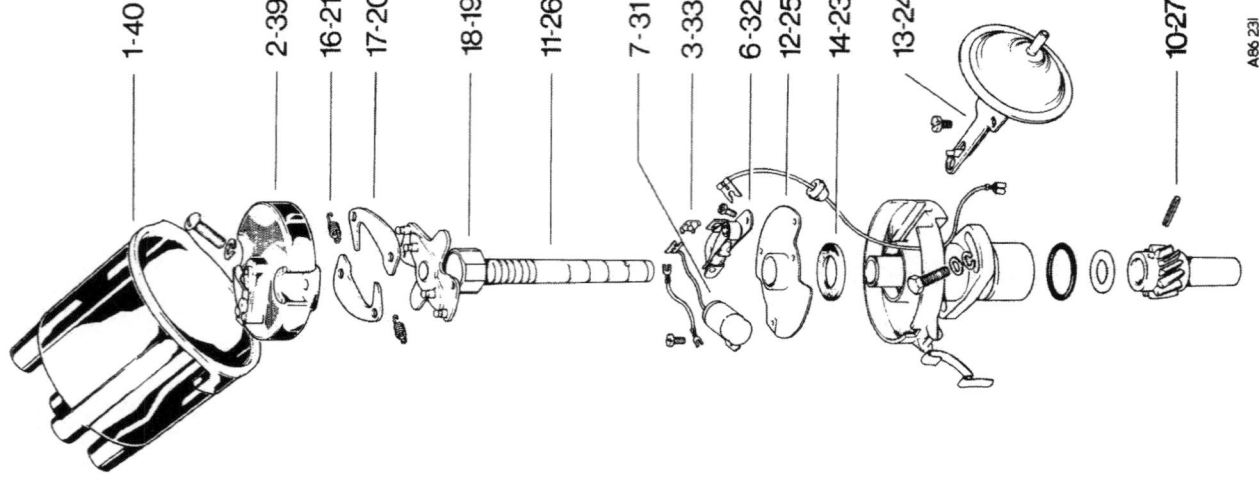

A86 23l

IGNITION DISTRIBUTOR – DELCO REMY

Overhaul 86.35.26

NOTE: Instructions 8, 9, 28, 29 and 30 apply to distributors fitted with cam lubrication sponge only.

Dismantling

1 Remove the cover.
2 Remove two screws and spring washers. Lift off the rotor.
3 Note the position of the two wire eyelets on the terminal post.
4 Push the moving contact spring away from the terminal post and slip two wire eyelets along the post to release.
5 Rotate the shaft to position the weights for the best access to the cross-headed screws. The screws are cross-headed to provide a choice of screwdriver position.
6 Remove two cross-headed screws and spring washers. Lift out the contact assembly.
7 Remove the screw and lift out the condenser.
8 Squeeze the two sides of the cam lubrication post together and withdraw the sponge.
9 Remove the sponge from the post.
10 Tap out the roll pin. Remove the drive gear and thrust washer.
11 Ensure that the shaft is burr-free. Withdraw the assembly.
12 Remove the special circlip and lift off the plate.
13 Remove two screws and lift off the earth lead and vacuum advance unit.
14 Carefully prise out the felt washer.
15 Remove the rubber grommet upwards and withdraw the wire assembly.
16 Remove the control springs, exercising great care not to distort the springs.
17 Lift off the weights.
18 Remove the cam unit by withdrawing down the shaft.

Reassembling

19 Lubricate the shaft with engine oil. Fit the cam unit to the shaft.
20 Position the weights.

21 Fit the control springs, exercising great care not to distort the springs.
22 Insert the wire assembly downwards and fit the rubber grommet.
23 Saturate the felt washer with engine oil and position in the base recess.
24 Fit the vacuum advance unit. Include the earth lead tag under the appropriate screw head.
25 Lubricate the plate bearing with engine oil. Fit the plate and secure it with the special circlip.
26 Ensure that the shaft is adequately lubricated with engine oil. Insert the shaft assembly.
27 Fit the thrust washer and drive gear. Secure with the roll pin.
28 Work an amount of Shell 'Alvania No. 2' grease or equivalent into the sponge.
29 Fit the sponge to the post.
30 Squeeze the two sides of the post together and insert the post. Ensure that the curved base surface faces outwards.
31 Fit the condenser. Include the earth lead tag under the screw head.
32 Position the contact assembly. Fit two cross-headed screws and spring washers finger tight.
33 Push the moving contact spring away from the terminal post and slip two wire eyelets along the post to secure in the positions noted at operation 3 above.
34 Rotate the shaft to position the contact heel on a cam peak and position the weights for the best access to the contacts.
35 Move the fixed contact about the pivot to adjust the contact gap to 0.015 in (0.38 mm). This may be facilitated by inserting a screwdriver in the slots and twisting to position the fixed contact.
36 Tighten two cross-headed screws.
37 Check the correct gap has been maintained.
38 Apply one drop of engine oil to each weight pivot post and each 'cam action' position.
39 Position the rotor with correct location of the keying. Secure with two screws and spring washers.
40 Fit the cover.

Callout references: 1-40, 2-39, 16-21, 17-20, 18-19, 11-26, 7-31, 3-33, 6-32, 12-25, 14-23, 13-24, 10-27

IGNITION COMPONENTS WITH
DELCO REMY CONVENTIONAL CONTACT SYSTEM

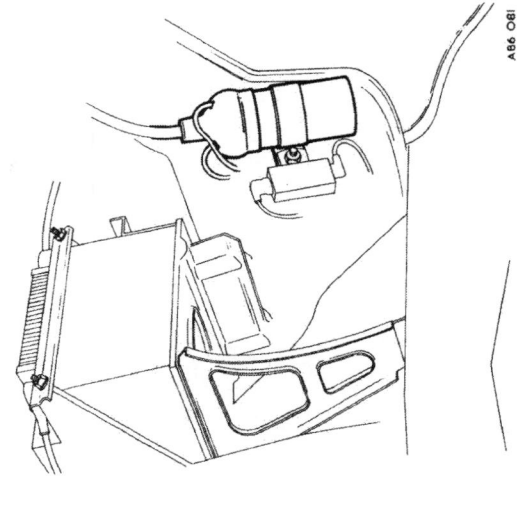

A86 081

BALLAST RESISTOR WIRE

Data

Resistance	1.3 to 1.5 ohm
Wire length	63 in (1600 mm)
Wire colour code	Pink/white

Description

This system is designed to assist engine starting under adverse conditions. A ballast resistor wire built into the harness is electrically positioned in series in the normal supply to the ignition coil. This wire causes a voltage drop in the circuit so that the 12 volt supply from the ignition switch may be employed to power the nominally rated 6 volt ignition coil.

During engine start the resistor is by-passed and the battery voltage (reduced from 12 volt by the starter motor load) is applied to the coil direct from the starter motor relay. This slight voltage overload provides an increased high tension voltage at the spark plugs.

IGNITION COIL

Data

Manufacturer	Lucas
Type	15C6
Lucas part number	45266
Triumph part number	UKC 2982
Primary winding resistance	1.3 to 1.45 ohm

IGNITION COIL

Remove and refit   86.35.32

Removing

1   Drive the vehicle onto a ramp.
2   Raise the ramp.
3   Locate the ignition coil mounted in the engine bay low down on the right-hand side of the bulkhead as shown.
4   Pull up the protective cover.
5   Pull off the high tension lead.
6   Disconnect two Lucar connectors.
7   Remove two nuts, spring washers and washers.
8   Remove the ignition coil from two body studs.

Refitting

9   Reverse 1 to 8.

IGNITION DISTRIBUTOR – LUCAS ELECTRONIC
– Triumph Part No. TKC 3328

Data

Manufacturer	Lucas
Type	47DE4
Lucas part number	41701
Triumph part number	TKC 3328
System	Opus electronic in built
Polarity	Negative earth only
Pick up air gap	0.014 to 0.016 in (0.35 to 0.40 mm)
Rotation—viewed on rotor	Anti-clockwise
Firing angle	90 ± 1 degree
Dwell angle	70—80 degrees
Engine firing order	1 – 3 – 4 – 2
To be used in conjunction with an external drive resistor of	10 ± 5% ohm

Centrifugal advance

Check at decelerating speeds

Distributor rev/min	Degs. distributor advance		Crankshaft rev/min	Degs. crankshaft advance	
	Minimum	Maximum		Minimum	Maximum
400	No advance to occur		800	No advance to occur	
650	1.0	4.0	1300	2	8
950	4.0	6.0	1900	8	12
1400	6.5	8.5	2800	13	17
1700	7.0	9.0	3400	14	18
2500	7.0	9.0	5000	14	18

IGNITION DISTRIBUTOR – LUCAS ELECTRONIC
– Triumph Part No. TKC 1204

Data

Manufacturer	Lucas
Type	47DE4
Lucas part number	41601
Triumph part number	TKC 1204
System	Opus electronic in-built
Polarity	Negative earth only
Pick-up air gap	0.014 to 0.016 in (0.35 to 0.40 mm)
Rotation—viewed on rotor	Anti-clockwise
Firing angle	90 ± 1 degree
Engine firing order	1 – 3 – 4 – 2
To be used in conjunction with an external resistor of	10 ± 5% ohm

Centrifugal advance

Check at increasing speeds

Distributor rev/min	Degrees distributor advance		Crankshaft rev/min	Degrees crankshaft advance	
	Minumum	Maximum		Minimum	Maximum
400	No advance to occur		800	No advance to occur	
500	0	1.0	1000	0	2
750	1.0	3.0	1500	2	6
950	2.5	4.5	1900	5	9
1100	3.5	5.5	2200	7	11
1750	6.0	8.0	3500	12	16
2100	7.0	9.0	4200	14	18
2750	7.0	9.0	5500	14	18

Retard unit

Check first with 11 inHg.   Increase to 15 inHg.   Finally decrease to 3 inHg.

Inches of mercury vacuum	Degrees distributor retard		Degrees crankshaft retard	
	Minimum	Maximum	Minimum	Maximum
3	No retard to occur			
11	5	7	10	14
15	5	7	10	14

IGNITION DISTRIBUTOR — LUCAS ELECTRONIC — Triumph Part No. TKC 1689

Data

Manufacturer	Lucas
Type	47DE4
Lucas Part No.	41603
Triumph Part No.	TKC 1689

System	Opus electronic in-built
Polarity	Negative earth only
Pick-up air gap	0.014 to 0.016 in (0.35 to 0.40 mm)
Rotation — viewed on rotor	Anti-clockwise
Firing angle	90 ± 1 degree
Engine firing order	1 – 3 – 4 – 2
To be used in conjuction with an external drive resistor of	10 ± 5% ohm

Centrifugal advance

Check at increasing speeds

Distributor rev/min	Degrees distributor advance		Crankshaft rev/min	Degrees crankshaft advance	
	Minimum	Maximum		Minimum	Maximum
440	No advance to occur		880	No advance to occur	
650	1.5	3.5	1300	3	7
750	3.0	5.0	1500	6	10
1050	4.5	6.5	2100	9	13
1900	8.5	10.5	3800	17	21
2250	10.0	12.0	4500	20	24
3000	10.0	12.0	6000	20	24

Retard unit

Check first with 11 inHg.   Increase to 15 inHg.   Finally decrease to 3 inHg.

Inches of mercury vacuum	Degrees distributor retard		Degrees crankshaft retard	
	Minimum	Maximum	Minimum	Maximum
3	No retard to occur		No retard to occur	
11	5	7	10	14
15	5	7	10	14

IGNITION DISTRIBUTOR — LUCAS ELECTRONIC — Triumph Part No. TKC 3330

Data

Manufacturer	Lucas
Type	47 DE4
Lucas part number	41700
Triumph part number	TKC 3330

System	Opus electronic in built
Polarity	Negative earth only
Pick-up air gap	0.014 to 0.016 in (0.35 to 0.40 mm)
Rotation-viewed on rotor	Anti-clockwise
Firing angle	90 ± 1 degree
Dwell angle	70–80 degrees
Engine firing order	1 – 3 – 4 – 2
To be used in conjunction with an external drive resistor of	10 ± 5% ohm

Centrifugal advance

Check at increasing speeds

Distributor rev/min	Degs. distributor advance		Crankshaft rev/min	Degrees crankshaft advance	
	Minimum	Maximum		Minimum	Maximum
400	No advance to occur		800	No advance to occur	
650	1.0	4.0	1300	2	8
950	4.0	6.0	1900	8	12
1400	6.5	8.5	2800	13	17
1700	7.0	9.0	3400	14	18
2500	7.0	9.0	5000	14	18

Retard Unit

Ins. of mercury vacuum	Degs. distributor retard		Degs. crankshaft retard	
	Minimum	Maximum	Minimum	Maximum
3	No retard to occur		No retard to occur	
11	5	7	10	14
15	5	7	10	14

Check first with 11 inHg. Increase to 15 inHg.
Finally decrease to 3 inHg.

IGNITION DISTRIBUTOR – LUCAS ELECTRONIC

Description   86.35.00

The 'Opus electronic in built' system consists of a conventional ignition coil and high tension circuit. The distributor contains a power transistor which manages the current flow through the ignition coil primary winding.

Distributor – deleted are the conventional cam, contacts and capacitor. These are replaced by an oscillator, timing rotor, pick up and amplifier. A conventional Lucas body, mechanical centrifugal advance and vacuum retard unit (when fitted) are retained.

Electronic circuit – the encapsulated oscillator supplies pulses to the pick up. The majority of these pulses are 'lost'. The timing rotor is carried on the rotating shaft and contains four ferrite rods. When one of the ferrite rods aligns with the pick up a pulse is 'caught' by the pick up and applied to the input of the encapsulated amplifier. The result is that the amplifier output switches the power transistor to the off condition.

Ignition coil and high tension circuit – the off condition of the power transistor collapses the ignition coil primary winding current. A spark occurs at the appropriate spark plug in the conventional manner.

Distributor with retard unit only:

Retard unit – the pick up is mounted on the moving plate. This assembly may be rotated through a limited angle by the vacuum retard unit. The ignition timing is thus modified by the vacuum retard unit by amending the relationship between the timing rotor and the pick up.

Drive resistor – this unit may be considered as a detached component of the amplifier. Its function is associated with the transistors in the amplifier. It is independently mounted due to its size and heat dissipating requirements.

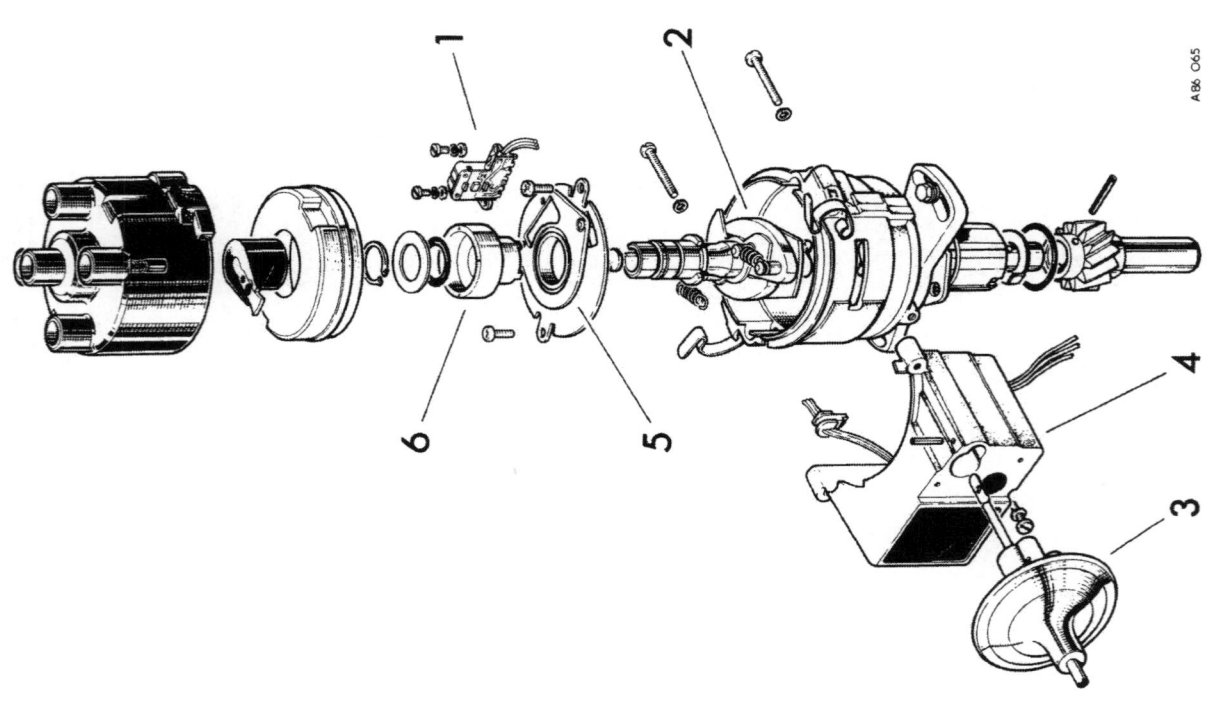

1 Pick-up
2 Centrifugal advance
3 Retard unit (when fitted)
4 Oscillator and amplifier
5 Moving plate
6 Timing rotor

A86 065

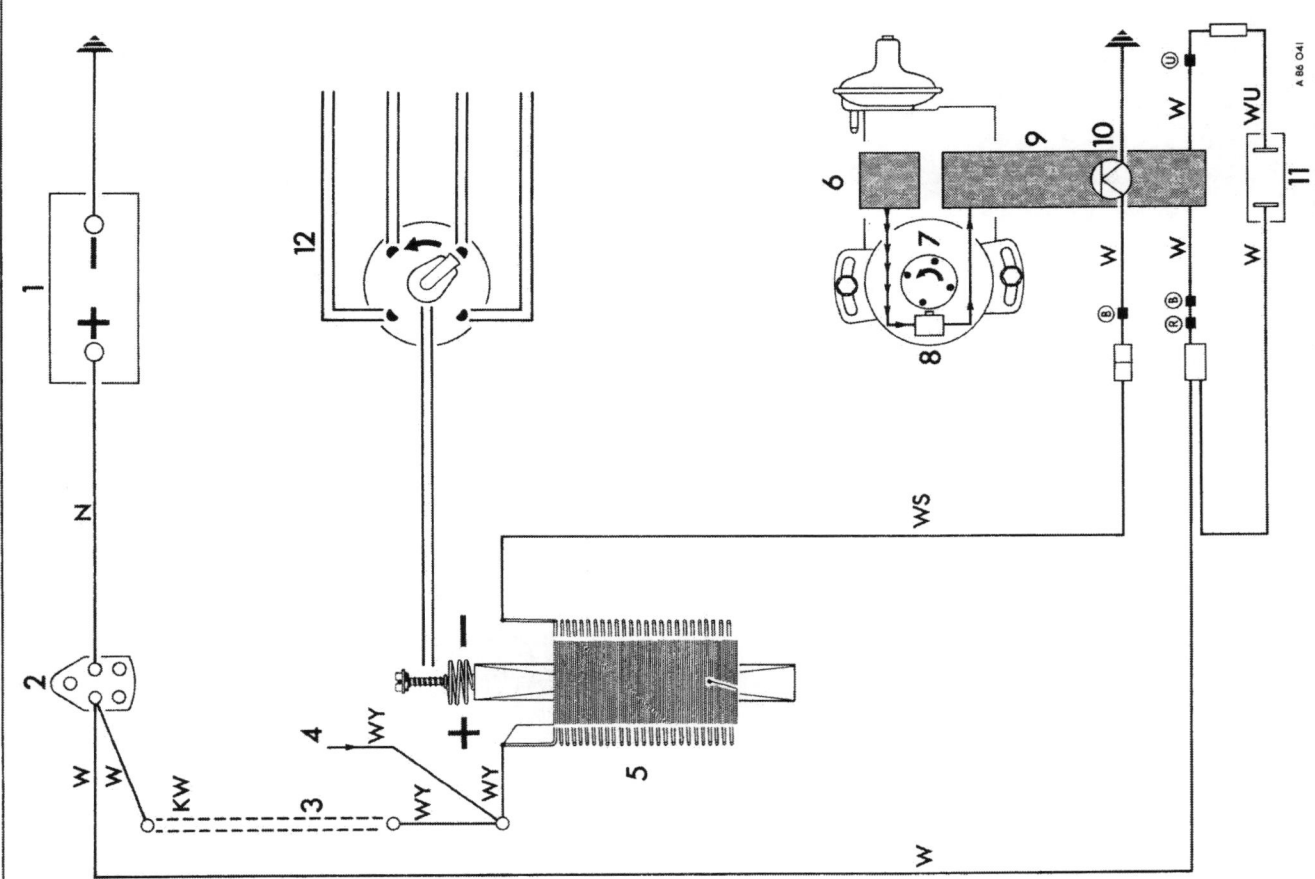

1 Battery
2 Ignition/starter switch
3 Ballast resistor wire
4 Start ignition supply from
  starter motor relay
5 Ignition coil
6 Oscillator
7 Timing rotor
8 Pick-up
9 Amplifier
10 Power transistor
11 Drive resistor
12 High tension circuit

Colour code

N   Brown
W   White
KW Pink/White
WY White/Yellow
WS White/Slate
WU White/Blue
Ⓑ   Black ident
Ⓡ   Red ident
Ⓤ   Blue ident

A 86 O4I

IGNITION DISTRIBUTOR – LUCAS ELECTRONIC

Ignition timing — adjust   86.35.15

The 'Opus electronic in-built' ignition system provides a beneficial long dwell period with a short open period. For this reason a static adjustment using a test lamp is not practicable. The test lamp would only flicker and would not provide an exact firing position.

If the engine can be run adjust dynamically as follows. If the engine cannot be run, adjust statically as follows.

Dynamic

1 Connect a tachometer to the engine as instructed by the manufacturer. NOTE: The vehicle instrument panel tachometer may be used if no other instrument is available.

2 Connect a timing light as instructed by the manufacturer. The engine is timed on number one cylinder which is at the front of the engine.

3 Distributor with retard unit only: Ensure that the retard unit pipe is connected.

4 Run the engine.

5 Position the timing light to illuminate the crankshaft pulley and timing cover scale.

6 Hold the speed at 700 to 900 rev/min. Nominal 800 rev/min.

7 The ignition timing at idle should now be as given in the chart, see 86.35.00.

8 If a correction is required, perform operations 9 to 13.

9 Stop the engine.

10 Use Service tool S 349 to slacken two distributor mounting bolts.

11 Rotate the distributor body slightly clockwise to advance the timing, or anti-clockwise to retard the timing.

12 Tighten two distributor mounting bolts.

13 Repeat operation 4 onwards.

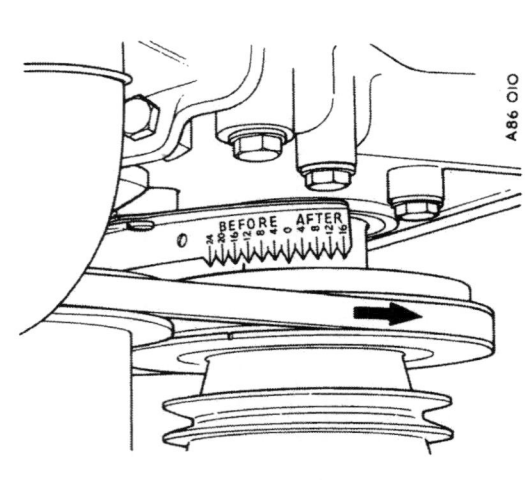

A86 010

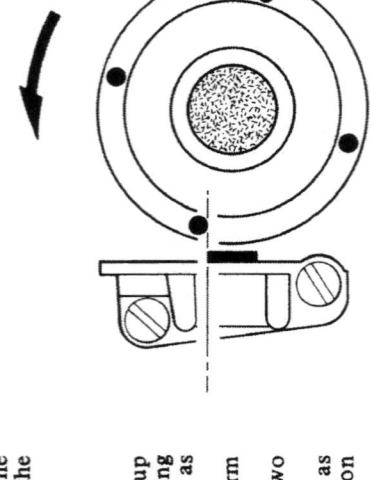

A86 063

Static

14 Isolate the battery.

15 Rotate the crankshaft in the engine run direction to align the mark on the pulley with the 10° B.T.D.C. on the timing cover scale.

16 Remove the distributor cover.

17 Pull off the rotor.

18 Remove the plastic anti-flash cover.

19 Inspect the relationship of the pick-up to the nearest ferrite rod on the timing rotor. This should be positioned as shown.

20 If a correction is required, perform operations 21 to 23.

21 Use Service tool S 349 to slacken two distributor mounting bolts.

22 Rotate the distributor body as required to achieve the position shown.

23 Tighten two distributor mounting bolts.

24 Fit the plastic anti-flash cover with the two recesses positioned adjacent to the clips.

25 Push on the rotor.

26 Fit the cover.

27 Connect the battery.

28 When the engine can be run, adjust dynamically as detailed above.

IGNITION DISTRIBUTOR – LUCAS ELECTRONIC

Lubrication   86.35.18

1 Remove the fresh air duct, see 80.15.31.
2 Remove the cover.
3 Pull off the rotor.
4 Remove the plastic anti-flash cover.
5 Apply a few drops of engine oil to the felt pad to lubricate the rotor carrier bearing.
6 Inject a few drops of engine oil through the apertures to lubricate the centrifugal timing control
7 Apply one drop of engine oil to each of the two lubrication apertures of the moving plate bearing.

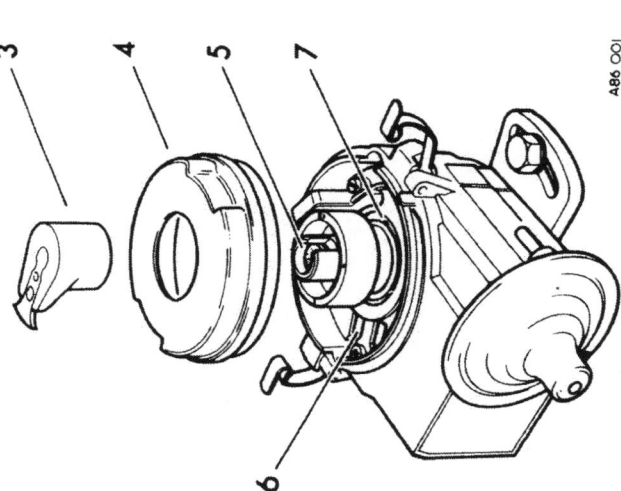

A86 OO1

IGNITION DISTRIBUTOR – LUCAS ELECTRONIC

Remove and refit   86.35.20

CAUTION: Do not connect the ignition distributor wires listed below direct to the battery positive supply –

White wire with Blue indent.
White wire with Black indent.

Removing

1 Isolate the battery.
2 Remove the fresh air duct. 80.15.31.
3 Remove the distributor cover.
4 Distributor with retard unit only: Pull off the retard unit pipe.
5 Disconnect three wire connectors.
6 Use Service tool S349 to remove two distributor mounting bolts, spring washers and washers.
7 Carefully withdraw and manoeuvre the distributor from the block.

Refitting

8 Ensure that the mounting plate is correctly fitted to the block. The mounting plate is symmetrical and may be fitted either way round.
9 Rotate the crankshaft in the engine run direction to bring number one piston to T.D.C. on the firing stroke and align the mark on the pulley with the 0 degree on the timing cover scale.
10 Distributor with retard unit only: Carefully manoeuvre and insert the distributor into the block with the retard unit facing exactly rearwards. Engage the drive gear so that the rotor is finally pointing approximately towards the rear manifold mounting bolt as shown.

11 Distributor with no retard unit only: Carefully manouvre and insert the distributor into the block with the oscillator and amplifier unit facing exactly rearwards. Engage the drive gear so that the rotor is finally pointing approximately towards the rear manifold mounting bolt as shown.
12 Fit two distributor mounting bolts, spring washers and washers.
13 Connect three wire connections as shown on illustration 86.35.00.
14 Distributor with retard unit only: Push on the retard unit pipe.
15 Fit the distributor cover.
16 Connect the battery.
17 Adjust ignition timing see, 86.35.16.
18 Fit the fresh air duct, see 80.15.31.

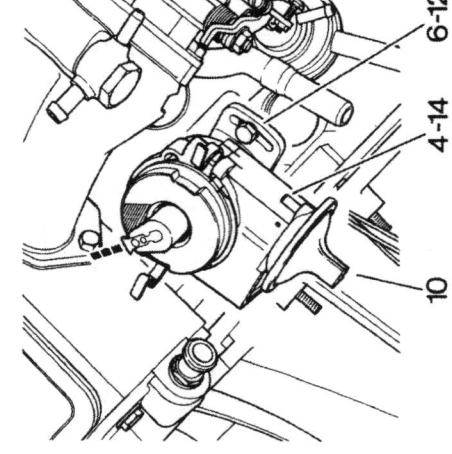

A86 OO9/I

IGNITION DISTRIBUTOR
– LUCAS ELECTRONIC

Overhaul   86.35.26

Dismantling

1 Remove the cover.
2 Pull off the rotor.
3 Remove the plastic anti flash cover.
4 Withdraw the felt pad.
5 Carefully remove two screws, lock washers and washers to release the pick up.
6 Remove two long screws and lock washers.
7 Hold the amplifier module in position. Remove one short screw, lock washer and washer.
8 Distributor with retard unit only:
   Hold the distributor body in one hand and the amplifier module in the other hand. Carefully manoeuvre to unhook the retard unit link from the moving plate pin. This operation will not be visible.
9 Hold the distributor body and amplifier module slighlty apart. Withdraw two clips.
10 Pull out the wire grommet. Remove the amplifier module and pick up joined together by the wires.
11 Distributor with retard unit only:
   Tap out the retard unit pin. Withdraw the retard unit.
12 Using a suitable pair of small circlip pliers remove the circlip.
13 Remove the plain washer.
14 Remove the rubber 'O' ring.
15 Carefully withdraw the timing rotor.
16 Remove two screws. Lift out the base plate.
17 Tap out the drive gear pin. Remove the drive gear and thrust washer. Ensure that the shaft is burr free and withdraw it.

18 Remove the metal distance collar.
19 Remove the control springs, exercising care not to distort the springs.
   NOTE: Do not attempt to dismantle the shaft and mechanism further.

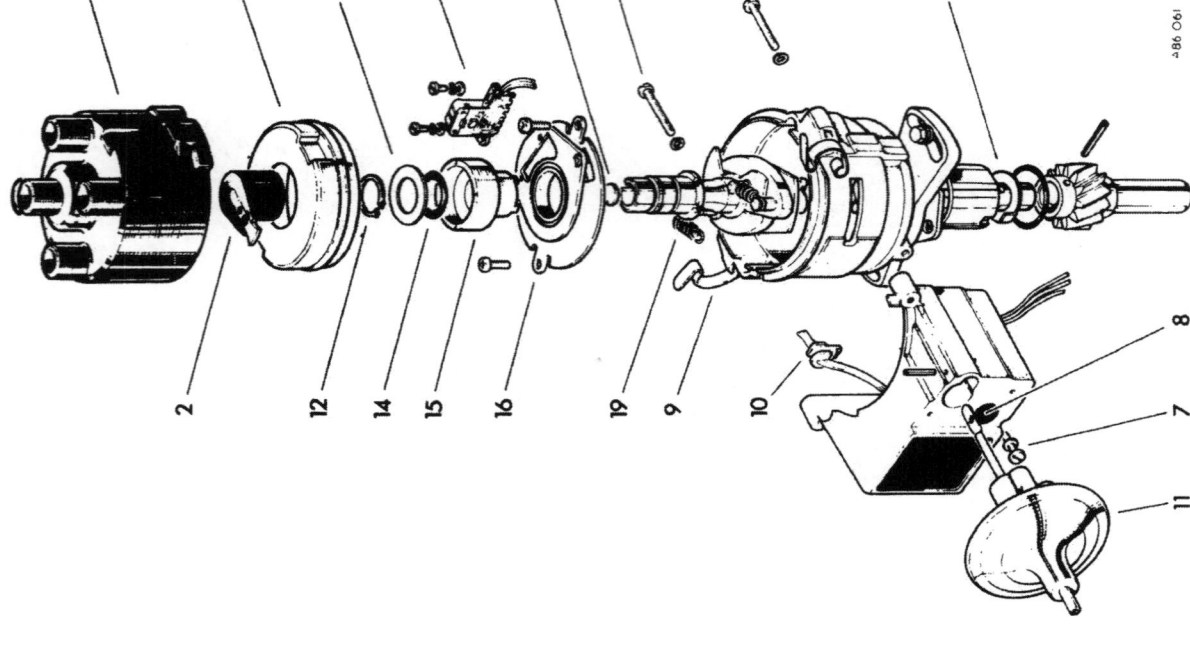

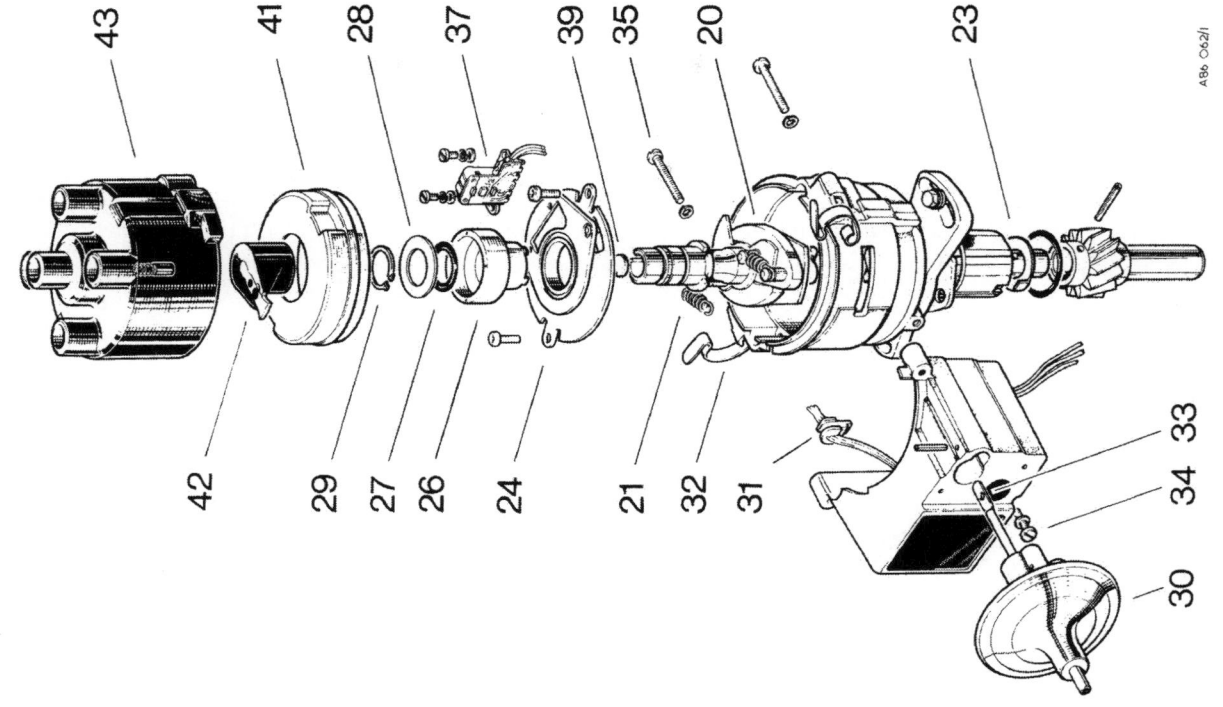

Reassembling

20 Lubricate the weight assembly working surfaces with Rocol 'Moly pad'.

21 Fit the control springs, exercising care not to distort the springs.

22 Fit the metal distance collar.

23 Lubricate the shaft with Rocol 'Moly pad' and insert it into the body. Fit the thrust washer and drive gear. Secure with the drive gear pin.

24 Distributor with retard unit only:
Lubricate the moving plate pin with Rocol 'Moly Pad'. Position the base plate so that the moving plate pin is correctly positioned for the retard unit link. Secure with two screws.

25 Distributor with no retard unit only:
Position the base plate so that the pick-up mounting is away from the grommet cut-out. Secure with two screws.

26 Carefully insert the timing rotor. Ensure that the master projection locates correctly in the master slot.

27 Fit the rubber 'O' ring.

28 Fit the plain washer.

29 Fit the circlip.

30 Distributor with retard unit only:
Insert the retard unit. Secure with the retard unit pin.

31 Hold the distributor body and amplifier module slightly apart. Push in the wire grommet.

32 Insert two clips.

33 Distributor with retard unit only:
Hold the distributor body in one hand and the amplifier module in the other hand. Carefully manouvre and slightly rotate the moving plate to hook the retard unit link to the moving plate pin. This operation will not be visible.

34 Hold the amplifier module in position. Fit one short screw, lock washer and washer finger-tight.

35 Fit two long screws and lock washer finger tight.

36 Ensure that the amplifier module and two wire grommets are correctly seated. Tighten three screws evenly.

37 Position the pick-up. Carefully fit two screws, lock washers and washers finger tight.

38 Adjust the pick-up air gap, see 86.35.31.

39 Insert the felt pad.

40 Lubricate, see 86.35.18.

41 Fit the plastic anti-flash cover with the two recesses positioned adjacent to the clips.

42 Push on the rotor.

43 Fit the cover.

IGNITION COMPONENTS WITH LUCAS—ELECTRONIC SYSTEM

IGNITION DISTRIBUTOR – LUCAS ELECTRONIC

Pick-up air gap — adjust   86.35.31

CAUTION: Do not insert a feeler gauge into the pick-up air gap when the ignition circuit is energized.

1 Isolate the battery.
2 Remove the fresh air duct, see 80.15.31.
3 Remove the cover.
4 Pull off the rotor.
5 Remove the anti-flash cover.
6 If the pick-up air gap is correct a 0.014 to 0.016 in (0.35 to 0.40 mm) feeler gauge will just slide between the contacts.
7 When the pick up air gap is correct instructions 8 to 11 may be ignored.
8 If a correction is required slacken two screws.
9 Move the pick-up about the pivot screw to adjust the gap.
10 Tighten two screws.
11 Check that the correct gap has been maintained.
CAUTION: Ensure that this operation is performed as the gap may change substantially when tightening the screws.

0·014 to 0·016 in
0·35 to 0·40mm

8–10

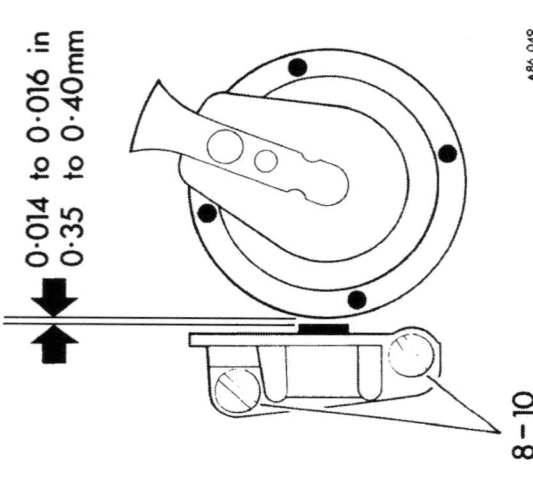

A86 049

BALLAST RESISTOR WIRE

Data

Resistance	1.3 to 1.5 ohm
Wire length	63 in (1600 mm)
Wire colour code	Pink/white

Description

This system is designed to assist engine starting under adverse conditions. A ballast resistor wire built into the harness is electrically positioned in series in the normal supply to the ignition coil. This wire causes a voltage drop in the circuit so that the 12 volt supply from the ignition switch may be employed to power the nominally rated 6 volt ignition coil.

During engine start the resistor is by-passed and the battery voltage (reduced from 12 volt by the starter motor load) is applied to the coil direct from the starter motor relay. This slight voltage overload provides an increased high tension voltage at the spark plugs.

continued

IGNITION COIL

Data

Manufacturer	Lucas
Type	15C6
Lucas part number	45266
Triumph part number	UKC 2982

Primary winding resistance .... 1.3 to 1.45 ohm

IGNITION COIL

Remove and refit   86.35.32

Removing

1 Drive the vehicle onto a ramp.
2 Raise the ramp.
3 Locate the ignition coil mounted in the engine bay low down on the right-hand side of the bulkhead as shown.
4 Pull up the protective cover.
5 Pull off the high tension lead.
6 Disconnect two Lucar connectors.
7 Remove two nuts, spring washers and washers.
8 Remove the drive resistor lug from the body stud.
9 Remove the ignition coil from two body studs.

Refitting

10 Reverse 1 to 9.

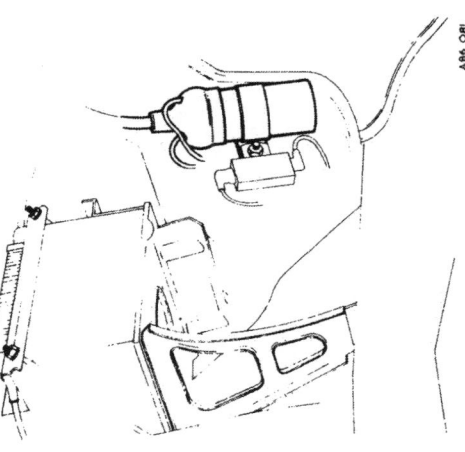

A86 081

DRIVE RESISTOR

Data

Manufacturer	Lucas
Lucas part number	54427556
Triumph part number	UKC 3908

Resistance .... 10 ± 5% ohm

Description

This unit may be considered as a detached component of the ignition distributor amplifier. Its function is associated with the transistors in the amplifier. It is independently mounted due to its size and heat dissipating requirements.

DRIVE RESISTOR

Remove and refit   86.35.37

Removing

1 Drive the vehicle onto a ramp.
2 Raise the ramp.
3 Locate the drive resistor mounted in the engine bay low down on the right hand side of the bulkhead as shown.
4 Disconnect two Lucar connectors.
5 Remove single nut, spring washer and washer.
6 Remove the drive resistor from the body stud.

Refitting

7 Reverse 1 to 6. The Lucar connectors may be fitted either way round.

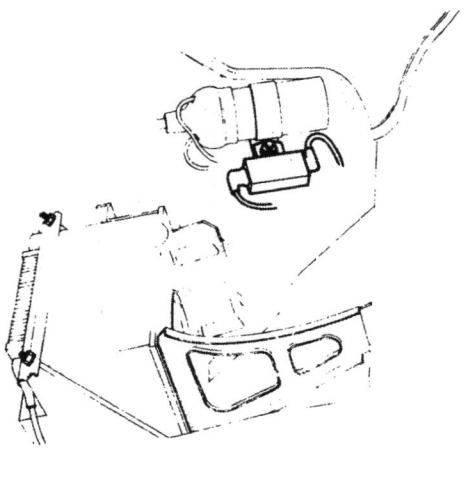

A86 082

IGNITION DISTRIBUTOR — DELCO REMY ELECTRONIC — Triumph Part No. PKC 1333

Data

Manufacturer	Delco Remy
Series	D 302
Delco Remy part number	9977215
Triumph part number	PKC 1333
System	Electronic — current controlled ignition system
Polarity	Negative earth only
Pulse generator	Reluctor
Air gap	Non-adjustable
Rotation — viewed on rotor	Anti-clockwise
Firing angle	90 ± 1 degree

Centrifugal advance

Distributor rev/min	Degrees distributor advance		Crankshaft rev/min	Degrees crankshaft advance	
	Minimum	Maximum		Minimum	Maximum
400	Nil	Nil	800	Nil	Nil
500	0	1.5	1000	0	3.0
600	0.7	3.4	1200	1.4	6.8
700	2.5	5.3	1400	5.0	10.6
800	3.4	5.5	1600	6.8	11.0
1000	4.6	6.6	2000	9.2	13.2
1200	5.7	7.8	2400	11.4	15.6
1400	6.8	8.9	2800	13.6	17.8
1500	7.4	9.5	3000	14.8	19.0
1800	9.5	Max.	3600	19.0	Max.

Retard unit

Millimetres of mercury vacuum	Degrees distributor retard		Degrees crankshaft retard	
	Minimum	Maximum	Minimum	Maximum
75	Nil	Nil	Nil	Nil
76	0	7.0	0	14.0
150	0	7.0	0	14.0
280	5.0	7.0	10.0	14.0
380	5.0	7.0	10.0	14.0

IGNITION DISTRIBUTOR — DELCO REMY ELECTRONIC — Triumph Part No. RKC 3773

Data

Manufacturer	Delco Remy
Series	D 302
Delco Remy part number	9977120
Triumph part number	RKC 3773
System	Electronic — current controlled ignition system
Polarity	Negative earth only
Pulse generator	Reluctor
Air gap	Non-adjustable
Rotation — viewed on rotor	Anti-clockwise
Firing angle	90 ± 1 degree

Centrifugal advance

Distributor rev/min	Degrees distributor advance		Crankshaft rev/min	Degrees crankshaft advance	
	Minimum	Maximum		Minimum	Maximum
400	Nil	Nil	800	Nil	Nil
500	0	1.3	1000	0	2.6
600	0.3	2.7	1200	0.6	5.4
700	1.7	4.1	1400	3.4	8.2
800	3.0	5.4	1600	6.0	10.8
900	4.4	6.8	1800	8.8	13.6
1000	5.7	8.2	2000	11.4	16.4
1100	7.1	9.5	2200	14.2	19.0
1200	8.5	10.9	2400	17.0	21.8
1250	9.2	11.6	2500	18.4	23.2
1600	11.6	Max.	3200	23.2	Max.

Retard unit

Millimetres of mercury vacuum	Degrees distributor retard		Degrees crankshaft retard	
	Minimum	Maximum	Minimum	Maximum
76	Nil	Nil	Nil	Nil
152	0	3.5	0	7.0
203	2.5	6.0	5.0	12.0
254	5.0	7.0	10.0	14.0
305	5.0	7.0	10.0	14.0
508	7.0	Max.	14.0	Max.

IGNITION DISTRIBUTOR — DELCO REMY ELECTRONIC — Triumph Part No. RKC 4722

Data

Manufacturer	Delco Remy
Series	D 302
Delco Remy part number	9977254
Triumph part number	RKC 4722
System	Electronic — current controlled ignition system
Polarity	Negative earth only
Pulse generator	Reluctor
Air gap	Non-adjustable
Rotation — viewed on rotor	Anti-clockwise
Firing angle	90 ± 1 degree

Centrifugal advance

Distributor rev/min	Degrees distributor advance		Crankshaft rev/min	Degrees crankshaft advance	
	Minimum	Maximum		Minimum	Maximum
300	Nil	Nil	600	Nil	Nil
400	0	0.4	800	0	0.8
500	0	1.2	1000	0	2.4
600	0	2.0	1200	0	4.0
700	0.6	2.8	1400	1.2	5.6
800	1.4	3.6	1600	2.8	7.2
900	2.2	4.4	1800	4.4	8.8
1000	3.0	5.2	2000	6.0	10.4
1200	4.0	6.0	2400	8.0	12.0
1400	4.8	6.9	2800	9.6	13.8
1600	5.7	7.8	3200	11.4	15.6
1800	6.6	8.7	3600	13.2	17.4
2000	7.5	9.6	4000	15.0	19.2
2400	9.6	Max.	4800	19.2	Max.

Retard unit

Millimetres of mercury vacuum	Degrees distributor retard		Degrees crankshaft retard	
	Minimum	Maximum	Minimum	Maximum
76	Nil	Nil	Nil	Nil
152	0	3.5	0	7.0
203	2.5	6.0	5.0	12.0
254	5.0	7.0	10.0	14.0
305	5.0	7.0	10.0	14.0
508	7.0	Max.	14.0	Max.

IGNITION DISTRIBUTOR —
DELCO REMY ELECTRONIC

Description   **86.35.00**

The Delco Remy electronic—current controlled ignition system consists of two units. A
pulse generator ignition distributor and an
ignition coil and electronic module assembly.

Distributor—an angle transducer consisting of
a timing rotor, static component, permanent
magnet and winding supply timing signal
pulses to the electronic module assembly. A
conventional AC Delco body, mechanical centrifugal advance and vacuum retard unit are
retained.

Retard unit—the static permanent magnet and
winding may be rotated through a limited
angle by the vacuum retard unit. The ignition
timing is thus modified by amending the relationship between the timing rotor and the static
assembly.

1   High tension rotor arm

2   Centrifugal advance mechanism

3   Angle transducer — timing rotor

4   — static component

5   — permanent magnet

6   — winding

7   Body

8   Drive gear

9   Retard unit

10 Plug to electronic module assembly

2379

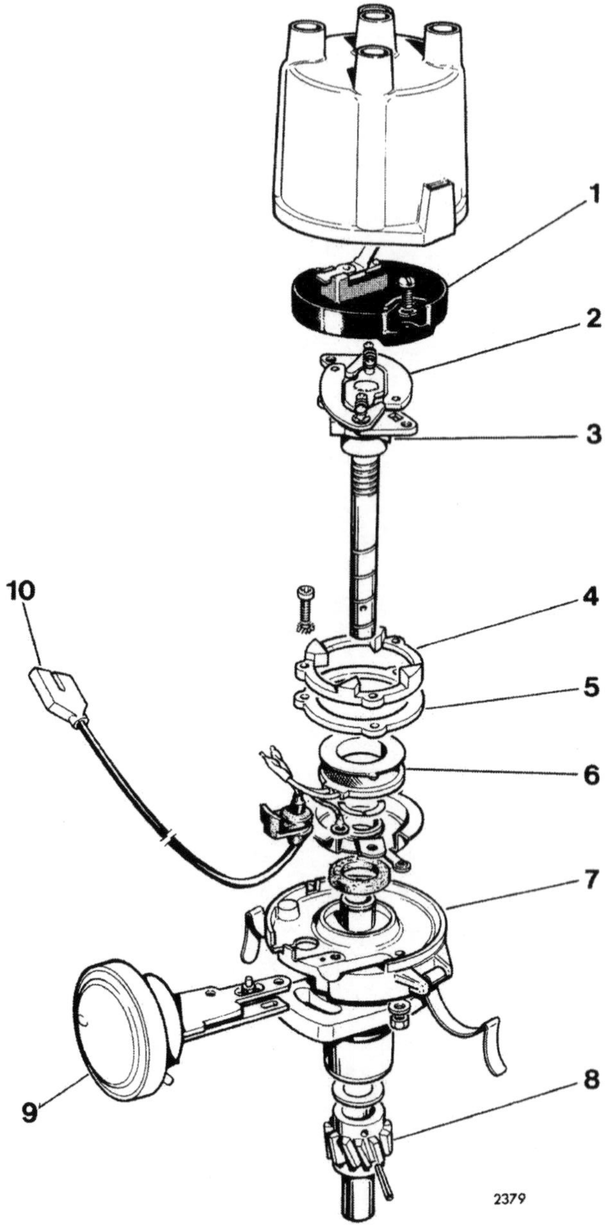

IGNITION COMPONENTS WITH
DELCO REMY—ELECTRONIC SYSTEM

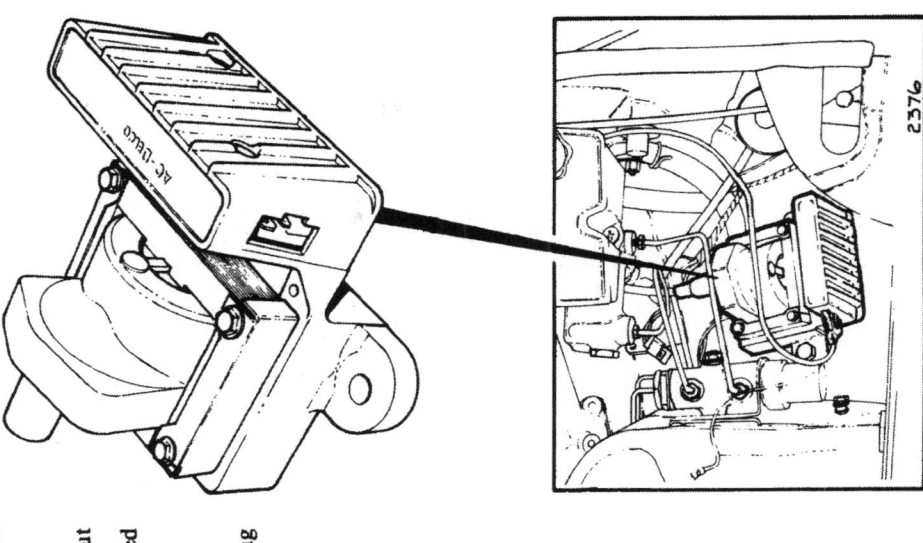

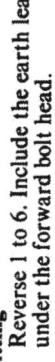

IGNITION COIL AND ELECTRONIC MODULE ASSEMBLY

Data

Manufacturer	AC Delco — France
AC Delco part number	3474214
Triumph part number	PKC 0478
System	Electronic — current controlled ignition system
Polarity	Negative earth only
Primary winding:	
Maximum current controlled at	5.5 amp
Resistance	0.75 ohm

Description

The unit consists of an ignition coil winding and an electronic module assembly mounted on a light alloy die casting.

The electronic module assembly receives timing pulses from the ignition distributor. The module amplifies the signal to control the on-off switching of a power transistor.

The 'off' condition of the power transistor collapses the ignition coil primary winding current. A spark occurs at the appropriate spark plug in the conventional manner.

A feature is that the module contains a current limiting circuit, the maximum current being controlled at 5.5 amp. The ignition coil primary winding is not responsible for current control and can therefore be of low resistance — 0.75 ohm.

This design allows the ignition coil to operate efficiently with a high kilovolt output at all engine speeds.

IGNITION COIL AND ELECTRONIC MODULE ASSEMBLY

Remove and refit   86.35.37

Removing
1 Depress the claw and pull off the pulse lead plug.
2 Pull off the high tension lead.
3 Disconnect the harness plug.
4 Remove the front bolt assembly — the nut is positioned under the front wing.
5 Remove the rear bolt — a cage nut is fitted to the mounting bracket.
6 Remove the unit from the vehicle.

Refitting
7 Reverse 1 to 6. Include the earth lead tag under the forward bolt head.

HEADLAMP

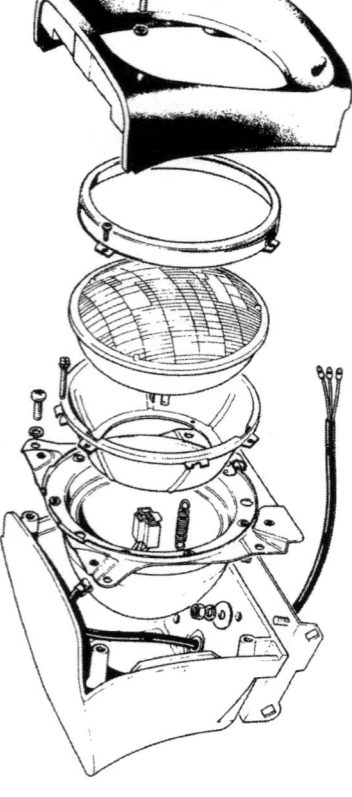

A86 006

A86 045

Data

Actuator

Manufacturer	Lucas
Type	15W
Lucas part number	75857
Triumph part number	RKC 0822
Polarity	Negative earth only
Running current – after 60 seconds from cold with link rod disconnected from crank	
Running speed – crank after 60 seconds from cold with link rod disconnected from crank	1.5 amp.
Armature end-float	46 to 52 rev/min
Brush length – new	0.002 to 0.008 in (0.05 to 0.20 mm)
renew if less than	0.250 in (6.35 mm)
	0.187 in (4.75 mm)
Brush spring pressure – when compressed so brush bottom is aligned with brush-box slot end	5 to 7 ozf (140 to 200 gf)

Description   86.40.00

A base bracket is bolted rigidly to the vehicle body. A substantial light alloy member is hinged to the base bracket. The light alloy member is traversed from one position to the other by an electric actuator. Mounted to the light alloy member is a 'body colour' box casting which contains the headlamp.

Actuator – this consists of a permanent magnet motor and a gearbox unit which drives a single direction rotating crank arm. The gearbox unit includes a limit switch.

Action – rotation of the actuator crank arm is converted to an up and down motion of the light alloy member by a link rod. The weight of the assembly is counter-balanced by a spring.

Box casting – with the headlamp in the close position the top surface of the box casting provides the visible panel which follows the vehicle body contours. In the open position the box casting forms the visible fairing. The headlamp is a conventional Lucas seven inch housing and light unit assembly.

Hand knob – the actuator is provided with a hand knob. This may be used to open or close a headlamp during service or if an actuator should fail. Rotate only in the direction shown.

WARNING: Exercise care when using the hand knob. If the battery is not isolated slight rotation of the hand knob may initiate a full cycle movement. Keep all limbs clear of the mechanism to avoid personal injury.

Design – to assist manufacture and service the base bracket, light alloy member, actuator and link rod assembly is not handed. To follow the vehicle body contours the box casting is handed.

Service – special precautions must be taken to avoid scratching the visible paint surfaces of the box casting. If the headlamp assembly is removed from the vehicle onto a bench, the bench should be covered with a thick protective cloth.

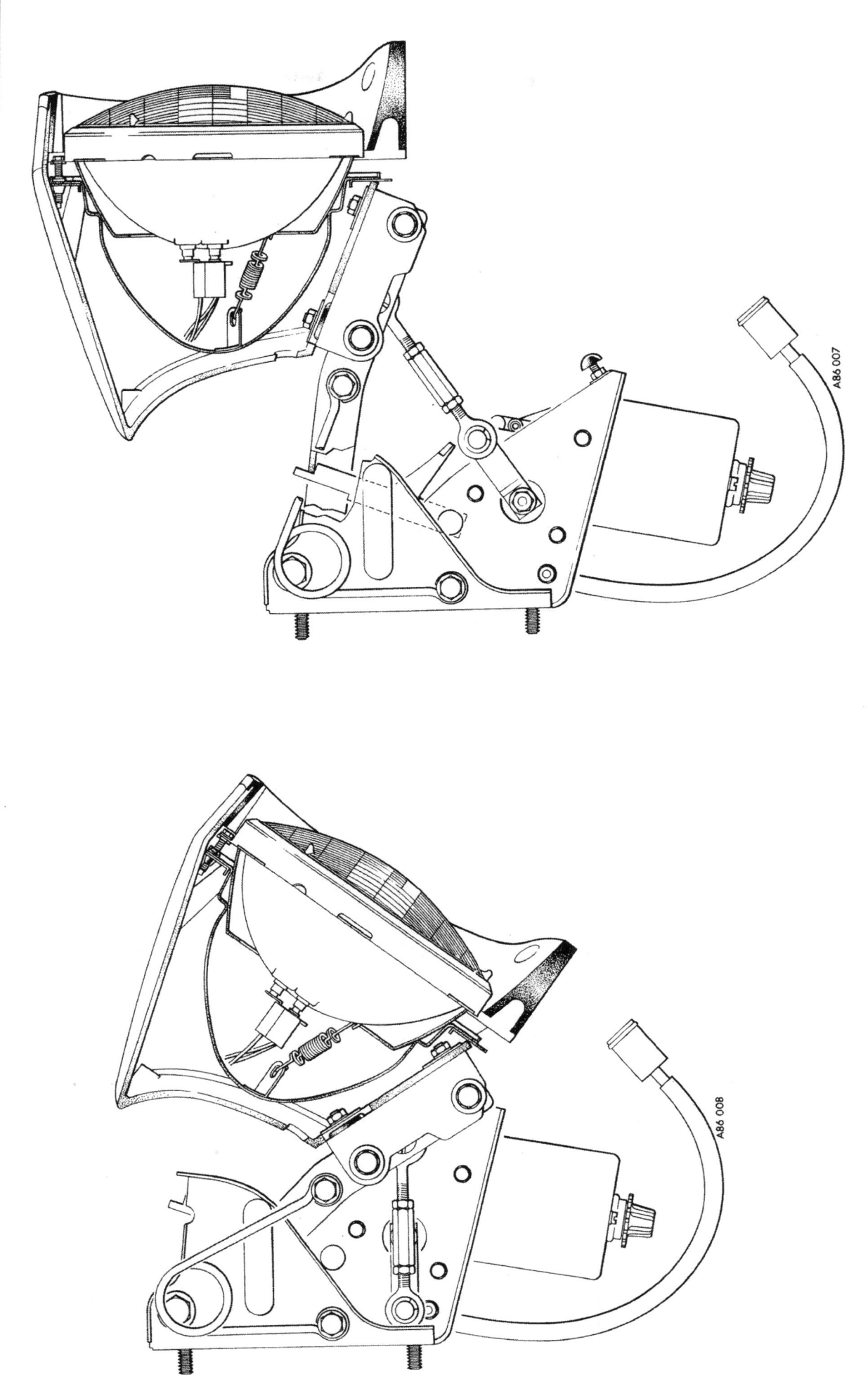

A86 007

A86 008

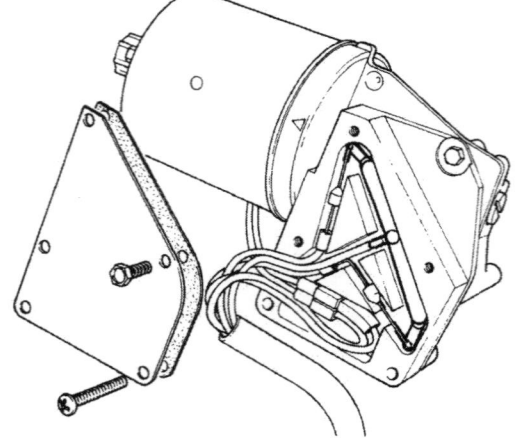

A86 055

Limit switch

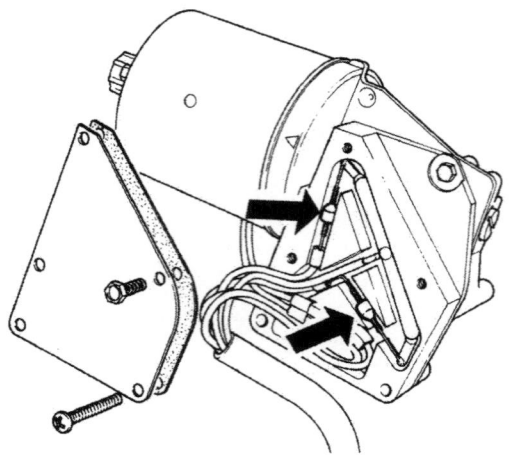

A86 054

Diodes

HEADLAMP
ELECTRICAL CIRCUIT
— U.K. and European

The circuit may be considered in two sections, the control circuit and the motor power circuit.

Control circuit — to manage the two run/stop relays for three operations.

Normal up selection — move the master light switch to headlamps. Supply to main/dip/flash switch for main or dip beam. Also supply via delay unit — terminal 2, diode D4 and terminal 1 to blue/purple up line. Circuit continues across each limit switch to appropriate run/stop relay winding. When a headlamp reaches the up position the circuit is broken by the limit switch.

Normal down selection — move the master light switch to parking lamps or off. Supply via normally closed contacts of flash relay to blue/brown down line. Circuit continues across each limit switch to appropriate run/stop relay winding. When a headlamp reaches the down position the circuit is broken by the limit switch.

Head flash selection — move the main/dip flash switch to head flash. Supply to main beams. Also signal on blue/white wire to delay unit — terminal 6 — to turn on transistor. Delay unit capacitor C1 will charge for later use. Flash relay winding will now pull in to energize blue/purple up line. Transistor base circuit earth and flash relay winding earth is via terminal 2, dip beam contacts — always closed when head flash is selected — and across dip beam to earth. When the switch is released capacitor C1 will discharge slowly through the transistor base circuit to hold the condition for approximately 4 seconds. This prevents excessive full cycle movements of the headlamps if the driver should flash the headlamps more than once.

Motor power circuit — supply through single circuit breaker. Each motor runs in a single direction only. An up selection causes the crank arm to rotate through 216 degrees. A down selection causes the crank arm to rotate through 144 degrees. When the control circuit de-energizes a relay the contacts drop to connect the motor to earth. This action causes regenerative braking of the armature which maintains consistent stopping of the crank arm.

Circuit breaker — if the motion of either headlamp is obstructed the motor will draw an excess current. This condition will be tolerated for a short time to allow the operational headlamp to complete its movement. A single Otter current/heat sensitive circuit breaker will then actuate to protect the motor power circuit. The circuit breaker is self resetting and has a quick recovery time.

Diodes — two diodes included in each limit switch prevent electrical interaction between the left-hand and right-hand side control circuits. During a motor run both the 'open stop' and the 'close stop' contacts are made. If the headlamp movements should get slightly out of phase—and the diodes were not included—the action would not be terminated. Also a selection to parking lamps or off — if the diodes were not included — would not extinguish the light units until both headlamps close.

1 Master light switch
2 Main/dip/flash switch
3 Main beam
4 Dip beam
5 L.H. actuator – limit switch
6 R.H. actuator – limit switch
7 L.H. run/stop relay
8 R.H. run/stop relay
9 Circuit reaker
10 L.H. actuator – motor
11 R.H. actuator – motor
12 Delay unit
13 Flash relay

Colour code

B	Black
B/LG	Black/light green
G	Green
N	Brown
NK	Brown/pink
N/LG	Brown/light green
NU	Brown/blue
P	Purple
R	Red
R/LG	Red/light green
U	Blue
UB	Blue/black
UG	Blue/green
UK	Blue/pink
U/LG	Blue/light gree
UN	Blue/brown
UO	Blue/orange
UP	Blue/purple
UR	Blue/red
US	Blue/slate
UW	Blue/white

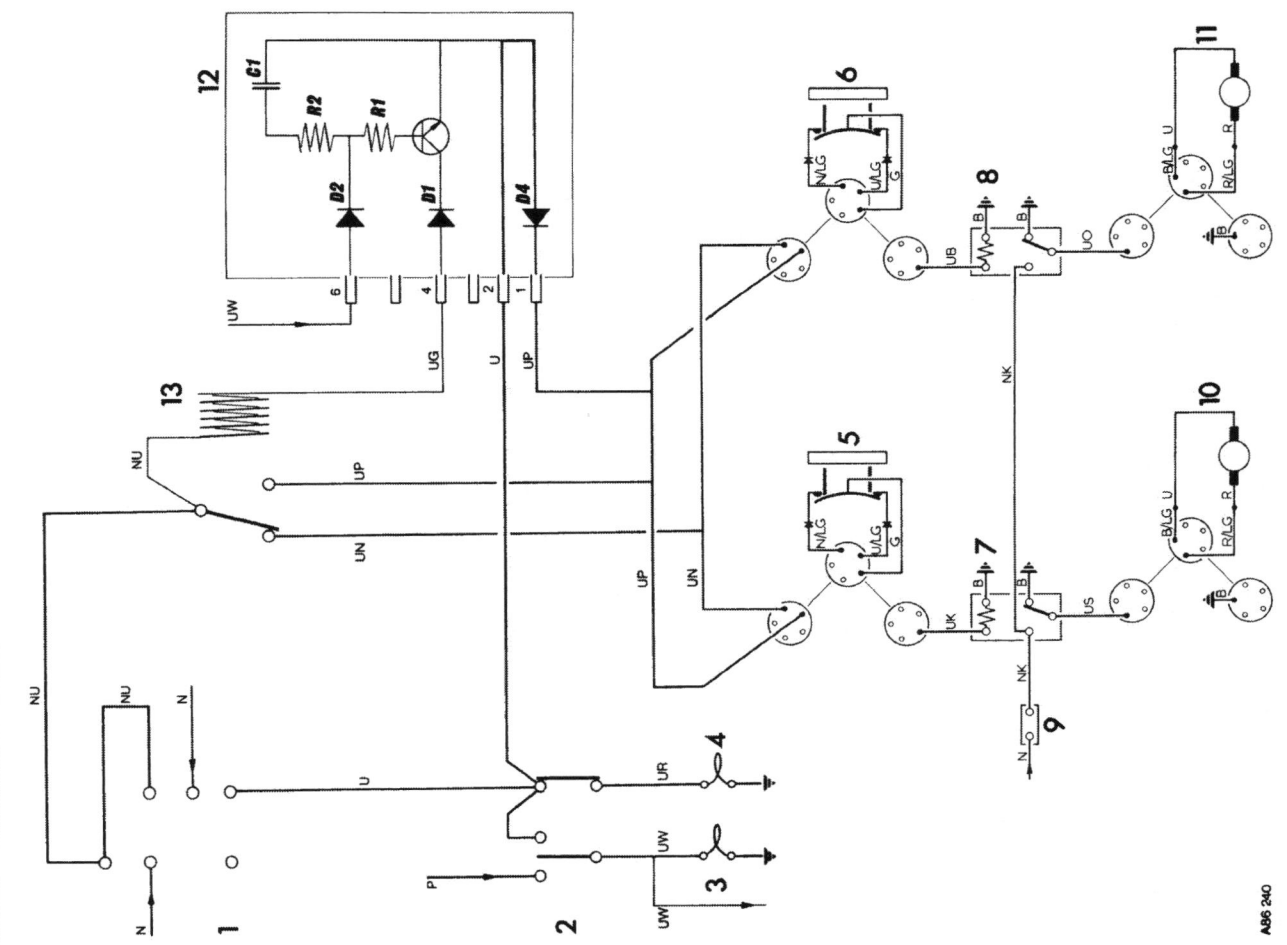

A86 240

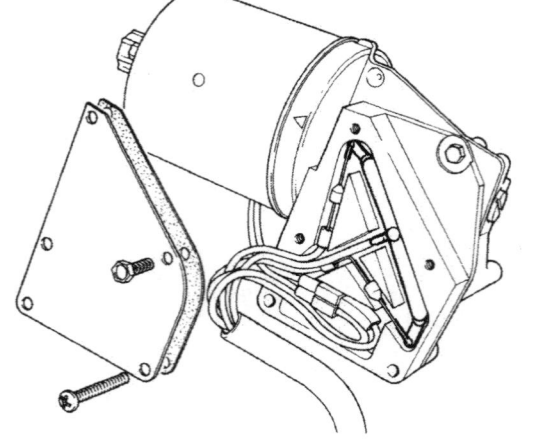

A86 055

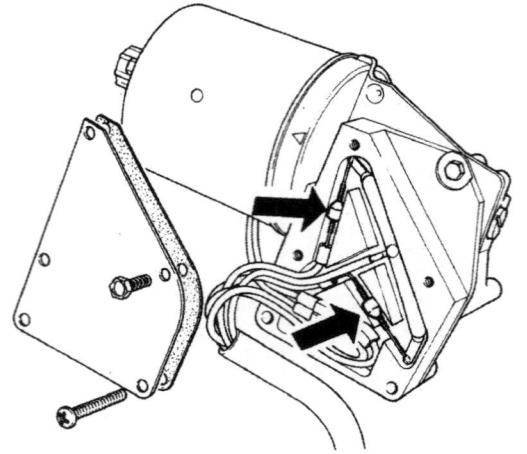

Limit switch

A86 054

Diodes

HEADLAMP ELECTRICAL CIRCUIT – U.S.A.

The circuit may be considered in two sections, the control circuit and the motor power circuit.

Control circuit – to manage the two run/stop relays for two operations.

Normal up selection – move the master light switch to headlamps. Supply to main/dip switch for main or dip beam. Also supply to blue up line. Circuit continues across each limit switch to appropriate run/stop relay winding. When a headlamp reaches the up position the circuit is broken by the limit switch.

Normal down selection – move the master light switch to parking lamps or off. Supply to blue/brown down line. Circuit continues across each limit switch to appropriate run/stop relay winding. When a headlamp reaches the down position the circuit is broken by the limit switch.

Motor power circuit – supply through single circuit breaker. Each motor runs in a single direction only. An up selection causes the crank arm to rotate through 216 degrees. A down selection causes the crank arm to rotate through 144 degrees. When the control circuit de-energizes a relay the contacts drop to connect the motor to earth. This action causes regenerative braking of the armature which maintains consistent stopping of the crankarm.

Circuit breaker – if the motion of either headlamp is obstructed the motor will draw an excess current. This condition will be tolerated for a short time to allow the operational headlamp to complete its movement. A single Otter current/heat-sensitive circuit breaker will then actuate to protect both left-hand and right-hand side motor power circuits. The circuit breaker is self resetting and has a quick recovery time.

Diodes – two diodes included in each limit switch prevent electrical interaction between the left-hand and right-hand side control circuits. During a motor run both the 'open stop' and the 'close stop' contacts are made. If the headlamp movement should get slightly out of phase – and the diodes were not included – the action would not be terminated. Also a selection to side or off – if the diodes were not included – would not extinguish the light units until both headlamps close.

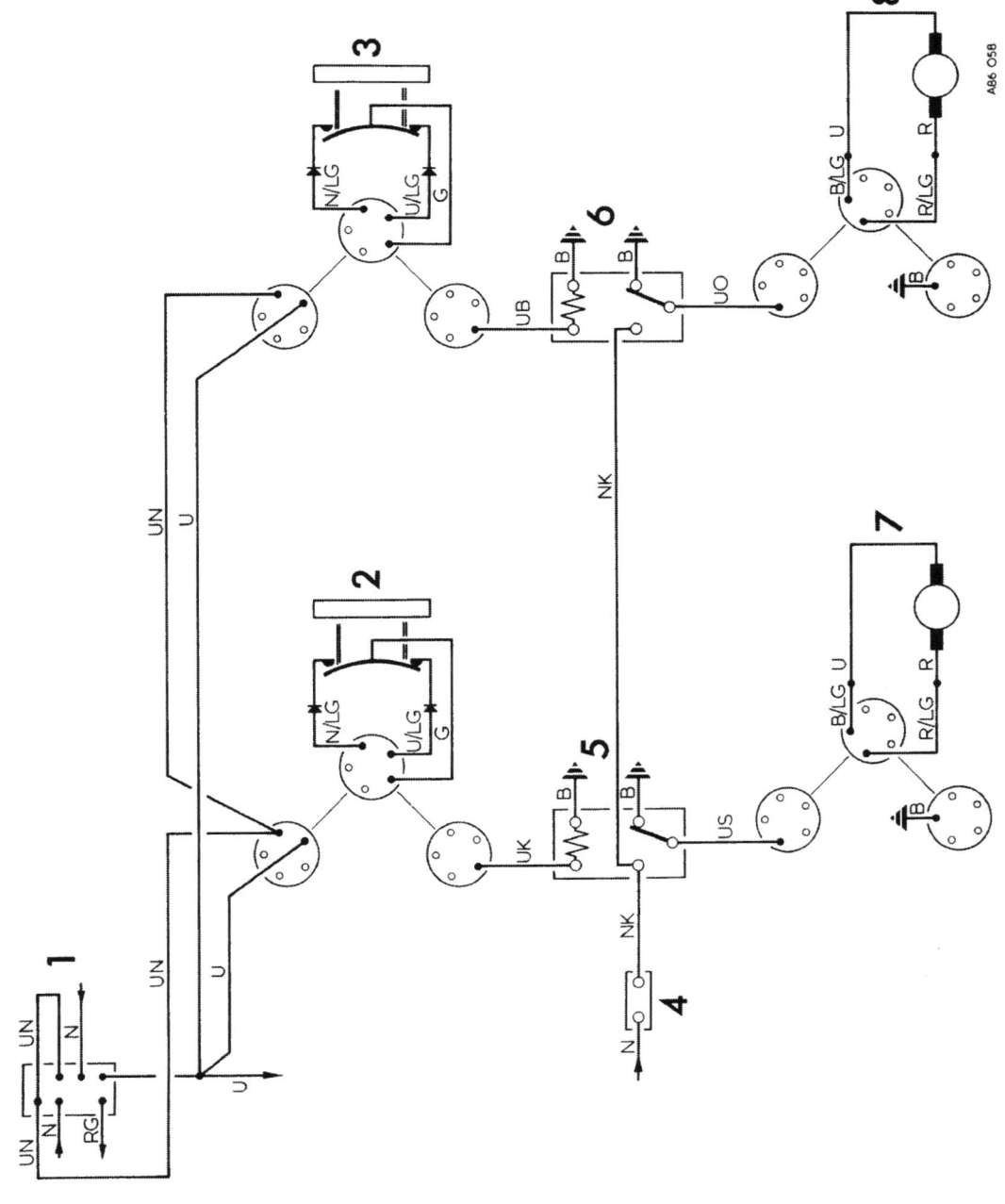

1   Master light switch
2   L.H. actuator – limit switch
3   R.H. actuator – limit switch
4   Circuit breaker
5   L.H. run/stop relay
6   R.H. run/stop relay
7   L.H. actuator – motor
8   R.H. actuator – motor

Colour code

B	Black
B/LG	Black/light green
G	Green
N	Brown
NK	Brown/pink
N/LG	Brown/light green
R	Red
RG	Red/green
R/LG	Red/light green
U	Blue
UB	Blue/black
UK	Blue/pink
U/LG	Blue/light green
UN	Blue/brown
UO	Blue/orange
US	Blue/slate

A86 O58

HEADLAMP RUBBER BEZEL

Remove and refit   86.40.01

Removing

1 Select the master light switch to raise the headlamps.
2 Isolate the battery to extinguish the headlamps.
3 Unscrew four Pozidriv screws and lock washers.
4 Pull the rubber bezel from the box casting.
5 Manoeuvre the rubber bezel downwards into the headlamp cavity. If necessary manoeuvre further downwards to remove from the vehicle. The rubber bezel may be distorted slightly to facilitate this operation.
6 Collect up four Pozidriv screws and lock washers.

Refitting

7 Reverse 1 to 5.

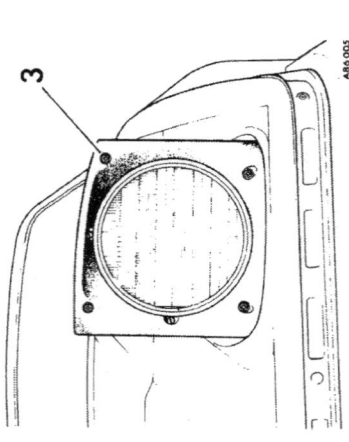

A86 005

HEADLAMP ASSEMBLY

Remove and refit   86.40.02

Removing

1 Remove the rubber bezel, see 86.40.01.
2 To assist refitting, note the actuator harness and headlamp wire runs relative to the components.
3 Disconnect the actuator harness plug.
4 Disconnect three headlamp snap connectors.
5 Support the weight of the headlamp assembly. Remove four nuts, lock washers and washers. Carefully manoeuvre the headlamp assembly upwards through the body aperture.

Refitting

6 Carefully manoeuvre the headlamp assembly downwards through the body aperture. Fit four washers, lock washers and nuts.
7 Connect three headlamp snap connectors. Ensure that the wire runs are as noted at operation 2 above. Connect the wires as follows:
   Blue/red wire to blue/red wire
   Blue/white wire to blue/white wire
   Black wire to black wire.
8 Connect the actuator harness plug. Ensure that the harness run is as noted at operation 2 above.
9 Inspect the actuator harness and headlamp wire runs to ensure that no foul occurs while using the actuator manual thumb screw to traverse the mechanism over its full travel.
10 Adjust the headlamp assembly, see 86.40.16.
11 Refit the rubber bezel, see 86.40.01.

A86 074

HEADLAMP LIGHT UNIT

Remove and refit   86.40.09

Removing

1 Remove the rubber bezel, see 86.40.01.
2 Remove three screws to release the retaining rim and light unit.
3 Pull the connector block from the light unit.

Refitting

4 Reverse 1 to 3.

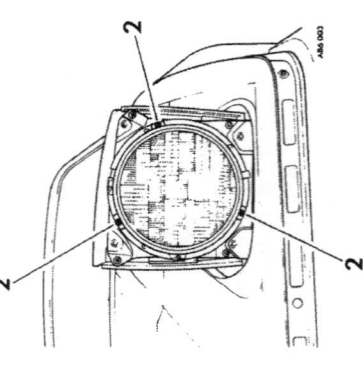

A86 003

HEADLAMP LINK ROD

Remove and refit   86.40.12

The upper end of the link rod contains a rubber bush. This provides a measure of compliance to the link rod alignment and to the primary and secondary adjustments.

After an extended period of service wear of the upper rubber bush and the lower Oilite bush may dictate renewal of the link rod.

Removing

1 Remove the headlamp assembly, see 86.40.02.
2 Perform 86.40.15 operations 2 to 11.

Refitting

3 Perform 86.40.15 operations 39 to 49.
4 Refit the headlamp assembly, see 86.40.02.

HEADLAMP ACTUATOR

Remove and refit   86.40.13

Removing

1 Remove the headlamp assembly, see 86.40.02.
2 Safely retain the spring by rotating the actuator manual thumb screw to position the light alloy member against the metal up stop on the base bracket.
3 Remove the circlip and washer.
4 Remove the nut, lock washer, washer and screw. Remove the harness 'P' clip.
5 Remove three screws and lock washers.
6 Manoeuvre the link rod from the bush.
7 Remove the bush from the crank arm.
8 Manoeuvre the crank arm through the aperture.

Refitting

9 Manoeuvre the crank arm through the aperture.
10 Lubricate the bush working surfaces with engine oil.
11 Fit the bush to the crank arm.
12 Position the link rod ends in the turnbuckle so that an equal number of threads are visible at each end.
13 Manoeuvre the link rod to the bush. It may be necessary to rotate the manual thumb screw to position the crank arm.
14 Position the actuator. It may be necessary to rotate the manual thumb screw to position the crank arm. Ensure that the actuator harness is looped up between the actuator and the base bracket. Secure with three screws and lock washers.
15 Position the harness 'P' clip. Secure with the screw, washer, lock washer and nut.
16 Fit the washer and circlip.
17 With the headlamp assembly removed from the vehicle perform the primary adjustment and the secondary adjustment, see 86.40.16.
18 Refit the headlamp assembly, see 86.40.02.

HEADLAMP ACTUATOR

Overhaul   86.40.14

CAUTION: The actuator operates in a hostile environment. After overhaul or disturbing any joint the unit must be sealed as detailed in operation 33.

Dismantling

1 Remove three hexagon screws and two Pozidriv screws. Lift off the cover and gasket.
2 Disconnect two Lucar connectors.
3 Remove one hexagon screw. Lift off the limit switch and harness.
4 Remove the nut. Withdraw the crank arm and washer.
5 Ensure that the shaft is burr-free and withdraw it. Remove the dished washer.
6 Using a large screwdriver blade carefully prise the hand knob from the armature shaft.
7 Remove the thrust screw or the thrust screw and locknut as fitted.
8 Remove the through bolts.
9 Carefully withdraw the cover and armature about 0.2 in (5 mm). Continue withdrawal, allowing the brushes to drop clear of the commutator. Ensure that the two brushes are not contaminated with grease.
10 Pull the armature from the cover against the action of the permanent magnet.
11 Remove two thrust washers.
NOTE: These may be on the armature shaft or in the cover bearing recess.
12 Remove three screws to release the brush assembly. Break the wire slot seal. Lift the assembly from the recess.

continued

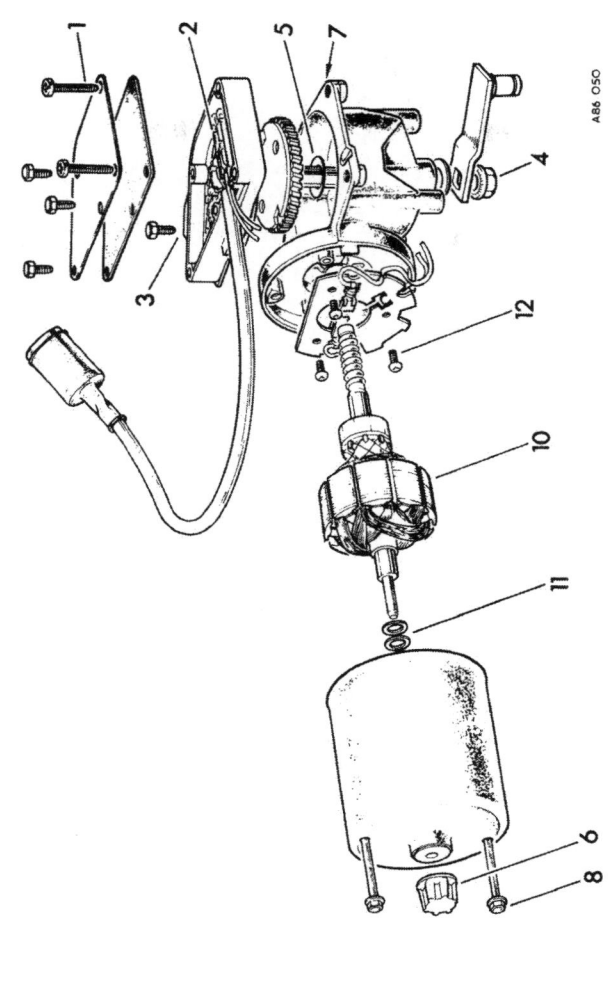

A86 050

Reassembling

NOTE: The following lubricants are required during assembly:

Molybdenum di-sulphide oil.
Shell Turbo 41 oil.
Ragosine Listate grease.

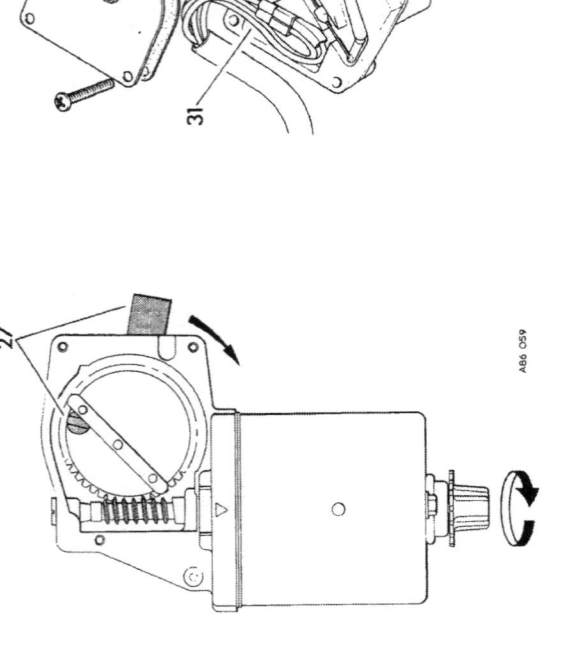

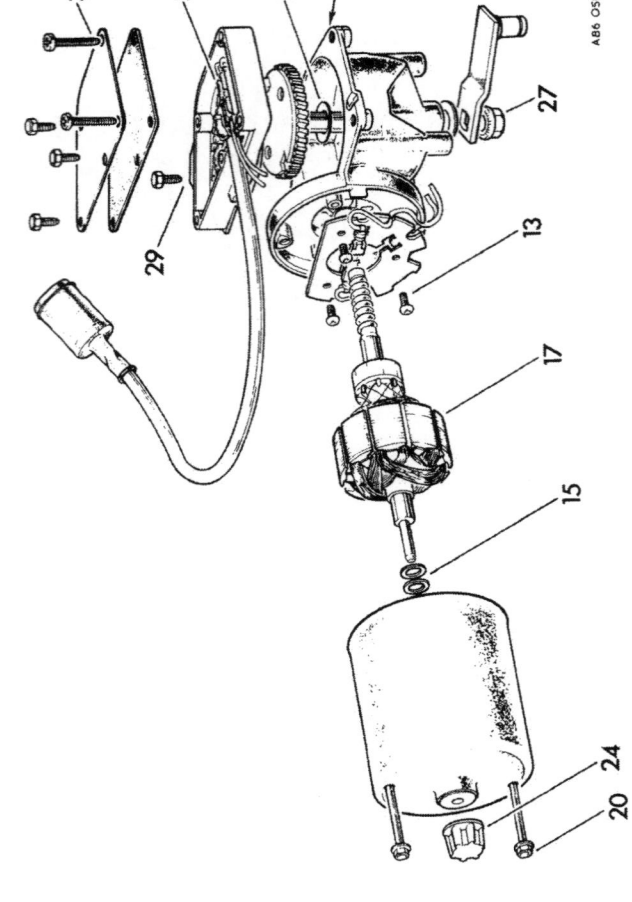

13 Position the brush assembly. Insert the wires in the slot. Secure with three screws.

14 Lubricate two thrust washers with Molybdenum di-sulphide oil.

15 Fit two thrust washers into the cover bearing recess.

16 Lubricate the cover bearing with Shell Turbo 41 oil.

17 Position the armature to the cover against the action of the permanent magnet. Ensure that the two thrust washers remain in position during this operation.

18 Lubricate the self-aligning bearing with Shell Turbo 41 oil.

19 Carefully insert the armature shaft through the bearing. Ensure that the brushes are not contaminated with lubricant. Push the two brushes back to clear the commutator.

20 Seat the cover against the gearbox. Turn the cover to align the marks shown. Fit the through-bolts.

21 Fit the thrust screw or the thrust screw and locknut as fitted.

22 If a non-adjustable thrust screw is fitted check the armature end-float as follows:
Position a feeler gauge between the armature shaft and the thrust screw. Push the armature towards the cover. End-float should be 0.002 to 0.008 in. In the unlikely event of adjustment being required end-float may be increased by fitting shim washer/washers under the thrust screw head or reduced by mounting the thrust screw in a lathe and removing metal from the underside of the head.

23 If an adjustable thrust screw and locknut is fitted adjust the armature end-float as follows:
Slacken the locknut. Screw the thrust screw in until resistance is felt. Screw the thrust screw out a quarter of a turn – maintain in this position and tighten the locknut.

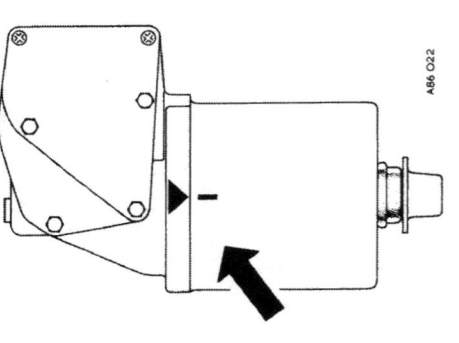

24 Push the hand knob onto the armature shaft.

25 Lubricate the final gear bushes with Shell Turbo 41 oil.

26 Fit the dished washer with its concave surface facing the final gear. Insert the shaft.

27 Fit the washer. Fit the crank arm. Ensure that the relationship of the crank arm to the final gear cam is as shown. Secure with the nut.

28 Lubricate the final gear cam with Ragosine Listate grease.

29 Position the limit switch and harness. Secure with one hexagon screw.

30 Connect two Lucar connectors as follows:
Red/light green wire to red wire.
Black/light green wire to blue wire.

31 Pack the wires into the limit switch recesses as shown.

32 Position the gasket and cover. Secure with three hexagon screws and two Pozidriv screws.

33 Seal the exterior of the unit by applying a rubberised sealing compound such as vehicle body underseal. Special attention must be given to disturbed joints and the wire slot seal.

HEADLAMP ASSEMBLY

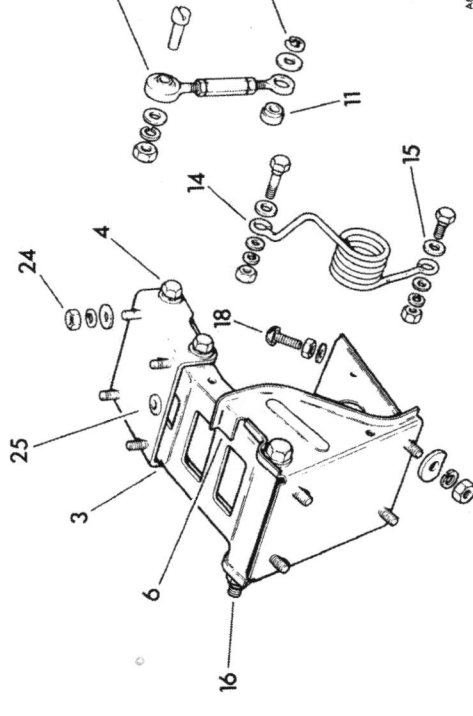

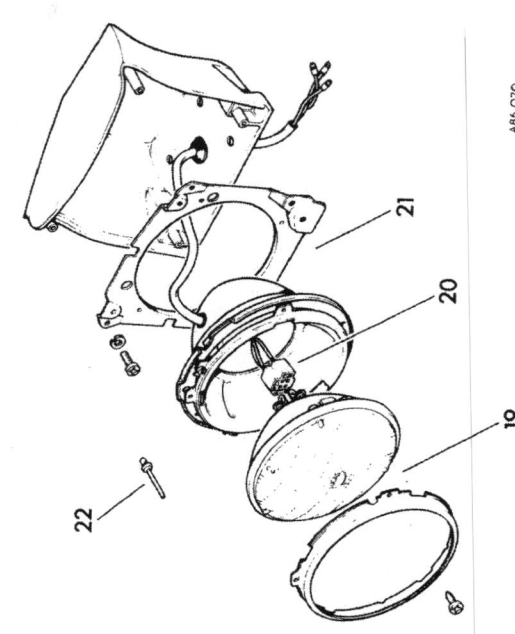

Overhaul 86.40.15

Dismantling

1 Remove the headlamp assembly, see 86.40.02.

2 Remove the nut, lock washer, washer and screw. Remove the harness 'P' clip.

3 To assist refitting, scribe the outline of the mounting bracket sides onto the light alloy member.

4 Remove four bolts, lock washers and washers. Separate the two assemblies.

5 Withdraw the headlamp harness from the light alloy member.

6 Safely restrain the spring by rotating the actuator hand knob to position the light alloy member against the metal up stop on the base bracket.

7 Remove the circlip and washer.

8 Remove the nut, lock washer, washer and special screw.

9 Slide the upper end of the link rod from the light alloy member.

10 Remove the link rod from the crank arm.

11 Remove the bush from the crank arm.

12 Remove three screws and lock washers. Manoeuvre the crank arm through the aperture and remove the actuator.

13 Ensure that the spring is safely restrained and extended to its weakest working position by checking that the light alloy member is against the metal up stop on the base bracket.

14 Retain the spring by strong hand pressure. Carefully remove the nut, lock washer, small washer, large washer and special bolt.

15 Remove the nut, lock washer, small washer, large washer and special bolt. Lift away the spring.

16 Remove the nut, washer, washer and bolt. Withdraw the light alloy member.

17 Withdraw the hinge pin.

18 Slacken the locknut. Remove the rubber down stop including the locknut and washer.

19 Remove three screws to release the retaining rim and light unit.

20 Pull the connector block from the light unit.

21 Remove four screws and lock washers. Withdraw the housing and plate.

22 If necessary drill out four 'pop rivets' to separate the housing plate.

23 To assist refitting, scribe the outline of the mounting bracket onto the box casting.

24 Remove four nuts, lock washers and washers. Remove the mounting bracket.

25 Remove the grommet from the mounting bracket to release the headlamp harness.

continued

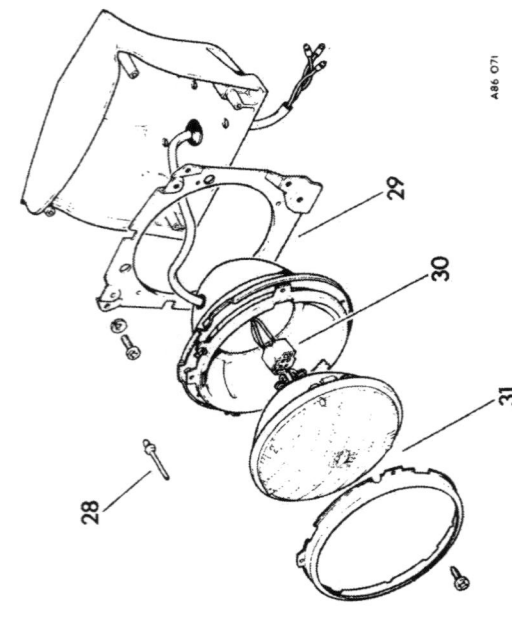

A86 071

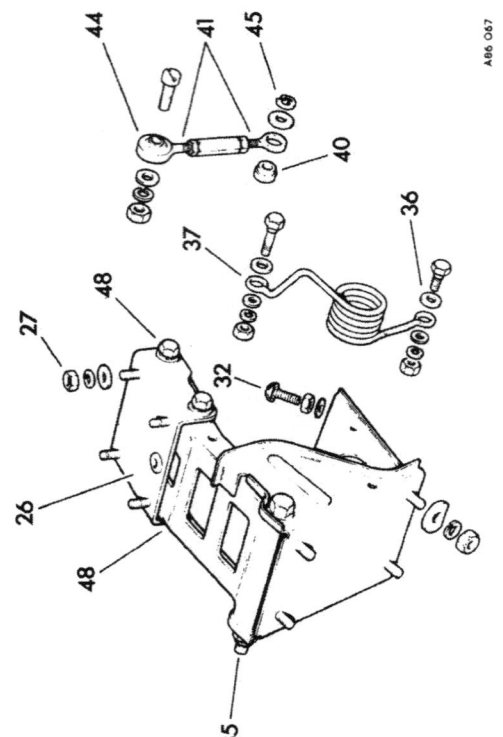

A86 067

Reassembling

26 Position the headlamp harness and fit the grommet to the mounting bracket.

27 Position the mounting bracket to the scribe lines on the box casting. Secure with four nuts, lock washers and washers.

28 If necessary, fit four 'pop rivets' to unite the housing and plate.

29 Insert the housing and plate. Secure with four screws and lock washers.

30 Push the connector block on to the light unit.

31 Position the retaining rim and light unit. Secure with three screws.

32 Fit the rubber down stop including the locknut and washer.

33 Lubricate the hinge pin working surfaces with P.B.C. (Poly Butyl Cuprysil) grease.

34 Insert the hinge pin into the light alloy member.

35 Insert the light alloy member into the base bracket. Secure with the bolt, washer, washer and nut.

36 Position the spring. Secure with the special bolt, large washer, small washer, lock washer and nut.

37 Retain the spring by strong hand pressure. Secure with the special bolt, large washer, small washer, lock washer and nut.

38 Manoeuvre the crank arm through the aperture and position the actuator. Ensure that the actuator harness is looped up between the actuator and the base bracket. Secure with three screws and lock washers.

39 Lubricate the bush working surfaces with engine oil.

40 Fit the bush to the crank arm.

41 Position the link rod ends in the turnbuckle so that an equal number of threads are visible at each end.

42 Fit the link rod to the bush.

43 Slide the upper end of the link rod to the light alloy member.

44 Fit the special screw, washer, lock washer and nut.

45 Fit the washer and circlip.

46 With the headlamp assembly removed from the vehicle perform the primary and secondary adjustment, see 86.40.16.

47 Insert the headlamp harness through the light alloy member.

48 Position the mounting bracket to the scribe lines on the light alloy member. Secure with four bolts, lock washers and washers.

49 Position the harness 'P' clip. Secure with the screw, washer, lock washer and nut.

50 Fit the headlamp assembly, see 86.40.02.

HEADLAMP ASSEMBLY

Adjust   86.40.16

Primary adjustment

The primary adjustment is to ensure that the light alloy member is forced hard against the metal up stop on the base bracket when the crank arm stops for the up position. This condition is achieved by adjusting the length of the link rod.

This adjustment may be made with the headlamp assembly in situ or removed from the vehicle.

1   *Headlamp assembly in situ only:*
    Select the master light switch to raise the headlamps.

2   *Headlamp assembly removed from the vehicle only:*
    Using the actuator hand knob rotate the crank arm to obtain the T.D.C. position as shown.

3   Slacken two link rod lock nuts. Note that the upper lock nut has a left-hand thread.

4   Rotate the turnbuckle by hand – do not use a spanner – until slight resistance is felt as the light alloy member contacts the metal up stop on the base bracket. This is the datum point.

5   Rotate a further 4½ flats (270 degrees) using a spanner.

    NOTE: This will provide a 'crowd' of 1.20 to 1.40 mm to the length of the link rod. Correct pre-load will then be applied to the up stop.

6   Hold the turnbuckle in this position and tighten two lock nuts.

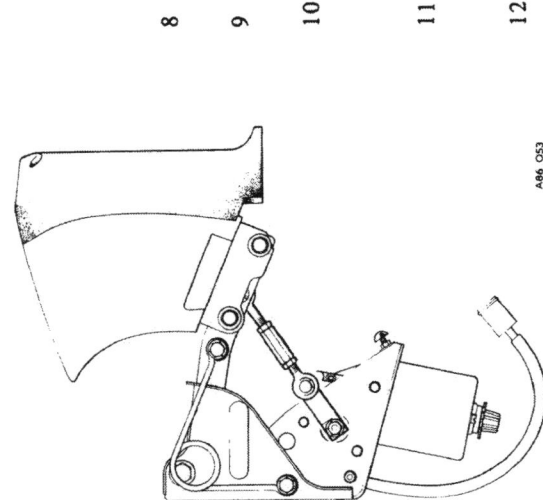

A86 O53

Secondary adjustment

The secondary adjustment is to ensure that the rubber down stop mounted on the base bracket is suitably compressed by the light alloy member when the crank arm stops for the down position. This condition is achieved by adjusting the position of the rubber down stop.

This adjustment may be made with the headlamp assembly in situ or removed from the vehicle.

7   Perform the primary adjustment, see 86.40.16.

    CAUTION: The position the light alloy member assumes in the down position is dependent on the length of the link rod. A correct secondary adjustment cannot be achieved until the primary adjustment is correctly set.

8   Slacken the rubber down stop lock nut. Screw the rubber down stop to its lowest position.

9   *Headlamp assembly in situ only:*
    Select the master light switch to retract the headlamps.

10 *Headlamp assembly removed from vehicle only:*
    Using the actuator hand knob rotate the crank arm to obtain B.D.C. position as shown.

11 Screw the rubber down stop out by hand until it just contacts the light alloy member. This is the datum point.

12 Screw out a further 1⅓ turns (480 degrees).

    NOTE: This will provide a 'crowd' of 1.00 to 1.20 mm to the downstop.

13 Hold the rubber down stop in this position and tighten the lock nut.

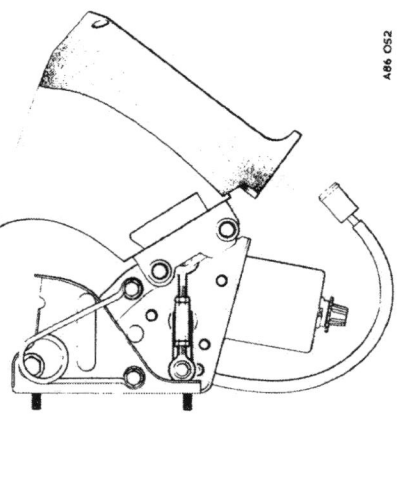

A86 O52

HEADLAMP CIRCUIT BREAKER

Remove and refit   86.40.19

Removing

1   Open the cubby box lid.
2   Remove the two Pozidriv screws. Withdraw the lower panel to obtain access to the component mounting plate.
3   Refer to 86.55.00, Component mounting plate. Locate the circuit breaker for the appropriate market and vehicle.
4   Pull off two electrical connectors to detach the circuit breaker from the vehicle.

Refitting

5   Push on two electrical connectors. The connectors may be fitted either way round.
6   Stow the circuit breaker in a suitable position.
7   Reverse 1 to 2.

HEADLAMP

Beam aiming   86.40.17

Beam aiming can best be accomplished using equipment such as Lucas 'Beamsetter', 'Lev-L-Lite' or 'Beam tester'. This service is available at Triumph distributors or dealers and will ensure maximum road illumination with minimum discomfort to other road users.

With the headlamps in the up position the adjustment is achieved in the same way as for conventional solid mounted Lucas headlamp units. One screw positions the beam in the horizontal plane while a second screw controls beam height.

1   Select the master light switch to raise the headlamps.
2   Ensure that the headlamp assembly is correctly adjusted, see 86.40.16.
3   Gain access to the beam aiming screws by inserting a screwdriver through the 'cut outs' provided in the rubber bezel.
4   Screw 'A' positions the beam in the horizontal plane.
5   Screw 'B' controls beam height.

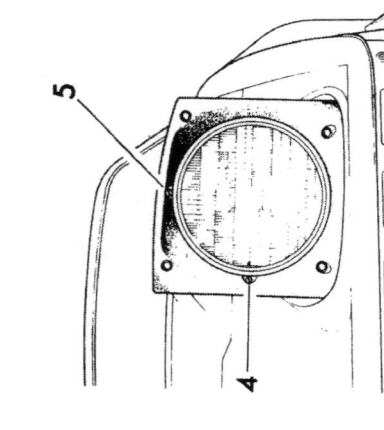

A86.002

Box casting adjustment

The box casting adjustment is to ensure that the top surface of the box casting is correctly aligned with the vehicle body contours when the headlamp is retracted. This condition is achieved by adjusting the position of components.

This adjustment may only be made with the headlamp assembly in situ.

14   Perform the primary and secondary adjustment, see 86.40.16.

CAUTION: The position the light alloy member assumes in the down position is dependent on the length of the link rod. A correct box casting adjustment cannot be achieved until the primary adjustment is correctly set.

15   Ensure that the headlamps are in the retracted position.
16   Slacken four nuts securing the base bracket to the vehicle body.
17   Move the complete headlamp assembly to align the top surface of the box casting with the vehicle body contours.
18   Hold the headlamp assembly in this position and tighten four nuts.
19   If sufficient adjustment is not available to achieve alignment perform operations 20 to 22.
20   Slacken four bolts securing the mounting bracket to the light alloy member.
21   Adjust the relationship of the components to facilitate the operation.
22   Hold the components in position and tighten four bolts.
23   Repeat operation 15 onwards.

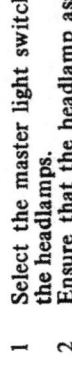

20–22

16–18

A86 072

FRONT PARKING AND FLASHER LAMP

Remove and refit   **86.40.26**

Removing

1. Remove the lamp harness from the body clip.
2. Disconnect three snap connectors.
3. Remove two Pozidriv screws and washers. Withdraw the clear lens and the amber plate lens.
4. Remove the lens gasket.
5. Remove two bulbs from the bayonet fittings.
6. Remove two nuts, spring washers and washers.
7. Withdraw the lamp base and gasket.

Refitting

8. Insert the lamp base and gasket. Ensure that it is the correct way up with the lens securing tappings horizontal.
9. Fit two nuts, spring washers and washers.
10. Fit two bulbs to the bayonet fittings.
11. Fit the lens gasket.
12. Position the amber plate lens to the clear lens. Ensure that the assembly is the correct way up with the screw holes horizontal and the amber plate lens the correct end.
13. Insert the lens assembly. Secure with two Pozidriv screws and washers.
14. Connect three snap connectors as follows:
    Left-hand lamp only —
    Red wire to red wire.
    Green/red wire to green wire.
    Black wire to black wire.
    Right-hand lamp only—
    Red wire to red wire.
    Green/white wire to green wire.
    Black wire to black wire.
15. Fit the lamp harness to the body clip.

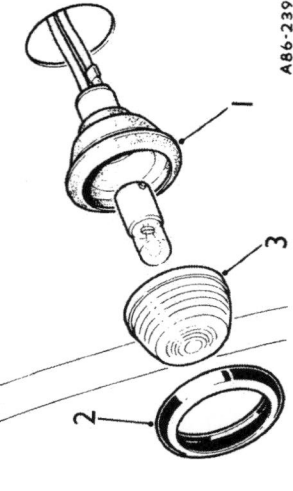

A86 024

FRONT FLASHER REPEATER LAMP

Remove and refit   **86.40.53**

Removing

1. The lamp unit is attached by a groove in the rubber component of the lamp locating in an aperture provided in the vehicle body. Carefully manoeuvre the rubber to allow the complete lamp unit to be withdrawn outwards.
2. Pull off the metal bezel.
3. Remove the lens.
4. Remove the bulb from the bayonet fitting.
5. *Early vehicles only:*
   Locate the terminations of the green wire and the black wire below the headlamp assembly.
6. *Later vehicles only:*
   Locate the terminations of the green wire and the black wire in the engine bay behind the headlamp mounting position.
7. Disconnect two electrical connections.
8. Provide a length of slave cord about 2 metres long.
9. Attach the cord to the two wire ends.
10. Attach the other end of the cord to the vehicle body to prevent it being pulled completely through.
11. Carefully withdraw the lamp wires from the vehicle wing cavity.
12. Detach the cord from the two wire ends.

Refitting

13. Reverse 1 to 12. Connect two wires as follows:
    Left-hand lamp only —
    Light green wire to green wire.
    Black wire to black wire.
    Right-hand lamp only —
    Green/white wire to green wire.
    Black wire to black wire.

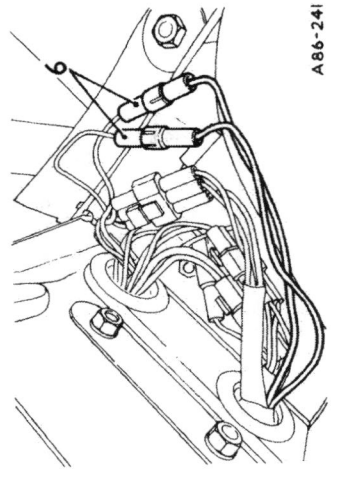

A86-239

A86-241

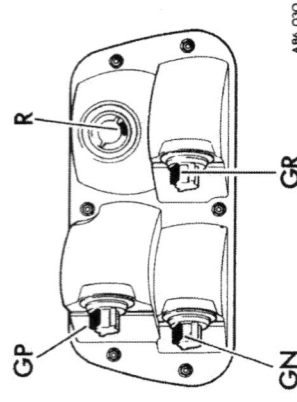

A86 027

FRONT MARKER LAMP

Remove and refit   86.40.59

Removing

1 Select the master light switch to raise the headlamps.
2 Isolate the battery to extinguish the headlamps.
3 Pull the bulb holder from the lamp base.
4 Pull the bulb from the bulb holder.
5 Disconnect two Lucar connectors.
6 Remove two nuts, spring washers and washers.
7 Withdraw the lamp assembly. Do not attempt to disassemble the lens from the lamp base.

Refitting

8 Ensure that the rubber gasket is secured to vehicle body.
9 Reverse 1 to 7.

A86 025

REAR MARKER LAMP

Remove and refit   86.40.64

Removing

1 Open the luggage boot lid.
2 Remove two nuts, spring washers and washers.
3 Remove the clamp cover.
4 Pull the bulb holder from the lamp base.
5 Pull the bulb from the bulb holder.
6 Disconnect two Lucar connectors.
7 Withdraw the lamp assembly. Do not attempt to disassemble the lens from the lamp base.

Refitting

8 Ensure that the rubber gasket is secured to the vehicle body.
9 Reverse 1 to 7.

A86 026

REAR LAMP ASSEMBLY

Remove and refit   86.40.70

Removing

1 Open the luggage boot lid.
2 Turn back the floor mat on the appropriate side.
3 Remove two trim panel top longer Pozidriv screws.
4 Remove two trim panel bottom shorter Pozidriv screws.
5 Remove the trim panel.
6 Rotate four bulb holders anti-clockwise and remove from the bayonet fittings.
7 Remove four bulbs from the bayonet fittings.
8 Remove one nut and spring washer.
9 Remove the harness earth tag.
9 Remove five nuts, spring washers and washers.
10 Withdraw the lens and lens gasket. The lens is a one piece assembly. The lens section may not be replaced individually.
11 Withdraw the lamp base and lamp base gasket.

Refitting

12 Reverse 1 to 11. Fit the four bulb holders so that the wire colour codes are as the left-hand assembly shown. On a right-hand assembly the last wire is GW Green/White.

A86 030

GP	Green/Purple
R	Red
GN	Green/Brown
GR	Green/Red

PLATE ILLUMINATION LAMP

Remove and refit   **86.40.86**

Removing

1   Open the luggage boot lid to obtain improved access.
2   Remove two Pozidriv screws.
3   Manoeuvre the lamp from the body panel aperture. Take care not to break the festoon bulb.
4   Carefully remove the festoon bulb.
5   Remove two Lucar connectors.

Refitting

6   Reverse 1 to 5. The two Lucar connectors may be fitted either way round.

REAR FOG LAMP ASSEMBLY

Remove and refit   **86.40.99**

Removing

1   From inside the luggage compartment disconnect the lamp leads. Pass the leads through the body grommet to hang loose below the lamp.
2   Remove two bolts, nuts and washers securing the lamp to the bracket.

Refitting

3   Reverse instructions 1 and 2

A86 028

ROOF LAMP

Remove and refit   **86.45.02**

Early vehicles only

Removing

1   Isolate the battery.
2   Gently squeeze the lens adjacent to the clip projections and remove the lens.
3   Carefully remove the festoon bulb.
4   Remove two Pozidriv screws.
5   Withdraw the lamp base.
6   Note the wire colour codes and positions.
7   Disconnect two terminal ends.

Refitting

8   Reverse 1 to 7. Insert the lamp base with the switch facing forward. Ensure that the right-hand screw makes a good earth connection to the vehicle body.

A86 036

MAP/COURTESY LAMP

Remove and refit   **86.45.10**

Later vehicles only:

Removing

1   Isolate the battery.
2   Carefully prise the rearward edge of the lamp outwards to free it from the door trim pad.
3   Carefully remove the festoon bulb.
4   Note the wire colour codes and positions.
5   Remove the three Lucar connectors.

Refitting

6   Reverse 1 to 5.

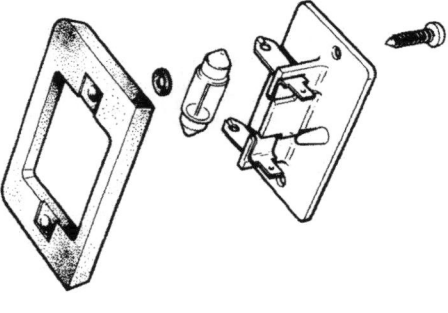

A86230

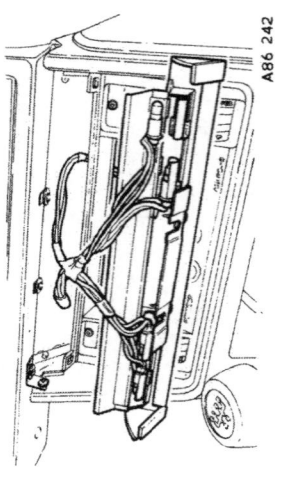

A86 254

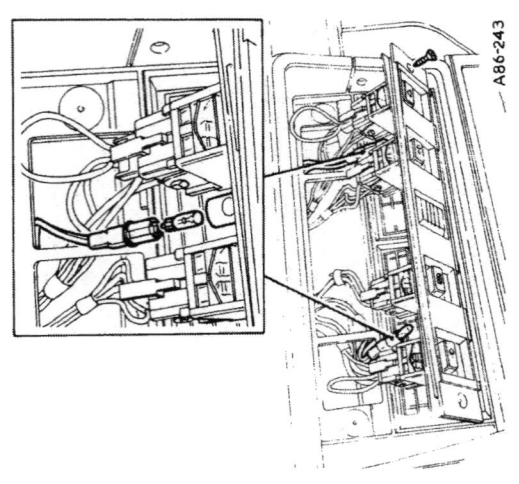

A86 242

A86-243

INSTRUMENT ILLUMINATION

Remove and refit   **86.45.32**

The four instrument illumination asemblies may be considered as a composite part of the instrument panel. Each instrument illumination assembly consists of three parts. The bulb and bulb holder which may best be removed from the concealed side of the instrument panel. The green dome cover which will not normally require to be removed.

Removing

All operations:

1. Isolate the battery.
2. Remove the fascia centre grille, see 76.55.14.
3. Remove the fascia instrument cowl, see 76.46.17.
4. Read the remainder of this operation and decide the best approach for the specific operation that is to be performed.

Any bulb and bulb holder may be removed as follows:

5. At the concealed side of the instrument panel proceed as follows: Rotate the appropriate bulb holder anti-clockwise and carefully withdraw from the bayonet fitting.
6. If satisfactory access is not available at the concealed side of the instrument panel proceed as follows: Perform 88.20.01 operations 3 to 9. Withdraw the instrument panel as shown. Rotate the appropriate bulb holder anti-clockwise and carefully withdraw from the bayonet fitting.
7. Pull the bulb from the bulb holder.

Any green dome cover may be removed as follows:

8. Remove three Pozidriv screws and washers.
9. Carefully slide the lens upwards following the path of its natural arc.
10. Lift out the face panel.
11. Remove the speedometer, see 88.30.01 or the tachometer, see 88.30.21 to obtain access to the appropriate green dome cover.
12. Remove the green dome cover from the housing claws. Take care not to break a claw.

Refitting

13. Reverse all operations performed.

HEATER CONTROL ILLUMINATION

Remove and refit   **86.45.44**

Removing

1. Remove two Pozidriv screws.
2. Lower the panel downwards.
3. Any of the four bulb holders may now be removed by tilting the panel and sliding out a bulb holder.
4. Remove the bulb from the bayonet fitting.

Refitting

5. Reverse 1 to 4.

FASCIA SWITCH PANEL ILLUMINATION

Remove and refit   **86.45.47**

Removing

1. Isolate the battery.
2. Remove two Pozidriv screws and washers.
3. Withdraw the panel.
4. Either of the two bulb holders may now be removed by carefully pulling from the housing.
5. Pull the bulb from the bulb holder.

Refitting

6. Reverse 1 to 5.

A86 073

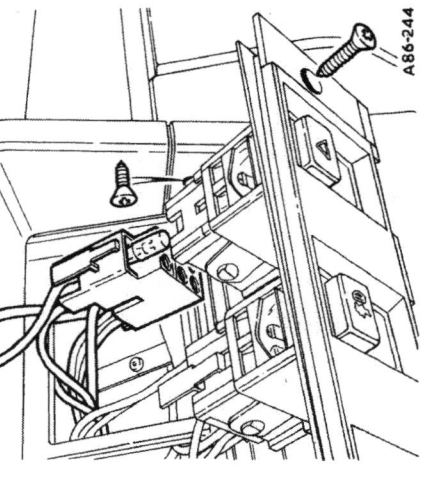

A86-244

WARNING LIGHT

Remove and refit   86.45.60

The warning light assemblies may be
considered as a composite part of the
instrument panel. Each warning light
assembly consists of three parts. The bulb
holder which may only be removed from
the concealed side of the instrument panel.
The bulb which may be removed from
either side of the instrument panel. The
annotated lens which may only be removed
from the exposed side of the instrument
panel.

Removing

All operations:
1 Isolate the battery.
2 Remove the fascia centre grille, see
   76.55.14.
3 Remove the fascia instrument cowl,
   see 76.46.17.
4 Read the remainder of this operation
   and decide the best approach for the
   specific operation that is to be
   performed.

Any bulb holder may be removed as
follows:

5 At the concealed side of the
   instrument panel proceed as follows:
   Rotate the appropriate bulb holder
   anti-clockwise and carefully withdraw
   from the bayonet fitting.
6 If satisfactory access is not available at
   the concealed side of the instrument
   panel proceed as follows:
   Perform 88.20.01 operations 3 to 9.
   Withdraw the instrument panel as
   shown. Rotate the appropriate bulb
   holder anti-clockwise and carefully
   withdraw from the bayonet fitting.
7 Pull the bulb from the bulb holder.

Any bulb or annotated lens may be
removed as follows:
8 Remove three Pozidriv screws and
   washers.
9 Carefully slide the lens upwards
   following the path of its natural arc.
10 Lift out the face panel.
11 Lift out the appropriate annotated
    lens.
12 Pull the bulb from the bulb holder.

Refitting
13 Reverse all operations performed.

HAZARD WARNING LIGHT

Remove and refit   86.45.76

Removing
1 Isolate the battery.
2 Remove two Pozidriv screws and
   washers.
3 Withdraw the panel.
4 Disconnect the hazard switch harness
   plug.
5 Pull the bulb from the harness plug.

Refitting
6 Reverse 1 to 5.

DOOR SPEAKER

Remove and refit   86.50.13

When fitted

Removing
1 Remove the door trim pad, see
   76.34.01.
2 Remove the four Pozidriv screws and
   spring clips securing the speaker to the
   trim pad.
3 Withdraw the speaker.

Refitting
4 Reverse instructions 1 to 3.

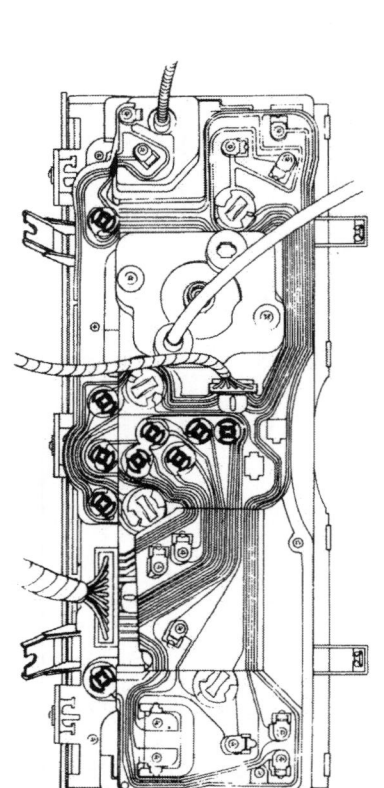

A86 064

COMPONENT MOUNTING PLATE
– U.K. – R.H. Steering

Early vehicles

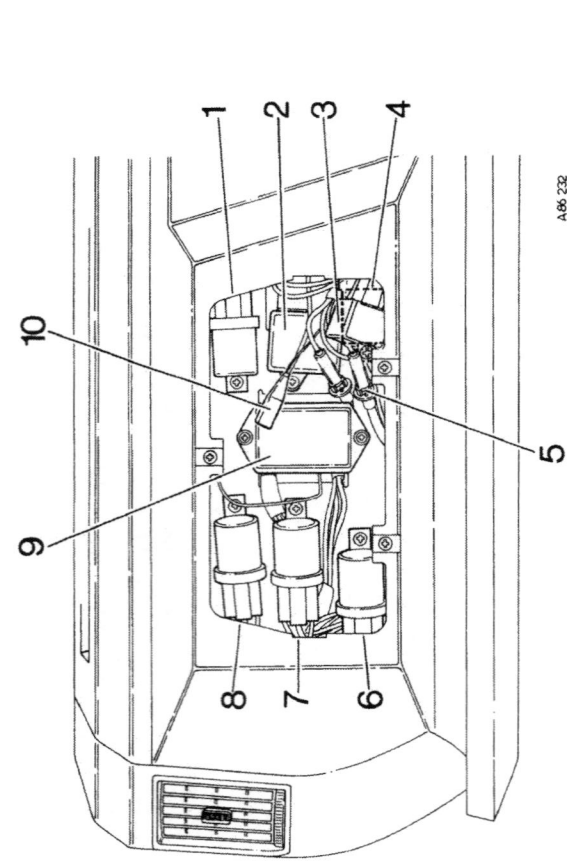

A86 232

1 Starter motor relay
2 Headlamp – delay unit
3 Hazard flasher unit
4 Headlamp – R.H. run/stop relay
5 Fuses – in line
6 Headlamp – L.H. run/stop relay
7 Horn relay
8 Headlamp – flash relay
9 Fuse box
10 Headlamp – circuit breaker

Later vehicles

A86 233

1 Headlamp – run/stop relay
2 Headlamp – delay unit
3 Headlamp – flash relay
4 Hazard flasher unit
5 Headlamp – circuit breaker
6 Fuse box
7 Horn relay
8 Starter motor relay
9 Headlamp – run/stop relay

COMPONENT MOUNTING PLATE
– European – L.H. Steering

Early vehicles

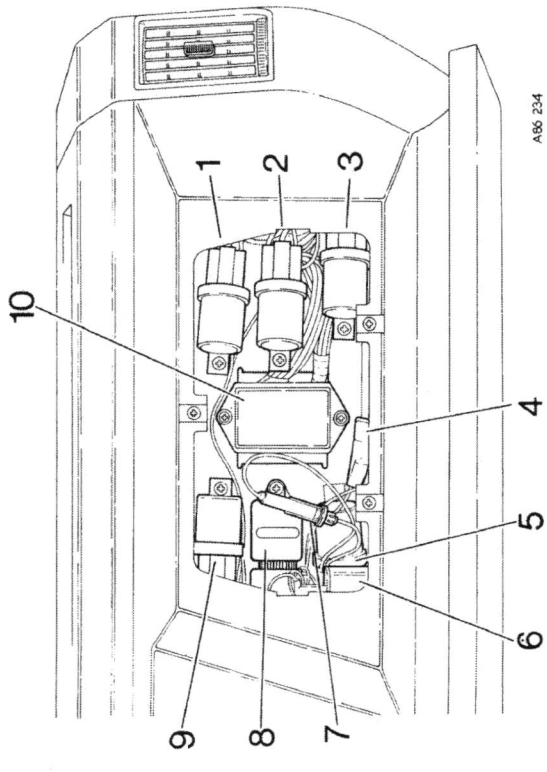

1 Headlamp – flash relay
2 Horn relay
3 Headlamp – R.H. run/stop relay
4 Headlamp – circuit breaker
5 Headlamp – L.H. run/stop relay
6 Hazard flasher unit
7 Fuses – in line
8 Headlamp – delay unit
9 Starter motor relay

Later vehicles

1 Headlamp – R.H. run/stop relay
2 Starter motor relay
3 Horn relay
4 Fuse box
5 Headlamp – circuit breaker
6 Hazard flasher unit
7 Headlamp – flash relay
8 Headlamp – delay unit
9 Headlamp – L.H. run/stop relay

COMPONENT MOUNTING PLATE – U.S.A.

Early vehicles

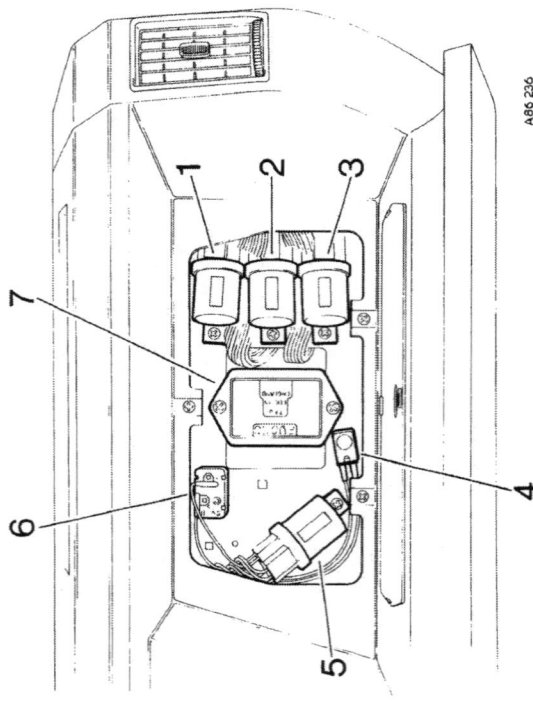

A86 236

1 Interlock starter motor relay
2 Air conditioning – control relay
3 Headlamp – R.H. run/stop relay
4 Headlamp – circuit breaker
5 Headlamp – L.H. run/stop relay
6 Hazard flasher unit
7 Fuse box

Intermediate vehicles

A86 237

1   Starter motor relay
2   Air conditioning – control relay
3   Headlamp – R.H. run/stop relay
4   Headlamp – circuit breaker
5   Headlamp – L.H. run/stop relay
6   Hazard flasher unit
7   Fuse – in line
8   Seat belt – timer/buzzer module
9   Horn relay
10 Fuse box

COMPONENT MOUNTING PLATE – U.S.A.

Later vehicles

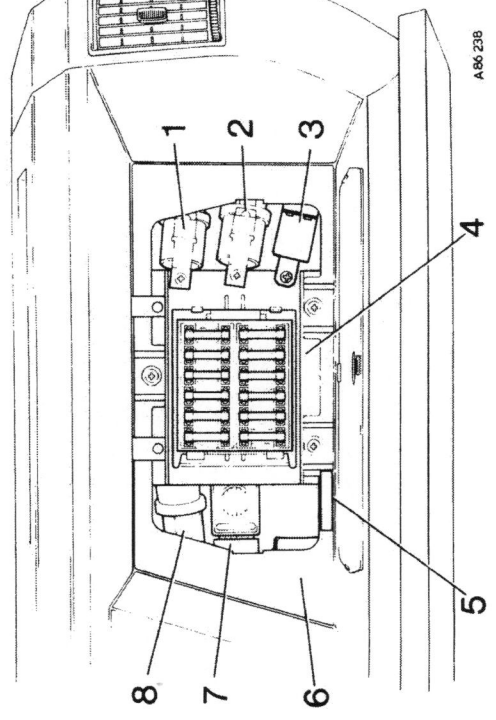

A86 238

1   Headlamp – R.H. run/stop relay
2   Starter motor relay
3   Horn relay
4   Fuse box
5   Headlamp – circuit breaker
6   Hazard flasher unit
7   Seat belt – timer/buzzer module
8   Headlamp – L.H. run/stop relay

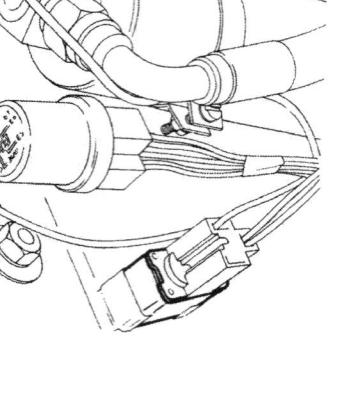

A86 098

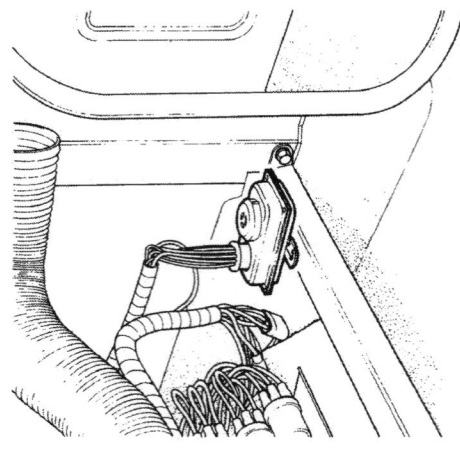

A86 032

TURN SIGNAL FLASHER UNIT 86.55.11

Remove and refit

Early vehicles only

Removing

1 Locate the flasher unit mounted in a clip attached to the fascia support rail forward of the choke and bonnet release controls.
2 Pull the flasher unit from the clip.
3 Disconnect two Lucar connectors.

Refitting

4 Reverse 1 to 3. Connect two Lucar connectors as follows:
  Light green/slate wire to terminal B.
  Light green/brown wire to terminal L.

AIR CONDITIONING—DELAY CIRCUIT FLASHER UNIT 86.55.31

Remove and refit

Early vehicles only

Removing

1 Open the bonnet.
2 Locate the flasher unit mounted in a clip attached to a forward engine bay panel.
3 Pull the flasher unit from the clip.
4 Disconnect the harness plug.

Refitting

5 Connect the harness plug. Ensure that the flasher unit Lucar blades are fitted into the harness plug operational sockets.
6 Reverse 1 to 3.

INTERLOCK MODULE 86.57.07

Remove and refit

Early U.S.A. vehicles only

Removing

1 Locate the interlock module clipped to the fascia rail at the extreme right-hand end.
2 Wriggle the interlock module forwards and sideways to disengage the two clips.
3 Disconnect the multi-pin harness plug.

Refitting

4 Reverse instructions 1 to 3. The multi-pin harness plug is keyed and may only be fitted in the correct position.

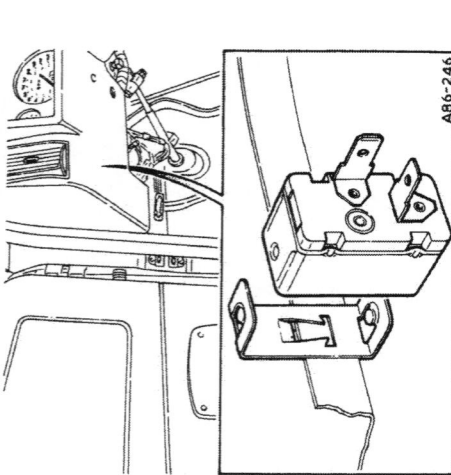

A86-246

A86 087

AIR CONDITIONING— DELAY CIRCUIT RELAY 86.55.30

Remove and refit

Early vehicles only

Removing

1 Open the bonnet.
2 Locate the relay attached to a forward engine bay panel.
3 Remove the Pozidriv screw.
4 Disconnect the harness plug.

Refitting

5 Reverse 1 to 4. Ensure that the harness earth tag is included in the screw assembly.

STARTER MOTOR

86.60.00

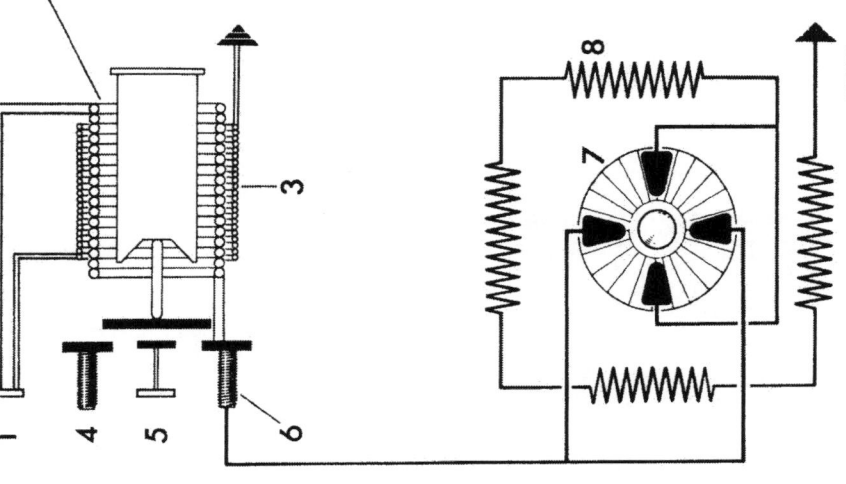

NT0170

1. Unmarked 'WR wire' connector
2. Pull-in winding
3. Hold-in winding
4. Solenoid battery terminal
5. IGN connector for ballast ignition
6. Solenoid motor terminal
7. Brushes and commutator
8. Field windings

Data

Manufacturer	Lucas
Type	2M100 PE
Lucas part number	25703
Triumph part number	TKC 0020

Motor

Yoke diameter	4 in (101.60 mm)
Light running — speed	6,000 rev/min
current	40 amp.
torque	Not stated
Load running — speed	1,000 rev/min
current	300 amp.
torque	7.3 lbf ft (1.01 kgf m)
Locked — speed	Nil
current	463 amp.
torque	14.4 lbf ft (1.99 kgf m)
Commutator minimum skimming	
thickness	0.140 in (3.56 mm)
Brush length — new	0.710 in (18.03 mm)
renew if less than. ...	0.375 in (9.53 mm)
Brush spring tension	36 ozf (1000 gf)
Shaft end-float: maximum between bush	
and Spire retaining ring	0.010 in (0.25 mm)
Bearing renewal mandrel diameter:	
Commutator end cover bearing. ...	0.4377 in (11.118 mm)
Drive end bracket bearing ...	0.4729 in (12.012 mm)

Solenoid

Pull-in winding resistance — measured	
between unmarked 'WR wire' connector	
and 'STA' terminal	0.25 to 0.27 ohm
Hold-in winding resistance — measured	
between unmarked 'WR wire' connector	
and unit body	0.76 to 0.80 ohm

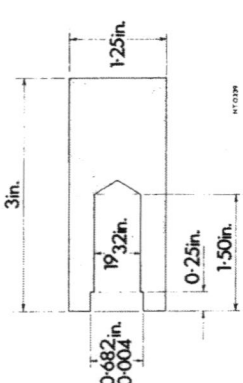

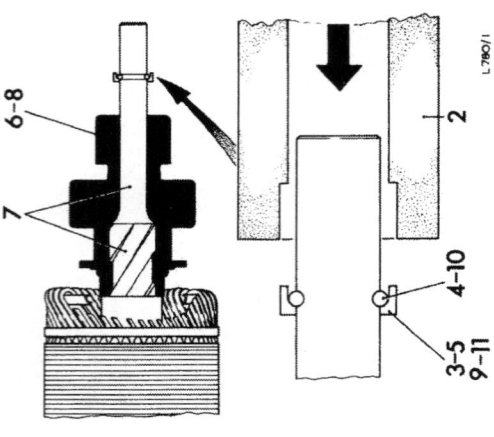

STARTER MOTOR

Remove and refit   86.60.01

Removing

1. Drive the vehicle onto a ramp.
2. Isolate the battery.
3. Raise the ramp.
4. Lower the complete exhaust system. It is not necessary to remove it from the vehicle.
   - a. Remove two bolts, spring washers and washers at the gearbox bracket.
   - b. Remove two nuts, spring washers, washers and bolts at the bell-housing bracket.
   - c. Unhook two rubber rings at the front silencer hanger.
   - d. Unhook two rubber rings at the tail pipe hanger.
   - e. Remove three nuts, spring washers and washers at the manifold flange.
5. Unclip the heat shield from the starter solenoid.
6. Swing the front of the exhaust pipe under the engine and temporarily secure under the right-hand side of the vehicle.
7. Disconnect the Lucar connector.
8. Remove the nut and spring washer. Disconnect the battery lead from the solenoid.
9. Slacken one bolt indicated at the bell-housing exhaust bracket.
10. Remove the lower mounting bolt, spring washer and nut.
11. Remove the middle mounting bolt, cable clip, spring washer and nut.
12. Remove the upper mounting bolt, spring washer and nut.
    NOTE: This bolt may be removed with the starter motor tilted.
13. Manoeuvre the starter motor downwards from the vehicle.

Refitting

14. Position the starter motor upwards to the vehicle.
15. Fit the upper mounting bolt, spring washer and nut finger-tight.
    NOTE: This bolt may be inserted with the starter motor tilted.
16. Fit the middle mounting bolt, cable clip, spring washer and nut finger-tight.
17. Fit the lower mounting bolt, spring washer and nut finger-tight. Include the exhaust bell-housing bracket in the assembly.
18. Tighten the upper bolt assembly.
19. Tighten the middle bolt assembly.
20. Tighten the lower bolt assembly.
21. Tighten one bolt indicated at the bell-housing exhaust bracket.
22. Connect the battery lead to the solenoid. Fit the spring washer and nut.
23. Connect the Lucar connector.
24. Swing the front of the exhaust pipe under the engine and position to the manifold.
25. Clip the heat shield to the starter solenoid.
26. Reverse operation 4. Fit a new exhaust manifold gasket.
27. Lower the ramp.
28. Ensure that the electrical leads are stowed along the inside edge of the heat shield.
29. Connect the battery.

STARTER MOTOR

Roller clutch drive — remove and refit   86.60.07

Removing

1. Dismantle the starter motor, see 86.60.13.
2. Provide a special punch as shown.
3. Position the special punch over the shaft end and tap the thrust collar from the jump ring towards the roller clutch drive.
4. Prise the jump ring from the shaft groove.
5. Remove the thrust collar.
6. Remove the roller clutch drive.

Refitting

7. Lubricate the splines and pinion bearing with grease. Shell SB 2628 for home market and cool climates. Shell Retinax A for hot climates.
8. Fit the roller clutch drive with the engaging lever convex surface facing the solenoid.
9. Fit the thrust collar with the open side facing the shaft end as shown.
10. Prise the jump ring into the shaft groove.
11. Force the thrust collar over the jump ring.

STARTER MOTOR

Overhaul   86.60.13

Dismantling

NOTE: Dismantling of the starter motor will necessitate the destruction of one Spire retaining ring. Ensure that a new Spire retaining ring for the armature shaft is available before proceeding further. This item is included in the sundry parts kit, Lucas part no. 54246438 or Triumph part no. 520466.

1　Remove the nut, spring washer and washer to free the connector link from the solenoid.

2　Carefully prise off the metal end cap.

3　Use a small chisel to cut a number of claws and remove the Spire retaining ring. Do not prise off the Spire retaining ring without cutting a number of claws as such action may damage the bearing end face, armature shaft and bearing surface when the shaft is withdrawn.

4　Remove two through bolts and spring washers.

5　Withdraw the yoke and commutator end cover assembly.

6　Remove the thrust washer.

7　Remove the rubber seal block.

8　Employ a second operator to support the yoke by hand. Use a length of wood of approximately 0.75 in (20

mm) diameter to tap the commutator end cover from the yoke.

9　Lift out two field winding brushes from the brush box to separate the commutator end cover from the yoke.

10　Tap out the pivot pin. The staking will fold inwards during withdrawal.

11　Remove two bolts and spring washers. Withdraw the solenoid leaving the plunger attached to the engaging lever.

12　Remove the return spring.

13　Withdraw the armature, roller clutch drive and plunger assembly from the drive end bracket.

14　Unhook the plunger complete with the solenoid seal moulding from the engaging lever.

Bearings

15　Inspect the porous bronze bearing bushes for wear.

16　If necessary renew either bush as follows:

Extract the bush using a suitable press and mandrel. Prepare the porous bronze bush by immersing it in thin engine oil for 24 hours or thin engine oil heated to 100° C for two hours. Allow the bush to cool in the oil. Fit the bush using a suitable press and a highly polished, shouldered mandrel of the appropriate dimension given in Data. Do not ream the bush after fitting or its porosity may be impaired.

Brushes

17　Clean the brushes and brush box with a petrol-moistened cloth.

18　Check that the brushes move freely in the brush box.

19　Check the brush spring pressure as shown. Position a new brush so that the top protrudes 0.060 in (1.50 mm) above the brush box. Brush spring pressure should be as given in Data. Repeat for the remaining three springs. If the pressure is low renew the commutator end bracket assembly.

20　Check the brush length. Renew the brushes if less than the length given in Data.

21　If necessary renew the commutator end cover brushes. Brushes are supplied attached to a new connector link. Withdraw two brushes from the brush box. Withdraw the connector link. Position new brushes as shown. Retain the longer flexible under the flap.

22　If necessary renew the field winding brushes. Brushes are supplied attached to a common flexible. Cut the old flexibles 0.250 in (6 mm) from the joint. Solder the new flexible to the ends of the old flexible. Do not attempt to solder direct to the field winding strip as the strip may be produced from aluminium.

NTa214.

Commutator

23 Clean the commutator with a petrol-moistened cloth. If the commutator is in good condition it will be smooth and free from pits or burned spots.

24 If necessary polish the commutator with fine glass-paper.

25 If necessary skim the commutator. Separate the armature from the roller clutch drive by performing 86.60.07. Mount the armature in a lathe and rotate at high speed. Using a very sharp tool, take a light cut. Polish with fine glass-paper. Do not cut below the minimum skimming thickness given in Data. Do not undercut insulators between segments.

Roller clutch drive

26 Do not wash the roller clutch in petrol as such action would remove lubricant from the sealed unit. It may be cleaned by wiping with a petrol-moistened cloth.

27 Check that the clutch locks in one direction and rotates smoothly in the other. The unit should move freely round and along the armature shaft splines.

28 The roller clutch is a sealed unit. If the above conditions are not met repair by replacement of the roller clutch unit.

Solenoid

29 Assembly of the starter solenoid involves soldering and sealing complications. It is therefore not advisable to attempt to service this unit. If the solenoid operation is suspect, repair by replacement of the solenoid unit.

30 The plunger is matched with the solenoid body. The spares unit of purchase is a matched solenoid and plunger and the box also contains a return spring. All three items should be fitted as a set.

Reassembling

31 Ensure that the bearing surfaces on the armature shaft are burr-free.

32 Hook the plunger complete with the solenoid seal moulding onto the engaging lever.

33 Insert the armature, roller clutch drive and plunger assembly into the drive end bracket.

34 Fit the return spring to the solenoid.

35 Fit the solenoid so the 'STA' terminal is adjacent to the yoke. Secure with two bolts and spring washers. Ensure that the plunger does not unhook during this operation.

36 Lightly grease the pivot pin. Align the holes and insert the pivot pin. Secure by staking. Ensure that the plunger does not unhook during this operation.

37 Insert two field winding brushes into the brush box with flexibles positioned as shown.

38 Position the commutator end cover to the yoke.

39 Position the rubber seal block.

40 Fit the thrust washer.

41 Holding the commutator end cover firmly to the yoke, insert the assembly.

42 Fit two through bolts and spring washers.

43 If necessary adjust the position of the rubber seal block.

44 Fit a new Spire retaining ring to the armature shaft.

45 Fit the metal end cap.

46 Fit washer, spring washer and nut to secure the connector link to the solenoid.

SWITCHES

A86 O47

A86 O48

A86 O46

Data		86.65.00

Ignition/starter switch

Normal vehicles only

View on switch harness plug:

Position 0	Off	No connections
Position 1	Auxiliary	N to WK
Position 2	Ignition	N to WK to W
Position 3	Start	N to W to WR

Ignition starter switch

Key warning system vehicles only

View on switch harness plug:

Position 0	Lock	N to NR
Position 1	Auxiliary	N to NR to WK
Position 2	Ignition	N to WK to W
Position 3	Start	N to W to WR

The black/green wire included in the switch harness is associated with the key warning system. A single Lucar connects to the key switch built into the steering column lock assembly.

Steering column multi-purpose switch—headlamp/turn signal/horn unit.

View on switch harness plug:

Position	Head main	U to UW
Position	Head dip	U to UR
Position	Head flash	P left hand to UW
Position	L.H. turn signal	LG/N to GR
Position	R.H. turn signal	LG/N to GW
Position	Horn	P right hand to PB

Steering column multi-purpose switch—washer/wiper unit

View on switch harness plug:

Position 0	Off	N/LG to R/LG
Position 1	Normal speed	G to R/LG
Position 2	High speed	G to U/LG
Push knob	Washers	G to L/GB

Master light switch

Position	Off	N left hand to UN left hand
Position	Side	N left hand to RG and N right hand to UN right hand
Position	Head	N left hand to RG and N right hand to U

Hazard switch

Position	Off	G to LG/S
Position	Hazard	LG/K to GR to GW to LG/K

Heated backlight switch

Position	Off	No connections
Position	On	G to WB

Oil pressure switch

Emission control – anti run on system vehicles only

Position	Engine static	WN to B
Position	Engine run	WP to B

IGNITION/STARTER SWITCH

Remove and refit   86.65.02

Removing

1 Isolate the battery.
2 Unscrew two long Pozidriv screws and remove the nacelle upper and lower halves.
   NOTE: The screws have a long threaded length of approximately 20 mm. A long 'unscrew time' should be expected.
3 Note the switch harness wire run.
4 Disconnect one harness plug.
5 Remove two small Pozidriv screws.
6 Remove the switch complete with its harness from the vehicle.

Refitting

7 Position the switch harness wire run as noted at operation 3 above. Insert the switch into the steering column lock assembly. Note the keyway and ensure that the lock shaft and switch shaft align correctly.
8 Fit two small Pozidriv screws.
9 Connect one harness plug.
10 Position the nacelle upper and lower halves. Secure with two long Pozidriv screws.
11 Connect the battery.

MASTER LIGHT SWITCH

Remove and refit   86.65.09

— Remove and refit

Removing

1 Remove the fascia switch panel, see 86.65.66.
2 Using a small screwdriver carefully prise off two Spire clips.
3 Remove the face panel and the switch identification strip assembly.
4 Push inwards one plastic clip on the switch and withdraw the switch from the panel.

Refitting

5 Reverse 1 to 4. Insert the switch so that the 'symbol' is at the lower edge.

DOOR SWITCH

Remove and refit   86.65.14

Removing

1 Open the appropriate door.
2 Remove the single screw.
3 Withdraw the switch.
4 Disconnect one Lucar connector.

Refitting

5 Reverse 1 to 4.

FRONT FOG LAMP SWITCH

Remove and refit   86.65.19

When fitted

Removing

1 Remove the fascia switch panel, see 86.65.66.
2 Using a small screwdriver carefully prise off two Spire clips.
3 Remove the face panel and the switch identification strip assembly.
4 Push inwards one plastic clip on the switch and withdraw the switch from the panel.

Refitting

5 Reverse 1 to 4. Insert the switch so that the 'symbol' is at the lower edge.

PANEL RHEOSTAT

Remove and refit   86.65.12

Removing

1 Isolate the battery.
2 Pull out the centre console tray.
3 Locate the hole in the knob. Insert a suitable probe into the hole and while depressing pull the knob from the shaft.
4 Unscrew the bezel.
5 Withdraw the panel rheostat downwards from the centre console panel.
6 Remove the spring washer.
7 Note the wire colour codes and positions.
8 Disconnect two Lucar connectors.

Refitting

9 Reverse 1 to 8.

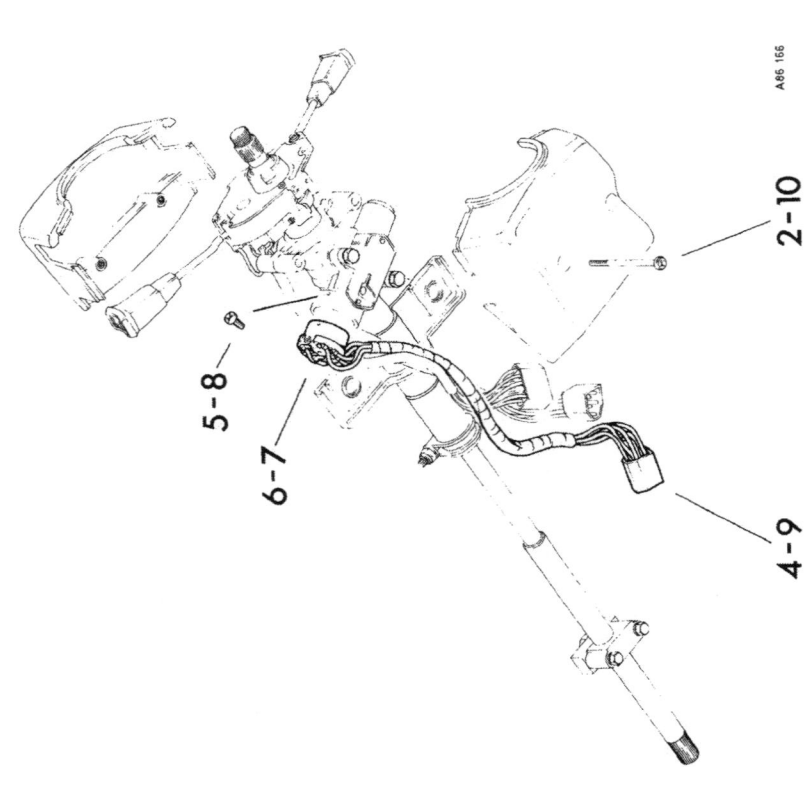

A86.166

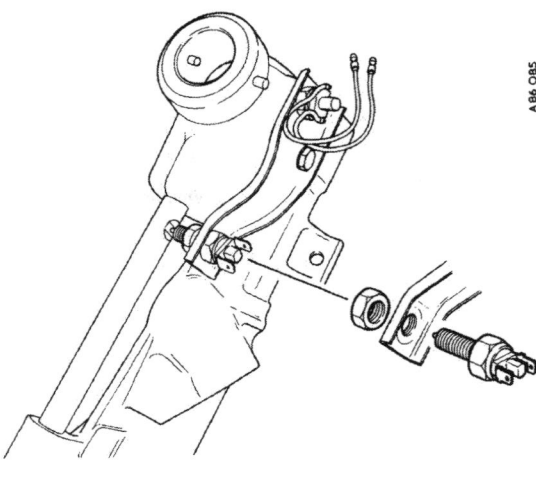

A86 085

REVERSE LAMP SWITCH

Remove and refit   86.65.20

Four speed gearbox only

Removing

1 Drive the vehicle onto a ramp.
2 Raise the ramp.
3 Disconnect two snap connectors.
4 Unscrew the switch from the gearbox extension.
5 Collect up the distance washer.

Refitting

6 Fit the distance washer to the switch.
7 Screw the switch into the gearbox extension and tighten lightly. **NOTE:** No further adjustment is required.
8 Connect two snap connectors. The connectors may be fitted either way round.
9 Perform a function test as follows: Switch on ignition. Select reverse. The reverse lamps should now be illuminated. Select any other gear. The reverse lamps should now be off.

Five speed gearbox only

Removing

10 Drive the vehicle onto a ramp.
11 Unscrew the gear lever knob.
12 Lift off the gear lever gaiter.
13 Remove four Pozidriv screws and washers. Lift out the draught excluder and plate.
14 Raise the ramp.
15 Disconnect two snap connectors.
16 Lower the ramp.
17 Slacken the locknut.
18 Unscrew the switch from the gearbox extension.

Refitting

19 Ensure that the locknut is fitted to the switch.
20 Screw the switch into the gearbox extension.
21 Adjust the switch position as follows: Provide a test lamp circuit as shown. Select reverse gear. Screw the switch inwards until the lamp just illuminates. This is the datum position. Screw the switch inwards a further 3 flats (180 degrees). Hold the switch in this position and tighten the locknut.
22 Raise the ramp.
23 Connect two snap connectors. The connectors may be fitted either way round.
24 Lower the ramp.
25 Perform a function test as follows: Switch on ignition. Select reverse. The reverse lamps should now be illuminated. Select any other gear. The reverse lamps should now be off.
26 Reverse 11 to 13.

INTERLOCK GEARBOX SWITCH

Remove and refit   86.65.28

Early U.S.A. vehicles only

Removing

1 Drive the vehicle onto a ramp.
2 Raise the ramp.
3 Locate the appropriate switch on the gearbox extension.
4 Disconnect two Lucar connectors.
5 Slacken the locknut.
6 Unscrew the switch from the tabbed bracket and locknut.
7 Collect up the locknut.

Refitting

8 Screw the switch partially into the tapped bracket.
9 Screw the locknut onto the switch.
10 Adjust the switch position as follows: Select any gear other than neutral. Screw the switch inwards until the switch plunger just contacts the selector shaft. This is the datum point. Screw the switch inwards a further 6 flats (360 degrees). Hold the switch in this position and tighten the locknut.
11 Connect two Lucar connectors. The connectors may be fitted either way round.
12 Perform a function test as follows: Sit in either the driver's or passenger's seat. Do not fasten the belt. Switch on ignition. Select any gear. The Fasten Belts warning light and buzzer should now be on. Select neutral: The visual and audible warnings should now be off.

A86 141

ELECTRICAL SYSTEM   463

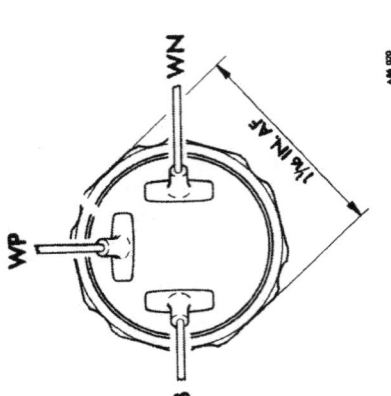

OIL PRESSURE SWITCH

Remove and refit   **86.65.30**

U.S.A. only

Removing

1   Locate the switch on the right-hand side of the engine adjacent to the dipstick.

2   Disconnect three Lucar connectors.

3   Using a spanner, unscrew the switch from the oil transfer adaptor.

Refitting

4   Screw the switch into the oil transfer adaptor. The thread is tapered. Do not overtighten.

5   Connect the three Lucar connectors as shown.

NOTE: Later vehicles have a moulded plug which can be fitted one way only. Wire colours may not conform to illustration.

WN

WP

1¼ in. AF

B

B   Black
WP   White/purple
WN   White/brown

SEAT SWITCH

Remove and refit   **86.65.29**

Removing

1   Remove the appropriate seat.

2   Unhook two front diaphragm attachment clips.

3   Note the switch position and wire run.

4   Withdraw the wires through the diaphragm hole.

5   Withdraw the switch.

Refitting

6   Reverse 1 to 5.

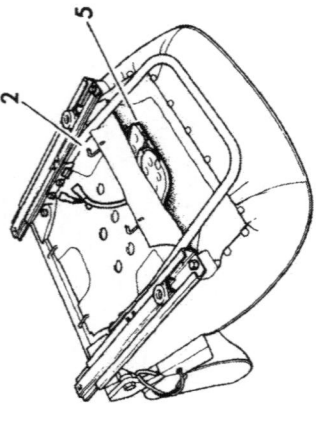

OIL PRESSURE SWITCH

Remove and refit   **86.65.30**

UK and Europe only

Removing

1   Locate the switch on the right-hand side of the engine adjacent to the dipstick tube.

2   Disconnect the Lucar connector.

3   Using a spanner, unscrew the switch from the oil transfer adaptor.

Refitting

4   Screw the switch into the oil transfer adaptor. The thread is tapered. Do not overtighten.

5   Connect the Lucar connector.

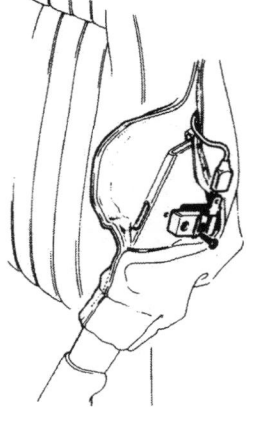

A86 031

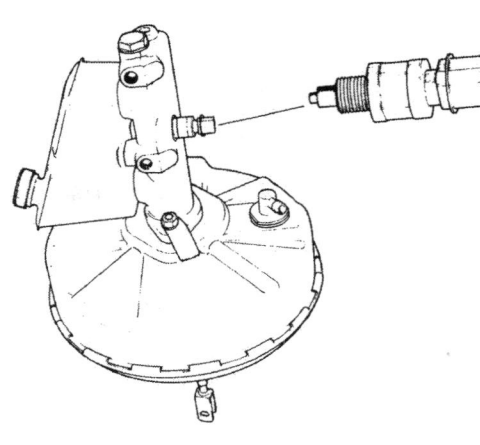

HANDBRAKE SWITCH   86.65.45

Remove and refit

Removing

1 Remove the console assembly, see 76.25.01.
2 Pull apart the Velcro 'touch and close' fastener strips along the top edge of the hand brake gauntlet.
3 Remove the single Pozidriv screw and detach the switch.
4 Disconnect the Lucar connector.

Refitting

5 Reverse 1 to 4.

BRAKE LINE FAILURE SWITCH   86.65.47

Remove and refit

Removing

1 Locate the brake line failure switch on the brake master cylinder.
2 Release the harness plug claws and disconnect the harness plug from the switch.
3 Using a spanner on the nylon switch body carefully unscrew the switch.

Refitting

4 Carefully screw the switch to the brake master cylinder. Do not overtighten. Torque load to only 15 lbf in (0,17 kgf m).
5 Connect the harness plug. The harness plug may be fitted either way round.

A86 035

BELT SWITCH

Driver's — Remove and refit   86.65.31

Passenger's — Remove and refit 86.65.32

Removing

1 Remove the driver's seat, see 76.70.04 or the passenger's seat, see 76.70.05.
2 Remove single bolt to release the integral buckle and switch unit.
3 Collect up the wavy washer, flange bush and distance piece.

Refitting

4 Reverse 1 to 3.

HEATED BACK LIGHT SWITCH   86.65.36

Remove and refit

Removing

1 Remove the fascia switch panel, see 86.65.66.
2 Using a small screwdriver carefully prise off two Spire clips.
3 Remove the face panel and the switch identification strip assembly.
4 Push inwards two spring clips on the switch and withdraw the switch from the panel.

Refitting

5 Reverse 1 to 4.

HAZARD SWITCH

Remove and refit   **86.65.50**

Removing

1   Remove the fascia switch panel, see 86.65.66.
2   Using a small screwdriver carefully prise off two Spire clips.
3   Remove the face panel and the switch identification strip assembly.
4   Push inwards one plastic clip on the switch and withdraw the switch from the panel.

Refitting

5   Reverse 1 to 4. Insert the switch so that the 'symbol' is at the lower edge.

NOTE: The hazard warning light built into the switch has a bulb housed in the switch harness plug.

STOP LAMP SWITCH

Remove and refit   **86.65.51**

Removing

1   Locate the switch adjacent to the brake pedal arm attachment to the brake servo.
2   Disconnect two Lucar connectors.
3   Slacken the large hexagon nut.
4   Push the brake pedal forward and remove the nut and washer/washers.
    CAUTION: Do not attempt to rotate the switch in the bracket as the switch has a locating flat.
5   Remove the switch from the bracket.

Refitting

6   Position the switch to the bracket.
7   Push the brake pedal forward and fit the washer/washers and nut finger-tight.
8   Tighten the nut lightly. Do not overtighten the nut on the plastic threads or the switch may be damaged.
9   Connect two Lucar connectors. The connectors may be fitted either way round.

CHOKE SWITCH

Remove and refit   **86.65.53**

Manual choke vehicles only

Removing

1   Locate the choke switch attached to the choke cable adjacent to the hand knob.
2   Using a small screwdriver remove the small screw.
3   Slide the clip from the switch and remove both items.
4   Disconnect one Lucar connector.

Refitting

5   Connect one Lucar connector.
6   Position the switch and clip over the reduced diameter of the cable. Slide the clip onto the switch.
7   Position the assembly so that the switch plunger is located in the hole provided in the outer cable housing. Secure with the small screw.

CIGARETTE LIGHTER

Remove and refit   **86.65.60**

Removing

1 Isolate the battery.
2 Pull out the centre console tray.
3 Withdraw the cigarette lighter heating unit.
4 Pull the purple wire 3 mm connector from the centre terminal.
5 Carefully insert a pair of long nosed pliers into the inner well to locate on the stronger cross piece as shown. Holding the outer well, unscrew the inner well from the outer well.
6 Remove the illumination ring.
7 Disconnect the black earth wire Lucar connector.
8 Disconnect the red/white wire single pin harness plug.
9 If necessary renew the bulb as follows: Squeeze the sides of the bulb cowl and withdraw. Unclip the bulb cowl from the bulb holder. Remove the bulb from the bayonet fitting.

Refitting

10 Reverse 1 to 9. Fit the cigarette lighter so that the bulb cowl is suitably positioned.

P10205

STEERING COLUMN MULTI-PURPOSE SWITCH

Remove and refit   **86.65.64**

Removing

1 Isolate the battery.
2 Unscrew two long Pozidriv screws and remove the nacelle upper and lower halves.
NOTE: The screws have a long threaded length of approximately 20 mm. A long 'unscrew time' should be expected.
3 Remove the steering wheel, see 57.60.01.
4 Note the switch harness wire runs.
5 Remove the Insuloid harness clip securing the switch harnesses to the fascia rail support strut. The clip is released by squeezing the projection as shown.
6 Disconnect two harness plugs.
7 Slacken the switch clamp screw.
8 Withdraw the switch complete with its harnesses from the column.

Individual switch renew

The multi-purpose switch is initially fitted as a complete unit. In service either half of the switch may be renewed as follows:

9 Do not slacken or remove two hexagon headed screws.
10 Drill out two rivets.
11 Remove one hexagon headed screw and washer.
12 Discard the defective switch.
13 Position the new switch.
14 Fit two bolts and nuts supplied with the new switch.
15 Fit one hexagon headed screw and washer. Do not fully tighten as the screw head is required to move with the switch arm.

continued

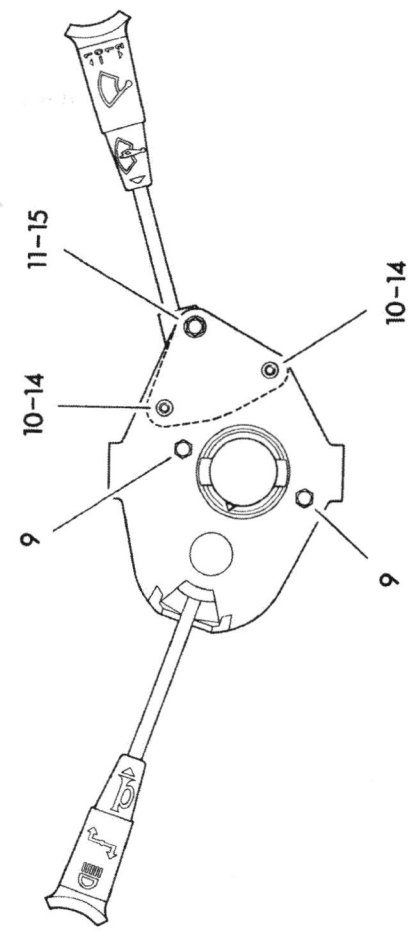

A 86 165

11–15

10–14

10–14

9

9

Refitting

16 Insert the switch harnesses into position. Position the switch to the column with the switch tongue located into the outer tube assembly slot.

17 Push the switch against the outer tube assembly and tighten the switch clamp screw.

18 Position the switch harness wire runs as noted at operation 4 above.

19 Connect two harness plugs.

20 Fit the Insuloid harness clip to secure the switch harnesses to the fascia rail support strut.

21 Fit the steering wheel, see 57.60.01. **NOTE:** The turn signal cancelling collar must be correctly aligned at this stage. Refer to 57.60.01.

22 Position the nacelle upper and lower halves. Secure with two long Pozidriv screws.

23 Connect the battery.

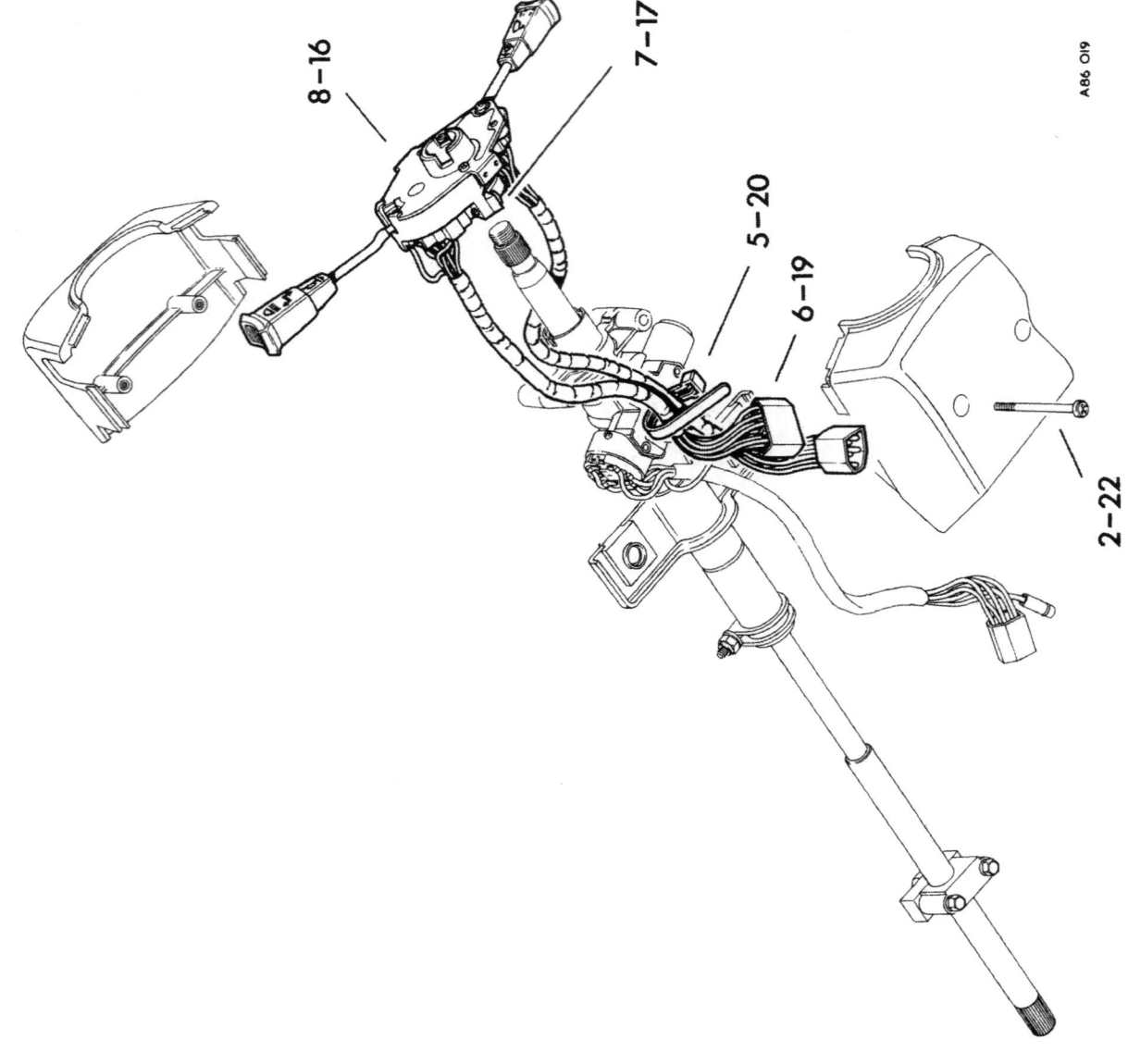

8–16

7–17

5–20

6–19

2–22

A86 019

REAR FOG LAMP SWITCH

Remove and refit   86.65.65

When fitted

Removing

1   Remove the fascia switch panel, see
    86.65.66.
2   Using a small screwdriver carefully
    prise off two Spire clips.
3   Remove the face panel and the switch
    identification strip assembly.
4   Push inwards two spring clips on the
    switch and withdraw the switch from
    the panel.

Refitting

5   Reverse 1 to 4.

FASCIA SWITCH PANEL

Remove and refit   86.65.66

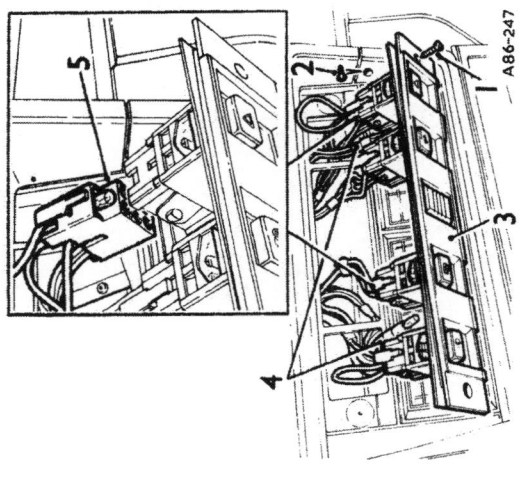

Removing

1   Remove two Pozidriv screws.
2   Remove one Pozidriv screw securing
    the instrument cowl
3   Push the instrument cowl up slightly
    to clear the top corner of the panel.
    Withdraw the fascia switch panel.
4   Pull out two switch identification strip
    bulb holders.
5   Disconnect all switch harness plugs.
6   Remove the fascia switch panel from
    the vehicle.

Refitting

7   Reverse 1 to 6.

BATTERY CONDITION INDICATOR 88.10.00

Data

Manufacturer	Smith's
Type	Bi-metal resistance
Smith's part number	BV 8115/00
Triumph part number	UKC 0512

Illumination . . . . Remote by instrument panel illumination

Description

The Smith's 'bi-metal resistance' battery condition indicator measures the system voltage. Instrument response is slow to damp out short period variations. The indicator produces no radio interference and no suppression equipment is required.

The battery condition indicator contains a bi-metal strip surrounded by a heater series winding. Current flow through the series winding heats the bi-metal strip which consequently distorts. The pointer is suspended between the moving end of the bi-metal strip and a spring blade. This arrangement causes the pointer to take up a position over the scale that is related to current flow through the indicator. Current flow through the indicator is related to system voltage.

BATTERY CONDITION INDICATOR

Remove and refit 88.10.07

Removing

1 Remove the lens, see 88.20.17.
2 Lift away the face panel.
3 Remove one Pozidriv screw.
4 Carefully withdraw the battery condition indicator.

Refitting

5 Reverse 1 to 4.

CLOCK

Data

Manufacturer	Smith's—made in France
Type	Transistor
Smith's part number	CTJ 3702/00
Triumph part number	UKC 2408

CLOCK

Adjust 88.15.04

Set the hands to the correct time—

Locate the adjustment knob below the fascia and to the left of the speedometer trip reset knob. Push the clock adjustment knob upwards and rotate to set the hands.

Regulate the clock—

The clock is precision regulated during manufacture and no further adjustment is possible in service. If the clock is gaining or losing less than five minutes per week the clock should be periodically reset to the correct time as detailed above. If the clock is gaining or losing more than five minutes per week the clock should be replaced.

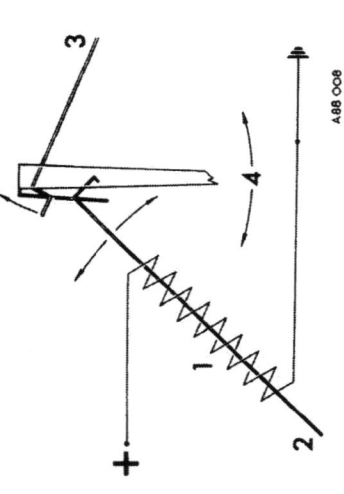

A88 008

† Supply voltage
1 Heater series winding
2 Bimetal strip
3 Spring blade
4 Pointer

CLOCK

Remove and refit 88.15.07

Removing

1 Remove the lens, see 88.20.17.
2 Lift away the face panel.
3 Unscrew the knurled nut. Withdraw the clock cable.
4 Remove two Pozidriv screws.
5 Withdraw the clock.

Refitting

6 Reverse 1 to 5.

INSTRUMENT PANEL

Description   88.20.00

The instrument panel is an independent unit which contains a set of instruments and a comprehensive set of warning lights. These are enclosed in a plastic housing. The exposed side of the instrument panel is finished with a face panel and a one-piece curved lens produced from ICI Acrylic. The individual instruments therefore require no bodies or glasses.

Electrical connections from the vehicle harness to the printed circuit attached to the concealed side of the instrument panel is by two multi-contact harness plugs.

The mechanism of the individual instruments are screw mounted into the housing. Electrical input to the instruments is via the instrument pillars. The electrical path from the printed circuit to the instrument pillars is by metal clips screwed down against exposed sections of the printed circuit. This design allows any instrument to be removed and refitted without making any conscious electrical connections.

The warning light bulbs are retained in bulb holders which are fitted into the concealed side of the instrument panel by bayonet fittings. The warning light annotated lens blocks are positioned by housing dowels and are retained by being sandwiched between the housing and the face panel. The warning light electrical connections are made automatically by two bulb holder strips making direct contact against exposed sections of the printed circuit.

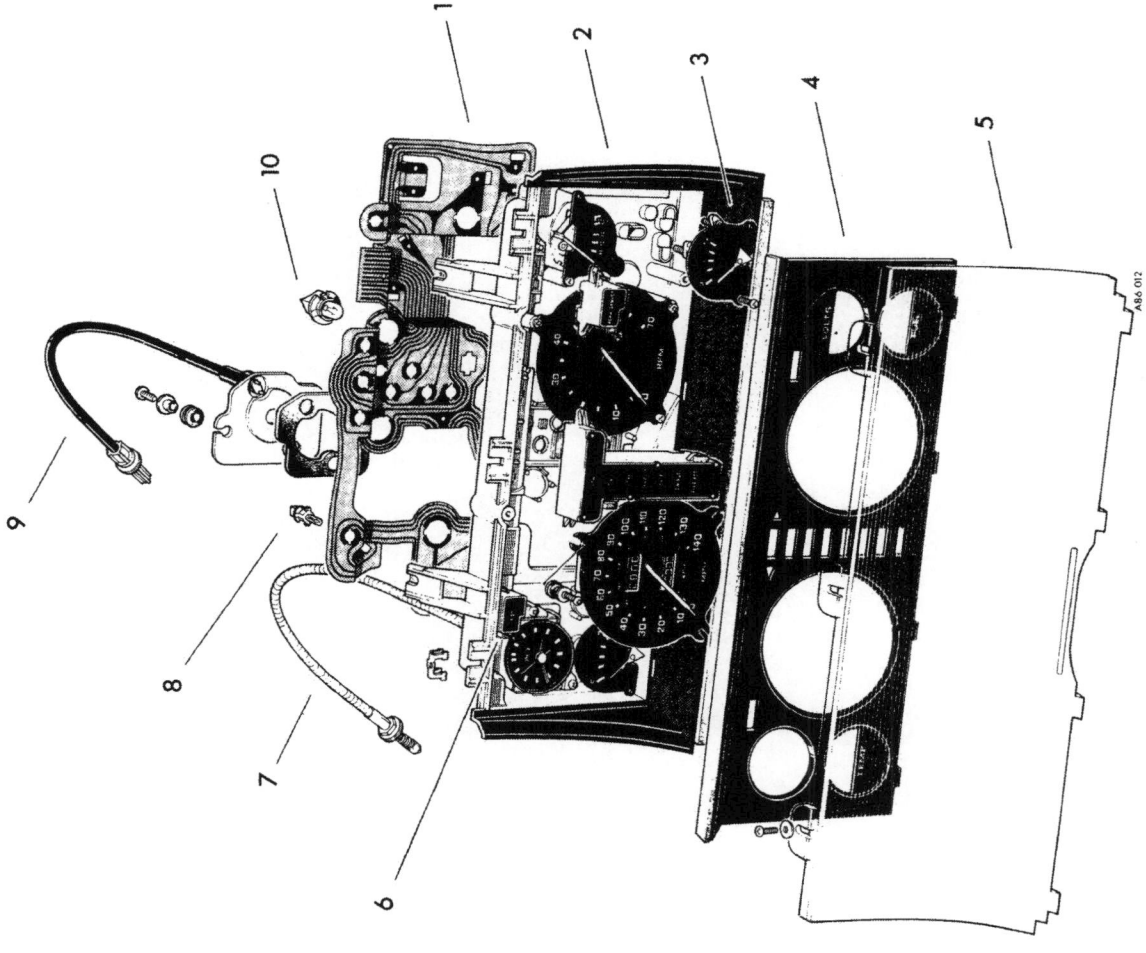

1 Printed circuit
2 Housing
3 Instrument
4 Face panel
5 Lens
6 Annotated lens block
7 Clock cable
8 Warning light
9 Speedometer trip
   reset cable
10 Instrument illumination

A86 012

INSTRUMENT PANEL

Remove and refit   88.20.01

Removing

1   Remove the fascia centre grille, see 76.55.14.
2   Remove the fascia instrument cowl, see 76.46.17.
3   Unscrew two long Pozidriv screws and remove the nacelle upper and lower halves.
    NOTE: The screws have a long threaded length of approximately 20 mm. A long 'unscrew time' should be expected.
4   Slacken the speedometer trip reset cable knurled nut. Withdraw the cable from the bracket slot.
5   Slacken the clock cable knurled nut. Withdraw the cable from the bracket slot.
6   Depress the lever to release the catch from the annular groove in the boss. Pull the speedometer cable from the instrument.
7   Remove two upper Pozidriv screws and washers.
8   Remove two lower Pozidriv screws and washers.
9   Withdraw the instrument panel slightly.
10 Disconnect two harness multi-contact plugs.
11 Remove the instrument panel from the vehicle.

Refitting

12 Ensure that two lower Spire nuts are correctly fitted.
13 Position the instrument panel with the clock cable and the speedometer trip reset cable inserted either side of the fascia rail support strut and harnesses.
14 Connect two harness multi-contact plugs.
15 Insert the instrument panel to its correct position.
16 To help establish the correct position, fit two upper Pozidriv screws and washers finger-tight.
17 Fit two lower Pozidriv screws and washers.
18 Tighten two upper Pozidriv screws and washers.
19 Push the speedometer cable onto the instrument. Ensure that the catch engages into the annular groove in the boss.
20 Insert the clock cable into the appropriate bracket slot. Hand tighten the knurled nut.
21 Insert the speedometer trip reset cable into the appropriate bracket slot. Hand tighten the knurled nut.
22 Position the nacelle upper and lower halves. Secure with two long Pozidriv screws.
23 Fit the fascia instrument cowl, see 76.46.17.
24 Fit the fascia centre grille, see 76.55.14.

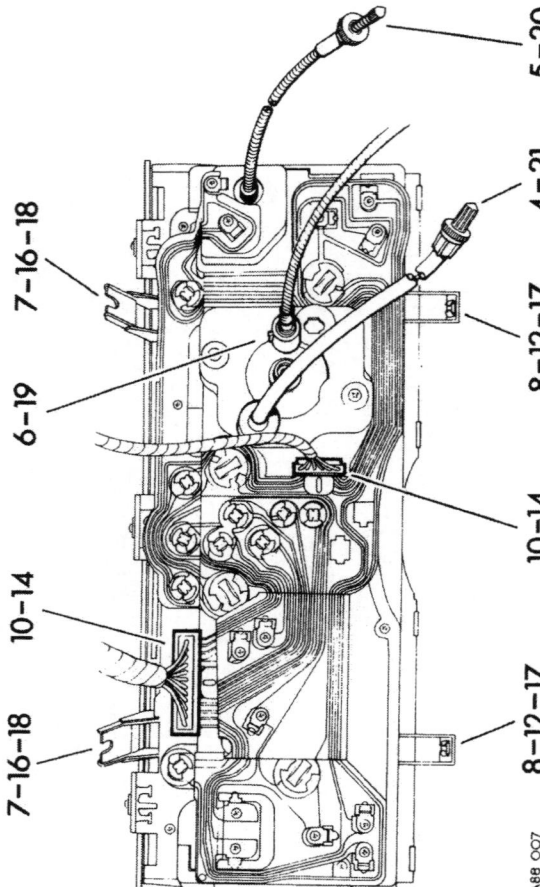

A86 O34

A88 OO7

5–20
4–21
7–16–18
6–19
8–12–17
10–14
7–16–18
10–14
8–12–17

INSTRUMENT PANEL

Lens — remove and refit   88.20.17

Removing

1 Remove the fascia centre grille, see 76.55.14.
2 Remove the fascia instrument cowl, see 76.46.17.
3 Remove three Pozidriv screws and washers.
4 Carefully slide the lens upwards following the path of its natural arc.

Refitting

5 Reverse 1 to 4. If difficulty is experienced to engage the four lens tongues, slacken two lower Pozidriv screws and slightly reposition the instrument panel.

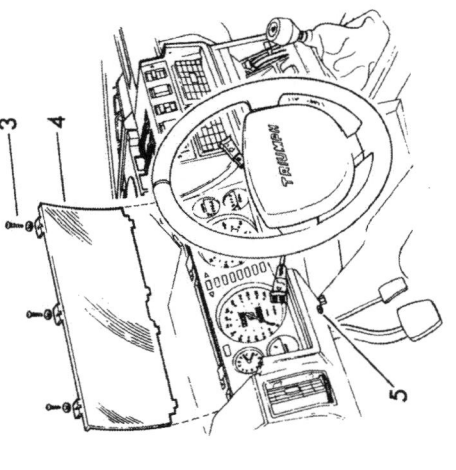

A 88 003

INSTRUMENT PANEL

Printed circuit — remove and refit   88.20.19

Removing

1 Remove the instrument panel, see 88.20.01.
2 Remove a number of small Pozidriv screws.
3 Lift out a number of contact clips.
4 Rotate four large bulb holders anti-clockwise and lift from the bayonet fittings.
5 Rotate a number of small bulb holders anti-clockwise and lift from the bayonet fittings.
6 Use a small screwdriver to carefully prise up two plastic press clips. Take care not to damage the printed circuit.
7 Release any sticky tape.
8 Lift away the printed circuit.

Refitting

9 Reverse 1 to 8.

FUEL AND TEMPERATURE INDICATION   88.25.00

Data

Fuel indicator

Manufacturer	Smiths
Type	Air cored
Smiths part number	ACF 8103/00
Triumph part number	UKC 0511
Body	None—assembled into instrument panel
Illumination	Remote by instrument panel illumination

Fuel tank unit

Manufacturer	Smiths
Smiths part number	TBS 5232/000EC
Triumph part number	TKC 0147

Temperature indicator

Manufacturer	Smiths
Type	Air cored
Smiths part number	ACT 8102/00
Triumph part number	UKC 0510
Body	None—assembled into instrument panel
Illumination	Remote by instrument panel illumination

Temperature transmitter

Manufacturer	Smiths
Type	Semi-conductor
Smiths part number	TT 4803/00A
Triumph part number	150843
Colour code	Black
Indication range	50 to 140 deg. centigrade
Thread	⅜ in—18 UNF

FUEL AND TEMPERATURE INDICATION

Description   88.25.00

The Smith's 'air cored' indication system is suitable for rugged environments and able to withstand high levels of vibration. Instrument response is rapid. The system is self-compensating for variation in voltage supply and no voltage stabilizer is required. The system produces no radio interference and no suppression equipment is required.

The 'air cored' indicator consists of three individual coil windings positioned relative to each other as shown. A central shaft carries a magnet bar which is free to swing in the area enclosed by the coils. The end of the shaft carries the pointer.

The magnetic field direction produced by any one coil is fixed. The magnetic field strength produced by any one coil may be varied by adjusting the current through the appropriate coil. The final magnetic field direction is the resultant of the currents through all three coils.

The design is that two of the coils receive a constant current. The third coil receives a current managed by a variable resistor which is the appropriate system sensor. The sensor therefore controls the final magnetic field direction. The magnet bar aligns itself with this magnetic field direction and the pointer is positioned to indicate the correct dial reading.

Switch off – when the circuit supply is switched off a small permanent magnet located in the assembly influences the magnet bar and the pointer returns to the zero position. The effect of this 'pull off' magnet is allowed for when calibrating the instrument during manufacture.

The circuit diagram for the fuel indication system and the temperature indication system is shown. Coils: 'A' and 'B' receive an almost constant current. In this circuit the current through coils 'A' and 'B' will vary but to a small amount compared to the variation through coil 'C'. Coil 'C' receives a current managed by the fuel tank unit or the temperature transmitter. A ballast resistor and calibration resistor are included in the circuit as shown.

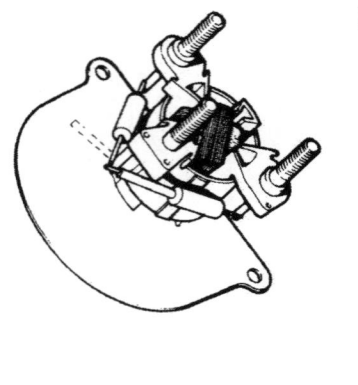

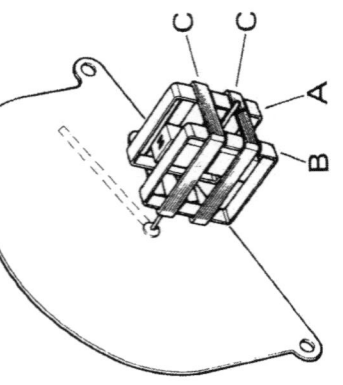

A88 005

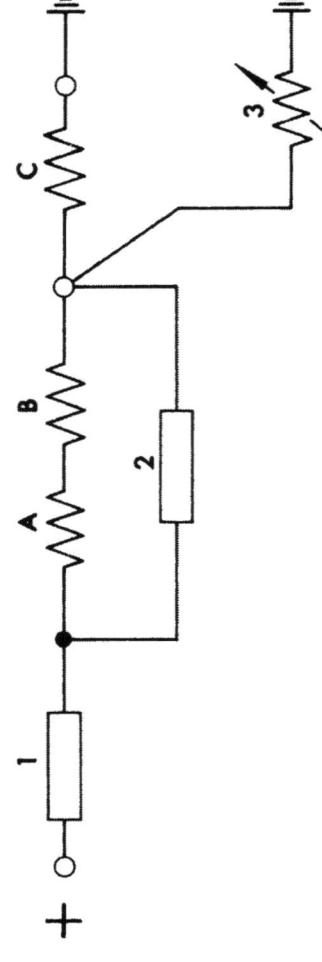

A88 006

1 Ballast resistor
2 Calibration resistor
A Coil 'A'
B Coil 'B'
C Coil 'C'
3 System sensor

A88 004

TEMPERATURE INDICATOR

Remove and refit   **88.25.14**

Removing

1   Remove the lens, see 88.20.17.
2   Lift away the face panel.
3   Remove one Pozidriv screw.
4   Carefully withdraw the temperature indicator.

Refitting

5   Reverse 1 to 4.

TEMPERATURE TRANSMITTER

Remove and refit   **88.25.20**

Removing

1   Drain part of the coolant, see 26.10.01.
2   Locate the transmitter on the inlet manifold.
3   Disconnect the Lucar connector.
4   Unscrew the transmitter from the inlet manifold.

Refitting

5   Reverse 1 to 4. Fit a new sealing washer if available.

FUEL INDICATOR

Remove and refit   **88.25.26**

Removing

1   Remove the lens, see 88.20.17.
2   Lift away the face panel.
3   Remove one Pozidriv screw.
4   Carefully withdraw the fuel indicator.

Refitting

5   Reverse 1 to 4.

FUEL TANK UNIT

Remove and refit   **88.25.32**

Removing

1   Drive the vehicle onto a ramp.
2   Estimate the quantity of fuel in the fuel tank.
3   Provide a suitable container to receive the quantity.
4   Raise the ramp.
5   Disconnect three Lucar connectors.
6   Prepare for fuel spillage. Pull off the rubber fuel outlet pipe and drain the tank contents into the container.
7   Release the locking ring by tapping anti-clockwise. Remove the locking ring.
   NOTE: This operation may be facilitated by employing a service tool — Churchill number 18G 1001.
8   Carefully withdraw the tank unit.
9   Remove the sealing washer.

Refitting

10   Reverse 1 to 9. Fit a new sealing washer if available. Connect the Lucar connectors as follows:
   Green/black wire to terminal T.
   Green/orange wire to terminal W.
   Black wire to earth terminal.

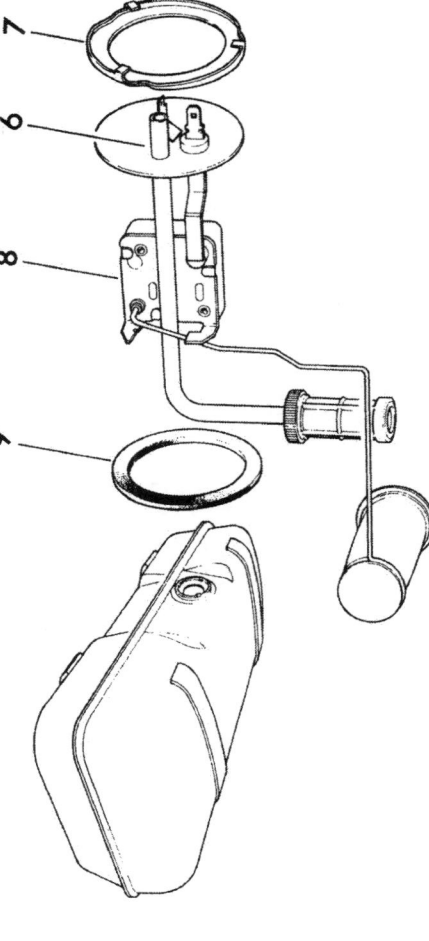

A 88 001

5–7

4–6

3–9

A88 002

SPEEDOMETER

Remove and refit   **88.30.01**

Removing

1 Remove the lens, see 88.20.17.
2 Lift away the face panel.
3 Depress the lever to release the catch from the annular groove in the boss. Pull the speedometer cable from the instrument.
4 Remove three Pozidriv screws.
5 Withdraw the speedometer.

Refitting

6 To assist engagement of the speedometer trip reset cable rotate the control to pre-set the alignment.
7 Insert the speedometer.
8 Fit three Pozidriv screws.
9 Push the speedometer cable onto the instrument. Ensure that the catch engages into the annular groove in the boss.
10 Position the face panel.
11 Fit the lens, see 88.20.17.

SPEEDOMETER

Trip reset cable — remove and refit   **88.30.02**

Removing

1 Remove the speedometer, see 88.30.01.
2 Note the run of the trip reset cable.
3 Slacken the trip reset cable knurled nut. Withdraw the cable from the bracket slot.
4 To assist withdrawal of the trip reset cable rotate the control to pre-set the alignment.
5 Using a small screwdriver release the trip reset cable claws. Withdraw the trip reset cable attachment from the instrument panel housing.

Refitting

6 To assist insertion of the trip reset cable rotate the control to pre-set the alignment.
7 Insert the trip reset cable attachment into the instrument panel housing. Ensure that the claws engage correctly.
8 Ensure that the trip reset cable run is as noted at operation 2 above.
9 Insert the trip reset cable into the bracket slot. Hand tighten the knurled nut.
10 Fit the speedometer, see 88.30.01.

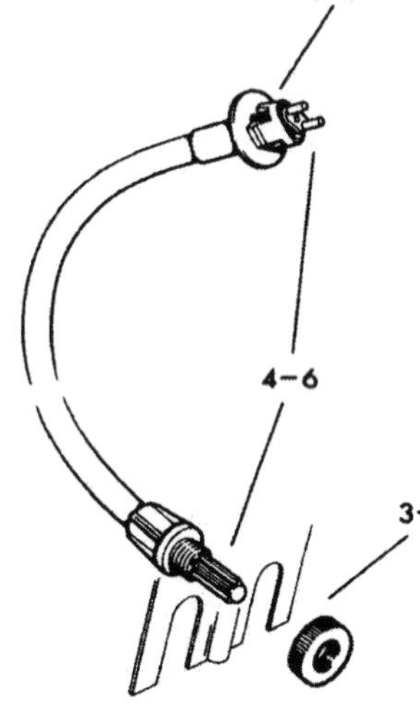

TACHOMETER

Remove and refit   **88.30.21**

Removing

1 Remove the lens, see 88.20.17.
2 Lift away the face panel.
3 Remove three Pozidriv screws.
4 Carefully withdraw the tachometer.

Refitting

5 Reverse 1 to 4.

All Service Tools mentioned in this Manual must be obtained direct from the manufacturers:
Messrs. V. L. Churchill & Co. Ltd.
P.O. Box No. 3
London Road
Daventry, Northants.
England NN11 4NF

Tool No.	Description
18G 47-1	Layshaft cluster bearings remover adaptor.
18G 47-3	Constant pinion remover/replacer adaptor.
18G 47 BD	Differential carrier bearings remover adaptor.
18G 47 BP	Mainshaft bearing and speedo gear remover/replacer adaptor.
18G 55 A (38U 3)	Piston ring compressor.
18G 106	Valve spring compressor.
18G 134	Bearing and oil seal replacer.
18G 134 DH (550)	Differential bearings replacer adaptor.
18G 191	Bevel pinion setting gauge.
18G 191 M	Dummy pinion.
18G 207 (S 98A)	Preload gauge.
18G 284	Impulse extractor – U.N.F.
18G 284 AAA (S 4235-A2)	First motion shaft remover adaptor.
18G 304	Front and rear hub remover.
18G 1197	Mainshaft bearing and speedometer drive gear replacer.
18G 1198	Gearbox mainshaft circlip replacer.
18G 1198A	Gearbox mainshaft circlip replacer adaptor sleeve.
18G 1199 (S 145)	Gearbox mainshaft circlip remover.
18G 1205 (S 337 RG 421)	Propeller shaft flange wrench.
18G 1208	Dummy layshaft.
18G 1256 A (S 114A)	Torx screw wrench.
18G 1261	Steering rack and pinion retainer spanner.
18G 1269	First motion shaft oil seal protector sleeve.

Tool No.	Description
18G 1311	Crankshaft spigot bearing remover.
18G 1312	Crankshaft spigot needle roller bearing.
47(S 4221A) 60A	Multi-purpose hand press.
	Valve guide remover/replacer.
S 60A-2A	Valve guide remover/replacer adaptor.
S 60A-7	Valve guide replacer adaptor.
S 60A-8	Valve guide replacer adaptor.
S 60A-9	Valve guide replacer adaptor.
MS 68	Torx screw wrench.
S 101	Differential case spreader.
S 101-1	Adaptor.
S 304	Rear hub bearing replacer.
S 314	Mainshaft ball bearing replacer.
S 348	Water pump overhaul kit.
S 349	Distributor wrench.
S 350	Cylinder head stud remover/replacer.
S 352	Valve spring compressor adaptor.
S 353	Carburetter adjusting tool.
S 356C	Front and rear hub remover.
S 356C-5	Retaining nuts.
S 357A	Plug spanner.
RTR 359	Front suspension closure nut wrench.
RTR 360	Retaining washer holding wrench.
3072 (S 4221A-10)	Slide hammer.
S 4221A-17	Differential bearing remover adaptor.
	Pinion head bearing remover/replacer adaptor.
S 4235A-1	Axle shaft remover.
S 4235A-10	Water pump assembly remover.
P 5045 (18G 1276)	Adjustable coil spring retainers.

5 SPEED TRANSMISSION

Tool No.	Description
18G 47 AJ	Pinion bearing remover/replacer adaptor.
18G 284 AAH	Mainshaft pilot bearing outer track remover adaptor.
18G 705-1	Fifth speed gear remover adaptor.
18G 1271	Axle shaft inner oil seal remover.
18G 1272	Pinion nut wrench and preload adaptor.
18G 1273	Pinion oil seal protector sleeve.
S 4221A-16	Outer taper bearing remover/replacer adaptor.

AUTOMATIC TRANSMISSION

Tool No.	Description
CBW 1C (18G 502)	Hydraulic test equipment.
CBW 1C-2	Pressure test adaptor.
18G 1307	Rear servo adjuster and special locknut front adaptor.
CBW 33	Mainshaft end-float gauge.
CBW 37A (18G 1016)	Clutch spring compressor.
CBW 41A (18G 702)	Rear clutch piston replacer.
CBW 42A (18G 1107)	Front clutch piston replacer.
CBW 60	Bench cradle.
CBW 62	Throttle cable mounting seal remover.
CBW 547A-50	Tension wrench.
CBW 547A-50-2A (18G 537B)	Rear servo adjuster adaptor.
CBW 548 (18G 681)	Torque screwdriver.

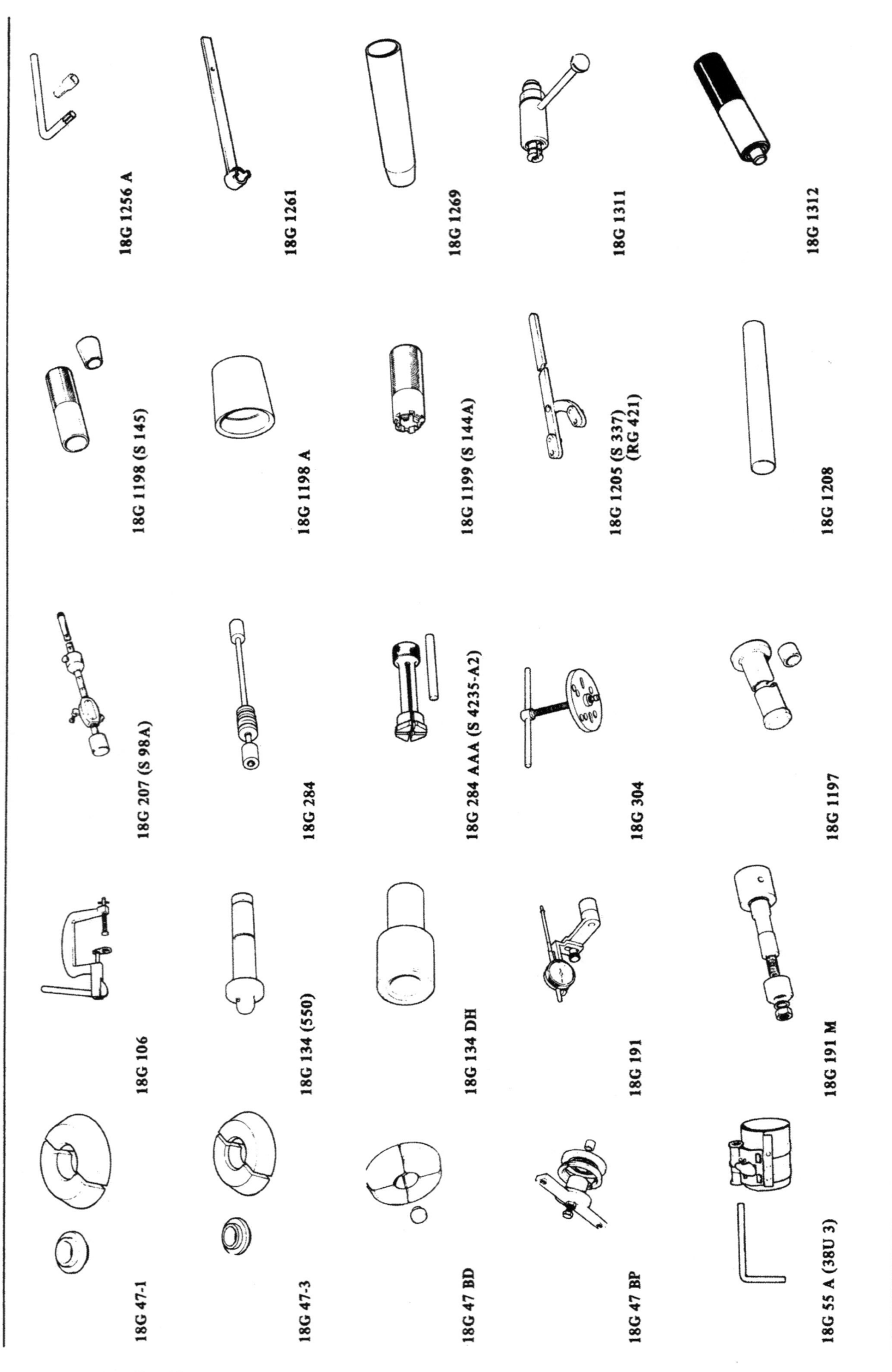

18G 1256 A

18G 1261

18G 1269

18G 1311

18G 1312

18G 1198 (S 145)

18G 1198 A

18G 1199 (S 144A)

18G 1205 (S 337) (RG 421)

18G 1208

18G 207 (S 98A)

18G 284

18G 284 AAA (S 4235-A2)

18G 304

18G 1197

18G 106

18G 134 (550)

18G 134 DH

18G 191

18G 191 M

18G 47-1

18G 47-3

18G 47 BD

18G 47 BP

18G 55 A (38U 3)

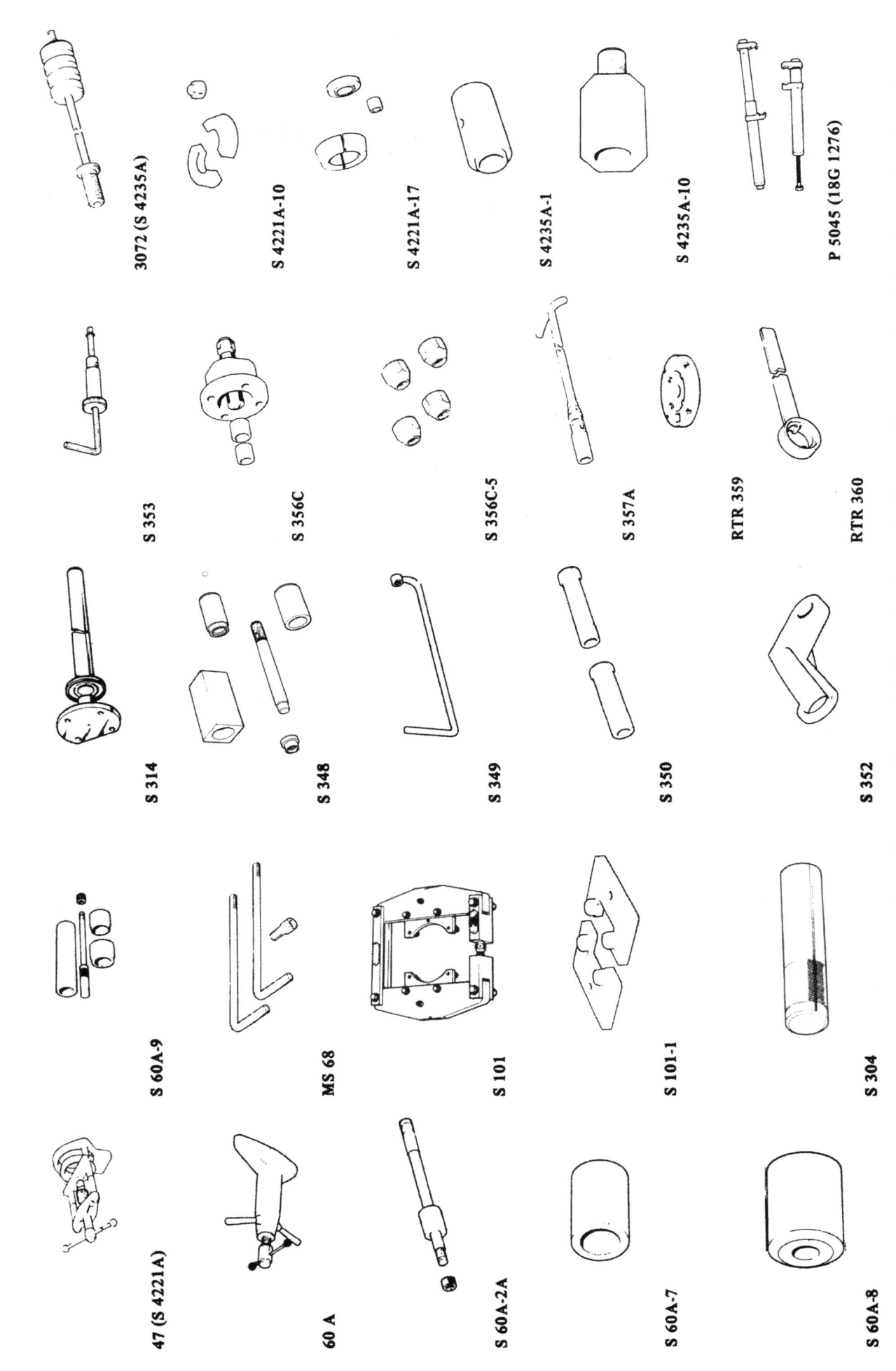

3072 (S 4235A)

S 4221A-10

S 4221A-17

S 4235A-1

S 4235A-10

P 5045 (18G 1276)

S 353

S 356C

S 356C-5

S 357A

RTR 359

RTR 360

S 314

S 348

S 349

S 350

S 352

S 60A-9

MS 68

S 101

S 101-1

S 304

47 (S 4221A)

60 A

S 60A-2A

S 60A-7

S 60A-8

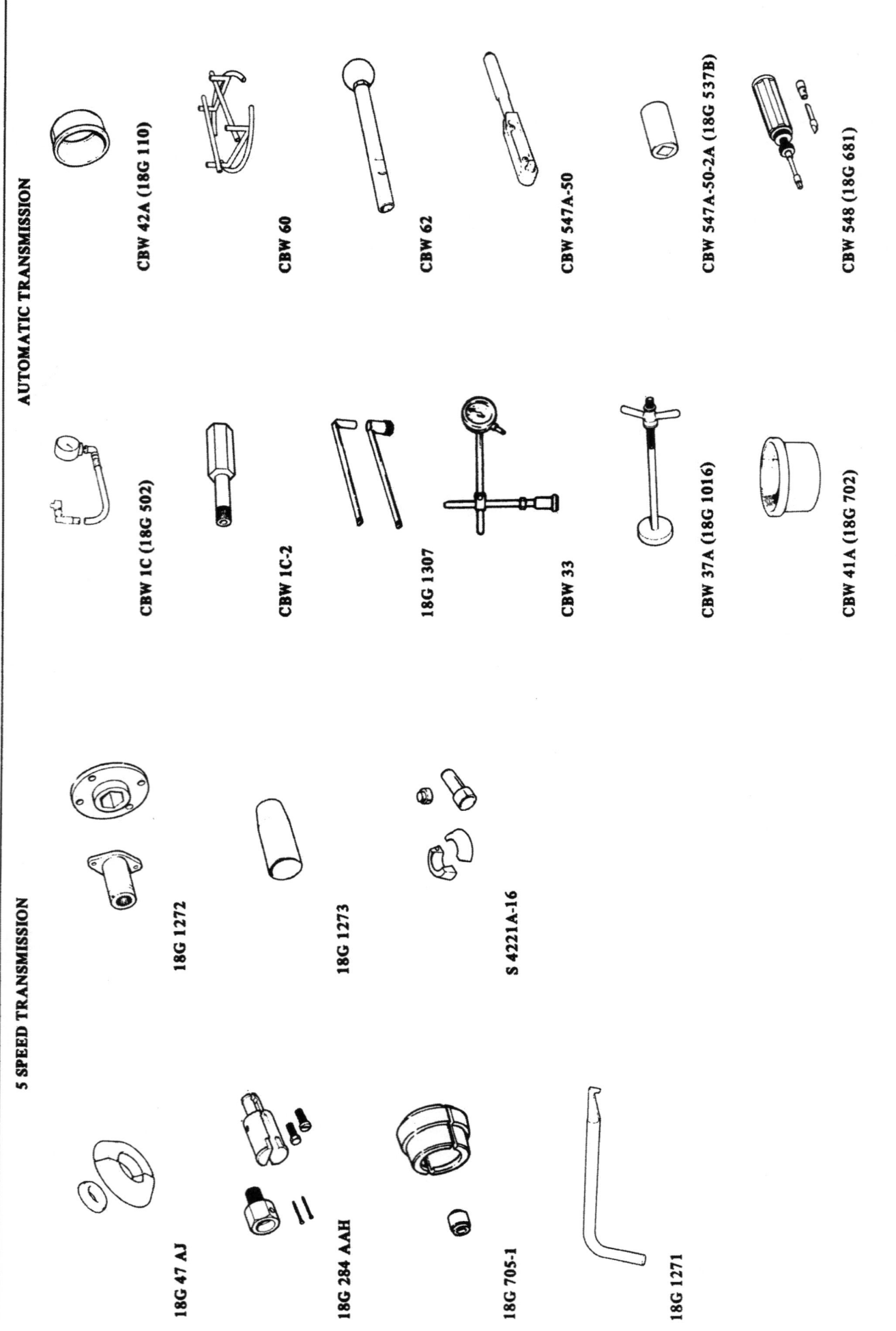

AUTOMATIC TRANSMISSION

CBW 42A (18G 110)

CBW 60

CBW 62

CBW 547A-50

CBW 547A-50-2A (18G 537B)

CBW 548 (18G 681)

CBW 1C (18G 502)

CBW 1C-2

18G 1307

CBW 33

CBW 37A (18G 1016)

CBW 41A (18G 702)

5 SPEED TRANSMISSION

18G 1272

18G 1273

S 4221A-16

18G 47 AJ

18G 284 AAH

18G 705-1

18G 1271

Service

**To be used with TR7 Repair Operation
Manual - AKM 3079B**

Publication Part No. AKM 3079/1
Published by BL Cars - Service
© BL Cars Limited, 1980

TRIUMPH
TR7
REPAIR
OPERATION
MANUAL
Supplement

This supplement is intended for use with the TR7 Repair Operation Manual AKM 3079B and provides additional information, changes to vehicle specifications and revisions to repair procedures.

CONTENTS

GENERAL FITTING INSTRUCTIONS

Vehicle Identification Number

Location
The vehicle identification number (V.I.N.) is stamped on a plate on the R.H. front suspension tower and should be quoted in full.
A sample V.I.N. is shown below:

TP A D V 7 A A 402027

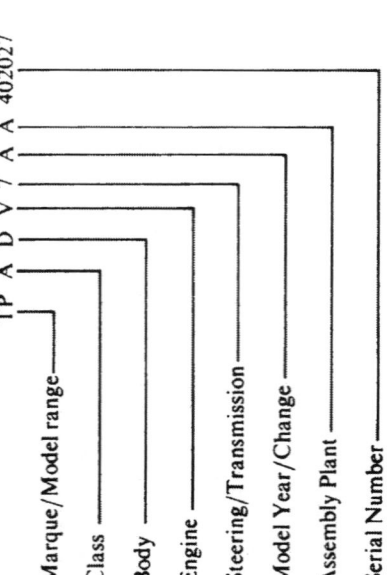

- Marque/Model range
- Class
- Body
- Engine
- Steering/Transmission
- Model Year/Change
- Assembly Plant
- Serial Number

GENERAL SPECIFICATION DATA

GEARBOX — 5 speed from VIN 402027

Ratios
Fifth (top) .... 0.792 : 1
Fourth .... 1.00 : 1
Third .... 1.40 : 1
Second .... 2.09 : 1
First .... 3.32 : 1
Reverse .... 3.43 : 1

Overall ratios UK:
Fifth (top) .... 3.09 : 1
Fourth .... 3.90 : 1
Third .... 5.46 : 1
Second .... 8.15 : 1
First .... 12.96 : 1
Reverse .... 13.38 : 1

Overall ratios Europe, USA and Canada:
Fifth (top) .... 2.73 : 1
Fourth .... 3.45 : 1
Third .... 4.83 : 1
Second .... 7.21 : 1
First .... 11.45 : 1
Reverse .... 11.83 : 1

GEARBOX—AUTOMATIC — from VIN 402027

Type .... Borg Warner 66

	3rd	2nd	1st	Rev.
Overall ratios to 1	3.08–5.88	4.47–8.53	7.36–14.05	6.44–12.30
Road speed corresponding to 1000 r.p.m.				
m.p.h.	21.9–11.47			
km.p.h.	35.2–18.43			

WEIGHTS (APPROXIMATE) — Coupé. From VIN 402027

	Manual gearbox	Automatic gearbox
*Showroom: Minimum	2258 lb (1024 kg)	2251 lb (1021 kg)
Maximum	2335 lb (1059 kg)	2328 lb (1056 kg)
*Unladen: Minimum	2348 lb (1065 kg)	2341 lb (1062 kg)
Maximum	2425 lb (1100 kg)	2418 lb (1097 kg)
*Gross vehicle weight	2954 lb (1340 kg)	2954 lb (1340 kg)
*Maximum axle load: Front	1576 lb (715 kg)	1576 lb (715 kg)
Rear	1466 lb (665 kg)	1466 lb (665 kg)
*Towing capacity — braked trailer	2240 lb (1016 kg)	2240 lb (1016 kg)

WEIGHTS (APPROXIMATE) — Convertible. From VIN 402027

	Manual gearbox	Automatic gearbox
*Showroom: Minimum	2249 lb (1020 kg)	2240 lb (1016 kg)
Maximum	2326 lb (1055 kg)	2317 lb (1051 kg)
*Unladen: Minimum	2339 lb (1061 kg)	2330 lb (1057 kg)
Maximum		
*Gross vehicle weight	2954 lb (1340 kg)	2954 lb (1340 kg)
*Maximum axle load: Front	1576 lb (715 kg)	1576 lb (715 kg)
Rear	1466 lb (665 kg)	1466 lb (665 kg)
*Towing capacity — braked trailer	2240 lb (1016 kg)	2240 lb (1016 kg)

* These figures must be taken as a guide only and vary according to market, model year and equipment fitted.

AUTOMATIC TRANSMISSION SHIFT SPEEDS

Throttle position	Zero throttle	Light throttle		Part throttle	
Selector	1	D	D	D	D
Shift	2-1	1-2	2-3	3-2	2-1
Road speed m.p.h.	28-39	7-13	12-19	27-43	12-22
km.p.h.	45-63	11-21	19-31	43-69	19-35

Throttle position	Kickdown				
Selector	D	D	D	1	D
Shift	1-2	2-3	3-2	2-1	3-1
Road speed m.p.h.	38-48	70-80	60-72	39-50	25-38
km.p.h.	61-77	112-128	96-116	63-81	40-61

FINAL DRIVE — from VIN 402027

Ratios: Used with 5 speed gearbox

U.K. .... 3.90 : 1
Europe, USA and Canada .... 3.45 : 1

Used with Automatic gearbox

Ratio .... 3.08 : 1

TYRES

Size:

Automatic Transmission (from VIN 402027) .... 185/70 SR 13

5 Speed Transmission

This information supersedes that which is given in the Repair Operation Manual.

UK and Europe .... 185/70 HR 13
USA and Canada .... 185/70 SR 13

CAPACITIES (NOMINAL)

This information supersedes that which is given in the Repair Operation Manual.

	USA	Imperial	Metric
Fuel tank	14.4 gals	12 gals	54.5 litres
Rear axle from dry	2 pts	1.6 pts	0.9 litres
Windscreen washer reservoir	3.3 pts	2.75 pts	1.6 litres
Air conditioning system	2.5 lbs	1.1 kg. of refrigerant 12	

ENGINE TUNING DATA — CANADA from VIN 402027

WARNING: Before commencing work on an ignition system, all high tension terminals, adaptors and diagnostic equipment for testing should be inspected to ensure that they are adequately insulated and shielded, to prevent accidental personal contact and minimize the risk of shock.

Wearers of surgically implanted pacemaker devices should not be in close proximity to ignition circuits or diagnostic equipment.

ENGINE
Type	O.h.c. in line 4 cylinder
Capacity	122 in³ (1998 cm³)
Compression ratio	8.0 : 1
Firing order	1–3–4–2
Number one cylinder	Front
Idle speed	800 ± 100 rev/min
Ignition timing:	
Static	10° B.T.D.C.
Dynamic at idle	2° A.T.D.C.
Location of ignition timing marks	Scale on front cover — notch on pulley
Valve clearance (engine cold):	
Inlet	0.008 in (0.2 mm)
Exhaust	0.018 in (0.5 mm)
Valve clearance adjustment	Pallets between valve and cam follower
Inlet opens 16° B.T.D.C.	
Inlet closes 56° A.B.D.C.	
Exhaust opens 56° B.B.D.C.	
Exhaust closes 16° A.T.D.C.	

IGNITION DISTRIBUTOR
See 86.35.00

SPARK PLUGS
Make/type	Champion N12Y or Unipart GSP 131
Gap	0.024 to 0.026 in (0.61 to 0.66 mm).

IGNITION COIL
Make/type	Lucas 15C6 or A.C. Delco 3474214
Primary resistance at 20°C (68°F)	1.3 to 1.5 ohms

CARBURETTERS
Make	Twin Zenith Stromberg
Type	175 CD SEVX
Needle	B1DH

ENGINE TUNING DATA — Low Compression Engine

WARNING: Before commencing work on an ignition system, all high tension terminals, adaptors and diagnostic equipment for testing should be inspected to ensure that they are adequately insulated and shielded, to prevent accidental personal contact and minimize the risk of shock.

Wearers of surgically implanted pacemaker devices should not be in close proximity to ignition circuits or diagnostic equipment.

ENGINE
Type	O.h.c. in line 4 cylinder
Capacity	122 in³ (1998 cm³)
Compression ratio	8.0 : 1
Firing order	1–3–4–2
Number one cylinder	Front
Idle speed	650 to 850 rev/min
Ignition timing:	
Static	10° B.T.D.C.
Dynamic	10° B.T.D.C. at 650 to 850 rev/min
Location of ignition timing marks	Scale on front cover — notch on pulley
Valve clearance (engine cold):	
Inlet	0.008 in (0.2 mm)
Exhaust	0.018 in (0.5 mm)
Valve clearance adjustment	Pallets between valve and cam follower
Valve timing:	
Inlet opens 16° B.T.D.C.	
Inlet closes 56° A.B.D.C.	
Exhaust opens 56° B.B.D.C.	
Exhaust closes 16° A.T.D.C.	

IGNITION DISTRIBUTOR
See 86.35.00

SPARK PLUGS
Make/type	Champion N12Y
Gap	0.024 to 0.026 in (0.61 to 0.66 mm).

IGNITION COIL
Make/type	Lucas 15C6
Primary resistance at 20°C (68°F)	1.3 to 1.5 ohms

CARBURETTERS
Make/type	Twin SU HS6
Needle	BBF

TORQUE WRENCH SETTINGS

These instructions supersede those given in the Repair Operation Manual.

AIR CONDITIONING

Operation	Description	Nm	lbf ft	kgf m
			Specified torque	
Hoses — Flare Type				
Compressor to Condenser	¾″ Crimp Back Nut	40	30	4,0
Condenser to Receiver Drier	⅝″ Crimp Back Nut	28	21	2,9
Evaporator to Compressor	⅞″ Crimp Back Nut	50	37	5,1
Evaporator to Receiver Drier	⅝″ Crimp Back Nut	28	21	2,9
Ranco Valve to Receiver Drier	⁷⁄₁₆″ Flare Nut	12	9	1,2
Rotalock Valve to Compressor	1″ UNS	50	37	5,1
Hoses — 'O' Ring Type				
Compressor to Condenser				
Compressor end	1″ UNS Gasket Nut	27	20	2,7
Condenser end	¾″ Gasket Nut	27	20	2,7
Evaporator to Compressor				
Compressor end	1″ UNS Gasket Nut	27	20	2,7
Evaporator end	⅞″ UNF Nut	37	27	3,7
Condenser to Receiver Drier	⅝″ UNF Gasket Nut	18	13	1,8
Receiver Drier to Evaporator	⅝″ UNF Nut	18	13	1,8
Ranco Valve to Receiver Drier	⁷⁄₁₆″ UNF Gasket Nut	9	7	0,9

ANTI-FREEZE SOLUTIONS — ALL MARKETS

These instructions supersede those given in the Repair Operation Manual.

The overall anti-freeze concentration should not fall below 30% by volume to ensure that the anti-corrosion properties of the coolant are maintained.

Use UNIPART Universal anti-freeze to protect the cooling system.

If this is not available, use an ethylene glycol based anti-freeze (containing no methanol) with non-phosphate corrosion inhibitors suitable for use in mixed metal engines to ensure the protection of the cooling system against frost and corrosion.

CAUTION: No other universal anti-freeze should be used with UNIPART Universal Anti-freeze.

RECOMMENDED LUBRICANTS & ANTI-FREEZE SOLUTIONS — BRITISH ISLES — ALL SEASONS

This information supersedes that given in the Repair Operation Manual

(THE PRODUCTS RECOMMENDED ARE NOT LISTED IN ORDER OF PREFERENCE)

COMPONENT	PER-FORMANCE LEVEL	UNIPART	BP	CASTROL	DUCKHAMS	ESSO	MOBIL	PETROFINA	TEXACO	SHELL
Engine Carburetter and Oil Can	BL Cars Ltd specification BLS 22.01.02	Unipart Super Motor Oil 15W/50	BP Super Visco-Static 20/50	Castrol GTX 20W/50	Duckhams Q Motor Oil 20W/50	Esso Uniflo 15W/50 or Esso Super-lube 10W/40	Mobil Super Motor Oil 15W/40	Fina Supergrade Motor Oil 15W/40	Havoline Motor Oil 15W/40	Shell Super Motor Oil 15W/40
Manual Gearbox	ATF meeting specification M2C 33G		BP Autran G	Castrol TQF	Duckhams Q-matic	Essoglide Type G	Mobil ATF 210	Fina Purfimatic 33G	Texamatic Type G	Shell Donex TF
Automatic Gearbox	ATF meeting Specification M2C 33G		BP Autran G	Castrol TQF	Duckhams Q-matic	Essoglide Type G	Mobil ATF 210	Fina Purfimatic 33G	Texamatic Type G	Shell Donax TF
Final Drive Unit*	MIL-L-2105 API GL4		BP Gear Oil 90 EP	Castrol Hypoy 90 EP	Duckhams Hypoid 90	Esso Gear Oil GX 85W/140	Mobilube HD 90	Fina Pontonic MP 80W/90	Texaco Multigear Lubricant 90 EP	Shell Spirax 90 EP
Grease Points Brake Cables Steering Rack and Rear Hubs†	NLGI-2 Multi-purpose Lithium based grease		BP Energrease L2	Castrol LM Grease	Duckhams LB 1D	Esso Multi-purpose	Mobil MP	Fina Marson HIL 2 Grease	Marfak All Purpose Grease	Shell Retinax A
Brake and Clutch Reservoirs	Unipart Universal Brake Fluid or other Brake Fluids having a minimum boiling point of 260°C (500°F) and complying with FMVSS 116 DOT 3									
Cooling system	Unipart Universal Anti-Freeze									
Windscreen Washers	Unipart All-Seasons Washer Fluid									

* If final drive unit is completely drained refill with oil meeting BL Cars specification BLS 22.OL.03 or MIL-L-2105B.
† Front Hubs. Mobilgrease Super.

RECOMMENDED LUBRICANTS AND ANTI-FREEZE SOLUTIONS — OVERSEAS MARKETS

This information supersedes that given in the Repair Operation Manual

SERVICE CLASSIFICATION	PERFORMANCE LEVEL	S.A.E. VISCOSITY	AMBIENT TEMPERATURE °C (−30 to +20)
ENGINE CARBURETTER DASH POTS OIL CAN	Use UNIPART Super Multigrade Motor Oil OR other oils meeting BL Cars specification BL 22.OL.02 OR the requirements of the CCMC OR API-SE	5W/20, 5W/30, 5W/40, 10W/30, 10W/40, 10W/50, 15W/40, 15W/50, 20W/40, 20W/50	(viscosity/temperature range chart)
FINAL DRIVE UNIT* TOP UP ONLY	MIL-L-2105 API GL4	Hypoid 90, Hypoid 80W	(chart)
MANUAL GEARBOX	ATF meeting specification M2C 33G		(chart)
AUTOMATIC GEARBOX	ATF meeting specification M2C 33G		
REAR HUBS GREASE GUN BRAKE CABLES STEERING RACK	NLGI-2 Multi-purpose lithium based grease	Front hubs NLGI-2 High Melting Point Grease	
BRAKE AND CLUTCH RESERVOIRS	UNIPART UNIVERSAL BRAKE FLUID or other Brake Fluids having a minimum boiling point of 260°C (500°F) and complying with FMVSS 116 DOT 3		
COOLING SYSTEM	UNIPART UNIVERSAL ANTI-FREEZE		
WINDSCREEN WASHER	UNIPART ALL-SEASONS SCREEN WASHER FLUID		

* Final Drive Unit if drained MUST be filled with an oil meeting BL Cars specification BLS 22.OL.03 or having a minimum performance level of MIL-L-2 105B

MAINTENANCE SUMMARY, UK & EUROPE

This information supersedes that given in the Repair Operation Manual.

After Sales Service = 1,000 miles / 1500 km

Intermediate Service = Every 6 months or 6,000 miles / 10 000 km

Main Service = Every 12 months or 12,000 miles / 20 000 km

Main Service (24 denotes every 24 months, 24,000 miles (40 000) km)

● ACTION   x OPERATION

Operation	After Sales Service	Intermediate Service	Main Service
Fit car protection kit	●	●	●
Check condition and security of seats and seat belts	x		x
Drive on lift. Stop engine	●	●	●
Check operation of lamps	x	x	x
Check operation of horns	x	x	x
Check operation of warning indicators	x	x	x
Check/adjust operation of screen washers	x	x	x
Check operation of screen wipers	x	x	x
Check security/operation of foot and hand brake: release fully after checking	x	x	x
Open bonnet: fit wing covers	●	●	●
Disconnect battery			●
Raise lift to convenient working height with wheels free to rotate	●	●	●
Remove hub/wheel nut caps	●	●	●
Mark stud to wheel relationship front wheels	●	●	●
Mark stud to wheel relationship rear wheels	●		●
Remove front wheels	●	●	●
Remove rear wheels	●		●
Inspect road wheels for damage	x	x	x
Check tyre tread depth	x	x	x
Check tyres visually for external cuts in fabric, exposure of ply or cord structure, lumps or bulges	x	x	x
Check tyres for uneven wear	x		x
Check/adjust tyre pressures	x	x	x
Inspect brake pads for wear and discs for condition. Renew pads if necessary	x	x	x
Adjust front hub bearing end-float	x		x
Remove brake drums, wash out dust, inspect shoes for wear and drums for condition. Renew shoes if necessary. Refit drums	x		x
Inspect for fluid leaks from dampers	x		x
Check condition and security of steering unit, joints and gaiters	x	x	x
Refit road wheels in original position	●	●	●
Check tightness of road wheel fastenings	x	x	x
Refit hub/wheel nut caps	●	●	●
Raise lift to convenient working height	●	●	●
Drain engine oil	x	x	x
Check/top-up gearbox oil	x	x	x

Main Service (24 denotes every 24 months, 24,000 miles (40 000) km)

● ACTION   x OPERATION

Operation	After Sales Service	Intermediate Service	Main Service
Check/top-up rear axle oil	x		x
Check visually brake hoses, pipes and unions for chafing, cracks, leaks and corrosion	x		x
Check visually fuel and clutch pipes and unions for chafing, leaks and corrosion	x	x	x
Check exhaust system for condition, leakage and security	x	x	x
Adjust handbrake cable (where accessible from below)	x	x	x
Check security of accessible engine mountings	x		x
Check security and condition of suspension joints and fixings	x		x
Renew engine oil filter element (where accessible from below)	x	x	x
Clean and refit drain plug	x	x	x
Check for oil leaks from engine and transmission	x	x	x
Lubricate headlamp fitting mechanism pivots	●	●	●
Lower lift	●	●	●
Fit exhaust extractor pipe			
Check/adjust torque of cylinder head nuts/bolts			
Renew engine oil filter element (where accessible from above)	x	x	x
Fill engine with oil	x	x	x
Lubricate all pedal pivots and control linkages	x		x
Top-up carburetter piston dampers	x		x
Renew air cleaner element(s)	x		x
Check security of accessible engine mountings	x		x
Check driving belts, adjust or renew	x	x	x
Renew spark plugs	x		x
Check/top-up battery electrolyte	x		
Clean and grease battery connections	x		
Check battery condition	x	●	●
Reconnect battery	●	●	●
Check/top-up clutch fluid reservoir	x	x	x
Check/top-up brake fluid reservoir	x	x	x
Check operation of brake fluid level warning light switch (where fitted)	x	x	x
Check brake servo hose for security and condition	x		x
Check/top-up screen washer reservoir	x	x	x
Check/top-up cooling system	x	x	x
Pressure test cooling and heater system for leaks	x		x
Renew fuel line filter (where fitted)	x		x
Check visually crankcase breathing system for leaks and hoses for security and condition	24	24	24
Renew engine breather filter (where fitted)	24		24
Start engine and check sealing of oil filter	x	x	x
Stop engine	●	●	●
Check visually distributor contact points, adjust or renew	x	x	x
Check throttle and choke operation	x		x

MAINTENANCE SUMMARY, UK & EUROPE

This information supersedes that given in the Repair Operation Manual.

After Sales Service = 1,000 miles / 1500 km
Intermediate Service = Every 6 months or 6,000 miles / 10 000 km
Main Service = Every 12 months or 12,000 miles / 12,000 miles / 20 000 km

● ACTION   × OPERATION

After Sales Service	Intermediate Service	Main Service (24 denotes every 24 months, 24,000 miles (40 000) km)	OPERATION
●	●	●	Start engine
×	×	×	Check ignition distributor characteristics and timing, using electronic equipment. Adjust as necessary
●			Stop engine
×	×	×	Set to fast idle; leave engine running
×	×	×	Lubricate all locks, hinges and door check mechanisms (not steering lock)
×	×	×	Check operation of all door, bonnet and boot locks
×	×	×	Check operation of window controls
×	●	●	Check/adjust carburetter for engine idle speed and emissions settings
●	●	●	Stop engine, disconnect instruments
●	●	●	Start engine (auto only)
×	×	×	Check/top-up automatic gearbox fluid
●	●	●	Stop engine
×	×	×	Re-check tension if alternator driving belt has been renewed
●	●	●	Remove wing covers
●	●	●	Fill in details and fix appropriate Unipart underbonnet stickers
●	●	●	Close bonnet
●	●	●	Remove exhaust extractor pipe
×	×	×	Remove spare wheel
×	×	×	Inspect wheel for damage
×	×	×	Check tyre tread depth
×	×	×	Check tyre visually for external cuts in fabric, exposure of ply or cord structure, lumps or bulges
×	×	×	Check tyre for uneven wear
×	×	×	Check/adjust tyre pressure
●	●	●	Refit spare wheel
●	●	●	Drive off lift
×	×	×	Check headlamp alignment
		×	Check/adjust front wheel alignment
×	×	×	Check front wheel alignment
×	●	×	Report additional work required
×	×	×	Remove car protection kit
×	×	×	Ensure cleanliness of controls, door handles, etc.
×	×	×	Carry out road or roller test

Road Test

● ACTION   × OPERATION

After Sales Service	Intermediate Service	Main Service (24 denotes every 24 months, 24,000 miles (40 000) km)	OPERATION
	●	●	Fit trade plates to vehicle
	×	×	Check starter operation and inhibitor switch—Automatic
	×	×	Check operation of lights, horns, indicators, wipers and washers
	×	×	Check indicators self-cancel
	×	×	Check operation of all warning indicators
	×	×	Check foot and hand brakes
	×	×	Check engine noise levels, performance and throttle operation
	×	×	Check clutch for free play, slipping and judder
	×	×	Check gear selection and noise level in all gears. Check engagement of auto box parking pawl
	×	×	Check steering for noise, effort required, free play, wander and self-centring
	×	×	Check alignment of steering wheel spokes
	×	×	Check suspension for noise, irregularity in ride (e.g. dampers) and wheel imbalance
	×	×	Check foot brake pedal effort, travel, braking efficiency, pulling and binding
	×	×	Check speedometer for steady operation, noise and operation of mileage recorder
	×	×	Check operation of all instruments
	×	×	Check for abnormal body noises
	×	×	Check operation of seat belts, including operation of inertia reels
	×	×	Check handbrake ratchet and hold
	×	×	Adjust engine idle speed while engine is hot
	●	●	Position car on lift
	●	●	Raise lift
	●	●	Inspect engine and transmission for oil leaks
	×	×	Check exhaust system for condition, leakage and security
	×	×	Lower lift and drive vehicle off
	×	×	Report on road test findings
	×	×	Remove car protection kit
	●	●	Ensure cleanliness of controls, door handles, etc.
	●	●	Remove trade plates

This Maintenance Summary was produced from Leycare Supplementary Job Sheet SMD 2553. Job Sheets used by BL Cars' Dealers operating Leycare Service are updated as modifications affecting routine maintenance are introduced, and the content of this maintenance summary may differ from that currently used by Leycare Service operatives.

BRAKE PREVENTATIVE MAINTENANCE

In addition to the recommended periodical inspection of brake components it is advisable as the car ages and as a precaution against the effects of wear and deterioration, to make a more searching inspection and renew parts as necessary.

It is recommended that:

1 Disc brake pads, drum brake linings, hoses and pipes should be examined at intervals no greater than those laid down in the Maintenance Summary.

2 Under normal operating conditions brake fluid should be changed completely every 18 months or 18,000 miles (30 000 km) whichever is the sooner. If the vehicle is frequently subjected to severe driving or operating conditions, it may be necessary to change the brake fluid at shorter intervals.

3 All fluid seals in the hydraulic system and all flexible hoses should be examined and renewed if necessary every three years or 60 000 km whichever is sooner. At the same time the working surface of the pistons and of the bores of the master cylinder, wheel cylinders and other slave cylinders should be examined and new parts fitted where necessary.

Care must be taken always to observe the following points:

a At all times use the recommended brake fluid.

b Never leave the fluid in unsealed containers; it absorbs moisture quickly and can be dangerous if used in your braking system in this condition.

c Fluid drained from the system or used for bleeding should be discarded.

d The necessity for absolute cleanliness throughout cannot be over-emphasized.

MANUAL GEARBOX — 5 SPEED

GEAR-CHANGE REMOTE CONTROL ASSEMBLY

Overhaul 37.16.20

These instructions supersede those given in the Repair Operation Manual.

Dismantling

1 Remove the remote control assembly from the gearbox.
2 Remove the two bolts and two countersunk screws securing the bias spring bridge plates.
3 Remove the two bridge plates, bridge plate liners and the bias spring.
4 Remove the bias spring adjusting bolts and locknuts.
5 Remove the two bolts and washers securing the reverse baulk plate assembly and withdraw the reverse baulk plate, springs and spacers.
6 Remove the four bolts and washers securing the bottom cover plate.
7 Remove the bottom cover plate.
8 Remove the reverse light switch and locknut.
9 Remove the square-headed pinchbolt securing the selector shaft elbow.
10 Remove the selector shaft elbow.
11 Withdraw the selector shaft.
12 Press out the two selector shaft bushes in the remote control casing.
13 Remove the circlips securing the pivot ball and bushes in the selector shaft elbows and press out the bushes and pivot balls.

Assembling

14 Press in new selector shaft bushes in the remote control casing.
15 Fit new bushes, pivot balls and circlips to the selector shaft elbow.
16 Fit the selector shaft to the casing.
17 Fit the rear elbow and secure with the square-headed pinchbolt.
18 Fit the baulk plate assembly.
19 Fit the reverse switch and locknut.
20 Fit the bottom cover plate.
21 Fit the bias spring adjusting bolts and locknuts.
22 Fit the bias spring, bridge plate liners and bridge plates.

23 Fit the remote control assembly to the gearbox.
  Operations to be carried out following the fitting of the remote control assembly to the gearbox.
24 Fit the gear lever.

Adjusting the reverse baulk plate

Adjustment of the reverse baulk plate must be carried out on a complete gearbox assembly.
25 Remove the bottom cover plate of the gear lever remote control assembly.
26 Locate the gear lever in neutral in a vertical position.
27 Slacken the baulk plate adjusting bolts and locknuts until the baulk plate is in contact with the backing plate.
28 Tighten the adjusting bolts *equally* until they just start to move the baulk plate out of contact with the backing plate.
29 Adjustment should be such that an effort of 30 to 35 lbf (13.6 to 15.9 kgf) is required to overcome the resistance of the baulk plate. This may be checked using a spring balance attached to the threaded end of the gear lever (gear knob end). Adjust by tightening or slackening the two adjacent bolts and locknuts located on the right-hand side of the reverse baulk plate.
  NOTE: A minimum clearance of 0.010 in (0.254 mm) must exist between the upper face of the baulk plate and the lower edge of the gear lever bush.

Adjustment of 1st/2nd gate stop

This operation must be carried out following the adjustment of the reverse baulk plate.
30 Engage 1st gear.
31 Check the clearance between the side of the gear lever and the edge of the baulk plate. This should be 0.010 to 0.049 in (0.25 to 1.25 mm). Adjust by adding or removing shims as necessary.
32 Engage 2nd gear and repeat the above operation.
33 Fit bottom cover plate.

Adjustment of gear lever bias spring

34 Unit completely assembled, engage 3rd gear.
35 Adjust the screws to position both legs of spring 0.5 mm clear of lever crosspin.

36 Apply a light load to gear lever in L.H. direction taking up play. Adjust R.H. screw downward until R.H. spring leg just makes contact with crosspin.
37 Repeat instruction 36 on the other side. Play will still be present but at extremes of gear lever travel the crosspin should make contact with the spring legs.
38 Return lever to neutral and rock across gate several times. Lever should return to 3rd/4th gate.
39 Tighten the locknuts.
40 Adjust the reverse switch, see 86.65.20.

WINDSCREEN WIPERS AND WASHERS

WINDSCREEN WIPER DELAY UNIT

Remove and refit 84.25.31

Removing

1 Disconnect both multi-pin plugs from the delay unit.
2 Remove the mounting screws and nuts, and withdraw the delay unit and insulating plate.

Refitting

3 Reverse instructions 1 and 2, ensuring that the earth lead is fitted to one of the mounting screws.

WIRING DIAGRAM — 1981 UK AND EUROPEAN MARKET   RIGHT-HAND AND LEFT-HAND STEERING

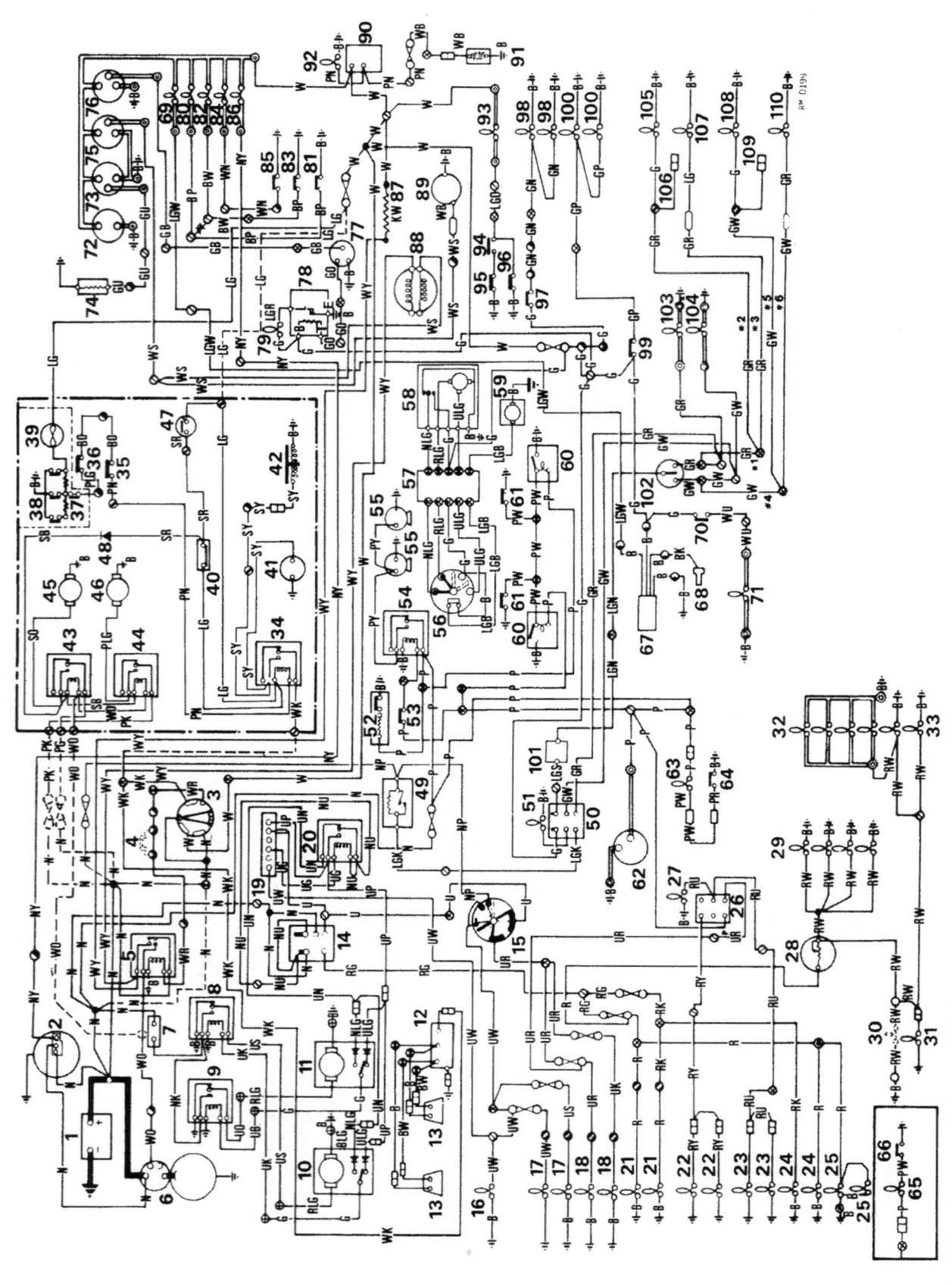

1 Battery
2 Alternator
3 Ignition/starter switch
4 Start inhibit switch (automatic transmission only)
5 Starter relay
6 Starter motor
7 Headlamp motor circuit breaker
8 Headlamp relay — L.H.
9 Headlamp relay — R.H.
10 Headlamp motor — L.H.
11 Headlamp motor — R.H.
12 Radio
13 Speaker
14 Master light switch
15 Main/dip/flash switch
16 Main beam warning light
17 Main beam
18 Dip beam
19 Headlamp flash unit
20 Headlamp flash relay
21 Front parking lamp
22 Front fog lamp
23 Rear fog guard lamp
24 Tail lamp
25 Number plate illumination lamp
26 Fog switch
27 Rear fog guard lamp warning light
28 Panel rheostat

29 Heater control illumination
30 Selector panel illumination (automatic transmission only)
31 Cigarette lighter illumination
32 Panel illumination
33 Switch panel illumination
34 Clutch relay
35 Air conditioning cut-out switch
36 Full throttle cut-out switch
37 Thermostat
38 Blower motor switch
39 Blower motor
40 Pressure cut in switch
41 Clutch
42 Throttle jack
43 Condenser fan relay — L.H.
44 Condenser fan relay — R.H.
45 Condenser fan — L.H.
46 Condenser fan — R.H.
47 Radiator thermostat
48 Diode
49 Hazard flasher unit
50 Hazard switch
51 Hazard warning light
52 Cigarette lighter
53 Horn-push
54 Horn relay
55 Horn
56 Windscreen wash/wipe switch

57 Wiper delay unit
58 Windscreen wiper motor
59 Windscreen washer motor
60 Map/courtesy lamp
61 Door switch
62 Clock
63 Luggage boot lamp
64 Luggage boot lamp switch } R.H. steering
65 Luggage boot lamp
66 Luggage boot lamp switch } L.H. steering
67 Coolant low indicator unit
68 Coolant low sensor
69 Coolant low warning light
70 Choke switch
71 Choke warning light
72 Voltmeter
73 Temperature gauge
74 Temperature transmitter
75 Tachometer
76 Fuel gauge
77 Tank unit
78 Low fuel delay unit
79 Low fuel warning light
80 Brake warning light
81 Brake pressure differential switch
82 Handbrake warning light
83 Handbrake switch
84 Oil pressure warning light
85 Oil pressure switch

86 Ignition warning light
87 Ballast resistor wire
88 Ignition coil — 6 volt
89 Ignition distributor
90 Heated rear screen switch
91 Heated rear screen
92 Heated rear screen warning light
93 Seat belt warning light
94 Passenger seat switch
95 Passenger belt switch
96 Driver belt switch
97 Reverse lamp switch
98 Reverse lamp
99 Stop lamp switch
100 Stop lamp
101 Direction indicator flasher unit
102 Direction indicator switch
103 Indicator warning light — L.H.
104 Indicator warning light — R.H.
105 Front flasher lamp — L.H.
106 Front flasher repeater lamp connection — L.H.
107 Rear flasher lamp — L.H.
108 Front flasher lamp — R.H.
109 Front flasher repeater lamp connection — R.H.
110 Rear flasher lamp — R.H.

COLOUR CODE

B	Black	N	Brown	S	Slate
G	Green	O	Orange	U	Blue
K	Pink	P	Purple	W	White
LG	Light green	R	Red	Y	Yellow

WIRE COLOUR CODES OF FLASHER LAMP CIRCUIT

Wire identity	Item	Right-hand steering		Left-hand steering	
		Heater vehicles	Air conditioning vehicles	Heater vehicles	Air conditioning vehicles
*1	L.H. supply	G/LG	GR	LG/G	GR
*2	L.H. front lamp	G/LG	GR	LG/G	GR
*3	L.H. rear lamp	GW	GR	GR and LG	GR and LG
*4	R.H. supply	LG/G	GW	G/LG	GW
*5	R.H. front lamp	LG/G	GW	G/LG	GW
*6	R.H. rear lamp	GR and LG	GW and LG	GW	GW

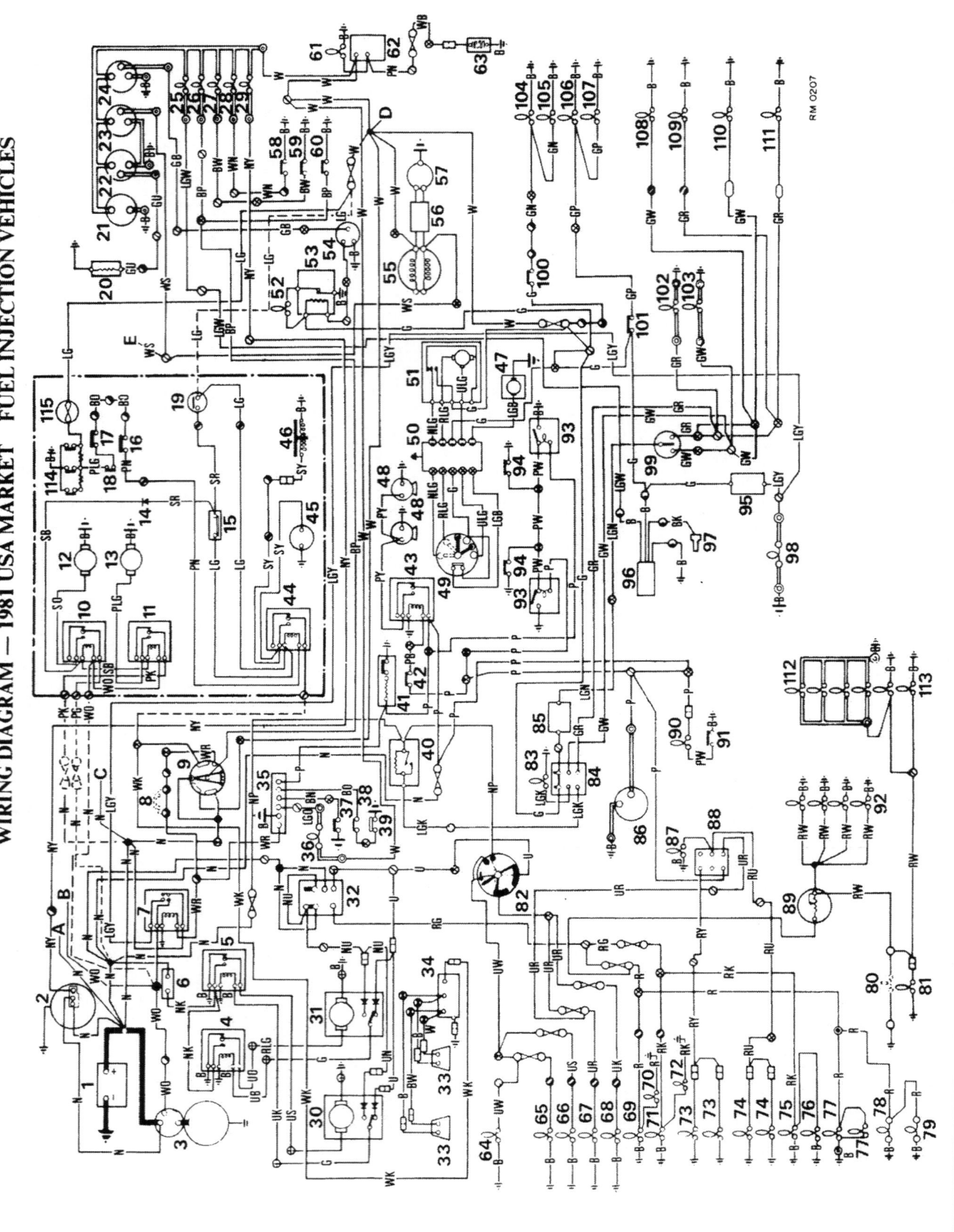

WIRING DIAGRAM — 1981 USA MARKET   FUEL INJECTION VEHICLES

RM 0207

494

1 Battery
2 Alternator
3 Starter motor
4 Headlamp relay — R.H.
5 Headlamp relay — L.H.
6 Headlamp motor circuit breaker
7 Starter relay
8 Starter inhibitor switch (automatic transmission only)
9 Ignition/starter switch
10 Condenser fan relay — L.H.
11 Condenser fan relay — R.H.
12 Condenser fan — L.H.
13 Condenser fan — R.H.
14 Diode
15 Pressure cut in switch
16 Air conditioning cut-out switch
17 Full throttle cut-out switch
18 Thermostat
19 Radiator thermostat
20 Temperature transmitter
21 Voltmeter
22 Temperature gauge
23 Tachometer
24 Fuel gauge
25 Coolant low warning light
26 Brake warning light
27 Handbrake warning light
28 Oil pressure warning light

29 Ignition warning light
30 Headlamp motor — L.H.
31 Headlamp motor — R.H.
32 Master light switch
33 Speaker
34 Radio
35 Seat belt timer/buzzer unit
36 Seat belt warning light
37 Belt switch
38 Door switch
39 Audible warning switch
40 Hazard flasher unit
41 Cigarette lighter
42 Horn-push
43 Horn relay
44 Clutch relay
45 Clutch
46 Engine air solenoid valve
47 Windscreen washer motor
48 Horn
49 Windscreen wash/wipe switch
50 Wiper delay unit
51 Windscreen wiper motor
52 Low fuel warning light
53 Low fuel delay unit
54 Tank unit
55 Ignition coil
56 Amplifier
57 Ignition distributor

58 Oil pressure switch
59 Handbrake switch
60 Brake pressure differential switch
61 Heated back-light warning light
62 Heated back-light switch
63 Heated back-light
64 Main beam warning light
65 Main beam — R.H.
66 Main beam — L.H.
67 Dip beam — R.H.
68 Dip beam — L.H.
69 Front marker lamp — R.H.
70 Front parking lamp — R.H.
71 Front marker lamp — L.H.
72 Front parking lamp — L.H.
73 Front fog lamp
74 Rear fog guard lamp
75 Tail lamp — L.H.
76 Rear marker lamp — L.H.
77 Number plate illumination lamp
78 Rear marker lamp — R.H.
79 Tail lamp — R.H.
80 Selector panel illumination (automatic transmission only)
81 Cigarette lighter illumination
82 Main/dip/flash switch
83 Hazard warning light
84 Hazard switch
85 Turn signal flasher unit

86 Clock
87 Rear fog guard warning light
88 Fog switch
89 Panel rheostat
90 Luggage boot lamp
91 Luggage boot lamp switch
92 Heater control illumination
93 Map/courtesy lamp
94 Door switch
95 Service interval counter
96 Coolant low indicator unit
97 Coolant low sensor
98 Oxygen sensor warning light
99 Turn signal switch
100 Reverse lamp switch
101 Stop lamp switch
102 Turn signal warning light — L.H.
103 Turn signal warning light — R.H.
104 Reverse lamp — R.H.
105 Reverse lamp — L.H.
106 Stop lamp — R.H.
107 Stop lamp — L.H.
108 Front flasher lamp — R.H.
109 Front flasher lamp — L.H.
110 Rear flasher lamp — R.H.
111 Rear flasher lamp — L.H.
112 Instrument illumination
113 Switch panel illumination
114 Blower motor switch
115 Blower motor

A To injector and ECU relay
B To diode resistor pack
C To fuel pump relay
D To diode resistor pack
E Fuel injection timing signal

See also Fuel Injection Wiring Diagram

COLOUR CODE

B	Black	N	Brown	S	Slate
G	Green	O	Orange	U	Blue
K	Pink	P	Purple	W	White
LG	Light green	R	Red	Y	Yellow

WIRING DIAGRAM   FUEL INJECTION — 1981

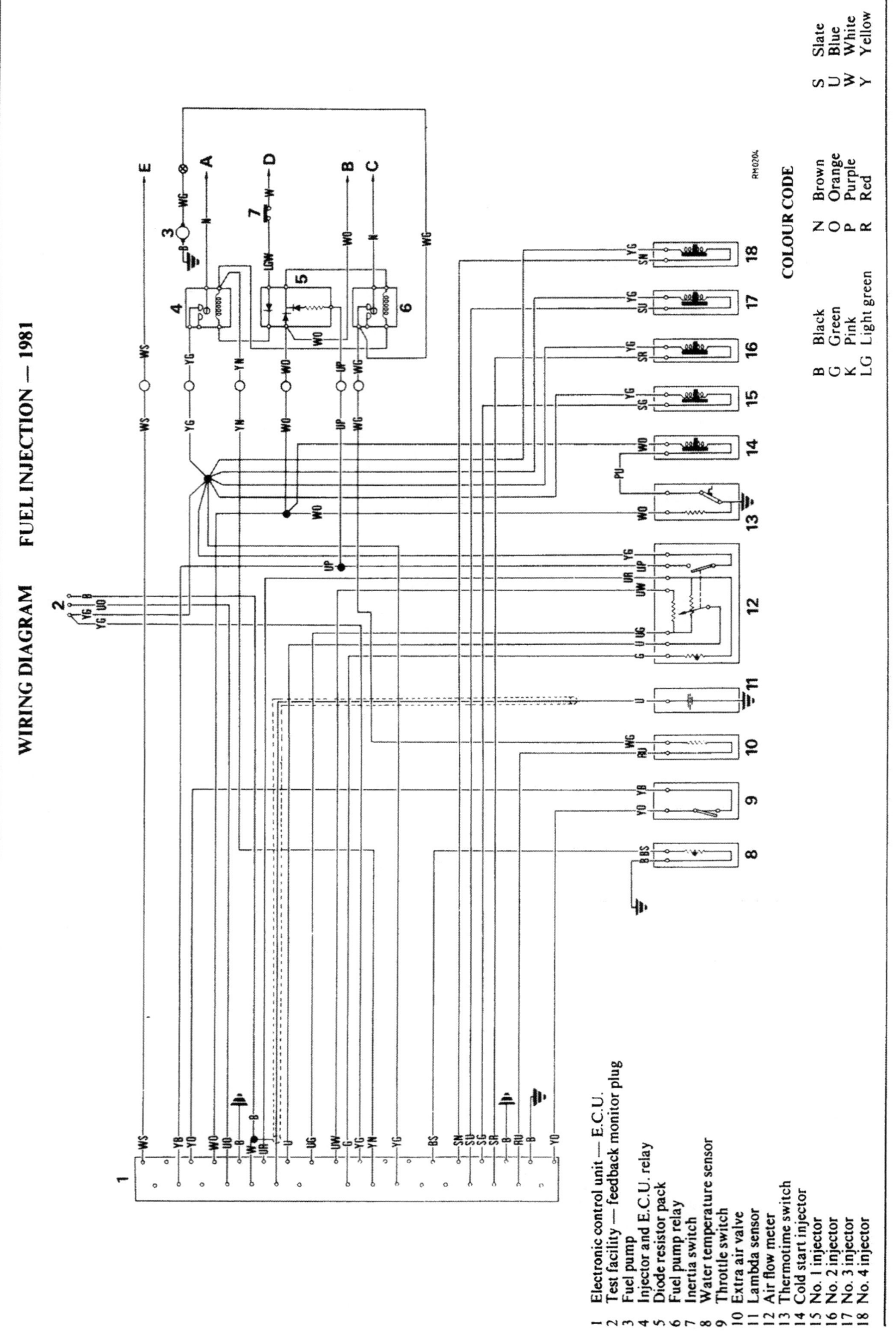

RM0204

COLOUR CODE

B	Black	N	Brown	S	Slate
G	Green	O	Orange	U	Blue
K	Pink	P	Purple	W	White
LG	Light green	R	Red	Y	Yellow

1 Electronic control unit — E.C.U.
2 Test facility — feedback monitor plug
3 Fuel pump
4 Injector and E.C.U. relay
5 Diode resistor pack
6 Fuel pump relay
7 Inertia switch
8 Water temperature sensor
9 Throttle switch
10 Extra air valve
11 Lambda sensor
12 Air flow meter
13 Thermotime switch
14 Cold start injector
15 No. 1 injector
16 No. 2 injector
17 No. 3 injector
18 No. 4 injector

IGNITION DISTRIBUTOR APPLICABILITY, IGNITION TIMING AND FEATURES CHART 1981

	LOW COMPRESSION ENGINE	CANADA
	Carburetter	Carburetter
	1981	1981
Triumph Part No.	RKC 5525	RKC 4722
Lucas Part No.	X	X
Delco Remy Part No.	9977370	9977254
Ignition timing — static	10° B.T.D.C.	10 degrees B.T.D.C.
Ignition timing — at idle	10° B.T.D.C	2 degrees A.T.D.C. Retard pipe connected
Idle speed	800 rev/min	800 rev/min
Conventional points ignition	✓	X
Electronic Ignition	X	✓
Centrifugal Advance	✓	✓
Vacuum Advance	✓	X
Retard Unit	X	✓

IGNITION DISTRIBUTOR — DELCO REMY

Data

Manufacturer	AC Delco
Series	D308
Delco Remy part no.	9977370
Stanpart No.	RKC 5525
Contact gap	0.014 to 0.016 in
Rotation — viewed on rotor	Anti-clockwise
Firing angles	90 ± 1 degree
Dwell angle	39 ± 1 degree
Open angle	51 ± 1 degree
Moving contact spring tension	19 to 24 ozf
Condenser capacity	0.18 to 0.23 mfd
Engine firing order	1-3-4-2

Centrifugal advance

Distributor r.p.m.	Degs. distributor advance		Crankshaft r.p.m.	Degrees crankshaft advance	
	Minimum	Maximum		Minimum	Maximum
300	No advance to occur		600	No advance to occur	
550	5	6.5	1100	10	13
1000	9.5	11	2000	19	22
1500	12	14	3000	24	28

Vacuum advance

Ins. of mercury vacuum	Degs. distributor advance		Degs. crankshaft advance	
	Minimum	Maximum	Minimum	Maximum
3	No advance to occur		No advance to occur	
5	0	4.5	0	9
7	4	7.5	8	15
8	6.5	7.5	13	15

TRIUMPH OFFICIAL TECHNICAL BOOKS

Brooklands Technical Books has been formed to supply owners, restorers and professional repairers with official factory literature.

Workshop Manuals

TR2 & TR3	502602	9780948207693
TR4 & TR4A	510322	9780948207952
TR5, TR250 & TR6 (Glove Box Autobooks Manual)		
		9781855201835
TR5-PI Supplement	545053	9781869826024
TR6 inc. TC & PI	545277/E2	9781869826130
TR7	AKM3079B	9781855202726
TR7 - Autobooks Manual 9781783181506		
TR8	AKM3981A	9781783180615
Spitfire Mk 1, 2 & 3 & Herald 1200, 12/50,		
13/60 & Vitesse 6	511243	9780946489992
Herald 948, 1200, 12/50, 13/60 - Autobooks Manual		
		9781783181513
Spitfire Mk 4	545254H	9781869826758
Spitfire 1500	AKM4329	9781869826666
Spitfire Mk 3, 4, 1500 (Glove Box Autobooks Manual)		
		9781855201248
2000 & 2500	AKM3974	9781869826086
GT6 Mk 1, 2, 3 & Vitesse 2 Litre		
	512947	9780907073901
GT6 Mk 2, GT6+ & Mk 3 & Vitesse 2 Litre Mk 2 1969-1973		
- Autobooks Manual		9781783181322
Stag	AKM3966	9781855200135
Stag - Autobooks Manual		9781783181490
Dolomite Sprint	AKM3629	9781855202825

Parts Catalogues

TR2 & TR3 501653		9780907073994
TR4	510978	9780907073949
TR4A	514837	9780907073956
TR250 US	516914	9781869826819
TR6 Sports Car 1969-1973	517785A	9780948207426
TR6 1974-1976	RTC9093A	9780907073932
TR7 1975-1978	RTC9814CA	9781855207943
TR7 1979 onwards	RTC9828CC	9781870642231
TR7 & TR8	RTC9020B	9781870642651
Herald 13/60	517056	9781869826154
Vitesse 2 Litre Mk 2	517786	9781869826147
Stag	519579	9781870642996
GT6 Mk 1 and Mk 2 /GT6+	515754/2	9781783180448
GT6 Mk 3	520949/A	9780948207938
Spitfire Mk 3	516282	9781870642873
Spitfire Mk 4 & Spitfire 1500 1973-1974		
	RTC 9008A	9781869826659
Spitfire 1500 1975-1980	RTC9819CB	9781870642187
Dolomite Range 1976 on	RTC9822CB	9781855202764

Owners Handbooks

Triumph Competition Preparation Manual		
TR250, TR5 and TR6		9781783180011
TR4	510326	9780948207662
TR4A	512916	9780948207679
TR5 PI	545034/2	9781855208544
TR250 (US)	545033	9780948207273
TR6	545078/1	9780948207402
TR6-PI	545078/2	9781855201750
TR6 (US 73)	545111/73	9781855204348
TR6 (US 75)	545111/75	9780948207150
TR7	AKM4332	9781870642736
TR8 (US)	AKM4779	9781855202832
Spitfire Mk 3	545017	9780948207181
Spitfire Mk 4	545220	9781870642439
Spitfire Mk 4 (US)	545189	9781855207967
Spitfire 1500	RTC9221	9781870642453
Spitfire Competition Preparation Manual		9781870642606
GT6	512944	9781855201583
GT6 Mk 2 & GT6+	545057	9781855201422
GT6 Mk 3	545186	9780946489848
GT6, GT6+ & 2000 Competition Preparation Manual		
		9781855200678
2000, 2500 TC and 2500S	AKM3617/2	9781855202788
Herald 1200 12/50	512893/6	9781855200616
Herald 13/60	545037	9781855201415
Vitesse 2 Litre	545006	9781855200746
Vitesse Mk 2	545070/2	9781855200418
Vitesse 6	511236/5	9781855207974

Carburetters

SU Carburetters Tuning Tips & Techniques	
	9781855202559
Solex Carburetters Tuning Tips & Techniques	
	9781855209770
Weber Carburettors Tuning Tips and Techniques	
	9781855207592

Truimph - Road Test Books

Triumph Herald 1959-1971	9781855200517
Triumph Vitesse 1962-1971	9781855200500
Triumph 2000 / 2.5 / 2500 1963-1977	9780946489237
Triumph GT6 Gold Portfolio 1966-1974	9781855202443
Triumph TR6 Road Test Portfolio	9781855209268
Triumph Spitfire Road Test Portfolio	9781855209534
Triumph Stag Road Test Portfolio	9781855208933

From Triumph specialists, Amazon or, in case of difficulty, from the distributor.

Brooklands Books Ltd., P.O. Box 146, Cobham, Surrey,
KT11 1LG, England, UK
Phone: +44 (0) 1932 865051   info@brooklands-books.com
www.brooklands-books.com

www.brooklandsbooks.com

Printed in Great Britain
by Amazon

46508064R00275